LEARNING AIDS

MANAGERIAL
ACCOUNTING

Tenth Canadian Edition

Ray H. Garrison, D.B.A., CPA
Professor Emeritus
Brigham Young University

Theresa Libby, Ph.D., CPA, CA
University of Waterloo

Alan Webb, Ph.D., FCPA, FCA
University of Waterloo

Eric W. Noreen, Ph.D., CMA
(Co-Author, U.S. Edition)
Professor Emeritus
University of Washington

Peter C. Brewer, Ph.D., CPA
(Co-Author, U.S. Edition)
Wake Forest University—Winston-Salem, North Carolina

McGraw-Hill
Ryerson

McGraw-Hill
Ryerson

MANAGERIAL ACCOUNTING
Tenth Canadian Edition

Copyright © 2015, 2012, 2009, 2004, 2001, 1999 by McGraw-Hill Ryerson Limited. Copyright © 2012, 2010, 2008, 2006, 2003, 2000, 1997, 1994, 1991, 1988, 1985, 1982, 1979, 1976 by McGraw-Hill Education LLC. All rights reserved. No part of this publication may be reproduced or transmitted in any form or by any means, or stored in a data base or retrieval system, without the prior written permission of McGraw-Hill Ryerson Limited, or in the case of photocopying or other reprographic copying, a license from The Canadian Copyright Licensing Agency (Access Copyright). For an Access Copyright license, visit www.accesscopyright.ca or call toll free to 1-800-893-5777.

Statistics Canada information is used with the permission of Statistics Canada. Users are forbidden to copy the data and redisseminate them, in an original or modified form, for commercial purposes, without permission from Statistics Canada. Information on the availability of the wide range of data from Statistics Canada can be obtained from Statistics Canada's Regional Offices, its World Wide Web site at www.statcan.gc.ca, and its toll-free access number 1-800-263-1136.

The Internet addresses listed in the text were accurate at the time of publication. The inclusion of a website does not indicate an endorsement by the authors or McGraw-Hill Ryerson, and McGraw-Hill Ryerson does not guarantee the accuracy of the information presented at these sites.

ISBN-13: 978-1-25-902490-0
ISBN-10: 1-25-902490-3

1 2 3 4 5 6 7 8 9 10 TCP 1 9 8 7 6 5

Printed and bound in Canada.

Care has been taken to trace ownership of copyright material contained in this text; however, the publisher will welcome any information that enables it to rectify any reference or credit for subsequent editions.

Director of Product Management: Rhondda McNabb
Product Manager: Keara Emmett
Executive Marketing Manager: Joy Armitage Taylor
Product Developer: Amy Rydzanicz
Senior Product Team Associate: Stephanie Giles
Supervising Editor: Jessica Barnoski
Photo/Permissions Editor: Indu Arora
Copy Editor/Proofreader: Julia Cochrane
Plant Production Coordinator: Sheryl MacAdam
Manufacturing Production Coordinator: Lena Keating
Cover Design: Katherine Strain
Cover Image: Steven Hayes/Getty Images
Interior Design: Katherine Strain
Page Layout: Aptara®, Inc.
Printer: Transcontinental Printing Group

Library and Archives Canada Cataloguing in Publication

Garrison, Ray H., author
    Managerial accounting / Ray H. Garrison, D.B.A., CPA, Professor Emeritus, Brigham Young University, Theresa Libby, Ph.D., CPA, CA, University of Waterloo, Alan Webb, Ph.D., FCPA, FCA, University of Waterloo, Eric W. Noreen, Ph.D., CMA (Co-Author, U.S. Edition), Professor Emeritus, University of Washington, Peter C. Brewer, Ph.D., CPA (Co-Author, U.S. Edition), Wake Forest University—Winston-Salem, North Carolina. — Tenth Canadian edition.

Revision of Managerial accounting / Ray H. Garrison . . . [et al.]. — 9th Canadian ed. — [Toronto]: McGraw-Hill Ryerson, [2011], ©2012. Includes bibliographical references and index. ISBN 978-1-25-902490-0 (bound)

    1. Managerial accounting—Textbooks. I. Libby, Theresa, 1963-, author II. Webb, Alan (Professor), author III. Noreen, Eric W., author IV. Brewer, Peter C., author V. Title.

HF5657.4.M38 2014   658.15'11   C2014-903642-6

Dedication

To our families, and the students and instructors who will use this book.

About the Authors

Ray H. Garrison is Emeritus Professor of Accounting at Brigham Young University, Provo, Utah. He received his B.S. and M.S. degrees from Brigham Young University and his D.B.A. degree from Indiana University. As a certified public accountant, Professor Garrison has been involved in management consulting work with both national and regional accounting firms. He has published articles in *The Accounting Review*, *Management Accounting*, and other professional journals. Innovation in the classroom has earned Professor Garrison the Karl G. Maeser Distinguished Teaching Award from Brigham Young University.

Theresa Libby is a Professor of Accounting in the School of Accounting and Finance, University of Waterloo. She received her Ph.D. from the University of Waterloo and a B. Comm. from the University of Windsor. Professor Libby is also a chartered professional accountant. Her research interests include the manager's use of accounting information for decision making, the effects of budgeting processes on performance, and accounting ethics. She has published articles in *CA Magazine* and *CMA Management*, as well as in leading research journals including *The Accounting Review*, *Contemporary Accounting Research*, *Business Ethics Quarterly*, and the *Journal of Management Accounting Research*. Professor Libby sits on the editorial boards of *Contemporary Accounting Research* and *Management Accounting Research* and has served as the editor of *Behavioral Research in Accounting*. In 2014, Professor Libby was awarded the L. S. Rosen Outstanding Educator Award by the Canadian Academic Accounting Association.

Alan Webb is a Professor in the School of Accounting and Finance at the University of Waterloo. He is a graduate of Mount Allison University and the University of Alberta, with B. Comm. and Ph.D. degrees. His primary research interests are in the areas of incentives, goal-setting, and performance measurement. Professor Webb has presented his work throughout North America and he is an editor of *Contemporary Accounting Research*. His research publications appear in *The Accounting Review*, *Journal of Accounting Research*, *Journal of Management Accounting Research*, *Contemporary Accounting Research*, *Issues in Accounting Education*, *CA Magazine*, and *CMA Management* magazine. He is a chartered professional accountant and has volunteered in numerous professional activities both in Canada and abroad. In 2011, Professor Webb was awarded the L. S. Rosen Outstanding Educator Award by the Canadian Academic Accounting Association and was named a Fellow of the Institute of Chartered Professional Accountants of Ontario for his outstanding career accomplishments.

Eric W. Noreen (Co-author, U.S. Edition) is Professor Emeritus of Accounting at the University of Washington and was Visiting Price Waterhouse Professor of Management Information & Control at INSEAD, an international graduate school of business located in France, and a professor at the Hong Kong University of Science and Technology. He received his B.A. degree from the University of Washington and M.B.A. and Ph.D. degrees from Stanford University. A Certified Management Accountant, he was awarded a Certificate of Distinguished Performance by the Institute of Certified Management Accountants. Professor Noreen has served as Associate Editor of *The Accounting Review* and the *Journal of Accounting and Economics*. He has published numerous articles in academic journals and has won a number of awards for his teaching.

Peter C. Brewer (Co-author, U.S. Edition) is a Lecturer in the Department of Accountancy at Wake Forest University. Prior to joining the faculty at Wake Forest, he was an accounting professor at Miami University for 19 years. He holds a B.S. degree in accounting from Penn State University, an M.S. degree in accounting from the University of Virginia, and a Ph.D. from the University of Tennessee. He has published numerous articles in a variety of journals. Professor Brewer has received Miami University's Richard T. Farmer School of Business Teaching Excellence Award and has been recognized on two occasions by the Miami University Associated Student Government for "making a remarkable commitment to students and their educational development." He is a leader in undergraduate management accounting curriculum innovation and the use of the case method for teaching undergraduate management accounting courses. He is a frequent presenter at various professional and academic conferences and meetings.

Brief Contents

Contents

Garrison/Libby/Webb:

For centuries, the lighthouse has stood as a beacon of guidance for mariners at sea. More than an aid to navigation, the lighthouse symbolizes safety, permanence, reliability, and the comforts of the familiar.

For this reason, we continue to illustrate the tenth Canadian edition of our flagship accounting publication, *Managerial Accounting* by Garrison, Libby, and Webb, with an image that we feel encapsulates the greatest strengths of this market-leading text.

Garrison is your guide through the challenges of learning managerial accounting. It identifies the three functions that managers must perform within their organizations—plan operations, control activities, and make decisions—and explains the managerial accounting information necessary for these functions, how to collect or prepare it, and how to interpret it. To achieve this, the tenth Canadian edition of *Managerial Accounting* focuses, now as in the past, on three qualities:

Your guide through the challenges of learning managerial accounting

Relevance. Every effort is made to help students relate the concepts in this book to the decisions made by managers in practice. With chapter openers based on real-world scenarios, in-chapter examples providing practical applications, knowledge in action summaries, and extensive end-of-chapter material, a student reading Garrison should never have to ask, "Why am I learning this?"

Balance. Garrison provides extensive examples and end-of-chapter material covering the breadth of business types found in practice, including manufacturing, service, retail, wholesale organizations, and not-for-profit entities. In the tenth Canadian edition, material related to the adoption of International Financial Reporting Standards (IFRS) continues to be highlighted with icons in the margins of the text.

Clarity. Generations of students have praised Garrison for the accessibility and readability of its writing, but that's just the beginning. Discussions of technical material have been simplified, chapters have been reordered, more specialized topics have been moved to online appendices, and the entire book has been thoroughly revised with the objective of making learning and teaching from Garrison as easy as possible. Key term definitions and icons signifying ethics, writing, and Excel assignments continue to add clarity for both students and instructors. In addition, students and instructors will work with clear, well-written supplements that employ consistent terminology.

The authors' steady focus on these three core elements has led to tremendous results.

What makes Garrison such a powerful learning tool?

Managerial Accounting is full of pedagogy designed to make studying productive. On the following pages, you will see the kind of engaging, helpful pedagogical features that make Garrison a favourite among both instructors and students.

Section Overviews
The tenth Canadian edition is divided into five sections. One-page overviews map the chapters included and how they are related.

Opening Vignettes
These chapter openers, based on real-world scenarios, introduce the chapter and highlight some of the issues, concepts, and decisions faced by managers that are discussed in the ensuing pages.

SECTION 2

COSTING

Chapters 5 through 8

Chapters 5 through 8 provide a comprehensive description of how costs are associated with manufacturing and other activities. In addition, these costing systems can be applied to service organizations and not-for-profit organizations. To permit costing for such specialized situations, two costing systems, job-order costing and process costing, can be mixed and matched.

Chapter 5 begins with the most basic and widely used costing system, *job-order costing*. Job-order costing permits costs to be assigned to specific outcomes, termed *jobs*, so that costs can be accumulated for what a company produces. In addition, manufacturing overhead—a term often shortened to just *overhead*—is assigned by a process of averaging to estimate its amount before actual overhead costs are known.

Chapter 6 introduces an averaging calculation used for costing similar units of product, termed *process costing*. The ordering of costs learned in financial

partially finished inventory. Chapter overhead methods gated to departme permit better man more accurate cos

Chapter 7 introdu way to disaggrego ing costs. Cost ob activities are cost driver. By doing t proved and mano activities rather th ing importance of types of organizat agement of overhe

Chapter 8 comp describing variabl only variable man

CHAPTER 5

Learning Objectives

After studying Chapter 3, you should be able to

1. Distinguish between process costing and job-order costing, and identify the production or service processes that fit with each costing method.

2. Recognize the flow of costs through a job-order costing system.

3. Compute predetermined overhead rates, and explain why estimated overhead costs (rather than actual overhead costs) are used in the costing process.

4. Record the journal entries that reflect the flow of costs in a job-order costing system.

5. Apply overhead cost to work in process using a predetermined

SYSTEMS DESIGN: JOB-ORDER COSTING

▪ **CUSTOM DESIGN AT ICEJERSEYS.COM**

Sport BUFF is dedicated to off best selection of officially sports merchandise and ap Montreal. Customers know tha ter what team they support, Sp will have a jersey in stock Internet and online shopping more popular, the store launched the website htt IceJerseys.com and began offe tom team outfitting services f teams at all skill levels. Custo an online tool called "JerseyB choose colours and styles, and t provide a team logo or the I com staff will design a logo

Individual team members' names and numbers and the team logo are p stitched on each jersey to meet customer specifications.

Accurately pricing custom-designed jerseys depends critically on the costing information available to managers at companies like IceJerseys.com, on the prices charged by competitors. The price quoted by IceJerseys.com tom batch of hockey jerseys must adequately cover costs and allow for an profit margin while remaining price-competitive. Costs might include th devoted to designing custom logos and other artwork; the cost of materials a

Learning Aids
These pedagogical boxes emphasize and summarize key content for students.

LEARNING AID

Key Formulas for Contribution Format Income Statements

Operating income = Unit CM × Q – Fixed expenses

CM = Sales – Variable expenses

CM per unit = Per unit sales – Per unit variable expenses

CM ratio = Total CM ÷ Total sales or CM ratio = Per unit CM ÷ Per unit sales

Variable expense ratio = Variable expenses ÷ Sales

In these formulas, CM = contribution margin and Q = quantity of goods sold in units.

IN BUSINESS

When deciding whether to bid for a major sporting event such as the Olympic Games, the potential host would perform a careful analysis of the expected differential revenues and differential costs. For example, according to some estimates, the differential costs to British Columbia of hosting the Vancouver 2010 Olympics were about $1.5 billion. Differential costs are those that were incurred *only* as a result of hosting the games. Examples are the cost of facilities such as the speed-skating arena that would not have been built if Vancouver had not won the Olympic bid, security for the events, and galas sponsored by the provincial government. Costs that would have been incurred even if British Columbia had not hosted the Olympics, such as upgrades to the Sea-to-Sky Highway leading to Whistler, are *not* considered differential costs.

A large source of differential revenue for British Columbia will be the money received in the years following the games as the result of tourists visiting the province after watching the Olympics on television. Some experts estimated that the 2010 Olympics could result in an additional 1.1 million to 2.7 million tourists for British Columbia in the five years following the games. According to a 2014 report prepared by Tourism BC, total tourism revenues for British Columbia in 2012 increased 2.5% compared to 2011 and 40.5% compared to 2002, suggesting estimates of the differential revenues

In Business

These helpful boxed features offer a glimpse into how real companies use the managerial accounting concepts discussed in the chapter. Every chapter contains several of these current examples.

Generally Accepted Accounting Principles

Financial accounting statements prepared for external users must be prepared in accordance with generally accepted accounting principles (GAAP). External users must have some assurance that the reports have been prepared in accordance with some common set of ground rules. Beginning January 1, 2011, Canada joined more than 100 other countries, including Australia, New Zealand, and European Union member countries, in adopting International Financial Reporting Standards (IFRS) for publicly accountable enterprises. As of that date, in Canada, IFRS became GAAP for public companies. The purpose of IFRS is simple: to enhance the comparability and clarity of financial information on a global basis. Given the increasing degree of globalization of the economy and the interconnectedness of capital markets, accounting standard setters in Canada concluded that it was crucial to adopt IFRS.[2] Private companies and not-for-profit organizations are not required to adopt IFRS but instead can use accounting standards for private enterprises (ASPE). While the common ground rules established by IFRS will enhance comparability across external reporting jurisdictions, they do not necessarily lead to the type of reports that would be most useful

IFRS Icon

The IFRS icon continues to identify where changes as a result of IFRS adoption in Canada are affecting managerial accounting.

Knowledge in Action

New to the tenth edition, these summaries provide examples of how key concepts covered in the chapter are applied by managers in practice. They are intended to reinforce the practical relevance of the material being learned.

KNOWLEDGE IN ACTION
Managers can apply their knowledge about cost behaviour when
· Calculating sales needed to achieve break-even profit levels
· Estimating sales needed to achieve desired profit targets
· Estimating the impact of sales volume changes on profit
· Costing products
· Preparing budgets and analyzing differences between actual and budgeted results
· Deciding whether to keep or drop a product
· Deciding whether to make a product internally or outsource production

Managerial Accounting has earned a reputation for the best practice material of any text on the market. The tenth Canadian edition includes both new and revised exercises, problems, and cases. Features include:

NEW

Instant Quiz 2-3
If a merchandising company has cost of goods sold of $250,000, beginning merchandise inventory of $50,000, and ending merchandise inventory of $40,000, calculate the amount of inventory purchases for the period.

Instant Quizzes
New to the tenth edition, these short questions are designed to allow students to test their understanding of key topics as they work through each chapter. Each question is intended to take only a few minutes at most to complete. Several instant quizzes are included in each chapter, starting with Chapter 2. To provide feedback for the instant quizzes, solutions for all questions are provided at the end of each chapter.

Review Problems & Solutions

REVIEW PROBLEM: COST–VOLUME–PROFIT RELATIONSHIPS

Networks Company manufactures wireless routers. The company's contribution format income statement for the most recent year is given below:

	Total	Per Unit	Percentage of Sales
Sales (25,000 units).........	$2,500,000	$100	100%
Less variable expenses.............	1,500,000	60	? %
Contribution margin..............	1,000,000	$ 40	? %
Less fixed expenses..............	800,000		
Operating income.................	$ 200,000		

NEW

DISCUSSION CASE

DISCUSSION CASE 3-1
Despite the numerous benefits of developing an accurate understanding of cost behaviour discussed in this chapter, research indicates that surprisingly few companies use quantitative techniques such as the high-low method or regression analysis to separate mixed costs into fixed and variable components.

Required:
Discuss reasons why companies might not use quantitative techniques (high-low method or regression analysis) to develop an accurate understanding of cost behaviour.

Discussion Cases
New to the tenth edition, these short cases focus on one or more of the concepts covered in the chapter. They are designed to provoke careful thought about key topics and to generate in-class discussion. One case has been developed for each chapter.

QUESTIONS

2-1 Would costs related to the building used only by administrative personnel, such as heat and lights, property taxes, and insurance, be considered part of manufacturing overhead? Why or why not?
2-2 Distinguish between the following: (a) direct materials, (b) indirect materials, (c) direct labour, (d) indirect labour, and (e) manufacturing overhead.
2-3 Are product costs always expensed in the period in which they are incurred? Explain.
2-4 What are marketing or selling costs? How are they treated on the income statement?
2-5 Describe the schedule of cost of goods manufactured. How does it tie into the income

Questions

NEW

Foundational Exercises
New to the tenth Canadian edition of Garrison! Each chapter now contains one Foundational exercise that includes "building block" questions related to one concise set of data. These exercises can be used for in-class discussion or as homework assignments. The Foundational Exercises are available on Connect.

EXERCISES   **connect**

EXERCISE 2-1 Classifying Manufacturing Costs [LO1]
The costs below all relate to Sounds Good, a company based in Alberta that manufactures high-end audio equipment such as speakers, receivers, CD players, turntables, and home theatre systems. The company owns all of the manufacturing facilities (building and equipment) but rents the space used by the non-manufacturing employees (accounting, marketing, sales, human resources).

Required:
For each cost, indicate whether it would most likely be classified as a direct labour, direct

Exercises

Problems ————————————————

Excel Simulations

NEW

New to the tenth Canadian edition of Garrison! Simulated Excel questions, assignable within Connect, allow students to practise their Excel skills—such as using basic formulas and formatting—within the context of managerial accounting. These questions feature animated, narrated Help and Show me tutorials (when enabled), as well as automatic feedback and grading for both students and professors.

Applying Excel

This feature links the power of Excel with managerial accounting concepts by illustrating how Excel functionality can be used to better understand accounting data. Applying Excel goes beyond plugging numbers into a template by providing students with an opportunity to build their own Excel worksheets and formulas. Students are then asked "what if" questions in which they analyze not only how related pieces of accounting data affect each other, but what they do. Applying Excel is integrated with McGraw-Hill's Connect, allowing students to practise their skills online with algorithmically generated datasets.

Cases ————————————————

CASES　　　　　　　　　**■ connect**

CASE 2–27 [LO1, LO2, LO3, LO4]
John Ranton, president and founder of Running Mate, could hardly contain his excitement over the operating results for his company's second year of operations. Running Mate is an online retailer of a GPS running watch that records distance, time, speed, heart rate, and a number of other statistics. Ranton's company does not manufacture the watches, but instead purchases them directly from the manufacturer based in China and resells them through its online shopping site. During the first two years of operation, Ranton decided to hold the selling price of the watch constant at $100 per unit in an effort to attract business. He was also able to negotiate a deal with the supplier to hold Running Mate's cost per watch constant at $80 per unit for the two years.

Operating expenses for each of the first two years of operation consist only of advertising expenses and the salaries paid to the website designer/administrator and the company's book-keeper. Because Ranton is busy with his numerous other business ventures, the bookkeeper also looks after the day-to-day operations of Running Mate and has sole signing authority to

EXERCISE 2–12 Classification of Labour Costs [LO1]
Greg Powers is employed by Gussie Company, where he assembles a component part for one of the company's products. Greg is paid $14 per hour for regular time, and he is paid time and a half (i.e., $21 per hour) for all work in excess of 40 hours per week.

Required:
1. Assume that during a given week Greg is idle for three hours due to machine breakdowns and that he is idle for two more hours due to material shortages. No overtime is recorded for the week. Allocate Greg's wages for the week between direct labour and manufacturing overhead cost.
2. Assume that during a following week Greg works a total of 49 hours. He has no idle time for the week. Allocate Greg's wages for the week between direct labour cost and manufacturing overhead cost.
3. Greg's company provides an attractive package of benefits for its employees. This package includes a retirement program and a health insurance program. Explain two ways that the company could handle the costs of its direct labourers' employee benefits in its cost records.

Writing Assignments
These encourage students to practise critical thinking and effective writing.

CASE 5–31 Ethics and the Manager [LO3, LO5, LO7]
Emily Carrigan was recently transferred to the Appliances Division of Delancy Corporation. Shortly after taking over her new position as divisional controller, Carrigan was asked to de-velop the division's predetermined overhead rate for the upcoming year. The accuracy of the rate is important. Delancy Corporation uses direct labour-hours in all of its divisions as the allocation base for manufacturing overhead.

To compute the predetermined overhead rate, Carrigan divided her estimate of the total manufacturing overhead for the coming year by the production manager's estimate of the total direct labour-hours for the coming year. She took her computations to the division's general manager for approval but was quite surprised when he suggested a modification in the base. Her conversation with the general manager of the Appliances Division, Harry Dafoe, went like this:

Carrigan: Here are my calculations for next year's predetermined overhead rate. If you approve, we can enter the rate into the computer on January 1 and be up and running in the

Ethics Assignments
These serve as a reminder that ethical conduct is just as important as profits in business.

Focus on the Tenth Canadian Edition

Book Philosophy and Structure

Developing and improving a textbook on a topic as broad as managerial accounting is an ongoing challenge requiring a guiding philosophy.

The authors of the tenth Canadian edition use the framework established by Garrison, Noreen, and Brewer in their fourteenth U.S. edition as a starting point. Although we rely on this framework in guiding our general approach, we have developed a text that distinctly reflects the Canadian business and education setting. Our main objectives are to make the various topics as easy to learn for students as possible and to provide the flexibility necessitated by the varied requirements of our Canadian users. We have developed a text that can be covered in a single-term course and that also provides students with a useful resource for subsequent courses in managerial accounting.

In the first two chapters we describe the key responsibilities of managers, their need for managerial accounting information, and the role of professional ethics for management accountants. We also address the major differences between financial and managerial accounting and cover key cost terms and classifications. Next, we cover two major topic areas that support the information needs of managerial accounting: cost behaviour and analysis, and the costing of products and services. This foundation material is the basis for Chapters 3 and 4, which focus on cost behaviour patterns, cost prediction models, and cost–volume–profit analysis. The remaining foundation material is covered in Chapters 5 through 8, which examine the major types of costing systems used by organizations.

In Chapters 9 through 11, we build on this foundation in our coverage of planning and control topics. Chapters 9 and 10 explore how managers can use predetermined costs in the form of budgets and standard costs both in planning for the future and in evaluating past performance. Chapter 11 covers a variety of management control techniques, including responsibility centre reporting and evaluation and performance measurement.

The second major application of the foundation material is examined in Chapters 12 and 13, which focus on short-term and long-term decision analysis. In Chapter 12, we cover relevant costs and analysis techniques used for short-term decisions, and in Chapter 13, we present the approaches used to analyze long-term capital budgeting decisions. Because the analysis required for short- and long-term decisions requires estimates of future costs, a thorough understanding of the cost behaviour concepts covered in Chapters 3 and 4 is essential. The book concludes with online Chapter 14 on financial statement analysis, which we view as an extension of both the control topics covered in earlier chapters and the decision analysis material presented in Chapters 12 and 13.

Each chapter provides an extensive set of exercises, problems, and cases that cover manufacturing, service, and not-for-profit organizations, as well as international businesses. This material has been developed to give students an appreciation for the types of situations faced by a wide variety of actual businesses. Feedback from our users indicates that while there is variety in the set of topics covered in any single course and the order in which they are covered, the structure and flexibility offered by our book makes it well suited to meet their needs.

Overall, our book is written in a way that facilitates understanding at the conceptual level and provides a sound basis for application.

What's New in the Tenth Edition

The tenth Canadian edition has been reviewed extensively to identify improvements over previous editions. The results of peer reviews and the authors' efforts are reflected in the revisions, reorganization, and new content development throughout the book. We have reordered the material in the tenth edition, placing the chapters on cost behaviour (Chapter 3) and cost–volume–profit (Chapter 4) concepts *before* the chapters on costing systems (Chapters 5 through 8). This reordering reflects our belief that understanding cost behaviour and analysis techniques is very helpful when studying costing systems. To demonstrate the practical application of the topics covered in the book, a new Knowledge in Action summary has been developed for each chapter after Chapter 1. These bullet point summaries give examples of how managers actually use the concepts covered in the chapter. Many exercises, problems, cases, and research questions have been revised and new ones created. We have also created a new Discussion Case at the end of each chapter. These short cases are designed to stimulate in-class discussion of a particular topic and require students to think more deeply about one or more key concepts. To further facilitate learning, we have developed new Instant Quizzes in most chapters that are designed to give students an opportunity to test their understanding of each major topic as they work through the chapter. The quizzes are short questions covering a single topic. To provide students with feedback, solutions to the Instant Quizzes are provided at the end of each chapter. Additionally, in several chapters, we have updated or created new Learning Aids to emphasize key materials and to reinforce students' understanding of the decision-making approach used for certain analysis techniques. We are confident that, collectively, these changes will enhance students' understanding and application of key managerial accounting topics.

The specific changes in each of the individual chapters of the tenth edition are summarized below:

- **Chapter 1** has been revised to improve clarity and to remove content deemed too advanced for an introductory text. Most notably the section on process management has been considerably shortened and the section on business plans removed. New In Business segments have been added.

- **Chapter 2** has a new opening vignette based on an actual service company, and several In Business segments have been revised or replaced with more current material. Exhibit 2–6 has been revised to clarify the cost flow example. Exhibits 2–7 and 2–9 have been replaced with Learning Aids. Seven Instant Quizzes have been included and a Knowledge in Action summary added.

- In **Chapter 3**, new examples have been developed to illustrate key cost behaviour concepts, and the related graphs have been revised. Several of the In Business segments have been revised or replaced to reflect more current material. Five Instant Quizzes have been included and a Knowledge in Action summary added.

- **Chapter 4** has a new opening vignette illustrating the use of the break-even concept in practice. Several In Business segments have been updated or replaced to reflect more current material. A new section on calculating multi-product break-even units has been developed, including a new Exhibit 4–6. The Learning Aid on multi-product cost–volume–profit analysis has been updated to include break-even units. Nine Instant Quizzes have been included and a Knowledge in Action summary added.

- **Chapter 5** has an updated opening vignette to reflect more current information, and several new examples of the use of job-order costing in service industries have been added. A new In Business segment has been added to describe job-order costing in a non-profit organization. References to paper copies of job tickets, cost sheets, and so on have been removed in favour of screen shots from a computerized database and discussion of how costs accumulate electronically in computerized costing systems. The discussion of disposition of over/underapplied overhead in the body of the chapter as well as the material included in Appendix 5A has been expanded to consider the impact of *International Accounting Standard (IAS) 2* on external reporting of product/service costs. Five Instant Quizzes have been included and a Knowledge in Action summary added.

- **Chapter 6** includes a new opening vignette illustrating the type of production process for which process costing is ideal. The main example built and elaborated upon throughout the chapter has been revised and refreshed. The appendix on service department cost allocation has been moved to online Appendix 11A: Transfer Pricing, Quality Costs, and Service Department Cost Allocation (see also Chapter 11 below) since users expressed the view that the material is better suited to being online. Finally, four Instant Quizzes and a Knowledge in Action summary have been added.

- **Chapter 7** includes a new opening vignette illustrating the usefulness of activity-based costing (ABC) in the auto industry. In addition, three new In Business segments have been added to illustrate the use of ABC in the travel and service industries. The review problem has been refreshed and a new review problem has been added that compares costs under traditional and ABC systems. Five Instant Quizzes have been included and a Knowledge in Action summary added.

- **Chapter 8** includes a new opening vignette illustrating a real-life example of managers' motivation to build inventory under an absorption costing system and how variable costing avoids this problem. In addition, the discussion of lean accounting has been enhanced, and a new In Business segment illustrating how lean accounting can be used to improve cost management in hospitals is included. Five Instant Quizzes and a Knowledge in Action summary are also included.

- **Chapter 9** has a new opening vignette that builds on the vignette developed for Chapter 2. A new example has been developed to illustrate the preparation of the master budget and its supporting components and the use of flexible budgets. The cash budget section has been revised to utilize the approach for calculating and paying interest expense employed in practice. The discussion of the financing section of the cash budget has been clarified to enhance understandability and a new formula has been included to simplify the calculation of borrowings and loan repayments. New In Business segments have been developed. Eight Instant Quizzes have been included and the Knowledge in Action summary added.

- **Chapter 10** includes one new and one updated In Business segment describing examples in the service industry. The Sales Variance Analysis Appendix has been added to the end of Chapter 10 as Appendix 10C (was Appendix 11A in the ninth edition) as the material fits better with the material in this chapter. Five Instant Quizzes and a Knowledge in Action summary have been added.

- **Chapter 11** now includes an updated version of the opening vignette as well as two new In Business segments concerning the using of the balanced scorecard in Canadian organizations. In addition, the coverage of material in this chapter has been reduced to better reflect knowledge necessary for an introductory course on managerial accounting. To facilitate coverage of more complex material by some instructors (e.g., transfer pricing, cost of quality, and profitability analysis), these topics have been included in the new online Appendix 11A: Transfer Pricing, Quality Costs, and Service Department Cost Allocation. Four Instant Quizzes and a Knowledge in Action summary have been included.

- **Chapter 12** has a new opening vignette concerning relevant costing in the airline industry, and a new In Business segment on relevant costs in the decision to lay off employees has been added. Six Instant Quizzes and a Knowledge in Action summary have been included.

- In **Chapter 13**, the opening vignette has been updated. All examples have been revised to discontinue the use of present value tables in performing the calculations. Instead, all present value amounts are now based on the use of formulas available in Microsoft Excel. The discussion of present value concepts has also been revised as needed to incorporate the use of formulas from Microsoft Excel. In keeping with these changes, the present value factor appendices have been removed. The discussion of the weighted-average cost of capital has been revised to improve clarity. New In Business segments have been developed. Six Instant Quizzes have been included and a Knowledge in Action summary added.

- In **Chapter 14**, an online chapter, some of the examples have been revised to reflect current values from publicly available sources of financial information. The discussion has been revised to identify the various users of the different analyses described in the chapter. Exhibit 14–5 has been transformed into a Learning Aid. What is now Exhibit 14–5 has been updated to provide current website addresses for information sources. A Knowledge in Action summary has been added.

Teaching and Learning with Technology

Get Connect Accounting. Get Results.

McGraw-Hill Connect™ is a digital teaching and learning environment that gives students the means to better connect with their coursework, with their instructors, and with the important concepts that they will need to know for success now and in the future. With Connect, instructors can deliver assignments, quizzes, and tests easily online. Students can practice important skills at their own pace and on their own schedule.

Key Features of Garrison Connect

Simple Assignment Management and Smart Grading

- Spend more time teaching and less time managing
- Create and deliver assignments easily with selectable end-of-chapter questions, test bank items, and more.
- Go paperless with online submission and grading of student assignments.
- Have assignments graded automatically, giving students immediate feedback on their work and comparisons with correct answers.
- Reinforce classroom concepts with practice tests and instant quizzes.

Online Assignments

- Assign text end-of-chapter exercises, problems, and cases, algorithmic questions, test bank items, Excel simulations, Applying Excel questions, Foundational exercises, and more.

Intelligent Response Technology (IRT)

IRT is a redesigned student interface for the Garrison Connect end-of-chapter assessment content. The benefits include improved answer acceptance to reduce students' frustration with formatting issues (such as rounding). Select questions have been redesigned to test students' knowledge more fully. They now include tables for students to work through rather than requiring that all calculations be done offline.

Instructor Library

The Connect Instructor Library provides all of the critical resources instructors need to build their course including access to the eBook version of the text, PowerPoint slides, Solutions Manual, Instructor's Manual, Test Bank, and more. The Connect Instructor Library also allows instructors to upload their own files.

eBook

The Connect eBook allows for anytime, anywhere access to the text. Capabilities like highlighting, note sharing, and bookmarking provide students with a convenient tool for comprehensive review. A powerful search function allows students to pinpoint and connect key concepts in a snap.

LearnSmart

LEARNSMART LearnSmart uses intelligent adaptive technology to deliver results in boosting grades, increasing course retention, and strengthening memory recall. The proven LearnSmart engine has helped over 2 million student users answer nearly 1.5 billion questions since 2009. LearnSmart builds a unique learning experience for each student's individual needs. It starts by identifying the topics a student knows and does not know. As the student progresses, LearnSmart adapts and adjusts the content based on his or her individual strengths, weaknesses, and confidence, ensuring that every minute spent studying with LearnSmart is the most efficient and productive study time possible.

SmartBook

SMARTBOOK As the first and only adaptive reading experience, SmartBook is changing the way students read and learn. SmartBook creates a personalized reading experience by highlighting the most important concepts a student needs to learn at that moment in time. As a student engages with SmartBook, the reading experience continuously adapts by highlighting content based on what each student knows and doesn't know. This ensures that he or she is focused on the content needed to close specific knowledge gaps, while simultaneously promoting long-term learning. The LearnSmart questions are integrated within the SmartBook, allowing students to practice and reinforce what they have read.

Connect Insight

connect INSIGHT NEW to the tenth Canadian edition of Garrison! Visualized data tailored to your needs as an instructor make it possible to quickly confirm early signals of success, or identify early warning signs regarding student performance or concept mastery—even while on the go.

Services and Support

Instructor Support

The following instructor resources are available online on Connect:

Instructor's Manual The *Instructor's Manual* includes chapter overviews, assignment grids featuring levels of difficulty, and chapter-by-chapter lists of service examples.

Solutions Manual This supplement contains completely worked out solutions to all assignment material and a general discussion of the use of group exercises. In addition, the manual contains suggested course outlines and a listing of exercises, problems, and cases scaled according to difficulty.

Computerized Test Bank Nearly 2,000 questions are organized by chapter and include true/false, multiple-choice, and essay questions, plus computational problems. Use it to make different versions of the same test, change the answer order, edit and add questions, and conduct online testing. Technical support for this software is available. The files are also available in RTF for printing.

Microsoft PowerPoint Slides Available on Connect, these slides offer a great visual complement for your lectures. A complete set of slides covers each chapter.

Microsoft Excel Templates These are the solutions to the Microsoft Excel templates offered online.

Superior Solutions and Support

The McGraw-Hill Ryerson team is ready to help you assess and integrate any of our products, technology, and services into your course for optimal teaching and learning performance. Whether it's helping your students improve their grades, or putting your entire course online, the McGraw-Hill Ryerson team is here to help you. Contact your Learning Solutions Consultant today to learn how to maximize all of McGraw-Hill Ryerson's resources!

For more information on the latest technology and Learning Solutions offered by McGraw-Hill Ryerson and its partners, please visit us online: **www.mheducation.ca/he/solutions.**

 McGraw-Hill Ryerson

Solutions that make a difference. Technology that fits.

MH-Campus
LMS Integration

Connect
Course Management

LearnSmart
Adaptive Learning

Tegrity
Lecture Capture

Custom
Print & Digital

Reviewers

The efforts of many people are needed to develop and improve a text. Among these people are the reviewers and consultants who point out areas of concern, cite areas of strength, and make recommendations for change. In this regard, the professors named on this page provided feedback that was enormously helpful in preparing the tenth Canadian edition of *Managerial Accounting*.

Suggestions have been received from many of our colleagues across Canada and throughout the world who have used the prior editions of *Managerial Accounting*. This is vital feedback that we rely on in each edition. Each of those who have offered comments and suggestions has our thanks.

Bharat Aggarwal, *Sheridan Institute of Technology*

George Boland, *Queen's University*

Gillian Bubb, *University of the Fraser Valley*

Tammy Crowell, *Dalhousie University*

Elliot Currie, *University of Guelph*

Shujun Ding, *University of Ottawa*

Ian Feltmate, *Acadia University*

Mark Gandey, *Bishop's University*

Barbara Katz, *Kwantlen Polytechnic University*

Amy Kwan, *University of Toronto*

Glenn Leonard, *University of New Brunswick, Fredericton*

Winston Marcellin, *George Brown College*

Bonnie Martel, *Niagara College*

Ann Overton, *Centennial College*

Pamela Quon, *Athabasca University*

Todd Rose, *Memorial University*

Pina Salvaggio, *Dawson College*

John Siambanopoulos, *Western University*

Acknowledgements

The tenth Canadian edition of *Managerial Accounting* has benefited from the assistance of numerous individuals and groups. This assistance was invaluable in providing us with materials, review comments and suggestions, and technical assistance. Commissioned reviewers across Canada assisted with suggestions and clarifications that reflect their views of the materials they examined.

Materials were provided by the American Accounting Association, CGA-Canada and CMA-Canada (both now part of CPA Canada), and SAP Canada. In each case, an acknowledgement is included when the material is used in the textbook. The U.S. authors acknowledge materials provided by the AICPA, the Institute of Certified Management Accountants, and the Chartered Institute of Management Accountants (United Kingdom).

We also received invaluable input and support through the years from present and former colleagues and students. We are indebted to the following individuals who helped adapt, critique, and shape the ancillary package for the Canadian market: Shannon Butler, Western University; Susan Cohlmeyer, Memorial University; Robert Ducharme, University of Waterloo; Kathy Falk, University of Toronto, Mississauga; Ian Feltmate, Acadia University; Bonnie Martel, Niagara College; Don Smith, Georgian College; and Mike Meehan, Sheridan College.

The extraordinary efforts of a talented group of individuals at McGraw-Hill Ryerson made all of this come together. We especially thank Keara Emmett, for her guidance throughout this project; Amy Rydzanicz, for initiating the developmental work for this edition and for tirelessly following the whole process through until the final printing; Jessica Barnoski, who managed the final production of this book; and all the marketing and sales people who helped bring this book to both instructors and students. We also thank all those who worked behind the scenes to ensure the successful completion of this book. Special thanks to Julia Cochrane for her careful editing and proofreading of the entire textbook.

Despite the assistance we received, we acknowledge our responsibility for the contents of this book. We appreciate suggestions and questions from our audience.

MANAGERIAL
ACCOUNTING

Tenth Canadian Edition

OVERVIEW AND FOUNDATION

Chapters 1 through 4

Chapters 1 and 2 present an overview of background matter for subsequent chapters and also provide information on technical topics that appear in later chapters. Chapters 3 and 4 focus on cost behaviour patterns, cost prediction models, and cost–volume–profit analysis. These topics provide the foundation for later chapters on costing techniques, budgeting, standard costs, and decision analysis. Thus, it is important to study these chapters carefully to be prepared.

Chapter 1 describes what managers do and how managerial accounting can serve these needs. The chapter highlights the key differences between financial and managerial accounting. The importance of ethics for accountants is also covered, and some key managerial concepts important in today's organizations are discussed.

Chapter 2 begins by describing how costs are classified and explains the distinction between product and period costs. Next, the steps involved in calculating the cost of goods sold and the cost of goods manufactured are presented. These calculations

provide a structure for the costing methods covered in subsequent chapters.

Chapter 2 also presents a basic discussion of cost behaviour, which is important to numerous topics in later chapters. The chapter concludes with two topics important to cost control and decision analysis. First, direct costs are distinguished from indirect costs, which will be important when special-purpose performance reports are discussed later in the book. Second, different types of "decision-focused costs" are presented: differential costs, opportunity costs, and sunk costs. Understanding these concepts is critical to decision-making analysis, which is covered in Chapter 12.

Chapter 3 describes the details of cost behaviour and how costs that contain a mix of behaviours can be identified and analyzed.

Chapter 4 builds on the idea of cost behaviour and incorporates revenues to provide commonly used tools for analysis and short-term decisions, including cost–volume–profit analysis and break-even analysis.

MANAGERIAL ACCOUNTING AND THE BUSINESS ENVIRONMENT

THE ROLE OF THE MANAGEMENT ACCOUNTANT IN VALUE CREATION

The role of management accountants has evolved considerably over the past few decades. No longer considered to be just "bean-counters" who compile and report information internally in organizations, today's management accountants are expected to have expertise in cost management, performance measurement, and risk management. Moreover, they play a key role in decision making across the various functional areas of an organization. From operational-level decisions related to quality control to strategic planning decisions about the products to offer and the markets in which the company will compete, management accountants can add value. Moreover, given the growing emphasis on social and environmental responsibility, management accountants have to be more aware of the needs and concerns of a broader set of stakeholders than ever before. Identifying, understanding, and addressing the expectations of suppliers, customers, employees, and the communities in which the organization operates are now central to the role of management accountants.

In fulfilling their complex responsibilities, management accountants are expected to adhere strictly to a high standard of professional ethics. Indeed, the ethical behaviour of accountants in organizations has come under increasing scrutiny in recent years with the spate of corporate scandals in North America and elsewhere. Codes of professional ethics for management accountants typically contain standards related to competence, confidentiality, integrity, and credibility. Serious breaches of one or more of these standards can result in severe consequences, including expulsion from the professional body that granted the professional accountant's designation.

Given the breadth of responsibilities, the expertise requirements, and the challenge of working in an increasingly global marketplace, managerial accounting offers the potential for a very rewarding career.

Source: Certified Management Accountants, *What Is a CMA?* http://www.cma-canada.org/index.cfm?ci_id=4442&la_id=1; and Giuseppe Valiante, "Data Tracker Makes Tracks," *Financial Post*, November 2, 2009.

Managerial accounting concerns providing information to managers—that is, people inside an organization who direct and control its operations. In contrast, **financial accounting** concerns providing information to shareholders, creditors, and others who are outside an organization. Managerial accounting provides data that help organizations run more efficiently. Financial accounting provides the scorecard by which a company's past performance is judged.

Managerial accounting concerns determining and developing internal accounting information as a tool for helping managers make business decisions that satisfy customers while continuously monitoring costs and improving efficiencies. This requires management accountants to prepare a variety of reports. Some reports compare actual results to plans and to benchmarks focusing on how well managers or business units have performed. Other reports provide timely updates on key indicators, such as orders received, capacity utilization, customer satisfaction, and sales. Reports may also be prepared as needed to help investigate specific problems, such as a decline in profitability of a product line, or to help decide whether to outsource some of the business operations. In contrast, financial accounting focuses on producing a limited set of specific quarterly and annual financial statements in accordance with generally accepted accounting principles (GAAP) and government regulations.

Because managerial accounting is manager oriented, its study must be preceded by some understanding of what managers do, the information managers need, and the general business environment. Accordingly, the purpose of this chapter is to briefly examine these subjects.

Managerial accounting
The form of accounting concerning providing information to managers for use in planning and controlling operations and for decision making.

Financial accounting
The form of accounting concerning providing information to shareholders, creditors, and others outside the organization.

THE WORK OF MANAGERS AND THEIR NEED FOR MANAGERIAL ACCOUNTING INFORMATION

Every organization—large and small—has managers who perform several major activities—*planning, directing and motivating, controlling,* and *decision making.* **Planning** involves establishing goals and specifying how to achieve them. **Directing and motivating** involve mobilizing people to carry out plans and run routine operations. **Controlling** involves gathering feedback to ensure that the plan is being properly executed or modified as circumstances change. **Decision making** involves selecting a course of action from competing alternatives. Managerial accounting information plays a vital role in these basic management activities; below we take a closer look at each.

Planning

Assume that you work for TD Canada Trust and that you are in charge of the company's campus recruiting for all undergraduate business majors. In this example, your planning process begins by establishing a goal such as this: to recruit the best and brightest university and college graduates. The next stage of the planning process requires specifying how to achieve this goal by answering numerous questions:

- How many students do we need to hire in total and from each major?
- What schools do we plan to include in our recruiting efforts?
- How will we compare students to one another to decide who will be extended job offers?
- What salary will we offer our new hires?
- How much money can we spend on our recruiting efforts?

Plans are often accompanied by a **budget.** A budget is a detailed plan for the future that is usually expressed in formal quantitative terms. As the head of campus recruiting at TD Canada Trust, your budget includes two key components. First, you

LEARNING OBJECTIVE
Describe the functions performed by managers.

Planning
Developing goals and specifying how to achieve them.

Directing and motivating
Mobilizing people to carry out plans and run routine operations.

Controlling
Gathering feedback to ensure that the plan is being properly executed or modified as necessary.

Decision making
Selecting a course of action from among alternatives.

Budget
A quantitative plan for acquiring and using financial and other resources over a specified future time period.

Controller
The manager in charge of the accounting department in an organization.

must work with other senior managers inside the company to establish a budgeted amount of total salaries that can be offered to all new hires. Second, you must create a budget that quantifies how much you intend to spend on your campus recruiting activities. Budgets are usually prepared on an annual basis under the overall direction of the **controller**, who is the manager in charge of the accounting department. Chapter 9 examines the budget preparation process in detail.

Directing and Motivating

In addition to planning for the future, managers must oversee day-to-day activities and keep the organization functioning smoothly. This requires motivating and directing people. Managers assign tasks to employees, arbitrate disputes, answer questions, solve on-the-spot problems, and make many small decisions that affect customers and employees. For example, managers at TD Canada Trust need to assign specific employees the task of scheduling and conducting student interviews. Other employees are charged with determining the appropriate salary level for new hires. Moreover, managers need to establish procedures for resolving differences in opinion that inevitably arise when deciding which students should receive job offers. In effect, directing is the part of managers' activities that deals with the routine and the here and now. Managerial accounting data, such as daily sales reports, are often used in this type of day-to-day decision making.

Controlling

Once you have established and started implementing TD Canada Trust's recruiting plan, you transition to the control process. This process involves gathering, evaluating, and responding to feedback to ensure that this year's recruiting process meets expectations. It also includes evaluating the feedback to find ways to run a more effective recruiting campaign next year. The control process involves answering questions such as these:

- Did we succeed in hiring the planned number of students within each major and at each school?
- Is our method of comparing students to one another working?
- Did we stay within our budget for total salary commitments to new hires?
- Did we stay within our budget for spending on recruiting activities?

Performance reports
Detailed reports prepared on a periodic basis that compare budgeted data to actual data.

As you can see, many questions need to be answered as part of the control process. When answering these questions, your goal is to go beyond simple yes or no answers to find out why performance exceeded or failed to meet expectations. Part of the control process includes preparing **performance reports**. A performance report compares budgeted data to actual data on a periodic basis, usually monthly, to identify and learn from excellent performance and to identify and eliminate sources of unsatisfactory performance. Performance reports can also be used as one of many inputs to help evaluate and reward employees. Chapters 9, 10, and 11 include examples of different types of performance reports used by organizations.

Although our example focused on TD Canada Trust's campus recruiting efforts, we could have described how planning enables companies such as BCE, Rogers, and Telus to continuously improve their cellular networks, or how it helped NAD Electronics develop and market its home audio systems. We could have discussed how the control process helps Pfizer and Eli Lilly ensure that their pharmaceutical drugs are produced in conformance with rigorous quality standards, or how Sobeys relies on the control process to keep its grocery shelves stocked. We could also have looked at planning and control failures such as BP's massive oil spill in the Gulf of Mexico. In short, all managers perform planning and controlling activities.

EXHIBIT 1–1   Examples of Decisions

What should we be selling?	Whom should we be serving?	How should we execute?
What products and services should be the focus of our marketing efforts?	Who should be the focus of our marketing efforts?	How should we supply our parts and services?
What new products and services should we offer?	Whom should we start serving?	How should we expand our capacity?
What prices should we charge for our products and services?	Who should pay price premiums or receive price discounts?	How should we reduce our capacity?
What products and services should we discontinue?	Whom should we stop serving?	How should we improve our efficiency and effectiveness?

Decision Making

Perhaps the most basic managerial skill is the ability to make intelligent, data-driven decisions. Broadly speaking, many of those decisions revolve around the following three questions. *What* should we be selling? *Whom* should we be serving? *How* should we execute? Exhibit 1–1 provides examples of decisions pertaining to each of these three categories.

The left-hand column of Exhibit 1–1 suggests that every company must make decisions related to the products and services that it sells. For example, each year Rogers must decide how to allocate its marketing budget across the various products and services it sells. Air Canada must decide what ticket prices to establish for each of its approximately 1,500 flights per day. Paradigm Electronics must decide whether to discontinue certain models of home theatre speakers.

The middle column of Exhibit 1–1 indicates that all companies must make decisions related to the customers that they serve. For example, Sears Canada must decide how to allocate its marketing budget between products that tend to appeal to male versus female customers. FedEx must decide whether to expand its services into new markets across the globe. Royal Bank of Canada must decide whether to discontinue customers that may be unprofitable.

The right-hand column of Exhibit 1–1 shows that companies also make decisions related to how they execute. For example, Bombardier must decide whether to rely on outside vendors to manufacture many of the parts used to make its airplanes. In an economic downturn, a manufacturer might have to decide whether to eliminate one eight-hour shift at three plants or to close one plant. Finally, all companies have to decide among competing improvement opportunities. For example, a company may have to decide whether to implement a new software system, to upgrade a piece of equipment, or to provide extra training to its employees.

The Planning and Control Cycle

The work of management discussed in this part of the chapter is summarized in the model shown in Exhibit 1–2. The model, which depicts the **planning and control cycle**, illustrates the smooth flow of management activities from planning through directing and motivating, controlling, and then back to planning again. All of these activities involve decision making, so it is depicted as the hub around which the other activities revolve.

Managerial accounting can help serve the information needs of managers in all phases of the planning and control cycle. The management accountant can prepare detailed reports that managers need to make both day-to-day and long-term decisions, and also prepare budgets to help direct resources toward the organization's goals. Later, the management accountant compares actual costs and revenues with

Planning and control cycle
The flow of management activities through planning, directing and motivating, and controlling, and then back to planning again.

EXHIBIT 1-2 The Planning and Control Cycle

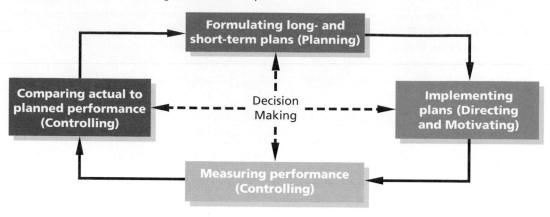

the budgeted figures and prepares reports to inform management about any significant variances from budget. Management information needs vary from business to business, but as you work your way through this book, you will be introduced to many of the tools that management accountants use to meet these needs.

Strategy

As a fundamental element of the planning and control cycle, companies must have a viable *strategy* for succeeding in the marketplace. A **strategy** is a game plan that enables a company to attract and retain customers by distinguishing itself from competitors. The focal point of a company's strategy should be its target customers. A company can succeed only if it creates a reason for customers to choose it over a competitor. These reasons, or what are more formally called *customer value propositions*, are the essence of strategy.

Customer value propositions tend to fall into three broad categories—*customer intimacy, operational excellence*, and *product leadership*. Companies that adopt a *customer intimacy* strategy are in essence saying to their target customers, "You should choose us because we understand and respond to your individual needs better than our competitors do." Cisco Systems, The Keg Steakhouse & Bar, and Dell Computer Corporation rely primarily on a customer intimacy value proposition for their success. Companies that pursue the second customer value proposition, called *operational excellence*, are saying to their target customers, "You should choose us because we can deliver products and services faster, more conveniently, and at a lower price than our competitors." WestJet, Winners, and Canadian National Railway are examples of companies that succeed first and foremost because of their operational excellence. Companies pursuing the third customer value proposition, called *product leadership*, are saying to their target customers, "You should choose us because we offer higher-quality products than our competitors." Cervélo, SABIAN Cymbals, and NAD Electronics are examples of companies that succeed because of their product leadership. Although a company may offer its customers a combination of these three customer value propositions, one usually outweighs the others in terms of importance.[1]

Managerial accounting plays a critical role in providing information to management to facilitate implementing and monitoring strategy. For example, many companies employ sophisticated performance measurement systems, such as the balanced scorecard (discussed in Chapter 11), that track performance on key metrics that management believes are critical to the success of the chosen strategy. Given that the focal point of strategy is the target customers, not surprisingly many of the metrics used by organizations focus on the target customers (e.g., customer satisfaction, number of new products available to customers, number of customer complaints) and on key internal processes that relate to serving customers (e.g., research and development, delivery time).

IN BUSINESS

Some planning decisions made by managers require considerable financial resources to implement and thus require very careful consideration before deciding to proceed. For example, Canadian Pacific, a railway company, announced in May 2013 that capital spending plans for 2013 had been increased by $100 million, bringing the total planned spending to over $1 billion for the year. Much of the planned spending by Canadian Pacific in 2013 was for track upgrades and improvements to signal systems in response to strong demand for its rail shipping services. In deciding to proceed with the capital spending plans, management at Canadian Pacific would have considered the estimated costs involved and the anticipated benefits of the increased demand for its services.

Source: Reuters, "CP Rail to Increase 2013 Spending by up to C$100 Million," http://www.reuters.com/article/2013/05/07/cprailway-spending-idUSL2N0DO2GY20130507, May 7, 2013; *Canadian Pacific*, http://www.cpr.ca/en/news-and-media/news/Pages/cp-increases-2013-capital-investment-program.aspx.

◼ COMPARISON OF FINANCIAL AND MANAGERIAL ACCOUNTING

Financial accounting reports are prepared for external parties, such as shareholders and creditors, whereas managerial accounting reports are prepared for managers inside the organization. This contrast results in a number of major differences between financial and managerial accounting, even though both financial and managerial accounting typically rely on the same underlying financial data. These differences are summarized in Exhibit 1–3.

LEARNING OBJECTIVE 2
Identify the major differences and similarities between financial and managerial accounting.

As shown in Exhibit 1–3, in addition to the reports being prepared for different people, financial and managerial accounting also differ in their emphasis between the past and the future, in the type of data provided to users, and in several other ways. These differences are discussed in the following sections.

Emphasis on the Future

Since *planning* is such an important part of the manager's job, managerial accounting has a strong future orientation. In contrast, financial accounting primarily summarizes past financial transactions. These summaries may be useful in planning, but only to a point. The future is not simply a reflection of what has happened in the past. Changes are constantly taking place in economic conditions, customer needs and desires, competitive conditions, and so on. All of these changes demand that managers' planning be based in large part on estimates of what will happen rather than on summaries of what has already happened.

Relevance of Data

Financial accounting data are expected to be objective and verifiable. However, for internal use, the manager wants information that is relevant even if it is not completely objective or verifiable. By relevant, we mean *appropriate for the problem at hand*. For example, it is difficult to verify estimated sales volumes for a new product, but this is exactly the type of information that is most useful to managers in their decision making. Managerial accounting should be flexible enough to provide whatever data are relevant for a particular decision.

Less Emphasis on Precision

Making sure that amounts are accurate down to the last dollar takes time and effort. While that kind of accuracy is desirable for external reports, most managers would

EXHIBIT 1–3   Comparison of Financial and Management Accounting

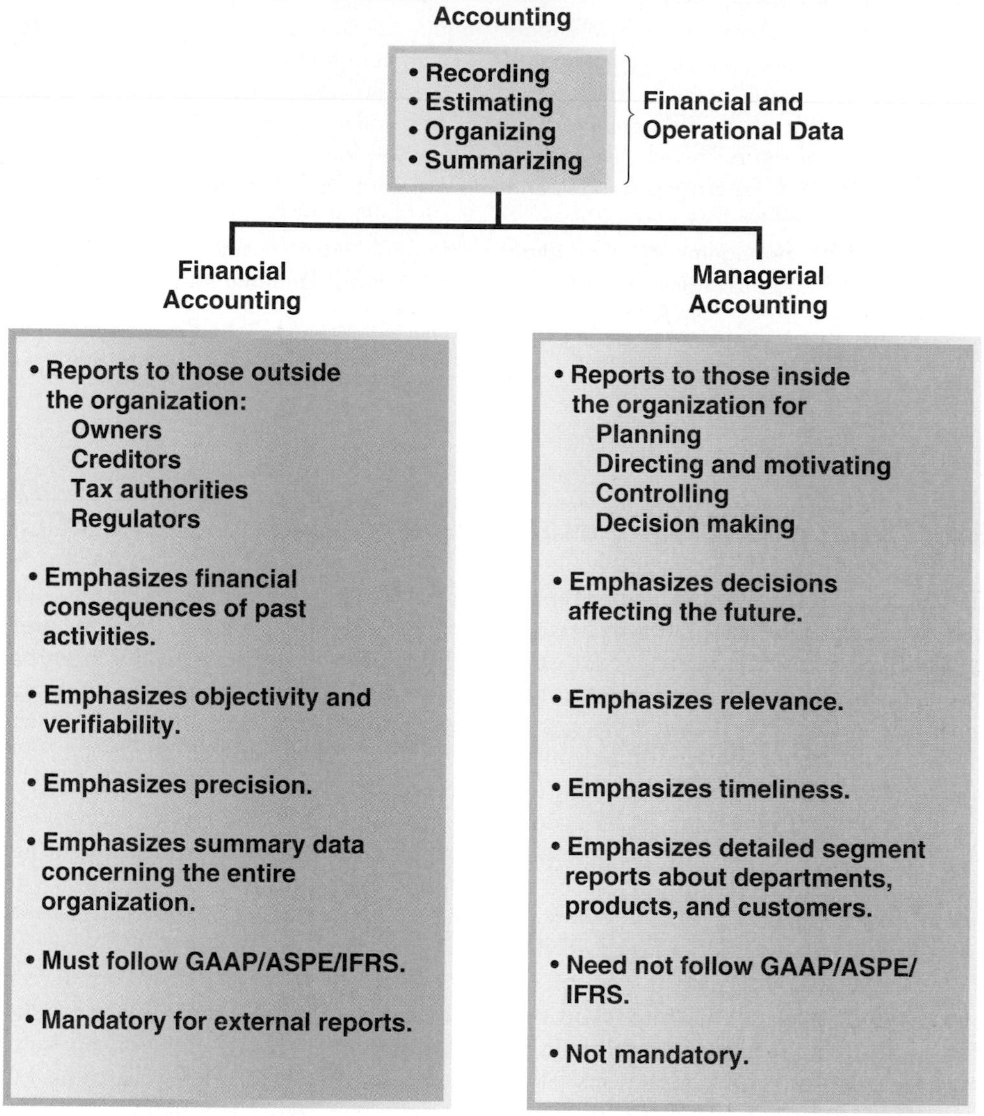

Accounting

- Recording
- Estimating
- Organizing
- Summarizing

Financial and Operational Data

Financial Accounting

- **Reports to those outside the organization:**
  Owners
  Creditors
  Tax authorities
  Regulators

- **Emphasizes financial consequences of past activities.**

- **Emphasizes objectivity and verifiability.**

- **Emphasizes precision.**

- **Emphasizes summary data concerning the entire organization.**

- **Must follow GAAP/ASPE/IFRS.**

- **Mandatory for external reports.**

Managerial Accounting

- **Reports to those inside the organization for**
  Planning
  Directing and motivating
  Controlling
  Decision making

- **Emphasizes decisions affecting the future.**

- **Emphasizes relevance.**

- **Emphasizes timeliness.**

- **Emphasizes detailed segment reports about departments, products, and customers.**

- **Need not follow GAAP/ASPE/IFRS.**

- **Not mandatory.**

rather have an immediate estimate than wait for a more precise answer. For this reason, management accountants often place less emphasis on precision than do financial accountants. For example, in a decision involving hundreds of millions of dollars, estimates that are rounded to the nearest million dollars are probably good enough. In addition to placing less emphasis on precision than financial accounting, managerial accounting places more importance on non-financial data. For example, data about customer satisfaction gathered through surveys or focus groups may be routinely used in managerial accounting reports.

Segments of an Organization

Financial accounting is primarily concerned with reporting for the company as a whole. By contrast, managerial accounting focuses much more on the parts, or **segments**, of a company. These segments can be evaluated independently from other parts of the organization and may be product lines, customers, sales territories, divisions, departments, or any other categorization of the company's activities for which management finds it useful to have financial data. Financial accounting does require some breakdowns of revenues and costs by major segments in external

Segments
Any parts of an organization that can be evaluated independently of other parts and about which the manager seeks financial data.

reports, but this is a secondary emphasis. In managerial accounting, segment reporting is the primary emphasis.

Generally Accepted Accounting Principles

Financial accounting statements prepared for external users must be prepared in accordance with generally accepted accounting principles (GAAP). External users must have some assurance that the reports have been prepared in accordance with some common set of ground rules. Beginning January 1, 2011, Canada joined more than 100 other countries, including Australia, New Zealand, and European Union member countries, in adopting International Financial Reporting Standards (IFRS) for publicly accountable enterprises. As of that date, in Canada, IFRS became GAAP for public companies. The purpose of IFRS is simple: to enhance the comparability and clarity of financial information on a global basis. Given the increasing degree of globalization of the economy and the interconnectedness of capital markets, accounting standard setters in Canada concluded that it was crucial to adopt IFRS.[2] Private companies and not-for-profit organizations are not required to adopt IFRS but instead can use accounting standards for private enterprises (ASPE). While the common ground rules established by IFRS will enhance comparability across external reporting jurisdictions, they do not necessarily lead to the type of reports that would be most useful in internal decision making since they are still based on historical information.

Because managerial accounting is not bound by GAAP, managers are free to determine the content and form of internal reports to best suit the needs of the organization. The only constraint is that the expected benefits from using the information should outweigh the costs of collecting, analyzing, and summarizing the data. Nevertheless, as we will see in subsequent chapters, financial reporting requirements have heavily influenced managerial accounting practice.

Managerial Accounting—Not Mandatory

Financial accounting is mandatory; that is, it must be done. Various outside parties, such as the provincial and territorial securities regulators and the tax authorities, require periodic financial statements. Managerial accounting, on the other hand, is not mandatory. A company is completely free to do as much or as little as it wishes. No regulatory bodies or other outside agencies specify what is to be done or, for that matter, whether anything is to be done at all. Since managerial accounting is completely optional, the important question is always "Is the information useful?" rather than "Is the information required?"

■ ORGANIZATIONAL STRUCTURE

Management must accomplish its objectives by working with and relying on employees. This is done by creating an organizational structure that permits effective *decentralization* of management decisions.

Decentralization

Decentralization is the delegation of decision making throughout an organization by providing managers at various operating levels with the authority to make key decisions relating to their areas of responsibility. Some organizations are more decentralized than others.

We will use the organizational structure depicted in Exhibit 1–4 of a hypothetical company, Metro Coffee, to illustrate the key concepts in this section. Metro Coffee's president (often synonymous with the term *chief executive officer* or *CEO*) sets the broad strategy for the company and makes major strategic decisions (such as

LEARNING OBJECTIVE ❸
Describe the role of management accountants in an organization.

Decentralization
The delegation of decision making throughout an organization by providing managers at various operating levels with the authority to make key decisions relating to their areas of responsibility.

EXHIBIT 1–4   Organization Chart: Metro Coffee Inc.

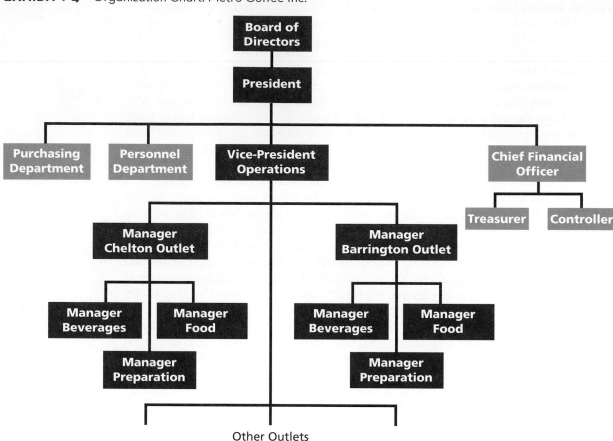

Other Outlets

those related to opening stores in new markets), but much of the remaining decision-making authority is delegated to managers on various levels throughout the organization. Metro Coffee has a number of outlets, each of which has a store manager as well as a separate manager for each major aspect of the store's operations, such as beverages, food, and preparation. In addition, the company has support departments, such as a central Purchasing Department and a Personnel Department, that provide services for all outlets.

    The arrangement of boxes shown in Exhibit 1–4 is called an **organization chart**. The purpose of an organization chart is to show how responsibility has been divided among managers and to show formal lines of reporting and communication, or the *chain of command*. Each box depicts an area of management responsibility, and the lines between the boxes show the lines of formal authority between managers. The chart tells us, for example, that the store managers are responsible to the operations vice-president. In turn, the latter is responsible to the company president, who in turn is responsible to the board of directors. Following the lines of authority and communication on the organization chart, we can see that the manager of the Chelton outlet would ordinarily report to the operations vice-president rather than directly to the president of the company.

Line and Staff Relationships

An organization chart also depicts *line* and *staff* positions in an organization. A person in a **line position** is *directly* involved in achieving the basic objectives of the organization. A person in a **staff position**, by contrast, is only *indirectly* involved in achieving those basic objectives. Staff positions *support* or provide assistance to line positions or other parts of the organization, but they do not have direct authority

Organization chart
A diagram of a firm's organizational structure that depicts formal lines of reporting, communication, and responsibility between managers.

Line position
A job position that is directly related to the achievement of the organization's basic objectives.

Staff position
A job position that is only indirectly related to the achievement of the organization's basic objectives. Such positions are supportive in nature in that they provide service or assistance to line positions or to other staff positions.

over line positions. Refer again to the organization chart in Exhibit 1–4. Since the basic objective of Metro Coffee is to sell food and beverages at a profit, those managers whose areas of responsibility are directly related to the sales effort occupy line positions. These positions, which are shown in a darker colour in the exhibit, include the managers of the various departments in each outlet, the outlet managers, the operations vice-president, and members of top management.

By contrast, the manager of the central Purchasing Department occupies a staff position, since the only function of the Purchasing Department is to support and serve the line departments by doing their purchasing for them. However, both line and staff managers have authority over the employees in their own departments.

The Controller

In Canada, the manager in charge of the Accounting Department is usually known as the *controller*. The controller reports to the *chief financial officer* (CFO). Both the controller and the CFO are staff positions. The CFO is the member of the top-management team who is responsible for providing relevant and timely data to support planning and control activities and for preparing financial statements for external users. The controller is responsible for the more technical details of accounting and finance, provides leadership to other professionals in her or his department, and analyzes new and evolving situations. An effective controller is able to work well with top managers from other disciplines and can communicate technical information in a simple and clear manner.

■ BUSINESS PROCESS MANAGEMENT

A key challenge for managers is to continuously improve the *business processes* that serve customers. A **business process** is a series of steps that are followed to carry out some task or activity in a business. It is quite common for the linked set of steps making up a business process to span departmental boundaries. The term *value chain* is often used when we look at how the functional departments of an organization interact with one another to form business processes. A **value chain**, as shown in Exhibit 1–5, consists of the major business functions that add value to a company's products and services. The customer's needs are most effectively met by coordinating the business processes that span these functions.

This section briefly discusses three topics related to managing and improving business processes—lean production, enterprise systems, and risk management. Although each topic is unique, they all share the common theme of focusing on managing and improving business processes.

Lean Production

Lean production is a management approach that organizes resources such as people and machines around the flow of business processes and that only produces units in response to customer orders. It is often called **just-in-time (JIT) production** because products are only manufactured in response to customer orders and they are completed just in time to be shipped to customers. Lean thinking differs from traditional manufacturing methods, which organize work departmentally and encourage those

EXHIBIT 1–5 Business Functions Making up the Value Chain

Research and Development	Product Design	Manufacturing	Marketing	Distribution	Customer Service

IN BUSINESS

Tesco, a grocery retailer in Britain, used lean thinking to improve its replenishment process for cola products. Tesco and Britvic (its cola supplier) traced the cola delivery process from "the checkout counter of the grocery store through Tesco's regional distribution center (RDC), Britvic's RDC, the warehouse at the Britvic bottling plant, the filling lines for cola destined for Tesco, and the warehouse of Britvic's can supplier." Each step of the process revealed enormous waste. Tesco implemented numerous changes, such as electronically linking its point-of-sale data from its grocery stores to its RDC. This change let customers pace the replenishment process, and it helped increase store delivery frequency to every few hours around the clock. Britvic also began delivering cola to Tesco's RDC in wheeled dollies that could be rolled directly into delivery trucks and then to point-of-sale locations in grocery stores.

These changes reduced the total product "touches" from 150 to 50, thereby cutting labour costs. The elapsed time from the supplier's filling line to the customer's cola purchase dropped from 20 days to 5 days. The number of inventory stocking locations declined from five to two, and the supplier's distribution centre was eliminated.

Source: Ghostwriter, "Teaching the Big Box New Tricks," *Fortune*, November 14, 2005, pp. 208B–208F.

departments to maximize their output even if it exceeds customer demand and bloats inventories. Because lean thinking only allows production in response to customer orders, the number of units produced tends to equal the number of units sold, resulting in minimal inventory. The lean approach also results in fewer defects, less wasted effort, and quicker customer response times than traditional production methods.

Enterprise Systems

Historically, companies often implemented specific software programs to support specific business functions. For example, the accounting department would select its own software applications to meet its needs, while manufacturing would select different software programs to support its needs. The separate systems were usually not integrated, so data could not easily be exchanged between them. The result was data duplication, inconsistencies, and errors, coupled with lengthy customer response times and high costs.

An **enterprise system** is designed to overcome these problems by integrating data across an organization into a single software system that enables all employees to have simultaneous access to a common set of data. The data integration inherent in an enterprise system has two elements. First, all data are recorded only once in the company's centralized digital data repository, the *database*. When data are added to the database or are changed, the new information is simultaneously and immediately available to everyone across the organization that has access to the system. Second, the unique data elements contained within the database can be linked. For example, one data element, such as a customer identification number, can be related to other data elements, such as that customer's address, billing history, shipping history, merchandise returns history, and so on. The ability to establish such relationships among data elements explains why this type of database is called a *relational database*.

Data integration helps employees communicate with one another and with their suppliers and customers. For example, consider how the *customer relationship management* process improves when enterprisewide information resides in one location. Whether meeting the customer's needs requires accessing information related to billing (an accounting function), delivery status (a distribution function), price quotes (a marketing function), or merchandise returns (a customer service function), the required information is readily available to the employee interacting

Enterprise system
A software system designed to overcome problems in data duplication, inconsistencies, and errors by integrating data across an organization into a single software system.

with the customer. Although data integration is expensive, its benefits have led many companies to invest in enterprise systems.

Risk Management

Businesses face risks every day. Some risks are foreseeable. For example, a company could reasonably be expected to foresee the possibility of a natural disaster or a fire destroying its centralized data storage facility. Companies respond to this type of risk by maintaining off-site backup data storage facilities. Other risks are unforeseeable. As an example, in March 2010, Bauer Hockey Corp. announced a recall of 13 different models of its junior and youth hockey sticks, most of which were manufactured in China prior to 2008. The reason for the recall was that the yellow paint used on the sticks contained lead in excess of allowable limits. Lead can cause adverse health consequences if ingested by children. Estimates indicate that worldwide, as many as 100,000 of these sticks were sold between 2006 and 2010, including nearly 70,000 in Canada.[3] The financial consequences of such recalls can be significant and could include Bauer's cost of replacing the sticks returned by customers, potential lost sales due to consumer concerns about the safety of the product, and lawsuits arising from health issues related to product use.

Every business strategy or decision involves risks. **Enterprise risk management** is a process used by a company to proactively identify and manage those risks.

Enterprise risk management
A process used by a company to proactively identify and manage foreseeable risks.

Identifying and Controlling Business Risks   Companies should identify foreseeable risks before they occur rather than react to unfortunate events that have already happened. The left-hand column of Exhibit 1–6 provides 12 examples of

---

EXHIBIT 1–6   Identifying and Controlling Business Risks

Examples of Business Risks	Examples of Controls to Reduce Business Risks
• Intellectual assets being stolen from computer files	• Create firewalls that prohibit computer hackers from corrupting or stealing intellectual property.
• Products harming customers	• Develop a formal and rigorous new product–testing program.
• Losing market share due to the unforeseen actions of competitors	• Develop an approach for legally gathering information about competitors' plans and practices.
• Poor weather conditions shutting down operations	• Develop contingency plans for overcoming weather-related disruptions.
• A website malfunctioning	• Thoroughly test the website before going "live" on the Internet.
• A supplier strike halting the flow of raw materials	• Establish a relationship with two companies capable of providing needed raw materials.
• A poorly designed incentive scheme causing employees to make bad or high-risk decisions	• Create a balanced set of performance measures that motivate the desired behaviour.
• Financial statements inaccurately reporting the value of inventory	• Count the physical inventory on hand to make sure that it agrees with the accounting records.
• An employee stealing assets	• Segregate duties so that the same employee does not have physical custody of an asset and the responsibility of accounting for it.
• An employee accessing unauthorized information	• Create password-protected data access that prevents employees from obtaining information not needed to do their jobs.
• Inaccurate budget estimates causing excessive or insufficient production	• Implement a rigorous budget review process.
• Failing to comply with equal employment opportunity laws	• Create a report that tracks key metrics related to compliance with the laws.

IN BUSINESS

Some business risks cannot easily be controlled. For example, General Motors had to halt production at its plant in Oshawa, Ontario, in late 2012 because of a strike at one of its key suppliers, Lear Corp. General Motors had no ready alternative source of supply for the seats supplied by Lear Corp. that are used in many of its vehicles. As a result, the strike at Lear Corp. had the unfortunate consequence of disrupting production at General Motors. Risks such as an interruption in the supply of raw materials can have serious negative effects on a company and its employees. At General Motors, over 4,000 employees were affected by the halt in production, and while it was ongoing, some had their wages reduced by 35%.

Source: Dana Flavelle, "GM Plant in Oshawa Hit by Supplier Strike," *thestar.com, Business,* http://www.thestar.com/business/2012/10/29/gm_plant_in_oshawa_hit_by_supplier_strike.html, October 29, 2012; Greg Keenan, "GM Halts Oshawa Plant over Strike at Supplier Lear," *The Globe and Mail,* http://www.theglobeandmail.com/globe-investor/gm-halts-oshawa-plant-over-strike-at-supplier-lear/article4727800/.

business risks. This list is not exhaustive; rather its purpose is to illustrate the diverse nature of business risks that companies face. Whether the risks relate to the weather, computer hackers, complying with the law, employee theft, financial reporting, or strategic decision making, they all have one thing in common: if the risks are not managed effectively, they can impair a company's ability to meet its goals.

Once a company identifies its risks, it can respond to them in various ways, such as accepting, avoiding, sharing, or reducing the risk. Perhaps the most common risk management tactic is to reduce risks by implementing specific controls. The right-hand column of Exhibit 1–6 provides an example of a control that could be implemented to help reduce each of the risks mentioned in the left-hand column of the exhibit.

In conclusion, a sophisticated enterprise risk management system cannot guarantee that all risks are eliminated. Nonetheless, many companies understand that managing risks is superior to reacting, perhaps too late, to unfortunate events.

ETHICS, CORPORATE GOVERNANCE, AND CORPORATE SOCIAL RESPONSIBILITY

LEARNING OBJECTIVE 5
Explain the nature and importance of ethics for accountants, the role of corporate governance, and corporate social responsibility.

A series of high-profile financial scandals in the public and private sectors have raised deep concerns about ethics in business and government.[4] There are good reasons for companies to be concerned about their ethical reputation. A company that is not trusted by its customers, employees, and suppliers will eventually suffer. In the short run, virtue is sometimes its own reward, but in the long run, business ethics should be taken seriously because the very survival of the company may depend on the level of trust held by its stakeholders.

Professional accounting organizations are given the right of association and certain rights of self-government by provincial and territorial governments in Canada. One inherent requirement of such rights is an expression of public service in the form of a code of ethics. Each accounting organization is then permitted to operate according to the laws of the country, using its code of ethics as an operating guideline. Typically, these codes contain details of how members should conduct themselves in their dealings with the public, their association, and other members. For example, accountants must maintain a level of competence appropriate to their designation. Confidentiality is essential because of the importance of the information they analyze. Integrity is maintained by avoiding conflicts of interest with their employers or clients, by communicating the limits of professional competence, and by not accepting favours that would compromise their judgment. Objectivity must be present in communications, so that recipients can receive both favourable and unfavourable information.

EXHIBIT 1–7   Professional Misconduct and Code of Professional Ethics Regulation

All Members, Students and Firms will adhere to the following Code of Professional Ethics of CMA Ontario:

(1) A Member, Student or Firm will act at all times with:

(a) responsibility for and fidelity to public needs;

(b) fairness and loyalty to such Member's, Student's or Firm's associates, clients and employers; and

(c) competence through devotion to high ideals of personal honour and professional integrity.

(2) A Member, Student or Firm will:

(a) maintain at all times independence of thought and action;

(b) not express an opinion on financial reports or statements without first assessing her or his relationship with her or his client to determine whether such Member, Student or Firm might expect her or his opinion to be considered independent, objective and unbiased by one who has knowledge of all the facts; and

(c) when preparing financial reports or statements or expressing an opinion on financial reports or statements, disclose all material facts known to such Member, Student or Firm in order not to make such financial reports or statements misleading, acquire sufficient information to warrant an expression of opinion and report all material misstatements or departures from generally accepted accounting principles.

(3) A Member, Student or Firm will:

(a) not disclose or use any confidential information concerning the affairs of such Member's, Student's or Firm's employer or client unless authorized to do so or except when such information is required to be disclosed in the course of any defence of himself or herself or any associate or employee in any lawsuit or other legal proceeding or against alleged professional misconduct by order of lawful authority of the Board or any committee of CMA Ontario in the proper exercise of their duties but only to the extent necessary for such purpose and only as permitted by law;

(b) inform his or her employer or client of any business connections or interests of which such Member's, Student's or Firm's employer or client would reasonably expect to be informed;

(c) not, in the course of exercising his or her duties on behalf of such Member's, Student's or Firm's employer or client, hold, receive, bargain for or acquire any fee, remuneration or benefit without such employer's or client's knowledge and consent;

(d) take all reasonable steps, in arranging any engagement as a consultant, to establish a clear understanding of the scope and objectives of the work before it is commenced and will furnish the client with an estimate of cost, preferably before the engagement is commenced, but in any event as soon as possible thereafter.

(4) A Member, Student or Firm will:

(a) conduct himself or herself toward other Members, Students and Firms with courtesy and good faith;

(b) not commit an act discreditable to the profession;

(c) not engage in or counsel any business or occupation which, in the opinion of CMA Ontario, is incompatible with the professional ethics of a management accountant.

(5) A Member, Student or Firm will:

(a) at all times maintain the standards of competence expressed by the Board from time to time;

(b) disseminate the knowledge upon which the profession of management accounting is based to others within the profession and generally promote the advancement of the profession;

(c) undertake only such work as he or she is competent to perform by virtue of his or her training and experience and will, where it would be in the best interests of an employer or client, engage, or advise the employer or client to engage, other specialists.

Source: Adapted from Certified Management Accountants of Ontario, *Professional Misconduct and Code of Professional Ethics Regulation*, updated August 20, 2011. Reprinted by permission of Certified Management Accountants of Ontario.

Professional accountants must be familiar with their code of ethics because the rules for competence, confidentiality, integrity, and objectivity are complex in real situations. In addition, procedures for resolving complex situations should be known. Some codes of ethics give more extensive guidance than others. For example, the code shown in Exhibit 1–7 provides clear guidance concerning what professional ethical standards to follow.[5] Notice how the details of this code address the concepts of confidentiality, integrity, and objectivity discussed above.

Businesses are organizations comprising employees pursuing objectives (sometimes termed *missions*). These organizations have formal relationships among their employees, as illustrated by the organization chart earlier in this chapter. However, informal relationships and activities are also present that must focus on achieving the objectives of a wide group of people known as *stakeholders*. Stakeholders are people within and outside the organization who have an interest in the activities of the organization. Employees, shareholders, and creditors have an obvious interest in what the organization does, but so do the customers, the suppliers, the competitors, and the communities in which the organization operates. All of these stakeholders can benefit from the organization's undertakings, but they can also be harmed by these activities.

To reduce the likelihood that employees will engage in undesirable activities that may harm various stakeholders, many companies prepare a formal code of conduct to reflect their values and moral system. The document specifies what is expected of permanent and temporary employees in their dealings with the various stakeholders. Thus, the code reflects what the company stands for when it interacts through its employees with other stakeholders. Public companies often make their code of conduct available online. For example, the code of conduct for the Canadian Imperial Bank of Commerce (CIBC) provides standards for honesty and integrity, respect, conflicts of interest, community activities, and safeguarding information and assets. Moreover, codes of conduct often contain guidance on what employees should do upon observing a violation of one or more standards by a co-worker or superior. Through its code of conduct, a company can provide its members with specific guidance as to how their activities should be conducted to reflect the values needed to achieve the objectives of the organization.

Corporate Governance

Corporate governance
A system by which a company is directed and controlled.

Effective *corporate governance* enhances shareholders' confidence that a company is being run in their best interests rather than in the interests of top managers. Recent financial scandals have also increased the emphasis being placed on the development of good governance practices. **Corporate governance** is the system by which a company is directed and controlled. If properly implemented, the corporate governance system should provide incentives for the board of directors and top management to pursue objectives that are in the interests of the company's owners, and it should provide for effective monitoring of performance.[6] Many would argue that in addition to protecting the interests of shareholders, an effective corporate governance system should also protect the interests of the company's other stakeholders—its customers, creditors, employees, suppliers, and the communities within which it operates.

Unfortunately, history has repeatedly shown that unscrupulous top managers, if unchecked, will sometimes exploit their power to defraud stakeholders. This unpleasant reality became all too clear in 2001 when the fall of Enron kicked off a wave of corporate scandals involving financial reporting fraud and misuse of corporate funds at the very highest levels—including CEOs and CFOs. Collectively, these scandals are estimated to have cost shareholders billions of dollars. While this was disturbing in itself, it also indicated that the institutions intended to prevent such abuses weren't working, thus raising fundamental questions about the adequacy of the existing corporate governance system. In an attempt to respond to these concerns, the U.S. Congress passed the most important reform of corporate governance in many decades—*The Sarbanes-Oxley Act of 2002*. The Act applies to all publicly traded companies in the United States, including Canadian companies such as Barrick Gold, whose shares trade on a U.S. stock exchange. Some of the key aspects of the legislation are as follows:

- Requires the CEO and CFO to certify in writing that the financial statements fairly represent the results of operations. Certifying financial statements known to contain misrepresentations can lead to jail time for the CEO or CFO.

- Places the power to hire, compensate, and terminate the public accounting firm that audits a company's financial reports in the hands of the audit committee of the board of directors.
- Restricts the nature and extent of non-auditing services that can be provided by public accounting firms to companies that are their audit clients. Provision of non-audit services such as consulting can impair a public accounting firm's ability to act objectively when auditing the financial statements.
- Requires a company's annual report to contain an internal control report. Internal controls are established by management to assure shareholders and prospective investors that the financial statements are reliable. The report must contain a statement by management about the effectiveness of the internal controls.

The hope is that the provisions of the *Sarbanes-Oxley Act of 2002* will reduce the incidence of fraudulent financial reporting that so seriously shook the public's confidence in securities markets worldwide.

Corporate Social Responsibility

Companies are responsible for producing financial results that satisfy shareholders, but this must be balanced against the need to conduct operations and dealings in an ethical and morally responsible fashion. Organizations have a corporate social responsibility to serve other stakeholders—such as customers, employees, suppliers, communities, and environmental and human rights advocates—whose interests are tied to the company's performance. **Corporate social responsibility** (CSR) is a concept whereby organizations consider the needs of all stakeholders when making decisions. CSR extends beyond legal compliance to include voluntary actions that satisfy stakeholder expectations. Numerous companies, such as the Royal Bank of Canada, Unilever Canada, and Tim Hortons, prominently describe issues related to environmental sustainability and social responsibility

Corporate social responsibility
A concept whereby organizations consider the needs of all stakeholders when making decisions.

IN BUSINESS

Canada has had its share of corporate scandals in recent years, including the highly publicized events at Livent Inc., a theatre production company based in Toronto, Ontario. After a lengthy legal battle, Garth Drabinsky and Myron Gottlieb, co-founders of Livent Inc., were sentenced in August 2009 to jail for seven and six years, respectively, for their role in an accounting fraud that cost investors an estimated $500 million. The fraud, which involved misrepresentation of revenues and expenses in Livent Inc.'s financial statements, was perpetrated over several years, from 1993 to 1998. The fraud came to light beginning in August 1998 after Drabinsky and Gottlieb lost control of the financially troubled theatre company and the new management team began conducting an internal investigation. Despite having what appeared to be a strong board of directors and the fact that its financial statements were audited annually by a reputable accounting firm, Drabinsky and Gottlieb, both directly and indirectly through their influence on company employees, were still able to conceal their wrongdoing for an extended period. As Ontario Superior Court Justice Mary Lou Benotto noted during the sentencing hearing, "Mr. Drabinsky and Mr. Gottlieb presided over a corporation whose corporate culture was one of dishonesty."

Source: Theresa Tedesco, "The Final Act? Garth Drabinsky Faces the Music in Canada's First Major Prosecution of Alleged Accounting Fraud," May 3, 2008, *Financial Post*; Barbara Schecter, "Drabinsky Gets 7 Years, Gottlieb 6 for Fraud," August 5, 2009, *Financial Post*; Michel Magnan, Denis Cormier, and Pascale Lapointe-Antunes, "Corporate Fraud's Red Flag: Arrogance," December 1, 2009, *Financial Post*.

EXHIBIT 1–8   Examples of Corporate Social Responsibilities

Companies should provide *customers* with
- Safe, high-quality products that are fairly priced.
- Competent, courteous, and rapid delivery of products and services.
- Full disclosure of product-related risks.
- Easy-to-use information systems for shopping and tracking orders.

Companies should provide *suppliers* with
- Fair contract terms and prompt payments.
- Reasonable time to prepare orders.
- Hassle-free acceptance of timely and complete deliveries.
- Cooperative rather than unilateral actions.

Companies should provide *shareholders* with
- Competent management.
- Easy access to complete and accurate financial information.
- Full disclosure of enterprise risks.
- Honest answers to knowledgeable questions.

Companies and their suppliers should provide *employees* with
- Safe and humane working conditions.
- Non-discriminatory treatment and the right to organize and file grievances.
- Fair compensation.
- Opportunities for training, promotion, and personal development.

Companies should provide *communities* with
- Payment of fair taxes.
- Honest information about plans, such as plant closings.
- Resources that support charities, schools, and civic activities.
- Reasonable access to media sources.

Companies should provide *environmental and human rights advocates* with
- Greenhouse gas emissions data.
- Recycling and resource conservation data.
- Child labour transparency.
- Full disclosure of suppliers located in developing countries.

initiatives on their websites and prepare annual CSR reports that provide extensive details regarding these activities.

Exhibit 1–8 presents examples of CSRs that are of interest to six stakeholder groups. Many companies are paying increasing attention to these types of broadly defined responsibilities for four reasons. First, socially responsible investors control trillions of investment capital dollars. Companies that want access to this capital must excel in terms of their social performance. Second, a growing number of employees want to work for a company that recognizes and responds to its social responsibilities. If companies hope to recruit and retain these highly skilled employees, then they must offer fulfilling careers that serve the needs of broadly defined stakeholders. Third, many customers seek to purchase products and services from socially responsible companies. The Internet enables these customers to readily locate competing products, making it even easier to avoid doing business with undesirable companies. Fourth, non-government organizations (NGOs) and activists are more capable than ever of tarnishing a company's reputation by publicizing its environmental or human rights missteps. The Internet has enabled environmental and human rights advocacy groups to better organize their resources, spread negative information, and take coordinated actions against offending companies.[7]

IN BUSINESS

A survey conducted by Hewitt Associates, a human resources consulting and outsourcing company, shows that employees who believe their employer has a good record for CSR are more engaged in their work and more committed to their employer. Employers are also aware of this, as results from the same survey indicate that they believe the top three benefits for undertaking CSR initiatives are a positive organizational reputation, higher employee engagement, and a positive impact on the environment. A similar view of the importance of an organization's reputation for CSR to prospective employees is echoed by Mario Paron, chief human resources officer for KPMG LLG in Canada. He notes that "When [young recruits] are assessing their choices as to what type of organization they want to be associated with, the entire [CSR] and green aspects are definitely things they ask us about."

Sources: Hewitt Associates, "Research from Best Employers in Canada Study Builds Business Case for Investment in Corporate Social Responsibility," *Canada News Wire*, Ottawa, January 25, 2010; and Derek Sankey, "Jobs Blooming from Companies' Growing Green Focus," *National Post*, April 22, 2009.

It is important to understand that a company's social performance can affect its financial performance. For example, if a company's poor social performance alienates customers, then its revenues and profits will suffer. This explains why companies use enterprise risk management, as described earlier in this chapter, to meet the needs of all stakeholders.

SUMMARY

- Managerial accounting assists managers in carrying out their responsibilities, which include planning, directing and motivating, controlling, and decision making. **[LO1]**
- Managerial accounting differs substantially from financial accounting in that it is oriented more toward the future, places less emphasis on precision, emphasizes segments of an organization (rather than the organization as a whole), is not governed by generally accepted accounting principles, and is not mandatory. **[LO2]**
- Most organizations are decentralized to some degree. An organization chart depicts who works for whom in the organization, and which units perform the various staff and line functions. Accountants perform a staff function—they support and provide assistance to others inside the organization. **[LO3]**
- Lean production organizes resources around business processes and pulls units through those processes in response to customer orders. The result is lower inventories, fewer defects, less wasted effort, and quicker customer response times. **[LO4]**
- An enterprise system integrates data from across the organization in a single software system that makes the same data available to all managers. Risk management involves proactively identifying and managing key risks faced by an organization. **[LO4]**
- Many organizations prepare a code of conduct to reflect their values and the moral system under which they operate. Professional accounting organizations also have their own code of professional ethics to provide guidance for members, regardless of their place of employment. As an extension of the concept of organizational ethics, many companies have embraced corporate social responsibility, whereby the needs of numerous stakeholders are considered when making decisions. **[LO5]**

GLOSSARY

Review key terms and definitions on Connect.

DISCUSSION CASE

DISCUSSION CASE 1–1
Companies such as CIBC have developed a detailed code of conduct for their employees and often make this information publicly available by providing a copy of the code online. For example, the CIBC code of conduct can be found at http://www.cibc.com/ca/inside-cibc/governance/governance-practices/code-of-conduct.html.

Required:
If you are an employee at CIBC, what are some benefits of having such a detailed code of conduct? Might there be any disadvantages to CIBC in having such a detailed code of conduct?

QUESTIONS

1–1 What are the major differences between financial and managerial accounting?
1–2 Describe the four major activities of a manager.
1–3 What is a budget?
1–4 Describe the three broad categories of customer value propositions.
1–5 What are the four steps in the planning and control cycle?
1–6 Describe the responsibilities of the controller.
1–7 Distinguish between line and staff positions in an organization.
1–8 What is decentralization?
1–9 What are the six business functions that make up the value chain?
1–10 What are some examples of things socially responsible organizations should provide for their employees?
1–11 What is an enterprise system supposed to accomplish?
1–12 Why should companies be careful to maintain a good ethical reputation?
1–13 Why do companies prepare a code of conduct?
1–14 What are the four key aspects of the *Sarbanes-Oxley Act of 2002?*
1–15 Briefly describe what is meant by *enterprise risk management.*
1–16 What are some examples of common business risks faced by companies?

EXERCISES

EXERCISE 1–1 Functions Performed by Managers [LO1]
Each of the following independent examples involves one or more of the four major activities carried out by managers at Sights and Sounds, a manufacturer of high-quality televisions and audio equipment for home use: planning, directing and motivating, controlling, and decision making.

   i. Sales managers are developing estimates of next year's demand for the company's newest line of LCD televisions. This information will be used in preparing the annual budget.
  ii. In reviewing the monthly quality control reports, the production manager for home theatre systems has noticed that an unusually high number of units were discovered to have manufacturing defects. She is putting together a team of employees to investigate the problem.
 iii. Managers in the research and development department are developing a recommendation as to which of two alternative design choices the company should use for its line of floor speakers.
  iv. The most recent monthly performance report shows disappointing results for sales of the company's line of plasma televisions in May. Sales are well below budget, and the product manager for plasma televisions is evaluating several issues, including how retailers can be motivated to improve sales; the production schedule for the next three months; and, longer term, the possibility of discontinuing this product line.

Required:
For each example, select which of the four activities managers are carrying out and briefly explain the basis for your choice(s). Some examples may include more than one type of activity.

EXERCISE 1–2 Financial and Managerial Accounting [LO2]

Each of the following is primarily either financial accounting or managerial accounting in nature.

   i. Preparing an income statement for use in filing the company's annual corporate tax return with the Canada Revenue Agency.

  ii. Preparing an analysis of the profitability of each of the company's three major product lines for the past three months. The analysis will be used to make decisions related to resource allocation, potential changes in marketing strategy, and production scheduling.

 iii. Preparing a detailed schedule of accounts receivables balances that are more than 120 days past due to determine the allowance for doubtful accounts to be used in the year-end financial statements.

  iv. Estimating customer satisfaction by calculating the dollar value of all products returned in the past month and comparing it to returns in the same month last year.

   v. Preparing a detailed schedule of accounts receivables balances that are more than 120 days past due for only those customers who regularly purchase the company's products. The purpose of the analysis is to identify potential changes to the credit terms offered to regular customers (e.g., payment due dates, interest on overdue balances).

Required:

For each item above, briefly explain whether it is primarily financial accounting or primarily managerial accounting in nature.

EXERCISE 1–3 Risk Management and the Value Chain [LO4]

Sights and Sounds, a manufacturer of high-quality televisions and audio equipment for home use, has implemented the following controls as part of managing business risks.

   i. Security features on their online shopping website to prevent unauthorized access to customer credit card information.

  ii. Inspection of raw materials purchased from suppliers to reduce the likelihood of defective or substandard materials being used in production.

 iii. A licensing system for the company's products whereby to be a certified distributor, a retailer must satisfy several requirements related to location (e.g., total population), industry experience, store size, number of salespeople, etc.

  iv. Database firewalls that prevent hackers from accessing sensitive information on new products being developed.

   v. The use of consumer focus groups to pilot test new advertising campaigns to assess their appeal, clarity of messaging, and impact.

  vi. Rigorous testing protocols to ensure all new products are designed to comply with safety regulations before being put into production.

Required:

For each item, identify which of the six business functions that make up the value chain the control relates to most directly.

PROBLEMS

PROBLEM 1–4 Ethics in Business [LO5]

John Brigley, CPA, is the controller of Baden Foods, a large privately owned food processing company located in southern Ontario. Brigley received his designation as a certified professional accountant several years ago and has been working his way up the corporate ladder at Baden Foods. As controller, Brigley is responsible for coordinating the preparation of the annual operating budget, which includes projections of revenues and expenses for the coming year. Once the budget is approved by James Davis, the president of Baden Foods, it is used in the monthly performance report, which compares actual results to the budget projections.

To provide an incentive for the senior management team to make decisions that benefit the company as a whole, last year Davis established a bonus plan. In any month that the company's actual operating income (revenues minus expenses) is better than the budgeted amount, all members of the senior management team, including the CFO, the controller, the vice-president of Production, and the vice-president of Marketing, receive a bonus. Last year was the first year the new bonus plan was used, and bonuses were paid out in 5 of the 12 months of the fiscal year.

Late Friday afternoon, as Brigley was working on finalizing the operating budget for the upcoming fiscal year, he received a call from Jan Robson, the CFO at Baden Foods. The conversation went as follows:

Robson: Hi John, how goes the budgeting process? We have the review with James Davis next week so I just want to be sure we're good to go.

Brigley: Really well, Jan. I'm just putting the final touches on the budget projections and will have a draft version for your review first thing Monday morning.

Robson: Great, glad to hear it. How do the operating income numbers look compared to last year's actual results?

Brigley: They look great. With the success of some of our new products last year, our new marketing campaign, and the tainted food scandal that has plagued one of our key competitors, I'm budgeting significant increases in operating income each month compared to last year.

Robson: Significant increases every month? Are you sure about this?

Brigley: Well, as sure as one can ever be when projecting what revenues and expenses will be in the future. But I'm confident that the budget is based on reasonable expectations. I've talked to all the key managers in production and marketing, and they agree that my estimates are very reasonable.

Robson: Sounds like you've done your homework, as usual. I'm thinking though that maybe being a bit more conservative in *our* budget estimates might be a better way to go.

Brigley: I don't quite follow. It's not that the estimates are aggressive. As I said, all the key managers think the budget is reasonable, and attainable if we work hard.

Robson: Right, I understand that. I'm just saying that given the new bonus plan that Davis introduced last year, maybe we should be developing monthly budgets that we are sure we can meet or beat. Do you follow?

Brigley: Wait a minute—are you suggesting that we intentionally lowball the budget numbers just so we can get our bonuses each month?

Robson: I prefer to think of it as conservative budgeting as opposed to lowballing. Plus, it's not like I'm asking you to misstate the actual revenues and expenses that get reported each month. That would be unethical since the actual numbers get used by our creditors and by the tax authorities.

Brigley: I don't know, Jan. Intentionally developing budgets that we know we can beat just to get our bonuses seems just as unethical as misstating the actual results.

Robson: I disagree. The budgets are used only for internal purposes. What's the harm in being a little conservative? Besides, we all work hard and we deserve the monthly bonuses. Davis will never know because he's so busy with his charitable foundations these days that he really doesn't have a good idea of what's realistic when it comes to the budget each year. As you know he basically approves whatever we recommend without much discussion.

Brigley: But won't he get suspicious when actual results are better than the budget every month?

Robson: Heck no, he'll just be delighted that we're doing better than expected! It's a win–win situation, John. We'll get our bonuses and Davis will be happy the company is doing so well. I've got to run, but I look forward to seeing those conservative budget projections first thing Monday morning.

Required:
1. In deciding whether to comply with Robson's request for a "conservative budget," what aspects of the code of professional ethics featured in Exhibit 1–7 should guide Brigley's behaviour?
2. What would you recommend that Brigley do, and why?

PROBLEM 1–5 Planning and Control Activities [LO1]

The Sports Network (TSN), a Canadian television network, broadcasts a variety of content, including sporting events (e.g., baseball, basketball, football, golf, hockey), feature programs (e.g., "That's Hockey"), and news broadcasts (e.g., "Sports Desk"). Managing a major television network such as TSN very frequently involves planning, directing and motivating, controlling, and decision making. Indeed, networks such as TSN deliver new program content to viewers on a daily basis, with some content, such as sports news broadcasts, changing as the day unfolds. Managing this type of organization is highly challenging and dynamic.

Required:
For each of the four functions performed by managers (planning, directing and motivating, controlling, and decision making), identify three examples of activities managers at a television network such as TSN would likely engage in.

PROBLEM 1-6 Ethics in Business [LO5]

Anna Williams, CPA, was recently hired as assistant controller of GroChem Inc., which processes chemicals for use in fertilizers. Williams was selected for this position because of her past experience in chemical processing. During her first month on the job, Williams made a point of getting to know the people responsible for the plant operations and learning how things are done at GroChem.

During a conversation with the plant supervisor, Williams asked about the company procedures for handling toxic waste materials. The plant supervisor replied that he was not involved with the disposal of wastes and suggested that Williams might be wise to ignore this issue. This response strengthened Williams's determination to probe this area further to be sure that the company was not vulnerable to litigation.

On further investigation, Williams discovered evidence that GroChem was using a nearby residential landfill to dump toxic wastes—an illegal activity. It appeared that some members of GroChem's management team were aware of this situation and may have been involved in arranging for this dumping; however, Williams was unable to determine whether her superior, the controller, was involved.

Uncertain how she should proceed, Williams began to consider her options by outlining the following two alternative courses of action:

- Seek the advice of her superior, the controller.
- Anonymously release the information to the local newspaper.

Required:
1. Discuss why Williams has an ethical responsibility to take some action in the matter of GroChem Inc. and the dumping of toxic wastes. Refer to the code of professional ethics in Exhibit 1-7 to support your answer.
2. For each of the two alternative courses of action that Williams has outlined, explain whether or not the action is appropriate according to the guidelines presented in Exhibit 1-7.
3. Assume that Williams sought the advice of her superior, the controller, and discovered that the controller was involved in the dumping of toxic wastes. Describe the steps that Williams should take to resolve this situation.

(CMA, adapted)

PROBLEM 1-7 Corporate Governance and Corporate Social Responsibility [LO5]

Problems experienced by Toyota Motor Corporation beginning in 2010 with accelerator pedals sticking and brakes malfunctioning in some of its vehicle models illustrate how important it is to identify and control business risks, even for highly reputable companies. Among other things, Toyota was criticized for not acting quickly enough in implementing recalls, which according to some estimates involve 14 million vehicles worldwide. Also, reports suggest that Toyota did not tell federal regulators in Canada about a possible problem with the accelerator pedal when the company first learned of the issue. Instead Toyota waited until after the recall notice had been issued to inform regulators about the problem. Some have suggested that Toyota's rapid growth in worldwide production and sales compromised its focus on maintaining high standards of quality. In response to the crisis, Toyota temporarily closed some plants in Britain and France as a result of lower demand because of the recalls. The company also offered significant discounts to win back lost customers in North America. In December 2012, Toyota announced that it will pay over $1 billion to settle hundreds of lawsuits related to the accelerator problems.

Required:
1. Identify stakeholders that were probably negatively affected by the problems experienced by Toyota.
2. What role does effective corporate governance play in reducing the likelihood that companies will experience the types of problems faced by Toyota?

PROBLEM 1–8 Line and Staff Positions; Organization Chart [LO3]
The Association of Medical Personnel (AMP) is a membership-education organization that serves a wide range of individuals who work for medical institutions, including hospitals, clinics, and medical practices. The membership is composed of doctors, nurses, medical assistants, and professional administrators. The purpose of the organization is to provide individuals in the medical field with a professional organization that offers educational and training opportunities through local chapters, a monthly magazine (*AMP Review*), continuing-education programs, seminars, self-study courses, and research publications.

AMP is governed by a board of directors, who are members elected to these positions by the membership. The chairperson of the board is the highest-ranking volunteer member and presides over the board; the board establishes policy for the organization. The policies are administered and carried out by AMP's paid professional staff. The president's chief responsibility is to manage the operations of the professional staff. Like any organization, the professional staff of AMP is composed of line and staff positions. A partial organization chart of the AMP professional staff is shown in Exhibit 1–A.

EXHIBIT 1–A   Partial Organization Chart for the Association of Medical Personnel

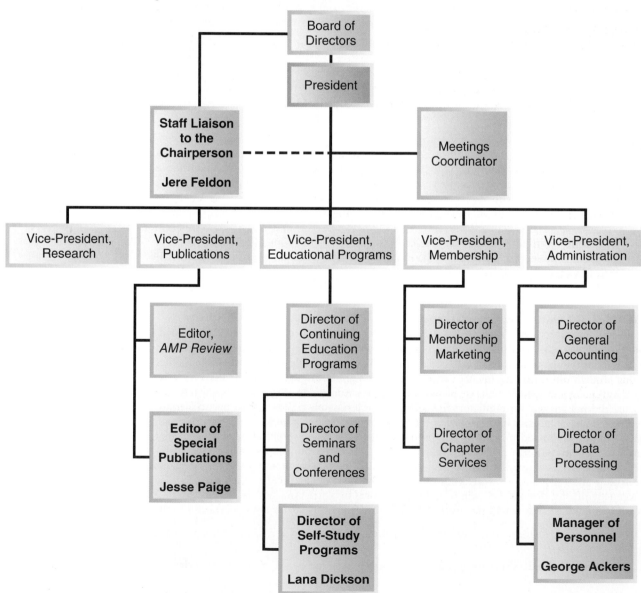

Four of the positions appearing in the organization chart are described below.

Jere Feldon, Staff Liaison to the Chairperson
Feldon is assigned to work with the chairperson of AMP by serving as an intermediary between the chairperson and the professional staff. All correspondence to the chairperson is funnelled through Feldon. Feldon also works very closely with the president of AMP, especially on any matters that have to be brought to the attention of the chairperson and the board.

Lana Dickson, Director of Self-Study Programs
Dickson is responsible for developing and marketing the self-study programs offered by AMP. Self-study courses consist of DVDs and a workbook. Most of the courses are developed by outside contractors who work under her direction. Dickson relies on the director of membership marketing to help her market these courses.

Jesse Paige, Editor of Special Publications
Paige is primarily responsible for the publication and sale of any research monographs generated by the research department. In addition, he coordinates the publication of any special projects prepared by any other AMP committees or departments. Paige also works with AMP's Publication Committee, which sets policy on the types of publications that AMP should publish.

George Ackers, Manager of Personnel
Ackers works with all of the departments of AMP in hiring professional and clerical staff. The individual departments screen and interview prospective employees for professional positions, but Ackers is responsible for advertising open positions. Ackers plays a more active role in the hiring of clerical personnel by screening individuals before they are sent to the departments for interviews. In addition, Ackers coordinates the employee performance evaluation program and administers AMP's salary schedule and fringe benefit program.

Required:
1. Distinguish between line positions and staff positions in an organization by defining each. Include in your discussion the role, purpose, and importance of each.
2. Conflicts will often arise between line and staff managers in organizations. Discuss the characteristics of line and staff managers that may cause conflicts between the two.
3. For each of the four individuals identified by name in the text,
   a. Identify whether the individual's position is a line or staff position and explain why.
   b. Identify potential problems that could arise in each individual's position, either due to the type of position (i.e., line or staff) or to the location of the individual's position within the organization.

(CMA, adapted)

PROBLEM 1–9 Value Chain Analysis [LO4]
Some companies that manufacture multiple products perform a comprehensive assessment of individual product profitability by collecting the costs incurred for each of the major business functions in the value chain and comparing them to the revenues generated by each of their major product offerings. For example, a manufacturer of home electronics equipment employing this type of analysis would separately track the research and development, product design, manufacturing, marketing, distribution, and customer service costs for each of its major product lines, such as televisions, home theatre systems, and speakers. Revenues for each of these product lines would also be separately identified, allowing managers to calculate profitability on a product-by-product basis.

Required:
1. Identify some benefits and challenges of performing the type of value chain analysis described above in a company that has multiple product lines.
2. What might cause some of the costs for the specific functions making up the value chain to increase or decrease over the life of a product (i.e., from the early to mature stages of a product's life)?

Mc Graw Hill Education connect®   Mc Graw Hill Education LEARNSMART®   Mc Graw Hill Education SMARTBOOK™

For more information on the resources available from McGraw-Hill Ryerson, go to www.mheducation.ca/he/solutions.

COST TERMS, CONCEPTS, AND CLASSIFICATIONS

■ UNDERSTANDING COSTS

Stephen Kamperman owns and operates a successful landscaping and snow-removal business, The Lawn Guy Limited, based near Halifax, Nova Scotia. For Stephen, understanding costs is an important part of running his company. For example, to determine the appropriate amount to charge a client for lawn care, Stephen needs to know the direct costs that are incurred. These include costs directly related to doing the work for the client, such as the gas used by the mowers and other equipment; any material costs, such as fertilizer; and the hourly wages paid to the employees he hires to do the work. In evaluating the overall profitability of the landscaping business, Stephen also needs to consider costs that aren't directly related to a particular client but must be incurred to run the business, such as the original cost of the lawn mowers to calculate depreciation, and the insurance on the equipment. When making planning decisions such as estimating cash flows, he needs to think about how costs will change in response to changes in the activity level of his business. Some costs, such as gas for the mowers, will increase proportionately with the number of hours spent mowing lawns, while other costs, such as insurance and registration on the trucks used to get his employees and equipment to the client's location, will not.

Stephen's business has two distinct services, landscaping and snow removal. To determine the profitability of each service, he needs to identify costs that are directly related to landscaping (e.g., insurance on lawn mowers) versus snow removal (e.g., gas for snow blowers). He also has to decide how to allocate administrative costs that are common to both services, such as wages paid to the office staff, and the costs of any office equipment used for the business.

Finally, successful entrepreneurs such as Stephen are often looking for new business opportunities. If such an opportunity comes along, Stephen will need to consider the potential benefits of investing his time and money in the new business versus continuing to operate The Lawn Guy Limited. If he decides to keep his existing company, he will have to forgo any financial benefits related to the new business; these forgone benefits represent an opportunity cost of that decision. As part of the consideration of new opportunities, Stephen will have to determine which costs incurred by his current company are relevant to the decision of whether he should continue with it, or instead start a new business. To make a good decision, Stephen will need to focus only on those costs that differ between the alternatives of keeping his existing business and starting a new one, and ignore all costs that do not.

The above example shows some of the many cost concepts that are critical to understand when managing a business. The chapter builds on this example by examining the different ways of classifying costs, the flow of costs through the financial statements, cost behaviour basics, and additional cost concepts that are critical to effective decision making.

Source: Discussions with Stephen Kamperman, owner of The Lawn Guy Limited.

■ GENERAL COST CLASSIFICATIONS

All types of organizations incur costs—businesses such as manufacturing, merchandising, or service companies; not-for-profit organizations such as Hockey Canada; and government agencies such as Statistics Canada. Generally, the kinds of costs that are incurred and the way these costs are classified depend on the type of organization involved. However, managerial accounting is applicable to all types of organizations. For this reason, our discussion of cost characteristics considers a variety of organizations—manufacturing, merchandising, and service.

Our initial focus in this chapter is on manufacturing companies, since their basic activities include most of the activities found in other types of business organizations. Manufacturing companies such as MEGA Brands, Bombardier, and CCM acquire raw materials, produce finished goods, market, distribute, bill, and incur costs. Therefore, an understanding of costs in a manufacturing company can be very helpful in understanding costs in other types of organizations. Categories that are not applicable to a certain type of organization can be omitted.

Manufacturing Costs

Most manufacturing companies divide manufacturing costs into three broad categories: direct materials, direct labour, and manufacturing overhead. A discussion of each of these categories follows.

Direct Materials   The materials that go into the final product are called *raw materials*. This term is somewhat misleading, since it seems to imply unprocessed natural resources like wood pulp or iron ore. Actually, *raw materials* refer to any materials that are used in the final product, and the finished product of one company can become the raw materials of another company. For example, car batteries produced by Magna International are a raw material used by BMW in some of its automobiles.

Raw materials may include both direct and indirect materials. **Direct materials** are those materials that become an integral part of the finished product and that can be physically and conveniently traced to it. Examples include the seats Bombardier purchases from subcontractors to install in its passenger trains and the components NAD Electronics uses in its stereo amplifiers.

Sometimes it is not worth the effort to trace the costs of relatively insignificant materials to the end products. Such minor items include the solder used to make electrical connections in a Sony TV and the glue used in a pair of Saucony running shoes. Materials such as solder and glue are called **indirect materials** and are included as part of manufacturing overhead, which is discussed later in this section. Indirect materials can still be thought of as raw materials, but they are not treated as direct materials because the costs of directly tracing them to the finished products exceed the benefits of doing so.

Direct Labour   **Direct labour** consists of labour costs that can be easily (i.e., physically and conveniently) traced to individual units of product. The labour costs of assembly-line workers at Bauer Hockey, for example, are direct labour costs, as are the labour costs of welders at Irving Shipbuilding and equipment operators at Cervélo.

LEARNING OBJECTIVE ❶
Identify and give examples of each of the three basic manufacturing cost categories.

Direct materials
Those materials that become an integral part of a finished product and can be conveniently traced to it.

Indirect materials
Small items of material that may become an integral part of a finished product but whose costs of tracing exceed the benefits.

Direct labour
Those factory labour costs that can be traced easily to individual units of product.

Indirect labour
The labour costs of janitors, supervisors, materials handlers, and other factory workers that cannot be conveniently traced directly to particular products.

Labour costs that cannot be physically traced to the creation of products, or that can be traced only at great cost and inconvenience, are termed **indirect labour** and treated as part of manufacturing overhead, along with indirect materials. Indirect labour includes the labour costs of janitors, supervisors, materials handlers, and security personnel. Although the efforts of these workers are essential to production, it would be either impractical or impossible to accurately trace their costs to specific units of product. Hence, such labour costs are treated as indirect labour.

Manufacturing overhead
All costs associated with manufacturing except direct materials and direct labour.

Manufacturing Overhead   **Manufacturing overhead**, the third element of manufacturing costs, includes all costs of manufacturing except direct materials and direct labour. Manufacturing overhead includes items such as indirect materials, indirect labour, maintenance and repairs on production equipment, heat and light, property taxes, depreciation, and insurance on manufacturing facilities. A company also incurs costs associated with its selling and administrative functions (for heat and light, property taxes, insurance, depreciation, and so forth), but these costs are not included as part of manufacturing overhead. Only those costs associated with *operating the production facility (factory)* are included in the manufacturing overhead category. Various terms are used to describe manufacturing overhead, such as *indirect manufacturing cost, factory overhead*, and *factory burden*. All of these terms are synonymous with *manufacturing overhead*.

Conversion cost
Direct labour cost plus manufacturing overhead cost.

Manufacturing overhead combined with direct labour is called **conversion cost**. This term stems from the fact that direct labour costs and overhead costs are incurred to convert materials into finished products. Direct labour combined with direct materials is called **prime cost**, which, following from the discussion above about direct and indirect costs, groups the two types of direct costs into one category.

Prime cost
Direct materials cost plus direct labour cost.

Classification of Manufacturing Labour Costs

The classification of direct labour and indirect labour costs is relatively straightforward. Janitorial wages are usually classified as overhead because they represent an indirect cost, as do payroll costs for supervisors, security personnel, and maintenance workers. However, the appropriate classification of idle time and overtime premiums of production workers is less obvious. For example, if three hours of a production worker's time are idle (i.e., not spent on production activities) and each hour costs $20, then $60 of idle time cost is usually charged to overhead if management feels that the cost is a general cost of all production. However, if a specific job results in idle time, such as waiting for materials because of a product design change demanded by the customer, then the idle time could be charged to the direct labour costs of that job. Whether the customer will pay for the charge depends on the prevailing market conditions (e.g., degree of competition) or the details of the contract with the customer.

Overtime premiums
The extra hourly wage rate paid to workers who must work more than their normal time requirements.

Overtime premiums represent the extra hourly wage rate paid to production workers who must work above their normal time requirements. For example, a worker might be paid time and a half for five overtime hours. Thus, if $20 is the base rate, the five hours will have an overtime premium of $10 per hour × 5 hours, or $50. Classification of the overtime as direct labour or overhead depends on the cause of the overtime. A job-specific reason (e.g., a rush order) dictates a direct job cost, whereas a normal overtime cost resulting from general conditions, such as peak production needs, dictates an overhead (indirect) charge to all jobs completed during that peak period.

Employee benefits, such as employment taxes, extended medical coverage, and pension costs paid by the employer, can be as much as 30% to 40% of base pay. Employee benefit costs for indirect labour are obviously classified as indirect overhead. However, the employee benefit costs for direct labour are typically added to the base direct labour rate in calculating a total direct labour cost, including benefits.

Non-manufacturing Costs

Generally, non-manufacturing costs are divided into two categories: (1) marketing or selling costs and (2) administrative costs.

Marketing or selling costs include all costs necessary to secure customer orders and get the finished product or service to the customer. These costs are often called *order-getting and order-filling costs.* Examples of marketing costs are order-getting costs such as those for advertising, sales travel, and sales salaries or commissions. Order-filling costs include packing, shipping, and the costs of finished goods warehouses.

Administrative costs include all executive, organizational, and clerical costs associated with the *general management* of an organization rather than with manufacturing, marketing, or selling. Examples of administrative costs are executive compensation; accounting; human resources; public relations; and other costs involved in the overall, general administration of the organization *as a whole.*

Managerial accounting concepts and techniques apply to both non-manufacturing and manufacturing activities. Service organizations such as public accounting firms use cost concepts in analyzing and costing their services. Banks use cost analysis to determine the cost of offering such services as chequing accounts, consumer loans, and credit cards, and insurance companies determine the cost of servicing customers by geographic location, age, marital status, and occupation. This type of cost analysis provides data for controlling selling and administrative functions in the same way that manufacturing cost analysis provides data for controlling manufacturing functions.

Marketing or selling costs
All costs necessary to secure customer orders and get the finished product or service to the customer.

Administrative costs
All executive, organizational, and clerical costs associated with the general management of an organization rather than with manufacturing, marketing, or selling.

Instant Quiz 2-1
Which of the following is *not* a manufacturing cost for a company that makes running shoes: the cost of the thread used in stitching for the shoes, the salary of the manager who supervises the inspection of finished goods, or the salaries of the personnel in the Accounts Payable Department?

IN BUSINESS

Industry Canada, a department of the Canadian federal government, has a website containing a wealth of cost data and other statistics for Canadian industries. The information is organized according to whether the industry is in the goods-producing sector or the service-producing sector, and within each of these categories are more refined subcategories. For example, categories of goods-producing industries include manufacturing, utilities, construction, and agriculture. Service-producing industries include transportation, finance, real estate, and retail, and subcategories are provided for each industry.

The site also includes separate information for small and medium-sized enterprises (SMEs), which can be useful for managers of smaller organizations seeking comparative data. For example, cost of sales and labour cost details for several categories of manufacturing companies are show below:

Industry	Category	Cost of Sales	Labour as a Percentage of Sales
Manufacturing	Frozen Food	56.9%	7.0%
Manufacturing	Clothing	59.9%	13.8%
Manufacturing	Paper	64.4%	13.8%

The above data show that cost of sales percentages and labour cost percentages vary across different categories of manufacturing companies. Paper manufacturers have the highest cost of sales, at over 64%, while frozen food manufacturers have the lowest, at about 57%. Moreover, frozen food manufacturers have the lowest labour costs as a percentage of sales, likely due to more extensive use of automated manufacturing processes for those companies.

Source: Industry Canada, *Canadian Industry Statistics,* http://www.ic.gc.ca/eic/site/cis-sic.nsf/eng/Home.

PRODUCT COSTS VERSUS PERIOD COSTS

In addition to the distinction between manufacturing and non-manufacturing costs, there are other ways to categorize costs. For instance, they can also be classified as either *product costs* or *period costs*. To understand the difference between product costs and period costs, the matching principle from financial accounting is helpful.

Generally, costs are recognized as expenses on the income statement in the period that benefits from the cost. For example, if a company pays for two years of liability insurance in advance, the entire amount is not considered an expense of the year in which the payment is made. Instead, one-half of the cost is recognized as an expense each year. The reason is that both years—not just the first year—benefit from the insurance payment. The unexpensed portion of the insurance payment is carried on the balance sheet as an asset called *prepaid insurance*. The *matching principle* is based on the accrual concept and states that *costs incurred to generate a particular revenue should be recognized as expenses in the same period that the revenue is recognized*. This means that if a cost is incurred to acquire or produce something that will eventually be sold, then the cost should be recognized as an expense only when the sale takes place, that is, when the benefit occurs. Such costs are called *product costs*.

Product Costs

Product costs
All costs that are involved in the purchase or manufacture of goods. In the case of manufactured goods, these costs consist of direct materials, direct labour, and manufacturing overhead. They are also called inventoriable costs.

For financial accounting purposes, **product costs** include all costs involved in acquiring or making a product. In the case of manufactured goods, these costs consist of direct materials, direct labour, and manufacturing overhead. Product costs "attach" to units of product as the goods are purchased or manufactured, and they remain attached as the goods go into inventory awaiting sale. Product costs are initially assigned to an inventory account on the balance sheet. When the goods are sold, the costs are released from inventory as expenses (typically called *cost of goods sold*) and matched against sales revenue. Since product costs are initially assigned to inventories, they are also known as *inventoriable costs*. This means that a product cost such as direct materials or direct labour might be incurred during one period but not treated as an expense until a following period when the completed product is sold. Thus, product costs will be present in inventories and cost of goods sold.

Period Costs

Period costs
All costs that are expensed on the income statement in the period in which they are incurred or accrued. Selling (marketing) and administrative expenses are period costs.

Period costs are all those costs not included in product costs. These costs are expensed on the income statement in the period in which they are incurred, using the usual rules of accrual accounting. Period costs are not included as part of the cost of either purchased or manufactured goods. Sales commissions and advertising are examples of period costs. Neither sales commissions nor advertising are included as part of the cost of purchased or manufactured goods. Rather, both items are treated as expenses on the income statement in the period in which they are incurred.

As discussed above, *all selling and administrative expenses are period costs*. Therefore, advertising, executive salaries, sales commissions, public relations, and other non-manufacturing costs discussed earlier are all period costs. They will appear on the income statement as expenses in the period in which they are incurred. Careful analysis of the purpose of costs is necessary to separate product from period costs. Exhibit 2–1 summarizes the cost terms that we have introduced so far.

EXHIBIT 2-1   Summary of Cost Terms

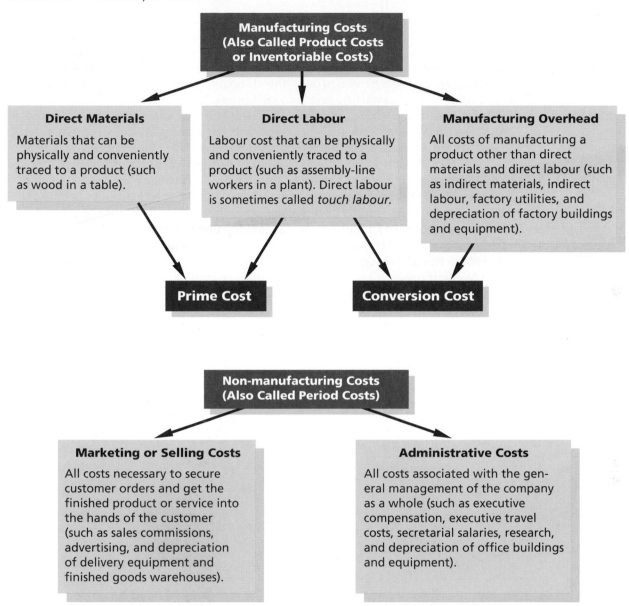

COST CLASSIFICATIONS ON FINANCIAL STATEMENTS

In this section, we examine the cost classifications used on the financial statements of manufacturing and merchandising companies. Financial statements prepared by a *manufacturing* company are more complex than the statements prepared by a merchandising company because the manufacturing company must account for the production of its goods as well as for the marketing of them. The production process gives rise to many costs that do not exist in a merchandising company, and these costs must be accounted for on the manufacturing company's financial statements. Conversely, merchandising companies such as retail stores simply purchase goods from suppliers for resale to customers. In this section, we focus on how accounting similarities and differences between manufacturing and merchandising companies affect the details included in the balance sheet and income statement.

The Balance Sheet

The balance sheet of a manufacturing company is generally similar to that of a merchandising company. For example, both have assets such as cash, accounts receivable, and prepaid expenses and liabilities such as accounts payable and loans payable. However, the key difference relates to the inventory accounts. A merchandising company has only one class of inventory—goods purchased from suppliers that are awaiting resale to customers. By contrast, manufacturing companies have three classes of inventories—raw (direct) materials, work in process, and finished goods. **Raw (direct) materials inventory**, discussed earlier, represents the materials used to make a product that have not yet been placed into production. **Work in process inventory** consists of units of product that are partially complete and require additional work before they are ready to sell to a customer. **Finished goods inventory** consists of complete units of product that have not yet been sold to customers. Typically, only the sum of these three categories of inventory is shown on the balance sheet of external reports. However, the notes to the financial statements often provide more detail about the amounts in each category.

We will use two hypothetical companies—Graham Manufacturing and Reston Bookstore—to illustrate the concepts discussed in this section. Graham Manufacturing is located in Victoria, British Columbia, and makes precision brass fittings for yachts. Reston Bookstore is a small bookstore in Moncton, New Brunswick, specializing in selling books about Atlantic Canada.

The footnotes to Graham Manufacturing's annual report reveal the following information concerning its inventories:

Raw (direct) materials inventory
Materials used to make a product that have not yet been placed into production.

Work in process inventory
Inventory consisting of units of product that are only partially complete and will require further work before they are ready for sale to a customer.

Finished goods inventory
Inventory consisting of units of product that have been completed but have not yet been sold to customers.

Graham Manufacturing Corporation Inventory Accounts		
	Beginning Balance	**Ending Balance**
Raw Materials	$ 60,000	$ 50,000
Work in Process	90,000	60,000
Finished Goods	125,000	175,000
Total inventory accounts	$275,000	$285,000

Graham Manufacturing's raw materials inventory consists largely of brass rods and brass blocks. The work in process inventory consists of partially completed brass fittings. The finished goods inventory consists of brass fittings that are ready to be sold to customers.

In contrast, the Inventory account at Reston Bookstore consists entirely of the costs of books the company has purchased from publishers for resale to the public. In merchandising companies like Reston, these inventories may be called *merchandise inventories*. The beginning and ending balances in this account appear as follows:

Reston Bookstore Inventory Account		
	Beginning Balance	**Ending Balance**
Merchandise inventory	$100,000	$150,000

EXHIBIT 2-2   Comparative Income Statements: Merchandising and Manufacturing Companies

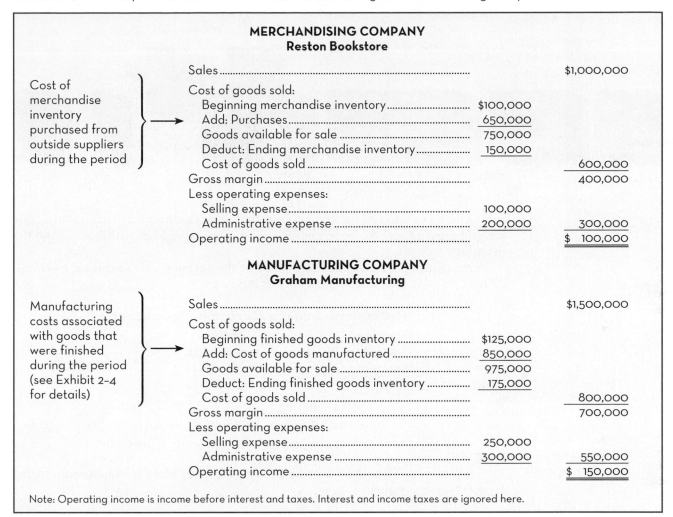

MERCHANDISING COMPANY
Reston Bookstore

Sales		$1,000,000
Cost of goods sold:		
Beginning merchandise inventory	$100,000	
Add: Purchases	650,000	
Goods available for sale	750,000	
Deduct: Ending merchandise inventory	150,000	
Cost of goods sold		600,000
Gross margin		400,000
Less operating expenses:		
Selling expense	100,000	
Administrative expense	200,000	300,000
Operating income		$ 100,000

Cost of merchandise inventory purchased from outside suppliers during the period

MANUFACTURING COMPANY
Graham Manufacturing

Sales		$1,500,000
Cost of goods sold:		
Beginning finished goods inventory	$125,000	
Add: Cost of goods manufactured	850,000	
Goods available for sale	975,000	
Deduct: Ending finished goods inventory	175,000	
Cost of goods sold		800,000
Gross margin		700,000
Less operating expenses:		
Selling expense	250,000	
Administrative expense	300,000	550,000
Operating income		$ 150,000

Manufacturing costs associated with goods that were finished during the period (see Exhibit 2-4 for details)

Note: Operating income is income before interest and taxes. Interest and income taxes are ignored here.

The Income Statement

Exhibit 2-2 compares the income statements of Reston Bookstore and Graham Manufacturing. For illustration, these statements contain more detail about cost of goods sold than you will generally find in published financial statements.

At first glance, the income statements of merchandising and manufacturing firms like Reston Bookstore and Graham Manufacturing are very similar. The only apparent difference is in the labels of some of the entries that go into the computation of the cost of goods sold figure. In Exhibit 2-2, the computation of cost of goods sold relies on the following basic equation for inventory accounts:

> **LEARNING OBJECTIVE 3**
> Prepare an income statement, including the calculation of cost of goods sold.

Basic Equation for Inventory Accounts

$$\text{Beginning balance} + \text{Additions to inventory} = \text{Ending balance} + \text{Withdrawals from inventory}$$

The logic of this equation, which applies to any inventory account, is illustrated in Exhibit 2-3. At the beginning of the period, the inventory contains a beginning balance. During the period, additions are made to the inventory through purchases or other means. The sum of the beginning balance and the additions to the account is the total amount of inventory available for sale. During the period, withdrawals are made from inventory. Whatever is left at the end of the period after these withdrawals

EXHIBIT 2-3   Inventory Flow

Beginning balance + Additions   =   Total available   −   Withdrawals   =   Ending balance

is the ending balance. At the end of the period, all of the inventory that was available for sale must either still be in ending inventory or have been withdrawn from the inventory account.

These concepts are applied to determine the cost of goods sold for a merchandising company like Reston Bookstore as follows:

Cost of Goods Sold in a Merchandising Company

$$\text{Beginning balance inventory} + \text{Purchases} = \text{Ending merchandise inventory} + \text{Cost of goods sold}$$

or

$$\text{Cost of goods sold} = \text{Beginning merchandise inventory} + \text{Purchases} - \text{Ending merchandise inventory}$$

The cost of goods sold for a manufacturing company like Graham Manufacturing is determined as follows:

Cost of Goods Sold in a Manufacturing Company

$$\text{Beginning finished goods inventory} + \text{Cost of goods manufactured} = \text{Ending finished goods inventory} + \text{Cost of goods sold}$$

or

$$\text{Cost of goods sold} = \text{Beginning finished goods inventory} + \text{Cost of goods manufactured} - \text{Ending finished goods inventory}$$

To determine the cost of goods sold in a merchandising company like Reston Bookstore, we need to know only the beginning and ending balances in the merchandise inventory account and the purchases. Total purchases can be determined easily in a merchandising company by simply adding together all purchases from suppliers.

To determine the cost of goods sold in a manufacturing company like Graham Manufacturing, we need to know the *cost of goods manufactured* and the beginning and ending balances in the finished goods inventory account. The **cost of goods manufactured** consists of the manufacturing costs associated with goods that were *finished* during the period. The cost of goods manufactured figure for Graham Manufacturing is derived in Exhibit 2–4, which contains a *schedule of cost of goods manufactured.*

Instant Quiz 2-3
If a merchandising company has cost of goods sold of $250,000, beginning merchandise inventory of $50,000, and ending merchandise inventory of $40,000, calculate the amount of inventory purchases for the period.

Cost of goods manufactured
Costs that include the direct materials, direct labour, and manufacturing overhead used for the products finished during the period.

EXHIBIT 2-4   Graham Manufacturing Schedule of Cost of Goods Manufactured

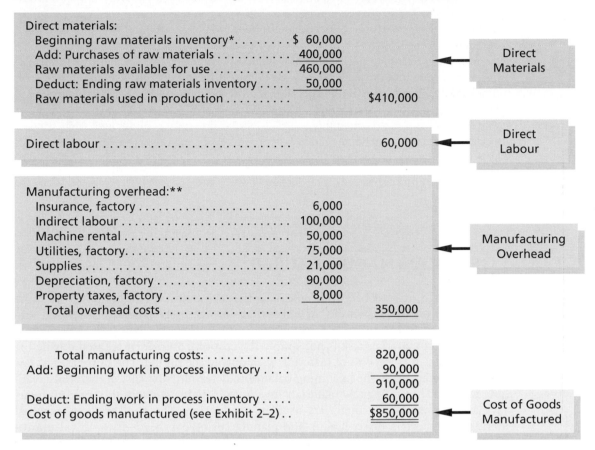

Direct materials:
  Beginning raw materials inventory*. . . . . $ 60,000
  Add: Purchases of raw materials 400,000   Direct
  Raw materials available for use 460,000   Materials
  Deduct: Ending raw materials inventory   50,000
  Raw materials used in production $410,000

Direct labour   60,000   Direct
                                                                                              Labour

Manufacturing overhead:**
  Insurance, factory   6,000
  Indirect labour   100,000
  Machine rental   50,000
  Utilities, factory.   75,000   Manufacturing
  Supplies   21,000   Overhead
  Depreciation, factory   90,000
  Property taxes, factory   8,000
    Total overhead costs   350,000

    Total manufacturing costs: 820,000
  Add: Beginning work in process inventory   90,000
                                                                        910,000
  Deduct: Ending work in process inventory   60,000   Cost of Goods
  Cost of goods manufactured (see Exhibit 2–2) . . $850,000   Manufactured

*We assume in this example that the Raw Materials Inventory account contains only direct materials and that indirect materials are carried in a separate Supplies account. Using a Supplies account for indirect materials is common practice among companies. In Chapter 5, we discuss the procedure to be followed if *both* direct and indirect materials are carried in a single account.

**In Chapter 5 we will see that the manufacturing overhead section of the schedule of cost of goods manufactured can be simplified considerably by using what is called a *predetermined overhead rate*.

IN BUSINESS

An example of a common supplementary income statement disclosure made by public companies such as BlackBerry, a manufacturer of smartphones, is shown below:

	Fiscal Year-End		
	2013	**2012**	**2011**
Revenue.	100.0%	100.0%	100.0%
Cost of sales.	69.0	64.3	55.7
Gross margin.	31.0%	35.7%	44.3%
Expenses			
Research and development	13.6%	8.4%	6.8%
Selling and administration.	19.1	14.1	12.1
Amortization.	6.4	3.1	2.2
Impairment of Goodwill.	3.0	1.9	0.0
Total expenses.	42.1%	27.5%	21.1%
Operating income (loss)	11.1%	8.2%	23.2%

This income statement format expresses all product and period costs as a percentage of revenue, allowing financial statement users such as BlackBerry managers, investors, or analysts to readily evaluate performance trends over time. In the case of BlackBerry, the cost of sales (product costs) has been steadily increasing since 2011, resulting in a gross margin of only 31% in 2013 compared to 44.3% in 2011. Period expenses such as research and development and selling and administration are also considerably higher as a percentage of revenue in 2013 than they were in 2011. Financial statement users would want to know the reasons for any significant trends. For example, is the declining gross margin percentage due to downward pressure on prices because of increased competition from other smartphone manufacturers, or is it due to increases in production costs? In the case of operating expense percentages, further analysis of BlackBerry's results would show that the increases are due to a sharp decline in sales since 2011 of about 44%, while spending on research and development and selling, marketing, and administration has changed little over this same period.

Source: BlackBerry, 2013 *Annual Report*. Reprinted with permission.

SCHEDULE OF COST OF GOODS MANUFACTURED

LEARNING OBJECTIVE 4
Prepare a schedule of cost of goods manufactured.

Schedule of cost of goods manufactured
A schedule showing the direct materials, direct labour, and manufacturing overhead costs incurred for a period and assigned to work in process and completed goods.

Total manufacturing costs
Costs that represent the direct materials, direct labour, and manufacturing overhead used to perform the production work for finished or unfinished products for the period.

The **schedule of cost of goods manufactured** in Exhibit 2–4 contains the three elements of product costs discussed earlier—direct materials, direct labour, and manufacturing overhead.

The direct materials cost is not simply the cost of materials purchased during the period—rather it is the cost of materials *used* during the period. The purchases of raw materials are added to the beginning balance to determine the cost of materials available for use. The ending raw materials inventory is deducted from this amount to arrive at the cost of raw materials used in production. The sum of the three cost elements—materials, direct labour, and manufacturing overhead—is the **total manufacturing costs** of $820,000. However, this is *not* the same thing as the cost of goods manufactured for the period of $850,000. The subtle distinction between the *total manufacturing cost* and the *cost of goods manufactured* is very easy to miss. Some of the materials, direct labour, and manufacturing overhead costs incurred during the period relate to goods that are not yet completed. As stated above, the cost of goods manufactured consists of the manufacturing cost associated with the goods that were *finished* during the period. Consequently, adjustments need to be made to the total manufacturing costs of the period for the partially completed goods that were in process at the beginning and at the end of the period. The costs that relate to goods that are not yet completed are shown in the work in process inventory figures at the bottom of the schedule. Note that the beginning work in process inventory must be added to the manufacturing costs of the period, and the ending work in process inventory must be deducted, to arrive at the cost of goods manufactured. The $30,000 decline in the Work in Process account during the year ($90,000 − $60,000) explains the $30,000 difference between the total manufacturing cost and the cost of goods manufactured.

Financial statements intended for users external to the organization, such as shareholders and lenders, often summarize information so that the detail shown in Exhibits 2–2 and 2–4 is not provided. In particular, the details shown in Exhibit 2–4 for direct materials and manufacturing overhead are not disclosed for external reporting purposes. External users do not need this level of reporting detail to evaluate a company's profitability, and it is not required by GAAP. However, financial statements generated for internal use by management would typically provide the detail shown in these exhibits.

Product Costs—A Closer Look

Earlier in the chapter, we defined product costs as consisting of those costs incurred to either purchase or manufacture goods. For manufactured goods, these costs consist of direct materials, direct labour, and manufacturing overhead. To understand product

EXHIBIT 2-5   Cost Flows and Classifications in a Manufacturing Company

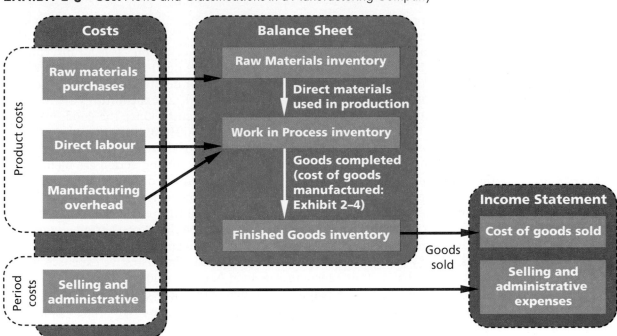

costs more fully, it is helpful to look briefly at the flow of costs in a manufacturing company. This will help us understand how product costs move through the various accounts and how they affect the balance sheet and the income statement.

Exhibit 2-5 illustrates the flow of costs in a manufacturing company. Raw materials purchases are recorded in the raw materials inventory account. When raw materials are used in production, their costs are transferred to the Work in Process Inventory account as direct materials. Notice that direct labour cost and manufacturing overhead cost are added directly to work in process. Work in process can be viewed as products on an assembly line. The direct materials, direct labour, and manufacturing overhead costs added to work in process in Exhibit 2-5 are the costs needed to complete these products as they move along this assembly line.

Notice from Exhibit 2-5 that as goods are completed, their cost is transferred from work in process to finished goods, where they will await sale to a customer. As goods are sold, their cost is transferred from finished goods to cost of goods sold. At this point, the various costs required to make the product are finally recorded as an expense.

Inventoriable Costs

As stated earlier, product costs are often called *inventoriable costs*. The reason is that these costs go directly into inventory accounts as they are incurred (first into work in process and then into finished goods), rather than going into expense accounts, hence the term *inventoriable costs. This is a key concept, since such costs can end up on the balance sheet as assets if goods are either partially completed or unsold at the end of a period.* To illustrate this point, refer again to Exhibit 2-5. At the end of the period, the materials, labour, and overhead costs that are associated with the units in the Work in Process and Finished Goods Inventory accounts will appear on the balance sheet as part of the company's assets. These costs will not become expenses until the goods are completed and sold.

Selling and administrative expenses are not involved in making a product. For this reason, they are not treated as product costs but rather as period costs that are expensed as they are incurred, as shown in Exhibit 2-5.

An Example of Cost Flows

Exhibit 2–6 builds on Exhibit 2–5 by providing an example of cost flows through the balance sheet and income statement in a manufacturing company using t-accounts for the key accounts involved. As goods are being worked on, costs for direct materials, direct labour, and manufacturing overhead are debited to work in process inventory. In our example, we show the total amount debited to work in process of $800,000, but in practice individual entries are made as expenditures are incurred for each of the three categories of manufacturing costs. Once the goods are complete, work in process inventory is credited for $800,000, with the corresponding debit to finished goods inventory. Note that both of these accounts are inventory accounts, so their related balances at the end of a reporting period are included on the balance sheet. Finally, when the goods are sold, finished goods inventory is credited for the cost of the items, with the corresponding debit to cost of goods sold, an income statement account. Importantly, it is not until the goods are sold that the direct material, direct labour, and manufacturing overhead costs originally debited to work in process inventory get expensed on the income statement through cost of goods sold. By contrast, the $150,000 of selling and administrative expenses are expensed immediately to the income statement in the period incurred.

Thus far, we have been mainly concerned with classifications of manufacturing costs to determine inventory valuations on the balance sheet and cost of goods sold on the income statement of external financial reports. However, costs are used for many purposes, and each purpose requires a different classification of costs. We will consider several different purposes for cost classifications in the remaining sections

> **Instant Quiz 2–4**
> Calculate the cost of goods manufactured for a company that has direct material costs of $205,000, direct labour costs of $30,000, manufacturing overhead costs of $175,000, beginning work in process inventory of $45,000, and ending work in process inventory of $30,000.

EXHIBIT 2-6   An Example of Cost Flows in a Manufacturing Company

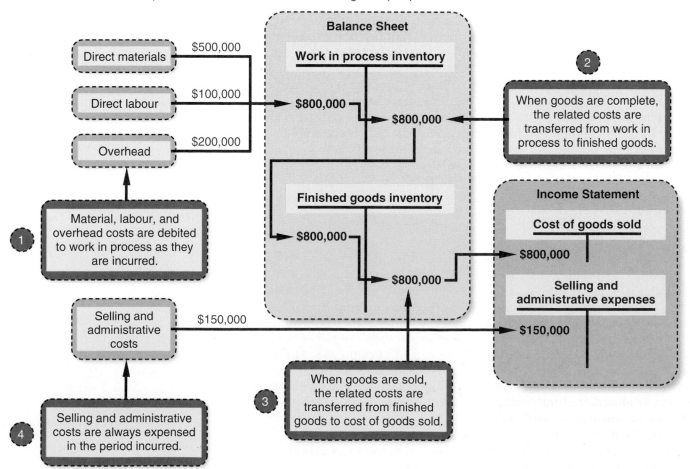

LEARNING AID

Summary of Cost Classifications

Purpose of Cost Classification	Cost Classifications

Preparing external financial statements	• Product costs (inventoriable)
	  • Direct materials
	  • Direct labour
	  • Manufacturing overhead
	 • Period costs (expensed)
	  • Non-manufacturing costs
	   • Marketing or selling costs
	   • Administrative costs

Predicting cost behaviour in response to changes in activity	• Variable cost (proportional to activity) • Fixed cost (constant in total)
Assigning costs to cost objects such as departments or products	• Direct cost (can easily be traced) • Indirect cost (cannot easily be traced; must be allocated)
Making decisions	• Differential cost (differs between alternatives) • Sunk cost (past cost not affected by a decision) • Opportunity cost (forgone benefit)

of this chapter. To help keep the big picture in mind, we suggest that you refer back to the Learning Aid above as you progress through the rest of this chapter.

◼ COST CLASSIFICATIONS FOR PREDICTING COST BEHAVIOUR

Quite frequently, it is necessary to predict how a certain cost will behave in response to a change in activity. **Cost behaviour** refers to how a cost reacts or responds to changes in the level of activity. As the activity level rises and falls, a particular cost may rise and fall as well—or it may remain constant. For planning purposes, a manager must be able to anticipate which of these will happen, and if a cost can be expected to change, the manager must know by how much it will change. To help make such distinctions, costs are often categorized as *variable* or *fixed*. As you will see throughout the textbook, understanding cost behaviour is critical for management accountants when preparing reports (Chapter 3), analyzing profits (Chapter 4), developing budgets (Chapter 9), and making short-term (Chapter 12) and long-term (Chapter 13) decisions. We briefly introduce the topic of cost behaviour in this chapter but return to it in greater detail in Chapter 3.

LEARNING OBJECTIVE ❺
Explain the differences between variable and fixed costs.

Cost behaviour
The way in which a cost reacts or responds to changes in the level of activity.

Variable Cost

A **variable cost** is a cost that varies, in total, in direct proportion to changes in the level of activity. The activity can be expressed in many ways, such as units produced, units sold, kilometres driven, beds occupied, lines of print, or hours worked. A good example of a variable cost is direct materials. The cost of direct materials used during a period will vary, in total, in direct proportion to the number of units that are produced. To illustrate this idea, consider the Nova Bus Corporation. Each bus requires one battery. As the output of buses increases and decreases, the number of batteries used will increase and decrease proportionately. If bus production goes up 10%, then the number of batteries used will also go up 10%. The concept of a variable cost is shown graphically in Exhibit 2–7.

Variable cost
A cost that varies, in total, in direct proportion to changes in the level of activity. A variable cost is constant per unit.

EXHIBIT 2-7   Variable and Fixed Cost Behaviour

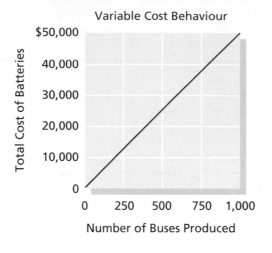

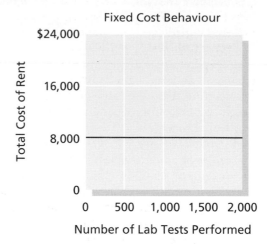

The graph on the left-hand side of Exhibit 2-7 illustrates that the *total variable cost* rises and falls as the activity level rises and falls. This idea is presented below, assuming that a battery costs $50:

Number of Buses Produced	Cost per Battery	Total Variable Cost— Batteries
1...	$50	$ 50
500...	50	25,000
1,000...	50	50,000

Although total variable costs change as the activity level changes, it is important to note that a variable cost is constant if expressed on a *per unit* basis. Observe from the tabulation above that the per unit cost of batteries remains constant at $50 even though the total cost of the batteries increases and decreases with activity levels.

There are many examples of costs that are variable with respect to the products and services provided by a company. In a manufacturing company, variable costs include items such as direct materials; shipping costs; sales commissions; and some elements of manufacturing overhead, such as indirect materials. For now, we will also assume that direct labour is a variable cost, although as we will see in Chapter 3, direct labour may act more like a fixed cost in many situations. In a merchandising company, variable costs include items such as cost of goods sold and commissions to salespeople. In a hospital, the variable costs of providing health care services to patients include the costs of the supplies, drugs, meals, and perhaps nursing services.

When we say that a cost is variable, we usually mean that it is variable with respect to the products and services the organization produces or provides. However, costs can be variable with respect to other activities. For example, the wages paid to employees at a Future Shop retail outlet depend on the number of hours the store is open and not strictly on the number of products sold. In this case, wage costs are variable with respect to the hours of operation. Nevertheless, when we say that a cost is variable, we ordinarily mean it is variable with respect to the volume of revenue-generating output—in other words, how many bicycles are produced, how many DVDs are rented, how many patients are treated, and so on.

Fixed cost
A cost that remains constant, in total, regardless of changes in the level of activity within the relevant range. If a fixed cost is expressed on a per unit basis, it varies inversely with the level of activity.

Fixed Cost

A **fixed cost** is a cost that remains constant, in total, regardless of changes in the level of activity. Unlike variable costs, fixed costs are not affected by changes in activity. Consequently, as the activity level rises and falls, the fixed costs remain constant in total amount unless influenced by some outside force, such as price changes. Rent is a good example of a fixed cost. Suppose the Saskatchewan Health Clinic rents a machine for $8,000 per month that tests blood samples for the presence of leukemia cells. The $8,000 monthly rental cost is incurred regardless of the number of tests performed during the month. The concept of a fixed cost is shown graphically on the right-hand side of Exhibit 2–7.

Very few costs are completely fixed. Most will change if there is a large enough change in activity. For example, suppose that the capacity of the leukemia diagnostic machine at the Saskatchewan Health Clinic is 2,000 tests per month. If the clinic needs to perform more than 2,000 tests in a month, it will be necessary to rent an additional machine, which will cause an increase in the fixed costs. When we say a cost is fixed, we mean it is fixed within some *relevant range*. The **relevant range** is the range of activity within which the assumptions about variable and fixed costs are valid. For example, the assumption that the rent for diagnostic machines is $8,000 per month is valid within the relevant range of 0 to 2,000 tests per month.

Relevant range
The range of activity within which assumptions about variable and fixed cost behaviour are valid.

Fixed costs can create confusion if they are expressed on a per unit basis because the average fixed cost per unit increases and decreases *inversely* with changes in activity. For the Saskatchewan Health Clinic, the average cost per test falls as the number of tests performed increases. This is because the $8,000 rental cost is spread over more tests. Conversely, as the number of tests performed in the clinic declines, the average cost per test rises as the $8,000 rental cost is spread over fewer tests. This concept is illustrated in the table below:

Monthly Rental Cost	Number of Tests Performed	Average Cost per Test
$8,000	10	$800
8,000	500	16
8,000	2,000	4

Note that if the Saskatchewan Health Clinic performs only 10 tests each month, the rental cost of the equipment averages $800 per test. But if 2,000 tests are performed each month, the average cost drops to only $4 per test. More will be said later about the problems created for both the accountant and the manager by this variation in unit costs.

Examples of fixed costs are straight-line depreciation, insurance, property taxes, rent, supervisory salaries, administrative salaries, and advertising.

Some costs contain variable and fixed cost elements; these are called **mixed costs**. An example is the total wages paid to sales staff. A portion of these wages is usually a fixed salary and does not vary with the level of selling activity. However, quite often a portion (sales commissions) of the total wages varies directly with the amount of sales generated by the salesperson. Mixed costs are quite common, but we defer further discussion of their behaviour and analysis until Chapter 3.

A summary of both variable and fixed cost behaviour is presented in the Learning Aid below.

Mixed costs
Costs that contain both variable and fixed cost elements.

Instant Quiz 2–5
Using the information from the Saskatchewan Clinic example, if 1,000 tests are performed in a month, calculate the total machine rental costs and average machine rental costs per test. If 4,000 tests are performed in a month, calculate the total machine rental costs.

LEARNING AID

Summary of Variable and Fixed Cost Behaviour

Cost	Behaviour of the Cost (within the relevant range)	
	In Total	**Per Unit**
Variable cost	Total variable cost increases and decreases in proportion to changes in the activity level.	Variable costs remain constant per unit.
Fixed cost	Total fixed cost is not affected by changes in the activity level within the relevant range.	Fixed costs decrease per unit as the activity level rises and increase per unit as the activity level falls.

■ COST CLASSIFICATIONS FOR ASSIGNING COSTS TO COST OBJECTS

Cost object
Anything for which cost data are desired.

Direct cost
A cost that can be easily and conveniently traced to the particular cost object under consideration.

Indirect cost
A cost that cannot be easily and conveniently traced to the particular cost object under consideration.

Common cost
A cost that is incurred to support a number of cost objects but cannot be traced to any of them individually.

Costs are assigned to objects for a variety of purposes including pricing, profitability analysis, and cost management. A **cost object** is anything for which cost data are desired—including products, customers, jobs, and organizational subunits. For assigning costs to cost objects, costs are classified as either *direct* or *indirect*.

Direct Cost

A **direct cost** is a cost that can be easily and conveniently traced to the particular cost object under consideration. The concept of direct cost extends beyond just direct materials and direct labour. For example, if Roots is assigning costs to its various regional and national sales offices, then the salary of the sales manager in its Alberta office is a direct cost of that office.

Indirect Cost

An **indirect cost** is a cost that cannot be easily and conveniently traced to the particular cost object under consideration. For example, a Moosehead Breweries factory may produce many varieties of beer. The factory manager's salary is an indirect cost of a particular variety, such as Premium Dry. This is because the factory manager's salary is not caused by any one variety of beer but rather is incurred as a consequence of running the entire factory. *To be directly traced to a cost object such as a particular product, the cost must be caused by the cost object.* The factory manager's salary is called a *common cost* of producing the various products of the factory. A **common cost** is a cost that is incurred to support a number of cost objects but cannot be traced to any of them individually. A common cost is a type of indirect cost.

A particular cost may be direct or indirect, depending on the cost object. While the salary of the manager of the Moosehead Breweries factory is an *indirect* cost of manufacturing Premium Dry beer, it is a *direct* cost of the manufacturing division. In the first case, the cost object is the brand of beer. In the second case, the cost object is the entire manufacturing division.

■ COST CLASSIFICATIONS FOR DECISION MAKING

Differential cost
A difference in cost between any two alternatives.

Differential revenue
A difference in revenue between any two alternatives.

Incremental cost
An increase in cost between two alternatives.

Costs are an important feature of many business decisions. In making decisions, it is essential to have a clear understanding of the concepts of *differential cost, opportunity cost*, and *sunk cost*.

Differential Cost and Revenue

Decisions involve choosing among alternatives. In business decisions, each alternative has certain costs and benefits that must be compared to the costs and benefits of the other available alternatives. A difference in costs between any two alternatives is known as a **differential cost**. A difference in revenues between any two alternatives is known as **differential revenue**.

A differential cost is also known as an **incremental cost**, although technically an incremental cost should refer only to an increase in cost from one alternative to another; decreases in cost should be referred to as *decremental costs*. Differential cost is a broader term, encompassing both cost increases (incremental costs) and cost decreases (decremental costs) between alternatives.

The accountant's differential cost concept is similar to the economist's marginal cost concept. When referring to changes in cost and revenue, economists employ the terms *marginal cost* and *marginal revenue*. The revenue that can be obtained from selling one more unit of product is called *marginal revenue*, and the cost involved in producing one more unit of product is called *marginal cost*. Thus, the economist's marginal cost concept is basically the same as the accountant's differential cost concept, but it is applied to a single unit of output.

Differential costs can be either fixed or variable. To illustrate, assume that Nature Way Cosmetics Inc. is thinking about changing its marketing method from distribution through retailers to distribution by a network of neighbourhood sales representatives. Present costs and revenues are compared to projected costs and revenues in the following table:

	Retailer Distribution (present)	Sales Representatives (proposed)	Differential Costs and Revenues
Revenues............................	$700,000	$800,000	$100,000
Cost of goods sold (V)..............	350,000	400,000	50,000
Advertising (F)......................	80,000	45,000	(35,000)
Commissions (V)...................	–0–	40,000	40,000
Warehouse depreciation (F).........	50,000	80,000	30,000
Other expenses (F).................	60,000	60,000	–0–
Total............................	540,000	625,000	85,000
Operating income..................	$160,000	$175,000	$ 15,000

V = Variable; F = Fixed.

According to the preceding analysis, the differential revenue is $100,000 and the differential costs total $85,000, leaving a positive differential operating income of $15,000 under the proposed marketing plan.

The decision of whether Nature Way Cosmetics should stay with the present retail distribution or switch to sales representatives could be made on the basis of the operating incomes of the two alternatives. As we see in the above analysis, the

IN BUSINESS

When deciding whether to bid for a major sporting event such as the Olympic Games, the potential host would perform a careful analysis of the expected differential revenues and differential costs. For example, according to some estimates, the differential costs to British Columbia of hosting the Vancouver 2010 Olympics were about $1.5 billion. Differential costs are those that were incurred *only* as a result of hosting the games. Examples are the cost of facilities such as the speed-skating arena that would not have been built if Vancouver had not won the Olympic bid, security for the events, and galas sponsored by the provincial government. Costs that would have been incurred even if British Columbia had not hosted the Olympics, such as upgrades to the Sea-to-Sky Highway leading to Whistler, are *not* considered differential costs.

A large source of differential revenue for British Columbia will be the money received in the years following the games as the result of tourists visiting the province after watching the Olympics on television. Some experts estimated that the 2010 Olympics could result in an additional 1.1 million to 2.7 million tourists for British Columbia in the five years following the games. According to a 2014 report prepared by Tourism BC, total tourism revenues for British Columbia in 2012 increased 2.5% compared to 2011 and 40.5% compared to 2002, suggesting estimates of the differential revenues likely to result from the Olympics may have been reasonable.

Source: *The Value of Tourism in British Columbia, Trends from 2002 to 2012*, Tourism BC, http://www.destinationbc.ca/getattachment/Research/Industry-Performance/Value-of-Tourism/Value-of-Tourism-in-British-Columba-(2012)/2012-Value-of-Tourism_Full-Report.pdf.aspx. Material reprinted with the express permission of National Post Inc.

operating income under the present distribution method is $160,000, whereas the operating income under sales representatives is estimated to be $175,000. Therefore, using sales representatives is preferred, since it would result in $15,000 higher operating income. Note that we would have arrived at exactly the same conclusion by simply focusing on the differential operating income rather than individually examining differential revenues and differential costs, which of course also show a net $15,000 advantage for sales representatives.

In general, only the differences between alternatives are relevant in decisions. Those items that are the same under all alternatives and that are not affected by the decision can be ignored. For example, in the Nature Way Cosmetics example, the Other Expenses category, which is $60,000 under both alternatives, can be ignored, since it has no effect on the decision. If it was removed from the calculations, the sales representatives would still be preferred by $15,000. This is an extremely important principle in managerial accounting that we will return to in later chapters.

Opportunity Cost

Opportunity cost is the potential benefit that is given up when one alternative is selected over another. To illustrate this important concept, consider the following examples:

Example 1

Vicki, a university student, has a part-time job that pays her $200 per week. She would like to spend a week at the beach during the study break, and her employer has agreed to give her the time off, but without pay. The $200 in lost wages would be an opportunity cost of taking the week off to be at the beach.

Example 2

Suppose that The Bay is considering investing a large sum of money in land that may be a site for a future store. Rather than invest the funds in land, the company could deposit the funds in an interest-bearing account with its bank. If the land is acquired, the opportunity cost will be the interest income that could have been earned if the funds had been deposited at the bank.

Example 3

Steve is employed with a company that pays him a salary of $40,000 per year. He is thinking about leaving the company and returning to school. Since returning to school would require that he give up his $40,000 salary, the forgone salary is an opportunity cost of getting further education.

Opportunity costs are not usually entered in the accounting records of an organization, but they must be explicitly considered in every decision a manager makes. Virtually every alternative has an associated opportunity cost. In Example 3 above, for instance, if Steve decides to stay at his job, an opportunity cost is still involved—the higher income that could be realized in future years as a result of returning to school.

Sunk Cost

A **sunk cost** is a cost *that has already been incurred* and that cannot be changed by any decision made now or in the future. Since sunk costs cannot be changed and thus will never differ under any alternative courses of action being considered, they are not differential costs. And because only differential costs are relevant in a decision, sunk costs should *always* be ignored.

To illustrate a sunk cost, assume that a company paid $50,000 several years ago for a special-purpose machine. The machine was used to make a product that is now obsolete and can no longer be sold at a price sufficient to generate a profit. Even though in hindsight the purchase of the machine may have been unwise, the $50,000 cost has been incurred and cannot be undone. Moreover, it would be foolish to continue making the obsolete product in a misguided attempt to "recover" the original cost of the machine. In short, the $50,000 originally paid for the machine is a sunk cost that should be ignored in current decisions.

KNOWLEDGE IN ACTION

Managers can apply their knowledge of cost terms, concepts, and classifications when
· Preparing financial statements
· Preparing a schedule of cost of goods manufactured
· Predicting costs
· Assigning costs to cost objects such as products, customers, jobs, or departments
· Deciding between various alternative courses of action

SUMMARY

- Manufacturing costs can be divided into three broad categories: direct materials, direct labour, and manufacturing overhead. Non-manufacturing costs are usually classified as either marketing/selling costs or administrative costs. **[LO1]**
- When valuing inventories and determining expenses for the balance sheet and income statement, costs are classified as either product costs or period costs. Product costs are assigned to inventory and considered assets until the products are sold. At the point of sale, product costs become cost of goods sold on the income statement. In contrast, period costs are expensed in the period in which they are incurred. **[LO2]**
- In a manufacturing company, cost of goods sold on the income statement is calculated by adding cost of goods manufactured to beginning finished goods inventory and then deducting the ending finished goods inventory. In a merchandising company, cost of goods sold is calculated by adding cost of goods purchased to beginning merchandise inventory and then deducting the ending merchandise inventory. Selling and administrative expenses are treated as period costs for both manufacturing and merchandising companies. **[LO3]**
- For manufacturing companies, the cost of goods manufactured must be calculated as part of the determination of cost of goods sold. Total manufacturing cost incurred is the sum of direct materials used in production, direct labour incurred, and total overhead costs for the period. Total manufacturing cost is added to beginning work in process inventory, and ending work in process inventory is then deducted to arrive at the cost of goods manufactured for the period. Work in process consists of goods started but not yet complete. **[LO4]**
- To predict cost behaviour, managers commonly classify costs into two categories, variable and fixed. Variable costs, in total, are strictly proportional to activity, but variable cost per unit is constant within a relevant range. Total fixed costs remain the same for changes in activity occurring within the relevant range. However, average fixed cost per unit decreases (increases) as the number of units increases (decreases). **[LO5]**
- To assign costs to cost objects such as products or departments, costs are classified as direct or indirect. Direct costs can conveniently be traced to the cost objects. Indirect costs cannot conveniently be traced to cost objects. **[LO6]**
- When making decisions, the concepts of differential cost and revenue, opportunity cost, and sunk cost are of vital importance. Differential costs and revenues are those items that differ between alternatives. Opportunity cost is the benefit that is forgone when one alternative is selected over another. Sunk cost is a cost that occurred in the past and cannot be altered. Differential cost and opportunity cost should be carefully considered in decisions. Sunk costs are always irrelevant in decision making and should be ignored. **[LO7]**

REVIEW PROBLEM 1: COST TERMS

Many new cost terms have been introduced in this chapter. It will take you some time to learn what each term means and how to properly classify costs in an organization. To assist in this learning process, consider the following example. RTW Company manufactures acoustic and electric guitars. Selected costs associated with the manufacture of the acoustic guitars and the general operations of the company are given below:

1. The guitars use metal for the frets and tuning knobs that costs $10 per guitar.
2. Wages for employees who handcraft the guitars total $175 per guitar.
3. Insurance on the manufacturing facilities totals $5,000 per year.

4. Glue used in the assembly process amounts to $3 per guitar.
5. The annual depreciation cost of the machines used to cut and finish the wood in the guitars totals $15,000.
6. The salary of the vice-president of marketing at RTW is $125,000 per year.
7. The salary of the manager responsible for manufacturing operations is $130,000 per year.
8. The total costs of an advertising campaign paid at the beginning of the current fiscal year that has now been discontinued were $75,000.
9. Instead of producing the acoustic guitars, RTW Company could use the manufacturing facilities to increase production of electric guitars that would generate operating income of $100,000 per year.

In the following tabulation, these costs are classified according to various cost terms used in the chapter. *Carefully study the classification of each cost.* If you don't understand why a particular cost is classified the way it is, reread the section of the chapter discussing the particular cost term. The terms *variable cost* and *fixed cost* refer to how costs behave with respect to the number of acoustic guitars produced in a year.

Solution to Review Problem 1

Selected Cost	Variable Cost	Fixed Cost	Period (Selling and Administrative) Cost	Product Cost			To Units of Product		Sunk Cost	Opportunity Cost
				Direct Materials	Direct Labour	Manufacturing Overhead	Direct	Indirect		
1. Metal/knobs used in guitar ($10 per guitar)	X			X			X			
2. Wages to handcraft a guitar ($175 per guitar)	X				X		X			
3. Insurance on manufacturing facilities ($5,000 per year)		X				X		X		
4. Glue used in assembly process ($3 per guitar)	X					X		X		
5. Depreciation on machines used to produce guitars ($15,000 per year)		X				X		X	X*	
6. Salary of the marketing VP ($125,000 per year)		X	X							
7. Salary of manufacturing operations manager ($130,000 per year)		X	X			X		X		
8. Discontinued advertising campaign ($75,000)		X	X						X†	
9. Operating income forgone on manufacturing facilities ($100,000 per year)										X‡

*This is a sunk cost, since the outlay for the equipment on which the depreciation is based was made in a previous period.

†This is a sunk cost because the advertising expenditures have already been incurred.

‡This is an opportunity cost, since it represents the potential benefit that is lost or sacrificed as a result of using the manufacturing facilities to produce guitars. Opportunity cost is a special category of cost that is not ordinarily recorded in an organization's accounting books. To avoid possible confusion with other costs, we will not attempt to classify this cost in any other way except as an opportunity cost.

REVIEW PROBLEM 2: SCHEDULE OF COST OF GOODS MANUFACTURED AND INCOME STATEMENT

Fisher Limited is a manufacturer that produces a single product. The following information has been taken from the company's production, sales, and cost records for the just-completed year:

Production in units..	30,000
Sales in units...	?
Ending finished goods inventory in units	?
Sales in dollars..	$650,000
Costs:	
Advertising...	$50,000
Direct labour..	$80,000
Indirect labour	$60,000
Raw materials purchased..	$160,000
Building rent (production uses 80% of the space; administrative	
and sales offices use the rest)	$50,000
Utilities, factory	$35,000
Royalty paid for use of production patent, $1 per unit produced.......................	?
Maintenance, factory...	$25,000
Rent for special production equipment, $6,000 per year plus $0.10 per unit produced ...	?
Selling and administrative salaries..	$140,000
Other factory overhead costs	$11,000
Other selling and administrative expenses...................................	$20,000

	Beginning of Year	End of Year
Inventories:		
Raw materials..	$20,000	$10,000
Work in process	$30,000	$40,000
Finished goods..	$0	?

The finished goods inventory is being carried at the average unit production cost for the year. The selling price of the product is $25 per unit.

Required:
1. Prepare a schedule of cost of goods manufactured for the year.
2. Compute the following:
   a. The number of units in the finished goods inventory at the end of the year.
   b. The cost of the units in the finished goods inventory at the end of the year.
3. Prepare an income statement for the year.

Solution to Review Problem 2

1.   **FISHER LIMITED**
                          Schedule of Cost of Goods Manufactured
                                For the year ended xxxx

Direct materials:		
Raw materials inventory, beginning..	$ 20,000	
Add: Purchases of raw materials	160,000	
Raw materials available for use...	180,000	
Deduct: Raw materials inventory, ending..................................	10,000	
Raw materials used in production..		$170,000
Direct labour..		80,000
Manufacturing overhead:		
Indirect labour	60,000	
Building rent (80% × $50,000)..	40,000	
Utilities, factory	35,000	
Royalty on patent ($1 per unit × 30,000 units)...........................	30,000	
Maintenance, factory...	25,000	

continued

Rent on equipment: $6,000 + ($0.10 per unit × 30,000 units)...............	9,000	
Other factory overhead costs	11,000	
Total overhead costs...		210,000
Total manufacturing costs..		460,000
Add: Work in process inventory, beginning.................................		30,000
		490,000
Deduct: Work in process inventory, ending.................................		40,000
Cost of goods manufactured..		$450,000

2. *a.* To compute the number of units in the finished goods inventory at the end of the year, we must first compute the number of units sold during the year:

$$\frac{\text{Total sales}}{\text{Unit selling price}} = \frac{\$650,000}{\$25 \text{ per unit}} = 26,000 \text{ units sold}$$

Units in the finished goods inventory, beginning	0
Units produced during the year..	30,000
Units available for sale...	30,000
Units sold during the year (above)	26,000
Units in the finished goods inventory, ending...................................	4,000

b. The average production cost per unit during the year is

$$\frac{\text{Cost of goods manufactured}}{\text{Number of units produced}} = \frac{\$450,000}{30,000 \text{ units}} = \$15 \text{ per unit}$$

Thus, the cost of the units in the finished goods inventory at the end of the year is 4,000 units × $15 per unit = $60,000.

3.

FISHER LIMITED
Income Statement
For the year ended xxxx

Sales		$650,000
Cost of goods sold:		
Finished goods inventory, beginning.......................................	$ 0	
Add: Cost of goods manufactured	450,000	
Goods available for sale..	450,000	
Finished goods inventory, ending	60,000	390,000
Gross margin		260,000
Selling and administrative expenses:		
Advertising..	50,000	
Building rent (20% × $50,000)..	10,000	
Selling and administrative salaries	140,000	
Other selling and administrative expense..................................	20,000	220,000
Operating income..		$ 40,000

GLOSSARY

 Review key terms and definitions on Connect.

DISCUSSION CASE

DISCUSSION CASE 2–1

Understanding cost terms and concepts is considerably more important in larger organizations with complex operations and multiple products or services being offered. In smaller and simpler companies that manufacture or sell only a single product, or for companies that have only a single service, the topics covered in this chapter have limited importance or relevance.

Required:
Do you agree with this statement? Why or why not?

QUESTIONS

2-1 Would costs related to the building used only by administrative personnel, such as heat and lights, property taxes, and insurance, be considered part of manufacturing overhead? Why or why not?

2-2 Distinguish between the following: (a) direct materials, (b) indirect materials, (c) direct labour, (d) indirect labour, and (e) manufacturing overhead.

2-3 Are product costs always expensed in the period in which they are incurred? Explain.

2-4 What are marketing or selling costs? How are they treated on the income statement?

2-5 Describe the schedule of cost of goods manufactured. How does it tie into the income statement?

2-6 What are prime costs and conversion costs?

2-7 What is the difference between total manufacturing costs incurred and the cost of goods manufactured?

2-8 Is it possible for costs such as salaries or depreciation to end up as assets on the balance sheet? Explain.

2-9 What is a mixed cost?

2-10 As the level of activity increases, on a per unit basis, explain what happens to variable costs and fixed costs.

2-11 What is the relevant range, and why is it important to understand this when predicting costs?

2-12 Why is manufacturing overhead considered an indirect cost of a unit of product?

2-13 In deciding whether to replace an existing machine with a newer, more cost effective machine, the original cost of the existing machine should be compared to the cost of the new machine. Do you agree? Explain.

2-14 Only variable costs can be differential costs. Do you agree? Explain.

2-15 Rick Johnstone is employed by Westin Company. Last week he worked 46 hours assembling one of the company's products. Westin's employees work a standard 40-hour week, and Johnstone is paid $18 per hour. Employees are paid time and a half for any hours worked in excess of the standard 40 hours. Assuming the overtime is the result of an overall spike in demand for all products, allocate Johnstone's earnings for the week between direct labour cost and manufacturing overhead cost.

2-16 Pat Campbell operates a moulding press at Barrie Fabrication Company. Last week Pat worked 35 hours and was idle 5 hours due to scheduled maintenance on the equipment. Her basic wage rate is $26 per hour. Allocate Pat's wages for the week between direct labour cost and manufacturing overhead cost.

EXERCISES

EXERCISE 2-1 Classifying Manufacturing Costs [LO1]

The costs below all relate to Sounds Good, a company based in Alberta that manufactures high-end audio equipment such as speakers, receivers, CD players, turntables, and home theatre systems. The company owns all of the manufacturing facilities (building and equipment) but rents the space used by the non-manufacturing employees (accounting, marketing, sales, human resources).

Required:

For each cost, indicate whether it would most likely be classified as a direct labour, direct material, manufacturing overhead, marketing and selling, or administrative cost.

1. Depreciation, taxes, and insurance on the manufacturing facilities.
2. Rent on the office space used by the non-manufacturing staff.
3. Salaries paid to the employees who produce the audio equipment.
4. Cost of the glue used to fasten the company's logo to the grill used on all of its speakers.
5. The cost of online advertising.
6. Salaries paid to the accounting employees.
7. Salary paid to the production manager who supervises the manufacturing activities for all products.
8. Cost of the plastic used for turntable dust covers.
9. Bonuses paid to sales staff for meeting their monthly sales goals.
10. Salary paid to the manager of the human resources department.

EXERCISE 2-2 Classification of Costs as Period or Product Costs [LO2]

Suppose that you have a summer job at Remotely Speaking, a company that manufactures sophisticated portable two-way radio transceivers for remote-controlled military reconnaissance missions. The company, which is privately owned, has approached a bank for a loan to help finance its tremendous growth. The bank requires financial statements before approving such a loan. You have been asked to help prepare the financial statements and are given the following list of costs:

1. Depreciation on salespeople's cars.
2. Rent on equipment used in the factory.
3. Lubricants used for machine maintenance.
4. Salaries of personnel who work in the finished goods warehouse.
5. Soap and paper towels used by factory workers at the end of a shift.
6. Factory supervisors' salaries.
7. Heat, water, and power consumed in the factory.
8. Materials used for boxing company products for shipment overseas. (Units are not normally boxed.)
9. Advertising costs.
10. Workers' Compensation Insurance for factory employees.
11. Depreciation on chairs and tables in the factory lunchroom.
12. The wages of the receptionist in the administrative offices.
13. Cost of leasing the corporate jet used by the company's executives.
14. The cost of renting rooms at a British Columbia resort for the annual sales conference.
15. The cost of packaging the company's product.

Required:

Classify the above costs as either product (inventoriable) costs or period (non-inventoriable) costs for preparing the financial statements for the bank.

EXERCISE 2-3 Constructing an Income Statement [LO3]

Home Entertainment, a retailer of CDs and DVDs, provided the following information for the month of June:

Sales	$150,000
Selling expenses	40,000
Administrative expenses	25,000
Merchandise inventory, beginning balance	12,000
Merchandise inventory, ending balance	22,000
Merchandise purchases	90,000

Required:

Prepare an income statement for the company for the month.

EXERCISE 2-4 Prepare a Schedule of Cost of Goods Manufactured [LO4]

Acromould Fabrication manufactures a variety of products in its factory. Data for the most recent month's operations appear below:

Beginning raw materials inventory	$ 66,000
Purchases of raw materials	528,000
Ending raw materials inventory	78,000
Direct labour	258,000
Manufacturing overhead	456,000
Beginning work in process inventory	228,000
Ending work in process inventory	264,000

Required:

Prepare a schedule of cost of goods manufactured for the company for the month.

EXERCISE 2-5 Fixed and Variable Costs [LO5]

Urban Auto Glass specializes in the repair and replacement of windshields for passenger vehicles. Variable and fixed costs related to installation activities for the most recent month (July) are listed below:

Item	
Number of windshields installed	1,000
Variable expenses:	
Direct materials..	$200,000
Direct labour (1 hour per installation)	30,000
Indirect materials	10,000
Fixed expenses:	
Installation supervisor's wages...	$4,000
Installation scheduler's wages	2,000
Warehouse expenses	5,000

Required:
1. Calculate the per unit amounts for each of the variable expense and fixed expense items in July.
2. Management expects that 1,200 windshields will be installed in August and that this level of activity is within the relevant range for all variable and fixed expenses. Calculate
   a. The total expense for each of the variable and fixed cost items above.
   b. The per unit amounts for each of the variable and fixed cost items above. Explain any differences in the per unit amounts between July and August.
3. Identify some factors that might cause variable costs per unit to change if the actual level of activity in a given month falls above or below the relevant range.

EXERCISE 2–6 Identifying Examples of Direct and Indirect Costs [LO6]
The Royal Hotel is located in central Alberta and has, among others, the following cost objects:

1. Hotel guests.
2. Hotel restaurant.
3. Hotel fitness centre and pool.
4. Hotel business centre (computers, printer, fax machine).

Required:
For each of the above cost objects, identify two examples of a direct cost and two examples of an indirect cost.

EXERCISE 2–7 Differential, Opportunity, and Sunk Costs [LO7]
The Sorrento Hotel is a four-star hotel in downtown Montreal. The hotel's operations vice-president would like to replace the hotel's antiquated computer terminals at the registration desk with attractive state-of-the-art flat-panel displays. The new displays would take less space; consume less power; and provide additional security, since they can be viewed only from a restrictive angle. The new computer displays would not require any new wiring. The hotel's chef believes the funds would be better spent on a new bulk freezer for the kitchen.

Required:
For each of the items below, indicate by placing an X in the appropriate column whether it should be considered a differential cost, an opportunity cost, or a sunk cost in the decision to replace the old computer terminals with new flat-panel displays. If none of the categories apply for a particular item, leave all columns blank. The first item has been completed as an example:

	Item	Differential Cost	Opportunity Cost	Sunk Cost
Ex.	Cost of electricity to run the terminals	X		
1.	Cost of the new flat-panel displays			
2.	Cost of the old computer terminals			
3.	Rent on the space occupied by the registration desk			
4.	Wages of registration desk personnel			
5.	Benefits from a new freezer			
6.	Costs of maintaining the old computer terminals			
7.	Cost of removing the old computer terminals............			
8.	Cost of existing registration desk wiring			

EXERCISE 2-8 Opportunity Costs and Sunk Costs [LO7]

Johnson Company manufactures sporting goods. One of its products is generating very low operating income, and management is trying to decide whether it should keep or drop that product. Five years ago, the company paid $1,500,000 for the building in which the product is manufactured and $500,000 for the land. The net book value (original cost less accumulated depreciation) for the building is $1,375,000. Management paid the annual property taxes and insurance on the building two weeks ago ($30,000 total). The manufacturing equipment used to make the product was also purchased five years ago at a cost of $300,000 and has a net book value of $150,000. Management was recently approached by an individual who offered to pay $1,000,000 for the land, building and equipment. Two weeks later, a second individual contacted management and offered to rent the manufacturing facilities for $20,000 per month.

Required:

Which of the above costs are opportunity costs with respect to deciding whether or not to continue to manufacture the product, and which are sunk costs? Explain your answers.

EXERCISE 2-9 Product Cost Flows; Product versus Period Costs [LO2, LO3]

Gelinas Computer Company was organized on May 1. On that date, the company purchased 22,000 USB flash drives to be sold with personal computers, each pre-loaded with the company's product information brochures. The front of the USB flash drives displays the company's name and an attractive corporate logo. Each USB flash drive cost Gelinas $6.

During May, 19,500 USB flash drives were drawn from the raw materials inventory account. Of these, 500 were taken by the sales manager to an important sales meeting with prospective customers and handed out as advertising. The remaining USB flash drives drawn from inventory were sold by bundling them with units of the company's product that were being manufactured during May. Of the units of product that were bundled with the USB flash drive during May, 95% were completed and transferred from work in process to finished goods. Of the units completed during the month, 80% were sold and shipped to customers.

Required:

1. Determine the cost of flash drives that would be in each of the following accounts at May 31:
   a.   Raw Materials.
   b.   Work in Process.
   c.   Finished Goods.
   d.   Cost of Goods Sold.
   e.   Advertising Expense.
2. Specify whether each of the above accounts would appear on the balance sheet or on the income statement at May 31.

EXERCISE 2-10 Preparation of a Schedule of Cost of Goods Manufactured and Cost of Goods Sold [LO1, LO3, LO4]

Tiessen Limited provided the following information for the year ended December 31:

Costs incurred:	
Marketing expense	$300,000
Direct labour cost	270,000
Raw material purchases	396,000
Rent, manufacturing building	240,000
Indirect labour	168,900
Sales commissions	105,000
Utilities, manufacturing	27,000
Depreciation, manufacturing equipment	72,000
Supplies, manufacturing	2,100
Depreciation, office equipment	24,000
Repairs, manufacturing equipment	120,000

Inventories:	Beginning of Year	End of Year
Raw materials.......................................	$24,000	$30,000
Work in process	15,000	60,000
Finished goods.....................................	210,000	75,000

Required:
1. Prepare a schedule of cost of goods manufactured.
2. Prepare the cost of goods sold section of Tiessen Limited's income statement for the year.

EXERCISE 2–11 Classification of Costs as Variable or Fixed, and as Selling and Administrative or Product [LO2, LO5]
Below are listed various costs that are found in organizations:

1. The costs of turn signal switches used at a General Motors plant. These are installed in the steering columns assembled at the plant.
2. The salary of the manager in charge of production at BlackBerry.
3. Salespeople's commissions at Avon Products, a company that sells cosmetics door to door.
4. Insurance on one of Bombardier's factory buildings.
5. The costs of shipping brass fittings from Graham Manufacturing's plant in British Columbia to customers in California.
6. Depreciation on the bookshelves at Reston Bookstore.
7. The costs of X-ray film at the Toronto General Hospital's radiology lab.
8. The cost of leasing a toll-free telephone number at Staples Canada. The monthly charge for the toll-free number is independent of the number of calls taken.
9. The depreciation on the playground equipment at a McDonald's outlet.
10. The cost of mozzarella cheese used at a Pizza Hut outlet.

Required:
Classify each cost as either variable or fixed with respect to the volume of goods or services produced and sold by the organization. Also classify each cost as a selling and administrative cost or as a product cost. Prepare your answer sheet as shown below. Place an X in the appropriate columns to show the proper classifications of each cost.

	Cost Behaviour		Selling and	Product
Cost Item	**Variable**	**Fixed**	**Administrative Cost**	**Cost**

EXERCISE 2–12 Classification of Labour Costs [LO1]

Greg Powers is employed by Gussie Company, where he assembles a component part for one of the company's products. Greg is paid $14 per hour for regular time, and he is paid time and a half (i.e., $21 per hour) for all work in excess of 40 hours per week.

Required:
1. Assume that during a given week Greg is idle for three hours due to machine breakdowns and that he is idle for two more hours due to material shortages. No overtime is recorded for the week. Allocate Greg's wages for the week between direct labour cost and manufacturing overhead cost.
2. Assume that during a following week Greg works a total of 49 hours. He has no idle time for the week. Allocate Greg's wages for the week between direct labour cost and manufacturing overhead cost.
3. Greg's company provides an attractive package of benefits for its employees. This package includes a retirement program and a health insurance program. Explain two ways that the company could handle the costs of its direct labourers' employee benefits in its cost records.

PROBLEMS

PROBLEM 2-13 Cost Classification [LO2, LO5, LO6]

Cycle Business manufactures and sells road and mountain bikes through a network of retail outlets in western Canada. Below is a partial list of expense items incurred in the most recent month (November), when 1,000 bicycles were manufactured, shipped, and sold. There was no beginning or ending work in process or finished goods inventory in November:

Item	October	November
Units produced and sold	900	1,000
Sales	$900,000	$1,000,000
Leather used for the bicycle seats	27,000	30,000
Production manager's salary	6,000	6,000
Life insurance for the company president	200	200
Electricity used in the production facilities*	1,000	1,100
Sales commissions	45,000	50,000
Internet advertising	1,000	1,000
Employee benefits for the production workers†	18,000	20,000
Property taxes on the production facilities	1,000	1,000
Shipping costs	45,000	50,000
Salary of the chief financial officer	10,000	10,000

*Each month, regardless of how much electricity is used, Cycle Business pays a $100 base charge to the utilities company.
†Employee benefits total 20% of the wages paid to production workers, who on average earn $20 per hour. Each bicycle requires 5 hours of direct labour.

Required:
1. With respect to the partial list of November expenses, answer the following:
   a.   Which items represent variable manufacturing costs?
   b.   Which items represent fixed manufacturing costs?
   c.   If the bicycle is the cost object, which items from (a) and (b) above are direct costs and which are indirect costs?
   d.   Which items would be classified as selling expenses?
   e.   Which items would be classified as administrative expenses?
2. Assume that 1,200 bicycles will be manufactured and sold in December. For the items you classified as manufacturing costs in (1), estimate the cost for December. Assume that there will be no change in unit costs for any direct materials, hourly wages will remain the same, and employee benefits will continue at 20% of wages.

PROBLEM 2-14 Classification of Labour Costs [LO1]

Big Sky Equipment manufactures and sells camping equipment. Employees in the production department are paid $30 per hour but receive $45 per hour for each hour worked in excess of 40 hours per week.

Required:
1. Calculate the total wages for the week if an employee works 50 hours. Of the total, how much would the company allocate to direct labour cost? To manufacturing overhead cost?
2. In a different week, suppose an employee works 45 hours but is idle for 3 hours during the week due to a shortage of direct materials used in production. Calculate the employee's total wages for the week. How much of this amount would be allocated to direct labour cost? To manufacturing overhead cost?
3. Big Sky provides employee benefits that cost $9 for each hour the employee works (either regular time or overtime). During a particular week, an employee works 52 hours but is idle for 6 hours due to an equipment breakdown. Calculate the employee's total wages and employee benefits for the week. If employee benefits are considered by the company to be part of manufacturing overhead cost, how much of the total wages and employee benefits for the week would be allocated to direct labour cost? To manufacturing overhead cost?
4. Refer to the data in (3) above. If the company treats that part of employee benefits relating to direct labour as added direct labour cost, how much of the wages and employee benefits for the week will be allocated to direct labour cost? To manufacturing overhead cost?

PROBLEM 2–15 Cost Classification [LO1, LO2, LO5, LO7]

Several years ago, Wallace Company purchased a small building adjacent to its manufacturing plant in order to have room for expansion when needed. Since the company had no immediate need for the extra space, it rented out the building to another company for a rental revenue of $35,000 per year. The renter's lease will expire soon, and rather than renewing the lease, Wallace Company has decided to use the building itself to manufacture a new product.

Direct materials cost for the new product will total $50 per unit. It will be necessary to hire a supervisor to oversee production. His salary will be $3,000 per month. Workers will be hired to manufacture the new product, with direct labour cost amounting to $22 per unit. Manufacturing operations will occupy all of the building space, so it will be necessary to rent space in a warehouse nearby to store finished units of product. The rental cost will be $1,500 per month. In addition, the company will need to rent equipment for use in producing the new product; the rental cost will be $2,200 per month. The company will continue to depreciate the building on a straight-line basis, as in past years. Depreciation on the building is $7,000 per year.

Advertising costs for the new product will total $28,000 per year. Costs of shipping the new product to customers will be $7 per unit. Electrical costs of operating machines will be $4 per unit.

To have funds to purchase materials, meet payrolls, and so forth, the company will have to liquidate some temporary investments. These investments are yielding a return of $5,000 per year.

Required:
Prepare an answer sheet with the following column headings:

Name of the Cost	Variable Cost	Fixed Cost	Product Cost			Period (Selling and Administrative) Cost	Opportunity Cost	Sunk Cost
			Direct Materials	Direct Labour	Manufacturing Overhead			

List the different costs associated with the new product decision down the left column (under Name of the Cost). Then place an X under each heading that describes the type of cost involved. There may be X's under several column headings for a single cost. (For example, a cost may be a fixed cost, a period cost, and a sunk cost; you would place an X under each of these column headings opposite the cost.)

PROBLEM 2–16 Classification of Costs as Variable or Fixed and Direct or Indirect [LO1, LO2, LO5, LO6]

Listed below are costs found in various organizations.

1. Depreciation, executive jet.
2. Costs of shipping finished goods to customers.
3. Wood used in manufacturing furniture.
4. Sales manager's salary.
5. Electricity used in manufacturing furniture.
6. Salary of the secretary to the company president.
7. Aerosol attachment placed on a spray can produced by the company.
8. Billing costs.
9. Packing supplies for shipping products overseas.
10. Sand used in manufacturing concrete.
11. Supervisor's salary, factory.
12. Executive life insurance.
13. Sales commissions.
14. Employee benefits, assembly-line workers.
15. Advertising costs.
16. Property taxes on warehouses used to store finished goods.
17. Lubricants for production equipment.

Required:
Prepare an answer sheet with column headings as shown below. For each cost item, indicate whether it would be variable or fixed with respect to the number of units produced and sold, and then whether it would be a selling cost, an administrative cost, or a product cost. If it is a product cost, indicate whether it would typically be treated as a direct or an indirect cost with respect to units of product. Three sample answers are provided for illustration:

Cost Item	Variable or Fixed	Selling Cost	Administrative Cost	Product Cost	
				Direct	Indirect
Direct labour	V			X	
Executive salaries	F		X		
Factory rent	F				X

PROBLEM 2-17 Schedule of Cost of Goods Manufactured; Income Statement; Cost Behaviour [LO1, LO2, LO3, LO4, LO5]
Various cost and sales data for Medco Inc. are given for the just-completed year:

Purchases of raw materials	$ 90,000
Raw materials inventory, beginning	10,000
Raw materials inventory, ending	17,000
Depreciation, factory	42,000
Insurance, factory	5,000
Direct labour	60,000
Maintenance, factory	30,000
Administrative expenses	70,000
Sales	450,000
Utilities, factory	27,000
Supplies, factory	1,000
Selling expenses	80,000
Indirect labour	65,000
Work in process inventory, beginning	7,000
Work in process inventory, ending	30,000
Finished goods inventory, beginning	10,000
Finished goods inventory, ending	40,000

Required:
1. Prepare a schedule of cost of goods manufactured.
2. Prepare an income statement.
3. Assume that the company produced the equivalent of 10,000 units of product during the year. What was the average cost per unit for direct materials? What was the average cost per unit for factory depreciation?
4. Assume that the company expects to produce 15,000 units of product during the coming year. What average cost per unit and what total cost would you expect the company to incur for direct materials at this level of activity? For factory depreciation? (In preparing your answer, assume that direct materials is a variable cost and that depreciation is a fixed cost; also assume that depreciation is computed on a straight-line basis.)
5. As the manager responsible for production costs, explain to the president any difference in the average costs per unit between (3) and (4) above.
6. Assuming the company produced 20,000 fully and partially finished units during the year, determine the cost components of the finished goods inventory, which is composed of 4,000 finished units.

PROBLEM 2-18 Classification of Salary Cost as a Period or Product Cost [LO2]
You have just been hired by EduRom Company, which was organized on January 2 of the current year. The company manufactures and sells a variety of educational DVDs for personal computers. It is your responsibility to supervise the employees who take orders from customers over the phone and to arrange for shipping orders via Federal Express, Canada Post, and other freight carriers.

The company is unsure how to classify your annual salary in its cost records. The company's cost analyst says that your salary should be classified as a manufacturing (product) cost, the controller says that it should be classified as a selling expense, and the president says that it doesn't matter which way your salary cost is classified.

Required:
1. Which viewpoint is correct? Why?
2. From the point of view of the reported operating income for the year, is the president correct in saying that it doesn't matter which way your salary cost is classified? Explain.

PROBLEM 2-19 Classification of Various Costs [LO1, LO2, LO5, LO7]

Todd Radford has invented a new type of low-friction broom. After giving the matter much thought, Todd is pretty sure he will quit his $2,000 per month job with a janitorial service and produce and sell the brooms full time. Todd will rent a small building and use it as a production plant. The rent will be $1,500 per month. Todd will rent production equipment at a cost of $550 per month.

The cost of materials for each broom will be $11.50. Todd will hire workers to produce the brooms. They will be paid $4.25 for each completed unit. Todd will rent a room in the house next door for use as his sales office. The rent will be $250 per month. He has arranged for the telephone company to add voicemail to his home phone to get after-hours messages from customers. The addition of voicemail will increase his monthly phone bill by $5.

Todd has some money in savings that is earning interest of $1,100 per year. These savings will be withdrawn and used for about a year to get the business going. To sell his brooms, Todd will advertise heavily in the local area. Advertising costs will be $450 per month. In addition, Todd will pay a sales commission of $0.80 for each broom sold. For the time being, Todd does not intend to draw any salary from the new company. Todd has already paid the legal and filing fees to incorporate his business. These fees amounted to $1,500.

Required:

1.   Prepare an answer sheet with the following column headings:

Name of the Cost	Variable Cost	Fixed Cost	Product Cost			Period (Selling and Administrative) Cost	Opportunity Cost	Sunk Cost
			Direct Materials	Direct Labour	Manufacturing Overhead			

List the different costs associated with the new company down the left column (under Name of Cost). Then place an X under each heading that describes the type of cost involved. There may be X's under several column headings for a single cost. (That is, a cost may be a fixed cost, a period cost, and a sunk cost; you would place an X under each of these column headings opposite the cost.) Under the variable cost column, list only those costs that would be variable with respect to the number of low-friction brooms that are produced and sold.

2.   All of the costs you have listed above, except one, are differential costs between the alternatives of Todd producing brooms or staying with the janitorial service. Which cost is *not* differential? Explain.

PROBLEM 2-20 Cost Classification and Cost Behaviour [LO2, LO5, LO6, LO7]

Heritage Company manufactures a beautiful bookcase that is very popular. The company has sufficient demand to keep production going indefinitely at the plant's full capacity of 4,000 bookcases per year. Annual cost data at full capacity follow:

Direct materials used (wood and glass).....................................	$430,000
General office salaries	110,000
Factory supervision...	70,000
Sales commissions...	60,000
Depreciation, factory building..	105,000
Depreciation, office equipment...	2,000
Indirect materials, factory...	18,000
Factory labour (cutting and assembly).....................................	90,000
Advertising	100,000
Insurance, factory	6,000
General office supplies (billing)..	4,000
Property taxes, factory...	20,000
Utilities, factory..	45,000

Required:

1.   Prepare an answer sheet with the column headings shown below. Enter each cost item on your answer sheet, placing the dollar amount under the appropriate headings. As examples, this has already been done for the first two items in the list above. Note that each cost item is classified in two ways: first, as either variable or fixed with respect to the

number of units produced and sold and, second, as either a selling and administrative cost or a product cost. (If the item is a product cost, it should also be classified as either direct or indirect, as shown.)

Cost Item	Cost Behaviour		Selling or Administrative Cost	Product Cost	
	Variable	Fixed		Direct	Indirect*
Direct materials used	$430,000			$430,000	
General office salaries		$110,000	$110,000		

*To units of product.

2. Total the dollar amounts in each of the columns in (1) above. Compute the average product cost per bookcase.
3. Due to a recession, assume that production drops to only 2,000 bookcases per year. Would you expect the average product cost per bookcase to increase, decrease, or remain unchanged? Explain. No computations are necessary.
4. Refer to the original data. The president's next-door neighbour has considered making herself a bookcase and has priced the necessary materials at a building supply store. As an alternative, she has asked the president whether she could purchase a bookcase from the Heritage Company "at cost," and the president has agreed to let her do so.
   a. Would you expect any disagreement between the two over the price the neighbour should pay? Explain. What price does the president probably have in mind? The neighbour?
   b. Since the company is operating at full capacity, what cost term used in the chapter might be justification for the president to charge the full regular price to the neighbour and still be selling "at cost"? Explain.

PROBLEM 2–21 Variable and Fixed Costs; Subtleties of Direct and Indirect Costs [LO5, LO6]
The Central Area Well-Baby Clinic provides a variety of health services to newborn babies and their parents. The clinic is organized into a number of departments, one of which is the Immunization Centre. A number of costs of the clinic and the Immunization Centre are listed below.
Example: The cost of polio immunization tablets.
a. The salary of the head nurse in the Immunization Centre.
b. Costs of incidental supplies consumed in the Immunization Centre, such as paper towels.
c. The cost of lighting and heating the Immunization Centre.
d. The cost of disposable syringes used in the Immunization Centre.
e. The salary of the Central Area Well-Baby Clinic's information systems manager.
f. The costs of mailing letters soliciting donations to the Central Area Well-Baby Clinic.
g. The wages of nurses who work in the Immunization Centre.
h. The cost of medical malpractice insurance for the Central Area Well-Baby Clinic.
i. Depreciation on the fixtures and equipment in the Immunization Centre.

Required:
For each cost listed above, indicate whether it is a direct or indirect cost of the Immunization Centre, whether it is a direct or indirect cost of immunizing particular patients, and whether it is variable or fixed with respect to the number of immunizations administered. Use the form shown below for your answer:

Item Description	Direct or Indirect Cost of the Immunization Centre		Direct or Indirect Cost of Particular Patients		Variable or Fixed with Respect to the Number of Immunizations Administered	
	Direct	Indirect	Direct	Indirect	Variable	Fixed
Example: The cost of polio immunization tablets	X		X		X	

PROBLEM 2–22 Schedule of Cost of Goods Manufactured; Income Statement
[LO1, LO2, LO3, LO4]
Veekay Company was organized on November 1 of the previous year. After seven months of start-up losses, management had expected to earn a profit during June, the most recent month. Management was disappointed, however, when the income statement for June also showed a loss. June's income statement follows:

VEEKAY COMPANY Income Statement For the Month Ended June 30		
Sales...		$660,000
Less operating expenses:		
Selling and administrative salaries.....................	$ 39,000	
Rent on facilities	40,000	
Purchases of raw materials...........................	209,000	
Insurance..	10,000	
Depreciation, sales equipment........................	11,000	
Utilities costs...	55,000	
Indirect labour..	119,000	
Direct labour	99,000	
Depreciation, factory equipment......................	13,000	
Maintenance, factory..................................	8,000	
Advertising..	88,000	691,000
Operating loss...		$ (31,000)

After seeing the $31,000 loss for June, Veekay's president stated, "I was sure we'd be profitable within six months, but after eight months we're still spilling red ink. Maybe it's time for us to throw in the towel. To make matters worse, I just heard that Debbie won't be back from her surgery for at least six more weeks."

Debbie is the company's controller; in her absence, the statement above was prepared by a new assistant who has had little experience in manufacturing operations. Additional information about the company follows:

a. Only 85% of the rent on facilities applies to factory operations; the remainder applies to selling and administrative activities.
b. Inventory balances at the beginning and end of June were as follows:

	June 1	June 30
Raw materials	$19,000	$46,000
Work in process...............................	77,000	94,000
Finished goods	22,000	66,000

c. Some 90% of the insurance and 80% of the utilities cost apply to factory operations; the remaining amounts apply to selling and administrative activities.

The president has asked you to check over the above income statement and recommend whether the company should continue operations.

Required:
1. As one step in gathering data for a recommendation to the president, prepare a schedule of cost of goods manufactured for June.
2. As a second step, prepare a new income statement for the month.
3. Based on your statements prepared in (1) and (2) above, would you recommend that the company continue operations?

PROBLEM 2–23 Ethics and the Manager [LO2]
The top management of General Electronics Inc. is well known for "managing by the numbers." With an eye on the company's desired growth in overall net profit, the company's CEO sets target profits at the beginning of the year for each of the company's divisions. The CEO has stated her policy as follows: "I won't interfere with operations in the divisions. I am available

for advice, but the division vice-presidents are free to do anything they want as long as they hit the target profits for the year."

In November, Stan Richart, the vice-president in charge of the Smartphone Technologies Division, saw that making the current year's target profit for his division was going to be very difficult. Among other actions, he directed that discretionary expenditures be delayed until the beginning of the new year. On December 30, he was angered to discover that a warehouse clerk had ordered $350,000 of smartphone parts earlier in December, even though the parts weren't really needed by the assembly department until January or February. Contrary to common accounting practice, the General Electronics Inc. *Accounting Policy Manual* states that such parts are to be recorded as an expense when delivered. To avoid recording the expense, Richart asked that the order be cancelled, but the Purchasing Department reported that the parts had already been delivered and the supplier would not accept returns. Since the bill had not yet been paid, Richart asked the Accounting Department to correct the clerk's mistake by delaying recognition of the delivery until the bill is paid in January.

Required:
1. Are Richart's actions ethical? Explain why they are or are not ethical.
2. Do the general management philosophy and accounting policies at General Electronics encourage or discourage ethical behaviour? Explain.

PROBLEM 2-24 Schedule of Cost of Goods Manufactured; Income Statement; Cost Behaviour [LO1, LO2, LO3, LO4, LO5]
Carlton Manufacturing Company provided the following details about operations in February:

Purchases of raw materials	$130,000
Maintenance, factory	37,000
Direct labour	32,500
Depreciation, factory equipment	55,000
Indirect materials, factory	3,000
Selling and administrative salaries	42,500
Utilities, factory	26,000
Sales commissions	17,500
Insurance, factory equipment	4,000
Depreciation, sales equipment	20,000
Advertising expenses	107,500
Rent, factory building	?

The company also provided details regarding the balances in the inventory accounts at the beginning and end of the month as follows:

	Beginning of Month	End of Month
Raw materials	$25,000	?
Work in process	24,000	?
Finished goods	15,000	?

Raw materials used in production cost $135,000, total overhead costs for the year were $170,000, the goods available for sale totalled $360,000, and the cost of goods sold totalled $317,500.

Required:
1. Prepare a schedule of cost of goods manufactured and the cost of goods sold section of the company's income statement for the year.
2. Assume that the dollar amounts given above are for the equivalent of 15,000 units produced during the year. Compute the average cost per unit for direct materials used, and compute the average cost per unit for rent on the factory building.
3. Assume that in the following year the company expects to produce 20,000 units. What average cost per unit and total cost would you expect to be incurred for direct materials, and for rent on the factory building? Direct materials are a variable cost and rent is a fixed cost.
4. As the manager in charge of production costs, explain to the president the reason for any difference in the average costs per unit between (2) and (3) above.

PROBLEM 2-25 Working with Incomplete Data from the Income Statement and Schedule of Cost of Goods Manufactured [LO3, LO4]

Supply the missing data in the four cases that follow. Each case is independent of the others:

	Case			
	1	2	3	4
Schedule of Cost of Goods Manufactured				
Direct materials..	$ 5,600	$ 10,400	$ 6,600	$ 7,600
Direct labour..	1,600	4,600	?	2,900
Manufacturing overhead	8,000	?	7,700	20,000
Total manufacturing costs.............................	?	28,800	19,800	?
Beginning work in process inventory.................	?	1,200	2,200	?
Ending work in process inventory.....................	3,200	4,000	?	1,900
Cost of goods manufactured...........................	14,400	?	17,600	29,900
Income Statement				
Sales..	$20,000	46,000	33,000	47,500
Beginning finished goods inventory....................	4,800	?	7,700	8,600
Cost of goods manufactured...........................	14,400	?	17,600	29,900
Goods available for sale	?	?	?	?
Ending finished goods inventory.......................	7,200	4,600	?	6,700
Cost of goods sold......................................	?	30,500	19,800	?
Gross margin	?	?	?	?
Selling and administrative expenses	4,800	?	?	9,500
Operating income..	?	6,300	3,300	?

PROBLEM 2-26 Income Statement; Schedule of Cost of Goods Manufactured [LO1, LO2, LO3, LO4]

The following information was taken from the accounting records of Mitchell Company for last year:

Selling expenses	$ 140,000
Raw materials inventory, January 1....................................	90,000
Raw materials inventory, December 31................................	60,000
Utilities, factory..	36,000
Direct labour cost..	150,000
Depreciation, factory..	162,000
Purchases of raw materials...	750,000
Sales...	2,500,000
Insurance, factory	40,000
Supplies, factory...	15,000
Administrative expenses	270,000
Indirect labour..	300,000
Maintenance, factory	87,000
Work in process inventory, January 1.................................	180,000
Work in process inventory, December 31..............................	100,000
Finished goods inventory, January 1...................................	260,000
Finished goods inventory, December 31...............................	210,000

Management wants to organize these data into a better format so that financial statements can be prepared for the year.

Required:
1. Prepare a schedule of cost of goods manufactured as in Exhibit 2–4.
2. Compute the cost of goods sold.
3. Using data as needed from (1) and (2) above, prepare an income statement.
4. Assuming production of finished and semi-finished goods amounted to 412,500 units for the past year, calculate the cost components of the ending finished goods inventory of 55,176 units. (*Hint:* The categories of costs in the ending inventory are the same as the total manufacturing costs; only the amounts are different.)

CASES

CASE 2-27 [LO1, LO2, LO3, LO4]

John Ranton, president and founder of Running Mate, could hardly contain his excitement over the operating results for his company's second year of operations. Running Mate is an online retailer of a GPS running watch that records distance, time, speed, heart rate, and a number of other statistics. Ranton's company does not manufacture the watches, but instead purchases them directly from the manufacturer based in China and resells them through its online shopping site. During the first two years of operation, Ranton decided to hold the selling price of the watch constant at $100 per unit in an effort to attract business. He was also able to negotiate a deal with the supplier to hold Running Mate's cost per watch constant at $80 per unit for the two years.

Operating expenses for each of the first two years of operation consist only of advertising expenses and the salaries paid to the website designer/administrator and the company's book-keeper. Because Ranton is busy with his numerous other business ventures, the bookkeeper also looks after the day-to-day operations of Running Mate and has sole signing authority to make expenditures on the company's behalf. To motivate his website designer to create a web-site that is easy to use and appealing to customers, Ranton decided to pay her a commission equal to 1% of annual sales in both 2015 and 2016. The salaries paid to the website administrator and the bookkeeper were the same in both years and totalled $92,000. Annual advertising expenses of $8,000 were also the same in both years.

After reviewing the operating results for 2015 (shown below), Ranton roughly calculated the expected sales and expenses for 2016 based on anticipated sales of 10,000 watches at a price of $100 per unit and a cost of $80 per unit. He calculated expected operating expenses in 2016 based on the 2015 cost per unit of $13.75 ($110,000 ÷ 8,000). Based on his calculations (shown below), Ranton expected a 25% improvement in 2016 operating income, in keeping with the increase in unit sales. So, when Running Mate's bookkeeper provided Ranton with the actual results shown below for 2016, he was thrilled. Operating income had improved 50% compared to 2015 on sales growth of 25%.

	2015	2016 Expected	2016 Actual
Sales (units)	8,000	10,000	10,000
Sales	$800,000	$1,000,000	$1,000,000
Cost of goods sold	640,000	800,000	800,000
Gross margin	160,000	200,000	200,000
Operating expenses	110,000	137,500	125,000
Operating income	$ 50,000	$ 62,500	$ 75,000

Ranton has always been an entrepreneur at heart but has no formal training in financial accounting or management accounting. He has always had the bookkeeper prepare annual financial statements.

Required:

1. Explain the nature of the error made by Ranton when calculating expected operating income for 2016.
2. Based on the information provided in the case, recalculate the expected results for 2016. For Ranton's benefit, provide details on the specific items included in operating expenses (advertising, salaries, and commissions). Based on your calculations of the expected results for 2016, are the actual results for 2016 as good as Ranton originally thought? Explain.
3. Compare the expected operating expenses per your calculations in (2) to the actual results shown above for 2016. If you were Ranton, what follow-up questions would you have for the bookkeeper about 2016 operations?

CASE 2-28 Differential Revenues and Costs, Opportunity Costs, and Sunk Costs [LO7]

Performance Edge (PE) is a consulting company with offices in all major Canadian cities; its cor-porate headquarters are in Hamilton, Ontario. The company specializes in developing employee reward and recognition programs for its clients, which range from manufacturing companies to reservation centres for hotel chains. One of the most popular programs developed by PE involves working with its clients' management teams to establish performance goals for employees.

Once the performance goals are established, PE develops a reward program whereby employees receive points instead of cash for attaining the goals set by management. The more difficult the goal, the greater the number of points received by the employee for goal attainment. The points can be redeemed for prizes such as bicycles; barbecues; computers; cameras; vacations; and gift certificates to restaurants, clothing and jewellery stores, and so on. PE has developed a catalogue of prizes that is distributed to employees so that they can see what they will be able to redeem their points for should they attain their performance goals for the period.

As part of the service offered to its clients, PE maintains an inventory of the prizes that can be purchased by its clients' employees with their points. PE purchases the prizes directly from manufacturers and wholesalers but maintains a reasonably large inventory of most items offered in its catalogue to ensure that they are available to clients on a timely basis. The inventory is kept in a warehouse at Stoney Creek, a community that is part of the city of Hamilton. The warehouse was purchased several years ago, and PE has grown considerably since then. Indeed, in recent months, delays have occurred in getting prizes to some clients because the warehouse is no longer large enough to maintain sufficient quantities of all items.

About a month ago, Reg White, the facilities manager at PE, became aware of a larger warehouse in nearby Burlington that is available for a long-term lease. The lease would qualify as an operating lease, so the monthly lease payments would be expensed. Although the warehouse in Burlington is larger than the current facility in Stoney Creek, White estimates that the utility costs will be lower because it is more modern and energy efficient. Another benefit of moving to the new warehouse will be that PE won't have to pay property taxes or building insurance since it won't own the building. Also, because the new warehouse is larger than PE currently requires to maintain an adequate inventory of prizes, it will be able to sublet about 15% of the total space to another tenant, at least for the next few years until it needs to take over the entire facility.

White also believes that it shouldn't be too hard to sell the existing warehouse in Stoney Creek based on conversations he has had with a commercial property real estate agent who already has clients interested in making an offer. Because the existing warehouse isn't yet fully depreciated, White also thinks that selling it will help PE's bottom line because the company will no longer have to charge the depreciation expense to the income statement. Another benefit of selling the existing warehouse is that PE will no longer incur the maintenance and repair costs, or the salary of the building maintenance manager, who will be let go if the company decides to rent the new facility. Maintenance costs of the new warehouse will be paid by the building's owner, unless the repairs are the result of damage caused by PE, in which case PE will be responsible for the costs. White thinks that insurance on the inventory of prizes and the costs of security personnel on-site 24/7 will not change if PE decides to move to the new warehouse.

One drawback in selling the existing warehouse is that PE will no longer earn the operating income associated with the small parking lot it had on one corner of the property. PE rented parking spaces to employees of a business on an adjacent property that did not have its own parking. Net of the annual costs of maintaining the parking lot (snow removal, repairs, security cameras, etc.), PE made a small operating profit each year.

Required:
1. Identify the differential revenues and costs related to keeping the existing warehouse in Stoney Creek versus renting the new facility in Burlington.
2. Are there any opportunity costs associated with selling the old warehouse?
3. What kind of cost is the depreciation expense on the old warehouse? Should it be considered in deciding whether to stay in the existing location or rent the new facility? Why or why not?

INSTANT QUIZ SOLUTIONS

2-1
The accounts payable personnel are not involved in manufacturing activities and so their salaries are not manufacturing costs.

2-2
The chief financial officer's wages are considered a period cost because he or she is typically not involved in the production of the product.

2-3

Cost of goods sold = Beginning inventory + Purchases − Ending inventory
Rearranging to solve for purchases:
     Purchases = Cost of goods sold − Beginning inventory + Ending inventory
Purchases = $250,000 − $50,000 + $40,000
Purchases = $240,000

2-4

Cost of goods manufactured = Direct materials + Direct labour + Manufacturing overhead +
     Beginning work in process inventory − Ending work in process inventory
Cost of goods manufactured = $205,000 + $30,000 + $175,000 + $45,000 − $30,000
Cost of goods manufactured = $425,000

2-5

Total machine rental costs: $8,000
Average machine rental costs per test: $8,000 ÷ 1,000 tests = $8 per test
Total machine rental costs if number of tests is 4,000 per month will likely be $16,000 ($8,000 ×
2 machines). Two machines will be needed, since each machine can only perform 2,000 tests per
month.

2-6

Net book value is a sunk cost since it simply represents the amount of the original cost (a sunk
cost) that has not yet been expensed through depreciation.

2-7

The salvage value is an opportunity cost since it represents a potential benefit that would be
given up if the equipment were not sold.

CHAPTER 3

Learning Objectives

After studying Chapter 3, you should be able to

1 Describe how fixed and variable costs behave and how to use them to predict costs.

2 Analyze mixed costs using various approaches.

3 Prepare an income statement using the contribution format.

4 (Appendix 3A) Analyze a mixed cost using the least-squares regression method.

COST BEHAVIOUR: ANALYSIS AND USE

■ COSTLY BEHAVIOUR REQUIRED

Cervélo Cycles manufactures racing bike frames and has its headquarters in Toronto, Ontario. Founded in 1996, the company is now the world's largest manufacturer of triathlon and time-trial bikes. Before deciding to introduce a new model to its current lineup of bikes, Cervélo's management must estimate the profits that will be generated. Developing profit estimates will require management to forecast unit sales for the new model, set the selling price, and estimate the incremental costs that will be incurred. Predicting some of the incremental costs, such as raw materials, is easy, since they tend to vary in direct proportion with the estimated number of units to be produced. However, other costs, such as direct labour, are tougher to predict, since management must consider whether additional production employees have to be hired or whether production for the new model can be met with the existing workforce. Other costs may be even more difficult to predict. For example, if introducing a new model requires Cervélo to expand its production facilities, some of the costs related to maintaining the new plant, such as indirect materials, will vary with production volume. However, other types of maintenance costs, such as the salary of the maintenance supervisor, will remain constant across a fairly wide range of production volumes. Thus, it is important to break down some categories of costs, such as maintenance, into fixed and variable components to estimate how they will behave in total.

It is clear from the discussion above that Cervélo's management must thoroughly understand how a wide variety of costs behave. Moreover, they must use this understanding of cost behaviour to predict the total costs that will be incurred under different assumptions about the demand for the new model. Analyzing the profit implications of new product development is just one of many examples of how a detailed knowledge of cost behaviour can help management make sound decisions.

What are the different cost behaviour patterns that management should understand? What approaches can be used to develop cost-prediction models? These key topics are covered in this chapter.

Source: http://www.cervelo.com.

In Chapter 2, we explained that costs can be classified by behaviour. *Cost behaviour* refers to how a cost will react or change as changes take place in the level of business activity. An understanding of cost behaviour is key to many decisions in an organization. Managers who understand how costs behave are better able to predict what costs will be under various operating circumstances. Attempts at decision making without a thorough understanding of cost behaviour patterns can lead to problems. For example, a decision to drop a particular product line might result in far lower cost savings than managers had assumed—leading to a decline in profits. To avoid such problems, a manager must be able to accurately predict what costs will be at various activity levels.

This chapter briefly reviews the definitions of variable costs and fixed costs and then discusses the behaviour of these costs in greater depth than in Chapter 2. We also introduce a third type of cost behaviour pattern, known as a *mixed* or *semi-variable* cost. All three cost behaviour patterns—variable, fixed, and mixed—are found in most organizations. The relative proportion of each type of cost present in a firm represents the firm's **cost structure**. For example, an organization might have many fixed costs but few variable or mixed costs. Alternatively, it might have many variable costs but few fixed or mixed costs. A firm's cost structure can have a significant effect on its decisions. In this chapter, we will concentrate on gaining a fuller understanding of the behaviour of each type of cost. In Chapter 4, we will more fully discuss how cost structure can affect decision making. We conclude the chapter by introducing a new income statement format—called the *contribution format*—in which costs are organized by behaviour rather than by the traditional functions of production, sales, and administration.

Cost behaviour, as presented in this chapter, introduces the description and analytical techniques needed for many areas of managerial accounting, including costing, planning and control, and decision making. The descriptions and techniques presented here are simplified so that they are easily understandable, but the ideas are appropriate for analyzing more complex situations that will appear in later chapters.

Cost structure
The relative proportion of fixed, variable, and mixed costs found in an organization.

■ TYPES OF COST BEHAVIOUR PATTERNS

Variable Costs

LEARNING OBJECTIVE ❶
Describe how fixed and variable costs behave and how to use them to predict costs.

We explained in Chapter 2 that a variable cost is one whose *total dollar* amount varies in direct proportion to changes in the activity level. This means that if the activity level doubles, the total dollar amount of the variable costs also doubles. If the activity level increases by only 10%, then the total dollar amount of the variable costs increases by 10% as well, and so on.

We also learned in Chapter 2 that a variable cost remains constant if expressed on a *per unit* basis. For example, consider Sledding Adventures, a small company based in Whistler, British Columbia, that provides dog sled tours. After every tour, which lasts about two hours, the company gives each customer a drink (coffee, tea, or hot chocolate) and a light snack. The drinks and snacks ("refreshments") cost Sledding Adventures $10 per person. If we look at the cost of the refreshments on a *per person* basis, the cost is constant at $10. This $10 cost per person will not change, regardless of how many customers are served by Sledding Adventures. The behaviour of this variable cost, on both a per unit and a total basis, is tabulated as follows:

Number of Customers	Refreshment Cost per Customer	Total Cost of Refreshments
100	$10	$ 1,000
200	10	2,000
400	10	4,000
800	10	8,000

EXHIBIT 3-1   Variable Cost Behaviour

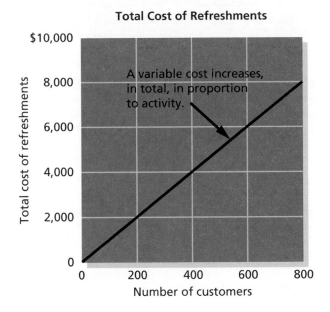

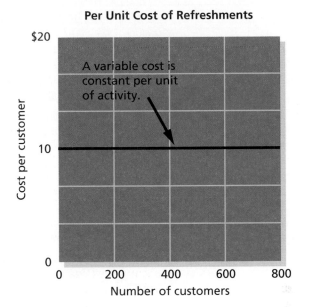

The idea that a variable cost is constant per unit but varies in total with the activity level is crucial to an understanding of cost behaviour patterns. We will rely on this concept repeatedly in this chapter and in subsequent chapters. However, it is possible for the variable cost per unit to change once activity levels are outside the relevant range. In the above example, if Sledding Adventures needed 1,500 refreshments, the unit cost might drop below $10 per refreshment if a quantity discount is provided by the supplier of the drinks or snacks. Similarly, if fewer than 100 refreshments were required, the unit cost per refreshment might be more than $10.

Exhibit 3–1 illustrates variable cost behaviour graphically. Note that the graph of the total refreshment costs slopes upward to the right. This is because the total cost of refreshments is directly proportional to the number of customers. In contrast, the graph of the per unit cost of refreshments is flat because the cost of refreshments per customer is constant at $10.

The Activity Base   For a cost to be variable, it must be variable *with respect to something*. That "something" is its *activity base*. An **activity base** is a measure of whatever causes a variable cost to be incurred. Some of the most common activity bases are direct labour-hours, machine-hours, units produced, and units sold. Other examples of activity bases are the number of kilometres driven by salespeople, the number of kilograms of laundry processed by a hotel, the number of calls handled by a customer service department, and the number of occupied beds in a hospital.

To plan and control variable costs, a manager must be well acquainted with the various activity bases within the firm. People sometimes think that if a cost doesn't vary with production or with sales, then it is not really a variable cost. This is incorrect. As suggested by the range of bases or drivers listed above, costs are caused by many different activities within an organization. Whether a cost is considered to be variable depends on whether it is caused by the activity under consideration. For example, if a manager is analyzing the cost of service calls for a product warranty, the relevant activity measure is the number of service calls made. Those costs that vary in total with the number of service calls made are the variable costs of making service calls.

Nevertheless, unless stated otherwise, you can assume that the activity base under consideration is the total volume of goods and services produced or sold by the

Activity base
A measure of whatever causes a variable cost to be incurred. For example, the total cost of direct materials in a bicycle manufacturing company will increase as the number of bicycles produced increases. Therefore, the number of bicycles produced is an activity base for explaining the total cost of direct materials.

IN BUSINESS

The Sporthotel Theresa (http://www.theresa.at/), owned and operated by the Egger family, is a four-star hotel located in Zell im Zillertal, Austria. The hotel features access to hiking, skiing, biking, and other activities in the Ziller Alps as well as its own fitness facility and spa.

Three full meals a day are included in the hotel room charge. Breakfast and lunch are served buffet-style, while dinner is a more formal affair with as many as six courses. The chef, Stefan Egger, believes that food costs are roughly proportional to the number of guests staying at the hotel; that is, they are a variable cost. He must order food from suppliers two or three days in advance, but he adjusts his purchases to the number of guests who are currently staying at the hotel and their consumption patterns. In addition, guests choose from the dinner menu early in the day, which helps Stefan plan which foodstuffs will be required for dinner. Consequently, he is able to prepare just enough food so that all guests are satisfied and yet waste is held to a minimum.

Source: Conversation with Stefan Egger, chef at the Sporthotel Theresa.

---

organization. So, for example, if we ask whether the cost of direct materials at Cervélo is a variable cost, the answer is yes, since the cost of direct materials is variable with respect to Cervélo's total volume of production. We will specify the activity base only when it is something other than total production or sales.

Extent of Variable Costs   The number and type of variable costs present in an organization depend in large part on the organization's structure and purpose. A public utility like Hydro One, with large investments in equipment, tends to have few variable costs. Most of the costs are associated with its plant, and these costs tend to be insensitive to changes in levels of service provided. A manufacturing company like Paradigm, by contrast, often has many variable costs; these costs are associated with both manufacturing and distributing its products to customers.

Merchandising companies like Future Shop and Canadian Tire usually have a high proportion of variable costs in their cost structure. In most merchandising companies, the cost of merchandise purchased for resale, a variable cost, constitutes a very large component of total cost. Service companies, by contrast, have diverse cost structures. Some service companies, such as the restaurant chain Harvey's, have significant variable costs because of their raw material costs. On the other hand, service companies involved in consulting, auditing, engineering, dental, medical, software development, and architectural activities have very large fixed costs in the form of expensive facilities and highly trained salaried employees.

Some of the more frequently encountered variable costs are listed in Exhibit 3–2. This exhibit is not a complete listing of all costs that can be considered variable. Moreover, some of the costs listed in the exhibit may behave more like fixed than variable costs in some organizations and in some circumstances. We will see some examples of this later in the chapter. Nevertheless, Exhibit 3–2 is a useful list of many of the costs that are normally considered variable with respect to the volume of output.

True Variable versus Step-Variable Costs

Not all variable costs have exactly the same behaviour pattern. Some variable costs behave in a *true variable* or *proportionately variable* pattern. Other variable costs behave in a *step-variable* pattern.

True Variable Costs   Direct materials is a true or proportionately variable cost because the amount used during a period varies in direct proportion to the level of

EXHIBIT 3-2   Examples of Variable Costs

Type of Organization	Costs That Are Normally Variable with Respect to Volume of Output
Merchandising company	Cost of goods (merchandise) sold

Manufacturing company	Manufacturing costs:
	  Direct materials
	Variable portion of manufacturing overhead:
	  Indirect materials, such as lubricants or supplies
	  Power

Both merchandising and manufacturing companies	Selling, general, and administrative costs:
	  Sales commissions
	  Clerical costs, such as billing
	  Shipping costs

Service organizations	Supplies, travel, clerical

production activity. Moreover, any amounts purchased but not used can be stored and carried forward to the next period as inventory.

Step-Variable Costs   The cost of a resource that is obtainable only in large amounts (such as maintenance workers) and that increases or decreases only in response to fairly wide changes in activity is known as a **step-variable cost**. For example, the wages of maintenance workers are often considered to be a variable cost, but this labour cost doesn't behave in quite the same way as the cost of direct materials. Unlike direct materials, the time of maintenance workers is obtainable only in large blocks. Moreover, any maintenance time not utilized cannot be stored as inventory and carried forward to the next period. If the time is not used effectively, it is gone forever. Furthermore, a maintenance crew can work at a fairly leisurely pace if there is limited work to do but intensify its efforts if things get busy. For this reason, small changes in the level of production may have no effect on the number of maintenance workers employed by the company.

The behaviour of a step-variable cost is contrasted with the behaviour of a true variable cost in Exhibit 3–3. Notice that the need for maintenance help changes only with fairly wide changes in volume and that when additional maintenance time is obtained, it comes in large, indivisible chunks. The strategy of management

Step-variable cost
A cost (such as the cost of a maintenance worker) that is obtainable only in large amounts and that increases and decreases only in response to fairly wide changes in the activity level.

IN BUSINESS

Majestic Ocean Kayaking, of Ucluelet, British Columbia, is owned and operated by Tracy and Ted Eeftink. The company offers a number of guided kayaking excursions ranging from three-hour tours of the Ucluelet harbor to six-day kayaking and camping trips in Clayoquot Sound. One of the company's excursions is a four-day kayaking and camping trip to The Broken Group Islands in the Pacific Rim National Park Reserve. Special regulations apply to trips in the park—including a requirement that one certified guide must be assigned for every five guests or fraction thereof. For example, a trip with 12 guests must have at least three certified guides. Guides are not salaried and are paid on a per-day basis. Therefore, the cost to the company of the guides for a trip is a step-variable cost rather than a fixed cost or a true variable cost. One guide is needed for 1 to 5 guests, two guides for 6 to 10 guests, three guides for 11 to 15 guests, and so on.

Source: Tracy Eeftink, co-owner, Majestic Ocean Kayaking. For more information about the company, see http://www.oceankayaking.com.

EXHIBIT 3-3 True Variable versus Step-Variable Costs

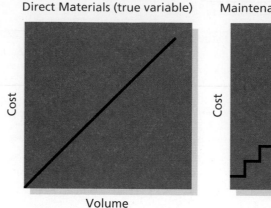

Direct Materials (true variable)

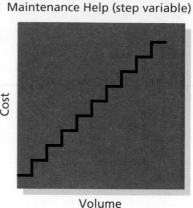

Maintenance Help (step variable)

in dealing with step-variable costs must be to obtain the fullest use of services possible for each separate step. Great care must be taken in working with these kinds of costs to prevent unneeded resources from building up in an organization. There may be a tendency to employ additional help more quickly than needed, and there is a natural reluctance to lay off people when volume declines.

The Linearity Assumption and the Relevant Range

In dealing with variable costs, we have assumed a strictly linear relationship between cost and volume, except in the case of step-variable costs. Economists correctly point out that many costs classified by accountants as variable actually behave in a *curvilinear* fashion. The behaviour of **curvilinear costs** is shown in Exhibit 3–4.

Curvilinear costs
Costs that show a curved relationship between cost and activity rather than a straight-line relationship.

Although many costs are not strictly linear, a curvilinear cost can be reasonably approximated with a straight line within the band of activity known as the *relevant range*. The relevant range is that range of activity within which the assumptions made about cost behaviour are valid. For example, note that the dashed line in Exhibit 3–4 can be used as an accurate approximation to the curvilinear cost within the shaded relevant range. However, outside the relevant range, this particular straight line is a poor approximation to the curvilinear cost relationship. Managers should always keep in mind that a particular assumption about cost behaviour may be invalid if activity falls outside the relevant range.

EXHIBIT 3-4 Curvilinear Costs and the Relevant Range

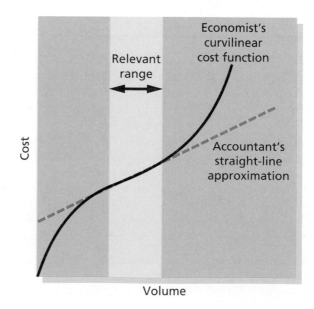

EXHIBIT 3-5   Fixed Cost Behaviour

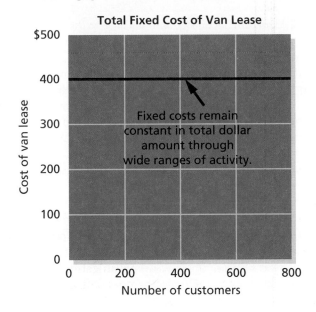

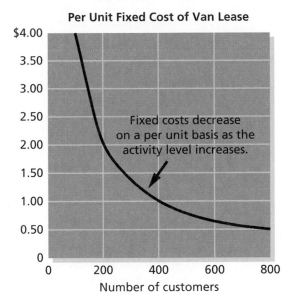

Fixed Costs

In our discussion of cost behaviour patterns in Chapter 2, we stated that total fixed costs remain constant within the relevant range of activity. To continue the Sledding Adventures example, assume the company decides to lease a van for $400 per month to pick up customers at their hotel and return them there after the tour. The *total* amount of the lease payments is the same regardless of the number of customers the company takes on its sledding tours during any given month. This cost behaviour pattern is shown graphically in Exhibit 3–5.

Since fixed costs remain constant in total, the average fixed cost *per unit* becomes progressively smaller as the level of activity increases. If Sledding Adventures has only 100 customers in a month, the $400 fixed rental cost amounts to an average of $4 per customer. If there are 800 customers, the fixed rental cost averages only 50 cents per customer. This aspect of the behaviour of fixed costs is also displayed in Exhibit 3–5. Note that as the number of customers increases, the average unit cost drops, but it drops at a decreasing rate. The first customers have the greatest impact on the average fixed costs per unit.

It is sometimes necessary to express fixed costs on an average per unit basis. For example, in Chapter 2 we showed how unit product costs computed for use in external financial statements contain both variable and fixed costs. However, we caution against expressing fixed costs on an average per unit basis in internal reports because it creates the false impression that fixed costs actually change as the level of activity changes. To avoid confusion in internal reporting and decision-making situations, fixed costs should be expressed in total rather than on a per unit basis.

> **Instant Quiz 3-2**
> Based on Exhibit 3-5, what is the average lease cost per customer if there are 200 customers in a month? What are the total lease costs if there are 200 customers in a month?

Types of Fixed Costs

Fixed costs are sometimes referred to as *capacity costs*, since they result from outlays made for buildings, equipment, skilled employees, and other resources required to provide the basic capacity for sustained operations. For planning purposes, fixed costs can be viewed as being either *committed* or *discretionary*.

Committed Fixed Costs   **Committed fixed costs** are those investments in facilities, equipment, and the basic organizational structure that cannot be significantly reduced, even for short time periods, without making fundamental changes that would

Committed fixed costs
Fixed costs that are difficult to adjust in the short term and that relate to the investment in facilities, equipment, and the basic organizational structure of a firm.

IN BUSINESS

A growing number of companies and individuals are becoming more sensitive to the amount of greenhouse gas emissions for which they are responsible. Numerous online resources are now available for calculating the quantity of these emissions, known as the *carbon footprint* (e.g., The Greenhouse Gas Protocol, http://www.ghgprotocol.org). Increasingly, companies are recognizing that reducing their carbon footprint can be a win–win situation. Not only does improving energy conservation, reducing wastage, and so on, have environmental benefits, but companies are learning that going green can have positive effects on profits as well. For example, companies can significantly reduce electricity costs by switching to energy-efficient light bulbs, turning down thermostats, and switching off equipment not being used. Travel expenses can be reduced by using video-conferencing facilities such as Skype, and office expenses can be reduced by double-sided printing, or using only electronic versions of documents. These are just a few examples of the potential that going green has for reducing variable and fixed costs alike. Experts estimate that implementing such simple strategies to reduce the size of the carbon footprint can improve profits by nearly 40% for larger companies. A survey conducted by the Canadian Federation of Independent Business, which represents over 100,000 small businesses in Canada, indicates that environmental awareness is not just about the bottom line. About 50% of respondents indicated that cost savings is one factor that motivated them to "go green." However, over 80% responded that they are actively trying to reduce their carbon footprint because it is the right thing to do for the well-being of the environment.

Source: Chris Young, "A Recession Is a Good Time to Go Green," *Financial Post*, October 7, 2009.

impair a firm's ability to attain its long-term objectives. Examples are depreciation of buildings and equipment, property taxes, insurance expenses, and salaries of top management and operating personnel. Even if operations are temporarily interrupted or activity levels reduced, committed fixed costs remain largely unchanged in the short term. Once a decision is made to acquire committed fixed resources, the company may be locked into that decision for many years. Consequently, such commitments should be made only after carefully analyzing the available alternatives. Long-term investment decisions involving committed fixed costs will be examined in Chapter 13.

Discretionary fixed costs
Fixed costs arising from annual decisions by management to spend in certain areas, such as advertising and research.

Discretionary Fixed Costs
Discretionary fixed costs, often called *managed fixed costs*, are those costs that arise from annual decisions by management to spend in certain fixed cost areas. Examples of discretionary fixed costs are advertising, research and development, and management training programs.

Two key differences exist between discretionary and committed fixed costs. First, the planning horizon for a discretionary fixed cost is short term—usually a single year. By contrast, committed fixed costs have a planning horizon that extends several years. Second, unlike committed costs, discretionary fixed costs can be reduced in the short run with minimal damage to the long-run organizational objectives. For example, spending on management training programs can be reduced because of poor economic conditions. Although some unfavourable consequences may result from the reduction, they are unlikely to be as severe as those that would result if the company decided to reduce committed fixed costs by laying off key personnel.

Whether a particular cost is regarded as committed or discretionary may depend on management's strategy. For example, during recessions when the level of home building is down, some construction companies lay off most of their workers and have a minimal level of operations. Conversely, other construction companies retain large numbers of employees on the payroll, even though the workers have little or no work to do. While these latter companies may be faced with short-term cash flow

IN BUSINESS

The trend of companies having a relatively large proportion of their total costs made up by committed fixed costs related to the employment of knowledge workers has considerable implications for an organization's planning and control system. For example, at a software development company such as Enflick, based in Waterloo, Ontario, knowing that the majority of their expenses are the fixed wages paid to their programmers makes developing accurate expense budgets quite easy. This is because unless new programmers are hired or existing ones leave, the majority of Enflick's expenses will stay the same from one month to the next. However, a big challenge for companies like Enflick is deciding how many programmers to hire, particularly when the business is first starting to grow. When dealing with committed fixed costs related to knowledge workers, acquiring the appropriate amount of this human capital resource is critical to the success of an organization. The goal is to avoid having too many or too few committed fixed costs relative to what is necessary to meet the demand for the products or services. Given how difficult it is to reduce committed fixed costs such as knowledge workers in the short run, determining and maintaining appropriate staffing levels has become a very important issue for companies in the high-tech sector.

problems, it will be easier for them to respond quickly when economic conditions improve. The most important characteristic of discretionary fixed costs is that management is not locked into its decisions regarding such costs. Discretionary costs can be adjusted from year to year or even perhaps during the course of a year if necessary.

The Trend toward Fixed Costs   The trend in many companies is toward greater fixed costs relative to variable costs. Tasks that used to be performed by hand have been taken over by machines. For example, grocery clerks at Loblaws and Sobeys used to key in prices by hand on cash registers. Now, stores are equipped with bar code readers that enter price and other product information automatically, and many have self-checkout stations where customers pay for their purchases without the involvement of store personnel. In general, competition has created pressure to give customers more value for their money—a demand that can often be satisfied only by automating business processes. For example, H&R Block used to fill out tax returns for customers mainly by hand, and the advice given to a customer largely depended on the knowledge of that particular employee. Now, sophisticated computer software based on the accumulated knowledge of many experts is used to complete tax returns, and the software provides the customer with tax planning and other advice tailored to their needs.

As the extent of automation has grown, so too has the demand for *knowledge workers*—those who work primarily with their minds rather than their hands. Knowledge workers tend to be salaried, highly trained, and difficult to replace; the costs of compensating knowledge workers are often relatively fixed and are committed rather than discretionary costs. This trend toward companies having a higher proportion of committed fixed costs is likely to continue for the foreseeable future.

Fixed Costs and the Relevant Range

The concept of the relevant range discussed earlier is also important in understanding fixed costs. The relevant range of activity for a fixed cost is the range of activity over which the graph of the cost is flat, as in Exhibit 3–6. As a company expands its level of activity, it may outgrow its facilities, or the key management team may need to be expanded. The result, of course, will be increased committed fixed costs as larger facilities are built and as new management positions are created.

One reaction to the step pattern depicted in Exhibit 3–6 is to say that fixed costs are really just a type of step-variable costs. To some extent this is true, since almost

EXHIBIT 3-6 Fixed Costs and the Relevant Range

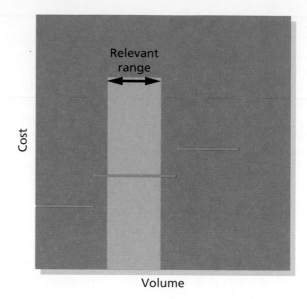

all costs can be adjusted in the long run. However, there are two major differences between the step-variable costs depicted earlier in Exhibit 3–3 and the fixed costs depicted in Exhibit 3–6. First, step-variable costs can often be adjusted quickly as conditions change, whereas once fixed costs have been set, they often cannot be changed easily. For example, a step-variable cost such as maintenance labour can easily be adjusted upward or downward by hiring and laying off maintenance workers. By contrast, once a company has signed a lease for a building, it is locked into that level of lease cost for the life of the contract.

Second, the *width of the steps* depicted for step-variable costs is much narrower than the width of the steps depicted for the fixed costs in Exhibit 3–6. The width of the steps relates to the volume or level of activity. For step-variable costs, the width of a step may be 40 hours of activity or less when dealing with a cost such as maintenance labour. However, for fixed costs, the width of a step may be *thousands* or even *tens of thousands* of hours of activity when dealing with a committed cost related to production equipment. Because the width of the steps for step-variable costs is generally so narrow, these costs can be treated as variable costs for most purposes. Conversely, the width of the steps for fixed costs is so wide that these costs must generally be treated as being fixed within the entire relevant range of activity.

Mixed Costs

A mixed cost contains both variable and fixed cost elements. Mixed costs are also known as *semi-variable costs*. To continue the Sledding Adventures example, the company pays $400 per month in van lease payments plus $0.20 per kilometre to operate the van. If the company drives 1,000 kilometres in a month, the total vehicle costs will be $600, made up of $400 in fixed cost plus $200 in variable cost. Exhibit 3–7 shows the behaviour of this mixed cost.

Even if Sledding Adventures fails to attract any customers in a particular month and does not use the van to pick up clients (or for any other purpose), the company will still have to pay the $400 fixed lease cost for the van. This is why the cost line in Exhibit 3–7 intersects the vertical cost axis at the $400 point. For every kilometre the van is driven, costs will increase by $0.20. Therefore, the total cost line slopes upward as the variable cost element is added to the fixed cost element.

Since the mixed cost in Exhibit 3–7 is represented by a straight line, the following equation for a straight line can be used to express the relationship between mixed cost and the level of activity:

$$Y = a + bX$$

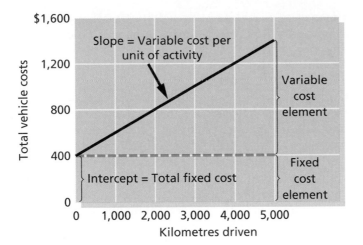

EXHIBIT 3-7 Mixed Cost Behaviour

In this equation,

Y = The total mixed cost
a = The total fixed cost (the vertical intercept of the line)
b = The variable cost per unit of activity (the slope of the line)
X = The level of activity

Because the variable cost per unit equals the slope of the straight line, the steeper the slope, the higher the variable cost per unit.

In the case of the total vehicle cost paid by Sledding Adventures, the equation is written as follows:

$$Y = \$400 + \$0.20X$$

| Total mixed cost | Total fixed cost | Variable cost per unit of activity | Activity level |

This equation makes it very easy to calculate what the total mixed cost would be for any level of activity within the relevant range. For example, suppose that the company expects to drive the van 3,000 kilometres next month. Then the total vehicle costs will be $1,000, calculated as follows:

$$Y = \$400 + (\$0.20 \text{ per kilometre} \times 3,000 \text{ kilometres})$$
$$= \$1,000$$

> **Instant Quiz 3-3**
> Cool Gadgets pays all sales staff a fixed salary of $2,000 per month plus a 5% commission on sales. What type of cost are total sales staff wages at Cool Gadgets? Write the equation for total monthly sales staff wages.

ANALYZING MIXED COSTS

Mixed costs are very common. For example, the cost of providing X-ray services to patients at southwestern Ontario's Grand River Hospital is a mixed cost. The costs of equipment depreciation and radiologists' and technicians' salaries are fixed, but the costs of X-ray film, power, and supplies are variable. At Air Canada facilities across Canada, maintenance costs are a mixed cost. The company must incur fixed costs for renting maintenance facilities and for keeping skilled mechanics on the payroll, but the costs of replacement parts, lubricating oils, tires, and so forth, are variable with respect to how often and how far the company's aircraft are flown.

The fixed portion of a mixed cost represents the basic minimum cost of having an activity *ready and available* for use. The variable portion represents the cost incurred for *actual consumption* of the activity. The variable element varies in proportion to the amount of activity that is consumed.

LEARNING OBJECTIVE ❷
Analyze mixed costs using various approaches.

How does management go about actually estimating the fixed and variable components of a mixed cost? Common methods used in practice are *account analysis* and the *engineering approach*.

In **account analysis**, each account under consideration is classified as either variable or fixed, based on the analyst's prior knowledge of how the cost in the account behaves, which is often developed by analyzing past records of cost and activity data. For example, direct materials are classified as variable because they vary in direct proportion with the number of units produced, while a building lease cost is classified as fixed because over the relevant range of activity it does not vary. The total fixed cost is the sum of the costs for the accounts that have been classified as fixed. The variable cost per unit is estimated by dividing the sum of the costs for the accounts that have been classified as variable by the total activity.

The **engineering approach** to cost analysis involves a detailed analysis of what cost behaviour *should* be, based on an industrial engineer's evaluation of the production methods to be used, the materials specifications, labour requirements, equipment usage, efficiency of production, power consumption, and so on. The engineering approach may be used in conjunction with developing standard costs for each unit produced, which is discussed in detail in Chapter 10. For example, Pizza Hut might use the engineering approach to estimate the cost of serving a particular take-out pizza. The cost of the pizza is estimated by carefully costing the specific ingredients used to make the pizza, the power consumed to cook the pizza, and the cost of the container in which the pizza is delivered. The engineering approach is typically used in situations where no past experience is available on activity and costs.

Account analysis
A method for analyzing cost behaviour in which each account under consideration is classified as either variable or fixed based on the analyst's prior knowledge of how the cost in the account behaves.

Engineering approach
A detailed analysis of cost behaviour based on an industrial engineer's evaluation of the inputs required to carry out a particular activity and of the prices of those inputs.

Diagnosing Cost Behaviour with a Scattergram Plot

James Ng, the chief financial officer of the Hamilton Hotel, began his analysis of electrical costs by collecting cost and activity data for a number of recent months. These data are as follows:

Month	Activity Level: Occupancy-Days	Electrical Costs
January	2,600	$6,260
February	2,850	6,550
March	3,530	8,000
April	1,440	4,000
May	540	2,300
June	1,120	3,600
July	3,160	7,300
August	3,610	8,100
September	1,260	3,700
October	190	1,773
November	1,080	3,320
December	2,050	5,200

The first step in analyzing the cost and activity data is to plot the data on a scattergram. This plot immediately reveals any non-linearities or other problems with the data. Scattergrams can easily be produced using software packages such as Microsoft Excel using the charts commands. The scattergram of electrical costs versus occupancy-days at the Hamilton Hotel is reproduced in the first panel of Exhibit 3–8. Two things should be noted about this scattergram:

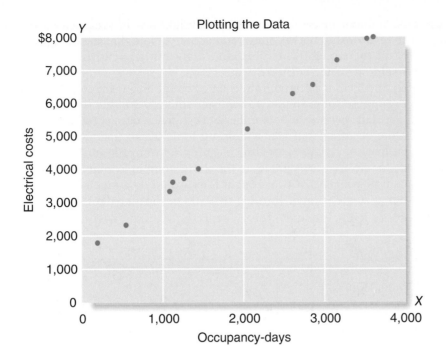

Plotting the Data

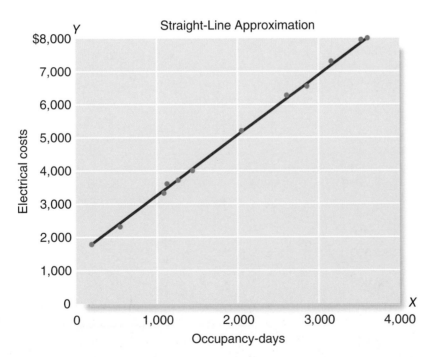

Straight-Line Approximation

EXHIBIT 3-8   Scattergram
Method of Cost Analysis

1. The total electrical cost, Y, is plotted on the vertical axis. Cost is known as the **dependent variable**, since the amount of cost incurred during a period depends on the level of activity for the period. That is, as the level of activity increases, total cost also ordinarily increases.
2. The activity, X (occupancy-days in this case), is plotted on the horizontal axis. Activity is known as the **independent variable**, since it causes variations in the cost.

From the scattergram, it is evident that electrical costs do increase with the number of occupancy-days. In addition, the scattergram reveals that the relationship between electrical costs and occupancy-days is approximately *linear*. In other words, the points lie more or less along a straight line. Such a straight line has been drawn in the second panel of Exhibit 3–8 using the *add trendline* chart option in Excel.

Dependent variable
A variable that responds to some causal factor; total cost is the dependent variable, as represented by the letter Y in the equation $Y = a + bX$.

Independent variable
A variable that acts as a causal factor; activity is the independent variable, as represented by the letter X in the equation $Y = a + bX$.

Linear cost behaviour
Cost behaviour where the relationship between cost and activity can be reasonably approximated by a straight line.

Linear cost behaviour occurs whenever a straight line is a reasonable approximation for the relationship between cost and activity. Note that the data points do not fall exactly on the straight line. This almost always happens in practice; the relationship is seldom perfectly linear.

Plotting the data on a scattergram is an essential diagnostic step that is too often overlooked. Suppose, for example, we had been interested in the relationship between total cleaning staff wages and the number of occupancy-days at the hotel. The permanent, full-time cleaning staff can handle up to 1,500 occupancy-days in a month. Beyond that level of activity, part-time cleaning staff must be utilized. The cost and activity data for cleaning are plotted on the scattergram in Exhibit 3–9. Looking at that scattergram, it is evident that two straight lines would do a much better job of fitting the data than a single straight line. Up to 1,500 occupancy-days, total cleaning staff

EXHIBIT 3-9 More Than One Relevant Range

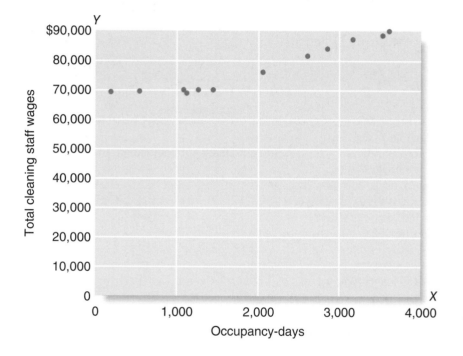

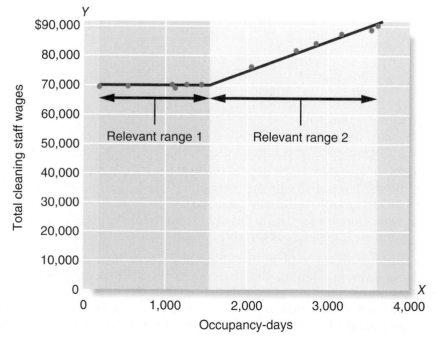

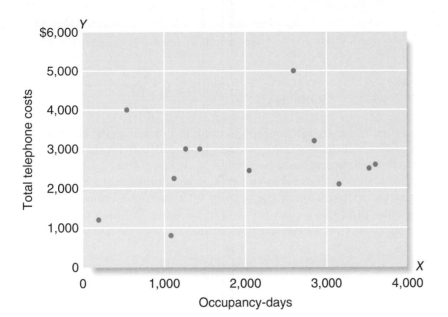

EXHIBIT 3-10   A Diagnostic Scattergram Plot

wages are essentially a fixed cost. Above 1,500 occupancy-days, total cleaning staff wages are a mixed cost. This happens because, as stated above, the permanent full-time cleaning staff can handle up to 1,500 occupancy-days in a month. Above that level, part-time cleaning staff are called in to help, which adds to the cost. Consequently, two straight lines (and two equations) are used to represent total cleaning staff wages—one for the relevant range of 0 to 1,500 occupancy-days and one for the relevant range of 1,501 to 4,000 occupancy-days.

As another example, suppose that Hamilton Hotel management is interested in the relationship between the hotel's telephone costs and occupancy-days. Guests are billed directly for their use of telephones, so those costs do not appear on the hotel's cost records. The telephone costs of concern to management are the charges for the staff's use of telephones. The data for this cost are plotted in Exhibit 3–10. It is evident from that plot that while the telephone costs do vary from month to month, they are not related to occupancy-days. Something other than occupancy-days is driving the telephone costs. Therefore, it does not make sense to analyze these costs any further by attempting to estimate a variable cost per occupancy-day for telephone costs. Plotting the data helps diagnose such situations.

The High–Low Method

Assuming that the scattergram plot indicates a linear relationship between cost and activity, the fixed and variable cost elements of a mixed cost can be estimated using the *high–low method* or the *least-squares regression method*. The **high–low method** is based on the rise-over-run formula for the slope of a straight line. If the relationship between cost and activity can be represented by a straight line, then the slope of the straight line is equal to the variable cost per unit of activity. Consequently, the following formula, using basic algebra, can be used to estimate the variable cost:

High–low method
A method of separating a mixed cost into its fixed and variable elements by analyzing the change in cost between the high and low levels of activity.

$$\text{Variable cost} = \text{Slope of the line} = \frac{\text{Rise}}{\text{Run}} = \frac{Y_2 - Y_1}{X_2 - X_1}$$

To analyze mixed costs with the high–low method, begin by identifying the period with the lowest level of activity and the period with the highest level of activity. For the above formula, select the period with the lowest activity as the first point and the period with the highest activity as the second point. Consequently, the formula becomes

$$\text{Variable cost} = \frac{Y_2 - Y_1}{X_2 - X_1} = \frac{\text{Cost at the high activity level} - \text{Cost at the low activity level}}{\text{High activity level} - \text{Low activity level}}$$

or

$$\text{Variable cost} = \frac{\text{Change in cost}}{\text{Change in activity}}$$

Therefore, when the high–low method is used, the variable cost is estimated by dividing the difference in cost between the high and low levels of activity by the change in activity between those two points.

Using the high–low method to analyze the relation between electrical costs and occupancy-days, we first identify the periods with the highest and lowest *activity*—in this case, August and October, per the data in the table. We then use the activity and cost data from these two periods to estimate the variable cost component as follows:

	Occupancy-Days	Electrical Cost Incurred
High activity level (August).....................	3,610	$8,100
Low activity level (October)...................	190	1,773
Change......................................	3,420	$6,327

$$\text{Variable cost} = \frac{\text{Change in cost}}{\text{Change in activity}} = \frac{\$6{,}327}{3{,}420} = \$1.85 \text{ per occupancy-day}$$

Having determined that the variable rate for electrical costs is $1.85 per occupancy-day, we can now determine the amount of fixed cost. This is done by taking total cost at *either* the high or the low activity level and deducting the variable cost element. In the computation below, total cost at the high activity level is used to compute the fixed cost element:

Fixed cost element = Total cost − Variable cost element

= $8,100 − ($1.85 per occupancy-day × 3,610 occupancy-days)

= $1,421.50

Both the variable and fixed cost elements have now been isolated. The electrical costs can be expressed as $1,421.50 per month plus $1.85 per occupancy-day.

The total electrical costs can also be expressed in terms of the equation for a straight line as follows:

$$Y = \$1{,}421.50 + \$1.85X$$

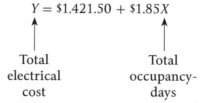

Total
electrical
cost

Total
occupancy-
days

Sometimes the high and low levels of activity don't coincide with the high and low amounts of cost. For example, the period that has the highest level of activity may not have the highest amount of cost. Nevertheless, the highest and lowest levels of *activity* are always used to analyze a mixed cost under the high–low method. This is because the analyst would like to use data that reflect the greatest possible variation in activity.

The high–low method is very simple to apply, but it suffers from a major (and sometimes critical) defect—it utilizes only two data points. Generally, two points are not enough to produce accurate results. Additionally, the periods with the highest and lowest activity tend to be unusual in that they represent the two extremes. A cost formula that is estimated solely using data from these unusual periods may seriously misrepresent the true cost relationship that holds during normal periods. For these reasons, other methods of cost analysis that utilize a greater number of points, such as *least-squares regression*, are generally more accurate than the high–low method. If managers choose to use the high–low method, they should do so with full awareness of its limitations.

Fortunately, computer software makes it very easy to use sophisticated statistical cost estimation methods that use all of the data and are capable of providing much more information than just the estimates of variable and fixed costs. The details of these statistical methods are beyond the scope of this text, but the least-squares regression method is discussed in the appendix to this chapter. Regardless of the cost estimation approach used, it is always a good idea to first plot the data in a scattergram. By simply looking at the scattergram, you can quickly verify whether it makes sense to fit a straight line to the data using least-squares regression or some other method.

> **Instant Quiz 3-4**
> Using the equation for total electrical costs developed for the Hamilton Hotel, predict total electrical costs for a month when total occupancy-days are expected to be 3,000.

▇ THE CONTRIBUTION FORMAT

Separating costs into fixed and variable elements helps to predict costs and provide benchmarks. As we will see in later chapters, separating costs into fixed and variable elements is often crucial in making decisions. This crucial distinction between fixed and variable costs is at the heart of the **contribution approach** to constructing income statements. The unique thing about the contribution approach is that it provides managers with an income statement that clearly distinguishes between fixed and variable costs and therefore facilitates planning, control, and decision making.

LEARNING OBJECTIVE
Prepare an income statement using the contribution format.

Contribution approach
An income statement format where costs are separated into variable and fixed categories.

Why a New Income Statement Format?

An income statement prepared using the *traditional approach*, as illustrated in Chapter 2, is organized in a "functional" format—emphasizing the functions of production, administration, and sales. No attempt is made to distinguish between fixed and variable costs. Under the heading Administrative Expense, for example, both variable and fixed costs are lumped together.

Although an income statement prepared in the functional format may be useful for external reporting, it has serious limitations when used for internal purposes. Internally, the manager needs cost data organized in a format that will facilitate planning, control, and decision making. As we will see in later chapters, these tasks are much easier when cost data are available in a fixed and variable format. The contribution approach to the income statement was developed in response to this need.

The Contribution Approach

Exhibit 3–11 illustrates the contribution approach to the income statement with a simple example based on assumed data, along with the traditional approach discussed in Chapter 2.

Notice that the contribution approach separates costs into fixed and variable categories, first deducting variable expenses from sales to obtain what is known as the *contribution margin*. The **contribution margin** is the amount remaining from sales revenues after variable expenses have been deducted. This amount *contributes* toward covering fixed expenses and then toward profits for the period.

The simplified contribution approach income statement makes a common assumption that can cause confusion. The variable production expenses assume production equals sales in terms of units. Thus, the expenses for production, like those for selling and administrative costs, use sales volume as the driver. A more complete income statement needs to show beginning and ending inventory levels so that variable production costs can use production volume activity as the cost driver.

Contribution margin
The amount remaining from sales revenues after all variable expenses have been deducted.

EXHIBIT 3-11   Comparison of the Contribution Income Statement with the Traditional Income Statement

Traditional Approach (costs organized by function)			Contribution Approach (costs organized by behaviour)		
Sales.....................		$12,000	Sales.......................		$12,000
Less cost of goods sold.............		6,000*	Less variable expenses:		
Gross margin......................		6,000	Variable production.............	$2,000	
Less operating expenses:			Variable selling	600	
Selling........................	$3,100*		Variable administrative..........	400	3,000
Administrative.................	1,900*	5,000	Contribution margin...............		9,000
Operating income		$ 1,000	Less fixed expenses:		
			Fixed production	4,000	
			Fixed selling....................	2,500	
			Fixed administrative	1,500	8,000
			Operating income.................		$ 1,000

*Contains both variable and fixed expenses. This is the income statement for a manufacturing company; thus, when the income statement is placed in the contribution format, the cost of goods sold figure is divided between variable production costs and fixed production costs. If this was the income statement for a *merchandising* company (which simply purchases completed goods from a supplier), then the cost of goods sold would be *all* variable.

Instant Quiz 3-5
Based on Exhibit 3-11, what would you expect total variable costs to be if sales were $24,000? What would you expect total fixed costs to be if sales were $24,000?

The contribution format income statement is used as an internal planning and decision-making tool. Its emphasis on cost behaviour facilitates cost–volume–profit analysis (the topic of the next chapter), management performance appraisals, and budgeting. Moreover, the contribution approach helps managers organize data relevant to numerous decisions, such as product-line analysis, pricing, use of scarce resources, and make or buy analysis. All of these topics are covered in later chapters.

KNOWLEDGE IN ACTION

Managers can apply their knowledge about cost behaviour when
- Calculating sales needed to achieve break-even profit levels
- Estimating sales needed to achieve desired profit targets
- Estimating the impact of sales volume changes on profit
- Costing products
- Preparing budgets and analyzing differences between actual and budgeted results
- Deciding whether to keep or drop a product
- Deciding whether to make a product internally or outsource production

---

SUMMARY

- Three major classifications of costs were discussed in this chapter: variable, fixed, and mixed. [LO1]
- Mixed costs are a combination of variable and fixed elements and can be expressed in equation form as $Y = a + bX$, where Y is the cost, a is the fixed cost element, b is the variable cost per unit of activity, and X is the activity. [LO1]
- The first step in analyzing a mixed cost is to prepare a scattergram to permit a visual inspection of the relationship between the cost and the activity. Costs are plotted on the vertical axis and activity levels on the horizontal axis of the scattergram. [LO2]
- If the scattergram indicates that the relationship between cost and activity is linear, the variable and fixed components of the mixed cost can be estimated using the high–low method or the least-squares regression method. [LO2]

- The high–low method estimates the variable and fixed cost components by analyzing the change in cost between the high and low levels of activity. The method is based on the rise-over-run formula for the slope of a straight line. [LO2]
- To facilitate decision making, the income statement can be prepared in a contribution format. The contribution format classifies costs on the income statement by cost behaviour (i.e., variable versus fixed) rather than by functional areas such as production, administration, and sales. [LO3]

REVIEW PROBLEM 1: COST BEHAVIOUR

Indie Scooters operates a scooter rental service. Consider the following costs of the company over the relevant range of 6,000 to 9,000 hours of operating time for its scooters:

	Hours of Operating Time			
	6,000	7,000	8,000	9,000
Total costs:				
Variable costs.....................	$ 27,000	$?	$?	$?
Fixed costs	252,000	?	?	?
Total costs	$279,000	$?	$?	$?
Cost per hour:				
Variable cost......................	$?	$?	$?	$?
Fixed cost	?	?	?	?
Total cost per hour..................	$?	$?	$?	$?

Required:
Compute the missing amounts, assuming that cost behaviour patterns remain unchanged within the relevant range of 6,000 to 9,000 hours.

Solution to Review Problem 1

The variable cost per hour can be computed as follows:

$$\$27,000 \div 6,000 \text{ hours} = \$4.50 \text{ per hour}$$

Therefore, the missing amounts are as follows:

	Hours of Operating Time			
	6,000	7,000	8,000	9,000
Total costs:				
Variable costs				
(@ $4.50 per hour)...........	$ 27,000	$ 31,500	$ 36,000	$ 40,500
Fixed costs.....................	252,000	252,000	252,000	252,000
Total costs	$279,000	$283,500	$288,000	$292,500
Cost per hour:				
Variable cost	$ 4.50	$ 4.50	$ 4.50	$ 4.50
Fixed cost......................	42.00	36.00	31.50	28.00
Total cost per hour	$ 46.50	$ 40.50	$ 36.00	$ 32.50

Observe that the total variable costs increase in proportion to the number of hours of operating time, but that these costs remain constant at $4.50 if expressed on a per hour basis. In contrast, the total fixed costs do not change with changes in the level of activity. They remain constant at $252,000 within the relevant range. With increases in activity, however, the fixed cost per hour decreases, dropping from $42.00 per hour when the scooters are operated 6,000 hours per period to only $28.00 per hour when they are operated 9,000 hours per period. *Because of this troublesome aspect of fixed costs, they are most easily (and most safely) dealt with on a total basis, rather than on a unit basis, in cost analysis work.*

REVIEW PROBLEM 2: HIGH–LOW METHOD

The CFO of Hamilton Hotel would like a cost formula that relates the hotel maintenance costs for a month to the number of occupancy-days for that month. Monthly maintenance costs and occupancy-days for the past seven months are shown below:

Month	Occupancy Days	Maintenance Costs
January	5,600	$7,900
February	7,100	$8,500
March	5,000	$7,400
April	6,500	$8,200
May	7,300	$9,100
June	8,000	$9,800
July	6,200	$7,800

Required:
1. Use the high–low method to establish the fixed and variable components of maintenance costs.
2. Express the fixed and variable components of maintenance costs as a cost formula in the form $Y = a + bX$.

Solution to Review Problem 2

1. The first step in the high–low method is to identify the periods of the lowest and highest activity. These periods are March (5,000 occupancy-days) and June (8,000 occupancy-days).
   The second step is to compute the variable cost per unit using those two data points:

Month	Occupancy Days	Maintenance Costs
High activity level (June)	8,000	$9,800
Low activity level (March)	5,000	7,400
Change	3,000	$2,400

$$\text{Variable cost} = \frac{\text{Change in cost}}{\text{Change in activity}} = \frac{\$2,400}{3,000} = \$0.80 \text{ per occupancy-day}$$

The third step is to compute the fixed cost element by deducting the variable cost element from the total cost at either the high or low activity level. In the computation below, the high point of activity is used:

$$
\begin{aligned}
\text{Fixed cost element} &= \text{Total cost} - \text{Variable cost element} \\
&= \$9,800 - (\$0.80 \text{ per occupancy-day} \times 8,000 \text{ occupancy days}) \\
&= \$3,400
\end{aligned}
$$

2. The cost formula is $Y = \$3,400 + \$0.80X$.

GLOSSARY

Review key terms and definitions on Connect.

DISCUSSION CASE

DISCUSSION CASE 3-1
Despite the numerous benefits of developing an accurate understanding of cost behaviour discussed in this chapter, research indicates that surprisingly few companies use quantitative techniques such as the high–low method or regression analysis to separate mixed costs into fixed and variable components.

Required:
Discuss reasons why companies might not use quantitative techniques (high–low method or regression analysis) to develop an accurate understanding of cost behaviour.

QUESTIONS

3-1   Identify some examples of variable costs for a manufacturing company.
3-2   What effect does a decrease in volume have on
    a.   Unit fixed costs?
    b.   Unit variable costs?
    c.   Total fixed costs?
    d.   Total variable costs?
3-3   Define the following terms: (*a*) cost behaviour and (*b*) relevant range.
3-4   What are curvilinear costs? What are some examples of costs that might behave in a curvilinear fashion?
3-5   Define a step-variable cost and give an example.
3-6   Managers often assume a strictly linear relationship between cost and volume. How can this practice be defended in light of the fact that many costs are curvilinear?
3-7   Is advertising a discretionary fixed cost or a committed fixed cost? Explain.
3-8   Classify the following fixed costs as normally being either committed or discretionary:
    a.   Insurance on buildings.
    b.   Advertising.
    c.   Travel.
    d.   Long-term equipment leases.
    e.   Pension payments to a company's retirees.
    f.   Training.
3-9   Does the concept of the relevant range apply to fixed costs? Explain.
3-10   What is the engineering approach to cost analysis? In what situations might this approach be used?
3-11   What is the purpose of preparing a scattergram?
3-12   Why does the high–low method use the high–low activity levels instead of the high–low cost levels?
3-13   Give the general formula for a mixed cost. Which term represents the variable cost? The fixed cost?
3-14   How is the contribution margin calculated?

EXERCISES

Mc Graw Hill Education **connect**

EXERCISE 3-1 Fixed and Variable Cost Behaviour [LO1]
Goes-Down-Smooth operates a number of smoothie bars in busy suburban malls. The fixed weekly expense of a smoothie bar is $2,500, and the variable cost per smoothie served is $0.75.

Required:
1.   Fill in the following table with your estimates of total costs and cost per smoothie at the indicated levels of activity for a smoothie bar. Round off the cost of a smoothie to the nearest tenth of a cent.

	Smoothies Served in a Week		
	2,100	2,800	3,500
Fixed cost	?	?	?
Variable cost..................................	?	?	?
Total cost......................................	?	?	?
Cost per smoothie served....................	?	?	?

2. Does the cost per smoothie increase, decrease, or remain the same as the number of smoothies served in a week increases? Explain.

EXERCISE 3-2 Scattergram Analysis [LO2]

The data below have been taken from the cost records of the Halifax General Hospital. The data relate to the costs of admitting patients at various levels of patient activity:

Month	Number of Patients Admitted	Admitting Department Costs
May	3,600	$29,400
June	3,800	$30,400
July	2,900	$27,400
August	3,200	$28,000
September	3,300	$28,600
October	2,600	$26,200
November	2,200	$25,600
December	3,500	$29,200

Required:
1. Use Microsoft Excel to prepare a scattergram using the above data. Plot admitting department costs on the vertical axis and the number of patients admitted on the horizontal axis.
2. Does it appear that admitting department costs are related to the number of patients admitted? Explain.

EXERCISE 3-3 High-Low Method [LO2]

Refer to the data in Exercise 3-2 for the Halifax General Hospital.

Required:
1. Using the high-low method, estimate the fixed cost of admitting patients per month and the variable cost of admissions per patient.
2. What factors other than the number of patients admitted are likely to affect changes in admitting department costs from month to month?

EXERCISE 3-4 Contribution Format Income Statement [LO3]

The Rhythm Shop is a large retailer of acoustic, electric, and bass guitars. An income statement for the company's acoustic guitar department for a recent quarter is presented below:

THE RHYTHM SHOP Income Statement—Acoustic Guitar Department For the Quarter Ended March 31		
Sales..		$1,600,000
Cost of goods sold...........................		800,000
Gross margin.................................		800,000
Selling and administrative expenses:		
Selling expenses.........................	$400,000	
Administrative expenses	200,000	600,000
Operating income............................		$ 200,000

The guitars sell, on average, for $800 each. The department's variable selling expenses are $75 per guitar sold. The remaining selling expenses are fixed. The administrative expenses are 25% variable and 75% fixed. The company purchases its guitars from several suppliers at an average cost of $400 per guitar.

Required:
1. Prepare an income statement for the quarter using the contribution approach.
2. What was the contribution toward fixed expenses and profits from each guitar sold during the quarter? (State this figure in a single dollar amount per guitar.)
3. If The Rhythm Shop sells 100 more guitars in the quarter ending June 30 than it did in the quarter ending March 31, and fixed costs remain the same, by how much will operating income increase?

EXERCISE 3-5 Cost Behaviour; Contribution Format Income Statement [LO1, LO3]
Parker Company manufactures and sells a single product. A partially completed schedule of the company's total and per unit costs over a relevant range of 60,000 to 100,000 units produced and sold each year is given below:

	Units Produced and Sold		
	60,000	80,000	100,000
Total costs:			
Variable costs...........................	$150,000	?	?
Fixed costs	360,000	?	?
Total costs.................................	$510,000	?	?
Cost per unit:			
Variable cost............................	?	?	?
Fixed cost	?	?	?
Total cost per hour........................	?	?	?

Required:
1. Complete the schedule of the company's total and unit costs above.
2. Assume that the company produces and sells 90,000 units during the year at a selling price of $7.50 per unit. Prepare a contribution format income statement for the year.

EXERCISE 3-6 High-Low Method [LO2]
Zerbel Company, a wholesaler of large, custom-built air-conditioning units for commercial buildings, has noticed considerable fluctuation in its shipping expense from month to month, as shown below:

Month	Units Shipped	Total Shipping Expense
January	4	$2,200
February.......................	7	$3,100
March	5	$2,600
April...........................	2	$1,500
May	3	$2,200
June	6	$3,000
July	8	$3,600

Required:
1. Using the high-low method, estimate the cost formula for shipping expense.
2. What factors, other than the number of units shipped, are likely to affect the company's shipping expense? Explain.

EXERCISE 3-7 Cost Behaviour; High-Low Method [LO2]
Prompt Parcel Service operates a fleet of delivery trucks in a large metropolitan area. A careful study by the company's cost analyst has determined that if a truck is driven 120,000 kilometres during a year, the average operating cost is 11.6 cents ($0.116) per kilometre. If a truck is

driven only 80,000 kilometres during a year, the average operating cost increases to 13.6 cents ($0.136) per kilometre.

Required:
1. Using the high–low method, estimate the variable and fixed cost elements of the annual cost of truck operation.
2. Express the variable and fixed costs in the form $Y = a + bX$.
3. If a truck was driven 100,000 kilometres during a year, what total cost would you expect to be incurred?

EXERCISE 3–8 High–Low Method; Predicting Cost [LO2]
The number of blood tests performed and the related costs over the last nine months in Brentline Hospital are given below:

Month	Blood Tests Performed	Blood Test Costs
January	3,125	$14,000
February	3,500	$14,500
March	2,500	$ 11,500
April	2,125	$10,000
May	2,250	$ 11,000
June	1,500	$ 8,500
July	1,550	$ 8,400
August	2,750	$12,000
September	2,875	$13,000

Required:
1. Using the high–low method, estimate the cost formula for blood tests.
2. Using the cost formula you derived above, what blood test costs would you expect to be incurred during a month in which 2,300 blood tests are performed?

EXERCISE 3–9 Scattergram Analysis; High–Low Method [LO2]
Refer to the data in Exercise 3–8 for Brentline Hospital.

Required:
1. Using Microsoft Excel, prepare a scattergram using the data from Exercise 3–8. Plot cost on the vertical axis and activity on the horizontal axis. Use the "add trendline" feature of Microsoft Excel to fit a line through the points on your scattergram.
2. Scrutinize the points on your graph, and explain why the high–low method would or would not yield an accurate cost formula in this situation.

EXERCISE 3–10 High–Low Method; Predicting Cost [LO2]
Great Eastern Inns has a total of 2,000 rooms in its chain of motels located in eastern Canada. On average, 70% of the rooms are occupied each day. The company's operating costs are $42 per occupied room per day at this occupancy level, assuming a 30-day month. This $42 figure contains both variable and fixed cost elements. During February, the occupancy rate dropped to only 45%. A total of $1,584,000 in operating cost was incurred during February.

Required:
1. Estimate the variable cost per occupied room per day.
2. Estimate the total fixed operating costs per month.
3. Assume that the occupancy rate increases to 50% during March. What total operating costs would you expect the company to incur during March?

PROBLEMS

PROBLEM 3–11 Contribution Format versus Traditional Income Statement [LO3]
Home Entertainment is a small, family-owned business that purchases LCD televisions from a reputable manufacturer and sells them at the retail level. The televisions sell, on average, for $1,500 each. The average cost of a television from the manufacturer is $900.

Home Entertainment has always kept careful accounting records, and the costs that it incurs in a typical month are as follows:

Costs	Cost Formula
Selling:	
Advertising	$950 per month
Delivery of televisions.....................	$40 per television sold
Sales salaries and commissions	$2,900 per month, plus 4% of sales
Utilities	$400 per month
Depreciation of sales facilities.............	$3,000 per month
Administrative:	
Executive salaries........................	$8,000 per month
Depreciation of office equipment..........	$500 per month
Clerical	$1,500 per month, plus $40 per television sold
Insurance.................................	$400 per month

During April, the company sold and delivered 150 televisions.

Required:
1. Prepare an income statement for April using the traditional format with costs organized by function.
2. Redo (1) above, this time using the contribution format with costs organized by behaviour. Show costs and revenues on both a total and a per unit basis down through contribution margin.
3. Refer to the income statement you prepared in (2) above. Why might it be misleading to show the fixed costs on a per unit basis?

PROBLEM 3–12 Traditional and Contribution Format Income Statement [LO3]
Haaki Shop Inc. is a large retailer of surfboards. The company assembled the information shown below for the quarter ended May 31:

	Amount
Total sales revenue	$800,000
Selling price per surfboard	400
Variable selling expense per surfboard................................	50
Variable administrative expense per surfboard........................	20
Total fixed selling expense...	150,000
Total fixed administrative expense.....................................	120,000
Merchandise inventory, beginning balance	80,000
Merchandise inventory, ending balance...............................	100,000
Merchandise purchases..	320,000

Required:
1. Prepare a traditional income statement for the quarter ended May 31.
2. Prepare a contribution format income statement for the quarter ended May 31.
3. What was the contribution toward fixed expenses and profits for each surfboard sold during the quarter? (State this figure in a single dollar amount per surfboard.)

PROBLEM 3–13 Identifying Cost Behaviour Patterns [LO1]
A number of graphs displaying cost behaviour patterns are shown below. The vertical axis on each graph represents total cost, and the horizontal axis represents the level of activity (volume).

Required:
1. For each of the following situations, identify the graph that illustrates the cost behaviour pattern involved. Any graph may be used more than once.

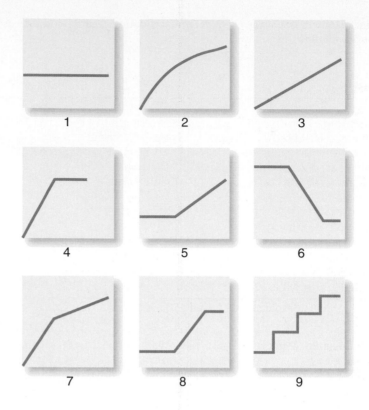

a. Charges for data usage on a smartphone plan—a flat fixed charge for the first 500 MB, plus a variable cost per megabyte for usage above 500 MB.
b. Wages for software development staff, all of whom are paid a fixed monthly salary.
c. Licensing fees paid to the provincial government to operate dog sled tours. A fee of $10 per tour is paid for the first 1,000 tours, with no additional fees paid if tours exceed 1,000.
d. Cost of raw materials, where the cost starts at $7.50 per unit and then decreases by 5 cents per unit for each of the first 100 units purchased, after which it remains constant at $2.50 per unit.
e. Cost of a monthly high-speed Internet plan, where $50 is charged for 0–250 MB usage, $75 for 251 to 500 MB usage, $100 for 501 to 750 MB usage, and $125 for 751 MB usage and above.
f. Wage expense paid to tree planters who receive $0.10 per tree planted.
g. Rent on a factory building donated by the county, where the agreement calls for rent of $100,000 less $1 for each direct labour-hour worked in excess of 200,000 hours, but a minimum rental payment of $20,000 must be paid.
h. Wages paid to sales staff who receive a fixed salary per month and sales commissions equal to 5% of sales for every sales dollar they generate above $250,000. No additional commissions are paid for sales above $1,000,000.
i. Raw materials costs, where the first 1,000 units cost $1 per unit, with the unit cost dropping to $0.80 per unit for quantities above 1,000.

2. How would a knowledge of cost behaviour patterns such as those above help a manager analyze the cost structure of his or her company?

(CPA, adapted)

PROBLEM 3–14 High–Low Method; Scattergram Analysis [LO2]
Davidson Engine Repairs provides maintenance and repair services for small engines such as those found in lawn mowers, power saws, and snow throwers. The repair shop costs include the salaries for the mechanics, insurance and depreciation on the repair equipment, materials and parts used for the jobs, and utilities. The repair shop manager would like to develop a model for predicting repair costs and over the past 10 months has carefully recorded the total repair

costs incurred, along with the number of maintenance and repair jobs completed each month. The data are shown below:

Month	Jobs	Repair Costs
January......................	220	$22,000
February......................	180	$ 18,000
March........................	160	$ 17,600
April.........................	200	$20,000
May	260	$24,000
June	240	$22,400
July	140	$ 16,000
August......................	120	$ 12,800
September	100	$ 13,600
October......................	80	$ 9,600

Required:
1. Using Microsoft Excel, prepare a scattergram by plotting jobs performed and repair costs on a graph. Fit a straight line to the plotted points using the "add trendline" feature in Microsoft Excel. Do repair costs appear to be related to the number of jobs completed in a month? Explain.
2. Using the high–low method, estimate a cost formula for repair costs. Express the formula in the form $Y = a + bX$.
3. Now assume the manager wants to predict costs for a month where 600 jobs will be completed. Should you use the formula developed above to predict costs for a 600-job month? Why or why not?

PROBLEM 3–15 High–Low Method; Predicting Cost [LO1, LO2]
Prince Company's total overhead costs at various levels of activity are presented below:

Month	Direct Labour- Hours	Total Overhead Cost
September	100,000	$388,000
October.....................	80,000	$340,400
November	135,000	$485,600
December...................	140,000	$483,200

Assume that the overhead cost above consists of utilities, supervisory salaries, depreciation, and maintenance. The breakdown of these costs at the 80,000-machine-hour level of activity in October is as follows:

Utilities (variable)	$104,000
Supervisory salaries	
and depreciation (fixed).................	120,000
Maintenance (mixed)	116,400
Total overhead cost.........................	$340,400

The company wants to break down the maintenance cost into its variable and fixed cost elements.

Required:
1. Estimate how much of the $483,200 of overhead cost in December was maintenance cost. (*Hint:* To do this, first determine how much of the $483,200 consisted of utilities and supervisory salaries. Think about the behaviour of variable and fixed costs within the relevant range.)
2. Using the high–low method, estimate a cost formula for maintenance.
3. Express the company's total overhead cost in the form $Y = a + bX$.
4. What total overhead cost would you expect to be incurred at an activity level of 90,000 machine-hours?

PROBLEM 3–16 High–Low Method; Cost of Goods Manufactured [LO1, LO2]
Nurally Inc. manufactures a single product. Selected data from the company's cost records for two recent months are given below:

	Level of Activity	
	July–Low	October–High
Number of units produced	9,000	12,000
Cost of goods manufactured.............................	$285,000	$390,000
Work in process inventory, beginning	14,000	22,000
Work in process inventory, ending........................	25,000	15,000
Direct materials cost per unit............................	15	15
Direct labour cost per unit	6	6
Manufacturing overhead cost, total.......................	?	?

The company's manufacturing overhead cost consists of both variable and fixed cost elements. To have data available for planning, management wants to determine how much of the overhead cost is variable with units produced and how much of it is fixed per year.

Required:
1. For both July and October, estimate the amount of manufacturing overhead cost added to production. The company had no underapplied or overapplied overhead in either month. (*Hint:* Construct a schedule of cost of goods manufactured.)
2. Using the high–low method, estimate a cost formula for manufacturing overhead. Express the variable portion of the formula in terms of a variable rate per unit of product.
3. If 9,500 units are produced during a month, what will the cost of goods manufactured be? (Assume that the company's beginning work in process inventory for the month is $16,000 and that its ending work in process inventory is $19,000. Also assume that there is no underapplied or overapplied overhead cost for the month.)

PROBLEM 3–17 High–Low Method; Predicting Cost [LO1, LO2]
Echeverria S.A. is an Argentinian manufacturing company whose total factory overhead costs fluctuate somewhat from year to year, according to the number of machine-hours worked in its production facility. These costs (in Argentinian pesos) at high and low levels of activity over recent years are given below:

	Level of Activity	
	Low	High
Machine-hours.....................................	60,000	80,000
Total factory overhead costs......................	274,000 pesos	312,000 pesos

The factory overhead costs above consist of indirect materials, rent, and maintenance. The company has analyzed these costs at the 60,000 machine-hours level of activity as follows:

Indirect materials (variable).................................	90,000 pesos
Rent (fixed)..	130,000
Maintenance (mixed)	54,000
Total factory overhead costs...............................	274,000 pesos

For planning purposes, the company wants to break down the maintenance cost into its variable and fixed cost elements.

Required:
1. Estimate how much of the factory overhead cost of 312,000 pesos at the high level of activity consists of maintenance cost. (*Hint:* First determine how much of the 312,000 pesos cost consists of indirect materials and rent. Think about the behaviour of variable and fixed costs.)

2. Using the high–low method, estimate a cost formula for maintenance.
3. What *total* overhead costs would you expect the company to incur at an operating level of 65,000 machine-hours?

CASES

CASE 3–18 Scattergram Analysis; Selection of an Activity Base; High–Low Method [LO2]
Waverley Welding Company provides welding services for a variety of industrial customers in the manufacturing, aerospace, and electronics industries. The number of jobs completed from one month to the next varies considerably, and jobs differ in terms of the complexity of the welding requirements. More complex jobs can take significantly longer to complete. Management knows that overhead costs have a fixed and a variable component but, until now, has not attempted to determine which measure of activity should be used for planning and forecasting.

The table below shows data for the most recent fiscal year. Management believes that either the number of jobs completed each month or the number of direct labour-hours incurred each month could be used as the activity base. However, they are not sure which is more appropriate:

Month	Overhead	Direct Labour-Hours	Jobs
January	$75,045	4,781	500
February	$69,491	3,548	350
March	$71,993	3,990	400
April	$81,217	5,466	550
May	$60,162	1,914	200
June	$68,364	3,157	250
July	$78,351	5,000	500
August	$81,582	6,114	600
September	$77,691	5,108	500
October	$68,355	3,624	350
November	$69,886	3,900	400
December	$83,434	5,700	510

Overhead includes costs such as the maintenance supervisor's salary, depreciation on the welding equipment, and indirect materials used on each job. Electricity costs are also included in overhead and are significant since welding equipment consumes a relatively high amount of energy. Waverley Welding also employs a mix of experienced and inexperienced welders. Experienced welders are paid a higher hourly wage but are more efficient and tend to incur less wastage of indirect materials. Inexperienced welders are of course paid less on a per hour basis but work more slowly and use more indirect materials.

Required:
1. Prepare a scattergram with overhead costs on the vertical axis and direct labour-hours on the horizontal axis.
2. Prepare a scattergram with overhead costs on the vertical axis and number of jobs on the horizontal axis.
3. Which activity measure should be used as the activity base for predicting overhead costs?
4. For the activity measure you recommended in (3) above, use the high–low method to estimate a cost formula for maintenance.

CASE 3–19 Mixed Cost Analysis and the Relevant Range [LO1, LO2]
The Ramon Company is a manufacturer that is interested in developing a cost formula to estimate the fixed and variable components of its monthly manufacturing overhead costs.

The company wishes to use machine-hours as its measure of activity and has gathered the data below for this year and last year:

| | Last Year | | This Year | |
| | Machine-Hours | Overhead Costs | Machine-Hours | Overhead Costs |
Month				
January............................	21,000	$84,000	21,000	$86,000
February...........................	25,000	99,000	24,000	93,000
March...............................	22,000	89,500	23,000	93,000
April................................	23,000	90,000	22,000	87,000
May.................................	20,500	81,500	20,000	80,000
June................................	19,000	75,500	18,000	76,500
July.................................	14,000	70,500	12,000	67,500
August.............................	10,000	64,500	13,000	71,000
September	12,000	69,000	15,000	73,500
October	17,000	75,000	17,000	72,500
November	16,000	71,500	15,000	71,000
December..........................	19,000	78,000	18,000	75,000

The company leases all of its manufacturing equipment. The lease arrangement calls for a flat monthly fee up to 19,500 machine-hours. If the machine-hours used exceed 19,500, then the fee becomes strictly variable with respect to the total number of machine-hours used during the month. Lease expense is a major element of overhead cost.

Required:
1. Using the high–low method, estimate a manufacturing overhead cost formula.
2. Prepare a scattergram using all of the data for the two-year period. Describe the cost behaviour pattern revealed by your scattergram plot.
3. Based on (2), do you have any concerns about the accuracy of the high–low estimates that you computed?
4. Assume that the company consumes 22,500 machine-hours during a month. Using the high–low method, estimate the total overhead cost that would be incurred at this level of activity. Be sure to consider only the data points contained in the relevant range of activity when performing your computations.

CASE 3–20 Analysis of Mixed Costs in a Pricing Decision [LO1, LO2, LO3]
Christine Dandra owns a catering company that serves food and beverages at exclusive parties and business functions. Dandra's business is seasonal, with a heavy schedule during the summer months and holidays and a lighter schedule at other times.

One of the major events that Dandra's customers request is a cocktail party. She offers a standard cocktail party and has estimated the cost per guest for this type of party as follows:

Food and beverages	$19.00
Labour (0.5 hour @ $15.00 per hour)...................................	7.50
Overhead (0.5 hour @ $20.50 per hour)...............................	10.25
Total cost per guest...	$36.75

This standard cocktail party lasts three hours, and Dandra hires one worker for every six guests, which is one half-hour of labour per guest. These workers are hired only as needed and are paid only for the hours they actually work.

Dandra ordinarily charges $50 per guest. She is confident about her estimates of the costs of food and beverages and labour but is not as comfortable with the estimate of overhead cost. The $20.50 overhead cost per labour-hour was determined by dividing total overhead expenses for the past 12 months by total labour-hours for the same period. Monthly data concerning overhead costs and labour-hours appear below.

Dandra has received a request to bid on a 200-guest fundraising cocktail party to be given next month by an important local charity. (The party would last the usual three hours.) She would like to win this contract because the guest list for this charity event includes many prominent

Month	Labour-Hours	Overhead Expenses
January	1,500	$ 48,400
February	1,560	47,620
March	1,800	52,800
April	2,520	56,320
May	2,700	58,960
June	3,300	62,480
July	3,900	65,120
August	4,500	67,750
September	4,200	66,000
October	2,700	59,840
November	1,860	54,560
December	3,900	64,240
Total	34,440	$704,090

individuals that she would like to land as future clients. Dandra is confident that these potential customers will be favourably impressed by her company's services at the charity event.

Required:
1. Estimate the contribution to profit of a standard 200-guest cocktail party if Dandra charges her usual price of $50 per guest. (In other words, by how much would her overall profit increase?)
2. How low could Dandra bid for the charity event, in terms of a price per guest, and still not lose money on the event itself?
3. The individual who is organizing the charity's fundraising event has indicated that he has already received a bid under $45 from another catering company. Do you think Dandra should bid below her normal $50 per guest price for the charity event? Why or why not?

(CMA, adapted)

INSTANT QUIZ SOLUTIONS

3–1
It is a true variable cost because it will change in direct proportion to the level of activity—the number of trees planted.

3–2
The average lease cost per customer is $2 ($400 ÷ 200 customers). Total lease costs are $400 when there are 200 customers, as the lease represents a fixed monthly cost.

3–3
Total sales staff wages are a mixed cost because there is both a fixed portion ($2,000) and a variable portion (5% of sales).
The cost equation is $Y = \$2,000 + 0.05X$, where Y = total monthly sales staff wages and X = monthly sales dollars.

3–4
The cost equation is $Y = \$1,421.50 + \$1.85X$.
When total occupancy-days are 3,000, electrical costs will be $\$1,421.50 + \$1.85(3,000) = \$6,971.50$.

3–5
Total variable costs are 25% of sales: $3,000 ÷ $12,000.
If sales are $24,000, total variable costs will be $6,000 ($24,000 × 0.25).
In the absence of information that $24,000 is outside the relevant range of activity, total fixed costs will be $8,000, as per the contribution format income statement.

■ APPENDIX 3A: LEAST-SQUARES REGRESSION CALCULATIONS

LEARNING OBJECTIVE **4**
Analyze a mixed cost
using the least-squares
regression method.

**Least-squares regression
method**
A method of separating a mixed
cost into its fixed and variable
elements by fitting a regression
line that minimizes the sum of
the squared errors.

The **least-squares regression method**, unlike the high–low method discussed in the chapter, uses all the data to separate a mixed cost into its fixed and variable components. A *regression line* of the form $Y = a + bX$ is fitted to the data, where a represents the total fixed cost and b represents the variable cost per unit of activity. The basic idea of the least-squares regression method is illustrated in Exhibit 3A–1 using hypothetical data points. Notice from the exhibit that the deviations from the plotted points to the regression line are measured vertically on the graph. These vertical deviations are called the *regression errors* and represent the difference between the estimated cost and the actual cost at a given level of activity. A regression line that perfectly explains the relationship between X and Y has all the points on the line. The least-squares regression method computes the regression line that minimizes the sum of these squared errors. The formulas that accomplish this are as follows:[1]

$$b = \frac{n(\Sigma XY) - (\Sigma X)(\Sigma Y)}{n(\Sigma X^2) - (\Sigma X)^2}$$

$$a = \frac{(\Sigma X) - b(\Sigma X)}{n}$$

where

X = The level of activity (independent variable)
Y = The total mixed cost (dependent variable)
a = The total fixed cost (the vertical intercept of the line)
b = The variable cost per unit of activity (the slope of the line)
n = The number of observations
Σ = The sum across all n observations

Manually performing the calculations required by the formulas is tedious and prone to errors. Fortunately, statistical software packages such as SPSS and SAS are widely available that quickly and accurately perform the calculations automatically. Spreadsheet software, such as Microsoft Excel, can also be used to do least-squares regression, as can some handheld calculators. In addition to estimates of the intercept (fixed cost) and slope (variable cost per unit), least-squares regression software ordinarily provides a number of other very useful statistics. One of these statistics is

EXHIBIT 3A–1　The Concept
of Least-Squares Regression

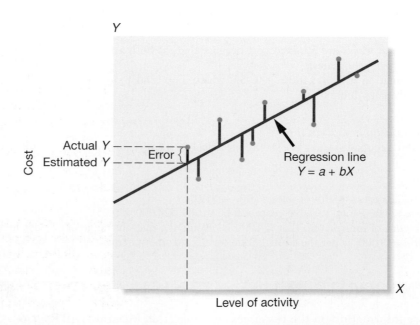

Month	Occupancy-Days	Electrical Costs
January	2,600	$ 6,260
February	2,850	6,550
March	3,530	8,000
April	1,440	4,000
May	540	2,300
June	1,120	3,600
July	3,160	7,300
August	3,610	8,100
September	1,260	3,700
October	190	1,773
November	1,080	3,320
December	2,050	5,200
Intercept	$ 1,364	
Slope	$ 1.87	
RSQ	1.00	

EXHIBIT 3A–2 The Least-Squares Regression Worksheet for the Hamilton Hotel

the R^2, which is a measure of *goodness of fit*. The R^2 tells us the percentage of the variation in the dependent variable (cost) that is explained by variation in the independent variable (activity). The R^2 varies from 0% to 100%, and the higher the percentage, the better. A regression line that fits the data perfectly would have an R^2 of 1 (100%), but R^2 would be 0 in a situation where no fit was achieved by the regression line.

To illustrate how Microsoft Excel can be used to calculate the intercept a, the slope b, and the R^2, we will use the Hamilton Hotel data for electrical costs that appear in Exhibit 3A–2. The table in Exhibit 3A–2 reproduces the data and shows the results of the regression analysis conducted using Microsoft Excel.

The slope, intercept, and R^2 are computed using the Microsoft Excel functions INTERCEPT, SLOPE, and RSQ. For each function you must specify the range of cells containing the Y values (electrical costs) and the X values (occupancy days).[2] According to the calculations carried out by Microsoft Excel, the fixed electrical cost (Intercept) is $1,364 per month and the variable cost (Slope) is $1.87 per occupancy-day. Therefore, the cost formula for electrical cost is

$$Y = a + bX$$
$$Y = \$1,364 + \$1.87X$$

Note the R^2 (RSQ) of 1.00, which is very high, indicating that all of the variation in electrical costs is explained by the variation in occupancy-days. This is a perfect fit of the regression line to the actual data. On the other hand, a low R^2 is an indication of a poor fit.

Even when using the regression method, you should always plot the data in a scattergram, but it is particularly important to check the data visually when the R^2 is low. A quick look at the scattergram can reveal the strength of the relationship between the cost and the activity, or that the relationship is something other than a simple straight line. In such cases, additional analysis is required. Plotting the data to create a scattergram is easy in Microsoft Excel, the results of which appear in Exhibit 3A–3. Consistent with the high R^2 value of 1.00, the relationship between cost and activity is approximately linear, so it is reasonable to fit a straight line to the data as we have done with the least-squares regression.

Economic Plausibility

Statistical software packages and spreadsheets such as Excel can readily perform the calculations required for the least-squares regression method and provide fit statistics such as R^2 that permit evaluation of the model fit. But managers must also carefully consider the **economic plausibility** of the relationship between the activity chosen

Economic plausibility
A qualitative assessment of whether the relationship between the independent and dependent variables in a cost estimation model makes sense from an economic perspective.

EXHIBIT 3A-3   A Scattergram
Plot of the Hamilton Hotel Data

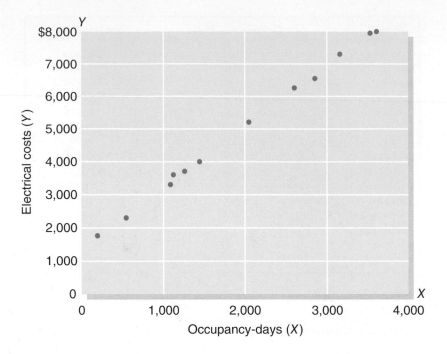

as the independent variable and the cost being predicted. The question that managers must think about in assessing economic plausibility is whether it makes *economic* sense that a change in the activity level of the independent variable would cause a change in the dependent variable. In our example above, it is economically plausible that an increase in occupancy-days would cause an increase in electrical costs at the Hamilton Hotel. More occupancy-days would lead to increased use of the various electronic devices in a hotel room, such as the lights, television, radio, air conditioner, and heater, which of course would increase the use of electricity. However, using the number of cleaning staff employed at the hotel as the independent variable would have lower economic plausibility. One would not expect a strong association between electrical costs and the number of cleaning staff. That said, the R^2 of a regression model using the number of cleaning staff as the independent variable instead of the number of occupancy-days might still be quite high, although likely lower than the 1.00 found above. Why? Because as the number of occupancy-days increases, more cleaning staff will eventually need to be hired, making it appear that the number of cleaning staff causes an increase in electrical costs. However, the real driver of electrical costs in this example is occupancy-days.

Because it is easy to generate cost estimation models with tools such as Microsoft Excel, managers might be tempted to use a "see what works" approach when selecting activities to use as independent variables. Therefore, applying the economic plausibility criterion, in addition to statistical criteria such as R^2, is always a good idea.

Multiple Regression Analysis

In the discussion thus far, we have assumed that a single factor, such as occupancy-days, drives the variable cost component of a mixed cost. This assumption is acceptable for many mixed costs, but in some situations there may be more than one causal factor driving the variable cost element. For example, shipping costs may depend on both the number of units shipped *and* the weight of the units. In a situation such as this, *multiple regression* is more appropriate to use. **Multiple regression** is an analytical method used when the dependent variable (e.g., cost) is caused by more than one activity. Although adding more activities, or independent variables, makes the computations more complex, the principles involved are the same as in the simple least-squares regression approach discussed above. The R^2 for multiple regression analysis represents the amount of variation in the dependent variable explained by

Multiple regression
An analytical method required in those situations where variations in a dependent variable are caused by more than one activity.

the *set* of independent variables included in the model and, as with simple regression, ranges from 0 to 1. Managers should also consider the economic plausibility of each independent variable included in the cost estimation model.

APPENDIX 3A SUMMARY

- The least-squares method is a superior approach for cost estimation because it incorporates all data points in the analysis. Computer software such as SPSS and SAS can perform the calculations required by the least-squares regression method. Regression analysis software also calculates other useful statistics, such as R^2, which quantifies the goodness of fit. Spreadsheet packages such as Microsoft Excel can also be used to perform least-squares regression calculations. **[LO4]**
- In addition to examining fit statistics such as R^2 and preparing a scattergram to visually assess the relationship between the independent and dependent variables, managers should also consider the economic plausibility of the relationship. This involves qualitatively assessing whether it makes economic sense for the independent and dependent variables to be causally related. **[LO4]**
- Multiple regression analysis involves the use of more than one independent variable in predicting the behaviour of a dependent variable. Fit statistics such as R^2 can be computed for multiple regression analysis, and economic plausibility is still important to evaluate. **[LO4]**

APPENDIX 3A EXERCISES, PROBLEMS, AND CASES McGraw Hill Education **connect**

EXERCISE 3A–1 Least-Squares Regression [LO4] *eXcel*
Spentz Company offers rental cars in several off-airport locations. Management would like to better understand the behaviour of the company's costs. One of these is the cost of cleaning cars. The company operates its own car wash and cleaning facilities in which each rental car that is returned is thoroughly cleaned before being released for rental to another customer. Management believes that the costs of operating the cleaning facilities should be related to the number of rental returns. Accordingly, the following data have been compiled:

Month	Rental Returns	Cleaning Costs
January	4,620	$15,170
February	4,906	$19,036
March	5,282	$16,358
April	5,748	$19,423
May	7,080	$23,001
June	9,722	$32,182
July	10,864	$31,905
August	10,536	$29,895
September	9,256	$32,790
October	7,480	$27,574
November	4,212	$14,745
December	4,990	$16,621

Required:
Using least-squares regression, estimate the fixed cost and variable cost elements of monthly car wash costs. Estimate the fixed cost element to the nearest dollar and the variable cost element to the nearest cent.

EXERCISE 3A–2 Least-Squares Regression [LO4] *eXcel*
The Hard Rock Mining Company is developing cost formulas for management planning and decision making. The company's cost analyst has concluded that utilities cost is a mixed cost, and he is attempting to find a base with which the cost might be closely correlated. The controller has

suggested that tonnes mined might be a good base to use in developing a cost formula. The production manager disagrees; she thinks that direct labour-hours would be a better base. The cost analyst has decided to try both bases and has assembled the following information:

Quarter	Tonnes Mined	Direct Labour-Hours	Utilities Cost
Year 1:			
First	15,000	5,000	$50,000
Second	11,000	3,000	45,000
Third	21,000	4,000	60,000
Fourth	12,000	6,000	75,000
Year 2:			
First	18,000	10,000	$100,000
Second	25,000	9,000	105,000
Third	30,000	8,000	85,000
Fourth	28,000	11,000	120,000

Required:
1.   Using tonnes mined as the independent (X) variable:
   a.   Determine a cost formula for utilities cost using the least-squares regression method. Calculate the R^2 as part of your analysis.
   b.   Prepare a scattergram and plot the tonnes mined and utilities cost.
2.   Using direct labour-hours as the independent (X) variable, repeat the computations in 1(a) and (b) above.
3.   Would you recommend that the company use tonnes mined or direct labour-hours as a base for planning utilities cost?

 EXERCISE 3A–3 Least-Squares Regression [LO4]
Serenity Living manufactures gas fireplaces for home use. Each unit produced goes through a complex quality control process. The company has observed quality control costs as follows over the past six weeks:

Week	Units Produced	Total Quality Control Costs
1.........................	24	$540
2.........................	15	$400
3.........................	30	$620
4.........................	12	$380
5.........................	18	$480
6.........................	27	$580

For planning purposes, the company's management wants to know the amount of variable quality control costs per unit and the total fixed quality control costs per week.

Required:
1.   Using the least-squares regression method, estimate the variable and fixed elements of the quality control cost.
2.   Express the cost data in (1) above in the form $Y = a + bX$.
3.   If the company produces 20 gas fireplaces next week, what are the expected total quality control costs?
4.   Evaluate the economic plausibility of using units produced to predict total quality control costs.

 PROBLEM 3A–4 Scattergram; Cost Behaviour; Least-Squares Regression Method [LO4]
Melody Baker has just been appointed director of recreation programs for Highland Park. In the past, the city has sponsored a number of softball leagues in the summer months. From

the city's cost records, Baker has found the following total costs associated with the softball leagues over the past five years:

Number of Leagues	Total Costs
5..................	$13,000
2..................	7,000
4..................	10,500
6..................	14,000
3..................	10,000

Each league requires its own paid supervisor and paid umpires as well as printed schedules and other copy work. Therefore, Baker knows that some variable costs are associated with the leagues. She would like to know the amount of variable cost per league and the total fixed cost per year associated with the softball program. This information would help her plan.

Required:
1. Using the least-squares regression method, estimate the variable cost per league and the total fixed cost per year for the softball program.
2. Express the cost data derived in (1) above in the form $Y = a + bX$.
3. Assume that Baker would like to expand the softball program during the coming year to involve a total of seven leagues. Compute the expected total cost for the softball program. Can you see any problem with using the cost formula from (2) above to derive this total cost figure? Explain.
4. Prepare a scattergram and fit a line to the plotted points using the cost formula expressed in (2) above.

PROBLEM 3A-5 Least-Squares Regression Analysis; Pricing Decision [LO4]
Tom Davis runs a guiding company, Chief Adventures, based in Squamish, British Columbia, that takes customers on guided tours 12 months a year. During peak season, Davis employs up to 30 guides, all of whom are paid on an hourly basis at an average rate of $20 per hour. While there is some variation, tours are typically three hours in length. Chief Adventures has considerable fixed costs, including insurance, vehicle rentals, property taxes on its office building and warehouse, provincial licensing fees, utilities, wireless communications, administrative staff, and advertising. Each guided tour also results in variable costs, such as snacks for the customers, tour booklets, and other minor expenses. Other than the wages paid to guides, Tom has been recording all of these other fixed and variable costs as guiding expenses.

For planning purposes, Tom would like to be able to separate the variable and fixed components of guiding expenses. He thinks that the variable costs related to each guided tour are likely to be closely related to the number of customers served during a month. To begin the analysis Tom has compiled monthly data for 2014 below. *Note:* The guiding expenses exclude the hourly wages paid to guides.

Month	Number of Customers	Guiding Expenses
January	1,500	$ 44,000
February....................................	1,680	47,400
March.......................................	1,800	48,000
April..	2,520	51,400
May	2,700	53,600
June	3,300	56,800
July	3,900	59,400
August......................................	4,500	61,600
September	4,200	60,000
October	2,700	54,600
November	1,860	49,600
December..................................	3,900	58,400
Total..	34,560	$644,800

Required:

1. Prepare a scattergram that plots the number of customers on the *X*-axis and guiding expenses on the *Y*-axis. What insights are revealed by your scattergram?
2. Is it economically plausible for variable guiding expenses to be related to the number of customers? Explain.
3. Use the least-squares regression method to estimate the fixed and variable components of guiding expenses.
4. Assume that a small group of six tourists wants to go on a three-hour tour that will require two guides. What is the minimum amount Chief Adventures can charge the group to cover the variable expenses of the tour?

(CMA, adapted)

PROBLEM 3A–6 Least-Squares Regression; Scattergram; Comparison of Activity Bases [LO2, LO4]

Green Care Limited (GCL) manufactures environmentally friendly electric lawn mowers, and demand has been growing rapidly. Management would like to develop cost formulas for planning and decision making. The company's cost analyst has concluded that utilities cost is a mixed cost, and she is attempting to find an activity base with which the cost might be closely related. The controller has suggested that units produced might be a good base to use in developing a cost formula. The production superintendent disagrees; he thinks that direct labour-hours would be a better base since different lawn mower models have different production requirements. The cost analyst has decided to try both bases and has assembled the following information for the past eight months:

Month	Units Produced	Direct Labour-Hours	Utilities Cost
January	60,000	15,000	$200,000
February	44,000	9,000	180,000
March	84,000	12,000	240,000
April	48,000	18,000	300,000
May	72,000	30,000	400,000
June	100,000	27,000	420,000
July	120,000	24,000	340,000
August	112,000	33,000	480,000

Required:

1. Using units produced as the independent (*X*) variable:
   a. Determine a cost formula for utilities cost using the least-squares regression method.
   b. Prepare a scattergram and plot the units produced and utilities cost. (Plot cost on the vertical axis and units produced on the horizontal axis.) Fit a straight line to the plotted points using the cost formula determined in (*a*) above.
2. Using direct labour-hours as the independent (*X*) variable, repeat 1(*a*) and (*b*) above.
3. Would you recommend that the company use units produced or direct labour-hours as a base for planning utilities cost?
4. Evaluate the economic plausibility of using units produced or direct labour-hours to predict utilities cost.

CHAPTER 4

COST–VOLUME–PROFIT RELATIONSHIPS

Learning Objectives

After studying Chapter 4, you should be able to

1 Explain how changes in activity affect contribution margin and operating income.

2 Prepare and interpret a cost–volume–profit graph.

3 Use the contribution margin ratio to compute changes in contribution margin and operating income resulting from changes in sales volume.

4 Show the effects on contribution margin of changes in variable costs, fixed costs, selling price, and volume.

5 Compute the break-even point in unit sales and sales dollars.

6 Determine the level of sales needed to achieve a desired target profit.

7 Compute the margin of safety and explain its significance.

8 Explain cost structure, compute the degree of operating leverage at a particular level of sales, and explain how operating leverage can be used to predict changes in operating income.

9 Compute the break-even point for a multi-product company in unit sales and sales dollars, and explain the effects of changes in the sales mix on the contribution margin and the break-even point.

10 (Online Appendix 4A) Conduct a cost–volume–profit analysis with uncertainty.

■ LOFTY ANALYSIS

A key metric tracked by airlines is the break-even load factor. This is the percentage of seats that must be sold for the airline to achieve a break-even level ($0) of profits. The break-even load factor depends on the level of fixed costs, the average price per ticket the airline is able to charge its customers, and the variable costs incurred for each flight. Fixed costs include aircraft maintenance, insurance, depreciation, the wages of administrative staff, and so on. Variable costs include items such as pilot and flight attendant wages, fuel expense per flight, the cost of complimentary on-board drinks and snacks and newspapers, and charges related to processing each ticket sold.

Bigger airlines typically have a higher break-even load factor since their total fixed costs are higher. For example, WestJet recently reported a break-even load factor of about 72% compared to around 79% for Air Canada. These are both considerably higher than the 55% break-even load factor reported by Porter Airlines, a small regional airline based in Toronto.

The actual load factor, which is the percentage of seats actually sold, can easily be compared to the break-even load factor to provide a quick glimpse of how well the airline is doing. In December 2012, Air Canada and WestJet both reported an actual load factor of about 82%, while Porter Airlines had a load factor of 64%. Each airline's actual load factor is above the break-even level, indicating they are generating positive operating income before taxes.

How is the break-even level of activity calculated? What information is required? What assumptions are necessary to perform the analysis? These and other issues related to understanding key relationships among cost, volume, and profit are the focus of this chapter.

Sources: Scott Deveau, "Porter Airline's Edge," *Financial Post*, October 23, 2011, http://business.financialpost.com/2011/10/23/porter-airlines-edge/; Ross Marowits, "Air Canada, Porter Airlines, Load Factors on the Rise to Finish 2012 on Upward Trajectory," *The Canadian Press*, January 7, 2013, http://www.huffingtonpost.ca/2013/01/07/air-canada-porter-airlines-load-factors_n_2423877.html; http://www.westjet.com/pdf/investorMedia/presentation_2011_agm.pdf.

C ost-volume–profit (CVP) analysis is a powerful tool that helps managers understand the relationships among cost, volume, and profit. CVP focuses on how profits are affected by the following five elements:

1. Prices of products.
2. Volume or level of activity.
3. Per unit variable costs.
4. Total fixed costs.
5. Mix of products sold.

Because CVP analysis helps managers understand how profits are affected by these key factors, it is a vital tool in many business decisions. These decisions include what products to manufacture and services to offer, what prices to charge, what marketing strategy to adopt, and what cost structures to implement. Careful study of the elements and assumptions, however, is needed to avoid mistakes and to know when to extend the ideas presented in this chapter to more complex situations.

To help understand the role of CVP analysis in business decisions, consider the hypothetical case of Acoustic Concepts Inc., a company founded by Prem Narayan. Narayan, a graduate engineering student at the time, started Acoustic Concepts to market a radical new speaker that he had designed for automobile sound systems. The speaker, called the Sonic Blaster, uses an advanced microprocessor chip to boost amplification to awesome levels. Narayan contracted with a Taiwanese electronics manufacturer to produce the speaker. With start-up money provided by his family, Narayan placed an order with the manufacturer for completed units and ran advertisements in auto magazines.

The Sonic Blaster was an almost immediate success, and sales grew to the point that Narayan moved the company's headquarters out of his apartment and into rented quarters in a neighbouring industrial park. He also hired a receptionist, an accountant, a sales manager, and a small sales staff to sell the speakers to retail stores. The accountant, Bob Luchinni, had worked for several small companies as a business advisor, accountant, and bookkeeper.

THE BASICS OF COST-VOLUME-PROFIT ANALYSIS

LEARNING OBJECTIVE ①
Explain how changes in activity affect contribution margin and operating income.

Narayan has asked Luchinni to analyze several things he has been thinking about, including the profit effect of a drop in sales volume or a change in variable cost per unit, the incremental sales necessary to justify a new advertising campaign under consideration, and the profit impact of dropping the selling price. As the first step in preparing the analyses, Luchinni looks at the contribution income statement. The contribution income statement emphasizes the behaviour of costs and therefore is extremely helpful to a manager in judging the impact on profits of changes in selling price, cost, or volume. Luchinni will base his analysis on the following contribution income statement he prepared last month:

ACOUSTIC CONCEPTS INC.		
Contribution Income Statement		
For the Month of June		
	Total	Per Unit
Sales (400 speakers)	$100,000	$250
Less variable expenses	60,000	150
Contribution margin	40,000	$100
Less fixed expenses	35,000	
Operating income*	$ 5,000	

*Operating income less interest expense less income tax expense equals net income.

This contribution format income statement was prepared for management's use and would not ordinarily be made available to those outside the company. Note that this statement reports sales, variable expenses, and CM on both a per unit basis and a total basis. These per unit figures are very helpful for performing the CVP analysis that we will be studying over the next several pages. Also, note that we use operating income as our measure of profit. We ignore income taxes throughout most of this chapter so that we can more easily focus on the central issues of CVP analysis.

Contribution Margin

As explained in Chapter 3, contribution margin (CM) is the amount remaining from sales revenue after variable expenses have been deducted. Thus, it is the amount available to cover fixed expenses and then to provide profits for the period. Notice the sequence here—CM is used *first* to cover the fixed expenses, and then whatever remains goes toward profits. If the CM is not sufficient to cover the fixed expenses, then a loss occurs for the period. To illustrate with an extreme example, assume that by the middle of a particular month Acoustic Concepts has sold only one speaker. At that point, the company's income statement will appear as follows:

	Total	Per Unit	Percentage of Sales
Sales (1 speaker).............................	$ 250	$250	100%
Less variable expenses.........................	150	150	60%
Contribution margin..........................	100	$100	40%
Less fixed expenses...........................	35,000		
Operating loss	$(34,900)		

For each additional speaker that the company sells during the month, $100 more in CM will become available to help cover the fixed expenses. If a second speaker is sold, for example, then the total CM will increase by $100 (to a total of $200) and the company's operating loss will decrease by $100, to $34,800:

	Total	Per Unit	Percentage of Sales
Sales (2 speakers).............................	$ 500	$250	100%
Less variable expenses.........................	300	150	60%
Contribution margin..........................	200	$100	40%
Less fixed expenses...........................	35,000		
Operating loss	$(34,800)		

If enough speakers are sold to generate $35,000 in CM, then all of the fixed costs will be covered and the company will have managed to at least *break even* for the month—that is, to show neither profit nor loss but just cover all of its expenses. To reach the break-even point, the company has to sell 350 speakers in a month, since each speaker sold yields $100 in CM:

	Total	Per Unit	Percentage of Sales
Sales (350 speakers)	$87,500	$250	100%
Less variable expenses.........................	52,500	150	60%
Contribution margin..........................	35,000	$100	40%
Less fixed expenses...........................	35,000		
Operating income.............................	$ –0–		

Break-even point
The level of sales at which profit is zero. The break-even point can also be defined as the point where total sales equals total expenses, or as the point where total contribution margin equals total fixed expenses. Sales — variable expenses — fixed expenses = $0.

Computation of the break-even point is discussed in detail later in the chapter; for now, note that the **break-even point** is the level of sales at which profit is zero.

Once the break-even point is reached, operating income will increase by the unit CM for each additional unit sold. If 351 speakers are sold in a month, for example, then we can expect that the operating income for the month to be $100, since the company will have sold 1 speaker more than the number required to break even:

	Total	Per Unit	Percentage of Sales
Sales (351 speakers)	$ 87,750	$250	100%
Less variable expenses	52,650	150	60%
Contribution margin	35,100	$100	40%
Less fixed expenses	35,000		
Operating income	$ 100		

If 352 speakers are sold (2 speakers above the break-even point), then the operating income for the month will be $200, and so forth. To estimate profit at any sales level above the break-even point, simply multiply the number of units sold in excess of the break-even point by the unit CM. The result represents the anticipated operating income for the period. Or, to estimate the effect of a planned increase in sales on profits, the manager can simply multiply the increase in units sold by the unit CM. The result will be the expected increase in operating income. To illustrate, if Acoustic Concepts is currently selling 400 speakers per month and plans to increase sales to 425 speakers per month, the anticipated effect on operating profits can be computed as follows:

Increased number of speakers to be sold	25
Contribution margin per speaker	×$100
Increase in operating income	$2,500

These calculations can be verified as follows:

	Sales Volume			
	400 Speakers	425 Speakers	Difference 25 Speakers	Per Unit
Sales	$100,000	$106,250	$6,250	$250
Less variable expenses	60,000	63,750	3,750	150
Contribution margin	40,000	42,500	2,500	$100
Less fixed expenses	35,000	35,000	–0–	
Operating income	$ 5,000	$ 7,500	$2,500	

Instant Quiz 4-1
Calculate the increase in operating income if Acoustic Concepts sells 500 speakers per month instead of 400.

To summarize, if sales are zero, the company's operating loss equals its fixed expenses. Each unit that is sold reduces the loss by the amount of the unit CM. Once the break-even point has been reached, each additional unit sold increases the company's operating profit by the amount of the unit CM.

The income statements shown above for Acoustic Concepts illustrate the fundamentals of CVP analysis but are based on some simplifying assumptions. For example, we assumed that selling price per unit, variable expenses per unit, and total fixed expenses remained constant even for large changes in sales volumes. Simplifications such as these make the analysis easier to prepare and permit a preliminary examination of the profit effects of alternative scenarios (e.g., increased sales volume, decreased selling price per unit). However, a more complex examination of CVP relationships that relaxes the simplifying assumptions can easily be handled by computer spreadsheet programs that permit more sophisticated forms of "what if" analysis.

COST–VOLUME–PROFIT RELATIONSHIPS IN GRAPHIC FORM

Relationships among revenue, cost, profit, and volume can be expressed graphically by preparing a **cost-volume-profit (CVP) graph**. A CVP graph highlights CVP relationships over wide ranges of activity. To help explain his analysis to Narayan, Luchinni prepared a CVP graph for Acoustic Concepts.

LEARNING OBJECTIVE **2**
Prepare and interpret a cost-volume-profit graph.

Preparing the Cost-Volume-Profit Graph

In a CVP graph (sometimes called a *break-even chart*), unit volume is commonly represented on the horizontal *x*-axis and dollars on the vertical *y*-axis. Preparing a CVP graph involves three steps, as depicted in Exhibit 4–1, and can easily be accomplished using software such as Microsoft Excel.

1. Plot the line parallel to the volume axis that represents total fixed expenses. For Acoustic Concepts, total fixed expenses are $35,000.
2. Plot the line representing total expenses (fixed plus variable) at various activity levels. For example, in Exhibit 4–1, total expenses at an activity level of 600 speakers are calculated as follows:

Fixed expenses	$ 35,000
Variable expenses (600 speakers × $150)	90,000
Total expenses	$125,000

Total expenses at other activity levels are calculated using this approach.
3. Plot the line representing total sales dollars at various activity levels. For example, in Exhibit 4–1, sales at an activity level of 600 speakers are $150,000 (600 speakers × $250 per speaker). Total sales at other activity levels are calculated using this approach.

Cost-volume-profit (CVP) graph
The relationships among revenues, costs, and level of activity presented in graphic form.

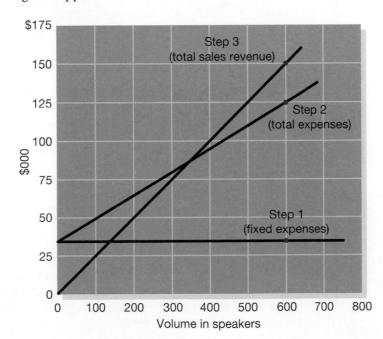

EXHIBIT 4-1   Preparing the CVP Graph

The interpretation of the completed CVP graph is given in Exhibit 4–2. The anticipated profit or loss at any given level of sales is measured by the vertical distance between the total revenue line (sales) and the total expenses line (variable expenses plus fixed expenses).

The break-even point is where the total revenue and total expenses lines intersect. The break-even point of 350 speakers in Exhibit 4–2 agrees with the break-even point computed earlier.

As discussed earlier, when sales are below the break-even point, in this case, 350 units, the company incurs a loss. Note that the loss (represented by the vertical distance between the total expense and total revenue lines) becomes larger as sales decline. When sales are above the break-even point, the company earns a profit and the amount of the profit (represented by the vertical distance between the total revenue and total expense lines) increases as sales increase.

A simpler form of the CVP graph, called a *profit graph*, is presented in Exhibit 4–3. That graph is based on the following equation:

$$\text{Profit} = \text{Unit CM} \times Q - \text{Fixed expenses}$$

where Q is the quantity of items sold.

In the case of Acoustic Concepts, the equation can be expressed as

$$\text{Profit} = \$100 \times Q - \$35,000$$

Because this is a linear equation, it plots profit as a single straight line. To plot the line, simply compute the profit at different sales volumes. For example, when the sales volume is zero (i.e., $Q = 0$), the profit is $-\$35,000$ (= $\$100 \times 0 - \$35,000$). When Q is 600, the profit is $\$25,000$ (= $\$100 \times 600 - \$35,000$). Profit at other sales volume levels is similarly calculated.

The break-even point on the profit graph is the volume of sales at which profit is zero and is indicated by the dashed line on the graph. Note that the profit steadily

---

Instant Quiz 4-2
Using the profit equation, verify that Acoustic Concepts will have a loss of $25,000, as shown in Exhibit 4–3, if sales volume is 100 speakers.

EXHIBIT 4-2   The Completed CVP Graph

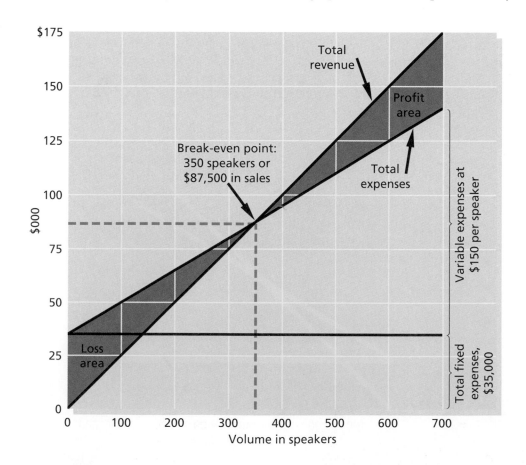

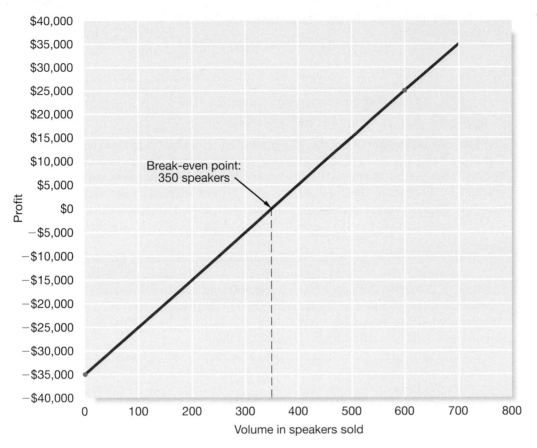

EXHIBIT 4-3   The Profit Graph

increases to the right of the break-even point as the sales volume increases and that the loss becomes increasingly larger to the left of the break-even point as the sales volume decreases.

▮ CONTRIBUTION MARGIN RATIO

In the previous section, we explored how CVP relationships can be visualized by using a CVP graph. In this section, we show how the CM ratio can be used in CVP calculations. As the first step, we have added a column to Acoustic Concepts' contribution income statement, in which sales revenues, variable expenses, and CM are expressed as a percentage of sales:

LEARNING OBJECTIVE ❸
Use the contribution margin ratio to compute changes in contribution margin and operating income resulting from changes in sales volume.

	Total	Per Unit	Percentage of Sales
Sales (400 speakers)	$100,000	$250	100%
Less variable expenses	60,000	150	60%
Contribution margin	40,000	$100	40%
Less fixed expenses	35,000		
Operating income	$ 5,000		

The CM expressed as a percentage of total sales is referred to as the **contribution margin (CM) ratio**. This ratio is computed as follows:

$$\text{CM ratio} = \frac{\text{Contribution margin}}{\text{Sales}}$$

Contribution margin (CM) ratio
The contribution margin as a percentage of total sales.

For Acoustic Concepts, the computations are as follows:

$$\frac{\text{Total contribution margin: } 40{,}000}{\text{Total sales: } \$100{,}000} = 40\%$$

or

$$\frac{\text{Per unit contribution margin: } \$100}{\text{Per unit sales: } \$250} = 40\%$$

The CM ratio shows how the CM is affected by a change in total sales. Acoustic Concepts has a CM ratio of 40%, meaning that for each dollar increase in sales, total CM will increase by 40 cents ($1 sales × CM ratio of 40%). Operating income will also increase by 40 cents, assuming that fixed costs are not affected by the increase in sales. The effect of a change in sales on the CM can be expressed in equation form as follows:

$$\text{Change in CM} = \text{CM ratio} \times \text{Change in sales}$$

As this illustration suggests, *the effect on operating income of any dollar change in total sales can be computed by simply applying the CM ratio to the dollar change.* For example, if Acoustic Concepts plans a $30,000 increase in sales during the coming month, the CM will increase by $12,000 ($30,000 increased sales × CM ratio of 40%). As we noted above, operating income will also increase by $12,000 if fixed costs do not change. This is verified by the following table:

	Sales Volume			Percentage of Sales
	Current	Expected	Increase	
Sales..................................	$100,000	$130,000	$30,000	100%
Less variable expenses................	60,000	78,000*	18,000	60%
Contribution margin....................	40,000	52,000	12,000	40%
Less fixed expenses....................	35,000	35,000	–0–	
Operating income......................	$ 5,000	$ 17,000	$ 12,000	

*$130,000 expected sales ÷ $250 per unit = 520 units. 520 units × $150 per unit = $78,000.

Instant Quiz 4-3
Calculate the effect on operating income if Acoustic Concepts has a $50,000 increase in sales, assuming fixed costs do not increase.

Some managers prefer to work with the CM ratio rather than the unit CM. The CM ratio is particularly valuable when trade-offs must be made between more dollar sales of one product and more dollar sales of another. Generally speaking, when trying to increase sales, products that yield the greatest amount of CM per dollar of sales should be emphasized.

SOME APPLICATIONS OF COST–VOLUME–PROFIT CONCEPTS

LEARNING OBJECTIVE 4
Show the effects on contribution margin of changes in variable costs, fixed costs, selling price, and volume.

Bob Luchinni, the accountant at Acoustic Concepts, wants to demonstrate how the concepts developed on the preceding pages of this chapter can be used to analyze some of the issues that the company's president, Prem Narayan, is worried about. Luchinni gathered the following basic data:

	Per Unit	Percentage of Sales
Sales price..	$250	100%
Less variable expenses.......................................	150	60%
Contribution margin	$100	40%

Recall that fixed expenses are $35,000 per month. Luchinni will use these data to show the effects of changes in variable costs, fixed costs, sales price, and sales volume on the company's profitability.

LEARNING AID

Key Formulas for Contribution Format Income Statements

Operating income = Unit CM × Q – Fixed expenses

CM = Sales – Variable expenses

CM per unit = Per unit sales – Per unit variable expenses

CM ratio = Total CM ÷ Total sales or CM ratio = Per unit CM ÷ Per unit sales

Variable expense ratio = Variable expenses ÷ Sales

In these formulas, CM = contribution margin and Q = quantity of goods sold in units.

Before proceeding further, however, we need to introduce another concept—the *variable expense ratio*. The **variable expense ratio** is the ratio of variable expenses to sales. It is computed by dividing the total variable expenses by the total sales, or, in a single-product analysis, it is computed by dividing the variable expenses per unit by the unit selling price. In the case of Acoustic Concepts, the variable expense ratio is 0.60; that is, variable expense is 60% of sales. Expressed as an equation, the variable expense ratio is

Variable expense ratio
The ratio of variable expenses to sales.

$$\text{Variable expense ratio} = \frac{\text{Variable expenses}}{\text{Sales}}$$

This leads to a useful equation that relates the CM ratio to the variable expense ratio as follows:

$$\text{CM ratio} = \frac{\text{Contribution margin}}{\text{Sales}}$$

$$\text{CM ratio} = \frac{\text{Sales} - \text{Variable expenses}}{\text{Sales}}$$

$$\text{CM ratio} = 1 - \text{Variable expense ratio}$$

Change in Fixed Cost and Sales Volume

Acoustic Concepts is currently selling 400 speakers per month at $250 per speaker, for total monthly sales of $100,000. The sales manager feels that a $10,000 increase in the monthly advertising budget would increase monthly sales by $30,000 to a total of $130,000. Should the advertising budget be increased? The following table shows the effect of the proposed change in monthly advertising budget:

| | Sales Volume | | | |
	Current Sales	Sales with Additional Advertising Budget	Difference	Percentage of Sales
Sales	$100,000	$130,000*	$30,000	100%
Less variable expenses	60,000	78,000†	18,000	60%
Contribution margin	40,000	52,000	12,000	40%
Less fixed expenses	35,000	45,000‡	10,000	
Operating income	$ 5,000	$ 7,000	$ 2,000	

*New unit sales: $130,000 ÷ $250 per unit = 520 units
†520 units × $150 per unit = $78,000
‡$35,000 plus additional $10,000 monthly advertising budget = $45,000

Assuming no other factors need to be considered, the increase in the advertising budget should be approved since it would lead to an increase in operating income of $2,000. There are two shorter ways to present this solution. The first alternative solution follows:

Alternative Solution 1

Expected total contribution margin:	
$130,000 × 40% CM ratio	$52,000
Current total contribution margin:	
$100,000 × 40% CM ratio	40,000
Incremental contribution margin	12,000
Change in fixed costs:	
Less incremental advertising expense	10,000
Increased operating income	$ 2,000

Since in this case only the fixed costs and the sales volume change, the solution can be presented in an even shorter format, as follows:

Alternative Solution 2

Incremental contribution margin:	
$30,000 × 40% CM ratio	$12,000
Less incremental advertising expense	10,000
Increased operating income	$ 2,000

Incremental analysis
An analytical approach that focuses only on those items of revenue, cost, and volume that will change as a result of a decision.

Notice that this approach does not require a knowledge of previous sales. Also notice that it is unnecessary under either alternative approach to prepare an income statement. Both approaches involve an **incremental analysis**—they consider only those items of revenue, cost, and volume that will change if the new program is implemented.[1] Although in each case a new income statement could have been prepared, the incremental approach is more direct and focuses attention on the specific items involved in the decision.

Change in Variable Costs and Sales Volume

Refer to the original data. Recall that Acoustic Concepts is currently selling 400 speakers per month. Management is contemplating the use of higher-quality components, which would increase variable costs (and thereby reduce the CM) by $10 per speaker. However, the sales manager predicts that the higher overall quality would increase sales to 480 speakers per month. Should the higher-quality components be used? The $10 increase in variable costs will decrease the unit CM by $10—from $100 to $90.

Solution

Expected total contribution margin with	
higher-quality components:	
480 speakers × $90 per speaker	$ 43,200
Current total contribution margin:	
400 speakers × $100 per speaker	40,000
Increase in total contribution margin	$ 3,200

According to this incremental analysis, the higher-quality components should be used. Since fixed costs will not change, the $3,200 increase in CM shown above should result in a $3,200 increase in operating income.

Change in Fixed Costs, Selling Price, and Sales Volume

Refer to the original data and recall again that the company is currently selling 400 speakers per month. To increase sales, the sales manager would like to reduce the selling price by $20 per speaker and increase the advertising budget by $15,000 per month. The sales manager argues that if these two actions are taken, unit sales will increase by

50% to 600 speakers per month. Should the changes be made? A decrease of $20 per speaker in the selling price will cause the unit CM to decrease from $100 to $80.

Solution

Expected total contribution margin with lower selling price:	
600 speakers × $80 per speaker..	$ 48,000
Current total contribution margin:	
400 speakers × $100 per speaker	40,000
Incremental contribution margin..	8,000
Change in fixed costs:	
Less incremental advertising expense..	15,000
Reduction in operating income...	$ (7,000)

According to this incremental analysis, the changes should not be made. The $7,000 reduction in operating income that is shown above can be verified by preparing comparative income statements as follows:

	Current 400 Speakers per Month		Expected 600 Speakers per Month		
	Total	**Per Unit**	**Total**	**Per Unit**	**Difference**
Sales	$100,000	$250	$138,000	$230	$38,000
Less variable expenses................	60,000	150	90,000	150	30,000
Contribution margin...................	40,000	$100	48,000	$ 80	8,000
Less fixed expenses..................	35,000		50,000*		15,000
Operating income (loss)...............	$ 5,000		$ (2,000)		$ (7,000)

*$35,000 + additional monthly advertising budget of $15,000 = $50,000.

Change in Variable Cost, Fixed Cost, and Sales Volume

Refer to the original data. As before, the company is currently selling 400 speakers per month. The sales manager would like to pay the salespeople a commission of $15 per speaker sold, rather than the flat salaries that now total $6,000 per month. The sales manager is confident that the change will increase monthly sales by 15% to 460 speakers per month. Should the change be made?

Solution

Changing the sales staff from a salaried basis to a commission basis will affect both fixed and variable costs. Fixed costs will decrease by $6,000, from $35,000 to $29,000. Variable costs per unit will increase by $15, from $150 to $165, and the unit CM will decrease from $100 to $85:

Expected total contribution margin with sales staff on commission:	
460 speakers × $85 per speaker	$39,100
Current total contribution margin:	
400 speakers × $100 per speaker	40,000
Decrease in total contribution margin...	(900)
Change in fixed costs:	
Add salaries avoided if a commission is paid	6,000
Increase in operating income	$ 5,100

According to this incremental analysis, the change should be made. Again, the same answer can be obtained by preparing comparative income statements:

	Current 400 Speakers per Month		Expected 460 Speakers per Month		Difference: Increase or (Decrease) in Net Income
	Total	Per Unit	Total	Per Unit	
Sales.............................	$100,000	$250	$115,000	$250	$15,000
Less variable expenses.............	60,000	150	75,900	165	(15,900)
Contribution margin...............	40,000	$100	39,100	$ 85	(900)
Less fixed expenses...............	35,000		29,000		6,000
Operating income.................	$ 5,000		$ 10,100		$ 5,100

Change in Regular Selling Price

Refer to the original data, where Acoustic Concepts is currently selling 400 speakers per month. The company has an opportunity to make a bulk sale of 150 speakers to a wholesaler if an acceptable price can be worked out. This sale would not affect the company's regular sales and would not impact total fixed expenses. What price per speaker should be quoted to the wholesaler if Acoustic Concepts wants to increase its monthly profits by $3,000?

Variable cost per speaker..	$150
Desired profit per speaker:	
$3,000 ÷ 150 speakers..	20
Quoted price per speaker..	$170

Notice that no fixed expenses are included in the computation. This is because fixed expenses are not affected by the bulk sale, so all of the additional revenue that is in excess of variable costs goes to increasing the profits of the company.

Importance of the Contribution Margin

As stated in the introduction to this chapter, CVP analysis seeks the most profitable combination of variable costs, fixed costs, selling price, and sales volume. The above examples show that the effect on the CM is a major consideration in deciding on the most profitable combination of these factors. We have seen that profits can sometimes be improved by reducing the CM if fixed costs can be reduced by a greater amount. More commonly, however, we have seen that the way to improve profits is to increase the total CM. Sometimes this can be done by reducing the selling price and thereby increasing volume, sometimes it can be done by increasing the fixed costs (such as advertising) and thereby increasing volume, and sometimes it can be done by trading off variable and fixed costs with appropriate changes in volume. Many other combinations of factors are possible.

   The amount of the unit CM figure (and the size of the CM ratio) has a significant influence on the actions a company is willing to take to improve profits. For example, the greater the unit CM, the greater the amount the company may be willing to spend in order to increase unit sales. This explains in part why companies with high unit CMs (such as auto manufacturers) advertise so heavily, while companies with low unit CMs (such as dishware manufacturers) tend to spend much less for advertising. In short, the effect on the CM is critical to many operating decisions.

LEARNING AID

COST-VOLUME-PROFIT ANALYSIS

Changes Affecting
- Selling price per unit
- Variable unit costs
- Fixed costs
- Volume

Decision Rule:

Make change if   Increase in contribution margin > Increase in fixed costs or
                        Decrease in contribution margin < Decrease in fixed costs

Do not make change if Increase in contribution margin < Increase in fixed costs or
                        Decrease in contribution margin > Decrease in fixed costs

■ BREAK-EVEN ANALYSIS

Break-even analysis is an aspect of CVP analysis that is designed to answer questions such as how far sales could drop before the company begins to lose money.

Break-Even Computations

Earlier in the chapter, we defined the break-even point to be the level of sales at which the company's profit (operating income) is zero. The break-even point can be computed using either the *equation method* or the *formula method*—the two methods are equivalent.

The Equation Method   The **equation method** translates the contribution format income statement illustrated earlier in the chapter into an equation form, as follows:

$$\text{Profits} = (\text{Sales} - \text{Variable expenses}) - \text{Fixed expenses}$$

Rearranging this equation yields the following equation, which is widely used in CVP analysis:

$$\text{Sales} = \text{Variable expenses} + \text{Fixed expenses} + \text{Profits}$$

At the break-even point, profits are zero. Therefore, the break-even point can be computed by finding that point where sales just equal the total of the variable expenses plus the fixed expenses. For Acoustic Concepts, the break-even point in unit sales, Q, can be computed as follows:

$$\text{Sales} = \text{Variable expenses} + \text{Fixed expenses} + \text{Profits}$$

$$\$250Q = \$150Q + \$35{,}000 + \$0$$
$$\$100Q = \$35{,}000$$
$$Q = \$35{,}000 \div \$100$$
$$Q = 350 \text{ speakers}$$

where

$$Q = \text{Number (quantity) of speakers sold}$$
$$\$250 = \text{Unit sales price}$$
$$\$150 = \text{Unit variable expenses}$$
$$\$35{,}000 = \text{Total fixed expenses}$$

LEARNING OBJECTIVE ⑤
Compute the break-even point in unit sales and sales dollars.

Equation method
A method of computing break-even sales using the contribution format income statement.

The break-even point in sales dollars can be computed by multiplying the break-even level of unit sales by the selling price per unit:

$$350 \text{ speakers} \times \$250 = \$87,500$$

The break-even point in total sales dollars, X, can also be directly computed as follows:

$$\text{Sales} = \text{Variable expenses} + \text{Fixed expenses} + \text{Profits}$$
$$X = 0.60X + \$35,000 + \$0$$
$$0.40X = \$35,000$$
$$X = \$35,000 \div 0.40$$
$$X = \$87,500$$

where

$$X = \text{Total sales dollars}$$
$$0.60 = \text{Variable expenses as a percentage of sales}$$
$$\$35,000 = \text{Total fixed expenses}$$

Note that in the above analysis, the *variable expense ratio*, defined earlier in the chapter, is used. Also note that using the ratios in the above analysis yields a break-even point expressed in sales dollars rather than in units sold. If desired, the break-even point in units sold can be computed as follows:

$$\$87,500 \div \$250 = 350 \text{ speakers}$$

It is worth noting that while the solutions for the examples used in this chapter always work out to round numbers, this will of course not always be the case in practice. When necessary, managers should round up to get the sales levels needed to at least break even or achieve the desired target profit.

Formula method
A method of computing the break-even point where the fixed expenses are divided by the contribution margin per unit.

The Formula Method   The **formula method** is a shortcut version of the equation method already described. The approach centres on the idea discussed earlier that each unit sold provides a certain amount of CM that goes toward covering fixed costs. To find how many units must be sold to break even, we simply rearrange the profit equation to divide total fixed costs by the unit CM:[2]

$$\text{Break-even point in units sold} = \frac{\text{Fixed expenses}}{\text{Unit contribution margin}}$$

Each speaker generates a CM of $100 ($250 selling price, less $150 variable expenses). Since the total fixed expenses are $35,000, the break-even point is as follows:

$$\frac{\text{Fixed expenses}}{\text{Unit contribution margin}} = \frac{\$35,000}{\$100 \text{ per speaker}} = 350 \text{ speakers}$$

A variation of this method uses the CM ratio instead of the unit CM. The result is the break-even in total sales dollars rather than in total units sold:

$$\text{Break-even point in total sales dollars} = \frac{\text{Fixed expenses}}{\text{CM ratio}}$$

Instant Quiz 4-4
Calculate the break-even point in units and sales dollars assuming Acoustic Concepts' fixed costs are $40,000 and the CM remains the same at $100 per unit.

In the Acoustic Concepts example, the calculations are as follows:

$$\frac{\text{Fixed expenses}}{\text{CM ratio}} = \frac{\$35,000}{40\%} = \$87,500$$

This approach, based on the CM ratio, is useful when a company has multiple product lines and wishes to compute a single break-even point for the company as a whole. We will return to this concept later in the chapter.

■ TARGET OPERATING PROFIT ANALYSIS

CVP formulas can be used to determine the sales volume needed to achieve a target operating profit. Suppose that Prem Narayan of Acoustic Concepts would like to earn a target operating profit of $40,000 per month. How many speakers would have to be sold?

LEARNING OBJECTIVE ⑥
Determine the level of sales needed to achieve a desired target profit.

The Equation Method

One approach is to use the equation method. Instead of solving for the unit sales where operating profits are zero, you instead solve for the unit sales where operating profits are $40,000:

$$\text{Sales} = \text{Variable expenses} + \text{Fixed expenses} + \text{Profits}$$
$$\$250Q = \$150Q + \$35{,}000 + \$40{,}000$$
$$\$100Q = \$75{,}000$$
$$Q = \$75{,}000 \div \$100$$
$$Q = 750 \text{ speakers}$$

where

$Q =$ Number of speakers sold
$\$250 =$ Unit sales price
$\$150 =$ Unit variable expenses
$\$35{,}000 =$ Total fixed expenses
$\$40{,}000 =$ Target operating profit

Thus, the target operating profit can be achieved by selling 750 speakers per month, which represents $187,500 in total sales ($250 × 750 speakers).

The Formula Method

The second approach involves expanding the formula used to determine break-even units to include the target operating profit as follows:

$$\text{Units sold to attain the target profit} = \frac{\text{Fixed expenses} + \text{Target operating profit}}{\text{Unit contribution margin}}$$

$$\frac{\$35{,}000 \text{ fixed expenses} + \$40{,}000 \text{ target operating profit}}{\$100 \text{ contribution margin per speaker}} = 750 \text{ speakers}$$

This approach gives the same answer as the equation method since it is simply a shortcut version of the equation method. The problem of computing the dollar sales level required to achieve a target operating profit is very similar to the problem of finding a break-even point. The dollar sales needed to attain the target operating profit can be computed as follows:

$$\text{Dollar sales to attain target profit} = \frac{\text{Fixed expenses} + \text{Target operating profit}}{\text{CM ratio}}$$

$$= \frac{\$35{,}000 + \$40{,}000}{0.40}$$

$$= \$187{,}500$$

Instant Quiz 4-5
Calculate the sales units and sales dollars required if Acoustic Concepts has a target profit of $55,000. Assume fixed costs are $35,000 and the CM per unit is $100.

After-Tax Analysis

Operating profit in the preceding analysis has ignored income taxes, but for-profit organizations are required to pay corporate income taxes. In general, operating profit after taxes can be computed as a fixed percentage of income before taxes. To calculate income taxes, we multiply the tax rate (t) by the operating profit before taxes (B). Therefore, after-tax profit is equal to profit before taxes $\times\ (1 - t)$ and is derived as follows:

$$\text{Profit after taxes} = \text{Before-tax profit} - \text{Taxes}$$
$$= B - t(B)$$
$$= B(1 - t)$$

Dividing both sides by $(1 - t)$, income before taxes is equal to profit after taxes divided by 1 minus the tax rate $(1 - t)$:

$$B = \frac{\text{Profit after taxes}}{(1 - t)}$$

Using the previous example, assume that the tax rate is 30% and the target operating profit is $49,000 *after* taxes. The target profit can be achieved by selling 1,050 speakers. The appropriate formula to use is

$$\frac{\text{Fixed expenses} + [(\text{Target after-tax profit})/(1 - \text{tax rate})]}{\text{Contribution margin per unit}}$$

$$\frac{\$35,000 + [\$49,000/(1 - 0.3)]}{\$100} = 1,050 \text{ speakers}$$

Instant Quiz 4-6
How many speakers must Acoustic Concepts sell to earn an after-tax profit of $56,000? Assume fixed expenses are $35,000, CM is $100 per unit, and the tax rate is 30%.

LEARNING AID

SINGLE-PRODUCT CVP ANALYSIS

Break-Even (Formula Method)
- **Units:**

$$\text{Break-even point in units sold} = \frac{\text{Fixed expenses}}{\text{Unit contribution margin}}$$

- **Sales Dollars:**

$$\text{Break-even point in total sales dollars} = \frac{\text{Fixed expenses}}{\text{CM ratio}}$$

Target Operating Profit (Formula Method)*
- **Units:**

$$\text{Units sold to attain target profit} = \frac{\text{Fixed expenses} + \left[\dfrac{\text{Target after-tax profit}}{1 - \text{Tax rate}}\right]}{\text{Unit contribution margin}}$$

- **Sales Dollars:**

$$\text{Dollar sales to attain target profit} = \frac{\text{Fixed expenses} + \left[\dfrac{\text{Target after-tax profit}}{1 - \text{Tax rate}}\right]}{\text{CM ratio}}$$

*In cases where taxes are ignored, replace "Target after-tax profit/(1 − Tax rate)" with "Target profit."

Whenever target operating profit is expressed on an after-tax basis, the equation method can be used as described earlier, except that target operating profit must be restated to a pre-tax basis.

THE MARGIN OF SAFETY

The **margin of safety** is the excess of budgeted (or actual) sales over the break-even volume of sales. It states the amount by which sales can drop before losses begin to be incurred. The higher the margin of safety, the lower the risk of not breaking even. The formula for its calculation is as follows:

LEARNING OBJECTIVE 7
Compute the margin of safety and explain its significance.

Margin of safety = Total budgeted (or actual) sales − Break-even sales

The margin of safety can also be expressed in percentage form. This percentage is obtained by dividing the margin of safety in dollar terms by total sales:

$$\text{Margin of safety percentage} = \frac{\text{Margin of safety in dollars}}{\text{Total budgeted (or actual) sales}}$$

Margin of safety
The excess of budgeted (or actual) sales over the break-even volume of sales.

The calculations for the margin of safety for Acoustic Concepts are as follows:

Sales (at the current volume of 400 speakers) (a)	$100,000
Break-even sales (350 speakers)	87,500
Margin of safety (in dollars) (b)	$ 12,500
Margin of safety as a percentage of sales, (b) ÷ (a)	12.5%

This margin of safety means that with the company's current prices and costs, a reduction in sales of $12,500, or 12.5% from the current level, would result in just breaking even.

In a single-product firm like Acoustic Concepts, the margin of safety can also be expressed in terms of the number of units sold by dividing the margin of safety in dollars by the selling price per unit. In this case, the margin of safety is 50 speakers ($12,500 ÷ $250 per speaker = 50 speakers).

Instant Quiz 4-7
Assume Acoustic Concepts has a current sales volume of $150,000 and break-even sales of $100,000. Calculate the margin of safety in dollars and the margin of safety percentage.

COST–VOLUME–PROFIT CONSIDERATIONS IN CHOOSING A COST STRUCTURE

Cost structure refers to the relative proportion of fixed and variable costs in an organization. An organization often has some latitude in trading off between fixed and variable costs. For example, fixed investments in automated equipment can reduce variable labour costs. In this section, we discuss the choice of a cost structure, focusing on the effect of cost structure on profit stability, in which *operating leverage* plays a key role.

LEARNING OBJECTIVE 8
Explain cost structure, compute the degree of operating leverage at a particular level of sales, and explain how operating leverage can be used to predict changes in operating income.

Cost Structure and Profit Stability

Which cost structure is better—high variable costs and low fixed costs, or the opposite? No single answer to this question is possible: either structure has its advantages. To show what we mean, refer to the contribution format income statements given below for two blueberry farms. Bogside Farm depends on temporary foreign workers to pick its berries by hand, whereas Sterling Farm has invested in expensive berry-picking machines. Consequently, Bogside Farm has higher variable costs, but Sterling Farm has higher fixed costs:

	Bogside Farm		Sterling Farm	
	Total	Percentage	Total	Percentage
Sales...	$100,000	100%	$100,000	100%
Less variable expenses........................	60,000	60%	30,000	30%
Contribution margin	40,000	40%	70,000	70%
Less fixed expenses...........................	30,000		60,000	
Operating income.............................	$ 10,000		$ 10,000	

Which farm has the better cost structure? The answer depends on many factors, including the long-run trend in sales, year-to-year fluctuations in the level of sales, and the attitude of the owners toward risk. If sales are expected to be above $100,000 in the future, then Sterling Farm probably has the better cost structure. This is because its CM ratio is higher, and its operating income will therefore increase more rapidly as sales increase. To illustrate, assume that each farm experiences a 10% increase in sales without any increase in fixed costs. The new income statements are as follows:

	Bogside Farm		Sterling Farm	
	Total	Percentage	Total	Percentage
Sales...	$110,000	100%	$110,000	100%
Less variable expenses........................	66,000	60%	33,000	30%
Contribution margin	44,000	40%	77,000	70%
Less fixed expenses...........................	30,000		60,000	
Operating income.............................	$ 14,000		$ 17,000	

Sterling Farm has experienced a greater increase in operating income due to its higher CM ratio, even though the increase in sales was the same for both farms.

What if sales drop below $100,000? What are the break-even points of the two farms? What are their margins of safety? The computations needed to answer these questions are carried out as follows, using the formula method:

	Bogside Farm	Sterling Farm
Fixed expenses	$ 30,000	$ 60,000
Contribution margin ratio......................................	÷40%	÷70%
Break-even in total sales dollars.................................	$ 75,000	$ 85,714
Total current sales (a)...	$100,000	$100,000
Break-even sales...	75,000	85,714
Margin of safety in sales dollars (b).............................	$ 25,000	$ 14,286
Margin of safety as a percentage of sales, (b) ÷ (a)..............	25.0%	14.3%

Bogside Farm is less vulnerable to downturns than Sterling Farm for two reasons. First, due to its lower fixed expenses, Bogside Farm has a lower break-even point and a higher margin of safety, as shown by the computations above. Therefore, it will not incur losses as quickly as Sterling Farm in periods of sharply declining sales. Second, due to its lower CM ratio, Bogside Farm will not lose CM as rapidly as Sterling Farm when sales fall off. Thus, Bogside Farm's income will be less volatile. We saw earlier that this is a drawback when sales increase, but it provides more protection when sales drop. And, because its break-even point is lower, Bogside Farm can suffer a larger sales decline before losses emerge.

IN BUSINESS

In recent years, computer chip manufacturers have poured more than $75 billion into constructing new manufacturing facilities to meet the growing demand for digital devices such as iPhones and BlackBerrys. Because 70% of the costs of running these facilities are fixed, a sharp drop in customer demand forces these companies to choose between two undesirable options. They can slash production levels and absorb large amounts of unused capacity costs, or they can continue producing large volumes of output in spite of shrinking demand, thereby flooding the market with excess supply and lowering prices. Either choice distresses investors who tend to shy away from computer chip makers in economic downturns.

Source: Bruce Einhorn, "Chipmakers on the Edge," *BusinessWeek*, January 5, 2009, pp. 30–31.

To summarize, without knowing the future, it is not obvious which cost structure is better. Both have advantages and disadvantages. Sterling Farm, with its higher fixed costs and lower variable costs, will experience wider swings in operating income as changes take place in sales, with greater profits in good years and greater losses in bad years. Bogside Farm, with its lower fixed costs and higher variable costs, will enjoy greater stability in operating income and will be more protected from losses during bad years, but at a cost of lower operating income in good years.

Operating Leverage

A lever is a tool for multiplying force. Using a lever, a massive object can be moved with only a modest amount of force. In business, *operating leverage* serves a similar purpose. **Operating leverage** is a measure of how sensitive operating income is to percentage changes in sales. Operating leverage acts as a multiplier. If operating leverage is high, a small percentage increase in sales can produce a much larger percentage increase in operating income.

Operating leverage can be illustrated by returning to the data given above for the two blueberry farms. We previously showed that a 10% increase in sales (from $100,000 to $110,000 for each farm) results in a 70% increase in the operating income of Sterling Farm (from $10,000 to $17,000) and only a 40% increase in the operating income of Bogside Farm (from $10,000 to $14,000). Thus, for a 10% increase in sales, Sterling Farm experiences a much greater percentage increase in profits than does Bogside Farm. Therefore, Sterling Farm has greater operating leverage than Bogside Farm.

The **degree of operating leverage** is a measure, at a given level of sales, of how a percentage change in sales volume will affect profits. It is computed by the following formula:

$$\text{Degree of operating leverage} = \frac{\text{Contribution margin}}{\text{Operating income}}$$

To illustrate, the degree of operating leverage for the two farms at a $100,000 sales level is as follows:

$$\text{Bogside Farm} = \frac{\$40,000}{\$10,000} = 4$$

$$\text{Sterling Farm} = \frac{\$70,000}{\$10,000} = 7$$

Since the degree of operating leverage for Bogside Farm is 4, the farm's operating income grows four times as fast as its sales. Similarly, Sterling Farm's operating income grows seven times as fast as its sales. Thus, if sales increase by 10%, then we can expect the operating income of Bogside Farm to increase by four times this

Operating leverage
A measure of how sensitive operating income is to a given percentage change in sales. It is computed by dividing the contribution margin by operating income.

Degree of operating leverage
A measure, at a given level of sales, of how a percentage change in sales volume will affect profits. The degree of operating leverage is computed by dividing contribution margin by operating income.

amount, or 40%, and the operating income of Sterling Farm to increase by seven times this amount, or 70%. In general, this relation between the percentage change in operating income is given by the following formula:

$$\text{Percentage change in operating income} =$$
$$\text{Degree of operating leverage} \times \text{Percentage change in sales}$$

Bogside Farm: Percentage change in operating income = 4 × 10% = 40%

Sterling Farm: Percentage change in operating income = 7 × 10% = 70%

What is responsible for the higher operating leverage at Sterling Farm? The only difference between the two farms is their cost structure. If two companies have the same total revenue and same total expense but different cost structures, then the company with the higher proportion of fixed costs in its cost structure will have higher operating leverage. Referring back to the original example, while both farms have sales of $100,000 and total expenses of $90,000, one-third of Bogside Farm's costs are fixed but two-thirds of Sterling Farm's costs are fixed. As a consequence, Sterling's degree of operating leverage is higher than Bogside's.

The degree of operating leverage is greatest at sales levels near the break-even point and decreases as sales and profits rise. The following table shows the degree of operating leverage for Bogside Farm at various sales levels. (Data used earlier for Bogside Farm are shown in colour.)

Sales	$75,000	$80,000	$100,000	$150,000	$225,000
Less variable expenses	45,000	48,000	60,000	90,000	135,000
Contribution margin (a)	30,000	32,000	40,000	60,000	90,000
Less fixed expenses	30,000	30,000	30,000	30,000	30,000
Operating income (b)	$ –0–	$ 2,000	$ 10,000	$ 30,000	$ 60,000
Degree of operating leverage, (a) ÷ (b)	∞	16	4	2	1.5

Instant Quiz 4-8
Assume Bogside Farm has current sales of $80,000 and a degree of operating leverage of 16, as shown in the table. If sales increase by 25%, calculate the percentage change in operating income, and calculate the new operating income in dollars.

Thus, a 10% increase in sales increases operating profits by only 15% (10% × 1.5) if the company is operating at a $225,000 sales level, as compared to the 40% increase we computed earlier at the $100,000 sales level. The degree of operating leverage continues to decrease the more the company increases sales from its break-even

IN BUSINESS

The effects of the 2007–2008 recession were widespread, hitting manufacturing and service companies alike. In the United States, an estimated 22,000 legal jobs were lost as a result of layoffs and firm closures. However, Canadian law firms operating in the United States did not fare nearly as badly with respect to job losses, in part due to their considerably lower operating leverage. According to one senior executive of a Canadian law firm with headquarters in Montreal and offices in the United States, the degree of operating leverage averages 1.5 to 2 for Canadian firms, compared to 5 for many U.S. law firms. The larger degree of operating leverage for U.S. firms is in part due to much higher fixed overhead costs relative to Canadian firms. The higher overhead costs relate to the larger number of administrative and support staff typically employed at U.S. firms. When tough economic times hit, firms with a high degree of operating leverage (and high fixed costs) are sometimes forced to cut costs through a reduction in the size of their workforce.

Source: Julius Melnitzer, "Canadian Firms in U.S. Avoiding Big Layoff Hits," *Financial Post*, April 29, 2009, p. 3.

point. At the break-even point, the degree of operating leverage is infinitely large ($30,000 CM ÷ $0 operating income = ∞).

A manager can use the degree of operating leverage to quickly estimate what effect various percentage changes in sales will have on profits, without needing to prepare detailed income statements. As shown by our examples, the effects of operating leverage can be dramatic. If a company is near its break-even point, then even small percentage increases in sales can yield large percentage increases in profits. *This explains why management will often work very hard for only a small increase in sales volume.* If the degree of operating leverage is 5, then a 6% increase in sales translates into a 30% increase in profits.

Indifference Analysis

We have seen that CVP analysis can be used as input for decisions about the profitability of individual products. CVP analysis is also useful for aiding decisions about the comparative profitability of alternative products or methods of production. The analysis focuses on cost behaviour in relation to changes in activity level. Relative profitability depends on activity level. A product with a high level of fixed costs requires a higher sales activity level to generate a profit than a product with low fixed costs and comparatively high variable costs. CVP analyses facilitate the comparison of alternatives with different fixed and variable cost structures.

To illustrate, assume that Goodwin Company has decided to introduce a new product that can be manufactured by either a labour-intensive production (LIP) system or a capital-intensive production (CIP) system. The manufacturing method will not affect the quality of the product. The estimated manufacturing costs of a LIP system and a CIP system are as follows:

	LIP System		CIP System	
Selling price per unit sold............................		$40.00		$40.00
Direct material*....................................		6.00		5.00
Direct labour-hours (DLH).........................	0.8 DLH @ $15	12.00	0.5 DLH @ $20	10.00
Variable overhead.................................	0.8 DLH @ $10	8.00	0.5 DLH @ $10	5.00
Variable selling expense...........................		2.00		2.00
Total variable costs................................		28.00		22.00
Contribution margin...............................		$ 12.00		$ 18.00
Fixed overhead†..................................		$ 1,200,000		$3,000,000
Fixed selling expenses.............................		$ 600,000		$ 600,000
Break-even sales..................................		$6,000,000		$8,000,000
Break-even units..................................		150,000		200,000

*The LIP system results in higher direct material costs per unit because of more wastage of materials.
†These costs are directly traceable to the new product line. They would not be incurred if the new product were not produced.

We can calculate the point at which Goodwin will be indifferent about using a LIP system versus a CIP system as follows:

1. Determine the unit CM multiplied by the number of units (Q) minus the total fixed costs of each alternative.
2. Set up an equation with each alternative on opposite sides of the equal sign.
3. Solve for Q the indifference point:

$$\$12Q - \$1,800,000 = \$18Q - \$3,600,000$$

$$\$6Q = \$1,800,000$$

$$Q = 300,000 \text{ units}$$

Note from line 2 of the equation that the $6 difference in CM is on the left-hand side of the equation, and the $1,800,000 on the right-hand side of the equation is the difference in fixed costs. The indifference point can therefore be found quickly by dividing the difference in fixed costs by the difference in CMs between the two alternatives:

$$\frac{\text{Fixed cost of CIP} - \text{Fixed cost of LIP}}{\text{CM of CIP} - \text{CM of LIP}} = \frac{\$3,600,000 - \$1,800,000}{\$18 - \$12} = 300,000 \text{ units}$$

At sales below the indifference point of 300,000 units, profitability will be higher for LIP. Sales above the indifference point will generate higher profitability for CIP, because CIP generates a higher CM per unit than LIP does.

■ SALES MIX

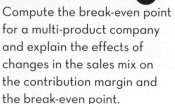

LEARNING OBJECTIVE 9

Compute the break-even point for a multi-product company and explain the effects of changes in the sales mix on the contribution margin and the break-even point.

Sales mix
The relative proportions in which a company's products are sold. Sales mix is computed by expressing the sales of each product as a percentage of total sales.

Before concluding our discussion of CVP concepts, we consider the effect of changes in sales mix on a firm's profits.

The Definition of Sales Mix

The term **sales mix** refers to the relative proportions in which a company's products are sold. Managers try to achieve the combination, or mix, that will yield the greatest amount of profits. Most companies have several products, and often these products are not equally profitable; therefore, profits depend to some extent on the company's sales mix. Profits will be greater if high-margin rather than low-margin items make up a relatively large proportion of total sales.

Changes in the sales mix can cause considerable variation in a company's profits. A shift in the sales mix from high-margin items to low-margin items can cause total profits to decrease even though total sales may increase. Conversely, a shift in the sales mix from low-margin items to high-margin items can cause the opposite effect—total profits may increase even though total sales decrease. It is one thing to achieve a particular sales volume, but it is quite another to sell the most profitable mix of products.

IN BUSINESS

For companies such as BlackBerry, managing profits in an extremely competitive operating environment is a constant challenge. With several different smartphone models available, BlackBerry managers need a detailed understanding of how introducing a new model will impact profits. For example, when a new model such as the BlackBerry Q10 is introduced, determining the net effect on total CM is not simply a matter of estimating the demand for the new product and the per unit CM. Companies that offer multiple product choices for consumers must also estimate the extent to which sales of a new model will affect sales of existing models. So, as sales increase for a new model, declines are to be expected for older models, which must be taken into account when evaluating the incremental effects on profit from new product introductions. This is especially true for manufacturers of high-tech products, since consumers almost always want the newest models.

Moreover, in light of increasing competition for products such as smartphones and tablets, BlackBerry, Samsung, Apple Inc., and other manufacturers have responded by offering new models with lower selling prices and lower CMs. This ever-evolving product mix must be monitored continuously to ensure that the company generates a return on investment that is acceptable to its shareholders. Adding to this complexity are the different market segments and geographic regions served by companies such as BlackBerry. For example, the functionality demanded by business users of their smartphones can differ from that of personal users, as can their willingness and ability to pay for those features. Understanding the fundamentals of CVP relationships is essential in such a dynamic multi-product environment.

Sources: Bloomberg News, "No Easy Fix for Apple's Squeezed Profit Margins," http://business. financialpost.com/2013/02/11/no-easy-fix-for-apples-squeezed-profit-margins/?_lsa=6003-a9c5, February 11, 2013; David Friend, Canadian Press, "Clash of the Smartphones? How Samsung's latest Galaxy Handset Could Throw a Wrench Into BlackBerry's U.S. Z10 Launch," http:// business.financialpost.com/2013/03/12/samsung-galaxy-s4-blackberry-z10/?_lsa=6003-a9c5, March 12, 2013; http://ca.blackberry.com/smartphones.html#.

Sales Mix and Break-Even Analysis

If a company sells more than one product, break-even analysis is somewhat more complex than has been discussed to this point. This is because different products have different selling prices, different costs, and different CMs. Consequently, the break-even point depends on the mix in which the various products are sold. To illustrate, consider Sound Unlimited, a small company that imports DVDs from France. At present, the company distributes the following to retailers: the Le Louvre DVD, a multimedia free-form tour of the famous art museum in Paris, and the Le Vin DVD, which features the wines and wine-growing regions of France. Both multimedia products have audio, photos, video clips, and sophisticated software. The company's September sales, expenses, and break-even point in total sales dollars are shown in Exhibit 4–4. As shown in the exhibit, the break-even point is $60,000 in sales, which was computed by dividing the fixed costs by the company's *overall* CM ratio of 45%.

Exhibit 4–5 shows an approach to calculating the break-even point in units when a company sells more than one product. The approach is based on calculating a weighted-average CM per unit for the multiple products based on the existing unit sales mix and the individual CM per unit for each product. For Sound Unlimited, the weighted-average CM of $11.25 per unit is based on the existing sales mix of 20% Le Louvre DVDs (800 units) and 80% Le Vin DVDs (3,200 units), and the individual CM per unit of the two products respectively of $6.25 and $12.50, as shown in Exhibit 4–5. Note that the sales mix percentages are based on the unit sales of each product as a percentage of total sales. For example, the sales mix percentage for Le Louvre DVDs of 20% is calculated as 800 ÷ 4,000. To determine the total number of DVDs that must be sold at the current sales mix, the final step is to divide total fixed costs by the weighted-average CM per unit. As shown in Exhibit 4–5, for Sound Unlimited the total number of units that must be sold to break even for both products is 2,400 ($27,000 ÷ $11.25). The number of units of each product that must be sold to break even at the current sales mix can then be calculated as follows:

Le Louvre:	2,400 × 20% = 480 units
Le Vin:	2,400 × 80% = 1,920 units

Also, the sales in dollars of each product that must be sold to break even at the current sales mix can be calculated as follows:

Le Louvre:	480 × $25 per unit = $12,000
Le Vin:	1,920 × $25 per unit = $48,000

EXHIBIT 4-4 Multi-Product Break-Even Analysis in Sales Dollars

SOUND UNLIMITED
Contribution Income Statement
For the Month of September

	Le Louvre DVD		Le Vin DVD		Total	
	Amount	Percentage	Amount	Percentage	Amount	Percentage
Sales...........................	$20,000	100%	$80,000	100%	$100,000	100%
Variable expenses..................	15,000	75%	40,000	50%	55,000	55%
Contribution margin..................	$ 5,000	25%	$40,000	50%	45,000	45%
Fixed expenses........................					27,000	
Operating income					$ 18,000	

Computation of the break-even point:

$$\frac{\text{Fixed expenses}}{\text{Overall CM ratio}} = \frac{\$27,000}{0.45} = \$60,000$$

Verification of the break-even point:

	Le Louvre DVD	Le Vin DVD	Total
Current dollar sales......................	$20,000	$80,000	$100,000
Percentage of total dollar sales..........	20%	80%	100%
Sales at the break-even point	$12,000	$48,000	$60,000

	Le Louvre DVD		Le Vin DVD		Total	
	Amount	Percentage	Amount	Percentage	Amount	Percentage
Sales.................................	$12,000	100%	$48,000	100%	$60,000	100%
Variable expenses....................	9,000	75%	24,000	50%	33,000	55%
Contribution margin..................	$ 3,000	25%	$24,000	50%	$ 27,000	45%
Fixed expenses........................					27,000	
Operating income					$ 0	

EXHIBIT 4-5 Multi-Product Break-Even Analysis in Units

	Le Louvre DVD		Le Vin DVD		
	Total (800 units)	Per Unit	Total (3,200 units)	Per Unit	Total (4,000 units)
Sales.........................	$20,000	$25.00	$80,000	$25.00	$100,000
Less variable expenses.........	15,000	18.75	40,000	12.50	55,000
Contribution margin	$ 5,000	$ 6.25	$40,000	$ 12.50	45,000
Less fixed expenses............					27,000
Operating income					$ 18,000

	(1)	(2)	(3) (1) × (2)	(4)	(4) ÷ (3)
	CM Per Unit	Sales Mix %*	Weighted CM Per Unit	Total Fixed Expenses	Break-Even Units
Le Louvre DVD	$ 6.25	20%	$ 1.25		
Le Vin DVD	$12.50	80%	$10.00		
Total...........................			$ 11.25	$27,000	2,400

*Le Louvre: 800 units ÷ 4,000 units; Le Vin: 3,200 units ÷ 4,000.

Note that these sales dollars amounts are the same as shown in Exhibit 4–4, which uses the formula approach to calculate break-even sales dollars in total and then determines sales amounts for each product. The two methods of calculating break-even values in a multi-product company shown in Exhibits 4–4 and 4–5 are both valid approaches. The method that managers adopt will likely be a function of whether they prefer to think about break-even amounts in units or in dollars.

The $60,000 in sales dollars, or 2,400 units, represents the break-even point for Sound Unlimited as long as the sales mix does not change. *If the sales mix changes, then the break-even point (dollars or units) will also change.* This is illustrated by the results for October, in which the sales mix shifted away from the more profitable Le Vin DVD (which has a 50% CM ratio) toward the less profitable Le Louvre DVD (which has only a 25% CM ratio). These results appear in Exhibit 4–6.

In Exhibit 4–6, although total sales have remained unchanged at $100,000, the sales mix is exactly the reverse of what it was in Exhibits 4–4 and 4–5, with most of the sales now coming from the less profitable Le Louvre DVD. Notice that this shift in the sales mix has caused both the overall CM ratio and total profits to drop sharply from the prior month—the overall CM ratio has dropped from 45% in September to only 30% in October, and operating income has dropped from $18,000 to only $3,000. In addition, with the drop in the overall CM ratio, the company's break-even point is no longer $60,000 in sales. Since the company is now realizing a lower average CM per dollar of sales, it takes more sales to cover the same amount of fixed costs. Thus, the break-even point has increased from $60,000 to $90,000 in sales per year, or from 2,400 total units to 3,600 total units.

In preparing a break-even analysis, some assumptions must be made concerning the sales mix. Usually the assumption is that it will not change. However, if the manager knows that changes in the operating environment (consumer tastes, market share, competitors' actions, etc.) are likely to cause changes in the sales mix, then these factors must be explicitly considered in any CVP computations. Otherwise, the manager may make decisions on the basis of outdated data.

> **Instant Quiz 4–9**
> Assume that the sales mix for Sound Unlimited changes such that unit sales are 40% from Le Louvre and 60% from Le Vin. Fixed costs are the same at $27,000 and the CM per unit for each product is the same as per Exhibit 4–5. Calculate the new weighted-average CM per unit and the total number of units that need to be sold to break even.

EXHIBIT 4-6   Multi-Product Break-Even Analysis: A Shift in Sales Mix (see Exhibits 4–4 and 4–5)

SOUND UNLIMITED
Contribution Income Statement
For the Month of October

	Le Louvre DVD		Le Vin DVD		Total	
Units	3,200		800		4,000	
	Amount	**Percentage**	**Amount**	**Percentage**	**Amount**	**Percentage**
Sales	$80,000	100%	$20,000	100%	$100,000	100%
Less variable expenses	60,000	75%	10,000	50%	70,000	70%
Contribution margin	$20,000	25%	$10,000	50%	30,000	30%
Less fixed expenses					27,000	
Operating income					$ 3,000	

Computation of the break-even point in total sales dollars:

$$\frac{\text{Fixed expenses}}{\text{Overall CM ratio}} = \frac{\$27,000}{0.30} = \$90,000$$

Computation of the break-even point in total unit sales:*

$$\frac{\text{Fixed expenses}}{\text{Weighted-average CM per unit}} = \frac{\$27,000}{(0.8 \times \$6.25) + (0.2 \times \$12.50)} = 3,600 \text{ units}$$

*The only difference from Exhibit 4–5 is the change in sales mix to reflect 80% for Le Louvre and 20% for Le Vin.

LEARNING AID

MULTI-PRODUCT CVP ANALYSIS
Overall Contribution Margin Ratio

$$\text{Overall CM ratio} = \frac{\text{Total CM, all products}}{\text{Total sales, all products}}$$

Weighted-Average Contribution Margin per Unit

$$(\text{Product 1: CM per unit} \times \text{Sales mix \%}) + (\text{Product 2: CM per unit} \times \text{Sales mix \%}) + \cdots \text{ for each product}$$

Break-Even (Formula Method)
Sales Dollars

$$\text{Total sales dollars to break even} = \frac{\text{Fixed expenses}}{\text{Overall CM ratio}}$$

Sales Units

$$\text{Total sales units to break even} = \frac{\text{Fixed expenses}}{\text{Weighted-average CM per unit}}$$

Target Operating Profit (Formula Method)
Sales Dollars

$$\text{Dollar sales to attain target profit} = \frac{\text{Fixed expenses} + \left[\dfrac{\text{Target after-tax profit}}{1 - \text{Tax rate}} \right]}{\text{Overall CM ratio}}$$

ASSUMPTIONS OF CVP ANALYSIS

A number of assumptions typically underlie CVP analysis:

1. Selling price is constant throughout the entire relevant range. The price of a product or service does not change as volume changes.
2. Costs are linear throughout the entire relevant range, and they can accurately be divided into variable and fixed elements. The variable element is constant per unit, and the fixed element is constant in total over the entire relevant range.
3. In multi-product companies, the sales mix is constant.
4. In manufacturing companies, inventories do not change. The number of units produced equals the number of units sold (this assumption is considered further in Chapter 8).

While some of these assumptions may be violated in practice, the results of CVP analysis are often "good enough" to be quite useful. For example, in most multi-product companies, the sales mix is constant enough that the results of CVP analysis are reasonably accurate. Perhaps the greatest danger lies in relying on simple CVP analysis when a manager is contemplating a large change in volume that lies outside the relevant range. For example, a manager might consider increasing the level of sales far beyond what the company has previously experienced. However, even in these situations, a manager can adjust the model as we have done in this chapter to take into account anticipated changes in selling prices, fixed costs, and the sales mix that would otherwise violate the assumptions. For example, in a decision that would affect fixed costs, the change in fixed costs can explicitly be taken into account, as illustrated earlier in this chapter in the Acoustic Concepts example.

KNOWLEDGE IN ACTION

Managers can apply CVP techniques when
- Considering the impact of changes to selling prices, variable costs, or fixed costs on profits
- Identifying how cost structure affects the relation between changes in sales and changes in profit
- Calculating sales levels required to break even or achieve target profits in single- or multi-product settings
- Considering changes to the sales mix in a multi-product setting
- Considering the profit impact of adding new products or discontinuing existing products
- Preparing budgets

SUMMARY

- Cost–volume–profit (CVP) analysis is based on a simple model of how contribution margin (CM) and operating income respond to changes in selling prices, costs, and volume. The analysis is based on the contribution income statement approach and requires a detailed understanding of cost behaviour. [LO1]
- A CVP graph depicts the relationships between sales volume in units and fixed expenses, variable expenses, total expenses, total sales, and profits. The CVP graph is useful for developing intuition about how costs and profits respond to changes in sales volume. [LO2]
- The CM ratio is the ratio of the total CM to total sales. This ratio can be used to estimate the effect of a change in total sales on operating income. [LO3]
- The techniques of CVP analysis can be used to estimate the effects on CM and operating profit of changes to sales volume, fixed costs, variable costs per unit, and selling prices. A useful aspect of the analysis is that managers can evaluate the profit impact of the trade-offs inherent to many operating decisions, such as increasing advertising costs to boost sales volumes. [LO4]
- The break-even point is the level of sales (in units or in dollars) at which the company generates zero profits. The break-even point can be computed using several different techniques that are all based on the simple profit equation. [LO5]
- The profit equation can also be used to compute the level of sales required to attain a target profit. [LO6]
- The margin of safety is the amount by which the company's current sales exceed break-even sales. [LO7]
- The degree of operating leverage measures the effect of a percentage change in sales on the company's operating income. The higher the degree of operating leverage, the more sensitive operating income will be to a change in sales. The degree of operating leverage is not constant—it depends on the company's current level of sales. [LO8]
- The profits of a multi-product company are affected by its sales mix. Changes in the sales mix can affect the break-even point, margin of safety, and other critical measures. [LO9]

REVIEW PROBLEM: COST–VOLUME–PROFIT RELATIONSHIPS

Networks Company manufactures wireless routers. The company's contribution format income statement for the most recent year is given below:

	Total	Per Unit	Percentage of Sales
Sales (25,000 units)...............	$2,500,000	$100	100%
Less variable expenses.............	1,500,000	60	?%
Contribution margin................	1,000,000	$ 40	?%
Less fixed expenses................	800,000		
Operating income..................	$ 200,000		

Management believes operating income can be further improved and would like you to prepare the following analysis.

Required:

1. Compute the company's CM ratio and variable expense ratio.
2. Compute the company's break-even point in both units and sales dollars. Use the equation method.
3. Assume that sales increase by $600,000 next year. If cost behaviour patterns remain unchanged, by how much will the company's operating income increase? Use the CM ratio to determine your answer.
4. Refer to the original data. Assume that next year, management wants the company to earn a minimum profit of $500,000. How many units will have to be sold to meet this target profit figure?
5. Refer to the original data. Compute the company's margin of safety in both dollar and percentage form.
6. *a.* Compute the company's degree of operating leverage at the current level of sales.
    b. Assume that, through a more intense effort by the sales staff, the company's sales increase by 12% next year. By what percentage would you expect operating income to increase? Use the operating leverage concept to obtain your answer.
    c. Verify your answer to (*b*) by preparing a new income statement showing a 12% increase in sales.
7. In an effort to increase sales and profits, management is considering using a higher-quality microprocessor in the router. The higher-quality microprocessor would increase variable costs by $8 per unit, but management could eliminate one quality inspector, who is paid a salary of $40,000 per year. The sales manager estimates that the higher-quality microprocessor would increase annual sales by at least 10%.
    a. Assuming that changes are made as described above, prepare a projected income statement for next year. Show data on a total, per unit, and percentage basis.
    b. Compute the company's new break-even point in both units and dollars of sales. Use the formula method.
    c. Would you recommend that the changes be made? Why or why not?

Solution to Review Problem

1. CM ratio: Variable expense ratio:

$$\frac{\text{CM}}{\text{Selling price}} = \frac{\$40}{\$100} = 40\% \qquad \frac{\text{Variable expenses}}{\text{Selling price}} = \frac{\$60}{\$100} = 60\%$$

2.   Sales = Variable expenses + Fixed expenses + Profits
    $$\$100Q = \$60Q + \$800,000 + \$0$$
    $$\$40Q = \$800,000$$
    $$Q = 20,000 \text{ units, or, at } \$100 \text{ per unit, } \$2,000,000$$

    Alternative solution where *X* equals the break-even level of sales in dollars:

    $$X = 0.60X + \$800,000$$
    $$0.40X = \$800,000$$
    $$X = \$2,000,000, \text{ or, at } \$100 \text{ per unit, } 20,000 \text{ units}$$

3. | | |
    |---|---:|
    | Increase in sales .... | $600,000 |
    | Multiply by the contribution margin ratio .... | × 40% |
    | Expected increase in contribution margin.............. | $240,000 |

    Since the fixed expenses are not expected to change, operating income will increase by the entire $240,000 increase in CM computed above.

4. Equation method:
    $$\text{Sales} = \text{Variable expenses} + \text{Fixed expenses} + \text{Profits}$$
    $$\$100Q = \$60Q + \$800,000 + \$500,000$$
    $$\$40Q = \$1,300,000$$
    $$Q = 32,500 \text{ units}$$

    Formula method:

    $$\frac{\text{Fixed expenses} + \text{Target profit}}{\text{CM per unit}} = \frac{\$800,000 + \$500,000}{\$40} = 32,500 \text{ units}$$

5.

$$\text{Total sales} - \text{Break-even sales} = \text{Margin of safety in dollars}$$

$$\$2,500,000 - \$2,000,000 = \$500,000$$

$$\frac{\text{Margin of safety in dollars}}{\text{Total sales}} = \frac{\$500,000}{\$2,500,000} = 20\%$$

6. *a.*

$$\frac{\text{CM}}{\text{Operating income}} = \frac{\$1,000,000}{\$200,000} = 5 \text{ times}$$

b.

Expected increase in sales......................	12%
Degree of operating leverage	×5
Expected increase in operating income.............	60%

c. If sales increase by 12%, then 28,000 units (25,000 × 1.12) will be sold next year. The new income statement will be as follows:

	Total	Per Unit	Percentage of Sales
Sales (28,000 units)...........................	$2,800,000	$100	100%
Less variable expenses.........................	1,680,000	60	60%
Contribution margin...........................	1,120,000	$ 40	40%
Less fixed expenses...........................	800,000		
Operating income.............................	$ 320,000		

The $320,000 expected operating income for next year represents a 60% increase over the $200,000 operating income earned during the current year:

$$\frac{\$320,000 - \$200,000}{\$200,000} = 60\%$$

Note from the income statement above that the increase in sales from 25,000 to 28,000 units has resulted in increases in *both* total sales and total variable expenses. It is a common error to overlook the increase in variable expenses when preparing a projected income statement.

7. *a.* A 10% increase in sales would result in 27,500 units being sold next year: 25,000 units × 1.10 = 27,500 units.

	Total	Per Unit	Percentage of Sales
Sales (27,500 units)...........................	$2,750,000	$100	100%
Less variable expenses.........................	1,870,000	68*	68%*
Contribution margin...........................	880,000	$32	32%
Less fixed expenses...........................	760,000†		
Operating income.............................	$ 120,000		

*$60 + $8 = $68; $68 ÷ $100 = 68%.
†$800,000 − $40,000 = $760,000.

Note that the change in per unit variable expenses results in a change in both the per unit CM and the CM ratio.

b. Break-even point in units:

$$\frac{\text{Fixed expenses}}{\text{CM per unit}} = \frac{\$760,000}{\$32} = 23,750 \text{ units}$$

Break-even point in sales dollars:

$$\frac{\text{Fixed expenses}}{\text{CM ratio}} = \frac{\$760,000}{0.32} = \$2,375,000$$

    c.   No. Based on these data, the changes should not be made. The company's operating income will decrease from the current $200,000 to $120,000 per year. Also, the changes will result in a higher break-even point (23,750 units compared to the current 20,000 units). Finally, the margin of safety will be reduced from $500,000 as calculated in (5) above to

$$\text{Margin of safety in dollars} = \text{Total sales} - \text{Break-even sales}$$
$$\$2,750,000 - \$2,375,000 = \$375,000$$

Overall, this change would not be good for the company.

GLOSSARY

 Review key terms and definitions on Connect.

DISCUSSION CASE

DISCUSSION CASE 4–1

Critics of CVP analysis claim that the assumptions underlying the analysis are almost certain to be violated in practice, thus severely limiting the practical value of the various techniques covered in this chapter. Moreover, say the critics, in the highly competitive environment in which many companies operate, the assumptions necessary for CVP analysis are even more likely to be violated. Arguably, companies that face stiff competition and thus could benefit most from CVP analysis may be the least likely to be able to use the techniques because of the restrictive assumptions.

Required:
Do you agree with the claims made by the critics of CVP analysis regarding its limited value in practice? Why or why not?

QUESTIONS

4-1   How is the CM per unit calculated? How is this value useful in planning business operations?

4-2   Where is the break-even point on a CVP graph?

4-3   Often the most direct route to a business decision is to perform an incremental analysis. What is meant by an incremental analysis?

4-4   What is meant by the term *operating leverage*?

4-5   What is meant by the term *margin of safety*?

4-6   If a company experiences a decrease in its CM ratio, what will be the impact on its break-even level of sales?

4-7   Name three approaches to break-even analysis. Briefly explain how each approach works.

4-8   In a CVP graph, what is the impact on the break-even level of sales if the slope of the total revenue line gets steeper, assuming no change to the total expense line? What is the impact on the break-even level of sales if the slope of the total expenses line gets steeper, assuming no change to fixed expenses or to the slope of the total revenue line?

4-9   What effect would a 30% income tax rate have on the CVP formula?

4-10   What is meant by the term *cost structure*?

4-11   Companies X and Y are in the same industry. Company X is highly automated, whereas Company Y relies primarily on labour to make its products. If sales and total expenses in the two companies are about the same, which company would you expect to have the lower margin of safety? Why?

4-12   What is meant by the term *sales mix*? What assumption is usually made concerning sales mix in CVP analysis?

4-13   Assume that Company Z, which sells two products, has changed its sales mix so that it sells a higher proportion of the product with the higher CM. What will be the impact on the break-even level of sales? Explain your answer.

EXERCISES

EXERCISE 4–1 Preparing a Contribution Format Income Statement [LO1]

White Limited's most recent income statement is shown below:

	Total	Per Unit
Sales (6,000 units).....................	$312,000	$52.00
Variable expenses.....................	216,000	36.00
Contribution margin...................	96,000	$16.00
Fixed expenses.......................	84,000	
Operating income....................	$ 12,000	

Required:

Prepare a new contribution format income statement under each of the following conditions (consider each case independently):

1. The sales volume increases by 200 units.
2. The sales volume declines by 200 units.
3. The sales volume is 5,250 units.

EXERCISE 4–2 Prepare a Profit Graph [LO2]

Capricio Enterprises distributes a single product whose selling price is $19 and whose variable expense is $15 per unit. The company's fixed expense is $12,000 per month.

Required:

1. Prepare a profit graph for the company up to a sales level of 4,000 units.
2. Estimate the company's break-even point in unit sales using your profit graph.

EXERCISE 4–3 Computing and Using the Contribution Margin Ratio; Computing the Break-Even Point [LO3, LO5]

In March, Mitchell Limited had sales of $250,000 (50,000 units), total variable expenses of $190,000, and total fixed expenses of $36,000.

Required:

1. What is the company's CM ratio?
2. Using the CM ratio, calculate the break-even level of sales in dollars.
3. Estimate the change in the company's operating income if it increased its total sales by $20,000.

EXERCISE 4–4 Changes in Variable Costs, Fixed Costs, Selling Price, and Volume [LO4]

Data for Moorefield Corporation are shown below:

	Per Unit	Percentage of Sales
Selling price............................	$90	100%
Variable expenses.....................	63	70%
Contribution margin...................	$27	30%

Fixed expenses are $65,000 per month, and the company is selling 2,750 units per month.

Required:

1. The marketing manager argues that a $5,000 increase in the monthly advertising budget would increase monthly sales by $12,000. Should the advertising budget be increased?
2. Refer to the original data. Management is considering using higher-quality components that would increase the variable cost by $4 per unit. The marketing manager believes the higher-quality product would increase sales by 20% per month. Should the higher-quality components be used?

EXERCISE 4–5 Compute the Break-Even Point [LO5]
Mackson Products distributes a single product, a woven basket; its selling price is $8 and its variable cost is $6 per unit. The company's monthly fixed expense is $5,500.

Required:
1. Solve for the company's break-even point in unit sales using the equation method.
2. Solve for the company's break-even point in sales dollars using the equation method and the CM ratio.
3. Solve for the company's break-even point in unit sales using the formula method.
4. Solve for the company's break-even point in sales dollars using the formula method and the CM ratio.

EXERCISE 4–6 Compute the Level of Sales Required to Attain a Target Profit [LO6]
Ng Corporation produces and sells only one product; its selling price is $100 and its variable cost is $80 per unit. The company's monthly fixed expense is $20,000.

Required:
1. Using the equation method, solve for the unit sales that are required to earn a target profit before taxes of $3,000.
2. Using the formula method, solve for the dollar sales that are required to earn a target profit before taxes of $4,000.
3. Using the formula method, calculate the number of units that need to be sold to earn an after-tax income of $6,000, assuming a tax rate of 25%.

EXERCISE 4–7 Compute the Margin of Safety [LO7]
Mohan Corporation is a distributor of a sun umbrella used at resort hotels. Data concerning the next month's budget appear below:

Selling price.....................................	$25 per unit
Variable expense................................	$15 per unit
Fixed expense	$8,500 per month
Unit sales...	1,000 units per month

Required:
1. Compute the company's margin of safety.
2. Compute the company's margin of safety as a percentage of its sales.

EXERCISE 4–8 Compute and Use the Degree of Operating Leverage [LO8]
Entergo Company installs home theatre systems. The company's most recent monthly contribution format income statement appears below:

	Amount	Percentage of Sales
Sales....................................	$120,000	100%
Variable expenses......................	84,000	70%
Contribution margin....................	36,000	30%
Fixed expenses	24,000	
Operating income......................	$ 12,000	

Required:
1. Compute the company's degree of operating leverage.
2. Using the degree of operating leverage, estimate the impact on operating income of a 10% increase in sales.
3. Verify your estimate from (2) above by constructing a new contribution format income statement for the company, assuming a 10% increase in sales.

EXERCISE 4–9 Compute the Break-Even Point for a Multi-Service Company; Compute Sales for a Target Profit [LO6, LO9]
Gulf Shore Lawn and Garden Maintenance provides two general outdoor services: lawn maintenance and garden maintenance. The company charges customers $15 per hour for each type of service, but lawn maintenance has higher variable costs ($7 per hour) than garden maintenance

($3 per hour) because of fuel expenses incurred to operate lawn-mowing equipment. All employees are paid a fixed monthly salary. A contribution format income statement for a recent month for the two services appears below. During the month, 6,000 hours of lawn maintenance services and 2,000 hours of garden maintenance were provided:

	Lawn Maintenance	Per Hour	Garden Maintenance	Per Hour	Total
Sales..................	$90,000	$15	$30,000	$15	$120,000
Variable expenses.......	42,000	7	6,000	3	48,000
Contribution margin.....	$48,000	$ 8	$24,000	$12	72,000
Fixed expenses					54,000
Operating income.......					$ 18,000

Required:
1. Compute the overall CM ratio for the company.
2. Compute the overall break-even point for the company in sales dollars.
3. Compute the weighted-average CM per hour for the company.
4. Calculate the overall break-even point for the company in hours.
5. At the overall break-even point in total hours, how many hours of each service must be provided for the company to break even?
6. Calculate the overall sales in dollars required to earn an after-tax profit of $42,000 if the tax rate is 30%.

EXERCISE 4–10 Break-Even and Target Profit Analysis [LO3, LO4, LO5, LO6]
Super Sales Company is the exclusive distributor for a high-quality knapsack. The product sells for $60 per unit and has a CM ratio of 40%. The company's fixed expenses are $360,000 per year. The company plans to sell 17,000 knapsacks this year.

Required:
1. What are the variable expenses per unit?
2. Use the equation method.
   a. What is the break-even point in units and in sales dollars?
   b. What sales level in units and in sales dollars is required to earn an annual profit of $90,000?
   c. What sales level in units is required to earn an annual after-tax profit of $90,000 if the tax rate is 25%?
   d. Assume that through negotiation with the manufacturer, Super Sales Company is able to reduce its variable expenses by $3 per unit. What is the company's new break-even point in units and in sales dollars?
3. Repeat (2) above using the formula method.

EXERCISE 4–11 Break-Even Analysis; Cost–Volume–Profit Graphing [LO2, LO4, LO5]
Horace Society is planning its annual Western Fair Raceway Gala. The Gala committee has assembled the following expected costs for the event:

Dinner (per person)	$10
Gaming tokens and program (per person)..............	$2
Prize payouts	$4,300
Tickets and advertising..............................	$800
Private box suite rental..............................	$1,700
Lottery licences.....................................	$200

The committee members would like to charge $40 per person for the evening's activities.

Required:
1. Compute the break-even point for the Gala (in terms of the number of people that must attend).
2. Assume only 200 people attended the Gala last year. If the same number attend this year, what price per ticket must be charged to break even?
3. Using the $40 ticket price per person amount, prepare a CVP graph for the Gala from 0 tickets up to 600 tickets sold.

EXERCISE 4–12 Using a Contribution Format Income Statement [LO1, LO4]
Kelly Company's most recent contribution format income statement is shown below:

	Total	Per Unit
Sales (60,000 units)	$600,000	$10
Variable expenses..................	360,000	6
Contribution margin................	240,000	$4
Fixed expenses	100,000	
Operating income..................	$ 140,000	

Required:
Prepare a new contribution format income statement under each of the following conditions (consider each case independently):
1. The number of units sold increases by 30%.
2. The selling price decreases by $1 per unit, and the number of units sold increases by 20%.
3. The selling price increases by $1 per unit, fixed expenses increase by $20,000, and the number of units sold decreases by 10%.
4. Variable expenses increase by 60 cents per unit, the selling price increases by 15%, and the number of units sold decreases by 15%.

EXERCISE 4–13 Missing Data; Basic Cost–Volume–Profit Concepts [LO1, LO2]
Fill in the missing amounts in each of the eight case situations below. Each case is independent of the others. (*Hint:* One way to find the missing amounts is to prepare a contribution format income statement for each case, enter the known data, and then compute the missing items.)
a. Assume that only one product is being sold in each of the following four case situations:

Case	Units Sold	Sales	Variable Expenses	Contribution Margin per Unit	Fixed Expenses	Operating Income (Loss)
1	9,000	$270,000	$162,000	$?	$90,000	$?
2	?	$350,000	?	$15	$170,000	$40,000
3	20,000	?	$280,000	$ 6	?	$35,000
4	5,000	$160,000	?	?	$82,000	$(12,000)

b. Assume that more than one product is being sold in each of the following four case situations:

Case	Sales	Variable Expenses	Average Contribution Margin (percentage)	Fixed Expenses	Operating Income (Loss)
1	$450,000	$?	40%	$?	$ 65,000
2	$200,000	$130,000	?	$ 60,000	?
3	?	?	80%	$470,000	$ 90,000
4	$300,000	$ 90,000	?	?	$ (15,000)

EXERCISE 4–14 Break-Even and Target Profit Analysis [LO3, LO4, LO5, LO6]
Memtech Company is the exclusive distributor of a high-speed computer memory chip. The product sells for $50 per unit and has a CM ratio of 30%. The company's fixed expenses are $240,000 per year.

Required:
1. What are the variable expenses per unit?
2. Using the equation method:

a. What is the break-even point in units and in sales dollars?
b. What sales level in units and in sales dollars is required to earn an operating income of $75,000?
c. Assume that through negotiation with the manufacturer, Memtech Company is able to reduce its variable expenses by $5 per unit. What is the company's new break-even point in units and in sales dollars?
3. Repeat (2) above using the formula method.
4. Referring to the original data, what sales level in dollars is required to earn an annual profit of $75,000 after taxes if the company's tax rate is 20%?

EXERCISE 4–15 Operating Leverage [LO4, LO8]

Supreme Door Company sells pre-hung doors to home builders. The doors are sold for $60 each. Variable costs are $42 per door, and fixed costs total $450,000 per year. The company is currently selling 30,000 doors per year.

Required:
1. Prepare a contribution format income statement for the company at the current level of sales, and compute the degree of operating leverage.
2. Management is confident that the company can sell 37,500 doors next year (an increase of 7,500 doors, or 25%, over current sales). Compute the following:
    a. The expected percentage increase in operating income for next year.
    b. The expected operating income for next year. (Do not prepare an income statement; use the degree of operating leverage to compute your answer.)

EXERCISE 4–16 Break-Even and Target Profit Analysis [LO4, LO5, LO6]

Bait-N-Tackle sells fishing equipment. One of the company's products, a basic tackle box, sells for $48 per unit. Variable expenses are $36 per tackle box, and fixed expenses associated with the tackle box total $18,000 per month.

Required:
1. Compute the company's break-even point in number of tackle boxes and in total sales dollars.
2. If the variable expenses per tackle box increase as a percentage of the selling price, will it result in a higher or a lower break-even point? Why? (Assume that the fixed expenses remain unchanged.)
3. At present, the company is selling 2,600 tackle boxes per month. The sales manager is convinced that a 12.5% reduction in the selling price will result in a 20% increase in the number of tackle boxes sold each month. Prepare two contribution income statements, one under current operating conditions, and one as operations would appear after the proposed changes. Show both total and per unit data on your statements.
4. Refer to the data in (3) above. How many tackle boxes would have to be sold at the new selling price to yield a minimum operating income of $14,400 per month?
5. Refer to the data in (3) above. How many tackle boxes would have to be sold at the new selling price to generate after-tax operating income of $16,800 if the tax rate is 30%?

EXERCISE 4–17 Multi-Product Break-Even Analysis [LO9]

Gogan Company manufactures and sells two products: Basic and Deluxe. Monthly sales, CM ratios, and the CM per unit for the two products are shown below:

	Product		
	Basic	Deluxe	Total
Sales..................................	$600,000	$400,000	$1,000,000
Contribution margin ratio	60%	35%	?
Contribution margin per unit	$9.00	$11.50	?

The company's fixed expenses total $400,000 per month.

Required:
1. Prepare a contribution format income statement for the company as a whole.
2. Compute the overall break-even point in dollars for the company based on the current sales mix.

3. Compute the overall break-even point in units for the company based on the current sales mix.
4. If sales increase by $50,000 per month, by how much would you expect operating income to increase? What are your assumptions?
5. If sales increase by 5,000 units per month, by how much would you expect operating income to increase? What are your assumptions?

PROBLEMS

PROBLEM 4–18 Basic Cost-Volume-Profit Analysis [LO1, LO3, LO4, LO5, LO8]
Klein Company distributes a high-quality bird feeder that sells for $30 per unit. Variable costs are $12 per unit, and fixed costs total $270,000 annually.

Required:
Answer the following independent questions:
1. What is the product's CM ratio?
2. Use the CM ratio to determine the break-even point in sales dollars.
3. The company estimates that sales will increase by $60,000 during the coming year due to increased demand. By how much should operating income increase?
4. Assume that the operating results for last year were as follows:

Sales	$600,000
Variable expenses	240,000
Contribution margin	360,000
Fixed expenses	270,000
Operating income	$ 90,000

   a. Compute the degree of operating leverage at the current level of sales.
   b. The president expects sales to increase by 16% next year. By how much should operating income increase?
5. Refer to the original data. Assume that the company sold 23,000 units last year. The sales manager is convinced that a 12% reduction in the selling price, combined with a $40,000 increase in advertising expenditures, would cause annual sales in units to increase by 30%. Prepare two contribution format income statements, one showing the results of last year's operations and one showing what the results of operations would be if these changes were made. Would you recommend that the company do as the sales manager suggests?
6. Refer to the original data. Assume again that the company sold 23,000 units last year. The president feels that it would be unwise to change the selling price. Instead, he wants to increase the sales commission by $4 per unit. He thinks that this move, combined with some increase in advertising, would increase annual unit sales by 50%. By how much could advertising be increased with profits remaining unchanged? Do not prepare an income statement; use the incremental analysis approach.

PROBLEM 4–19 Basic Cost-Volume-Profit Analysis [LO1, LO3, LO4, LO5, LO6]
Stratford Company distributes a lightweight lawn chair that sells for $15 per unit. Variable expenses are $6 per unit, and fixed expenses total $180,000 annually. Results for last year are as follows:

Sales (24,000 units)	$360,000
Variable expenses	144,000
Contribution margin	216,000
Fixed expenses	180,000
Operating income	$ 36,000

Required:
Answer the following independent questions:
1. Calculate the company's CM ratio and its break-even point in sales dollars and in units.
2. If sales increase by $45,000 during the coming year due to increased demand, by how much should operating income increase? Use the incremental approach in preparing your answer.

3. Refer to the original data. The sales vice-president is convinced that a 10% decrease in the selling price, combined with a $100,000 increase in marketing expenditures, would increase annual unit sales by 75%. Prepare a new contribution format income statement assuming these changes occur. Should the company proceed with the changes?

4. Refer to the original data. The president feels that it would be unwise to change the selling price. Instead, she wants to increase the sales commission by $2 per unit. She thinks that this move, combined with some increase in advertising, would increase sales to 48,000 units compared to 24,000 last year. By how much could advertising be increased with profits remaining unchanged? Do not prepare an income statement; use the incremental analysis approach.

PROBLEM 4–20 Sales Mix; Multi-Product Break-Even Analysis [LO9]
Smithen Company, a wholesale distributor, has been operating for only a few months. The company sells three products—sinks, mirrors, and vanities. Budgeted sales by product and in total for the coming month are shown below based on planned unit sales as follows:

	Units	Percentage
Sinks	1,000	50%
Mirrors	500	25%
Vanities	500	25%
Total	2,000	100%

	Sinks		Mirrors		Vanities		Total	
Percentage of total sales.	48%		20%		32%		100%	
Sales	$240,000	100%	$100,000	100%	$160,000	100%	$500,000	100%
Variable expenses	72,000	30%	80,000	80%	88,000	55%	240,000	48%
Contribution margin	$168,000	70%	$ 20,000	20%	$ 72,000	45%	260,000	52%
Contribution margin per unit	$ 168		$ 40		$ 144			
Fixed expenses							223,600	
Operating income							$ 36,400	

$$\text{Break-even point in sales dollars} = \frac{\text{Fixed expenses}}{\text{Overall CM ratio}} = \frac{\$223,600}{0.52} = \$430,000$$

Break-even point in unit sales:

$$\frac{\text{Total Fixed expenses}}{\text{Weighted-average CM per unit}} = \frac{\$223,600}{\$130^*} = 1,720 \text{ units}$$

$$*(\$168 \times 0.50) + (\$40 \times 0.25) + (\$144 \times 0.25)$$

As shown by these data, operating income is budgeted at $36,400 for the month, break-even sales dollars at $430,000, and break-even unit sales at 1,720.

Assume that actual sales for the month total $504,000 (2,100 units), with the CM ratio and per unit amounts the same as budgeted. Actual fixed expenses are the same as budgeted, $223,600. Actual sales by product are as follows: sinks, $126,000 (525 units); mirrors, $210,000 (1,050 units); and vanities, $168,000 (525 units).

Required:

1. Prepare a contribution format income statement for the month based on actual sales data. Present the income statement in the format shown above.
2. Compute the break-even point in sales dollars for the month, based on the actual data.
3. Calculate the break-even point in unit sales for the month, based on the actual data.
4. Considering the fact that the company exceeded its $500,000 sales budget for the month, the president is shocked at the results shown on your income statement in (1) above. Prepare a brief memo for the president explaining why both the operating results and the break-even point in sales dollars are different from what was budgeted.

PROBLEM 4-21 Basic Cost-Volume-Profit Analysis; Graphing [LO1, LO2, LO4, LO5]
The Tops national chain of shirt stores carry many styles of shirts that are all sold at the same price. To encourage sales personnel to step up their sales efforts, the company pays a generous sales commission on each shirt sold. Sales personnel also receive a small basic salary.

The following table contains cost and revenue data for the Bradbury store. These data are typical of the company's many outlets:

	Per Shirt
Selling price...........................	$40.00
Variable expenses:	
Invoice cost........................	$ 18.00
Sales commission..................	7.00
Total variable expenses...............	$25.00
	Annual
Fixed expenses:	
Advertising	$ 80,000
Rent.............................	150,000
Salaries..........................	70,000
Total fixed expenses.................	$300,000

Tops is a fairly new company. The company has asked you, as a member of its planning group, to assist in some basic analysis of its stores and company policies.

Required:
1. Calculate the annual break-even point in dollar sales and in unit sales for the Bradbury store.
2. Prepare a CVP graph showing cost and revenue data for the Bradbury store from 0 shirts up to 30,000 shirts sold each year. Clearly indicate the break-even point on the graph.
3. If 19,000 shirts are sold in a year, what will be the Bradbury store's operating income or loss?
4. The company is considering paying the Bradbury store manager an incentive commission of $3 per shirt (in addition to the salesperson's commissions). If this change is made, what will be the new break-even point in dollar sales and in unit sales?
5. Refer to the original data. As an alternative to (4) above, the company is considering paying the store manager a $3 commission on each shirt sold in excess of the break-even point. If this change is made, what will be the store's operating income or loss if 23,500 shirts are sold in a year?
6. Refer to the original data. The company is considering eliminating sales commissions entirely in its stores and increasing fixed salaries by $107,000 annually.
   a. If this change is made, what will be the new break-even point in dollar sales and in unit sales in the Bradbury store?
   b. Would you recommend that the change be made? Explain.

PROBLEM 4-22 Break-Even Analysis; Pricing [LO1, LO4, LO5]
Whitney Sewing and Alterations has just introduced a new line of alteration services for men's suits for which the company is trying to determine an optimal selling price. Marketing studies suggest that the company can increase sales by 2,000 units for each $2 per unit reduction in the selling price. The company's current selling price is $45 per unit, and variable expenses are $27 per unit. Fixed expenses are $111,600 per year. The current annual sales volume (at the $45 selling price) is 6,000 units.

Required:
1. What is the current yearly operating income or loss?
2. What is the current break-even point in units and in dollar sales?
3. Assuming that the marketing studies are correct, what is the *maximum* profit that the company can earn yearly? At how many units and at what selling price per unit would the company generate this profit?

4.   What would be the break-even point in units and in dollar sales using the selling price you determined in (3) above (i.e., the selling price at the level of maximum profits)? Why is this break-even point different from the break-even point you computed in (2) above?

PROBLEM 4–23 Graphing; Incremental Analysis; Operating Leverage [LO2, LO4, LO5, LO6, LO8]

Teri Hall recently opened Sheer Elegance Inc., a store specializing in fashionable stockings. Hall has just completed a course in managerial accounting, and she believes that she can apply certain aspects of the course to her business. She is particularly interested in adopting the CVP approach to decision making. Thus, she has prepared the following analysis:

Sales price per pair of stockings	$10.00
Variable expense per pair of stockings	4.00
Contribution margin per pair of stockings	$ 6.00
Fixed expense per year:	
Building rental	$ 48,000
Equipment depreciation	12,000
Selling	120,000
Administrative	60,000
Total fixed expense	$240,000

Required:

1.   How many pairs of stockings must the store sell to break even? What does this represent in total dollar sales?
2.   Prepare a CVP graph for the store from 0 pairs up to 60,000 pairs of stockings sold each year. Indicate the break-even point on the graph.
3.   How many pairs of stockings must the store sell to earn a $15,000 target profit for the first year?
4.   Hall now has one full-time and one part-time salesperson working in the store. It will cost her an additional $20,000 per year to convert the part-time position to a full-time position. Hall believes that the change would bring in an additional $40,000 in sales each year. Should she convert the position? Use the incremental approach. (Do not prepare an income statement.)
5.   Refer to the original data. Actual operating results for the first year are as follows:

Sales	$600,000
Variable expenses	240,000
Contribution margin	360,000
Fixed expenses	240,000
Operating income	$ 120,000

a.   What is the store's degree of operating leverage?
b.   Hall is confident that with some effort she can increase sales by 20% next year. What would be the expected percentage increase in operating income? Use the degree of operating leverage concept to compute your answer.

PROBLEM 4–24 Break-Even and Target Profit Analysis [LO5, LO6]

The Marbury Stein Shop sells steins from all parts of the world. The owner of the shop, Clint Marbury, is thinking of expanding his operations by hiring local college and university students, on a commission basis, to sell steins at the local post-secondary schools. The steins will bear the school emblem.

These steins must be ordered from the manufacturer three months in advance, and because of the unique emblem of each school, they cannot be returned. The steins would cost Marbury $15 each, with a minimum order of 200 steins. Any additional steins would have to be ordered in increments of 50.

Since Marbury's plan would not require any additional facilities, the only costs associated with the project would be the cost of the steins and the cost of sales commissions. The selling price of the steins would be $30 each. Marbury would pay the students a commission of $6 for each stein sold.

Required:

1. To make the project worth his time, Marbury requires a $7,200 operating income for the first six months of the venture. What level of sales in units and dollars is required to attain this target operating income? Show all computations.
2. What level of sales dollars is required to generate $12,000 in after-tax operating income if the tax rate is 20%?
3. Assume that the venture is undertaken and an order is placed for 200 steins. What is Marbury's break-even point in units and in sales dollars? Show all computations, and explain the reasoning behind your answer.

PROBLEM 4–25 Sales Mix; Multi-Product Break-Even Analysis; Target Profit; Margin of Safety [LO6, LO7, LO9]

Warm Hands, a small company based in Prince Edward Island, manufactures and sells two types of lightweight gloves for runners—Warm and Cozy. Current revenue, cost, and unit sales data for the two products appear below:

	Warm	Cozy
Selling price per pair	$8.00	$12.00
Variable expenses per pair	$2.00	$ 6.00
Number of pairs sold monthly	600 units	200 units

Fixed expenses are $2,250 per month.

Required:

1. Assuming the sales mix above, do the following:
   a. Prepare a contribution format income statement showing both dollars and percentage columns for each product and for the company as a whole.
   b. Compute the break-even point in dollars for the company as a whole and the margin of safety in both dollars and percentage of sales.
   c. Compute the break-even point in units for the company as a whole and the margin of safety in both units (pairs of gloves) and percentage of sales.
   d. Compute how many pairs of gloves must be sold overall if the company wants to make an after-tax target profit of $4,725 and the tax rate is 30%. Assume that the sales mix remains the same as shown above.
2. The company has developed another type of gloves that provide better protection in extreme cold, Toasty, which the company plans to sell for $20 per pair. At this price, the company expects to sell 200 pairs per month of the product. The variable expense would be $16 per pair. The company's fixed expenses would not change.
   a. Prepare another contribution format income statement, including sales of Toasty (sales of the other two products would not change).
   b. Compute the company's new break-even point in dollars for the company as a whole and the new margin of safety in both dollars and percentage of sales.
3. The president of the company is puzzled by your analysis. He does not understand why the break-even point has gone up even though there has been no increase in fixed expenses and the addition of the new product has increased the total CM. Explain to the president what happened.

PROBLEM 4–26 Sales Mix; Multi-Product Break-Even Analysis [LO9]

MediaSol Inc. produces affordable, high-quality personal multimedia entertainment devices. The company's Video Division manufactures three portable video players—the Standard, the Deluxe, and the Pro—that are widely used by the younger generation. Selected information on the portable video players is given below:

	Standard	Deluxe	Pro
Selling price per video player................	$80.00	$120.00	$180.00
Variable expenses per video player:			
Production............................	44.00	54.00	63.00
Selling (10% of selling price).............	8.00	12.00	18.00

All sales are made through the company's own retail outlets. The Video Division has the following fixed costs:

	Per Month
Fixed production costs..................	$ 90,000
Advertising expense.....................	75,000
Administrative salaries	37,500
Total	$202,500

Sales, in units, over the past two months have been as follows:

	Standard	Deluxe	Pro	Total
April	1,000	500	2,500	4,000
May..................	3,750	750	1,500	6,000

Required:
1. Using the contribution approach, prepare an income statement for April and an income statement for May, with the following headings:

Standard		Deluxe		Pro		Total	
Amount	%	Amount	%	Amount	%	Amount	%

Sales.........

Etc. ....

Place the fixed expenses only in the Total column. Do not show percentages for the fixed expenses.
2. On seeing the income statements in (1) above, the president said, "I can't believe this! We sold 50% more portable video players in May than in April, yet profits went down. It's obvious that costs are out of control in that division." What other explanation can you give for the drop in operating income?
3. Compute the Video Division's break-even point in dollar sales for April.
4. Has May's break-even point in dollar sales gone up or down from April's break-even point? Explain without computing a break-even point for May.
5. Assume that sales of the Standard video player increase by $35,000. What would be the effect on operating income? What would be the effect if Pro video player sales increased by $35,000? Do not prepare income statements; use the incremental analysis approach in determining your answer.

PROBLEM 4–27 Changes in Cost Structure; Break-Even Analysis; Operating Leverage; Margin of Safety [LO4, LO5, LO6, LO7, LO8]
Frieden Company's contribution format income statement for last month is shown below:

Sales (40,000 units)................................	$800,000
Variable expenses....................................	560,000
Contribution margin.................................	240,000
Fixed expenses	192,000
Operating income	$ 48,000

Competition is intense, and Frieden Company's profits vary considerably from one year to the next. Management is exploring opportunities to increase profitability.

Required:
1. Frieden's management is considering a major upgrade to the manufacturing equipment, which would result in fixed expenses increasing by $240,000 per month. However, variable expenses would decrease by $6 per unit. Selling price would not change. Prepare two contribution

format income statements, one showing current operations and one showing how operations would appear if the upgrade is completed. Show an Amount column, a Per Unit column, and a Percentage column on each statement. Do not show percentages for the fixed expenses.

2.   Refer to the income statements in (1) above. For both current operations and the proposed new operations, compute (*a*) the degree of operating leverage, (*b*) the break-even point in dollars, and (*c*) the margin of safety in both dollar and percentage terms.

3.   Calculate the unit sales per month at which Frieden management will be indifferent between doing the major upgrade to the manufacturing equipment and not doing the upgrade. Based on this analysis, should Frieden proceed with the major upgrade? Why or why not?

4.   Refer to the original data. Instead of doing the major upgrade to the equipment, management is considering introducing a new advertising campaign that will increase fixed expenses by $20,000 per month. Management believes the new advertisements will increase monthly unit sales by 10%. Should Frieden proceed with the new advertising campaign?

PROBLEM 4–28 Interpretive Questions on the Cost–Volume–Profit Graph [LO2, LO5]
A CVP graph, as illustrated below, is a useful tool for showing relationships between an organization's costs, volume, and profits:

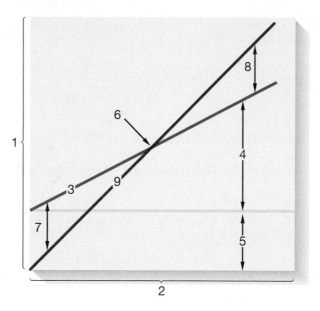

Required:
1.   Identify the numbered components in the CVP graph.
2.   State the effect of each of the following actions on line 3, line 9, and the break-even point. For line 3 and line 9, state whether the action will cause the line to
  • Remain unchanged.
  • Shift upward.
  • Shift downward.
  • Have a steeper slope (i.e., rotate upward).
  • Have a flatter slope (i.e., rotate downward).
  • Shift upward *and* have a steeper slope.
  • Shift upward *and* have a flatter slope.
  • Shift downward *and* have a steeper slope.
  • Shift downward *and* have a flatter slope.
In the case of the break-even point, state whether the action will cause the break-even point to
  • Remain unchanged.
  • Increase.
  • Decrease.
  • Probably change, but the direction is uncertain.
Treat each case independently.
Example: Fixed costs are decreased by $90,000 each period.
  Answer (see choices above):   Line 3: Shift downward.
                                        Line 9: Remain unchanged.
                                        Break-even point: Decrease.

a.   The unit selling price increases from $100 to $110.
b.   The per unit variable costs decrease from $40 to $36.
c.   The total fixed costs increase by $80,000.
d.   Two thousand more units are sold during the period than were budgeted.
e.   Due to paying salespeople a commission rather than a flat salary, fixed costs decrease by $21,000 per period, and unit variable costs increase by $6.
f.   As a result of an increase in the cost of materials, both unit variable costs and the selling price increase by $6.
g.   Advertising costs increase by $50,000 per period, but unfortunately the number of units sold does not change.
h.   Upgrades to manufacturing equipment increase fixed costs by $40,000 per period, but variable costs per unit decrease by $2 per unit.

PROBLEM 4–29 Changes in Fixed and Variable Costs; Break-Even and Target Profit Analysis [LO4, LO5, LO6]
Novelties Inc. produces and sells faddish products directed at the pre-teen market. A new product has come onto the market that the company is anxious to produce and sell. Enough capacity exists in the company's plant to produce 30,000 units each month. Variable costs to manufacture and sell one unit would be $1.60, and fixed costs would total $40,000 per month.

The Marketing Department predicts that demand for the product will exceed the 30,000 units that the company is able to produce. Additional production capacity can be rented from another company at a fixed cost of $2,000 per month. Variable costs in the rented facility would total $1.75 per unit, due to somewhat less efficient operations than in the main plant. The product would sell for $2.50 per unit.

Required:
1.   Compute the monthly break-even point for the new product in units and in total dollar sales. Show all computations in good form.
2.   How many units must be sold each month to make a monthly operating income of $9,000?
3.   If the sales manager receives a bonus of 15 cents for each unit sold in excess of the break-even point, how many units must be sold each month to earn a return of 25% on the monthly investment in fixed costs?

PROBLEM 4–30 Changes in Cost Structure; Break-Even Analysis; Operating Leverage; Margin of Safety [LO4, LO5, LO7, LO8]

Duchamp Company's contribution format income statement for the most recent month is given below:

Sales (30,000 units).........................	$900,000
Variable expenses...........................	630,000
Contribution margin.........................	270,000
Fixed expenses	180,000
Operating income...........................	$ 90,000

The industry in which Duchamp Company operates is quite sensitive to cyclical movements in the economy. Thus, profits vary considerably from year to year according to general economic conditions. The company has a large amount of unused capacity and is studying ways of improving profits.

Required:
1.   New equipment has come on the market that would allow Duchamp Company to automate a portion of its operations. Variable costs would be reduced by $9 per unit. However, fixed costs would increase to a total of $450,000 each month. Prepare two contribution format income statements, one showing current operations and one showing how operations would appear if the new equipment is purchased. Show an Amount column, a Per Unit column, and a Percentage column on each statement. Do not show percentages for the fixed costs.
2.   Refer to the income statements in (1) above. For both current operations and the proposed new operations, compute (*a*) the degree of operating leverage, (*b*) the break-even point in dollars, and (*c*) the margin of safety in both dollar and percentage terms.
3.   Refer again to the data in (1) above. As a manager, what factor would be paramount in your mind in deciding whether to purchase the new equipment? (You may assume that ample funds are available to make the purchase.)

4. Refer to the original data. Rather than purchase new equipment, the marketing manager argues that the company's marketing strategy should be changed. Instead of paying sales commissions, which are included in variable expenses, the marketing manager suggests that salespeople be paid fixed salaries and that the company invest heavily in advertising. The marketing manager claims that this new approach would increase unit sales by 60% without any change in selling price, the company's new monthly fixed expenses would be $247,500, and its operating income would increase by 25%. Compute the break-even point in dollar sales for the company under the new marketing strategy. Do you agree with the marketing manager's proposal?

PROBLEM 4–31 Changes in Cost Structure; Break-Even Analysis; Indifference [LO4, LO5, LO6]
Lockhart Manufacturing Co. is manufacturing a new product for the following costs:

Direct materials per unit	$9
Direct labour per unit	1.2 DLH @ $14/DLH
Variable overhead per unit	0.75 of direct labour costs
Fixed manufacturing costs	$1,108,000
Fixed selling and administrative costs	$1,685,000
Selling price per unit	$60
Variable selling costs per unit	$4

The production manager feels that savings could be achieved by automating the plant. If the plant was automated, the costs would change as follows:

Direct materials cost per unit	$7.50
Direct labour per unit	0.75 DLH @ $18/DLH
Variable overhead per unit	0.6 of direct labour costs
Fixed manufacturing costs	$1,494,000

There would be no change to any other costs or to the selling price.

Required
1. Calculate the break-even point in annual unit sales for the new product if Lockhart Manufacturing uses the
    a. Current method of production.
    b. Automated method of production.
2. Calculate the annual number of unit sales at which Lockhart Manufacturing would be indifferent about which manufacturing method is used. If demand exceeds this amount, which method of production should be used?
3. Identify four factors that Lockhart Manufacturing might consider before selecting either the current method of production or the automated method of production.
                                                                          (CGA–Canada adapted)

PROBLEM 4–32 Changes in Cost Structure; Break-Even Analysis; Target Profit [LO5, LO6, LO8]
Alliance Enterprises is considering extensively modifying their manufacturing equipment. The modifications will result in less wastage of materials, which will reduce variable manufacturing costs and introduce changes to the production process that will improve product quality. This will allow Alliance to increase the selling price of the product. Annual fixed costs are expected to increase to $750,000 if the modifications are made. Expected fixed and variable costs as well as the selling prices are shown below:

Cost Item	Existing Equipment	Modified Equipment
Selling price per unit	$36	$40
Variable cost per unit	$28	$25
Fixed costs	$330,000	$750,000

Required
1. Determine Alliance Enterprises' break-even point in units with the existing equipment and with the modified equipment.
2. Determine the sales level in units at which the modified equipment will achieve a 25% target profit-to-sales ratio (ignore taxes).
3. Determine the sales level in units at which the modified equipment will achieve $63,000 in after-tax operating income. Assume a tax rate of 30%.
4. Determine the sales level at which profits will be the same for either the existing or modified equipment.

CASES

CASE 4–33 Multi-Product Cost–Volume–Profit Analysis and Target Profit [LO9]
Karges Coffee Inc. manufactures a line of single-cup brewing machines for home and office use that brew a cup of coffee, tea, or hot chocolate in less than a minute. The machines use specially packaged portions of coffee, tea, or hot chocolate that can be purchased online directly from Karges or at specialty coffee shops licensed to distribute the company's products. The appeal of the brewing machines is twofold. First, they offer a high level of convenience. The use of prepackaged coffee servings means no grinding of coffee beans and no mess. Also, the brewing machines have a water reservoir that for some models is large enough to make up to 20 cups of coffee. Second, the taste of each cup of coffee, tea, or hot chocolate is very consistent. The brewers' pressurized system uses the same amount of water for each cup, and the airtight seal used in the individual portions keeps the product fresh.

The company has three models of brewers that offer different features, such as the size of the water reservoir, the number of brewing sizes, and the types of filtering devices used in the machine. Data from the most recent fiscal year for the three models are shown below:

	Model		
	Home Brewer	**Office Basic**	**Office Deluxe**
Sales volume (units)...........................	12,000	30,000	6,000
Unit selling price..............................	$150	$200	$300
Variable cost per unit.........................	120	140	180
Contribution margin per unit..................	$ 30	$ 60	$120

Fixed costs are $1,500,000 per year. The company has no work in process or finished goods inventories. The company is facing increased levels of competition from manufacturers using similar brewing technologies and believes there is no room for any increases in unit selling prices.

Required:
1. Calculate the company's overall break-even point in sales dollars and in units.
2. Calculate the overall sales dollars required to earn a target profit of $1,500,000 (ignore taxes). Assume the sales mix does not change.
3. Calculate the
   a. Sales dollars required for each product at the overall break-even level of sales calculated in (1) above.
   b. Unit sales of each product at the overall break-even level of sales units calculated in (1) above.
4. What impact would doubling the number of Office Basic units sold next year have on the overall break-even point in sales dollars? Assume that there will be no changes to the Home Brewer or Office Deluxe unit sales, that unit selling prices and variable costs will remain the same for each model, and that total fixed costs will be unchanged.
5. The company is considering a new advertising campaign to raise overall consumer awareness of the product offerings. The total cost of the year-long campaign would be $180,000. By how much would unit sales need to increase overall for the company to be able to justify the new campaign? How many units of each product must be sold to justify the new campaign? Assume no change to the current product mix.

6. Suppose that instead of being designed to increase total sales volume, the new $180,000 advertising campaign will focus on getting customers who would have purchased the Office Basic model to buy the Office Deluxe model instead. To justify the cost of the new advertising, how many customers must purchase the Deluxe model instead of the Basic model? Assume that the new advertising campaign will have no impact on sales of the Home Brewer model.

7. The company is considering adding a new product to its line of brewers targeted at the office-use market. The new brewer, the Office Plus, would sell for $250 per unit and would have variable unit costs of $160. Introducing the new model would increase fixed costs by $102,000 annually and would reduce annual unit sales of the Office Basic and Office Deluxe models by 10% each. Assuming no change to the sales of the Home Brewer model, how many units of the Office Plus model would need to be sold to justify its addition to the product line next year?

CASE 4–34 Cost Structure; Break-Even Point; Target Profits [LO4, LO5, LO6]

Crescent Corporation manufactures multi-function photocopiers that are sold to businesses through a network of independent sales agents located in the United States and Canada. These sales agents sell a variety of products to businesses in addition to Crescent's multi-function photocopiers. The sales agents are currently paid a 19% commission on sales, and this commission rate was used when Crescent's management prepared the following budgeted income statement for the upcoming year:

Sales		$15,000,000
Cost of goods sold:		
Variable	$8,400,000	
Fixed	1,400,000	9,800,000
Gross margin		5,200,000
Selling and administrative expenses:		
Commissions	2,850,000	
Fixed advertising expense	400,000	
Fixed administrative expense	1,600,000	4,850,000
Operating income		$ 350,000

Since the completion of the above statement, Crescent's management has learned that the independent sales agents are demanding an increase in the commission rate to 22% of sales for the upcoming year. This would be the third increase in commissions demanded by the independent sales agents in five years. As a result, Crescent's management has decided to investigate the possibility of hiring its own sales staff to replace the independent sales agents.

Crescent's controller estimates that the company would have to hire six salespeople to cover the current market area, and the total annual payroll cost of these employees would be about $350,000, including benefits. The salespeople would also be paid commissions of 12% of sales. Travel and entertainment expenses are expected to total about $200,000 for the year. The company would also have to hire a sales manager and support staff, whose salaries and benefits would total $100,000 per year. To make up for the promotions that the independent sales agents had been running on behalf of Crescent, management believes that the company's budget for fixed advertising expenses should be increased by $250,000.

Required:
1. Assuming sales of $15,000,000, construct a budgeted contribution format income statement for the upcoming year for each of the following alternatives:
   a. The independent sales agents' commission rate remains unchanged at 19%.
   b. The independent sales agents' commission rate increases to 22%.
   c. The company employs its own sales force.
2. Calculate Crescent Corporation's break-even point in sales dollars for the upcoming year assuming the following:
   a. The independent sales agents' commission rate remains unchanged at 19%.
   b. The independent sales agents' commission rate increases to 22%.
   c. The company employs its own sales force.

3. Refer to your answer to 1(*b*) above. If the company employs its own sales force, what volume of sales would be necessary to generate the operating income the company would realize if sales are $15,000,000 and the company continues to sell through agents (at a 22% commission rate)?

4. Determine the volume of sales at which operating income would be equal regardless of whether Crescent Corporation sells through agents (at a 22% commission rate) or employs its own sales force.

5. Prepare a profit graph on which you plot the profits for both of the following alternatives:
    a. The independent sales agents' commission rate increases to 22%.
    b. The company employs its own sales force.
    On the graph, use total sales revenue as the measure of activity.

6. Write a memo to the president of Crescent Corporation in which you recommend whether the company should continue to use independent sales agents (at a 22% commission rate) or employ its own sales force. Fully explain the reasons for your recommendation in the memo.

(CMA, adapted)

CASE 4–35 Break-Even Levels for Individual Products in a Multi-Product Company [LO6, LO9]

Jasmine Richards met her boss, Rick McNeil, at the pop machine in the lobby. McNeil is the vice-president of marketing at Down East Lures Corporation. Richards was puzzled by some calculations she had been doing, so she initiated this conversation:

Richards: Rick, I'm not sure how to go about answering the questions that came up at the meeting with the president yesterday.

McNeil: What's the problem?

Richards: The president wanted to know the break-even point for each of the company's products, but I'm having trouble figuring them out.

McNeil: I'm sure you can handle it, Jasmine. And, by the way, I need your analysis on my desk tomorrow morning at 8:00 A.M. sharp so I can look at it before the follow-up meeting at 9:00.

Down East Lures makes three fishing lures in its manufacturing facility in Prince Edward Island. Data concerning these products appear below:

	Frog	Minnow	Worm
Normal annual sales volume (units)................	100,000	200,000	300,000
Unit selling price.....................................	$2.00	$1.40	$0.80
Variable cost per unit...............................	$1.20	$0.80	$0.50

Total fixed expenses for the entire company are $282,000 per year. All three products are sold in highly competitive markets, so the company is unable to raise its prices without losing unacceptable numbers of customers. The company has no work in process or finished goods inventories due to an extremely effective lean manufacturing system.

Required:

1. What is the company's overall break-even point in total sales dollars?

2. Of the total fixed costs of $282,000, $18,000 relate directly to the Frog lure product, $96,000 relate directly to the Minnow lure product, and $60,000 relate directly to the Worm lure product. The remaining fixed expenses of $108,000 consist of common fixed costs such as administrative salaries, rent on the factory building, and advertising expenses for the company as a whole. These common fixed expenses are not directly related to any particular product but must be incurred as part of operating the business.
    a. What is the break-even point in units for each product? *Note:* Management insists that Richards separately calculate the break-even point for each product using its CM per unit and only the fixed expenses that relate directly to that product.
    b. If the company sells exactly the break-even quantity of each product calculated in (*a*), calculate the overall profit of the company. Explain this result to management.
    c. Calculate the company's overall break-even point in units using the weighted-average CM approach. How many units of each product must be sold at the break-even level? Comment on any significant differences you see between these results and those of (*a*) above.

INSTANT QUIZ SOLUTIONS

4–1
$(500 - 400) \times \$100$ per speaker $= \$10,000$ increase in operating income

4–2
Profit = Unit CM $\times$ Q $-$ Fixed expenses
Profit = $(\$100 \times 100) - \$35,000$
Loss = $\$(25,000)$

4–3
Change in CM = CM ratio $\times$ Change in sales
Change in CM = $40\% \times \$50,000$
Change in CM = $\$20,000$

4–4
$$\text{Break-even point in units sold} = \frac{\text{Fixed expenses}}{\text{Unit CM}}$$

Break-even point in units sold = $\$40,000 \div \$100$
Break-even point in units sold = 400

$$\text{Break-even point in total sales dollars} = \frac{\text{Fixed expenses}}{\text{CM ratio}}$$

Break-even in total sales dollars = $\$40,000 \div 40\%$
Break-even in total sales dollars = $\$100,000$

4–5
$$\text{Units sold to attain the target profit} = \frac{\text{Fixed expenses} + \text{Target operating profit}}{\text{Unit CM}}$$

$$= \frac{\$35,000 + \$55,000}{\$100} = 900$$

$$\text{Dollars sales to attain target profit} = \frac{\text{Fixed expenses} + \text{Target operating profit}}{\text{CM ratio}}$$

$$= \frac{\$35,000 + \$55,000}{40\%} = \$225,000$$

4–6
$$\text{Units sold to attain target profit} = \frac{\text{Fixed expenses} + \left[\dfrac{\text{Target after-tax profit}}{1 - \text{Tax rate}}\right]}{\text{Unit CM}}$$

$$= \frac{\$35,000 + [\$56,000/(1 - 0.3)]}{\$100} = 1,150 \text{ speakers}$$

4–7
Margin of safety = Total budgeted (or actual) sales $-$ Break-even sales
Margin of safety = $\$150,000 - \$100,000$
Margin of safety = $\$50,000$

$$\text{Margin of safety percentage} = \frac{\text{Margin of safety in dollars}}{\text{Total budgeted (or actual) sales}}$$

Margin of safety percentage = $\$50,000 \div \$150,000$
Margin of safety percentage = 33.3%

4–8
Percentage change in operating income = Degree of operating leverage $\times$ Percentage change in sales
Percentage change in operating income = $16 \times 25\%$
Percentage change in operating income = 400%
New operating income in dollars:
$\quad \$2,000 + (\$2,000 \times 4) = \$10,000$

4-9
Weighted-average CM per unit:
$(0.4 \times \$6.25) + (0.6 \times \$12.50) = \$10$ per unit

$$\text{Total sales units to break even} = \frac{\text{Fixed expenses}}{\text{Weighted-average CM per unit}}$$

$$\text{Total sales units to break even} = \frac{\$27,000}{\$10} = 2,700$$

■ APPENDIX 4A: COST–VOLUME–PROFIT ANALYSIS WITH UNCERTAINTY

 Appendix available on Connect.

![McGraw Hill Education] connect®   ![McGraw Hill Education] LEARNSMART®   ![McGraw Hill Education] SMARTBOOK™

For more information on the resources available from McGraw-Hill Ryerson, go to www.mheducation.ca/he/solutions.

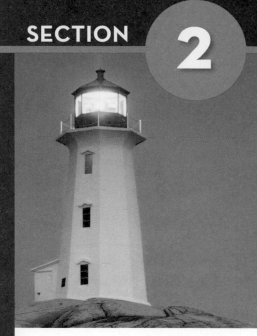
COSTING

Chapters 5 through 8

Chapters 5 through 8 provide a comprehensive description of how costs are associated with manufacturing and other activities. In addition, these costing systems can be applied to service organizations and not-for-profit organizations. To permit costing for such specialized situations, two costing systems, job-order costing and process costing, can be mixed and matched.

Chapter 5 begins with the most basic and widely used costing system, *job-order costing*. Job-order costing permits costs to be assigned to specific outcomes, termed *jobs*, so that costs can be accumulated for what a company produces. In addition, manufacturing overhead—a term often shortened to just *overhead*—is assigned by a process of averaging to estimate its amount before actual overhead costs are known.

Chapter 6 introduces an averaging calculation used for costing similar units of product, termed *process costing*. The ordering of costs learned in financial accounting (namely, average and FIFO) can be applied. The idea of equivalent units is explained, so that

partially finished work in process can be valued in inventory. Chapter 6 also presents an elaboration of overhead methods so that overhead can be disaggregated to departments (the cost object in this case) to permit better management control of overhead and more accurate costing.

Chapter 7 introduces activity-based costing, another way to disaggregate overhead and non-manufacturing costs. Cost objects are defined as activities, and activities are costed by identifying a relevant cost driver. By doing this, overhead costing can be improved and management can focus on managing activities rather than outcomes. Given the increasing importance of overhead costs incurred in some types of organizations, methods to improve the management of overhead costs are important.

Chapter 8 completes the costing segment by describing variable costing. Variable costing assigns only variable manufacturing costs to production as opposed to all manufacturing costs, as was described in earlier chapters under the term *absorption costing*.

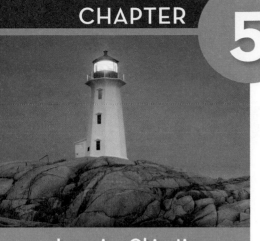

SYSTEMS DESIGN: JOB-ORDER COSTING

▌ CUSTOM DESIGN AT ICEJERSEYS.COM

Sport BUFF is dedicated to offering the best selection of officially licensed sports merchandise and apparel in Montreal. Customers know that no matter what team they support, Sport BUFF will have a jersey in stock. As the Internet and online shopping became more popular, the store owners launched the website http://www.IceJerseys.com and began offering custom team outfitting services to hockey teams at all skill levels. Customers use an online tool called "JerseyBuilder" to choose colours and styles, and they either provide a team logo or the IceJerseys.com staff will design a logo for them. Individual team members' names and numbers and the team logo are printed or stitched on each jersey to meet customer specifications.

Accurately pricing custom-designed jerseys depends critically on the quality of costing information available to managers at companies like IceJerseys.com, as well as on the prices charged by competitors. The price quoted by IceJerseys.com for a custom batch of hockey jerseys must adequately cover costs and allow for an adequate profit margin while remaining price-competitive. Costs might include the labour devoted to designing custom logos and other artwork; the cost of materials and labour involved in manufacturing the custom batches of jerseys (or the cost of purchasing them from outside suppliers); and the costs of the manufacturing, printing, and stitching equipment used to produce the jerseys to customer specifications (called *manufacturing overhead*). Since this equipment will be used to produce several different batches of custom jerseys in any one year, managers at IceJerseys.com must find a way to divide these costs between batches so they can estimate the total cost per jersey in each batch. In this chapter, we will examine methods of accurately estimating the total cost per unit for specifically identifiable products and services such as custom jerseys, and we will explore why this information is key to setting prices and to identifying opportunities for cost control for many firms.

Source: IceJerseys.com Team Outfitting: team.icejerseys.com. Reprinted with permission.

Absorption costing
A costing method that includes all manufacturing costs—direct materials, direct labour, and both variable and fixed overhead—as part of the cost of a finished unit of product; synonymous with *full costing*.

Full costing
Another name for *absorption costing*.

Understanding how products and services are costed is vital to managers because costing methods can have an important impact on reported profits and on key management decisions such as pricing and outsourcing. Nevertheless, external financial reporting and tax reporting regulations heavily influence how costs are accumulated and summarized in managerial reports. Managers believe it is easier and less expensive to use a single method of costing for both external and internal purposes. Since regulations require use of absorption costing to determine product costs, it has become the most popular costing approach.

In **absorption costing**, *all* manufacturing costs, fixed and variable, are assigned to units of product—units are said to *fully absorb manufacturing costs*. The absorption costing approach is also known as **full costing**. Later, in Chapter 8, we look at product costing from a different point of view called *variable costing*. In Chapter 8 we also discuss the strengths and weaknesses of the two approaches.

■ JOB-ORDER AND PROCESS COSTING

LEARNING OBJECTIVE 1
Distinguish between process costing and job-order costing, and identify the production or service processes that fit with each costing method.

In computing the cost of a product or a service, managers face a difficult problem. Many costs (such as rent) do not change much from month to month, while production levels will go up in one month and then down in another. In addition to variations in the level of production, several different products or services may be produced in the same period. Under these conditions, how is it possible to accurately determine the cost of a product or service? In practice, assigning costs to products and services involves averaging some cost types across time periods and across products or services. The way this averaging is carried out depends heavily on the method used to produce the product or provide the service.

Process Costing

Process costing system
A costing system used in those manufacturing situations where a single, homogeneous product (such as cement or oil) flows in a continuous stream out of the production process.

A **process costing system** is used in situations where the company produces many units of a single product (such as frozen orange juice concentrate) for long periods at a time. Examples are mixing cement at St. Marys Cement, refining oil at Petro-Canada, mixing and bottling beverages at Coca-Cola, and making wieners at J. M. Schneider Inc. (owned by Maple Leaf Foods Inc.). All of these industries are characterized by an essentially homogeneous product that flows evenly through the production process on a continuous basis.

Process costing systems accumulate costs in a particular operation or department for an entire period (month, quarter, or year) and then divide this total cost by the number of units produced during the period. The basic formula for process costing is as follows:

$$\frac{\text{Unit product cost}}{\text{(per litre, kilogram, bottle)}} = \frac{\text{Total manufacturing cost}}{\text{Total units produced (litres, kilograms, bottles)}}$$

Since one unit of product (litre, kilogram, bottle) is indistinguishable from any other unit of product, each unit is assigned the same average cost. This costing technique results in a broad average unit cost figure that applies to homogeneous units flowing in a continuous stream out of the production process.

Job-Order Costing

Job-order costing system
A costing system used in situations where many different products, jobs, or services are produced each period.

A **job-order costing system** is used in situations where many *different* products or services are produced each period. For example, a Levi Strauss clothing factory may make many different types of jeans for both men and women during a month. A particular order might consist of 1,000 stonewashed men's blue denim jeans, style number A312, with a 32-inch waist and a 30-inch inseam. This order of 1,000 jeans is called a *batch* or a *job*. In a job-order costing system, costs are traced and allocated to jobs, and then the costs of the job are divided by the number of units in the job to arrive at an average cost per unit.

Other examples of situations where job-order costing is used are large-scale construction projects managed by Bechtel Corporation, commercial aircraft produced by Bombardier, greeting cards designed and printed by Hallmark, and airline meals prepared by Cara. All of these examples are characterized by diverse outputs. Each Bechtel project is different from every other—the company could be simultaneously constructing a dam in Zaire and a bridge in Indonesia. Likewise, each airline orders a different type of meal from Cara's catering service.

Job-order costing is also used extensively in service industries and not-for-profit organizations. Hospitals, social service agencies, law firms, movie studios, accounting firms, and advertising agencies all use a variation of job-order costing to accumulate costs for accounting, billing, and performance evaluation. For example, the production of the British Open golf broadcast by TSN and the accumulation of treatment-related costs for each patient admitted to hospital are both suitable job-order costing projects.

Although the detailed example of job-order costing provided in the following section deals with a manufacturing firm, the same basic concepts and procedures are used by many service organizations. The essential difference for service organizations is the lack of raw materials in the cost of their services. For example, a public accounting firm has cost elements involving direct labour and overhead but not raw materials, because the firm does not make a physical item. However, to avoid duplicating the discussion that follows, the more comprehensive manufacturing environment will be presented, with the service application addressed in exercises and problems.

The record-keeping and cost assignment problems are more complex when a company sells many different products and services than when it has only a single product. Since the products are different, the costs are typically different. Consequently, cost records must be maintained for each distinct product or job. For example, a lawyer in a large criminal law practice would ordinarily keep separate records of the costs of advising and defending each of her clients. The Levi Strauss factory mentioned earlier would keep the costs of filling orders for particular styles, sizes, and colours of jeans separately. Thus, a job-order costing system requires more effort than a process costing system. Nevertheless, job-order costing is used by more than half the manufacturers in North America.

In this chapter, we focus on the design of a job-order costing system. In the following chapter, we focus on process costing and also look more closely at the similarities and differences between the two costing methods.

> **Instant Quiz 5-1**
> Identify which of the following products is likely to be costed using a job-order costing system and which by a process costing system: paper towels, legal services, auto repairs, house paint, engagement rings, household cleaners, Caribbean cruises, 4 × 8 sheets of plywood.

■ JOB-ORDER COSTING—AN OVERVIEW

To introduce job-order costing, we will follow a specific job as it progresses through the manufacturing process. This job consists of two experimental couplings that ABY Precision Machining has agreed to produce for Loops Unlimited, a manufacturer of roller coasters. Couplings connect the cars on the roller coaster and are a critical component in the performance and safety of the ride. Before we begin our discussion, recall from Chapter 2 that companies generally classify manufacturing costs into three broad categories: (1) direct materials, (2) direct labour, and (3) manufacturing overhead. As we study the operation of a job-order costing system, we will see how each of these three types of costs is recorded and accumulated. You may wish to refer to the summary of document flows presented in Exhibit 5–5 later in the chapter as you work through the example below.

> **LEARNING OBJECTIVE** ②
> Recognize the flow of costs through a job-order costing system.

Measuring Direct Materials Cost

Bill of materials
A record that lists the type and quantity of each major item of the materials required to make a product.

ABY Precision Machining requires four G7 connectors and two M46 housings to make the two experimental couplings for Loops Unlimited. If this were a standard product, there would be a *bill of materials* for the product. A **bill of materials** is a record that lists the type and quantity of each item of the materials needed to complete a unit of product. In this case, ABY's production staff determined from the blueprints that each coupling requires two connectors and one housing; therefore, to make two couplings, four connectors and two housings are required.

A *production order* is issued when an agreement has been reached with the customer concerning the quantities, prices, and shipment date for the order. The Production Department then prepares a *materials requisition form*. The **materials requisition form** is a document that (1) specifies the type and quantity of materials to be drawn from the storeroom and (2) identifies the job to which the costs of the materials are to be charged. The form controls the flow of materials into production and also makes entries in the accounting records. A sample materials requisition form is provided in Exhibit 5–1.

Materials requisition form
A detailed source document that specifies the type and quantity of materials that are to be drawn from the storeroom and identifies the job to which the costs of materials are to be charged.

The ABY Precision Machining materials requisition form in Exhibit 5–1 shows that the company's Milling Department has requisitioned two M46 housings and four G7 connectors for the Loops Unlimited order, which has been designated as Job 2B47.

Previously, we used the terms *direct materials* and *raw materials*. This distinction should be clarified. Direct materials represent materials that are directly traced to the product or service. Raw materials are ingredients that are converted into a finished product. Semi-finished materials, or supplies for a service job, could be considered direct materials if they were important enough to be directly traced to the job, but they are not raw materials. In summary, raw materials can be direct materials, but not all direct materials are necessarily raw materials.

Job Cost Sheet

Job cost sheet
A form prepared for each job that records the materials, labour, and overhead costs charged to the job.

After being notified that the production order has been issued, the Accounting Department prepares a *job cost sheet* similar to the one presented in Exhibit 5–2. A **job cost sheet** is a form prepared for each separate job that records the materials, labour, and overhead costs charged to the job.

After direct materials are issued, the Accounting Department's job-order costing software automatically generates a job cost sheet like the one in Exhibit 5–2. Note

EXHIBIT 5-1 Materials Requisition Form

Materials Requisition Number	14873		Date	March 2

Job Number to Be Charged	2B47

Department	Milling

Description	Quantity	Unit Cost	Total Cost
M46 Housing	2	$124	$248
G7 Connector	4	$103	412
			$660

JOB COST SHEET ▫ ◻ ✖

Job Number	2B47 ▾		Date Initiated	March 2
Department	Milling		Date Completed	
Item	Special order coupling		Units Completed	
For Stock				

	Direct Materials		Direct Labour			Manufacturing Overhead		
	Req. No.	Amount	Ticket	Hours	Amount	Hours	Rate	Amount
	14873	$660	843	5	$75			

Cost Summary			Units Shipped		
Direct Materials	$		Date	Number	Balance
Direct Labour		$			
Manufacturing Overhead	$				
Total Cost	$				
Unit Product Cost	$				

EXHIBIT 5-2 Job Cost Sheet

that the $660 cost for direct materials shown earlier on the materials requisition form has been charged to Job 2B47 on its job cost sheet. The requisition number 14873 is also recorded on the job cost sheet to make it easier to identify the source for the direct materials charge.

In addition to serving as a means for charging costs to jobs, the job cost sheet is also a key part of a firm's accounting records. Job cost sheets are a subsidiary ledger to the Work in Process account because the detailed records that they provide for the jobs in process add up to the balance in work in process.

Measuring Direct Labour Cost

Direct labour cost is handled in much the same way as direct materials cost. Direct labour consists of labour charges that are easily traced to a particular job. Labour charges that cannot be easily traced directly to any job are treated as part of manufacturing overhead. As discussed in Chapter 2, this latter category of labour costs is termed *indirect labour* and includes tasks such as maintenance, supervision, and cleanup.

Today many companies rely on computerized systems (rather than paper and pencil) to maintain employee *time tickets*. A completed **time ticket** is an hour-by-hour summary of the employee's activities throughout the day. One computerized approach to creating time tickets uses bar codes to capture data. Each employee and each job has a unique bar code. When beginning work on a job, the employee scans three bar codes using a handheld device much like the bar code readers at grocery store checkout stands. The first bar code indicates that a job is being

Time ticket
A detailed source document that is used to record an employee's hour-by-hour activities during a day.

EXHIBIT 5-3   Employee
Time Ticket

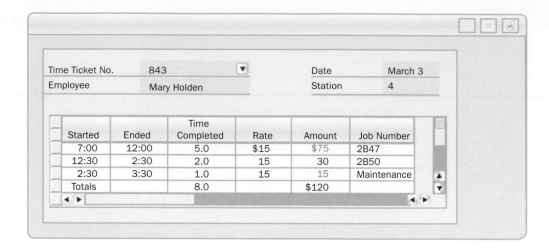

started, the second is the unique bar code on the employee's identity badge, and the third is the unique bar code of the job itself. This information is fed automatically via an electronic network to a computer that notes the time and records all of the data. When the task is completed, the employee scans a bar code indicating the task is complete, the bar code on his or her identity badge, and the bar code attached to the job. This information is relayed to the computer, which again notes the time, and a time ticket, such as the one shown in Exhibit 5–3, is automatically prepared. Because all of the source data are already in computer files, the labour costs can be automatically posted to job cost sheets. For example, Exhibit 5–3 shows $75 of direct labour cost related to Job 2B47. This amount is automatically posted to the job cost sheet shown in Exhibit 5–2. The time ticket in Exhibit 5–3 also shows $15 of indirect labour costs related to performing maintenance. This cost is treated as part of manufacturing overhead and does not get posted on a job cost sheet.

Computers, coupled with technology such as bar codes, can eliminate much of the drudgery involved in routine bookkeeping activities while at the same time increasing timeliness and accuracy.

IN BUSINESS

The design was straightforward—59 black and white bars used to speed up the grocery checkout line and give supermarkets a new tool to track their stock. But the Universal Product Code has become much more than that since it was first used to read the price on a pack of gum in 1974. Today, bar codes are scanned more than 10 billion times a day around the world for many different purposes, including tracking grocery sales and inventory, loading aircraft, and tracking packages.

Although more expensive to implement, radio-frequency identification devices (RFIDs) are beginning to replace bar code scanning systems. The addition of RFID tags can be costly but can increase workflow efficiency. For example, Kumho Tire, of South Korea, places RFID tags in all of the tires it produces. Tags are implanted inside the inner liner of each tire, allowing Kumho to track information about quality, performance, and time to manufacture. Kumho expects to cut about $9.5 million in annual production, quality control, and logistics costs using RFID technology.

Sources: Adapted from "A Grocery Store Icon Turns 35: Bar Code Birthday," *National Post*, June 29, 2009, p. FP4; "Kumho now including RFID tags in all tires," *Tire Review*, June 19, 2013, http://www.tirereview.com/Article/114971/kumho_now_including_rfid_tags_in_all_tires.aspx.

COMPUTING PREDETERMINED OVERHEAD RATES

Manufacturing overhead must be included with direct materials and direct labour on the job cost sheet, since manufacturing overhead is also a product cost. However, assigning manufacturing overhead to units of product can be a difficult task. There are four reasons for this:

LEARNING OBJECTIVE
Compute predetermined overhead rates, and explain why estimated overhead costs (rather than actual overhead costs) are used in the costing process.

1. Manufacturing overhead costs are indirect costs. This means that it is either impossible or difficult to trace these costs directly to a particular product or job.
2. Manufacturing overhead consists of many different items, ranging from the grease used in machines to the annual salary of the production manager.
3. Even though output may fluctuate due to seasonal or other factors, manufacturing overhead costs tend to remain relatively constant due to the presence of fixed costs.
4. The timing of payment of manufacturing overhead costs often varies. Some items, such as property taxes for the land on which the factory is built, may be paid once per year, while other items are paid for quarterly, monthly, or as acquired. But we produce finished items continuously and rather uniformly all year long.

Given these problems, about the only way to assign overhead costs to products is to use an allocation process. This allocation of overhead costs is accomplished by selecting an *allocation base* that is common to all of the company's products and services. An **allocation base** is a measure, such as direct labour-hours (DLH) or machine-hours (MH), that is used to assign overhead costs to products and services.

Allocation base
A measure of activity, such as direct labour-hours or machine-hours, that is used to assign costs to cost objects.

The most widely used allocation bases are direct labour-hours and direct labour cost, with machine-hours and even units of product (where a company has only a single product) also used to some extent.

Manufacturing overhead is commonly applied to products using a *predetermined overhead rate*. The **predetermined overhead rate** is computed by dividing the total estimated manufacturing overhead cost for the period by the estimated total amount of the allocation base as follows:

$$\text{Predetemined overhead rate} = \frac{\text{Estimated total manufacturing overhead cost}}{\text{Estimated total units in the allocation base}}$$

Predetermined overhead rate
A rate used to charge overhead costs to jobs; the rate is established in advance for each period using estimates of total manufacturing overhead cost and of the total allocation base for the period.

Note that the predetermined overhead rate is based on *estimated* rather than actual results. This is because the *predetermined* overhead rate is computed *before* the period begins and is used to *apply* overhead cost to jobs throughout the period. The process of assigning overhead cost to jobs is called **overhead application**. The formula for determining the amount of overhead cost to apply to a particular job is

$$\begin{array}{c}\text{Overhead applied to}\\\text{a particular job}\end{array} = \begin{array}{c}\text{Predetermined}\\\text{overhead rate}\end{array} \times \begin{array}{c}\text{Amount of the allocation}\\\text{base incurred by the job}\end{array}$$

Overhead application
The process of charging manufacturing overhead cost to job cost sheets and to the Work in Process account.

For example, if the predetermined overhead rate is $8 per direct labour-hour, then $8 of overhead is *applied* to a job for each direct labour-hour incurred by the job. When the allocation base is direct labour-hours, the formula becomes

$$\begin{array}{c}\text{Overhead applied to}\\\text{a particular job}\end{array} = \begin{array}{c}\text{Predetermined}\\\text{overhead rate}\end{array} \times \begin{array}{c}\text{Actual direct labour-hours}\\\text{charged to the job}\end{array}$$

Using the Predetermined Overhead Rate   To illustrate the steps involved in computing and using a predetermined overhead rate, let's return to ABY Precision Machining. The company has estimated its total manufacturing overhead costs will be $320,000 for the year and its total direct labour-hours will be

40,000. Its predetermined overhead rate for the year is $8 per direct labour-hour, shown as follows:

$$\text{Predetermined overhead rate} = \frac{\text{Estimated total manufacturing overhead cost}}{\text{Estimated total units in the allocation base}}$$

$$\frac{\$320,000}{40,000 \text{ direct labour-hours}} = \$8 \text{ per direct labour-hour}$$

The job cost sheet in Exhibit 5–4 indicates that 27 direct labour-hours were charged to Job 2B47. Therefore, a total of $216 of overhead cost is applied to the job:

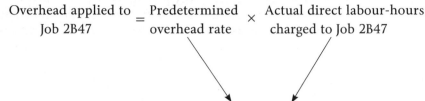

$$\begin{matrix} \text{Overhead applied to} \\ \text{Job 2B47} \end{matrix} = \begin{matrix} \text{Predetermined} \\ \text{overhead rate} \end{matrix} \times \begin{matrix} \text{Actual direct labour-hours} \\ \text{charged to Job 2B47} \end{matrix}$$

$216 of overhead applied to Job 2B47 = $8/DLH × 27 direct labour-hours

This amount of overhead has been entered on the job cost sheet in Exhibit 5–4. Note that this is *not* the actual amount of overhead caused by the job. There is no attempt to trace actual overhead costs to jobs—if that could be done, the costs would be direct costs, not overhead. The overhead assigned to the job is simply a share of the total overhead that was estimated at the beginning of the year. When a company applies overhead cost to jobs as we have done—that is, by multiplying actual activity by the predetermined overhead rate—it is called a **normal cost system**.

Normal cost system
A costing system in which overhead costs are applied to jobs by multiplying a predetermined overhead rate by the actual amount of the allocation base incurred by the job.

EXHIBIT 5-4   A Completed Job Cost Sheet

JOB COST SHEET

Job Number	2B47		Date Initiated	March 2
Department	Milling		Date Completed	March 8
Item	Special-order coupling			
For Stock			Units Completed	2

Direct Materials		Direct Labour			Manufacturing Overhead		
Req. No.	Amount	Ticket	Hours	Amount	Hours	Rate	Amount
14873	$ 660	843	5	$ 75	27	$8/DLH	$216
14875	506	846	8	80			
14912	238	850	4	45			
	$1,404	851	10	120			
			27	$320			

Cost Summary		Units Shipped		
Direct Materials	$ 1,404	Date	Number	Balance
Direct Labour	$ 320	March 8	—	2
Manufacturing Overhead	$ 216			
Total Product Cost	$ 1,940			
Unit Product Cost	$ 970*			

*$1,940 ÷ 2 units = $970 per unit.

The overhead may be applied when direct labour-hours are charged to jobs, or all of the overhead can be applied at once when the job is completed. The choice is up to the company. If a job is not completed at year-end, however, overhead should be applied to jobs so as to value the work in process inventory.

The Need for a Predetermined Rate   Instead of using a predetermined rate based on estimates, a company could wait until the end of the accounting period to compute an actual overhead rate based on the actual total manufacturing costs and the actual total units in the allocation base for the period. However, managers cite several reasons for using predetermined overhead rates instead of actual overhead rates:

1. Managers would like to know the accounting system's valuation of completed jobs *before* the end of the accounting period. Suppose, for example, that ABY Precision Machining waits until the end of the year to compute its overhead rate. Then the cost of goods sold for Job 2B47 will not be known until the close of the year, even though the job was completed and shipped to the customer in March.
2. If actual overhead rates are computed frequently, seasonal factors in overhead costs or in the allocation base can produce fluctuations in the overhead rates. For example, the costs of heating and cooling a production facility in Halifax will be highest in the winter and summer months and lowest in the spring and fall. If an overhead rate is computed each month or each quarter, the predetermined overhead rate will go up in the winter and summer and down in the spring and fall. Two identical jobs, one completed in the winter and one completed in the spring, will be assigned different costs if the overhead rate is computed on a monthly or quarterly basis. Managers generally feel that such fluctuations in overhead rates and costs serve no useful purpose and are misleading.
3. The use of a predetermined overhead rate simplifies record-keeping. To determine the overhead cost to apply to a job, the accounting staff at ABY Precision Machining simply multiply the direct labour-hours recorded for the job by the predetermined overhead rate of $8 per direct labour-hour.

For these reasons, most companies use predetermined overhead rates rather than actual overhead rates in their cost accounting systems.

Choice of an Allocation Base for Overhead Cost

Ideally, the allocation base used in the predetermined overhead rate should *drive* the overhead cost. A **cost driver** is a factor that causes overhead costs, such as machine-hours, beds occupied, computer time, or flight-hours. If a base is used to compute overhead rates that does not "drive" overhead costs, then the result will be inaccurate overhead rates and distorted product costs. For example, if direct labour-hours are used to allocate overhead, but in reality, overhead has little to do with direct labour-hours, then products with high direct labour-hour requirements will be allocated too much overhead and will be overcosted.

Most companies use direct labour-hours or direct labour cost as the allocation base for manufacturing overhead. However, major shifts are taking place in the structure of costs in many industries. In the past, direct labour accounted for up to 60% of the cost of many products, with overhead cost making up only a small portion of the remainder. This situation has been changing for two reasons. First, sophisticated automated equipment has taken over functions that used to be performed by direct labour workers. Since the costs of acquiring and maintaining such equipment are classified as overhead, this increases overhead while decreasing direct labour-hours. Second, products are themselves becoming more sophisticated and complex and change more frequently. This increases the need for highly skilled indirect workers such as engineers. As a result of these two trends, direct labour cost is decreasing relative to overhead as a component of product costs.

Instant Quiz 5-2
The managers at Automated Systems Inc. (ASI) estimate that $350,000 of overhead cost will be incurred this year related to 4,000 hours of run time for specialized machinery and equipment. Assuming ASI uses machine hours as the allocation base, calculate the predetermined overhead rate that will be used to apply overhead to jobs. If the specialized machinery is run for 250 hours to produce the components making up Job 427B, calculate the amount of overhead that will be applied to that job.

Cost driver
A factor that causes overhead costs, such as machine-hours, beds occupied, computer time, or flight-hours.

In companies where direct labour and overhead costs have been moving in opposite directions, it is difficult to argue that direct labour "drives" overhead costs. Accordingly, in recent years, managers in some companies have used *activity-based costing* principles to redesign their cost accounting systems. Activity-based costing is a costing technique that is designed to reflect more accurately the demands that products, customers, and other cost objects make on overhead resources. The activity-based approach is discussed in more detail in Chapter 7.

Although direct labour may not be an appropriate allocation base in some industries, in others it continues to be a significant driver of manufacturing overhead. Indeed, most manufacturing companies in North America continue to use direct labour as the primary or secondary allocation base for manufacturing overhead. The key point is that the allocation base used by the company should really drive, or cause, overhead costs, and direct labour is not always an appropriate allocation base.

Computation of Unit Costs

With the application of ABY Precision Machining's $216 manufacturing overhead to the job cost sheet in Exhibit 5–4, the job cost sheet is almost complete. There are two final steps. First, the totals for direct materials, direct labour, and manufacturing overhead are transferred to the Cost Summary section of the job cost sheet and added together to obtain the total cost for the job. Then the total cost ($1,940) is divided by the number of units (2) to obtain the unit cost ($970). As indicated earlier, *this unit cost is an average cost and should not be interpreted as the cost that would actually be incurred if another unit was produced.* Much of the actual overhead would not change at all if another unit was produced, so the incremental cost of an additional unit is something less than the average unit cost of $970.

The completed job cost sheet will serve as the basis for valuing unsold units in ending inventory and determining cost of goods sold.

> **Instant Quiz 5–3**
> Explain why some production costs must be assigned to products through an allocation process.

Summary of Document Flows

The sequence of events discussed above is summarized in Exhibit 5–5. A careful study of the flow of documents in this exhibit provides a good overview of the overall operation of a job-order costing system.

EXHIBIT 5-5   The Flow of Documents in a Job-Order Costing System

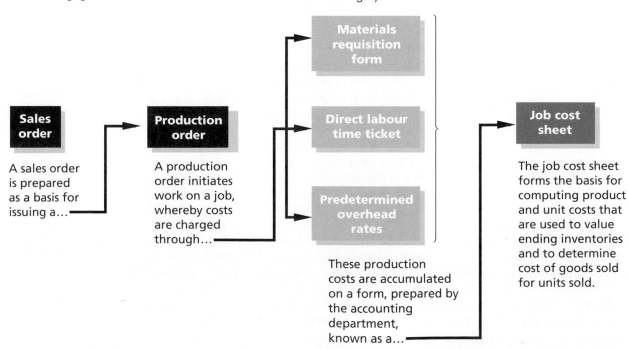

■ JOB-ORDER COSTING—THE FLOW OF COSTS

We are now ready to take a more detailed look at the flow of costs through the company's formal accounting system. To illustrate, we will consider a single month's activity for Rand Company, a producer of gold and silver commemorative medallions. We will work through the example step by step and then summarize our work in Exhibits 5-9, 5-10, and 5-11.

LEARNING OBJECTIVE ❹
Record the journal entries that reflect the flow of costs in a job-order costing system.

Rand Company has two jobs in process during April, the first month of its fiscal year. Job A, a special minting of 1,000 gold medallions commemorating the 100th anniversary of the Calgary Stampede, was started during March and had $30,000 in manufacturing costs already accumulated on April 1. Job B, an order for 10,000 silver medallions commemorating the same event, was started in April.

The Purchase and Issue of Materials

On April 1, Rand Company had $7,000 in raw materials on hand. During the month, the company purchased an additional $60,000 in raw materials. The purchase is recorded in journal entry (1) below:

(1)

Raw Materials Inventory	60,000	
Accounts Payable		60,000

As explained in Chapter 2, Raw Materials Inventory is an asset account. Thus, when raw materials are purchased, they are initially recorded as an asset—not as an expense.

Issue of Direct and Indirect Materials   During April, $52,000 in raw materials was requisitioned from the storeroom for use in production. These raw materials include $50,000 of direct materials and $2,000 of indirect materials. Entry (2) records the issue of the materials to the production departments:

(2)

Work in Process Inventory	50,000	
Manufacturing Overhead	2,000	
Raw Materials Inventory		52,000

The materials charged to Work in Process Inventory represent direct materials for specific jobs. As these materials are entered into the Work in Process account, they are also recorded on the appropriate job cost sheets. This point is illustrated in Exhibit 5-6, where $28,000 of the $50,000 in direct materials is charged to Job A's cost sheet and the remaining $22,000 is charged to Job B's cost sheet. (In this example, all data are presented in summary form, and the job cost sheet is abbreviated.)

The $2,000 charged to Manufacturing Overhead in entry (2) represents indirect materials used in production during April. Observe that the Manufacturing Overhead account is separate from the Work in Process account. The purpose of the Manufacturing Overhead account is to accumulate all manufacturing overhead costs as they are incurred during a period.

Before leaving Exhibit 5-6, note that the job cost sheet for Job A contains a beginning balance of $30,000. We stated earlier that this balance represents the cost of work done during March that has been carried forward to April. Also note that the Work in Process account contains the same $30,000 balance. *The reason the $30,000 appears in both places is that the Work in Process account is a control account and the job cost sheets form a subsidiary ledger. Thus, the Work in Process account contains a summarized total of all costs appearing on the individual job cost sheets for all jobs in process at any given point in time.* (Since Rand Company had only Job A in process at the beginning of April, Job A's $30,000 balance on that date is equal to the balance in the Work in Process account.)

Issue of Direct Materials Only   Sometimes the materials drawn from the Raw Materials Inventory account are all direct materials. In this case, the entry to record the issue of the materials into production is as follows:

EXHIBIT 5-6   Raw Materials Cost Flows

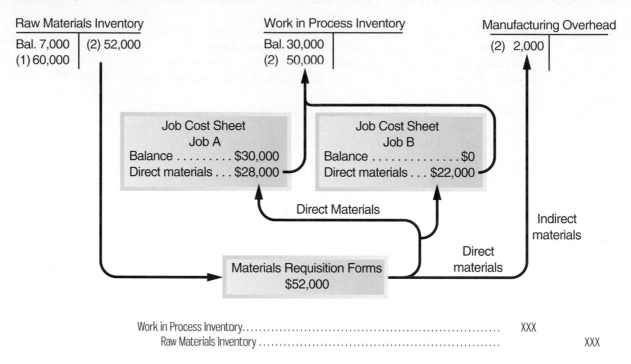

| Work in Process Inventory.. | XXX | |
| Raw Materials Inventory .... | | XXX |

Labour Cost

As work is performed in various departments of Rand Company from day to day, employees' time worked is recorded and forwarded to the Accounting Department. In the Accounting Department, the hours worked are costed according to the various employee wage rates, and the resulting costs are classified as either direct or indirect labour. In April, $60,000 was recorded for direct labour and $15,000 for indirect labour, resulting in the following summary entry:

(3)

Work in Process Inventory..	60,000	
Manufacturing Overhead	15,000	
Salaries and Wages Payable..		75,000

Only direct labour is added to the Work in Process account. For Rand Company, this amounted to $60,000 for April.

At the same time that direct labour costs are added to Work in Process, they are also added to the individual job cost sheets, as shown in Exhibit 5-7. During April, $40,000 of direct labour cost was charged to Job A, and the remaining $20,000 was charged to Job B.

The labour costs charged to Manufacturing Overhead ($15,000) represent the indirect labour costs of the period, such as supervision, janitorial work, and maintenance.

Manufacturing Overhead Costs

Recall that all costs of operating the factory other than direct materials and direct labour are classified as manufacturing overhead costs. These costs are entered directly into the Manufacturing Overhead account as they are incurred. To illustrate, assume that Rand Company incurred the following general factory costs during April:

Utilities (heat, water, and power).....................................	$21,000
Rent on factory equipment	16,000
Miscellaneous factory costs	3,000
Total	$40,000

EXHIBIT 5-7   Labour Cost Flows

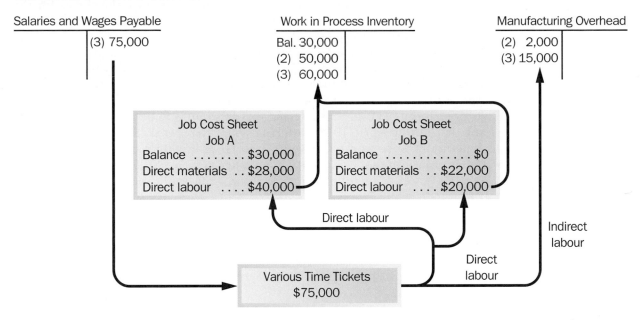

The following entry records the incurrence of these costs:

(4)

Manufacturing Overhead..	40,000	
Accounts Payable...		40,000

In addition, assume that during April, Rand Company recognized $13,000 in accrued property taxes and that $7,000 in prepaid insurance expired on factory buildings and equipment. The following entry records these items:

(5)

Manufacturing Overhead..	20,000	
Property Taxes Payable...		13,000
Prepaid Insurance...		7,000

Finally, assume that the company recognized $18,000 in depreciation on factory equipment during April. The following entry records the accrual of this depreciation:

(6)

Manufacturing Overhead..	18,000	
Accumulated Depreciation...		18,000

In short, *all* manufacturing overhead costs are recorded directly into the Manufacturing Overhead account as they are incurred day by day throughout a period. It is important to understand that Manufacturing Overhead is a control account for many—perhaps thousands of—subsidiary accounts, such as Indirect Materials, Indirect Labour, and Factory Utilities. As the Manufacturing Overhead account is debited for costs during a period, the various subsidiary accounts are also debited. In the example above and also in the assignment material for this chapter, we omit the entries to the subsidiary accounts for the sake of brevity.

▇ THE APPLICATION OF MANUFACTURING OVERHEAD

LEARNING OBJECTIVE
Apply overhead cost to work in process using a predetermined overhead rate.

Since actual manufacturing overhead costs are charged to the Manufacturing Overhead control account rather than to Work in Process, how are manufacturing overhead costs assigned to Work in Process? The answer is, by means of the predetermined overhead rate. Recall from our discussion earlier in the chapter that a predetermined overhead rate is established at the beginning of each year. The rate is calculated by dividing the estimated total manufacturing overhead cost for the year by the estimated total units in the allocation base (measured in machine-hours, direct labour-hours, or some other base). The predetermined overhead rate is then used to apply overhead costs to jobs. For example, if direct labour-hours is the allocation base, overhead cost is applied to each job by multiplying the number of direct labour-hours charged to the job by the predetermined overhead rate.

To illustrate, assume that Rand Company has used machine-hours in computing its predetermined overhead rate and that this rate is $6 per machine-hour. Also assume that during April, 10,000 machine-hours were worked on Job A and 5,000 machine-hours were worked on Job B (a total of 15,000 machine-hours). Thus, $90,000 in overhead cost (15,000 machine-hours × $6 = $90,000) would be applied to Work in Process. The following entry records the application of Manufacturing Overhead to Work in Process:

(7)

Work in Process..	90,000	
Manufacturing Overhead		90,000

The flow of costs through the Manufacturing Overhead account is detailed in Exhibit 5–8.

The "actual overhead costs" in the Manufacturing Overhead account shown in Exhibit 5–8 are the costs that were added to the account in entries (2) through (6). Observe that the incurrence of these actual overhead costs [entries (2) through (6)] and the application of overhead to Work in Process [entry (7)] represent two separate and entirely distinct processes.

The Concept of a Clearing Account   The Manufacturing Overhead account operates as a clearing account. As we have noted, actual factory overhead costs are debited to the accounts as they are incurred day by day throughout the year. At certain intervals during the year, usually when a job is completed, overhead cost is released

EXHIBIT 5–8   The Flow of Costs in Overhead Application

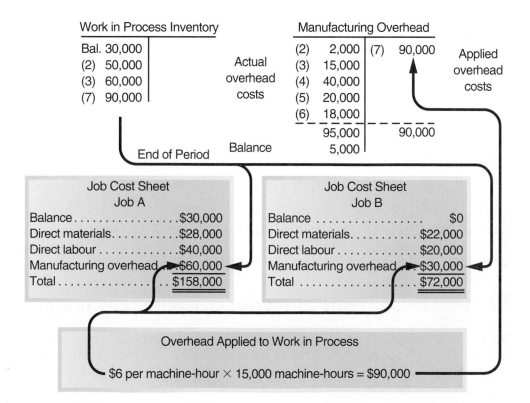

from the Manufacturing Overhead account and is applied to the Work in Process account by means of the predetermined overhead rate. Work in Process is debited and Manufacturing Overhead is credited. This sequence of events is illustrated as follows:

Manufacturing Overhead
(a clearing account)

Actual overhead costs are charged to the account as these costs are incurred day by day throughout the period. $\longrightarrow$

$\longrightarrow$ Overhead is applied to Work in Process using the predetermined overhead rate.

The actual overhead costs incurred and shown as debits in the Manufacturing Overhead account are a result of many different types of overhead costs. A brief list of some of the different types is presented in the journal entries, numbers 4, 5 and 6, or in the schedule of cost of goods manufactured, shown in Exhibit 5–11 or previously in Exhibit 2–4. The clearing account concept actually represents a general ledger control account for a subsidiary ledger that contains the detailed information on each type of overhead cost.

As we emphasized earlier, the predetermined overhead rate is based entirely on estimates of what overhead costs are *expected* to be, and it is established before the year begins. As a result, the overhead cost applied during a year will almost certainly turn out to be more or less than the overhead cost that is actually incurred. For example, notice from Exhibit 5–8 that Rand Company's actual overhead costs for the period are $5,000 greater than the overhead cost that was applied to Work in Process, resulting in a $5,000 debit balance in the Manufacturing Overhead account. We will reserve discussion of what to do with this $5,000 balance until a later section in this chapter, Complications of Overhead Application.

For the moment, we can conclude by noting from Exhibit 5–8 that the cost of a completed job consists of the actual materials cost of the job, the actual labour cost of the job, and the overhead cost *applied* to the job. Pay particular attention to the following subtle but important point: *Actual overhead costs are not charged to jobs; actual overhead costs do not appear on the job cost sheet, nor do they appear in the Work in Process account. Only the applied overhead cost, based on the predetermined overhead rate, appears on the job cost sheet and in the Work in Process account.* Study this point carefully.

> **Instant Quiz 5-4**
> Explain why companies use predetermined overhead rates rather than actual manufacturing overhead costs to apply overhead to jobs.

Non-manufacturing Costs

In addition to manufacturing costs, companies also incur marketing and selling costs. As explained in Chapter 2, these costs should be treated as period expenses and charged directly to the income statement. *Non-manufacturing costs should not go into the Manufacturing Overhead account.* To illustrate the correct treatment of non-manufacturing costs, assume that Rand Company incurred $30,000 of selling and administrative salaries during April. The following entry records these salaries:

(8)

Salaries Expense..	30,000	
Salaries and Wages Payable......................................		30,000

Assume that depreciation on office equipment during April was $7,000. The entry is as follows:

(9)

Depreciation Expense...	7,000	
Accumulated Depreciation..		7,000

Pay particular attention to the difference between this entry and entry (6), where we recorded depreciation on factory equipment. In journal entry (6), depreciation on factory equipment was debited to Manufacturing Overhead and is therefore a product cost. In journal entry (9) above, depreciation on office equipment was debited to Depreciation Expense. Depreciation on office equipment is considered to be a period expense rather than a product cost.

Finally, assume that advertising was $42,000 and that other selling and administrative expenses in April totalled $8,000. The following entry records these items:

(10)

Advertising Expense...	42,000	
Other Selling and Administrative Expense...	8,000	
Accounts Payable*..		50,000

*Other accounts, such as Cash, may be credited.

Because the amounts in entries (8) through (10) all go directly into expense accounts, they have no effect on product costs. The same is true of any other selling and administrative expenses incurred during April, including sales commissions, depreciation on sales equipment, rent on office facilities, insurance on office facilities, and related costs.

The distinction between manufacturing overhead costs and non-manufacturing costs such as selling and administrative expenses is sometimes difficult because of the type of cost. For example, depreciation and salaries should be classified as product costs if related to manufacturing but are classified as period costs and expensed if related to non-manufacturing activities. In practice, the classification has to be based on what the firm does to incur the costs. If it sells or markets, then this is not production and the distinction is clear. If it involves administration, then the distinction depends on what is administered and how important it is to decision making to separate production administration from overall administration. For example, if all the company does is produce the Hibernia oil platform, then administration is production (manufacturing) overhead. However, if the company is administering many jobs and marketing new jobs at the same time, it may not be able to distinguish overhead from administrative time on the part of senior management. Thus, unless costs are needed for a cost-recovery billing, administration salaries expense may be the expeditious way to treat the salaries.

■ COST OF GOODS MANUFACTURED

LEARNING OBJECTIVE 6
Prepare schedules of cost of goods manufactured and cost of goods sold.

When a job is completed, the finished output is transferred from the production departments to the finished goods warehouse. By this time, the Accounting Department will have charged the job with direct materials and direct labour cost, and manufacturing overhead will have been applied using the predetermined rate. A transfer of these costs must be made within the costing system that *parallels* the physical transfer of the goods to the finished goods warehouse. The costs of the completed job are transferred out of the Work in Process account and into the Finished Goods account. The sum of all amounts transferred between these two accounts represents the cost of goods manufactured for the period.

In the case of Rand Company, assume that Job A was completed during April. The following entry transfers the cost of Job A from Work in Process to Finished Goods:

(11)

Finished Goods Inventory..	158,000	
Work in Process Inventory..		158,000

The $158,000 represents the completed cost of Job A, as shown on the job cost sheet in Exhibit 5–8. Since Job A was the only job completed during April, the $158,000 also represents the cost of goods manufactured for the month.

Job B was not completed by month-end, so its cost will remain in the Work in Process account and carry over to the next month. If a balance sheet is prepared at the end of April, the cost accumulated thus far on Job B will appear as "Work in Process Inventory" in the assets section.

Cost of Goods Sold

As units in finished goods are shipped to customers, their cost is transferred from the Finished Goods account into the Cost of Goods Sold account. If a complete job is shipped, as in the case where a job has been done to a customer's specifications, then it is a simple matter to transfer the entire cost appearing on the job cost sheet into the Cost of Goods Sold account. In most cases, however, only a portion of the units involved in a particular job will be immediately sold. In these situations, the unit cost must be used to determine how much product cost should be removed from Finished Goods and charged to Cost of Goods Sold.

For Rand Company, we will assume that 750 of the 1,000 gold medallions in Job A were shipped to customers by the end of the month, for total sales revenue of $225,000. Since 1,000 units were produced and the total cost of the job from the job cost sheet was $158,000, the unit product cost was $158. The following journal entries record the sale (all sales are on account):

(12)

Accounts Receivable..	225,000	
Sales...		225,000

(13)

Cost of Goods Sold..	118,500	
Finished Goods Inventory..		118,500
($158 per unit × 750 units = $118,500)		

With entry (13), the flow of costs through our job-order costing system is completed.

Summary of Cost Flows

To pull the entire Rand Company example together, journal entries (1) through (13) are summarized in Exhibit 5–9. The flow of costs through the accounts is presented in T-account form in Exhibit 5–10.

Exhibit 5–11 presents a schedule of cost of goods manufactured and a schedule of cost of goods sold for Rand Company. Note particularly from Exhibit 5–11 that the manufacturing overhead cost on the schedule of cost of goods manufactured is the overhead applied to jobs during the month—not the actual manufacturing overhead costs incurred. The reason for this can be traced back to journal entry (7) and the T-account for Work in Process that appears in Exhibit 5–10. Under a normal costing system as illustrated in this chapter, applied—not actual—overhead costs are assigned to jobs and thus to Work in Process Inventory. In contrast, in Chapter 2, actual overhead costs were assigned to Work in Process and included in the schedule of cost of goods manufactured. This is because we had not introduced the concept of normal costing in that chapter. Note also that the cost of goods manufactured for the month ($158,000) agrees with the amount transferred from Work in Process to Finished Goods for the month, as recorded earlier in entry (11). Also note that this $158,000 figure is used in computing the cost of goods sold for the month.

An income statement for April is presented in Exhibit 5–12. Observe that the cost of goods sold figure on this statement ($123,500) is carried down from Exhibit 5–11.

EXHIBIT 5-9 Summary of
Rand Company Journal Entries

(1)		
Raw Materials	60,000	
Accounts Payable		60,000
(2)		
Work in Process	50,000	
Manufacturing Overhead	2,000	
Raw Materials		52,000
(3)		
Work in Process	60,000	
Manufacturing Overhead	15,000	
Salaries and Wages Payable		75,000
(4)		
Manufacturing Overhead	40,000	
Accounts Payable		40,000
(5)		
Manufacturing Overhead	20,000	
Property Taxes Payable		13,000
Prepaid Insurance		7,000
(6)		
Manufacturing Overhead	18,000	
Accumulated Depreciation		18,000
(7)		
Work in Process	90,000	
Manufacturing Overhead		90,000
(8)		
Salaries Expense	30,000	
Salaries and Wages Payable		30,000
(9)		
Depreciation Expense	7,000	
Accumulated Depreciation		7,000
(10)		
Advertising Expense	42,000	
Other Selling and Administrative Expense	8,000	
Accounts Payable		50,000
(11)		
Finished Goods	158,000	
Work in Process		158,000
(12)		
Accounts Receivable	225,000	
Sales		225,000
(13)		
Cost of Goods Sold	118,500	
Finished Goods		118,500

EXHIBIT 5–10   Summary of Cost Flows—Rand Company

Raw Materials				
Bal.	7,000	(2)	52,000	
(1)	60,000			
Bal.	15,000			

Work in Process				
Bal.	30,000	(11)	158,000	
(2)	50,000			
(3)	60,000			
(7)	90,000			
Bal.	72,000			

Finished Goods				
Bal.	10,000	(13)	118,500	
(11)	158,000			
Bal.	49,500			

Manufacturing Overhead				
(2)	2,000	(7)	90,000	
(3)	15,000			
(4)	40,000			
(5)	20,000			
(6)	18,000			
Bal.	5,000			

Accumulated Depreciation			
		XX	
	(6)	18,000	
	(9)	7,000	

Cost of Goods Sold		
(13)	118,500	

Accounts Payable			
		XX	
	(1)	60,000	
	(4)	40,000	
	(10)	50,000	

Salaries and Wages Payable			
		XX	
	(3)	75,000	
	(8)	30,000	

Property Taxes Payable			
		XX	
	(5)	13,000	

Accounts Receivable			
XX*			
(12)	225,000		

Prepaid Insurance			
XX			
	(5)	7,000	

Capital Stock	
	XX

Retained Earnings	
	XX

Sales		
	(12)	225,000

Salaries Expense		
(8)	30,000	

Depreciation Expense		
(9)	7,000	

Advertising Expense		
(10)	42,000	

Other Selling and Administrative Expense		
(10)	8,000	

Explanation of entries:
(1) Raw materials purchased.
(2) Direct and indirect materials issued into production.
(3) Direct and indirect factory labour cost incurred.
(4) Utilities and other factory costs incurred.
(5) Property taxes and insurance incurred on the factory.
(6) Depreciation recorded on factory assets.
(7) Overhead cost applied to Work in Process.
(8) Administrative salaries expense incurred.
(9) Depreciation recorded on office equipment.
(10) Advertising and other expense incurred.
(11) Cost of goods manufactured transferred into finished goods.
(12) Sale of job A recorded.
(13) Cost of goods sold recorded for job A.

*XX = Normal balance in the account (for example, Accounts Receivable normally carries a debit balance).

EXHIBIT 5-11 Schedules of Cost of Goods Manufactured and Cost of Goods Sold

Cost of Goods Manufactured

Direct materials:

Raw materials inventory, beginning..............	$ 7,000	
Add: Purchases of raw materials	60,000	
Total raw materials available	67,000	
Deduct: Raw materials inventory, ending.........	15,000	
Raw materials used in production	52,000	
Less indirect materials included in manufacturing overhead.....................................	2,000	$ 50,000
Direct labour		60,000
Manufacturing overhead applied to work in process .		90,000
Total manufacturing costs		200,000
Add: Beginning work in process inventory...........		30,000
		230,000
Deduct: Ending work in process inventory...........		72,000
Cost of goods manufactured.......................		$158,000

Cost of Goods Sold

Finished goods inventory, beginning................		$ 10,000
Add: Cost of goods manufactured..................		158,000
Goods available for sale...........................		168,000
Deduct: Finished goods inventory, ending...........		49,500
Unadjusted cost of goods sold		118,500
Add: Underapplied overhead*......................		5,000
Adjusted cost of goods sold........................		$123,500

*The underapplied overhead is added to cost of goods sold. If overhead was overapplied, it would be deducted from costs of goods sold.

EXHIBIT 5-12 Income Statement

RAND COMPANY
Income Statement
For the Month Ending April 30

Sales..		$225,000
Less cost of goods sold ($118,500 + $5,000).............		123,500
Gross margin		101,500
Less selling and administrative expenses:		
Salaries expense.....................................	$30,000	
Depreciation expense	7,000	
Advertising expense.................................	42,000	
Other expense.....................................	8,000	87,000
Net income		$ 14,500

■ COMPLICATIONS OF OVERHEAD APPLICATION

LEARNING OBJECTIVE 7

Compute underapplied or overapplied overhead cost, and prepare the journal entry to close the balance in manufacturing overhead to the appropriate accounts.

We need to consider two complications relating to overhead application. These are (1) the computation of underapplied and overapplied overhead and (2) the disposition of any balance remaining in the Manufacturing Overhead account at the end of a period.

Underapplied and Overapplied Overhead

Since the predetermined overhead rate is established before a period begins and is based entirely on estimated data, there will generally be a difference between the amount of overhead cost applied to Work in Process and the amount of overhead cost actually incurred during a period. In the case of Rand Company, for example, the predetermined overhead rate of $6 per hour resulted in $90,000 of overhead cost being applied to Work in Process, whereas actual overhead costs for April proved to be $95,000 (as shown in Exhibit 5-8). The difference between the overhead cost applied to Work in Process and the actual overhead costs of a period is termed either **underapplied overhead** or **overapplied overhead**. For Rand Company, overhead was underapplied because the applied cost ($90,000) was $5,000 less than the actual cost ($95,000). If the situation had been reversed and the company had applied $95,000 in overhead cost to Work in Process while incurring actual overhead costs of only $90,000, then the overhead would have been overapplied.

What causes underapplied or overapplied overhead? The causes can be complex, and a full explanation will have to wait for Chapter 10. The basic problem is that the method of applying overhead to jobs using a predetermined overhead rate assumes that actual overhead costs will be proportional to the actual amount of the allocation base incurred during the period. If, for example, the predetermined overhead rate is $6 per machine-hour, then it is assumed that actual overhead costs incurred will be $6 for every machine-hour that is actually worked. There are at least two reasons why this may not be true. First, much of the overhead consists of fixed costs that do not change as the number of machine-hours incurred goes up or down. Second, spending on overhead items may or may not be under control. A fuller explanation of the causes of underapplied and overapplied overhead will have to wait for later chapters.

To illustrate what can happen, suppose that two companies—Turbo Crafters and Black & Howell—have prepared the following estimated data for the coming year:

	Company	
	Turbo Crafters	**Black & Howell**
Predetermined overhead rate based on	Machine-hours	Direct materials cost
Estimated manufacturing overhead (a)	$300,000	$120,000
Estimated amount of allocation base (b)...............	75,000	80,000
Predetermined overhead rate, (a) ÷ (b)	$4 per machine-hour	150% of direct materials cost

Note that when the allocation base is dollars—such as direct materials cost in the case of Black & Howell—the predetermined overhead rate is a *percentage* of the allocation base. When dollars are divided by dollars, the result is a *percentage*.

Now assume that because of unexpected changes in overhead spending and changes in demand for the companies' products, the *actual* overhead cost and the *actual* activity recorded during the year in each company are as follows:

	Company	
	Turbo Crafters	**Black & Howell**
Actual manufacturing overhead costs...................	$290,000	$130,000
Actual amount of allocation base	68,000	$ 90,000

For each company, note that the actual data for both cost and the allocation base differ from the estimates used in computing the predetermined overhead rate. This results in underapplied and overapplied overhead as follows:

	Company	
	Turbo Crafters	**Black & Howell**
Actual manufacturing overhead cost....................	$290,000	$130,000
Manufactured overhead cost applied to Work in Process during the year:		
Predetermined overhead rate (a).....................	$4 per machine-hour	150% of direct material cost
Actual total amount of allocation base (b)............	68,000 machine-hours	$90,000 direct material cost
Manufacturing overhead applied (a) × (b)..............	$ 272,000	$135,000
Underapplied (overapplied) manufacturing overhead...	$ 18,000	$ (5,000)

Underapplied overhead
A debit balance in the Manufacturing Overhead account that arises when the amount of overhead cost actually incurred is greater than the amount of overhead cost applied to Work in Process during a period.

Overapplied overhead
A credit balance in the Manufacturing Overhead account that arises when the amount of overhead cost applied to Work in Process is greater than the amount of overhead cost actually incurred during a period.

For Turbo Crafters, notice that the amount of overhead cost applied to Work in Process ($272,000) is less than the actual overhead cost for the year ($290,000). Therefore, overhead is underapplied. Also notice that the original estimate of overhead in Turbo Crafters ($300,000) is not directly involved in this computation. Its impact is felt only through the $4 predetermined overhead rate that is used.

For Black & Howell, the amount of overhead cost applied to Work in Process ($135,000) is greater than the actual overhead cost for the year ($130,000), so overhead is overapplied.

Disposition of Underapplied or Overapplied Overhead Balances

What disposition should be made of any underapplied or overapplied balance remaining in the Manufacturing Overhead account at the end of a period? Under current accounting standards applicable in Canada (IAS 2):

> *Unallocated overheads are recognised as an expense in the period in which they are incurred. In periods of abnormally high production, the amount of fixed overhead allocated to each unit of production is decreased so that inventories are not measured above cost.*

Note that IAS 2 is a financial reporting standard that is not necessarily required to be followed for internal purposes. Even so, most companies treat accounting for inventory costs consistently for both financial reporting and internal management decision making for simplicity's sake. Thus, the balance in the account must be treated in one of two ways depending on whether it was under- or overapplied during the year:

1. If overhead was underapplied, the remaining balance is closed out to Cost of Goods Sold.
2. If overhead was overapplied, the remaining balance is allocated among Work in Process, Finished Goods, and Cost of Goods Sold in proportion to the overhead applied during the current period in the ending balances of these accounts.

> **Instant Quiz 5-5**
> Explain conceptually why it makes sense to close out underapplied overhead to Cost of Goods Sold but then to allocate overapplied overhead between Work in Process and Finished Goods Inventory accounts on the Balance Sheet and Cost of Goods Sold on the Income Statement.

Close out Underapplied Overhead to Cost of Goods Sold   As mentioned above, closing out the balance in Manufacturing Overhead to Cost of Goods Sold is simpler than the allocation method. Returning to the example of Rand Company, the entry to close the $5,000 of underapplied overhead to Cost of Goods Sold is as follows:

(14)

Cost of Goods Sold...	5,000	
Manufacturing Overhead..		5,000

Note that since there is a debit balance in the Manufacturing Overhead account, Manufacturing Overhead must be credited to close out the account. This has the effect of increasing Cost of Goods Sold for April to $123,500:

Unadjusted cost of goods sold [from entry (13)]	$ 118,500
Add underapplied overhead [entry (14) above]	5,000
Adjusted cost of goods sold	$123,500

After this adjustment is made, Rand Company's income statement for April will appear as was shown earlier in Exhibit 5–12.

Allocate Overapplied Overhead among Accounts   Allocation of overapplied overhead assigns overhead costs to where they would have gone in the first place had it not been for the errors in the estimates going into the predetermined overhead rate.

For illustrative purposes, assume the $5,000 remaining balance in the Manufacturing Overhead account of Rand Company was overapplied. First, it is necessary to determine the amount of overhead applied during April in each of the accounts. The computations are as follows:

Overhead applied in work in process inventory, April 30............................	$30,000	33.33%
Overhead applied in finished goods inventory, April 30		
($60,000 ÷ 1,000 units = $60 per unit) × 250 units	15,000	16.67%
Overhead applied in cost of goods sold, April		
($60,000 ÷ 1,000 units = $60 per unit) × 750 units..........................	45,000	50.00%
Total overhead applied	$90,000	100.00%

Based on the above percentages, the overapplied overhead (i.e., a credit balance in Manufacturing Overhead) is allocated as in the following journal entry:

Manufacturing Overhead	5,000.00	
Work in Process (33.33% × $5,000)..		1,666.50
Finished Goods (16.67% × $5,000)...		833.50
Cost of Goods Sold (50.00% × $5,000)..		2,500.00

Note that the first step in the allocation was to determine the amount of overhead applied in each account. For Finished Goods, for example, the total amount of overhead applied to Job A, $60,000, was divided by the total number of units in Job A, 1,000 units, to arrive at the average overhead applied of $60 per unit. Since 250 units from Job A were still in ending finished goods inventory, the amount of overhead applied in the Finished Goods Inventory account was $60 per unit multiplied by 250 units, or $15,000 in total.

An alternative but less accurate way to allocate overapplied overhead among Work in Process, Finished Goods, and Cost of Goods Sold is to use the entire cost of manufacturing in each account.

Had we chosen this method to allocate the overapplied overhead in the Rand Company example, the computations and entry would have been as follows:

Work in process inventory, April 30		$ 72,000	36.00%
Finished goods inventory, April 30.		49,500	24.75%
Cost of goods sold..	$118,500		
Less: Work in process inventory, April 1.............................	30,000		
Less: Finished goods inventory, April 1..............................	10,000	78,500	39.25%
Total...		$200,000	100.00%
Manufacturing Overhead	5,000		
Work in Process (36.0% × $5,000).................................		1,800	
Finished Goods (24.75% × $5,000)		1,237	
Cost of Goods Sold (39.25% × $5,000)............................		1,963	

A comparison of the percentages above with those using only overhead suggests that total manufacturing costs and overhead were not in the same proportions in each account. This difference is the inaccuracy in the problem resulting from using total manufacturing costs to conduct the allocation.

The rationale for deducting the beginning work in process and finished goods inventories from the cost of goods sold is to permit the allocation to be based on costs from the current period. By doing so, the 39.25% in the Rand Company example reflects only total manufacturing costs from April and thus corresponds to the period in which the overapplied overhead occurred. Without this adjustment, cost of goods sold would be assigned the overhead difference based on costs carried over from March and thus bear a disproportionate amount of the overapplied overhead.

A summary of the concepts discussed in this section is presented in a Learning Aid.

LEARNING AID

SUMMARY OF OVERHEAD CONCEPTS

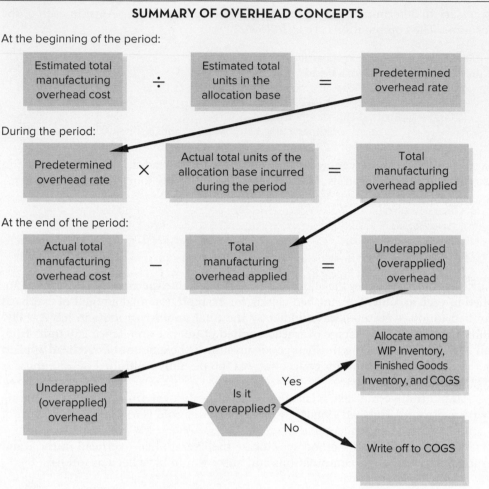

At the beginning of the period:

Estimated total manufacturing overhead cost ÷ Estimated total units in the allocation base = Predetermined overhead rate

During the period:

Predetermined overhead rate × Actual total units of the allocation base incurred during the period = Total manufacturing overhead applied

At the end of the period:

Actual total manufacturing overhead cost − Total manufacturing overhead applied = Underapplied (overapplied) overhead

Underapplied (overapplied) overhead → Is it overapplied?

Yes → Allocate among WIP Inventory, Finished Goods Inventory, and COGS

No → Write off to COGS

A General Model of Product Cost Flows

The flow of costs in a product costing system is presented in the form of a T-account model in Exhibit 5–13. This model applies as much to a process costing system as it does to a job-order costing system. Examination of this model can be very helpful in gaining a perspective as to how costs enter a system, flow through it, and finally end up as Cost of Goods Sold on the income statement.

Variations from the General Model of Product Cost Flow

Costing systems can vary from what is reflected by the general model. While the general model is the most complete description, circumstances may make such a complete system too costly. For example, a system variation known as *backflush costing* can permit labour charges to be made directly to manufacturing overhead. Then overhead is applied to the cost of completed jobs along with raw materials, so that the need to keep work in process records can be avoided. Such a minimal treatment of work in process is justified in a mechanized lean manufacturing (JIT) environment. Cost of completed jobs still reflects the material and overhead (including labour), but the record-keeping system reflects the simplified needs of the production environment.

EXHIBIT 5-13   A General Model of Cost Flows

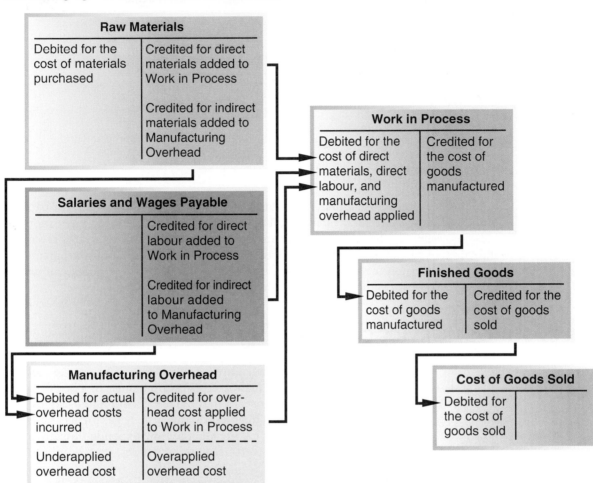

Multiple Predetermined Overhead Rates

Our discussion of overhead in this chapter has assumed that there is a single predetermined overhead rate for an entire factory called a **plantwide overhead rate**. This is, in fact, common practice—particularly in smaller companies. But in larger companies, *multiple predetermined overhead rates* are often used. In a **multiple predetermined overhead rate** system, there is usually a different overhead rate for each production department. Such a system, while more complex, is considered to be more accurate because it can reflect differences across departments in how overhead costs are incurred. For example, overhead might be allocated based on direct labour-hours in departments that are relatively labour intensive and based on machine-hours in departments that are relatively machine intensive. When multiple predetermined overhead rates are used, overhead is applied in each department according to its own overhead rate as a job proceeds through the department.

To illustrate, refer to the data in the following table, where Cook Company has two departments (A and B) and several jobs in process. Data are provided for two of these jobs (X and Y). If the company uses a plantwide overhead rate of $12 ($336,000 ÷ 28,000 DLH), then the overhead costs applied to Job X and Job Y will be $8,400 ($12 × 700 hours + $12 × 0) and $12 ($12 × 0 hours + $12 × 1 hour), respectively. However, if overhead is applied using department overhead rates, then Job X will be assigned $2,800 ($4 × 700 direct labour-hours) and Job Y will be assigned $8,400 ($12 × 700 machine-hours):

Plantwide overhead rate
A single predetermined overhead rate used throughout a plant.

Multiple predetermined overhead rate
A costing system in which there are multiple overhead cost pools with a different predetermined rate for each cost pool, rather than a single predetermined overhead rate for the entire company. Frequently, each production department is treated as a separate overhead cost pool.

Cook Company	Department A	Department B	Total
Overhead cost	$84,000	$252,000	$336,000
Direct labour-hours	21,000	7,000	28,000 DLH
Machine-hours	7,000	21,000	28,000 MH
Overhead cost driver	21,000 DLH	21,000 MH	
Overhead rate: Plantwide			$12 per DLH
By department	$ 4/DLH	$12/MH	
Direct labour-hours—Job X	700	0	
Direct labour-hours—Job Y	0	1	
Machine-hours—Job X	1	0	
Machine-hours—Job Y	0	700	

The decision to use a plantwide rate versus separate rates for each department comes down to costs versus benefits. It is cheaper to use a plantwide rate, since the costs of gathering and analyzing information are lower, but separate rates are more informative when the activities that drive overhead costs differ among departments. Improved decision making resulting from more accurate overhead data can justify the added costs of gathering separate departmental overhead data.

JOB-ORDER COSTING IN SERVICE COMPANIES

Job-order costing is used in service organizations, such as law firms, movie studios, hospitals, and repair shops, as well as in manufacturing companies. In a law firm, for example, each client is a "job," and the costs of that job are accumulated day by day on a job cost sheet as the client's case is handled by the firm. Legal forms and similar inputs represent the direct materials for the job; the time expended by attorneys is like direct labour; and the costs of secretaries and legal aides, rent, depreciation, and so forth, represent the overhead.

In a movie studio such as Columbia Pictures, each film produced by the studio is a "job," and costs of direct materials (costumes, props, film, etc.) and direct labour

IN BUSINESS

The Royal Ontario Museum, Science World British Columbia, and the Maritime Museum of the Atlantic all have permanent exhibits that can be seen year round. In addition, they mount time-limited special exhibits to bring in new patrons and to encourage regular patrons to attend more often. But how much does a museum special exhibit cost? According to Mark Walhimer, Managing Partner of Museum Planning, LLC, the answer depends on the type of artifacts displayed and the complexity of the exhibit's design. "An Art exhibit of mostly flat art work, little mount making or rigging can start at $75 per square foot including graphics. An interactive Science Center exhibition with a high density of interactive exhibits can reach $550 per square foot and beyond. When Disney does preliminary estimates of their attractions they budget $650 per square foot," says Walhimer in a blog posting. While job-order costing was developed to deal with specialized and identifiable manufacturing "jobs," job-order costing techniques can also be usefully applied to estimating the cost to mount special artistic or cultural exhibits. Costing these exhibits is important to other related decisions, including pricing of special exhibit tickets, and to fundraising through current museum patrons and government programs to ensure the exhibits are both culturally and financially successful.

Source: http://museumplanner.org/how-much-do-exhibits-cost/.

(actors, directors, and extras) are charged to each film's job cost sheet. A share of the studio's overhead costs, such as utilities, depreciation of equipment, and wages of maintenance workers, is also charged to each film.

In sum, job-order costing is a versatile and widely used costing method that may be encountered in virtually any organization that provides diverse products or services.

■ USE OF INFORMATION TECHNOLOGY

Earlier in the chapter, we discussed how bar code technology can be used to record labour time—reducing the drudgery in that task and increasing accuracy. Bar codes have many other uses.

In a company with a well-developed bar code system, the manufacturing cycle begins with the receipt of a customer's order in electronic form. Until very recently, the order would have been received via electronic data interchange (EDI), which involves a network of computers linking organizations. An EDI network allows companies to electronically exchange business documents and other information that extends into all areas of business activity, from ordering raw materials to shipping completed goods. EDI was developed in the 1980s and requires significant investment in programming and networking hardware. Recently, EDI has been challenged by far cheaper Internet-based alternatives— XML (Extensible Markup Language), which is an extension of HTML (Hypertext Markup Language), and JSON (JavaScript Object Notation). HTML tells the browser how to display information on your screen, but the computer doesn't know what the information is—it just displays it. XML and JSON provide additional tags that identify the kind of information that is being exchanged. For example, price data might be coded as <price> 14.95 <price>. When the computer reads this piece of data and sees the tag <price> surrounding 14.95, it immediately knows that this is a price. These tags can designate many different kinds of information—customer orders, medical records, bank statements, and so on—and the tags indicate to the computer how to display, store, and retrieve the information. Office Depot was an early adopter of XML, which it is using to facilitate e-commerce with its big customers.

Once an order has been received via EDI or over the Internet in the form of an XML or JSON file, the computer draws up a list of required raw materials and sends out electronic purchase orders to suppliers. When materials arrive at the company's plant from the suppliers, bar codes that have been applied by the suppliers are scanned to update inventory records and to trigger payment for the materials.

Goods ready to be shipped are packed into containers, which are bar-coded with information that includes the customer number, the type and quantity of goods being shipped, and the order number. This bar code is then used to prepare billing information and track the packed goods until they are placed on a carrier for shipment to the customer. Some customers require that the packed goods be bar-coded with point-of-sale labels that can be scanned at retail checkout counters. These scans allow the retailer to update inventory records, verify price, and generate a customer receipt.

In short, bar code technology is being integrated into all areas of business activity. When combined with EDI or web-based data interchange, it eliminates a lot of clerical drudgery and allows companies to capture and exchange more data and to analyze and report information much more quickly and completely and with less error than with manual systems.

An enterprise resource planning (ERP) system represents a real-time computer system using a single uniform database that is coupled with modules for accounting, logistics, and human resources. Full use of these modules permits an integrated system response for Internet-based orders in XML or JSON, supplier purchases and payables, inventory management, production, sales and receivables, treasury, and capital (fixed) assets management. Major suppliers of such ERP systems include Oracle, SAP, and Epicor. Other companies provide certified software that is compatible with these systems.

KNOWLEDGE IN ACTION

Managers can apply their knowledge about job-order costing when
- Calculating the product/service cost when many different products/services are produced in the year
- Setting prices to ensure the price exceeds the cost to produce the product or service
- Estimating the amount of overhead cost to apply to each of the various products or services produced
- Calculating the value of inventory included on the Balance Sheet and the Cost of Goods Sold disclosed on the Income Statement

---

SUMMARY

- Job-order costing and process costing are widely used to track costs. Job-order costing is used in situations where the organization offers many different products or services, such as in furniture manufacturers, hospitals, and legal firms. [LO1]
- Process costing is used where units of product are homogeneous, such as in flour milling or cement production. [LO1]
- Materials requisition forms and labour time tickets are used to assign direct materials and direct labour costs to jobs in a job-order costing system. Manufacturing overhead costs are assigned to jobs through use of a predetermined overhead rate. These costs are recorded in the general ledger using journal entries that reflect the cost flows through the job-order system. [LO2, LO3, LO4]
- The predetermined overhead rate is established before the period begins by dividing the estimated total manufacturing overhead cost for the period by the estimated total allocation base for the period. The most frequently used allocation bases are direct labour-hours and machine-hours. Overhead is applied to jobs by multiplying the predetermined overhead rate by the actual amount of the allocation base used by the job. [LO3, LO5]
- Since the predetermined overhead rate is based on estimates, the actual overhead cost incurred during a period may be more or less than the amount of overhead cost applied to production. Such a difference is referred to as *underapplied* or *overapplied overhead*. [LO7]
- The schedules of Cost of Goods Manufactured and Cost of Goods Sold summarize the flow of costs through the job-order costing system. Any under- or overapplied overhead for a period can be (1) closed out to Cost of Goods Sold; (2) allocated among Work in Process, Finished Goods, and Cost of Goods Sold; or (3) carried forward to the end of the year. [LO6, LO7]
- When overhead is underapplied, manufacturing overhead costs have been understated and therefore inventories and/or expenses must be adjusted upward. When overhead is overapplied, manufacturing overhead costs have been overstated and therefore inventories and/or expenses must be adjusted downward. [LO7]

REVIEW PROBLEM: JOB-ORDER COSTING

Hogle Company is a manufacturing firm that uses job-order costing. On January 1, the beginning of its fiscal year, the company's inventory balances were as follows:

Raw materials	$20,000
Work in process	15,000
Finished goods	30,000

The company applies overhead cost to jobs on the basis of machine-hours worked. For the current year, the company estimated that it would work 75,000 machine-hours and incur $450,000 in manufacturing overhead cost. The following transactions were recorded for the year:

a.   Raw materials were purchased on account: $410,000.

b.   Raw materials were requisitioned for use in production: $380,000 ($360,000 direct materials and $20,000 indirect materials).

c.   The following costs were incurred for employee services: direct labour, $75,000; indirect labour, $110,000; sales commissions, $90,000; and administrative salaries, $200,000.

d.   Sales travel costs were incurred: $17,000.

e.   Utility costs were incurred in the factory: $43,000.

f.   Advertising costs were incurred: $180,000.

g.   Depreciation was recorded for the year: $350,000 (80% relates to factory operations, and 20% relates to selling and administrative activities).

h.   Insurance expired during the year: $10,000 (70% relates to factory operations, and the remaining 30% relates to selling and administrative activities).

i.   Manufacturing overhead was applied to production. Due to greater than expected demand for its products, the company worked 80,000 machine-hours during the year.

j.   Goods costing $900,000 to manufacture according to their job cost sheets were completed during the year.

k.   Goods were sold on account to customers during the year at a total selling price of $1,500,000. The goods cost $870,000 to manufacture according to their job cost sheets.

Required:
1.   Prepare journal entries to record the preceding transactions.
2.   Post the entries in (1) above to T-accounts (don't forget to enter the opening balances in the inventory accounts).
3.   Is Manufacturing Overhead underapplied or overapplied for the year?
4.   Prepare a Schedule of Cost of Goods Manufactured and Cost of Goods Sold for the year. Prepare the appropriate journal entry to dispose of under/overapplied overhead at year-end. If overhead is overapplied, allocate based on the entire cost of manufacturing in each of Work in Process, Finished Goods, and Cost of Goods Sold.
5.   Prepare an Income Statement for the year.

Solution to Review Problem

1.	*a.* Raw Materials..	410,000	
	Accounts Payable		410,000
	b. Work in Process..	360,000	
	Manufacturing Overhead..	20,000	
	Raw Materials		380,000
	c. Work in Process..	75,000	
	Manufacturing Overhead..	110,000	
	Sales Commissions Expense	90,000	
	Administrative Salaries Expense.....................................	200,000	
	Salaries and Wages Payable		475,000
	d. Sales Travel Expense...	17,000	
	Accounts Payable		17,000
	e. Manufacturing Overhead.......................................	43,000	
	Accounts Payable		43,000
	f. Advertising Expense	180,000	
	Accounts Payable		180,000
	g. Manufacturing Overhead.......................................	280,000	
	Depreciation Expense...	70,000	
	Accumulated Depreciation.......................................		350,000
	h. Manufacturing Overhead.......................................	7,000	
	Insurance Expense	3,000	
	Prepaid Insurance..		10,000

i.   The predetermined overhead rate for the year is computed as follows:

$$\frac{\text{Estimated manufacturing overhead, } \$450,000}{\text{Estimated machine-hours, } 75,000} = \$6 \text{ per machine-hour}$$

Based on the 80,000 machine-hours actually worked during the year, the company would apply $480,000 in overhead cost to production: 80,000 machine-hours × $6 = $480,000. The following entry records this application of overhead cost:

Work in Process..	480,000	
Manufacturing Overhead.....................................		480,000
j. Finished Goods...	900,000	
Work in Process..		900,000
k. Accounts Receivable...	1,500,000	
Sales		1,500,000
Cost of Goods Sold	870,000	
Finished Goods...		870,000

2.

Raw Materials

Bal.	20,000	(*b*)	380,000
(*a*)	410,000		
Bal.	50,000		

Work in Process

Bal.	15,000	(*j*)	900,000
(*b*)	360,000		
(*c*)	75,000		
(*i*)	480,000		
Bal.	30,000		

Finished Goods

Bal.	30,000	(*k*)	870,000
(*j*)	900,000		
Bal.	60,000		

Cost of Goods Sold

(*k*)	870,000		

Manufacturing Overhead

(*b*)	20,000	(*i*)	480,000
(*c*)	110,000		
(*e*)	43,000		
(*g*)	280,000		
(*h*)	7,000		
	460,000		480,000
		Bal.	20,000

Prepaid Insurance

		(*h*)	10,000

Sales Commissions Expense

(*c*)	90,000		

Accumulated Depreciation

		(*g*)	350,000

Accounts Receivable

(*k*)	1,500,000		

Administrative Salary Expense

(*c*)	200,000		

Sales Travel Expense

(*d*)	17,000		

Accounts Payable

		(*a*)	410,000
		(*d*)	17,000
		(*e*)	43,000
		(*f*)	180,000

Sales

		(*k*)	1,500,000

Advertising Expense

(*f*)	180,000		

Depreciation Expense

(*g*)	70,000		

Salaries and Wages Payable

		(*c*)	475,000

Insurance Expense

(*h*)	3,000		

3.   Manufacturing overhead is overapplied for the year.

4.

HOGLE COMPANY
Schedule of Cost of Goods Manufactured and Cost of Goods Sold
For the Year Ended December 31

Cost of Goods Manufactured

Direct Materials:

Raw materials inventory, January 1.........................	$ 20,000	
Add: Purchases of raw materials	410,000	
Total raw materials available	430,000	
Deduct: Raw materials inventory, December 31.................	50,000	
Raw materials used in production............................	380,000	
Less: Indirect materials	20,000	
Direct materials used in production.........................		$360,000
Direct labour		75,000
Manufacturing overhead applied to work in process		480,000
Total manufacturing costs		915,000
Add: Beginning work in process inventory....................		15,000
		930,000
Deduct: Ending work in process inventory		(30,000)
Cost of goods manufactured.................................		$900,000

Cost of Goods Sold

Finished goods inventory, January 1.........................		$ 30,000
Add: Cost of goods manufactured.............................		900,000
Goods available for sale....................................		930,000
Deduct: Finished goods inventory, December 31...............		(60,000)
Unadjusted cost of goods sold..............................		870,000
Deduct: Overapplied overhead*..............................		(18,000)
Adjusted cost of goods sold		$852,000

*The entry to dispose of the overapplied overhead is as follows:

Work in Process Inventory, December 31		$30,000	3%
Finished Goods Inventory, December 31		$60,000	7%
Unadjusted Cost of Goods Sold	$870,000		
Less Work in Process Inventory, January 1	$ (15,000)		90%
Less Finished Goods Inventory, January 1	$(30,000)	$825,000	
Total		$915,000	100%
Manufacturing Overhead	$20,000		
Work in Process ($20,000 × 3%)		$ 600	
Finished Goods ($20,000 × 7%)		1,400	
Cost of Goods Sold ($20,000 × 90%)		18,000	

5.

HOGLE COMPANY
Income Statement
For the Year Ended December 31

Sales...		$1,500,000
Less cost of goods sold.....................................		852,000
Gross margin...		648,000
Less selling and administrative expenses:		
Sales commissions expense	$ 90,000	
Administrative salaries expense............................	200,000	
Sales travel expense.......................................	17,000	
Advertising expense.......................................	180,000	
Depreciation expense	70,000	
Insurance expense...	3,000	560,000
Operating income		$ 88,000

GLOSSARY

 Review key terms and definitions on Connect.

DISCUSSION CASE

DISCUSSION CASE 5-1

Although job-order costing was originally developed for use in manufacturing environments, it is equally applicable in organizations that provide services rather than manufactured goods. A public accounting firm is one such organization.

Required:

Develop a list of "products" provided by the employees and partners of a typical public accounting office in your area. Next, develop a list of costs that would be incurred to provide each product/service in your first list. Consider which of these costs are direct and which are indirect (i.e., overhead), and identify an appropriate cost driver for each overhead type. How might this information be used to determine the price to charge one client of the public accounting firm for audit services in the coming year?

QUESTIONS

5-1 Why aren't actual overhead costs traced to jobs just as direct materials and direct labour costs are traced to jobs?

5-2 When would job-order costing be used instead of process costing?

5-3 What is the purpose of the job cost sheet in a job-order costing system?

5-4 What is a predetermined overhead rate, and how is it computed?

5-5 Explain how a sales order, a production order, a job cost sheet, a materials requisition form, and a labour time ticket are involved in producing and costing products.

5-6 What factors should be considered in selecting a base to be used in computing the predetermined overhead rate?

5-7 Define the term *cost driver* and indicate how it is used in job-order costing.

5-8 If a company fully allocates all of its overhead costs to jobs, does this guarantee that a profit will be earned for the period?

5-9 What account is credited when overhead cost is applied to work in process? Would you expect the amount applied for a period to equal the actual overhead costs of the period? Why or why not?

5-10 What is underapplied overhead? Overapplied overhead? What disposition is made of these amounts at the end of the period?

5-11 Provide two reasons why overhead might be underapplied in a given year.

5-12 What adjustment is made for underapplied overhead on the schedule of cost of goods sold? What adjustment is made for overapplied overhead?

5-13 Gorman Company applies overhead cost to jobs on the basis of direct labour cost. Job A, which was started and completed during the current period, shows charges of $6,000 for direct materials, $15,000 for direct labour, and $7,500 for overhead on its job cost sheet. Job B, which is still in process at year-end, shows charges of $2,500 for direct materials and $4,000 for direct labour. Should any overhead cost be added to Job B at year-end? Explain and calculate the amount, if necessary.

5-14 A company assigns overhead cost to completed jobs on the basis of 150% of direct labour cost. The job cost sheet for Job 313 shows that $12,000 in direct materials was used on the job and that $16,000 in direct labour cost was incurred. If 750 units were produced in Job 313, what is the unit product cost?

5-15 What is a plantwide overhead rate? Why are multiple overhead rates, rather than a plantwide overhead rate, used in some companies?

5-16 Under what conditions would direct labour be a poor allocation base to use in allocating manufacturing overhead?

5-17 "Predetermined overhead rates smooth product costs." Do you agree? Why?

5-18 Explain clearly why a portion of overapplied overhead for an interim period should be carried to the balance sheet. What conceptual factor is assumed in the argument?

5-19 Why does the calculation of the percentages for overapplied overhead reduce the costs of goods sold by the opening inventories? What would happen if such a deduction were not made?

EXERCISES

EXERCISE 5-1 Process Costing and Job-Order Costing [LO1]
Which would be more appropriate in each of the following organizations—job-order costing or process costing?

a.   A custom home builder.
b.   A golf course designer.
c.   A textbook publisher.
d.   A business consultant.
e.   An oil refinery.
f.   A soft-drink bottler.
g.   A film studio.
h.   A firm that supervises bridge construction projects.
i.   A manufacturer of fine custom jewellery.
j.   A paint factory.
k.   An auto repair shop.
l.   A factory making frozen orange juice concentrate.

EXERCISE 5-2 Computing Job Costs [LO2]
Weaver Company's predetermined overhead rate is $18.00 per direct labour-hour, and its direct labour wage rate is $12.00 per hour. The following information pertains to Job A-200:

Direct materials	$200
Direct labour	$ 120

Required:
1.   What is the total manufacturing cost assigned to Job A-200?
2.   If Job A-200 consists of 50 units, what is the average cost assigned to each unit included in the job?

EXERCISE 5-3 Compute the Predetermined Overhead Rate [LO3]
Logan Products computes its predetermined overhead rate annually on the basis of direct labour-hours. At the beginning of the year, it estimated that its total manufacturing overhead would be $586,000 and the total direct labour would be 40,000 hours. Its actual total manufacturing overhead for the year was $713,400 and its actual total direct labour was 41,000 hours.

Required:
Compute the company's predetermined overhead rate for the year, calculate the total overhead applied, and determine the amount of under- or overapplied overhead in the year.

EXERCISE 5-4 Prepare Journal Entries [LO4]
Lancaster Company recorded the following transactions for the just-completed month:

a. $45,000 in raw materials was purchased on account.
b. $125,000 in raw materials was requisitioned for use in production. Of this amount, $70,000 was for direct materials and the remainder was for indirect materials.
c.   Total labour wages of $212,000 were incurred. Of this amount, $183,000 was for direct labour and the remainder was for indirect labour.
d.   Additional manufacturing overhead costs of $189,000 were incurred.

Required:
Record the above transactions in journal entries.

EXERCISE 5-5 Apply Overhead [LO5]
Carera Corporation uses a predetermined overhead rate of $23.10 per direct labour-hour. This predetermined rate was based on 12,000 estimated direct labour-hours and $277,200 of estimated total manufacturing overhead.

The company incurred actual total manufacturing overhead costs of $266,000 and 12,600 total direct labour-hours during the period.

Required:
Determine the amount of manufacturing overhead applied to units of product during the period as well as the amount of over- or underapplied overhead for the period.

EXERCISE 5–6 Applying Overhead; Cost of Goods Manufactured [LO5, LO6, LO7]
The following cost data relate to the manufacturing activities of Black Company during the just-completed year:

Manufacturing overhead costs:	
Property taxes, factory..	$ 3,000
Utilities, factory...	5,000
Indirect labour..	10,000
Depreciation, factory..	24,000
Insurance, factory..	6,000
Total actual manufacturing overhead costs............................	$48,000
Other costs incurred:	
Purchases of raw materials...	$32,000
Direct labour cost...	$40,000
Inventories:	
Raw materials, beginning..	$ 8,000
Raw materials, ending..	$ 7,000
Work in process, beginning...	$ 6,000
Work in process, ending...	$ 7,500

The company uses a predetermined overhead rate to apply overhead cost to production. The rate for the year was $5 per machine-hour; a total of 10,000 machine-hours were recorded for the year. All raw materials ultimately become direct materials—none are classified as indirect materials.

Required:
1. Compute the amount of underapplied or overapplied overhead cost for the year.
2. Prepare a schedule of cost of goods manufactured for the year.

EXERCISE 5–7 Prepare T-Accounts [LO4, LO6]
Granger Products recorded the following transactions for the just-completed month. The company had no beginning inventories:

a. $75,000 in raw materials was purchased for cash.
b. $73,000 in raw materials was requisitioned for use in production. Of this amount, $67,000 was for direct materials and the remainder was for indirect materials.
c. Total wages of $152,000 were incurred and paid. Of this amount, $134,000 was for direct labour and the remainder was for indirect labour.
d. Additional manufacturing overhead costs of $126,000 were incurred and paid.
e. Manufacturing overhead costs of $178,000 were applied to jobs using the company's predetermined overhead rate.
f. All of the jobs in process at the end of the month were completed and shipped to customers.
g. If overhead is underapplied in the period, it is closed out to cost of goods sold. If overhead is overapplied in the period, it is allocated among appropriate accounts on the basis of the cost of manufacturing in each account.

Required:
1. Post the above transactions to T-accounts.
2. Determine the cost of goods sold for the period.

EXERCISE 5–8 Underapplied and Overapplied Overhead [LO7]
Cretin Enterprises uses a predetermined overhead rate of $21.40 per direct labour-hour. This predetermined rate was based on 16,000 estimated direct labour-hours and $342,400 of estimated total manufacturing overhead.

The company incurred actual total manufacturing overhead costs of $345,000 and 16,500 total direct labour-hours during the period. There were no beginning inventories, and all goods produced in the period were shipped out to customers before period-end.

Required:
1. Determine the amount of underapplied or overapplied manufacturing overhead for the period.
2. What is the effect on gross margin for the period?

EXERCISE 5–9 Applying Overhead in a Service Company [LO2, LO3, LO5]

Drew Architectural Design began operations on January 2. The following activity was recorded in the company's Work in Process account for the first month of operations:

Work in Process

Costs of subcontracted work	90,000	To completed projects	570,000
Direct staff costs	200,000		
Studio overhead	320,000		

Drew Architectural Design is a service firm, so the names of the accounts it uses are different from the names used in manufacturing companies. Costs of Subcontracted Work is comparable to Direct Materials, Direct Staff Costs is the same as Direct Labour, Studio Overhead is the same as Manufacturing Overhead, and Completed Projects is the same as Finished Goods. Apart from the difference in terms, the accounting methods used by the company are identical to the methods used by manufacturing companies.

Drew Architectural Design uses a job-order costing system and applies studio overhead to Work in Process on the basis of direct staff costs. At the end of January, only one job was still in process. This job (the Kareen Corporation Headquarters project) had been charged with $13,500 in direct staff costs.

Required:
1. Compute the predetermined overhead rate that was in use during January.
2. Complete the following job cost sheet for the partially completed Kareen Corporation Headquarters project:

Job Cost Sheet
Kareen Corporation Headquarters Project
As of January 31

Costs of subcontracted work	$?
Direct staff costs	?
Studio overhead	?
Total cost to January 31.........................	$?

EXERCISE 5–10 Schedules of Cost of Goods Manufactured and Cost of Goods Sold; Income Statement [LO6]

The following data from the just-completed year are taken from the accounting records of Eccles Company:

Sales	$643,000
Direct labour cost...	90,000
Raw material purchases..	132,000
Selling expenses	100,000
Administrative expenses..	43,000
Manufacturing overhead applied to work in process........................	210,000
Actual manufacturing overhead costs.....................................	220,000

Inventory	Beginning of Year	End of Year
Raw materials..	$8,000	$10,000
Work in process...	5,000	20,000
Finished goods..	70,000	25,000

Required:
1. Prepare a schedule of cost of goods manufactured. Assume all raw materials used in production were direct materials.
2. Prepare a schedule of cost of goods sold.
3. Prepare an income statement.

EXERCISE 5–11 Applying Overhead in a Service Company; Journal Entries [LO4, LO5, LO7]
Local Landscaping uses a job-order costing system to track the costs of its landscaping projects. The company provides complete garden design and landscaping services. The following table provides data concerning the three landscaping projects that were in process during May. There was no work in process at the beginning of May:

	Project		
	Williams	**Chandler**	**Nguyen**
Designer-hours....................	200	80	120
Direct materials cost.............	$4,800	$1,800	$3,600
Direct labour cost................	$2,400	$1,000	$1,500

Actual overhead costs were $16,000 for May. Overhead costs are applied to projects on the basis of designer-hours since most of the overhead is related to the costs of the garden design studio. The predetermined overhead rate is $45 per designer-hour. The Williams and Chandler projects were completed in May; the Nguyen project was not completed by the end of the month. No other jobs were in process during May.

Required:
1. Compute the amount of overhead cost that would have been charged to each project during May.
2. Prepare a journal entry showing the completion of the Williams and Chandler projects and the transfer of costs to the Completed Projects (i.e., Finished Goods) account.
3. What is the balance in the Work in Process account at the end of the month?
4. What is the balance in the Overhead account at the end of the month? What is this balance called?

EXERCISE 5–12 Varying Predetermined Overhead Rates [LO3, LO5]
Jacarda Company makes a composting bin that is subject to wide seasonal variations in demand. Unit product costs are computed on a quarterly basis by dividing each quarter's manufacturing costs (materials, labour, and overhead) by the quarter's production in units. The company's estimated costs, by quarter, for the coming year are given below:

	Quarter			
	First	**Second**	**Third**	**Fourth**
Direct materials..........................	$240,000	$120,000	$ 60,000	$180,000
Direct labour	96,000	48,000	24,000	72,000
Manufacturing overhead.................	228,000	204,000	192,000	216,000
Total manufacturing costs...............	$564,000	$372,000	$276,000	$468,000
Number of units to be produced..........	80,000	40,000	20,000	60,000
Estimated unit product cost..............	$7.05	$9.30	$13.80	$7.80

Management finds the variation in unit product costs to be confusing and difficult to work with. It has been suggested that the problem lies with manufacturing overhead, since it is the largest element of cost. Accordingly, you have been asked to find a more appropriate way of assigning manufacturing overhead cost to units of product. After some analysis, you have determined that the company's overhead costs are mostly fixed and therefore show little sensitivity to changes in the level of production.

Required:
1. The company uses a job-order costing system. How would you recommend that manufacturing overhead cost be assigned to production? Be specific, and show computations.
2. Recompute the company's unit product costs in accordance with your recommendations in (1) above.

EXERCISE 5–13 Applying Overhead; Journal Entries; Disposition of Underapplied or Overapplied Overhead [LO4, LO5, LO7]
The following information is taken from the accounts of Foster Corp. The entries in the T-accounts are summaries of the transactions that affected those accounts during the year:

Manufacturing Overhead				Work in Process			
(a)	380,000	(b)	410,000	Bal.	105,000	(c)	760,000
		Bal.	30,000		210,000		
					115,000		
				(b)	410,000		
				Bal.	80,000		

Finished Goods				Cost of Goods Sold			
Bal.	160,000	(d)	820,000	(d)	820,000		
(c)	760,000						
Bal.	100,000						

The overhead applied to production during the year is distributed among the ending balances in the accounts as follows:

Work in Process, ending..	$ 32,800
Finished Goods, ending.	41,000
Cost of Goods Sold.	336,200
Overhead applied...	$410,000

For example, of the $80,000 ending balance in Work in Process, $32,800 was overhead applied during the year.

Required:
1. Identify the reasons for entries (*a*) through (*d*).
2. The company allocates any balance in the Manufacturing Overhead account to the other accounts in proportion to the overhead applied during the year that is in the ending balance in each account. Prepare the necessary journal entry, with supporting computations.

EXERCISE 5–14 Departmental Overhead Rates [LO3, LO5]
Grange Company has two departments, Stamping and Assembly. The company uses a job-order costing system and computes a predetermined overhead rate in each department. The Stamping Department bases its rate on machine-hours, and the Assembly Department bases its rate on direct labour cost. At the beginning of the year, the company made the following estimates:

	Department	
	Stamping	Assembly
Direct labour-hours.......................	40,000	125,000
Machine-hours............................	300,000	15,000
Manufacturing overhead cost.............	$2,550,000	$4,000,000
Direct labour cost	$360,000	$3,200,000

Required:
1. Compute the predetermined overhead rate to be used in each department.
2. Assume that the overhead rates you computed in (1) above are in effect. The job cost sheet for Job 407, which was started and completed during the year, shows the following:

	Department	
	Stamping	**Assembly**
Direct labour-hours.........................	25	100
Machine-hours.............................	450	20
Materials requisitioned....................	$400	$1,850
Direct labour cost.........................	$250	$800

Compute the total overhead cost applied to Job 407.

3.   Would you expect substantially different amounts of overhead cost to be charged to some jobs if the company used a plantwide overhead rate based on direct labour cost instead of using departmental rates? Explain. No computations are necessary.

EXERCISE 5–15 Applying Overhead; T-Accounts; Journal Entries [LO3, LO4, LO5, LO7]
Medusa Products uses a job-order costing system. Overhead costs are applied to jobs on the basis of machine-hours. At the beginning of the year, management estimated that the company would incur $170,000 in manufacturing overhead costs for the year and work 85,000 machine-hours.

Required:
1.   Compute the company's predetermined overhead rate.
2.   Assume that during the year the company actually works only 80,000 machine-hours and incurs the following costs in the Manufacturing Overhead and Work in Process accounts:

Manufacturing Overhead				Work in Process	
Utilities	14,000	?		Direct materials	530,000
Insurance	9,000			Direct labour	85,000
Maintenance	33,000			Overhead	?
Indirect materials	7,000				
Indirect labour	65,000				
Depreciation	40,000				

Copy the data in the T-accounts above onto your answer sheet. Compute the amount of overhead cost that would be applied to Work in Process for the year, and make the entry in your T-accounts.
3.   Compute the amount of underapplied or overapplied overhead for the year, and show the balance in your Manufacturing Overhead T-account. Prepare a journal entry to properly dispose of the balance.
4.   Explain why the manufacturing overhead was underapplied or overapplied for the year.

EXERCISE 5–16 Overhead Application [LO3, LO5]
Sportway Inc. produces high-quality tennis racquets and golf clubs using a patented forming process and high-quality hand-finishing. Products move through two production departments: Forming and Finishing. The company uses departmental overhead rates to allocate overhead costs. Overhead is allocated based on machine-hours in Forming and direct labour cost in Finishing. Information related to costs for last year is provided below:

	Tennis Racquets	**Golf Clubs**
Annual production and sales.................	5,000	8,000
Direct materials per unit.....................	$4.50	$3.50
Direct labour cost per unit:		
Forming Department	$8.00	$3.50
Finishing Department........................	$3.50	$4.00
Machine hours per unit:		
Forming Department	0.75	0.25
Finishing Department........................	0.25	0.50

In addition, the firm budgets manufacturing overhead at $52,000 in the Forming Department and $45,000 in the Finishing Department.

Required:
1. Determine the overhead application rate for each department.
2. Determine the total cost per unit of tennis racquets and golf clubs.

PROBLEMS

PROBLEM 5–17 Comprehensive Problem [LO3, LO4, LO5, LO7]
Regal Millwork Ltd. produces reproductions of antique residential mouldings at a plant located in Manchester, England. Since there are hundreds of products, some of which are made only to order, the company uses a job-order costing system. On July 1, the start of the company's fiscal year, inventory account balances were as follows:

Raw Materials	£10,000
Work in Process	£4,000
Finished Goods	£8,000

The company applies overhead cost to jobs on the basis of machine-hours. For the fiscal year starting July 1, it was estimated that the plant would operate 45,000 machine-hours and incur £99,000 in manufacturing overhead cost. During the year, the following transactions were completed:
a. Raw materials were purchased on account: £160,000.
b. Raw materials were requisitioned for use in production: £140,000 (materials costing £120,000 were chargeable directly to jobs; the remaining materials were indirect).
c. Costs for employee services were incurred as follows:

Direct labour	£90,000
Indirect labour	£60,000
Sales commissions	£20,000
Administrative salaries	£50,000

d. Prepaid insurance expired during the year: £18,000 (£13,000 of this amount related to factory operations, and the remainder related to selling and administrative activities).
e. Utility costs were incurred in the factory: £10,000.
f. Advertising costs were incurred: £15,000.
g. Depreciation was recorded on equipment: £25,000 (£20,000 of this amount was on equipment used in factory operations; the remaining £5,000 was on equipment used in selling and administrative activities).
h. Manufacturing overhead cost was applied to jobs: £ ? (the company recorded 50,000 machine-hours of operating time during the year).
i. Goods that had cost £310,000 to manufacture according to their job cost sheets were completed.
j. Sales (all on account) to customers during the year totalled £498,000. These goods cost £308,000 to manufacture according to their job cost sheets.

Required:
1. Prepare journal entries to record the transactions for the year.
2. Prepare T-accounts for inventories, Manufacturing Overhead, and Cost of Goods Sold. Post relevant data from your journal entries to these T-accounts (don't forget to enter the opening balances in your inventory accounts). Compute an ending balance in each account.
3. Is Manufacturing Overhead underapplied or overapplied for the year? Prepare a journal entry to properly dispose of any balance in the Manufacturing Overhead account.
4. Prepare an income statement for the year. (Do not prepare a schedule of cost of goods manufactured; all of the information needed for the income statement is available in the journal entries and T-accounts you have prepared.)

PROBLEM 5–18 Journal Entries; T-Accounts; Cost Flows [LO4, LO5, LO7]

Ravsten Company uses a job-order costing system. On January 1, the beginning of the current year, the company's inventory balances were as follows:

Raw Materials......................................	$ 16,000
Work in Process	$ 10,000
Finished Goods	$30,000

The company applies overhead cost to jobs on the basis of machine-hours. For the current year, the company estimated that it would work 36,000 machine-hours and incur $153,000 in manufacturing overhead cost. The following transactions were recorded for the year:

a. Raw materials were purchased on account: $200,000.
b. Raw materials were requisitioned for use in production: $190,000 (80% direct and 20% indirect).
c. The following costs were incurred for employee services:

Direct labour.......................................	$160,000
Indirect labour.....................................	$ 27,000
Sales commissions.................................	$ 36,000
Administrative salaries	$ 80,000

d. Heat, power, and water costs were incurred in the factory: $42,000.
e. Prepaid insurance expired during the year: $10,000 (90% relates to factory operations, and 10% relates to selling and administrative activities).
f. Advertising costs were incurred, $50,000.
g. Depreciation was recorded for the year: $60,000 (85% relates to factory operations, and 15% relates to selling and administrative activities).
h. Manufacturing overhead cost was applied to production. The company recorded 40,000 machine-hours for the year.
i. Goods that cost $480,000 to manufacture according to their job cost sheets were transferred to the finished goods warehouse.
j. Sales for the year totalled $700,000 and were all on account. The total cost to manufacture these goods according to their job cost sheets was $475,000.

Required:
1. Prepare journal entries to record the transactions given above.
2. Prepare T-accounts for inventories, Manufacturing Overhead, and Cost of Goods Sold. Post relevant data from your journal entries to these T-accounts (don't forget to enter the opening balances in your inventory accounts). Compute an ending balance in each account.
3. Is Manufacturing Overhead underapplied or overapplied for the year? Prepare a journal entry to properly dispose of any balance in the Manufacturing Overhead account.
4. Prepare an income statement for the year. (Do not prepare a schedule of cost of goods manufactured; all of the information needed for the income statement is available in the journal entries and T-accounts you have prepared.)

PROBLEM 5–19 T-Accounts; Applying Overhead [LO3, LO5, LO7]

Durham Company's trial balance as of January 1, the beginning of the current year, is shown below:

Cash	$ 8,000	
Accounts Receivable	13,000	
Raw Materials..	7,000	
Work in Process...	18,000	
Finished Goods..	20,000	
Prepaid Insurance..	4,000	
Plant and Equipment.......................................	230,000	
Accumulated Depreciation		$ 42,000
Accounts Payable...		30,000
Capital Stock		150,000
Retained Earnings...		78,000
Total	$300,000	$300,000

Durham Company uses a job-order costing system. During the year, the following transactions took place:

a.   Raw materials were purchased on account: $45,000.

b.   Raw materials were requisitioned for use in production: $40,000 (80% direct and 20% indirect).

c.   Factory utility costs were incurred: $14,600.

d.   Depreciation was recorded on plant and equipment: $28,000. Three-fourths of the depreciation relates to factory equipment, and the remainder relates to selling and administrative equipment.

e.   Costs for salaries and wages were incurred as follows:

Direct labour.	$40,000
Indirect labour	$18,000
Sales commissions.	$10,400
Administrative salaries	$25,000

f.   Prepaid insurance expired during the year: $3,000 (80% relates to factory operations, and 20% relates to selling and administrative activities).

g.   Miscellaneous selling and administrative expenses were incurred: $18,000.

h.   Manufacturing overhead was applied to production. The company applies overhead on the basis of 150% of direct labour cost.

i.   Goods that cost $130,000 to manufacture according to their job cost sheets were transferred to the finished goods warehouse.

j.   Goods that had cost $120,000 to manufacture according to their job cost sheets were sold on account for $200,000.

k.   Collections from customers during the year totalled $197,000.

l.   Payments to suppliers on account during the year totalled $100,000; payments to employees for salaries and wages totalled $90,000.

Required:

1.   Prepare a T-account for each account in the company's trial balance, and enter the opening balances shown above.

2.   Record the transactions above directly into the T-accounts. Prepare new T-accounts as needed. Key your entries to the letters (*a*) through (*l*) above. Find the ending balance in each account.

3.   Is manufacturing overhead underapplied or overapplied for the year? Make an entry in the T-accounts to properly dispose of any balance in the Manufacturing Overhead account.

4.   Prepare an income statement for the year. (Do not prepare a schedule of cost of goods manufactured; all of the information needed for the income statement is available in the T-accounts you have prepared.)

PROBLEM 5–20 Cost Flows; T-Accounts; Income Statement [LO3, LO5, LO7]

PQB Inc. designs and fabricates movie props such as mock-ups of star fighters and cybernetic robots. The company's balance sheet as of January 1, the beginning of the current year, appears below.

Since each prop is a unique design and may require anything from a few hours to a month or more to complete, PQB uses a job-order costing system. Overhead in the fabrication shop is charged to props on the basis of direct labour cost. The company estimated that it would incur $80,000 in manufacturing overhead and $100,000 in direct labour cost during the year. The following transactions were recorded during the year:

a.   Raw materials, such as wood, paints, and metal sheeting, were purchased on account: $80,000.

b.   Raw materials were issued to production: $90,000 ($5,000 of this amount was for indirect materials).

c.   Payroll costs were incurred and paid: direct labour, $120,000; indirect labour, $30,000; and selling and administrative salaries, $75,000.

d.   Fabrication shop utilities costs were incurred: $12,000.

e.   Depreciation was recorded for the year: $30,000 ($5,000 on selling and administrative assets; $25,000 on fabrication shop assets).

f.   Prepaid insurance expired: $4,800 ($4,000 related to fabrication shop operations, and $800 related to selling and administrative activities).

g.   Shipping expenses were incurred: $40,000.

h.   Other manufacturing overhead costs were incurred: $17,000 (credit Accounts Payable).

i.   Manufacturing overhead was applied to production. Overhead is applied on the basis of direct labour cost.

j.   Movie props that cost $310,000 to produce according to their job cost sheets were completed.
k.   Sales for the year totalled $450,000 and were all on account. The total cost to produce these movie props was $300,000 according to their job cost sheets.
l.   Collections on account from customers totalled $445,000.
m.   Payments on account to suppliers totalled $150,000.

PQB Inc.
Balance Sheet
January 1

Assets

Current assets:		
Cash..		$ 15,000
Accounts receivable.......................................		40,000
Inventories:		
Raw materials..	$ 25,000	
Work in process...	30,000	
Finished goods (props awaiting shipment)................	45,000	100,000
Prepaid insurance...		5,000
Total current assets......................................		160,000
Buildings and equipment..................................	500,000	
Less accumulated depreciation...........................	210,000	290,000
Total assets..		$450,000

Liabilities and Shareholders' Equity

Accounts payable...		$ 75,000
Capital stock..	$250,000	
Retained earnings...	125,000	375,000
Total liabilities and shareholders' equity................		$450,000

Required:

1.   Prepare a T-account for each account on the company's balance sheet, and enter the beginning balances.
2.   Make entries directly into the T-accounts for the transactions given above. Create new T-accounts as needed. Determine an ending balance for each T-account.
3.   Was manufacturing overhead underapplied or overapplied for the year? Assume that the company allocates any overhead balance among the Work in Process, Finished Goods, and Cost of Goods Sold accounts, using the overall balances in each account. Prepare a journal entry to show the allocation. (Round allocation percentages to one decimal place.)
4.   Prepare an income statement for the year. (Do not prepare a schedule of cost of goods manufactured; all of the information needed for the income statement is available in the T-accounts.)

PROBLEM 5–21 T-Accounts; Overhead Rates; Journal Entries [LO3, LO4, LO5, LO7]
Kenworth Company uses a job-order costing system. Only three jobs—Job 105, Job 106, and Job 107—were worked on during November and December. Job 105 was completed on December 10; the other two jobs were still in production on December 31, the end of the company's operating year. Data from the job cost sheets of the three jobs follow:

	Job Cost Sheet		
	Job 105	Job 106	Job 107
November costs incurred:			
Direct materials	$16,500	$9,300	$0
Direct labour	$13,000	$7,000	$0
Manufacturing overhead.................	$20,800	$11,200	$0
December costs incurred:			
Direct materials	$0	$8,200	$21,300
Direct labour	$4,000	$6,000	$10,000
Manufacturing overhead.................	?	?	?

The following additional information is available:

a.   Manufacturing overhead is applied to jobs on the basis of direct labour cost.
b.   Balances in the inventory accounts at November 30 were as follows:

Raw Materials.....................................	$40,000
Work in Process	?
Finished Goods	$85,000

Required:

1.   Prepare T-accounts for Raw Materials, Work in Process, Finished Goods, and Manufacturing Overhead. Enter the November 30 inventory balances given above; in the case of Work in Process, compute the November 30 balance and enter it into the Work in Process T-account.

2.   Prepare journal entries for *December* as follows:

   a.   Prepare an entry to record the issue of materials into production, and post the entry to appropriate T-accounts. (In the case of direct materials, it is not necessary to make a separate entry for each job.) Indirect materials used during December totalled $4,000.

   b.   Prepare an entry to record the incurrence of labour cost, and post the entry to appropriate T-accounts. (In the case of direct labour cost, it is not necessary to make a separate entry for each job.) Indirect labour cost totalled $8,000 for December.

   c.   Prepare an entry to record the incurrence of $19,000 in various actual manufacturing overhead costs for December (credit Accounts Payable). Post this entry to the appropriate T-accounts.

3.   What apparent predetermined overhead rate does the company use to assign overhead cost to jobs? Using this rate, prepare a journal entry to record the application of overhead cost to jobs for December (it is not necessary to make a separate entry for each job). Post this entry to the appropriate T-accounts.

4.   As stated earlier, Job 105 was completed during December. Prepare a journal entry to show the transfer of this job off the production line and into the finished goods warehouse. Post the entry to the appropriate T-accounts.

5.   Determine the balance at December 31 in the Work in Process inventory account. How much of this balance consists of costs charged to Job 106? Job 107?

PROBLEM 5–22 Multiple Departments; Overhead Rates; Underapplied or Overapplied Overhead [LO3, LO5, LO7]

Winder, Knotter, and Nale is a small law firm that has 10 partners and 10 support people. The firm employs a job-order costing system to accumulate costs chargeable to each client, and it is organized into two departments—the Research and Documents Department and the Litigation Department. The firm uses predetermined overhead rates to charge the costs of these departments to its clients. At the beginning of the current year, the firm's management made the following estimates for the year:

	Department	
	Research and Documents	**Litigation**
Research-hours	20,000	–
Direct lawyer-hours.................................	9,000	16,000
Materials and supplies..............................	$18,000	$5,000
Direct lawyer cost..................................	$430,000	$800,000
Departmental overhead cost	$700,000	$320,000

The predetermined overhead rate in the Research and Documents Department is based on research-hours, and the rate in the Litigation Department is based on direct lawyer cost.

   The costs charged to each client are made up of three elements: materials and supplies used, direct lawyer costs incurred, and an applied amount of overhead from each department in which work is performed on the case.

   Case 618-3 was initiated on February 10 and completed on June 30. During this period, the following costs and time were recorded on the case:

	Department	
	Research and Documents	**Litigation**
Research-hours	18	—
Direct lawyer-hours................................	9	42
Materials and supplies............................	$50	$30
Direct lawyer cost.................................	$410	$2,100

Required:
1. Compute the predetermined overhead rate used during the year in the Research and Documents Department. Compute the rate used in the Litigation Department.
2. Using the rates you computed in (1) above, compute the total overhead cost applied to Case 618-3.
3. What is the total cost charged to Case 618-3? Show computations by department and in total for the case.
4. At the end of the year, the firm's records revealed the following *actual* cost and operating data for all cases handled during the year:

	Department	
	Research and Documents	**Litigation**
Research-hours	23,000	—
Direct lawyer-hours................................	8,000	15,000
Materials and supplies............................	$19,000	$6,000
Direct lawyer cost.................................	$400,000	$725,000
Departmental overhead cost	$770,000	$300,000

Determine the amount of underapplied or overapplied overhead cost in each department for the year.

PROBLEM 5–23 Journal Entries; T-Accounts; Disposition of Underapplied or Overapplied Overhead; Income Statement [LO3, LO4, LO5, LO7]
Heavenly Displays Inc. puts together large-scale fireworks displays—primarily for Canada Day celebrations sponsored by corporations and municipalities. The company assembles and orchestrates complex displays using pyrotechnic components purchased from suppliers throughout the world. The company has built a reputation for safety and for the awesome power and brilliance of its computer-controlled shows. Heavenly Displays builds its own launch platforms and its own electronic controls. Because of the company's reputation, customers order shows up to a year in advance. Since each show is different in terms of duration and components used, Heavenly Displays uses a job-order costing system.

Heavenly Displays' trial balance as of January 1, the beginning of the current year, is given below:

Cash	$ 9,000	
Accounts Receivable	30,000	
Raw Materials......................................	16,000	
Work in Process	21,000	
Finished Goods	38,000	
Prepaid Insurance...................................	7,000	
Buildings and Equipment	300,000	
Accumulated Depreciation		$128,000
Accounts Payable...................................		60,000
Salaries and Wages Payable		3,000
Capital Stock		200,000
Retained Earnings...................................		30,000
Total...	$421,000	$421,000

The company charges manufacturing overhead costs to jobs on the basis of direct labour-hours. (Each customer order for a complete fireworks display is a separate job.) Management estimated that the company would incur $135,000 in manufacturing overhead costs in the fabrication and electronics shops and would work 18,000 direct labour-hours during the year. The following transactions occurred during the year:

a.   Raw materials, consisting mostly of skyrockets, mortar bombs, flares, wiring, and electronic components, were purchased on account: $820,000.

b.   Raw materials were issued to production: $830,000 ($13,000 of this amount was for indirect materials, and the remainder was for direct materials).

c.   Fabrication and electronics shop payrolls were accrued: $200,000 (70% direct labour and 30% indirect labour). A total of 20,800 direct labour-hours were worked during the year.

d.   Selling and administrative salaries were accrued: $150,000.

e.   The company prepaid additional insurance premiums of $38,000 during the year. Prepaid insurance expiring during the year was $40,000 (only $600 relates to selling and administrative; the other $39,400 relates to the fabrication and electronics shops because of the safety hazards involved in handling fireworks).

f.   Marketing cost was incurred: $100,000.

g.   Depreciation charges for the year totalled $40,000 (70% relates to fabrication and electronics shop assets, and 30% relates to selling and administrative assets).

h.   Property taxes were accrued on the shop buildings: $12,600 (credit Accounts Payable).

i.   Manufacturing overhead cost was applied to jobs.

j.   Jobs completed during the year had a total production cost of $1,106,000 according to their job cost sheets.

k.   Revenue (all on account) was $1,420,000. Cost of Goods Sold (before any adjustment for underapplied or overapplied overhead) was $1,120,000.

l.   Cash collections on account from customers totalled $1,415,000.

m.   Cash payments on accounts payable totalled $970,000. Cash payments to employees for salaries and wages totalled $348,000.

Required:

1.   Prepare journal entries for the year's transactions.

2.   Prepare a T-account for each account in the company's trial balance, and enter the opening balances given above. Post your journal entries to the T-accounts. Prepare new T-accounts as needed. Compute the ending balance in each account.

3.   Is manufacturing overhead underapplied or overapplied for the year? Prepare the necessary journal entry to dispose of the balance in the Manufacturing Overhead account.

4.   Prepare an income statement for the year. (Do not prepare a statement of cost of goods manufactured; all of the information needed for the income statement is available in the T-accounts.)

PROBLEM 5–24 Multiple Departments; Applying Overhead [LO3, LO5, LO7]
WoodGrain Technology makes home office furniture from fine hardwoods. The company uses a job-order costing system and predetermined overhead rates to apply manufacturing overhead cost to jobs. The predetermined overhead rate in the Preparation Department is based on machine-hours, and the rate in the Fabrication Department is based on direct materials cost. At the beginning of the year, the company's management made the following estimates for the year:

	Department	
	Preparation	**Fabrication**
Machine-hours.......................................	80,000	21,000
Direct labour-hours................................	35,000	65,000
Direct materials cost	$ 190,000	$400,000
Direct labour cost..................................	$280,000	$530,000
Manufacturing overhead cost......................	$ 416,000	$720,000

Job 127 was started on April 1 and completed on May 12. The company's cost records show the following information concerning the job:

	Department	
	Preparation	Fabrication
Machine-hours......................................	350	70
Direct labour-hours...............................	80	130
Direct materials cost	$940	$1,200
Direct labour cost.................................	$ 710	$ 980

Required:

1. Compute the predetermined overhead rate used during the year in the Preparation Department. Compute the rate used in the Fabrication Department.
2. Compute the total overhead cost applied to Job 127.
3. What would be the total cost recorded for Job 127? If the job contained 25 units, what would be the unit product cost?
4. At the end of the year, the records of WoodGrain Technology revealed the following *actual* cost and operating data for all jobs worked on during the year:

	Department	
	Preparation	Fabrication
Machine-hours......................................	73,000	24,000
Direct labour-hours...............................	30,000	68,000
Direct materials cost	$ 165,000	$420,000
Manufacturing overhead cost.....................	$390,000	$ 740,000

What was the amount of underapplied or overapplied overhead in each department at the end of the year?

PROBLEM 5–25 T-Account Analysis of Cost Flows [LO3, LO6, LO7]
Selected ledger accounts for Realm Company are given below for the just-completed year:

Raw Materials

Bal. 1/1	30,000	Credits	?
Debits	420,000		
Bal. 31/12	60,000		

Manufacturing Overhead

Debits	385,000	Credits	?

Work in Process

Bal. 1/1	70,000	Credits	810,000
Direct materials	320,000		
Direct labour	110,000		
Overhead	400,000		
Bal. 31/12	?		

Factory Wages Payable

Debits	179,000	Bal. 1/1	10,000
		Credits	175,000
		Bal. 31/12	6,000

Finished Goods

Bal. 1/1	40,000	Credits	?
Debits	?		
Bal. 31/12	130,000		

Cost of Goods Sold

Debits	?	

Required:

1. What was the cost of raw materials put into production during the year?
2. How much of the materials in (1) consisted of indirect materials?

3. How much of the factory labour cost for the year consisted of indirect labour?
4. What was the cost of goods manufactured for the year?
5. What was the cost of goods sold for the year (before considering underapplied or overapplied overhead)?
6. If overhead is applied to production on the basis of direct materials cost, what rate was in effect during the year?
7. Was manufacturing overhead underapplied or overapplied? By how much?
8. Compute the ending balance in the Work in Process inventory account. Assume that this balance consists entirely of goods started during the year. If $32,000 of this balance is direct materials cost, how much of it is direct labour cost? Manufacturing overhead cost?

PROBLEM 5–26 Schedule of Cost of Goods Manufactured; Overhead Analysis [LO3, LO5, LO6, LO7]

The Pacific Manufacturing Company operates a job-order costing system and applies overhead cost to jobs on the basis of direct labour cost. In computing an overhead rate for the year, the company's estimates were as follows: manufacturing overhead cost, $126,000, and direct labour cost, $84,000. The company has provided the data in the following table:

	Beginning	Ending
Raw Materials	$ 21,000	$ 16,000
Work in Process	$ 44,000	$ 40,000
Finished Goods	$68,000	$60,000

The following actual costs were incurred during the year:

Purchase of raw materials (all direct)	$133,000
Direct labour cost	$ 80,000
Manufacturing overhead costs	123,000

Required:
1. *a.* Compute the predetermined overhead rate for the year.
   b. Compute the amount of underapplied or overapplied overhead for the year.
2. Prepare a schedule of cost of goods manufactured for the year.
3. Compute the cost of goods sold for the year. (Do not include any underapplied or overapplied overhead in your cost of goods sold figure.) How is overapplied (underapplied) overhead disposed of at year-end?
4. Job 137 was started and completed during the year. What price would have been charged to the customer if the job required $3,200 in materials and $4,200 in direct labour cost and the company priced its jobs at 40% above the job's cost according to the accounting system?
5. Direct labour made up $8,000 of the $40,000 ending Work in Process inventory balance. Supply the information missing below:

Direct materials.....................................	$?
Direct labour..	8,000
Manufacturing overhead	?
Work in process inventory	$40,000

PROBLEM 5–27 Predetermined Overhead Rate; Disposition of Underapplied or Overapplied Overhead [LO3, LO7]

Savallas Company is highly automated and uses computers to control manufacturing operations. The company uses a job-order costing system and applies manufacturing overhead cost to products on the basis of computer-hours. The following estimates were used in preparing the predetermined overhead rate at the beginning of the year:

Computer-hours......................................	85,000
Manufacturing overhead cost	$1,530,000

During the year, a severe economic recession resulted in cutting back production and a buildup of inventory in the company's warehouse. The company's cost records revealed the following actual cost and operating data for the year:

Computer-hours......................................	60,000
Manufacturing overhead cost	$1,350,000
Inventories at year-end:	
Raw materials...................................	$ 400,000
Work in process	$ 160,000
Finished goods..................................	$1,040,000
Cost of goods sold...............................	$2,800,000

Required:
1. Compute the company's predetermined overhead rate for the year.
2. Compute the underapplied or overapplied overhead for the year.
3. Assume that the company closes any underapplied or overapplied overhead directly to Cost of Goods Sold. Prepare the appropriate entry.
4. Assume that the company allocates any overapplied overhead to Work in Process, Finished Goods, and Cost of Goods Sold on the basis of the amount of overhead applied during the year that remains in each account at the end of the year. These amounts are $43,200 for Work in Process, $280,800 for Finished Goods, and $756,000 for Cost of Goods Sold. Underapplied overhead is charged directly to Cost of Goods Sold. Prepare the journal entry to show the disposal of under/overapplied overhead.

PROBLEM 5-28 Comprehensive Problem: Journal Entries; T-Accounts; Financial Statements [LO3, LO4, LO5, LO6, LO7]
Southworth Company uses a job-order costing system and applies manufacturing overhead cost to jobs on the basis of the cost of direct materials used in production. At the beginning of the current year, the following estimates were made to compute the predetermined overhead rate: manufacturing overhead cost, $248,000, and direct materials cost, $155,000. The following transactions took place during the year (all purchases and services were acquired on account):
a. Raw materials were purchased: $142,000.
b. Raw materials were requisitioned for use in production (all direct materials): $150,000.
c. Utility bills were incurred in the factory: $21,000.
d. Costs for salaries and wages were incurred as follows:

Direct labour...	$216,000
Indirect labour.......................................	$90,000
Selling and administrative salaries	$145,000

e. Maintenance costs were incurred in the factory: $15,000.
f. Advertising costs were incurred: $130,000.
g. Depreciation was recorded for the year: $50,000 (90% relates to factory assets, and the remainder relates to selling and administrative assets).
h. Rental cost was incurred on buildings: $90,000 (80% of the space is occupied by the factory, and 20% is occupied by sales and administration).
i. Miscellaneous selling and administrative costs were incurred: $17,000.
j. Manufacturing overhead cost was applied to jobs: $?.
k. Cost of goods manufactured for the year was $590,000.
l. Sales for the year (all on account) totalled $1,000,000. These goods cost $600,000 according to their job cost sheets.
   The balances in the inventory accounts at the beginning of the year were as follows:

Raw Materials.......................................	$18,000
Work in Process	$24,000
Finished Goods	$35,000

Required:
1. Prepare journal entries to record the above data.
2. Post your entries to T-accounts. (Don't forget to enter the opening inventory balances above.) Determine the ending balances in the inventory accounts and in the Manufacturing Overhead account.

3. Prepare a schedule of cost of goods manufactured.
4. Prepare a journal entry to properly dispose of any balance in the Manufacturing Overhead account. Prepare a schedule of cost of goods sold.
5. Prepare an income statement for the year.
6. Job 218 was one of many jobs started and completed during the year. The job required $3,600 in direct materials and 400 hours of direct labour time at a rate of $11 per hour. If the job contained 500 units and the company billed at 75% above the unit product cost on the job cost sheet, what price per unit would have been charged to the customer?

PROBLEM 5–29 Plantwide versus Departmental Overhead Rates; Underapplied or Overapplied Overhead [LO3, LO5, LO7]

"Don't tell me we've lost another bid!" exclaimed Janice Hudson, president of Prime Products Inc. "I'm afraid so," replied Doug Martin, the operations vice-president. "One of our competitors underbid us by about $10,000 on the Hastings job." "I just can't figure it out," said Hudson. "It seems we're either too high to get the job or too low to make any money on half the jobs we bid. What's happened?"

Prime Products manufactures specialized goods to customers' specifications and operates a job-order costing system. Manufacturing overhead cost is applied to jobs on the basis of direct labour cost. The following estimates were made at the beginning of the year:

	Department			
	Cutting	Machining	Assembly	Total Plant
Direct labour..	$300,000	$200,000	$400,000	$900,000
Manufacturing overhead	$540,000	$800,000	$100,000	$1,440,000

Jobs require varying amounts of work in the three departments. The Hastings job, for example, would have required manufacturing costs in the three departments as follows:

	Department			
	Cutting	Machining	Assembly	Total Plant
Direct material..............................	$12,000	$900	$5,600	$18,500
Direct labour.................................	$6,500	$1,700	$13,000	$21,200
Manufacturing overhead	?	?	?	?

The company uses a plantwide overhead rate to apply manufacturing overhead cost to jobs.

Required:
1. Assuming the use of a plantwide overhead rate:
   a. Compute the rate for the current year.
   b. Determine the amount of manufacturing overhead cost that would have been applied to the Hastings job.
2. Suppose that instead of using a plantwide overhead rate, the company had used a separate predetermined overhead rate in each department. Under these conditions:
   a. Compute the rate for each department for the current year.
   b. Determine the amount of manufacturing overhead cost that would have been applied to the Hastings job.
3. Explain the difference between the manufacturing overhead that would have been applied to the Hastings job using the plantwide rate in 1(b) above and using the departmental rates in 2(b).
4. Assume that it is customary in the industry to bid jobs at 150% of total manufacturing cost (direct materials, direct labour, and applied overhead). What was the company's bid price on the Hastings job? What would the bid price have been if departmental overhead rates had been used to apply overhead cost?
5. At the end of the year, the company assembled the following *actual* cost data relating to all jobs worked on during the year:

	Cutting	Machining	Assembly	Total Plant
		Department		
Direct material............................	$760,000	$ 90,000	$ 410,000	$1,260,000
Direct labour..............................	$320,000	$ 210,000	$340,000	$ 870,000
Manufacturing overhead	$560,000	$830,000	$ 92,000	$1,482,000

Compute the underapplied or overapplied overhead for the year (*a*) assuming that a plant-wide overhead rate is used, and (*b*) assuming that departmental overhead rates are used.

CASES

Case 5–30 Critical Thinking; Interpretation of Manufacturing Overhead Rates [LO3, LO5]
Sharpton Fabricators Corporation manufactures a variety of parts for the automotive industry. The company uses a job-order costing system with a plantwide predetermined overhead rate based on direct labour-hours. On December 10, 2015, the company's controller made a preliminary estimate of the predetermined overhead rate for 2016. The new rate was based on the estimated total manufacturing overhead cost of $3,402,000 and the estimated 63,000 total direct labour-hours for 2016:

$$\text{Predetermined overhead rate} = \frac{\$3,402,000}{63,000 \text{ hours}}$$

$$= \$54 \text{ per direct labour-hour}$$

This new predetermined overhead rate was communicated to top managers in a meeting on December 11. The rate did not cause any comment because it was within a few cents of the overhead rate that had been used during 2015. One of the subjects discussed at the meeting was a proposal by the production manager to purchase an automated milling machine centre built by Central Robotics. The president of Sharpton Fabricators, Kevin Reynolds, agreed to meet with the regional sales representative from Central Robotics to discuss the proposal.

On the day following the meeting, Reynolds met with Jay Warner, Central Robotics' sales representative. The following discussion took place:

Reynolds: Lisa Winter, our production manager, asked me to meet with you since she's interested in installing an automated milling machine centre. Frankly, I'm skeptical. You're going to have to show me this isn't just another expensive toy for Lisa's people to play with.

Warner: That shouldn't be too difficult, Kevin. The automated milling machine centre has three major advantages. First, it's much faster than the manual methods you're using. It can process about twice as many parts per hour as your current milling machines. Second, it's much more flexible. There are some up-front programming costs, but once those have been incurred, almost no setup is required on the machines for standard operations. You just punch in the code of the standard operation, load the machine's hopper with raw material, and the machine does the rest.

Reynolds: Yeah, but what about cost? Having twice the capacity in the milling machine area won't do us much good. That centre is idle much of the time, anyway.

Warner: I was getting there. The third advantage of the automated milling machine centre is lower cost. Winters and I looked over your present operations, and we estimated that the automated equipment would eliminate the need for about 6,000 direct labour-hours a year. What is your direct labour cost per hour?

Reynolds: The wage rate in the milling area averages about $32 per hour. Fringe benefits raise that figure to about $41 per hour.

Warner: Don't forget your overhead.

Reynolds: Next year the overhead rate will be about $54 per direct labour-hour.

Warner: So including fringe benefits and overhead, the cost per direct labour-hour is about $95.

Reynolds: That's right.

Warner: Since you can save 6,000 direct labour-hours per year, the cost savings would amount to about $570,000 a year, and our 60-month lease plan would require payments of only $348,000 per year.

Reynolds: Sold! When can you install the equipment?

Shortly after this meeting, Reynolds informed the company's controller of the decision to lease the new equipment, which would be installed over the Christmas vacation period. The controller realized that this decision would require a recomputation of the predetermined overhead rate for 2016, since the decision would affect both the manufacturing overhead and the direct labour-hours for the year. After talking with both the production manager and the sales representative from Central Robotics, the controller discovered that in addition to the annual lease cost of $348,000, the new machine would also require a skilled technician/ programmer who would have to be hired at a cost of $50,000 per year to maintain and program the equipment. Both of these costs would be included in factory overhead. There would be no other changes in total manufacturing overhead cost, which is almost entirely fixed. The controller assumed that the new machine would result in a reduction of 6,000 direct labour-hours for the year from the levels that had initially been planned.

When the revised predetermined overhead rate for 2016 was circulated among the company's top managers, there was considerable dismay.

Required:

1. Recompute the predetermined rate assuming that the new machine will be installed. Explain why the new predetermined overhead rate is higher (or lower) than the rate that was originally estimated for 2016.
2. What effect (if any) would this new rate have on the cost of jobs that do not use the new automated milling machine?
3. Why would managers be concerned about the new overhead rate?
4. After seeing the new predetermined overhead rate, the production manager admitted that he probably wouldn't be able to eliminate all of the 6,000 direct labour-hours. He had been hoping to accomplish the reduction by not replacing workers who retire or quit, but that would not be possible. As a result, the real labour savings would only be about 2,000 hours—one worker. In the light of this additional information, evaluate the original decision to acquire the automated milling machine from Central Robotics.

CASE 5–31 Ethics and the Manager [LO3, LO5, LO7]

Emily Carrigan was recently transferred to the Appliances Division of Delancy Corporation. Shortly after taking over her new position as divisional controller, Carrigan was asked to develop the division's predetermined overhead rate for the upcoming year. The accuracy of the rate is important. Delancy Corporation uses direct labour-hours in all of its divisions as the allocation base for manufacturing overhead.

To compute the predetermined overhead rate, Carrigan divided her estimate of the total manufacturing overhead for the coming year by the production manager's estimate of the total direct labour-hours for the coming year. She took her computations to the division's general manager for approval but was quite surprised when he suggested a modification in the base. Her conversation with the general manager of the Appliances Division, Harry Dafoe, went like this:

Carrigan: Here are my calculations for next year's predetermined overhead rate. If you approve, we can enter the rate into the computer on January 1 and be up and running in the job-order costing system right away for this year.

Dafoe: Thanks for coming up with the calculations so quickly. They look just fine. There is, however, one slight modification I'd like to see. Your estimate of the total direct labour-hours for the year is 110,000 hours. How about cutting that to about 105,000 hours?

Carrigan: I don't know if I can do that. The production manager says she will need about 110,000 direct labour-hours to meet the sales projections for next year. Besides, there will be over 108,000 direct labour-hours during the current year, and sales are projected to be higher next year.

Dafoe: Emily, I know all of that. I would still like to reduce the direct labour-hours in the base to something like 105,000 hours. You probably don't know that I had an agreement with your predecessor as divisional controller to shave 5% or so off the estimated direct labour-hours every year. That way, we kept a reserve that usually resulted in a big boost to operating income at the end of the fiscal year in December. We called it our Christmas bonus. Corporate headquarters always seemed as pleased as punch that we could pull off such a miracle at the end of the year. This system has worked well for many years, and I don't want to change it now.

Required:

1. Explain how shaving 5% off the estimated direct labour-hours in the base for the predetermined overhead rate usually results in a big boost in operating income at the end of the fiscal year.
2. Should Carrigan go along with the general manager's request to reduce the direct labour-hours in the predetermined overhead rate computation to 105,000 direct labour-hours?

CASE 5–32 Single versus Multiple Overhead Application Rates [LO3, LO5]

Foster Appliance Repair has developed a reputation over many years of providing high-quality, reliable repair services at a fair price. The company has grown from a two-person operation (run by Victor Foster and his wife Sally Jones) to a much larger company employing Foster and Jones as well as four skilled repair personnel and two service technicians. Jones manages the front office and prepares all accounting-related records for the company. Recently, Jones has noticed a decline in profits generated by the repair business. Foster has also noticed some decline in the number of repairs completed over the past few months. He believes this reduction may be due to increased competition from a new repair shop in the area. Since pricing is based to a large degree on the cost of repairs, Foster asked Jones to spend some time analyzing how repair costs were charged to jobs, to better understand the problem. He was quick to remind Jones that he was committed to keeping all personnel on fixed salaries since he believes this allows him to keep good employees and encourages loyalty to the company.

Jones collected the following information about the costing system:

*   Direct materials used in repairs are charged directly to the job.
*   The four repair personnel are paid a fixed salary of $50,000 per year, and the two technicians are paid a fixed salary of $38,000 per year. Jones estimates that each of the six repair personnel works 1,750 hours per year on customer jobs.
*   Other budgeted indirect support costs for the year (e.g., rent, insurance, utilities, supplies, repair van maintenance, repair van depreciation) total $178,450, including Foster's and Jones's salaries.
*   The price for each job is calculated on a cost-plus basis. Customers pay the total cost to complete the job plus a markup of 10%.
*   The total cost for each job is calculated as follows: total direct material cost plus the "shop rate" × number of repair hours to complete the job. The shop rate is applied to all types of repair jobs. The shop rate is calculated as the sum of the repair personnel salaries plus budgeted indirect support costs for the year divided by the estimated total hours to be worked on customer jobs for the year.
*   Jones noted that about 65% of total indirect costs related to complex repairs over the last couple of years, while the other 35% of total indirect costs related to simpler repairs. Even so, about half of the total time worked on customer jobs by repair personnel and technicians was related to complex repairs, while the other half was related to simple repairs. While Jones believed this was important information, she realized it was not taken into account when calculating the overall shop rate for the year.

Required:

1. Calculate the shop rate for the year based on the above information gathered by Jones.
2. Use the information gathered by Jones about the proportion of complex and simple repairs each year to calculate different shop rates that could be applied to complex and simple repair work.
3. Consider Job 1246 completed by Foster Appliance Repair last month. The job cost sheet indicates $115 cost of direct materials plus 6 hours of labour time × the shop rate.
    a. Calculate the total price charged to the customer, assuming a 10% markup on cost.
    b. By doing a little more digging, Jones was able to determine that 2 of the 6 hours spent on Job 1246 were related to complex repairs, while 4 of the 6 hours spent on the job were related to simple repairs. Use this information and the two shop rates calculated in (2) above to estimate the price that would have been charged for Job 1246 under this new system.
4. Using all of the information gathered to this point, explain why Foster Appliance Repair may be selling fewer repairs, resulting in lower profitability.

INSTANT QUIZ SOLUTIONS

5-1

Job-order: legal services, auto repairs, engagement rings, Caribbean cruises; Process: paper towels, house paint, household cleaners, 4 × 8 sheets of plywood.

5-2

Predetermined overhead rate = $350,000 ÷ 4,000 MH = $87.50 per MH. Overhead applied to Job 427B = 250 MH × $87.50 = $21,875.

5-3

Some production costs, such as a factory manager's salary, cannot be traced to a particular product or job but rather are incurred as a result of overall production activities. In addition, some production costs, such as indirect materials, cannot easily be traced to jobs. If these costs are to be assigned to products, they must be allocated to the products.

5-4

If actual manufacturing overhead cost is applied to jobs, then the company must wait until the end of the accounting period to apply overhead and to cost jobs. If the company computes actual overhead rates more frequently to get around this problem, the rates may fluctuate widely. Overhead cost tends to be incurred somewhat evenly from month to month (due to the presence of fixed costs), whereas production activity often fluctuates. The result is high overhead rates in periods with low activity and low overhead rates in periods with high activity. For these reasons, most companies use predetermined overhead rates to apply manufacturing overhead costs to jobs.

5-5

When actual overhead turns out to be less than estimated (i.e., overhead is overapplied), this amount should not all be charged to income this period since inventory will be undervalued on the balance sheet. These actual costs, if allocated to WIP and Finished Goods inventory, will then be charged against income when the related goods are sold, better satisfying the matching principle.

APPENDIX 5A: THE PREDETERMINED OVERHEAD RATE AND CAPACITY

LEARNING OBJECTIVE 8

Explain the implications of basing the predetermined overhead rate on activity at full capacity rather than on estimated activity for the period.

Companies typically base their predetermined overhead rates on the estimated, or budgeted, amount of the allocation base for the upcoming period. This is the method that is used in the chapter, but it is a practice that has recently come under severe criticism. An example will be very helpful in understanding why. Harmony Corporation manufactures music CDs for local recording studios. The company has a CD-duplicating machine that can produce a new CD every 10 seconds from a master CD. The company leases the CD-duplicating machine for $180,000 per year, and this is the company's only manufacturing overhead. With allowances for setups and maintenance, the machine is theoretically capable of producing up to 900,000 CDs per year. However, due to weak retail sales of CDs, the company's commercial customers are unlikely to order more than 600,000 CDs next year. The company uses machine time as the allocation base for applying manufacturing overhead. These data are summarized below:

Harmony Corporation Data	
Total manufacturing overhead cost...	$180,000 per year
Allocation base: Machine time per CD..	10 seconds per CD
Capacity..	900,000 CDs per year
Budgeted output for next year	600,000 CDs

If Harmony follows common practice and computes its predetermined overhead rate using estimated, or budgeted, figures, then its predetermined overhead rate for next year will be $0.03 per second of machine time, computed as follows:

$$\frac{\text{Estimated total manufacturing overhead cost, \$180,000}}{\text{Estimated total units in the allocation base, 600,000 CDs} \times \text{10 seconds per CD}} = \$0.03 \text{ per second}$$

Since each CD requires 10 seconds of machine time, each CD will be charged $0.30 of overhead cost.

Critics charge that there are two problems with this procedure. First, if predetermined overhead rates are based on budgeted activity, then the unit product costs will fluctuate, depending on the budgeted level of activity for the period. For example, if the budgeted output for the year was only 300,000 CDs, the predetermined overhead rate would be $0.06 per second of machine time or $0.60 per CD rather than $0.30 per CD. In general, if budgeted output falls, the overhead cost per unit will increase; it will appear that the CDs cost more to make. Managers may then be tempted to increase prices at the worst possible time—just as demand is falling.

Second, critics charge that under the traditional approach, products are charged for resources that they do not use. When the fixed costs of capacity are spread over estimated activity, the units produced must shoulder the costs of unused capacity. That is why the applied overhead cost per unit increases as the level of activity falls. The critics argue that products should be charged only for the capacity that they use; they should not be charged for the capacity they do not use. This can be accomplished by basing the predetermined overhead rate on capacity as follows:

$$\frac{\text{Total manufacturing overhead cost at capacity, \$180,000}}{\text{Total units in the allocation base at capacity, 900,000 CDs} \times \text{10 seconds per CD}} = \$0.02 \text{ per second}$$

Since the predetermined overhead rate is $0.02 per second, the overhead cost applied to each CD will be $0.20. This charge is constant and is not affected by the level of activity during a period. If output falls, the charge will still be $0.20 per CD.

The use of capacity will almost certainly result in underapplied overhead. If actual output at Harmony Corporation is 600,000 CDs, then only $120,000 of overhead cost will be applied to products ($0.20 per CD × 600,000 CDs). Since the actual overhead cost is $180,000, there will be underapplied overhead of $60,000. In another departure from tradition, the critics suggest that the underapplied overhead that results from idle capacity should be separately disclosed on the income statement as the Cost of Unused Capacity—a period expense. Disclosing this cost as a lump sum on the income statement, rather than burying it in Cost of Goods Sold or ending inventories, makes it much more visible to managers.

Official pronouncements (IAS 2) now prohibit basing predetermined overhead rates on capacity for external reports, although predetermined overhead rates based on capacity could be used for internal reporting. If so, managers would need to judge the benefits in terms of improved decision making against the potential cost of having to calculate inventory values and the Cost of Goods Sold using one method for external reporting and a different method for internal reporting.

APPENDIX 5A SUMMARY

- In this chapter, we have calculated the overhead application rate using a denominator equal to budgeted or estimated amount of the allocation base for the period. [LO8]
- Critics argue that this means the application rate for manufacturing overhead will fluctuate as the budgeted amount of the allocation base fluctuates from period to period. [LO8]
- Instead, it is suggested that the predetermined overhead rate should be based on total units of the allocation base at capacity. [LO8]
- The result will almost always be underapplied overhead, since most firms do not operate at full capacity all of the time. [LO8]
- Managers may wish to separate out underapplied overhead resulting from idle capacity in the income statement as the Cost of Unused Capacity, making it much more visible to managers and reminding them that unused capacity could be managed better in the next period. [LO8]

APPENDIX 5A QUESTIONS, EXERCISES, PROBLEMS, AND CASES

5A-1 If the plant is operated at less than capacity and the predetermined overhead rate is based on the estimated total units in the allocation base at capacity, will overhead ordinarily be overapplied or underapplied?

5A-2 Define the Cost of Unused Capacity and discuss why it might be calculated.

EXERCISE 5A-1 Overhead Rates and Capacity Issues [LO3, LO5, LO7, LO8]
Estate Pension Services helps clients set up and administer pension plans that comply with tax laws and regulatory requirements. The firm uses a job-order costing system in which overhead is applied to clients' accounts on the basis of professional staff-hours charged to the accounts. Data concerning two previous years appear below:

	2013	2014
Estimated professional staff-hours to be charged to clients' accounts....................	2,400	2,250
Estimated overhead cost............................	$144,000	$144,000
Professional staff-hours available....................	3,000	3,000

"Professional staff-hours available" is a measure of the capacity of the firm. Any hours available that are not charged to clients' accounts represent unused capacity.

Required:

1. Jennifer Miyami is an established client whose pension plan was set up many years ago. In both 2013 and 2014, only five hours of professional staff time were charged to Miyami's account. If the company bases its predetermined overhead rate on the estimated overhead cost and the estimated professional staff-hours to be charged to clients, how much overhead cost would have been applied to Miyami's account in 2013? In 2014?

2. Suppose that the company bases its predetermined overhead rate on the estimated overhead cost and the estimated professional staff-hours to be charged to clients as in (1) above. Also suppose that the actual professional staff-hours charged to clients' accounts and the actual overhead costs turn out to be exactly as estimated in both years. By how much would the overhead be underapplied or overapplied in 2013? In 2014?

3. Refer back to the data concerning Miyami in (1) above. If the company bases its predetermined overhead rate on the estimated overhead cost and the professional staff-hours available, how much overhead cost would have been applied to Miyami's account in 2013? In 2014?

4. Suppose that the company bases its predetermined overhead rate on the estimated overhead cost and the professional staff-hours available as in (3) above. Also suppose that the actual professional staff-hours charged to clients' accounts and the actual overhead costs turn out to be exactly as estimated in both years. By how much would the overhead be underapplied or overapplied in 2013? In 2014?

PROBLEM 5A–2 Predetermined Overhead Rate and Capacity [LO3, LO5, LO7, LO8]
Alderberry Recording Inc. is a small audio recording studio. The company handles work for advertising agencies—primarily for radio ads—and has a few singers and bands as clients. Alderberry Recording handles all aspects of recording, from editing to making a digital master from which CDs can be copied. The competition in the audio recording industry has always been tough, but it has been getting even tougher over the last several years. The studio has been losing customers to newer studios that are equipped with more up-to-date equipment and are able to offer very attractive prices and excellent service. Summary data concerning the last two years of operations follow:

	2013	2014
Estimated hours of studio service......................	1,000	750
Estimated studio overhead cost........................	$90,000	$90,000
Actual hours of studio service provided	900	600
Actual studio overhead cost incurred	$90,000	$90,000
Hours of studio service at capacity	1,800	1,800

The company applies studio overhead to recording jobs on the basis of the hours of studio service provided. For example, 30 hours of studio time were required to record, edit, and master the *Fire* music CD for a local band. All of the studio overhead is fixed, and the actual overhead cost incurred was exactly as estimated at the beginning of the year in both 2013 and 2014.

Required:

1. Alderberry Recording computes its predetermined overhead rate at the beginning of each year based on the estimated studio overhead and the estimated hours of studio service for the year. How much overhead would have been applied to the *Fire* job if it had been done in 2013? In 2014? By how much would overhead have been underapplied or overapplied in 2013? In 2014?

2. The president of Alderberry Recording has heard that some companies in the industry have changed to a system of computing the predetermined overhead rate at the beginning of each year based on the estimated studio overhead for the year and the hours of studio service that could be provided at capacity. He would like to know what effect this method would have on job costs. How much overhead would have been applied using this method to the *Fire* job if it had been done in 2013? In 2014? By how much would overhead have been underapplied or overapplied in 2013 using this method? In 2014?

3. How would you interpret the underapplied or overapplied overhead that results from using studio-hours at capacity to compute the predetermined overhead rate?

4. What fundamental business problem is Alderberry Recording facing? Which method of computing the predetermined overhead rate is likely to be more helpful in facing this problem? Explain.

CASE 5A–3 Ethics; Predetermined Overhead Rate and Capacity [LO5, LO8]

Melissa Loester, the new controller of PowerDrives Inc., has just returned from a seminar on the choice of the activity level in the predetermined overhead rate. Even though the subject did not sound exciting at first, she found that there were some important ideas presented that should get a hearing at her company. After returning from the seminar, she arranged a meeting with the production manager, Jan Laird, and the assistant production manager, Lonny Lee.

Loester: I ran across an idea that I wanted to check out with both of you. It's about the way we compute predetermined overhead rates.

Laird: We're all ears.

Loester: We compute the predetermined overhead rate by dividing the estimated total factory overhead for the coming year by the estimated total units produced for the coming year.

Lee: We've been doing that as long as I've been with the company.

Laird: And it has been done that way at every other company I've worked at, except at most places they divide by direct labour-hours.

Loester: We use units because it is simpler and we basically make one product with minor variations. But, there's another way to do it. Instead of dividing the estimated total factory overhead by the estimated total units produced for the coming year, we could divide by the total units produced at capacity.

Lee: Oh, the Marketing Department will love that. It will drop the costs on all of our products. They'll go wild over there cutting prices.

Loester: That is a worry, but I wanted to talk to both of you first before going over to Marketing.

Laird: Aren't you always going to have a lot of underapplied overhead?

Loester: That's correct, but let me show you how we would handle it. Here's an example based on our budget for next year:

Budgeted (estimated) production...................................	80,000 units
Budgeted sales..	80,000 units
Capacity..	100,000 units
Selling price..	$70 per unit
Variable manufacturing cost......................................	$18 per unit
Total manufacturing overhead cost (all fixed).....................	$2,000,000
Selling and administrative expenses (all fixed)...................	$ 1,950,000
Beginning inventories..	$0

Traditional approach to computing the predetermined overhead rate:

$$\text{Predetermined overhead rate} = \frac{\text{Estimated total manufacturing overhead cost}}{\text{Estimated total amount of the allocation base}}$$

$$= \frac{\$2,000,000}{80,000 \text{ units}} = \$25 \text{ per unit}$$

Budgeted Income Statement		
Revenue (80,000 units × $70 per unit)...........................		$5,600,000
Cost of goods sold:		
Variable manufacturing (80,000 units × $18 per unit)...........	$1,440,000	
Manufacturing overhead applied		
(80,000 units × $25 per unit).............................	2,000,000	3,440,000
Gross margin..		2,160,000
Selling and administrative expenses............................		1,950,000
Operating income...		$ 210,000

New approach to computing the predetermined overhead rate using capacity in the denominator:

$$\text{Predetermined overhead rate} = \frac{\text{Estimated total manufacturing overhead cost at capacity}}{\text{Estimated total amount of the allocation base at capacity}}$$

$$= \frac{\$2,000,000}{100,000 \text{ units}} = \$20 \text{ per unit}$$

Budgeted Income Statement		
Revenue (80,000 units × $70 per unit)		$5,600,000
Cost of goods sold:		
Variable manufacturing (80,000 units × $18 per unit).......	$1,440,000	
Manufacturing overhead applied		
(80,000 units × $20 per unit).........................	1,600,000	3,040,000
Gross margin..		2,560,000
Cost of unused capacity [(100,000 units – 80,000 units)		
× $20 per unit]...		400,000
Selling and administrative expenses.........................		1,950,000
Operating income		$ 210,000

Laird: Whoa!! I don't think I like the looks of that "Cost of unused capacity." If that thing shows up on the income statement, someone from headquarters is likely to come down here looking for some people to lay off.

Lee: I'm worried about something else, too. What happens when sales are not up to expectations? Can we pull the "hat trick"?

Loester: I'm sorry, I don't understand.

Laird: Lonny's talking about something that happens fairly regularly. When sales are down and profits look like they are going to be lower than the president told the owners they were going to be, the president comes down here and asks us to deliver some more profits.

Lee: And we pull them out of our hat.

Laird: Yeah, we just increase production until we get the profits we want.

Loester: I still don't understand. You mean you increase sales?

Laird: Nope, we increase production. We're the production managers, not the sales managers.

Loester: I get it. Since you have produced more, the sales force has more units it can sell.

Laird: Nope, the marketing people don't do a thing. We just build inventories and that does the trick.

Required:

In all of the questions below, assume that the predetermined overhead rate under the traditional method is $25 per unit, and under the new method it is $20 per unit. Also assume that under the traditional method (used for internal reporting), any underapplied or overapplied overhead is taken directly to the income statement as an adjustment to Cost of Goods Sold. Assume the company has decided to use these overhead methods for internal reporting.

1. Suppose actual production is 80,000 units. Compute the operating incomes that would be realized under the traditional and new methods if actual sales are 75,000 units and everything else turns out as expected.
2. How many units would have to be produced under each of the methods in order to realize the budgeted operating income of $210,000 if actual sales are 75,000 units and everything else turns out as expected?
3. What effect does the new method based on capacity have on the volatility of operating income?
4. Will the "hat trick" be easier or harder to perform if the new method based on capacity is used?
5. Do you think the "hat trick" is ethical?

SYSTEMS DESIGN: PROCESS COSTING

■ COSTING THE "QUICKER-PICKER-UPPER"

If you have ever spilled milk, there is a good chance that you used Bounty paper towels to clean up the mess. Procter & Gamble (P&G) manufactures Bounty in two main processing departments—Paper Making and Paper Converting. In the Paper Making Department, wood pulp is converted into paper and then spooled into 2,000-pound (900-kg) rolls. In the Paper Converting Department, two of the rolls of paper are simultaneously unwound into a machine that creates a two-ply paper towel that is decorated, perforated, and embossed to create texture. The large sheets of paper towels that emerge from this process are wrapped around a cylindrical cardboard core measuring eight feet (2.5 m) in length. Once enough sheets wrap around the core, the eight-foot roll is cut into individual rolls of Bounty that are sent down a conveyor to be wrapped, packed, and shipped.

In this type of manufacturing environment, costs cannot be readily traced to individual rolls of Bounty; however, given the homogeneous nature of the product, the total costs incurred in the Paper Making Department can be spread uniformly across its output of 2,000-pound rolls of paper. Similarly, the total costs incurred in the Paper Converting Department (including the cost of the 2,000-pound rolls that are transferred in from the Paper Making Department) can be spread uniformly across the number of cases of Bounty produced.

P&G uses a similar costing approach for many of its products, such as Tide laundry detergent, Crest toothpaste, and Pringles chips.

Source: Conversation with Brad Bays, formerly a Procter & Gamble financial executive.

A s explained in Chapter 5, there are two basic costing systems in use: job-order costing and process costing. A job-order costing system is used in situations where many different jobs or products are worked on each period. Examples of industries that typically use job-order costing are furniture manufacturers; special-order printers; shipbuilders; and many types of service organizations, such as repair shops and professional accounting services.

By contrast, process costing is most commonly used in industries that produce essentially homogeneous (i.e., uniform) products on a continuous basis, such as bricks, corn flakes, pop, and paper. Process costing is particularly used in companies that convert basic raw materials into homogeneous products, such as Alcan (aluminum ingots), Kimberly-Clark (toilet paper), Dover Industries (flour), Imperial Oil (gasoline and lubricating oils), and Christie (crackers). A form of process costing may also be used by utilities that produce gas, water, and electricity. As suggested by the length of this list, process costing is in very wide use.

Our purpose in this chapter is to extend the discussion of product costing to include a process costing system.

■ COMPARISON OF JOB-ORDER AND PROCESS COSTING

Much of what you learned in the preceding chapter about costing and cost flows applies equally well to process costing in this chapter. We are not throwing out all that you have learned about costing and starting from scratch with a whole new system. The similarities that exist between job-order and process costing can be summarized as follows:

1. Both systems have the same basic purposes—to assign materials, labour, and overhead costs to products and to provide a mechanism for computing unit costs.

2. Both systems use the same basic manufacturing accounts, including Manufacturing Overhead, Raw Materials, Work in Process, and Finished Goods.

3. The flow of costs through the manufacturing accounts is basically the same in both systems.

The differences between job-order and process costing arise from two factors. The first is that the flow of units in a process costing system is more or less continuous, and the second is that these units are indistinguishable from one another. Under process costing, it makes no sense to try to identify materials, labour, and overhead costs with a particular order from a customer (as we did with job-order costing), since each order is just one of many that are filled from a continuous flow of virtually identical units from the production line. Under process costing, we accumulate costs *by department*, rather than by order, and assign these costs equally to all units that pass through the department during a period.

A further difference between the two costing systems is that the job cost sheet is not used in process costing, since the focal point of that method is departments. Instead of using job cost sheets, a document known as a **production report** is prepared for each department in which work is done on products. The production report serves several functions. It summarizes the number of units moving through a department during a period, and it also provides a computation of unit costs. In addition, it shows what costs were charged to the department and how these costs were disposed. The department production report is the key document in a process costing system.

The major differences between job-order and process costing are summarized in Exhibit 6–1.

Production report
A report that summarizes all activity in a department's Work in Process account during a period and that contains three parts: a quantity schedule and a computation of equivalent units, a computation of total and unit costs, and a cost reconciliation.

EXHIBIT 6-1   Differences between Job-Order and Process Costing

Job-Order Costing	Process Costing
1. Many different jobs are worked on during each period, with each job having different production requirements.	1. A single product is produced either on a continuous basis or in long production runs. All units of product are identical.
2. Costs are accumulated by individual job, regardless of the accounting period during which the work is done.	2. Costs are accumulated by department, during an accounting period.
3. The *job cost sheet* is the key document controlling the accumulation of costs by a job.	3. The *department production report* is the key document showing the accumulation and disposition of costs by a department.
4. Unit costs are computed *by job* on the job cost sheet.	4. Unit costs are computed *by department* on the department production report.

■ PROCESS COST FLOWS

Before presenting a detailed example of process costing, it is useful to see how manufacturing costs flow through a process costing system.

Processing Departments

Processing department
Any location in an organization where work is performed on a product and where materials, labour, or overhead costs are added to the product.

A **processing department** is part of an organization where work is performed on a product and where materials, labour, or overhead costs are added to the product. For example, a potato chip factory operated by Frito-Lay might have three processing departments—one for preparing potatoes, one for cooking, and one for inspecting and packaging. A brick factory might have two processing departments—one for mixing and moulding clay into brick form and one for firing the moulded brick. A company can have as many or as few processing departments as are needed to complete a product or service. Some products and services may go through several processing departments, while others may go through only one or two. Regardless of the number of departments involved, all processing departments have two essential features: First, the activity performed in the processing department must be performed uniformly on all of the units passing through it. Second, the output of the processing department must be identical.

Products in a process costing environment, such as bricks or potato chips, typically flow in a sequence from one department to another, as shown in Exhibit 6–2.

IN BUSINESS

In 2013, **Coca-Cola Company** sold almost $47 billion of products in over 200 countries. Some of the key processing steps in its bottling process are washing and rinsing bottles, mixing and blending ingredients, filling and capping bottles, and labelling and packaging bottles. Raw material costs are added at various stages during this process. For example, sugar, filtered water, carbon dioxide, and syrup are added during the filling and capping stage, and labels are added during the labelling and packaging stage.

Coca-Cola's manufacturing process is well suited for process costing because it produces a continuous stream of identical bottles of pop. The material costs and conversion costs incurred at the various stages of the production process can be assigned to products by spreading them evenly over the total production volume.

Source: The Coca-Cola Company 2013 *Annual Report* and http://www.coca-colacompany.com.

EXHIBIT 6-2   Sequential Processing Departments

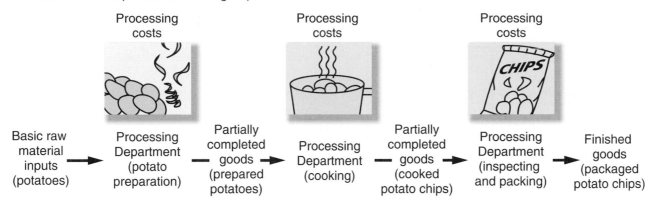

Basic raw material inputs (potatoes) → Processing Department (potato preparation) → Partially completed goods (prepared potatoes) → Processing Department (cooking) → Partially completed goods (cooked potato chips) → Processing Department (inspecting and packing) → Finished goods (packaged potato chips)

The Flow of Materials, Labour, and Overhead Costs

Cost accumulation is simpler in a process costing system than in a job-order costing system. In a process costing system, instead of having to trace costs to hundreds of different jobs, costs are traced to only a few processing departments. In a process costing system, production costs are not identified with specific units or batches of product. Instead, an average unit cost is computed by dividing total production costs for the period by the number of units produced during the same period.

A T-account model of materials, labour, and overhead cost flows in a process costing system is given in Exhibit 6-3. Several key points should be noted from this exhibit. First, note that a separate Work in Process account is maintained for *each processing department*. In contrast, in a job-order costing system there may be only a single Work in Process account for the entire company. Second, note that the completed production of the first processing department (Department A in the exhibit) is transferred into the Work in Process account of the second processing department (Department B), where it undergoes further work. After this further work, the completed units are transferred into Finished Goods. (In Exhibit 6-3, we show only two processing departments, but a company may have many processing departments.)

LEARNING OBJECTIVE ①
Record the flow of materials, labour, and overhead through a process costing system.

IN BUSINESS

The Trappist monks of St. Sixtus monastery in Belgium have been brewing beer since 1839. Customers must make an appointment with the monastery to buy a maximum of two 24-bottle cases per month. The scarce and highly prized beer sells for between €30 and €40 per case depending on the type. The monk's brewing ingredients include water, malt, hops, sugar, and yeast. The sequential steps of the beer-making process include grinding and crushing, brewing, filtering, boiling, fermentation, storage, and bottling.

Unlike growth-oriented for-profit companies, the monastery has not expanded its production capacity since 1946, seeking instead to sell just enough beer to sustain the monks' modest lifestyle. The celebrated beer—often called the best in the world—is usually only available for sale at the abbey, located in the Belgian countryside, but in December 2012, the monks exported a limited amount of beer to other countries in North America and Europe to raise money needed for renovations to the abbey. Mark Bode, spokesman for the abbey, suggests this won't happen again any time soon. "They say, 'We are monks, we don't want to be too commercial. We needed some money to help us buy the new abbey and that's it,'" Bode explains. "Back to normal again."

Source: John W. Miller, "Trappist Command: Thou Shalt Not Buy Too Much of Our Beer," *The Wall Street Journal*, November 29, 2007, pp. A1 and A14, http://online.wsj.com/news/articles/SB119628388037006909; http://www.sintsixtus.be/eng/brouwerij.htm; http://www.npr.org/blogs/thesalt/2012/12/12/166987378/a-sign-from-above-needing-new-roof-monks-sell-rare-beer-in-u-s.

EXHIBIT 6-3 T-Account Model of Process Costing Flows

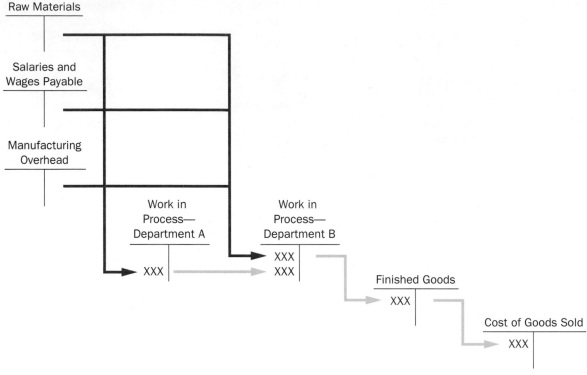

Transferred-in costs
Costs attached to products that
have been received from a prior
processing department.

Finally, note that materials, labour, and overhead costs can be added in *any* processing department—not just the first. Costs in Department B's Work in Process account consist of the materials, labour, and overhead costs incurred in Department B plus the costs attached to partially completed units transferred in from Department A (called **transferred-in costs**).

Materials, Labour, and Overhead Cost Entries

To complete our discussion of cost flows in a process costing system, in this section we show journal entries relating to materials, labour, and overhead costs at Standard Products Co., a producer of Green Clean, a multi-purpose household cleaner. The company has two processing departments—Mixing and Filling. In the Mixing Department, the various ingredients are checked for quality and then mixed to create bulk liquid cleaner. In the Filling Department, bottles are checked for defects, filled with cleaner, capped, and labelled, and then the bottles are packed for shipping.

Materials Costs   As in job-order costing, materials are drawn from the storeroom using a materials requisition form. Materials can be added in any processing department, although it is not unusual for materials to be added only in the first processing department, with subsequent departments adding only labour and overhead costs as the partially completed units move along toward completion.

At Standard Products Co., some materials (water, cleaning agents, and fragrances) are added in the Mixing Department, and other materials (bottles, caps, labels, and packing materials) are added in the Filling Department. The journal entry for placing materials into process in the first department is as follows:

Work in Process—Mixing.......................	20,000	
Raw Materials............................		20,000

The journal entry to record the materials used in the second processing department, the Filling Department, is as follows:

Work in Process—Filling.......................	10,000	
Raw Materials............................		10,000

Labour Costs   In process costing, labour costs are traced to departments, not to individual jobs. The following entry records the labour costs in the Mixing Department at Standard Products Co.:

Work in Process—Mixing......................	7,500	
Salaries and Wages Payable..............		7,500

Overhead Costs   If production is stable from period to period and if overhead costs are incurred uniformly over the year, actual overhead costs can be charged to departments. However, if production levels fluctuate or if overhead costs are not incurred uniformly, charging products with actual overhead costs will result in unit product costs that vary randomly from one period to the next. In such a situation, predetermined overhead rates should be used to charge overhead cost to products, the same as in job-order costing. When predetermined overhead rates are used, each department has its own separate rate, with the rates being computed as discussed in Chapter 5. Overhead cost is then applied to units of product as the units move through the various departments. Since predetermined overhead rates are widely used in process costing, we will assume their use throughout the remainder of this chapter.

The following journal entry is used to apply overhead costs to units of product for the Mixing Department:

Work in Process—Mixing......................	12,000	
Manufacturing Overhead.................		12,000

Completing the Cost Flows   Once processing has been completed in a department, the product units are transferred to the next department for further processing, as illustrated earlier in the T-accounts in Exhibit 6–3. The following journal entry is used to transfer the costs of partially completed units from the Mixing Department to the Filling Department:

Work in Process—Filling.......................	39,500	
Work in Process—Mixing		39,500

After processing has been completed in the Filling department, the costs of the completed units are then transferred to the Finished Goods inventory account:

Finished Goods................................	49,500	
Work in Process—Filling..................		49,500

Finally, when a customer's order is filled and units are sold, the cost of the units is transferred to Cost of Goods Sold:

Cost of Goods Sold............................	49,500	
Finished Goods..........................		49,500

To summarize, the cost flows between accounts are basically the same in a process costing system as they are in a job-order costing system. The only noticeable difference at this point is that a process costing system has a separate Work in Process account for each department.

We now turn our attention to Tropic Breeze, a company that manufactures two models of an efficient and reliable industrial fan for use in large factory spaces. Tropic Breeze uses process costing to determine its unit product cost. The company's production process includes three processing departments, the Housings Department, the Electrics and Testing Department, and the Inspection and Packing Department. The basic idea in process costing is to add together all of the costs incurred in a department during a period and then spread these costs uniformly across the units processed in that department during that period. As we will see, applying this simple idea involves a few complications.

EQUIVALENT UNITS OF PRODUCTION

LEARNING OBJECTIVE
Compute the equivalent units of production using the weighted-average method.

Equivalent units
The product of the number of partially completed units and their percentage of completion with respect to a particular cost. Equivalent units are the number of complete whole units one could obtain from the materials and effort contained in partially completed units.

FIFO method
A method of accounting for cost flows in a process costing system in which equivalent units and unit costs relate only to work done during the current period.

Weighted-average method
A method of process costing that blends together units and costs from both the current and prior periods.

Equivalent units of production (weighted-average method)
The units transferred to the next department (or to finished goods) during the period plus the equivalent units in the department's ending work in process inventory.

After materials, labour, and overhead costs have been accumulated in a department, the department's output must be determined so that unit costs can be computed. In the simplest case, average unit cost can be computed by dividing total manufacturing costs by the number of units produced during a given time period. The difficulty is that a department usually has some partially completed units in its ending inventory. This is because the production schedule does not necessarily match the accounting schedule. Companies want to value their inventory on hand at the end of each accounting period (typically, each month), but production scheduling is tied more directly to customer orders than to accounting periods. Therefore, there will typically be incomplete units in inventory at the end of an accounting period; we deal with this issue by counting them in "equivalent units." It does not seem reasonable to count these partially completed units as equivalent to fully completed units when counting the department's output. Therefore, Tropic Breeze mathematically converts these partially completed units into an *equivalent* number of fully completed units. In process costing, this is done using the following formula:

Equivalent units = Number of partially completed units × Percentage completion

As the formula states, **equivalent units** are defined as the product of the number of partially completed units and the percentage completion of those units. Equivalent units are the number of complete units that could have been obtained from the materials and effort that went into the partially completed units.

For example, suppose the Housings Department at Tropic Breeze has 500 units in its ending work in process inventory that are 60% complete. These 500 partially complete units are equivalent to 300 fully complete units (500 × 60% = 300). Therefore, the ending work in process inventory contains 300 equivalent units. These equivalent units are added to any fully completed units to determine the period's output for the department—called the *equivalent units of production*.

Equivalent units of production for a period can be computed in two different ways. Accounting standards (IAS 2) allow for inventory costing using either the weighted-average or the FIFO method. In this chapter, we discuss the *weighted-average method*. In Appendix 6A, we discuss the *FIFO (first in, first out) method*. In the **FIFO method** of process costing, equivalent units and unit costs relate only to work done during the current period. In contrast, the **weighted-average method** blends together units and costs from the current period with units and costs from the prior period. The **equivalent units of production (weighted-average method)** for a department are the number of units transferred to the next department (or to finished goods) plus the equivalent units in the department's ending work in process inventory.

Weighted-Average Method

Under the weighted-average method, a department's equivalent units are computed as follows:

Instant Quiz 6-2
Suppose there are 5,000 full-time students and 1,250 part-time students (taking approximately half of the regular class load) in the Faculty of Management at Westly University. Using the concept of equivalent units, how many full-time equivalent students are enrolled in the Faculty of Management?

Weighted–Average Method
(a separate calculation is made for each cost category in each processing department)

$$\begin{array}{c}\text{Equivalent units} \\ \text{of production}\end{array} = \begin{array}{c}\text{Units transferred to the next} \\ \text{department or to finished goods}\end{array} + \begin{array}{c}\text{Equivalent units in ending} \\ \text{work in process inventory}\end{array}$$

Note that computation of the equivalent units of production involves adding the number of units transferred out of the department to the equivalent units in the department's ending inventory. There is no need to compute the equivalent units for the units transferred out of the department—they are 100% complete with respect to the work done in that department or they would not be transferred out. In other words, each unit transferred out of the department is counted as one equivalent unit.

Consider the Electrics and Testing Department at Tropic Breeze. This department uses computerized machines to ensure the electrical integrity of the industrial fans produced. Efficiency and reliability are a key to Tropic Breeze Fans' competitive advantage; the company has invested in specialized testing equipment to ensure customer satisfaction with the end product. The following activity took place in the department in May:

		Percentage Completed	
Electrics and Testing Department	**Units**	**Materials**	**Conversion**
Work in process, May 1...	200	55%	30%
Units started into production during May	5,000		
Units completed during May and			
transferred to the next department	4,800	100%*	100%*
Work in process, May 31..	400	40%	25%
*It is always assumed that units transferred out of a department are 100% complete with respect to the processing done in that department.			

Note the use of the term *conversion* in the above table. Conversion cost, as defined in Chapter 2, is direct labour cost plus manufacturing overhead cost. In process costing, conversion cost is often—but not always—treated as a single element of product cost.

Note that the May 1 beginning work in process was 55% complete with respect to materials costs and 30% complete with respect to conversion costs. This means that 55% of the materials costs required to complete the units had already been incurred. Likewise, 30% of the conversion costs required to complete the units had already been incurred.

Two equivalent unit figures must be computed—one for materials and one for conversion. These computations are shown in Exhibit 6–4.

Note that the computations in Exhibit 6–4 ignore the fact that the units in the beginning work in process inventory were partially complete. For example, the 200 units in beginning inventory were already 30% complete with respect to conversion costs. The 4,800 units transferred to the next department consist of 200 units in the beginning inventory plus 4,600 units started and completed during the current period. The weighted-average method is concerned only with the equivalent units that are in the ending inventories and in units transferred to the next department—it is not concerned with the fact that the beginning inventory was already partially complete. In other words, the 4,900 equivalent units computed using the weighted-average method include work that was accomplished in prior periods. This is a key point regarding the weighted-average method, and it is easy to overlook.

Instant Quiz 6-3
Of materials, labour, and overhead, which types of cost make up conversion costs?

EXHIBIT 6-4   Equivalent Units of Production: Weighted-Average Method

	Materials	Conversion
Units transferred to the next department.................	4,800	4,800
Work in process, May 31:		
400 units × 40% complete with respect to materials	160	
400 units × 25% complete with respect to conversion......		100
Equivalent units of production	4,960	4,900

EXHIBIT 6-5 Visual Perspective of Equivalent Units of Production

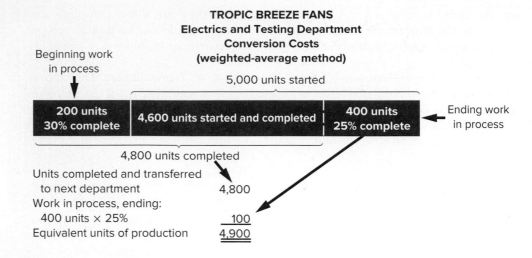

TROPIC BREEZE FANS
Electrics and Testing Department
Conversion Costs
(weighted-average method)

Beginning work in process

5,000 units started

| 200 units 30% complete | 4,600 units started and completed | 400 units 25% complete |

Ending work in process

4,800 units completed

Units completed and transferred
  to next department   4,800
Work in process, ending:
  400 units × 25%   100
Equivalent units of production   4,900

Averages, in general, hide the details of the elements that make up the average. For example, the average of 2 + 4 is 3. The average of 1 + 5 is 3. If the manager is not interested in the details of the elements, then the average provides all of the information needed. If costs from one period to the next are approximately equal (for example, 3 + 3), the average is also a reasonable representation of the results. A third explanation for the use of the average approach is the relative size of the beginning inventory of work in process compared to the current production. For example, if the beginning inventory is only one-tenth of the current production, the average (weighted) of $(\frac{1}{10})(1) + (\frac{9}{10})(5) = 4.60$ is very accurate. In addition to the advantage of ease of computation, another advantage of the weighted-average method is that it generates very accurate results when costs are relatively stable from one period to the next or when the size of current production dominates the beginning inventory. All of these factors are common characteristics of process costing environments!

Exhibit 6–5 provides an alternative way of looking at the computation of equivalent units of production. Study this exhibit carefully before going on.

■ COMPUTE AND APPLY COSTS

LEARNING OBJECTIVE 3

Compute the cost per equivalent unit using the weighted-average method.

In the last section we computed the equivalent units of production for materials and for conversion at Tropic Breeze Fans. In this section, we will compute the cost per equivalent unit for materials and for conversion. We will then use these costs to value ending work in process and finished goods inventories. Exhibit 6–6 displays all of the data concerning May's operations in the Electrics and Testing Department that we will need to complete these tasks.

Cost per Equivalent Unit—Weighted-Average Method

In the weighted-average method, the cost per equivalent unit is computed as follows:

Weighted—Average Method
(a separate calculation is made for each cost category in each processing department)

$$\text{Cost per equivalent unit} = \frac{\text{Cost of beginning work in process inventory} + \text{Cost added during the period}}{\text{Equivalent units of production}}$$

Work in process, beginning:	
Units in process	200
Stage of completion with respect to materials	55%
Stage of completion with respect to conversion	30%
Costs in the beginning inventory:	
Materials cost	$ 9,600
Conversion cost	5,575
Total cost in the beginning inventory.................	$ 15,175
Units started into production during the period	5,000
Units completed and transferred out...................	4,800
Costs added to production during the period:	
Materials cost	$368,600
Conversion cost	350,900
Total cost added in the department...................	$ 719,500
Work in process, ending:	
Units in process	400
Stage of completion with respect to materials	40%
Stage of completion with respect to conversion	25%

EXHIBIT 6–6   Electrics and Testing Department Data for May Operations

Note that the numerator is the sum of the cost of beginning work in process inventory and the cost added during the period. Thus, the weighted-average method blends together costs from the prior and current periods. That is why it is called the weighted-average method: it averages together units and costs from both the prior and current periods.

The costs per equivalent unit for materials and for conversion are computed below for the Electrics and Testing Department for May:

Instant Quiz 6-4
Mike Jones, Director of Accounting at Acme Brands, has calculated that there are 6,250 equivalent units of production for materials in the Mixing Department at the end of the current month. Assuming beginning work in process inventory costs for materials were $7,250, and $10,750 of additional materials costs was added in the period, calculate the cost per equivalent unit for materials for the Mixing Department using the weighted-average method.

Electrics and Testing Department **Costs per Equivalent Unit**	**Materials**	**Conversion**
Cost of beginning work in process inventory	$ 9,600	$ 5,575
Costs added during the period	368,600	350,900
Total cost (a)..	$378,200	$356,475
Equivalent units of production (see the computations in		
Exhibit 6–4) (b)..	4,960	4,900
Cost per equivalent unit (a) ÷ (b)..	$76.25	$72.75

■ APPLYING COSTS—WEIGHTED-AVERAGE METHOD

The costs per equivalent unit are used to value units in ending inventory and units that are transferred to the next department. For example, each unit transferred out of Tropic Breeze's Electrics and Testing Department to the Inspection and Packing Department will carry with it a cost of $149 ($76.25 for materials cost and $72.75 for conversion cost). Since 4,800 units were transferred out in May to the next department, the total cost assigned to these units is $715,200 (4,800 units × $149 per unit).

A complete accounting of the costs of both ending work in process inventory and the units transferred out follows:

LEARNING OBJECTIVE ④
Assign costs to units using the weighted-average method.

Electrics and Testing Department **Costs of Ending Work in Process Inventory and the Units Transferred Out**			
	Materials	Conversion	Total
Ending work in process inventory:			
Equivalent units of production (a)			
400 units × 40% complete with respect to materials	160		
400 units × 25% complete with respect to conversion..............		100	
Cost per equivalent unit (see above) (b)...........................	$76.25	$72.75	
Cost of ending work in process inventory (a) × (b)................	$12,200	$7,275	$19,475
Units completed and transferred out:			
Units transferred to the next department (a).......................	4,800	4,800	
Cost per equivalent unit (see above) (b)...........................	$76.25	$72.75	
Cost of units transferred out (a) × (b)............................	$366,000	$349,200	$715,200

In each case, the equivalent units are multiplied by the cost per equivalent unit to determine the cost assigned to the units. This is done for each cost category—in this case, materials and conversion. The equivalent units for the units completed and transferred out are simply the number of units transferred to the next department because they would not have been transferred unless they were complete.

The costs assigned to ending work in process inventory and to the units transferred out reconcile with the costs we started with in Exhibit 6–6, as shown below:

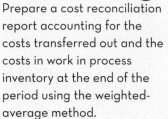

LEARNING OBJECTIVE 5

Prepare a cost reconciliation report accounting for the costs transferred out and the costs in work in process inventory at the end of the period using the weighted-average method.

Electrics and Testing Department **Cost Reconciliation**	
Costs to be accounted for:	
Cost of beginning work in process inventory (Exhibit 6–6)...	$ 15,175
Costs added to production during the period (Exhibit 6–6)	719,500
Total cost to be accounted for...	$734,675
Costs accounted for as follows:	
Cost of ending work in process inventory (see above)...	$ 19,475
Cost of units transferred out (see above)...	715,200
Total cost accounted for	$734,675

The $715,200 cost of the units transferred to the next department, Inspection and Packing, is accounted for in that department as "costs transferred in." It is treated in the process costing system as just another category of costs, like materials or conversion costs. The only difference is that the costs transferred in are always 100% complete with respect to the work done in the Inspection and Packing Department. When the products are completed in this last department, their costs are transferred to finished goods.

Summary of Tropic Breeze Fans Costing

Exhibit 6–7 displays a production report for the Electrics and Testing Department costs calculated on the previous pages. The production activity in units is displayed in the Quantity Schedule. This schedule summarizes the activity for the month of May and is used to begin the calculation of equivalent units of production. The schedule of costs per equivalent unit summarizes the production costs for the month of May plus the beginning work in process for May. These costs are used together with the equivalent units from the quantity schedule to compute the weighted unit costs. Finally, the production report is completed by computing the cost reconciliation. The total costs to be accounted for are tested against the total of

EXHIBIT 6–7   Production Report—Weighted-Average Method

TROPIC BREEZE FANS
Electrics and Testing Department Production Report
(weighted-average method)

Quantity Schedule and Equivalent Units

	Quantity Schedule		
Units to be accounted for:			
Work in process, May 1 (materials 55% complete; conversion 30% complete)	200		
Started into production	5,000		
Total units.................................	5,200		

	Quantity Schedule	Equivalent Units (EU)	
		Materials	Conversion
Units accounted for as follows:			
Transferred to the next department	4,800	4,800	4,800
Work in process, May 31 (materials 40% complete; conversion 25% complete	400	160*	100†
Total units and equivalent units of production (see Exhibit 6-4)	5,200	4,960	4,900

Costs per Equivalent Unit

	Total Cost	Materials	Conversion	Whole Unit
Cost to be accounted for:				
Work in process, May 1	$ 15,175	$ 9,600	$ 5,575	
Cost added in the Electrics and Testing Department.................................	719,500	368,600	350,900	
Total cost (a)	$734,675	$378,200	$356,475	
Equivalent units of production (b) (see above)		4,960	4,900	
Cost per EU,‡ (a) ÷ (b)		$ 76.25 +	$ 72.75 =	$149.00

Cost Reconciliation

	Total Cost	Materials	Conversion
Cost accounted for as follows:			
Transferred to next department:			
4,800 units × $149.00 each.....................	$715,200	4,800	4,800
Work in process, May 31:			
Materials, at $76.25 per EU	12,200	160	
Conversion, at $72.75 per EU....................	7,275		100
Total work in process, May 31	19,475		
Total cost.......................................	$734,675		

*40% × 400 units = 160 equivalent units.
†25% × 400 units = 100 equivalent units.
‡EU = Equivalent unit.

EXHIBIT 6–8   Schedule of Cost of Goods Manufactured

Tropic Breeze Fans Schedule of Cost of Goods Manufactured	
Cost of goods manufactured:	
Total manufacturing costs	$719,500
Add: Beginning work in process inventory	15,175
	734,675
Deduct: Ending work in process inventory	19,475
Cost of goods manufactured	$715,200

the cost of units transferred to the next department and the work in process costs at May 31 to ensure all costs have been properly accounted for.

It is worth noting at this point the relationship of the costs reflected in the production report to the schedules of cost of goods manufactured presented in Chapters 2 and 5 and the work in process general ledger account. Exhibit 5–11 in Chapter 5 will help you picture the relationships.

Exhibit 6–8 provides an example calculation of the cost of goods manufactured for Tropic Breeze Fans. The cost of the beginning work in process inventory, $15,175, is the beginning general ledger balance for work in process. The total manufacturing costs of $719,500 represent the cost of raw material used, the cost of direct labour used, and the manufacturing overhead applied during May. These three types of costs, at $719,500, increase the Work in Process account for May. The cost of goods manufactured is $715,200, which represents what is transferred out of work in process for May, leaving the ending work in process balance in the general ledger of $19,475. A careful tracing of the description of these costs to the schedule of costs of goods manufactured as shown in Exhibit 5–11 will help you visualize how the costs from the production report for process costs link to the general ledger.

■ OPERATION COSTING

The costing systems discussed in Chapter 5 and in this chapter represent the two ends of a continuum. On one end, we have job-order costing, which is used by companies that produce many different items—generally to customer specifications. On the other end, we have process costing, which is used by companies that produce basically homogeneous products in large quantities. Between these two extremes, there are many hybrid systems that include characteristics of both job-order and process costing. One of these hybrids is called *operation costing*.

Operation costing

A hybrid costing system used when products are manufactured in batches and when the products have some common characteristics and some individual characteristics. This system handles materials the same way as in job-order costing and labour and overhead the same way as in process costing.

Operation costing is used in situations where products have some common characteristics and also some individual characteristics. Shoes, for example, have common characteristics in that all styles involve cutting and sewing that can be done on a repetitive basis, using the same equipment and following the same basic procedures. Shoes also have individual characteristics—some are made of expensive leathers and others may be made using inexpensive synthetic materials. In a situation such as this, where products have some common characteristics but also must be handled individually, operation costing may be used to determine product costs.

As mentioned above, operation costing is a hybrid system that employs aspects of both job-order and process costing. Products are typically handled in batches when operation costing is in use, with each batch charged for its own specific materials. In this sense, operation costing is similar to job-order costing. However, labour and overhead costs are accumulated by operation or by department, and these costs are assigned to units as in process costing. If shoes are being produced, for example, each shoe is charged the same per unit conversion cost, regardless of the style involved, but it is charged with its specific materials cost. Thus, the company is able to distinguish between styles in terms of materials, but it is able to employ the simplicity of a process costing system for labour and overhead costs.

Examples of other products for which operation costing may be used are electronic equipment (such as semiconductors), textiles, clothing, and jewellery (such as rings, bracelets, and medallions). Products of this type are typically produced in batches, but they can vary considerably from model to model or from style to style in terms of the cost of raw material inputs. Therefore, an operation costing system is well suited for providing cost data.

■ FLEXIBLE MANUFACTURING SYSTEMS

A plant that uses a flexible manufacturing system (FMS) is heavily automated, and its activities are organized around cells, or islands, of automated equipment. The FMS concept is having a major impact on costing in several ways. One of these is through allowing companies to switch their systems from the more costly job-order approach to a less costly process or operation approach. This switching is made possible because FMS is proving to be highly efficient in reducing the setup time required between products and jobs. With setup time only a small fraction of previous levels, companies are able to move between products and jobs with about the same speed as if they were working in a continuous, process-type environment. The result is that these companies are able to employ process costing techniques in situations that previously required job-order costing. As the use of FMS grows (and becomes even more efficient), some managers predict that job-order costing will slowly disappear except in a few select industries.

A further impact of FMS is through its focus on cells rather than on departments. Although production reports are still prepared in FMS settings, these reports are either much broader, including the entire production process (many cells), or much narrower, including only a single cell or workstation. If JIT is practised, then the production report becomes greatly simplified, regardless of the level at which it is prepared.

KNOWLEDGE IN ACTION

Managers can apply their knowledge about process costing when
- Calculating the product/service cost when many units of relatively uniform products/services are produced in the year
- Setting prices to ensure the price exceeds the cost to produce the product or service
- Calculating the value of inventory included on the balance sheet and the cost of goods sold disclosed on the income statement

SUMMARY

- Process costing is used in situations where homogeneous products or services are produced on a continuous basis. Costs flow through the manufacturing accounts in basically the same way in a process costing system as in a job-order costing system. However, costs are accumulated by department rather than by job in process costing. [LO1]
- In process costing, the equivalent units of production must be determined for each cost category in each department. Under the weighted-average method, the equivalent units of production equals the number of units transferred out to the next department or to finished goods plus the equivalent units in ending work in process inventory. The equivalent units in ending inventory equal the product of the number of partially completed units in ending work in process inventory and their percentage of completion with respect to the specific cost category. [LO2]

- • Under the weighted-average method, the cost per equivalent unit for a specific cost category is computed by adding the cost of beginning work in process inventory and the cost added during the period and then dividing the result by the equivalent units of production (i.e., calculating the average). [LO3]
- • The cost per equivalent unit is then used to value the ending work in process inventory and the units transferred out to the next department or to finished goods. [LO4]
- • Costs are transferred from one department to the next until the last processing department. At that point, the cost of completed units is transferred to finished goods. At the end of the period, a cost reconciliation is prepared to account for the costs transferred out and costs in work in process inventory at the end of the period. [LO5]

REVIEW PROBLEM 1: PROCESS COST FLOWS AND REPORTS

Lanyard Home Paint Company produces exterior latex paint, which it sells in four-litre containers. The company has two processing departments—Base Fab and Finishing. White paint, which is used as a base for all of the company's paints, is mixed from raw ingredients in the Base Fab Department. In the Finishing Department, pigments are added to the basic white paint, the pigmented paint is squirted under pressure into four-litre containers, and the containers are labelled and packed for shipping. Information relating to the company's operations for April is as follows:

a. Raw materials were issued for use in production: Base Fab Department, $851,000; Finishing Department, $629,000.

b. Direct labour costs were incurred: Base Fab Department, $330,000; Finishing Department, $270,000.

c. Manufacturing overhead cost was applied: Base Fab Department, $665,000; Finishing Department, $405,000.

d. Paint that had been prepared for shipping was transferred from the Finishing Department to Finished Goods: $3,200,000.

Required:

1. Prepare journal entries to record items (*a*) through (*d*) above.

2. Post the journal entries from (1) above to T-accounts. The balance in the Base Fab Department's Work in Process account on April 1 was $150,000; the balance in the Finishing Department's Work in Process account was $70,000. After posting entries to the T-accounts, find the ending balance in each department's Work in Process account.

3. Prepare a production report for the Base Fab Department for April. The following additional information is available regarding production in the Base Fab Department during April:

Production data for four-litre containers of paint:

Units (containers) in process, April 1: 100% complete as to materials, 60% complete as to labour and overhead...	30,000
Units (containers) started into production during April	420,000
Units (containers) completed and transferred to the Finishing Department	370,000
Units (containers) in process, April 30: 50% complete as to materials, 25% complete as to labour and overhead...	80,000

Cost data:

Work in process inventory, April 1:

Materials..	$ 92,000
Labour..	21,000
Overhead..	37,000
Total cost...	$150,000

Cost added during April:

Materials..	$851,000
Labour..	330,000
Overhead..	665,000

4. Prepare the journal entry to record the transfer of basic white paint from the Base Fab Department to the Finishing Department, and post it to the appropriate T-accounts (*Hint:* The dollar amount of the transfer was determined in (3) above).

Solution to Review Problem 1

1. *a.* Work in Process—Base Fab Department.................................... 851,000
   Work in Process—Finishing Department..................................... 629,000
      Raw Materials 1,480,000
   b. Work in Process—Base Fab Department.................................... 330,000
   Work in Process—Finishing Department..................................... 270,000
      Salaries and Wages Payable... 600,000
   c. Work in Process—Base Fab Department.................................... 665,000
   Work in Process—Finishing Department..................................... 405,000
      Manufacturing Overhead... 1,070,000
   d. Finished Goods.. 3,200,000
      Work in Process—Finishing Department............................... 3,200,000

2.

Raw Materials

| Bal. | XXX | (*a*) | 1,480,000 |

Salaries and Wages Payable

| | | (*b*) | 600,000 |

Work in Process— Base Fab Department

Bal.	150,000	(Part 4)	1,850,000
(*a*)	851,000		
(*b*)	330,000		
(*c*)	665,000		
Bal.	146,000		

Manufacturing Overhead

| (Various actual costs) | | (*c*) | 1,070,000 |

Work in Process— Finishing Department

Bal.	70,000	(*d*)	3,200,000
(*a*)	629,000		
(*b*)	270,000		
(*c*)	405,000		
(*d*)	1,850,000		
Bal.	24,000		

Finished Goods

| Bal. | | | XXX |
| (*d*) | 3,200,000 | | |

3.

LANYARD HOME PAINT COMPANY
Production Report—Base Fab Department
For the Month Ended April 30

Quantity Schedule and Equivalent Units

Quantity Schedule

Units (four-litre containers) to be accounted for:
  Work in process, April 1
   (all materials, 60% labour and
   overhead added last month) 30,000
  Started into production 420,000
    Total units............................. 450,000

| | Equivalent Units (EU) | | |
	Materials	Labour	Overhead
Units (four-litre containers) accounted for as follows:			
Transferred to Finishing			
Department............................. 370,000	370,000	370,000	370,000
Work in process, April 30 (materials			
50% complete; labour and			
overhead 25% complete)................. 80,000	40,000*	20,000*	20,000*
Total units and equivalent			
units of production................... 450,000	410,000	390,000	390,000

*Materials: 80,000 units × 50% = 40,000 equivalent units; labour and overhead: 80,000 units × 25% = 20,000 equivalent units.

Costs per Equivalent Unit (EU)

	Total Cost	Materials	Labour	Overhead	Whole Unit
Cost to be accounted for:					
Work in process, April 1................	$ 150,000	$ 92,000	$ 21,000	$ 37,000	
Cost added by the Base Fab					
Department.......................	1,846,000	851,000	330,000	665,000	
Total cost (a).....................	$1,996,000	$943,000	$351,000	$702,000	
Equivalent units of production (b)........	—	410,000	390,000	390,000	
Cost per EU, (a) ÷ (b)..................	—	$2.30 +	$0.90 +	$1.80 =	$5.00

Cost Reconciliation

	Total Cost	Materials	Labour	Overhead
Cost accounted for as follows:				
Transferred to				
Finishing Department:				
370,000 units, at $5.00 each........	$1,850,000	370,000	370,000	370,000
Work in process, April 30:				
Materials, at $2.30 per EU...........	92,000	40,000		
Labour, at $0.90 per EU.............	18,000		20,000	
Overhead, at $1.80 per EU...........	36,000			20,000
Total work in process	146,000			
Total cost.........................	$1,996,000			

4. Work in Process—Finishing				
Department		1,850,000		
Work in Process—Base Fab				
Department...................			1,850,000	

REVIEW PROBLEM 2: UNITS AND COST ASSIGNMENT

Power Company passes its product through several departments, the last of which is the Finishing Department. Conversion costs are added evenly throughout the process in this department. One-fourth of direct materials is added at the beginning of the process, and the remaining three-fourths is added when the process is 50% complete with respect to conversion costs.

During June, 475,000 units of product were transferred to finished goods. Of these units, 100,000 units were 40% complete with respect to conversion costs at the beginning of the period and 375,000 were started and completed during the period. At the end of June, the work in process inventory comprised 225,000 units that were 30% complete with respect to conversion costs. Total costs to account for include $949,375 for conversion costs and $616,250 for direct materials.

Required:

1. Determine the equivalent units of production with respect to conversion costs and with respect to direct materials for the Finishing Department.
2. Compute the conversion cost and the direct materials cost per equivalent unit.
3. Compute the amount of conversion cost and the amount of the direct materials cost assigned to the units completed and to the ending work in process inventory.

Solution to Review Problem 2

1. Equivalent unit calculations:

		Equivalent Units (EU)	
		Materials	Conversion
Units accounted for as follows:			
Transferred to the next department.........................	475,000	475,000	475,000
Work in process, June 30:			
Material, 25% complete; conversion, 30% complete	225,000	56,250	67,500
Total units accounted for.........................	700,000	531,250	542,500

2. Unit cost calculations:

Conversion cost per equivalent unit = \$949,375 ÷ 542,500 units = \$1.75
Direct materials cost per equivalent unit = \$616,250 ÷ 531,250 units = \$1.16

3. Allocation of materials and conversion cost to products:

	Equivalent Units	Per Unit Cost	Allocated Cost
Transferred out:			
Materials	475,000	\$1.16	\$ 551,000
Conversion costs	475,000	1.75	831,250
			\$1,382,250 (a)
Work in Process			
Materials (225,000 × 0.25).....................	56,250	\$1.16	\$ 65,250
Conversion (225,000 × 0.3).....................	67,500	1.75	118,125
			183,375 (b)
Total cost accounted for: (a) + (b).............................			\$1,565,625

GLOSSARY

Review key terms and definitions on Connect.

DISCUSSION CASE

DISCUSSION CASE 6–1

Process costing methods rely extensively on managers' estimates of percentage of completion for both costing products and calculating equivalent units of production. While most managers understand the importance of accurate estimates to the integrity of their process costing systems, they also have incentives to produce profits for their shareholders.

Required:

Discuss how incorrect estimates could be used to artificially boost profits, considering the issue from the perspectives of both managers and shareholders.

QUESTIONS

6–1   Under what conditions is it appropriate to use a process costing system?
6–2   In what ways are job-order and process costing different?
6–3   Why is cost accumulation easier in a process costing system than it is in a job-order costing system?
6–4   How many Work in Process accounts are maintained in a company that uses process costing?

6–5   Assume that a company has two processing departments—Mixing and Firing. Prepare a journal entry to show a transfer of partially completed units from the Mixing Department to the Firing Department.

6–6   Assume that a company has two processing departments—Mixing followed by Firing. Explain what costs might be added to the Firing Department's Work in Process account during a period.

6–7   What is meant by the term *equivalent units of production* when the weighted-average method is used?

6–8   "The increasing use of flexible manufacturing systems will result in a reduction in the importance of process costing over time." Do you agree or disagree and why?

6–9   If FIFO is a more accurate costing method, why would a manager choose to use the weighted-average method instead? List at least three reasons.

EXERCISES

EXERCISE 6–1 Process Costing Journal Entries [LO1]

Arizona Brick Corporation produces bricks in two processing departments—Moulding and Firing. Information relating to the company's operations in March follows:

a.   Raw materials were issued for use in production: Moulding Department, $28,000; Firing Department, $5,000.

b.   Direct labour costs were incurred: Moulding Department, $18,000; Firing Department, $5,000.

c.   Manufacturing overhead was applied: Moulding Department, $24,000; Firing Department, $37,000.

d.   Unfired, moulded bricks were transferred from the Moulding Department to the Firing Department. According to the company's process costing system, the cost of the unfired, moulded bricks was $67,000.

e.   Finished bricks were transferred from the Firing Department to the finished goods warehouse. According to the company's process costing system, the cost of the finished bricks was $108,000.

f.   Finished bricks were sold to customers. According to the company's process costing system, the cost of the finished bricks sold was $106,000.

Required:
Prepare journal entries to record items (*a*) through (*f*) above.

EXERCISE 6–2 Computation of Equivalent Units—Weighted-Average Method [LO2]

Lindex Company manufactures a product that goes through three processing departments. Information relating to activity in the first department during October is given below:

		Percentage Completed	
	Units	Materials	Conversion
Work in process, October 1..........	25,000	90%	60%
Work in process, October 31.........	15,000	70%	50%

The department started 195,000 units into production during the month and transferred 205,000 completed units to the next department.

Required:
Compute the equivalent units of production for the first department for October, assuming that the company uses the weighted-average method of accounting for units and costs.

EXERCISE 6–3 Cost per Equivalent Unit—Weighted-Average Method [LO3]

Ainsley Industries uses the weighted-average method in its process costing system. Data for the Assembly Department for May appear below:

	Materials	Labour	Overhead
Work in process, May 1............................	$ 14,550	$23,620	$118,100
Cost added during May............................	$88,350	$14,330	$ 71,650
Equivalent units of production....................	1,200	1,100	1,100

Required:
Compute the cost per equivalent unit for materials, for labour, for overhead, and in total.

EXERCISE 6–4 Assigning Costs to Units—Weighted-Average Method [LO4]
Data concerning a recent period's activity in the Prep Department, the first processing department in a company that uses process costing, appear below:

	Materials	Conversion
Equivalent units of production in ending work in process	300	100
Cost per equivalent unit	$31.56	$9.32

A total of 1,300 units were completed and transferred to the next processing department during the period.

Required:
Compute the cost of the units transferred to the next department during the period and the cost of ending work in process inventory.

EXERCISE 6–5 Process Costing Journal Entries [LO1]
Faber Brot is a bread-baking company located in Aachen, Germany, near the Dutch border. The company uses a process costing system for its single product—a popular pumpernickel bread. Faber Brot has two processing departments—Mixing and Baking. The T-accounts below show the flow of costs through the two departments in April (all amounts are in euros: €):

Work in Process—Mixing

Balance 1/4	10,000	Transferred out	760,000
Direct materials	330,000		
Direct labour	260,000		
Overhead	190,000		

Work in Process—Baking

Balance 1/4	20,000	Transferred out	980,000
Transferred in	760,000		
Direct labour	120,000		
Overhead	90,000		

Required:
Prepare journal entries showing the flow of costs through the two processing departments during April.

EXERCISE 6–6 Equivalent Units and Cost per Equivalent Unit—Weighted-Average Method [LO2, LO3]
Healthcheck Corp. manufactures an antacid product that passes through two departments. Data for June for the first department follow:

	Litres	Materials	Labour	Overhead
Work in process, June 1	80,000	$68,600	$30,000	$48,000
Litres started in process	760,000			
Litres transferred out	790,000			
Work in process, June 30	50,000			
Cost added during June		$907,200	$370,000	$592,000

The beginning work in process inventory was 80% complete with respect to materials and 75% complete with respect to labour and overhead. The ending work in process inventory was 60% complete with respect to materials and 20% complete with respect to labour and overhead.

Required:
Assume that the company uses the weighted-average method of accounting for units and costs.
1. Compute the equivalent units for June's activity for the first department.
2. Determine the costs per equivalent unit for June.

EXERCISE 6-7 Equivalent Units—Weighted-Average Method [LO2]
Green House Inc. processes cleaning fluid used as a base for household cleaning products produced by various distributors. Two departments are involved: Mixing and Heating. Data relating to litres of cleaning fluid processed in the Mixing Department during October are provided below:

	Litres of Cleaning Fluid	Percentage Completed*
Work in process, October 1.........................	25,000	35%
Work in process, October 31........................	5,000	70%

*Labour and overhead only.

A total of 25,000 litres of cleaning fluid were started into processing during October. All materials are added at the beginning of processing in the Mixing Department.

Required:
Compute the equivalent units for October for the Mixing Department, assuming that the company uses the weighted-average method of accounting for units.

EXERCISE 6-8 Equivalent Units and Cost per Equivalent Unit—Weighted-Average Method [LO2, LO3, LO4, LO5]
Grand River Company produces a high-quality insulation material that passes through two production processes. Data for November for the first process follow:

	Units	Completion with Respect to Materials	Completion with Respect to Conversion
Work in process inventory, November 1................	80,000	50%	25%
Work in process inventory, November 30..............	60,000	45%	20%
Materials cost in work in process inventory, November 1.............................		$76,600	
Conversion cost in work in process inventory, November 1.............................		$34,900	
Units started into production..........................		300,000	
Units transferred to the next process...................		320,000	
Materials cost added during November		$410,000	
Conversion cost added during November		$234,500	

Required:
1. Assume that the company uses the weighted-average method of accounting for units and costs. Determine the equivalent units for November for the first process.
2. Compute the costs per equivalent unit for November for the first process.
3. Determine the total cost of ending work in process inventory and the total cost of units transferred to the next process in November.

EXERCISE 6-9 Cost Reconciliation—Weighted-Average Method [LO5]
The Shop Supply Company produces rolls of disposable shop towels that it supplies to auto
parts outlets and industrial cleaning supplies distributors. Shop towels are similar to paper
towels, but they are thicker and more durable and textured to deal more effectively with
grease and grime than the traditional paper towel sold for home use. The continuous sheet
of paper material is run through the Sizing and Rolling Department, where the paper is cut
to the appropriate length and rolled onto cardboard tubes. The rolls then move on to the
Packaging Department, where they are shrink-wrapped and packed into cases for delivery
to customers.

During March, the Sizing and Rolling Department transferred 45,000 rolls of paper to the
Packaging Department. The ending inventory in March in the Sizing and Rolling Department
consisted of 4,000 rolls that were 100% complete with respect to materials and 80% complete
with respect to conversion. The costs per equivalent unit for the month were materials, $10.50,
and conversion, $4.00.

Required:
Prepare the cost reconciliation portion of the Sizing and Rolling Department's production
report for March.

PROBLEMS

**PROBLEM 6-10 Equivalent Units, Cost per Equivalent Unit, Assigning Costs—
Weighted-Average Method [LO2, LO3, LO4, LO5]**
CloverSweet Inc. manufactures a product that goes through two departments prior to completion. The information shown in the table below is available about work in the first department,
the Mixing Department, during June:

	Units	Percentage Complete	
		Materials	Conversion
Work in process, beginning	50,000	75%	30%
Started into production	430,000		
Completed and transferred out	380,000		
Work in process, ending	100,000	60%	40%

	Materials	Conversion
Work in process, beginning	$ 45,500	$25,000
Costs added during June	$425,500	$145,000

Required:
Assume that the company uses the weighted-average method.
1. Determine the equivalent units for June for the first process.
2. Compute the costs per equivalent unit for June for the first process.
3. Determine the total cost of ending work in process inventory and the total cost of units
    transferred to the next process in June.
4. Prepare a report that reconciles the total costs assigned to the ending work in process
    inventory and the units transferred out with the costs in beginning inventory and costs
    added during the period.

**PROBLEM 6-11 Equivalent Units; Assigning Costs—Weighted-Average Method
[LO2, LO3, LO4, LO5]**
The WireOne Company manufactures high-quality coated electrical wire in two departments,
Weaving and Coating. Materials are introduced at various points during work in the Weaving
Department. After the weaving is completed, the materials are transferred into the Coating
Department, where specialty plastic coating is applied.

Selected data relating to the Weaving Department during May are given below:

Production data:

Kilograms in process, May 1 (materials 100% complete; conversion 80% complete)	85,000
Kilograms started into production during May	365,000
Kilograms completed and transferred to Coating	?
Kilograms in process, May 31 (materials 65% complete; conversion 30% complete)	55,000

Cost data:

Work in process inventory, May 1:	
Materials cost	$ 101,000
Conversion cost	$51,000
Cost added during May:	
Materials cost	$462,000
Conversion cost	$213,000

The company uses the weighted-average method.

Required:
1. Compute the equivalent units of production.
2. Compute the costs per equivalent unit for May.
3. Determine the cost of ending work in process inventory and of the units transferred to the Coating Department.
4. Prepare a cost reconciliation between the costs determined in (3) above and the cost of beginning inventory and costs added during the period.

PROBLEM 6-12 Interpreting a Report—Weighted-Average Method [LO2, LO3, LO4]
Parandah Electronics Ltd., located in England, assembles a standard electrical component from parts it purchases from various suppliers. The production process consists of several steps, starting with assembly, which takes place in the Assembly Department. The company recently hired a new accountant, who prepared the following report for the department for May, using the weighted-average method:

Quantity Schedule

Units to be accounted for:	
Work in process, May 1 (materials 90% complete; conversion 80% complete)	8,000
Started into production	26,000
Total units	34,000
Units accounted for as follows:	
Transferred to next department	28,000
Work in process, May 31 (materials 75% complete; conversion 50% complete)	6,000
Total units	34,000

Cost Reconciliation

Cost to be accounted for:	
Work in process, May 1	£ 13,400
Cost added in the department	87,800
Total cost to be accounted for	£101,200
Cost accounted for as follows:	
Work in process, May 31	£ 12,450
Transferred to next department	88,750
Total cost accounted for	£101,200

The company's management would like some additional information about May's operation in the Assembly Department. (The currency in England is the pound, denoted by the symbol £.)

Required:
1. How many units were started and completed during May?
2. What were the equivalent units for May for materials and conversion costs?
3. What were the costs per equivalent unit for May? The following additional data are available concerning the department's costs:

	Materials	Conversion	Total
Work in process, May 1.................	£9,000	£4,400	£13,400
Costs added during May................	£56,000	£31,250	£87,250

4. Verify the accountant's ending work in process inventory figure (£12,450) given in the report.
5. The new manager of the Assembly Department is asked to estimate the incremental cost of processing an additional 1,000 units through the department. He takes the unit cost for an equivalent whole unit that you computed in (3) above and multiplies this figure by 1,000. Will this method yield a valid estimate of incremental cost? Explain.

PROBLEM 6–13 Analysis of Work in Process T-Account—Weighted-Average Method
[LO1, LO2, LO3, LO4, LO5]
Brady Products manufactures a silicone paste wax that goes through three processing departments—Cracking, Blending, and Packing. All of the raw materials are introduced at the start of work in the Cracking Department. The Work in Process T-account for the Cracking Department for May follows:

Work in Process—Cracking Department

Inventory, May 1 (35,000 kilograms, conversion ⁴⁄₅ complete)	63,700	Completed and transferred to Blending (? kilograms)	?
May costs added:			
Raw materials (280,000 kilograms)	397,600		
Conversion costs	189,700		
Inventory, May 31 (45,000 kilograms, conversion ²⁄₃ complete)	?		

The May 1 work in process inventory consists of $43,400 in materials cost and $20,300 in conversion cost. The company uses the weighted-average method.

Required:
1. Determine the equivalent units of production for May.
2. Determine the costs per equivalent unit for May.
3. Determine the cost of the units completed and transferred to Blending during May and the cost of ending work in process inventory.
4. What criticism can be made of the unit costs that you have computed if they are used to evaluate how well costs have been controlled?

PROBLEM 6–14 Equivalent Units; Costing of Inventories; Journal Entries—Weighted-Average Method [LO1, LO2, LO3, LO4]
Zap Rap Inc. is a manufacturer of audio CDs. The company's chief financial officer is trying to verify the accuracy of the December 31 work in process and finished goods inventories prior to closing the books for the year. He strongly suspects that the year-end dollar balances are incorrect, but he believes that all the other data are accurate. The year-end balances shown on Zap Rap's books are as follows:

	Units	Costs
Work in process, December 31 (materials 100% complete; conversion 50% complete)..	30,000	$95,000
Finished goods, December 31..	50,000	$201,000

There were no finished goods inventories at the beginning of the year. The company uses the weighted-average method of process costing. There is only one processing department.

A review of the company's inventory and cost records has disclosed the following data:

		Costs	
	Units	Materials	Conversion
Work in process, January 1 (materials 100% complete; conversion 80% complete)	20,000	$22,000	$48,000
Started into production......................................	800,000		
Costs added during the year		$880,000	$2,367,000
Units completed during the year............................	790,000		

Required:

1. Determine the equivalent units and the costs per equivalent unit for materials and conversion for the year.
2. Determine the amount of cost that should be assigned to the ending work in process and finished goods inventories.
3. Prepare the necessary correcting journal entry to adjust the work in process and finished goods inventories to the correct balances as of December 31.
4. Determine the cost of goods sold for the year, assuming that there is no underapplied or overapplied overhead.

(CPA, adapted)

PROBLEM 6–15 Comprehensive Process Costing Problem [LO1, LO2, LO3, LO4, LO5]
Fryer's Choice produces a specially blended vegetable oil widely used in restaurant deep fryers. The blending process creates a cooking oil that can be heated to a high temperature, but does not smoke or smell. The oil is produced in two departments: Blending and Bottling. Raw materials are introduced at various points in the Blending Department.

The following incomplete Work in Process T-account is available for the Blending Department for March:

Work in Process—Blending

March 1 balance (20,000 litres; materials 100% complete; labour and overhead 90% complete)	$38,000	Completed and transferred to Bottling (___?___ litres)	$???
March costs added:			
Oils (390,000 litres)	495,000		
Direct labour	72,000		
Overhead	181,000		
March 31 inventory (40,000 litres; materials 75% complete, labour and overhead 25% complete)	$???		

The March 1 beginning inventory in the Blending Department consists of the following cost elements: raw materials, $25,000; direct labour, $4,000; and overhead, $9,000.

Costs incurred during March in the Bottling Department were materials used, $115,000; direct labour, $18,000; and overhead cost applied to production, $42,000. The company uses the weighted-average method in its process costing.

Required:

1. Prepare journal entries to record the cost incurred in both the Blending Department and the Bottling Department during March. Key your entries to the items (*a*) through (*f*) below:
   a. Raw materials were issued for use in production.
   b. Direct labour costs were incurred.
   c. Manufacturing overhead costs for the entire factory were incurred: $225,000. (*Hint:* Credit Accounts Payable.)
   d. Manufacturing overhead cost was applied to production using a predetermined overhead rate.

    e.   Units that were complete with respect to processing in the Bottling Department were transferred to finished goods: $950,000.

    f.   Completed units were sold on account: $1,500,000. The cost of goods sold was $890,000.

2.   Post the journal entries from (1) above to T-accounts. The following account balances existed at the beginning of March. (*Note:* The beginning balance in the Blending Department's Work in Process account is given above.)

Raw materials.	$681,000
Work in Process—Bottling Department.	65,000
Finished Goods	20,000

After posting the entries to the T-accounts, find the ending balance in the inventory accounts and the manufacturing overhead accounts.

3.   Prepare a production report for the Blending Department for March.

4.   Prepare the journal entry to record the transfer of finished goods from the Blending Department to the Bottling Department and post to the appropriate T-accounts prepared in (2) above.

CASES

CASE 6–16 Ethics and the Manager; Understanding the Impact of Percentage Completion on Profit [LO2, LO3, LO4]

Jason Bieler and Nancy Delirion are production managers in the Appliances Division of Meester Corporation, which has several dozen plants scattered in locations throughout the world. Delirion manages the plant in Toronto, while Bieler manages the plant in Vancouver. Production managers are paid a salary and get an additional bonus equal to 10% of their base salary if the entire division meets or exceeds its target profits for the year. The bonus is determined in March after the company's annual report has been prepared and issued to shareholders.

    Late in February, Delirion received a phone call from Bieler that went like this:

Bieler: How's it going, Nancy?

Delirion: Fine, Jason. How's it going with you?

Bieler: Great! I just got the preliminary profit figures for the division for last year and we are within $62,500 of making the year's target profits. All we have to do is to pull a few strings, and we'll be over the top!

Delirion: What do you mean?

Bieler: Well, one thing that would be easy to change is your estimate of the percentage completion of your ending work in process inventories.

Delirion: I don't know if I should do that, Jason. Those percentage completion numbers are supplied by Marita Janovski, my lead supervisor. I have always trusted her to provide us with good estimates. Besides, I have already sent the percentage completion figures to corporate headquarters.

Bieler: You can always tell them there was a mistake. Think about it, Nancy. All of us managers are doing as much as we can to pull this bonus out of the hat. You may not want the bonus cheque, but the rest of us sure could use it.

    The final processing department in Delirion's production facility began the year with no work in process inventories. During the year, 270,000 units were transferred in from the prior processing department and 250,000 units were completed and sold. Costs transferred in from the prior department totalled $49,221,000. No materials are added in the final processing department. A total of $16,320,000 of conversion cost was incurred in the final processing department during the year.

Required:

1.   Janovski estimated that the units in ending inventory in the final processing department were 25% complete with respect to the conversion costs of the final processing department. If this estimate of the percentage completion is used, what will be the cost of goods sold for the year?

2.   Does Bieler want Delirion to increase or decrease the estimated percentage completion? Explain why.

3.   What percentage completion figure would result in increasing the reported operating income by $62,500 over the operating income that would be reported if the 25% figure were used?

4.   Do you think Delirion should go along with the request to alter estimates of the percentage completion? Why or why not?

CASE 6–17 Effect of Incorrect Costing across Departments—Weighted-Average Method [LO2, LO3, LO4, LO5]

Tavia Limited manufactures a plastic gasket that is used in automobile engines. The gaskets go through three processing departments: Mixing, Forming, and Stamping. The company's accountant (who is very inexperienced) has prepared a summary of production and costs for the Forming Department for October, as follows:

Work in process inventory, October 1 (8,000 units; materials 100% complete; conversion $7/8$ complete)	$ 22,420*
Costs transferred in from the Mixing Department	81,480
Material added during October (added when processing is 50% complete in the Forming Department)	27,600
Conversion costs added during October	96,900
Total departmental costs	$228,400
Forming Department costs assigned to:	
Units completed and transferred to the Stamping Department (100,000 units at $2.284 each)	$228,400
Work in process inventory, October 31 (5,000 units, conversion $2/5$ complete)	–
Total departmental costs assigned	$228,400

*Consists of cost transferred in, $8,820; materials cost, $3,400; and conversion costs, $10,200.

After mulling over the data above, Tavia's president commented, "I can't understand what's happening here. Despite a concentrated effort at cost reduction, our unit cost actually went up in the Forming Department last month. With that kind of performance, year-end bonuses are out of the question for the people in that department."

The company uses the weighted-average method in its process costing.

Required:
1. Prepare a report for the Forming Department for October showing how much cost should have been assigned to the units completed and transferred to the Stamping Department and to the ending work in process inventory.
2. Explain to the president why the unit cost appearing on the report prepared by the accountant is so high.

CASE 6–18 Inventory Valuation under Process Costing—Weighted-Average Method [LO2, LO3, LO4, LO5]

Using an old family recipe, Rachel Archer started a company that produces root beer. Archer opened the doors of Rachel's Real Root Beer on January 1. The company struggled for the first few months, but by the end of September, the customer list was expanding rapidly. Archer realized that bottling by hand was becoming more and more difficult as the orders continued to come in. To purchase the automated equipment needed to expand further, Archer realized it would be necessary to borrow money.

Archer was disappointed to find that few banks were willing to make a loan to such a small company, but she finally found a bank that would consider her loan application. However, Archer was informed that she would have to supply up-to-date financial statements with her loan application.

Archer had not bothered with formal financial statements so far—she felt that as long as the balance in the company's chequing account kept increasing, the company was doing fine. She wondered how she was going to determine the value of the root beer in the work in process and finished goods inventories to put on her company's balance sheet.

Archer approached Ed Switzer, an old friend currently working for a local accounting firm. After talking with Archer and touring her production facility, Switzer suggested a process costing system (using the weighted-average method) since Archer's company produces only one standard product in a continuous production process. During the plant tour, Switzer noted that Archer ran the operation as one department. At the beginning of the process, the various ingredients were checked for quality and then mixed and injected with carbon dioxide to create bulk root beer. Then bottles were checked for defects, filled with root beer, capped, visually inspected again for defects, and then packed into cases (12 bottles per case) for shipping. At this point, completed cases were transferred to finished goods.

Archer asked Switzer to help her calculate the work in process and finished goods inventory cost to put on the company balance sheet at the end of August. To get started, Switzer asked Archer to collect several pieces of information. Details collected by Archer are listed below:

a. Approximately 75% of raw materials cost is added at the beginning of the process, and 25% is added when the product is 85% complete. Conversion costs are added evenly throughout the process.

b. Archer estimated there were 550 units of product that were 75% complete for raw materials and 60% complete for conversion on August 1. From her bank records, she calculated that the raw materials cost added to the opening inventory was about $650 and conversion cost was about $430.

c. During August, 3,000 units of product were started into production, and 2,400 of these were completed and transferred to finished goods. Costs added to production during August were $3,840 for materials and $3,480 for conversion.

d. At the end of August, the work in process inventory was made up of 1,150 units that were 75% complete for materials and 50% complete for conversion costs.

Using this information, Switzer agreed to prepare a report indicating the cost of both work in process and finished goods inventory that Archer would need to report on her balance sheet as at August 30.

Required:

Take on the role of Switzer and prepare the report for Archer. Be sure to provide all details, including a full production report, to help Archer understand how costs were calculated.

INSTANT QUIZ SOLUTIONS

6-1

Since the products are identical and are produced and sold in large batches, process costing is the most appropriate costing method.

6-2

The number of full-time equivalent students is $5,000 + 50\% \times 1,250 = 5,625$.

6-3

Recall from Chapter 2 that conversion costs include labour and overhead added during production.

6-4

Cost per equivalent unit $= (\$7,250 + \$10,750) \div 6,250 = \$2.88$.

■ connect®   ■ LEARNSMART®   ■ SMARTBOOK™

For more information on the resources available from McGraw-Hill Ryerson, go to www.mheducation.ca/he/solutions.

■ APPENDIX 6A: FIFO METHOD

The FIFO method of process costing differs from the weighted-average method in two ways: (1) the computation of equivalent units, and (2) the way in which costs of beginning inventory are treated. The FIFO method is generally considered to be more accurate than the weighted-average method, but it is more complex. The complexity is not a problem for computers, but the FIFO method is a little more difficult to understand and to learn than the weighted-average method.

Equivalent Units—FIFO Method

LEARNING OBJECTIVE **6**
Compute the equivalent units of production using the FIFO method.

The computation of equivalent units under the FIFO (or first in, first out) method differs in two ways from computation under the weighted-average method.

First, the "units transferred out" is divided into two parts. One part consists of the units from the beginning inventory that were completed and transferred out, and the other part consists of the units that were both *started* and *completed* during the current period.

Second, full consideration is given to the amount of work expended during the current period on units in the *beginning* work in process inventory as well as on units in the ending inventory. Thus, under the FIFO method, both beginning and ending inventories are converted to an equivalent units basis. For the beginning inventory, the equivalent units represent the work done to *complete* the units; for the ending inventory, the equivalent units represent the work done to bring the units to a stage of partial completion at the end of the period (the same as with the weighted-average method).

The formula for computing the equivalent units of production under the FIFO method is more complex than under the weighted-average method:

FIFO Method
(a separate calculation is made for each cost category in each processing department)

Equivalent units of production = Equivalent units to complete beginning work in process inventory*
+ Units started and completed during the period
+ Equivalent units in ending work in process inventory

$$
\begin{array}{l}
\text{*Equivalent units to} \\
\text{complete beginning work} = \\
\text{in process inventory}
\end{array}
\begin{array}{l}
\text{Units in beginning} \\
\text{work in process} \\
\text{inventory}
\end{array}
\times
\left(
100\% -
\begin{array}{l}
\text{Percentage completion} \\
\text{of beginning work in} \\
\text{process inventory}
\end{array}
\right)
$$

The equivalent units of production can also be determined as follows:

Equivalent units of production = Units transferred out
+ Equivalent units in ending work in process inventory
− Equivalent units in beginning work in process inventory

To illustrate the FIFO method, refer again to the data for the Electrics and Testing Department at Tropic Breeze Fans. The department completed and transferred

	Materials	Conversion
To complete beginning work in process:		
Materials: 200 units × (100% − 55%*)...............	90	
Conversion: 200 units × (100% − 30%*)		140
Units started and completed during the period..........	4,600[†]	4,600[†]
Ending work in process:		
Materials: 400 units × 40% complete	160	
Conversion: 400 units × 25% complete		100
Equivalent units of production	4,850	4,840

EXHIBIT 6A–1 Equivalent Units of Production: FIFO Method

*This is the work needed to complete the units in beginning inventory.
[†]5,000 units started − 400 units in ending work in process = 4,600 units started and completed. This can also be computed as 4,800 units completed and transferred to the next department − 200 units in beginning work in process inventory. The FIFO method assumes that the units in beginning inventory are finished first.

4,800 units to the Inspection and Packing Department during May. Since 200 of these units came from the beginning inventory, the Electrics and Testing Department must have started and completed 4,600 units during May. The 200 units in the beginning inventory were 55% complete with respect to materials and only 30% complete with respect to conversion costs when the month started. Thus, to complete these units the department must have added another 45% of materials costs (100% − 55% = 45%) and another 70% of conversion costs (100% − 30% = 70%). Following this line of reasoning, the equivalent units for the department for May are computed as shown in Exhibit 6A–1.

Comparison of Equivalent Units of Production under the Weighted-Average and FIFO Methods

Stop at this point and compare the data in Exhibit 6A–1 with the data in Exhibit 6–4 in the chapter, which shows the computation of equivalent units under the weighted-average method. Also refer to Exhibit 6A–2, which compares the two methods.

The essential difference between the two methods is that the weighted-average method blends work and costs from the prior period with work and costs in the current period, whereas the FIFO method separates the two periods. To see this more clearly, consider the following reconciliation of the two calculations of equivalent units:

Electrics and Testing Department	Materials	Conversion
Equivalent units—weighted-average method....................	4,960	4,900
Less equivalent units in beginning inventory:		
200 units × 55%...	110	
200 units × 30%...		60
Equivalent units of production—FIFO method..................	4,850	4,840

From the above, it is evident that the FIFO method removes the equivalent units that were already in beginning inventory from the equivalent units as defined using the weighted-average method. Thus, the FIFO method isolates the equivalent units due to work performed during the current period. The weighted-average method, on the other hand, blends the equivalent units already in beginning inventory with the equivalent units due to work performed in the current period.

EXHIBIT 6A-2   Visual Perspective of Equivalent Units of Production—Conversion

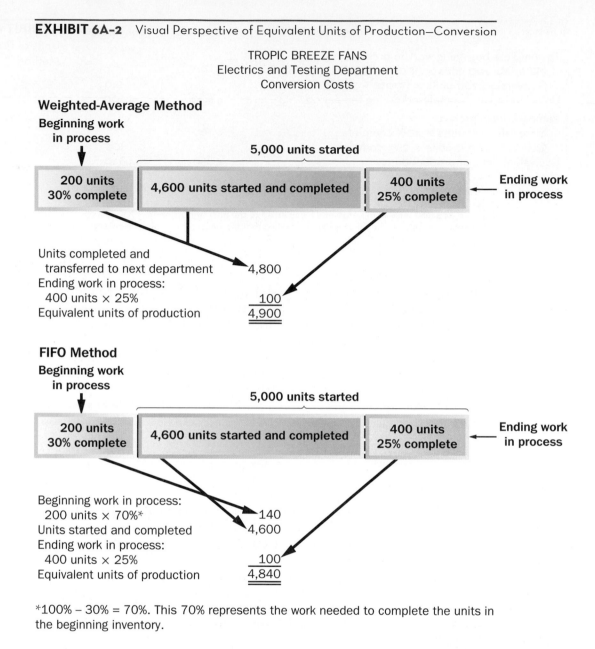

TROPIC BREEZE FANS
Electrics and Testing Department
Conversion Costs

Weighted-Average Method

Beginning work in process

5,000 units started

| 200 units 30% complete | 4,600 units started and completed | 400 units 25% complete |

Ending work in process

Units completed and
 transferred to next department   4,800
Ending work in process:
 400 units × 25%   100
Equivalent units of production   4,900

FIFO Method

Beginning work in process

5,000 units started

| 200 units 30% complete | 4,600 units started and completed | 400 units 25% complete |

Ending work in process

Beginning work in process:
 200 units × 70%*   140
Units started and completed   4,600
Ending work in process:
 400 units × 25%   100
Equivalent units of production   4,840

*100% – 30% = 70%. This 70% represents the work needed to complete the units in the beginning inventory.

PRODUCTION REPORT—FIFO METHOD

The steps followed to prepare a production report under the FIFO method are the same as those discussed earlier for the weighted-average method. However, since the FIFO method distinguishes between units in the beginning inventory and units started during the year, the cost reconciliation portion of the report is more complex under the FIFO method. To illustrate the FIFO method, we will again use the data for Tropic Breeze Fans.

Step 1: Prepare a quantity schedule and compute the equivalent units. There is only one difference between a quantity schedule prepared under the FIFO method and one prepared under the weighted-average method. This difference relates to units transferred out. As explained earlier in our discussion of equivalent units, the FIFO method divides units transferred out into two parts. One part consists of the units in the beginning inventory, and the other part consists of the units started and completed during the current period.

A quantity schedule showing this format for units transferred out is presented in Exhibit 6A–3, along with a computation of equivalent units for the month. We explained

EXHIBIT 6A-3   Production Report—FIFO Method

TROPIC BREEZE FANS
Electrics and Testing Department Production Report
(FIFO method)

Quantity Schedule and Equivalent Units

	Quantity Schedule		

Units to be accounted for:			
Work in process, May 1 (materials 55% complete; conversion 30% complete)	200		
Started into production	5,000		
Total units	5,200		

		Equivalent Units (EU)	
		Materials	Conversion
Units accounted for as follows:			
Transferred to the next department			
From beginning inventory*	200	90	140
Started and completed in the month†	4,600	4,600	4,600
Work in process, May 31 (materials 40% complete; conversion 25% complete)	400	160	100
Total units and equivalent units of production	5,200	4,850	4,840

Costs per Equivalent Unit

	Total Cost	Materials	Conversion	Whole Unit
Cost to be accounted for:				
Work in process, May 1	$ 15,175			
Cost added in the department (a)	719,500	368,600	350,900	
Total cost	$734,675			
Equivalent units of production (b) (see above)		4,850	4,840	
Cost per EU, (a) ÷ (b)		$76.00 +	$72.50 =	$148.50

Cost Reconciliation

	Total Cost	Equivalent Units	
		Materials	Conversion
Cost accounted for as follows:			
Transferred to next department:			
From beginning inventory:			
Cost in beginning inventory	$ 15,175		
Cost to complete these units			
Materials at $76.00 per EU	6,840	90	
Conversion at $72.50 per EU	10,150		140
Total cost from beginning inventory	$ 32,165		
Units started and completed this month at $148.50 per EU	$683,100	4,600	4,600
Total cost transferred out	$ 715,265		
Work in process, May 31:			
Materials, at $76.25 per EU	$ 12,160	160	
Conversion, at $72.75 per EU	7,250		100
Total work in process, May 31	19,410		
Total cost	$ 734,675		

*Materials: 200 × (100% − 55%) = 90 EU. Conversion: 200 × (100% − 30%) = 140 EU.
†5,000 units started − 400 units in ending inventory = 4,600 units started and completed.

earlier that in computing equivalent units under the FIFO method, we must first show the amount of work required *to complete* the units in the beginning inventory. We then show the number of units started and completed during the period, and finally we show the amount of work *completed* on the units still in process at the end of the period. Carefully trace through these computations in Exhibit 6A–3.

LEARNING OBJECTIVE 7
Compute the cost per equivalent unit using the FIFO method.

Step 2: Compute the cost per equivalent unit. In computing unit costs under the FIFO method, we use only those costs that were incurred during the current period, and we ignore any costs in the beginning work in process inventory. Under the FIFO method, *unit costs relate only to work done during the current period* as follows:

FIFO Method
(a separate calculation is made for each cost category in each processing department)

$$\text{Cost per equivalent unit} = \frac{\text{Cost added during the period}}{\text{Equivalent units of production}}$$

The costs per equivalent unit computed in Exhibit 6A–3 are used to cost units of product transferred to the next department; in addition, they are used to show the cost attached to partially completed units in the ending work in process inventory.

The costs per equivalent unit are used to value units in ending inventory and units that are transferred to the next department. For example, each unit transferred out of the Electrics and Testing Department to the Inspection and Packing Department will carry with it a cost of $148.50—$76.00 for materials cost and $72.50 for conversion cost for work done in the current period. Since 4,600 units were started and transferred out in May to the next department, the total cost assigned to these units is $683,100 (4,600 units × $148.50 per unit).

LEARNING OBJECTIVE 8
Prepare a cost reconciliation report accounting for the costs transferred out and the costs in work in process inventory at the end of the period using the FIFO method.

Step 3: Prepare a cost reconciliation. The purpose of the cost reconciliation is to show how the costs charged to a department during a period are accounted for. With the FIFO method, two cost elements are associated with the units in the beginning work in process inventory. The first element is the cost carried over from the prior period ($15,175 from Exhibit 6A–3). The second element is the cost needed to complete these units ($6,840 of materials plus $10,150 of conversion costs in Exhibit 6A–3).

For units started and completed in the month, we simply multiply the number of units started and completed by the total cost per unit to determine the amount transferred out. This is $683,100 for the department (see Exhibit 6A–3).

Finally, the amount of cost attached to the ending work in process inventory is computed by multiplying the cost per equivalent unit figures for the month by the number of equivalent units for materials and conversion costs in ending inventory.

Note that the $715,265 cost of the units transferred to the next department, Inspection and Packing, are accounted for in that department as "costs transferred in." As in the weighted-average method, this cost is treated in the process costing system as just another category of costs, like materials or conversion costs. The only difference is that the costs transferred in are always 100% complete with respect to the work done in the Inspection and Packing Department. Costs are passed on from one department to the next in this fashion, until they are transferred to finished goods.

A Comparison of Costing Methods

In most situations, the weighted-average and FIFO methods produce very similar unit costs. If there are never any ending inventories, as in an ideal lean production (JIT) environment, the two methods will produce identical results. This is because, without any ending inventories, no costs can be carried forward into the next period, and the weighted-average method bases the unit costs on only the current period's costs—just as in the FIFO method. If there *are* ending inventories, either erratic input prices or erratic production levels are also required to generate much of a difference in unit costs under the two methods. This is because the weighted-average method blends the unit costs from the prior period with the unit costs of the current period. Unless these unit costs differ greatly, the blending does not make much difference.

Nevertheless, from the standpoint of cost control, the FIFO method is superior to the weighted-average method. Current performance should be measured in relation to costs of the current period only, and the weighted-average method mixes costs of the current period with costs of the prior period. Thus, under the weighted-average method, the manager's apparent performance in the current period is influenced by what happened in the prior period. This problem does not arise under the FIFO method because the FIFO method makes a clear distinction between costs of prior periods and costs incurred during the current period. For the same reason, the FIFO method also provides more up-to-date cost data for decision making.

On the other hand, the weighted-average method is simpler to apply than the FIFO method, but computers can handle the additional calculations with ease once they have been appropriately programmed. A detailed comparison of the weighted-average and FIFO methods is provided in the Learning Aid that follows:

LEARNING AID

COMPARISON OF PROCESS COSTING METHODS

Weighted Average	FIFO
1. Equivalent units of production are calculated at the end of each period by adding together the completed units transferred out and the equivalent units in ending work in process inventory.	1. Equivalent units of production are calculated at the end of each period by adding together the completed units transferred out and the equivalent units in ending work in process inventory *less equivalent units in beginning work in process inventory.*
2. Cost per equivalent unit is calculated by adding the cost of beginning work in process inventory and the costs added during the period and dividing the total by the equivalent units of production (i.e., taking the weighted average).	2. Cost per equivalent unit is calculated by dividing the costs added during the period by the equivalent units of production.
3. Total cost for the period is calculated as the cost per equivalent unit times the equivalent units of production.	3. Total cost for the period is calculated as the cost per equivalent unit times the equivalent units of production.

APPENDIX 6A SUMMARY

- Under the FIFO method of process costing, both beginning and ending inventories are converted to an equivalent units basis. For the beginning inventory, the equivalent units represent the work done to *complete* the units; for the ending inventory, the equivalent units represent the work done to bring the units to a stage of partial completion at the end of the period (the same as with the weighted-average method). [LO6]
- Under the FIFO method, for the cost per equivalent unit, we use only those costs that were incurred during the current period, and we ignore any costs in the beginning work in process inventory. Under the FIFO method, *unit costs relate only to work done during the current period.* [LO7]
- The cost per equivalent unit is then used to value the ending work in process inventory and the units transferred out to the next department or to finished goods. Costs are transferred from one department to the next until the last processing department. At that point, the cost of completed units is transferred to finished goods. At the end of the period, a cost reconciliation is prepared to account for the costs transferred out and costs in work in process inventory at the end of the period. [LO8]

APPENDIX 6A QUESTIONS, EXERCISES, PROBLEMS, AND CASES

6A-1 How does the computation of equivalent units under the FIFO method differ from the computation of equivalent units under the weighted-average method?

6A-2 From the standpoint of cost control, why is the FIFO method superior to the weighted-average method?

EXERCISE 6A-1 Computation of Equivalent Units—FIFO Method [LO6]

QualityCo produces wine bottles for vintners in a process that starts in the Melt and Mould Department. Data concerning that department's operations in the most recent period appear below:

Beginning work in process:	
Units in process..	400
Stage of completion with respect to materials	75%
Stage of completion with respect to conversion............................	25%
Units started into production during the month...............................	42,600
Units completed and transferred out	42,500
Ending work in process:	
Units in process..	500
Stage of completion with respect to materials	80%
Stage of completion with respect to conversion............................	30%

Required:

QualityCo uses the FIFO method in its process costing system. Compute the equivalent units of production for the period for the Melt and Mould Department.

EXERCISE 6A-2 Cost per Equivalent Unit—FIFO Method [LO7]

Tolerin Company uses the FIFO method in its process costing system. Data for the Assembly Department for May appear below:

	Materials	Labour	Overhead
Cost added during May...........................	$41,280	$26,460	$66,150
Equivalent units of production....................	8,000	7,000	7,000

Required:

Compute the cost per equivalent unit for materials, for labour, for overhead, and in total.

EXERCISE 6A-3 Assigning Costs to Units—FIFO Method [LO8]

Data concerning a recent period's activity in the Mixing Department, the first processing department in a company that uses process costing, appear below:

	Materials	Conversion
Cost of work in process inventory at the beginning of the period.................	$2,700	$380
Equivalent units of production in the ending work in process inventory	800	200
Equivalent units of production required to complete the beginning work in process inventory...	400	700
Cost per equivalent unit for the period...	$4.40	$1.30

A total of 8,000 units were completed and transferred to the next processing department during the period. Beginning work in process inventory consisted of 1,000 units, and ending work in process inventory consisted of 2,000 units.

Required:

Compute the FIFO cost of the units transferred to the next department during the period and the cost of ending work in process inventory.

EXERCISE 6A–4 Equivalent Units and Cost per Equivalent Unit—FIFO Method [LO6, LO7]

Refer to the data for Healthcheck Corp. in Exercise 6–6.

Required:

Assume that the company uses the FIFO method of accounting for units and costs.
1. Compute the equivalent units for June's activity for the first processing department.
2. Determine the costs per equivalent unit for June.

EXERCISE 6A–5 Equivalent Units; Assigning Costs—FIFO Method [LO6, LO7]

Krollon Company uses the FIFO method in its process costing system. The following data are for the most recent month of operations in one of the company's processing departments:

Units in beginning inventory	400
Units started into production	4,300
Units in ending inventory	300
Units transferred to the next department	4,400

	Materials	Conversion
Percentage completion of beginning inventory	70%	30%
Percentage completion of ending inventory	80%	40%

The cost of beginning inventory according to the company's costing system was $7,886, of which $4,897 was for materials and the remainder was for conversion cost. The costs added during the month amounted to $181,652. The costs per equivalent unit for the month were as follows:

	Materials	Conversion
Cost per equivalent unit	$18.20	$23.25

Required:

1. Compute the total cost per equivalent unit for the month.
2. Compute the equivalent units of material and of conversion costs in the ending inventory.
3. Compute the equivalent units of material and of conversion costs that were required to complete the beginning inventory.
4. Determine the number of units started and completed during the month.
5. Determine the costs of ending inventory and units transferred out.

EXERCISE 6A–6 Equivalent Units—FIFO Method [LO6]

Refer to the data for Green House Inc. in Exercise 6–7.

Required:

Compute the equivalent units for October for the Cleaning Department, assuming that the company uses the FIFO method of accounting for units.

PROBLEM 6A–7 Equivalent Units; Cost per Equivalent Unit; Assigning Costs—FIFO Method [LO6, LO7, LO8]

Refer to the data for the Mixing Department in CloverSweet Inc. in Problem 6–10. Assume that the company uses the FIFO method rather than the weighted-average method in its process costing system.

Required:

1. Determine the equivalent units for June for the first process.
2. Compute the costs per equivalent unit for June for the first process.
3. Determine the total cost of ending work in process inventory and the total cost of units transferred to the next process in June.
4. Prepare a report that reconciles the total costs assigned to the ending work in process inventory and the units transferred out with the costs in beginning inventory and costs added during the period.

PROBLEM 6A-8 Equivalent Units; Applying Costs—FIFO Method [LO6, LO7, LO8]
Jones Company manufactures a single product and uses process costing (FIFO method). The company's product goes through two processing departments, Etching and Wiring. The following activity was recorded in the Etching Department during July:

Production data:	
Units in process, July 1 (materials 60% complete; conversion 30% complete).........................	50,000
Units started into production...	500,000
Units in process, July 31 (materials 80% complete; conversion 40% complete)	60,000
Cost data:	
Work in process inventory, July 1:	
Materials cost...	$17,000
Conversion cost	$3,000
Cost added during July:	
Materials cost...	$ 457,200
Conversion cost	$349,300

Materials are added at several stages during the etching process. The company uses the FIFO method.

Required:
1. Compute the equivalent units of production.
2. Compute the costs per equivalent unit for July.
3. Determine the cost of ending work in process inventory and of the units transferred to the Wiring Department.
4. Prepare a cost reconciliation between the costs determined in (3) above and the cost of beginning inventory and costs added during the period.

CASE 6A-9 Effect of Incorrect Costing across Departments—FIFO Method [LO6, LO7, LO8]
Refer to the data for Tavia Limited in Case 6–17. Assume that the company uses the FIFO method.

Required:
1. Prepare a report for the Forming Department for October showing how much cost should have been assigned to the units completed and transferred to the Stamping Department and to the ending work in process inventory.
2. Assume that in order to remain competitive, the company undertook a major cost-cutting program during October. Would the effects of this cost-cutting program tend to show up more under the weighted-average method or under the FIFO method? Explain your answer.

CASE 6A-10 Inventory Valuation under Process Costing—FIFO Method [LO6, LO7, LO8]
Refer to the data for Rachel's Real Root Beer in Case 6–18. Assume the company uses the FIFO method.

Required:
Take on the role of Switzer and prepare the report for Archer. Be sure to provide all details, including a full production report, to help Archer understand how costs were calculated.

APPENDIX 6B: SHRINKAGE AND LOST UNITS

   Appendix available on Connect.

ACTIVITY-BASED COSTING: A TOOL TO AID DECISION MAKING

■ MEASURING THE COST OF PRODUCT COMPLEXITY

Increasing product variety and supply chain complexity can lead to increased fixed as well as variable costs. Fixed overhead costs, such as procurement costs, material handling costs, and inventory control costs, all increase as product variety and supply chain complexity increase. Toyota Motor Corp. has recently identified this issue as a key target for future cost control initiatives. For example, Toyota has decided to use 10 rather than 50 different types of airbags and 21 rather than 100 different types of radiators across its product line. According to estimates from Toyota, a program to narrow down the number of different components used in vehicles as well as sourcing more components from fewer suppliers has reduced time and cost to create new models by at least 30%. The next goal is to reduce the number of different cylinder sizes used from 18 to 6 by 2016. Traditional job-order and process costing systems discussed in the previous chapters are designed to spread manufacturing overhead evenly across units of product and to ignore non-manufacturing overhead costs, such as procurement and inventory control costs, altogether. This design potentially masks the increased cost due to product variety and product complexity. To the contrary, activity-based costing (ABC) is designed to provide managers with cost information that can be used to manage both types of overhead, allowing for better-informed decisions related to product pricing, cost management, capacity utilization, and customer profitability.

How do companies decide which activity measures to use? What are the different types of activity cost pools? How are costs allocated to the various pools? How are activity costs assigned to cost objects? These are the key questions addressed in this chapter.

Source: "Toyota targets fewer parts, complexity to speed product creation," *Automotive News*, June 15, 2013, http://www.autonews.com/apps/pbcs.dll/article?AID=/20130615/OEM/306159999#ixzz2YmgrOPIV.

Activity-based costing (ABC)
A costing method based on activities that is designed to provide managers with cost information for strategic and other decisions that potentially affect capacity and therefore fixed costs.

This chapter introduces the concept of *activity-based costing*, which has been embraced by manufacturing, service, and not-for-profit organizations including Purolator Courier, RONA Inc., Coca-Cola, and Toronto's Hospital for Sick Children. **Activity-based costing (ABC)** is a costing method that is designed to provide managers with cost information for strategic and other decisions that potentially affect capacity and therefore fixed as well as variable costs. ABC is typically used as a supplement to, rather than as a replacement for, a company's usual costing system. Most organizations that use ABC have two costing systems—the official costing system, which is used to prepare external financial reports, and the ABC system, which is used for internal decision making and for managing activities.

This chapter focuses primarily on ABC applications in manufacturing to contrast with the material presented in earlier chapters. More specifically, Chapters 4, 5, and 6 focused on traditional absorption costing systems used by manufacturing companies to calculate unit product costs for valuing inventories and determining cost of goods sold for external financial reports. In contrast, this chapter explains how manufacturing companies can use ABC rather than traditional methods to calculate unit product costs for managing overhead and making decisions. Because of the broad role that ABC can play in facilitating decisions related to product pricing, cost management, capacity utilization, and customer profitability, it is important that both accountants and non-accountants understand its purpose and application.

■ THE TREATMENT OF COSTS UNDER THE ACTIVITY-BASED COSTING MODEL

LEARNING OBJECTIVE ❶
Explain the activity-based costing model and how it differs from a traditional costing system.

Overhead cost pools
Groups of overhead cost elements.

As noted above, traditional absorption costing is designed to provide data for external financial reports. In contrast, ABC is designed for use in internal decision making. As a consequence, ABC differs from traditional cost accounting in several ways. In ABC,

1. Non-manufacturing as well as manufacturing costs may be assigned to products, but only on a cause-and-effect basis.
2. Some manufacturing costs may be excluded from product costs.
3. Numerous **overhead cost pools** are used, each of which is allocated to products and other cost objects using its own unique measure of activity.
4. Overhead rates, or activity rates, may be based on the level of activity at capacity rather than on the budgeted level of activity.

Each of these departures from traditional cost accounting practices will be discussed in turn.

Non-manufacturing Costs and Activity-Based Costing

In traditional cost accounting, only manufacturing costs are assigned to products. Selling and administrative expenses are treated as period expenses and are not assigned to products. However, many of these non-manufacturing costs are also part of the costs of producing, selling, distributing, and servicing products. For example, commissions paid to salespeople, shipping costs, and warranty repair costs can easily be traced to individual products. In this chapter, we will use the term *overhead* to refer to non-manufacturing costs as well as to indirect manufacturing costs. In ABC, products are assigned all of the overhead costs—non-manufacturing as well as manufacturing—that they can reasonably be estimated to have caused. In essence, we will be determining the entire cost of a product rather than just its manufacturing cost. The focus in Chapters 5 and 6 was on determining just the manufacturing cost of a product.

Manufacturing Costs Excluded under Activity-Based Costing

In traditional cost accounting, *all* manufacturing costs are assigned to products—even manufacturing costs that are not caused by the products. For example, in Chapter 5 we learned that a predetermined plantwide overhead rate is computed by dividing all budgeted manufacturing overhead costs by a measure of budgeted activity such as direct labour-hours. This approach spreads *all* manufacturing overhead costs across products based on each product's direct labour-hours (commonly called the "peanut butter–spreading" approach). In contrast, ABC systems assign costs to a product only if there is good reason to believe that the cost would be affected by decisions concerning the product. Recall that manufacturing overhead costs include all costs of manufacturing other than direct materials and direct labour. Some of these costs, for example, the plant controller's salary or the factory security guard's wages, are actually unaffected by product-related decisions and are therefore treated as period expenses instead of product costs under ABC.

Additionally, in a traditional absorption costing system, the costs of unused, or idle, capacity are assigned to products. If the budgeted level of activity declines, the overhead rate and unit product costs increase as the increasing costs of idle capacity are spread over a smaller base. In contrast, in ABC, products are only charged for the costs of the capacity they use—not for the costs of the capacity they don't use. This provides more stable unit product costs and is consistent with the goal of assigning to products only the costs of the resources that they use. Instead of assigning the costs of idle capacity to products, in ABC, these costs are considered to be period costs that flow through to the income statement as an expense of the current period. This treatment highlights the cost of idle capacity rather than burying it in inventory and cost of goods sold.

As will be seen in the example presented in this chapter, this departure from traditional costing approaches represents one of the key benefits of ABC, as it results in better information for decision making.

Overhead Cost Pools, Allocation Bases, and Activity-Based Costing

Throughout the 19th and early 20th centuries, costing system designs were simple and satisfactory. Typically, either one plantwide overhead cost pool or a number of departmental overhead cost pools were used to assign overhead costs to products. The plantwide and departmental approaches always had one thing in common—they relied on allocation bases such as direct labour-hours and machine-hours to allocate overhead costs to products. In labour-intensive production processes, direct labour was the most common choice for an overhead allocation base because it represented a large component of product costs; direct labour-hours were closely tracked; and many managers believed that direct labour-hours, the total volume of units produced, and overhead costs were highly correlated. Given that most companies at the time were producing a very limited variety of products that required similar resources to produce, allocation bases such as direct labour-hours, or even machine-hours, worked fine because in fact there was probably little difference in the overhead costs attributable to different products.

In the early 1990s, conditions began to change. Many tasks previously done by direct labourers were being performed by automated equipment—a component of overhead. Companies began creating new products and services at an ever-accelerating rate that differed in volume, batch size, and complexity. As illustrated in Exhibit 7–1, managing and sustaining this product diversity required investing in many more overhead resources, such as production schedulers and

EXHIBIT 7–1   Indirect Costs Are Displacing Direct Costs

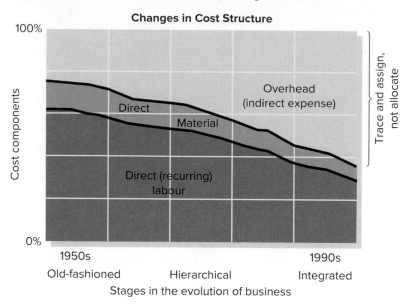

Source: Institute of Management Accountants Statements on Management Accounting.

Activity
Any event that causes the consumption of overhead resources.

Activity cost pool
A "bucket" in which costs are accumulated that relate to a single activity measure in the activity-based costing system.

Activity measure
An allocation base in an activity-based costing system; ideally, a measure of the amount of activity that drives the costs in an activity cost pool; also called a cost *driver*.

Transaction driver
A simple count of the number of times an activity occurs.

Duration driver
A measure of the amount of time required to perform an activity.

Instant Quiz 7-1
Identify and explain the four main differences between ABC and traditional product costing approaches.

product design engineers, that had no obvious connection to direct labour-hours or machine-hours. In this new environment, continuing to rely exclusively on a limited number of overhead cost pools and traditional allocation bases posed the risk that reported unit product costs would be distorted and, therefore, misleading when used for decision making. Thanks to advances in information technology that make more complex costing systems feasible, the ABC approach has appeal in today's business environment. ABC uses more cost pools and unique measures of activity to better understand the costs of managing and sustaining product diversity.

In ABC, an **activity** is any event that causes the consumption of overhead resources. An **activity cost pool** is a "bucket" in which costs are accumulated that relate to a single activity measure in the ABC system. An **activity measure** is an allocation base in an ABC system. The term *cost driver* is also used to refer to an activity measure because the activity measure should "drive" the cost being allocated. The two most common types of activity measures are *transaction drivers* and *duration drivers*. A **transaction driver** is a simple count of the number of times an activity occurs, such as the number of bills sent out to customers. A **duration driver** measures the amount of time required to perform an activity, such as the time spent preparing individual bills for customers. In general, duration drivers are more accurate measures of resource consumption than transaction drivers, but they take more effort to record. For that reason, transaction drivers are more often used in practice.

Many companies throughout the world continue to base overhead allocations on cost drivers that vary with volume of production or service provided. In situations where overhead costs and direct labour-hours are highly correlated or in situations where the goal of the overhead allocation process is mainly to prepare external financial reports, this practice makes sense. However, if plantwide overhead costs do not move in tandem with plantwide direct labour-hours or machine-hours, product costs will be distorted. ABC addresses this issue by defining five levels of activity—unit-level, batch-level, product-level, customer-level, and organization-sustaining—which largely do *not* relate to the volume of units produced or services provided. These levels are described as follows:[1]

1. **Unit-level activities** are performed each time a unit is produced. The costs of unit-level activities should be proportional to the number of units produced. For example, providing power to run processing equipment is a unit-level activity since power tends to be consumed in proportion to the number of units produced.

2. **Batch-level activities** are performed each time a batch is handled or processed, regardless of how many units are in the batch. For example, tasks such as placing purchase orders, setting up equipment, and arranging for shipments to customers are batch-level activities. They are incurred once for each batch (or customer order). Costs at the batch level depend on the number of batches processed rather than on the number of units produced, the number of units sold, or other measures of volume. For example, the cost of setting up a machine for batch processing is the same regardless of whether the batch contains 100 or 10,000 items.

3. **Product-level activities** relate to specific products and typically must be carried out regardless of how many batches are run or units of product are produced or sold. For example, activities such as designing a product, advertising a product, and maintaining a product manager and staff are all product-level activities.

4. **Customer-level activities** relate to specific customers and include activities such as sales calls, catalogue mailings, and general technical support that are not tied to any specific product.

5. **Organization-sustaining activities** are carried out regardless of which customers are served, which products are produced, how many batches are run, or how many units are made. This category includes activities such as heating the factory, cleaning executive offices, providing a computer network, arranging for loans, and preparing annual reports to shareholders.

Unit-level activities
Activities that arise as a result of the total volume of goods produced and services performed each time a unit is produced.

Batch-level activities
Activities performed each time a batch of goods is handled or processed, regardless of how many units are in a batch. The amount of resources consumed depends on the number of batches run rather than on the number of units in the batch.

Product-level activities
Activities that relate to specific products that must be carried out regardless of how many units are produced and sold or batches run.

Customer-level activities
Activities that are carried out to support customers but that are not related to any specific product.

IN BUSINESS

The Club Med—Bora Bora of Tahiti is a resort owned and operated by the French company Club Med. Most guests buy all-inclusive packages that include lodging, participation in the resort's many activities, a full range of beverages, and sumptuous buffet meals. The resort's guests come from around the world. The international nature of the club's guests poses challenges for the kitchen staff—for example, Japanese breakfasts feature miso soup, stewed vegetables in soy sauce, and rice porridge, whereas Germans are accustomed to cold cuts, cheese, and bread for breakfast. Moreover, the number of guests varies widely from 300 in the high season to 20 in the low season. The chefs in the kitchen must ensure that food in the correct quantities and variety is available to please the club's varied clientele. To make this possible, a report is prepared each day that lists how many Japanese guests, German guests, French guests, Polish guests, U.S. guests, and so forth, are currently registered. This information helps the chefs prepare the appropriate quantities of specialized foods. In essence, costs in the kitchen are driven not by the number of guests alone, but by how many guests are Japanese, how many German, how many French, and so on. The costs are driven by multiple drivers

Source: Conversation with Dominique Tredano, Chef de Village (i.e., general manager), Club Med—Bora Bora. For information about Club Med, see http://www.clubmed.com.

IN BUSINESS

Canadian River Expeditions runs river rafting trips on the Nahanni River. A seven-day trip down the Nahanni River in the Northwest Territories is one of the most popular. Guests travel over 240 kilometres from Virginia Falls to Nahanni Butte. The company runs trips of one or two rafts, with a guaranteed ratio of one guide for every four guests. The company provides all meals on the trip.

In terms of the hierarchy of activities, a guest can be considered as a unit and a raft as a batch. In that context, the wages paid to the guides are a batch-level cost because each raft requires a guide regardless of the number of guests in the raft. Imagine that each guest is given a mug to use during the trip and to take home at the end of the trip as a souvenir. The cost of the mug is a unit-level cost because the number of mugs given away is strictly proportional to the number of guests on a trip.

What about the costs of food served to guests and guides—is this a unit-level cost, a batch-level cost, a product-level cost, or an organization-sustaining cost? At first glance, it might be thought that food costs are a unit-level cost—the greater the number of guests, the higher the food costs. However, that is not quite correct. Imagine how all of the food needed for the trip is packed. It isn't always practical to finely adjust the amount of food for the actual number of guests planned to be on a trip—most of the food comes prepackaged in large lots. For example, a shrimp cocktail menu item may call for two large bags of frozen shrimp per raft, so that many bags will be packed regardless of how many guests are expected on the raft. Consequently, the costs of food are not a unit-level cost that varies with the number of guests actually on a trip. Instead, the costs of food are a batch-level cost.

Source: http://nahanni.com/about-us/.

Organization-sustaining activities
Activities that are carried out regardless of which customers are serviced, which products are produced, how many batches are run, or how many units are made.

Instant Quiz 7-2
Provide one specific example of a unit-level, a batch-level, a product level, a customer-level, and an organization-sustaining activity.

Activity Rates Based on Capacity, Not Budget

In a traditional absorption costing system, predetermined overhead rates are computed by dividing budgeted overhead costs by a measure of budgeted activity such as budgeted direct labour-hours. This practice results in applying the costs of unused, or idle, capacity to products, and it results in unstable unit product costs. If budgeted activity falls, the overhead rate increases because the fixed components of overhead are spread over a smaller base, resulting in increased unit product costs.

In ABC, products are charged for the costs of capacity they use—not for the costs of capacity they do not use. In other words, the costs of idle capacity are not charged to products. This results in more stable unit costs and is consistent with the objective of assigning only those costs to products that are actually caused by the products. Instead of assigning the costs of idle capacity to products, in ABC, these costs are considered to be period costs that flow through to the income statement as an expense of the current period. This treatment highlights the cost of idle capacity rather than burying it in inventory and cost of goods sold.

DESIGNING AN ACTIVITY-BASED COSTING SYSTEM

There are three essential characteristics of a successful ABC implementation. First, top managers must strongly support the implementation because their leadership is instrumental in properly motivating all employees to accept the need for change. Second, top managers should ensure that ABC data are linked to how people are

EXHIBIT 7-2   Classic Brass Income Statement

Classic Brass
Income Statement
Year Ended December 31, 2013

Sales...		$3,200,000
Cost of goods sold:		
Direct materials.........................	$ 975,000	
Direct labour............................	351,250	
Manufacturing overhead*................	1,000,000	2,326,250
Gross margin...............................		873,750
Selling and administrative expenses:		
Shipping expenses.......................	65,000	
Marketing expenses	300,000	
General administrative expenses.........	510,000	875,000
Operating income		$ (1,250)

*The company's traditional costing system allocates manufacturing overhead to products using a plantwide overhead rate and machine-hours as the allocation base. Inventory levels did not change during the year.

evaluated and rewarded. If employees continue to be evaluated and rewarded using traditional (non-ABC) cost data, they will quickly get the message that ABC is not important and will ignore the information provided by the system. Third, a cross-functional team should be created to design and implement the ABC system. The team should include representatives from each area that will use ABC data, such as marketing, production, engineering, and accounting departments. These cross-functional employees possess detailed knowledge of many parts of an organization's operations that is crucial for designing an effective ABC system. Moreover, utilizing the knowledge of cross-functional managers reduces their resistance to change because they feel involved in the ABC implementation process. Time after time, when accountants have attempted to implement an ABC system on their own without top-management support and cross-functional involvement, the results have been ignored.

To illustrate the design and use of an ABC system, we use Classic Brass Inc., a company that makes two main product lines for luxury yachts—standard stanchions and custom compass housings. The president of the company, John Towers, is concerned about the company's poor financial results (see Exhibit 7–2). He is concerned that the price for standard stanchions might be too high, but Tom Olafson, the marketing manager, believes competitors may be setting their prices very low, maybe even below cost, in order to increase market share. Mary Johns, the accounting manager, wonders if Classic Brass is incorrectly calculating the cost of standard stanchions and thinks ABC might help. Like most other ABC implementations, the new ABC system would supplement, rather than replace, the existing cost accounting system, which would continue to be used for external financial reports. The new ABC system would be used to prepare special reports for management decisions such as bidding on new business.

The accounting manager drew the chart in Exhibit 7–3 to explain the general structure of the ABC model. Cost objects, such as products, give rise to activities. For example, a customer order for a compass housing requires the activity of preparing a production order. Such an activity consumes resources. A production order uses a sheet of paper and takes time to fill out, and the consumption of resources causes costs. The greater the number of sheets used to fill out production orders and the greater the amount of time devoted to filling out such orders,

EXHIBIT 7-3   The Activity-Based Costing Model

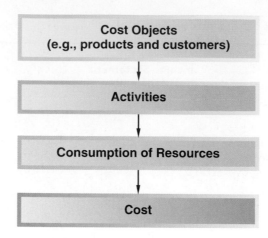

the greater the cost. ABC analyzes these types of relationships to identify how products and customers affect costs.

As in most companies, the ABC team at Classic Brass felt that the company's traditional cost accounting system adequately measured the direct material and direct labour costs of products since these costs are directly traced to products. Therefore, the ABC system would be concerned solely with manufacturing overhead and selling and administrative costs.

The team felt it was important to carefully plan how it would go about implementing the new ABC system at Classic Brass. Accordingly, the implementation process was broken down into five basic steps:

1. Identify and define activities, activity cost pools, and activity measures.
2. Assign overhead costs to activity cost pools.
3. Calculate activity rates.
4. Assign overhead costs to cost objects using the activity rates and activity measures.
5. Prepare management reports.

Step 1: Identify and Define Activities, Activity Cost Pools, and Activity Measures

The first major step is to identify the activities that will form the foundation for the system. This can be difficult and time-consuming and involves a great deal of judgment. A common procedure is for the individuals on the ABC implementation team to interview people who work in overhead departments and ask them to describe their major activities. Ordinarily, this results in a very long list of activities.

The length of such lists can be a problem. On one hand, the greater the number of activities tracked in the ABC system, the more accurate the costs are likely to be. On the other hand, it is costly to design, implement, maintain, and use a complex system involving large numbers of activities. Consequently, the original lengthy list of activities is usually reduced to a smaller number by combining similar activities. For example, several actions may be involved in handling and moving raw materials—from receiving raw materials on the loading dock to sorting them into the appropriate bins in the storeroom. All of these activities might be combined into a single activity called *materials handling*.

When combining activities in an ABC system, activities should be grouped together at the appropriate level. Batch-level activities should not be combined with unit-level activities, or product-level activities with batch-level activities, and so on.

In general, it is best to combine only those activities that are highly correlated with each other within a level. For example, the number of customer orders received is likely to be highly correlated with the number of completed customer orders shipped, so these two batch-level activities (receiving and shipping orders) can usually be combined with little loss of accuracy.

At Classic Brass, the ABC team, in consultation with top managers, selected the following *activity cost pools* and *activity measures*:

Activity Cost Pools at Classic Brass	
Activity Cost Pool	**Activity Measure**
Customer Orders	Number of customer orders
Product Design	Number of product designs
Order Size	Machine-hours
Customer Relations	Number of active customers
Other	Not applicable

The Customer Orders cost pool is assigned all costs of resources that are consumed by taking and processing customer orders, including costs of processing paperwork and any costs involved in setting up machines for specific orders. The activity measure for this cost pool is simply the number of customer orders received. This is a *batch-level activity*, since each order generates work that occurs regardless of whether the order is for 1 unit or 1,000 units.

The Product Design cost pool is assigned all costs of resources consumed in designing products. The activity measure for this cost pool is the number of products designed. This is a *product-level activity*, since the amount of design work on a new product does not depend on the number of units ultimately ordered or batches ultimately run.

The Order Size cost pool is assigned all costs of resources consumed as a consequence of the number of units produced, including the costs of miscellaneous factory supplies, power to run machines, and some equipment depreciation. This is a *unit-level activity*, since each unit requires some of these resources. The activity measure for this cost pool is machine-hours.

The Customer Relations cost pool is assigned all costs associated with maintaining relations with customers, including the costs of sales calls and the costs of entertaining customers. The activity measure for this cost pool is the number of customers the company has on its active customer list. The Customer Relations cost pool represents a *customer-level* activity.

The Other cost pool is assigned all overhead costs that are not associated with customer orders, product design, production units, or customer relations. These costs mainly consist of *organization-sustaining costs* and the *costs of unused, idle capacity*. Recall that these types of costs should *not* be assigned to products since they represent resources that are *not* consumed by products.

Step 2: Assign Overhead Costs to Activity Cost Pools

After the ABC system is designed, the team is ready to begin the process of actually computing the costs of products, customers, and other objects of interest. As shown in Exhibit 7–4, assigning costs to cost objects under ABC is a two-stage process. In the first stage, manufacturing and non-manufacturing overhead is allocated to the activity cost pools. In the second stage, the costs for the activities are allocated to the various cost objects. As with the traditional costing systems discussed in Chapters 5 and 6, direct costs are traced directly to cost objects. We begin our discussion of the mechanics of ABC with the first-stage allocations.

LEARNING OBJECTIVE 2
Assign costs to cost pools using a first-stage allocation, and compute activity rates.

EXHIBIT 7-4   Activity-Based Costing Two-Stage Cost Allocation Process

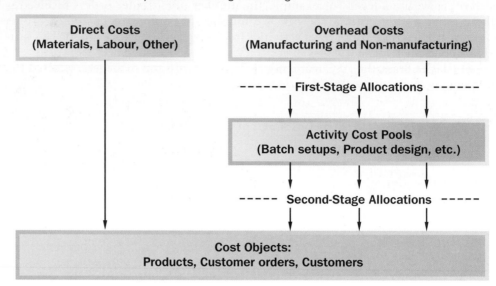

Exhibit 7-5 shows the annual overhead costs (both manufacturing and non-manufacturing) that Classic Brass intends to assign to its activity cost pools. Notice that the data in the exhibit are organized by department (e.g., Production, General Administrative, and Marketing). This is because the data have been extracted from the company's general ledger. General ledgers usually classify costs within the departments where the costs are incurred. For example, salaries, supplies, rent, and so forth incurred in the marketing department are charged to that department. The functional orientation of the general ledger mirrors the presentation of costs in the absorption income statement in Exhibit 7-2. In fact, you'll notice that the total costs for the Production Department in Exhibit 7-5 ($1,000,000) equal the total manufacturing overhead costs from the income statement in Exhibit 7-2. Similarly, the total costs for the General Administrative and Marketing Departments in Exhibit 7-5 ($510,000 and $300,000) equal the marketing and general and administrative expenses shown in Exhibit 7-2.

EXHIBIT 7-5   Annual Overhead Costs (Both Manufacturing and Non-manufacturing) at Classic Brass

Production Department:		
Indirect factory wages.....................	$500,000	
Factory equipment depreciation...........	300,000	
Factory utilities...........................	120,000	
Factory building lease	80,000	$1,000,000
General Administrative Department:		
Administrative wages and salaries..........	400,000	
Office equipment depreciation.............	50,000	
Administrative building lease..............	60,000	510,000
Marketing Department:		
Marketing wages and salaries..............	250,000	
Selling expenses..........................	50,000	300,000
Total overhead cost........................		$ 1,810,000

Three costs included in the income statement in Exhibit 7–2—direct materials, direct labour, and shipping—are excluded from the costs shown in Exhibit 7–5. The ABC team purposely excluded these costs from Exhibit 7–5 because the existing costing system can accurately trace direct materials, direct labour, and shipping costs to products.

Classic Brass's ABC system will divide the nine types of overhead costs in Exhibit 7–5 among its activity cost pools via an allocation process called *first-stage alloca-tion*. The **first-stage allocation** in an ABC system is the process of assigning functionally organized overhead costs derived from a company's general ledger to the activity cost pools.

First-stage allocation
The process by which overhead costs are assigned to activity cost pools in an activity-based costing system.

First-stage allocations are usually based on the results of interviews with employees who have first-hand knowledge of the activities. For example, Classic Brass needs to allocate $500,000 of indirect factory wages to its five activity cost pools. These allocations will be more accurate if the employees who are classi-fied as indirect factory workers (e.g., supervisors, engineers, and quality inspectors) are asked to estimate what percentage of their time is spent dealing with customer orders, with product design, with processing units of product (i.e., order size), and with customer relations. Departmental managers are typically interviewed to determine how the non-personnel costs should be distributed across the activity cost pools. For example, the Classic Brass production manager would be interviewed to determine how the $300,000 of factory equipment depreciation (shown in Exhibit 7–5) should be allocated to the activity cost pools. The key question that the production manager would need to answer is, "What percentage of the available machine capacity is consumed by each activ-ity, such as the number of customer orders or the number of units processed (i.e., size of orders)?"

The results of the interviews at Classic Brass are displayed in Exhibit 7–6. For example, factory equipment depreciation is distributed 20% to Customer Orders, 60% to Order Size, and 20% to the Other cost pool. The resource in this instance is machine time. According to the estimates made by the production manager, 60% of the total available machine time was used to actually process units to fill orders. This percentage is entered in the Order Size column. Each customer order requires setting up, which also requires machine time. This activity consumes 20% of the total available machine time and is entered under the Customer Orders column. The remaining 20% of available machine time represents idle time and is entered under the Other column.

We will not go into the details of how all of the percentages in Exhibit 7–6 were determined. However, note that 100% of the factory building lease has been assigned to the Other cost pool. Classic Brass has a single production facility. It has no plans to ex-pand or to sublease any excess space. The cost of this production facility is treated as an organization-sustaining cost because there is no way to avoid even a portion of this cost if a particular product or customer is dropped. (Remember that organization-sustaining costs are assigned to the Other cost pool and are not allocated to products.) In contrast, some companies have separate facilities for manufacturing specific products. The costs of these separate facilities could be directly traced to the specific products.

Once the percentage distributions in Exhibit 7–6 have been established, it is easy to allocate costs to the activity cost pools. The results of this first-stage alloca-tion are displayed in Exhibit 7–7. Each cost is allocated across the activity cost pools by multiplying it by the percentages in Exhibit 7–6. For example, the indirect fac-tory wages of $500,000 are multiplied by the 25% entry under Customer Orders in Exhibit 7–6 to arrive at the $125,000 entry under Customer Orders in Exhibit 7–7. Similarly, the indirect factory wages of $500,000 are multiplied by the 40% entry under Product Design in Exhibit 7–6 to arrive at the $200,000 entry under Product Design in Exhibit 7–7. All of the entries in Exhibit 7–7 are computed in this way.

Now that the first-stage allocations to the activity cost pools have been com-pleted, the next step is to compute the activity rates.

EXHIBIT 7–6   Results of Interviews: Distribution of Resource Consumption across Activity Cost Pools

	Activity Cost Pools					
	Customer Orders	Product Design	Order Size	Customer Relations	Other	Totals
Production Department:						
Indirect factory wages	25%	40%	20%	10%	5%	100%
Factory equipment depreciation	20%	0%	60%	0%	20%	100%
Factory utilities	0%	10%	50%	0%	40%	100%
Factory building lease...............	0%	0%	0%	0%	100%	100%
General Administrative Department:						
Administrative wages and salaries ...	15%	5%	10%	30%	40%	100%
Office equipment depreciation	30%	0%	0%	25%	45%	100%
Administrative building lease	0%	0%	0%	0%	100%	100%
Marketing Department:						
Marketing wages and salaries	22%	8%	0%	60%	10%	100%
Selling expenses	10%	0%	0%	70%	20%	100%

EXHIBIT 7–7   First-Stage Allocations to Activity Cost Pools

	Activity Cost Pools					Totals Taken from General Ledger
	Customer Orders	Product Design	Order Size	Customer Relations	Other	
Production Department:						
Indirect factory wages	$ 125,000	$200,000	$ 100,000	$ 50,000	$ 25,000	$500,000
Factory equipment depreciation	60,000	0	180,000	0	60,000	300,000
Factory utilities	0	12,000	60,000	0	48,000	120,000
Factory building lease..............	0	0	0	0	80,000	80,000
General Administrative Department:						
Administrative wages and salaries ..	60,000	20,000	40,000	120,000	160,000	400,000
Office equipment depreciation	15,000	0	0	12,500	22,500	50,000
Administrative building lease	0	0	0	0	60,000	60,000
Marketing Department:						
Marketing wages and salaries	55,000	20,000	0	150,000	25,000	250,000
Selling expenses	5,000	0	0	35,000	10,000	50,000
Total	$320,000	$ 252,000	$380,000	$367,500	$490,500	$1,810,000

> Exhibit 7-6 shows that Customer Orders consume 25% of the resources represented by the $500,000 of indirect factory wages:
>
> $$25\% \times \$500{,}000 = \$125{,}000$$
>
> Other entries in the spreadsheet are computed in a similar fashion.

EXHIBIT 7–8   Computation of Activity Rates

Activity Cost Pools	(a) Total Cost*	(b) Total Activity	(a) ÷ (b) Activity Rate
Customer orders.....	$320,000	1,000 orders	$320 per order
Product design.......	$252,000	400 designs	$630 per design
Order size..........	$380,000	20,000 MHs	$19 per MH
Customer relations...	$367,500	250 customers	$1,470 per customer
Other	$490,500	Not applicable	Not applicable

*From Exhibit 7-7.

Step 3: Calculate Activity Rates

The activity rates that will be used for assigning overhead costs to products and customers are computed in Exhibit 7–8. The ABC team determined the total activity for each cost pool that would be required to produce the company's current product mix and to serve its present customers. These numbers are listed in Exhibit 7–8. For example, the ABC team found that 400 new product designs are required each year to serve the company's current customers. The activity rates are computed by dividing the *total* cost for each activity by its *total* activity. For example, the $320,000 total annual cost for the Customer Orders cost pool is divided by the total of 1,000 customer orders per year to arrive at the activity rate of $320 per customer order. Similarly, the $252,000 *total* cost for the Product Design cost pool is divided by the *total* number of designs (i.e., 400 product designs) to determine the activity rate of $630 per design. Note that activity rates are not computed for the Other category of costs. This is because the Other cost pool consists of organization-sustaining costs and costs of idle capacity that are not allocated to products and customers.

The entries in Exhibit 7–8 indicate that on average a customer order consumes resources that cost $320, a product design consumes resources that cost $630, an order consumes resources that cost $19 per machine-hour, and maintaining relations with a customer consumes resources that cost $1,470. Note that these are *average* figures. Some members of the ABC design team at Classic Brass argued that it would be unfair to charge all new products the same $630 product design cost regardless of how much design time they actually require. After discussing the pros and cons, the team concluded that it would not be worth the effort to keep track of actual design time spent on each new product. They felt that the benefits of increased accuracy would not be great enough to justify the higher cost of implementing and maintaining the more detailed costing system. Similarly, some team members were uncomfortable assigning the same $1,470 cost to each customer because different customers place different demands on the resources of the company. However, while everyone agreed with this concern, the data that would be required to measure individual customers' demands on resources were not currently available. Rather than delay implementation of the ABC system, the team decided to defer such refinements.

Before proceeding, it would be helpful to review the overall process of assigning costs to products and other cost objects in an ABC system. Exhibit 7–9 summarizes the ABC system at Classic Brass. We recommend that you carefully go over this exhibit. In particular, two things about Exhibit 7–9 are important to keep in mind. First, direct materials, direct labour, and shipping costs are included because they are all direct costs of the cost objects and must be considered when analyzing total costs related to products, customer orders, and customers. These costs were not included in the first-stage allocations because that process deals with assigning overhead costs to activity cost pools. Second, the Other category, which contains organization-sustaining costs and costs of idle capacity, is not allocated to products or customers.

Instant Quiz 7-3
Vikram Company identified $25,200 of overhead costs to be assigned to the order-processing cost pool. A total of 350 orders were processed in the year. Calculate the activity rate to be used to assign costs from this cost pool to the customer orders cost object.

EXHIBIT 7-9   The Activity-Based Costing Model at Classic Brass

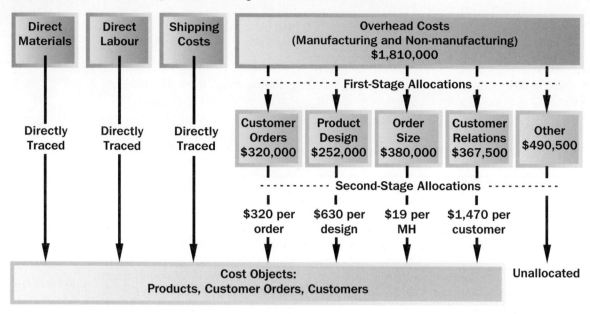

SECOND-STAGE ALLOCATION OF OVERHEAD COSTS

LEARNING OBJECTIVE ③

Assign costs to a cost object using a second-stage allocation.

Second-stage allocation
The process by which activity rates are used to apply costs to products and customers in activity-based costing.

The fourth step in the implementation of ABC is called *second-stage allocation*. In the **second-stage allocation**, activity rates are used to apply overhead costs to products and customers.

Step 4: Assign Overhead Costs to Cost Objects Using the Activity Rates and Activity Measures

First, we will illustrate how to assign costs to products, followed by an example of how to assign costs to customers. The data needed by the ABC team to assign overhead costs to Classic Brass's two products—standard stanchions and custom compass housings—are as follows:

Standard Stanchions

1. This product line does not require any new design resources.
2. 30,000 units were ordered during the year, making up 600 separate orders.
3. Each stanchion requires 35 minutes of machine time, for a total of 17,500 machine-hours.

Custom Compass Housings

1. This is a custom product that requires new design resources.
2. There were 400 orders for custom compass housings. Orders for this product are placed separately from orders for standard stanchions.
3. There were 400 custom designs prepared. One custom design was prepared for each order.
4. Since some orders were for more than one unit, a total of 1,250 custom compass housings were produced during the year. A custom compass housing requires an average of 2 machine-hours, for a total of 2,500 machine-hours.

Notice that 600 customer orders were placed for standard stanchions and 400 customer orders were placed for custom compass housings, for a total of 1,000 customer orders. All 400 product designs related to custom compass housings; none related to standard stanchions. Producing 30,000 standard stanchions required 17,500 machine-hours, and producing 1,250 custom compass housings required 2,500 machine-hours, for a total of 20,000 machine-hours.

Exhibit 7–10 illustrates how overhead costs are assigned to the standard stanchions and custom compass housings. For example, the exhibit shows that $192,000 of overhead costs is assigned from the Customer Orders activity cost pool to the standard stanchions ($320 per order × 600 orders). Similarly, $128,000 of overhead costs is assigned from the Customer Orders activity cost pool to the custom compass housings ($320 per order × 400 orders). The Customer Orders cost pool contained a total of $320,000 (see Exhibit 7–7 or 7–8), and this total amount has been assigned to the two products ($192,000 + $128,000 = $320,000).

Exhibit 7–10 shows that a total of $952,000 of overhead costs is assigned to Classic Brass's two product lines—$524,500 to standard stanchions and $427,500 to custom compass housings. This amount is less than the $1,810,000 of overhead costs included in the ABC system. Why? The total amount of overhead assigned to products does not match the total amount of overhead cost in the ABC system, because the ABC team purposely did not assign the $367,500 of Customer Relations and $490,500 of Other costs to products. The Customer Relations activity is a customer-level activity and the Other activity is an organization-sustaining activity—neither activity is caused by products. As shown below, when the Customer Relations and Other activity costs are added to the $952,000 of overhead costs assigned to products, the total is $1,810,000:

	Standard Stanchions	Custom Compass Housings	Total
Overhead Costs Assigned to Products			
Customer orders	$192,000	$128,000	$ 320,000
Product design	0	252,000	252,000
Order size	332,500	47,500	380,000
Subtotal	$524,500	$427,500	952,000
Overhead Costs Not Assigned to Products			
Customer relations			367,500
Other			490,500
Subtotal			858,000
Total overhead cost			$1,810,000

Next, we describe another aspect of second-stage allocations—assigning activity costs to customers. The data needed by the design team to assign overhead costs to one of its company's customers—Windward Yachts—are as follows:

Windward Yachts

1. The company placed a total of three orders.
   a. Two orders were for 150 standard stanchions per order.
   b. One order was for a single custom compass housing unit.
2. A total of 177 machine-hours were used to fulfill the three customer orders.
   a. The 300 standard stanchions required 175 machine-hours.
   b. The custom compass housing required 2 machine-hours.
3. Windward Yachts is one of 250 customers served by Classic Brass.

EXHIBIT 7–10   Assigning
Overhead Costs to Products

Overhead Cost for the Standard Stanchions

Activity Cost Pools	(a) Activity Rate*	(b) Activity	(a) × b) ABC Cost
Customer orders........	$320 per order	600 orders	$192,000
Product design	$630 per design	0 designs	0
Order size..............	$ 19 per MH	17,500 MHs	332,500
Total...................			$524,500

Overhead Cost for the Custom Compass Housing

Activity Cost Pools	(a) Activity Rate*	(b) Activity	(a) × (b) ABC Cost
Customer orders	$320 per order	400 orders	$128,000
Product design	$630 per design	400 designs	252,000
Order size..............	$ 19 per MH	2,500 MHs	47,500
Total...................			$427,500

*From Exhibit 7–8.

As shown in Exhibit 7–11, the ABC team calculated that $6,423 of overhead costs should be assigned to Windward Yachts. The exhibit shows that Windward Yachts is assigned $960 ($320 per order × 3 orders) of overhead costs from the Customer Orders activity cost pool, $630 ($630 per design × 1 design) from the Product Design cost pool, $3,363 ($19 per machine-hour × 177 machine-hours) from the Order Size cost pool, and $1,470 ($1,470 per customer × 1 customer) from the Customer Relations cost pool.

With second-stage allocations complete, the ABC design team was ready to turn its attention to creating reports that would help explain the company's first-ever operating loss.

■ PRODUCT AND CUSTOMER MARGINS

LEARNING OBJECTIVE ④

Use activity-based costing to compute product and customer margins.

The most common management reports prepared with ABC data are product and customer profitability reports. These reports help companies channel their resources to their most profitable growth opportunities, while at the same time highlighting products and customers that drain profits. We begin by illustrating a product profitability report, followed by a customer profitability report.

EXHIBIT 7–11   Assigning
Overhead Costs to Customers

Overhead Cost for Windward Yachts

Activity Cost Pools	(a) Activity Rate*	(b) Activity	(a) × (b) ABC Cost
Customer orders............	$ 320 per order	3 orders	$ 960
Product design	$ 630 per design	1 designs	630
Order size.................	$ 19 per MH	177 MHs	3,363
Customer relations.........	$1,470 per customer	1 customer	1,470
Total overhead cost assigned to customer................			$6,423

*From Exhibit 7–8.

Step 5: Prepare Management Reports

The Classic Brass ABC team realized that the profit from a product, also called the *product margin*, is a function of the product's sales and the direct and indirect costs that the product incurs. The ABC cost allocations shown in Exhibit 7–10 summarize only each product's indirect (i.e., overhead) costs. Therefore, to compute a product's profit (i.e., product margin), the design team needed to gather each product's sales and direct costs in addition to the overhead costs previously computed. The pertinent sales and direct cost data for each product are shown below. Notice that the numbers in the total column agree with the income statement in Exhibit 7–2:

	Standard Stanchions	Custom Compass Housings	Total
Sales.............................	$2,660,000	$540,000	$3,200,000
Direct costs:			
Direct materials..................	905,500	69,500	975,000
Direct labour....................	263,750	87,500	351,250
Shipping........................	60,000	5,000	65,000

Having gathered the above data, the design team created the product profitability report shown in Exhibit 7–12. The report reveals that standard stanchions are profitable, with a positive product margin of $906,250, whereas the custom compass housings are unprofitable, with a negative product margin of $49,500. Keep in mind that the product profitability report purposely does not include the costs in the Customer Relations and Other activity cost pools. These costs, which total $858,000, are excluded from the report because they are not caused by the products. Customer Relations costs are caused by customers, not products. The Other costs are organization-sustaining costs that are not caused by any particular product or customer.

The product margins can be reconciled with the company's operating income as follows:

	Standard Stanchions	Custom Compass Housings	Total
Sales (see Exhibit 7–12)...	$2,660,000	$540,000	$3,200,000
Total costs (see Exhibit 7–12).....................................	1,753,750	589,500	2,343,250
Product margins (see Exhibit 7–12)...............................	$ 906,250	$ (49,500)	856,750
Overhead costs not assigned to products:			
Customer relations (see Exhibit 7–8).........................			367,500
Other (see Exhibit 7–8)...			490,500
Total..			858,000
Operating income...			$ (1,250)

Next, the design team created a customer profitability report for Windward Yachts. Similar to the product profitability report, the design team needed to gather data concerning sales to Windward Yachts and the direct material, direct labour, and shipping costs associated with those sales. These data are presented below:

	Windward Yachts
Sales...............................	$11,350
Direct costs:	
Direct material costs...............	2,123
Direct labour costs	1,900
Shipping costs	205

EXHIBIT 7-12   Product Margins—Activity-Based Costing

	Standard Stanchions	Custom Compass Housing
Sales............................	$2,660,000	$540,000
Costs:		
Direct materials	$905,500	$ 69,500
Direct labour	263,750	87,500
Shipping costs	60,000	5,000
Customer orders (from Exhibit 5-9)...	192,000	128,000
Product design (from Exhibit 5-9)...		252,000
Order size (from Exhibit 5-9)	332,500	47,500
Total cost..........................	1,753,750	589,500
Product margin	$ 906,250	$ (49,500)

EXHIBIT 7-13   Customer Margin—Activity-Based Costing

		Windward Yachts
Sales..		$11,350
Costs:		
Direct materials	$2,123	
Direct labour.................................	1,900	
Shipping	205	
Customer orders (from Exhibit 5-10)	960	
Product design (from Exhibit 5-10).............	630	
Order size (from Exhibit 5-10)	3,363	
Customer relations (from Exhibit 5-10)	1,470	10,651
Customer margin		$ 699

Instant Quiz 7-5
Household Supply Company produces and sells a variety of natural home cleaning products. This year, Mitchell Hardware has ordered 1,200 cases (50 cases per order) of ZipClean, Household Supply's most popular all-purpose cleaner. Each case contains 24 bottles of ZipClean and sells for $72. Each bottle contains $0.95 of direct materials and $0.40 of direct labour. Overhead is assigned on the basis of $1.10 per bottle and $250 per order processed. Compute the customer margin for Mitchell Hardware.

Using these data and the data from Exhibit 7–11, the design team created the customer profitability report shown in Exhibit 7–13. The report revealed that the customer margin for Windward Yachts is $699. A similar report could be prepared for each of Classic Brass's 250 customers, thereby enabling the company to cultivate relationships with its most profitable customers, while taking steps to reduce the negative impact of unprofitable customers.

COMPARISON OF TRADITIONAL AND ACTIVITY-BASED COSTING PRODUCT COSTS

The ABC team used a two-step process to compare its traditional and ABC product costs. First, the team reviewed the product margins reported by the traditional costing system. Then they looked at the differences between the traditional and ABC product margins.

Product Margins Computed Using the Traditional Costing System

Classic Brass's traditional costing system assigns only manufacturing costs to products—this includes direct materials, direct labour, and manufacturing overhead. Selling and administrative costs are not assigned to products. Exhibit 7–14 shows the product margins reported by Classic Brass's traditional costing system. We will explain how these margins were calculated in three steps. First, the sales and direct materials and direct labour cost data are the same numbers used by the ABC team to prepare Exhibit 7–12. In other words, the traditional costing system and the ABC system treat these three pieces of revenue and cost data identically.

> **LEARNING OBJECTIVE** **5**
> Compare product costs computed using traditional and activity-based costing methods.

Second, the traditional costing system uses a plantwide overhead rate to assign manufacturing overhead costs to products. The numerator for the plantwide overhead rate is $1,000,000, which is the total amount of manufacturing overhead shown on the income statement in Exhibit 7–2. The footnote in Exhibit 7–2 mentions that the traditional costing system uses machine-hours to assign manufacturing overhead costs to products. The Order Size activity in Exhibit 7–8 used 20,000 machine-hours as its level of activity. These same 20,000 machine-hours would be used in the denominator of the plantwide overhead rate, which is computed as follows:

$$\text{Plantwide overhead rate} = \frac{\text{Total estimated manufacturing overhead}}{\text{Total estimated machine–hours}}$$

$$= \frac{\$1,000,000}{20,000 \text{ machine–hours}}$$

$$= \$50 \text{ per machine–hour}$$

Since 17,500 machine-hours were worked on standard stanchions, this product line is assigned $875,000 (17,500 machine-hours × $50 per machine-hour) of manufacturing overhead cost. Similarly, the custom compass housings required 2,500 machine-hours, so this product line is assigned $125,000 (2,500 machine-hours × $50 per machine-hour) of manufacturing overhead cost. The sales of each product minus its cost of goods sold equals the product margin of $615,750 for standard stanchions and $258,000 for custom compass housings.

Notice that the operating loss of $1,250 shown in Exhibit 7–14 agrees with the loss reported in the income statement in Exhibit 7–2. The company's *total* sales, *total* costs, and resulting operating loss are the same regardless of whether you are

---

EXHIBIT 7–14 Product Margins—Traditional Costing System

Product Margins—Traditional Cost System	Standard Stanchions		Custom Compass Housings		Total	
Sales........................		$2,660,000		$540,000		$3,200,000
Cost of goods sold:						
Direct materials	$905,500		$ 69,500		$ 975,000	
Direct labour..............	263,750		87,500		351,250	
Manufacturing overhead ..	875,000	2,044,250	125,000	282,000	1,000,000	2,326,250
Product margin		$ 615,750		$258,000		873,750
Selling and administrative..						875,000
Operating income						$ (1,250)

looking at the absorption income statement in Exhibit 7–2 or the traditional product profitability analysis in Exhibit 7–14. Although the "total pie" remains constant across the traditional and ABC systems, what differs is how the pie is divided between the two product lines. The traditional product margin calculations suggest that standard stanchions are generating a product margin of $615,750 and the custom compass housings a product margin of $258,000. However, these product margins differ from the ABC product margins reported in Exhibit 7–12. Indeed, the traditional costing system is sending misleading signals to Classic Brass's managers about each product's profitability. We explain why in the next section.

The Differences between Activity-Based Costs and Traditional Product Costs

The changes in product margins caused by switching from the traditional costing system to the ABC system are shown below:

	Standard Stanchions	Custom Compass Housings
Product margins—traditional (from Exhibit 7–14).................	$ 615,750	$ 258,000
Product margins—ABC (from Exhibit 7–12).......................	906,250	(49,500)
Change in reported product margins	$290,500	$(307,500)

The traditional costing system overcosts the standard stanchions and consequently reports an artificially low product margin for this product. The switch to an activity-based view of product profitability increases the product margin on standard stanchions by $290,500. In contrast, the traditional costing system undercosts the custom compass housings and reports an artificially high product margin for this product. The switch to ABC decreases the product margin on custom compass housings by $307,500.

The reasons for the change in reported product margins between the two costing methods are revealed in Exhibit 7–15. The top portion of the exhibit shows each product's direct and indirect cost assignments as reported by the traditional costing system in Exhibit 7–14. For example, Exhibit 7–15 includes the following costs for standard stanchions: direct materials, $905,500; direct labour, $263,750; and manufacturing overhead, $875,000. Each of these costs corresponds to those reported in Exhibit 7–14. Notice that the selling and administrative costs of $875,000 are purposely not allocated to products because these costs are considered to be period costs. Similarly, the bottom portion of Exhibit 7–15 summarizes the direct and indirect cost assignments as reported by the ABC system in Exhibit 7–12. The only new information in Exhibit 7–15 is shown in the two columns of percentages. The first column of percentages shows the percentage of each cost assigned to standard stanchions. For example, the $905,500 of direct materials cost traced to standard stanchions is 92.9% of the company's total direct materials cost of $975,000. The second column of percentages does the same thing for custom compass housings.

The traditional costing system and the ABC system report different product margins for three reasons:

1. The traditional costing system allocates *all* manufacturing costs to products regardless of whether they consumed those costs. The ABC system does not assign manufacturing overhead costs to products for either Customer Relations activities or Other (organization-sustaining) activities because they are not caused by any particular product. From an ABC point of view, assigning these costs to products is inherently arbitrary and counterproductive.

EXHIBIT 7-15   A Comparison of Traditional and Activity-Based Cost Assignments

	Standard Stanchions		Custom Compass Housings		Total
	(a) Amount	(a) ÷ (c) %	(b) Amount	(b) ÷ (c) %	(c) Amount
Traditional Costing System					
Direct materials	$ 905,500	92.9%	$ 69,500	7.1%	$ 975,000
Direct labour	263,750	75.1%	87,500	24.9%	351,250
Manufacturing overhead.................	875,000	87.5%	125,000	12.5%	1,000,000
Total cost assigned to products...........	$2,044,250		$282,000		2,326,250
Selling and administrative................					875,000
Total cost					$ 3,201,250
ABC System					
Direct costs:					
Direct materials.......................	$ 905,500	92.9%	$ 69,500	7.1%	$ 975,000
Direct labour..........................	263,750	75.1%	87,500	24.9%	351,250
Shipping	60,000	92.3%	5,000	7.7%	65,000
Indirect costs:					
Customer orders	192,000	60.0%	128,000	40.0%	320,000
Product design........................	0	0.0%	252,000	100.0%	252,000
Order size	332,500	87.5%	47,500	12.5%	380,000
Total cost assigned to products...........	$ 1,753,750		$589,500		2,343,250
Costs not assigned to products:					
Customer relations					367,500
Other...........................					490,500
Total cost					$ 3,201,250

2. The traditional costing system allocates *all* manufacturing overhead costs using machine-hours, a volume-related allocation base that may or may not reflect what actually causes these costs. The ABC system uses unique activity measures (most of which are *not* volume-related) to allocate the cost of each activity cost pool selected on the basis of management's assessment of the driver of overhead costs for that activity. For example, the traditional costing system assigns 87.5% of the Product Design activity to standard stanchions even though that product caused none of these costs. Conversely, all of the Product Design activity costs should be assigned to custom compass housings, not just the 12.5% under the traditional system. The overall effect is that traditional costing systems overcost high-volume products (such as custom compass housings) and undercost low-volume products (such as standard stanchions) because they assign batch-level and product-level costs using volume-related allocation bases (such as machine hours).

3. The ABC system assigns non-manufacturing overhead costs such as shipping to products on a cause-and-effect basis. The traditional costing system excludes these costs because they are classified as period costs.

The ABC design team presented the results of its work in a meeting attended by all of the top managers of Classic Brass, including the president, John Towers; the production manager, Susan Richter; the marketing manager, Tom Olafson; and the accounting manager, Mary Goodman. The ABC team brought with them copies of the chart showing the ABC design (Exhibit 7–7) and the table comparing the traditional and ABC cost assignments (Exhibit 7–15). After the formal presentation by the ABC team, the following discussion took place:

Towers: I would like to personally thank the ABC team for all of the work they have done and for an extremely interesting presentation. I am now beginning to wonder about a lot of the decisions we have made in the past using our old cost accounting system.

According to the ABC analysis, we had it all backward. We are losing money on the custom products and making a fistful on the standard products.

Goodman: I have to admit that I had no idea that the Product Design work for custom compass housings was so expensive! I knew burying these costs in our plantwide overhead rate was penalizing standard stanchions, but I didn't understand the magnitude of the problem.

Richter: I never did believe we were making a lot of money on the custom jobs. You ought to see all of the problems they create for us in production.

Olafson: I hate to admit it, but the custom jobs always seem to give us headaches in marketing, too.

Towers: If we are losing money on custom compass housings, why not suggest to our customers that they go elsewhere for that kind of work?

Olafson: Wait a minute, we would lose a lot of sales.

Richter: So what? We would save a lot more costs.

Goodman: Maybe yes, maybe no. Some of the costs would not disappear if we were to drop the custom business.

Olafson: Like what?

Goodman: Well Tom, I believe you said that about 10% of your time is spent dealing with new products. As a consequence, 10% of your salary was allocated to the Product Design cost pool. If we were to drop all of the products requiring design work, would you be willing to take a 10% pay cut?

Olafson: I trust you're joking.

Goodman: Do you see the problem? Just because 10% of your time is spent on custom products doesn't mean that the company would save 10% of your salary if the custom products were dropped. Before we take drastic action like dropping the custom products, we should identify which costs are really relevant.

Towers: I think I see what you are driving at. We wouldn't want to drop a lot of products only to find that our costs really haven't changed much. It is true that dropping the products would free up resources like Tom's time, but we had better be sure we have some good use for those resources *before* we take such an action.

As the discussion among Classic Brass managers illustrates, caution should be exercised before taking action based on an ABC analysis such as that shown in Exhibits 7–14 and 7–15. The product and customer margins computed in those exhibits are a useful starting point for further analysis, but managers need to know what costs are really affected before taking any action such as dropping a product or customer or changing the prices of products or services.

IN BUSINESS

COMPARING ACTIVITY-BASED AND TRADITIONAL PRODUCT COSTS

Airco Heating and Air Conditioning (Airco), located in Van Buren, Arkansas, implemented an ABC system to better understand the profitability of its products. The ABC system assigned $4,458,605 of overhead costs to eight activities as follows:

Activity Cost Pool	Total Cost	Total Activity	Activity Rate
Machines.................	$ 435,425	73,872 machine-hours	$ 5.89
Data record maintenance..	132,597	14 products administered	$ 9,471.21
Material handling.........	1,560,027	16,872 products	$ 92.46
Product changeover.......	723,338	72 setup hours	$10,046.36
Scheduling...............	24,877	2,788 production runs	$ 8.92
Raw material receiving....	877,107	2,859 receipts	$ 306.79
Product shipment.........	561,014	13,784,015 miles	$ 0.04
Customer service.........	144,220	2,533 customer contacts	$ 56.94
Total....................	$4,458,605		

Airco's managers were surprised by the fact that 55% [($1,560,027 + $877,107) ÷ $4,458,605] of its overhead resources were consumed by the material handling and raw material receiving activities. They responded by reducing the raw material and part transport distances within the facility. In addition, they compared the traditional and ABC product margin percentages (computed by dividing each product's margin by the sales of the product) for the company's seven product lines of air conditioners as summarized below:

	5-Ton	**6-Ton**	**7.5-Ton**	**10-Ton**	**12.5-Ton**	**15-Ton**	**20-Ton**
				Product			
Traditional product margin % ..	−20%	4%	40%	−4%	20%	42%	70%
ABC product margin %	−15%	−8%	50%	1%	−6%	40%	69%

In response to the ABC data, Airco decided to explore the possibility of raising prices on 5-ton, 6-ton, and 12.5-ton air conditioners while at the same time seeking to reduce overhead consumption by these products (1 ton equals approximately 900 kg).

Source: Copyright 2004 from Heather Nachtmann and Mohammad Hani Al-Rifai, "An Application of Activity-Based Costing in the Air Conditioner Manufacturing Industry," *The Engineering Economist 49*, Issue 3, 2004, pp. 221–236. Reproduced by permission of Taylor & Francis Group, LLC, www.taylorandfrancis.com.

Targeting Process Improvements

The ABC model illustrated in the preceding sections can readily be used to identify areas that would benefit from process improvements. Indeed, managers often cite this as the major benefit of ABC.[2] **Activity-based management (ABM)** is used in conjunction with ABC to improve processes and reduce costs. ABM is used in organizations as diverse as manufacturing companies, hospitals, and the Canadian Coast Guard.[3] When "forty percent of the cost of running a hospital involves storing, collecting and moving information," there is obviously a great deal of room for eliminating waste and for improvement.[4]

The first step in any improvement program is to decide what to improve. The theory of constraints approach, which is discussed in Chapter 12, is a powerful tool for targeting the area in an organization where improvement will yield the greatest benefit. ABM provides another approach. The activity rates computed in ABC can provide valuable clues concerning where there is waste and scope for improvement in an organization. For example, managers at Classic Brass were surprised at the high cost of customer orders. Some customer orders are for less than $100 worth of products, and yet it costs, on average, $320 to process an order according to the activity rates calculated in Exhibit 7–8. This seemed very expensive for an activity that adds no value to the product. As a consequence, the customer order processing activity was targeted for improvement.

Benchmarking is another way to utilize the information in activity rates. **Benchmarking** is a systematic approach to identifying the activities with the greatest room for improvement. It is based on comparing the performance of some aspect of an organization's operations (e.g., quality control) with the performance of other, similar organizations known for their outstanding performance. Using outside organizations as the basis for comparison is known as *external benchmarking*. Some companies also use *internal benchmarking*, where one division's operations (e.g., customer order processing) is compared to other divisions that are performing well on that activity. If a particular part of the organization performs well below the external or internal benchmark, managers will likely target that area for improvement.

Activity-based management (ABM)
A management approach that, in conjunction with activity-based costing, improves processes and reduces costs.

Benchmarking
A systematic approach of comparing the performance of some aspect of an organization's operations to that of outstanding external companies or to other divisions within the same organization.

Activity-Based Costing and External Reports

Although ABC generally provides more accurate product costs than traditional costing methods, it is infrequently used for external reports for a number of reasons. First, external reports are less detailed than internal reports prepared for decision making. On the external reports, individual product costs are not reported. Cost of goods sold and inventory valuations are disclosed, but there is no breakdown of these accounts by product. If some products are undercosted and some are overcosted, the errors tend to offset each other when the product costs are added together.

Second, it is often very difficult to make changes in a company's accounting system. The official cost accounting systems in most large companies are usually embedded in complex computer applications that have been modified in-house over the course of many years. It is extremely difficult to make changes in such applications without causing numerous bugs, which can lead to errors in the resulting information.

Third, an ABC system such as the one described in this chapter does not conform to GAAP. As discussed in Chapter 2, product costs computed for external reports must include all of the manufacturing costs and only manufacturing costs; however, in an ABC system as described in this chapter, product costs exclude some manufacturing costs and include some non-manufacturing costs. It is possible to adjust the ABC data at the end of the period to conform to GAAP, but that requires more work. Appendix 7A presents an approach for using a modified form of ABC for external reporting purposes.

Fourth, auditors are likely to be uncomfortable with allocations based on interviews with the company's personnel. Such subjective data can easily be manipulated by management to make earnings and other key variables look more favourable.

For all of these reasons, most companies confine their ABC efforts to special studies for management and do not attempt to integrate ABC into their formal cost accounting systems.

LEARNING AID

ACTIVITY-BASED COSTING VERSUS TRADITIONAL PRODUCT COSTING

Item	ABC	Traditional
1. Number of cost pools.	1. Numerous, based on key activities involved in product/service.	1. Small number, based on key production/service departments.
2. Treatment of manufacturing overhead (MOH).	2. Allocated to products only if *caused* by products.	2. All MOH allocated to products.
3. Activity measures used for applying overhead.	3. Mix of unit-level (e.g., labour-hours) and non-unit-level (e.g., batches). Vary by activity.	3. Typically unit-level (e.g., labour-hours). Vary by department.
4. Treatment of non-manufacturing overhead (e.g., shipping costs).	4. Allocated to products or customers if *caused* by products or customers.	4. Expensed as period costs.
5. Treatment of direct materials and labour.	5. Directly traced to cost objects.	5. Directly traced to cost objects
6. Use for external financial reporting.	6. Usually requires modification because of items 2 and 4 (see Appendix 7A).	6. Typically no modifications required as it conforms to GAAP.

■ THE LIMITATIONS OF ACTIVITY-BASED COSTING

Implementing an ABC system is a major undertaking, requiring substantial resources. And, once implemented, an ABC system is more costly to maintain than a traditional costing system—data concerning numerous activity measures must be collected, checked, and entered into the system. The benefits of increased accuracy may not outweigh these costs.

ABC produces numbers, such as product margins, that may be at odds with the numbers produced by traditional costing systems. But managers are accustomed to using traditional costing systems to run their operations, and traditional costing systems are often used in performance evaluations. Essentially, ABC changes the rules of the game. It is well established that changes in organizations—particularly those that alter the rules of the game—inevitably face resistance. This underscores the importance of top-management support and the full participation of line managers, as well as the accounting staff, in any ABC initiative. If ABC is viewed as an accounting initiative that does not have the full support of top management, it is doomed to failure.

In practice, most managers insist on fully allocating all costs to products, customers, and other cost objects in an ABC system—including the costs of idle capacity and organization-sustaining costs. This results in overstated costs and understated margins and mistakes in pricing and other critical decisions.[5]

ABC data can easily be misinterpreted and must be used with care in making decisions. Costs assigned to products, customers, and other cost objects are only *potentially* relevant. Before making any significant decisions using ABC data, managers must identify which costs are really relevant for the decision at hand.

As discussed in the previous section, reports generated by the best ABC systems do not conform to GAAP. Consequently, an organization involved in ABC should have two costing systems—one for internal use and one for preparing external reports. This is costlier than maintaining just one system and may cause confusion about which system is to be believed and relied on.

IN BUSINESS

In a survey of large manufacturing companies in Canada, nearly 66% of the respondents indicated they believed an ABC system could potentially add value to their organization. However, despite acknowledging its perceived usefulness, only 39% of the responding companies had actually implemented an ABC system across all business units in the organization. Kaplan and Anderson (2007) provide some possible reasons for this relatively low adoption rate:

- High implementation and maintenance costs of ABC systems.
- Inaccuracies in activity costs due to the need for subjective estimates of the amount of time spent on various activities.
- Inability of ABC systems to completely capture the complexity of actual operations.
- Difficulties integrating ABC data from multiple business units across the organization.

Although ABC offers the potential for more accurate product costs, managers must carefully consider all costs of implementing, maintaining, and using the system. Further, some of the reasons cited by Kaplan and Anderson (2007) suggest that implementing a more complex costing system will not automatically result in more accurate costs. Only if estimated benefits exceed all estimated costs should the ABC implementation proceed.

Sources: Alnoor Bhimani, Maurice Gosselin, Mthuli Ncube, and Hiroshi Okano, "Activity-Based Costing: How Far Have We Come Internationally?" *Cost Management*, May–June 2007, pp. 12–17; Robert Kaplan and Steven Anderson, "The Innovation of Time-Driven Activity-Based Costing," *Cost Management*, March–April 2007, pp. 5–15.

KNOWLEDGE IN ACTION

Managers can apply their knowledge about ABC when
- Calculating the product/service cost when the firm produces a variety of products or when products are highly customized and the design and production process is complex. These are the conditions under which applying overhead uniformly to products is likely to cause the greatest distortion in product/service cost.
- Setting prices to ensure the price exceeds the cost to produce the product or service
- Identifying activities that would benefit from process improvement (e.g., eliminating waste, decreasing processing time, reducing defects and rework)

SUMMARY

- Under traditional cost accounting methods, all manufacturing costs—even those not caused by specific products—are allocated to products. Non-manufacturing costs that are caused by products are not assigned to products. Traditional costing methods also allocate the costs of idle capacity to products, which, in effect, charges them for resources not used. [LO1]
- Traditional costing methods rely on unit-level allocation bases, such as direct labour-hours and machine-hours. This results in overcosting high-volume products and undercosting low-volume products and can lead to mistakes when making decisions. [LO1]
- Activity-based costing (ABC) estimates the costs of the resources consumed by cost objects such as products and customers. The approach taken in ABC recognizes that cost objects generate the need for activities that in turn consume costly resources. Activities form the link between costs and cost objects. [LO1, LO2]
- ABC is concerned with overhead—both manufacturing overhead and selling and administrative overhead. The accounting for direct labour and direct materials is usually unaffected by the use of ABC. [LO1, LO2]
- To develop an ABC system, companies typically choose a small set of activities that summarize much of the work performed in overhead departments. Associated with each activity is an activity cost pool. Where possible, overhead costs are directly traced to these activity cost pools. Remaining overhead costs are assigned to the activity cost pools in the first-stage allocation. [LO2]
- An activity rate is computed for each cost pool by dividing the costs assigned to the cost pool by the measure of activity for the cost pool. In the second-stage allocation, activity rates are used to apply costs to cost objects such as products and customers. [LO3, LO4]
- Activity-based management (ABM) utilizes information from the ABC system to target activities in need of process improvements. Benchmarking performance against world-class organizations or other high-performing divisions within the same organization can help identify activities most in need of improvement. [LO4]
- Product costs computed under ABC are often quite different from the costs generated by a company's traditional cost accounting system because ABC assigns only costs caused by products, uses activity measures that are not necessarily volume related, and assigns non-manufacturing costs such as shipping on a cause-and-effect basis. [LO5]

REVIEW PROBLEM 1: ACTIVITY-BASED COSTING

Advanced Products Corporation produces a fire-resistant commercial filing cabinet that it sells to office furniture distributors. The company has a simple ABC system that it uses for internal decision-making purposes. The company has two overhead departments, whose costs are listed below:

Overhead Costs	
Manufacturing overhead.................	$500,000
Selling and administrative overhead	300,000
Total overhead costs....................	$800,000

The company's ABC system has the following activity cost pools and activity measures:

Activity Cost Pool	Activity Measure
Assembling units...................	Number of units
Processing orders	Number of customer orders
Customer support	Number of customers
Other	These costs are not allocated to products or customers

Costs assigned to the "Other" activity cost pool have no activity measure; they consist of the costs of unused capacity and organization-sustaining costs, neither of which are assigned to orders, customers, or the product.

Advanced Products distributes the costs of manufacturing overhead and selling and administrative overhead to the activity cost pools based on interviews with employees as reported below:

	Assembling Units	Processing Orders	Customer Support	Other	Total
Manufacturing overhead	50%	35%	5%	10%	100%
Selling and administrative overhead..	10%	45%	25%	20%	100%
Total activity......................	1,000 units	250 orders	100 customers		

Required:
1. Prepare a report showing the first-stage allocations of overhead costs to the activity cost pools. (Use Exhibit 7–7 as a guide.)
2. Compute the activity rates for the activity cost pools. (Use Exhibit 7–8 as a guide.)
3. Prepare a report showing the overhead costs attributable to Shenzhen Enterprises, one of Advanced Products' customers. Last year, Shenzhen ordered filing cabinets four different times. Shenzhen ordered 80 filing cabinets in total during the year. (Use Exhibit 7–11 as a guide.)
4. The selling price of a filing cabinet is $595. The cost of direct materials is $180 per filing cabinet, and direct labour is $50 per filing cabinet. What is the customer margin of Shenzhen Enterprises? (Use Exhibit 7–13 as a guide.)

Solution to Review Problem 1

1. The first-stage allocation is as follows:

	Assembling Units	Processing Orders	Customer Support	Other	Total
Manufacturing overhead	$250,000	$ 175,000	$ 25,000	$50,000	$500,000
Selling and administrative overhead..	30,000	135,000	75,000	60,000	300,000
Total overhead costs..............	$280,000	$310,000	$100,000	$110,000	$800,000

Example: According to the distribution of resources across activities, 50% of the $500,000 manufacturing overhead cost is attributable to assembling units activities:

$$\$500,000 \times 50\% = \$250,000$$

Other entries in the table are determined in a similar manner.

2. Computation of activity rates:

Activity Cost Pools	(a) Total Cost	(b) Total Activity	(a) ÷ (b) Activity Rate
Assembling units......................	$280,000	1,000 units	$ 280 per unit
Processing orders.....................	$ 310,000	250 orders	$1,240 per order
Customer support	$ 100,000	100 customers	$1,000 per customer

3. Computation of the overhead costs attributable to Shenzhen Enterprises:

Activity Cost Pools	(a) Activity Rate	(b) Activity	(a) × (b) ABC Cost
Assembling units....................	$280 per unit	80 units	$22,400
Processing orders..................	$1,240 per order	4 orders	4,960
Customer support	$1,000 per customer	1 customer	$ 1,000
Total...............................			$28,360

4. The customer margins for Shenzhen can be computed as follows:

Sales (80 units × $595 per unit)...............................		$47,600
Costs:		
Direct materials (80 units × $180 per unit)..................	$14,400	
Direct labour (80 units × $50 per unit).....................	4,000	
Assembling units...	22,400	
Processing orders..	4,960	
Customer support	1,000	46,760
Customer margin		$ 840

REVIEW PROBLEM 2: COMPARISON OF TRADITIONAL COSTING AND ACTIVITY-BASED COSTING

Rocky Mountain Corporation makes two types of hiking boots—Xactive and Pathbreaker. Data concerning these two product lines appear below:

	Xactive	Pathbreaker
Selling price per unit	$127.00	$89.00
Direct materials per unit	$64.80	$51.00
Direct labour per unit	$18.20	$13.00
Direct labour-hours per unit.......................	1.4 DLHs	1.0 DLHs
Estimated annual production and sales	25,000 units	75,000 units

The company has a traditional costing system in which manufacturing overhead is applied to units based on direct labour-hours. Data concerning manufacturing overhead and direct labour-hours for the upcoming year appear below:

Estimated total manufacturing overhead..........................	$2,200,000
Estimated total direct labour-hours...............................	110,000 DLHs

Required:
1. Using Exhibit 7–14 as a guide, compute the product margins for the Xactive and Pathbreaker products under the company's traditional costing system.
2. The company is considering replacing its traditional costing system with an ABC system that would assign its manufacturing overhead to the following four activity cost pools (the Other cost pool includes organization-sustaining costs and idle capacity costs):

Cost Pools and Activity Measures	Estimated Overhead Cost	Xactive	Pathbreaker	Total
Supporting direct labour (direct labour-hours)	$ 797,500	35,000	75,000	110,000
Batch setups (setups)	680,000	250	150	400
Product-sustaining (number of products)	650,000	1	1	2
Other	72,500	NA	NA	NA
Total manufacturing overhead cost	$2,200,000			

Using Exhibit 7–12 as a guide, compute the product margins for the Xactive and Pathbreaker products under the ABC system.
3. Using Exhibit 7–15 as a guide, prepare a quantitative comparison of the traditional and activity-based cost assignments. Explain why the traditional and activity-based cost assignments differ.

Solution to Review Problem 2

1. Under the traditional direct labour-hour based costing system, manufacturing overhead is applied to products using the predetermined overhead rate computed as follows:

$$\text{Predetermined overhead rate} = \frac{\text{Estimated total manufacturing overhead cost}}{\text{Estimated total direct labour–hours}}$$

$$= \frac{\$2,200,000}{110,000 \text{ DLHs*}} = \$20.00 \text{ per DLH}$$

*25,000 units of Xactive @ 1.4 DLH per unit + 75,000 units of Pathbreaker @ 1.0 DLH per unit = 35,000 DLHs + 75,000 DLHs = 110,000 DLHs.

Consequently, the product margins using the traditional approach are computed as follows:

	Xactive	Pathbreaker	Total
Sales..	$3,175,000	$6,675,000	$9,850,000
Direct materials	1,620,000	3,825,000	5,445,000
Direct labour	455,000	975,000	1,430,000
Manufacturing overhead applied @ $20.00 per direct labour-hour.........................	700,000	1,500,000	2,200,000
Total manufacturing cost..........................	2,775,000	6,300,000	9,075,000
Product margin..................................	$ 400,000	$ 375,000	$ 775,000

Note that all of the manufacturing overhead cost is applied to the products under the company's traditional costing system.

2. The first step is to determine the activity rates:

Activity Cost Pools*	(a) Total cost	(b) Total Activity	(a) ÷ (b) Activity Rate
Supporting direct labour	$797,500	110,000 DLHs	$7.25 per DLH
Batch setups	$680,000	400 setups	$1,700 per setup
Product-sustaining.........................	$650,000	2 products	$325,000 per product

*The Other activity cost pool is not shown above because it includes organization-sustaining and idle capacity costs that should not be assigned to products.

Under the ABC system, the product margins are computed as follows:

	Xactive	Pathbreaker	Total
Sales	$3,175,000	$6,675,000	$9,850,000
Direct materials	1,620,000	3,825,000	5,445,000
Direct labour	455,000	975,000	1,430,000
Supporting direct labour-hour	253,750	543,750	797,500
Batch setups	425,000	255,000	680,000
Product-sustaining	325,000	325,000	650,000
Total cost	3,078,750	5,923,750	9,002,500
Product margin	$ 96,250	$ 751,250	$ 847,500

3.   The quantitative comparison is as follows:

	Xactive		Pathbreaker		Total
	(a)	(a) ÷ (c)	(b)	(b) ÷ (c)	(c)
Traditional Costing System	Amount	%	Amount	%	Amount
Direct materials	$1,620,000	29.8%	$ 3,825,000	70.2%	$5,445,000
Direct labour	455,000	31.8%	975,000	68.2%	1,430,000
Manufacturing overhead	700,000	31.8%	1,500,000	68.2%	2,200,000
Total cost assigned to products	$2,775,000		$6,300,000		$9,075,000
ABC System					
Direct costs:					
Direct materials	$ 1,620,000	29.8%	$3,825,000	70.2%	$5,445,000
Direct labour	455,000	31.8%	975,000	68.2%	1,430,000
Indirect costs:					
Supporting direct labour	253,750	31.8%	543,750	68.2%	797,500
Batch setups	425,000	62.5%	255,000	37.5%	680,000
Product-sustaining	325,000	50.0%	325,000	50.0%	650,000
Total cost assigned to products	$3,078,750		$5,923,750		9,002,500
Costs not assigned to products:					
Other					72,500
Total cost					$9,075,000

The traditional and activity-based cost assignments differ for two reasons. First, the traditional system assigns all $2,200,000 of manufacturing overhead to products. The ABC system assigns only $2,127,500 of manufacturing overhead to products. The ABC system does not assign the $72,500 of Other activity costs to products because they represent organization-sustaining and idle capacity costs. Second, the traditional system uses one unit-level activity measure, direct labour-hours, to assign 31.8% of all overhead to the Xactive product line and 68.2% of all overhead to the Pathbreaker product line. The ABC system assigns 62.5% of Batch setup costs (a batch-level activity) to the Xactive product line and 37.5% to the Pathbreaker product line. The ABC system assigns 50% of product-sustaining costs (a product-level activity) to each product line.

GLOSSARY

   Review key terms and definitions on Connect.

DISCUSSION CASE

DISCUSSION CASE 7-1
Implementing an ABC system should proceed only if management believes the benefits of doing so will exceed the costs. The costs of an ABC system are not difficult to quantify. They include identifying the key activities, developing an information system to record and report information, collecting data for activity measures, and maintaining the system. More difficult to quantify are the benefits of adopting an ABC system.

Required:
Can you identify some qualitative benefits of adopting ABC? Can any of these be quantified? How could management deal with uncertainty related to any potential benefits of adopting an ABC system?

QUESTIONS

7-1 How are non-manufacturing costs related to selling, shipping, and distribution activities treated under the ABC approach?

7-2 Why is direct labour a poor base for allocating overhead in many companies?

7-3 Why are overhead rates in ABC based on the level of activity at capacity rather than on the budgeted level of activity?

7-4 What is an activity cost pool?

7-5 What are unit-level, batch-level, product-level, customer-level, and organization-sustaining activities?

7-6 What types of costs should not be assigned to products in an ABC system?

7-7 Why are transaction drivers typically used more often than duration drivers in practice?

7-8 Why is the first stage of the allocation process in ABC often based on interviews?

7-9 What is benchmarking?

7-10 When ABC is used, why are manufacturing overhead costs often shifted from high-volume products to low-volume products?

7-11 What is the second-stage allocation in ABC?

7-12 What are the two chief limitations of ABC?

7-13 Why is ABC as described in the chapter unacceptable for external reporting purposes?

EXERCISES

To help identify which exhibits to refer to when working on the exercises, problems, and cases, use the following guide: (*a*) first-stage allocations to activity cost pools: Exhibit 7-7; (*b*) computation of activity rates: Exhibit 7-8; (*c*) assigning overhead costs to products: Exhibit 7-10; (*d*) assigning overhead costs to customers: Exhibit 7-11; (*e*) product margins: Exhibit 7-12; and (*f*) customer margins: Exhibit 7-13.

EXERCISE 7-1 Activity-Based Costing Cost Hierarchy [LO1]
The following activities occur at Greenwich Corporation, a company that manufactures a variety of products:

a.   Various individuals manage the parts inventories.
b.   A clerk in the factory issues purchase orders for a job.
c.   The Personnel Department trains new production workers.
d.   The factory's general manager meets with other department heads, such as marketing, to coordinate plans.
e.   Direct labour workers assemble products.
f.   Engineers design new products.
g.   The materials storekeeper issues raw materials to be used in jobs.
h.   The Maintenance Department performs periodic preventive maintenance on general-use equipment.

Required:
Classify each of the activities above as a unit-level, a batch-level, a product-level, or an organization-sustaining activity.

EXERCISE 7–2 First-Stage Allocation in a Service Company [LO2]

MobileCash Corporation operates a fleet of armoured cars that make scheduled pickups and deliveries for its customers. The company is implementing an ABC system that has four activity cost pools: Travel, Pickup and Delivery, Customer Service, and Other. The activity measures are kilometres for the Travel cost pool, number of pickups and deliveries for the Pickup and Delivery cost pool, and number of customers for the Customer Service cost pool. The Other cost pool has no activity measure. The following costs will be assigned using the ABC system:

Driver and guard wages	$ 840,000
Vehicle operating expense	270,000
Vehicle depreciation	150,000
Customer representative salaries and expenses	180,000
Office expenses..	40,000
Administrative expenses	340,000
Total cost...	$1,820,000

The distribution of resource consumption across the activity cost pools is as follows:

	Travel	Pickup and Delivery	Customer Service	Other	Totals
Driver and guard wages	40%	45%	10%	5%	100%
Vehicle operating expense	75%	5%	0%	20%	100%
Vehicle depreciation	70%	10%	0%	20%	100%
Customer representative salaries and expenses	0%	0%	85%	15%	100%
Office expenses.....................................	0%	25%	35%	40%	100%
Administrative expenses	0%	5%	55%	40%	100%

Required:

Carry out the first-stage allocations of costs to activity cost pools as illustrated in Exhibit 7–7.

EXERCISE 7–3 First-Stage Allocation in a Manufacturing Company [LO2]

MovieTime Corporation produces furniture and fixtures for home theatre installations. John Jones, the owner of the company, recognized a trend in home theatre installations starting about three years ago and began working with local design firms and home builders to offer affordable yet high-quality furnishings for new construction and renovation markets. The company's most popular product is a leather upholstered recliner with a cup holder and snack tray built into each chair's arms. Last year, John decided to implement an ABC system to better understand the overall cost structure and to ensure he was charging competitive prices that would also allow the firm to remain profitable over the longer term.

The ABC system is designed to allow direct material and direct labour to be traced directly to each of the company's four main products. The system also includes four activity cost pools for overhead: Quality Control and Inspection, Order Processing, Delivery and Installation, and Other. The activity measures are units produced for Quality Control and Inspection, number of orders for Order Processing, and number of deliveries for Delivery and Installation. The Other cost pool has no activity measure. The following costs will be assigned using the ABC system:

Indirect factory salaries	$ 520,000
Delivery crew wages expense...	140,000
Delivery vehicle operating expenses and depreciation......................	95,000
Procurement and order processing salaries expense.......................	103,000
Office expenses...	25,000
Other administrative expenses	225,000
Total cost..	$1,108,000

The distribution of resource consumption across the activity cost pools is as follows:

	Quality Control and Inspection	Delivery and Installation	Order Processing	Other	Totals
Indirect factory salaries...............................	50%	25%	20%	5%	100%
Delivery crew wages expense.........................	0%	75%	10%	15%	100%
Delivery vehicle operating expenses and depreciation ..	0%	80%	10%	10%	100%
Procurement and order processing salaries and expenses............................	10%	10%	65%	15%	100%
Office expenses.......................................	15%	15%	35%	35%	100%
Other administrative expenses	15%	5%	40%	40%	100%

Required:
Carry out the first-stage allocations of costs to activity cost pools as illustrated in Exhibit 7–7.

EXERCISE 7–4 Compute Activity Rates and Assign to a Cost Object [LO3]
(This exercise is a continuation of Exercise 7–3; it should be assigned *only* if Exercise 7–3 is also assigned.) The ABC system at MovieTime contains the following activity cost pools and activity rates this year:

Activity	Total Activity
Quality control and inspection.............................	4,800 units produced
Delivery and installation..................................	1,200 deliveries
Order processing	920 orders processed
Other	None

Activity data have also been supplied for the leather recliner product line:

Activity	Total Activity for the Leather Recliner Product Line
Quality control and inspection.................	1,200 units produced
Delivery and installation......................	300 deliveries
Order processing	230 orders processed

Required:
1. Using the first-stage allocation from Exercise 7–3 and the above data, compute the activity rates for the ABC system. (Use Exhibit 7–8 as a guide). Round to the nearest whole cent.
2. Determine the total overhead cost that would be assigned to the leather recliner product line using the ABC system.

EXERCISE 7–5 Compute Activity Rates and Assign to a Cost Object [LO2, LO3]
Brookside Property Management is a property management service company for small shopping malls that uses ABC to estimate costs for pricing and other purposes. The owner of the company believes that costs are driven primarily by the area of outdoor maintenance (parking lots, sidewalks, and gardens), the area of indoor tenant space in the shopping mall, the distance to travel to the shopping mall, and the number of shopping malls managed. In addition, the costs of managing the indoor tenant space depend on whether the tenants are located on the main level or other levels of the mall. Accordingly, the company uses the five activity cost pools listed below:

Activity Cost Pool	Activity Measure
Management of outdoor areas	Square metres of outdoor areas
Management of indoor mall space—main level	Square metres of main level mall space
Management of indoor mall space—other levels	Square metres of non–main level mall space
Travel to jobs	Kilometres
Customer billing and service	Number of shopping malls

The company has already carried out its first-stage allocations of costs. The company's annual costs and activities are summarized as follows:

Activity Cost Pool	Estimated Overhead Cost	Expected Activity
Management of outdoor areas	$ 69,850	127,000 square metres of outdoor areas
Management of indoor mall space—main level	$ 114,400	104,000 square metres of main level mall space
Management of indoor mall space—other levels ..	$307,500	246,000 square metres of non–main level mall space
Travel to jobs	$ 6,600	22,000 kilometres
Customer billing and service	$ 13,800	8 shopping malls

Parker Hills Shopping Mall is one of Brookside's oldest clients. Details concerning the mall's layout, outdoor space, and distance from Brookside's head office are as follows:

Activity	Total Activity for Parker Hills Mall
Management of outdoor areas	16,000 square metres of outdoor areas
Management of indoor mall space—main level	25,000 square metres of main level mall space
Management of indoor mall space—other levels	0, as mall only has one level
Travel to jobs	2,500 kilometres travelled
Customer billing and service	1 shopping mall

Required:
1. Compute the activity rate for each of the activity cost pools.
2. Determine the total overhead cost that would be assigned to the Parker Hills Shopping Mall using the ABC system.

EXERCISE 7–6 Second-Stage Allocation [LO3]
Larner Corporation is a diversified manufacturer of industrial goods. The company's ABC system contains the following six activity cost pools and activity rates:

Activity Cost Pool	Activity Rates
Supporting direct labour	$7.00 per direct labour-hour
Machine processing	$3.00 per machine-hour
Machine setups	$40.00 per setup
Production orders	$160.00 per order
Shipments	$120.00 per shipment
Product-sustaining	$800.00 per product

Activity data have been supplied for the following products:

	Total Expected Activity	
	J78	W52
Direct labour-hours	1,000	40
Machine-hours	3,200	30
Machine setups	5	1
Production orders	5	1
Shipments	10	1
Product-sustaining	1	1

Required:
Determine the total overhead cost that would be assigned to each of the products listed above in the ABC system.

EXERCISE 7–7 Product and Customer Profitability Analysis [LO3, LO4]
PWC Systems Inc. makes personal watercraft for sale through specialty sporting goods stores. The company has a standard model but also makes custom-designed models. Management has designed an ABC system with the following activity cost pools and activity rates:

Activity Cost Pool	Activity Rates
Supporting manufacturing	$22 per direct labour-hour
Order processing	$212 per order
Custom design processing	$243 per custom design
Customer service	$307 per customer

Management would like an analysis of the profitability of a particular customer, WaveRider, which has ordered the following products over the last 12 months:

	Standard Model	Custom Design
Number of watercraft	16	3
Number of orders	2	3
Number of custom designs	0	3
Direct labour-hours per watercraft	24.5	28.0
Selling price per watercraft	$10,600	$13,200
Direct materials cost per watercraft	$ 7,950	$ 9,240

The company's direct labour rate is $24 per hour.

Required:
Using the company's ABC system, compute the customer margin of WaveRider.

EXERCISE 7–8 Activity Measures [LO1]
Various activities at Husang Corporation, a manufacturing company, are listed below:

Activity

a. Direct labour workers assemble a product.
b. Products are designed by engineers.
c. Equipment is set up to process a batch.
d. Machines are used to shape and cut materials.
e. Monthly bills are sent out to regular customers.
f. Materials are moved from the receiving dock to production lines.
g. All completed units are inspected for defects.
h. Diversity training is provided to all employees in the company.

Required:
1. Classify each activity as unit-level, batch-level, product-level, customer-level, or organization-sustaining.
2. For each activity, provide an example of one transaction driver and one duration driver that might be used in Husang Corporation's ABC system.

EXERCISE 7–9 Computing Activity-Based Costing Product Costs [LO2, LO3]
High-Calibre Products Corporation makes two products: titanium rims and posts. Data regarding the two products follow:

	Direct Labour-Hours per Unit	Annual Production
Rims.......................	0.40	20,000 units
Posts......................	0.20	80,000 units

Additional information about the company follows:

a. Rims require $17 in direct materials per unit, and posts require $10.
b. The direct labour wage rate is $16 per hour.
c. Rims are more complex to manufacture than posts, and they require special equipment.
d. The ABC system has the following activity cost pools:

Activity Cost Pool	Activity Measure	Estimated Overhead Cost	Activity Rims	Activity Posts	Activity Total
Machine setups................	Number of setups	$ 21,600	100	80	180
Special processing.............	Machine-hours	$ 180,000	4,000	0	4,000
General factory................	Direct labour-hours	$288,000	8,000	16,000	24,000

Required:

1. Compute the activity rate for each activity cost pool.
2. Determine the unit cost of each product according to the ABC system, including direct materials and direct labour.

EXERCISE 7–10 First-Stage Allocations [LO2]

The operations vice-president of the Regal Bank of Canada, Kristin Wu, has been interested in investigating the efficiency of the bank's operations. She has been particularly concerned about the costs of handling routine transactions at the bank and would like to compare these costs at the bank's various branches. If the branches with the most efficient operations can be identified, their methods can be studied and then replicated elsewhere. While the bank maintains meticulous records of wages and other costs, there has been no attempt thus far to show how those costs are related to the various services provided by the bank. Wu has asked for your help in conducting an ABC study of bank operations. In particular, she would like to know the cost of opening an account, the cost of processing deposits and withdrawals, and the cost of processing other customer transactions.

The Windsor branch of the Regal Bank of Canada submitted the following cost data for last year:

Teller wages	$150,000
Assistant branch manager salary.............	70,000
Branch manager salary	85,000
Total.......................................	$305,000

Virtually all of the other costs of the branch—rent, depreciation, utilities, and so on—are organization-sustaining costs that cannot be meaningfully assigned to individual customer transactions, such as depositing cheques.

In addition to the cost data above, the employees of the Windsor branch have been interviewed concerning how their time was distributed last year across the activities included in the ABC study. The results of those interviews appear below:

	Distribution of Resource Consumption across Activities				
	Opening Accounts	Processing Deposits and Withdrawals	Processing Other Customer Transactions	Other Activities	Totals
Teller wages	0%	75%	15%	10%	100%
Assistant branch manager salary	10%	15%	25%	50%	100%
Branch manager salary ..	0%	0%	20%	80%	100%

Required:
Prepare the first-stage allocation for Wu as illustrated in Exhibit 7–7.

EXERCISE 7–11 Computing and Interpreting Activity Rates [LO3]

(This exercise is a continuation of Exercise 7–10; it should be assigned *only* if Exercise 7–10 is also assigned.) The manager of the Windsor branch of the Regal Bank of Canada has provided the following data concerning the transactions of the branch during the past year:

Activity	Total Activity at the Windsor Branch
Opening accounts	200 accounts opened
Processing deposits and withdrawals	50,000 deposits and withdrawals
Processing other customer transactions...............	1,000 other customer transactions

The lowest costs reported by other branches for these activities are displayed below:

Activity	Lowest Cost among All Regal Bank of Canada Branches
Opening accounts	$24.35 per account opened
Processing deposits and withdrawals	$2.72 per deposit or withdrawal
Processing other customer transactions...............	$48.90 per other customer transaction

Required:
1.   Using the first-stage allocation from Exercise 7–10 and the above data, compute the activity rates for the ABC system. (Use Exhibit 7–8 as a guide.) Round all computations to the nearest whole cent.
2.   What do these results suggest to you concerning operations at the Windsor branch?

EXERCISE 7–12 Second-Stage Allocation to an Order [LO3]

Transvaal Mining Tools Ltd. of South Africa makes specialty tools used in the mining industry. The company uses an ABC system for internal decision making. The company has four activity cost pools, as listed below. The currency in South Africa is the rand, denoted here by R:

Activity Cost Pool	Activity Measure	Activity Rate
Order size	Number of direct labour-hours	R17.60 per direct labour-hour
Customer orders	Number of customer orders	R360.00 per customer order
Product testing........................	Number of testing hours	R79.00 per testing hour
Selling.................................	Number of sales calls	R1,494.00 per sales call

The managing director of the company would like information concerning the cost of a recently completed order for hard-rock drills. The order required 150 direct labour-hours, 18 hours of product testing, and three sales calls.

Required:
Prepare a report showing the overhead cost of the order for hard-rock drills according to the ABC system. What is the total overhead cost assigned to the order?

EXERCISE 7–13 Cost Hierarchy [LO1]

Green Glider Corporation makes golf carts that it sells directly to golf courses throughout the world. Several basic models are available, which are modified to suit the needs of each particular golf course. A golf course located in British Columbia, for example, would typically specify that its golf carts come equipped with retractable rain-proof covers. In addition, each customer (i.e., golf course) customizes its golf carts with its own colour scheme and logo. The company typically makes all of the golf carts for a customer before starting work on the next customer's golf carts.

Below are listed a number of activities and costs at Green Glider Corporation:

a.   The purchasing department orders the colour of paint specified by the customer from the company's supplier.
b.   A steering wheel is installed in a golf cart.
c.   An outside lawyer draws up a new generic sales contract for the company, limiting Green Glider's liability in case of accidents that involve its golf carts.

d.   The company's paint shop makes a stencil for a customer's logo.
e.   A sales representative visits a previous customer to check on how the company's golf carts are working out and to try to make a new sale.
f.   The accounts receivable department prepares the bill for a completed order.
g.   Electricity is used to heat and light the factory and the administrative offices.
h.   A golf cart is painted.
i.   The company's engineer modifies the design of a model to eliminate a potential safety problem.
j.   The marketing department has a catalogue printed and then mails copies to golf course managers.
k.   Completed golf carts are individually tested on the company's test track.
l.   A new model golf cart is shipped to the leading golfing trade magazine to be evaluated for the magazine's annual rating of golf carts.

Required:
Classify each of the costs or activities above as unit-level, batch-level, product-level, customer-level, or organization-sustaining. In this case, customers are golf courses, products are the various models of the golf cart, a batch is a specific order from a customer, and units are individual golf carts.

EXERCISE 7–14 Second-Stage Allocation and Margin Calculations [LO3, LO4]
Roll Board Inc. manufactures several models of high-quality skateboards. The company's ABC system has four activity cost pools, which are listed below along with their activity measures and activity rates:

Activity Cost Pool	Activity Measure	Activity Rate
Supporting direct labour	Number of direct labour-hours	$14 per direct labour-hour
Batch processing	Number of batches	$98 per batch
Order processing	Number of orders	$173 per order
Customer service	Number of customers	$1,320 per customer

The company just completed a single order from SkateCo for 3,200 entry-level skateboards. The order was produced in 27 batches. Each skateboard required 0.7 direct labour-hours. The selling price was $125 per skateboard, the direct materials cost was $77.50 per skateboard, and the direct labour cost was $17.50 per skateboard. This was the only order from SkateCo for the year.

Required:
Using Exhibit 7–13 as a guide, prepare a report showing the customer margin on sales to SkateCo for the year.

EXERCISE 7–15 Cost Hierarchy and Activity Measures [LO1]
Various activities at Companhia de Textils S.A., a manufacturing company located in Brazil, are listed below. The company makes a variety of products.
a.   Preventive maintenance is performed on general-purpose production equipment.
b.   Products are assembled by hand.
c.   Reminder notices are sent to customers who are late in making payments.
d.   Purchase orders are issued for materials to be used in production.
e.   Modifications are made to product designs.
f.   New employees are hired by the personnel office.
g.   Machine settings are changed between batches of different products.
h.   Parts inventories are maintained in the storeroom. (Each product requires its own unique parts.)
i.   Insurance costs are incurred on the company's facilities.

Required:
1.   Classify each of the activities as unit-level, batch-level, product-level, customer-level, or organization-sustaining.
2.   Where possible, name one or more activity measures that could be used to assign costs generated by the activity to products or customers.

EXERCISE 7–16 Comprehensive Activity-Based Costing Exercise [LO2, LO3, LO4]
Cancico Communications has supplied the following data for use in its ABC system:

Overhead Costs

Wages and salaries	$262,500
Other overhead costs............	150,000
Total overhead costs.............	$ 412,500

Activity Cost Pool	Activity Measure	Total Activity
Direct labour support	Number of direct labour-hours	7,500 DLHs
Order processing	Number of orders	600 orders
Customer support	Number of customers	120 customers
Other............................	These costs are not allocated to products or customers.	NA

Distribution of Resource Consumption across Activity Cost Pools

	Direct Labour Support	Order Processing	Customer Support	Other	Total
Wages and salaries	20%	40%	30%	10%	100%
Other overhead costs	15%	25%	25%	35%	100%

During the year, Cancico Communications completed an order for special telephone equipment for a new customer, HurnTel. This customer did not order any other products during the year. Data concerning that order follow:

Selling price....................................	$220 per unit
Units ordered..................................	115 units
Direct materials................................	$ 195 per unit
Direct labour-hours	0.6 DLH per unit
Direct labour rate.............................	$ 22 per DLH

Required:
1. Using Exhibit 7–7 as a guide, prepare a report showing the first-stage allocations of overhead costs to the activity cost pools.
2. Using Exhibit 7–8 as a guide, compute the activity rates for the activity cost pools.
3. Prepare a report showing the overhead costs for the order from HurnTel, including customer support costs.
4. Using Exhibit 7–13 as a guide, prepare a report showing the customer margin for HurnTel.

EXERCISE 7–17 Calculating and Interpreting Activity-Based Costing Data [LO2, LO3]
Jane's Cookhouse is a popular restaurant located in a scenic setting. The owner of the restaurant has been trying to better understand costs at the restaurant and has hired a student intern to conduct an ABC study. The intern, in consultation with the owner, identified three major activities. The intern then completed the first-stage allocations of costs to the activity cost pools, using data from last month's operations. The results appear below:

Activity Cost Pool	Activity Measure	Total Cost	Total Activity
Serving a party of diners..................	Number of parties served	$12,000	5,000 parties
Serving a diner	Number of diners served	$90,000	12,000 diners
Serving a drink...........................	Number of drinks ordered	$26,000	10,000 drinks

The above costs include all of the costs of the restaurant except for organization-sustaining costs such as rent, property taxes, and top-management salaries. A group of diners who ask to sit at the same table are counted as a party. Some costs, such as the costs of cleaning linen, are the same whether one person is at a table or the table is full. Other costs, such as washing dishes, depend on the number of diners served.

Prior to the ABC study, the owner knew very little about the costs of the restaurant. She knew that the total cost for the month (including organization-sustaining costs) was $180,000 and that 12,000 diners had been served. Therefore, the average cost per diner was $15.

Required:
1. According to the ABC system, what is the total cost of serving each of the following parties of diners?
   a. A party of four diners that orders three drinks in total.
   b. A party of two diners that does not order any drinks.
   c. A lone diner who orders two drinks.
2. Convert the total costs you computed in (1) above to costs per diner. In other words, what is the average cost per diner for serving each of the following parties?
   a. A party of four diners that orders three drinks in total.
   b. A party of two diners that does not order any drinks.
   c. A lone diner who orders two drinks.
3. Why do the costs per diner for the three different parties differ from each other and from the overall average cost of $15.00 per diner?

EXERCISE 7–18 Customer Profitability Analysis [LO3, LO4, LO5]

Med Max distributes medical supplies to doctors' offices and clinics throughout Alberta. Med Max sets its prices by marking up its cost of goods sold by 5%. For example, if Med Max paid $100 to buy supplies from manufacturers, Med Max would charge its customers $105 to purchase these supplies.

For years, Med Max believed that the 5% markup covered its selling and administrative expenses and provided a reasonable profit. However, in the face of declining profits, Med Max decided to implement an ABC system to help improve its understanding of customer profitability. The company broke its selling and administrative expenses into five activities, as shown below:

Activity Cost Pool	Activity Measure	Total Cost	Total Activity
Customer deliveries...........................	Number of deliveries	$ 400,000	5,000 deliveries
Manual order processing.....................	Number of manual orders	300,000	4,000 orders
Electronic order processing..................	Number of electronic orders	200,000	12,500 orders
Line item picking.............................	Number of line items picked	500,000	400,000 line items
Other organization-sustaining costs...........	NA	600,000	
Total selling and administrative expense.......		$2,000,000	

Med Max gathered the data below for two of the many clinics that it serves—City Clinic and County Clinic (both clinics purchased a total quantity of medical supplies that had cost Med Max $30,000 to buy from its manufacturers):

		Activity	
Activity Measure		City Clinic	County Clinic
Number of deliveries		10	20
Number of manual orders		0	40
Number of electronic orders.........		10	0
Number of line items picked.........		100	260

Required:
1. Compute the total revenue that Med Max would receive from City Clinic and County Clinic.
2. Compute the activity rate for each activity cost pool.
3. Compute the total activity costs that would be assigned to City Clinic and County Clinic.
4. Compute Med Max's customer margin for City Clinic and County Clinic. (*Hint:* Do not overlook the $30,000 cost of goods sold that Med Max incurred serving each clinic.)
5. Describe the purchasing behaviours that are likely to characterize Med Max's least profitable customers.

PROBLEMS

PROBLEM 7–19 Evaluating the Profitability of Services [LO2, LO3, LO4]

Kenosha Winter Services is a small family-owned snow-removal business. For its services, the company has always charged a flat fee per hundred square metres of snow removal. The current fee is $12.75 per hundred square metres. However, there is some question about whether the company is actually making any money on jobs for some customers—particularly those located on more remote properties that require considerable travel time. The owner's daughter, home from school for the summer, has suggested investigating this question using ABC. After some discussion, a simple system consisting of four activity cost pools seemed to be adequate. The activity cost pools and their activity measures appear below:

Activity Cost Pool	Activity Measure	Activity for the Year
Snow removal	Square metres cleaned (00s)	32,000 hundred square metres
Travel to jobs	Kilometres driven	15,000 kilometres
Job support	Number of jobs	400 jobs
Other (costs of idle capacity and organization-sustaining costs).	None	NA

The total cost of operating the company for the year is $390,000, which includes the following costs:

Wages.	$150,000
Supplies.	40,000
Snow removal equipment depreciation.	20,000
Vehicle expenses	40,000
Office expenses.	60,000
President's compensation.	80,000
Total cost.	$390,000

Resource consumption is distributed across the activities as follows:

	Distribution of Resource Consumption across Activity Cost Pools				
	Snow Removal	Travel to Jobs	Job Support	Other	Total
Wages.	80%	10%	0%	10%	100%
Supplies	100%	0%	0%	0%	100%
Snow removal equipment depreciation.	80%	0%	0%	20%	100%
Vehicle expenses	0%	60%	0%	40%	100%
Office expenses.	0%	0%	45%	55%	100%
President's compensation.	0%	0%	40%	60%	100%

Job support consists of receiving calls from potential customers at the home office, scheduling jobs, billing, resolving issues, and so on.

Required:

1. Using Exhibit 7–7 as a guide, prepare the first-stage allocation of costs to the activity cost pools.
2. Using Exhibit 7–8 as a guide, compute the activity rates for the activity cost pools.
3. The company recently completed a 3,500-square-metre snow removal job at Hometown Hardware—a 75-kilometre round-trip journey from Kenosha's offices. Compute the cost of this job using the ABC system.

4. The revenue from the Hometown Hardware job was $446.25 (3,500 square metres at $12.75 per hundred square metres). Using Exhibit 7–13 as a guide, prepare a report showing the margin from this job.

5. What do you conclude concerning the profitability of the Hometown Hardware job? Explain.

6. What advice would you give the president concerning pricing jobs in the future?

PROBLEM 7–20 Activity-Based Costing and Bidding on Jobs [LO2, LO3]

Vance Asbestos Removal Company removes potentially toxic asbestos insulation and related products from buildings. The company's estimator has been involved in a long-simmering dispute with the on-site work supervisors. The on-site supervisors claim that the estimator does not adequately distinguish between routine work, such as removal of asbestos insulation around heating pipes in older homes, and non-routine work, such as removing asbestos-contaminated ceiling plaster in industrial buildings. The on-site supervisors believe that non-routine work is far more expensive than routine work and should bear higher customer charges. The estimator sums up his position in this way: "My job is to measure the area to be cleared of asbestos. As directed by top management, I simply multiply the square metres by $4,000 per thousand square metres to determine the bid price. Since our average cost is only $3,000 per thousand square metres, that leaves enough cushion to take care of the additional costs of non-routine work that shows up. Besides, it is difficult to know what is routine or not routine until you actually start tearing things apart."

To shed light on this controversy, the company initiated an ABC study of all of its costs. Data from the ABC system follow:

Activity Cost Pool	Activity Measure	Total Activity
Removing asbestos	Thousands of square metres	500,000 m²
Estimating and job setup	Number of jobs	200 jobs*
Working on non-routine jobs	Number of non-routine jobs	25 non-routine jobs
Other (costs of idle capacity and organization-sustaining costs)	Not applicable; these costs are not allocated to jobs.	

*The total number of jobs includes non-routine jobs as well as routine jobs. Non-routine jobs as well as routine jobs require estimating and setup work.

Wages and salaries	$ 200,000
Disposal fees	600,000
Equipment depreciation	80,000
On-site supplies	60,000
Office expenses	190,000
Licensing and insurance	370,000
Total cost	$1,500,000

	Distribution of Resource Consumption across Activity Cost Pools				
	Removing Asbestos	Estimating and Job Setup	Working on Non-routine Jobs	Other	Total
Wages and salaries	40%	10%	35%	15%	100%
Disposal fees	70%	0%	30%	0%	100%
Equipment depreciation	50%	0%	40%	10%	100%
On-site supplies	55%	15%	20%	10%	100%
Office expenses	10%	40%	30%	20%	100%
Licensing and insurance	50%	0%	40%	10%	100%

Required:

1. Using Exhibit 7–7 as a guide, perform the first-stage allocation of costs to the activity cost pools.
2. Using Exhibit 7–8 as a guide, compute the activity rates for the activity cost pools.
3. Using the activity rates you have computed, determine the total cost and the average cost per thousand square metres of each of the following jobs according to the ABC system:
   a. A routine 2,000-square-metre asbestos removal job.
   b. A routine 4,000-square-metre asbestos removal job.
   c. A non-routine 2,000-square-metre asbestos removal job.
4. Given the results you obtained in (3) above, do you agree with the estimator that the company's present policy for bidding on jobs is adequate?

PROBLEM 7–21 Second-Stage Allocations and Product Margins [LO3, LO4]

AnimPix Inc. is a small company that creates computer-generated animations for films and television. Much of the company's work consists of short commercials for television, but the company also does realistic computer animations for special effects in movies.

The young founders of the company have become increasingly concerned with the economics of the business—particularly since many competitors have sprung up recently in the local area. To help understand the company's cost structure, an ABC system has been designed. Three major activities are carried out in the company: animation concept, animation production, and contract administration. The animation concept activity is carried out at the contract proposal stage when the company bids on projects. This is an intensive activity that involves individuals from all parts of the company in creating storyboards and prototype stills to be shown to the prospective client. After the client has accepted a project, the animation goes into production and contract administration begins. Technical staff do almost all of the work involved in animation production, whereas administrative staff are largely responsible for contract administration. The activity cost pools and their activity measures and rates are listed below:

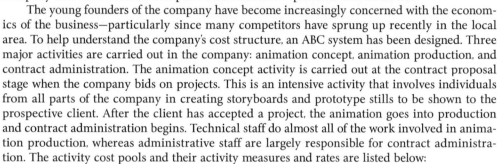

Activity Cost Pool	Activity Measure	Activity Rate
Animation concept...........................	Number of proposals	$6,000 per proposal
Animation production........................	Minutes of animation	$ 7,700 per minute of animation
Contract administration.....................	Number of contracts	$6,600 per contract

These activity rates include all of the costs of the company, except for the costs of idle capacity and organization-sustaining costs. There are no direct labour or direct materials costs.

Preliminary analysis using these activity rates has indicated that the local commercials segment of the market may be unprofitable. This segment is highly competitive. Producers of local commercials may ask several companies like AnimPix to bid, which results in an unusually low ratio of accepted contracts to bids. Furthermore, the animation sequences tend to be much shorter for local commercials than for other work. Since animation work is billed at standard rates according to the running time of the completed animation, the revenues from these short projects tend to be below average. Data concerning activity in the local commercials market appear below:

Activity Measure	Local Commercials
Number of proposals.........................	20
Minutes of animation	12
Number of contracts.........................	8

The total sales for local commercials amounted to $240,000.

Required:

1. Determine the cost of the local commercials market. (Think of the local commercials market as a product.)
2. Prepare a report showing the product margin of the local commercials market. (Remember, this company has no direct materials or direct labour costs.)
3. What would you recommend to management concerning the local commercials market?

PROBLEM 7-22 Activity Rates and Activity-Based Management [LO2, LO3]

Onassis Catering is a Greek company that provides passenger and crew meals to airlines operating out of two international airports in Athens and Corfu. The operations at the two airports are managed separately, and top management believes that there may be benefits to greater sharing of information between the two operations.

To better compare the two operations, an ABC system has been designed with the active participation of the managers at both airports. The ABC system is based on the following activity cost pools and activity measures:

Activity Cost Pool	Activity Measure
Meal preparation..	Number of meals
Flight-related activities..	Number of flights
Customer service..	Number of customers
Other (costs of idle capacity and organization-sustaining costs)..........	NA

The operation at Athens International Airport (AIA) serves 1 million meals annually on 5,000 flights for 10 different airlines. (Each airline is considered one customer.) The annual cost of running the AIA airport operation, excluding only the costs of raw materials for meals, totals €3,675,000. *Note:* The currency in Greece is the euro, denoted by €.

Annual Cost of the AIA Operation	
Cooks and delivery personnel wages	€3,000,000
Kitchen supplies	37,500
Chef salaries.................................	225,000
Equipment depreciation........................	75,000
Administrative wages and salaries	187,500
Building costs.................................	150,000
Total cost....................................	€3,675,000

To help determine the activity rates, employees were interviewed and asked how they divided their time among the four major activities. The results of employee interviews at AIA are displayed below:

	Distribution of Resource Consumption across Activities at the AIA Operation				
	Meal Preparation	Flight-Related	Customer Service	Other	Total
Cooks and delivery personnel wages.................	75%	20%	0%	5%	100%
Kitchen supplies.....................	100%	0%	0%	0%	100%
Chef salaries........................	30%	20%	40%	10%	100%
Equipment depreciation..............	60%	0%	0%	40%	100%
Administrative wages and salaries	0%	20%	60%	20%	100%
Building costs.......................	0%	0%	0%	100%	100%

Required:
1. Perform the first-stage allocation of costs to the activity cost pools. (Use Exhibit 7-7 as a guide.)
2. Compute the activity rates for the activity cost pools. (Use Exhibit 7-8 as a guide.) Do not round off.

3. The Corfu operation has already concluded its ABC study and has reported the following activity rates: 2.48 per meal for meal preparation; 144.50 per flight for flight-related activities; and 12,000 for customer service. Comparing the activity rates for the AIA operation you computed in (2) above to the activity rates for Corfu, do you have any suggestions for the top management of Onassis Catering?

PROBLEM 7–23 Comparing Traditional and Activity-Based Costing Product Margins [LO1, LO3, LO4]

Modern Tools makes two types of chain saws—High Grade and Professional. Data concerning these two product lines appear below:

	High Grade	Professional
Selling price per unit	$215.50	$387.00
Direct materials per unit	$ 83.50	$212.00
Direct labour per unit	$ 30.00	$ 45.00
Direct labour-hours per unit	1.0 DLHs	1.5 DLHs
Estimated annual production and sales	75,000 units	25,000 units

The company has a traditional costing system in which manufacturing overhead is applied to units based on direct labour-hours. Data concerning manufacturing overhead and direct labour-hours for the upcoming year appear below:

Estimated total manufacturing overhead.	$1,350,000
Estimated total direct labour-hours	112,500 DLHs

Required:

1. Using Exhibit 7–14 as a guide, compute the product margins for the High Grade and the Professional products under the company's traditional costing system.
2. The company is considering replacing its traditional costing system with an ABC system that would assign its manufacturing overhead to the following four activity cost pools (the Other cost pool includes organization-sustaining costs and idle capacity costs):

		Expected Activity		
Activities and Activity Measures	**Estimated Overhead Cost**	**High Grade**	**Professional**	**Total**
Supporting direct labour (direct labour-hours)	$ 573,750	75,000	37,500	112,500
Batch setups (setups)	621,250	75	275	350
Product-sustaining (number of products)	110,000	1	1	2
Other	45,000	NA	NA	NA
Total manufacturing overhead cost	$1,350,000			

Using Exhibit 7–12 as a guide, compute the product margins for the High Grade and Professional products under the ABC system.

3. Explain why and how the traditional and activity-based cost assignments differ.

CASES

CASE 7–24 Comprehensive Activity-Based Costing [LO2, LO3, LO5]

Kolbec Community College (KCC) has 4,000 full-time students and offers a variety of academic programs in three areas: professional studies, arts, and technology. The professional studies programs prepare students for administrative and clerical jobs in a variety of professional settings, including accounting, medicine, and law. The arts program's offerings are wide ranging and include graphic design, digital animation, culinary arts, cosmetology, and music arts. The technology programs are also varied, including information technology, medical laboratory technology, electrical engineering technology, pharmacy technology, and natural resources technology.

The chief financial officer of KCC, Lynn Jones, has consistently emphasized to other members of the senior management team the importance of understanding the costs of delivering the various academic programs. To that end, the costing system used at KCC tracks the direct costs of each program, which are shown below on an annual basis, along with the number of full-time students:

Item	Professional Studies	Arts	Technology	Total
Full-time students....................	2,000	1,000	1,000	4,000
Professors' salaries	$1,260,000	$ 650,000	$ 780,000	$2,690,000
Administrative salaries	105,000	70,000	70,000	245,000
Supplies.............................	40,000	150,000	50,000	240,000
Teaching support	160,000	100,000	80,000	340,000
Facilities............................	275,000	150,000	175,000	600,000
Total direct cost	$1,840,000	$1,120,000	$1,155,000	$ 4,115,000

It is very important to understand the overhead costs consumed by each academic program at KCC in determining the full cost of operating the programs. Central administration at KCC allocates financial resources to academic programs based on the estimated full cost per student of delivering the program. The overhead costs at KCC are significant, totalling over 60% of direct costs. Total annual overhead costs at KCC are as follows:

	Cost
Administrative salaries	$900,000
Facility costs.................................	1,300,000
Office expenses..............................	300,000
Total overhead costs........................	$2,500,000

Traditionally, KCC has allocated overhead costs to academic programs on the basis of the number of full-time students in each program. This approach was deemed appropriate since Jones reasoned that increasing the number of students at KCC would result in higher overhead costs (e.g., more facilities would be needed, more indirect support costs would be incurred, etc.). However, Jones is beginning to question the accuracy of the traditional approach since it results in a similar full cost per student for the arts and technology programs, which she feels doesn't make sense. Based on her knowledge of the programs, Jones feels that the technology program is probably more expensive to deliver than the arts program, but this does not come through in the traditional costing approach.

Jones recently attended a seminar on management techniques being used by leading educational institutions that, among other topics, covered the basics of the ABC approach. She likes the idea of being able to assign indirect costs to academic programs on the basis of how much of the support activity resources are consumed by each program. If Jones's instincts are correct in that some programs consume more resources of certain activities than others, this could have a significant impact on the overhead costs assigned to each under the ABC approach.

Upon returning to KCC, Jones decides to implement ABC. She, along with Assistant CFO James West, begins by identifying the key activities used to support the teaching programs. Rather than getting too detailed with respect to identifying activities in the initial implementation, Jones decides to keep the process manageable and comes up with six key activities. Next, based on a series of interviews with various KCC employees who work in the departments covered by the identified activities, Jones and West estimate the percentage of the total administrative, facility, and office expense resources consumed by each activity. Again, to keep the process efficient, Jones rounds all percentages to the nearest 5%, figuring that a "close enough" approach will suffice for this initial implementation and recognizing that the estimates are subjective to begin with. The results are shown below:

	Resource Distribution across Activities		
Activity	**Administrative**	**Facilities**	**Office**
Central administration	20%	5%	15%
Information systems technology................	20%	15%	15%
Student counselling services	5%	5%	10%
Human resources..............................	10%	5%	10%
Library operations.............................	20%	60%	30%
Registrar's office..............................	25%	10%	20%
Total......................................	100%	100%	100%

Working with key personnel from each of the six activities shown above, Jones and West then identify the activity measure and the quantity of that measure used for each teaching program. Fortunately, KCC implemented an enterprise resource planning system a few years ago, which is already tracking much of the information needed regarding the activity measures and the specific quantities for each academic program:

Activity	Measure	Professional	Arts	Technology
Central administration	Hours spent on program	6,000	7,000	7,000
Information systems technology......	Processing hours	6,000	3,000	12,000
Student counselling services	Number of students counselled	180	115	205
Human resources....................	Number of admin. staff and faculty members	21	15	14
Library operations	Number of library circulations	6,000	3,000	3,000
Registrar's office....................	Full-time students	2,000	1,000	1,000

Required:
1. Using the traditional approach to assigning overhead costs to academic programs:
    a. Calculate the predetermined overhead rate.
    b. Assign the overhead costs to each academic program using the predetermined rate.
    c. Calculate the total cost per student (direct costs plus overhead) of operating each academic program.
2. Using ABC, complete the following requirements:
    a. Using Exhibit 7–7 as a guide, complete the first-stage allocation of overhead costs to academic programs.
    b. Using Exhibit 7–8 as a guide, calculate the activity rates for each of the activity cost pools.
    c. Using the activity rates calculated in (*b*), complete the second-stage allocation of overhead to academic programs.
3. Based on the results of (2), calculate the total cost per student (direct costs plus overhead) of operating each academic program.
4. Draft a memo to Jones explaining the key reasons for differences in the total cost per student of operating each academic program that arise between the traditional costing approach and ABC.

CASE 7–25 Activity-Based Costing and Pricing [LO2, LO3, LO4, LO5]

Oxford Concrete Inc. (OCI) processes and distributes various types of cement. The company buys quarried local rock, limestone, and clay from around the world and mixes, blends, and packages the processed cement for resale. OCI offers a large variety of cement types that it sells in one-kilogram bags to local retailers for small do-it-yourself jobs. The major cost of the cement is raw materials. However, the company's predominantly automated mixing, blending, and packaging processes require a substantial amount of manufacturing overhead. The company uses relatively little direct labour.

Some of OCI's cement mixtures are very popular and sell in large volumes, while a few of the recently introduced cement mixtures sell in very low volumes. OCI prices its cements at manufacturing cost plus a 25% markup, with some adjustments made to keep the company's prices competitive.

For the coming year, OCI's budget includes estimated manufacturing overhead cost of $4,400,000. OCI assigns manufacturing overhead to products on the basis of direct labour-hours. The expected direct labour cost totals $1,200,000, which represents 100,000 hours of direct labour time. Based on the sales budget and expected raw materials costs, the company will purchase and use $10,000,000 of raw materials (mostly quarried rock, limestone, and clay) during the year.

The expected costs for direct materials and direct labour for one-kilogram bags of two of the company's cement products appear below:

	Normal Portland	High Sulphate Resistance
Direct materials...........................	$9.00	$5.80
Direct labour (0.02 hours per bag)..........	$0.24	$0.24

OCI's controller believes that the company's traditional costing system may be providing misleading cost information. To determine whether this is the case, the controller has prepared an analysis of the year's expected manufacturing overhead costs, as shown in the following table:

Activity Cost Pool	Activity Measure	Expected Activity for the Year	Expected Cost for the Year
Purchasing	Purchase orders	4,000 orders	$ 1,120,000
Materials handling	Number of setups	2,000 setups	386,000
Quality control................	Number of batches	1,000 batches	180,000
Mixing	Mixing hours	190,000 mixing hours	2,090,000
Blending......................	Blending hours	64,000 blending hours	384,000
Packaging	Packaging hours	48,000 packaging hours	240,000
Total manufacturing overhead cost....................			$4,400,000

Data regarding the expected production of Normal Portland and High Sulphate Resistance cement mixes are presented below:

	Normal Portland	High Sulphate Resistance
Expected sales............................	160,000 kilograms	8,000 kilograms
Batch size	10,000 kilograms	500 kilograms
Setups	4 per batch	4 per batch
Purchase order size........................	20,000 kilograms	500 kilograms
Mixing time per 100 kilograms	3 mixing hours	3 mixing hours
Blending time per 100 kilograms............	1 blending hour	1 blending hour
Packaging time per 100 kilograms..........	0.6 packaging hours	0.6 packaging hours

Required:
1. Using direct labour-hours as the base for assigning manufacturing overhead cost to products, do the following:
    a. Determine the predetermined overhead rate that will be used during the year.
    b. Determine the unit product cost of one kilogram of the Normal Portland cement and one kilogram of the High Sulphate Resistance cement.
2. Using ABC as the basis for assigning manufacturing overhead cost to products, do the following:
    a. Determine the total amount of manufacturing overhead cost assigned to the Normal Portland cement and to the High Sulphate Resistance cement for the year.

    b.   Using the data developed in 2(*a*) above, compute the amount of manufacturing overhead cost per kilogram of the Normal Portland cement and the High Sulphate Resistance cement. Round all computations to the nearest whole cent.

    c.   Determine the unit product cost of one kilogram of the Normal Portland cement and one kilogram of the High Sulphate Resistance cement.

3.   Write a brief memo to the president of OCI explaining what you found in (1) and (2) above, and discuss the implications to the company of using direct labour as the base for assigning manufacturing overhead cost to products.

INSTANT QUIZ SOLUTIONS

7–1

The four main differences between traditional costing and ABC are (1) both manufacturing and non-manufacturing costs may be assigned to products on a cause-and-effect basis under ABC but not traditional product costing; (2) some manufacturing costs that would be included in the predetermined overhead rate under traditional costing would not be applied to cost objects under ABC because they do not drive the cost of that cost object; (3) while departmental or plantwide overhead rates are used in traditional costing, ABC uses many different cost pools that are based on activities that drive cost, not departmental organization; and (4) activity rates are often calculated based on activity at capacity, while under traditional costing, budgeted levels of activity are used in the denominator of predetermined overhead rates.

7–2

One good example is a company that produces and sells flat-screen TVs. A unit-level activity is installing the digital receiver in each TV produced. A batch-level activity is ordering stands in three different colours to use for each of three different models of TVs produced. A product-level activity is the design of a new model of TV with next-generation electronics. A customer-level activity is a salesperson visiting a customer to ensure he or she is pleased with the product quality and delivery specifications. An organization-sustaining activity is seeking outside legal advice on the terms of the top manager's employment contracts.

7–3

Total overhead costs related to order processing = $25,200; a total of 350 orders were processed in the year; therefore, the activity rate to assign order processing costs to the customer orders cost object is $25,200 ÷ 350 = $72 per order.

7–4

Total overhead applied to Product Q43 = (120 DLH × $7 per DLH) + (43 MH × $2 per MH) + (4 setups × $63 per setup) + (5 shipments × $12 per shipment) = $1,238.

7–5

Customer margin for Mitchell Hardware is as follows:

Revenue	1,200 cases × $72 per case	$86,400
Less expenses:		
Direct material	(1,200 cases × 24 bottles) × $0.95	27,360
Direct labour	(1,200 cases × 24 bottles) × $0.40	11,520
Unit-level overhead applied	(1,200 cases × 24 bottles) × 1.10	31,680
Order processing	1,200 cases at 50 cases per order = 24 orders × $250 per order	6,000
Customer margin		$9,840

connect **LEARNSMART** **SMARTBOOK**

For more information on the resources available from McGraw-Hill Ryerson, go to www.mheducation.ca/he/solutions.

APPENDIX 7A: USING A MODIFIED FORM OF ACTIVITY-BASED COSTING TO DETERMINE PRODUCT COSTS FOR EXTERNAL REPORTS

LEARNING OBJECTIVE **6**

Use activity-based costing techniques to compute unit product costs for external reports.

This chapter has emphasized using ABC information in internal decisions. However, a modified form of ABC can also be used to develop product costs for external financial reports. For this purpose, product costs include *all* manufacturing overhead costs—including organization-sustaining costs and the costs of idle capacity—and exclude all non-manufacturing costs, even costs that are clearly caused by the products.

The simplest absorption costing systems as described in Chapter 5 assign manufacturing overhead costs to products using a single plantwide predetermined overhead rate based on direct labour-hours or machine-hours. When ABC is used to assign manufacturing overhead costs to products, a predetermined overhead rate is computed for each activity cost pool. An example will make this difference clear.

Maxtar Industries manufactures high-quality smoker/barbecue units. The company has two product lines—Premium and Standard. The company has traditionally applied manufacturing overhead costs to these products using a plantwide predetermined overhead rate based on direct labour-hours. Exhibit 7A–1 details how the unit product costs of the two product lines are computed using the company's traditional costing system. The unit product cost of the Premium product line is $71.60, and the unit product cost of the Standard product line is $53.70, according to this traditional costing system.

Maxtar Industries has recently experimented with an ABC approach to determining its unit product costs for external reporting purposes. The company's ABC system has three activity cost pools: (1) supporting direct labour, (2) setting up machines, and (3) parts administration. The top of Exhibit 7A–2 displays basic data concerning these

EXHIBIT 7A–1 Maxtar Industries' Traditional Costing System

Basic Data		
Total estimated manufacturing overhead cost	$1,520,000	
Total estimated direct labour-hours..................	400,000 DLHs	

	Premium	Standard
Direct materials per unit...........	$40.00	$30.00
Direct labour per unit	$24.00	$18.00
Direct labour-hours per unit	2.0 DLHs	1.5 DLHs
Units produced	50,000 units	200,000 units

Computation of the Predetermined Overhead Rate

$$\text{Predetermined overhead rate} = \frac{\text{Total estimated manufacturing overhead}}{\text{Total estimated amount of the allocation base}}$$

$$= \frac{\$1,520,000}{400,000} = 3.80 \text{ per DLH}$$

Traditional Unit Product Costs

	Premium	Standard
Direct materials....................................	$40.00	$30.00
Direct labour	24.00	18.00
Manufacturing overhead (2.0 DLHs × $3.80 per DLH; 1.5 DLHs × $3.80 per DLH)	7.60	5.70
Unit product cost	$ 71.60	$ 53.70

EXHIBIT 7A-2 Maxtar
Industries' ABC System

Basic Data

1. Activities and Activity Measures	Estimated Overhead Cost	Expected Activity		
		Premium	Standard	Total
Supporting direct labour (DLHs)........	$ 800,000	100,000	300,000	400,000
Setting up machines (setups)...........	480,000	600	200	800
Parts administration (part types)	240,000	140	60	200
Total manufacturing overhead cost	$1,520,000			

2. Computation of Activity Rates

Activities	(a) Estimated Overhead Cost	(b) Total Expected Activity	(a) ÷ (b) Activity Rate
Supporting direct labour.......	$800,000	400,000 DLHs	$2 per DLH
Setting up machines...........	$480,000	800 setups	$600 per setup
Parts administration...........	$240,000	200 part types	$1,200 per part type

3. Assigning Overhead Costs to Products

Overhead Cost for the Premium Product

Activity Cost Pools	(a) Activity Rate	(b) Activity	(a) × (b) ABC Cost
Supporting direct labour.......	$2 per DLH	100,000 DLHs	$200,000
Setting up machines...........	$600 per setup	600 setups	360,000
Parts administration...........	$1,200 per part type	140 part types	168,000
Total			$728,000

Overhead Cost for the Standard Product

Activity Cost Pools	(a) Activity Rate	(b) Activity	(a) × (b) ABC Cost
Supporting direct labour.......	$2 per DLH	300,000 DLHs	$600,000
Setting up machines...........	$600 per setup	200 setups	120,000
Parts administration...........	$1,200 per part type	60 part types	72,000
Total			$ 792,000

4. ABC Product Costs

	Premium	Standard
Direct materials..	$40.00	$30.00
Direct labour	24.00	18.00
Manufacturing overhead ($728,000 ÷ 50,000 units; $792,000 ÷ 200,000 units).................................	14.56	3.96
Unit product cost	$78.56	$ 51.96

activity cost pools. Note that the total estimated overhead cost in these three cost pools, $1,520,000, agrees with the total estimated overhead cost in the company's traditional costing system. The company's ABC system simply provides an alternative way to allocate the company's manufacturing overhead across the two products.

The activity rates for the three activity cost pools are computed in the second table in Exhibit 7A-2. For example, the total cost in the "Setting up machines" activity cost pool, $480,000, is divided by the total activity associated with that cost pool, 800 setups, to determine the activity rate of $600 per setup.

The activity rates are used to allocate overhead costs to the two products in the third table in Exhibit 7A-2. For example, the activity rate for the "Setting up machines" activity cost pool, $600 per setup, is multiplied by the Premium product line's

600 setups to determine the $360,000 machine setup cost allocated to the Premium product line. The overhead cost per unit is determined at the bottom of this table by dividing the total overhead cost by the number of units produced. For example, the Premium product line's total overhead cost of $728,000 is divided by 50,000 units to determine the $14.56 overhead cost per unit.

The table at the bottom of Exhibit 7A–2 displays the ABC unit product costs. Note that these unit product costs differ from those computed using the company's traditional costing system in Exhibit 7A–1. Because the ABC system contains both a batch-level (setting up machines) and a product-level (parts administration) activity cost pool, the unit product costs under ABC follow the usual pattern in which overhead costs are shifted from the high-volume to the low-volume product. The unit product cost of the Standard product line, the high-volume product, has gone down from $53.70 under the traditional costing system to $51.96 under ABC. In contrast, the unit product cost of the Premium product line, the low-volume product, has increased from $71.60 under the traditional costing system to $78.56 under ABC. Instead of arbitrarily assigning most of the costs of setting up machines and of parts administration to the high-volume product, the ABC system more accurately assigns these costs to the two products.

APPENDIX 7A SUMMARY

- A modified form of activity-based costing (ABC) can be used for external financial reporting. However, when used for external reports, product costs include only manufacturing costs and exclude all non-manufacturing costs. [LO6]

APPENDIX 7A EXERCISES, PROBLEMS, AND CASES

EXERCISE 7A–1 Activity-Based Costing Product Costs for External Reports [LO6]
Data concerning Cranur Architects Corporation's two major business lines are given below:

	Commercial	Residential
Direct materials per square metre..............	$6.00	$4.50
Direct labour per square metre.................	$48	$36
Direct labour-hours per square metre..........	0.1 DLHs	0.075 DLHs
Estimated annual output......................	40,000 m²	280,000 m²

The company has a traditional costing system in which architecture department overhead is applied to units (square metres of architectural drawings) based on direct labour-hours. Data concerning architecture department overhead and direct labour-hours for the upcoming year appear below:

Estimated total architecture department overhead	$670,000
Estimated total direct labour-hours................................	25,000 DLHs

Required:
1. Determine the unit costs of the Commercial and Residential products under the company's traditional costing system.
2. The company is considering replacing its traditional costing system for determining unit product costs for external reports with an ABC system. The ABC system would have the following three activity cost pools:

Activities and Activity Measures	Estimated Overhead Cost	Expected Activity		
		Commercial	Residential	Total
Supporting direct labour (direct labour-hours)	$600,000	4,000	21,000	25,000
Drawing software modifications (changes)...................	60,000	100	25	125
Quality review and technical checks (tests).................	10,000	80	20	100
Total service department overhead cost.................	$670,000			

Determine the unit costs (cost per square metre of architectural drawings) of the Commercial and Residential lines of business under the ABC system.

EXERCISE 7A–2 Activity-Based Costing Product Costs for External Reports [LO6]
Krunkel Company makes two products and uses a traditional costing system in which a single plantwide predetermined overhead rate is computed based on direct labour-hours. Data for the two products for the upcoming year follow:

	Mercon	Wurcon
Direct materials cost per unit.....................	$ 10.00	$ 8.00
Direct labour cost per unit	$ 3.00	$ 3.75
Direct labour-hours per unit	0.20	0.25
Number of units produced	10,000	40,000

These products are customized to some degree for specific customers.

Required:
1. The company's manufacturing overhead costs for the year are expected to be $336,000. Using the company's traditional costing system, compute the unit product costs for the two products.
2. Management is considering an ABC system in which half of the overhead would continue to be allocated on the basis of direct labour-hours and half would be allocated on the basis of engineering design time. The Mercon product and the Wurcon product are expected to need 4,000 engineering design hours each. Compute the unit product costs for the two products using the proposed ABC system.
3. Explain why the unit product costs differ between the two systems.

PROBLEM 7A–3 Activity-Based Costing as an Alternative
to Traditional Product Costing [LO6]
Rehm Company manufactures a product that is available in both a deluxe model and a regular model. The company has manufactured the regular model for years. The deluxe model was introduced several years ago to tap a new segment of the market. Since introduction of the deluxe model, the company's profits have steadily declined, and management has become increasingly concerned about the accuracy of its costing system. Sales of the deluxe model have been increasing rapidly.

Manufacturing overhead is assigned to products on the basis of direct labour-hours. For the current year, the company has estimated that it will incur $6,000,000 in manufacturing overhead cost and produce 15,000 units of the deluxe model and 120,000 units of the regular model. The deluxe model requires 1.6 hours of direct labour time per unit, and the regular model requires 0.8 hours. Material and labour costs per unit are as follows:

	Model	
	Deluxe	Regular
Direct materials.................	$154	$112
Direct labour...................	$ 16	$ 8

Required:
1. Using direct labour-hours as the base for assigning manufacturing overhead cost to products, compute the predetermined overhead rate. Using this rate and other data from the problem, determine the unit product cost of each model.
2. Management is considering using ABC to apply manufacturing overhead costs to products for external financial reports. The ABC system would have the following four activity cost pools:

Activity Cost Pool	Activity Measure	Estimated Overhead Costs
Purchase orders...............................	Number of purchase orders	$ 252,000
Scrap/rework orders...........................	Number of scrap/rework orders	648,000
Product testing................................	Number of tests	1,350,000
Machine-related	Machine-hours	3,750,000
Total overhead cost...........................		$6,000,000

Activity Measure	Expected Activity		
	Deluxe	Regular	Total
Number of purchase orders....................	400	800	1,200
Number of scrap/rework orders	500	400	900
Number of tests	6,000	9,000	15,000
Machine-hours................................	20,000	30,000	50,000

Using Exhibit 7–8 as a guide, compute the predetermined overhead rates (i.e., activity rates) for each of the four activity cost pools.
3. Using the predetermined overhead rates computed in (2) above, do the following:
   a. Compute the total amount of manufacturing overhead cost that would be applied to each model using the ABC system. After you have computed these totals, determine the amount of manufacturing overhead cost per unit for each model.
   b. Compute the unit product cost of each model (materials, labour, and manufacturing overhead).
4. From the data you developed in (1) through (3) above, identify factors that may account for the company's declining profits.

PROBLEM 7A–4 Activity-Based Costing as an Alternative to Traditional Product Costing [LO6]
For many years, Sinclair Graphic Design has provided design and digital-printing services for indoor banners. The nylon banners, which come in a standard size, are used for a variety of purposes, including trade shows, sporting events, and other promotional activities. Three years ago, the company introduced a second printing and production service for outdoor banners that have become increasingly popular. The outdoor banners are a more complex product than the indoor banners, requiring weatherproof vinyl materials and a different printing process to improve the visibility of the text and graphics content. Moreover, outdoor banners are printed in smaller production runs because of less frequent orders; the setup of the printing equipment takes longer; and, since higher durability is needed to withstand the elements, more quality inspections are needed. Under the traditional costing approach, overhead costs are assigned to the products on the basis of direct labour-hours.

Despite the introduction of the new outdoor banners, profits have declined steadily over the past three years. Management is beginning to believe that the company's costing system may be at fault. Unit costs for materials and labour for the two products follow:

	Indoor Banners	Outdoor Banners
Direct materials..............................	$ 9	$26
Direct labour ($20 per hour).................	$20	$60

Management estimates that the company will incur $600,000 in overhead costs during the current year and that 10,000 indoor banners and 2,000 outdoor banners will be produced and sold.

Required:

1. Compute the predetermined overhead rate assuming that the company continues to apply overhead cost to products on the basis of direct labour-hours. Using this rate and other data from the problem, determine the unit product cost of each product.
2. Management is considering using ABC to apply overhead cost to products for external financial reports. Some preliminary work has been done, and the data that have been collected are displayed below. Using these data, calculate the predetermined overhead rate for each activity cost pool identified below:

	Estimated Total Overhead Costs	Activity Measures		
		Indoor Banners	Outdoor Banners	Total
Order processing (orders received).............	$150,000	500	500	1,000
Print setup (number of batches)................	50,000	800	200	1,000
Artwork and graphic design (labour-hours)	350,000	7,000	7,000	14,000
Quality control (number of inspections)	50,000	400	400	800
Total overhead cost............................	600,000			

3. Using the predetermined manufacturing overhead rates that you computed in (2) above, do the following:
   a. Determine the total amount of manufacturing overhead cost that would be applied to each product using the ABC system. After you have computed these totals, determine the amount of overhead cost per unit of each product.
   b. Compute the unit product cost of each product.
4. Based on your calculations in (1) through (3) above, in terms of overhead cost, what factors make the outdoor banners more costly to produce than the indoor banners? Are the outdoor banners as profitable as the company thinks they are? Explain.

PROBLEM 7A–5 Activity-Based Costing as an Alternative to Traditional Product Costing [LO6]

Erte Inc. manufactures two models of high-pressure steam valves, the XR7 model and the ZD5 model. Data regarding the two products follow:

Product	Direct Labour-Hours	Annual Production	Total Direct Labour-Hours
XR7...............	0.2 DLHs per unit	20,000 units	4,000 DLHs
ZD5...............	0.4 DLHs per unit	40,000 units	16,000 DLHs
			20,000 DLHs

Additional information about the company follows:
a. Product XR7 requires $35 in direct materials per unit, and product ZD5 requires $25.
b. The direct labour rate is $20 per hour.
c. The company has always used direct labour-hours as the base for applying manufacturing overhead cost to products. Manufacturing overhead totals $1,480,000 per year.
d. Product XR7 is more complex to manufacture than product ZD5 and requires the use of a special milling machine.
e. Because of the special work required in (d) above, the company is considering the use of ABC to apply overhead cost to products. Three activity cost pools have been identified, and the first-stage allocations have been completed. Data concerning these activity cost pools appear below:

Activity Cost Pool	Activity Measure	Estimated Total Cost	Estimated Total Activity		
			XR7	ZD5	Total
Machine setups..................	Number of setups	$ 180,000	150	100	250
Special milling....................	Machine-hours	300,000	1,000	0	1,000
General factory..................	Direct labour-hours	1,000,000	4,000	16,000	20,000
		$1,480,000			

Required:
1. Assume that the company continues to use direct labour-hours as the base for applying overhead cost to products.
   a. Compute the predetermined overhead rate.
   b. Determine the unit product cost of each product.
2. Assume that the company decides to use ABC to apply overhead cost to products.
   a. Compute the activity rate for each activity cost pool. Also compute the amount of overhead cost that would be applied to each product.
   b. Determine the unit product cost of each product.
3. Explain why overhead cost shifted from the high-volume product to the low-volume product under ABC.

CASE 7A–6 Contrasting Activity-Based Costing and Traditional Costing [LO2, LO3, LO4, LO6]
"Wow! Is that R-92 model ever a loser! It's time to cut back its production and shift our resources toward the new T-95 model," said Graham Thomas, executive vice-president of Thomas Products Inc. "Just look at this income statement I've received from accounting. The T-95 is generating over eight times as much profit as the R-92 on one-sixth of the unit sales. I'm convinced that our future depends on the T-95." The year-end statement to which Thomas was referring is shown below:

	Total	Model	
		R-92	T-95
Sales	$ 11,125,000	$9,000,000	$2,125,000
Cost of goods sold	6,900,000	5,490,000	1,410,000
Gross margin	4,225,000	3,510,000	715,000
Less selling and administrative expenses	3,675,000	3,450,000	225,000
Operating income	$ 550,000	$ 60,000	$490,000
Number of units produced and sold		30,000	5,000

"The numbers sure look that way," replied Julie Williams, the company's sales manager. "But why isn't the competition more excited about the T-95? I know we've been producing the model for only three years, but I'm surprised that more of our competitors haven't recognized what a cash cow it is."

"I think it's our new automated plant," replied Thomas. "Now it takes only two direct labour-hours to produce a unit of the R-92 and three direct labour-hours to produce a unit of the T-95. That's considerably less than it used to take us."

"I agree that automation is wonderful," replied Williams. "I suppose that's how we're able to hold down the price of the T-95. Taylor Company in England tried to bring out a T-95 but discovered they couldn't touch our price. But Taylor is killing us on the R-92 by undercutting our price with some of our best customers. I suppose they'll pick up all of our R-92 business if we move out of that market. But who cares? We don't even have to advertise the T-95; it just seems to sell itself."

"My only concern about automation is how our manufacturing overhead rate has shot up," said Thomas. "Our total manufacturing overhead cost is $2,700,000. That comes out to be a hefty amount per direct labour-hour, but Dianne down in accounting has been using direct labour-hours as the base for computing overhead rates for years and doesn't want to change. I don't suppose it matters as long as costs get assigned to products."

"I've never understood that debit and credit stuff," replied Williams. "But I think you've got a problem in production. I had lunch with Janet, our plant manager, yesterday and she complained about how complex the T-95 is to produce. Apparently they have to do a lot of setups, special soldering, and other work on the T-95 just to keep production moving. And they have to inspect every single unit."

"It'll have to wait," said Thomas. "I'm writing a proposal to the board of directors to phase out the R-92. We've got to increase our bottom line or we'll all be looking for jobs."

Required:
1. Compute the predetermined overhead rate based on direct labour-hours that the company used during the year. (There was no underapplied or overapplied overhead for the year.)
2. Direct materials and direct labour costs per unit for the two products are as follows:

	R-92	T-95
Direct materials..................	$75	$120
Direct labour.....................	$36	$ 54

Using these data and the rate computed in (1) above, determine the unit product cost of each product under the company's traditional costing system.

3. Assume that the company's $2,700,000 in manufacturing overhead cost can be assigned to six activity cost pools, as follows:

	Estimated Overhead Costs	Expected Activity		
Activity Cost Pool (and Activity Measure)		Total	R-92	T-95
Machine setups (number of setups).................	$ 312,000	1,600	1,000	600
Quality control (number of inspections)	540,000	9,000	4,000	5,000
Purchase orders (number of orders).................	135,000	1,200	840	360
Soldering (number of solder joints)..................	675,000	200,000	60,000	140,000
Shipments (number of shipments)..................	198,000	600	400	200
Machine-related (machine-hours)....................	840,000	70,000	30,000	40,000
	$2,700,000			

Given these data, would you support a recommendation to expand sales of the T-95? Explain your position.

4. From the data you prepared in (3) above, why do you suppose the T-95 "just seems to sell itself"?

5. If you were president of Thomas Products Inc., what strategy would you follow from this point forward to improve the company's overall profits?

VARIABLE COSTING: A TOOL FOR MANAGEMENT

BIG 3 AUTOMAKERS BUILD INVENTORY BEFORE BAILOUT

In a study of accounting practices in the auto industry before the 2008 financial crisis and resulting auto industry government bailout, a team of three researchers found evidence that the Big 3 North American automakers were building many more vehicles than they could sell. Data collected and analyzed as part of this study indicate that from 2005 to 2006, managers at General Motors Co., Ford Motor Co., and Chrysler Group LLC felt pressured to generate short-term profits even at the expense of long-term corporate stability. Due to absorption costing methods required for financial reporting and pressure for short-term profits, managers were strongly tempted to build inventories and increase profits without increasing sales. How can this be done? It seems logical that producing more units will have no impact on profits unless the units are sold, right? Wrong! As we will discover in this chapter, *absorption costing*—the most widely used method of determining product costs—can artificially increase profits by increasing the quantity of units produced. Another approach, called *variable costing,* is preferred by some managers for internal decision making and must be used when an income statement is prepared in the contribution format. Ordinarily, absorption costing and variable costing produce different figures for operating income, and the difference can be quite large. In addition to showing how these two methods differ, we will consider the arguments for and against each costing method and show how management decisions can be affected by the costing method chosen.

Source: A. Brüggen, R. Krishnan, and K. L. Sedatole (2011). Drivers and Consequences of Short-Term Production Decisions: Evidence from the Auto Industry. *Contemporary Accounting Research, 28*(1), 83–123.

I n Chapters 3 and 4, we mainly assumed inventories were insignificant or that production equals sales at the end of the period. This assumption is reasonable in some situations, as will be shown later in this chapter when we discuss lean production. However, inventories are rarely zero, and the level of inventory held at the end of the period can have a significant effect on reported income under the absorption costing approach.

OVERVIEW OF ABSORPTION AND VARIABLE COSTING

LEARNING OBJECTIVE 1
Identify how variable costing differs from absorption costing, and compute unit product costs under each method.

In Chapters 3 and 4, we learned that the contribution format income statement and cost–volume–profit (CVP) analysis are valuable management tools for internal decision making. Both of these tools emphasize cost behaviour and require that managers carefully distinguish between variable and fixed costs. Absorption costing, which was discussed in Chapter 2 and used in Chapters 5 and 6 and Appendix 7A, is different in that it assigns both variable and fixed costs to products—mingling them in a way that makes it difficult for managers to distinguish between them. While absorption costing is useful, and it is actually required for external financial reporting, variable costing is often more useful for internal management decisions as it focuses on *cost behaviour*, clearly separating fixed from variable costs and making it easier to apply the CVP concepts (e.g., "how many units must we sell to break even?") discussed in the preceding chapters.

Absorption Costing

In Chapter 5, we learned that absorption costing treats *all* manufacturing costs as product costs, regardless of whether they are variable or fixed. The cost of a unit of product under the absorption costing method therefore consists of direct materials, direct labour, and *both* variable and fixed manufacturing overhead. Thus, absorption costing allocates a portion of fixed manufacturing overhead cost to each unit of product, along with the variable manufacturing costs. Because absorption costing includes all manufacturing costs as product costs, it is frequently referred to as full costing.

Variable Costing

Under **variable costing**, only those manufacturing costs that vary with output are treated as product costs. This generally includes direct materials, direct labour, and the variable portion of manufacturing overhead. Fixed manufacturing overhead is not treated as a product cost under this method. Rather, fixed manufacturing overhead is treated as a period cost, and, like selling and administrative expenses, it is expensed in its entirety against revenue each period. Consequently, the cost of a unit of product in inventory or in cost of goods sold under the variable costing method does not contain any fixed overhead cost.

Variable costing is sometimes referred to as **direct costing** or **marginal costing**. The term *direct costing* was popular for many years, but it is slowly disappearing from day-to-day use. The term *variable costing* is more descriptive of the way in which product costs are computed when a contribution format income statement is prepared.

Variable costing
A costing method that includes only variable manufacturing costs—direct materials, direct labour, and variable manufacturing overhead—in the cost of a unit of product.

Direct costing
Another name for *variable costing.*

Marginal costing
Another name for *variable costing.*

Selling and Administrative Expenses

To complete this summary comparison of absorption and variable costing, we need to consider briefly the handling of selling and administrative expenses. These expenses are rarely treated as product costs, regardless of the costing method in use.

EXHIBIT 8–1 Cost Classifications: Absorption versus Variable Costing

Absorption Costing		Variable Costing
Product costs	Direct materials	**Product costs**
	Direct labour	
	Variable manufacturing overhead	
	Fixed manufacturing overhead	
Period costs	Variable selling and administrative expenses	**Period costs**
	Fixed selling and administrative expenses	

Thus, under either absorption or variable costing, selling and administrative expenses are always treated as period costs (expenses) and deducted from revenues as incurred.

Exhibit 8–1 summarizes the classification of costs under both absorption and variable costing.

Unit Cost Computations

To illustrate the computation of unit product costs under both absorption and variable costing, consider Boley Company, a small company that produces a single product and has the following cost structure:

Number of units produced each year	6,000
Variable costs per unit:	
Direct materials	$ 2
Direct labour	4
Variable manufacturing overhead	1
Variable selling and administrative expenses	3
Fixed costs per year:	
Fixed manufacturing overhead	30,000
Fixed selling and administrative expenses	10,000

Under the absorption costing method, *all* manufacturing costs, variable and fixed, are included when determining the unit product cost. Thus, if the company sells a unit of product and absorption costing is being used, then $12 (consisting of $7 variable cost and $5 fixed cost) will be deducted on the income statement as cost of goods sold. Similarly, any unsold units will be carried as inventory on the balance sheet at $12 each:

Absorption Costing	
Direct materials	$ 2
Direct labour	4
Variable manufacturing overhead	1
Total variable production cost	7
Fixed manufacturing overhead ($30,000 ÷ 6,000 units of product)	5
Unit product cost	$12

Under the variable costing method, only the variable manufacturing costs are included in product costs. Therefore, if the company sells a unit of product, only $7 will be deducted as cost of goods sold, and unsold units will be carried in the balance sheet inventory account at only $7 each:

Variable Costing

Direct materials..	$2
Direct labour...	4
Variable manufacturing overhead..	1
Unit product cost...	$7

(The $30,000 fixed manufacturing overhead in variable costing will be expensed in total against income as a period expense, along with the selling and administrative expenses.)

■ INCOME COMPARISON OF ABSORPTION AND VARIABLE COSTING

Income statements prepared under the absorption and variable costing approaches are shown in Exhibit 8–2. In preparing these statements, we use the data for Boley Company presented earlier, along with other information about the company, as given below:

LEARNING OBJECTIVE ❷
Prepare income statements using both variable and absorption costing.

Units in beginning inventory...	–0–
Units produced...	6,000
Units sold	5,000
Units in ending inventory	1,000
Selling price per unit..	$ 20
Selling and administrative expenses:	
Variable per unit...	$ 3
Fixed per year..	$10,000

Unit cost computations for absorption and variable costing:

	Absorption Costing	Variable Costing
Unit product cost:		
Direct materials	$ 2	$2
Direct labour	4	4
Variable manufacturing overhead	1	1
Fixed manufacturing overhead ($30,000 ÷ 6,000 units)	5	—
Unit product cost	$12	$7

Several points can be made about the financial statements in Exhibit 8–2:

1. Under the absorption costing method, if there is an ending inventory, the fixed manufacturing costs associated with the inventory will be carried forward as a balance sheet account, Inventory, rather than being treated as a period cost. Such a deferral of costs is known as **fixed manufacturing overhead cost deferred in inventory**. The process can be explained by referring to the data for Boley Company. During the current period, Boley Company produced 6,000 units but sold only 5,000 units, leaving 1,000 unsold units in the ending inventory.

Fixed manufacturing overhead cost deferred in inventory
The portion of the fixed manufacturing overhead cost of a period that goes into inventory under the absorption costing method as a result of production exceeding sales.

Under the absorption costing method, each unit produced is assigned $5 in fixed overhead cost (see the unit cost computations above). Therefore, each of the 1,000 units going into inventory at the end of the period has $5 in fixed manufacturing overhead cost attached to it, or a total of $5,000 for the 1,000 units. *This fixed manufacturing overhead cost of the current period is deferred in inventory to the next period, when, it is hoped, these units will be taken out of inventory and sold.* The deferral of $5,000 of fixed manufacturing overhead costs can be seen clearly by analyzing the ending inventory under the absorption costing method:

Variable manufacturing costs: 1,000 units × $7......................................	$ 7,000
Fixed manufacturing overhead costs: 1,000 units × $5	5,000
Total inventory value	$12,000

In summary, under absorption costing, of the $30,000 in fixed manufacturing overhead costs incurred during the period, only $25,000 (5,000 units sold × $5) has been included on the income statement in cost of goods sold. The remaining

---

EXHIBIT 8–2 Comparison of Absorption and Variable Costing—Boley Company

Absorption Costing

Sales (5,000 units × $20 per unit)			$100,000
Less cost of goods sold:			
Beginning inventory	$ –0–		
Add cost of goods manufactured			
(6,000 units × $12 per unit)	72,000		
Goods available for sale...................	72,000		
Deduct ending inventory			
(1,000 units × $12 per unit)...............	12,000		
Cost of goods sold............................		60,000	
Gross margin...................................		40,000	
Less selling and administrative expenses			
(5,000 units × $3 variable			
per unit + $10,000 fixed)		25,000	
Operating income		$ 15,000	

Note the difference in ending inventories. Fixed manufacturing overhead cost at $5 per unit is included under the absorption approach. This explains the difference in ending inventory and in operating income (1,000 units × $5 per unit = $5,000).

Variable Costing

Sales (5,000 units × $20 per unit)..........			$100,000
Less variable expenses:			
Variable cost of goods sold:			
Beginning inventory	$ –0–		
Add variable manufacturing costs			
(6,000 units × $7 per unit)..............	42,000		
Goods available for sale................	42,000		
Deduct ending inventory			
(1,000 units × $7 per unit)	7,000		
Variable cost of goods sold	35,000		
Variable selling and administrative			
expenses (5,000 units × $3 per unit)....	15,000	50,000	
Contribution margin..........................		50,000	
Less fixed expenses:			
Fixed manufacturing overhead...........	30,000		
Fixed selling and administrative			
expenses	10,000	40,000	
Operating income		$ 10,000	

$5,000 (1,000 units *not* sold × $5) has been deferred in inventory to the next period.

2. Under the variable costing method, the entire $30,000 in fixed manufacturing overhead costs has been treated as an expense of the current period (see the bottom portion of the variable costing income statement).

3. The ending inventory figure under the variable costing method is $5,000 less than it is under the absorption costing method. This is because under variable costing, only the variable manufacturing costs are assigned to units of product and therefore included in inventory:

Variable manufacturing costs: 1,000 units × $7 .... $7,000

The $5,000 difference in ending inventories explains the difference in operating income reported between the two costing methods. Operating income is $5,000 *more* under absorption costing since, as already explained, $5,000 of fixed manufacturing overhead cost has been deferred in inventory to the next period under that costing method.

4. The absorption costing income statement makes no distinction between fixed and variable costs; therefore, it is not well suited for CVP computations, which are important for good planning and control. To generate data for CVP analysis, it is necessary to spend time reworking and reclassifying costs on the absorption statement.

5. The variable costing approach to costing units of product blends very well with the contribution approach to the income statement, since both concepts are based on the idea of classifying costs by behaviour. The variable costing data in Exhibit 8–2 can be used immediately in CVP computations.

Careful reading of the previous two sections, unit cost calculations and income comparisons of absorption and variable costing, may have created confusion when the fixed overhead unit cost was calculated. In Chapter 5, the Learning Aid and Appendix 5A suggest the use of a predetermined overhead rate. Such a rate is applicable to the unit cost of fixed overhead and the unit cost of variable overhead used here. However, in the examples in this chapter, we use actual overhead rates rather than predetermined ones in order to reduce unneeded complexity. What is illustrated about the effects of inventory on the difference in operating income will hold, regardless of the use of actual or predetermined overhead rates.

Essentially, the difference between the absorption costing method and the variable costing method centres on timing. Advocates of variable costing say that fixed manufacturing costs should be expensed immediately in total, whereas advocates of absorption costing say that fixed manufacturing costs should be charged against revenues bit by bit as units of product are sold. Any units of product not sold under absorption costing result in fixed costs being inventoried and carried forward as *assets* to the next period. We will defer discussing the arguments presented by each side in this dispute until after we have a better understanding of the two methods. Nevertheless, as we will see in the discussion of Emerald Isle Knitters, the use of absorption costing can sometimes produce strange effects on income statements.

> **Instant Quiz 8-1**
> Are selling and administrative expenses treated as product or period costs under absorption costing? Under variable costing?

■ EXTENDED COMPARISON OF INCOME DATA

Emerald Isle Knitters Ltd., located in the Republic of Ireland, is a small company that manufactures traditional wool fishermen's sweaters. The company's basic data appear in the first part of Exhibit 8–3, and the absorption costing income statements as reported to the bank for the last three years appear in the first part of the conclusion of Exhibit 8–3. Sean MacLafferty, the company accountant, decided to try using the variable costing approach to see what effect that might have on operating

LEARNING OBJECTIVE 3
Reconcile variable costing and absorption costing operating incomes, and explain why the two amounts differ.

income. The variable costing income statements for the last three years appear in the lower part of the conclusion of Exhibit 8-3.

Note that Emerald Isle Knitters maintained a steady rate of production per year of 25,000 sweaters. However, sales varied from year to year. In year 1, production and sales were equal. In year 2, production exceeded sales due to a cancelled order. In year 3, sales recovered and exceeded production. As a consequence, inventories did not change during year 1, inventories increased during year 2, and inventories decreased during year 3. *The change in inventories during the year is the key to understanding how absorption costing differs from variable costing.* Note that when inventories increase in year 2, absorption costing operating income exceeds variable costing operating income. When inventories decrease in year 3, the opposite occurs—variable costing operating income exceeds absorption costing operating income. And when there is no change in inventories, as in year 1, there is no difference in operating income between the two methods. Why is this? The reasons are discussed below and are briefly summarized in the Learning Aid below:

1.   When production and sales are equal, as in year 1 for Emerald Isle Knitters, operating income will generally be the same regardless of whether absorption or variable costing is used. This is because the *only* difference that can exist between absorption and variable costing operating incomes is the amount of fixed manufacturing overhead recognized as expense on the income statement. When everything that is produced in the year is sold, all of the fixed manufacturing overhead assigned to units of product under absorption costing becomes part of the current year's cost of goods sold. Under variable

---

EXHIBIT 8-3   Absorption and Variable Costing Data—Emerald Isle Knitters Ltd.

Basic Data

Selling price per unit sold	€ 20
Variable manufacturing cost per unit produced	7
Fixed manufacturing overhead costs per year	150,000
Variable selling and administrative expenses per unit sold	1
Fixed selling and administrative expenses per year	90,000

	Year 1	Year 2	Year 3	Three Years Together
Units in beginning inventory	–0–	–0–	5,000	–0–
Units produced	25,000	25,000	25,000	75,000
Units sold	25,000	20,000	30,000	75,000
Units in ending inventory	–0–	5,000	–0–	–0–

Unit Product Costs

	Year 1	Year 2	Year 3
Under variable costing (variable manufacturing costs only)	€ 7	€ 7	€ 7
Under absorption costing:			
Variable manufacturing costs	€ 7	€ 7	€ 7
Fixed manufacturing overhead costs (€150,000 spread over the number of units produced in each year)	6	6	6
Total absorption cost per unit	€ 13	€ 13	€ 13

continued

EXHIBIT 8-3   concluded

Absorption Costing

	Year 1		Year 2		Year 3		Three Years Together	
Sales		€500,000		€400,000		€600,000		€1,500,000
Less cost of goods sold:								
Beginning inventory	€ -0-		€ -0-		€ 65,000		€ -0-	
Add cost of goods manufactured (25,000 units × €13 per unit)	325,000		325,000		325,000		975,000	
Goods available for sale	325,000		325,000		390,000		975,000	
Less ending inventory (5,000 units × €13 per unit)	-0-		65,000		-0-		-0-	
Cost of goods sold		325,000		260,000		390,000		975,000
Gross margin		175,000		140,000		210,000		525,000
Less selling and administrative expenses		115,000*		110,000*		120,000*		345,000
Operating income		€ 60,000		€ 30,000		€ 90,000		€ 180,000

*The selling and administrative expenses are computed as follows:
Year 1: 25,000 units × €1 per unit variable + €90,000 fixed = €115,000.
Year 2: 20,000 units × €1 per unit variable + €90,000 fixed = €110,000.
Year 3: 30,000 units × €1 per unit variable + €90,000 fixed = €120,000.

Variable Costing

	Year 1		Year 2		Year 3		Three Years Together	
Sales		€500,000		€400,000		€600,000		€1,500,000
Less variable expenses:								
Variable cost of goods sold:								
Beginning inventory	€ -0-		€ -0-		€ 35,000		€ -0-	
Add variable manufacturing costs (25,000 units × €7 per unit)	175,000		175,000		175,000		525,000	
Goods available for sale	175,000		175,000		210,000		525,000	
Less ending inventory (5,000 units × €7 per unit)	-0-		35,000		-0-		-0-	
Variable cost of goods sold	175,000*		140,000*		210,000*		525,000	
Variable selling and administrative expenses (€1 per unit sold)	25,000		20,000		30,000		75,000	
		200,000		160,000		240,000		600,000
Contribution margin		300,000		240,000		360,000		900,000
Less fixed expenses:								
Fixed manufacturing overhead	150,000		150,000		150,000		450,000	
Fixed selling and administrative expenses	90,000		90,000		90,000		270,000	
		240,000		240,000		240,000		720,000
Operating income		€ 60,000		€ -0-		€ 120,000		€ 180,000

*The variable cost of goods sold could have been computed more simply as follows:
Year 1: 25,000 units sold × €7 per unit = €175,000.
Year 2: 20,000 units sold × €7 per unit = €140,000.
Year 3: 30,000 units sold × €7 per unit = €210,000.

LEARNING AID

COMPARATIVE INCOME EFFECTS OF ABSORPTION AND VARIABLE COSTING

Relationship between Production and Sales for the Period	Effect on Inventories	Relationship between Absorption and Variable Costing Operating Incomes
Production = Sales	No change in inventories	Absorption costing operating income = Variable costing operating income
Production > Sales	Inventories increase	Absorption costing operating income > Variable costing operating income*
Production < Sales	Inventories decrease	Absorption costing operating income < Variable costing operating income†

*Operating income is higher under absorption costing, since fixed manufacturing overhead cost is *deferred* in inventory under absorption costing as inventories increase.
†Operating income is lower under absorption costing, since fixed manufacturing overhead cost is *released* from inventory under absorption costing as inventories decrease.

costing, the total fixed manufacturing overhead flows directly to the income statement as an expense. So, under either method, when production equals sales (and hence there is no change in inventories), all of the fixed manufacturing overhead incurred during the year flows through to the income statement as expense. Therefore, the operating income under the two methods is the same.

2. When production exceeds sales (see year 2 in Exhibit 8–3), the operating income reported under absorption costing will generally be greater than the operating income reported under variable costing. This occurs because under absorption costing, part of the fixed manufacturing overhead costs of the current period is deferred in inventory. In year 2, for example, €30,000 of fixed manufacturing overhead costs (5,000 units × €6 per unit) has been applied to units in ending inventory. These costs are excluded from cost of goods sold.

Under variable costing, however, *all* of the fixed manufacturing overhead costs of year 2 have been immediately expensed. As a result, the operating income for year 2 under variable costing is €30,000 *less* than it is under absorption costing. Exhibit 8–4 contains a reconciliation of the variable costing and absorption costing operating income figures.

3. When production is less than sales (see year 3 in Exhibit 8–3), the operating income reported under the absorption costing approach will generally be less than the operating income reported under the variable costing approach. This happens because as inventories are drawn down, the fixed manufacturing overhead costs that were previously deferred in inventory under absorption costing are released and charged against income (known as **fixed manufacturing overhead cost released from inventory**). In year 3, for example, the €30,000 in fixed manufacturing overhead costs deferred in inventory under the absorption approach from year 2 to year 3 is released from inventory because these units were sold. As a result, the cost of goods sold for year 3 contains not only all of

Fixed manufacturing overhead cost released from inventory
The portion of the fixed manufacturing overhead cost of a prior period that becomes an expense of the current period under the absorption costing method as a result of sales exceeding production.

	Year 1	Year 2	Year 3
Variable costing operating income	€60,000	€-0-	€120,000
Add fixed manufacturing overhead costs deferred in inventory under absorption costing (5,000 units × €6 per unit)	-0-	30,000	-0-
Deduct fixed manufacturing overhead costs released from inventory under absorption costing (5,000 units × €6 per unit)	-0-	-0-	(30,000)
Absorption costing operating income..........	€60,000	€30,000	€90,000

EXHIBIT 8-4   Reconciliation of Variable Costing and Absorption Costing—Operating Income Data from Exhibit 8-3

the fixed manufacturing overhead costs for year 3 (since all that was produced in year 3 was sold in year 3) but €30,000 of fixed manufacturing overhead costs from year 2 as well.

By contrast, under variable costing, only the fixed manufacturing overhead costs of year 3 have been charged against year 3. The result is that operating income under variable costing is €30,000 *more* than it is under absorption costing. Exhibit 8-4 reconciles the variable costing and absorption costing operating income figures for year 3.

Careful reading of Exhibit 8-3 will raise the following question: Why is operating income not influenced by changes in inventories when variable costing is used? The reason is that variable costing releases variable costs from inventory to cost of goods sold in amounts that are based on the volume of sales. So production does not influence the cost of goods sold because fixed manufacturing overhead is fixed and not released as cost of goods sold as it was with absorption costing.

4. Over an *extended* period of time, the cumulative operating income figures reported under absorption costing and variable costing tend to be the same. This is because over the long run, sales cannot exceed production, nor can production much exceed sales. The shorter the time period, the more the operating income figures will tend to differ.

> **Instant Quiz 8-2**
> Parker Company had $5,000,000 in sales and reported a $300,000 profit in its annual report to shareholders. According to a CVP analysis prepared for management's use, $5,000,000 in sales is the break-even point for the company. Did the company's inventory level increase, decrease, or remain unchanged? Explain.

Effect of Changes in Production on Operating Income

In the Emerald Isle Knitters example in the preceding section, production was constant and sales fluctuated over the three-year period. Since sales fluctuated, the income statements that MacLafferty presented in Exhibit 8-3 allowed us to see the effect of changes in sales on operating income under both variable and absorption costing.

To further investigate the differences between variable and absorption costing, MacLafferty next put together the hypothetical example in Exhibit 8-5. In this example, sales are constant and production fluctuates (the opposite of Exhibit 8-3). The purpose of Exhibit 8-5 is to illustrate the effect of changes in *production* on operating income under both variable and absorption costing.

Variable Costing

Operating income is *not* affected by changes in production under variable costing. Notice from Exhibit 8-5 that operating income is the same for all three years under the variable costing approach, although production exceeds sales in one year and is less than sales in another year. In short, a change in production has no effect on operating income when variable costing is used.

Absorption Costing

Operating income *is* affected by changes in production under absorption costing. As shown in Exhibit 8–5, operating income under the absorption approach goes up in year 2, in response to the increase in production for that year, and then goes down in year 3, in response to the drop in production for that year. Note particularly that operating income goes up and down between these two years *even though the same number of units is sold in each year*. The reason for this effect can be traced to the shifting of fixed manufacturing overhead costs between periods under the absorption costing method as a result of changes in inventory.

As shown in Exhibit 8–5, production exceeds sales in year 2, resulting in an increase of 10,000 units in inventory. Each unit produced during year 2 has €6 in fixed manufacturing overhead costs attached to it (see the unit cost computations at the top of Exhibit 8–5). Therefore, €60,000 (10,000 units × €6) of the fixed manufacturing overhead costs of year 2 are not charged against that year but rather are added to the inventory account (along with the variable manufacturing costs). The operating income of year 2 rises sharply, because these costs are deferred in inventories, even though the same number of units is sold in year 2 as in the other years.

The reverse effect occurs in year 3. Since sales exceed production in year 3, that year is forced to cover all of its own fixed manufacturing overhead costs as well as the fixed manufacturing overhead costs carried forward in inventory from year 2. A substantial drop in operating income during year 3 results from the release of fixed manufacturing overhead costs from inventories, despite the fact that the same number of units is sold in that year as in the other years.

EXHIBIT 8–5   Sensitivity of Costing Methods to Changes in Production—Hypothetical Data

Basic Data

Selling price per unit sold...	€ 25
Variable manufacturing cost per unit produced	10
Fixed manufacturing overhead costs per year	300,000
Variable selling and administrative expenses per unit sold.....................	1
Fixed selling and administrative expenses per year................................	200,000

	Year 1	Year 2	Year 3
Units in beginning inventory	–0–	–0–	10,000
Units produced..	40,000	50,000	30,000
Units sold	40,000	40,000	40,000
Units in ending inventory	–0–	10,000	–0–

Unit Product Costs

	Year 1	Year 2	Year 3
Under variable costing (variable manufacturing costs only)	€ 10.00	€ 10.00	€ 10.00
Under absorption costing:			
Variable manufacturing costs..	€ 10.00	€ 10.00	€ 10.00
Fixed manufacturing overhead costs (€300,000 spread over the number of units produced in each year)............................	7.50	6.00	10.00
Total absorption cost per unit...	€ 17.50	€ 16.00	€ 20.00

continued

EXHIBIT 8-5 *concluded*

Absorption Costing

	Year 1	Year 2	Year 3
Sales (40,000 units)	€1,000,000	€1,000,000	€1,000,000
Less cost of goods sold:			
Beginning inventory	€ -0-	€ -0-	€ 160,000
Add cost of goods manufactured	700,000*	800,000*	600,000*
Goods available for sale	700,000	800,000	760,000
Less ending inventory	-0-	160,000†	-0-
Cost of goods sold	700,000	640,000	760,000
Gross margin	300,000	360,000	240,000
Less selling and administrative expenses (40,000 units × €1 per unit + €200,000)	240,000	240,000	240,000
Operating income	€ 60,000	€ 120,000	€ -0-

*Cost of goods manufactured:
Year 1: 40,000 units × €17.50 per unit = €700,000.
Year 2: 50,000 units × €16.00 per unit = €800,000.
Year 3: 30,000 units × €20.00 per unit = €600,000.
†Ending inventory year 2: 10,000 units × €16 per unit = €160,000.

Variable Costing

	Year 1	Year 2	Year 3
Sales (40,000 units)	€1,000,000	€1,000,000	€1,000,000
Less variable expenses:			
Variable cost of goods sold:			
Beginning inventory	€ -0-	€ -0-	€ 100,000
Add variable manufacturing costs at €10 per unit produced	400,000	500,000	300,000
Goods available for sale	400,000	500,000	400,000
Less ending inventory	-0-	100,000*	-0-
Variable cost of goods sold	400,000	400,000	400,000
Variable selling and administrative expenses	40,000	40,000	40,000
Contribution margin	560,000	560,000	560,000
Less fixed expenses:			
Fixed manufacturing overhead	300,000	300,000	300,000
Fixed selling and administrative expenses	200,000	200,000	200,000
Operating income	€ 60,000	€ 60,000	€ 60,000

*Ending inventory, year 2: 10,000 units × €10 per unit = €100,000.

EXHIBIT 8–6 Reconciliation of Variable Costing and Absorption Costing—Operating Income Data from Exhibit 8–5

	Year 1	Year 2	Year 3
Variable costing operating income	€60,000	€ 60,000	€ 60,000
Add fixed manufacturing overhead costs deferred in inventory under absorption costing (10,000 units × €6 per unit)	–0–	60,000	–0–
Deduct fixed manufacturing overhead costs released from inventory under absorption costing (10,000 units × €6 per unit)	–0–	–0–	(60,000)
Absorption costing operating income	€60,000	€120,000	€ –0–

Instant Quiz 8-3
Fill in the blanks: Under variable costing, _____ drives operating income, while under absorption costing, _____ and _____ drive operating income.

The variable costing and absorption costing operating incomes are reconciled in Exhibit 8–6. This exhibit shows that the differences in operating income can be traced to the effects of changes in inventories on absorption costing operating income. Under absorption costing, fixed manufacturing overhead costs are deferred in inventory when inventories increase and are released from inventory when inventory decreases.

CHOOSING A COSTING METHOD

The Impact on the Manager

LEARNING OBJECTIVE 4
Explain the advantages and disadvantages of both variable and absorption costing.

Opponents of absorption costing argue that shifting fixed manufacturing overhead cost between periods can be confusing and can lead to misinterpretations and even to faulty decisions. Look again at the data in Exhibit 8–5. A manager might wonder why operating income went up substantially in year 2 under absorption costing when sales remained the same as in the prior year. Was it a result of lower selling costs or more efficient operations, or was some other factor involved? A manager cannot determine this by simply looking at the absorption costing income statement. Then, in year 3, operating income drops sharply, even though again the same number of units is sold as in the other two years. Why would income rise in one year and then drop in the next? The figures seem erratic and contradictory and can lead to confusion and a loss of confidence in the integrity of the statement data.

By contrast, the variable costing income statements in Exhibit 8–5 are clear and easy to understand. Sales remain constant over the three-year period covered in the exhibit, so both contribution margin and operating income also remain constant. The statements are consistent with what managers would expect to happen under the circumstances, so they tend to generate confidence rather than confusion.

Under variable costing, revenue essentially drives operating income. Under absorption costing, both revenue and production drive operating income. The two drivers create confusion for the user of operating income because it is difficult to perceive income without first selling what is produced, something absorption costing does.

Instant Quiz 8-4
Explain how fixed manufacturing overhead costs are shifted from one period to another under absorption costing.

To avoid mistakes when absorption costing is used, readers of financial statements should be alert to changes in inventory levels. Under absorption costing, if inventories increase, fixed manufacturing overhead costs are deferred in inventories and operating income increases. If inventories decrease, fixed manufacturing overhead costs are released from inventories and operating income decreases. Thus, fluctuations in operating income can be due to changes in inventories rather than to changes in sales.

Cost–Volume–Profit Analysis and Absorption Costing

Absorption costing is widely used for both internal and external reports. Many firms use the absorption approach exclusively because of its focus on *full* costing of units of product. A weakness of the method, however, is its inability to dovetail well with CVP analysis.

To illustrate, refer again to Exhibit 8–3. Let us compute the break-even point for Emerald Isle Knitters. To obtain the break-even point, we divide total fixed costs by the contribution margin per unit:

Selling price per unit	€ 20
Variable costs per unit	8
Contribution margin per unit	€ 12
Fixed manufacturing overhead costs.	€ 150,000
Fixed selling and administrative costs.	90,000
Total fixed costs	€ 240,000

$$\frac{\text{Total fixed costs}}{\text{Contribution margin per unit}} = \frac{€240,000}{€12} = 20,000 \text{ units}$$

The break-even point is 20,000 units. Notice from Exhibit 8–3 that in year 2, the firm sold exactly 20,000 units, the break-even volume. Under the contribution approach, using variable costing, the firm does break even in year 2, showing zero operating income. *Under absorption costing, however, the firm shows a positive operating income of €30,000 for year 2.* How can this be? How can absorption costing produce a positive operating income when the firm sold exactly the break-even volume of units?

The answer lies in the fact that €30,000 in fixed manufacturing overhead costs were deferred in inventory during year 2 under absorption costing and therefore did not appear as expenses. By deferring these fixed manufacturing overhead costs in inventory, the income statement shows a profit even though the company sold exactly the break-even volume of units. Absorption costing runs into similar kinds of difficulty in other areas of CVP analysis, which assumes that variable costing is being used.

Absorption break-even analysis requires the analysis of two drivers, sales and production. By determining various levels for each driver, a zero operating income could be determined. But as in mathematics, a single equation does not provide a unique solution when there are two unknowns. Various possible sales and production levels that can create a break-even operating income are what *break-even* means here. For example, see year 3 of Exhibit 8–5, where 40,000 units were sold and 30,000 units were produced. Operating income is zero, or break even.

Decision Making

A basic problem with absorption costing is that fixed manufacturing overhead costs appear to be variable with respect to the number of units sold, but they are not. For example, in Exhibit 8–3, the absorption unit product cost is €13, but the variable portion of this cost is only €7. Since the product costs are stated on a per unit basis, managers may mistakenly believe that if another unit is produced, it will cost the company €13.

The misperception that absorption unit product costs are variable can lead to many managerial problems, including inappropriate pricing decisions and decisions to drop products that are in fact profitable. We will discuss these problems with absorption costing product costs more fully in later chapters.

External Reporting, Income Taxes, and Management Performance Evaluation

Practically speaking, absorption costing is required for external reports in the United States and is the predominant method used in Canada. In Canada, *International Accounting Standard 2, Inventories* requires a company to assign to work in process and finished goods inventory the laid-down cost of materials plus the cost of direct labour and the applicable share of overhead expenses. For income tax purposes in Canada, the Canada Revenue Agency's *Interpretation Bulletin IT473R, Inventory Valuation* permits both variable and absorption costing for determining taxable income.

Even if a company uses absorption costing for its external reports, a manager can use variable costing statements for internal reports. No particular accounting problems are created by using *both* costing methods—the variable costing method for internal reports and the absorption costing method for external reports. As we demonstrated earlier in Exhibits 8–5 and 8–6, the adjustment from variable costing operating income to absorption costing operating income is a simple one that can be made easily at year-end. Computer systems such as those described in Chapter 5 can make the conversion, as long as the information is contained in the supporting database.

Top executives of publicly held corporations are typically evaluated based on the earnings reported in the external financial reports presented to shareholders. This creates a problem for top executives who might otherwise favour using variable costing for internal reports. They may feel that since their performance evaluation and any potential bonuses they might earn are based on meeting profit targets and profits are defined using absorption costing, their everyday decisions should also be based on absorption costing data.

Advantages of Variable Costing and the Contribution Approach

As stated earlier, even if the absorption approach is used for external reporting purposes, variable costing, together with the contribution format income statement, is an appealing alternative for internal reports. The advantages of variable costing can be summarized as follows:

1. Data required for CVP analysis can be taken directly from a contribution format income statement. These data are not available on a conventional absorption costing statement.
2. Under variable costing, the profit for a period is not affected by changes in inventories. Other things remaining equal (e.g., selling prices, costs, sales mix), profits move in the same direction as sales when variable costing is used.
3. Managers often assume that unit product costs are variable costs. This is a problem under absorption costing because unit product costs are a combination of both fixed and variable costs. Under variable costing, unit product costs do not contain fixed costs.
4. The impact of fixed costs on profits is emphasized under the variable costing and contribution approach. The total amount of fixed costs appears explicitly on the income statement, highlighting that the whole amount of fixed costs must be covered for the company to be truly profitable. Under absorption costing, the fixed costs are mingled with the variable costs and are buried in cost of goods sold and in ending inventories.
5. Variable costing data make it easier to estimate the profitability of products, customers, and other segments of the business. With absorption costing, profitability is obscured by arbitrary allocations of fixed costs. We will discuss these issues in later chapters.
6. Variable costing ties in with cost control methods such as standard costs and flexible budgets, which we will cover in later chapters.

7. Variable costing operating income is closer to net cash flow than absorption costing operating income. This is particularly important for companies with potential cash flow problems.

With all of these advantages, one might wonder why absorption costing continues to be used almost exclusively for external reporting and why it is the predominant choice for internal reports as well. This is partly due to tradition, but absorption costing is also attractive to many accountants and managers because they believe it better matches costs with revenues—it is consistent with the matching principle.

Advocates of absorption costing argue that *all* manufacturing costs must be assigned to products to properly match the costs of producing units of product with the revenues from the units when they are sold. The fixed costs of depreciation, taxes, insurance, supervisory salaries, and so on, are just as essential to manufacturing products as are the variable costs.

Advocates of variable costing argue that fixed manufacturing costs are not really the costs of any particular unit of product. These costs are incurred in order to have the *capacity* to make products during a particular period and will be incurred even if nothing is made during the period. Moreover, whether a unit is made or not, the fixed manufacturing costs will be exactly the same. Therefore, variable costing advocates argue that fixed manufacturing costs are not part of the costs of producing a particular unit of product and thus the matching principle dictates that fixed manufacturing costs should be charged to the current period.

Another downside of absorption or full costing is that it can be used by an unethical manager to deliberately mislead others. This is possible because reported profits are affected by inventory buildups or draw-downs if fixed costs are included in inventory. During periods of inventory buildup, less than a year's fixed costs will be expensed, and during years in which inventory is reduced, more than a year's fixed costs will be expensed. An unethical manager whose bonus is based on operating income, for example, could make profits appear higher by simply building up inventory levels, since there is a direct relationship between ending inventory and operating income. Those responsible for performance evaluation should look beyond the bottom line to identify such abuses.

One restriction on the unethical use of absorption costing to increase operating income by building ending inventories is the application of the generally accepted accounting principle of lower of cost or market. The ending inventory has to be examined for its saleability by determining its market value. If market is below cost, then a loss is recorded in the income statement of the current period. Thus, if the excess inventory could not be sold, a write-down is expected, which would reduce but not necessarily eliminate the operating income resulting from the inventory buildup. Whether the result would make absorption operating income equal to variable operating income is a question of the specifics, and thus they are unlikely to be exactly equal.

At any rate, absorption costing is a generally accepted method for preparing mandatory external financial reports. Probably because of the cost and possible confusion of maintaining two separate costing systems—one for external reporting and one for internal reporting—most companies use absorption costing for both external and internal reports, although decreasing information processing costs may result in more firms using two costing systems in the future.

There may also be important strategic reasons for using absorption costing. Senior management, for example, may fear that variable costing will result in an overemphasis on contribution margin and lead to insufficient attention to the management of fixed costs. Decision makers may focus too much on short-run profitability and bring long-run harm to the company. For example, long-term profitability will suffer if managers, lured by the attractiveness of high contribution margins, set product prices too low because of blindness to the existence of fixed costs. This is a particular risk in those industries in which the trend has been for cost structures to shift away from variable costs. Judging from

> **Instant Quiz 8–5**
> What arguments can be advanced in favour of treating fixed manufacturing overhead costs as product costs?

the dominant use of absorption costing, it appears that managers have generally concluded that the incremental benefits of variable costing information are outweighed by these strategic factors and the additional costs of maintaining parallel systems.

IMPACT OF LEAN PRODUCTION

As discussed in this chapter, variable and absorption costing will produce different operating income figures whenever the number of units produced is different from the number of units sold—in other words, whenever there is a change in the number of units in inventory. We have also learned that the absorption costing operating income figure can be erratic, sometimes moving in a direction that is opposite from the movement in sales.

When companies use lean production (JIT) methods, these problems are reduced. The erratic movement of operating income under absorption costing and the difference in operating income between absorption and variable costing occur because of changes in the number of units in inventory. As noted in Chapter 1, lean thinking only allows production in response to customer orders, so the number of units produced tends to equal the number of units sold, thereby resulting in minimal inventory. Under lean production, goods are produced to customers' orders, and the goal is to eliminate finished goods inventories entirely and reduce work in process inventory to almost nothing. In addition to minimizing inventory holding costs, lean production reduces the ability of an unethical manager to manage reported earnings by building inventory. Recall our discussion above indicating that when inventories build under absorption costing, less than a year's fixed costs will be expensed, thus artificially boosting income. If, on the other hand, there is very little inventory, then changes in inventories will be very small and both variable and absorption costing will show basically the same operating income figure. In that case, absorption costing operating income will move in the same direction as movements in sales.

Of course, the cost of a unit of product will still be different between variable and absorption costing, as explained earlier in the chapter. But when lean production is used, the differences in operating income will largely disappear.

IN BUSINESS

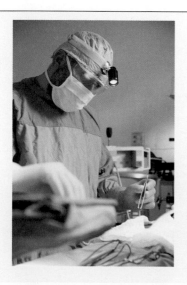

Conmed, a surgical device maker in Utica, New York, switched to lean manufacturing by replacing its assembly lines with U-shaped production cells. It also started producing only enough units to satisfy customer demand rather than producing as many units as possible and storing them in warehouses. The company calculated that its customers use one of its disposable surgical devices every 90 seconds, so that is precisely how often it produces a new unit. Its assembly area for fluid-injection devices used to occupy 3,300 square feet (300 m²) of space and contained $93,000 worth of parts. Now the company produces its fluid-injection devices in 660 square feet (60 m²) of space while maintaining only $6,000 of parts inventory.

When Conmed adopted lean manufacturing, it substantially reduced its finished goods inventories. What impact do you think this initial reduction in inventories may have had on net operating income? Why?

Source: Pete Engardio, "Lean and Mean Gets Extreme," *Businessweek*, March 23 and 30, 2009, pp. 60–62.

KNOWLEDGE IN ACTION

Managers can apply their knowledge about variable costing when
- Performing CVP analysis to determine the number of units of product or service that must be sold in order for the firm to break even
- Explaining changes to net operating income since variable costing income statements are not affected by changes in inventory levels
- Identifying additional variable costs that will be incurred to make one more unit of product, which is important information for managers to consider when making decisions about expanding production
- Examining the impact of fixed costs on profits by highlighting the total amount of fixed costs that must be covered for the company to be truly profitable

SUMMARY

- Variable and absorption costing are alternative methods of determining unit product costs. [LO1]
- Under variable costing, only those production costs that vary with output are treated as product costs. This includes direct materials; variable overhead; and, ordinarily, direct labour. Fixed manufacturing overhead is treated as a period cost and charged off against revenue as it is incurred, the same as selling and administrative expenses. [LO1]
- Under absorption costing, fixed manufacturing overhead is treated as a product cost, along with direct materials, direct labour, and variable overhead; therefore, a portion of fixed manufacturing overhead is assigned to each unit as it is produced. When some goods remain unsold at the end of the period, some of the fixed manufacturing overhead cost is held in inventory and deferred to the period in which the related units of product are sold. Thus, under absorption costing, it is possible to defer a portion of the fixed manufacturing overhead cost of one period to the next period through the inventory account. [LO1]
- When preparing variable costing income statements, fixed manufacturing costs are expensed immediately and in total. When preparing absorption costing income statements, fixed manufacturing costs are charged against revenues bit by bit as units of product are sold. Any unsold units of product under absorption costing carry a portion of fixed manufacturing overhead with them into inventory as assets to the next period. [LO2]
- The shifting of fixed manufacturing overhead cost between periods under absorption costing can cause operating income to fluctuate erratically and can result in confusion and unwise decisions on the part of management. To guard against mistakes when they interpret income statement data, managers should be alert to any changes that may have taken place in inventory levels or in unit product costs during the period. [LO3]
- Practically speaking, variable costing cannot be used externally for financial reporting purposes in certain jurisdictions mainly because it does not conform to the matching principle (i.e., that revenues should be matched with the cost of generating those revenues). However, variable costing may be used internally for planning and is particularly useful when applying cost–volume–profit (CVP) concepts in profit planning and decision making. [LO4]

REVIEW PROBLEM: CONTRASTING VARIABLE AND ABSORPTION COSTING

Dexter Company produces and sells a single product, a fan housing unit used in commercial heating and cooling systems. Selected cost and operating data relating to the product for two years are given below:

Selling price per unit..............................	$ 50
Manufacturing costs:	
Variable per unit produced:	
Direct materials.............................	11
Direct labour................................	6
Variable overhead..........................	3
Fixed per year..................................	120,000
Selling and administrative costs:	
Variable per unit sold.........................	5
Fixed per year.................................	70,000

	Year 1	Year 2
Units in beginning inventory......................	–0–	2,000
Units produced during the year...................	10,000	6,000
Units sold during the year........................	8,000	8,000
Units in ending inventory.........................	2,000	–0–

Required:
1. Assume that the company uses absorption costing.
   - *a.* Compute the unit product cost in each year.
   - *b.* Prepare an income statement for each year.
2. Assume that the company uses variable costing.
   - *a.* Compute the unit product cost in each year.
   - *b.* Prepare an income statement for each year.
3. Reconcile the variable costing and absorption costing operating incomes.

Solution to Review Problem

1. *a.* Under absorption costing, all manufacturing costs, variable and fixed, are included in unit product costs:

	Year 1	Year 2
Direct materials...	$ 11	$ 11
Direct labour...	6	6
Variable manufacturing overhead.................................	3	3
Fixed manufacturing overhead		
($120,000 ÷ 10,000 units).....................................	12	
($120,000 ÷ 6,000 units)		20
Unit product cost..	$32	$40

  b. The absorption costing income statements follow:

		Year 1		Year 2
Sales (8,000 units × $50 per unit)...........................		$400,000		$ 400,000
Less cost of goods sold:				
Beginning inventory.......................................	$ –0–		$64,000	
Add cost of goods manufactured				
(10,000 units × $32 per unit)..........................	320,000			
(6,000 units × $40 per unit)...............................			240,000	
Goods available for sale...................................	320,000		304,000	
Less ending inventory				
(2,000 units × $32 per unit; 0 units)	64,000	256,000	–0–	304,000
Gross margin...		144,000		96,000
Less selling and administrative expenses....................		110,000*		110,000*
Operating income..		$ 34,000		$ (14,000)

*Selling and administrative expenses:	
Variable (8,000 units × $5 per unit)........................	$ 40,000
Fixed per year..	70,000
Total...	$110,000

2. *a.* Under variable costing, only the variable manufacturing costs are included in unit product costs:

	Year 1	Year 2
Direct materials	$ 11	$ 11
Direct labour	6	6
Variable manufacturing overhead	3	3
Unit product cost	$20	$20

b. The variable costing income statements follow. Notice that the variable cost of goods sold is computed in a simpler, more direct manner than in the examples provided earlier. On a variable costing income statement, either approach to computing the cost of goods sold followed in this chapter is acceptable.

	Year 1		Year 2	
Sales (8,000 units × $50 per unit)		$400,000		$400,000
Less variable expenses:				
Variable cost of goods sold				
(8,000 units × $20 per unit)	$160,000		$160,000	
Variable selling and administrative				
expenses (8,000 units × $5 per unit)	40,000		40,000	
Contribution margin		200,000		200,000
Less fixed expenses:				
Fixed manufacturing overhead	120,000		120,000	
Fixed selling and administrative expenses	70,000	190,000	70,000	190,000
Operating income		$ 10,000		$ 10,000

3. The reconciliation of the variable and absorption costing operating incomes follows:

	Year 1	Year 2
Variable costing operating income	$10,000	$ 10,000
Add fixed manufacturing overhead costs deferred in inventory under absorption costing (2,000 units × $12 per unit)	24,000	
Deduct fixed manufacturing overhead costs released from inventory under absorption costing (2,000 units × $12 per unit)		24,000
Absorption costing operating income	$34,000	$ (14,000)

GLOSSARY

Review key terms and definitions on Connect.

Mc Graw Hill Education connect°

DISCUSSION CASE

DISCUSSION CASE 8-1

Tough times can bring out the worst in people. When companies are desperate to stay in business or to report more favourable earnings to the market, some managers just can't seem to resist the temptation to manipulate reported profits. Unfortunately, inventory is sometimes a tempting target of such manipulation. While some companies may boost their own inventories to report higher profits, other companies use inventory manipulation in a more roundabout way: they produce excess inventory but then find ways to induce their customers to buy more product than they really need (known as "channel stuffing" or "trade loading").

Required:

Using the concepts discussed in this chapter, consider how the requirement to report for financial accounting purposes under absorption costing might play a role. Could a firm with sales below the break-even point still report profits?

QUESTIONS

8–1   What is the basic difference between absorption costing and variable costing?

8–2   Why is variable costing a better support for short-term planning and decision making than absorption costing?

8–3   If production and sales are equal, which method would you expect to show the higher operating income, variable costing or absorption costing? Why?

8–4   If production exceeds sales, which method would you expect to show the higher operating income, variable costing or absorption costing? Why?

8–5   If fixed manufacturing overhead costs are released from inventory under absorption costing, what does this tell you about the level of production in relation to the level of sales?

8–6   Delone Industries had $125,000 in sales and reported a $75,000 profit in its annual report to shareholders. According to a CVP analysis prepared for management's use, $125,000 in sales is the break-even point for the company. Did the company's inventory level increase, decrease, or remain unchanged? Explain.

8–7   How is the use of variable costing limited?

8–8   How does lean production reduce or eliminate the difference in reported operating income between absorption and variable costing?

EXERCISES

EXERCISE 8–1 Variable and Absorption Costing Unit Product Costs [LO1]
Bharat Bicycle, located in India, produces an inexpensive yet rugged bicycle for use on crowded city streets. The company sells the bicycle for 500 rupees. (Indian currency is denominated in rupees, denoted by R.) Selected data for the company's operations last year follow:

Units in beginning inventory	0
Units produced	10,000
Units sold	8,000
Units in ending inventory	2,000
Variable costs per unit:	
Direct materials	R120
Direct labour	R140
Variable manufacturing overhead	R50
Variable selling and administrative	R20
Fixed costs:	
Fixed manufacturing overhead	R600,000
Fixed selling and administrative	R400,000

Required:

1.   Assume that the company uses absorption costing. Compute the unit product cost for one bicycle.

2.   Assume that the company uses variable costing. Compute the unit product cost for one bicycle.

EXERCISE 8–2 Variable Costing Income Statement; Explanation of Difference in Operating Income [LO2]
Refer to the data in Exercise 8–1 for Bharat Bicycle. An absorption costing income statement prepared by the company's accountant appears below:

Sales (8,000 units × R500 per unit)...........................		R4,000,000
Cost of goods sold:		
Beginning inventory... R 0		
Add cost of goods manufactured		
(10,000 units × R ? per unit)......................	3,700,000	
Goods available for sale	3,700,000	
Less ending inventory		
(2,000 units × R ? per unit)........................	740,000	2,960,000
Gross margin		1,040,000
Selling and administrative expenses:		
Variable selling and administrative	160,000	
Fixed selling and administrative.............................	400,000	560,000
Operating income...		R 480,000

Required:

1. Determine how much of the ending inventory of R740,000 above consists of fixed manufacturing overhead cost deferred in inventory to the next period.

2. Prepare an income statement for the year using the variable costing method. Explain the difference in operating income between the two costing methods.

EXERCISE 8–3 Reconciliation of Absorption and Variable Costing Operating Incomes [LO3]

Sunrise Pools and Spas manufactures fibreglass forms for in-ground pools and swim spas for all-season use. The company uses variable costing for internal management reports and absorption costing for external reports to shareholders, creditors, and the government. The company has provided the data for their swim spa business in years 1, 2, and 3 shown below.

The company's fixed manufacturing overhead per unit was constant at $2,500 for all three years:

	Year 1	Year 2	Year 3
Inventories:			
Beginning (units).....................................	150	180	160
Ending (units)..	160	150	200
Variable costing operating income......................	$292,400	$269,200	$251,800

Required:

1. Determine each year's absorption costing operating income. Present your answer in the form of a reconciliation report, such as the one shown in Exhibit 8–6.

2. In year 4, the company's variable costing operating income was $240,200 and its absorption costing operating income was $205,200. Did inventories increase or decrease during year 4? How much fixed manufacturing overhead cost was deferred or released from inventory during year 4?

EXERCISE 8–4 Evaluating Absorption and Variable Costing as Alternative Costing Methods [LO4]

The following questions involve the same manufacturing company in two different sets of circumstances. In both, the cost structure of the company is constant from year to year. Selling prices, unit variable costs, and total fixed costs are the same in every year. However, unit sales and/or unit production levels may vary from year to year.

Required:

1. Consider the following data for scenario A:

	Year 1	Year 2	Year 3
Variable costing operating income......................	$16,847	$16,847	$16,847
Absorption costing operating income..................	$16,847	$29,378	$6,018

    a.   Were unit sales constant from year to year? Explain.

    b.   What was the relationship between unit sales and unit production levels in each year? For each year, indicate whether inventories grew or shrank.

2.   Consider the following data for scenario B:

	Year 1	Year 2	Year 3
Variable costing operating income (loss)...............	$16,847	$(18,153)	$(53,153)
Absorption costing operating income...................	$16,847	$17,583	$18,318

    a.   Were unit sales constant from year to year? Explain.

    b.   What was the relationship between unit sales and unit production levels in each year? For each year, indicate whether inventories grew or shrank.

3.   Given the patterns of operating income in scenarios A and B above, which costing method, variable costing or absorption costing, do you believe provides a better reflection of economic reality? Explain.

EXERCISE 8–5 Variable Costing Unit Product Cost and Income Statement; Break-Even [LO1, LO2]

Waterloo Storage Products makes a four-drawer plastic storage cabinet on casters meant for use in garages and workshops. Each cabinet sells for $35. Data for last year's operations follow:

Units in beginning inventory...............................	0
Units produced	25,000
Units sold...	21,500
Units in ending inventory................................	3,500
Variable costs per unit:	
Direct materials	$ 8
Direct labour..	10
Variable manufacturing overhead	2
Variable selling and administrative....................	4
Total variable cost per unit	$ 24
Fixed costs:	
Fixed manufacturing overhead	$ 75,000
Fixed selling and administrative.......................	110,000
Total fixed costs	$185,000

Required:
1.   Assume that the company uses variable costing. Compute the unit product cost for one storage cabinet.
2.   Assume that the company uses variable costing. Prepare a contribution format income statement for the year.
3.   What is the company's break-even point in terms of units sold?

EXERCISE 8–6 Absorption Costing Unit Product Cost; Income Statement [LO1, LO2]

Refer to the data in Exercise 8–5 for Waterloo Storage Products. Assume in this exercise that the company uses absorption costing.

Required:
1.   Compute the unit product cost for one storage cabinet.
2.   Prepare an income statement for the year.

EXERCISE 8–7 Variable and Absorption Costing Unit Product Costs; Income Statements [LO1, LO2]

Baxtell Company manufactures and sells a single product. The following costs were incurred during the company's first year of operations:

Variable costs per unit:		
Manufacturing:		
Direct materials..	$	25
Direct labour...		12
Variable manufacturing overhead...................		3
Variable selling and administrative.....................		5
Fixed costs per year:		
Fixed manufacturing overhead........................		200,000
Fixed selling and administrative expense...............		110,000

During the year, the company produced 25,000 units and sold 21,000 units. The selling price of the company's product is $65 per unit.

Required:
1. Assume that the company uses absorption costing.
    a. Compute the unit product cost.
    b. Prepare an income statement for the year.
2. Assume that the company uses variable costing.
    a. Compute the unit product cost.
    b. Prepare an income statement for the year.

EXERCISE 8–8 Inferring Costing Method; Unit Product Cost [LO1, LO4]
Sparn Limited incurs the following costs to produce and sell a single product:

Variable costs per unit:		
Direct materials	$	10
Direct labour...		5
Variable manufacturing overhead		2
Variable selling and administrative expenses		4
Fixed costs per year:		
Fixed manufacturing overhead........................		90,000
Fixed selling and administrative expenses..............		300,000

During the last year, 30,000 units were produced and 25,000 units were sold. The Finished Goods Inventory account at the end of the year shows a balance of $85,000 for the 5,000 unsold units.

Required:
1. Is the company using absorption costing or variable costing to cost units in the Finished Goods Inventory account? Show computations to support your answer.
2. Assume that the company wishes to prepare financial statements for the year to issue to its shareholders.
    a. Is the $85,000 figure for finished goods inventory the correct amount to use on these statements for external reporting purposes? Explain.
    b. At what dollar amount should the 5,000 units be carried in inventory for external reporting purposes?

EXERCISE 8–9 Variable Costing Income Statement; Reconciliation [LO2, LO3]
Morey Company has just completed its first year of operations. The company's absorption costing income statement for the year appears below:

MOREY COMPANY Income Statement		
Sales (40,000 units at $33.75 per unit)...............................		$1,350,000
Cost of goods sold:		
Beginning inventory...	$ 0	
Add cost of goods manufactured		
(50,000 units at $21 per unit).................................	1,050,000	
Goods available for sale	1,050,000	
Less ending inventory (10,000 units at $21 per unit)	210,000	840,000
Gross margin		510,000
Selling and administrative expenses		420,000
Operating income...		$ 90,000

The company's selling and administrative expenses consist of $300,000 per year in fixed expenses and $3 per unit sold in variable expenses. The company's $21 per unit product cost given above is computed as follows:

Direct materials..	$10
Direct labour...	4
Variable manufacturing overhead.......................................	2
Fixed manufacturing overhead ($250,000 ÷ 50,000 units)...............	5
Unit product cost..	$21

Required:
1. Redo the company's income statement in the contribution format using variable costing.
2. Reconcile any difference between the operating income on your variable costing income statement and the operating income on the absorption costing income statement above.

PROBLEMS

PROBLEM 8-10 Variable Costing Income Statement; Reconciliation [LO2, LO3]
During Durton Company's first two years of operations, the company reported absorption costing operating income as shown below. Production and cost data for the two years are given:

	Year 1	Year 2
Units produced	25,000	25,000
Units sold	20,000	30,000

	Year 1	Year 2
Sales (at $50 per unit)..	$1,000,000	$1,500,000
Cost of goods sold:		
Beginning inventory...	0	170,000
Add cost of goods manufactured (at $34 per unit)......................	850,000	850,000
Goods available for sale	850,000	1,020,000
Less ending inventory (at $34 per unit)................................	170,000	0
Cost of goods sold..	680,000	1,020,000
Gross margin	320,000	480,000
Selling and administrative expenses*......................................	310,000	340,000
Operating income..	$ 10,000	$ 140,000

*$3 per unit variable; $250,000 fixed each year.

The company's $34 unit product cost is computed as follows:

Direct materials..	$ 8
Direct labour...	10
Variable manufacturing overhead.......................................	2
Fixed manufacturing overhead ($350,000 ÷ 25,000 units)...............	14
Unit product cost..	$34

Required:
1. Prepare a variable costing income statement for each year in the contribution format.
2. Reconcile the absorption costing and variable costing operating income figures for each year.

PROBLEM 8–11 Variable and Absorption Costing Unit Product Costs and Income Statements; Explanation of Difference in Operating Income [LO1, LO2, LO3]

Coverall Inc. produces and sells a unique type of case for a standard size tablet computer that is guaranteed waterproof but still allows for regular functionality of the tablet. The company has just opened a new plant to manufacture these cases, and the following cost and revenue data have been provided for the first month of the plant's operation in the form of a worksheet:

Beginning inventory.	$ 0
Units produced	30,000
Units sold.	25,000
Selling price per unit	$75
Selling and administrative expenses:	
Variable per unit	$8
Fixed (total)	$525,000
Manufacturing costs:	
Direct materials cost per unit.	$18
Direct labour cost per unit	$8
Variable manufacturing overhead cost per unit.	$6
Fixed manufacturing overhead cost (total).	$630,000

Since the new case is unique in design, management is anxious to see how profitable it will be and has asked that an income statement be prepared for the month.

Required:
1. Assume that the company uses absorption costing.
   a. Determine the unit product cost.
   b. Prepare an income statement for the month.
2. Assume that the company uses variable costing.
   a. Determine the unit product cost.
   b. Prepare a contribution format income statement for the month.
3. Explain the reason for any difference in the ending inventory balances under the two costing methods and the impact of this difference on reported operating income.

PROBLEM 8–12 Comprehensive Problem with Labour Fixed [LO1, LO2, LO3, LO4]

eXcel

Zurgot Inc. has just organized a new division to manufacture and sell specially designed computer tables, using select hardwoods. The division's monthly costs are shown in the schedule below:

Manufacturing costs:	
Variable costs per unit:	
Direct materials.	$152
Variable manufacturing overhead	$10
Fixed manufacturing overhead costs (total).	$340,000
Selling and administrative costs:	
Variable.	15% of sales
Fixed (total)	$ 160,000

Zurgot regards all of its workers as full-time employees, and the company has a long-standing no-layoff policy. Furthermore, production is highly automated. Accordingly, the company includes its labour costs in its fixed manufacturing overhead. The tables sell for $400 each.

During the first month of operations, the following activity was recorded:

Units produced	4,000
Units sold.	3,200

Required:
1. Compute the unit product cost under
   a. Absorption costing.
   b. Variable costing.
2. Prepare an income statement for the month using absorption costing.
3. Prepare a contribution format income statement for the month using variable costing.
4. Assume that the company must obtain additional financing. As a member of top management, which of the statements that you have prepared in (2) and (3) above would you prefer to have with you when you negotiate with the bank? Why?
5. Reconcile the absorption costing and variable costing operating income figures in (2) and (3) above.

PROBLEM 8–13 Absorption and Variable Costing; Production Constant, Sales Fluctuate [LO1, LO2, LO3, LO4]

Leander Office Products Inc. produces and sells small storage and organizational products for office use. During the first month of operations, the products sold well. Andrea Leander, the owner of the company, was surprised to see a loss for the month on her income statement. This statement was prepared by a local bookkeeping service recommended to her by her bank manager. The statement follows:

LEANDER OFFICE PRODUCTS INC.		
Income Statement		
Sales (40,000 units)		$200,000
Variable expenses:		
Variable cost of goods sold*	$80,000	
Variable selling and administrative expenses	30,000	110,000
Contribution margin		90,000
Fixed expenses:		
Fixed manufacturing overhead	75,000	
Fixed selling and administrative expenses	20,000	95,000
Operating loss		$ (5,000)

*Consists of direct materials, direct labour, and variable manufacturing overhead.

Leander is discouraged over the loss shown for the month, particularly since she had planned to use the statement to encourage investors to purchase stock in the new company. A friend who is an accountant insists that the company should be using absorption costing rather than variable costing. He argues that if absorption costing had been used, the company would probably have reported a profit for the month.

Selected cost data relating to the product and to the first month of operations follow:

Units produced	50,000
Units sold	40,000
Variable costs per unit:	
Direct materials	$1.00
Direct labour	$0.80
Variable manufacturing overhead	$0.20
Variable selling and administrative expenses	$0.75

Required:
1. Complete the following.
   a. Compute the unit product cost under absorption costing.
   b. Redo the company's income statement for the month using absorption costing.
   c. Reconcile the variable and absorption costing operating income (loss) figures.
2. Was the accountant correct in suggesting that the company really earned a "profit" for the month? Explain.
3. During the second month of operations, the company again produced 50,000 units but sold 60,000 units. (Assume no change in total fixed costs.)

a. Prepare a contribution format income statement for the month using variable costing.

b. Prepare an income statement for the month using absorption costing.

c. Reconcile the variable costing and absorption costing operating income figures.

PROBLEM 8–14 Prepare and Reconcile Variable Costing Statements [LO1, LO2, LO3, LO4]
Audiophonics Limited manufactures and sells high-quality and durable ear buds for use with personal electronics that are custom moulded to each customer's ear. Cost data for the product follow:

Variable costs per unit:	
Direct materials..	$12
Direct labour...	24
Variable factory overhead..................................	8
Variable selling and administrative.....................	6
Total variable costs per unit...............................	$50
Fixed costs per month:	
Fixed manufacturing overhead............................	$240,000
Fixed selling and administrative.........................	180,000
Total fixed costs per month................................	$420,000

The product sells for $80 per unit. Production and sales data for May and June, the first two months of operations, are as follows:

	Units Produced	Units Sold
May	15,000	13,000
June..	15,000	17,000

Income statements prepared by the Accounting Department using absorption costing are presented below:

	May	June
Sales	$1,040,000	$1,360,000
Cost of goods sold:		
Beginning inventory......................................	0	120,000
Add cost of goods manufactured.....................	900,000	900,000
Goods available for sale................................	900,000	1,020,000
Less ending inventory...................................	120,000	0
Cost of goods sold.......................................	780,000	1,020,000
Gross margin	260,000	340,000
Selling and administrative expenses................	258,000	282,000
Operating income...	$ 2,000	$ 58,000

Required:
1. Determine the unit product cost under
    a. Absorption costing.
    b. Variable costing.
2. Prepare variable costing income statements for May and June using the contribution approach.
3. Reconcile the variable costing and absorption costing operating income figures.
4. The company's Accounting Department has determined the break-even point to be 14,000 units per month, computed as follows:

$$\frac{\text{Fixed cost per month}}{\text{Unit contribution margin}} = \frac{\$420,000}{\$30 \text{ per unit}} = 14,000 \text{ units}$$

On receiving this figure, the president commented, "There's something peculiar here. The controller says that the break-even point is 14,000 units per month. Yet we sold only 13,000 units in May, and the income statement we received showed a $2,000 profit. Which figure do we believe?" Prepare a brief explanation of what happened on the May income statement.

PROBLEM 8–15 Incentives Created by Absorption Costing; Ethics and the Manager [LO2, LO4]
Lydia Hartley, manager of UltraProducts' New Zealand Division, is trying to set the production schedule for the last quarter of the year. The New Zealand Division had planned to sell 100,000 units during the year, but current projections indicate sales will be only 78,000 units in total. By September 30, the following activity had been reported:

	Units
Inventory, January 1	0
Production	72,000
Sales	60,000
Inventory, September 30	12,000

Demand has been soft, and the sales forecast for the last quarter is only 18,000 units.

The division can rent warehouse space to store up to 30,000 units. The division should maintain a minimum inventory level of 1,500 units. Hartley is aware that production must be at least 6,000 units per quarter in order to retain a nucleus of key employees. Maximum production capacity is 45,000 units per quarter.

Due to the nature of the division's operations, fixed manufacturing overhead is a major element of product cost.

Required:
1. Assume that the division is using variable costing. How many units should be scheduled for production during the last quarter of the year? Show computations and explain your answer. Will the number of units scheduled for production affect the division's reported profit for the year? Explain.
2. Assume that the division is using absorption costing and that the divisional manager is given an annual bonus based on the division's operating income. If Hartley wants to maximize her division's operating income for the year, how many units should be scheduled for production during the last quarter? Explain.
3. Identify the ethical issues involved in the decision Hartley must make about the level of production for the last quarter of the year.

PROBLEM 8–16 Comparison of Costing Methods [LO1, LO2, LO3, LO4]
Canada Brewers Ltd. has just created a new division to manufacture and sell single-cup coffee makers under licence from a major single-cup coffee producer. The facility is highly automated and so has high monthly fixed costs, as shown in the following schedule of budgeted monthly costs. This schedule was prepared based on an expectation of a monthly production volume of 1,500 units.

During August, the following activity was recorded:

Units produced	1,500
Units sold	1,200
Selling price per unit	$55
Manufacturing costs:	
Variable cost per unit:	
Direct material	$10
Direct labour	8
Variable overhead	4
Total fixed overhead	$30,000
Selling and administrative costs:	
Variable	5% of sales
Fixed	8,000

Required:
1. Prepare an income statement for the month ended August 31, under absorption costing.
2. Prepare an income statement for the month ended August 31, under variable costing.
3. Beginning with absorption costing, reconcile the absorption costing and variable costing income figures for the month.
4. What are some of the arguments in favour of using variable costing? What are some of the arguments in favour of using absorption costing?

(CGA-Canada adapted)

PROBLEM 8-17 Comparison of Costing Methods [LO1, LO2, LO3, LO4]
The following information relates to Mucktar Ltd. during the first quarter of 2015:

	January	February	March
Unit sales...	12,000	14,000	18,000
Sales price per unit......................................	$12	$12	$12
Variable manufacturing cost per unit....................	5	5	5
Variable selling expense	2	2	2
Unit production..	15,000	18,000	13,000

Additional data:
a. On January 1, there were 2,000 units on hand.
b. Fixed overhead cost is $3.00 per unit and is applied to units of product on the basis of a production volume of 14,000 units per month. Costs of goods sold is adjusted for any overapplied or underapplied fixed manufacturing overhead.
c. Mucktar Ltd. uses FIFO inventory flow. Work in process inventories are not material and are to be ignored.
d. Fixed selling and administrative expenses total $22,000 per month.

Required:
1. Prepare quarterly income statements using
   a. Absorption costing.
   b. Variable costing.
2. Explain why, under absorption costing, monthly profits have moved erratically over the quarter and have not moved in correlation with changes in sales volume. Include a reconciliation of absorption and variable costing in your answer.
3. Identify the advantages and disadvantages of using variable costing for internal reporting purposes.

(CGA-Canada adapted)

PROBLEM 8-18 Prepare and Interpret Statements; Changes in Both Sales and Production; Lean Production [LO1, LO2, LO3, LO4]

ElectronPlus manufactures and sells a unique electronic part. Operating results for the first three years of activity were as follows (absorption costing basis):

	Year 1	Year 2	Year 3
Sales..	$1,000,000	$800,000	$1,000,000
Cost of goods sold:			
Beginning inventory..	0	0	280,000
Add cost of goods manufactured...............................	800,000	840,000	760,000
Goods available for sale	800,000	840,000	1,040,000
Less ending inventory..	0	280,000	190,000
Cost of goods sold...	800,000	560,000	850,000
Gross margin	200,000	240,000	150,000
Selling and administrative expenses	170,000	150,000	170,000
Operating income (loss)......................................	$ 30,000	$ 90,000	$ (20,000)

Sales dropped by 20% during year 2 due to the entry of several foreign competitors into the market. ElectronPlus had expected sales to remain constant at 50,000 units for the year; production was set at 60,000 units in order to build a buffer against unexpected spurts in demand. By the start of year 3, management could see that spurts in demand were unlikely and that the inventory was excessive. To work off the excessive inventories, ElectronPlus cut back production during year 3, as shown below:

	Year 1	Year 2	Year 3
Production in units	50,000	60,000	40,000
Sales in units	50,000	40,000	50,000

Additional information about the company follows:

a. The company's plant is highly automated. Variable manufacturing costs (direct materials, direct labour, and variable manufacturing overhead) total only $4 per unit, and fixed manufacturing overhead costs total $600,000 per year.

b. Fixed manufacturing overhead costs are applied to units of product on the basis of each year's planned production. (That is, a new fixed overhead rate is computed each year, as in Exhibit 8–5.)

c. Variable selling and administrative expenses are $2 per unit sold. Fixed selling and administrative expenses total $70,000 per year.

d. The company uses a FIFO inventory flow assumption.

Management of ElectronPlus can't understand why profits tripled during year 2 when sales dropped by 20%, and why a loss was incurred during year 3 when sales recovered to previous levels.

Required:
1. Prepare a contribution format income statement for each year using variable costing.
2. Refer to the absorption costing income statements above.
    a. Compute the unit product cost in each year under absorption costing. (Show how much of this cost is variable and how much is fixed.)
    b. Reconcile the variable costing and absorption costing operating income figures for each year.
3. Refer again to the absorption costing income statements. Explain why operating income was higher in year 2 than it was in year 1 under the absorption approach, in light of the fact that fewer units were sold in year 2 than in year 1.
4. Refer again to the absorption costing income statements. Explain why the company suffered a loss in year 3 but reported a profit in year 1, although the same number of units was sold in each year.
5. a. Explain how operations would have differed in year 2 and year 3 if the company had been using lean production, with the result that ending inventory was zero.
    b. If lean production had been in use during year 2 and year 3, what would the company's operating income (or loss) have been in each year under absorption costing? Explain the reason for any differences between these income figures and the figures reported by the company in the statements above.

CASES

CASE 8–19 Absorption Costing and Ethics [LO1, LO2, LO3, LO4]
"There must be something wrong with these statements!" exclaimed Hugh Richards, president of Ajax Inc. "They just don't make sense. We sold the same number of units this year as we did last year, yet our profits have tripled! Who messed up the calculations?"

Ajax Inc. is a medium-sized supplier of plastic components to the automobile industry and has been in business for 25 years. Sales forecasting has been relatively easy to do in the past since Ajax has had long-term, single-sourcing relationships with most of its customers.

In 2015, however, there was a threat of a strike at one of Ajax Inc.'s major raw materials suppliers. For that reason, Ajax management decided to purchase more raw materials and produce more components in 2015 than actually required, in anticipation of raw materials shortages in 2016. Manufacturing equipment was typically operated below capacity, so this boost in production was possible without incurring significant increased fixed manufacturing costs. The income statement and production reports to which Richards was referring are shown below:

	2014	2015
Sales (40,000 units each year)	$1,250,000	$1,250,000
Cost of goods sold	840,000	720,000
Gross margin	410,000	530,000
Selling and administrative expenses	350,000	350,000
Operating income	$ 60,000	$ 180,000

	2014	2015
Production in units	40,000	50,000
Sales in units	40,000	40,000
Variable manufacturing cost per unit produced	$6	$6
Variable selling and administrative expense per unit sold	$2	$2
Fixed manufacturing overhead costs (total)	$ 600,000	$600,000

Ajax Inc. uses absorption costing and applies fixed manufacturing overhead costs to its only product on the basis of each year's production. (Thus, a new fixed manufacturing overhead rate is computed each year, as in Exhibit 8–5.)

Required:
Take on the role of the CFO of Ajax Inc. Write a memo to Richards to explain why the operating income for 2015 was higher than for 2014 under absorption costing, although the same number of units was sold in each year. Make sure to include the following:
1.   A contribution format income statement for each year, using variable costing. Be sure to reconcile the variable costing and absorption costing operating income figures for each year.
2.   A brief discussion of the advantages and disadvantages of variable over absorption costing for internal reporting purposes.
3.   A discussion of the ramifications of returning to the "normal" level of production in the coming year.
4.   A recommendation: Should the company continue to "overproduce" in coming years to boost operating income?

CASE 8–20 Ethics and the Manager; Absorption Costing Income Statements [LO2, LO4]

Michael Lee was hired as chief executive officer (CEO) in late November by the board of directors of Hunter Electronics, a company that produces a state-of-the-art DVD drive for personal computers. The previous CEO was fired by the board due to a series of questionable business practices, including prematurely recording revenues on products that had not yet been shipped to customers.

Lee felt that his first priority on the job was to restore employee morale—which had suffered during the previous CEO's reign. He was particularly anxious to build a sense of trust between himself and the company's employees. His second priority was to prepare the budget for the coming year, which the board of directors wanted to review at their December 15 meeting.

After hammering out the details in meetings with key managers, Lee was able to put together a budget that he felt the company could realistically meet during the coming year. That budget appears below:

BASIC BUDGET DATA

Units in beginning inventory.	0
Units produced.	200,000
Units sold	200,000
Units in ending inventory	0
Variable costs per unit:	
Direct materials	$ 50
Direct labour	40
Variable manufacturing overhead	20
Variable selling and administrative	10
Total variable costs per unit.	$120
Fixed costs:	
Fixed manufacturing overhead	$ 8,400,000
Fixed selling and administrative	3,600,000
Total fixed costs	$12,000,000

HUNTER ELECTRONICS
Budgeted Income Statement
(Absorption Method)

Sales (200,000 units)		$40,000,000
Cost of goods sold:		
Beginning inventory	$ 0	
Add cost of goods manufactured (200,000 × $152 per unit)	30,400,000	
Goods available for sale	30,400,000	
Less ending inventory	0	30,400,000
Gross margin		9,600,000
Selling and administrative expenses:		
Variable selling and administrative	2,000,000	
Fixed selling and administrative	3,600,000	5,600,000
Operating income		$ 4,000,000

While the board of directors did not oppose the budget, they made it clear that the budget was not as ambitious as they had hoped. The most influential member of the board said, "Managers should have to really stretch to meet profit goals." After some discussion, the board decided to set a profit goal of $4,800,000 for the coming year. To provide strong incentives and a win–win situation, the board agreed to pay bonuses to top managers from a bonus pool of $200,000 if this profit goal was eventually met. Lee's share of the bonus pool would be $50,000. The bonus would be all-or-nothing: if actual operating income turned out to be $4,800,000 or more, the bonus would be paid; otherwise, no bonus would be allowed.

Required:
1. Assuming that the company does not build up its inventory (i.e., production equals sales) and its selling price and cost structure remain the same, how many units of the DVD drive would have to be sold to meet the target operating income of $4,800,000?
2. Verify your answer to (1) above by constructing a revised budget and budgeted absorption costing income statement that yields an operating income of $4,800,000.
3. Unfortunately, by October of the next year, it became clear that the company would not be able to make the $4,800,000 target profit. In fact, it looked like the company would wind up the year as originally planned, with sales of 200,000 units, no ending inventories, and a profit of $4,000,000.

   Several managers who were reluctant to lose their year-end bonuses approached Lee and suggested that the company could still show a profit of $4,800,000. The managers argued that at the current rate of sales, there was enough capacity to produce tens of thousands of additional DVD drives for the warehouse. Overtime costs might have to be incurred, but all of this additional cost would be assigned to the DVD drives in ending inventory.

If sales are 200,000 units for the year and the selling price and cost structure remain the same, how many units would have to be produced to show a profit of at least $4,800,000 under absorption costing? (Round your answer up to the nearest whole unit.)

4. Verify your answer to (3) above by constructing an absorption costing income statement.
5. Do you think Lee should approve the plan to build ending inventories in order to attain the target profit?
6. What advice would you give to the board of directors concerning how they determine bonuses in the future?

CASE 8–21 The Case of the Perplexed President; Lean Production [LO2, LO3, LO4]

John Ovard, president of Mylar Inc., is looking forward to receiving the company's second-quarter income statement. He knows that the sales budget of 20,000 units sold was met during the second quarter and that this represented a 25% increase in sales over the first quarter. He is especially happy about the increase in sales, since Mylar is about to approach its bank for additional loan money for expansion purposes. He anticipates that the strong second-quarter results will be a real plus in persuading the bank to extend the additional credit.

For this reason, Ovard is shocked when he receives the second-quarter income statement below, which shows a substantial drop in absorption costing operating income from the first quarter:

MYLAR INC. Income Statements For the First Two Quarters	First Quarter		Second Quarter	
Sales...		$1,600,000		$2,000,000
Cost of goods sold:				
Beginning inventory...........................	$ 210,000		$ 490,000	
Add cost of goods manufactured..............	1,400,000		980,000	
Goods available for sale......................	1,610,000		1,470,000	
Less ending inventory........................	490,000		70,000	
Cost of goods sold...........................	1,120,000		1,400,000	
Add underapplied overhead..................	0	1,120,000	240,000	1,640,000
Gross margin....................................		480,000		360,000
Selling and administrative expenses..............		310,000		330,000
Operating income...............................		$ 170,000		$ 30,000

Ovard is certain there is an error somewhere and immediately calls the controller into his office to find the problem. The controller states, "That operating income is correct, John. Sales went up during the second quarter, but the problem is in production. You see, we budgeted to produce 20,000 units each quarter, but a strike in one of our supplier's plants forced us to cut production back to only 14,000 units in the second quarter. That's what caused the drop in operating income."

Ovard is angered by the controller's explanation. "I call you in here to find out why income dropped when sales went up, and you talk about production! So what if production was off? What does that have to do with the sales that we made? If sales go up, then income ought to go up. If your statements can't show a simple thing like that, then we're due for some changes in your area!"

Budgeted production and sales for the year, along with actual production and sales for the first two quarters, are given below:

	Quarter			
	First	Second	Third	Fourth
Budgeted sales (units).........................	16,000	20,000	20,000	24,000
Actual sales (units).............................	16,000	20,000	—	—
Budgeted production (units)....................	20,000	20,000	20,000	20,000
Actual production (units).......................	20,000	14,000	—	—

The company's plant is heavily automated, so fixed manufacturing overhead costs total $800,000 per quarter. Variable manufacturing costs are $30 per unit. The fixed manufacturing overhead cost is applied to units of product at the rate of $40 per unit (based on the budgeted production shown above). Any underapplied or overapplied overhead is closed directly to cost of goods sold for the quarter.

The company had 3,000 units in inventory to start the first quarter and uses the FIFO inventory flow assumption. Variable selling and administrative expenses are $5 per unit sold.

Required:
1. What characteristic of absorption costing caused the drop in operating income for the second quarter, and what could the controller have said to explain the problem?
2. Prepare a contribution format income statement for each quarter, using variable costing.
3. Reconcile the absorption costing and the variable costing operating income figures for each quarter.
4. Identify and discuss the advantages and disadvantages of using the variable costing method for internal reporting purposes.
5. Assume that the company had introduced lean production methods at the beginning of the second quarter, resulting in zero ending inventory. (Sales and production during the first quarter were as shown above.)
   a. How many units would have been produced during the second quarter under lean production?
   b. Starting with the third quarter, would you expect any difference between the operating income reported under absorption costing and under variable costing? Explain why there would or would not be any difference.

CASE 8–22 Overproduction and Absorption Costing [LO2, LO3, LO4]
It is December 15 and Jane Jones, the plant manager at Acme Electric Fan Co., faces a difficult decision. The operation has been running steadily over the last 11 months. During that time, Jane worked with the production engineers to tweak the production machinery just enough to allow for a small increase in available capacity. The plant produced 18,000 fans between January and the end of November and is scheduled to produce 2,000 fans in the month of December. The sales manager indicates that all 20,000 fans will be sold by the end of the year. Jane realizes the extra investment in engineering costs will allow the plant to produce an extra 500 fans in December. Cost and pricing information are provided below:

Variable costs per unit:	
Raw material	$3
Direct labour	$2
Variable production costs	$1
Variable selling expenses	$1
Fixed manufacturing costs	$61,500
Beginning inventory	–0–
Selling price per unit	$12

Inventory holding costs are negligible, and customers have been known to place unexpected special orders that are typically difficult to fill. Jane figures a small safety stock of 500 fans would provide a cushion against future special orders. Even so, Jane is torn about the decision to produce the 500 additional fans. Her performance is evaluated mainly by the profit generated by the plant. In addition, her year-end bonus is based on profitability of the plant. Jane is worried that incurring the extra costs will have a negative effect on plant profitability.

Required:
Take on the role of the plant accountant and provide Jane with the analysis she needs to make an informed decision. Assuming the company utilizes absorption costing, analyze the effect of producing the additional 500 fans on plant profitability and on Jane's bonus, and recommend a course of action.

INSTANT QUIZ SOLUTIONS

8-1
Selling and administrative expenses are treated as period costs under absorption costing as well as under variable costing.

8-2
Inventory increased. The increase resulted in fixed manufacturing overhead cost being charged to ending inventory on the balance sheet. This reduced fixed manufacturing overhead cost, resulting in a profit even though the company operated at its break-even level of sales.

8-3
Under variable costing, *revenue* drives operating income, while under absorption costing, *revenue* and *production* drive operating income.

8-4
Under absorption costing, fixed manufacturing overhead costs are included in product costs, along with direct materials, direct labour, and variable manufacturing overhead. If some of the units are not sold by the end of the period, then they are carried into the next period as inventory. The fixed manufacturing overhead cost attached to the units in ending inventory follows the units into the next period. When the units are finally sold, the fixed manufacturing overhead cost that has been carried over with the units is included as part of that period's cost of goods sold.

8-5
Absorption costing advocates believe that absorption costing does a better job of matching costs with revenues than variable costing. They argue that all manufacturing costs must be assigned to products to properly match the costs of producing units of product with the revenues from the units when they are sold. They believe that no distinction should be made between variable and fixed manufacturing costs for matching costs and revenues.

■ connect   ■ LEARNSMART   ■ SMARTBOOK™

For more information on the resources available from McGraw-Hill Ryerson, go to www.mheducation.ca/he/solutions.

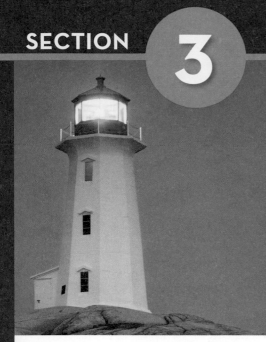

PLANNING AND CONTROL

Chapters 9, 10, and 11

Every organization needs to plan on a regular basis. **Chapter 9** describes the steps by which plans are translated into a master budget that can be used to allocate resources and coordinate activities across functional areas within the organization. To evaluate whether the plan is being achieved, many organizations employ a system of detailed performance standards, using the same reporting structure as the budgets presented in Chapter 9 and using one of the costing approaches described in Section 2.

Standard costing, described in **Chapter 10**, is an example of a tool that managers can use to monitor and control cost performance. Chapter 10 also applies the concept of flexible budgeting (introduced in Chapter 9) to overhead costs, which for many companies is now a major expense.

Chapter 11 completes our discussion of the approaches used by managers to control operations by introducing the concept of responsibility centres, which involves identifying subunits within the organization whose managers have well-defined control over costs, profits, and investment funds. In large organizations, responsibility centres often supply goods and services to each other, and Chapter 11 explores the pricing of these transactions. Key metrics used to evaluate the performance of responsibility centres are also presented in Chapter 11, as is the concept of the balanced scorecard, which incorporates both financial and non-financial measures.

BUDGETING

◼ BUDGETING BENEFITS

Most companies prepare budgets, regardless of their size or the nature of their business operations. As a quantified financial plan for the future, budgets are used internally by management and may also be used by parties external to the company, such as lenders. Manufacturing companies, merchandising companies, service businesses, and even government and not-for-profit organizations all apply the budgeting techniques described in this chapter to varying degrees. They do so because tangible benefits can result from preparing budgets and using them as a benchmark for evaluating actual performance throughout the year.

Recall our discussion of The Lawn Guy Limited from Chapter 2. The Lawn Guy Limited is a privately owned landscaping company based in Nova Scotia. Preparing a budget for the upcoming fiscal year will help the company's owner, Stephen Kamperman, in a number of ways. First, by budgeting revenues for landscaping services, Stephen will have a good idea of the resources required (and the related expenses) for the budgeted level of activity. In particular, he will be able to estimate the number of employees required to meet the demand for his company's services. For example, growth in the overall demand for his company's services may result in Stephen needing to hire additional employees. Second, developing a budget will help Stephen determine the resources needed for the different parts of his business. If relatively high growth is budgeted for lawn care services, he needs to make sure he has enough equipment, such as lawn mowers, to meet the demand. Third, quantifying in financial terms the budgeted revenues and related expenses for the upcoming year will give Stephen a clear picture of the expected profitability of his business. If he isn't satisfied with the anticipated level of profit, he can identify ways of making improvements, such as increasing advertising to generate more demand or finding ways to reduce costs. Finally, and often critical for small businesses, budgeting revenues and expenses will allow Stephen to estimate cash inflows and outflows for the coming year. This will allow him to make arrangements in advance with his bank to ensure he has access to short-term loans to cover any budgeted shortfalls in cash flow.

The above example provides a glimpse of how even small companies can benefit from budgeting, but numerous topics related to the preparation and use of budgets are important to consider. Who should participate in setting the budgets? How are the budget estimates determined? How is actual performance evaluated in comparison to the budget? These issues, along with others, are examined in this chapter.

Source: Discussions with Stephen Kamperman, owner of The Lawn Guy Limited.

Budgets are an important tool used by management to communicate financial objectives for the future, allocate resources, and coordinate activities across the different functional areas within the organization. Budgets can also be an important tool used by managers to periodically compare actual performance of revenues, expenses, and profits to the plan. When actual results are significantly better or worse than those in the budget, management will seek explanations as to the causes and take corrective action when necessary. In this chapter, we focus on the major steps involved in preparing budgets as well as some of the issues that influence how managers use and respond to budgets.

THE BASIC FRAMEWORK OF BUDGETING

Definition of Budgeting

A budget is a detailed plan for the future that is typically expressed in quantitative terms. The act of preparing a budget is called *budgeting*. The use of budgets to control a firm's activities is known as *budgetary control.*

The **master budget** summarizes a company's plans, setting specific targets for sales, production, distribution, administrative, and financing activities. It generally culminates in a cash budget, a budgeted income statement, and a budgeted balance sheet. In short, it represents a comprehensive financial expression of management's plans for the future and how these plans are to be accomplished.

Master budget
A summary of a company's plans in which specific targets are set for sales, production, distribution, administrative, and financing activities; it generally culminates in a cash budget, a budgeted income statement, and a budgeted balance sheet.

Budgets' Dual Role: Planning and Control

Budgets serve as both a planning tool and a control tool in organizations. Planning involves developing objectives and preparing various budgets to achieve these objectives. Control involves gathering feedback to assess the extent to which the objectives developed at the planning stage are being attained. An effective budgeting system provides for *both* planning and control. Good planning without effective control is time wasted.

Advantages of Budgeting

Organizations realize many benefits from budgets, including the following:

1. Budgets communicate management's plans throughout the organization, leading to a better understanding by all employees of the organization's goals and objectives.
2. Budgets force managers to *think about* and *plan for* the future. Without a budget, many managers would spend considerable time dealing with day-to-day emergencies.
3. The budgeting process provides a means of *allocating resources* to those parts of the organization where they can be used most effectively and are most needed.
4. The budgeting process can uncover potential **bottlenecks** before they occur, by identifying the demands that will be placed on key activities and processes. If necessary, changes can be made to any activity or process that does not currently have the capability or capacity to meet the budgeted level of activity on a timely basis.
5. Budgets *coordinate* the activities of the entire organization by *integrating* the plans of the various areas. Budgeting helps to ensure that everyone in the organization is pulling in the same direction.
6. Budgets define goals and objectives that can serve as *benchmarks* for evaluating subsequent actual performance. Periodic comparison of actual results to budgeted amounts allows management to determine whether the organization's goals are being met and to take corrective action as necessary.

Bottlenecks
Machines, activities, or processes that limit total output because they are operating at capacity.

Responsibility Accounting

Most of what we say in this chapter and in the next two chapters is concerned with *responsibility accounting*. The basic idea behind **responsibility accounting** is that managers should be held responsible for those items—and *only* those items—that they can actually influence to a significant extent. Each revenue or cost item in the budget is the responsibility of a manager who is held responsible for subsequent deviations between budgeted goals and actual results. In effect, responsibility accounting *personalizes* accounting information by holding individuals responsible for revenues and costs. This concept is central to any effective profit planning and control system. Someone must be held responsible for each cost or else no one will be responsible, and the cost may grow out of control.

Being held responsible for costs does not mean that the manager is penalized if the actual results do not measure up to the budgeted goals. However, the manager should take the initiative to correct any unfavourable discrepancies, should understand the source of significant favourable or unfavourable discrepancies, and should be prepared to explain discrepancies to top management. The point of an effective responsibility system is to make sure that nothing falls through the cracks and that the organization reacts quickly and appropriately to deviations from its plans and learns from the feedback it gets by comparing budgeted goals to actual results.

Choosing a Budget Period

Operating budgets ordinarily cover a one-year period corresponding to the company's fiscal year. Many companies divide their budget year into four quarters. The first quarter is then subdivided into months, and monthly budget figures are established. The last three quarters are carried in the budget at quarterly totals only. As the year progresses, the figures for the second quarter are broken down into monthly amounts, then the third-quarter figures are broken down, and so forth. This approach has the advantage of requiring periodic review of budget data throughout the year.

Continuous or *perpetual budgets* are used by many organizations. A **continuous or perpetual budget** is a 12-month budget that rolls forward one month (or quarter) as the current month (or quarter) is completed. In other words, one month (or quarter) is added to the end of the budget as each month (or quarter) comes to a close. This approach always keeps managers focused at least one year ahead so that they do not become too narrowly fixated on short-term results.

In this chapter, we will focus on one-year operating budgets. However, using basically the same techniques, operating budgets can be prepared for periods that extend over many years. It may be difficult to accurately forecast sales and expenses much beyond a year, but even rough estimates can help identify potential problems and opportunities that might otherwise be overlooked.

The Participative Budget

The success of a budget program is determined in large part by the way the budget is developed. The most successful budget programs allow managers to participate in preparing their own budget estimates—rather than having a budget imposed from above. This **participative budget** approach is particularly important if the budget is to be used to control and evaluate a manager's activities. If a budget is imposed on a manager from above, it may generate resentment rather than cooperation and increased productivity. Exhibit 9–1 illustrates this approach to budget preparation.

Participative budgets have a number of advantages:

1. Individuals at all levels of the organization are recognized as members of the team whose views and judgments are valued by top management.
2. Budget estimates prepared by front-line managers are often more accurate and reliable than estimates prepared by top managers, who have less detailed knowledge of market factors and day-to-day operations.

Responsibility accounting
A system of accountability in which managers are held responsible for those items of revenue and cost over which they can exert significant influence—and only those items. Managers are held responsible for differences between budgeted and actual results.

Continuous or perpetual budget
A 12-month budget that rolls forward one month (or quarter) as the current month (or quarter) is completed.

Participative budget
A method of preparing budgets in which managers prepare their own budget estimates. These budget estimates are then reviewed by the manager's supervisor, and any issues are resolved by mutual agreement, leading to a completed budget.

EXHIBIT 9-1   The Initial Flow of Budget Data in a Participative Budgeting System

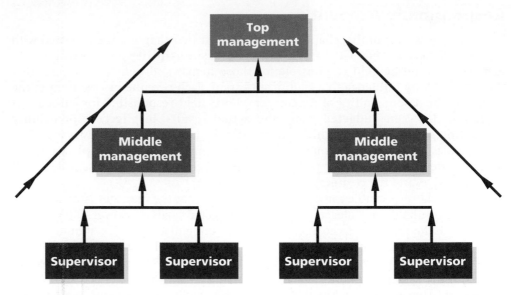

The initial flow of budget data in a participative system is from lower levels of responsibility to higher levels of responsibility. Each person with responsibility for revenue or cost items will prepare his or her own budget estimates and submit them to the next higher level of management. These estimates are reviewed and consolidated as they move upward in the organization.

3. Motivation is generally higher when individuals participate in setting their own goals than when the goals are imposed from above. Participative budgets create commitment to attaining the goal.
4. A manager who is not able to meet a budget that has been imposed from above can always say that the budget was unrealistic and impossible to meet. With a participative budget, this excuse is not available.

Budget estimates prepared by lower-level managers cannot necessarily be accepted without review by higher levels of management. If no review system is present, participative budgets may allow too much **budgetary slack**. Slack is the difference between the revenues and expenses a manager really believes can be achieved and the amounts included in the budget. Revenue budgets that are intentionally set at lower than expected levels and expense budgets that are set at higher than expected levels are said to contain slack.[1] Managers may attempt to create slack to increase the likelihood of obtaining rewards that are contingent on meeting or beating the budget or to reduce how hard they have to work during the period to attain their budgets. Slack can result in the misallocation of resources, inefficiencies, waste, and less effort by managers. Therefore, before budgets are accepted, they must be carefully reviewed by the manager's immediate superior. If changes from the original budget seem desirable, the items in question are discussed and modified as necessary by the mutual consent of the managers and their superiors.

All levels of an organization should work together to produce the budget. Since top management is generally unfamiliar with detailed day-to-day operations, it should rely on subordinates to provide detailed budget information. On the other hand, top management has a broader perspective on the goals for the company as a whole that is vital to budget preparation. Each level of responsibility in an organization should contribute in a *cooperative* effort to develop an integrated and realistic budget.

In an effort to ensure an effective budgeting process, many companies use a **budget committee**. This committee is typically responsible for overall policy matters related to the budget program and for coordinating the preparation of the budget itself. Committee membership usually consists of the president or CEO, heads of functional areas (e.g., sales, production, purchasing), and the

Budgetary slack
The difference between the revenues and expenses a manager believes can actually be achieved and the amounts included in the budget. Slack will exist when revenue budgets are intentionally set below expected levels and expense budgets are set above expected levels.

Budget committee
A group of key management personnel responsible for overall policy matters related to the budget program, coordinating the preparation of the budget, handling disputes related to the budget, and approving the final budget.

IN BUSINESS

A survey of 720 members of the Institute of Management Accountants yielded some interesting insights into corporate budgeting practices. About 70% of the respondents indicated that budget development occurs via a participative process, whereby the final budget is the result of negotiations between higher-level and lower-level managers. The majority of respondents also indicated that positive behavioural consequences of the budget development process include the support of continuous improvement processes, the provision of information that allows managers to react to changes in the operating environment, and better information sharing among business units. Also, contrary to some common criticisms of budgeting, most respondents did not believe that budgets cause managers to focus on short-term results or create undue pressure for employees to achieve performance targets. The survey results also showed that budgeting is not a stand-alone process but instead is often integrated with other management practices. For example, of the respondents using activity-based costing, 75% integrate it with the annual budgeting process.

Source: Reproduced with permission of INSTITUTE OF MANAGEMENT ACCOUNTANTS, from Karen Shastri and David Stout, "Budgeting: Perspectives from the Real World," *Management Accounting Quarterly*, Fall 2008, pp. 18–25; permission conveyed through Copyright Clearance Center, Inc.

controller. The budget committee handles any disagreements or problems that arise during the budgeting process, such as those between lower-level managers and their superiors when budget reviews are being conducted. Importantly, the budget committee also approves the final budget and receives periodic progress reports regarding the company's success in meeting its targets.

Despite the advantages of participative budgets, some companies still assign budgets to their employees. The process of assigning (or imposing) budgets is often more efficient since it typically does not involve negotiations or discussions between managers and subordinates, which can take a considerable amount of time and effort. Moreover, in some circumstances, management may assign tough budgets to employees in the belief that attaining the budgets is necessary for the company's survival. Since employees are often unwilling to set highly challenging goals for themselves, imposing budgets may be deemed necessary for the sake of the long-term viability of the company.

Behavioural Factors in Budgeting

Whether or not a budget program is accepted by lower management personnel will be reflective of the degree to which top management accepts the budget program as a vital part of the company's activities, and how top management uses budgeted data. If a budget program is to be successful, it must have the complete acceptance and support of the people who occupy key management positions. If lower- or middle-management personnel sense that top management simply tolerates budgeting as a necessary evil, then their own attitudes will reflect a similar lack of enthusiasm. If top management is not enthusiastic about and committed to the budget program, then it is unlikely that anyone else in the organization will be either.

In administering the budget program, it is particularly important that top management not use the budget to pressure or blame employees. Using budgets in such negative ways will breed hostility, tension, and mistrust rather than cooperation and productivity. Unfortunately, the budget is too often used as a pressure device, and excessive emphasis is placed on "meeting the budget" under all circumstances. Rather than being used as a weapon, the budget should be used as a positive instrument to assist in establishing goals, measuring operating results, and identifying areas that need attention.

IN BUSINESS

Many companies give employees cash bonuses for meeting or beating budget targets, but, increasingly, non-cash bonuses are being provided instead. Non-cash rewards take a variety of forms, including merchandise such as electronics, household items (e.g., barbecues, coffee makers), and sporting goods. Other companies provide non-cash rewards in the form of gift cards to allow employees more choice in what they will receive for attaining their budget targets. Interestingly, research shows that the type of reward (cash versus non-cash) influences how committed individuals will be to attaining their budget target and the difficulty level of the target they will set for themselves when allowed to participate in the budgeting process. For example, one recent study shows that employees eligible for non-cash rewards were more committed to attaining their budget targets than those eligible for cash rewards. However, employees eligible for non-cash rewards also set less challenging budget targets, in part to increase the likelihood of receiving the non-cash rewards, which they viewed as more attractive than cash rewards of equal value.

Source: Adam Presslee, Thomas Vance, and Alan Webb, "The Effect of Reward Type on Employee Goal Selection, Goal Commitment and Performance," *The Accounting Review*, 2013, pp. 1805–1831.

The human aspects of budgeting are extremely important. The remainder of the chapter deals with technical aspects of budgeting, but do not lose sight of the human aspects. The purpose of the budget is to motivate people and to coordinate their efforts. This purpose is undermined if managers become preoccupied with the technical aspects, or if the budget is used in a rigid and inflexible manner to control people.

A key issue related to the motivational aspect of budgets is the difficulty level of the budget targets. If the targets are too difficult, employees will quickly recognize that they are unattainable, and motivation and morale will suffer. If the targets are too easy, inefficiencies or less effort will result. Some experts argue that budget targets should be highly challenging and should require managers to stretch to meet them. A **stretch budget** is one that is highly difficult to attain and often requires significant changes to the way the related activities are performed. However, in practice, most companies set their budget targets at a "challenging but attainable" level.[2] Such targets can usually be met by competent managers exerting reasonable effort and are usually more motivating than stretch budgets.

Stretch budget
A budget that is highly difficult to achieve. Attainment of stretch budgets often requires considerable changes to the way activities are performed.

The difficulty level of budget targets becomes even more important when managers' bonuses are based on meeting or exceeding the budget. Under these commonly employed compensation schemes, a bonus is paid only if the budget is met. The bonus often increases when the budget target is exceeded, but it is usually capped at some maximum level. For obvious reasons, managers who work under such a bonus plan, or whose performance is evaluated based on meeting budget targets, usually prefer to have challenging but attainable budgets rather than stretch budgets. Moreover, highly achievable budgets may help build a manager's confidence and generate greater commitment to the budget and to the organization more generally. Finally, challenging but achievable budgets may result in less undesirable behaviour at the end of a budgetary period, such as excessive cost reductions by managers, since they will not have to struggle to meet their targets.

Zero-Base Budgeting

In the traditional approach to budgeting described in this chapter, the manager uses last year's budget and actual results as a basis for the current year's budget, making adjustments to revenues and costs based on anticipated changes in the operating environment. This is an incremental approach to budgeting in which the previous year's budget and actual results are used as a baseline.

Zero-base budgeting is an alternative approach used particularly in the government and not-for-profit sectors of the economy. Under a **zero-base budget**, managers are required to justify *all* budgeted expenditures, not just changes in the budget from the previous year. The baseline is zero rather than last year's budget. As a result, zero-base budgets can be an effective means of identifying operational inefficiencies and reducing costs dramatically.

The key problem with zero-base budgets is that they require considerable time and effort to prepare, so an important issue for companies that use this approach is deciding the frequency of the zero-base review. Critics argue that properly executed zero-base budgeting is too time-consuming and costly to justify on an annual basis. In addition, critics argue that annual reviews can become mechanical, limiting the benefits of zero-base budgeting. Whether a company should use an annual review is a matter of judgment. However, most managers agree that, on occasion, zero-base reviews can be very helpful.

Zero-base budget
A method of budgeting in which managers are required to justify all costs as if the activities involved were being proposed for the first time.

THE MASTER BUDGET: AN OVERVIEW

The master budget consists of a number of separate but interdependent budgets. Exhibit 9–2 is an overview of the various parts of the master budget and how they are related. Preparing a master budget for a manufacturing company is somewhat more complex than for other types of organizations (e.g., service companies, merchandising companies), so we focus on that setting in the example below. However, many of the steps described below for developing sales budgets, selling and administrative budgets, cash budgets, and so on, follow a similar approach regardless of the type of organization. To provide some variety in the examples, we use a merchandising company for the master budget review problem included at the end of the chapter.

LEARNING OBJECTIVE 2
Prepare the supporting components of a master budget and the budgeted financial statements.

The Sales Budget   A **sales budget** is a detailed schedule showing the expected sales for the budget period; typically, it is expressed in both dollars and units of product. An accurate sales budget is the key to the entire budgeting process. All of the other parts of the master budget depend on the sales budget in some way, as illustrated in Exhibit 9–2. So, if the sales budget is inaccurate, the rest of the budget will be inaccurate.

The sales budget helps determine how many units must be produced by manufacturing companies. For this reason, the production budget is prepared after the sales budget for manufacturing companies. The production budget in turn is used to determine the budgets for manufacturing costs, including the direct materials purchases budget, the direct labour budget, and the manufacturing overhead budget. These budgets are then combined with data from the sales budget and the selling and administrative expense budget to determine the cash budget. As shown in Exhibit 9–2, the selling and administrative expense budget is both dependent on and a determinant of the sales budget. This reciprocal relationship arises because sales will in part be determined by the funds committed for advertising and sales promotion.

Sales budget
A detailed schedule showing the expected sales for coming periods; these sales are typically expressed in both dollars and units.

The Cash Budget   Once the operating budgets (sales, production, etc.) have been established, the cash budget and other financial budgets can be prepared. A **cash budget** is a detailed plan that shows how cash resources will be acquired and used over some specified time period. Observe from Exhibit 9–2 that all of the operating budgets have an impact on the cash budget. In the case of the sales budget, the impact comes from the planned cash receipts to be received from sales. In the case of the other budgets, the impact comes from the planned cash expenditures within the budgets themselves.

Cash budget
A detailed plan showing how cash resources will be acquired and used over a specified time period.

EXHIBIT 9-2   The Master
Budget Interrelationships

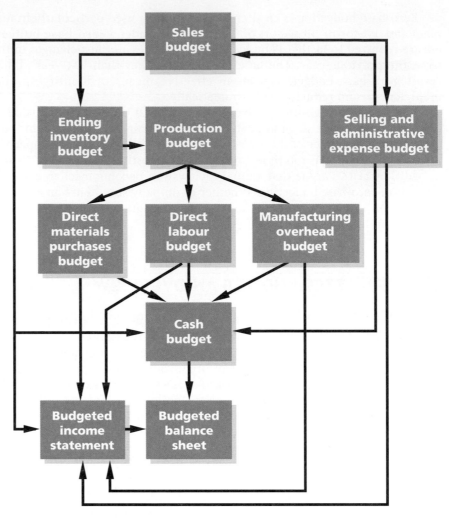

Note: For merchandising companies, the production budget is replaced by a merchandise purchases budget, and there is no manufacturing overhead budget.

Source: From SIROPOLIS. *SIROPOLIS SMALL BUS MGMT 5ED, 5E.* © 1994 South-Western, a part of Cengage Learning, Inc. Reproduced by permission. www.cengage.com/permissions.

Sales Forecasting—A Critical Step

The sales budget is usually based on the company's *sales forecast*. Sales from prior years are often used as a starting point in preparing the sales forecast. In addition, the managers will examine the company's unfilled orders, the company's pricing policy and marketing plans, trends in the industry, and general economic conditions. Some companies utilize complex statistical tools to analyze the data and build models that predict the company's sales in the coming year.

Preparing the Master Budget

We will use a hypothetical company, Patterson Framing Limited, to illustrate the preparation of a master budget. The company manufactures picture frames that it sells through an extensive distribution network in Canada and the United States. The following schedules will be prepared below in developing the master budget:

1. A sales budget, including a schedule of expected cash collections.
2. A production budget.
3. A direct materials purchases budget, including a schedule of expected cash disbursements for raw materials.

4. A direct labour budget.
5. A manufacturing overhead budget.
6. An ending finished goods inventory budget.
7. A selling and administrative expense budget.
8. A cash budget.
9. A budgeted income statement.
10. A budgeted balance sheet.

In the following sections, we will study each of these schedules. The balance sheet as at December 31, 2014, for Patterson Framing is shown below. As described below, some of these balance sheet amounts will be used in preparing the budget schedules for 2015:

PATTERSON FRAMING LIMITED
Balance Sheet December 31, 2014
Assets

Current assets:		
Cash.	$ 50,000	
Accounts receivable.	180,000	
Raw materials inventory (4,800 metres).	9,600	
Finished goods inventory (2,000 frames).	40,000	
Total current assets		$ 279,600
Plant and equipment:		
Land.	160,000	
Buildings and equipment	1,400,000	
Accumulated depreciation.	(584,000)	
Plant and equipment, net.		976,000
Total assets.		$1,255,600

Liabilities and Shareholders' Equity

Current liabilities:		
Accounts payable (raw materials).		$ 26,688
Shareholders' equity:		
Common shares	$ 600,000	
Retained earnings.	628,912	
Total shareholders' equity		1,228,912
Total liabilities and shareholders' equity		$1,255,600

The Sales Budget

The sales budget is the starting point in preparing the master budget. As shown earlier in Exhibit 9–2, all other items in the master budget, including production, purchases, inventories, and expenses, depend on it in some way.

The sales budget is constructed by multiplying the budgeted sales in units by the selling price. Schedule 1 contains the sales budget for Patterson Framing for the year 2015, by quarters. Notice from the schedule that the company plans to sell 200,000 picture frames during the year, with sales peaking in the third quarter.

A schedule of expected cash collections, such as the one that appears in Schedule 1 for Patterson Framing, is prepared after the sales budget. This schedule will be needed later to prepare the cash budget. Cash collections consist of collections on sales made to customers in prior periods plus collections on sales made in the current budget period. At Patterson Framing, experience has shown that 60% of sales is collected in the quarter in which the sale is made and the remaining 40% is collected in the following quarter. So, for example, 60% of the first-quarter sales of $600,000 (or $360,000) is collected during the first quarter and 40% (or $240,000) is collected during the second quarter.

Instant Quiz 9-1
Calculate third-quarter cash collections from sales for a company that expects to have credit sales of $100,000 in quarter 2 and $150,000 in quarter 3 and collects 80% in the quarter of sale and the remaining 20% in the following quarter.

SCHEDULE 1

PATTERSON FRAMING LIMITED
Sales Budget
For the Year Ending December 31, 2015

| | Quarter | | | | |
	1	2	3	4	Year
Budgeted sales (units).....................	20,000	60,000	80,000	40,000	200,000
Selling price per unit........................	× $30	× $30	× $30	× $30	× $30
Total budgeted sales..................	$600,000	$1,800,000	$2,400,000	$1,200,000	$6,000,000

Schedule of Expected Cash Collections

Accounts receivable 31/12/14*..............	$180,000				$180,000
First-quarter sales:†					
($600,000 × 60%, 40%)................	360,000	240,000			600,000
Second-quarter sales:					
($1,800,000 × 60%, 40%)................		1,080,000	720,000		1,800,000
Third-quarter sales:					
($2,400,000 × 60%, 40%)................			1,440,000	960,000	2,400,000
Fourth-quarter sales:‡					
($1,200,000 × 60%)...................				720,000	720,000
Total cash collections..................	$540,000	$1,320,000	$2,160,000	$1,680,000	$5,700,000

*Cash collections from last year's fourth-quarter sales. See the December 31, 2014, balance sheet.
†Cash collections from sales are as follows: 60% collected in the quarter of sale, and the remaining 40% collected in the following quarter.
‡Uncollected fourth-quarter sales appear as accounts receivable on the company's end-of-year balance sheet (see Schedule 10).

The Production Budget

Production budget
A detailed plan showing the number of units that must be produced during a period to meet both sales and inventory needs.

The **production budget** is prepared after the sales budget. The production budget lists the number of units that must be produced during each budget period to meet expected sales and to provide for the desired ending inventory. Production needs can be determined as follows:

Budgeted sales in units..	XXXX
Add desired ending inventory...	XXXX
Total needs	XXXX
Less beginning inventory	XXXX
Required production..	XXXX

Schedule 2 contains the production budget for Patterson Framing.

SCHEDULE 2

PATTERSON FRAMING LIMITED
Production Budget
For the Year Ending December 31, 2015

| | Quarter | | | | |
	1	2	3	4	Year
Budgeted sales (units).....................	20,000 10%	60,000 10%	80,000 10%	40,000	200,000
Add desired ending inventory*..............	6,000	8,000	4,000	3,000†	3,000
Total needs...........................	26,000	68,000	84,000	43,000	203,000
Less beginning inventory‡	2,000	6,000	8,000	4,000	2,000
Required production (units)..................	24,000	62,000	76,000	39,000	201,000

Note that production requirements for a quarter are influenced by the desired level of the ending inventory. Inventories should be carefully planned. Excessive inventories tie up working capital and create storage problems. On the other hand, insufficient inventories can lead to lost sales or last-minute, high-cost production efforts. At Patterson Framing, management believes that an ending inventory equal to 10% of the next quarter's sales strikes the appropriate balance.

*Ten percent of the next quarter's sales.
†Estimated.
‡The same as the prior quarter's ending inventory.

Instant Quiz 9-2
Calculate the required production for a company that expects to sell 10,000 units in quarter 2 and has a desired ending inventory of 2,000 units of finished goods and an opening inventory of 1,500 units.

Inventory Purchases—Merchandising Firm

Patterson Framing prepares a production budget, since it is a *manufacturing* firm. If it were a *merchandising* firm, then instead of a production budget, it would prepare a merchandise purchases budget showing the amount of goods to be purchased from its suppliers during the period. The merchandise purchases budget is in the same basic format as the production budget, except that it shows goods to be purchased rather than goods to be produced, as shown below:

Budgeted sales...	XXXX
Add desired ending merchandise inventory.................................	XXXX
Total needs	XXXX
Less beginning merchandise inventory	XXXX
Required purchases	XXXX

The merchandising firm prepares a merchandise purchases budget such as the one above for each item carried in inventory. The merchandise purchases budget can be expressed in terms of either units or the purchase cost of those units. So, for example, the budgeted sales shown in the table above can be expressed in terms of either the number of units sold or the purchase cost of the units sold. Some large retail organizations make such computations on a frequent basis (particularly at peak seasons) to ensure that adequate quantities are on hand to meet customer needs.

The Direct Materials Purchases Budget

After the production requirements have been computed, a **direct materials purchases budget** can be prepared. The direct materials purchases budget details the raw materials that must be purchased to meet the production budget and to provide for adequate inventories. The required purchases of raw materials are computed as follows:

Raw materials needed to meet the production schedule........................	XXXX
Add desired ending inventory of raw materials...............................	XXXX
Total raw materials needs...	XXXX
Less beginning inventory of raw materials	XXXX
Raw materials to be purchased	XXXX

Direct materials purchases budget
A detailed plan showing the amount of raw materials that must be purchased during a period to meet both production and inventory needs.

Schedule 3 contains the direct materials purchases budget for Patterson Framing. The only raw material included in that budget is a wood composite, which is the major material used to make the frame. The remaining raw materials, such as glue and finishing nails, are relatively insignificant and are included in variable manufacturing overhead. Notice that materials requirements are first determined in units (metres, kilograms, litres, and so on) and then translated into dollars by multiplying by the appropriate unit cost. Also note that the management of Patterson Framing wants to maintain ending inventories of raw materials equal to 10% of the following quarter's production needs.

The first line in the direct materials purchases budget contains the required production for each quarter, which is taken directly from the production budget (Schedule 2). Looking at the first quarter, the key elements of the budget are as follows:

- Total production needs: 24,000 frames × 1 metre per frame = 24,000 metres.
- Desired ending inventory: 10% × 62,000 metres (the following quarter's needs) = 6,200 metres.
- Total needs: 24,000 metres (production) + 6,200 (inventory) = 30,200 metres.

SCHEDULE 3

PATTERSON FRAMING LIMITED
Direct Materials Purchases Budget
For the Year Ending December 31, 2015

	Quarter 1	Quarter 2	Quarter 3	Quarter 4	Year
Required production—units (Schedule 2)........................	24,000	62,000	76,000	39,000	201,000
Raw materials needs per unit (1 metre).........................	1	1	1	1	1
Production needs (metres)...........	24,000	62,000	76,000	39,000	201,000
Add desired ending inventory.........	6,200	7,600	3,900	3,000	3,000
Total needs (metres).................	30,200	69,600	79,900	42,000	204,000
Less beginning inventory..............	2,400	6,200	7,600	3,900	2,400
Raw materials to be purchased........	27,800	63,400	72,300	38,100	201,600
Cost of raw materials to be purchased at $4.00 per metre......	$ 111,200	$ 253,600	$289,200	$152,400	$806,400

Schedule of Expected Cash Disbursements for Raw Materials

	Quarter 1	Quarter 2	Quarter 3	Quarter 4	Year
Accounts payable 31/12/14	$ 26,688				$ 26,688
First-quarter purchases: ($111,200 × 70%, 30%).............	77,840	$ 33,360			111,200
Second-quarter purchases: ($253,600 × 70%, 30%)...........		177,520	$ 76,080		253,600
Third-quarter purchases: ($289,200 × 70%, 30%)...........			202,440	$ 86,760	289,200
Fourth-quarter purchases: $152,400 × 70%).................				106,680	106,680
Total cash disbursements.............	$104,528	$ 210,880	$ 278,520	$193,440	$ 787,368

- Total purchases: 30,200 metres (total needed) − 2,400 (opening inventory) = 27,800 metres.
- Total purchase cost: 27,800 metres × $4.00 per metre = $111,200.

As with the production budget, the amounts listed under the Year column are not always the sum of the quarterly amounts. The desired ending inventory of raw materials for the year is the same as the desired ending inventory of raw materials for the fourth quarter. Likewise, the beginning inventory of raw materials for the year is the same as the beginning inventory of raw materials for the first quarter.

The direct materials purchases budget is usually accompanied by a schedule of expected cash disbursements for raw materials. This schedule is needed to prepare the overall cash budget. Disbursements for raw materials consist of payments for purchases on account in prior periods plus any payments for purchases in the current budget period. Schedule 3 contains such a schedule of cash disbursements.

Ordinarily, companies do not immediately pay their suppliers. At Patterson Framing, the policy is to pay for 70% of purchases in the quarter in which the purchase is made and 30% in the following quarter. So, while the company intends to purchase $111,200 worth of wood composite materials in the first quarter, the company will pay for only 70%, $77,840, in the first quarter and the remaining 30% in the second quarter. The company will also pay $26,688 in the first quarter for wood composite that was purchased on account in the previous quarter, but not yet paid for. This is the beginning balance in the accounts payable. Therefore, the total cash disbursements for wood composite in the first quarter are $104,528.

The Direct Labour Budget

The **direct labour budget** is also developed from the production budget. By knowing in advance what will be needed in terms of labour time throughout the budget year, the company can plan to adjust the labour force as required. Firms that neglect

Instant Quiz 9-3
Calculate the total cash disbursements in the second quarter for a company that needs to purchase 93,000 kilograms of raw materials at a cost of $0.60 per kilogram, where 50% of purchases are paid in the quarter the purchase is made and the remainder in the following quarter. Assume that 171,500 kilograms of raw material were purchased in the first quarter at a cost of $0.60 per kilogram.

Direct labour budget
A detailed plan showing labour requirements over a specified time period.

to budget face the risk of labour shortages or having to hire and lay off employees at awkward times. Erratic labour policies can lead to insecurity and inefficiency on the part of employees.

To compute direct labour requirements, the number of units of finished product to be produced each period (month, quarter, and so on) is multiplied by the number of direct labour-hours required to produce a single unit. For example, 24,000 frames are to be produced in the first quarter, and each frame requires 0.50 direct labour-hours, so a total of 12,000 direct labour-hours (24,000 frames × 0.50 direct labour-hours per frame) will be required. The direct labour requirements can then be translated into expected direct labour costs. How this is done will depend on the labour policy of the firm. In Schedule 4, the management of Patterson Framing has assumed that the direct labour force will be adjusted as the work requirements change from quarter to quarter. In that case, the total direct labour cost is computed simply by multiplying the direct labour-hour requirements by the direct labour rate per hour. For example, the direct labour cost in the first quarter is $240,000 (12,000 direct labour-hours × $20 per direct labour-hour).

SCHEDULE 4

PATTERSON FRAMING LIMITED
Direct Labour Budget
For the Year Ending December 31, 2015

	Quarter				
	1	2	3	4	Year
Units to be produced (Schedule 2)	24,000	62,000	76,000	39,000	201,000
Direct labour time per unit (hours)	0.5	0.5	0.5	0.5	0.5
Total direct labour-hours needed	12,000	31,000	38,000	19,500	100,500
Direct labour cost per hour.................	$ 20.00	$ 20.00	$ 20.00	$ 20.00	$ 20.00
Total direct labour cost*	$240,000	$620,000	$760,000	$390,000	$2,010,000

*This schedule assumes that the direct labour workforce will be fully adjusted to the workload (i.e., "Total direct labour-hours needed") each quarter.

Many companies have employment policies or union contracts that prevent them from laying off and rehiring workers as needed. Suppose, for example, that Patterson Framing has 40 workers who are classified as direct labour and each of them is guaranteed at least 420 hours of pay each quarter at a rate of $20 per hour. In that case, the minimum direct labour cost for a quarter is as follows:

$$40 \text{ workers} \times 420 \text{ hours} \times \$20 = \$336,000$$

Note that in this case, the direct labour costs for the first quarter would increase to $336,000.

The Manufacturing Overhead Budget

The **manufacturing overhead budget** provides a schedule of all costs of production other than direct materials and direct labour. Schedule 5 shows the manufacturing overhead budget for Patterson Framing. Note how the production costs are separated into variable and fixed components. The variable component is $2 per direct labour-hour. The fixed component is $251,250 per quarter. Because the variable component of the manufacturing overhead depends on direct labour, the first line in the manufacturing overhead budget consists of the budgeted direct labour-hours from the direct labour budget (Schedule 4). The budgeted direct labour-hours in each quarter are multiplied by the variable overhead rate to determine the variable component of manufacturing overhead. For example, the variable manufacturing overhead for the first quarter is

$$\$24,000 = 12,000 \text{ direct labour-hours} \times \$2.00 \text{ per direct labour-hour}$$

This is added to the fixed manufacturing overhead for the quarter to determine the total manufacturing overhead for the quarter as follows: $275,250 = $24,000 (variable) + $251,250 (fixed).

Manufacturing overhead budget
A detailed plan showing the indirect production costs that will be incurred over a specified time period.

SCHEDULE 5

PATTERSON FRAMING LIMITED Manufacturing Overhead Budget For the Year Ending December 31, 2015					
	Quarter				Year
	1	2	3	4	
Budgeted direct labour-hours (Schedule 4) ...	12,000	31,000	38,000	19,500	100,500
Variable overhead rate	$ 2.00	$ 2.00	$ 2.00	$ 2.00	$ 2.00
Variable manufacturing overhead.............	$ 24,000	$ 62,000	$ 76,000	$ 39,000	$201,000
Fixed manufacturing overhead................	251,250	251,250	251,250	251,250	1,005,000
Total manufacturing overhead................	275,250	313,250	327,250	290,250	1,206,000
Less depreciation	(30,000)	(30,000)	(30,000)	(30,000)	(120,000)
Cash disbursements for manufacturing overhead...................................	$245,250	$283,250	$297,250	$260,250	$1,086,000
Total manufacturing overhead (a)					$1,206,000
Budgeted direct labour-hours (b).............					100,500
Predetermined overhead rate for the year (a) ÷ (b).............................					$ 12.00

In most cases, fixed costs are the costs of supplying capacity to do things like make products, process purchase orders, handle customer calls, and so on. The amount of capacity that will be utilized depends on the expected level of activity for the period. If the expected level of activity is greater than the company's current capacity, then fixed costs may have to be increased. Or, if the expected level is appreciably below the company's current capacity, then it may be desirable to decrease fixed costs if possible. However, once the level of fixed costs has been determined in the budget, the costs really are fixed. Therefore, the time to adjust fixed costs is during the budgeting process. To determine the appropriate level of fixed costs at budget time, an activity-based costing system, as described in Chapter 7, can be very helpful. It can help answer questions like "How many clerks will we need to hire to process the anticipated number of purchase orders next year?" For simplicity, we assume in all of the budgeting examples in this book that the appropriate levels of fixed costs have already been determined for the budget with the aid of activity-based costing or some other method.

The last line of Schedule 5 for Patterson Framing shows its budgeted cash disbursements for manufacturing overhead. Since some of the overhead costs are not cash outflows, the total budgeted manufacturing overhead costs must be adjusted to determine the cash disbursements for manufacturing overhead. At Patterson Framing, the only significant non-cash manufacturing overhead cost is depreciation, which is $30,000 per quarter. These non-cash depreciation charges are deducted from the total budgeted manufacturing overhead to determine the expected cash disbursements. Patterson Framing pays all overhead costs involving cash disbursements in the quarter incurred. Note that the company's predetermined overhead rate for the year will be $12 per direct labour-hour, which is determined by dividing the total budgeted manufacturing overhead for the year by the total budgeted direct labour-hours for the year.

The Ending Finished Goods Inventory Budget

Ending finished goods inventory budget
A budget showing the dollar amount of cost expected to appear on the balance sheet for unsold units at the end of a period.

After Schedules 1 through 5 are completed, all of the data needed to compute unit product costs will be available. This computation is needed for two reasons: first, to determine cost of goods sold on the budgeted income statement and, second, to identify the amount to put on the balance sheet inventory account for unsold units. The carrying cost of the unsold units is computed on the **ending finished goods inventory budget**.

The unit product cost computations are shown in Schedule 6 based on absorption costing. For Patterson Framing, the absorption costing unit product cost is $20 per picture frame—consisting of $4 of direct materials, $10 of direct labour, and $6

PATTERSON FRAMING LIMITED
Ending Finished Goods Inventory Budget
(absorption costing basis)
For the Year Ending December 31, 2015

Item	Quantity	Cost	Total
Production cost per unit:			
Direct materials....................................	1.0 metre	$4.00 per metre	$ 4.00
Direct labour...	0.5 hours	$20.00 per hour	10.00
Manufacturing overhead	0.5 hours	$12.00 per hour	6.00
Unit product cost			$ 20.00
Budgeted finished goods inventory:			
Ending finished goods inventory in units (Schedule 2).....			3,000
Unit product cost (see above)...........................			× $20
Ending finished goods in dollars			$60,000

of manufacturing overhead. For convenience, the manufacturing overhead is applied to units of product on the basis of direct labour-hours. The budgeted carrying cost of the expected ending inventory is $60,000.

The Selling and Administrative Expense Budget

The **selling and administrative expense budget** lists the budgeted expenses for areas other than manufacturing. In large organizations, this budget is a compilation of many smaller, individual budgets submitted by department heads and other people responsible for selling and administrative expenses. For example, the marketing manager in a large organization would submit a budget detailing the advertising expenses for each budget period.

Schedule 7 contains the selling and administrative expense budget for Patterson Framing. Like the manufacturing overhead budget, the selling and administrative expense budget is divided into variable and fixed cost components. For Patterson Framing, the variable selling and administrative expense is $2.00 per frame. Consequently, budgeted sales in frames for each quarter are entered at the top of the schedule. These data are taken from the sales budget (Schedule 1). The budgeted variable selling and administrative expenses are determined by multiplying the budgeted frames sold by the variable selling and administrative expense per frame. For example, the budgeted variable selling and administrative expense for the first quarter is $40,000 (20,000 frames × $2.00 per frame). The fixed selling and administrative expenses (all given data) are then added to the variable selling and administrative expenses to arrive at the total budgeted selling and administrative expenses.

Finally, to determine the cash disbursements for selling and administrative expenses, the total budgeted expenses are adjusted by subtracting any non-cash items included in the budget and adding any cash expenditures not reflected in the budgeted amounts. As shown in Schedule 7, three items must be subtracted: depreciation of $4,000 per quarter because this is a non-cash expense; insurance of $19,000 per quarter because although this is an expense under accrual accounting, it does not represent an actual outflow of cash each quarter; and property taxes of $9,000 because this too is an expense under accrual accounting, but not a cash outflow each quarter. Two cash disbursements are added: the insurance premium payment of $76,000 in the third quarter, and the property tax payment of $36,000 in the fourth quarter. Each of these additions is necessary to reflect the actual timing of the cash outflows for insurance premiums and property taxes.

> **Instant Quiz 9-4**
> Calculate the unit product cost where each unit (a) requires 15 kilograms of raw materials that cost $0.20 per kilogram, (b) needs 0.4 hours of direct labour at a cost of $15 per hour, and (c) has manufacturing overhead applied on the basis of direct labour-hours with an overhead rate of $10 per hour.

Selling and administrative expense budget
A detailed schedule of planned expenses that will be incurred in areas other than manufacturing during a budget period.

SCHEDULE 7

			Quarter		
PATTERSON FRAMING LIMITED Selling and Administrative Expense Budget For the Year Ending December 31, 2015	**1**	**2**	**3**	**4**	**Year**
Budgeted sales in units (Schedule 1).........	20,000	60,000	80,000	40,000	200,000
Variable selling and administrative					
expenses per frame*....................	$ 2.00	$ 2.00	$ 2.00	$ 2.00	$ 2.00
Budgeted variable expense.................	$40,000	$120,000	$160,000	$80,000	$400,000
Budgeted fixed selling and administrative					
expenses					
Advertising..............................	20,000	20,000	20,000	20,000	80,000
Senior management salaries	50,000	50,000	50,000	50,000	200,000
Insurance...............................	19,000	19,000	19,000	19,000	76,000
Property taxes..........................	9,000	9,000	9,000	9,000	36,000
Depreciation...........................	4,000	4,000	4,000	4,000	16,000
Total budgeted fixed selling and					
administrative expenses................	102,000	102,000	102,000	102,000	408,000
Total budgeted selling and					
administrative expenses..............	142,000	222,000	262,000	182,000	808,000
Less depreciation expense	(4,000)	(4,000)	(4,000)	(4,000)	(16,000)
Less insurance expense.................	(19,000)	(19,000)	(19,000)	(19,000)	(76,000)
Add insurance premium payment.........			76,000		76,000
Less property tax expense	(9,000)	(9,000)	(9,000)	(9,000)	(36,000)
Add property tax paid...................				36,000	36,000
Cash disbursements for selling and					
administrative expenses..............	$110,000	$190,000	$306,000	$186,000	$792,000

*Commissions, clerical, and shipping.

The Cash Budget

As illustrated in Exhibit 9–2, the cash budget integrates much of the data developed in the preceding steps. It is a good idea to review Exhibit 9–2 to get the big picture firmly in mind before moving on.

The cash budget is composed of four major sections:

1. Receipts section.
2. Disbursements section.
3. Cash excess or deficiency section.
4. Financing section (borrowings, loan repayments, and interest expense)

The receipts section is a list of all of the cash inflows (except for financing) expected during the budget period. Generally, the major source of receipts is sales.

The disbursements section consists of all cash payments that are planned for the budget period. These payments include raw materials purchases (or inventory purchases for merchandising companies), direct labour payments, manufacturing overhead costs, and so on, as contained in their respective budgets. In addition, other cash disbursements, such as equipment purchases, dividends, and other cash withdrawals by owners, are included.

The cash excess or deficiency section is computed as follows:

Cash balance, beginning..	XXXX
Add receipts	XXXX
Total cash available before financing................................	XXXX
Less disbursements	XXXX
Excess (deficiency) of cash available over disbursements	XXXX

If there is a cash deficiency during any budget period, the company will need to borrow funds. If there is a cash excess during any budget period, after ensuring any targeted minimum cash balance is met, funds borrowed in previous periods may be repaid or the excess funds (i.e., above the targeted cash balance) can be invested.

The financing section provides a detailed account of the borrowings and loan repayments projected to take place during the budget period. It also includes the details of interest payments that will be due on money borrowed. A well-coordinated budgeting program eliminates uncertainty as to what the cash situation will be in two months, six months, or a year from now.

The cash budget should be broken down into time periods that are short enough to capture major fluctuations in cash balances. While a monthly cash budget is most common, many firms budget cash on a weekly or even daily basis, particularly start-up companies where cash needs are particularly high in the early months (or years) of operation. The cash budget for Patterson Framing, prepared on a quarterly basis, appears in Schedule 8. The cash budget builds on the earlier schedules and uses additional data provided as follows:

- The beginning cash balance is $50,000.
- Management plans to spend $80,000 during the year on equipment purchases: $20,000 in each quarter.
- The board of directors has approved cash dividends of $10,000 per quarter.
- Management would like to have a cash balance of at least $50,000 at the beginning of each quarter for contingencies.
- Patterson Framing has an open line of credit with a bank that enables the company to borrow funds as needed at a 4% annual interest rate to a maximum total loan balance of $500,000. To simplify the calculations in the example, all borrowing occurs at the beginning of quarters and all repayments are made at the end of quarters. We also assume that interest on total outstanding loan balances is paid quarterly. However, in practice, banks and other creditors typically require interest payments each month based on the average loan balance outstanding for that period.

The cash budget is prepared one quarter at a time, starting with the first quarter. The first step is to enter the beginning cash balance of $50,000 for the first quarter.

SCHEDULE 8

PATTERSON FRAMING LIMITED
Cash Budget
For the Year Ending December 31, 2015

	Schedule	1	2	3	4	Year
Cash balance, beginning.........		$50,000	$50,000	$50,000	$55,514	$50,000
Add collections from sales	1	540,000	1,320,000	2,160,000	1,680,000	5,700,000
Total cash available............		590,000	1,370,000	2,210,000	1,735,514	5,750,000
Less disbursements:						
Direct materials...............	3	104,528	210,880	278,520	193,440	787,368
Direct labour..................	4	240,000	620,000	760,000	390,000	2,010,000
Manufacturing overhead	5	245,250	283,250	297,250	260,250	1,086,000
Selling and administrative.....	7	110,000	190,000	306,000	186,000	792,000
Income taxes	9	89,400	89,400	89,400	89,400	357,600
Equipment purchases.........		20,000	20,000	20,000	20,000	80,000
Dividends....................		10,000	10,000	10,000	10,000	40,000
Total disbursements........		819,178	1,423,530	1,761,170	1,149,090	5,152,968
Excess (deficiency) of cash available over disbursements..		(229,178)	(53,530)	448,830	586,424	597,032
Financing:						
Borrowings (at beginning).....		281,998	107,424	0	0	389,422
Repayment (at end)		0	0	(389,422)	0	(389,422)
Interest*		(2,820)	(3,894)	(3,894)	0	(10,608)
Total financing		279,178	103,530	(393,316)	0	(10,608)
Cash balance, ending............		$50,000	$50,000	$55,514	$586,424	$586,424

*The interest payments relate to the total loan balance outstanding each quarter. Calculations for each quarter based on an annual interest rate of 4% are as follows:

Quarter 1: $281,998 × 4% × 0.25 = $2,820
Quarters 2 and 3: ($281,998 × 4% × 0.25) + ($107,424 × 4% × 0.25) = $3,894

This amount represents the cash balance shown on the December 31, 2014, balance sheet. The $540,000 in cash collections from customers is added to the beginning balance to arrive at the total cash available of $590,000. Since the total disbursements are $819,178 and the total cash available is only $590,000, there is a shortfall of $229,178. As management would like to have a beginning cash balance of at least $50,000 for the second quarter, the company will need to borrow $281,998. Note that the borrowing of $281,998 takes into account the fact that interest of 1% must be paid at the end of the quarter on the loan balance outstanding for the first quarter. Simple algebra can be used to solve for the borrowing required in the first quarter as follows:

$$\text{Excess cash (Deficiency)} + \text{Borrowing} - \text{Interest on borrowing}$$
$$= \text{Target cash balance}$$
$$\$(229,178) + X - 0.01X = \$50,000$$
$$X = \$281,998$$

Note that in the above formula, the amount of excess cash available in the period will be used whenever that amount is *less* than the target cash balance for the end of the period. For example, if excess cash available for Patterson Framing had been $40,000 at the end of the first quarter, that amount would have been used instead of the deficiency of $229,178. Also note that if there is excess cash available (but it is less than the target balance), that amount would be included in the above formula as a positive value whereas cash deficiency amounts are included as a negative value. Finally, in the above formula, X is the amount to be borrowed at the beginning of the quarter and $0.01\,X$ represents the interest (1% per quarter in our example) to be paid at the end of the quarter.

The second quarter of the cash budget is handled similarly. Note that the ending cash balance for the first quarter is brought forward as the beginning cash balance for the second quarter. Also note that additional borrowing is required in the second quarter because of the continuing cash shortfall. The same approach is used to solve for the required borrowing in the second quarter except that the amount of interest ($2,820) on the loan outstanding from the first quarter is now included in the formula below because it will have to be paid again at the end of the second quarter. The revised formula for solving the amount of required borrowing in the second quarter is as follows:

$$\$(53,530) - \$2,820 + X - 0.01X = \$50,000$$
$$X = \$107,424$$

In the third quarter, the cash flow situation improves dramatically and the excess cash available over disbursements is $448,830. This makes it possible for the company to repay its loans from the bank, which now total $389,422 ($281,998 + $107,424) along with the $3,894 interest for the third quarter ($389,422 × 1%), for a total of $393,316. The cash balance at the end of the third quarter after repaying the loans and the interest is $55,514, which exceeds the minimum required balance of $50,000.

In the case of Patterson Framing, all loans have been repaid by year-end. If all loans are not repaid and a budgeted income statement or balance sheet is being prepared, then interest must be accrued on the outstanding loans for the period since the last interest payment was made. For example, if interest is normally paid on the 15th of each month and monthly budgeted financial statements are prepared, an interest accrual will be required for the period between the 16th day of the month and the end of the month. This interest will *not* appear on the cash budget (since it has not yet been paid), but it will appear as part of interest expense on the budgeted income statement and as a liability (interest payable) on the budgeted balance sheet.

As with the production and raw materials budgets, the amounts under the Year column in the cash budget are not always the sum of the amounts for the four

---

Instant Quiz 9-5

A company has an opening cash balance of $40,000, expects cash receipts of $400,000 and cash disbursements of $425,000 for the first quarter, and desires an ending cash balance of at least $40,000. Assume an interest rate of 1% per quarter and that interest on outstanding loans must be paid at the end of each quarter. How much cash will the company need to borrow at the beginning of the first quarter?

quarters. In particular, the beginning cash balance for the year is the same as the beginning cash balance for the first quarter, and the ending cash balance is the same as the ending cash balance for the fourth quarter. Also, note that the beginning cash balance for any quarter is the same as the ending cash balance for the previous quarter.

Instant Quiz 9-6
Given your answer to Instant Quiz 9-5, calculate the amount of interest expense for the first quarter.

The Budgeted Income Statement

A budgeted income statement can be prepared from the data developed in Schedules 1 to 8. *The budgeted income statement is one of the key schedules in the budget process.* It shows the company's planned profit for the upcoming budget period, and it stands as a benchmark against which actual company performance can be measured. Schedule 9 contains the budgeted income statement for Patterson Framing.

SCHEDULE 9

PATTERSON FRAMING LIMITED Budgeted Income Statement For the Year Ending December 31, 2015	Schedule	
Sales	1	$6,000,000
Less cost of goods sold (200,000 frames at $20)	6	4,000,000
Gross margin		2,000,000
Less selling and administrative expenses	7	808,000
Operating income (before taxes and interest)		1,192,000
Income taxes (30% × $1,192,000)*		357,600
Interest expense	8	10,608
Net income		$ 823,792

*Income taxes would ordinarily be based on income *after* deducting interest expense. However, because income taxes are affected by the amount of interest expense, and both amounts affect the cash flow calculations in Schedule 8, we simplify the calculations by deducting interest expense after income taxes have been calculated on operating income.

The Budgeted Balance Sheet

The budgeted balance sheet is developed using the actual balance sheet at the end of the most recent fiscal period as the starting point (e.g., December 31, 2014, for Patterson Framing) and adjusting it for the data contained in the other budgets. Patterson Framing's budgeted balance sheet is presented in Schedule 10. It is important to point out that not all companies that prepare a master budget will necessarily prepare a budgeted balance sheet since responsibility accounting, discussed earlier in the chapter, largely focuses on comparing actual results for revenues and costs to budgeted amounts. As such, a budgeted income statement and a cash budget are commonly prepared, but practice varies with respect to budgeted balance sheets. However, external stakeholders, such as lenders, may require budgeted balance sheets as part of their assessment of the company's financial position for making decisions about credit terms such as interest rates, loan amounts, and maturity dates.

It is worth pointing out that we have simplified the treatment of income taxes on the income statement (Schedule 9) by assuming an effective rate of 30%. Most for-profit corporations in Canada are required to pay income taxes on taxable income, but calculating the effective rate is complex and is typically covered in introductory courses on taxation. However, companies that budget positive operating income calculate a budgeted effective tax rate and include income tax expense as an additional item on the budgeted income statement, as we have done in our example.

SCHEDULE 10

PATTERSON FRAMING LIMITED
Budgeted Balance Sheet
December 31, 2015
Assets

Current assets:

Cash	$ 586,424 (a)	
Accounts receivable	480,000 (b)	
Raw materials inventory	12,000 (c)	
Finished goods inventory	60,000 (d)	
Total current assets		$ 1,138,424

Plant and equipment:

Land	160,000 (e)	
Buildings, furniture and equipment	1,480,000 (f)	
Accumulated depreciation	(720,000) (g)	
Plant and equipment, net		920,000
Total assets		$2,058,424

Liabilities and Shareholders' Equity

Current liabilities:

Accounts payable	$ 45,720 (h)	

Shareholders' equity:

Common shares	600,000 (i)	
Retained earnings	1,412,704 (j)	
Total shareholders' equity		2,012,704
Total liabilities and shareholders' equity		$2,058,424

Explanation of December 31, 2015, budgeted balance sheet figures:
a.   The ending cash balance, as projected by the cash budget in Schedule 8.
b.   Forty percent of fourth-quarter sales, from Schedule 1 ($1,200,000 × 40% = $480,000).
c.   From Schedule 3, the ending raw materials inventory is 3,000 metres and costs $4.00 per metre. Therefore, the ending inventory in dollars is $12,000 (3,000 × $4).
d.   From Schedule 6.
e.   From the December 31, 2014, balance sheet (no change).
f.   The December 31, 2014, balance sheet indicated a balance of $1,400,000. During 2015, $80,000 in additional equipment will be purchased (see Schedule 8), bringing the December 31, 2015, balance to $1,480,000.
g.   The December 31, 2014, balance sheet indicated a balance of $584,000. During 2015, $136,000 of depreciation will be taken ($120,000 on Schedule 5 and $16,000 on Schedule 7), bringing the December 31, 2015, balance to $720,000.
h.   Thirty percent of the fourth-quarter raw materials purchases, from Schedule 3 ($152,400 × 30% = $45,720).
i.   From the December 31, 2014, balance sheet (no change).
j.   December 31, 2014, balance .... $ 628,912
     Add net income, from Schedule 9 823,792
     1,452,704
     Deduct dividends paid, from Schedule 8 ... 40,000
     December 31, 2015, balance $1,412,704

IN BUSINESS

The example presented in this chapter on preparing a master budget illustrates how much time and effort goes into the process. Imagine how much more effort would be required to prepare a master budget for a company with multiple divisions operating in different countries. Given the increasing complexity of organizations over the past few decades, many have questioned whether the benefits of preparing detailed operating budgets exceed the costs. A survey of 212 managers directly involved in the budgeting process at U.S. companies gathered evidence on their perceptions of both the benefits and limitations of budgets.

Over 70% of the respondents agreed that budgets are indispensable as a management tool. When respondents were asked to give the budgeting process an overall score with respect to the value added to the organization, the average grade assigned was 70 out of 100. Further, over 33% of the managers gave the budgeting process a grade of 80 or above. Importantly, managers were asked to assign this grade after taking into account the cost of preparing budgets (time and effort) and the dysfunctional consequences (e.g., budget slack) that might occur when budgets are used as a control tool.

Many of the key criticisms of the budgeting process identified by managers relate to how quickly it can become out of date if significant changes occur in the organization's operating environment. Nearly 50% of the respondents indicated that to combat this problem, they either prepare rolling budgets or use a form of flexible budget (discussed later in this chapter) in an effort to retain the control benefits of the budget process. Overall, while the budgeting process is not without its problems, this study showed that many managers continue to believe the benefits exceed the costs.

Source: Theresa Libby and Murray Lindsay, "Beyond Budgeting or Better Budgeting," *Strategic Finance*, August 2007, pp. 47–51.

■ FLEXIBLE BUDGET

The budgets presented in Schedules 1 to 10 are static budgets. A **static budget** is prepared only for the planned or budgeted level of activity. In our example, that level of activity was the forecast sales volume of 200,000 units. While this approach is suitable for planning, it can be inadequate for control if the actual level of activity during a period differs significantly from the budgeted level. Specifically, the problem that arises when a significant difference exists between actual and budgeted levels of activity is that it becomes very difficult to evaluate how well a manager did in generating revenues and controlling costs. For example, if actual activity levels are significantly higher than expected for Patterson Framing, actual revenues and variable costs will be considerably higher than static budget amounts. Should we conclude that the manager did a good job in generating revenues, but not so well in controlling costs? Clearly this is not a fair evaluation since the costs are above budget because the volume of actual activity exceeded the static budget amount. Thus, an alternative approach is needed to restore the usefulness of budgets as a control tool.

Flexible budgets take into account changes in revenues and costs expected to occur as a consequence of changes in activity. A **flexible budget** provides estimates of what revenues and costs should be for any level of activity within a specified range. When a flexible budget is used in performance evaluation, actual revenues and costs are compared to what the *revenues and costs should have been for the actual level of activity during the period* rather than to the planned budgeted revenues and costs from the static budget. This is a very important distinction—particularly for variable costs. If adjustments for the level of activity are not made, it is very difficult to interpret differences between actual and budgeted revenues and costs.

LEARNING OBJECTIVE 3
Prepare a flexible budget, and explain the need for the flexible budget approach

Static budget
A budget designed for only the planned level of activity.

Flexible budget
A budget that provides estimates of what revenues and costs should be for any level of activity within a specified range.

How a Flexible Budget Works

The basic idea of the flexible budget approach is that the budget is adjusted to show what revenues and costs *should be* for a specific level of activity. To illustrate how a flexible budget works, we build on the Patterson Framing master budget example to develop income statements for different levels of activity within a range of annual sales of 180,000 units to 220,000 units, or 10% below or above the static budget level. To simplify the example, we have omitted interest expense and income tax expense, although both could easily be included using the steps presented in preparing the static budget. Note that although Exhibit 9–3 presents an annual flexible budget, the same approach can be used in developing flexible budgets for shorter reporting periods, such as quarters or months. Also note that the flexible budget income statements in Exhibit 9–3 were prepared using the variable costing approach covered in Chapter 8. As a result, the operating income shown in

EXHIBIT 9-3   Flexible Budget Income Statement

PATTERSON FRAMING LIMITED
Flexible Budget
For the Year Ending December 31, 2015

	Budgeted Amount per Unit	Sales in Units		
		180,000	200,000	220,000
Sales..	$30.00	$5,400,000	$6,000,000	$6,600,000
Less variable expenses:				
Direct materials*.............................	4.00	720,000	800,000	880,000
Direct labour*................................	10.00	1,800,000	2,000,000	2,200,000
Variable manufacturing overhead#.............	1.00	180,000	200,000	220,000
Selling and administrative†...................	2.00	360,000	400,000	440,000
Total variable expenses......................	17.00	3,060,000	3,400,000	3,740,000
Contribution margin	$ 13.00	2,340,000	2,600,000	2,860,000
Less fixed expenses:				
Manufacturing overhead**....................		1,005,000	1,005,000	1,005,000
Selling and administrative##..................		408,000	408,000	408,000
Total fixed expenses		1,413,000	1,413,000	1,413,000
Operating income		$ 927,000	$ 1,187,000	$ 1,447,000

*Per unit amount as per Schedule 6.
#Variable overhead cost per hour (Schedule 5) multiplied by direct labour-hours per unit (Schedule 6): $2 × 0.5 = $1.00.
†Per unit amount as per Schedule 7.
**Total budgeted fixed overhead expense as per Schedule 5.
##Total budgeted fixed selling and administrative expenses as per Schedule 7.

Exhibit 9–3 for sales of 200,000 units is $1,187,000 while the operating income shown in Schedule 9 is $1,192,000. This difference of $5,000 arises because operating income in Schedule 9 was calculated using absorption costing and an additional 1,000 units of finished goods inventory were added in 2015 (Schedule 2). The additional manufacturing overhead deferred in finished goods inventory using absorption costing is $5,000: 1,000 units × $5.00 per unit of fixed overhead ($10 per hour × 0.5 hours per unit). The rate of $10 per hour for fixed overhead is based on the total rate of $12 per hour (Schedule 6) less $2 per hour for variable overhead (Schedule 5). We use variable costing to emphasize the revenue and cost behaviour patterns expected over this relevant range of activity. Specifically, the selling price and variable costs per unit are expected to remain constant, while total fixed costs are not expected to change over the relevant range.

The calculation of the revenues and expenses in Exhibit 9–3 is straightforward. The amounts *per unit* for sales and variable expenses are multiplied by the activity level (units) to arrive at the totals for the year. For example, for an activity level of 180,000 units, total sales are calculated as $30.00 × 180,000 = $5,400,000. Each of the variable expense line items is calculated in a similar fashion. Fixed costs are not expected to change over the relevant range of activity so they stay the same for each activity level shown in Exhibit 9–3. The flexible budget provides a useful tool in estimating operating income at different levels of activity using the cost–volume–profit concepts discussed in Chapter 4. As illustrated in Exhibit 9–3, a 20,000-unit change in sales volume, above or below the budgeted level of 200,000 units, causes a $260,000 change in operating income, which can be calculated as 20,000 units × $13.00 per unit contribution margin. Importantly, a flexible budget can be developed for any level of activity within the relevant range of activity. Thus, if actual sales volume for the year is 209,000 units, a flexible budget can be prepared showing what revenues and costs should have been for that level of activity.

USING THE FLEXIBLE BUDGETING CONCEPT IN PERFORMANCE EVALUATION

To demonstrate the control benefits of using the flexible budgeting approach to evaluate performance, we continue with our example of Patterson Framing. The flexible budget performance report shown in Exhibit 9–4 has three main components. First, it presents actual revenues and expenses for the year, given an actual sales volume of 220,000 units. Second, it contains a flexible budget based on actual sales of 220,000 units, using the revenues and expenses from Exhibit 9–3. Third, it shows the **flexible budget variance**, the difference between actual results and the flexible budget, with unfavourable and favourable variances labelled "U" and "F," respectively. As shown in Exhibit 9–4, actual operating income for 2015 was $1,087,400, while the flexible budget indicates that at an actual volume of 220,000 unit sales, $1,447,000 should have been earned. The flexible budget variances for the individual line items tell the story as to why the unfavourable operating income variance of $359,600 occurred. The largest contributing factor was the unfavourable sales variance of $330,000, so management will want to determine why the actual selling price of $28.50 per unit ($6,270,000 ÷ 220,000) differed from the budget of $30 per unit. Cost control also appears to have been a problem for many of the variable expenses at Patterson Framing, which in total were $28,600 above budget. As will be further explored in Chapter 10, the flexible budget variances for manufacturing costs (direct materials, direct labour, variable overhead) could have been caused by actual unit prices for production inputs differing from budget, or the actual quantities used in producing the 220,000 units differing from budget. Management will want to know the extent to which these two factors contributed to the variances shown in Exhibit 9–4.

LEARNING OBJECTIVE ❹
Prepare a performance report using the flexible budget approach

Flexible budget variance
The difference between actual and flexible budget amounts for revenues and expenses.

EXHIBIT 9-4   Flexible Budget Performance Report

PATTERSON FRAMING LIMITED
Flexible Budget Performance Report
For the Year Ending December 31, 2015

	Budgeted Amount per Unit	Actual (220,000 units)	Flexible Budget (220,000 units)	Flexible Budget Variance[††]	
Sales....................................	$30.00	$6,270,000	$6,600,000	$330,000	U
Less variable expenses:					
Direct materials*.....................	4.00	869,000	880,000	11,000	F
Direct labour*........................	10.00	2,244,000	2,200,000	44,000	U
Variable manufacturing overhead#....	1.00	228,800	220,000	8,800	U
Selling and administrative†...........	2.00	426,800	440,000	13,200	F
Total variable expenses..............	17.00	3,768,600	3,740,000	28,600	U
Contribution margin	$ 13.00	2,501,400	2,860,000	358,600	U
Less fixed expenses:					
Manufacturing overhead**...........		1,012,000	1,005,000	7,000	U
Selling and administrative##.........		402,000	408,000	6,000	F
Total fixed expenses		1,414,000	1,413,000	1,000	U
Operating income		$ 1,087,400	$ 1,447,000	$ 359,600	U

*Per unit amount as per Schedule 6.
#Variable overhead cost per hour (Schedule 5) multiplied by direct labour-hours per unit (Schedule 6): $2 × 0.5 = $1.00.
†Per unit amount as per Schedule 7.
**Total budgeted fixed overhead expense as per Schedule 5.
##Total budgeted fixed selling and administrative expenses as per Schedule 7.
††U = unfavourable variance; F = favourable variance.

EXHIBIT 9-5   Static Budget Performance Report

PATTERSON FRAMING LIMITED
Static Budget Performance Report
For the Year Ending December 31, 2015

	Budgeted Amount per Unit	Actual (220,000 units)	Static Budget (200,000 units)	Static Budget Variance[††]	
Sales..................................	$30.00	$6,270,000	$6,000,000	$270,000	F
Less variable expenses:					
Direct materials*.....................	4.00	869,000	800,000	69,000	U
Direct labour*........................	10.00	2,244,000	2,000,000	244,000	U
Variable manufacturing overhead#....	1.00	228,800	200,000	28,800	U
Selling and administrative†..........	2.00	426,800	400,000	26,800	U
Total variable expenses..............	17.00	3,768,600	3,400,000	368,600	U
Contribution margin	$ 13.00	2,501,400	2,600,000	98,600	U
Less fixed expenses:					
Manufacturing overhead**...........		1,012,000	1,005,000	7,000	U
Selling and administrative##..........		402,000	408,000	6,000	F
Total fixed expenses		1,414,000	1,413,000	1,000	U
Operating income		$ 1,087,400	$ 1,187,000	$ 99,600	U

*Per unit amount as per Schedule 6.
#Variable overhead cost per hour (Schedule 5) multiplied by direct labour-hours per unit (Schedule 6): $2 × 0.5 = $1.00.
†Per unit amount as per Schedule 7.
**Total budgeted fixed overhead expense as per Schedule 5.
##Total budgeted fixed selling and administrative expenses as per Schedule 7.
[††]U = unfavourable variance; F = favourable variance.

Static budget variance
The difference between actual and static budget amounts for revenues and expenses.

Instant Quiz 9-7
Assume a company prepares a static budget based on sales of 50,000 units and a contribution margin of $5 per unit. If actual sales are 60,000 units, calculate the contribution margin for the flexible budget.

Sales volume variance
The difference between flexible and static budget amounts for revenues and expenses caused by actual activity levels differing from static budget amounts.

The value of the flexible budget performance report for control purposes can be further illustrated by examining Exhibit 9–5, which presents a static budget performance report. The **static budget variances** in Exhibit 9–5 represent the differences between actual results at an activity level of 220,000 units and the static budget amounts at an activity level of 200,000 units. The sales variance is $270,000 favourable, suggesting that Patterson Framing had a good year overall. However, this sales variance is very misleading as it is attributable to selling 20,000 more units than planned per the static budget. While selling more units than planned is a good thing from a revenue perspective, the static budget variances for the variable expense items are all unfavourable because of this difference between the static budget level of activity and actual sales. Accordingly, the static budget variances for variable expenses are not useful in evaluating how well managers did at controlling costs at actual levels of activity. Hence, the key benefit of the flexible budget performance report shown in Exhibit 9–4 is that it removes the effects of any volume differences between actual results and the static budget. This allows for a much more meaningful analysis of how well managers did in generating revenue and controlling costs.

Finally, some companies integrate the information contained in Exhibits 9–4 and 9–5 in preparing a comprehensive performance report that includes actual results along with both flexible and static budget amounts. An example of this type of report is shown in Exhibit 9–6. Note that the total unfavourable static budget variance of $99,600 is the same as calculated in Exhibit 9–5, but Exhibit 9–6 shows that it consists of two components: (1) an unfavourable flexible budget variance of $359,600 from Exhibit 9–4 and (2) a favourable $260,000 *sales volume variance*. The **sales volume variance** represents the difference between the flexible and static budget amounts for revenues and expenses caused by actual activity levels differing from the static budget amounts. Because both the flexible and static budgets

EXHIBIT 9-6   Comprehensive Performance Report

PATTERSON FRAMING LIMITED
Comprehensive Performance Report[†]
For the Year Ending December 31, 2015

	Actual (220,000 units)	Flexible Budget Variance*	Flexible Budget (220,000 units)	Sales Volume Variance*	Static Budget (200,000 units)
Sales............................	$6,270,000	$330,000 U	$6,600,000	$600,000 F	$6,000,000
Less variable expenses:					
Direct materials................	869,000	11,000 F	880,000	80,000 U	800,000
Direct labour....................	2,244,000	44,000 U	2,200,000	200,000 U	2,000,000
Variable manufacturing					
overhead.....................	228,800	8,800 U	220,000	20,000 U	200,000
Selling and administrative[†]	426,800	13,200 F	440,000	40,000 U	400,000
Total variable expenses.........	3,768,600	28,600 U	3,740,000	340,000 U	3,400,000
Contribution margin	2,501,400	358,600 U	2,860,000	260,000 F	2,600,000
Less fixed expenses:					
Manufacturing overhead........	1,012,000	7,000 U	1,005,000	0	1,005,000
Selling and administrative.......	402,000	6,000 F	408,000	0	408,000
Total fixed expenses	1,414,000	1,000 U	1,413,000	0	1,413,000
Operating income	$ 1,087,400	$ 359,600 U	$ 1,447,000	$260,000 F	$ 1,187,000

$99,600 U
Total static budget variance

*U = unfavourable variance; F = favourable variance.
[†] All actual and flexible budget amounts as per Exhibit 9-4; all static budget amounts as per Exhibit 9-5.

are prepared using budgeted amounts per unit, the only difference that can arise between these two budgets relates to the actual level of activity differing from the static budget level. For example, the favourable sales volume variance of $600,000 for sales is calculated as follows: (220,000 units − 200,000 units) × $30 per unit. The sales volume variances for variable expenses are calculated in a similar fashion. Because total budgeted fixed expenses should be constant within the relevant range of activity, no differences between the flexible and static budgets arise for these items. The advantage of preparing a comprehensive report such as that shown in Exhibit 9-6 is that it helps managers isolate the part of the static budget variance caused solely by volume (activity) differences from the part caused by other factors, such as actual unit prices differing from budget. In Chapter 10, we will further explore the factors that can cause sales volume variances.

> **Instant Quiz 9-8**
> Given the details in Instant Quiz 9-7, calculate the flexible budget variance and sales volume variance if the actual contribution margin, based on selling 60,000 units, is $285,000.

IN BUSINESS

Most organizations determine the amounts to include in the master budget using an approach along the lines of that described in this chapter. However, in many professional sports, the budget for player salaries for each team is determined by the terms of the collective bargaining agreement (CBA) established between the players and team owners. For example, the 2013 CBA for the National Hockey League (NHL) established a maximum and minimum budget for player salaries for the 2013–2014 season of $64 million and $44 million, respectively. Each team had to set their total player salary budget within this range but it could not exceed the maximum level or be below the minimum. The salary budget is based on total hockey-related revenues projected for a season with 50% of that total used as the midpoint for the salary budget for each team. The minimum and maximum salary budget amounts are then set at 15% below and above the midpoint. So, if hockey-related revenues are estimated to be $120 million for a particular season, the maximum total salaries any team can pay are $69 million (15% above $60 million), with a minimum of $51 million. Although the budget for player salaries is imposed on each NHL team by the terms of the CBA, it is based on expected revenues, which, as we saw in this chapter, are also the starting point for developing a master budget. Moreover, as is the case with other types of organizations, budgets require NHL team management to plan for the future and to make resource allocation decisions. Carefully planning which players should be offered new contracts, the dollar amount of those contracts, and the length of the contracts, and identifying the areas where improvements are most needed (e.g., scoring, defence, goaltending), are all benefits that can arise as a result of having a budget for player salaries.

Source: Canadian Press, "NHL Labour Deal: The Nuts & Bolts," January 6, 2013, http://www.cbc.ca/sports/hockey/nhl/story/2013/01/06/sp-nhl-nhlpa-labour-deal-nuts-and-bolts.html.

◼ BUDGETING FOR NOT-FOR-PROFIT ENTITIES

LEARNING OBJECTIVE 5
Describe variations in the master budget process when applying it to not-for-profit situations.

Up to this point, we have discussed budgeting in the context of profit-seeking enterprises, where the sales estimate is the critical factor on which the rest of the master budget depends. Inaccurate sales estimates can create additional inaccuracies in many of the other budgets, given the intricate relationship between expenses and revenues in profit-oriented organizations. However, with not-for-profit (NFP) entities, there is often no relationship between expected revenues and expected expenditures. Examples of NFP entities are municipal, provincial, territorial, and federal governmental units; hospitals; universities; volunteer associations; and professional associations. The profit motive is replaced with a service orientation in NFP organizations. Budget information is gathered to assist in making decisions about what programs and expenditures the entity will undertake. The programs undertaken by an NFP are determined by its mission statement and can be very diverse in nature. For example, the United Way sponsors programs related to seniors' care, women's shelters, independent living, community centres, and so on. Having made decisions about the programs it will offer or support, the NFP entity then estimates the revenues needed to support these programs and the anticipated expenditures for each. Revenue sources may be in the form of grants, donations, special taxes, or membership fees. The viability of NFP organizations depends critically on their ability to generate revenues through their donors.

Accountability is of critical importance to most NFP entities. To ensure continued support from donors, it is advantageous to have a budgeting process in place to assist in planning how resources will be used effectively and efficiently. Budgets of NFP entities should be formally approved by the entity's governing body. A formally approved budget signals to employees and volunteers alike that the organization is committed to meeting its revenue and expenditure goals.

A budget can be prepared either on an expenditure basis or on a program basis. An expenditure-based budget simply lists the total expected costs of items such as rent, insurance, salaries, and depreciation without detailing how these various expenses relate to particular programs. However, many NFP organizations report budget information on the basis of programs rather than line-item expenses. Preparation of the budget on the basis of programs facilitates performance evaluation and allows for the comparison of the budgeted revenues and expenses of each program with the actual amounts on a periodic basis. This approach facilitates decision making about resource allocation among the various programs. Budgeting by program also facilitates the stewardship objective by providing information in a format that can determine whether funds designated by donors for specific purposes are being spent as intended.

IN BUSINESS

Many taxpayers evaluate the fiscal performance of a government, at least in part, based on the extent to which it establishes a "balanced budget"—one where budgeted revenues equal budgeted expenditures. As a result, it is not surprising that elected government officials focus time and effort during the budgeting process either to create a balanced budget or to minimize the extent of any budget deficits where expenditures exceed revenues. For example, the federal government's Budget 2014, tabled by the Honourable James Flaherty, Minister of Finance, projected a balanced budget by 2015–2016 after many years of large budget deficits.

Source: Excerpted from J. Flaherty, The Road to Balance: Creating Jobs and Opportunities; Economic Action Plan 2014, The Budget in Brief, February 11, 2014, http://www.budget.gc.ca/2014/docs/bb/pdf/brief-bref-eng.pdf.

KNOWLEDGE IN ACTION

Managers can apply their knowledge about budgeting when
- Deciding the extent to which employees responsible for attaining budget targets will participate in developing the budget
- Determining how difficult the budget targets should be to attain and whether or not rewards should be linked to attainment of those targets
- Making operational decisions such as planning inventory levels, staffing levels, and production scheduling
- Estimating cash inflows and outflows and arranging in advance for any short-term borrowing
- Evaluating actual performance compared to static budget amounts or flexible budget amounts
- Identifying the causes of differences between actual results and budgeted amounts (more on this in Chapter 10)

SUMMARY

- Budgets play a dual role in organizations (planning and control) and offer several benefits. These include the communication of management's plans, allocation of resources, coordination of activities, and establishment of goals and objectives that can be used to evaluate subsequent performance. [LO1]
- Budgets represent a key element of responsibility accounting systems, whereby managers are held responsible for revenue and cost items over which they have significant influence. The comparison of actual and budgeted results is a common feature of such systems. [LO1]
- Many companies employ a participative budgeting approach, whereby managers are allowed to participate in setting their own budgets. This approach can result in higher commitment to attaining the budget goals but is subject to potential problems if individuals try to set easy budgets through the creation of budget slack. [LO1]
- The preparation of a master budget involves numerous interrelated schedules and begins with the development of the sales budget, which is based on the sales forecast. For a manufacturing company, once the sales budget has been set, the production budget can be prepared since it depends on how many units are to be sold. The production budget determines how many units are to be produced. After it has been prepared, the various manufacturing cost budgets and selling and administrative budgets can be developed. [LO2]

- After the detailed budget schedules have been completed, the cash budget, budgeted income statement, and budgeted balance sheet can be prepared, which collectively provide an overall financial summary of the budget. [LO2]
- Some companies use flexible budgets to address the limitations that arise with static budgets when actual activity levels differ significantly from budgeted levels. Preparing flexible budgets involves restating the budget at the end of a reporting period using actual activity levels and budgeted per unit amounts for revenues and variable expenses. A flexible budget provides a better tool for evaluating managers' performance in generating revenue and controlling costs, given the actual volume of activity. [LO3]
- Preparing flexible budgets also permits companies to prepare performance reports that decompose the difference between actual results and the static budget into flexible budget variances and sales volume variances. This approach is helpful in isolating the cause of variances and forms the basis for further investigation. [LO4]
- Budgeting for not-for-profit (NFP) entities begins with a determination of the costs of undertaking the planned programs and activities. Then the revenues needed to support the programs and related expenditures are determined and budgeted. This approach is necessitated by the fact that in NFP entities there is often little relationship between revenues and expenditures because revenues often come from donors or other granting agencies. [LO5]

REVIEW PROBLEM: COMPLETING A MASTER BUDGET

The following data are for preparation of a second-quarter master budget for Rocket Company, a merchandising operation that prepares its master budget on a quarterly basis.

a. At the end of the previous quarter (March 31), the organization's balance sheet showed the following account balances:

Cash	$ 9,000	
Accounts receivable	48,000	
Inventory	12,600	
Buildings and equipment (net)	214,100	
Accounts payable		$ 18,300
Common shares		190,000
Retained earnings		75,400
	$283,700	$283,700

b. Actual sales for March and budgeted sales for April through July are as follows:

March (actual)	$60,000
April	$70,000
May	$85,000
June	$90,000
July	$50,000

c. Sales are 20% for cash and 80% on credit. All payments on credit sales are collected in the month following the sale. The accounts receivable at March 31 are a result of March credit sales.

d. The company's gross margin is 40% of sales. (In other words, the cost of goods sold is 60% of sales).

e. Monthly expenses are budgeted as follows: salaries and wages, $7,500 per month; shipping, 6% of sales; advertising, $6,000 per month; other expenses, 4% of sales. Depreciation, including depreciation on new assets acquired during the quarter, will be $6,000 for the quarter.

f. Each month's ending inventory should equal 30% of the following month's cost of goods sold.

g. Half of a month's inventory purchases are paid for in the month of purchase and half in the following month.

h. Equipment purchases during the quarter will be as follows: April, $11,500, and May $3,000.

i. Dividends totalling $3,500 will be declared and paid in June.

j. Management wants to maintain a minimum cash balance of $8,000. The company has an agreement with a local bank that allows the company to borrow necessary amounts at the beginning of each month, up to a total loan balance of $20,000. The interest rate is 1% per month. The company will, as far as it is able, repay the loan at the end of each month and must pay interest each month on the total loan balance outstanding for that month.

Required:

Using the data above, complete the following statements and schedules for the second quarter:

1. Sales budget and a schedule of expected cash collections:

	March (actual)	April	May	June	July
Sales Budget					
Total Sales.....................	$60,000	$70,000			
Cash (20%)...................	$ 12,000	$ 14,000			
Credit (80%).................	48,000	56,000			

All credit sales are collected in the month following the sale.

	April	May	June	Total
Schedule of Expected Cash Collections				
Cash sales............................	$ 14,000			
Credit sales...........................	48,000			
Total collections......................	$62,000			

2. *a.* Merchandise purchases budget:

	April	May	June	Total
Budgeted cost of goods sold...........	$42,000*	$51,000		
Add desired ending inventory...........	15,300†			
Total needs............................	57,300			
Less beginning inventory...............	12,600			
Required purchases....................	$ 44,700			

*$70,000 sales × 60% = $42,000.
†$51,000 × 30% = $15,300.

b. Schedule of expected cash disbursements for merchandise purchases:

	April	May	June	Total
For March purchases......................................	$ 18,300			$ 18,300
For April purchases.......................................	22,350	$22,350		44,700
For May purchases.......................................				
For June purchases.......................................				
Total cash disbursements for purchases................	$40,650			

3. Schedule of expected cash disbursements for selling and administrative expenses:

	April	May	June	Total
Salaries and wages..	$ 7,500			
Shipping..	4,200			
Advertising..	6,000			
Other expenses...	2,800			
Total cash disbursements for selling and administrative expenses...........................	$20,500			

4. Cash budget:

	April	May	June	Total
Cash balance, beginning...................................	$ 9,000			
Add cash collections..	62,000			
Total cash available..	71,000			
Less cash disbursements:				
For inventory purchases.............................	40,650			
For selling and administrative expenses..............	20,500			
For equipment purchases...........................	11,500			
For dividends...				
Total cash disbursements...............................	72,650			
Excess (deficiency) of cash.............................	$ (1,650)			
Financing				
Borrowings*..	9,747			
Repayments..	0			
Interest**..	(97)			
Total financing..	9,650			
Cash balance, ending.......................................	$ 8,000			

*April: ($1,650) + X − 0.01X = $8,000; X = $9,747 (rounded).
**April: $9,747 × 1% = $97.

5. Prepare an absorption costing income statement for the quarter ending June 30, as shown in Schedule 9.
6. Prepare a balance sheet as at June 30.

Solution to Review Problem

1. Sales budget:

	March (actual)	April	May	June	July
Total Sales......................	$60,000	$70,000	$85,000	$90,000	$50,000
Cash (20%)....................	$ 12,000	$ 14,000	$ 17,000	$ 18,000	$ 10,000
Credit (80%)...................	48,000	56,000	68,000	72,000	40,000

All credit sales are collected in the month following the sale.

Schedule of Expected Cash Collections				
	April	May	June	Total
Cash sales...	$ 14,000	$ 17,000	$ 18,000	$ 49,000
Credit sales...	48,000	56,000	68,000	172,000
Total collections..	$62,000	$ 73,000	$86,000	$221,000

2.   *a.*   Merchandise purchases budget:

	April	May	June	Total
Budgeted cost of goods sold	$42,000	$51,000	$54,000	$147,000
Add desired ending inventory*	15,300	16,200	9,000	9,000
Total needs	57,300	67,200	63,000	156,000
Less beginning inventory	12,600	15,300	16,200	12,600
Required purchases	$44,700	$51,900	$46,800	$143,400

*At April 30: $51,000 × 30% = $15,300.
At June 30: $50,000 July sales × 60% × 30% = $9,000.

b.   Schedule of cash disbursements for purchases:

	April	May	June	Total
For March purchases	$18,300			$18,300
For April purchases	22,350	$22,350		44,700
For May purchases		25,950	$25,950	51,900
For June purchases			23,400	23,400
Total cash disbursements	$40,650	$48,300	$49,350	$138,300

3.   Schedule of cash disbursements for selling and administrative expenses:

	April	May	June	Total
Salaries and wages	$ 7,500	$ 7,500	$ 7,500	$22,500
Shipping (6% of sales)	4,200	5,100	5,400	14,700
Advertising	6,000	6,000	6,000	18,000
Other expenses (4% of sales)	2,800	3,400	3,600	9,800
Total cash disbursements for selling and administrative expenses	$20,500	$22,000	$22,500	$65,000

4.   Cash budget:

	April	May	June	Total
Cash balance, beginning	$ 9,000	$ 8,000	$ 8,000	$ 9,000
Add cash collections	62,000	73,000	86,000	221,000
Total cash available	71,000	81,000	94,000	230,000
Less disbursements:				
For inventory purchases	40,650	48,300	49,350	138,300
For selling and administrative expenses	20,500	22,000	22,500	65,000
For equipment purchases	11,500	3,000	0	14,500
For dividends	0	0	3,500	3,500
Total disbursements	72,650	73,300	75,350	221,300
Excess (deficiency) of cash	(1,650)	7,700	18,650	8,700
Financing:				
Borrowings*	9,747	401	0	10,148
Repayments	0	0	(10,148)	(10,148)
Interest**	(97)	(101)	(101)	(299)
Total financing	9,650	300	(10,249)	(299)
Cash balance, ending	$ 8,000	$ 8,000	$ 8,401	$ 8,401

*April: ($1,650) + X − 0.01X = $8,000; X = $9,747 (rounded).
May: $7,700 + X − 0.01X − $97 (interest on April loan) = $8,000; X = $401 (rounded).
**April: $9,747 × 1% = $97; May and June: ($9,747 + $401) × 1% = $101.

5.   Income statement:

ROCKET COMPANY
Income Statement
For the Quarter Ended June 30

Sales		$245,000
Cost of goods sold (CGS):		
Beginning inventory (given)..	$ 12,600	
Add purchases (Part 2)...	143,400	
Goods available for sale...	156,000	
Ending inventory (Part 2)...	9,000	147,000
Gross margin		98,000
Selling and administrative expenses:		
Salaries and wages (Part 3)..	22,500	
Shipping (Part 3)...	14,700	
Advertising (Part 3)	18,000	
Depreciation	6,000	
Other expenses (Part 3)...	9,800	71,000
Operating income...		27,000
Less interest expense (Part 4)...		299
Net income..		$ 26,701

Note: CGS can also be computed as follows:
Sales of $245,000 × 60% = $147,000.

6.   Balance sheet:

ROCKET COMPANY
Balance Sheet
June 30

Assets

Current assets:		
Cash (Part 4)		$ 8,401
Accounts receivable (80% × $90,000).......................................		72,000
Inventory (Part 2)...		9,000
Total current assets..		89,401
Buildings and equipment, net ($214,100 + $14,500 − $6,000)...............		222,600
Total assets..		$ 312,001

Liabilities and Shareholders' Equity

Current liabilities:		
Accounts payable (Part 2: 50% × $46,800).............................		$ 23,400
Shareholders' equity:		
Common shares	$190,000	
Retained earnings*	98,601	288,601
Total liabilities and shareholders' equity		$ 312,001
*Retained earnings, beginning...	$ 75,400	
Add net income..	26,701	
Total..	102,101	
Less dividends	3,500	
Retained earnings, ending	$ 98,601	

GLOSSARY

McGraw Hill Education **connect**®   Review key terms and definitions on Connect.

DISCUSSION CASE

DISCUSSION CASE 9-1
Many consider intentionally creating budget slack to be unethical. Do you agree or disagree? Justify your answer. Are there any circumstances under which creating some budget slack might be acceptable, or even desirable, from the organization's perspective? Explain your answer.

QUESTIONS

9-1   What is a budget? What is budgetary control?
9-2   What is a bottleneck?
9-3   What is meant by the term *responsibility accounting*?
9-4   What is a master budget? Briefly describe its contents.
9-5   Why is the sales forecast the starting point in budgeting?
9-6   What is a budget committee? Why is it used by some companies?
9-7   What is a perpetual budget?
9-8   What is a participative budget? What are the major advantages of participative budgets?
9-9   What is budget slack? Why might managers be tempted to build slack into their budgets?
9-10 What is a stretch budget? What is a challenging but attainable budget?
9-11 What is the sales budget and why is so important in the budgeting process?
9-12 Which budget schedule replaces the production budget for merchandising companies?
9-13 Describe the difference between a static budget and a flexible budget.
9-14 What is a sales volume variance?

EXERCISES

EXERCISE 9-1 Schedule of Expected Cash Collections [LO2]
Peak sales for Northern Lift, a wholesale distributor of snow shovels, occur in November. The company's sales budget for the fourth quarter showing these peak sales is given below:

	October	November	December	Total
Budgeted sales (all on account).............	$400,000	$800,000	$700,000	$1,900,000

From past experience, the company has learned that 25% of a month's sales are collected in the month of sale, another 70% are collected in the month following sale, and the remaining 5% are collected in the second month following sale. Bad debts are negligible and can be ignored. August sales totalled $70,000, and September sales totalled $180,000.

Required:
1.   Prepare a schedule of expected cash collections from sales, by month and in total, for the third quarter.
2   Assume that the company will prepare a budgeted balance sheet as of September 30. Compute the accounts receivable as of that date.

EXERCISE 9-2 Sales and Production Budget [LO2]
The marketing department of Graber Corporation has submitted the following sales forecast for the upcoming fiscal year.

	First Quarter	Second Quarter	Third Quarter	Fourth Quarter
Budgeted unit sales....	16,000	15,000	14,000	15,000

The selling price of the company's product is $22.00 per unit. Management expects to collect 75% of sales in the quarter in which the sales are made and 20% in the following quarter, and 5% of sales are expected to be uncollectible. The beginning balance of accounts receivable, all of which is expected to be collected in the first quarter, is $66,000.

The company expects to start the first quarter with 3,200 units in finished goods inventory. Management desires an ending finished goods inventory in each quarter equal to 20% of the next quarter's budgeted sales. The desired ending finished goods inventory for the fourth quarter is 3,400 units.

Required:
1. Prepare the company's sales budget and schedule of expected cash collections.
2. Prepare the company's production budget for the upcoming fiscal year.

EXERCISE 9–3 Direct Materials Purchases Budget [LO2]

Micro Products Inc. has developed a very powerful electronic calculator. Each calculator requires three small chips that cost $3 each and are purchased from an overseas supplier. Micro Products has prepared a production budget for the calculator by quarters for year 2 and for the first quarter of year 3, as shown below:

	Year 2				Year 3
	First	Second	Third	Fourth	First
Budgeted production, in calculators..........	60,000	90,000	150,000	100,000	80,000

The chip used in production of the calculator is sometimes hard to get, so it is necessary to carry large inventories as a precaution against stock-outs. For this reason, the inventory of chips at the end of a quarter must be equal to 20% of the following quarter's production needs. A total of 36,000 chips will be on hand to start the first quarter of year 2.

Required:
Prepare a direct materials purchases budget for chips, by quarter and in total, for year 2. At the bottom of your budget, show the dollar amount of purchases for each quarter and for the year in total.

EXERCISE 9–4 Direct Labour Budget [LO2]

The manufacturing division manager of Davison Enterprises has submitted the following production forecast (in units) for each quarter of the next fiscal year. The plant produces seats for motorcycles:

	First Quarter	Second Quarter	Third Quarter	Fourth Quarter
Units to be produced	10,000	8,800	9,000	9,800

Each unit requires 0.50 direct labour-hours, and employees are paid $15 per hour.

Required:
1. Prepare the company's direct labour budget for the upcoming fiscal year, assuming that the direct labour workforce is adjusted each quarter to match the number of hours required to produce the forecasted number of units.
2. Prepare the company's direct labour budget for the next fiscal year, assuming that the direct labour workforce is *not* adjusted each quarter. Instead, assume that the company's direct labour workforce consists of permanent employees who are guaranteed to be paid for at least 4,500 hours of work each quarter. If the number of required direct labour-hours is less than this number, the workers are paid for 4,500 hours anyway. Any hours worked in excess of 4,500 hours in a quarter are paid at a rate of 1.5 times the normal hourly rate for direct labour.

EXERCISE 9–5 Manufacturing Overhead Budget [LO2]

The direct labour budget of Small Corporation for the upcoming fiscal year contains the following details concerning budgeted direct labour-hours:

	First Quarter	Second Quarter	Third Quarter	Fourth Quarter
Budgeted direct labour-hours	5,000	4,800	5,200	5,400

The company's variable manufacturing overhead rate is $1.75 per direct labour-hour, and the company's fixed manufacturing overhead is $35,000 per quarter. The only non-cash item included in the fixed manufacturing overhead is depreciation, which is $15,000 per quarter.

Required:
1. Prepare the company's manufacturing overhead budget for the upcoming fiscal year.
2. Compute the company's manufacturing overhead rate (including both variable and fixed manufacturing overhead) for the upcoming fiscal year. Round off to the nearest whole cent.

EXERCISE 9-6 Selling and Administrative Expense Budget [LO2]
The budgeted unit sales of Hirst Company for the upcoming fiscal year are provided below:

	First Quarter	Second Quarter	Third Quarter	Fourth Quarter
Budgeted unit sales...............	12,000	14,000	11,000	10,000

The company's variable selling and administrative expenses per unit are $2.75. Fixed selling and administrative expenses include advertising expenses of $12,000 per quarter, executive salaries of $40,000 per quarter, and depreciation of $16,000 per quarter. In addition, the company will make insurance payments of $6,000 in the second quarter and $6,000 in the fourth quarter. Finally, property taxes of $6,000 will be paid in the third quarter.

Required:
Prepare the company's selling and administrative expense budget for the upcoming fiscal year. Also include the cash disbursements for selling and administrative expenses as per Schedule 7.

EXERCISE 9-7 Cash Budget Analysis [LO2]
A cash budget, by quarter, is given below for a retail company (000 omitted). The company requires a minimum cash balance of $5,000 to start each quarter.

Required:
Fill in the missing amounts in the table that follows:

	Quarter				Year
	1	2	3	4	
Cash balance, beginning.	$ 6	$?	$?	$?	$?
Add collections from customers..................	?	?	96	?	323
Total cash available.	71	?	?	?	?
Less disbursements:					
Purchases of inventory.......................	35	45	?	35	?
Selling and administrative expenses..............	?	30	30	?	113
Equipment purchases.........................	8	8	10	?	36
Dividends..................................	2	2	2	2	?
Total disbursements	?	85	?	?	?
Excess (deficiency) of cash available over disbursements..........................	(2)	?	11	?	?
Financing:					
Borrowings	?	15	—	—	?
Repayments*................................	—	—	(?)	(16)	(?)
Total financing..............................	?	?	?	?	?
Cash balance, ending.	$?	$?	$?	$?	$?

*For this exercise assume there will be no interest on any borrowings.

EXERCISE 9-8 Preparing a Flexible Budget [LO3]
Auto Lavage is a Canadian company that owns and operates a large automatic carwash facility near Quebec. The following table provides data concerning the company's costs:

	Fixed Cost per Month	Cost per Car Washed
Cleaning supplies		$0.70
Electricity	$ 1,400	0.10
Maintenance		0.30
Wages and salaries	4,700	0.40
Depreciation	8,300	
Rent	2,100	
Administrative expenses	1,800	0.05

The company expects to charge customers an average of $5.90 per car washed.

Required:

Using Exhibit 9–3 as your guide, prepare a flexible budget for October assuming either 8,000 or 9,000 cars are washed.

EXERCISE 9–9 Flexible Budget Performance Report [LO3, LO4]

Refer to the data in Exercise 9–8. Auto Lavage's actual level of activity was 8,100 cars. The actual revenues and expenses for October are given below:

	Actual Data for 8,100 Cars
Sales	$49,300
Variable expenses:	
Cleaning supplies	6,075
Electricity	891
Maintenance	2,187
Wages and salary	3,402
Administrative	486
Fixed expenses:	
Electricity	1,450
Wages and salaries	4,700
Depreciation	8,300
Rent	2,100
Administrative	1,745

Required:

1. Prepare a flexible budget performance report for October using Exhibit 9–4 as your guide.
2. Prepare a comprehensive performance report for October using Exhibit 9–6 as your guide. Assume that the static budget for October was based on an activity level of 8,000 cars.

EXERCISE 9–10 Flexible Budget Performance Report [LO4]

Air Assurance Corporation provides on-site air quality testing services. The company has provided the following data concerning its operations:

	Fixed Component per Month	Variable Component per Job	Actuals for March
Revenue		$275	$24,750
Technician wages	$8,600		8,450
Mobile lab selling and administrative expenses	4,900	29	7,960 (5,216 fixed)
Office expenses	2,700	3	2,850 (2,556 fixed)
Advertising expenses	1,580		1,650
Insurance	2,870		2,870
Miscellaneous expenses	960	2	465 (269 fixed)

The company uses the number of jobs as its measure of activity. For example, mobile lab selling and administrative expenses should be $4,900 plus $29 per job, and the actual mobile lab operating expenses for March were $7,960. The company expected to work 100 jobs in March, but actually worked 98 jobs.

Required:
Prepare a comprehensive performance report for March using Exhibit 9–6 as your guide. Assume that the static budget for March was based on an activity level of 100 jobs.

PROBLEMS

PROBLEM 9–11 Integration of Sales, Production, and Direct Materials Budgets [LO2]
Crydon Inc. manufactures an advanced swim fin for scuba divers. Management is now preparing detailed budgets for the third quarter, July through September, and has assembled the following information to assist in preparing the budget:

a. The Marketing Department has estimated sales as follows for the remainder of the year (in pairs of swim fins):

July...	6,000
August..	7,000
September..	5,000
October...	4,000
November..	3,000
December	3,000

The selling price of the swim fins is $50 per pair.

b. All sales are on account. Based on past experience, sales are expected to be collected in the following pattern:

40% in the month of sale
50% in the month following sale
10% uncollectible

The beginning accounts receivable balance (excluding uncollectible amounts) on July 1 will be $130,000.

c. The company maintains finished goods inventories equal to 10% of the following month's sales. The inventory of finished goods on July 1 will be 600 pairs.

d. Each pair of swim fins requires 2 pounds of grelco compound. To prevent shortages, the company would like the inventory of grelco compound on hand at the end of each month to be equal to 20% of the following month's production needs. The inventory of grelco compound on hand on July 1 will be 2,440 kilograms.

e. Grelco compound costs $2.50 per kilogram. Crydon pays for 60% of its purchases in the month of purchase; the remainder is paid for in the following month. The accounts payable balance for grelco compound purchases will be $11,400 on July 1.

Required:
1. Prepare a sales budget, by month and in total, for the third quarter. (Show your budget in both pairs of swim fins and dollars.) Also prepare a schedule of expected cash collections, by month and in total, for the third quarter.
2. Prepare a production budget for each of the months July through October.
3. Prepare a direct materials budget for grelco compound, by month and in total, for the third quarter. Also prepare a schedule of expected cash disbursements for grelco compound, by month and in total, for the third quarter.

PROBLEM 9–12 Schedules of Expected Cash Collections and Disbursements [LO2]
Calgon Products, a distributor of organic beverages, needs a cash budget for September. The following information is available:

a. The cash balance at the beginning of September is $9,000.
b. Actual sales for July and August and expected sales for September are as shown below. Sales on account are collected over a three-month period as follows: 10% collected in the month of sale, 70% collected in the month following sale, and 18% collected in the second month following sale. The remaining 2% is uncollectible:

	July	August	September
Cash sales............................	$ 6,500	$ 5,250	$ 7,400
Sales on account....................	20,000	30,000	40,000
Total sales..........................	$26,500	$35,250	$47,400

c.   Purchases of inventory will total $25,000 for September. Twenty percent of a month's inventory purchases are paid for during the month of purchase. The accounts payable remaining from August's inventory purchases total $16,000, all of which will be paid in September.

d.   Selling and administrative expenses are budgeted at $13,000 for September. Of this amount, $4,000 is for depreciation.

e.   Equipment costing $18,000 will be purchased for cash during September, and dividends totalling $3,000 will be paid during the month.

f.   The company maintains a minimum cash balance of $5,000. An open line of credit is available from the company's bank to bolster the cash position as needed. Assume any borrowings occur at the beginning of the month and repayments occur at the end of the month. Interest on outstanding loan balances during the month must be paid at the end of each month. The monthly interest rate is 0.5%.

Required:
1.   Prepare a schedule of expected cash collections for September.
2.   Prepare a schedule of expected cash disbursements during September for inventory purchases.
3.   Prepare a cash budget for September. Indicate in the financing section any borrowing that will be needed during September.

PROBLEM 9–13 Behavioural Aspects of Budgeting; Ethics and the Manager [LO1]

Hayden Black, managing partner of the venture capital firm of Cole and Black, was dissatisfied with the top management of CompuDrive, a manufacturer of computer disk drives. Cole and Black had invested $20 million in CompuDrive, and the return on their investment had been unsatisfactory for several years. In a tense meeting of the board of directors of CompuDrive, Black exercised his firm's rights as the major equity investor in CompuDrive and fired CompuDrive's chief executive officer (CEO). He then quickly moved to have the board of directors of CompuDrive appoint him as the new CEO.

Black prided himself on his hard-driving management style. At a budget review meeting, he ripped up the departmental budgets that had been submitted for his review and yelled at the managers for their "gutless, do-nothing targets." He then ordered everyone to submit new budgets calling for at least a 40% increase in sales volume and announced that he would not accept excuses for results that fell below budget.

Kelly Catano, an accountant working for the production manager at CompuDrive, discovered toward the end of the following year that her boss had not been scrapping defective disk drives that had been returned by customers. Instead, he had been shipping them in new cartons to other customers to avoid booking losses. Quality control had deteriorated during the year as a result of the push for increased volume, and returns of defective drives were running as high as 15% of the new drives shipped. When she confronted her boss with her discovery, he told her to mind her own business. And then, to justify his actions, he said, "All of us managers are finding ways to hit Black's targets."

Required:
1.   Is Hayden Black using budgets as a planning and control tool?
2.   What are the behavioural consequences of the way budgets are being used at CompuDrive?
3.   What, if anything, do you think Catano should do?

PROBLEM 9–14 Production and Direct Materials Purchases Budgets [LO2]

Franklin Products Limited manufactures and distributes a number of products to retailers. One of these products, SuperStick, requires four kilograms of material D236 in the manufacture of each unit. The company is now planning raw materials needs for the third quarter—July, August, and September. Peak sales of SuperStick occur in the third quarter of each year. To keep production and shipments moving smoothly, the company has the following inventory requirements:

a.   The finished goods inventory on hand at the end of each month must be equal to 8,000 units plus 20% of the next month's sales. The finished goods inventory on June 30 is budgeted to be 22,000 units.

b.   The raw materials inventory on hand at the end of each month must be equal to 40% of the following month's production needs for raw materials. The raw materials inventory on June 30 for material D236 is budgeted to be 129,000 kilograms.
c.   The company maintains no work in process inventories.

A sales budget for SuperStick for the last six months of the year follows:

	Budgeted Sales in Units
July.	60,000
August.	75,000
September.	105,000
October.	53,000
November.	30,000
December	15,000

Required:
1.   Prepare a production budget for SuperStick for July, August, September, and October.
2.   Examine the production budget that you prepared. Why will the company produce more units than it sells in July and August and fewer units than it sells in September and October?
3.   Prepare a direct materials purchases budget showing the quantity of material D236 to be purchased for July, August, and September and for the quarter in total.

PROBLEM 9–15 Direct Materials Purchases and Direct Labour Budgets [LO2]
The production department of Taylor Company has submitted the following forecast of units to be produced by quarter for the upcoming fiscal year:

	First Quarter	Second Quarter	Third Quarter	Fourth Quarter
Units to be produced.	6,000	7,000	8,000	5,000

In addition, the beginning raw materials inventory for the first quarter is budgeted to be 3,600 kilograms and the beginning accounts payable for the first quarter is budgeted to be $11,775.

Each unit requires three kilograms of raw material that costs $2.50 per kilogram. Management wants to end each quarter with a raw materials inventory equal to 20% of the following quarter's production needs. The desired ending inventory for the fourth quarter is 3,700 kilograms. Management plans to pay for 70% of raw material purchases in the quarter acquired and 30% in the following quarter. Each unit requires 0.50 direct labour-hours, and direct labour-hour workers are paid $12 per hour.

Required:
1.   Prepare the company's direct materials purchases budget and schedule of expected cash disbursements for materials for the upcoming fiscal year.
2.   Prepare the company's direct labour budget for the upcoming fiscal year, assuming that the direct labour workforce is adjusted each quarter to match the number of hours required to produce the forecasted number of units produced.

PROBLEM 9–16 Direct Labour and Manufacturing Overhead Budgets [LO2]
The Bakery Department of Culbert Dessert Corporation has submitted the following forecast of fruit pies to be produced by quarter for the upcoming fiscal year.

	First Quarter	Second Quarter	Third Quarter	Fourth Quarter
Units to be produced.	8,000	11,000	9,000	13,000

Each unit requires 0.30 direct labour-hours, and direct labour-hour workers are paid $10.50 per hour.

In addition, the variable manufacturing overhead rate is $1.50 per direct labour-hour. The fixed manufacturing overhead is $23,000 per quarter. The only non-cash element of manufacturing overhead is depreciation, which is $7,000 per quarter.

Required:

1. Prepare the company's direct labour budget for the upcoming fiscal year, assuming that the direct labour workforce is adjusted each quarter to match the number of hours required to produce the forecasted number of units produced.
2. Prepare the company's manufacturing overhead budget. As per Schedule 5, your manufacturing overhead budget should also include the budgeted cash disbursements for overhead.

PROBLEM 9-17 Schedules of Expected Cash Collections and Disbursements; Income Statement; Balance Sheet [LO2]

Colerain Corporation is a merchandising company that is preparing a budget for the third quarter of the calendar year. The company's balance sheet as of June 30 is shown below:

COLERAIN CORPORATION **Balance Sheet** **June 30**	
Assets	
Cash.	$ 80,000
Accounts receivable.	126,000
Inventory.	52,000
Plant and equipment, net of depreciation.	200,000
Total assets.	$458,000
Liabilities and Shareholders' Equity	
Accounts payable.	$ 61,100
Common shares.	300,000
Retained earnings.	96,900
Total liabilities and shareholders' equity.	$458,000

Colerain's managers have made the following additional assumptions and estimates:

a. Estimated sales for July, August, September, and October will be $200,000, $220,000, $210,000, and $230,000, respectively.
b. All sales are on credit and all credit sales are collected. Each month's credit sales are collected 30% in the month of sale and 70% in the month following the sale. All of the accounts receivable at June 30 will be collected in July.
c. Each month's ending inventory must equal 40% of the cost of next month's sales. The cost of goods sold is 65% of sales. The company pays for 50% of its merchandise purchases in the month of the purchase and the remaining 50% in the month following the purchase. All of the accounts payable at June 30 will be paid in July.
d. Monthly selling and administrative expenses are always $65,000. Each month, $5,000 of this total amount is depreciation expense and the remaining $60,000 relates to expenses that are paid in the month they are incurred.
e. The company does not plan to borrow money or pay or declare dividends during the quarter ended September 30. The company does not plan to issue any common shares or repurchase its own shares during the quarter ended September 30.

Required:

1. Prepare a schedule of expected cash collections for July, August, and September. Also compute total cash collections for the quarter ended September 30.
2. a. Prepare a merchandise purchases budget for July, August, and September. Also compute total merchandise purchases for the quarter ended September 30.
   b. Prepare a schedule of expected cash disbursements for merchandise purchases for July, August, and September. Also compute total cash disbursements for merchandise purchases for the quarter ended September 30th.
3. Prepare an income statement for the quarter ended September 30. Use the absorption format shown in Schedule 9.
4. Prepare a balance sheet as of September 30.

PROBLEM 9-18 Cash Budget; Income Statement; Balance Sheet [LO2]

The balance sheet of Pixelize Inc., a photographic supplies distributor, as of May 31 is given below:

PIXELIZE INC.
Balance Sheet
May 31

Assets

Cash..	$ 8,000
Accounts receivable..	72,000
Inventory..	30,000
Buildings and equipment, net of depreciation	500,000
Total assets..	$610,000

Liabilities and Shareholders' Equity

Accounts payable	$ 90,000
Note payable...	15,000
Common shares	420,000
Retained earnings..	85,000
Total liabilities and shareholders' equity	$610,000

Pixelize Inc. has not budgeted previously, so it is limiting its master budget planning horizon to just one month ahead—namely, June. The company has assembled the following budget data relating to June:

a. Sales are forecast to be $250,000; $60,000 will be received in cash; the balance will be credit sales. One-half of the credit sales for a month are collected in the month of sale, and the balance is collected the next month. The entire May 31 accounts receivable balance will be collected in June.

b. Inventory purchases are expected to total $200,000 during the month of June. All of these purchases will be on account. Forty percent of all inventory purchases is paid for in the month of purchase with the other 60% paid the next month. The entire balance of the May 31 accounts payable to suppliers will be paid during June.

c. The inventory balance for June 30 is budgeted at $40,000.

d. The selling and administrative expenses budget for June is $51,000, excluding depreciation. All of these expenses will be paid in cash. The depreciation budget is $2,000 for the month.

e. The May 31 note payable that appears on the balance sheet will be paid in June. Interest expense for the month of June (all borrowings) will be $160, to be paid in cash.

f. Warehouse equipment totalling $9,000 will be acquired for cash in June.

g. In June, the company will borrow $18,000 from the bank by issuing a new note payable to the bank for that same amount. The new note will be due in one year.

Required:

1. Prepare a cash budget for June. Support your budget with a schedule of expected cash collections from sales and a schedule of expected cash disbursements for inventory purchases.

2. Prepare a budgeted income statement for June. Use the absorption costing income statement format as shown in Schedule 9.

3. Prepare a budgeted balance sheet as of June 30.

PROBLEM 9-19 Integration of Sales, Production, and Direct Materials Purchases Budgets [LO2]

Water Sport Inc. manufactures a small personal water tube used for children learning to swim. Management is now preparing detailed budgets for the third quarter, July through September, and has assembled the following information to assist:

a. The Marketing Department has estimated sales as follows for the remainder of the year (number of water tubes):

July	6,500	October.....................	3,000
August.......................	5,000	November..................	2,500
September	4,000	December..................	2,000

The selling price of the water tubes is $60.

b. All sales are on account. Based on past experience, sales are expected to be collected in the following pattern:

> 50% in the month of sale
> 45% in the month following sale
> 5% uncollectible

The beginning accounts receivable balance (excluding uncollectible amounts) on July 1 will be $160,000.

c. The company maintains finished goods inventories equal to 20% of the following month's sales. The inventory of finished goods on July 1 will be 1,300 units.

d. Each water tube requires 3 kilograms of synthetic polyisoprene rubber compound. To prevent shortages, the company would like the inventory of synthetic rubber compound on hand at the end of each month to be equal to 20% of the following month's production needs. The inventory of synthetic rubber compound on hand on July 1 will be 3,720 kilograms.

e. The synthetic rubber compound costs $3.50 per kilogram. Water Sport pays for 70% of its purchases in the month of purchase; the remainder is paid for in the following month. The accounts payable balance for synthetic rubber compound purchases will be $11,400 on July 1.

Required:

1. Prepare a sales budget, by month and in total, for the third quarter. (Show your budget in both units of water tubes and dollars.) Also prepare a schedule of expected cash collections, by month and in total, for the third quarter.
2. Prepare a production budget for each of the months July through October.
3. Prepare a direct materials purchases budget for synthetic rubber compound, by month and in total, for the third quarter. Also prepare a schedule of expected cash disbursements for synthetic rubber compound, by month and in total, for the third quarter.

PROBLEM 9-20 Completing a Master Budget [LO2]
The following data relate to the operations of Soper Company, a wholesale distributor of consumer goods, as of March 31:

Cash.	$ 8,000
Accounts receivable.	20,000
Inventory.	36,000
Building and equipment, net.	120,000
Accounts payable.	21,750
Common shares.	150,000
Retained earnings.	12,250

a. The gross margin is 25% of sales.
b. Actual and budgeted sales data are as follows:

March (actual).	$50,000
April.	60,000
May.	72,000
June.	90,000
July.	48,000

c. Sales are 60% for cash and 40% on credit. Credit sales are collected in the month following sale. The accounts receivable at March 31 are a result of March credit sales.
d. Each month's ending inventory should equal 80% of the following month's budgeted cost of goods sold.

e. One-half of a month's inventory purchases is paid for in the month of purchase; the other half is paid for in the following month. The accounts payable at March 31 are the result of March purchases of inventory.

f. Monthly expenses are as follows: commissions, 12% of sales; rent, $2,500 per month; other expenses (excluding depreciation), 6% of sales. Assume that these expenses are paid monthly. Depreciation is $900 per month (includes depreciation on new assets).

g. Equipment costing $1,500 will be purchased for cash in April.

h. The company must maintain a minimum cash balance of $4,000. An open line of credit is available at a local bank. All borrowing is done at the beginning of a month, and all repayments are made at the end of a month. The monthly interest rate is 1%. Interest must be paid at the end of each month based on the total loans outstanding for that month.

Required:

Using the data above, complete the following:

1. Schedule of expected cash collections:

	April	May	June	Quarter
Cash sales	$36,000			
Credit sales*	20,000			
Total collections	$56,000			

*40% of prior month's sales.

2. Merchandise purchases budget:

	April	May	June	Quarter
Budgeted cost of goods sold	$45,000*	$54,000		
Add desired ending inventory	43,200†			
Total needs	88,200			
Less beginning inventory	36,000			
Required purchases	$52,200			

*For April sales: $60,000 sales × 75% cost ratio = $45,000.
†$54,000 × 80% = $43,200.

Schedule of expected cash disbursements—Merchandise purchases:

	April	May	June	Quarter
March purchases	$21,750			$ 21,750
April purchases	26,100	$26,100		52,200
May purchases				
June purchases				
Total disbursements	$47,850			

3. Schedule of expected cash disbursements—Selling and administrative expenses:

	April	May	June	Quarter
Commissions	$ 7,200			
Rent	2,500			
Other expenses	3,600			
Total disbursements	$13,300			

4.   Cash budget:

	April	May	June	Quarter
Cash balance, beginning........................	$ 8,000			
Add cash collections	56,000			
Total cash available............................	$64,000	___	___	___
Less cash disbursements				
For inventory	$ 47,850			
For expenses	13,300			
For equipment	1,500			
Total cash disbursements	62,650	___	___	___
Excess (deficiency) of cash....................	$ 1,350	___	___	___
Financing:				
Etc.				

5.   Prepare an absorption costing income statement, similar to the one shown in Schedule 9, for the quarter ended June 30.
6.   Prepare a balance sheet as of June 30.

PROBLEM 9-21 Cash Budget with Supporting Schedules [LO2]

Scott Products Inc. is a merchandising company that sells binders, paper, and other school supplies. The company is planning its cash needs for the third quarter. In the past, Scott Products has had to borrow money during the third quarter to support peak sales of back-to-school materials, which occur during August. The following information has been assembled to assist in preparing a cash budget for the quarter:

a.   Budgeted monthly absorption costing income statements for July through October are as follows:

	July	August	September	October
Sales.....................................	$40,000	$70,000	$50,000	$45,000
Cost of goods sold.......................	24,000	42,000	30,000	27,000
Gross margin.............................	16,000	28,000	20,000	18,000
Selling and administrative expenses:				
Selling expense.......................	7,200	11,700	8,500	7,300
Administrative expense*...............	5,600	7,200	6,100	5,900
Total expenses	12,800	18,900	14,600	13,200
Operating income........................	$ 3,200	$ 9,100	$ 5,400	$ 4,800

*Includes $2,000 depreciation each month.

b.   Sales are 20% for cash and 80% on credit.
c.   Credit sales are collected over a three-month period, with 10% collected in the month of sale, 70% in the month following sale, and 20% in the second month following sale. May sales totalled $30,000, and June sales totalled $36,000.
d.   Inventory purchases are paid for within 15 days. Therefore, 50% of a month's inventory purchases is paid for in the month of purchase. The remaining 50% is paid in the following month. Accounts payable for inventory purchases at June 30 total $11,700.
e.   The company maintains its ending inventory levels at 75% of the cost of the merchandise to be sold in the following month. The merchandise inventory at June 30 is $18,000.
f.   Land costing $4,500 will be purchased in July.
g.   Dividends of $1,000 will be declared and paid in September.
h.   The cash balance on June 30 is $8,000; the company must maintain a cash balance of at least this amount at the end of each month.
i.   The company has an agreement with a local bank that allows the company to borrow up to a total loan balance of $40,000. The interest rate on these loans is 1% per month. All borrowing is done at the beginning of a month. The company would, as far as it is able, repay the loan at the end of each month. Interest must be paid at the end of each month based on the outstanding loans for that month. There are no loans outstanding as at June 30.

Required:
1. Prepare a schedule of expected cash collections for July, August, and September and for the quarter in total.
2. Prepare the following for merchandise inventory:
   a. A merchandise purchases budget for July, August, and September.
   b. A schedule of expected cash disbursements for merchandise purchases for July, August, and September and for the quarter in total.
3. Prepare a cash budget for July, August, and September and for the quarter in total.

PROBLEM 9–22 Cash Budget with Supporting Schedules; Changing Assumptions [LO2]
Refer to the data for Scott Products Inc. in Problem 9–21. The company's president is interested in knowing how reducing inventory levels and collecting accounts receivable sooner will impact the cash budget. He revises the cash collection and ending inventory assumptions as follows:

1. Sales continue to be 20% for cash and 80% on credit. However, credit sales from July, August, and September are collected over a three-month period, with 25% collected in the month of sale, 60% collected in the month following sale, and 15% in the second month following sale. Credit sales from May and June are collected during the third quarter using the collection percentages specified in Problem 9–21.
2. The company maintains its ending inventory levels for July, August, and September at 25% of the cost of merchandise to be sold in the following month. The merchandise inventory at June 30 remains $18,000 and accounts payable for inventory purchases at June 30 remains $11,700.

All other information from Problem 9–21 that is not referred to above remains the same.

Required:
1. Using the president's new assumptions in (1) above, prepare a schedule of expected cash collections for July, August, and September and for the quarter in total.
2. Using the president's new assumptions in (2) above, prepare the following for merchandise inventory:
   a. A merchandise purchases budget for July, August, and September.
   b. A schedule of expected cash disbursements for merchandise purchases for July, August, and September and for the quarter in total.
3. Using the president's new assumptions, prepare a cash budget for July, August, and September and for the quarter in total.
4. Briefly explain how the president's revised assumptions affect the cash budget.

PROBLEM 9–23 Integrated Operating Budgets [LO2]
The Western Division of Keltic Company manufactures a vital component that is used in one of Keltic's major product lines. The Western Division has been experiencing some difficulty in coordinating activities among its various departments, which has resulted in some shortages of the component at critical times. To overcome the shortages, the manager of the Western Division has decided to initiate a monthly budgeting system that is integrated among departments.

The first budget is to be for the second quarter of the current year. To assist in creating the budget, the divisional controller has accumulated the following information:

Sales. Sales through the first three months of the current year were 48,000 units. Actual sales in units for January, February, and March, and planned sales in units over the next five months, are given below:

January (actual)	9,000
February (actual)	15,000
March (actual)	24,000
April (planned)	30,000
May (planned)	53,000
June (planned)	75,000
July (planned)	68,000
August (planned)	45,000

In total, the Western Division expects to produce and sell 380,000 units during the current year.

Direct Materials. Two different materials are used in the production of the component. Data regarding these materials are given below:

Direct Materials	Units of Direct Materials per Finished Component	Cost per Unit	Inventory at March 31
No. 226	2 kilograms	$4.00	23,000 kilograms
No. 301	5 metres	$1.50	35,000 metres

Material No. 226 is sometimes in short supply. Therefore, the Western Division requires that enough of the material be on hand at the end of each month to provide for 60% of the following month's production needs. Material No. 301 is easier to obtain, so only 30% of the following month's production needs must be on hand at the end of each month.

Direct Labour. The Western Division has three departments through which the components must pass before they are completed. Information relating to direct labour in these departments is given below:

Department	Direct Labour-Hours per Finished Component	Cost per Direct Labour-Hour
Cutting	0.15	$16.00
Assembly	0.60	14.00
Finishing	0.10	18.00

Direct labour is adjusted to the workload each month.

Manufacturing Overhead. The Western Division manufactured 48,000 components during the first three months of the current year. The actual variable overhead costs incurred during this three-month period are shown below. The Western Division's controller believes that the variable overhead costs incurred during the last nine months of the year will be at the same rate per component as experienced during the first three months:

Utilities..	$ 63,000
Indirect labour	34,000
Supplies	18,000
Other...	9,800
Total variable overhead	$124,800

The actual fixed manufacturing overhead costs incurred during the first three months totalled $1,287,000. The Western Division has budgeted fixed manufacturing overhead costs for the entire year as follows:

Supervision	$ 785,000
Property taxes	129,000
Depreciation	2,619,000
Insurance	568,000
Other...	65,000
Total fixed manufacturing overhead	$4,166,000

Finished Goods Inventory. The desired monthly ending finished goods inventory is 20% of the next month's estimated sales. The Western Division has 6,000 units in finished goods inventory on March 31.

Required:
1. Prepare a production budget for the Western Division for the second quarter ending June 30. Show computations by month and in total for the quarter.
2. Prepare a direct materials purchases budget for each type of material for the second quarter ending June 30. Again show computations by month and in total for the quarter.

3. Prepare a direct labour budget for the second quarter ending June 30. This time it is *not* necessary to show monthly figures; show quarterly totals only. Assume that the workforce is adjusted as work requirements change.

4. Assume that the company plans to produce a total of 380,000 units for the year. Prepare a manufacturing overhead budget for the nine-month period ending December 31. (Do not compute a predetermined overhead rate.) Again, it is *not* necessary to show monthly figures.

(CMA, adapted)

PROBLEM 9–24 Completing a Master Budget [LO2]

The following data relate to the operations of Lim Corporation, a wholesale distributor of consumer goods:

Current assets as of December 31:

Cash	$ 6,000
Accounts receivable	36,000
Inventory	9,800
Buildings and equipment, net	110,885
Accounts payable	32,550
Common shares	100,000
Retained earnings	30,135

a. The gross margin is 30% of sales.
b. Actual and budgeted sales data are as follows:

December (actual)	$60,000
January	70,000
February	80,000
March	85,000
April	55,000

c. Sales are 40% for cash and 60% on credit. Credit sales are collected in the month following sale. The accounts receivable at December 31 are the result of December credit sales.

d. Each month's ending inventory should equal 20% of the following month's budgeted cost of goods sold.

e. One-quarter of a month's inventory purchases is paid for in the month of purchase; the other three-quarters is paid for in the following month. The accounts payable at December 31 are the result of December purchases of inventory.

f. Monthly expenses are as follows: commissions, $12,000; rent, $1,800; other expenses (excluding depreciation), 8% of sales. Assume that these expenses are paid monthly. Depreciation is $2,400 for the quarter and includes depreciation on new assets acquired during the quarter.

g. Equipment will be acquired for cash: $3,000 in January and $8,000 in February.

h. Management would like to maintain a minimum cash balance of $5,000 at the end of each month. The company has an agreement with a local bank that allows it to borrow up to a total loan balance of $50,000. The interest rate on these loans is 0.5% per month, and interest payments must be made at the end of each month. Assume all borrowing occurs at the beginning of a month. The company will, as far as it is able, repay outstanding loans at the end of each month.

Required:
Using the data above, complete the following:
1. Schedule of expected cash collections:

	January	February	March	Quarter
Cash sales	$28,000			
Credit sales	36,000			
Total collections	$64,000			

2.　Merchandise purchases budget:

	January	February	March	Quarter
Budgeted cost of goods sold.............	$49,000*			
Add desired ending inventory	11,200†	___	___	___
Total needs...............................	60,200			
Less beginning inventory................	9,800	___	___	___
Required purchases.....................	$50,400	___	___	___

*$70,000 sales × 70% = $49,000.
†$80,000 × 70% × 20% = $11,200.

Schedule of expected cash disbursements—Merchandise purchases:

	January	February	March	Quarter
December purchases.....................	$32,550*			$32,550
January purchases	12,600	$37,800		50,400
February purchases.....................				
March purchases	___			
Total disbursements.....................	$ 45,150	___	___	___

*Beginning balance of the accounts payable.

3.　Schedule of expected cash disbursements—Selling and administrative expenses:

	January	February	March	Quarter
Commissions.............................	$12,000			
Rent	1,800			
Other expenses..........................	5,600	___	___	___
Total disbursements.....................	$19,400	___	___	___

4.　Cash budget:

	January	February	March	Quarter
Cash balance, beginning..................	$ 6,000			
Add cash collections.....................	64,000	___	___	___
Total cash available	70,000	___	___	___
For inventory..........................	45,150			
For selling and administrative expenses...	19,400			
For equipment.........................	3,000	___	___	___
Total cash disbursements................	67,550			
Excess (deficiency) of cash...............	$ 2,450			
Financing				
Etc.				

5.　Prepare an absorption costing income statement, similar to the one shown in Schedule 9, for the quarter ended March 31.

6.　Prepare a balance sheet as of March 31.

PROBLEM 9-25 Applying the Flexible Budget Approach [LO3, LO4]
The Centrico Medical Laboratory, a government-sponsored charity, is located on the island of Ste. Lucretia. The laboratory has just finished its operations for September, which was a particularly busy month due to a chemical spill that affected a few neighbouring small islands,

causing many illnesses. The chemical spill and contamination largely bypassed Ste. Lucretia's water supply, but residents of Ste. Lucretia willingly donated supplies and the laboratory assisted in the medical testing to help people on other islands. As a consequence, the medical laboratory collected and processed over 25% more laboratory samples from potentially ill residents than had been originally planned for the month.

A report prepared by a government official comparing actual costs to costs included in the static budget for the medical laboratory appears below. (The currency in Ste. Lucretia is the East Caribbean dollar.) Continued support from the government depends on the lab's ability to demonstrate control over its costs:

CENTRICO MEDICAL LABORATORY Cost Control Report For the Month Ended September 30			
	Actual	Static Budget	Static Budget Variance
Laboratory samples collected	920	700	220
Variable costs:			
Medical supplies	$ 14,878	$ 10,640	$4,238
Lab tests	16,173	12,915	3,258
Refreshments for staff and volunteers	1,779	1,435	344
Administrative supplies	284	490	(206)
Total variable cost	33,114	25,480	7,634
Fixed costs:			
Staff salaries	19,800	19,800	0
Equipment depreciation	3,150	2,850	300
Rent	2,250	2,250	0
Utilities	486	450	36
Total fixed cost	25,686	25,350	336
Total cost	$58,800	$50,830	$ 7,970

The managing director of the medical laboratory is very unhappy with this report, claiming that his costs were higher than expected due to the emergency on the neighbouring islands. He also points out that the additional costs were fully covered by payments from grateful recipients on the other islands. The government official who prepared the report counters that all of the figures were submitted by the medical laboratory to the government; he was just pointing out that actual costs were considerably higher than promised in the budget.

Required:
1. Prepare a new performance report for September using the flexible budget approach. (*Note:* Even though there are no revenues in this setting, the flexible budget approach can still be used to prepare a flexible budget performance report. Use Exhibit 9–4 as your guide.)
2. Do you think any of the variances in the report you prepared should be investigated? Why?

CASES

CASE 9–26 The Challenges of Participative Budgeting [LO1]
Dave Ludwig is the chief financial officer (CFO) of a major sporting goods manufacturer, Playco. Playco manufactures four major product lines: golf equipment, hockey equipment, baseball equipment, and sporting apparel. All products are sold through an extensive network of independent retailers, some of which are major sporting goods outlets. Each product line is considered to be a separate division, headed up by a senior product manager who is responsible for all major day-to-day operating decisions, including pricing, product mix, production,

and managing and expanding dealer relationships. All of Playco's senior product managers have been with the company for at least 6 years, with experience ranging from 6 to 15 years.

In the past, Playco has always used a top-down approach to developing the master budget, whereby a senior management team, including the CEO, the CFO, and the vice-presidents of manufacturing and marketing, set the revenue and expense budgets each year for the four major product lines. These budgets have been based on the company's strategic plans; the team's analysis of the operating environment (including the key competitors); and other factors that could affect demand for sporting goods, such as expected inflation rates, interest rates, and changing demographics. Some input was sought from the senior product manager of each of the major product lines when developing the budget. However, this was limited to a one-on-one meeting between the manager and the CFO at the beginning of the budgeting process each year. These meetings typically lasted about an hour, during which the product managers were invited to provide input on the competitive environment, anticipated pricing issues, production plans (including any design changes), and so on. After these meetings had been completed, the senior management team typically met several times over a one-month period and finalized the budget. Each product manager was then assigned a detailed budget for all revenue and expense items under his or her control. The budget assignment was done during a meeting attended by all of the senior product managers and the senior management team. Each product manager's budget was presented by the CFO using a Microsoft PowerPoint presentation, so all managers were aware of each other's budgets. The product managers were free to comment on or react to their assigned budget at the meeting, but no negotiations took place. Typically, the managers said little other than to acknowledge their assigned budgets and perhaps discuss the challenges they presented.

Ludwig and the other members of the senior management team had always believed that their top-down approach was appropriate for several reasons. First, it was efficient since it didn't require extensive input from the senior product managers, other than the one-hour meetings with the CFO. Typically, the entire process took about a month. Second, it resulted in what Ludwig believed were consistently challenging and fair budgets across the four product lines. With some small variations, the revenue growth budgets and unit cost reduction targets were very consistent across the product lines each year. Ludwig believed this was important because the product managers' bonuses were influenced by how well they did compared to budget, and the top-down approach eliminated the problem of budget slack. Finally, since all of the members of the senior management team had been with the company for at least 10 years, and some input was solicited from the senior product managers, Ludwig felt that the budget was based on good information and thus was reasonably accurate.

Despite the perceived benefits of the top-down approach, Ludwig is beginning to hear some grumblings from the senior product managers that the process isn't fair and isn't resulting in accurate budgets. Ludwig isn't convinced that the process is unfair but acknowledges that there appear to be accuracy problems. Over the past five years, it has been common to see the revenues and expenses of the different product lines coming in considerably better or worse than budget. Some product lines did well in a given year and beat their budgets while others failed to meet their budgets. Moreover, some product lines did well one year and then poorly the next year compared to budget. There doesn't seem to be a predictable pattern to these results. Given this, Ludwig decides to attend an executive seminar on the use of participative budgeting to see if Playco might benefit from the approach.

After completing the seminar, Ludwig is convinced that the potential benefits arising from participative budgets, including more accurate budget estimates and greater commitment to the budgets by the senior product managers, justify trying the approach. He persuades the other members of the senior management team that Playco should try the participative approach in developing budgets for 2016. The process they agree on is as follows:

- Senior management will communicate the key strategic goals to the senior product managers (e.g., overall profit targets for the company) as well as key planning assumptions about inflation rates, unemployment rates, interest rates, etc.
- Based on the strategic goals and planning assumptions, the senior product managers will develop their own detailed revenue and expense budgets for 2016, providing written justification for any major assumptions and other key factors influencing their budgets (e.g., anticipated actions such as price cuts or new product introductions by key competitors).
- Senior management will review the budgets submitted by the senior managers and meet with them individually to discuss and negotiate the final amounts.

Richard Wood, senior product manager for the golf equipment line, is the first to have his budget review meeting with the senior management team. The attendees are Ludwig (CFO),

Lois Davis (CEO), Bill Stevens (VP Marketing), and Marita Delano (VP Production). Below are excerpts from the discussion at the meeting:

Wood: I just want to start off by saying how much I appreciate being given the chance to participate in setting my own budgets this year. My team has worked very hard in putting these estimates together. We have done extensive market research, talked to our distributors at length, and identified opportunities for improvements over last year. Overall I think that our revenue budget, which shows a 10% increase over last year, and our gross margin percentage, which is budgeted to improve by 3% despite higher costs on some raw materials, represent aggressive but attainable targets.

Ludwig: Well, Richard, we're glad to hear that you appreciate being permitted more involvement with the budget this year. We also think this is the right approach to use for many reasons and value your input in developing the budgets.

Davis: I echo Dave's sentiments about your participation but I must say, Richard, that overall we think your budget estimates for both revenues and expenses are a bit soft. We think you can do better.

Wood: I don't understand. As I stated earlier, my budget represents solid growth in revenues and effective cost management. If I achieve my budgets, the performance of the golf equipment product line in 2016 will be the best it's been in five years.

Stevens: There is no doubt that 10% revenue growth is a good starting point, but my sense of the golf equipment market for 2016 is that 15% growth is achievable. People are more health conscious than ever, and with longer golf seasons across the country because of climate change, we should see a nice spike in sales next year.

Delano: As for your expense budget, I commend you for budgeting a 3% improvement in gross margin percentage, but I think more can be done. I've crunched the numbers and talked to some of your production people, and I don't see why you can't budget a 5% improvement. You need to lean harder on suppliers for price reductions, use less overtime on the production line, and find other ways to cut costs next year.

Wood: This doesn't make any sense. If you guys think you know better than me what my budget should be, why did you ask me to participate in the first place? I've pushed my suppliers to the limit and I'm not willing to sacrifice quality to get lower unit costs. Overtime is unavoidable given scheduled shutdowns in the plant and the rush orders that inevitably occur. And, we're already running as lean as we can in production, so there isn't room to reduce costs more than I've budgeted without severely cutting corners.

Dave: Now hold on Richard; don't get defensive. Remember, as part of our new participative approach, we are here to negotiate the final budget with you to arrive at figures we're all comfortable with.

Wood: But this doesn't feel like a negotiation; it feels like I'm being told what my budget should be, despite the fact that I've assured you my numbers are solid. I've been with Playco 10 years—surely that gives me some credibility when it comes to developing a budget!

Davis: We didn't say the negotiations would be easy or that we don't trust you, Richard. But, you have to understand that from a companywide perspective, your budgets aren't good enough. We need more from you. And don't forget, because annual bonuses are linked to actual performance against budget, it's fair for us to demand that your budgets be very challenging.

Wood: I'm at a loss here; this isn't at all what I expected the process would be like. In some ways, I liked our old top-down approach better.

Ludwig: I think we've thrashed this out as much as we can. Richard; your mandate is clear. Do some fine-tuning of your estimates to come in with a revenue budget that is up 15% from 2015 and a gross margin budget that shows 5% improvement over last year. Because of our new participative approach, you are free to do whatever you need to make that happen in your budget.

Davis: Dave's right, take your time with these changes, Richard, and send us each a copy of your new budget within the next couple of weeks. I don't think we need to meet again since we all know what needs to be done. Thanks everyone; this has been a very efficient process.

The budget review meetings with the other senior product managers follow a similar pattern.

Required:
1. Why might the top-down approach have led to inaccurate budgets in prior years?
2. Identify the problems with the participative budgeting approach being used at Playco. What consequences may result from their approach?
3. What changes would you recommend be made to the participative budgeting approach at Playco?

CASE 9–27 Master Budget with Supporting Schedules [LO2]

Knockoffs Unlimited, a nationwide distributor of low-cost imitation designer necklaces, has an exclusive franchise on the distribution of the necklaces, and sales have grown so rapidly over the past few years that it has become necessary to add new members to the management team. To date, the company's budgeting practices have been inferior, and, at times, the company has experienced a cash shortage. You have been given responsibility for all planning and budgeting. Your first assignment is to prepare a master budget for the next three months, starting April 1. You are anxious to make a favourable impression on the president and have assembled the information below.

The necklaces are sold to retailers for $10 each. Recent and forecasted sales in units are as follows:

January (actual).............	20,000	June	50,000
February (actual)............	26,000	July	30,000
March (actual)...............	40,000	August...................	28,000
April........................	65,000	September	25,000
May	100,000		

The large buildup in sales before and during May is due to Mother's Day. Ending inventories should be equal to 40% of the next month's sales in units.

The necklaces cost the company $4 each. Purchases are paid for as follows: 50% in the month of purchase and the remaining 50% in the following month. All sales are on credit, with no discount, and payable within 15 days. The company has found, however, that only 20% of a month's sales are collected by month-end. An additional 70% is collected in the following month, and the remaining 10% is collected in the second month following sale. Bad debts have been negligible.

The company's monthly selling and administrative expenses are given below:

Variable:	
Sales commissions.....................................	4% of sales
Fixed:	
Advertising	$200,000
Rent..	18,000
Wages and salaries....................................	106,000
Utilities	7,000
Insurance...	3,000
Depreciation..	14,000

All selling and administrative expenses are paid during the month, in cash, with the exception of depreciation and insurance. Insurance is paid on an annual basis, in November of each year. The company plans to purchase $16,000 in new equipment during May and $40,000 in new equipment during June; both purchases will be paid in cash. The company declares dividends of $15,000 each quarter, payable in the first month of the following quarter. The company's balance sheet at March 31 is given below:

Assets

Cash	$ 74,000
Accounts receivable ($26,000 February sales;	
$320,000 March sales)................................	346,000
Inventory...	104,000
Prepaid insurance...	21,000
Fixed assets, net of depreciation	950,000
Total assets..	$1,495,000

Liabilities and Shareholders' Equity

Accounts payable..	$ 100,000
Dividends payable...	15,000
Common shares..	800,000
Retained earnings...	580,000
Total liabilities and shareholders' equity....................	$1,495,000

The company wants a minimum ending cash balance each month of $50,000. All borrowing is done at the beginning of the month, with any repayments made at the end of the month. The interest rate on these loans is 1% per month and must be paid at the end of each month based on the outstanding loan balance for that month.

Required:
Prepare a master budget for the three-month period ending June 30. Include the following detailed budgets:

1. *a.* A sales budget by month and in total.
    b. A schedule of expected cash collections from sales, by month and in total.
    c. A merchandise purchases budget in units and in dollars. Show the budget by month and in total.
    d. A schedule of expected cash disbursements for merchandise purchases, by month and in total.
2. A cash budget. Show the budget by month and in total.
3. A budgeted income statement for the three-month period ending June 30. Use the variable costing approach.
4. A budgeted balance sheet as of June 30.

CASE 9-28 Critiquing a Report; Preparing Spending Variances [LO3, LO4]

Farrar University offers an extensive continuing education program in many cities throughout the province. For the convenience of its faculty and administrative staff and to save costs, the university operates a motor pool. The motor pool operated with 20 vehicles until February, when an additional automobile was acquired at the request of the university administration. The motor pool furnishes gasoline, oil, and other supplies for its automobiles. A mechanic does routine maintenance and minor repairs. Major repairs are performed at a nearby commercial garage. Each year, the supervisor of the motor pool prepares an annual budget, which is reviewed by the university and approved after suitable modifications.

The following cost control report shows actual selling and administrative costs for March of the current year compared to one-twelfth of the annual budget:

FARRAR UNIVERSITY MOTOR POOL
Cost Control Report
For the Month Ended March 31

	Annual Budget	Monthly Budget (1/12 of Annual Budget)	March Actual	(Over) Under Budget
Kilometres...............................	600,000	50,000	58,000	
Autos	20	20	21	
Gasoline..................................	$ 96,000	$ 8,000	$ 8,970	$ (970)
Oil, minor repairs, parts.....................	30,000	2,500	2,840	(340)
Outside repairs	9,600	800	980	(180)
Insurance.................................	18,000	1,500	1,625	(125)
Salaries and benefits......................	103,320	8,610	8,610	0
Vehicle depreciation	48,000	4,000	4,200	(200)
Total	$304,920	$ 25,410	$ 27,225	$(1,815)

The annual budget was based on the following assumptions:

a. $0.16 per kilometre for gasoline.
b. $0.05 per kilometre for oil, minor repairs, and parts.
c. $480 per automobile per year for outside repairs.
d. $900 per automobile per year for insurance.
e. $8,610 per month for salaries and benefits.
f. $2,400 per automobile per year for depreciation.

The supervisor of the motor pool is unhappy with the report, claiming it paints an unfair picture of the motor pool's performance.

Required:

1. Prepare a flexible budget performance report for March. Use Exhibit 9-4 as a guide.
2. What are the deficiencies in the original cost control report? How does the report that you prepared in (1) above overcome these deficiencies?

(CMA, adapted)

CASE 9-29 Master Budget for a Manufacturer [LO3, LO4]

Garneau Manufacturing Ltd. produces and distributes a special type of chemical compound called Compound WX. The information below about Garneau's operations has been assembled to assist budget preparation. The company is preparing its master budget for the first quarter of 2016. The budget will detail each month's activity and the activity for the quarter in total. The master budget will be based on the following information:

a. Selling price is $60 per unit in 2015 and will not change for the first two quarters of 2016. Actual and estimated sales are as follows:

Actual 2015	Estimated 2016
November: 10,000 units	January: 11,000 units
December: 12,000 units	February: 10,000 units
	March: 13,000 units
	April: 11,000 units
	May: 10,000 units

b. The company produces enough units each month to meet that month's sales plus a desired inventory level equal to 20% of next month's estimated sales. Finished Goods inventory at the end of 2015 consisted of 2,200 units at a variable cost of $33 each.
c. The company purchases enough raw materials each month for the current month's production requirement and 25% of next month's production requirements. Each unit of product requires 5 kilograms of raw material at $0.60 per kilogram. There were 13,500 kilograms of raw materials in inventory at the end of 2015. Garneau pays 40% of raw material purchases in the month of purchase and the remaining 60% in the following month.
d. Each unit of finished product requires 1.25 labour-hours. The average wage rate is $16 per hour.
e. Variable manufacturing overhead is 50% of the direct labour cost.
f. Credit sales are 60% of total sales. The company collects 50% of the credit sales during the first month following the month of sale and 50% during the second month.
g. Fixed overhead costs (per month) are as follows:

Factory supervisor's salary	$75,000
Factory insurance	1,400
Factory rent	8,000
Depreciation of factory equipment	1,200

h. Total fixed selling and administrative expenses are as follows:

Advertising	$ 300
Depreciation	9,000
Insurance	250
Salaries	4,000
Other	14,550

i. Variable selling and administrative expenses consist of $4 for shipping and 10% of sales for commissions.
j. The company will acquire assets for use in the sales office at a cost of $300,000, which will be paid at the end of January 2016. The monthly depreciation expense on the additional capital assets will be $6,000.

k.   The balance sheet as of December 31, 2015, is as follows:

Assets

Cash		$ 80,000
Accounts receivable..............................		612,000
Inventory: Raw materials	$ 8,100	
Finished goods..................................	72,600	80,700
Plant and equipment............................	1,000,000	
Less accumulated depreciation..................	(100,000)	900,000
Total assets....................................		$1,672,700

Liabilities and Equity

Accounts payable................................	$ 24,000
6% long-term notes payable.....................	900,000
Common shares.................................	735,000
Retained earnings...............................	13,700
Total liabilities and shareholders' equity..........	$1,672,700

Additional information is as follows:
- All cash payments except purchases of raw materials are made monthly as incurred.
- All borrowings occur at the beginning of each month, and all repayments occur at the end of the month. Borrowings and repayments may occur in any amount.
- All interest on borrowed funds is paid at the end of each month at a rate of 0.5% per month.
- A minimum cash balance of $30,000 is required at the end of each month.

Required:
1. Prepare the following budgets for each of the first three months of 2016:
    a.   Sales budget.
    b.   Production budget.
    c.   Raw materials purchases budget.
    d.   Direct labour and manufacturing overhead budget.
    e.   Selling and administrative budget.
    f.   Cash budget.
2. Prepare a budgeted income statement for each of the first three months of 2016 and a budgeted balance sheet as at March 31, 2016.

INSTANT QUIZ SOLUTIONS

9–1

Cash collections from second-quarter sales: $100,000 × 20%	=	$ 20,000
Cash collections from third-quarter sales: $150,000 × 80%	=	120,000
Total cash collections in the third quarter		$140,000

9–2

Budgeted unit sales.....................	10,000
Add desired ending inventory	2,000
Total needs	12,000
Less beginning inventory...............	1,500
Required production	10,500

9–3

Payment for first-quarter purchases: 171,500 × $0.60 × 50%	=	$51,450
Payment for second-quarter purchases: 93,000 × $0.60 × 50%	=	27,900
Total cash disbursements in the second quarter		$79,350

9-4

Direct materials: 15 kilograms × $0.20 per kilogram	$ 3.00
Direct labour: 0.4 hours × $15 per hour	6.00
Manufacturing overhead: 0.4 hours × $10 per hour	4.00
Unit product cost	$13.00

9-5

Opening cash balance + Receipts − Disbursements = Excess cash (deficiency)

$40,000 + $400,000 − $425,000 = $15,000 excess

$15,000 is less than the target balance of $40,000, so they will need to borrow funds.

Formula:

$$\$15,000 + X - 0.01X = \$40,000$$
$$0.99X = \$25,000$$
$$X = \$25,253 \text{ (rounded)}$$

9-6

$25,253 × 1% = $253 (rounded)

9-7

60,000 × $5 = $300,000

9-8

Flexible budget variance = $285,000 − $300,000 = $15,000 unfavourable

Sales volume variance = $300,000 − $250,000 (50,000 × $5) = $50,000 favourable

APPENDIX 9A: INVENTORY DECISIONS

 Appendix available on Connect.

STANDARD COSTS AND OVERHEAD ANALYSIS

MANAGING DISTRIBUTION COSTS

Rising fuel costs in recent years have created pressure for many organizations to find ways to improve the management of the distribution function. For many manufacturing companies, the cost of shipping products to wholesalers, retailers, and the final customer represents a significant portion of their overall cost structure. To address these issues, Catalyst Paper Corporation, a pulp and paper manufacturer based in British Columbia, has developed a comprehensive approach to managing its distribution costs.

At Catalyst Paper, shipping products to customers involves a complex network of manufacturing plants, warehouses, transportation modes (e.g., rail versus truck), and carriers within transportation modes. To improve control over shipping expenses, analysts at Catalyst Paper have developed a model that they use to budget the cost of each shipment made to a customer throughout the year. The model is very elaborate and requires estimates of the transportation mode to be used for each shipment (e.g., rail, truck, container ship), the specific carrier that will be used within a transportation mode (e.g., ABC Trucking), the rates charged by that carrier, and the warehouse(s) that will be used to fill the order. Combining all of these estimates allows Catalyst to calculate the budgeted or "standard" cost for each shipment made to a customer. At the end of each month, company analysts compare the actual shipping costs to the standard amounts estimated by their model.

Variances between the actual and standard costs can be caused by several factors, including using different transportation modes (rail instead of truck), using different carriers (DEF Trucking instead of ABC Trucking), or using different warehouses to source the order, compared to the plan. The model developed by Catalyst Paper allows analysts to determine the portion of the total variance between actual and standard shipping expenses attributable to each of these factors. Once the causes of the variance have been identified, managers can identify follow-up actions aimed at eliminating or reducing unfavourable variances in future periods (e.g., switch to a less expensive transportation mode or carrier).

Prior to developing their analytical model, managers at Catalyst Paper could not pinpoint the cause of unfavourable variances in any given month. Thanks to the new approach, management believes they have a better understanding of the drivers of distribution costs. They also believe it has improved their ability to both plan and control distribution costs.

How are standards, such as those used by Catalyst Paper Corporation, set? How are the variances calculated and how do managers decide which ones to investigate? These are among the many topics examined in this chapter.

Source: Kevin Gaffney, Valeri Gladkikh, and Alan Webb, "A Case Study of a Variance Analysis Framework for Managing Distribution Costs," *Accounting Perspectives*, 6, 2007, pp. 167–190. Reprinted by permission of John Wiley and Sons via Rightslink.

Chapter 10 continues our three-chapter study of planning, control, and performance measurement. Quite often, these terms carry with them negative connotations. Indeed, performance measurements can be used counterproductively to create fear, to cast blame, and to punish. However, if used properly, as explained in the following examples, performance measurement serves a vital function in both daily life and in organizations. Consider the following situations:

> Imagine you want to improve your basketball shooting skill. You know that practice will help, so you go to the basketball court and start shooting toward the hoop. However, as soon as the ball gets close to the rim your vision goes blurry for a second, so that you cannot observe where the ball ended up in relation to the target (left, right, in front, too far back, inside the hoop?). It would be pretty difficult to improve under these conditions, and you would likely eventually lose interest in practising.
>
> Alternatively, imagine someone beginning a weight loss program. A normal step in such programs is to purchase a scale to track one's progress: Is this program working? Am I losing weight? A positive answer is encouraging and would motivate me to keep up the effort, while a negative answer might lead me to reflect on the process: Am I working on the right diet and exercise program? Am I doing everything I am supposed to? But, suppose you don't want to set up a sophisticated measurement system and decide to forgo the scale. You would still have some idea of how well you are doing from simple cues such as clothes feeling looser, a belt that fastens at a different hole, or simply via observation in a mirror! Now, imagine trying to sustain a weight loss program without any feedback on how well you are doing.
>
> In these examples, availability of quantitative measures of performance can yield two types of benefits: First, performance feedback can help improve the "production process" through a better understanding of what works and what doesn't; e.g., shooting this way works better than shooting that way. Second, feedback on performance can sustain motivation and effort, because it is encouraging and/or because it suggests that more effort is required for the goal to be met.[1]

In the same way, performance measurement can be helpful in an organization. It can provide feedback concerning what works and what does not work, and it can help motivate people to sustain their efforts.

Our study of performance measurement begins with the production function. In this chapter we see how various measures are used to control operations and to evaluate performance in this key operating area. Even though we are starting with an operational area, keep in mind that performance measures should be derived from the organization's overall strategy. For example, a company like Cervélo that bases its strategy on designing and producing world-class racing bicycles should use different performance measures than a company like Purolator Courier, where on-time delivery, customer convenience, and low cost are key competitive advantages. Cervélo may want to keep close track of the percentage of revenues from new models introduced within the last year, whereas Purolator may want to closely monitor the percentage of packages delivered on time. In Chapter 11, we will have more to say concerning the role of strategy in the selection of performance measures when we discuss the balanced scorecard. But first we will examine how *standard costs* are used by managers to help control costs.

Companies in highly competitive industries, such as Cenovus Energy, WestJet, Tim Hortons, and West Fraser Timber Company, must be able to provide high-quality goods and services at low cost. If they do not, their customers will buy from more efficient competitors. Operationally, managers must obtain inputs such as raw materials and electricity at the lowest possible prices and use them as effectively as possible while maintaining or increasing the quality of what they sell. If inputs are purchased at prices that are too high or greater quantities are used than is really necessary, higher costs will result.

How do managers control the prices that are paid for inputs and the quantities that are used? They could examine every transaction in detail, but this would obviously be an inefficient use of management time. For many companies, the answer to this control problem lies at least partially in *standard costs*. Standards represent specific elements of budgets (Chapter 9), such as direct materials or direct labour requirements, as well as overhead projections. As such, standards serve both a planning function and a control function. Whether or not organizations employ standard costs to formally cost jobs (Chapter 5) or processes (Chapter 6) is one of the decisions managers must make. If they decide to use actual costs for jobs or processes, they can still use standard costs for budgeting and operational planning.

Controlling overhead costs is also a major concern for managers in business, government, and not-for-profit organizations. Indeed, overhead is a major cost—if not *the* major cost—in many large organizations. Control of overhead costs poses special problems in part because they are more difficult to understand than direct materials and direct labour. Overhead is made up of numerous individual items, some of which are small in dollar amounts. Further, some overhead costs are variable and others are fixed. In this chapter we extend the concept of flexible budgets introduced in Chapter 9 to their use in controlling overhead costs. We also address the analysis and reporting of overhead costs within a standard costing system.

◼ STANDARD COSTS—MANAGEMENT BY EXCEPTION

A *standard* is a benchmark or "norm" for measuring performance. Standards are found everywhere. Your doctor evaluates your weight using standards that have been set for individuals of your age, height, and gender. The food we eat in restaurants must be prepared under specified standards of cleanliness. The buildings we live in must conform to standards set in building codes. Standards are also widely used in managerial accounting, where they relate to the *quantity* and *cost* of inputs used in manufacturing goods or providing services.

Quantity and cost standards are set for each major input, such as raw materials and labour time. *Quantity standards* specify how much of an input should be used to make a unit of product or provide a unit of service. *Cost (price) standards* specify how much should be paid for each unit of the input. Actual quantities and actual costs of inputs are periodically compared to these standards. If either the quantity or the cost of inputs departs significantly from the standards, managers investigate the discrepancy to find and eliminate the cause of the problem. This process is called **management by exception**.

In our daily lives, we operate in a management by exception mode most of the time. Consider what happens when you sit down in the driver's seat of a car. You put the key in the ignition, you turn the key, and the car starts. Your expectation (standard) that the car will start is met; you do not have to open the car hood and check the battery, the connecting cables, the fuel lines, and so on. If you turn the key and the car does not start, then you have a discrepancy (variance). Your expectations are not met, and you need to investigate why. Note that even if the car starts after a second try, it is wise to investigate anyway. The fact that the expectation was not initially met should be viewed as an opportunity to uncover the cause of the problem rather than as simply an annoyance. If the underlying cause is not discovered and corrected, the problem may recur and become much worse.

This basic approach to identifying and solving problems is used in the *variance analysis cycle*, which is illustrated in Exhibit 10–1. The cycle begins with the preparation of standard cost performance reports in the accounting department. These reports highlight the variances, which are the differences between actual results and what should have occurred according to the standards. The variances can raise numerous questions. Why did the variance occur? Why is this variance larger than it was last period? The significant variances are investigated to discover their root causes. Corrective actions are taken, and then the next period's operations are

Management by exception
A system of management in which standards are set for various operating activities that are then periodically compared to actual results. Any differences that are deemed significant are brought to the attention of management as "exceptions."

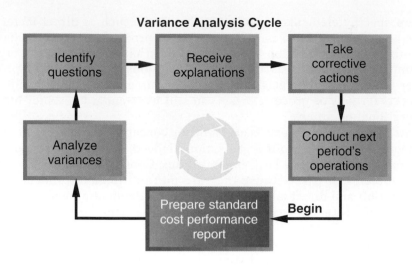

carried out. The cycle then begins again with the preparation of a new standard cost performance report for the most recent period. The emphasis should be on highlighting problems, finding their root causes, and taking corrective action. The goal is to improve operations—not to assign blame.

SETTING STANDARD COSTS

LEARNING OBJECTIVE ❶
Explain how direct materials standards and direct labour standards are set.

Setting price and quantity standards ideally combines the expertise of everyone who is responsible for purchasing and using inputs. In a manufacturing setting, this might include accountants, purchasing managers, engineers, production supervisors, line managers, and production workers. Past records of purchase prices and of input usage can be helpful in setting standards. In a service setting, time and service standards might also be set. However, the standards should be designed to encourage efficient *future* operations, not a repetition of *past* operations that may or may not have been efficient.

Who Uses Standard Costs?

Manufacturing, service, food, and not-for-profit organizations all use standards to some extent. Auto service centres like Canadian Tire, for example, often set specific labour time standards for the completion of certain work tasks, such as installing a water pump or changing a tire, and then measure actual performance against these standards. Fast-food outlets such as Harvey's have exacting standards as to the quantity of meat put into a sandwich, as well as standards for the cost of the meat. Hospitals have standard costs (for food, laundry, and other items) for each occupied bed per day, as well as standard time allowances for certain routine activities, such as laboratory tests. In short, you are likely to run into standard costs in virtually any line of business.

Manufacturing companies often have highly developed standard costing systems in which standards relating to materials, labour, and overhead are developed in detail for each separate product. A **standard cost record** shows the standard quantities and costs of the inputs required to produce a unit of a specific product. The cost is calculated by multiplying the standard quantity of each input required to produce one unit of output by the price or rate for that input. These records, which used to be recorded on file cards, are now electronically created and maintained as part of the company's accounting information system. In this section, we provide a detailed example of how standard costs are set in preparing the standard cost record.

Standard cost record
A detailed listing of the standard amounts of materials, labour, and overhead that should go into a unit of product or service, multiplied by the standard price or rate that has been set for each cost element.

Ideal versus Practical Standards

Should standards be attainable all of the time, part of the time, or almost none of the time? Opinions vary, but standards tend to fall into one of two categories—either ideal or practical.

Ideal standards are those that can be attained only under the best circumstances. They allow for no machine breakdowns or other work interruptions, and they call for a level of effort that can be attained only by the most skilled and efficient employees working at peak effort 100% of the time. Some managers feel that such standards have motivational value. They argue that even though employees know they will rarely meet the standard, it is a constant reminder of the need for ever-increasing efficiency and effort. However, few firms use ideal standards because most managers feel they are discouraging for even the most diligent workers. Moreover, when ideal standards are used, variances from the standards have little meaning. Large variances from the ideal are normal, so it is difficult to manage by exception.

Practical standards are defined as standards that are tight but attainable. They allow for normal machine downtime and employee rest periods, and they can be attained through reasonable, although highly efficient, efforts by the average employee. Variances from practical standards typically signal a need for management attention because they represent deviations that fall outside normal operating conditions. In addition to signalling abnormal conditions, they can also be used to forecast cash flows and plan inventory. By contrast, ideal standards cannot be used in normal budgets or plans; they do not allow for normal inefficiencies, so they result in unrealistic planning and forecasting figures.

Throughout the remainder of this chapter, we will assume the use of practical rather than ideal standards.

Ideal standards
Standards that allow for no machine breakdowns or other work interruptions and that require peak efficiency at all times.

Practical standards
Standards that allow for normal machine downtime and other work interruptions and can be attained through reasonable, although highly efficient, efforts by the average employee.

Setting Direct Materials Standards

We will use the hypothetical Heirloom Pewter Company to illustrate the development and application of a standard costing system. The company was organized a year ago, and its only product is a reproduction of an eighteenth-century pewter bookend. The bookend is made largely by hand, using traditional metal-working tools. Consequently, the manufacturing process is very labour-intensive and requires a high level of skill.

Heirloom Pewter has recently expanded its workforce to take advantage of unexpected demand for the bookends as gifts. The company started with a small group of experienced pewter workers but has had to hire less experienced workers as a result of the expansion. The president of the company, J. D. Wriston, has called a meeting to discuss production problems. Attending the meeting are Tom Kuchel, the production manager; Janet Warner, the purchasing manager; and George Hanlon, the corporate controller.

Wriston: I've got a feeling that we aren't getting the production we should out of our new people.

Kuchel: Give us a chance. Some of the new people have been with the company for less than a month.

Warner: Let me add that production seems to be wasting an awful lot of material—particularly pewter. That stuff is very expensive.

Kuchel: What about the shipment of defective pewter that you bought—the one with the iron contamination? That caused us major problems.

Warner: How was I to know it was off-grade? Besides, it was a great deal.

Wriston: Calm down, everybody. Let's get the facts before we start attacking each other.

Kuchel: I agree. The more facts the better.

Wriston: Okay, George, it's your turn. Facts are the controller's department.

Hanlon: I'm afraid I can't provide the answers off the top of my head, but if you give me about a week I can set up a system that can routinely answer questions relating to worker productivity, material waste, and input prices.

Wriston: Let's mark it on our calendars.

Standard price per unit
The price that should be paid for a single unit of materials, including shipping, receiving, and other such costs, net of any discounts allowed.

Hanlon's first task was to prepare price and quantity standards for the company's only significant raw material, pewter ingots. The **standard price per unit** for direct materials should reflect the final, delivered cost of the materials including shipping, receiving, and other such costs, net of any discounts taken. After consulting with Warner, the purchasing manager, Hanlon prepared the following documentation for the standard price of a kilogram of pewter in ingot form:

Purchase price, top-grade pewter..	$ 3.60
Freight, by truck, from the supplier's warehouse...........................	0.44
Receiving and handling..	0.05
Less purchase discount..	(0.09)
Standard price per kilogram...	$ 4.00

Notice that the standard price reflects a particular grade of material (top-grade) delivered by a particular type of carrier (truck). Allowances have also been made for handling and discounts. If everything proceeds according to these expectations, the net standard price of a kilogram of pewter should therefore be $4.

Standard quantity per unit
The amount of materials that should be required to complete a single unit of product, including allowances for normal waste, spoilage, and other inefficiencies.

The **standard quantity per unit** for direct materials should reflect the amount of material required for each unit of finished product, as well as an allowance for unavoidable waste, spoilage, and other normal inefficiencies. After consulting with Kuchel, the production manager, Hanlon prepared the following documentation for the standard quantity of pewter required for a pair of bookends:

Materials requirements as specified in the bill of materials for a pair of bookends, in kilograms.....................................	2.7
Allowance for waste and spoilage, in kilograms	0.2
Allowance for rejects, in kilograms	0.1
Standard quantity per pair of bookends, in kilograms......................	3.0

A bill of materials details the type and quantity of each item of material that should be used in a product. As shown above, it should be adjusted for waste and other factors when determining the standard quantity per unit of product. "Waste and spoilage" refers to materials that are wasted as a normal part of the production process or that spoil before they are used. "Rejects" refers to the direct materials contained in units that are defective and must be scrapped.

Although it is common to recognize allowances for waste, spoilage, and rejects when setting standard costs, this practice is often criticized because it contradicts the zero defects goal associated with improvement programs such as Six Sigma. If allowances for waste, spoilage, and rejects are built into the standard cost, the levels of those allowances should be periodically reviewed and reduced over time to reflect improved processes, better training, and better equipment.

Once the price and quantity standards have been set, the standard cost of materials per unit of finished product can be computed as

$$3.0 \text{ kilograms per unit} \times \$4 \text{ per kilogram} = \$12 \text{ per unit}$$

This $12 cost figure will appear as one item on the standard cost record of the product.

IN BUSINESS

Vale S.A., a Brazilian mining company, has built a fleet of 35 very large ships known as "Valemax" to carry iron ore mined in Brazil to ports in Asia. Vale initially built these ships to counteract the high cost of shipping iron ore, which at some points in 2007–2008 was higher per tonne ($88) than the average cost of a tonne of iron ore itself ($60). According to Tim Murray, an iron ore analyst with J Capital Research, shipping iron ore from Australia to China costs about $7 per tonne using the 180,000-tonne capacity Capesize ship, while the same-sized ship from Brazil is $17 per tonne. Vale believed the economies of scale provided by the larger Valemax ships would reduce the shipping cost per tonne of iron ore from Brazil to China enough to allow it to compete with its Australian rivals BHP Billiton and Rio Tinto.

Source: "A Tale of Two Countries," *SteelOrbis Blog*, April 13, 2013, http://blog.steelorbis.com/2013/04/15/a-tale-of-two-countries/; "Brazil's Iron Ore Ship Finally Comes in," *Little Red Blog China News and Analysis*, April 19, 2013, http://little-red-blog.com/brazils-iron-ore-ship-finally-comes-in/

Setting Direct Labour Standards

Direct labour price and quantity standards are usually expressed in terms of a labour rate and labour-hours. The **standard rate per hour** for direct labour includes not only wages earned but also employee benefits (e.g., Employment Insurance, extended medical insurance) and other labour costs. Using wage records and in consultation with the production manager, Hanlon determined the standard rate per hour at the Heirloom Pewter Company as follows:

Standard rate per hour
The labour rate that should be incurred per hour of labour time, including Employment Insurance, employee benefits, and other labour costs.

Basic average wage rate per hour	$15.00
Employment taxes at 10% of the basic rate	1.50
Employee benefits at 30% of the basic rate	4.50
Standard rate per direct labour-hour	$21.00

Many companies prepare a single standard rate for all employees in a department. This standard rate reflects the expected "mix" of workers, even though the actual wage rates may vary somewhat from individual to individual due to differing skills or seniority. According to the standard computed above, the direct labour rate for Heirloom Pewter should average $21 per hour.

The standard direct labour time required to complete a unit of product (generally called the **standard hours per unit**) is perhaps the single most difficult standard to determine. One approach for physical tasks is to break down each task into elemental body movements (such as reaching, pushing, and turning over). Published tables of standard times for such movements are available. Another approach is for an industrial engineer to do a time and motion study, which involves recording the time required for certain tasks. As stated earlier, the standard time should include allowances for breaks and personal needs of employees, cleanup, rejects, and machine downtime. After consulting with Kuchel, the production manager, Hanlon prepared the following documentation for the standard hours per unit:

Standard hours per unit
The amount of labour time that should be required to complete a single unit of product, including allowances for breaks, machine downtime, cleanup, rejects, and other normal inefficiencies.

Basic labour time per unit, in hours	1.9
Allowance for breaks and personal needs	0.1
Allowance for cleanup and machine downtime	0.3
Allowance for rejects	0.2
Standard labour-hours per unit of product	2.5

Once the rate and time standards have been set, the standard labour cost per unit of product can be computed as

$$2.5 \text{ hours per unit} \times \$21 \text{ per hour} = \$52.50 \text{ per unit}$$

This $52.50 cost figure appears along with direct materials as one item on the standard cost record of the product.

Standard labour-hours have declined in relative importance for some organizations. This is particularly true in highly automated manufacturing firms. However, for many service organizations and numerous other construction and processing organizations, labour remains an important input to the production and service activities. For these organizations, standard labour-hours inform workers and managers what is expected and how labour should be used. More specifically, standards and the resulting comparisons to actual labour-hours may serve to motivate workers and managers. Labour standards can influence individuals in setting their own goals.

Setting Variable Manufacturing Overhead Standards

As with direct labour, the price and quantity standards for variable manufacturing overhead are generally expressed in terms of rate and hours. The rate represents *the variable portion of the predetermined overhead rate* first discussed in Chapter 5. Developing the rate requires estimating both the unit cost of the variable overhead items used in production (indirect supplies, indirect labour, etc.) and the quantity required for the planned level of production. The unit costs are relatively straightforward to estimate and can be based on prior-year amounts or existing contractual agreements with suppliers that lock in prices. The quantities for variable overhead items can be estimated using actual results from prior periods. The hours relate to whatever activity base is used to apply overhead to units of product (usually machine-hours or direct labour-hours). At Heirloom Pewter, the variable portion of the predetermined overhead rate is $3 per direct labour-hour. Therefore, the standard variable manufacturing overhead cost per unit is computed as

$$2.5 \text{ hours per unit} \times \$3 \text{ per hour} = \$7.50 \text{ per unit}$$

Standard cost per unit
The standard cost of a unit of product as shown on the standard cost card; it is computed by multiplying the standard quantity or hours by the standard price or rate for each cost element.

This $7.50 cost figure appears along with direct materials and direct labour as one item on the standard cost record for variable production costs in Exhibit 10–2. Observe that the **standard cost per unit** is computed by multiplying the standard quantity or hours by the standard price or rate. We expand our discussion of standard costs to include fixed manufacturing overhead later in this chapter.

EXHIBIT 10-2   Standard Cost Record—Variable Production Cost

Inputs	(1) Standard Quantity or Hours	(2) Standard Price or Rate	(3) Standard Cost (1) × (2)
Direct materials	3.0 kilograms	$ 4.00	$12.00
Direct labour	2.5 hours	21.00	52.50
Variable manufacturing overhead	2.5 hours	3.00	7.50
Total standard variable cost per unit			$72.00

Are Standards the Same as Budgets?

Standards and budgets are very similar. The major distinction between the two terms is that a standard is a *unit* amount, whereas a budget is a *total* amount. The standard cost for materials at Heirloom Pewter is $12 per pair of bookends. If 1,000 pairs of bookends are to be manufactured during a budgeting period, then the budgeted cost of materials will be $12,000. In effect, *a standard can be viewed as the budgeted cost for one unit of product.*

A General Model for Variance Analysis

An important reason for separating standards into two categories—price and quantity—is that different managers are usually responsible for buying and for using inputs, and these two activities occur at different times. In the case of raw materials, for example, the purchasing manager is responsible for the price, and this responsibility is exercised at the time of purchase. In contrast, the production manager is responsible for the amount of the raw materials used, and this responsibility is exercised when the materials are used in production, which may be many weeks or months after the purchase date. It is important, therefore, that we separate discrepancies due to deviations from price standards from those due to deviations from quantity standards. Differences between *standard* prices and *actual* prices and *standard* quantities and *actual* quantities are called **variances**. The act of computing and interpreting variances is called *variance analysis*.

Variances
The differences between standard prices and quantities and actual prices and quantities.

A general model for computing standard cost variances for variable costs is presented in Exhibit 10–3. This model isolates price variances from quantity variances and shows how each of these variances is computed. We will use this model to compute variances for direct materials, direct labour, and variable manufacturing overhead. We will discuss the model for calculating and interpreting fixed overhead variances later in this chapter.

Four things should be noted from Exhibit 10–3. First, a price variance and a quantity variance can be computed for all three variable cost elements—direct materials, direct labour, and variable manufacturing overhead—even though the variance is not called by the same name in all cases. For example, a price variance is called a *materials price variance* in the case of direct materials but a *labour rate*

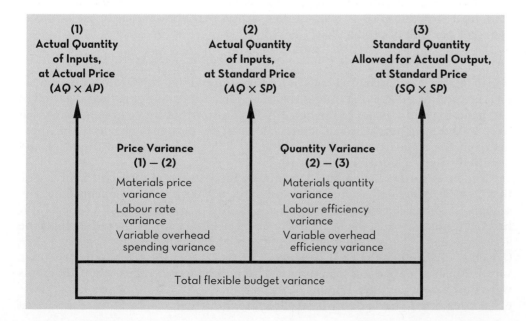

EXHIBIT 10-3   A General Model for Variance Analysis—Variable Production Costs

variance in the case of direct labour and an *overhead spending variance* in the case of variable manufacturing overhead.

Second, although the price variance may be called different names, it is computed in exactly the same way, regardless of whether one is dealing with direct materials, direct labour, or variable manufacturing overhead. The same is true with the quantity variance.

Third, the inputs represent the actual quantity of direct materials, direct labour, and variable manufacturing overhead used; the output represents the good production of the period, expressed in terms of the *standard quantity (or the standard hours) allowed for the actual output* (see column 3 in Exhibit 10–3). The **standard quantity allowed** or **standard hours allowed** means the amount of direct materials, direct labour, or variable manufacturing overhead *that should have been used* to produce the actual output of the period. This could be more or less than the materials, labour, or overhead that were *actually* used, depending on the efficiency or inefficiency of operations. The standard quantity allowed is computed by multiplying the actual output in units by the standard input allowed per unit.

Fourth, note that the amount in column 3 (*SQ × SP*) of Exhibit 10–3 represents the flexible budget for the period. In Chapter 9 we prepared a simplified version of a flexible budget based on the *actual* quantity of units produced for the period multiplied by the total *budgeted* cost per unit. When a standard costing system is being used, the flexible budget is based on the *standard quantity allowed* for the *actual* output achieved multiplied by the *standard price* per unit. As will be illustrated in the sections that follow, this revised approach to calculating the flexible budget permits the flexible budget variance introduced in Chapter 9 (Exhibit 9–4) for a period to be broken down into its price and quantity components.

With this general model as a foundation, we will now examine the price and quantity variances in more detail.

Standard quantity allowed
The amount of materials that should have been used to complete the period's output, as computed by multiplying the actual number of units produced by the standard quantity per unit.

Standard hours allowed
The time that should have been taken to complete the period's output, as computed by multiplying the actual number of units produced by the standard hours per unit.

■ USING STANDARD COSTS—DIRECT MATERIALS VARIANCES

LEARNING OBJECTIVE **2**
Compute the direct materials price and quantity variances, and explain their significance.

After determining Heirloom Pewter Company's standard costs for direct materials, direct labour, and variable manufacturing overhead, Hanlon's next step was to compute the company's variances for June, the most recent month. As discussed in the preceding section, variances are computed by comparing standard costs to actual costs. To facilitate this comparison, Hanlon referred to the standard cost data contained in Exhibit 10–2. This exhibit shows that the standard cost of direct materials per unit of product is

3.0 kilograms per unit × $4 per kilogram = $12 per unit

Heirloom Pewter's purchasing records for June showed that 6,500 kilograms of pewter were purchased at a cost of $3.80 per kilogram. This cost figure included freight and handling and was net of the quantity discount. All of the materials purchased were used during June to manufacture 2,000 pairs of pewter bookends. Using these data and the standard costs from Exhibit 10–2, Hanlon computed the price and quantity variances shown in Exhibit 10–4.

The three arrows in Exhibit 10–4 point to three different total cost figures. The first, $24,700, refers to the actual total cost of the pewter purchased during June. The second, $26,000, refers to what the actual quantity of pewter would have cost if it had been purchased at the standard price of $4.00 per kilogram rather than the actual price of $3.80 per kilogram. The difference between these two figures, $1,300 ($26,000 − $24,700), is the price variance. It exists because the actual purchase price was $0.20 per kilogram less than the standard purchase price. Since 6,500 kilograms were purchased, the total amount of the variance is $1,300 ($0.20 per kilogram × 6,500 kilograms). This variance is labelled *favourable* (denoted by F), since the actual

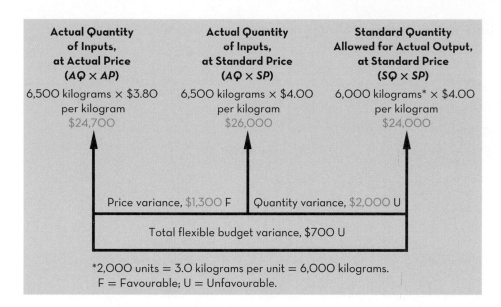

EXHIBIT 10-4 Variance Analysis—Direct Materials

purchase price was less than the standard purchase price. A price variance is labelled *unfavourable* (denoted by U) if the actual price exceeds the standard price.

The third arrow in Exhibit 10–4 points to $24,000 (i.e., the flexible budget amount). This would have been the cost of pewter had it been purchased at the standard price and only the amount allowed by the standard quantity had been used. The standard calls for 3 kilograms of pewter per unit. Since 2,000 pairs of bookends were produced, 6,000 kilograms of pewter should have been used. This is referred to as the *standard quantity allowed for the actual output*. If 6,000 kilograms of pewter had been purchased at the standard price of $4.00 per kilogram, the company would have spent $24,000. The difference between this figure, $24,000, and the figure at the end of the middle arrow in Exhibit 10–4, $26,000, is the quantity variance of $2,000.

To understand the quantity variance, note that the actual amount of pewter used in production was 6,500 kilograms. However, the standard amount of pewter allowed for the actual output is only 6,000 kilograms. Therefore, in total, 500 kilograms too much pewter was used to produce the actual output. To express this in dollar terms, multiply 500 kilograms by the standard price of $4.00 per kilogram to yield the quantity variance of $2,000. Why is the standard price, rather than the actual price, of the pewter used in this calculation? The production manager is ordinarily responsible for the quantity variance. If the actual price was used in the calculation of the quantity variance, the production manager would also be held responsible for the performance of the purchasing manager. Apart from being unfair, time-consuming debates between the production manager and purchasing manager could occur every time the actual price of an input is above its standard price. To avoid these debates, which can be an unproductive distraction to managers, the standard price is used when computing the quantity variance.

The quantity variance in Exhibit 10–4 is labelled *unfavourable* (denoted by U). This is because more pewter was used to produce the actual output than is called for by the standard. A quantity variance is labelled *favourable* if the actual quantity is less than the standard quantity.

The computations in Exhibit 10–4 reflect the fact that all of the material purchased during June was also used during June. How are the variances computed if a different amount of material is purchased than is used? To illustrate, assume that during June the company purchased 6,500 kilograms of materials, but used only 5,000 kilograms of material during the month and produced only 1,600 units. In this case, the price variance and quantity variance would be as shown in Exhibit 10–5.

There are two reasons that companies compute the materials price variance when materials are purchased rather than when they are used in production. First,

EXHIBIT 10-5 Variance Analysis—Direct Materials, When the Amount Purchased Differs from the Amount Used

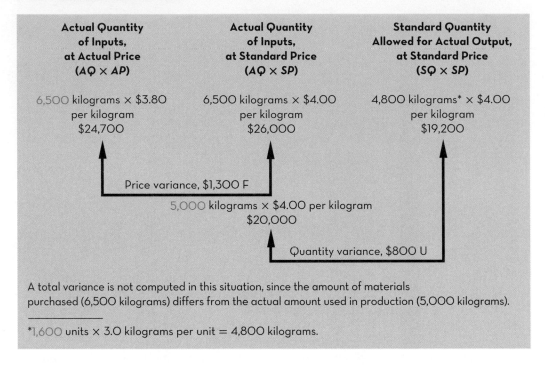

A total variance is not computed in this situation, since the amount of materials purchased (6,500 kilograms) differs from the actual amount used in production (5,000 kilograms).

*1,600 units × 3.0 kilograms per unit = 4,800 kilograms.

delaying the computation of the price variance until the materials are used would result in less-timely variance reports if there is a time gap between the purchase of materials and their use in production. Second, by computing the price variance at the time of purchase, materials can be carried in the inventory accounts at their standard cost. This greatly simplifies bookkeeping. Note, however, that the problem of determining the purchase price variance at a different time than the materials usage variance would not occur in a strict JIT environment. Appendix 10B at the end of the chapter explains how the simplified bookkeeping works in a standard costing system where inventories of direct materials exist.

Note from Exhibit 10-5 that the price variance is computed on the entire amount of material purchased (6,500 kilograms), as before, whereas the quantity variance is computed only on the portion of this material used in production during the month (5,000 kilograms). A quantity variance on the 1,500 kilograms of material purchased during the month but *not* used in production (6,500 kilograms purchased − 5,000 kilograms used = 1,500 kilograms unused) will be computed in a future period when these materials are drawn out of inventory and used in production. The situation illustrated in Exhibit 10-5 is common for companies that purchase materials well in advance of use and store the materials in warehouses while awaiting the production process.

Materials Price Variance—A Closer Look

Materials price variance
A measure of the difference between the actual unit price paid for an item and the standard price, multiplied by the quantity purchased.

A **materials price variance** measures the difference between what is paid for a given quantity of materials and what should have been paid according to the standard that has been set multiplied by the quantity purchased. From Exhibits 10-4 and 10-5, this difference can be expressed by the formula

$$\text{Materials price variance} = (AQ \times AP) - (AQ \times SP)$$

Actual   Actual   Standard
Quantity   Price   Price
Purchased

The formula can be factored into simpler form as follows:

$$\text{Materials price variance} = AQ(AP - SP)$$

This simpler formula permits variance computations to be made very quickly. Using the data from Exhibits 10–4 and 10–5 in this formula, we have

6,500 kilograms($3.80 per kilogram − $4.00 per kilogram) = −$1,300 F

Notice that the answer is the same as that yielded in Exhibit 10–4. Also note that because of the order of the calculation a negative variance is always labelled as *favourable* (F) and a positive variance is always labelled as *unfavourable* (U) when the formula approach is used. This is true of all variance formulas in this and later chapters.

Variance reports are often issued in a tabular format that shows the details and explanation of particular variances. Following is an example of such a report that has been provided by the purchasing manager:

	(1)	(2)	(3)	(4)	(5)	
HEIRLOOM PEWTER COMPANY						
Performance Report—Purchasing Department						
Item Purchased	**Quantity Purchased**	**Actual Price**	**Standard Price**	**Difference in Price (2) − (3)**	**Total Price Variance (1) × (4)**	**Explanation**
Pewter	6,500 kilograms	$3.80	$4.00	−$0.20	−$1,300 F	Negotiated for an especially favourable price.
F = Favourable						

Isolation of Variances   Variances should be isolated and brought to the attention of management as quickly as possible so that problems can be identified and corrected on a timely basis. The most significant variances should be viewed as red flags; an exception has occurred that requires explanation by the responsible manager and perhaps follow-up effort. The performance report itself may contain explanations for the variances, as illustrated above. In the case of Heirloom Pewter Company, the purchasing manager said that the favourable price variance resulted from negotiating an especially good price.

Responsibility for the Variance   Who is responsible for the materials price variance? Generally speaking, the purchasing manager has control over the price paid for goods and is therefore responsible for any price variances. Many factors influence the prices paid for goods, including how many units are ordered in a lot, how the order is delivered, whether the order is a rush order, and the quality of materials purchased. A deviation in any of these factors from what was assumed when the standards were set can result in a price variance. For example, purchase of second-grade materials rather than top-grade materials may result in a favourable price variance, since the lower-grade materials will generally be less costly (but perhaps less suitable for production).

However, someone other than the purchasing manager could be responsible for a materials price variance. Production may be scheduled in such a way, for example, that the purchasing manager must request delivery by air freight, rather than by truck. In these cases, the production manager bears responsibility for the resulting price variances.

A word of caution is in order. Variance analysis should not be used to assign blame. The emphasis must be on the control function in the sense of *supporting* the line managers and *assisting* them in meeting the goals that they have participated in setting for the company. In short, the emphasis should be positive rather than negative. Excessive focus on what has already happened, particularly in terms of assigning blame, can be destructive to the functioning of an organization.

Materials Quantity Variance—A Closer Look

Materials quantity variance
A measure of the difference between the actual quantity of materials used in production and the standard quantity allowed, multiplied by the standard price per unit of materials.

A **materials quantity variance** measures the difference between the quantity of materials used in production and the quantity that should have been used, according to the standard that has been set. Although the variance is concerned with the physical usage of materials, it is generally stated in dollar terms, as shown in Exhibit 10–4. The formula for the materials quantity variance is

$$\text{Materials quantity variance} = (AQ \times SP) - (SQ \times SP)$$

AQ = Actual Quantity Used

SP = Standard Price

SQ = Standard Quantity Allowed for Actual Output

Again, the formula can be factored into simpler terms:

$$\text{Materials quantity variance} = SP(AQ - SQ)$$

Using the data from Exhibit 10–4 in the formula, we have

$$\$4.00 \text{ per kilogram } (6{,}500 \text{ kilograms} - 6{,}000 \text{ kilograms*}) = \$2{,}000 \text{ U}$$

*2,000 units × 3.0 kilograms per unit = 6,000 kilograms.

The answer, of course, is the same as that yielded in Exhibit 10–4. The data might appear as follows if a formal performance report were prepared:

HEIRLOOM PEWTER COMPANY **Performance Report—Purchasing Department**						
	(1)	**(2)**	**(3)**	**(4)**	**(5)** **Total**	
Type of Materials	**Standard Price**	**Actual Quantity**	**Standard Quantity Allowed**	**Difference in Quantity (2) − (3)**	**Quantity Variance (1) × (4)**	**Explanation**
Pewter	$4.00	6,500 kg	6,000 kg	500 kg	$2,000 U	Low-quality materials unsuitable for production
U = Unfavourable						

The materials quantity variance is best isolated at the time that materials are placed into production. Materials are requisitioned for the number of units to be produced, according to the standard bill of materials for each unit. Any additional materials are usually drawn with an excess materials requisition, which is different from the normal requisition. This procedure calls attention to the excessive usage of materials *while production is still in process* and provides an opportunity for early identification and correction of any developing problem.

Excessive usage of materials can result from many factors, including faulty machines, inferior quality of materials, untrained workers, and poor supervision. Generally speaking, it is the responsibility of the production department to see that materials usage is kept in line with standards. There may be times, however, when the *purchasing* department is responsible for an unfavourable materials quantity variance. If the purchasing department obtains inferior-quality materials in an effort to reduce costs, the materials may be unsuitable for use and may result in excessive waste. Thus, purchasing rather than production will be responsible for the quantity variance. Indeed, at Heirloom Pewter, the production manager said that low-quality materials were the cause of the unfavourable materials quantity variance for June.

> **Instant Quiz 10-2**
> Using the information supplied for Toy Mountain in Instant Quiz 10-1, calculate the materials quantity variance and indicate a possible cause.

▮ USING STANDARD COSTS—DIRECT LABOUR VARIANCES

Hanlon's next step in determining Heirloom Pewter's variances for June was to compute the direct labour variances for the month. Recall from Exhibit 10-2 that the standard direct labour cost per unit of product is $52.50, computed as

LEARNING OBJECTIVE 3
Compute the direct labour rate and efficiency variances, and explain their significance.

$$\text{2.5 hours per unit} \times \$21 \text{ per hour} = \$52.50 \text{ per unit}$$

During June, the company paid its direct labour workers $108,000, including employment taxes and benefits, for 5,400 hours of work. This was an average of $20 per hour. Using these data and the standard costs from Exhibit 10-2, Hanlon computed the direct labour rate and efficiency variances that appear in Exhibit 10-6.

Notice that the column headings in Exhibit 10-6 are the same as those used in the prior two exhibits, except that in Exhibit 10-6 the terms *hours* and *rate* are used in place of the terms *quantity* and *price*.

Labour Rate Variance—A Closer Look

As explained earlier, the price variance for direct labour is commonly termed a **labour rate variance**. This variance measures any deviation from standard in the average hourly rate paid to direct labour workers. The formula for the labour rate variance is

Labour rate variance
A measure of the difference between the actual hourly labour rate and the standard rate, multiplied by the number of hours worked during the period.

$$\text{Labour rate variance} = (AH \times AR) - (AH \times SR)$$

$$\underset{\substack{\text{Actual} \\ \text{Hours}}}{\uparrow} \quad \underset{\substack{\text{Actual} \\ \text{Rate}}}{\uparrow} \quad \underset{\substack{\text{Standard} \\ \text{Rate}}}{\uparrow}$$

EXHIBIT 10-6 Variance Analysis—Direct Labour

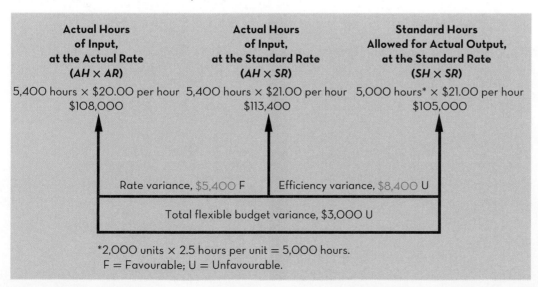

Actual Hours of Input, at the Actual Rate (AH × AR)	Actual Hours of Input, at the Standard Rate (AH × SR)	Standard Hours Allowed for Actual Output, at the Standard Rate (SH × SR)
5,400 hours × $20.00 per hour	5,400 hours × $21.00 per hour	5,000 hours* × $21.00 per hour
$108,000	$113,400	$105,000

Rate variance, $5,400 F   Efficiency variance, $8,400 U

Total flexible budget variance, $3,000 U

*2,000 units × 2.5 hours per unit = 5,000 hours.
F = Favourable; U = Unfavourable.

IN BUSINESS

Operations Workforce Optimization (OWO), now a unit of Accenture Ltd., provides software solutions to reduce labour inefficiency in retail settings. Borrowing from time-motion concepts first developed by scientific management pioneer Fredrick Taylor for steel mills and factory floors, OWO first breaks down tasks such as checking out a customer into quantified units and assigns standard times to complete them, called "engineered labour standards." Then it writes software to help the retail stores keep watch over the employee's work. Retailers including Gap Inc., Nike, and Toys "R" Us have implemented OWO software because it can reduce labour costs by 5 to 15%. By using engineered labour standards, OWO argues retailers can monitor worker performance and figure out how and where to reduce labour costs, the single biggest controllable expense in retail settings.

Source: Vanessa O'Connell, "Stores Count Seconds to Cut Labor Costs," The Wall Street Journal, November 13, 2008, pp. A1–A15.

The formula can be factored into simpler form as

$$\text{Labour rate variance} = AH(AR - SR)$$

Using the data from Exhibit 10–6 in the formula, we have

$$5{,}400 \text{ hours } (\$20.00 \text{ per hour} - \$21.00 \text{ per hour}) = -\$5{,}400 \text{ F}$$

In most companies, the rates paid to workers are quite predictable. Nevertheless, rate variances can arise through the way labour is used. Skilled workers with high hourly rates of pay may be given duties that require less skill and call for low hourly rates of pay. This will result in unfavourable labour rate variances, since the actual hourly rate of pay will exceed the standard rate specified for the particular task being performed. A reverse situation exists when unskilled or untrained workers are assigned to jobs that require higher levels of skill or training. The lower pay scale for these workers will result in favourable rate variances, although the workers may be less efficient. Finally, unfavourable rate variances can arise from overtime work paid at premium rates if any portion of the overtime premium is added to the direct labour account.

Who is responsible for controlling the labour rate variance? Since rate variances generally arise as a result of how labour is used, production supervisors are responsible for controlling them.

Labour Efficiency Variance—A Closer Look

Labour efficiency variance
A measure of the difference between the actual hours taken to complete a task and the standard hours allowed, multiplied by the standard hourly labour rate.

The quantity variance for direct labour, more commonly called the **labour efficiency variance**, measures the productivity of labour time. No variance is more closely watched by management, since it is widely believed that increasing the productivity of direct labour time is vital to reducing costs. The formula for the labour efficiency variance is

$$\text{Labour efficiency variance} = (AH \times SR) - (SH \times SR)$$

$$\begin{array}{ccc} \text{Actual} & \text{Standard} & \text{Standard} \\ \text{Hours} & \text{Rate} & \text{Hours} \\ & & \text{Allowed for} \\ & & \text{Actual Output} \end{array}$$

Factored into simpler terms, the formula is

$$\text{Labour efficiency variance} = SR(AH - SH)$$

Using the data from Exhibit 10–6 in the formula, we have

$21.00 per hour(5,400 hours − 5,000 hours*) = $8,400 U

*2,000 units × 2.5 hours per unit = 5,000 hours.

Possible causes of an unfavourable labour efficiency variance are poorly trained or motivated workers; poor-quality materials, requiring more labour time for processing; faulty equipment, causing breakdowns and work interruptions; poor supervision of workers; and inaccurate standards. The manager in charge of production is generally responsible for the labour efficiency variance. However, an unfavourable variance might be attributed to purchasing if the acquisition of lower-quality materials results in excessive labour processing time.

Insufficient demand for the company's products may be another important cause of an unfavourable labour efficiency variance. Managers in some companies argue that it is difficult, and perhaps unwise, to constantly adjust the workforce in response to changes in the amount of work that needs to be done. In such companies, the direct labour workforce is essentially fixed in the short run. If demand is insufficient to keep everyone busy, workers are not laid off. In this case, if demand falls below the level needed to keep everyone busy, an unfavourable labour efficiency variance will often be recorded because the actual quantity of hours for which employees are paid will exceed what is required for the actual output.

If the volume of customer orders is insufficient to keep employees busy, a manager has two options—either accept an unfavourable labour efficiency variance or utilize the employees to produce quantities of goods that exceed demand, resulting in a buildup of inventory.[2] A central principle of lean production (JIT) is that building inventory with no immediate prospect of sale is a bad idea. Excessive inventory—particularly work in process inventory—can lead to damaged or obsolete goods and therefore to generally inefficient operations. As a consequence, when the workforce is basically fixed in the short term, managers must be cautious about how labour efficiency variances are interpreted and used. Some advocate dispensing with labour efficiency variances entirely in such situations—at least for motivating and controlling workers on the shop floor.

> **Instant Quiz 10-3**
> Using the information supplied for Toy Mountain in Instant Quiz 10-1, calculate the direct labour rate and efficiency variances, and indicate possible causes for each.

USING STANDARD COSTS—VARIABLE MANUFACTURING OVERHEAD VARIANCES

The next step in Hanlon's analysis of Heirloom Pewter's variances for June is to compute the variable manufacturing overhead variances. The variable portion of manufacturing overhead can be analyzed with the same basic formulas used to analyze direct materials and direct labour. Recall from Exhibit 10-2 that the standard variable manufacturing overhead is $7.50 per unit of product, computed as follows:

 LEARNING OBJECTIVE 4
Compute the variable manufacturing overhead spending and efficiency variances, and explain their significance.

2.5 hours per unit × $3.00 per hour = $7.50 per unit

Heirloom Pewter's cost records showed that the total actual variable manufacturing overhead cost for June was $15,390. Recall from the earlier discussion of the direct labour variances that 5,400 hours of direct labour time was recorded during the month and that the company produced 2,000 pairs of bookends. Hanlon's analysis of this overhead data appears in Exhibit 10-7.

Notice the similarities between Exhibits 10-6 and 10-7. These similarities arise from the fact that direct labour-hours are being used as a base for allocating overhead cost to units of product; thus, the same hourly figures appear in Exhibit 10-7 for variable manufacturing overhead as in Exhibit 10-6 for direct labour. The main difference between the two exhibits is in the standard hourly rate being used, which in this company is much lower for variable manufacturing overhead. However, the format of the variance analysis for variable manufacturing overhead is the same if machine hours or material quantities or some other base is used.

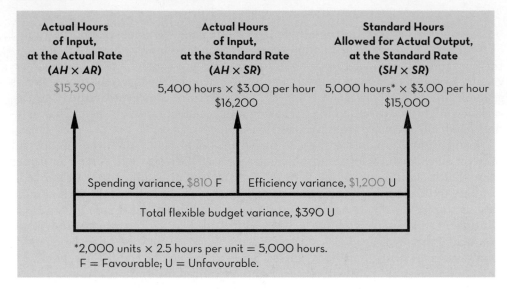

EXHIBIT 10-7   Variance Analysis—Variable Manufacturing Overhead

Actual Hours of Input, at the Actual Rate (AH × AR)	Actual Hours of Input, at the Standard Rate (AH × SR)	Standard Hours Allowed for Actual Output, at the Standard Rate (SH × SR)
$15,390	5,400 hours × $3.00 per hour $16,200	5,000 hours* × $3.00 per hour $15,000

Spending variance, $810 F | Efficiency variance, $1,200 U

Total flexible budget variance, $390 U

*2,000 units × 2.5 hours per unit = 5,000 hours.
F = Favourable; U = Unfavourable.

Variable Manufacturing Overhead Variances—A Closer Look

Variable overhead spending variance
The difference between the actual variable overhead cost incurred during a period and the standard cost that should have been incurred based on the actual activity of the period.

The formula for the **variable overhead spending variance** is

$$\text{Variable overhead spending variance} = (AH \times AR) - (AH \times SR)$$

AH = Actual Hours   AR = Actual Rate   SR = Standard Rate

Using the data from Exhibit 10–7, we have

$$(5,400 \times \$2.85) - (5,400 \times \$3.00) = -\$810 \text{ F}$$

Or, factored into simpler terms:

$$\text{Variable overhead spending variance} = AH(AR - SR)$$

Using the data from Exhibit 10–7 in the formula, we have

$$5,400 \text{ hours}(\$2.85 \text{ per hour*} - \$3.00 \text{ per hour}) = -\$810 \text{ F}$$

*$15,390 ÷ 5,400 hours = $2.85 per hour.

As will be explained below, the actual rate of $2.85 per hour incorporates both the price and the quantity of all actual variable overhead items used during the period. As such it represents a mixture of many individual actual rates (cost per kilogram of indirect materials, rate per hour of indirect labour, etc.) and cannot be interpreted in the same way as the actual price for direct materials or the actual rate for direct labour.

Variable overhead efficiency variance
The difference between the actual activity (direct labour-hours, machine-hours, or some other base) of a period and the standard activity allowed, multiplied by the variable part of the predetermined overhead rate.

The formula for the **variable overhead efficiency variance** is

$$\text{Variable overhead efficiency variance} = (AH \times SR) - (SH \times SR)$$

AH = Actual Hours   SR = Standard Rate   SH = Standard Hours Allowed for Actual Output

Or, factored into simpler terms:

$$\text{Variable overhead efficiency variance} = SR(AH - SH)$$

Again using the data from Exhibit 10–7, the computation of the variance is

$$\$3 \text{ per hour}(5,400 \text{ hours} - 5,000 \text{ hours*}) = \$1,200 \text{ U}$$

*2,000 units × 2.5 hours per unit = 5,000 hours.

Interpreting the Spending Variance   The variable overhead spending variance is most useful to managers when the cost driver for variable overhead really is the actual number of labour-hours or machine-hours worked. In other words, when the actual variable overhead costs vary in proportion with the actual number of hours worked in a period, the variable overhead spending variance can be informative. An overhead spending variance can occur if either (a) the actual purchase price of the variable overhead items differs from the standards or (b) the actual quantity of variable overhead items used differs from the standards.

To illustrate the two distinct components of the spending variance, we will further consider the Heirloom Pewter Company example. Assume that the variable manufacturing overhead rate of $3 per hour shown in Exhibit 10–2 is calculated as follows:

$$\text{Predetermined variable overhead rate} = \frac{\text{Estimated June total variable overhead cost}}{\text{Estimated June total direct labour-hours}}$$

$$\$3 = \$15,000 \div 5,000*$$

*2,000 units × 2.5 per hours per unit.

Further assume that the $15,000 of total variable manufacturing overhead costs consists of the following three items:

Indirect labour	$ 7,500
Indirect materials	5,000
Utilities	2,500
Total variable overhead	$15,000

The rate of $3 per hour incorporates estimates of both the *price* per unit that will be paid for each item included in variable overhead (e.g., indirect materials) and the *quantity* of those items that will be used for each direct labour-hour worked on the product.[3] For example, assume that Hanlon's estimate of $5,000 for indirect materials is based on expected usage of 200 kilograms of finishing materials at a cost of $25 per kilogram. This implies that 0.04 kilograms of indirect materials will be used for *each hour* worked on a pair of bookends (200 kilograms ÷ 5,000 hours). Given these characteristics of the predetermined overhead rate, two factors can cause the budgeted rate of $3 per hour to differ from the actual rate of $2.85 ($15,390 ÷ 5,400 hours) per hour implied by Exhibit 10–7. First, given the favourable spending variance for June, it may be that the actual cost of indirect materials was less than $25 per kilogram. Second, less than 0.04 kilograms of indirect materials may have been used per hour in producing 2,000 pairs of bookends in June. Of course, various combinations of these factors can also lead to the favourable spending variance, such as lower prices *and* more efficient use of indirect materials. Alternatively, higher prices could be more than offset by more efficient use of indirect materials.

In principle, the price and quantity components of the spending variance could be separately reported. However, this is seldom done because, typically, the price element is small so the variance is mainly influenced by how efficiently the quantities of variable overhead resources are used, such as indirect materials. Even though the price and quantity components are rarely broken out, the spending variance is useful to managers. For example, an unfavourable spending variance tells managers they must find ways to acquire overhead items at cheaper prices, use lower quantities of them, or both.

Interpreting the Efficiency Variance   Like the variable overhead spending variance, the variable overhead efficiency variance is useful only if the cost driver for variable overhead really is the actual hours worked. Then any increase or decrease in hours actually worked should result in an increase or decrease in variable overhead costs actually incurred. The variable overhead efficiency variance is an estimate of the effect on variable overhead costs of efficiencies or inefficiencies

> **Instant Quiz 10-4**
> OrderUp Company provides customer help centre services for online merchants. According to the company's standards, 0.15 direct labour-hours are required to fulfill a help request for one customer, and the variable overhead rate is $1.30 per direct labour-hour. This month, 35,000 help requests were responded to using 5,700 direct labour-hours. The company incurred a total of $7,125 in variable overhead costs.
> What variable overhead cost should have been incurred to fill the service requests for the 35,000 items? How much does this differ from the actual variable overhead cost?

in the use of the base (i.e., hours). In a sense, the term *variable overhead efficiency variance* is a misnomer. It seems to suggest that it measures the efficiency with which variable overhead resources were used. It does not. It is an estimate of the indirect effect on variable overhead costs of efficiency or inefficiency in the use of the activity base.

This point can be illustrated by looking again at Exhibit 10–7. During June, 400 more labour-hours were used than should have been used to produce the period's output. Each of these hours presumably required the incurrence of $3.00 of variable overhead cost, resulting in an unfavourable variance of $1,200 (400 hours × $3.00 = $1,200). Although this $1,200 variance is called an *overhead efficiency variance*, it could better be called a *labour-hours efficiency variance*, since it results from using too many labour-hours rather than from inefficient use of overhead resources. Accordingly, be careful to interpret the variance with a clear understanding of what it really measures. It is worth noting that the efficiency variance for variable overhead can be calculated only if a standard exists for hours (or other quantities) *allowed* for the actual quantity of output achieved for a period. In the absence of a quantity standard for inputs, only the spending variance can be calculated, as will be illustrated later in this chapter.

Control of the Efficiency Variance   Who is responsible for control of the overhead efficiency variance? Since the variance really reflects efficiency in the utilization of the base underlying the flexible budget, whoever is responsible for control of this base is responsible for control of the variance. If the base is direct labour-hours, then the supervisor or manager responsible for the use of labour time will be responsible for any overhead efficiency variance.

In preparation for the scheduled meeting to discuss his analysis of Heirloom Pewter's standard costs and variances, Hanlon distributed Exhibits 10–2 through 10–7 to the management group of Heirloom Pewter. This included Wriston, the president of the company; Kuchel, the production manager; and Warner, the purchasing manager. Wriston opened the meeting with the following question:

Wriston: George, I think I understand the report you distributed, but just to make sure, would you mind summarizing what you found?

Hanlon: As you can see, the biggest problems are the unfavourable materials quantity variance of $2,000 and the unfavourable labour efficiency variance of $8,400.

Wriston: Tom, you're the production boss. What do you think is causing the unfavourable labour efficiency variance?

Kuchel: It has to be the new production workers. Our experienced workers shouldn't have much problem meeting the standard of 2.5 hours per unit. We all knew that there would be some inefficiency for a while as we brought new people on board. My plan for overcoming the problem is to pair up each of the new workers with one of our old-timers and have them work together for a while. It would slow down our old-timers a bit, but I'll bet the unfavourable variance disappears and our new workers would learn a lot.

Wriston: Sounds good. Now, what about that $2,000 unfavourable materials quantity variance?

Hanlon: Tom, are the new workers generating a lot of scrap?

Kuchel: Yeah, I guess so.

Wriston: I think that could be part of the problem. Can you do anything about it?

Kuchel: I can watch the scrap closely for a few days to see where it's being generated. If it is the new workers, I can have the old-timers work with them on the problem when I team them up.

Wriston: Janet, the favourable materials price variance of $1,300 isn't helping us if it is contributing to the unfavourable materials quantity and labour efficiency variances. Let's make sure that our raw material purchases conform to our quality standards.

LEARNING AID

SUMMARY OF VARIANCE FORMULAS FOR VARIABLE COSTS

1. **Direct Materials**

   Price variance: $AQ^*(AP - SP)$
   Quantity variance: $SP(AQ - SQ)$

   where AQ^* = Actual quantity purchased, AP = Actual price, SP = Standard price, AQ = Actual quantity used, and SQ = Standard quantity.

2. **Direct Labour**

   Rate variance: $AH(AR - SR)$
   Efficiency variance: $SR(AH - SH)$

   where AH = Actual hours, AR = Actual direct labour rate, SR = Standard direct labour rate, and SH = Standard direct labour-hours.

3. **Variable Overhead**

   Spending variance: $AH^*(AR^* - SR^*)$
   Efficiency variance: $SR^*(AH^* - SH^*)$

   where AH^* = Actual hours of activity base, AR^* = Actual variable overhead rate, SR^* = Standard variable overhead rate, and SH^* = Standard hours of activity base.

Warner: Fair enough.

Wriston: Good. Let's reconvene in a few weeks to see what has happened. Hopefully, we can get those unfavourable variances under control.

Before proceeding further, we suggest that you pause at this point and go back and review the data contained in Exhibits 10–2 through 10–7. These exhibits and the accompanying text discussion provide a comprehensive, integrated illustration of standard setting and variance analysis.

Standard Costs and Variance in the Service Industry

While standard costing has its roots in the manufacturing industry, standard costing techniques can also help firms in the service industry understand and better manage their costs. The main differences between standard costing in the manufacturing and service industries are the terminology used and the manner in which the cost of goods sold account is constructed. A manufacturer's cost of goods manufactured is the sum of direct materials, direct labour, and manufacturing overhead cost. A merchandising company (e.g., a retail department store) calculates its cost of goods sold as the net purchase price paid for the products sold during the period. The cost of services provided in other service-based businesses mainly consists of labour, indirect overhead costs, and perhaps a small amount of direct materials incurred to provide services to customers/clients.

Variance analysis can also be useful in service companies, although direct materials might be the computers, office equipment, and office supplies necessary to provide the service and direct labour might be the salary paid to the employees providing the service. For example, a senior accountant's salary is considered direct labour in an accounting firm, while the office receptionist's salary is considered an overhead cost.

Although usually framed in terms of production, variance analysis can be very useful to managers of companies in the service industry. Labour variances are particularly useful since salaries and wages of the employees providing services usually make up the bulk of a service company's costs. Labour rate variances may indicate excessive overtime worked or the use of a greater proportion than expected of more senior staff that results in an increase in the overall average wage for the period. Labour efficiency variances occur when staff spend more than the standard time providing a particular service.

■ OVERHEAD RATES AND FIXED OVERHEAD ANALYSIS

LEARNING OBJECTIVE 5
Explain the significance of the denominator activity figure in determining the standard cost of a unit of product.

The detailed analysis of fixed overhead differs considerably from that of variable overhead discussed in the previous section, simply because of the difference in the nature of the costs involved. To provide a background for our discussion, we will first review briefly the need for, and computation of, predetermined overhead rates. This review will be helpful, since the predetermined overhead rate plays a major role in fixed overhead analysis. We will then show how fixed overhead variances are computed and discuss their usefulness to managers.

Flexible Budgets and Overhead Rates

Fixed costs come in large, discrete amounts that by definition do not change with changes in the level of activity within the relevant range. As we learned in Chapter 5, this creates a problem in product costing, since a given level of fixed overhead cost spread over a small number of units will result in a higher cost per unit than if the same costs are spread over a large number of units. Consider the data in the following table:

Month	(1) Fixed Overhead Cost	(2) Number of Units Produced	(3) Unit Cost (1) ÷ (2)
January	$6,000	1,000	$6.00
February......................	6,000	1,500	4.00
March	6,000	800	7.50

Notice that the large number of units produced in February results in a low unit cost ($4.00), whereas the small number of units produced in March results in a high unit cost ($7.50). This problem arises only in connection with the fixed portion of overhead, since by definition the variable portion of overhead remains constant on a per unit basis, with the total costs rising and falling in proportion to changes in the activity level. Most managers feel that the fixed portion of unit cost should be stabilized so that a single unit cost figure can be used throughout the year. As we learned in Chapter 5, this stability can be accomplished by using the predetermined overhead rate.

We will analyze the fixed overhead costs of Heirloom Pewter Company using the flexible budget of the company, as displayed in Exhibit 10–8. Note that the budgeted total fixed overhead costs amount to $300,000 within the relevant range of activity.

Denominator Activity   The formula that we used in Chapter 5 to compute the predetermined overhead rate is as follows (MH: machine-hours; DLH: direct labour-hours):

$$\text{Predetermined overhead rate} = \frac{\text{Estimated total manufacturing overhead cost}}{\text{Estimated total units in the base (MH, DLH, etc.)}}$$

Denominator activity
The activity figure used to compute the predetermined overhead rate.

The estimated total units in the base of the formula for the predetermined overhead rate is called the **denominator activity**. Recall from our discussion in Chapter 5 that once an estimated activity level (denominator activity) has been chosen, it remains unchanged throughout the year, even if the actual activity turns out to be

Overhead Costs	Cost Formula (per direct labour-hour)	Annual Activity (in direct labour-hours)		
		40,000	50,000	60,000
Variable overhead costs:				
Indirect labour..................	$ 1.50	$ 60,000	$ 75,000	$ 90,000
Lubricants......................	1.00	40,000	50,000	60,000
Power..........................	0.50	20,000	25,000	30,000
Total variable overhead cost..	$3.00	120,000	150,000	180,000
Fixed overhead costs:				
Depreciation		120,000	120,000	120,000
Supervisory salaries.............		144,000	144,000	144,000
Insurance		36,000	36,000	36,000
Total fixed overhead cost.....		300,000	300,000	300,000
Total overhead cost..............		$420,000	$450,000	$480,000

HEIRLOOM PEWTER COMPANY
Flexible Budgets at Various Levels of Activity

EXHIBIT 10–8   Flexible Budget Schedule

different from the original estimate. The reason for not changing the denominator is to maintain stability in the amount of overhead applied to each unit of product, regardless of when it is produced during the year.

Computing the Overhead Rate   When we discussed predetermined overhead rates in Chapter 5, we didn't explain how the estimated total manufacturing cost was determined. This figure can be derived from the flexible budget. Once the denominator level of activity is chosen, the flexible budget can be used to determine the total amount of overhead cost that should be incurred at that level of activity. The predetermined overhead rate can then be computed using the following variation on the basic formula for the predetermined overhead rate:

$$\frac{\text{Predetermined}}{\text{overhead rate}} = \frac{\text{Overhead from the flexible budget at the denominator level of activity}}{\text{Denominator level of activity}}$$

To illustrate, refer to Heirloom Pewter Company's flexible budget for manufacturing overhead in Exhibit 10–8. Suppose that the budgeted activity level for the year is 50,000 direct labour-hours (DLH) and that this will be used as the denominator activity in the formula for the predetermined overhead rate. The numerator in the formula is the estimated total overhead cost (variable and fixed) of $450,000 when the activity is 50,000 DLH. This figure is taken from the flexible budget in Exhibit 10–8. Therefore, the predetermined overhead rate for Heirloom Pewter Company is computed as follows:

$$\frac{\$450,000}{50,000\,\text{DLH}} = \$9.00 \text{ per direct labour-hour}$$

The company can also break its predetermined overhead rate down into variable and fixed elements rather than using a single combined figure:

$$\text{Variable element:} \frac{\$150,000}{50,000\,\text{DLH}} = \$3.00 \text{ per direct labour-hour}$$

$$\text{Fixed element:} \frac{\$300,000}{50,000\,\text{DLH}} = \$6.00 \text{ per direct labour-hour}$$

EXHIBIT 10–9 Standard Cost Record—Absorption Cost

Inputs	(1) Standard Quantity or Hours	(2) Standard Price or Rate	(3) Standard Cost (1) × (2)
Direct materials (from Exhibit 10-2)........	3.0 kilograms	$ 4.00	$12.00
Direct labour (from Exhibit 10-2)...........	2.5 hours	21.00	52.50
Variable manufacturing overhead (from Exhibit 10-2)	2.5 hours	3.00	7.50
Fixed manufacturing overhead............	2.5 hours	6.00	15.00
Total standard variable cost per unit....			$87.00

For every direct labour-hour of operation, work in process will be charged with $9.00 of overhead, of which $3.00 will be variable overhead and $6.00 will be fixed overhead. If a pair of bookends takes two and one-half direct labour-hours to complete, then its cost will include $7.50 variable overhead and $15 fixed overhead, as per the revised standard cost record shown in Exhibit 10–9, which now includes fixed manufacturing overhead.

In summary, the flexible budget provides the estimated overhead cost needed to compute the predetermined overhead rate. Thus, the flexible budget plays a key role in determining the amount of fixed and variable overhead cost that will be charged to units of product.

■ OVERHEAD APPLICATION AND FIXED OVERHEAD VARIANCES

LEARNING OBJECTIVE ❻
Compute and interpret the fixed overhead budget and volume variances.

To understand the fixed overhead variances, it is necessary first to understand how overhead is applied to work in process in a standard costing system. Therefore, we examine the details of the application process next.

Overhead Application in a Standard Costing System

In Chapter 5, recall that we applied overhead to work in process on the basis of actual hours of activity (multiplied by the predetermined overhead rate). This procedure was correct, since at the time we were dealing with a normal costing system that applies overhead using the actual levels of the activity base.[4] However, we are now dealing with a standard costing system. In such a system, overhead is applied to work in process on the basis of the *standard hours allowed for the actual output of the period* rather than on the basis of the actual number of hours worked. This point is illustrated in Exhibit 10–10. In a standard costing system, every unit of a particular

EXHIBIT 10–10 Applied Overhead Costs: Normal Costing System versus Standard Costing System

Normal Costing System Manufacturing Overhead		Standard Costing System Manufacturing Overhead	
Actual overhead costs incurred.	Applied overhead costs: Actual hours × Predetermined overhead rate.	Actual overhead costs incurred.	Applied overhead costs: Standard hours allowed for actual output × Predetermined overhead rate.
Under- or overapplied overhead		Under- or overapplied overhead	

product is charged with the same amount of overhead cost, regardless of how much time the unit actually requires for processing.

To illustrate the computation of fixed overhead variances, we again refer to the data for Heirloom Pewter Company:

Denominator activity in direct labour-hours	50,000
Budgeted annual fixed overhead costs....................................	$300,000
Fixed portion of the predetermined overhead rate (computed earlier)	$ 6

Let us assume that the following actual operating results were recorded for the month of June:

Actual direct labour-hours...	5,400
Standard direct labour-hours allowed*..	5,000
Actual fixed overhead costs:	
Depreciation..	$10,000
Supervisory salaries..	14,000
Insurance..	3,500
Total actual cost	$27,500

*For the actual production in June.

From these data, two variances can be computed for fixed overhead—a *budget variance* and a *volume variance*. The variances for the month of June are shown in Exhibit 10–11.

Notice from the exhibit that overhead has been applied to work in process on the basis of 5,000 standard hours allowed for the actual output of June rather than on the basis of 5,400 actual hours worked. As stated earlier, this keeps unit costs from being affected by any variations in efficiency.

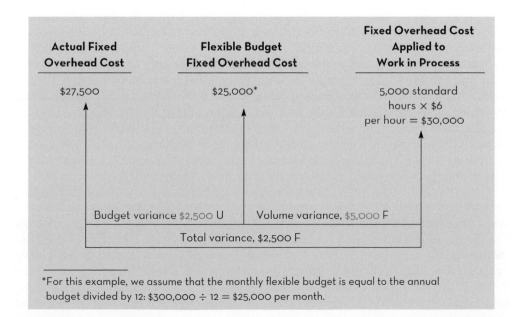

EXHIBIT 10–11   Computation of the June Fixed Overhead Variances

Actual Fixed Overhead Cost	Flexible Budget Fixed Overhead Cost	Fixed Overhead Cost Applied to Work in Process
$27,500	$25,000*	5,000 standard hours × $6 per hour = $30,000

Budget variance $2,500 U   Volume variance, $5,000 F

Total variance, $2,500 F

*For this example, we assume that the monthly flexible budget is equal to the annual budget divided by 12: $300,000 ÷ 12 = $25,000 per month.

Budget Variance

The **budget variance** is the difference between the actual fixed overhead costs incurred during the period and the budgeted fixed overhead costs as contained in the flexible budget. It can be computed as shown in Exhibit 10–11 or by using the formula

Budget variance = Actual fixed overhead cost − Flexible budget fixed overhead cost

Applying this formula to Heirloom Pewter Company, the budget variance is

$$\$27,500 - \$25,000 = \$2,500 \text{ U}$$

Budget variances for fixed overhead can be very useful, since they represent the difference between how much should have been spent (according to the flexible budget) and how much was actually spent. For the month of June, Heirloom Pewter's actual fixed costs were $2,500 higher than budget, and management may want to identify which specific fixed overhead items caused this variance. We will present a detailed performance report for overhead costs later in the chapter.

Volume Variance

The volume variance is a measure of utilization of plant facilities. The variance arises whenever the standard hours allowed for the actual output of a period are different from the denominator activity level that was planned when the period began. It can be computed as shown in Exhibit 10–11 or by the following formula:

$$\begin{matrix} \text{Volume} \\ \text{variance} \end{matrix} = \begin{matrix} \text{Fixed portion of} \\ \text{the predetermined} \\ \text{overhead rate} \end{matrix} \times \left(\begin{matrix} \text{Denominator} \\ \text{hours} \end{matrix} - \begin{matrix} \text{Standard hours} \\ \text{allowed} \end{matrix} \right)$$

Applying this formula to Heirloom Pewter Company, the volume variance is

$$\$6 \text{ per DLH}(4,167 - 5,000) = -\$4,998 \text{ F}$$

As discussed in Chapter 5, predetermined overhead rates are often prepared on an annual basis to avoid distortions in product costs caused by seasonal fluctuations in overhead items (e.g., heating costs). Heirloom Pewter's rate of $6 per hour for fixed overhead is based on estimated annual fixed costs of $300,000 and an annual denominator activity level of 50,000 labour-hours. However, to facilitate the calculation of a volume variance for the *month* of June, Hanlon assigned the annual denominator activity of 50,000 direct labour-hours evenly to each month. Therefore, denominator activity for June is 50,000 ÷ 12 = 4,167. Except for a $2 rounding difference, the favourable $4,998 volume variance above agrees with the amount of $5,000 shown in Exhibit 10–11. Importantly, when calculating the volume variance for the year, Hanlon will use the total annual denominator activity level of 50,000 hours and the standard hours allowed for the total production output for the year.

As stated earlier, the volume variance is a measure of utilization of available plant facilities. A favourable variance, as above, means that the company operated at an activity level *above* that planned for the period. An unfavourable variance means that the company operated at an activity level *below* that planned for the period.

It is important to note that the volume variance does not measure overspending or underspending. A company would normally incur the same dollar amount of fixed overhead cost regardless of whether the period's activity was above or below the planned (denominator) level because, after all, the costs are fixed over the relevant range of activity. Also note that fixed overhead does not have an efficiency variance because the fixed overhead budget for the actual direct labour-hours, 5,400, is the same as the fixed overhead budget for 5,000 standard direct labour-hours, namely $25,000. The volume variance occurs only as a result of the standard

(5,000) and denominator (4,167) direct labour-hours difference, 833 direct labour-hours. In short, the volume variance is an activity-related variance. It is explainable only by activity and is controllable only through activity.

To summarize:

1. If the denominator activity and the standard hours allowed for the actual output of the period are the same, then there is no volume variance.
2. If the denominator activity is greater than the standard hours allowed for the actual output of the period, then the volume variance is unfavourable, signifying an underutilization of available facilities.
3. If the denominator activity is less than the standard hours allowed for the actual output of the period, then the volume variance is favourable, signifying a higher utilization of available facilities than was planned.

Instant Quiz 10-5

Carlton Corporation uses a standard costing system that applies overhead to products based on the standard direct labour-hours allowed for the actual output of the period. Data concerning the most recent year appear below:

Total budgeted fixed overhead cost for the year	$400,000
Actual fixed overhead cost for the year	$ 394,000
Budgeted standard direct labour-hours (denominator level of activity)	50,000
Actual direct labour-hours	51,000
Standard direct labour-hours allowed for the actual output	48,000

Compute the fixed portion of the predetermined overhead rate for the year and the fixed overhead budget and volume variances.

Graphic Analysis of Fixed Overhead Variances

Some insights into the budget and volume variances can be gained through graphic analysis. A graph containing these variances is presented in Exhibit 10–12.

EXHIBIT 10–12   Graphic Analysis of Fixed Overhead Variances

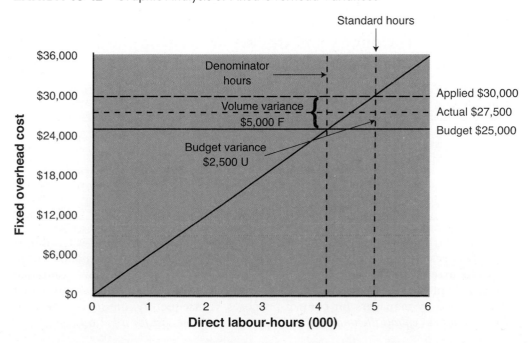

As shown in the graph, fixed overhead cost is applied to work in process at the predetermined rate of $6 for each standard hour of activity. (The applied cost line is the upward-sloping line on the graph.) Since a denominator level of 4,167 direct labour-hours was used for June, the applied cost line crosses the budget cost line at exactly the 4,167 direct labour-hours point. Thus, if the denominator hours and the standard hours allowed for the output are the same, there can be no volume variance, since the applied cost line and the budget cost line will be the same on the graph. It is only when the standard hours differ from the denominator hours that a volume variance can arise.

In this case, more standard hours are allowed for the actual June output (5,000 hours) than denominator hours (4,167 hours); the result is a favourable volume variance, since more cost was applied to production than was originally budgeted. If the situation had been reversed and fewer standard hours than denominator hours had been allowed for the actual output, then the volume variance on the graph would have been unfavourable.

Cautions in Fixed Overhead Analysis

A volume variance arises for fixed overhead because when applying the costs to work in process, we act *as if* the fixed costs were variable. This point can be seen from the graph in Exhibit 10–12. Notice from the graph that the fixed overhead costs are applied to work in process at a rate of $6 per hour *as if* they were variable. Treating these costs as if they were variable is necessary for product costing purposes, but there are some real dangers here. The manager can easily become misled and start thinking of the fixed costs as if they were *in fact* variable.

Keep in mind that fixed overhead costs come in large chunks. Expressing fixed costs on a unit or per hour basis, although necessary for product costing for external reports, is artificial. Increases or decreases in activity in fact have no effect on total fixed costs within the relevant range of activity. Even though fixed costs are expressed on a unit or per hour basis, they are *not* proportional to activity. In a sense, the volume variance is the error that occurs as a result of treating fixed costs as variable costs in the costing system.

Because of the confusion that can arise concerning the interpretation of the volume variance, some companies present the volume variance in physical units (hours) rather than in dollars, or express utilization as a percentage of capacity utilized.

Overhead Variances and Under- or Overapplied Overhead Cost

Four variances relating to overhead cost have been computed for Heirloom Pewter Company in this chapter. These four variances are as follows:

Variable overhead spending variance (Exhibit 10–7)	$ 810 F
Variable overhead efficiency variance (Exhibit 10–7)	1,200 U
Fixed overhead budget variance (Exhibit 10–11)	2,500 U
Fixed overhead volume variance (Exhibit 10–11)	5,000 F
Total overhead variance	$ 2,110 F

Recall from Chapter 5 that underapplied or overapplied overhead is the difference between the amount of overhead applied to products and the actual overhead costs incurred during a period. Basically, the overhead variances we have computed in this chapter break down the under- or overapplied overhead into variances that can be used by managers for control purposes. Consequently, *the sum of the overhead variances equals the under- or overapplied overhead cost for a period.*

Furthermore, in a standard costing system, unfavourable variances are equivalent to underapplied overhead, and favourable variances are equivalent to overapplied overhead. Unfavourable variances occur because more was spent on overhead than the standards allow. Underapplied overhead occurs when more was spent on overhead than was applied to products during the period. But in a standard costing system, the standard amount of overhead allowed is exactly the same as the amount of overhead applied to products. Therefore, in a standard costing system, unfavourable variances and underapplied overhead are the same thing, as are favourable variances and overapplied overhead.

For Heirloom Pewter Company, the total overhead variance was $2,110 favourable. Therefore, its overhead cost was overapplied by $2,110 for the year. To reinforce this concept, carefully study the review problem at the end of the chapter.

OVERHEAD REPORTING, VARIANCE INVESTIGATIONS, AND CAPACITY ANALYSIS

Hanlon completes his analysis of overhead spending at Heirloom Pewter Company in June by preparing the performance report shown in Exhibit 10–13. The report builds on the analysis of variable and fixed overhead presented, respectively, in Exhibits 10–7 and 10–11 by providing details on the individual items included in each category. This additional level of detail allows managers to determine the amount that each overhead item contributes to the spending (budget) and efficiency variances.

Two things should be noted about Exhibit 10–13. First, because Hanlon has developed a standard costing system and wants to report both the spending and efficiency variances for variable overhead costs, he has included budgeted costs for both the actual direct labour-hours used (5,400) and the standard direct labour-hours allowed (5,000) for the 2,000 units produced in June. As a result, the sum of the individual spending ($810 F) and efficiency ($1,200 U) variances reported in Exhibit 10–13 corresponds to the variances shown in Exhibit 10–7. The second issue to note in Exhibit 10–13 is that for fixed overhead costs, no efficiency variances are included; only budget variances are calculated. This is consistent with Exhibit 10–11, which illustrates that for fixed overhead, it is not possible to calculate an efficiency variance. As discussed earlier, this is because within the relevant range of activity, fixed costs do not change as the activity level changes. Therefore, the budget for each fixed overhead item is the same in columns (2) and (3) of Exhibit 10–13, even though the activity level differs by 400 hours (5,400 − 5,000) across these two columns. For control purposes, the budget variance for fixed overhead is the key tool. By comparing what was actually spent on each fixed overhead item to the budget, Hanlon can determine how well the managers responsible for these line items did in controlling costs.

Preparing an overhead performance report that contains both spending and efficiency variances is possible only if a standard costing system is in place. In the absence of a standard costing system, column (3) in Exhibit 10–13 would not exist since it represents the standard direct labour-hours allowed for the actual output achieved. However, even if a standard costing system is not being used, an overhead performance report can still be prepared, but it will include *only* the spending and budget variances. An example of this type of report is presented in Exhibit 10–14. Note that the spending and budget variances in Exhibit 10–14 are the same as those in Exhibit 10–13. The only difference between the two performance reports is that Exhibit 10–13, based on the standard costing system developed at Heirloom Pewter, also includes efficiency variances.

After preparing the performance report, managers still have to decide whether the variances that have been calculated require further action. For example, the $2,000 unfavourable fixed overhead budget variance for supervisory salaries is the largest single variance for the month of June. Should it be investigated? Should answers be sought as to the cause of the variance? Identifying which variances to

LEARNING OBJECTIVE 7

Prepare a performance report for manufacturing overhead, decide which variances to investigate, and perform an analysis of capacity utilization.

EXHIBIT 10-13   An Overhead Performance Report

HEIRLOOM PEWTER CORPORATION
Overhead Performance Report
For the Month Ended June 30

Actual production (units)	2,000
Actual direct labour-hours	5,400
Standard direct labour-hours allowed	5,000

> Budget allowances are based on the direct labour-hours that should have been used (5,000) to produce 2,000 units and the hours actually worked (5,400).

> This approach yields both a spending and an efficiency variance for variable manufacturing overhead.

	Cost Formula (per Direct Labour-Hour)	(1) Actual Costs 5,400 Direct Labour-Hours	(2) Budget Based on 5,400 Direct Labour-Hours*	(3) Budget Based on 5,000 Direct Labour-Hours*	Total Flexible Budget Variance (1) − (3)†	Breakdown of the Total Flexible Budget Variance — Spending (Budget) Variance (1) − (2)	Breakdown of the Total Flexible Budget Variance — Efficiency Variance (2) − (3)
Overhead Costs							
Variable overhead costs:							
Indirect labour	$1.50	$ 7,830	$ 8,100	$ 7,500	$ 330 U	$ 270 F	$ 600 U
Lubricants	1.00	5,022	5,400	5,000	22 U	378 F	400 U
Power	0.50	2,538	2,700	2,500	38 U	162 F	200 U
Total variable overhead cost	$3.00	15,390	16,200	15,000	390 U	810 F	1,200 U
Fixed overhead costs:							
Depreciation		10,000	10,000	10,000	0	0	–
Supervisory salaries		14,000	12,000	12,000	2,000 U	2,000 U	–
Insurance		3,500	3,000	3,000	500 U	500 U	–
Total fixed overhead cost		27,500	25,000	25,000	2,500 U	2,500 U	–
Total overhead cost		$42,890	$41,200	$40,000	$2,890 U	$1,690 U	$1,200 U

*Budget amounts for variable overhead costs are determined by multiplying budgeted direct labour-hours by the cost formula amount (per direct labour-hour). For example, indirect labour costs of $8,100 for 5,400 hours = $1.50 × 5,400.

†Total variable and fixed overhead variances as per Exhibits 10-7 (variable overhead) and 10-11 (fixed overhead).

EXHIBIT 10–14   An Overhead Performance Report with Only Spending or Budget Variances

HEIRLOOM PEWTER CORPORATION
Overhead Performance Report
For the Month Ended June 30

Actual production (units) 2,000
Actual direct labour-hours............... 5,400

Overhead Costs	Cost Formula (per Direct Labour-Hour)	(1) Actual Costs 5,400 Direct Labour-Hours	(2) Budget Based on 5,400 Direct Labour-Hours*	Spending (Budget) Variance (1) — (2)
Variable overhead costs:				
Indirect labour	$ 1.50	$ 7,830	$ 8,100	$ 270 F
Lubricants	1.00	5,022	5,400	378 F
Power	0.50	2,538	2,700	162 F
Total variable overhead cost.....	$3.00	15,390	16,200	810 F
Fixed overhead costs:				
Depreciation......................		10,000	10,000	0
Supervisory salaries		14,000	12,000	2,000 U
Insurance		3,500	3,000	500 U
Total fixed overhead cost........		27,500	25,000	2,500 U
Total overhead cost.................		$42,890	$41,200	$1,690 U

*Budget amounts for variable overhead costs are determined by multiplying budgeted direct labour-hours by the cost formula amount (per direct labour-hour). For example, indirect labour costs of $8,100 for 5,400 hours = $1.50 × 5,400.

target for investigation is an important part of the variance analysis cycle presented in Exhibit 10–1. In the next section, we examine how managers make these decisions.

Variance Investigation Decisions

Variance analysis and performance reports are important elements of *management by exception*, which focuses on those areas of responsibility where goals and expectations are not being met.

IN BUSINESS

Particularly in small companies, the controller may be the only person who understands concepts such as overhead variances and overapplied and underapplied overhead. Furthermore, a small-company controller may be able to both authorize cash disbursements and account for them. Since small, closely held companies often do not hire external auditors, these circumstances create an ideal environment for fraud.

Such was the case in a small manufacturing company with 100 employees and $30 million in annual sales. The controller embezzled nearly $1 million from the company over three years by writing cheques to himself. The consultant who uncovered the fraud was tipped off by the unusually high overhead variances that resulted from the controller recording fictitious expenses in the overhead accounts to offset his fraudulent cash withdrawals. After the fraud was exposed, the company implemented various controls to reduce the risk of future problems. These controls included hiring an internal auditor and requiring periodic review of overhead variances to identify and explain significant discrepancies.

Source: Reproduced with permission of INSTITUTE OF MANAGEMENT ACCOUNTANTS, and John B. MacArthur, Bobby E. Waldrup, and Gary R. Fane, "Caution: Fraud Overhead," *Strategic Finance*, October 2004, pp. 28–32; permission conveyed through Copyright Clearance Center, Inc.

The budgets and standards discussed in this chapter and in the preceding chapter reflect management's plans. If all goes according to plan, there will be little difference between actual results and the budgets and standards. However, if actual results do not conform to the budget and to standards, the performance reporting system sends a signal to the manager that an "exception" has occurred. This signal is in the form of a variance from the budget or standards.

However, are all variances worth investigating? The answer is no. Differences between actual results and what was expected will almost always occur. If every variance were investigated, management would spend a great deal of time tracking down immaterial differences. Variances may occur for any of a variety of reasons—only some of which warrant management attention. For example, hotter than normal weather in the summer may result in higher than expected electricity bills for air conditioning. Because of unpredictable random factors, every cost category will produce a variance of some kind.

How should managers decide which variances are worth investigating? One indicator is the dollar amount of the variance. A variance of $5 is probably not big enough to warrant attention, whereas a variance of $5,000 might well be worth investigating. Another indicator is the size of the variance relative to the amount of spending involved. A variance that is only 0.1% of spending on an item is likely due to random factors, while a variance of 10% of spending is more indicative that something is wrong and should be investigated.

Another approach is to plot variance data on a statistical control chart, as illustrated in Exhibit 10–15. The basic idea of a statistical control chart is that some random fluctuations in variances from period to period are to be expected even when costs are under control. A variance should be investigated only when it is unusual relative to the normal level of random fluctuation. Typically, the standard deviation of the variances is used as the measure of the normal level of fluctuations. Often a simple decision rule is adopted, such as "investigate all variances that are more than X standard deviations from zero." In the control chart in Exhibit 10–15, X is 1.0. That is, the decision rule in this company is to investigate all variances that are more than one standard deviation above (unfavourable) or below (favourable) zero. This means that the variances in weeks 7, 11, and 17 would have been investigated, but none of the others.

What value of X should be chosen? The greater the value of X, the wider the band of acceptable variances that would not be investigated. Thus, the greater the value of X, the less time will be spent tracking down variances, but the more likely it is that a truly out-of-control situation will be overlooked. Ordinarily, if X is selected to be 1.0, roughly 30% of all variances will trigger an investigation even when there is no real problem. If X is set at 1.5, the figure drops to about 13%. If X is set at 2.0, the figure drops to about 5%.

EXHIBIT 10–15 A Statistical Control Chart

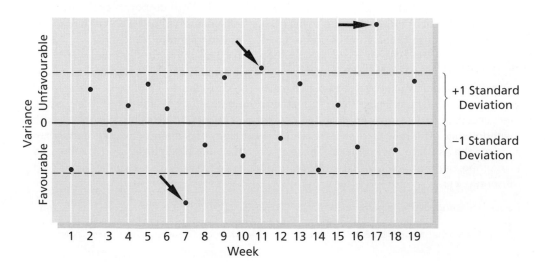

In addition to watching for unusually large variances, the pattern of the variances should be monitored. For example, a series of steadily increasing variances should trigger an investigation even if no variance is large enough by itself to warrant investigation.

Capacity Analysis

Capacity analysis allows managers to evaluate the financial impact of not fully utilizing available productive capacity, making it an important strategic tool for management. However, increasing the utilization of capacity by eliminating bottlenecks or increasing demand for products can take time. Similarly, reducing capacity because of insufficient long-term demand cannot be done overnight, so it is important that capacity analysis be conducted on an ongoing basis.

We use Heirloom Pewter Company to illustrate a basic approach to capacity analysis. Recall that the company has a budgeted production level of 20,000 pairs of bookends for the year. This denominator level of activity was used earlier in this chapter to determine a standard cost per pair of bookends of $87.00, based on 20,000 units or 50,000 direct labour-hours (see Exhibit 10–9). Assume now that the year has ended and 16,000 pairs of bookends have been sold.

If all available production time were used and no waste occurred, Heirloom Pewter could reach a level of capacity known as **theoretical capacity**. This level of capacity would require operations to be conducted around the clock, 365 days per year, with no downtime, similar to the definition of an ideal standard presented earlier in this chapter. If the denominator level of 20,000 units or 50,000 direct labour-hours represented 50% of the theoretical capacity, then Heirloom Pewter could produce 40,000 units (20,000 ÷ 0.50) in 100,000 hours.

Practical capacity represents what could be produced if unavoidable downtime were subtracted from theoretical capacity. Maintenance, breakdowns, and setup times for new operations are considered to be unavoidable downtime. If the denominator level were 80% of practical capacity, then 25,000 units (20,000 ÷ 0.80) could be produced using 62,500 direct labour-hours.

Capacity analysis proceeds by first examining the overhead cost (variable + fixed) at each level of capacity:

Theoretical capacity
The volume of activity resulting from operations conducted 24 hours per day, 7 days per week, 365 days per year, with no downtime.

Practical capacity
The productive capacity possible after subtracting unavoidable downtime from theoretical capacity.

	Total Overhead Costs
Theoretical.................................	(100,000 DLH × $3.00) × $300,000 = $600,000
Practical....................................	(62,500 DLH × $3.00) × $300,000 = $ 487,500
Denominator...............................	(50,000 DLH × $3.00) × $300,000 = $450,000
Actual	(40,000 DLH × $3.00) × $300,000 = $420,000

If Heirloom Pewter can sell all that it can produce at $105 per unit, then an indication of the opportunity cost incurred of not operating at the various levels of capacity can be computed as follows:

	Contribution Margin*	Total Overhead	Operating Income
Theoretical......................	40,000 units × ($105.00 − $64.50) −	$600,000	= $1,020,000
Practical........................	25,000 units × ($105.00 − $64.50) −	$ 487,500	= $ 525,000
Denominator....................	20,000 units × ($105.00 − $64.50) −	$450,000	= $ 360,000
Actual	16,000 units × ($105.00 − $64.50) −	$420,000	= $ 228,000

*$64.50 variable costs exclude $7.50 per unit variable overhead because it is included in the total overhead amount.

Note that $64.50 is composed of the standard materials cost of $12 per unit and the standard direct labour cost of $52.50 per unit shown in Exhibit 10–9. The remaining variable production cost of $7.50 per unit for overhead is included in the overhead charges calculated above.

To calculate the opportunity cost of operating at 16,000 units (a profit of $228,000), we begin by looking at what additional profit would have been possible at the theoretical capacity: $1,020,000 − $228,000, or $792,000 in lost profits. By examining marketing strategies or product design changes necessary to sell an additional 24,000 units (40,000 − 16,000), management might be able to significantly improve its profit picture. Analysis would also have to be conducted to evaluate the potential impact of any additional unit sales on setup costs, maintenance, wastage, etc. However, before making a decision to increase productive capacity, managers should conduct the type of analysis discussed in Chapter 13, where we examine capital budgeting decisions. Alternatively, if the long-term demand for bookends is expected to be only 16,000 units, management may consider reducing productive capacity, since only 64% (16,000 ÷ 25,000) of practical capacity is required to meet this level of demand. Reducing the fixed costs, such as insurance, taxes, and maintenance, associated with the unused capacity can lead to improvements in operating profits.

INTERNATIONAL USES OF STANDARD COSTS

Despite claims by some that standard costing systems are outdated, they continue to be used by companies worldwide. Survey evidence indicates that over 70% of companies in the United Kingdom use standard costing, while over 80% of companies in Japan use the approach. Moreover, recent surveys of managerial accounting practices show that the use of standard costing is far-reaching, and that the approach is commonly used in New Zealand (73%), Malaysia (70%), and Dubai (United Arab Emirates) (77%).[5]

Standard costs were first introduced in Japan after World War II. Nippon Electric Company (NEC) was one of the first Japanese companies to adopt standard costs for all of its products. Many other Japanese companies followed NEC's lead after the war and developed standard costing systems. Companies using standard costs commonly include them in the following processes:

- Cost control and performance evaluation.
- Product costing.
- Budgeting and forecasting.

According to managers who participated in the surveys reported above, the key variances used for control purposes, in order of importance, are fixed overhead budget variance, materials price variance, materials quantity variance, and direct labour efficiency variance. Overall, the evidence suggests that standard costing is far from obsolete and continues to play an important role in organizations worldwide.

EVALUATION OF CONTROLS BASED ON STANDARD COSTS

Advantages of Standard Costs

Standard costing systems have a number of advantages:

1. Standard costs are a key element in a management by exception approach. If costs remain within the standards, managers can focus on other issues. When costs fall significantly outside the standards, managers are alerted that problems may exist. This approach helps managers focus on important issues.

2. Standards that are viewed as reasonable by employees can promote efficiency. They provide benchmarks that individuals can use to judge their own performance.
3. Standard costs can greatly simplify bookkeeping. Instead of recording actual costs for each job, the standard costs for materials, labour, and overhead can be charged to jobs.
4. Standard costs fit naturally in an integrated system of responsibility accounting. The standards establish what costs should be, who should be responsible for them, and whether actual costs are under control.

Potential Problems with the Use of Standard Costs

The use of standard costs can present a number of potential problems:

1. Standard cost variance reports are usually prepared on a monthly basis and often are released days or even weeks after the end of the month. As a consequence, the information in the reports may be very outdated. Timely, frequent reports that are approximately correct are better than infrequent reports that are very precise but out of date by the time they are released. Some companies are now reporting variances and other key operating data daily or even more frequently.
2. If managers are insensitive and use variance reports to lay blame, morale may suffer. If variances are used to lay blame, subordinates may be tempted to cover up unfavourable variances or take actions that are not in the best interests of the company to make sure the variances are favourable. For example, workers may intensify their efforts to increase output at the end of the month to avoid an unfavourable labour efficiency variance. In the rush to increase output, quality may suffer.
3. Labour quantity standards and efficiency variances make two important assumptions. First, they assume that the production process is labour-paced: If labour works faster, output will go up. However, output in many companies is no longer determined by how fast labour works; rather, it is determined by the processing speed of machines. Second, the computations assume that labour is a variable cost. However, as discussed, direct labour may essentially be fixed in many companies. If labour is fixed, then an undue emphasis on labour efficiency variances creates pressure to build excess inventories.
4. In some cases, a favourable variance can be as bad as or worse than an unfavourable variance. For example, Harvey's has a standard for the amount of hamburger meat that should be in a burger. If there is a favourable variance, it means that less meat was used than the standard specifies. The result is a substandard burger and possibly a dissatisfied customer.
5. There may be a tendency with standard cost reporting systems to emphasize meeting the standards to the exclusion of other important objectives, such as maintaining and improving quality, on-time delivery, and customer satisfaction. This tendency can be reduced by using supplemental performance measures that focus on these other objectives.
6. Just meeting standards may not be sufficient; continuous improvement may be necessary to survive in the current competitive environment. For this reason, some companies focus on trends in standard cost variances—aiming for continuous improvement rather than just meeting the standards. In other companies, engineered standards are being replaced either by a rolling average of actual costs, which is expected to decline, or by very challenging target costs.

In summary, managers should exercise considerable care in their use of a standard costing system. It is particularly important that managers go out of their way to focus on the positive, rather than just on the negative, and to be aware of possible unintended consequences.

IN BUSINESS

Significant increases in health care costs over the past several decades in Canada, the United States, and other countries worldwide have prompted calls for new measures directed at improving cost control. Thibadoux, Scheidt, and Luckey (2007) explored the possible development and use of the standard costing methodology in the U.S. health care system. Developing standard costs would involve the use of evidence-based best practices (EBBP), which are clinical guidelines for diagnosis and treatment that are derived from scientific research. EBBP prescribe a standard approach to be followed by physicians in treating patients, involving the use of published checklists for every major diagnostic-related group (DRG). An example of a DRG is cardiac disease bypass surgery. By determining the cost of each step in the EBBP checklist for a particular DRG, a standard cost could be developed for diagnosing and treating each patient. Actual costs could then be compared to the standard cost and variances investigated.

Interviews with several practising physicians about the possible use of standard costs in the health care system suggest that the disadvantages may outweigh the benefits. While some interviewees indicated that a standard costing approach could be useful in identifying possible causes of cost increases, most had serious concerns about the concept. For example, many noted that being held responsible for adhering to standard costs could lead to decisions aimed more at controlling costs than ensuring the well-being of their patients. Similarly, others indicated that interpreting variances from standard costs could also be problematic in that a favourable cost variance could mean poor care had been given to the patient. Finally, some respondents stated that unlike manufacturing companies, where relatively precise standards can be developed for production, the approach used to treat a serious illness can vary considerably from one patient to the next. Therefore, they questioned whether meaningful standards could even be developed.

Whether or not U.S. health care administrators adopt the standard costing methodology remains to be seen. However, it is interesting to note the similarities between the standard costing problems identified by physicians and those noted earlier in this chapter.

Source: With kind permission from Springer Science + Business Media: *Journal of Business Ethics*, "Accounting and Medicine: An Exploratory Investigation into Physicians' Attitudes toward the Use of Standard Cost-Accounting Methods in Medicine," 75, 2007, pp. 137–149, Greg Thibadoux, Marsha Scheidt, and Elizabeth Luckey.

KNOWLEDGE IN ACTION

Managers prepare cost and quantity standards to evaluate the efficiency of their production or service provision processes. Standard costs are useful for the following reasons:

- By comparing actual to standard, managers can easily identify where to focus their cost control efforts.
- Standards that are viewed as reasonable by employees act as benchmarks by which employees can evaluate their own performance and potentially identify the need to work more efficiently.
- Analysis of variances fits with the idea of responsibility accounting, in which divisional managers' performance is evaluated relative to their ability to manage costs of the products produced or services provided by the division for which they are responsible.

SUMMARY

- A standard is a benchmark or norm for measuring performance. Standards are set for both the cost and the quantity of inputs needed to manufacture goods or to provide services. Quantity standards indicate how much of a cost element, such as labour time or raw materials, should be used in manufacturing a unit of product or in providing a unit of service. Cost standards indicate what the cost of the time or the materials should be. **[LO1]**
- Standards are normally practical in nature, meaning that they can be attained by reasonable, although highly efficient, efforts. Such standards are generally felt to have a favourable motivational impact on employees. Ideal standards are those attainable only under the best circumstances by the most skilled and efficient workers. While serving as a reminder that continuous improvement is needed, ideal standards can be discouraging. **[LO1]**
- The difference between actual cost and standard cost is referred to as a *variance*. Variances are computed for both the price and the quantity elements of materials, labour, and variable overhead. Price, rate, and spending variances for inputs are computed by taking the difference between the actual and standard prices of the inputs and multiplying the result by the amount of input purchased or used. Quantity and efficiency variances are computed by taking the difference between the actual amount of the input used and the amount of input that is allowed for the actual output, and then multiplying the result by the standard price of the input. **[LO2, LO3, LO4]**
- The denominator activity is the figure used to calculate the predetermined overhead rate for variable and fixed overhead. The overhead rate is used to determine the total standard cost per unit of a product by multiplying the rate by the quantity of the activity required to produce each unit. **[LO5]**
- Two variances exist for fixed overhead. The budget variance is simply the difference between the actual and budgeted amounts for total fixed overhead costs. The volume variance is the difference between the amount of fixed overhead cost applied to inventory and the total amount of fixed overhead that was originally budgeted for the period. **[LO6]**
- An overhead performance report provides details on each item that makes up total variable and fixed overhead. Both actual and budget figures are included in the report. Companies that use a standard costing system can prepare a performance report that includes both spending and efficiency variances for variable overhead and the budget variance for fixed overhead. Managers use the performance report to understand which specific overhead items are contributing the most to the overall variances for variable and fixed overhead. **[LO7]**
- Only unusual or particularly *significant* variances should be investigated—otherwise, a great deal of time could be spent investigating unimportant matters. Variance investigation decisions can be based on the dollar amount of the variance or the size of the variance relative to the amount of spending. A statistical control approach can also be employed, whereby only variances that are a certain number of standard deviations above or below zero are investigated. **[LO7]**
- Capacity analysis is a useful strategic tool that allows managers to evaluate the financial impact of operating at less than full productive capacity. Different definitions of "full capacity" exist, including theoretical capacity and practical capacity. Theoretical capacity is the volume of activity that would result from conducting operations with no downtime, 365 days a year, 24 hours per day. Practical capacity is determined by deducting unavoidable downtime from theoretical capacity. **[LO7]**

REVIEW PROBLEM: STANDARD COSTS

Fun Unlimited Corp. produces a toy called the Challenge. Overhead is applied to products on the basis of direct labour-hours. The company recently implemented a standard costing system to help control costs and has established the following standards for the Challenge toys:

Direct materials: 6 microns per toy at $0.50 per micron
Direct labour: 1.3 hours per toy at $15 per hour
Variable manufacturing overhead: 1.3 hours per toy at $4 per hour
Fixed manufacturing overhead: 1.3 hours per toy at $6 per hour

During July, the company produced 3,000 Challenge toys. The fixed overhead expense budget for July was $24,180, with 4,030 direct labour-hours as the denominator level of activity. Production data for the month on the toys follow:

> Direct materials: 25,000 microns were purchased at a cost of $0.48 per micron; 5,000 of these microns were still in inventory at the end of the month.
> Direct labour: 4,000 direct labour-hours were worked, at a cost of $64,000.
> Variable overhead: Actual cost in July was $17,000.
> Fixed overhead: Actual cost in July was $25,000.

Required:
1. Compute the materials, labour, variable manufacturing overhead, and fixed manufacturing overhead variances.
2. Calculate total overapplied or underapplied overhead for July.

Solution to Review Problem

1.   Materials variances:

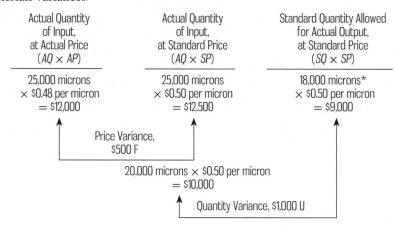

*3,000 toys × 6 microns per toy = 18,000 microns.

A total variance is not computed in this situation because the amount of materials purchased (25,000 microns) differs from the amount of materials used in production (20,000 microns).
   Using the formulas in the chapter, the same variances are computed as

$$\text{Materials price variance} = AQ(AP - SP)$$
$$25{,}000 \text{ microns}(\$0.48 \text{ per micron} - \$0.50 \text{ per micron}) = -\$500 \text{ F}$$

$$\text{Materials quantity variance} = SP(AQ - SQ)$$
$$\$0.50 \text{ per micron}(20{,}000 \text{ microns} - 18{,}000 \text{ microns}) = \$1{,}000 \text{ U}$$

Direct labour variances:

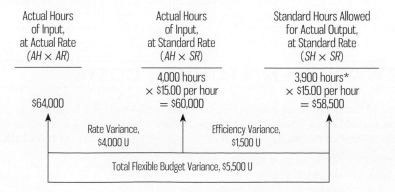

*3,000 toys × 1.3 hours per toy = 3,900 hours.

Using the formulas in the chapter, the same variances are computed as

$$\text{Labour rate variance} = AH(AR - SR)$$

$$4{,}000 \text{ hours}(\$16.00 \text{ per hour*} - \$15.00 \text{ per hour}) = \$4{,}000 \text{ U}$$

$$\text{*}\$64{,}000 \div 4{,}000 \text{ hours} = \$16.00 \text{ per hour}$$

$$\text{Labour efficiency variance} = SR(AH - SH)$$

$$\$15.00 \text{ per hour}(4{,}000 \text{ hours} - 3{,}900 \text{ hours}) = \$1{,}500 \text{ U}$$

Variable manufacturing overhead variances:

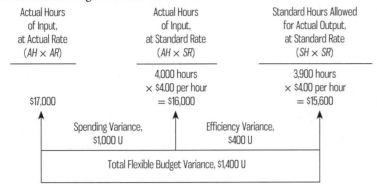

Using the formulas in the chapter, the same variances are computed as

$$\text{Variable overhead spending variance} = AH(AR - SR)$$

$$4{,}000 \text{ hours}(\$4.25 \text{ per hour*} - \$4.00 \text{ per hour}) = \$1{,}000 \text{ U}$$

$$\text{*}\$17{,}000 \div 4{,}000 \text{ hours} = \$4.25 \text{ per hour}$$

$$\text{Variable overhead efficiency variance} = SR(AH - SH)$$

$$\$4.00 \text{ per hour}(4{,}000 \text{ hours} - 3{,}900 \text{ hours}) = \$400 \text{ U}$$

Fixed manufacturing overhead variances:

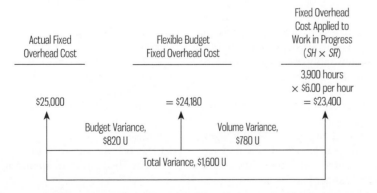

Using the formula in the chapter, the volume variance is computed as

$$\$6(4{,}030 - 3900) = \$780 \text{ U}$$

2. Actual overhead costs incurred:

Variable	$ 17,000
Fixed	25,000
Total	$42,000

Overhead costs applied:

Variable	$ 15,600
Fixed	23,400
Total	$39,000

Therefore, overhead is underapplied by $3,000 ($42,000 − $39,000).

DISCUSSION CASE

DISCUSSION CASE 10-1

Standard costing systems are helpful to managers, as they provide signals of poor quality or exceptional performance. Using standard costs on a management-by-exception basis can help managers to pinpoint areas that they need to pay particular attention to in the following periods, either in an attempt to improve performance or to better understand what is going well in that area that might be transferable to other areas in the organization. Even so, standard costing systems also facilitate other less positive outcomes, such as assigning blame and failing to work to improve efficiency beyond that dictated by the standard.

Required:

Discuss these and other potential negative consequences, as well as what can be done to overcome them when designing and utilizing standard costing systems.

GLOSSARY

   Review key terms and definitions on Connect.

QUESTIONS

10-1 What is a quantity standard? What is a price standard?

10-2 Distinguish between ideal and practical standards.

10-3 If employees are consistently unable to meet a standard, what effect would you expect this to have on their productivity?

10-4 What is the difference between a standard and a budget?

10-5 What is included in the standard rate per hour for direct labour?

10-6 Why are variances generally segregated in terms of a price variance and a quantity variance?

10-7 Who is generally responsible for the materials price variance? The materials quantity variance? The labour efficiency variance?

10-8 What are some possible causes of an unfavourable labour efficiency variance?

10-9 What does the term *standard hours allowed* mean?

10-10 What are the two factors that can cause a variable overhead spending variance?

10-11 What is meant by the term *denominator level of activity*?

10-12 Why do we apply overhead to work in process on the basis of standard hours allowed in Chapter 10, when we applied it on the basis of actual hours in Chapter 5? What is the difference in costing systems between the two chapters?

10-13 In a standard costing system, what two variances are computed for fixed manufacturing overhead?

10-14 What does the fixed overhead budget variance measure?

10-15 Under what circumstances would you expect the volume variance to be favourable? Unfavourable? Does the volume variance measure deviations in spending for fixed overhead items? Explain.

10-16 How might the volume variance be measured other than in dollars?

10-17 In Chapter 5, you became acquainted with the concept of under- or overapplied overhead. The under- or overapplied overhead can be broken down into what four variances?

10-18 "If factory overhead in total is underapplied, the overhead variances will be unfavourable." Do you agree? Why or why not?

10-19 How do managers decide which variances to investigate?

10-20 Why can undue emphasis on labour efficiency variances lead to excess work in process inventories?

10-21 What is the difference between theoretical capacity and practical capacity?

EXERCISES

EXERCISE 10-1 Setting Standards; Preparing a Standard Cost Card [LO1]

Swedish pharmaceutical company Davos Pharmacia makes an anticoagulant drug. The main ingredient in the drug is a raw material called Alpha SR40. Information concerning the purchase and use of Alpha SR40 follows:

Purchase of Alpha SR40: The raw material Alpha SR40 is purchased in 2-kilogram containers at a cost of 3,000 Kr per kilogram. (The Swedish currency is the krona, which is abbreviated as Kr.) A discount of 2% is offered by the supplier for payment within 10 days, and Davos Pharmacia takes all discounts. Shipping costs, which Davos Pharmacia must pay, amount to 1,000 Kr for an average shipment of ten 2-kilogram containers.

Use of Alpha SR40: The bill of materials calls for 6 grams of Alpha SR40 per capsule of the anticoagulant drug. (A kilogram equals 1,000 grams.) About 4% of all Alpha SR40 purchased is rejected as unsuitable and is not used to make the anticoagulant drug. Thus, on average the 6 grams of suitable Alpha SR40 required for each capsule represents 96% of the amount that initially goes into production.

Required:
1. Compute the standard purchase price for one gram of Alpha SR40.
2. Compute the standard quantity of Alpha SR40 (in grams) per capsule that passes final inspection. (Carry computations to two decimal places.)
3. Using the data from (1) and (2) above, prepare a standard cost card showing the standard cost of Alpha SR40 per capsule of the anticoagulant drug.

EXERCISE 10-2 Material Variances [LO2]
Fantastic Feeder Products Inc. manufactures high-quality wooden cutting boards sold to restaurants and gourmet home cooks. One of these boards, the CertiPro II, requires an expensive hardwood. During a recent month, the company manufactured 1,200 CertiPro II cutting boards using 540 metres of hardwood. The hardwood cost the company $2,970.

The company's standards for one CertiPro II cutting board are 0.4 metres of hardwood, at a cost of $5.00 per metre.

Required:
1. What cost for wood should have been incurred to make 1,200 CertiPro II cutting boards? How much greater or less is this than the cost that was incurred?
2. Break down the difference computed in (1) above into a materials price variance and a materials quantity variance.

EXERCISE 10-3 Direct Labour Variances [LO3]
SkyInc provides in-flight meals for a number of major airlines. One of the company's products is stuffed cannelloni with roasted pepper sauce, fresh baby corn, and spring salad. During the most recent week, the company prepared 6,000 of these meals, using 1,150 direct labour-hours. The company paid these direct labour workers a total of $11,500 for this work, or $10 per hour.

According to the standard cost card for this meal, it should require 0.20 direct labour-hours at a cost of $9.50 per hour.

Required:
1. What direct labour cost should have been incurred to prepare 6,000 meals? How much does this differ from the actual direct labour cost?
2. Break down the difference computed in (1) above into a labour rate variance and a labour efficiency variance.

EXERCISE 10-4 Variable Overhead Variances [LO4]
Claims Management Inc. provides claims processing services to several large health insurance providers. Customers who are covered by health insurance provided by one of Claims Management's partners submit their claims for health and dental services along with related documentation, and the employees at Claims Management compare their claims to the details of their benefit plans and calculate the value of the benefits owed. The company uses a predetermined variable overhead rate based on direct labour-hours.

In the month of September, 15,000 claims were processed using 4,500 direct labour-hours. The company incurred a total of $4,950 in variable overhead costs.

According to the company's standards, 0.25 direct labour-hours are required to process a claim, and the variable overhead rate is $1.20 per direct labour-hour.

Required:
1. What variable overhead cost should have been incurred to process the 15,000 claims? How much does this differ from the actual variable overhead cost?
2. Break down the difference computed in (1) above into a variable overhead spending variance and a variable overhead efficiency variance.

EXERCISE 10–5 Fixed Overhead Variances [LO5, LO6]

Happy Valley Pet Products uses a standard costing system that applies overhead to products based on standard direct labour-hours allowed for actual output of the period. During the recent year, the following data were collected:

Total budgeted fixed overhead cost for the year................................	$40,000
Actual fixed overhead cost for the year...	$38,000
Budgeted standard direct labour-hours...	10,000
Actual direct labour-hours...	12,000
Standard direct labour-hours allowed for the actual output.....................	9,000

Required:
1. Compute the fixed portion of the predetermined overhead rate for the year.
2. Compute the fixed overhead budget and volume variances.

EXERCISE 10–6 Variable Overhead Performance Report [LO7]

Hastings Company bases its variable overhead performance report on the actual direct labour-hours of the period. Data concerning the most recent year, which ended on December 31, are as follows:

Budgeted direct labour-hours	42,000
Actual direct labour-hours...	44,000
Standard direct labour-hours allowed	45,000
Cost formula (per direct labour-hour):	
Indirect labour	$ 0.90
Supplies	$ 0.15
Electricity...	$ 0.05
Actual costs incurred:	
Indirect labour..	$42,000
Supplies	$ 6,900
Electricity...	$ 1,800

Required:
Prepare a variable overhead performance report using the format in Exhibit 10–13. Compute both variable overhead spending and efficiency variances.

EXERCISE 10–7 Setting Standards [LO1]

Agnessa Premium Chocolate Ltd. produces specialty chocolate confections in England. The owner of the company is setting up a standard costing system; the following data is for one of the company's products, the Truffle Supreme, made with the finest white chocolate and various fillings. The data below pertain only to the white chocolate used in the product. (The currency in the United Kingdom is the British pound sterling, which is denoted by £.)

Material requirements, kilograms of white chocolate per dozen truffles	0.80 kilograms
Allowance for waste, kilograms of white chocolate per dozen truffles	0.02 kilograms
Allowance for rejects, kilograms of white chocolate per dozen truffles	0.03 kilograms
Purchase price, finest-grade white chocolate	£9.00 per kilogram
Purchase discount...	5% of purchase price
Shipping cost from the supplier in Belgium..	£0.20 per kilogram
Receiving and handling cost...	£0.05 per kilogram

Required:
1. Determine the standard price of a kilogram of white chocolate.
2. Determine the standard quantity of white chocolate for a dozen truffles.
3. Determine the standard cost of the white chocolate in a dozen truffles.

EXERCISE 10–8 Material and Labour Variances [LO2, LO3]

Camping Supply Company has developed a new camping lamp that runs on solar power. The solar cells charge in the sun all day and then the lamp is ready to run when the sun goes down. The company has a standard costing system to help control costs and has established the following standards related to the new camping lamp:

Direct materials: 3 small solar cells per lamp at $0.60 per cell
Direct labour: 0.75 hours per lamp at $12 per hour

During March, the company produced 4,000 camping lights. Production data for March are as follows:

Direct materials: 20,000 small solar cells were purchased at a cost of $0.65 per cell; 6,000 of these were still in inventory at the end of the month (there was no opening inventory).
Direct labour: 3,100 direct labour-hours were worked at a cost of $35,000.

Required:
1. Compute the following variances for March:
   a. Direct materials price and quantity variances.
   b. Direct labour rate and efficiency variances.
2. Prepare a brief explanation of the possible causes of each variance.

EXERCISE 10-9 Material and Labour Variances [LO2, LO3]
The direct materials and direct labour standards for one bottle of Clean-All spray cleaner are given below:

	Standard Quantity or Hours	Standard Price or Rate	Standard Cost
Direct materials...........	6.0 millilitres	$0.25 per millilitre	$1.50
Direct labour..............	0.2 hours	$12.00 per hour	$2.40

During the most recent month, the following activity was recorded:
a. 20,000 millilitres of material was purchased at a cost of $0.20 per millilitre.
b. All of the material was used to produce 3,000 bottles of Clean-All.
c. 625 hours of direct labour time was recorded at a total labour cost of $7,500.

Required:
1. Compute the direct materials price and quantity variances for the month.
2. Compute the direct labour rate and efficiency variances for the month.

EXERCISE 10-10 Material Variances [LO2]
Refer to the data in Exercise 10-9. Assume that instead of producing 3,000 bottles of Clean-All during the month, the company produced only 2,000 bottles, using 16,000 millilitres of material. (The rest of the material purchased remained in raw materials inventory.)

Required:
Compute the direct materials price and quantity variances for the month.

EXERCISE 10-11 Labour and Variable Manufacturing Overhead Variances [LO3, LO4]
Affordable Electronics Inc. manufactures medium-quality, reasonably priced DVD players. The company uses standards to control its costs. The labour standards that have been set for one player are as follows:

Standard Hours	Standard Rate per Hour	Standard Cost
12 minutes (0.2 hours)	$15.00	$3.00

During July, 3,400 hours of direct labour time were recorded to make 16,000 units. The direct labour cost totalled $49,300 for the month.

Required:
1. What direct labour cost should have been incurred to make the 16,000 DVD players? By how much does this differ from the cost that was incurred?
2. Break down the difference in cost from (1) above into a labour rate variance and a labour efficiency variance.
3. The budgeted variable manufacturing overhead rate is $4.00 per direct labour-hour. During July, the company incurred $15,640 in variable manufacturing overhead cost. Compute the variable overhead spending and efficiency variances for the month.

EXERCISE 10–12 Working Backward from Labour Variances [LO3]
Worldwide Credit Card Inc. uses standards to control the labour time involved in opening mail from cardholders and recording the enclosed remittances. Incoming mail is gathered into batches, and a standard time is set for opening and recording each batch. The labour standards relating to one batch are as follows:

	Standard Hours	Standard Rate	Standard Cost
Per batch.............	2.5	$12.00	$30.00

The record showing the time spent last week in opening batches of mail has been misplaced. However, the batch supervisor recalls that 168 batches were received and opened during the week, and the controller recalls the following variance data relating to these batches:

Total labour variance.................	$660 U
Labour rate variance.................	$300 F

Required:
1. Determine the number of actual labour-hours spent opening batches during the week.
2. Determine the actual hourly rate paid to employees for opening batches last week.

(*Hint:* A useful way to proceed is to work from known to unknown data, either by using the variance formulas or by using the columnar format shown in Exhibit 10–6.)

EXERCISE 10–13 Predetermined Overhead Rate; Overhead Variances [LO4, LO5, LO6]
The condensed form of Nordstrop Company's flexible budget for manufacturing overhead follows:

Overhead Costs	Cost Formula (per machine-hour)	Machine-Hours		
		8,000	9,000	10,000
Variable cost..........................	$1.05	$ 8,400	$ 9,450	$ 10,500
Fixed cost		24,800	24,800	24,800
Total overhead cost....................		$33,200	$34,250	$35,300

The following information is available for a recent period:
a. The denominator activity of 8,000 machine-hours was chosen to compute the predetermined overhead rate.
b. At the 8,000 standard machine-hours level of activity, the company should produce 3,200 units of product.
c. The company's actual operating results were as follows:

Number of units produced	3,500
Actual machine-hours.......................	8,500
Actual variable overhead costs	$ 9,860
Actual fixed overhead costs	$25,100

Required:
1. Compute the predetermined overhead rate and break it down into variable and fixed cost elements.
2. What were the standard hours allowed for the year's actual output?
3. Compute the variable overhead spending and efficiency variances and the fixed overhead budget and volume variances.

EXERCISE 10–14 Using Fixed Overhead Variances [LO5, LO6]
The standard cost card for the single product manufactured by Princess Company is given below:

Standard Cost Card—Per Unit

Direct materials, 2.1 metres at $6 per metre..	$ 12.60
Direct labour, 0.6 direct labour-hours at $27 per direct labour-hour..............................	16.20
Variable overhead, 0.6 direct labour-hours at $3.75 per direct labour-hour	2.25
Fixed overhead, 0.6 direct labour-hours at $9 per direct labour-hour............................	5.40
Total standard cost per unit..	$36.45

Last year, the company produced 7,500 units of product and worked 6,150 actual direct labour-hours. Manufacturing overhead cost is applied to production on the basis of direct labour-hours. Selected data relating to the company's fixed manufacturing overhead cost for the year are shown below:

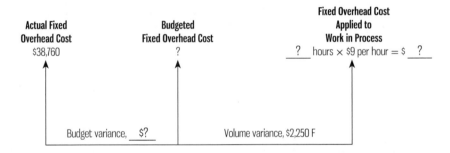

Actual Fixed Overhead Cost	Budgeted Fixed Overhead Cost	Fixed Overhead Cost Applied to Work in Process
$38,760	?	? hours × $9 per hour = $?

Budget variance, $?   Volume variance, $2,250 F

Required:
1. What were the standard hours allowed for the year's production?
2. What was the amount of budgeted fixed overhead cost for the year?
3. What was the budget variance for the year?
4. What denominator activity level did the company use in setting the predetermined overhead rate for the year?

EXERCISE 10–15 Fixed Overhead Variances [LO5, LO6]
Selected operating information on three different companies for a recent period is given below:

	Company		
	X	Y	Z
Full-capacity direct labour-hours.................................	20,000	9,000	10,000
Budgeted direct labour-hours*.................................	19,000	8,500	8,000
Actual direct labour-hours.......................................	19,500	8,000	9,000
Standard direct labour-hours allowed for actual output...........	18,500	8,250	9,500

*Denominator activity for computing the predetermined overhead rate.

Required:
For each company, state whether the volume variance would be favourable or unfavourable; also, explain in each case *why* the volume variance would be favourable or unfavourable.

EXERCISE 10–16 Overhead Performance Report with Both Spending and Efficiency Variances [LO4, LO7]

The cheque-clearing office of Pay Loans Company is responsible for processing all cheques that come to the company for payment. Managers at the company believe that variable overhead costs are essentially proportional to the number of labour-hours worked in the office, so labour-hours are used as the activity base when preparing variable overhead budgets and performance reports. Data for October, the most recent month, appear below:

Budgeted labour-hours....................................	1,300
Actual labour-hours.......................................	1,290
Standard labour-hours allowed for the	
actual number of cheques processed..................	1,320

	Cost Formula (per labour-hour)	Actual Costs Incurred in October
Variable overhead costs:		
Office supplies................................	$0.30	$ 219
Staff coffee lounge	0.10	186
Indirect labour................................	3.90	3,348
Total variable overhead cost..................	$4.30	$3,753

Fixed overhead at Pay Loans Company consists entirely of supervisory salaries and is applied at a rate of $6 per direct labour-hour. Actual fixed overhead costs totalled $6,300 in October, while the flexible budget was $6,000 for the month.

Required:

Prepare an overhead performance report for October for the cheque-clearing office that includes both spending and efficiency variances for variable overhead and the budget variance for fixed overhead. Use Exhibit 10–13 as a guide in preparing the performance report.

EXERCISE 10–17 Capacity Analysis [LO7]

Comfort Company produces leather office chairs. The standard cost per chair is as follows:

Direct materials..	$35
Direct labour...	15
Variable overhead (2 machine-hours at $4.00)*..........................	8
Fixed overhead (2 machine-hours at $8.00)*............................	16
Total standard cost per chair..	$ 74

*Overhead rates are based on a denominator activity level of 30,000 machine-hours.

During 2015, Comfort Company produced and sold 12,000 office chairs. Management believes that the denominator level of activity represents 75% of theoretical capacity and 80% of practical capacity.

Required:

1. Calculate the total overhead costs at the following levels of activity: theoretical, practical, denominator, and actual (2015).
2. Assuming Comfort Company can sell all of the chairs it can produce for $100 per unit, calculate the opportunity loss of producing 12,000 chairs in 2015 compared to the following capacity utilization alternatives: theoretical, practical, and denominator.

PROBLEMS

PROBLEM 10–18 Comprehensive Variance Analysis [LO2, LO3, LO4]

London Company's Forest City Plant produces precast ingots for industrial use. Anne-Marie Gosnell, who was recently appointed general manager of the Forest City Plant, has just been handed the plant's income statement for October. The statement is shown below.

Gosnell was shocked to see the poor results for the month, particularly since sales were exactly as budgeted. She stated, "I sure hope the plant has a standard costing system in operation. If it doesn't, I won't have the slightest idea of where to start looking for the problem."

	Budgeted	Actual
Sales (2,500 ingots).................................	$125,000	$125,000
Variable expenses:		
Variable cost of goods sold*.....................	40,000	45,455
Variable selling expenses..........................	10,000	10,000
Total variable expenses...............................	50,000	55,455
Contribution margin.................................	75,000	69,545
Fixed expenses:		
Manufacturing overhead..........................	30,000	29,500
Selling and administrative........................	37,500	37,500
Total fixed expenses.................................	67,500	67,000
Operating income (loss).............................	$ 7,500	$ 2,545

*Contains direct materials, direct labour, and variable manufacturing overhead.

The plant uses a standard costing system, with the standard variable cost per ingot details shown below:

	Standard Quantity or Hours	Standard Price or Rate	Standard Cost
Direct materials............................	2.0 kilograms	$1.25 per kilogram	$2.50
Direct labour..............................	0.54 hours	$10.00 per hour	5.40
Variable manufacturing overhead...........	0.27 hours*	$1.00 per hour	0.27
Total standard variable cost................			$ 8.17

*Based on machine-hours.

Gosnell has determined that during October the plant produced 2,500 ingots and incurred the following costs:
a. Purchased 6,300 kilograms of materials at a cost of $1.50 per kilogram. There were no raw materials in inventory at the beginning of the month.
b. Used 4,900 kilograms of materials in production. (Finished goods and work in process inventories are insignificant and can be ignored.)
c. Worked 1,800 direct labour-hours at a cost of $9.50 per hour.
d. Incurred a total variable manufacturing overhead cost of $1,080 for the month. A total of 900 machine-hours was recorded. It is the company's policy to close all variances to cost of goods sold on a monthly basis.

Required:
1. Compute the following variances for October:
   a. Direct materials price and quantity variances.
   b. Direct labour rate and efficiency variances.
   c. Variable manufacturing overhead spending and efficiency variances.
2. Summarize the variances that you computed in (1) above by showing the net overall favourable or unfavourable variance for October. What impact did this figure have on the company's income statement?
3. Pick out the two most significant variances that you computed in (1) above. Explain to Gosnell possible causes of these variances.

PROBLEM 10–19 Comprehensive Variance Analysis in a Hospital [LO2, LO3, LO4, LO5, LO6]

Marc Goudreau, administrator of Clearwater Hospital, was puzzled by the prior month's reports. "Every month, it's anyone's guess whether the lab will show a profit or a loss. Perhaps the only answer is to increase our lab fees again."

"We can't," replied Rhoda Groves, the controller. "There are still a lot of complaints about the last increase, particularly from the insurance companies and government health units. They're now paying only about 80% of what we bill. I'm beginning to think the problem is on the cost side."

To determine if the Clearwater lab costs are in line with those of other hospital labs, Goudreau has asked you to evaluate the costs for the past month. Groves has provided you with the following information:

a. Two basic types of tests are performed in the lab—smears and blood tests. During the past month, 2,700 smears and 900 blood tests were performed in the lab.

b. Small glass plates are used in both types of tests. During the past month, the hospital purchased 16,000 plates at a cost of $38,400. This cost is net of a 4% purchase discount. A total of 2,000 of these plates were unused at the end of the month; no plates were on hand at the beginning of the month.

c. During the past month, 1,800 hours of labour time were used in performing smears and blood tests. The cost of this labour time was $18,450.

d. The lab's variable overhead cost last month totalled $11,700.

e. Fixed overhead cost last month totalled $10,400.

Clearwater Hospital has never used standard costs. By searching industry literature, however, you have determined the following nationwide averages for hospital labs:

Plates: Three plates are required per lab test. These plates cost $2.50 each and are disposed of after the test is completed.

Labour: Each smear should require 0.3 hours to complete, and each blood test should require 0.6 hours to complete. The average cost of this lab time is $12 per hour.

Overhead: Overhead cost is based on direct labour-hours. The average rate of variable overhead is $6 per hour. The average rate of fixed overhead is $8 per hour. These rates are based on a denominator activity level of 1,250 hours per month.

Required:

1. Compute the materials price variance for the plates purchased last month, and compute a materials quantity variance for the plates used last month.

2. a. Compute a labour rate variance and a labour efficiency variance for the lab.
    b. In most hospitals, three-quarters of the workers in the lab are certified technicians and one-quarter are assistants. In an effort to reduce costs, Clearwater Hospital employs only one-half certified technicians and one-half assistants. Would you recommend that this policy be continued? Explain.

3. Compute the variable overhead spending and efficiency variances. Is there any relationship between the variable overhead efficiency variance and the labour efficiency variance? Explain.

4. Compute the fixed overhead budget and volume variances.

PROBLEM 10–20 Comprehensive Standard Cost Variances [LO2, LO3, LO4, LO5, LO6]

Clarissa McWhirter, vice-president of Cyprus Company, was pleased to see a small variance on the income statement after the trouble the company had been having in controlling manufacturing costs. She noted that the $12,250 overall manufacturing variance reported last period was well below the 3% limit that had been set for variances. The company produces and sells a single product. The standard cost card for the product follows:

Standard Cost Card—Per Unit

Direct materials, 4 metres at $3.50 per metre	$ 14
Direct labour, 1.5 direct labour-hours at $12 per direct labour-hour	18
Variable overhead, 1.5 direct labour-hours at $2 per direct labour-hour	3
Fixed overhead, 1.5 direct labour-hours at $6 per direct labour-hour	9
Standard cost per unit	$44

The following additional information is available for the year just completed:

a. The company manufactured 20,000 units of product during the year.

b. A total of 78,000 metres of material was purchased during the year at a cost of $3.75 per metre. All of this material was used to manufacture the 20,000 units. There were no beginning or ending inventories for the year.

c. The company worked 32,500 direct labour-hours during the year at a cost of $11.80 per hour.

d. Overhead cost is applied to products on the basis of standard direct labour-hours. Data relating to manufacturing overhead costs follow:

Denominator activity level (direct labour-hours).................................	25,000
Budgeted fixed overhead costs (from the flexible budget).......................	$150,000
Actual fixed overhead costs...	$148,000
Actual variable overhead costs...	$ 68,250

Required:

1. Compute the direct materials price and quantity variances for the year.
2. Compute the direct labour rate and efficiency variances for the year.
3. For manufacturing overhead, compute the following:
   a. The variable overhead spending and efficiency variances for the year.
   b. The fixed overhead budget and volume variances for the year.
4. Total the variances you have computed, and compare the net amount with the $12,250 mentioned by the vice-president. Do you think that everyone should be congratulated for a job well done? Explain.

PROBLEM 10–21 Applying Overhead; Overhead Variances [LO4, LO5, LO6]

The Scottish firm of Cullen and MacNeil produces a single product and uses a standard costing system to help control costs. Manufacturing overhead is applied to production on the basis of standard machine-hours. The Scottish currency is the British pound. According to the company's flexible budget, the following overhead costs should be incurred at an activity level of 18,000 machine-hours (the denominator activity level chosen for the year):

Variable manufacturing overhead cost..	£ 31,500
Fixed manufacturing overhead cost..	72,000
Total manufacturing overhead cost..	£103,500

During the year, the following operating results were recorded:

Actual machine-hours worked..	15,000
Standard machine-hours allowed...	16,000
Actual variable manufacturing overhead cost incurred...........................	£26,500
Actual fixed manufacturing overhead cost incurred..............................	£70,000

At the end of the year, the company's Manufacturing Overhead account contained the following data:

Manufacturing Overhead

Actual costs	96,500	Applied costs	92,000
	4,500		

Management would like to determine the cause of the £4,500 underapplied overhead.

Required:

1. Compute the predetermined overhead rate for the year. Break it down into variable and fixed cost elements.
2. Show how the £92,000 "Applied costs" figure in the manufacturing overhead account was computed.
3. Analyze the £4,500 underapplied overhead figure in terms of the variable overhead spending and efficiency variances and the fixed overhead budget and volume variances.
4. Explain the meaning of each variance that you computed in (3) above.

PROBLEM 10–22 Basic Variance Analysis [LO2, LO3, LO4]

VitalAid Inc. manufactures a vacuum-sealed high-protein food supplement that it sells to food aid organizations around the world. The company uses variable costing in conjunction with a standard costing system and has established the following standards for one package of VitalAid bars:

	Standard Quantity or Hours	Standard Price or Rate	Standard Cost
Direct materials.............................	350 grams	$12.00 per kg	$4.20
Direct labour...............................	0.25 hours	$13.00 per hour	$3.25
Variable manufacturing overhead...........	0.5 hours	$1.60 per hour	$0.80
Total standard variable cost................			$8.25

During October, the company recorded the following activity relative to production of VitalAid:

a. The company produced 4,000 packages during October.
b. A total of 1,800 kilograms of material was purchased at a cost of $19,800.
c. There was no beginning inventory of materials; however, at the end of the month, 300 kilograms of material remained in ending inventory.
d. The company employs 5 people to work on the production of VitalAid. During October, each employee worked an average of 185 hours at an average rate of $14.00 per hour.
e. Variable manufacturing overhead is assigned to VitalAid on the basis of direct labour-hours. Variable manufacturing overhead costs during October totalled $1,850.

The company's management is anxious to determine the efficiency of the VitalAid production activities.

Required:

1. a. Compute the price and quantity variances for direct materials used in the production of VitalAid.
   b. The materials were purchased from a new supplier who is anxious to enter into a long-term purchase contract. Would you recommend that the company sign the contract? Explain.

2. a. Compute the rate and efficiency variances for labour employed in the production of VitalAid.
   b. In the past, the 5 people employed in the production of VitalAid consisted of 3 senior workers and 2 assistants. During October, the company experimented with 4 senior workers and 1 assistant. Would you recommend that the new labour mix be continued? Explain.

3. Compute the variable overhead spending and efficiency variances. What relationship can you see between this efficiency variance and the labour efficiency variance?

PROBLEM 10–23 Overhead Performance Report [LO7]

Asper Company has recently introduced budgeting as an integral part of its corporate planning process. An inexperienced member of the accounting staff was given the assignment of constructing a flexible budget for manufacturing overhead costs and prepared it in the format that follows:

Percentage of Capacity	80%	100%
Machine-hours..	40,000	50,000
Utilities..	$ 41,000	$ 49,000
Supplies..	4,000	5,000
Indirect labour......................................	8,000	10,000
Maintenance..	37,000	41,000
Supervision..	10,000	10,000
Total manufacturing overhead cost.................	$100,000	$115,000

The company assigns manufacturing overhead costs to production on the basis of standard machine-hours. The cost formulas used to prepare the budgeted figures above are relevant over a range of 80% to 100% of capacity in a month. The managers who will be working under these budgets have control over both fixed and variable manufacturing overhead costs.

Required:
1. Use the high–low method (see Chapter 3) to separate fixed and variable costs.
2. Come up with a single cost formula for all overhead costs based on your analysis in (1) above. (*Hint:* Your cost formula should be of the form $y = a + bx$.)
3. During May, the company operated at 86% of machine-hour capacity. Actual manufacturing overhead costs incurred during the month were as follows:

Utilities	$ 42,540
Supplies	6,450
Indirect labour	9,890
Maintenance	35,190
Supervision	10,000
Total actual manufacturing overhead cost	$104,070

Fixed costs had no budget variances. Prepare an overhead performance report for May. Include both fixed and variable costs in your report (in separate sections). Structure your report so that it shows only a spending variance for variable overhead. The company originally budgeted to work 40,000 machine-hours during the month; standard hours allowed for the month's production totalled 41,000 machine-hours. (Use Exhibit 10–14 as a guide.)
4. Explain possible causes of the spending variance for supplies.

PROBLEM 10–24 Setting Standards [LO1]
Quintessence, a small cosmetics company in the south of France, plans to introduce a new body oil, called Dynamique, for which it needs to develop a standard product cost. The following information is available on the production of Dynamique:
a. The Dynamique base is made by mixing high-grade lanolin and alcohol. Both the lanolin and the alcohol lose some volume during the mixing process. As a result, each 100-litre batch of Dynamique base requires 100 litres of lanolin and 8 litres of alcohol.
b. After the base has been prepared, a highly concentrated jasmine powder is added to impart a pleasing scent. Only 200 grams of the powder is added to each 100-litre batch. The addition of the jasmine powder does not significantly change the total liquid volume.
c. Both the lanolin and the jasmine powder are subject to some contamination from naturally occurring materials. For example, the jasmine powder often contains some traces of insects that are not detected and removed when the jasmine petals are processed. Occasionally such contaminants interact in ways that result in an unacceptable product with an unpleasant odour. About one 100-litre batch in twenty is rejected as unsuitable for sale for this reason and is thrown away.
d. It takes a worker two hours to process one 100-litre batch of Dynamique. Employees work an eight-hour day, including two hours per day for lunch, rest breaks, and cleanup.

Required:
1. Determine the standard quantity for each of the raw materials needed to produce an acceptable 100-litre batch of Dynamique.
2. Determine the standard labour time allowed to produce an acceptable 100-litre batch of Dynamique.
3. The standard prices for direct materials and direct labour in euros (€) appear below:

Lanolin	€16 per litre
Alcohol	€2 per litre
Jasmine powder	€1 per gram
Direct labour cost	€12 per hour

Prepare a standard cost card for materials and labour for one acceptable 100-litre batch of Dynamique.

(CMA, adapted)

PROBLEM 10–25 Applying Overhead; Overhead Variances [LO4, LO5, LO6]
Ryder Company produces a single product, school backpacks made of a sturdy nylon fabric. The production of these bags requires a relatively large amount of labour time. Overhead cost is applied on the basis of standard direct labour-hours. The company's condensed flexible budget for manufacturing overhead is given below:

Overhead Costs	Cost Formula (per DLH)	Direct Labour-Hours 12,000	15,000	18,000
Variable manufacturing overhead cost..................	$1	$12,000	$ 15,000	$ 18,000
Fixed manufacturing overhead cost....................		75,000	75,000	75,000
Total manufacturing overhead cost.....................		$87,000	$90,000	$93,000

Each backpack requires 2 metres of direct material that has a standard cost of $1.50 per metre. The product requires 1.5 hours of direct labour time. The standard labour rate is $10 per hour.

During the year, the company had planned to operate at a denominator activity level of 15,000 direct labour-hours and to produce 10,000 units of product. Actual activity and costs for the year were as follows:

Number of units produced...	11,000
Actual direct labour-hours worked	17,500
Actual variable manufacturing overhead cost incurred..................	$ 15,750
Actual fixed manufacturing overhead cost incurred.....................	$76,500

Required:
1. Compute the predetermined overhead rate for the year. Break the rate down into variable and fixed components.
2. *a.* Compute the standard direct labour-hours allowed for the year's production.
    b. Complete the following manufacturing overhead T-account for the year:

Manufacturing Overhead

?	?
?	?

3. Determine the reason for the underapplied or overapplied overhead from (2) above by computing the variable overhead spending and efficiency variances and the fixed overhead budget and volume variances.
4. Suppose the company had chosen 18,000 direct labour-hours as the denominator activity rather than 15,000 hours. State which, if any, of the variances computed in (3) above would have changed, and explain how the variance(s) would have changed. No computations are necessary.

PROBLEM 10–26 Flexible Budget and Overhead Performance Report [LO4, LO5, LO6, LO7]
Groschl Company has had great difficulty in controlling manufacturing overhead costs. At a recent convention, the president heard about a control device for overhead costs known as a *flexible budget*, and he has hired you to implement this budgeting program in Groschl Company. After some effort, you have developed the following cost formulas for the company's Machining Department. These costs are based on a normal operating range of 10,000 to 20,000 machine-hours per month:

Overhead Cost	Cost Formula
Utilities	$0.70 per machine-hour
Lubricants	$1.00 per machine-hour plus $8,000 per month
Machine setup..	$0.20 per machine-hour
Indirect labour.......................................	$0.60 per machine-hour plus $120,000 per month
Depreciation..	$32,000 per month

During March, the first month after your preparation of the above data, the Machining Department worked 18,000 machine-hours and produced 9,000 units of product. The actual manufacturing overhead costs for March were as follows:

Utilities	$ 12,000
Lubricants	24,500
Machine setup	4,800
Indirect labour	132,500
Depreciation	32,000
Total manufacturing overhead cost	$205,800

Fixed costs had no budget variances. The department had originally been budgeted to work 20,000 machine-hours during March.

Required:
1. Prepare an overhead performance report for the Machining Department for the month of March. Include both variable and fixed costs in the report (in separate sections). Show only a spending variance on the report. (Use Exhibit 10–14 as your guide.)
2. What additional information would you need to compute an overhead efficiency variance for the department?

PROBLEM 10–27 Evaluating an Overhead Performance Report [LO5, LO6, LO7]
Timothy Hawkins, superintendent of Kal-Tubing Company's Machining Department, is very happy with his performance report for the past month. The report follows:

KAL-TUBING COMPANY **Overhead Performance Report—Machining Department**	Actual	Budget	Variance
Machine-hours	22,500	26,250	
Variable manufacturing overhead:			
Indirect labour	$ 59,100	$ 63,000	$ 3,900 F
Utilities	152,400	178,500	26,100 F
Supplies	37,800	42,000	4,200 F
Maintenance	74,700	84,000	9,300 F
Total variable manufacturing overhead	324,000	367,500	43,500 F
Fixed manufacturing overhead:			
Maintenance	$ 117,000	$ 117,000	0
Supervision	247,500	247,500	0
Depreciation	180,000	180,000	0
Total fixed manufacturing overhead	544,500	544,500	0
Total manufacturing overhead	$868,500	$912,000	$43,500 F

When he received a copy of this report, Wayne Lockhart, the production manager, commented, "I've been getting these reports for months now, and I still can't see how they help me assess efficiency and cost control in that department. I agree that the budget for the month was 26,250 machine-hours, but that represents 8,750 units of product, since it should take three hours to produce one unit. The department produced only 5,250 units during the month, and took 22,500 machine-hours to do it. Why do all the variances turn up favourable?"

Required:
1. In answer to Lockhart's question, why are all the variances favourable? Is the performance report useful? Explain.
2. Prepare a new overhead performance report that will help Lockhart assess efficiency and cost control in the Machining Department. (*Hint:* Exhibit 10–13 may be helpful in structuring your report.)

**PROBLEM 10–28 Selection of a Denominator; Overhead Analysis; Standard Cost Card
[LO1, LO4, LO5, LO6]**
Flores Company's condensed flexible budget for manufacturing overhead is as follows:

Overhead Costs	Cost Formula (per DLH)	Direct Labour-Hours		
		30,000	40,000	50,000
Variable manufacturing overhead cost............	$2.50	$ 75,000	$100,000	$125,000
Fixed manufacturing overhead cost..............		320,000	320,000	320,000
Total manufacturing overhead cost..............		$395,000	$420,000	$445,000

The company produces a single product that requires 2.5 direct labour-hours to complete. The direct labour wage rate is $20 per hour. Three metres of raw material are required for each unit of product, at a cost of $5 per metre.

Demand for the company's product differs widely from year to year. Expected activity for this year is 50,000 direct labour-hours; normal activity is 40,000 direct labour-hours per year.

Required:

1. Assume that the company chooses 40,000 direct labour-hours as the denominator level of activity. Compute the predetermined overhead rate, breaking it down into fixed and variable cost components.
2. Assume that the company chooses 50,000 direct labour-hours as the denominator level of activity. Repeat the computations in (1) above.
3. Complete two standard cost cards as outlined below:

Denominator Activity: 40,000 DLHs

Direct materials, 3 metres at $5 per metre	$15.00
Direct labour, ?..	?
Variable manufacturing overhead, ?............................	?
Fixed manufacturing overhead, ?..............................	?
Total standard cost per unit	$?

Denominator Activity: 50,000 DLHs

Direct materials, 3 metres at $5 per metre	$15.00
Direct labour, ?..	?
Variable manufacturing overhead, ?............................	?
Fixed manufacturing overhead, ?..............................	?
Total standard cost per unit	$?

4. Assume that 48,000 actual hours are worked during the year, and that 18,500 units are produced. Actual manufacturing overhead costs for the year are as follows:

Variable manufacturing overhead cost	$ 124,800
Fixed manufacturing overhead cost............................	321,700
Total manufacturing overhead cost	$446,500

a. Compute the standard hours allowed for the year's actual output.
b. Compute the missing items from the manufacturing overhead account below. Assume that the company uses 40,000 direct labour-hours (normal activity) as the denominator activity figure in computing overhead rates, as in (1) above:

Manufacturing Overhead

Actual costs	446,500	?	
	?	?	

c. Analyze your underapplied or overapplied overhead balance in terms of variable overhead spending and efficiency variances and fixed overhead budget and volume variances.

5. Looking at the variances that you have computed, what appears to be the major disadvantage of using normal activity rather than expected actual activity as a denominator in computing the predetermined overhead rate? What advantages can you see to offset this disadvantage?

PROBLEM 10-29 Developing Standard Costs [LO1]

Maxime S.A. is a small company that processes wild mushrooms found in the forests of central France. For many years, Maxime's products have had strong sales in France. However, companies from other countries in Europe, such as Italy and Spain, have begun marketing similar products in France, and price competition has become intense. Jean Gauthier, the company's controller, is planning to implement a standard costing system for Maxime and has gathered considerable information from the purchasing and production managers concerning production and material requirements for Maxime's products. Gauthier believes that the use of standard costing will allow Maxime to improve cost control and thereby better compete with the new entrants into the French market.

Maxime's most popular product is dried chanterelle mushrooms, which are sold in small vacuum-packed jars. Each jar contains 15 grams of dried mushrooms. Fresh mushrooms are purchased for €60 per kilogram in bulk from individuals who gather them from local forests. (€ stands for euro, the currency used in France.) Because of imperfections in the mushrooms and normal spoilage, one-quarter of the fresh mushrooms are discarded. Fifteen minutes is the direct labour time required for inspecting and sorting per kilogram of fresh mushrooms. After sorting and inspecting, the acceptable mushrooms are flash-dried, which requires 10 minutes of direct labour time per kilogram of acceptable, sorted, and inspected fresh mushrooms. The flash-drying removes most of the moisture content of the mushrooms and therefore reduces the weight of the acceptable mushrooms by 80%. As a consequence, a kilogram of *acceptable* fresh mushrooms yields only about 150 grams of dried mushrooms. After drying, the mushrooms are vacuum-packed in small jars and labels are applied.

Direct labour is paid at a rate of €12 per hour. The cost of the glass jars, lids, and labels is €10 per 100 jars. The labour time required to pack 100 jars is 10 minutes.

Required:
1. Develop the standard cost for the direct labour and materials cost components of a single jar of dried chanterelle mushrooms, including the costs of the mushrooms, inspecting and sorting, drying, and packing.
2. Gauthier wonders who should be held responsible—the purchasing manager or the production manager—for the following:
    a. The materials price variances for the chanterelle mushrooms. Explain.
    b. The materials quantity variances for the chanterelle mushrooms. Explain.

PROBLEM 10-30 Materials and Labour Variances; Computations from Incomplete Data [LO1, LO2, LO3]

Talia Company produces a single product. The company has set standards as follows for materials and labour:

	Direct Materials	Direct Labour
Standard quantity or hours per unit	? kilograms	1.25 hours
Standard price or rate	? per kilogram	$10 per hour
Standard cost per unit	?	$12.50

During the past month, the company purchased 3,000 kilograms of direct materials at a cost of $8,250. All of this material was used in the production of 700 units of product. Direct labour cost totalled $6,825 for the month. The following variances have been computed:

Materials quantity variance	$ 600 U
Total materials variance	$ 150 F
Labour efficiency variance	$2,250 F

Required:
1. For direct materials:
    a. Compute the standard price per kilogram for materials.
    b. Compute the standard quantity allowed for materials for the month's production.
    c. Compute the standard quantity of materials allowed per unit of product.
2. For direct labour:
    a. Compute the actual direct labour cost per hour for the month.
    b. Compute the labour rate variance.

(*Hint:* In completing the problem, it may be helpful to move from known to unknown data either by using the variance formulas or by using the columnar format shown in Exhibits 10–4 and 10–6.)

PROBLEM 10–31 Comprehensive Variance Analysis [LO2, LO3, LO4, LO5, LO6]
Helix Company produces costumes used in the television and movie industries. Recently the company received an ongoing order for Samurai robes to be worn in an upcoming Japanese historical action series made for television. The company uses a standard costing system to assist in the control of costs. According to the standards set for these robes, the factory has a denominator activity level of 780 direct labour-hours each month, which should result in the production of 1,950 robes. The standard costs associated with this level of production are as follows:

	Total	Per Unit of Product
Direct materials..	$35,490	$ 18.20
Direct labour...	$ 7,020	3.60
Variable manufacturing overhead*...............................	$ 2,340	1.20
Fixed manufacturing overhead*	$ 4,680	2.40
		$25.40

*Based on direct labour-hours

During April, the factory worked only 760 direct labour-hours and produced 2,000 robes. The following actual costs were recorded during the month:

	Total	Per Unit of Product
Direct materials (6,000 metres)	$36,000	$ 18.00
Direct labour...	$ 7,600	3.80
Variable manufacturing overhead.................................	$ 3,800	1.90
Fixed manufacturing overhead....................................	$ 4,600	2.30
		$26.00

At standard, each robe should require 2.8 metres of material. All of the materials purchased during the month were used in production.

Required:
Compute the following variances for April:
1. The materials price and quantity variances.
2. The labour rate and efficiency variances.
3. The variable manufacturing overhead spending and efficiency variances.
4. The fixed manufacturing overhead budget and volume variances.

PROBLEM 10–32 Overhead Performance Report [LO7]
Reagan Products Ltd., an Australian company, has the following cost formulas (expressed in Australian dollars) for variable overhead costs in one of its machine shops:

Variable Overhead Cost	Cost Formula (per machine-hour)
Supplies	$ 1.20
Power	2.10
Lubrication	0.90
Wearing tools	5.40
Total	$9.60

The flexible budget amounts for fixed overhead costs in July are as follows:

Fixed Overhead Cost	Flexible Budget
Depreciation	$17,500
Supervisory salaries	24,500
Maintenance	5,250
Total	$47,250

During July, the machine shop was scheduled to work 5,600 machine-hours and to produce 28,000 units of product. The standard machine time per unit of product is 0.2 hours. A severe storm during the month forced the company to close for several days, which reduced the level of output for the month. Actual results for July were as follows:

Actual machine-hours worked	4,700
Actual number of units produced	24,500

Actual costs for July were as follows:

Overhead Costs	Total Actual Cost	Per Machine-Hour
Variable overhead costs:		
Supplies	$ 5,593	$1.19
Power	10,199	2.17
Lubrication	4,512	0.96
Wearing tools	24,863	5.29
Total variable overhead	45,167	$9.61
Fixed overhead costs:		
Depreciation	17,500	—
Supervisory salaries	25,550	—
Maintenance	4,375	—
Total fixed overhead	47,425	—
Total overhead	$92,592	

Required:

Prepare an overhead performance report including both variable and fixed overhead for the machine shop for July. Use column headings in your report as shown below:

Overhead Costs	Cost Formula (per MH)	Actual Costs Incurred, 4,700 MHs	Flexible Budget Based on 4,700 MHs	Flexible Budget Based on Standard 4,900 MHs	Total Variance	Breakdown of the Total Variance	
						Spending Variance	Efficiency Variance

PROBLEM 10–33 Capacity Analysis [LO7]

The Yardman Company produces electric weed trimmers, among other products. The following standard costs per unit are associated with the trimmers:

Item	Quantity	Cost per Unit
Direct materials...	4 pieces at $5.00	$20.00
Direct labour...	2 hours at $12.00	24.00
Variable overhead.......................................	2 hours at $3.00	6.00
Fixed overhead..	2 hours at $5.00	10.00
Total...		$60.00

Normal activity of 60,000 hours was used as the denominator level. Other possible capacity levels were as follows:

Expected annual	55,000 hours
Practical annual.................................	75,000 hours
Theoretical annual	100,000 hours

An analysis of the difference between practical and theoretical capacity for the past year showed the following: 10,000 hours were not used because management decided not to employ two crews of workers. A further 5,000 hours of capacity had to be assigned to setup when machines were switched from one product to another. Another 5,000 hours were not used because scheduled maintenance of production equipment was required. Finally, the remaining 5,000 hours of theoretical capacity were not used because existing markets could not use all of the theoretical capacity without a substantial reduction in selling price. Management approached the Marketing Department to determine what pricing policy would be needed to move from the denominator level of activity (30,000 units) to practical capacity (37,500 units). Marketing suggested that a price reduction of 10% below the existing selling price of $80 would increase demand from 30,000 units to 37,500 units.

Marketing also indicated that to move from practical capacity (37,500 units) to theoretical capacity (50,000 units), two crews would need to be hired, setups eliminated, and maintenance deferred. A further 10% price reduction below the existing $80 would also be needed to increase demand by another 12,500 units.

Required:
Calculate gross profit at the following levels of capacity utilization: (*a*) expected annual, (*b*) denominator, (*c*) practical, and (*d*) theoretical. *Note:* Be sure to incorporate the selling price reductions necessary to sell all units produced at practical and theoretical levels of capacity utilization.

PROBLEM 10-34 Materials and Labour Variances; Computations from Incomplete Data [LO1, LO2, LO3]

Grand River Manufacturing produces a metal flange that it sells to several local home building supply retailers. The company has set standards as follows for materials and labour:

	Direct Materials	Direct Labour
Standard quantity or hours per unit	1.5 kilograms	? hours
Standard price or rate	$3 per kilogram	$? per hour
Standard cost per unit...	$4.50	$?

During the past month, the company purchased 1,500 kilograms of direct materials at a cost of $4,200. All of this material was used in the production of 840 units of product using 425 hours of direct labour. Direct labour cost totalled $4,675 for the month. The following variances have been computed:

Labour rate variance	$425 U
Total labour variance	$375 F
Materials quantity variance	$ 75 U

Required:
1. For direct labour:
    a. Compute the standard rate per hour for labour.
    b. Compute the standard quantity allowed for labour for the month's production.
    c. Compute the standard quantity of labour allowed per unit of product.

2. For direct materials:
    a. Compute the actual direct materials cost per kilogram for the month.
    b. Compute the materials price variance.

(*Hint:* In completing the problem, it may be helpful to move from known to unknown data either by using the variance formulas or by using the columnar format shown in Exhibits 10–4 and 10–6.)

CASES

CASE 10–35 Ethics and Possible Dysfunctional Consequences of Managing to Standards [LO1]

Road Gear manufactures accessories for road and mountain bicycles. The market for cycling accessories is very competitive, so Road Gear uses a standard costing system to control costs. The day-to-day management of each major line of accessories is the responsibility of a product line manager. These managers are responsible for all major production decisions, including purchasing direct materials, hiring and training production staff, scheduling production, and quality inspections. Monthly performance reports are prepared showing variances for direct materials, direct labour, variable overhead, and fixed overhead for each product line. The performance reports are prepared and distributed five business days after month-end and are reviewed at a monthly meeting attended by all of the product line managers, the vice-president of manufacturing, and the chief financial officer. The product line managers are responsible for explaining all significant unfavourable variances each month, and their annual performance review is based in part on how well they manage actual costs relative to the standard costs for their products. The performance reviews affect the managers' annual merit pay increases and bonus.

One of Road Gear's product lines is a high-quality bicycle computer, the Speed Tracker, that records speed, distance, time, cadence, and a variety of other metrics. Dan Roth is the product line manager for the Speed Tracker and has been with Road Gear for only about 14 months. Prior to joining the company, Roth worked at one of Road Gear's main competitors as a production foreman. Roth's first fiscal year at Road Gear was not very successful. Due to a variety of factors, the monthly variances for the Speed Tracker, particularly those for direct materials and direct labour, were unfavourable the majority of months. Even though Road Gear uses practical standards, Roth felt that the standard prices and quantities for direct materials, and the standard rates and hours for direct labour, were too tight. Moreover, increases in direct material costs during the year made matters worse, and as Roth repeatedly pointed out during the monthly meetings, he had no control over the prices charged by suppliers. Senior management was not convinced by Roth's explanations, so his merit pay increase was well below that of the average given to the other product line managers; his annual bonus was equally low.

In the current fiscal year, Roth decided to take a more active role in managing production costs for the Speed Tracker. He found a cheaper microprocessor, the Zip, for the Speed Tracker that cost 20% less per unit than the previous processor, the Zap, which was used in last year's model. Although Roth knew that the Zip was of lower quality and considerably less reliable than the Zap, he figured the trade-off was worth it since it would result in a favourable price variance for the Speed Tracker and would have no impact on the quantity variance. Moreover, since the causes of favourable variances typically weren't discussed at the monthly meetings, Roth was pretty sure he wouldn't have to explain the price–quality trade-off he had made. Roth also began hiring less-experienced production employees in an effort to eliminate the unfavourable labour rate variance for the Speed Tracker. Although the quality of workmanship was lower with these less-experienced workers and they took longer to produce each unit, the unfavourable labour efficiency variance was more than offset by the favourable rate variance.

Roth was pleased with his performance for the first three months of the current year. His variances for direct materials and direct labour were favourable in total, and senior management seemed satisfied that he was doing a better job managing costs. Although the number of Speed Trackers being returned under warranty was up nearly 15% over the same period last year, Roth attributed this to random events that likely wouldn't recur over the remaining months of the year.

Required:
1. Were the actions taken by Roth in the current fiscal year to improve his performance on direct materials and direct labour costs ethical? Explain.
2. What are some longer-term consequences of Roth's behaviour for Road Gear?
3. What steps could senior management at Road Gear take to reduce the type of behaviour exhibited by Roth?

CASE 10–36 Behavioural Impact of Standard Costs and Variances [LO1]
José Flores is the manufacturing supervisor of Newmarket Manufacturing Company, which produces a variety of plastic products. Some of these products are standard items that are listed in the company's catalogue, while others are made to customer specifications. Each month, Flores receives a performance report showing the budget for the month, the actual activity, and the variance between budget and actual. Part of Flores's annual performance evaluation is based on his department's performance against budget. Newmarket's purchasing manager, Adriana Goster, also receives monthly performance reports, and she, too, is evaluated in part on the basis of these reports.

The monthly reports for June had just been distributed when Flores met Goster in the hallway outside their offices. Scowling, Flores began the conversation, "I see we have another set of monthly performance reports hand-delivered by that not-very-nice junior employee in the budget office. He seemed pleased to tell me that I'm in trouble with my performance again."

Goster: I got the same treatment. All I ever hear about are the things I've done wrong. Now I'll have to spend a lot of time reviewing the report and preparing explanations. The worst part is that it's now July 21, so the information is almost a month old and we have to spend all this time on history.

Flores: My biggest gripe is that our production activity varies a lot from month to month, but we're given an annual budget that's written in stone. Last month we were shut down for three days when a strike delayed delivery of the basic ingredient used in our plastic formulation, and we had already exhausted our inventory. You know about that problem, though, because we asked you to call all over the country to find an alternative source of supply. When we got what we needed on a rush basis, we had to pay more than we normally do.

Goster: I expect problems like that to pop up from time to time—that's part of my job—but now we'll both have to take a careful look at our reports to see where the charges are reflected for that rush order. Every month I spend more time making sure that I really should be charged for each item reported than I do making plans for my department's daily work. It's really frustrating to see charges for things I have no control over.

Flores: The way we get information doesn't help, either. I don't get copies of the reports you get, yet a lot of what I do is affected by your department, and by most of our other departments. Why do the budget and accounting people assume that I should be told only about my operations, even though the president regularly gives us pep talks about how we all need to work together as a team?

Goster: I seem to get more reports than I need, and I am never asked to comment on them until top management calls me onto the carpet about my department's shortcomings. Do you ever hear comments when your department shines?

Flores: I guess they don't have time to review the good news. One of my problems is that all the reports are in dollars and cents. I work with people, machines, and materials. I need information to help me solve *this* month's problems—not another report of the dollars expended *last* month or the month before.

Required:
1. Based on the conversation between Flores and Goster, describe the likely motivation and behaviour of these two employees resulting from Newmarket Manufacturing Company's standard cost and variance reporting system.
2. When it is properly implemented, both employees and companies should benefit from a system involving standard costs and variances.
    a. Describe the benefits that can be realized from a standard costing system.
    b. Based on the situation presented above, recommend ways for Newmarket Manufacturing Company to improve its standard cost and variance reporting system so as to increase employee motivation.

(CMA, adapted)

CASE 10–37 Ethics and the Manager [LO7]
Lance Prating is the controller of the Colchester manufacturing facility of Tech Systems Incorporated. Among the many reports that must be filed with corporate headquarters is the annual overhead performance report. The report covers the year that ends on December 31 and is due at corporate headquarters shortly after the beginning of the new year. Prating does not like putting work off until the last minute, so just before Christmas, he put together a preliminary draft of the overhead performance report. Some adjustments would later be required for the few transactions that occur between Christmas and New Year's Day. A copy of the preliminary draft report, which Prating completed on December 21, is shown below:

COLCHESTER MANUFACTURING FACILITY
Overhead Performance Report
December 21 Preliminary Draft

Budgeted machine-hours.............. 100,000
Actual machine-hours................ 90,000

Overhead Costs	Cost Formula (per Machine-hour)	Actual Costs for 90,000 Machine-Hours	Flexible Budget Based on 90,000 Machine-Hours	Spending or Budget Variance
Variable overhead costs:				
Power	$0.03	$ 2,840	$ 2,700	$ 140 U
Supplies	0.86	79,060	77,400	1,660 U
Abrasives.......................	0.34	32,580	30,600	1,980 U
	$1.23	114,480	110,700	3,780 U
Fixed overhead costs:				
Depreciation....................		228,300	226,500	1,800 U
Supervisory salaries.............		187,300	189,000	1,700 F
Insurance.......................		23,000	23,000	0
Industrial engineering		154,000	160,000	6,000 F
Factory building lease		46,000	46,000	0
Total fixed overhead cost..........		638,600	644,500	5,900 F
Total overhead cost...............		$753,080	$755,200	$ 2,120 F

Tab Kapp, the general manager at the Colchester facility, asked to see a copy of the preliminary draft report at 4:45 P.M. on December 23. Prating carried a copy of the report to Kapp's office, where the following discussion took place:

Kapp: Wow! Almost all of the variances on the report are unfavourable. The only thing that looks good at all are the favourable variances for supervisory salaries and for industrial engineering. How did we have an unfavourable variance for depreciation?

Prating: Do you remember that milling machine that broke down because the wrong lubricant was used by the machine operator?

Kapp: Only vaguely.

Prating: It turned out we couldn't fix it. We had to scrap the machine and buy a new one.

Kapp: This report doesn't look good. I was raked over the coals last year when we had just a few unfavourable variances.

Prating: I'm afraid the final report is going to look even worse.

Kapp: Oh?

Prating: The line item for industrial engineering on the report is for work we hired Klein Engineering to do for us on a contract basis. The original contract was for $160,000, but we asked them to do some additional work that was not in the contract. Under the terms of the contract, we have to reimburse Klein Engineering for the costs of the additional work. The $154,000 in actual costs that appear on the preliminary draft report reflects only their billings through December 21. The last bill they had sent us was on November 28, and they completed the project just last week. Yesterday I got a call from Maria over at Klein and she said they would be sending us a final bill for the project before the end of the year. The total bill, including the reimbursements for the additional work, is going to be...

Kapp: I am not sure I want to hear this.

Prating: ... $176,000.

Kapp: Ouch!

Prating: The additional work we asked them to do added $16,000 to the cost of the project.

Kapp: No way can I turn in a performance report with an overall unfavourable variance. They'll really get on my back at corporate headquarters. Call Maria at Klein and ask her not to send the bill until after the first of the year. We have to have that $6,000 favourable variance for industrial engineering on the performance report.

Required:
What should Lance Prating do? Explain.

CASE 10–38 Working Backward from Variance Data [LO2, LO3, LO4, LO6]

You have recently graduated from university and have accepted a position with Sea-Jewels Inc., the manufacturer of a popular consumer product. During your first week on the job, the vice-president has been favourably impressed with your work. She has been so impressed, in fact, that yesterday she called you into her office and asked you to attend the executive committee meeting this morning to lead a discussion on the variances reported for last period. Anxious to favourably impress the executive committee, you took the variances and supporting data home last night on a memory stick to study.

Unfortunately, when you tried to open the files this morning some of them had become corrupted. All you could retrieve is shown below:

Standard Cost Card

Direct materials, 9 kilograms at $3 per kilogram	$27.00
Direct labour, 1.2 direct labour-hours at $15 per direct labour-hour	18.00
Variable manufacturing overhead, 1.2 direct labour-hours at $3 per direct labour-hour	3.60
Fixed manufacturing overhead, 1.2 direct labour-hours at $7 per direct labour-hour	8.40
Standard cost per unit	$57.00

	Total Standard Cost*	Variances Reported			
		Price or Rate	Spending or Budget	Quantity or Efficiency	Volume
Direct materials	$202,500	$3,450 F		$ 4,500 U	
Direct labour	$ 135,000	$7,275 U		$10,500 U	
Variable manufacturing overhead	$ 27,000		$650 F	$?† U	
Fixed manufacturing overhead	$ 63,000		$250 F		$7,000 U

*Applied to work in process during the period.
† Data corrupted.

You recall that manufacturing overhead cost is applied to production on the basis of direct labour-hours and that all of the materials purchased during the period were used in production. Since the company uses JIT to control work flows, work in process inventories are insignificant and can be ignored.

It is now 8:30 A.M. The executive committee meeting starts in just one hour; you realize that to avoid looking grossly incompetent, you must somehow generate the necessary "backup" data for the variances before the meeting begins. Without backup data, it will be impossible to lead the discussion or answer any questions.

Required:
1. How many units were produced last period? (Think hard about this one!)
2. How many kilograms of direct material were purchased and used in production?
3. What was the actual cost per kilogram of material?
4. How many actual direct labour-hours were worked during the period?
5. What was the actual rate paid per direct labour-hour?
6. How much actual variable manufacturing overhead cost was incurred during the period?
7. What is the total fixed manufacturing overhead cost in the company's flexible budget?
8. What were the denominator direct labour-hours for last period?

CASE 10–39 Full Variance Analysis: Variable Costing [LO3, LO4, LO5, LO6]

Anchorvale Electronics Limited manufactures and distributes transistors for electronics firms. In December 2014, Anchorvale required a bank loan and the bank manager insisted that Tracy Miller, Anchorvale's president, prepare a budget for 2015. In January 2016, Anchorvale needed an additional loan and Miller asked her accountant to prepare a budget for 2016 to show the bank manager. Miller was concerned because Anchorvale's profit for 2015 was considerably less than the 2015 budget figure given to the bank and she knew that the bank manager would want to know why. As a first step in analyzing the differences, Miller copied the 2015 actual figures onto the 2015 bank budget form shown below and prepared the standard cost details shown below the budget form:

ANCHORVALE ELECTRONICS LIMITED 2015
Budget Prepared for Bank Loan
Dollars in (000s)

	Static Budget	Actual	Variance
Sales—units................................	110,000	105,000	5,000 U
Sales—dollars..............................	$ 2,750	$ 2,520	$ 230 U
Cost of sales:			
Materials..................................	440	421	19 F
Labour....................................	880	845	35 F
Overhead.................................	220	205	15 F
Fixed factory overhead....................	300	303	3 U
	1,840	1,774	66 F
Gross profit...............................	910	746	164 U
Selling expenses:			
Variable..................................	220	209	11 F
Fixed	100	102	2 U
Administration—fixed.......................	200	197	3 F
	520	508	12 F
Profit before income tax....................	390	238	152 U
Income tax (40% of profit before tax)........	156	95	61 F
Net earnings..............................	$ 234	$ 143	$ 91 U

Standard Costs on Which Budget Is Based

		Standard per Unit
Sales price...		$25
Variable costs:		
Direct material..		$ 4
Labour, ½ hour at $16 per hour..................................		8
Overhead, ½ hour at $4 per hour................................		2
Fixed factory overhead:		
Depreciation.......................	$200,000	
Other..............................	100,000	
	$300,000	
Standard output 100,000 units at ½ hour = 50,000 direct labour-hours		
($300,000 ÷ 50,000) × ½ hour......................................		3
Selling expenses:		
Variable...		2
Fixed, $100,000 ÷ 100,000 units..................................		1
Administration:		
Fixed, $200,000 ÷ 100,000 units..................................		2
		$22

Standard costs were used for preparing bids, whereas the cost accounting system recorded actual costs.

Required:
1. Redraft the budget to show the 2015 static budget, flexible budget, actual, and variances from the flexible budget, with contribution margins separately identified. *Note:* See the standard cost details above.
2. Prepare a quantitative analysis to demonstrate to management the main causes for the variance from the flexible budget, as a basis both for taking corrective action and for explaining the variance from the static budget to the bank manager.

3. If expected 2016 operating results are similar to 2015, explain to the bank manager how much of the loan you would be able to repay from 2016 earnings. (Assume no changes in accounts receivable and accounts payable.)
4. If competition became intense in 2016 and Anchorvale was operating well below capacity at 85,000 units, explain with calculations the minimum bid you would make on an order for 10,000 units.
5. What changes to the management accounting and reporting system for Anchorvale Electronics would you propose?

(CGAC, Adapted)

INSTANT QUIZ SOLUTIONS

10-1

Materials price variance = $AQ(AP - SP)$, so 70,000 diodes($0.28 per diode − $0.30 per diode) = −$1,400 F.

The actual price paid per unit for the material was less than the standard price, which could occur if the company purchased a lower-grade material at a discount or bought an unusually large quantity to take advantage of quantity discounts. A favourable variance would also be experienced if the market price of the material changed or if the purchasing department did some particularly sharp bargaining.

10-2

Materials quantity variance = $SP(AQ - SQ)$, so $0.30 per diode(50,000 diodes − 40,000 diodes) = $3,000 U.

More materials were used to produce the actual output than were called for by the standard perhaps due to poorly trained or supervised workers, improperly adjusted machines, or defective materials.

10-3

Labour rate variance = $AH(AR - SR)$, so 6,400 hours($7.50* per hour − $7.00 per hour) = $3,200 U.
*$48,000 ÷ 6,400 hours = $7.50 per hour.

The average wage rate was higher than the standard wage rate. Possible explanations are an increase in wages that has not been reflected in the standards, unanticipated overtime, or a shift toward more highly paid workers.

Labour efficiency variance = $SR(AH - SH)$, so $7 per hour(6,400 hours − 6,000 hours) = $2,800 U. The actual number of labour-hours was greater than the standard labour-hours allowed for the actual output, which could be due to poor supervision, poorly trained workers, low-quality materials requiring more labour time to process, or machine breakdowns. In addition, if the direct labour force is essentially fixed, an unfavourable labour efficiency variance could be caused by a reduction in output due to decreased demand for the company's products.

10-4

Total direct labour-hours allowed = 35,000 requests × 0.15 standard direct labour-hours per request = 5,250 DLH
Standard variable overhead cost = 5,250 DLH × $1.30 per DLH = $6,825.
Actual variable overhead cost incurred = $7,125 − $6,825 = $300 U.

10-5

Fixed portion of the predetermined overhead rate = Fixed overhead ÷ Denominator level of activity = $400,000 ÷ 50,000 DLHs = $8.00 per DLH.
Budget variance = Actual fixed overhead cost − Flexible budget fixed overhead cost = $394,000 − $400,000 = −$6,000 F.
Volume variance = Fixed portion of predetermined rate × (Denominator hours − Standard hours) = $8.00 per DLH(50,000 DLHs − 48,000 DLHs) = $16,000 U.

connect   **LEARNSMART**   **SMARTBOOK**

For more information on the resources available from McGraw-Hill Ryerson, go to www.mheducation.ca/he/solutions.

APPENDIX 10A: FURTHER ANALYSIS OF MATERIALS VARIANCES

In this appendix, we will consider subcomponents of the materials quantity variance: a *materials mix* and *materials yield variance*. The extended model for calculating these variances is presented in Exhibit 10A–1.

The production of most goods generally requires more than one type of direct materials input. Chemical firms use varying proportions of interchangeable materials, and the same is true of food processing companies. For example, a company that produces flour with a mixture of red and white wheat may, on occasion, substitute one kind of wheat for another. When legally permitted, a manufacturer of canned fruit cocktail may substitute peaches for pears and a manufacturer of sausages may substitute beef for pork. The calculation of mix and yield variances is appropriate *only* if different types of materials can be substituted for one another. A **mix variance** results if the actual mix of materials inputs differs from the standard mix of materials. The standard mix reflects the proportional mix of materials that is expected to be used to produce a given product. A mix variance is calculated to determine the effects of a change in the materials mix on the total materials cost. The mix variance is favourable if the actual mix of materials inputs is cheaper than the standard mix. This means that a greater proportion of less-expensive materials was used in production. The mix variance is unfavourable if the actual mix of materials inputs is more expensive than the standard mix because a greater proportion of more-expensive materials was used. Where a manager has control over the composition of the mix, the mix variance can be a useful measure of the manager's performance.

A **yield variance** occurs when the total quantity of inputs actually used generates a different rate of output from what would have been achieved using standard quantities of inputs at the standard mix. To isolate the effects of the yield variance from the mix variance, the yield variance is calculated using the standard mix of materials inputs. By so doing, managers can calculate the dollar impact on total materials costs of the actual total quantity of inputs differing from the quantities that should have been used according to the standard costing system. A favourable yield variance means a lower total quantity of inputs was used than planned, while an unfavourable yield variance means more inputs were used in total than planned.

To illustrate the calculation of the mix and yield variances, assume that Cape Breton Chemical Company combines secret ingredients A and B to make a product known as Super-Cleaner Bjax. The standard mix calls for 2 kilograms of A and 3 kilograms of B to produce one unit of Bjax. The standard mix for A and B is therefore 2/5 and 3/5,

LEARNING OBJECTIVE
Compute the mix and yield variances for materials, and explain their significance.

Mix variance
The dollar effect on total materials cost of a difference between the actual mix of materials inputs and the standard mix of materials.

Yield variance
The dollar effect on total materials costs of the total quantity of inputs actually used generating a different output from what would have been achieved using standard quantities of inputs at the standard mix.

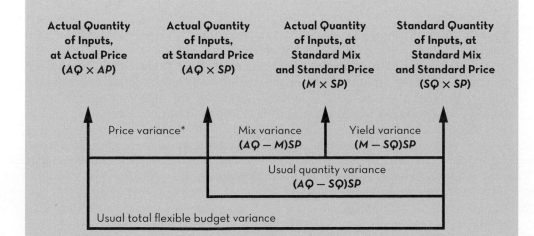

EXHIBIT 10A–1   Extended Model for Variance Analysis—Materials

Actual Quantity of Inputs, at Actual Price (AQ × AP)	Actual Quantity of Inputs, at Standard Price (AQ × SP)	Actual Quantity of Inputs, at Standard Mix and Standard Price (M × SP)	Standard Quantity of Inputs, at Standard Mix and Standard Price (SQ × SP)
Price variance*		Mix variance (AQ − M)SP	Yield variance (M − SQ)SP
		Usual quantity variance (AQ − SQ)SP	
Usual total flexible budget variance			

*Same as analysis presented in Exhibit 10–3.

respectively. Assume that 150 units were produced in July using 350 kilograms of A and 450 kilograms of B. Material A has a standard unit price of $1.50, and material B has a standard unit price of $2.50.

We begin by calculating the materials quantity variance for each type of material input and in total, using the formula presented earlier in the chapter: $SP(AQ - SQ)$:

Material A: $1.50(350 − 300*) = $75 U
Material B: $2.50(450 − 450*) = $ 0

*Material A: 2 kilograms per unit × 150 units;
Material B: 3 kilograms per unit × 150 units

Thus, the total quantity variance to be further analyzed into its mix and yield components is $75 unfavourable.

For each type of input, the mix variance can be calculated in two steps. First, multiply the budgeted mix percentage for that input by the actual *total* inputs of all types and subtract the result from the actual quantity of that input used in production for the period. This is the mix variance expressed in physical terms for each type of input. Second, multiply your answer from step one by the standard price of that input. The formula for the mix variance that is applied to *each* type of material input is shown below:

$$\text{Mix Variance} = \left[\text{Actual quantity} - \left(\text{Budgeted \%} \times \text{Total input} \right) \right] \times \text{Standard price}$$

or for each input used in production:

$$\text{Mix variance} = (AQ_A - M_A)SP_A$$

where

AQ_A is the actual quantity used of material A.
M_A is the standard mix of material A given the total quantity of material actually used.
SP_A is the standard price of material A.

For material A, the mix variance in July is

$$\left[350 - \frac{2}{5}(350 + 450) \right] \times \$1.50 = \$45 \text{ U}$$

Similarly, for material B, the mix variance in July is

$$\left[450 - \frac{3}{5}(350 + 450) \right] \times \$2.50 = \$75 \text{ F}$$

The result of multiplying the budgeted mix percentage for material A by the total quantity of inputs actually used in July is 320 kilograms [$\frac{2}{5}(350 + 450)$]. This is the amount of material A that would have been used if the budgeted mix had been adhered to. Since the amount of material actually used, 350 kilograms, exceeds the budgeted amount, the mix variance is unfavourable. If the budgeted mix had been adhered to for material B, 480 kilograms [$\frac{3}{5}(350 + 450)$] would have been used in July. Since the actual usage of material B was only 450 kilograms, the materials mix variance of material B is favourable. Note that the mix variances are calculated using the total quantity of materials inputs actually used (800 kilograms) and thus focus on the effects of the actual mix of inputs differing from the standard mix of inputs.

Overall, the mix variance is $30 favourable, which is the result of using a higher percentage of the less expensive material A in July (350 ÷ 800 = 43.75%) than planned in the budget (2 ÷ 5 = 40%). If the opposite had been true and a higher percentage of the more expensive material B had been used in July compared to the budgeted mix, the overall mix variance would have been unfavourable.

The yield variance is also calculated in two steps for each type of input. First, multiply the total quantity of all inputs used for the period by the standard mix percentage for that input, and, from this result, subtract the standard quantity of the input allowed for the output achieved. Note that this approach holds mix constant at the standard proportions, allowing the yield variance to be isolated from any differences between the actual and standard mix. Second, multiply the result of the first step by the standard price for that input. The formula for the yield variance that is applied to *each* type of material input is shown below:

Yield variance = [(Budgeted percentage × Total input) − Standard quantity] × Standard price

or, for each input used in production,

$$\text{Yield variance} = (M_A - SQ_A)SP_A$$

where

SQ_A is the standard quantity of material A, with the other items in the formula as defined above.

For material A, the yield variance in July is

$$\left[\frac{2}{5}(350 + 450) - 2(150)\right]\$1.50 = \$30 \text{ U}$$

Similarly, for material B, the yield variance in July is

$$\left[\frac{3}{5}(350 + 450) - 3(150)\right]\$2.50 = \$75 \text{ U}$$

Note that the yield variances are calculated using the standard mix of materials (40% A, 60% B) and thus focus on the effects of the actual quantity of inputs (at the standard mix) differing from the standard quantity of inputs. Overall, the yield variance for July is $105 unfavourable, comprising the individual amounts shown above. This indicates that, in total, more inputs were used for production than should have been according to the standards.

It is important to note how the sum of the mix and yield variances is equal to the total materials quantity variance calculated above:

Variance	Amount
Mix:	
Material A...	$ 45 U
Material B...	75 F
Total mix variance	$ 30 F
Yield:	
Material A...	$ 30 U
Material B...	75 U
Total yield variance	$105 U
Total mix and yield variances	$ 75 U

Collectively, the mix and yield variances explain why the total quantity variance occurred. In our example, using an actual mix of inputs that favoured the less expensive material A resulted in a favourable mix variance. However, this was offset by the fact that more inputs in total (particularly for material B) were required to produce the output for the period. Specifically, 800 kilograms of materials inputs was actually used (350 kilograms of material A and 450 kilograms of material B), while the standard amount allowed for the output achieved was 750 kilograms (300 kilograms of material A and 450 kilograms of material B). This resulted in a $105 unfavourable yield variance. It could be that the less expensive material A was more easily damaged, was harder to work with, or had other characteristics that led to the unfavourable yield variance. Whatever the reason, the manager's decision to increase the proportion of material A used in July production led to an unfavourable yield variance and an unfavourable total materials quantity variance. By separately examining the mix and yield components of the total quantity variance, the effects of the trade-offs between mix and yield effects can be detected. Moreover, there may be implications for other variances that arise from using an actual mix of inputs that differs from the standard. In our example, if material A is harder to work with, this could lead to an unfavourable labour efficiency variance if employees need to spend more time working with substandard material. So calculating the mix and yield variances may help managers understand the causes of other variances for the period.

Labour efficiency variances, described earlier in the chapter, can be analyzed in a similar manner if the composition of a work group is provided in the standard. The effects of departing from the standard mix of skilled and unskilled workers or experienced and less experienced employees can be broken down into mix and yield components. As with our example above, this allows managers to quantify the financial impact of changing the mix of labour inputs.

APPENDIX 10A SUMMARY

- When the production of a good requires more than one type of direct materials input, the total materials quantity variance can be further analyzed into mix and yield components if those inputs are substituted for each other. [LO8]
- A mix variance quantifies the dollar impact on materials costs of using an actual mix of inputs that differs from the standard mix. A yield variance quantifies the dollar impact of the actual total quantity of inputs differing from the standard quantity allowed for the output achieved. Because the yield variance is calculated using the standard mix of inputs, it permits the isolation of quantity differences (actual versus standard) from the mix differences (actual versus standard) calculated for the mix variance. [LO8]
- Calculating the mix and yield variances allows for a more complete evaluation of managers' decisions to change the mix of inputs in any given period. Because changing the mix of inputs can often affect the yield generated by those inputs, the dollar impact of this trade-off becomes clear after calculating the mix and yield variances. Changing the mix of inputs can also affect other variances, such as labour efficiency, and thus may help explain outcomes on those variances. [LO8]
- Mix and yield variances can also be calculated when different types of labour inputs are required to produce a product or deliver a service and can be substituted for each other. [LO8]

APPENDIX 10A EXERCISES AND PROBLEMS

EXERCISE 10A-1 Mix and Yield Variances [LO8]
The Grayson Company uses standard costs to account for its production of a specialty cleaning product called Green Clean. The standard cost of materials and direct labour to produce one bottle of Green Clean is as follows:

Material A............	1.5 litres at $0.80 per litre	$ 1.20
Material B	0.5 litres at $2.00 per litre	1.00
Direct labour.........	0.25 hours at $10.00 per hour	2.50

Both material A and material B are added at the start of the process. Production data for June 2016 are as follows:
a. Beginning work in process, 5,000 units, 25% complete.
b. Started during June, 18,000 units.
c. Ending work in process, 6,000 units, 60% complete.
d. No units were spoiled.

e. 28,000 litres of material A was issued to production.
f. 12,000 litres of material B was used during June.
g. Direct labour worked totalled 4,800 hours at a cost of $50,000 for the month.

Required:
Determine all of the material and labour variances possible from the preceding data for the month of June.

EXERCISE 10A-2 Mix and Yield Variances [LO8]
Davis Division uses three secret materials—A, B, and C—to produce its product, called Corzon. The materials are mixed in the following standard proportions to yield 100 litres of Corzon:

Secret Material	Quantity (litres)	Cost per Litre
A.....................................	80	$ 4.00
B.....................................	40	$ 8.00
C.....................................	30	$20.00

It requires 50 hours of direct labour at $20.00 per hour to produce 100 litres of Corzon.

On average, the division can produce and sell 200,000 litres of Corzon per month. In a recent month, the division used the following amounts of materials and labour to produce 175,000 litres of Corzon:

Secret Material	Quantity (litres)	Total Actual Cost
A...............................	159,000	$ 647,130
B...............................	72,000	580,204
C...............................	44,000	870,000
	275,000	$2,097,334
Direct labour.....................	91,000 hours	$1,380,000

Required:
1. Calculate the following materials variances for Corzon:
    a. Price.
    b. Quantity.
    c. Mix.
    d. Yield.
2. The supervisor of the Corzon product line argued that the workers were operating at standard, if not better, despite a large unfavourable labour efficiency variance of $52,500. Is the supervisor correct? Why or why not?

(SMAC, Adapted)

PROBLEM 10A-3 Mix and Yield Variances [LO8]
Dundas Company manufactures and sells two special-purpose cleaning solvents, Brill and Daz. The two products emerge from the same production process, which requires three materials: C12, D24, and E48. The division developed standard costs for these two solvents as shown below:

Joint Processing Costs		
Materials — C12...	12 kilograms at $4.80 per kilogram	$ 57.60
— D24...	8 kilograms at $8.40 per kilogram	67.20
— E48	2 kilograms at $10.30 per kilogram	20.60
Total materials input	22 kilograms	145.40
Labour (applied at $11.20 per kilogram × 22 kilograms)...		246.40
Overhead — Variable (applied at $5.60 per kilogram × 22 kilograms)................................		123.20
— Fixed (applied at $10.00 per kilogram × 22 kilograms)		220.00
Joint costs to produce 20 kilograms of good output		$735.00

Normal monthly volume is 22,000 kilograms of input materials processed or 20,000 kilograms of good output. Some variations of input quantities are permissible without affecting the quality of the finished products.

Costs Assigned to the Two Joint Products Using Market Value

Product	Good Output	Per Kilogram	Total	Joint* Costs	Standard Cost per Kilogram
Brill..............................	14 kilograms	$40	$560	$420.00	$30.00
Daz.............................	6 kilograms	70	420	315.00	52.50
	20 kilograms		$980	$735.00	

*Joint costs are allocated to the products on the basis of market value.

Materials are purchased from another division and are readily available; therefore, very little raw materials inventory is kept by Dundas Company. Materials prices are negotiated annually between the divisions. All production is finished daily; therefore, there are no work in process inventories.

Actual production of good output in July amounted to 22,800 kilograms. The production costs were calculated as follows:

Materials input—C12...........................	15,000 kilograms at $4.80 per kilogram	$ 72,000
—D24...........................	8,100 kilograms at $8.40 per kilogram	68,040
—E48...........................	2,200 kilograms at $10.30 per kilogram	22,660
Total Input.....................................	25,300 kilograms	$ 162,700
Labour for 25,300 kilograms processed..		$283,360

Good output: Brill, 15,800 kilograms
            Daz, 7,000 kilograms

Required:
Calculate the materials and labour cost variances in as much detail as the data permit for the Dundas Company for the month of July. Comment on the performance of the production function of the Dundas Company during July by explaining the significance of the variances you calculated.

(SMAC, Adapted)

APPENDIX 10B: GENERAL LEDGER ENTRIES TO RECORD VARIANCES

LEARNING OBJECTIVE 9
Prepare journal entries to record standard costs and variances.

Although standard costs and variances can be computed and used by management without being formally entered into the accounting records, most organizations prefer to make formal entries. Formal entry tends to give variances a greater emphasis than informal, off-the-record computations. This emphasis gives a clear signal of management's desire to keep costs within the standards that have been set. In addition, formal use of standard costs considerably simplifies the bookkeeping process. Inventories and cost of goods sold can be valued at their standard costs—eliminating the need to keep track of the actual cost of each unit.

Direct Materials Variances

To illustrate the general ledger entries needed to record standard cost variances, we will return to the data contained in the review problem at the end of the main body of the chapter. The entry to record the purchase of direct materials is as follows:

Raw materials (25,000 microns at $0.50 per micron)..............................	12,500	
Materials price variance (25,000 microns at $0.02 per micron F)...................		500
Accounts payable (25,000 microns at $0.48 per micron).......................		12,000

Notice that the price variance is recognized when purchases are made, rather than when materials are actually used in production. This permits the price variance to be isolated early, and it also permits the materials to be carried in the Inventory account at standard cost. As direct materials are later drawn from inventory and used in production, the quantity variance is isolated as follows:

Work in process (18,000 microns at $0.50 per micron)...........................	9,000	
Materials quantity variance (2,000 microns U at $0.50 per micron)................	1,000	
Raw materials (20,000 microns at $0.50 per micron)		10,000

Thus, direct materials enter into the Work in Process account at standard cost, in terms of both price and quantity. Notice that the favourable price variance is a credit and the unfavourable quantity variance is a debit.

The term *direct materials* is not the same as *raw materials*, even though they are often used interchangeably. Technically, *raw materials* refer to materials that are basic to the production process and usually no processing has been done that changes their nature. *Direct materials* refer to materials identified in the product as opposed to indirect supplies or materials that are not identified in the product. For example, oil is a direct material for the production of electricity and it is considered a raw material by most. Steel is a direct material in the production of automobiles. However, a car seat is a direct material, not a raw material. Because of the confusion, we will consider the two terms interchangeable unless an obvious distinction is necessary.

Direct Labour Variances

Referring again to the cost data in the review problem at the end of the chapter, the general ledger entry to record the incurrence of direct labour cost is as follows:

Work in process (3,900 hours at $15.00 per hour)................................	58,500	
Labour efficiency variance (100 hours U at $15.00 per hour)	1,500	
Labour rate variance (4,000 hours at $1.00 per hour U)...........................	4,000	
Wages payable (4,000 hours at $16.00 per hour)...............................		64,000

Thus, as with direct materials, direct labour costs enter into the Work in Process account at standard, both in terms of the rate and in terms of the hours allowed for the actual production of the period.

Variable and Fixed Manufacturing Overhead Variances

Referring to the cost data in the review problem at the end of the chapter, the entries to record actual overhead, the application of overhead, the overhead variances, and the disposition of underapplied overhead for July are shown below.

To record actual variable and fixed overhead for July:

Overhead costs ($17,000 + $25,000)	42,000	
Various credits, such as accounts payable............................		42,000

To record the application of variable overhead (3,900 × $4) and fixed overhead (3,900 × $6) in July:

Work in progress ($15,600 + $23,400)......................................	39,000	
Overhead costs..		39,000

To record the overhead variances and the disposition of underapplied overhead for July:

Variable overhead spending variance U......................................	1,000	
Variable overhead efficiency variance U.....................................	400	
Fixed overhead budget variance U	820	
Fixed overhead volume variance U..	780	
Overhead costs..		3,000

Cost Flows in a Standard Costing System

The flows of costs through the company's accounts are illustrated for direct materials and direct labour in Exhibit 10B–1. Note that entries into the various inventory accounts are made at standard cost—not actual cost. The differences between actual and standard costs are entered into special accounts that accumulate the various standard cost variances. Ordinarily, these standard cost variance accounts are closed out to cost of goods sold at the end of the period. Unfavourable variances increase cost of goods sold, and favourable variances decrease cost of goods sold.

EXHIBIT 10B–1   Cash Flows in a Standard Costing System

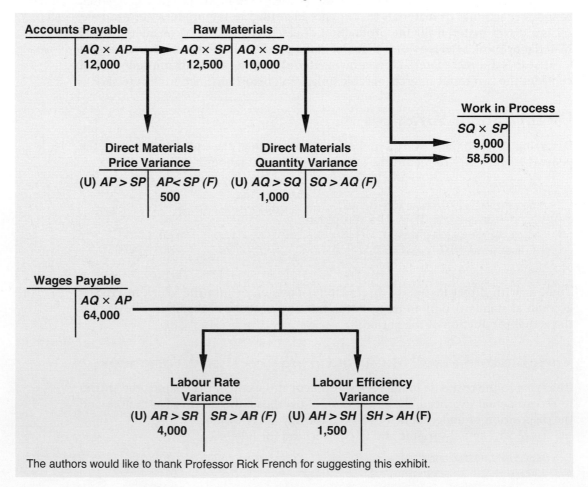

The authors would like to thank Professor Rick French for suggesting this exhibit.

APPENDIX 10B SUMMARY

- Entering standard costs and variances into the accounting records emphasizes management's desire to keep actual costs as close to standard as possible. It also simplifies the bookkeeping process because inventories and cost of goods sold can be valued at standard costs, negating the need to keep track of the actual costs of each unit. [LO9]
- Differences between the actual amounts paid for materials, labour, and overhead and standard costs are charged to accounts for price, rate, quantity, and efficiency variances. At the end of each reporting period, the variance accounts are closed out to cost of goods sold. Unfavourable variances increase cost of goods sold, while favourable variances decrease cost of goods sold. [LO9]

APPENDIX 10B EXERCISES AND PROBLEMS

EXERCISE 10B-1 Recording Variances in the General Ledger [LO9]

Wannabe Corporation makes a product with the following standard costs for direct materials and direct labour:

Direct materials: 1.90 metres at $6.70 per metre..............................	$12.73
Direct labour: 0.35 hours at $17.00 per hour	$ 5.95

During the most recent month, 10,000 units were produced. The costs associated with the month's production of this product were as follows:

Materials purchased: 19,500 metres at $7.00 per metre	$136,500
Materials used in production: 17,400 metres................................	—
Direct labour: 2,540 hours at $17.75 per hour................................	$ 45,085

The standard cost variances for direct materials and direct labour are as follows:

Materials price variance: 19,500 metres at $0.30 per metre U	$ 5,850 U
Materials quantity variance: 1,600 metres at $6.70 per metre F..............	$10,720 F
Labour rate variance: 2,540 hours at $0.75 per hour U	$ 1,905 U
Labour efficiency variance: 960 hours at $17.00 per hour F..................	$16,320 F

Required:
1. Prepare the journal entry to record the purchase of materials on account for the month.
2. Prepare the journal entry to record the use of materials for the month.
3. Prepare the journal entry to record the incurrence of direct labour cost for the month.

EXERCISE 10B-2 Materials and Labour Variances; Journal Entries [LO2, LO3, LO9]

Marmot Products began production of a new product on April 1. The company uses a standard costing system and has established the following standards for one unit of the new product:

	Standard Quantity or Hours	Standard Price or Rate	Standard Cost
Direct materials..............	3.5 metres	$6 per metre	$21
Direct labour.................	0.4 hours	$10 per hour	$ 4

During April, the following activity was recorded regarding the new product:
a. Purchased 7,000 metres of materials at a cost of $5.75 per metre.
b. Used 6,000 metres of materials to produce 1,500 units of the new product.
c. Worked 725 direct labour-hours on the new product at a cost of $8,120.

Required:

1. For direct materials:
   a.   Compute the direct materials price and quantity variances.
   b.   Prepare journal entries to record the purchase of materials and the use of materials in production.
2. For direct labour:
   a.   Compute the direct labour rate and efficiency variances.
   b.   Prepare journal entries to record the incurrence of direct labour cost for the month.
3. Post the entries you have prepared to the T-accounts below:

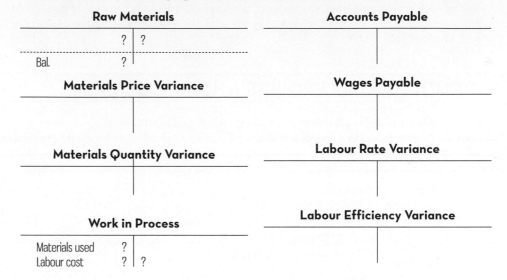

Raw Materials		Accounts Payable
?	?	

Bal.   ?

Materials Price Variance   **Wages Payable**

Materials Quantity Variance   **Labour Rate Variance**

Labour Efficiency Variance

Work in Process

Materials used   ?
Labour cost   ?   ?

PROBLEM 10B–3 Comprehensive Variance Analysis; Journal Entries [LO2, LO3, LO4, LO5, LO6, LO9]

Haliburton Mills Inc. is a large producer of men's and women's clothing. The company uses standard costs for all of its products. The standard costs and actual costs for a recent period are given below for one of the company's product lines (per unit of product):

	Standard Cost	Actual Cost
Direct materials:		
Standard: 4.0 metres at $3.60 per metre.	$ 14.40	
Actual: 4.4 metres at $3.35 per metre		$14.74
Direct labour:		
Standard: 1.6 hours at $4.50 per hour	7.20	
Actual: 1.4 hours at $4.85 per hour		6.79
Variable manufacturing overhead:		
Standard: 1.6 hours at $1.80 per hour.	2.88	
Actual: 1.4 hours at $2.15 per hour		3.01
Fixed manufacturing overhead:		
Standard: 1.6 hours at $3.00 per hour	4.80	
Actual: 1.4 hours at $3.05 per hour		4.27
Total cost per unit	$29.28	$28.81

Actual costs: 4,800 units at $28.81		$138,288
Standard costs: 4,800 units at $29.28		140,544
Difference in cost—favourable.		$ 2,256

During this period, the company produced 4,800 units of product. A comparison of standard and actual costs for the period on a total cost basis is also given above.

There was no inventory of materials on hand to start the period. During the period, 21,120 metres of materials was purchased and used in production. The denominator level of activity for the period was 6,860 hours.

Required:
1. For direct materials:
   a. Compute the price and quantity variances for the period.
   b. Prepare journal entries to record all activity relating to direct materials for the period.
2. For direct labour:
   a. Compute the rate and efficiency variances.
   b. Prepare a journal entry to record the incurrence of direct labour cost for the period.
3. Compute the variable manufacturing overhead spending and efficiency variances.
4. Compute the fixed overhead budget and volume variances.
5. On seeing the $2,256 total cost variance, the company's president stated, "It's obvious that our costs are well under control." Do you agree? Explain.
6. State possible causes of each variance that you have computed.

PROBLEM 10B–4 Comprehensive Variance Analysis with Incomplete Data; Journal Entries [LO2, LO3, LO4, LO5, LO6, LO9]
Topline Surf Boards manufactures a single product. The standard cost of one unit of this product is as follows:

Direct materials: 2 metres at $3 per metre	$ 6.00
Direct labour: 1 hour at $4.50 per hour	4.50
Variable manufacturing overhead: 1 hour at $3 per hour	3.00
Fixed manufacturing overhead: 1 hour at $5 per hour	5.00
Total standard variable cost per unit	$18.50

During October, 6,000 units were produced. Selected data relating to the month's production follow:

Materials purchased: 20,000 metres at $2.85 per metre	$57,000
Materials used in production: 12,650 metres	—
Direct labour: ? hours at $? per hour	$27,950
Variable manufacturing overhead cost incurred	$20,475
Variable manufacturing overhead efficiency variance	$ 1,500 U
Denominator level of activity for October	6,200 hours
Fixed manufacturing overhead budget variance	1,000 U

There was no beginning inventory of raw materials. The variable and fixed manufacturing overhead rates are based on direct labour-hours.

Required:
1. For direct materials:
   a. Compute the price and quantity variances for October.
   b. Prepare journal entries to record activity for October.
2. For direct labour:
   a. Compute the rate and efficiency variances for October.
   b. Prepare a journal entry to record labour activity for October.
3. For variable manufacturing overhead:
   a. Compute the spending variance for October, and verify the efficiency variance given above.
   b. If manufacturing overhead is applied to production on the basis of direct labour-hours, is it possible to have a favourable direct labour efficiency variance and an unfavourable variable overhead efficiency variance? Explain.
4. For fixed manufacturing overhead:
   a. Compute the volume variance for October.
   b. Compute actual costs for October.
5. State possible causes of each variance that you have computed.

◼ APPENDIX 10C: SALES VARIANCE ANALYSIS

Sales Variance Analysis

LEARNING OBJECTIVE ❿
Analyze variances from sales budgets.

The interaction of price and quantity represents important information for businesses to analyze to determine why the strategic goals and specific budgeted targets were not achieved. Managers want to know the effects of market volume changes, market penetration or share changes, sales mix changes, and price changes. Each of these elements can be isolated, but the true test of management is to reconstitute the combination needed for a new marketing strategy. Variances from previous results can provide a valuable starting point for this process.

To illustrate the nature of variance reporting in the revenue area, consider the following example for Ace Video Company:

Budget sales in units:	
Deluxe video game	10,000
Standard video game	5,000
Budget price:	
Deluxe	$ 60
Standard	$ 30
Market volume expected:	
Deluxe	70,000
Standard	90,000
Budget variable expense:	
Deluxe	$ 24
Standard	$ 15

The sales price for the deluxe video game was reduced to $54 from the anticipated $60. This resulted in a $48,000 increase in revenue. The standard video game price was increased by $3 per unit, resulting in a revenue decrease of $18,000. The reasoning behind the price and revenue changes is something marketing management should explain, so that a new pricing strategy can be considered.

Actual results for the period were as follows:

Unit sales:	
Deluxe	12,000
Standard	4,000
Sales prices:	
Deluxe	$ 54
Standard	$ 33
Market volume:	
Deluxe	75,000
Standard	85,000

Exhibit 10C–1 summarizes the relationships among budgeted and actual results. Revenue variance analysis can proceed as follows:

$$\text{Sales price variance} = \left[\text{Actual sales price} - \text{Budgeted sales price} \right] \times \text{Actual sales volume}$$

Deluxe: ($54 − $60) × 12,000 units = $72,000 U

Standard: ($33 − $30) × 4,000 units = $\underline{12,000 \quad F}$

Total sales price variance = $\underline{\$60,000\ U}$

Sales price variance
Actual sales price minus budgeted sales price, multiplied by actual sales quantity.

Note in Exhibit 10C–1 that the total $60,000 unfavourable **sales price variance** in contribution margin resulting from the change in sales price is calculated using actual sales volume in units times the difference in sales price (actual versus budget) because actual and budgeted variable costs per unit are the same.

EXHIBIT 10C-1   Actual and Budgeted Results—Ace Video Company

	Actual Results		Flexible Budget		Master Budget	
Revenue:						
Deluxe	(12,000 × $54)	$648,000	(12,000 × $60)	$720,000	(10,000 × $60)	$600,000
Standard	(4,000 × $33)	132,000	(4,000 × $30)	120,000	(5,000 × $30)	150,000
		780,000		840,000		750,000
Variable expenses:						
Deluxe	(12,000 × $24)	288,000	(12,000 × $24)	288,000	(10,000 × $24)	240,000
Standard	(4,000 × $15)	60,000	(4,000 × $15)	60,000	(5,000 × $15)	75,000
		348,000		348,000		315,000
Contribution margin		$432,000		$492,000		$435,000

	Sales Price Variance	Sales Volume Variance
Total variances	$60,000 U	$57,000 F

Firms often want to know how well they are performing compared to the market for their product. If the total market demand changes, they want to evaluate the impact on profits. Importantly, the variances that follow focus on the effects of volume, quantity, and mix changes on contribution margin. If these changes also affected the fixed costs, managers would also want to analyze these effects, but this is beyond the scope of our discussion. *Market volume variances* and *market share variances* can provide a method of seeing the contribution margin effects of market volume changes or changes in the portion of the market, termed *market share* or *market penetration*, captured by the firm.

We begin with the **market volume variance**, holding market share constant:

> **Market volume variance**
> Actual market volume minus budget market volume, times anticipated market share, multiplied by budgeted contribution margin.

$$\begin{array}{c} \text{Market} \\ \text{volume} \\ \text{varience} \end{array} = \left(\begin{array}{c} \text{Actual} \\ \text{market} \\ \text{volume} \end{array} - \begin{array}{c} \text{Budget} \\ \text{market} \\ \text{volume} \end{array} \right) \times \begin{array}{c} \text{Anticipated market} \\ \text{share percentage} \end{array} \times \begin{array}{c} \text{Budgeted} \\ \text{contribution} \\ \text{margin per unit} \end{array}$$

Deluxe: $(75,000 - 70,000) \times (10,000 \div 70,000) \times (\$60 - \$24) = \$25,714$ F

Standard: $(85,000 - 90,000) \times (5,000 \div 90,000) \times (\$30 - \$15) = \underline{\$\ 4,167}$ U

Total $\underline{\underline{\$21,547\ F}}$

The market volume variance represents the effect on contribution margin of the total market size (demand) differing from what was anticipated. Using Ace Video's budgeted market share percentages for each product, the analysis above indicates that the net effect of higher than anticipated total market demand for Deluxe video games and lower than anticipated total market demand for Standard video games is an increase in contribution margin of $21,547. This variance, although favourable, is not the result of any actions taken by Ace Video managers; instead it simply reflects the impact on contribution margin of the total market demand for video games differing from the estimates prepared by the company.

To calculate the impact on contribution margin of Ace Video's market share differing from budget, holding the effects of total market demand constant, we use the following **market share variance** approach:

> **Market share variance**
> Actual sales volume minus the anticipated portion of the actual market volume, multiplied by budgeted contribution margin per unit.

$$\begin{array}{c} \text{Market} \\ \text{share} \\ \text{variance} \end{array} = \begin{array}{c} \text{Actual} \\ \text{sales} \\ \text{quantity} \end{array} - \left(\begin{array}{c} \text{Actual} \\ \text{market} \\ \text{volume} \end{array} \times \begin{array}{c} \text{Anticipated} \\ \text{market share} \\ \text{percentage} \end{array} \right) \times \begin{array}{c} \text{Budgeted} \\ \text{contribution} \\ \text{margin per unit} \end{array}$$

Deluxe: $\{12,000 - [75,000 \times (10,000 \div 70,000)]\} \times (\$60 - \$24) = \$46,286$ F

Standard: $\{4,000 - [85,000 \times (5,000 \div 90,000)]\} \times (\$30 - \$15)\ \ = \underline{10,833\text{ U}}$

Total $\underline{\underline{\$35,453\text{ F}}}$

The favourable market share variance of $35,453 reflects the net effect of Ace Video enjoying a higher than budgeted market share for Deluxe video games (16% actual versus 14.3% budgeted) but a lower than budgeted market share for Standard video games (4.7% versus 5.6%).[6] The market share variance can be influenced by actions taken by managers. For example, the favourable market share variance for Deluxe video games is likely in part attributable to the $6 per unit price decrease. Another controllable factor that could influence the market share variance is a change to the company's marketing campaign.

Two aspects of the market volume variance and market share variance are worth emphasizing. First, each variance was calculated at the contribution margin level rather than individually analyzing revenues and variable expenses. This permits a direct evaluation of the profit effect of actual sales volumes differing from the master budget. Second, the use of the budgeted contribution margin per unit isolates the effects of volume variances from those of price (or cost) variances. The impact of actual selling prices differing from budget is captured by the sales price variance, while the impact of actual variable costs per unit differing from budget was analyzed in the main chapter text.

The market volume variance and the market share variance help managers understand why actual sales quantities were 12,000 units for Deluxe and 4,000 units for Standard compared to budgeted unit sales of 10,000 and 5,000, respectively. In total, these volume differences resulted in the following contribution margin variances:

Deluxe: $(12,000 - 10,000) \times (\$60 - \$24) = \$72,000$ F
Standard: $(4,000 - 5,000) \times (\$30 - \$15) = \underline{15,000\text{ U}}$
Total $\underline{\underline{\$57,000\text{ F}}}$

Composition: Market volume $= \$21,547$ F
             Market share $= \underline{35,453\text{ F}}$
                                                $\underline{\underline{\$57,000\text{ F}}}$

Sales mix variance
Quantifies the effects on contribution margin of selling the two products in a mix that differs from the original budget.

Sales quantity variance
Quantifies the effects on contribution margin of unit sales differing from the budget, holding constant the sales mix at the budgeted proportions.

An alternative view of sales volume variances can be generated by examining **sales mix variance** and **sales quantity variance** in terms of their relationship to the budgeted contribution margin. For this approach to be meaningful, management must be in a position to control the mix of products it sells in the market. While alternative formulations are possible using gross margins, sales prices, or weighted-average contribution margins, the straightforward use of contributions will be used in the illustration that follows, so that the principle can be understood:

$$\begin{array}{l}\text{Sales}\\\text{mix}\\\text{variance}\end{array} = \left(\begin{array}{l}\text{Actual}\\\text{sales}\\\text{quantity}\end{array} - \begin{array}{l}\text{Actual sales}\\\text{quantity at}\\\text{anticipated}\\\text{sales mix}\end{array}\right) \times \begin{array}{l}\text{Budgeted}\\\text{contribution}\\\text{margin per unit}\end{array}$$

Deluxe: $\{[12,000 - 16,000^* \times (10/15)]\} \times (\$60 - \$24) = \$48,000$ F

Standard: $\{[4,000 - 16,000 \times\ \ (5/15)]\} \times\ \ (\$30 - \$15) = \underline{20,000\text{ U}}$

Total sales mix variance $\underline{\underline{\$28,000\text{ F}}}$

*16,000 units = (12,000 + 4,000), 10/15 is the anticipated proportion of Deluxe sales, and 5/15 is the anticipated Standard mix proportion.

$$\begin{array}{l}\text{Sales}\\\text{quantity} =\\\text{variance}\end{array} \left\{\begin{array}{l}\left[\begin{array}{l}\text{Actual sales}\\\text{quantity at}\\\text{anticipated}\\\text{sales mix}\end{array}\right] - \begin{array}{l}\text{Anticipated}\\\text{sales}\\\text{quantity}\end{array}\right\} \times \begin{array}{l}\text{Budgeted}\\\text{contribution}\\\text{margin per unit}\end{array}$$

Deluxe: $\{[16{,}000 \times (10/15)] - 10{,}000\} \times (\$60 - \$24) = \$24{,}000$ F

Standard: $\{[16{,}000 \times (5/15)] - 5{,}000\} \times (\$30 - \$15) = \underline{\$\ 5{,}000\ \text{F}}$

Total sales quantity variance $\underline{\underline{\$29{,}000\ \text{F}}}$

The total sales volume variance is $57,000 favourable, composed of the following:

Sales mix	$28,000 F
Sales quantity	29,000 F
Total	$57,000 F

The sales mix variance quantifies the effects on contribution margin of selling the two products in a mix that differs from the original budget. As shown in the analysis above, Ace Video had a budgeted mix of 66.7% Deluxe games (10,000/15,000) and 33.3% Standard games (5,000/15,000). However, the actual mix turned out to be 75% Deluxe games (12,000/16,000) and 25% Standard games (4,000/16,000). Selling a higher proportion of Deluxe games generates a favourable total sales mix variance because Deluxe has a contribution margin of $36 per unit compared to $15 per unit for Standard. The sales quantity variance isolates the effects on contribution margin of unit sales differing from the budget, holding constant the sales mix at the budgeted proportions. Because total sales quantity was 16,000 units compared to the budget of 15,000 units, the total quantity variance is favourable.[7]

SUMMARY

- Increases in sales value do not necessarily equate to increases in profitability if selling and administrative costs related to providing the product that customers demand are higher than expected. [LO10]

APPENDIX 10C REVIEW PROBLEM: SALES VARIANCE ANALYSIS

The Leo Company produces and sells two product lines with budgeted revenues and expenses as follows:

	Spars	Masts
Expected total industry sales	48,000 units	85,000 units
Expected Leo Company sales	4,200 units	17,000 units
Expected selling price	$200 per unit	$300 per unit
Expected cost of manufacturing (40% fixed)	110 per unit	180 per unit
Expected selling and administrative costs (70% fixed)	60 per unit	70 per unit
Expected product profit margin	$30 per unit	$50 per unit
Actual results for 2015 included:		
Actual total industry sales	60,000 units	100,000 units
Actual Leo Company sales	6,000 units	18,000 units
Actual selling price	$180 per unit	$300 per unit

All costs behaved exactly as expected.

W. Gallant, vice-president of marketing and sales, has requested that the employees of his department be paid a bonus for the year based on the fact that they have been able to increase sales by 2,800 units over budget level for the year, an increase of over 13%.

Required:
1. Calculate the changes in overall company profits caused by the following factors:
    a. Sales price.
    b. Sales mix.
    c. Sales quantity.
    d. Market share.
    e. Market volume.

Solution to Appendix 10C Review Problem

1.

Budgeted Contribution Margin:	Spars	Masts
Selling price	$200	$300
Variable costs:		
Manufacturing	66	108
Selling and administrative	18	21
Total variable costs	84	129
Budgeted contribution margin per unit	$ 116	$ 171

a. **Sales Price Variance:**

Spars ($180 — $200) × 6,000	$ 120,000 U
Masts ($300 — $300) × 18,000	–0–
Total	$ 120,000 U

b. **Sales Mix Variance:**

Spars [6,000 — (4,200 ÷ 21,200 × 24,000)] × $116	$ 144,453 F
Masts [18,000 — (17,000 ÷ 21,200 × 24,000)] × $171	212,943 U
Total	$ 68,490 U

c. **Sales Quantity Variance:**

Spars [(4,200 ÷ 21,200 × 24,000) — 4,200] × $116	$ 64,347 F
Masts [(17,000 ÷ 21,200 × 24,000) — 17,000] × $171	383,943 F
Total	$448,290 F

d. **Market Share Variance:**

Spars [6,000 — (4,200 ÷ 48,000 × 60,000)] × $116	$ 87,000 F
Masts [18,000 — (17,000 ÷ 85,000 × 100,000)] × $171	342,000 U
Total	$255,000 U

e. **Market Volume Variance:**

Spars [(60,000 — 48,000) × (4,200 ÷ 48,000)] × $116	$ 121,800 F
Masts [(100,000 — 85,000) × (17,000 ÷ 85,000)] × $171	513,000 F
Total	$634,800 F

APPENDIX 10C QUESTIONS, EXERCISES, AND PROBLEMS ![McGraw Hill Education] connect®

10C–1   What is the *market share variance*, and is it controllable by managers?
10C–2   What is the *sales mix variance*, and is it controllable by managers?

EXERCISE 10C–1 Variance Analysis [LO10]
Johnston Company (JC) sells two types of bicycles with details as follows for 2016:

	Mountain	Road
Plan		
Expected total industry unit sales	96,000	170,000
Budgeted JC unit sales	8,400	34,000
Budgeted selling price per unit	$ 1,200	$ 1,600
Budgeted variable costs per unit	$968	$ 1,258
Actuals		
Actual total industry unit sales	120,000	200,000
Actual JC unit sales	12,000	36,000
Actual selling price per unit	$1,240	$ 1,575
Actual variable cost per unit	$1,000	$ 1,275

Required:
1. Calculate the budgeted contribution margin for each model.
2. Calculate the following variances:
   a. Sales price.   d. Sales mix.
   b. Market volume.   e. Sales quantity.
   c. Market share.

PROBLEM 10C-2 Variance Analysis [LO10]
Rest Easy produces two types of mattresses: Regular and Heavenly. Budgeted and actual data for 2015 were as follows:

	Master Budget		Actual	
	Regular	Heavenly	Regular	Heavenly
Price per unit.........................	$300	$ 800	$ 325	$ 700
Variable costs per unit..............	$220	$ 590	$ 238	$ 583
Unit sales...........................	4,500	5,500	7,200	4,800

Market Data for 2016:
Expected total market unit sales of mattresses: Regular 300,000; Heavenly 200,000
Actual total market sales of beds: Regular 444,444; Heavenly 222,223

Required:
1. Calculate the following variances:
   a. Sales price.
   b. Market volume.
   c. Market share.
   d. Sales mix.
   e. Sales quantity.
2. During 2016, Big Sleep, one of Rest Easy's key competitors, introduced an aggressive new marketing campaign that included online advertising. Big Sleep also reduced prices on its mattress that competes directly with Rest Easy's Heavenly model. Management at Rest Easy decided to follow suit by reducing the price on the Heavenly model but decided against changing the marketing approach. Using any of the variances that you believe are relevant from (1) above, evaluate the decisions made by Rest Easy's managers regarding the Heavenly model.

■ APPENDIX 10D: PREDICTION OF LABOUR TIME—LEARNING CURVE

 Appendix available on Connect.

REPORTING FOR CONTROL

MANAGING PERFORMANCE: HOW WELL ARE WE DOING?

A survey of professional accountants in industry was conducted to find out how well Canadian companies are doing at managing their financial and operational performance. In light of the amount of attention given in the business press to the development and use of more sophisticated performance measurement systems, such as the balanced scorecard, some of the findings are surprising. For example, when asked to rate the overall performance of their organization (e.g., revenues, profits), almost one-third of respondents indicated that it is *below* target. Of those companies attempting to use more comprehensive performance measurement systems that incorporate both financial and non-financial metrics (e.g., number of customer complaints), half indicated they still use more financial than non-financial performance metrics. Even so, those using more non-financial metrics indicated that they were getting good value from them. Unlike results of previous similar surveys, 68% of respondents indicated that their balanced scorecard systems helped improve organizational performance. These results suggest that despite the growing popularity of comprehensive performance measurement approaches, such as the balanced scorecard (discussed in this chapter), many companies are struggling to put the pieces together.

In this chapter, we will examine the common financial and non-financial measures used by organizations today for management control. In addition, we will attempt to better understand how strategic goals can drive the choice of performance measures, allowing organizations to do a better job of measuring the "right" aspects of performance given their strategies.

Source: Robert Angel, "Follow the Leaders," *CA Magazine*, October 2010. Article printed with permission from *CA Magazine*, published by the Canadian Institute of Chartered Accountants, Toronto.

Through a combination of feedback from actual results, comparisons to budgets, comparisons to results of previous periods, and even comparisons to other organizations, managers attempt to ensure that the organization moves in the planned direction, using *performance assessment* or *control.*

Managers control the organization using a variety of approaches. Accounting reports of financial results represent one important approach to controlling operations because such reports provide a means of obtaining comparisons to budgets, to previous results, and to the results of other organizations, as well as providing knowledge of actual financial results. Such financial comparisons also serve as a base for reward schemes or contracts used to motivate managers to work toward planned goals and objectives.

These financial performance reports can be constructed in various ways so that they better serve the specific control functions that management desires. As this chapter illustrates, segment reporting, responsibility centre reporting, and investment performance are commonly used reporting structures that provide somewhat different types of information. Each presents information in a manner that permits a different view of the organization and a different aspect of organizational control. Understanding how the aspects change and why managers would want these changes will permit you to integrate the concepts of control with reports about standard cost variances, cost of production, and flexible budget analyses described in earlier chapters.

The modern manufacturing environment has promoted the need for flexibility in management to accompany flexibility in production. Flexibility in management requires timely and accurate decisions by members of the organization ranging from top management to the production worker. Accounting formats often represent approaches that are not well understood by production workers. Increasingly, companies are using non-financial indicators of performance, such as scrap levels, rework efforts, market share, employee morale, pollutant discharges, and customer satisfaction. The process of collecting and presenting these data on a real-time basis is assisted by computer systems. Properly configured enterprise resource planning systems enable the operational and financial data to be maintained consistently by using a common interactive database.

◼ DECENTRALIZATION IN ORGANIZATIONS

In a **decentralized organization**, decision making is spread throughout the organization, rather than being confined to a few top executives. All large organizations are decentralized to some extent, out of necessity. At one extreme, a strongly decentralized organization is one in which there are few, if any, constraints on the freedom of even the lowest-level managers and employees to make decisions. At the other extreme, in a strongly centralized organization, lower-level managers have little freedom to make decisions. Most organizations fall somewhere between these two extremes.

Decentralized organization
An organization in which decision making is spread throughout the organization rather than being confined to a few top executives.

Decentralization and Segment Reporting

Effective decentralization requires *segment reporting* to permit analysis and evaluation of the decisions made by the segment managers. In addition to the companywide income statement, reports are needed for individual segments of the organization. A *segment* is defined as a part or activity of an organization about which managers would like cost, revenue, or profit data. A company's operations can be segmented in many ways. For example, a grocery store chain like Loblaws or Sobeys can segment its business by geographic region, by individual store, by the nature of the merchandise (i.e., fresh foods, canned goods, paper goods), by brand name, and so on. As we will see, it is possible to classify segments according to managers' ability to control revenues, costs, and profits. Importantly, the tools used to evaluate segment managers' performance depend directly on what they have control over.

SEGMENT REPORTING

To operate effectively, managers and decision makers must have a great deal more information available to them than the information provided by a single company-wide income statement. Whether prepared on a variable costing or absorption basis, such statements usually provide only a summary of overall operations; as such, they typically do not contain enough detail to allow the manager or investor to detect problems that may exist in the organization. For example, some product lines may be profitable while others are unprofitable; some sales territories may have a poor sales mix, or salespeople may be overlooking sales opportunities. Managers may want to analyze the results at a more detailed level to see if some salespeople are more effective than others, or to see if some producing divisions are effectively or ineffectively using their capacity and/or resources. To uncover such problems the manager may need not one but several income statements that focus on the segments of a company. The preparation of income statements of this type is known as *segmented reporting*.

An operating segment for financial accounting purposes is a component of an enterprise

- That engages in business activities from which it may earn revenues and incur expenses.
- Whose operating results are regularly reviewed by the enterprise's chief operating officer to make decisions about resources to be allocated to the segment and assess its performance.
- For which discrete financial information is available.

Different Levels of Segmented Statements

Segmented statements can be prepared for different levels of activity in an organization and in different formats; Exhibit 11–1 illustrates three levels of segmented statements for Cassalatta Inc., presented in a widely used format. The contribution format income statement for the entire company appears at the very top of the exhibit under the column labelled Total Company. Immediately to the right of this column are two columns—one for each of the two divisions. We can see that the Business Products Division's segment margin is $60,000 and the Consumer Products Division's is $40,000. These segment margins show the company's divisional managers how much each of their divisions is contributing to the company's profits.

Segmented income statements can be prepared for activities at many levels in a company. The divisions are segmented according to their major product lines. In the case of the Consumer Products Division, the product lines are computer animation and computer games. Going even further, each of the product lines is segmented according to how it is sold—in retail stores or by online sales. Notice that as we go from one segmented statement to another, we are looking at smaller and smaller pieces of the company. While not shown in Exhibit 11–1, segmented income statements could also have been prepared for the major product lines in the Business Products Division.

The benefits accruing to the manager from a series of statements such as those contained in Exhibit 11–1 are substantial. By carefully examining trends and results in each segment, the manager can gain considerable insight into the company as a whole and perhaps discover opportunities and courses of action that would otherwise have remained hidden from view. Advanced computer-based information systems make it easier to construct such statements and to keep them continuously current.

One obvious question becomes evident from a careful review of Exhibit 11–1: Why break down results by divisions first, product lines next, and then sales territories? The order of breakdown depends on what information is desired. Certainly it might be advantageous to begin with each sales territory. Then it would be possible to examine product lines for each sales territory, and then divisions for each product line. This alternative would permit a product-line comparison between divisions.

EXHIBIT 11–1   Cassalatta Inc.—
Segmented Income Statements
in the Contribution Format

Segments Defined as Divisions

	Total Company	Division	
		Business Products Division	Consumer Products Division
Sales	$500,000	$300,000	$200,000
Variable expenses:			
Variable cost of goods sold	180,000	120,000	60,000
Other variable expenses	50,000	30,000	20,000
Total variable expenses	230,000	150,000	80,000
Contribution margin	270,000	150,000	120,000
Traceable fixed expenses	170,000	90,000	80,000*
Divisional segment margin	100,000	$ 60,000	$ 40,000
Common fixed expenses not			
traceable to individual divisions	85,000		
Operating income	$ 15,000		

Segments Defined as Product Lines of the Consumer Products Division

	Consumer Products Division	Product Line	
		Computer Animation	Computer Games
Sales	$200,000	$75,000	$125,000
Variable expenses:			
Variable cost of goods sold	60,000	20,000	40,000
Other variable expenses	20,000	5,000	15,000
Total variable expenses	80,000	25,000	55,000
Contribution margin	120,000	50,000	70,000
Traceable fixed expenses	70,000	30,000	40,000
Product-line segment margin	50,000	$20,000	$ 30,000
Common fixed expenses not			
traceable to individual product lines	10,000		
Divisional segment margin	$ 40,000		

**Segments Defined as Sales Territories for One Product
Line—Computer Games—of the Consumer Products Division**

	Computer Games	Sales Territory	
		Online Sales	Retail Stores
Sales	$125,000	$100,000	$25,000
Variable expenses:			
Variable cost of goods sold	40,000	32,000	8,000
Other variable expenses	15,000	5,000	10,000
Total variable expenses	55,000	37,000	18,000
Contribution margin	70,000	63,000	7,000
Traceable fixed expenses	25,000	15,000	10,000
Sales channel segment margin	45,000	$ 48,000	$(3,000)
Common fixed expenses not			
traceable to individual sales channels	15,000		
Product-line segment margin	$ 30,000		

*Notice that this $80,000 in traceable fixed expenses is divided into two parts when the Consumer Products Division is broken down into product lines—$70,000 traceable and $10,000 common. The reasons for this are discussed later in the section "Traceable Costs Can Become Common."

What management wants to learn and the types of comparisons desired are factors used for deciding the order of the breakdown. The order of the breakdown should not affect the numbers, but it can alter what appears on a given report and the ease of review.

Assigning Costs to Segments

Segmented statements for internal use are typically prepared in the contribution format, as described in Chapter 3. The same costing guidelines are used in preparing these statements as are used in preparing a contribution statement generally, with one exception. This lies in the handling of fixed costs. Notice from Exhibit 11–1 that the fixed costs are divided into two parts on a segmented statement—one part labelled *traceable* and the other part labelled *common*. Only those fixed costs labelled *traceable* are charged to the various segments. If a fixed cost is not traceable directly to some segment, then it is treated as a common cost and kept separate from the segments themselves. Thus, under the contribution approach, a cost is never arbitrarily assigned to a segment of an organization.

In summary, two guidelines are followed in assigning costs to the various segments of a company under the contribution approach:

1. First, according to cost behaviour patterns (i.e., variable and fixed).
2. Second, according to whether the costs are directly traceable to the segments involved.

We now consider various aspects of Exhibit 11–1 in more depth.

Sales and Contribution Margin

To prepare segmented statements for management purposes, it is necessary to keep records of sales by individual segment, as well as in total for the organization. After deducting related variable expenses, a contribution margin (CM) figure can be computed for each segment, as illustrated in Exhibit 11–1.

Recall from our discussion of variable costing that the CM is an extremely useful piece of data for the manager—particularly for determining the effect on net income of increases or decreases in sales volume. If sales volume goes up or down, the effect on operating income can easily be computed by simply multiplying the unit CM by the change in units sold or by multiplying the change in sales dollars by the CM ratio. One assumption implicit here is that selling prices and variable costs do not change with changes in volume. Segmented statements give the manager the ability to make such computations on a product-by-product, division-by-division, or territory-by-territory basis, thereby providing the information needed to highlight areas of weakness or to capitalize on areas of strength.

The CM is basically a short-run planning tool. As such, it is especially valuable in decisions relating to temporary uses of capacity, to special orders, or to short-run product-line promotion. Decisions relative to the short run usually involve only variable costs and revenues, which of course are the very elements involved in CM. By carefully monitoring segment CM and segment CM ratios, the manager is in a position to make those short-run decisions that maximize each segment's contribution to the overall profitability of the organization. Such decisions will be discussed in detail in Chapter 12.

The Importance of Fixed Costs

The emphasis we place on the usefulness of the CM should not be taken as a suggestion that fixed costs are not important. Fixed costs are very important in any organization. What the contribution approach does imply is that *different costs are needed for different purposes*. For one purpose, variable costs and revenues alone may be adequate for a manager's needs; for another purpose, the manager's needs may encompass the fixed costs as well.

The breaking apart of fixed and variable costs also emphasizes to management that the costs are controlled differently and that these differences must be kept clearly in mind for both short-run and long-run planning. Moreover, the grouping of fixed costs under the contribution approach highlights the fact that, after the fixed costs have been covered, operating income increases to the extent of the CM generated on each additional unit sold. All of these concepts are useful to the manager *internally* for planning purposes.

Traceable and Common Fixed Costs

Traceable fixed costs can be defined as those fixed costs that can be identified with a particular segment and that arise because of the existence of the segment—if the segment had never existed, the fixed cost would not have been incurred, and/or if the segment were eliminated, the fixed cost would disappear. Only the traceable fixed costs are charged to particular segments. If a cost is not traceable to a segment, then it is not assigned to the segment. For example, the maintenance cost for the building in which a Challenger jet is assembled is a *traceable* fixed cost of the Challenger business segment of Bombardier Ltd.

A **common fixed cost** is a fixed cost that supports the operations of more than one segment but is not traceable in whole or in part to any one segment. Even if the segment were entirely eliminated, there would be no change in a true common fixed cost. Note the following:

- The salary of the Frito-Lay product manager at PepsiCo is a *traceable* fixed cost of the Frito-Lay business segment of PepsiCo.
- The salary of the CEO of General Motors Canada is a *common* fixed cost of the various divisions of General Motors Canada.
- The cost of the automatic bar-coding machine at Cassalatta is a *common* fixed cost of the Consumer Products Division and the Business Products Division.
- The cost of the receptionist's salary at an office shared by a number of doctors is a *common* fixed cost of the doctors. The cost is traceable to the office, but not to any one of the doctors individually.

Common fixed costs are not allocated to segments—the total amount is deducted to arrive at the income for the company as a whole (see Exhibit 11-1). The management accountant may contend that nothing is added to the overall usefulness of a segmented statement by allocating the common costs among segments. The accountant would argue that such allocations tend to reduce the usefulness of segmented statements. The reason is that arbitrary allocations draw attention away from those costs that are traceable to a segment and that should form a basis for appraising performance.

It is argued that any attempt to allocate common fixed costs among segments may result in misleading data or may obscure important relationships between segment revenues and segment earnings. Arbitrary allocation of common fixed costs often results in a segment appearing to be unprofitable, whereas it may be contributing substantially above its own traceable costs toward the overall profitability of a firm. In such cases, the allocated costs may lead to the unwise elimination of a segment and to a decrease in profits for the company as a whole because common costs do not disappear if the segment is closed down.

A word of caution is necessary here. Management reaction to common costs may help control the growth of such costs. Managers may use common cost allocation as a form of cost price or as a signal about the benefits received from headquarters and thus modify their actions for the common good of the organization. Empirical investigations suggest firms often allocate common costs to segments for a number of reasons. Rigorous analysis of the treatment of uncontrollable costs and

Traceable fixed costs
Fixed costs that can be identified with a particular segment and that arise because of the existence of the segment.

Common fixed cost
A fixed cost that supports the operations of more than one segment but is not traceable in whole or in part to any one segment.

allocated common costs suggests there may be some benefit to charging managers with uncontrollable costs or allocating common costs to segments. Managerial behaviour is complex, and investigation of it often finds results that were previously thought to be fallacious but may not be so.

Identifying Traceable Fixed Costs

The distinction between traceable and common fixed costs is crucial in segmented reporting, because traceable fixed costs are charged to the segments, but common fixed costs are not. In an actual situation, it is sometimes hard to determine whether a cost should be classified as traceable or common.

The general guideline is to treat as traceable costs *only those costs that would disappear over time if the segment itself disappeared.* For example, if the Consumer Products Division in Exhibit 11–1 were sold or discontinued, it would no longer be necessary to pay the division manager's salary. Therefore, the division manager's salary should be classified as a traceable fixed cost of the Consumer Products Division. On the other hand, the president of the company undoubtedly would continue to be paid even if the Consumer Products Division were dropped. In fact, he or she might even be paid more if dropping the division was a good idea. Therefore, the president's salary is common to both divisions and should not be charged to either division.

There will always be some costs that fall between the traceable and common categories, and considerable care and good judgment are required for their proper classification. The important point is to resist the temptation to allocate costs (such as depreciation of corporate facilities) that are clearly common and that will continue regardless of whether the segment exists or not. *Any allocation of common costs to segments reduces the value of the segment margin as a guide to long-run segment profitability and segment performance.*

Breakdown of Traceable Fixed Costs

In preparing segmented income statements, some managers like to separate the traceable fixed costs into two classes—discretionary and committed. As discussed in Chapter 3, discretionary fixed costs are under the immediate control of the manager, whereas committed fixed costs are not. Therefore, a breakdown of the traceable fixed costs into these two classes allows a company to distinguish between the performance of the segment manager and the performance of the segment as a long-term investment.

In some situations, this distinction in performance can be very important. A top-flight manager, for example, may be assigned to a division that has an antiquated plant or that is saddled with other committed fixed costs that are beyond the segment manager's control. Under these conditions, it is unfair to judge the segment manager's performance simply on the basis of overall margin generated by the segment. Rather, in these circumstances, the discretionary fixed costs should be separated from the committed fixed costs and deducted as a separate group from the segment's CM. The amount remaining after deducting the discretionary fixed costs, sometimes called a *segment performance margin*, should then be used as a basis for evaluating the segment manager's performance. This would be a valid measure of performance, as the amount involved would represent the margin generated by the segment after deducting all costs controllable by the segment manager. The committed fixed costs of a segment can be broken down in still other ways. However, the preceding discussion is adequate for our purposes.

Activity-Based Costing   Some costs are easy to identify as traceable costs. For example, the costs of advertising Procter & Gamble's Crest toothpaste on television are clearly traceable to Crest. A more difficult situation arises when a building, machine, or other resource is shared by two or more segments. For example, assume that a multi-product company leases warehouse space that is used for storing the full range of its products. Would the lease cost of the warehouse be a traceable or a common cost of the products? Managers familiar with activity-based costing (ABC) might argue that the lease is traceable and should be assigned to the products according to how much space the products use in the warehouse. In like manner, these managers would argue that order-processing costs, sales support costs, and other selling and administrative expenses should also be charged to segments according to the segments' consumption of selling and administrative resources.

To illustrate, consider the Holt Corporation, a company that manufactures concrete pipe for industrial uses. The company has three products—9-inch pipe, 12-inch pipe, and 18-inch pipe. Space is leased in a large warehouse on a yearly basis as needed. The lease cost of this space is $10 per square metre per year. The 9-inch pipe occupies 400 square metres of space, the 12-inch pipe occupies 1,600 square metres, and the 18-inch pipe occupies 2,000 square metres. The company also has an order-processing department that incurred $150,000 in order-processing costs last year. Management believes that order-processing costs are driven by the number of orders placed by customers in a year. Last year, 2,500 orders were placed, of which 1,200 were for 9-inch pipe, 800 were for 12-inch pipe, and 500 were for 18-inch pipe. Given these data, the following costs would be assigned to each product using the ABC approach:

Warehouse space cost:	
9-inch pipe: $10 × 400 square metres...	$ 4,000
12-inch pipe: $10 × 1,600 square metres.....................................	16,000
18-inch pipe: $10 × 2,000 square metres.....................................	20,000
Total cost assigned	$ 40,000
Order-processing costs:	
$150,000 ÷ 2,500 orders = $60 per order	
9-inch pipe: $60 × 1,200 orders...	$ 72,000
12-inch pipe: $60 × 800 orders..	48,000
18-inch pipe: $60 × 500 orders..	30,000
Total cost assigned	$150,000

This method of assigning costs combines the strength of ABC with the power of the contribution approach and greatly enhances the manager's ability to measure the profitability and performance of segments. However, managers must still ask themselves if the costs would in fact disappear over time if the segment itself disappeared. In the case of Holt Corporation, it is clear that the $20,000 in warehousing costs for 18-inch pipe would be eliminated if 18-inch pipe were no longer being produced. The company would simply rent less warehouse space the following year. However, suppose the company owns the warehouse. Then it is not so clear that the $20,000 of the cost of the warehouse would really disappear if 18-inch pipe were discontinued as a product. That part of the company warehouse might simply be empty while the costs of the warehouse continue to be incurred.

Traceable Costs Can Become Common

Fixed costs that are traceable to one segment may be common costs of another segment. This is because there are limits to how finely a cost can be separated without resorting to arbitrary allocation. The more finely segments are defined, the more costs they have in common.

This concept can be seen in Exhibit 11–2. Notice that when segments are defined as divisions, the Consumer Products Division has $80,000 in traceable fixed expenses. Only $70,000 of this amount remains traceable, however, when we narrow our definition to that of the product lines. Notice that the other $10,000 then becomes a common cost of these product lines of the Consumer Products Division.

EXHIBIT 11-2 Reclassification of Traceable Fixed Expenses from Exhibit 11-1

	Total Company	Segment	
		Business Products Division	Consumer Products Division
Contribution margin	$270,000	$150,000	$120,000
Traceable fixed expenses.............	170,000	90,000	80,000

	Consumer Products Division	Segment	
		Computer Animation	Computer Games
Contribution margin	$120,000	$50,000	$70,000
Traceable fixed expenses.............	70,000	30,000	40,000
Product-line segment margin	50,000	$20,000	$30,000
Common fixed expenses	10,000		
Divisional segment margin............	$ 40,000		

Why would $10,000 of traceable fixed cost become a common cost when the division is divided into product lines? The $10,000 is the monthly salary of the manager of the Consumer Products Division. This salary is a traceable cost of the division as a whole but is a common cost of the division's product lines. The manager's salary is a necessary cost of having the two product lines, but even if one of the product lines were discontinued entirely, the manager's salary would probably not be cut. Therefore, none of the manager's salary can really be traced to the individual products.

The $70,000 traceable fixed cost of the product lines consists of the cost of product-specific advertising. A total of $30,000 was spent on advertising animation software and $40,000 was spent on advertising computer games. These costs can clearly be traced to the individual product lines.

Segment Margin

Segment margin
A margin obtained by deducting a segment's traceable fixed costs from the segment's contribution margin.

Observe from Exhibit 11-1 that the **segment margin** is obtained by deducting a segment's traceable fixed costs from the segment's CM. It represents the margin available after a segment has covered all of its own costs. The segment margin is the best gauge of the long-run profitability of a segment, because it includes only those costs that are caused by the segment. The term *long-run* is applied here because fixed costs could be altered if the segment were eliminated. If a segment cannot cover its own costs, that segment should probably be dropped (unless it is essential to sales of other segments). Notice from Exhibit 11-1, for example, that the Retail Stores sales channel has a negative segment margin. This means that the segment is not generating enough revenue to cover its own costs. In fact, it is detracting from profits in that its $3,000 loss must be covered by other segments. Retention or elimination of product lines and other segments is covered in more depth in Chapter 12.

From a decision-making point of view, the segment margin is most useful in major decisions that affect capacity, such as dropping a segment. By contrast, as noted earlier, the CM is most useful in decisions relating to short-run changes, such as pricing of special orders that involve temporary use of existing capacity.

Segment Reporting for Financial Accounting

Differences in segment profits reports for internal management decision making and those required for external reporting are minimized given *International Financial Reporting Standard (IFRS) 8—Operating Segments*. This standard requires that segmented reports prepared for external users use the same methods and definitions used for internal segmented reports that are prepared to aid in making operating decisions. This is a very unusual requirement. Companies are not ordinarily required to report the same data to external users that are reported internally for decision-making purposes. This requirement has some serious drawbacks. First, segmented data are often highly sensitive, so companies are reluctant to release such data to the public for the simple reason that their competitors will then have access to the data. Second, segmented statements prepared in accordance with GAAP do not distinguish between fixed and variable costs and between traceable and common costs. Indeed, the segmented income statements illustrated earlier in this chapter do not conform to GAAP for that reason. To avoid the complications of reconciling non-GAAP segment earnings with GAAP consolidated earnings, it is likely that at least some managers will choose to construct their segmented financial statements to conform to GAAP. This will result in more occurrences of the problems discussed in the following section.

Hindrances to Proper Cost Assignment

Costs must be properly assigned to segments. All of the costs attributable to a segment— and only those costs—should be assigned to the segment. Unfortunately, companies often make mistakes when assigning costs to segments. They omit some costs, inappropriately assign traceable fixed costs, and arbitrarily allocate common fixed costs.

Omission of Costs   The costs assigned to a segment should include all costs attributable to that segment from the company's entire value chain, as discussed in Chapter 1. All of these functions, from research and development through product design, manufacturing, marketing, distribution, and customer service, are required to bring a product or service to the customer and generate revenues.

However, as discussed in Chapters 2, 5, and 8, only manufacturing costs are included in product costs under absorption costing, which is widely regarded as required for financial reporting. To avoid having to maintain two costing systems and to provide consistency between internal and external reports, many companies also use absorption costing for their internal reports, such as segmented income statements. As a result, such companies omit from their profitability analysis part or all of the *upstream* costs in the value chain, which consist of research and development and product design, and the *downstream* costs, which consist of marketing, distribution, and customer service. Yet these non-manufacturing costs are just as essential as manufacturing costs in determining product profitability. These upstream and downstream costs, which are usually included in selling and administrative expenses on the income statement, can represent half or more of the total costs of an organization. If either the upstream or downstream costs are omitted in profitability analysis, then the product is undercosted and management may unwittingly develop and maintain products that result in losses in the long run.

Inappropriate Methods for Assigning Traceable Costs among Segments   In addition to omitting costs, many companies do not correctly handle traceable fixed expenses on segmented income statements. First, they may not trace fixed expenses to segments even when it is feasible to do so. Second, they may use inappropriate allocation bases to allocate traceable fixed expenses to segments.

Failure to Trace Costs Directly   Costs that can be traced directly to a specific company segment should be charged directly to that segment. Failure to trace these costs directly results in these costs being placed in a companywide overhead pool. While a portion of these costs would then be allocated to the segment generating the costs, the rest would be incorrectly allocated to other segments. For example, the rent for a branch office of an insurance company should be charged directly against the branch to which it relates rather than included in a companywide overhead pool and then spread throughout the company.

Inappropriate Allocation Base   Some companies allocate costs to segments using arbitrary bases such as sales dollars or cost of goods sold. For example, under the sales dollars approach, costs are allocated to the various segments according to the percentage of company sales generated by each segment. Thus, if a segment generates 20% of the company's sales, it is allocated 20% of the company's selling and administrative expenses as its "fair share." This same basic procedure is followed if costs of goods sold or some other measure is used as the allocation base.

Costs should be allocated to segments for internal decision-making purposes only when the allocation base actually drives the cost being allocated (or is very highly correlated with the real cost driver). For example, sales should be used to allocate selling and administrative expenses only if a 10% increase in sales will result in a 10% increase in selling and administrative expenses. To the extent that selling and administrative expenses are not driven by sales volume, these expenses will be improperly allocated—with a disproportionately high percentage of the selling and administrative expenses assigned to the segments with the largest sales.

Arbitrarily Dividing Common Costs among Segments   Another business practice that leads to distorted segment costs is the practice of assigning non-traceable costs to segments. For example, some companies allocate the costs of the corporate headquarters building to products on segment reports. However, in a multi-product company, no single product is likely to be responsible for any significant amount of this cost. Even if a product were eliminated entirely, there would usually be no significant effect on any of the costs of the corporate headquarters building. In short, there is no cause-and-effect relationship between the cost of the corporate headquarters building and the existence of any one product. As a consequence, any allocation of the costs of the corporate headquarters building to the products must be arbitrary.

Common costs like the costs of the corporate headquarters building are necessary, of course, to have a functioning organization. The common practice of arbitrarily allocating these costs to segments is often justified on the grounds that "someone" has to "cover the common costs." While it is undeniably true that the common costs must be covered, arbitrarily allocating common costs to segments does not ensure that this will happen. In fact, adding a share of common costs to the real costs of a segment may make an otherwise profitable segment appear to be unprofitable. If a manager eliminates the apparently unprofitable segment, the real traceable costs of the segment will be saved, but its revenues will be lost. What happens to the common fixed costs that were allocated to the segment? They don't disappear; they are reallocated to the remaining segments of the company. That makes all of the remaining segments appear to be less profitable—possibly resulting in dropping other segments. The net effect will be to reduce the profits of the company as a whole and make it even more difficult to cover the common costs.

Additionally, common fixed costs are not manageable by the manager to whom they are arbitrarily allocated; they are the responsibility of higher-level managers. Allocating common fixed costs to responsibility centres is counterproductive in a responsibility accounting system. When common fixed costs are allocated to managers, they are held responsible for those costs even though they cannot control them.

In summary, the way many companies handle segment reporting results in cost distortion. This distortion results from three practices—the failure to trace costs directly to a specific segment when it is feasible to do so, the use of inappropriate bases for allocating costs, and the allocation of common costs to segments. The examples of segment reporting provided in Exhibits 11–1 and 11–2 avoid many of the problems encountered by companies that do not use variable costing. Variable costing permits a clearer allocation of costs to segments because it avoids the distortions created by the allocation of fixed manufacturing overhead that would be present with the use of absorption costing. Thus, our suggestions are to use variable costing for segment reports and allocate fixed manufacturing overhead as a period expense based on the criterion of traceability; that is, *fixed costs will disappear over time if the segment itself disappears.*

RESPONSIBILITY CENTRES

A **responsibility centre** is broadly defined as any part of an organization whose manager has control over and is accountable for cost, profit, or investments. The three primary types of responsibility centres are cost centres, profit centres, and investment centres.[1] As discussed below, organizations categorize responsibility centres into one of these three types based on the manager's authority to control cost, revenue, and investment funds.

Cost Centre   A **cost centre** is a business segment whose manager has control over costs but not over revenue or investment funds. Service departments, such as accounting, finance, selling and administrative, legal, and personnel, are usually considered to be cost centres. In addition, manufacturing facilities are often considered to be cost centres. The managers of cost centres are expected to minimize cost while providing the level of services or the amount of product demanded by the other parts of the organization. For example, the manager of a production facility would be evaluated at least in part by comparing actual costs to how much the costs should have been for the actual number of units produced during the period. Flexible budget variances and standard cost variances, discussed in Chapters 9 and 10, are often used to evaluate cost centre performance. However, managers should not be held accountable for controlling common costs arbitrarily allocated to their segment.

Profit Centre   In contrast to a cost centre, a **profit centre** is any business segment whose manager has control over both cost and revenue. Like a cost centre, however, a profit centre manager generally does not have control over investment funds. For example, the manager in charge of one of six resorts would be responsible for both the revenues and costs, and hence the profits, of the resort but might not have control over major investments in the resort. Profit centre managers are often evaluated by comparing actual profit to targeted or budgeted profit.

Investment Centre   An **investment centre** is any segment of an organization whose manager has control over cost, revenue, and investments in operating assets. For example, the president of General Motors Canada, a division of the General Motors Company, would have a great deal of discretion over investments in the division. The president of the division would be responsible for initiating investment proposals, such as funding research into more fuel-efficient engines for sport-utility vehicles. Once the proposal has been approved by General Motors Company's top-level executives and the board of directors, the president of General Motors Canada would then be responsible for making sure that the investment pays off. Investment centre managers are usually evaluated using return on investment or residual income measures, as discussed later in the chapter.

A partial organization chart for Universal Foods Corporation, a company in the snack food and beverage industry, appears in Exhibit 11–3. This partial organization chart indicates how the various business segments of the company are classified in terms of responsibility. Note that the cost centres are the departments and work centres that do not generate significant revenues by themselves. These are staff departments such as Finance, Legal, and Personnel, and operating units such as the bottling plant, warehouse, and beverage distribution centre. The profit centres are business segments that generate revenues and costs and include the Beverage, Salty Snacks, and Confections product segments. The vice-president of Operations oversees allocation of investment funds across the product segments and is also responsible for revenues and costs; therefore, Operations is treated as an investment centre. And, finally, corporate headquarters is an investment centre, since it is responsible for all revenues, costs, and investments.

LEARNING OBJECTIVE **2**
Differentiate among responsibility centres, such as cost centres, profit centres, and investment centres, and explain how performance is measured in each.

Responsibility centre
Any business segment whose manager has control over cost or profit or the use of investment funds.

Cost centre
A business segment whose manager has control over cost but has no control over revenue or the use of investment funds.

Profit centre
A business segment whose manager has control over cost and revenue but has no control over the use of investment funds.

Investment centre
A business segment whose manager has control over cost and revenue and also has control over the use of investment funds.

EXHIBIT 11-3   Business Segments Classified as Cost, Profit, and Investment Centres

EVALUATING INVESTMENT CENTRE PERFORMANCE—RETURN ON INVESTMENT

LEARNING OBJECTIVE **3**
Analyze the return on investment.

So far in this chapter we have focused on how to assign costs properly to responsibility centres. This is an important issue when evaluating cost and profit centres. However, evaluating an investment centre's performance requires more than accurate cost and segment margin reporting. In addition, an investment centre is responsible for earning an adequate return on investment. The next two sections of this chapter present two methods for evaluating this aspect of an investment centre's performance. The first method is called *return on investment (ROI)*. The second method is called *residual income*.

The Return on Investment Formula

Return on investment (ROI)
Operating income divided by average operating assets. ROI also equals margin multiplied by turnover.

The **return on investment (ROI)** is defined as operating income divided by average operating assets:

$$\text{Return on Investment} = \frac{\text{Operating income}}{\text{Average operating assets}}$$

The higher the ROI of a business segment, the greater the profit generated per dollar invested in the segment's operating assets.

Operating income
Income before interest and income taxes have been deducted.

Operating Income and Operating Assets Defined

Note that *operating income*, rather than net income, is used in the ROI formula. **Operating income** is income before interest and taxes and is sometimes referred to as *EBIT* (earnings before interest and taxes). The reason for using operating income in the formula is that the income figure used should be consistent with the base to which it is applied. Notice that the base (i.e., denominator) consists of *operating assets*. Thus, to be consistent we use operating income in the numerator because no debt is included in the denominator, and interest expense is paid for by the profits from the operating assets and thus is a distribution of those profits rather than an expense.

Operating assets include cash, accounts receivable, inventory, plant and equipment, and all other assets held for productive use in the organization and/ or the investment centre. Examples of assets that would not be included in the operating assets category (i.e., examples of non-operating assets) are land held for future use, an investment in another company, or a factory building rented to someone else. The operating assets base used in the formula is typically computed as the average of the operating assets between the beginning and the end of the year.

Operating assets
Cash, accounts receivable, inventory, plant and equipment, and all other assets held for productive use in an organization.

A major issue in ROI computations is the dollar amount of plant and equipment that should be included in the operating assets base. To illustrate the problem involved, assume that a company reports the following amounts for plant and equipment on its balance sheet:

Plant and equipment....................................	$3,000,000
Less accumulated depreciation........................	900,000
Net book value.......................................	$ 2,100,000

What dollar amount of plant and equipment should the company include with its operating assets in computing ROI? One widely used approach is to include only the plant and equipment's *net book value*—that is, the plant and equipment's original cost less accumulated depreciation ($2,100,000 in the example above). A second approach is to ignore depreciation and include the plant and equipment's entire *gross cost* in the operating assets base ($3,000,000 in the example above). Both of these approaches are used in actual practice, even though they will obviously yield very different operating asset, operating income, and ROI figures.

The following arguments can be raised for using net book value to measure operating assets and for using gross cost to measure operating assets in ROI computation.

Arguments for using net book value to measure operating assets in return on investment computations:
1. The net book value method is consistent with how plant and equipment are reported on the balance sheet (i.e., cost less accumulated depreciation to date).
2. The net book value method is consistent with the computation of operating income, which includes depreciation as an operating expense.

Arguments for using gross cost to measure operating assets in return on investment computations:
1. The gross cost method eliminates both the age of equipment and the method of depreciation as factors in ROI computations. (Under the net book value method, ROI tends to increase over time as net book value declines due to depreciation.)
2. The gross cost method does not discourage replacement of old, worn-out equipment. (Under the net book value method, replacing fully depreciated equipment with new equipment can have a dramatic adverse effect on ROI.)

Managers generally view consistency as the most important of the considerations above. As a result, a majority of companies use the net book value approach in ROI computations. In this text, we will also use the net book value approach unless a specific exercise or problem directs otherwise.

Understanding Return on Investment

The equation for ROI, operating income divided by average operating assets, does not provide much help to managers interested in taking action to improve their ROI. It offers only two levers for improving performance—operating income and average operating assets. Fortunately, ROI can also be expressed as follows:

$$\text{Return on Investment} = \text{Margin} \times \text{Turnover}$$

where

$$\text{Margin} = \frac{\text{Operating income}}{\text{Sales}}$$

and

$$\text{Turnover} = \frac{\text{Sales}}{\text{Average operating assets}}$$

Margin
Operating income divided by sales.

Turnover
The amount of sales generated in an investment centre for each dollar invested in operating assets. Sales divided by average operating assets.

The **margin** is a measure of management's ability to control operating expenses in relation to sales. The lower operating expenses are per dollar of sales, the higher the margin earned. **Turnover** is a measure of the sales that are generated for each dollar invested in operating assets. Note that the sales terms in the margin and turnover formulas cancel out when they are multiplied together, yielding the original formula for ROI stated in terms of operating income and average operating assets. So either formula for ROI will give the same answer. However, the margin and turnover formulation provides some additional insights.

From a manager's perspective, margin and turnover are very important concepts. Margin is ordinarily improved by increasing sales or reducing operating expenses, including cost of goods sold and selling and administrative expenses. Some managers tend to focus too much on margin and ignore turnover. However, turnover incorporates a crucial area of a manager's responsibility—the investment in operating assets. Excessive funds tied up in operating assets (e.g., cash, accounts receivable, inventories, plant and equipment, and other assets) depress turnover and lower ROI. In fact, inefficient use of operating assets can be just as much of a drag on profitability as excessive operating expenses, which depress margin.

Instant Quiz 11-2

Tamarind Services Company, a division of a major oil company, provides various services to the operators of an oil field in northern Alberta. Data concerning the most recent year are as follows:

Sales..	$ 12,000,000
Operating income	3,600,000
Average operating assets	24,000,000

Compute the margin, turnover, and ROI for Tamarind Services Company.

E.I. du Pont de Nemours and Company (better known as DuPont) pioneered the use of ROI and recognized the importance of looking at both margin and turnover in assessing a manager's performance. ROI is now widely used as the key measure of investment centre performance. ROI reflects in a single figure many aspects of the manager's responsibilities. It can be compared to the returns of other investment centres in the organization, the returns of other companies in the industry, and the past returns of the investment centre itself.

DuPont also developed the diagram that appears in the Learning Aid below. This diagram helps managers understand how they can improve ROI. Any increase in ROI must involve at least one of the following:

1. Increased sales.
2. Reduced operating expenses.
3. Reduced operating assets.

Many actions involve combinations of changes in sales, expenses, and operating assets. For example, a manager may make an investment in (i.e., increase) operating assets to reduce operating expenses or increase sales. Whether the net effect is favourable or not is judged in terms of its overall impact on ROI.

To illustrate how ROI is affected by various actions, we will use the Monthaven outlet of the Burger Grill chain as an example. Burger Grill is a small chain of upscale casual restaurants that has been rapidly adding outlets via franchising. The Monthaven franchise is owned by a group of local surgeons who have little time to devote to management and little expertise in business matters. Therefore, they delegate operating decisions—including decisions concerning investments in operating assets such as inventories—to a professional manager they have hired. The manager is evaluated largely based on the ROI the franchise generates.

The following data represent the results of operations for the most recent month:

Sales	$100,000
Operating expenses	90,000
Operating income	10,000
Average operating assets	50,000

LEARNING AID

ELEMENTS OF RETURN ON INVESTMENT

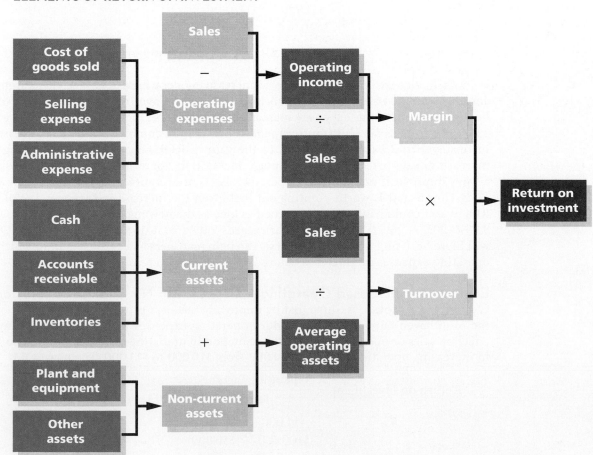

The ROI for the month is computed as follows:

$$\text{Return on Investment} = \frac{\text{Operating income}}{\text{Sales}} \times \frac{\text{Sales}}{\text{Average operating assets}}$$

$$= \frac{\$10,000}{\$100,000} \times \frac{\$100,000}{\$50,000}$$

$$= 10\% \times 2 = 20\%$$

Example 1: Increased Sales without Any Increase in Operating Assets

Assume that the manager of the Monthaven Burger Grill can increase sales by 10% without any increase in operating assets. The increase in sales will require additional operating expenses. However, operating expenses include some fixed expenses, which would probably not be affected by a 10% increase in sales. Therefore, the increase in operating expenses would probably be less than 10%; let's assume the increase is 7.8%. Under these assumptions, the new operating income would be $12,980, an increase of 29.8%, determined as follows:

Sales (1.10 × $100,000).................................	$110,000
Operating expenses (1.078 × $90,000)	97,020
Operating income......................................	$ 12,980

In this case, the new ROI would be

$$\text{Return on Investment} = \frac{\text{Operating income}}{\text{Sales}} \times \frac{\text{Sales}}{\text{Average operating assets}}$$

$$= \frac{\$12,980}{\$110,000} \times \frac{\$110,000}{\$50,000}$$

$$= 11.8\% \times 2.2 = 25.96\% \text{ (as compared to 20\% originally)}$$

When sales are increased *without* an increase in operating assets, both the margin and turnover are likely to be affected. In the example above, because sales increased by 10% and operating expenses increased by only 7.8%, the margin increased to 11.8% (up from 10%). This improvement in the margin, combined with the increase in turnover to 2.2 (up from 2), led to the gain in ROI. Clearly, if the percentage increase in sales exceeds the percentage increase in operating expenses, ROI will always improve, if no additional operating assets are required to generate the new sales. However, it is worth pointing out that given the increase in turnover, the old ROI of 20% could have been maintained as long as the new margin did not fall below 9.09% (20% ÷ 2.2). If the new margin exceeds 9.09%, as it does in the example, ROI will increase. Using this type of analysis can help managers assess the extent to which operating expenses can increase before ROI begins to decrease.

Example 2: Decreased Operating Expenses with No Change in Sales or Operating Assets

Assume that by improving business processes, the manager of the Monthaven Burger Grill can reduce operating expenses by $1,000 without any effect on sales or operating assets. This reduction in operating expenses would result in increasing operating income by $1,000, from $10,000 to $11,000. The new ROI is

$$\text{Return on Investment} = \frac{\text{Operating income}}{\text{Sales}} \times \frac{\text{Sales}}{\text{Average operating assets}}$$

$$= \frac{\$11,000}{\$100,000} \times \frac{\$100,000}{\$50,000}$$

$$= 11\% \times 2 = 22\% \text{ (as compared to 20\% originally)}$$

IN BUSINESS

In October 2013, Sears Canada announced the closure of their flagship Eaton Centre store in downtown Toronto, three other stores in Southwestern Ontario, and one in Richmond, British Columbia. Although each of these stores was in a top-performing shopping centre, the company accepted $400 million in exchange for the leases for these store locations. Sears Canada planned to reinvest these funds in a state-of-the-art distribution centre in Calgary to better serve e-commerce customers in western Canada and in continuing to improve existing stores across the country. According to Doug Campbell, CEO, the management team continuously looks at "... balancing the needs of the business in terms of capital investment and the need to build value for shareholders. Whenever we have an opportunity to produce higher return on investment, we've done that."

Source: Francine Kopun, "Sears Canada to close Toronto Eaton Centre store, four others; will Nordstrom move in?" *Toronto Star*, October 29, 2013.

When margins or profits are being squeezed, the first line of attack is often to cut costs. Discretionary fixed costs are particularly vulnerable to cuts. However, managers must be careful not to cut too much or in the wrong place. Inappropriate cost cutting can lead to decreased sales, increased costs elsewhere, and a drop in morale.

Example 3: Invest in Operating Assets to Increase Sales   Assume that the manager of the Monthaven Burger Grill invests $2,000 in a state-of-the-art soft-serve ice cream machine that can dispense a number of different flavours. This new machine will boost sales by $4,000 but will require additional operating expenses of $1,000. Thus, operating income will increase by $3,000, to $13,000. The new ROI is

$$\text{Return on Investment} = \frac{\text{Operating income}}{\text{Sales}} \times \frac{\text{Sales}}{\text{Average operating assets}}$$

$$= \frac{\$13,000}{\$104,000} \times \frac{\$104,000}{\$52,000}$$

$$= 12.5\% \times 2 = 25\% \text{ (as compared to 20\% originally)}$$

In this example, the investment had no effect on turnover, which remained at 2, so there had to be an increase in margin in order to improve the ROI.

Criticisms of Return on Investment

Although ROI is widely used in evaluating performance, it is not a perfect tool. The method is subject to the following criticisms:

1. Just telling managers to increase ROI may not be enough. Managers may not know how to increase ROI; they may increase ROI in a way that is inconsistent with the company's strategy; or they may take actions that increase ROI in the short run but harm the company in the long run (such as cutting back on research and development).
2. A manager who takes over a business segment typically inherits many committed costs over which the manager has no control. These committed costs may be relevant in assessing the performance of the business segment as an investment but make it difficult to fairly assess the performance of the manager relative to other managers.
3. As discussed in the next section, a manager who is evaluated based on ROI may reject profitable investment opportunities.

RESIDUAL INCOME

LEARNING OBJECTIVE ❹

Compute residual income, and describe the strengths and weaknesses of this method of measuring performance.

Residual income
The operating income that an investment centre earns above the required return on its operating assets.

Economic value added (EVA®)
A concept similar to residual income.

Another approach to measuring an investment centre's performance focuses on a concept known as *residual income*. **Residual income** is the operating income that an investment centre earns above the minimum required return on its operating assets. Thus, we use operating income as defined with ROI but reduce it by a special charge computed as a percentage of average operating assets. In equation form, residual income is calculated as follows:

$$\begin{array}{c}\text{Residual} \\ \text{income}\end{array} = \begin{array}{c}\text{Operating} \\ \text{income}\end{array} - \left(\begin{array}{c}\text{Average operating} \\ \text{assets}\end{array} \times \begin{array}{c}\text{Minimum required} \\ \text{rate of return}\end{array}\right)$$

Economic value added (EVA®) is a similar concept that differs in some details from residual income. EVA® has been popularized and trademarked by the consulting firm Stern, Stewart & Co. For example, under the economic value-added concept, funds used for research and development are treated as investments rather than as expenses. However, for our purposes, we will not draw any distinction between residual income and EVA®. We will illustrate residual income because the adjustments for EVA® are complex and would create more confusion than is appropriate for this introduction.

When residual income or EVA® is used to measure performance, the purpose is to maximize the total amount of residual income or EVA®, not to maximize overall ROI. Organizations as diverse as Loblaws, Quaker Oats, and Domtar have embraced some version of residual income in recent years.

For illustration, consider the following data for an investment centre—the Whitehorse Division of Yukon Marine Services Corporation:

YUKON MARINE SERVICES CORPORATION
Whitehorse Division
Basic Data for Performance Evaluation

Average operating assets	$100,000
Operating income	$ 20,000
Minimum required rate of return	15%

Yukon Marine Services Corporation has long had a policy of evaluating investment centre managers based on ROI but is considering a switch to residual income. The controller of the company, who is in favour of the change to residual income, has provided the following table, which shows how the performance of the division would be evaluated under each of the two methods:

YUKON MARINE SERVICES CORPORATION
Whitehorse Division
Alternative Performance Measures

	Return on Investment	Residual Income
Average operating assets	$100,000 (a)	$100,000
Operating income	$ 20,000 (b)	$ 20,000
Return on investment, (b) ÷ (a)	20%	
Minimum required return (15% × $100,000)		15,000
Residual income		$ 5,000

The reasoning underlying the residual income calculation is straightforward. The company is able to earn a rate of return of at least 15% on its investments. Since the company has invested $100,000 in the Whitehorse Division in the form of operating assets, the company should be able to earn at least $15,000 (15% × $100,000) on this investment. Since the Whitehorse Division's operating income is $20,000, the residual income exceeds the minimum required return by $5,000. If residual income is adopted as the performance measure to replace ROI, then the manager of the Whitehorse Division will be evaluated based on the growth from year to year in residual income.

Motivation and Residual Income

One of the primary reasons why the controller of Yukon Marine Services Corporation would like to switch from ROI to residual income has to do with how managers view new investments under the two performance measurement schemes. The residual income approach encourages managers to make investments that are profitable for the entire company but that would be rejected by managers who are evaluated by the ROI formula.

To illustrate this problem, suppose that the manager of the Whitehorse Division is considering purchasing a computerized diagnostic machine to aid in servicing marine diesel engines. The machine would cost $25,000 and is expected to generate additional operating income of $4,500 a year. From the standpoint of the company, this would be a good investment since it promises a rate of return of 18% ($4,500 ÷ $25,000), which is in excess of the company's minimum required rate of return of 15%.

If the manager of the Whitehorse Division is evaluated based on residual income, she would be in favour of the investment in the diagnostic machine evaluated below:

YUKON MARINE SERVICES CORPORATION Whitehorse Division Performance Evaluated Using Residual Income			
	Present	New Project	Overall
Average operating assets..................................	$100,000	$25,000	$125,000
Operating income..	$ 20,000	$ 4,500	$ 24,500
Minimum required return................................	15,000	3,750*	18,750
Residual income	$ 5,000	$ 750	$ 5,750

*$25,000 × 15% = $3,750.

Since the project would increase the residual income of the Whitehorse Division, the manager would want to invest in the new diagnostic machine.

Now suppose that the manager of the Whitehorse Division is evaluated based on ROI. The effect of the diagnostic machine on the division's ROI is computed below:

YUKON MARINE SERVICES CORPORATION Whitehorse Division Performance Evaluated Using Return on Investment			
	Present	New Project	Overall
Average operating assets (a)...........................	$100,000	$25,000	$125,000
Operating income (b)....................................	$ 20,000	$ 4,500*	$ 24,500
Return on investment, (b) ÷ (a)......................	20%	18%	19.6%

*$25,000 × 18% = $4,500.

The new project reduces the division's ROI from 20% to 19.6%. This happens because the 18% rate of return on the new diagnostic machine, while above the company's 15% minimum rate of return, is below the division's current ROI of 20%. Therefore, the new diagnostic machine would reduce the division's ROI, even though it would be a good investment from the standpoint of the company as a whole. If the manager of the division is evaluated based on ROI, she will be reluctant to even propose such an investment.

Generally, a manager who is evaluated based on ROI will want to reject any project whose rate of return is below the division's current ROI even if the rate of return on the project is above the minimum required rate of return for the entire company. In contrast, any project whose rate of return is above the minimum required rate of return for the company will result in an increase in residual income and thus add value for the shareholders. Since it is in the best interests of the company as a whole to accept any project whose rate of return is above the minimum required rate of return, managers who are evaluated based on residual income will tend to make better decisions concerning investment projects than managers who are evaluated based on ROI.

Divisional Comparison and Residual Income

The residual income approach has one major disadvantage. It cannot be used to compare the performance of divisions of different sizes. You would expect larger divisions to have more residual income than smaller divisions, not necessarily because they are better managed but simply because they are bigger.

As an example, consider the following residual income computations for Division X and Division Y:

	Division	
	X	Y
Average operating assets (a)	$1,000,000	$250,000
Operating income	$ 120,000	$ 40,000
Minimum required return: 10% × (a)	100,000	25,000
Residual income	$ 20,000	$ 15,000

Observe that Division X has slightly more residual income than Division Y, but that Division X has $1,000,000 in operating assets as compared to only $250,000 in operating assets for Division Y. Thus, Division X's greater residual income is probably more a result of its size than the quality of its management. In fact, it appears that the smaller division is better managed, since it has been able to generate nearly as much residual income with only one-fourth as much in operating assets with which to work. This problem can be reduced to some degree by focusing on the percentage change in residual income from year to year rather than on the absolute amount of the residual income.

Criticisms of Residual Income

As shown above, compared to ROI, the use of residual income can lead managers to make decisions more consistent with shareholders' objectives. Further, some claim that residual income is more closely related to shareholder returns than other metrics, such as sales growth, net income, and ROI. However, the following criticisms of residual income are worth noting:

1. Residual income is based on historical accounting data, which means that in particular, the accounting values used for capital assets can suffer from being out of date when costs are rising. This can lead to inflated amounts for residual income.

2. The residual income approach does not indicate what earnings *should* be for a particular business unit. A means of comparison is needed, which could involve using external benchmarks based on key competitors or evaluating trends in residual income over time (e.g., tracking the percentage change over several periods).
3. Calculating residual income requires numerous adjustments to financial information recorded using GAAP that can increase the cost of preparing the information.
4. Residual income is a financial metric that does not incorporate important leading non-financial indicators of success, such as employee motivation and customer satisfaction.

▌ BALANCED SCORECARD

A **balanced scorecard** consists of an integrated set of performance measures that is derived from the company's strategy and that supports the company's strategy throughout the organization. A strategy is essentially a theory about how to achieve the organization's goals and deals with issues such as how to attract customers, what products or services to sell, what markets to enter, and how to compete with rivals. According to some experts, there are three potentially successful generic strategic approaches to outperforming competitors:

LEARNING OBJECTIVE 5
Explain the use of balanced scorecards to assess performance.

Balanced scorecard
An integrated set of performance measures that is derived from and supports the organization's strategy.

1. **Cost leadership:** By maintaining low cost through efficiency relative to competitors, a company can make superior profits at current industry prices. Alternatively, the company can become a price leader because other firms are unable to undercut its prices. Low costs may also serve as a barrier against potential new market entrants and thereby protect long-term profitability. However, technological change or imitation of low-cost techniques by rivals can threaten the success of this strategy.
2. **Differentiation:** For products or services that are perceived as unique, customers will sometimes pay premium prices, giving the company higher profit margins. This cushion of higher profits reduces the effect of supplier or buyer power. Brand loyalty, however, may fail if the cost differential between the firm and the cost leader in the industry becomes too wide.
3. **Focus or niche:** By serving a narrow, strategic target market more effectively than rivals who are competing more broadly, a firm may be able to achieve superior profitability. The risk of being overtaken by broad-target firms who have economies of scale is a constant threat to the success of this strategy.

Under the balanced scorecard approach, top management translates its strategy into performance measures that employees can understand and can do something about. For example, the length of time passengers have to wait in line to have their baggage checked might be a performance measure for the supervisor in charge of the Air Canada check-in counter at the Vancouver airport. This performance measure is easily understood by the supervisor and can be improved by the supervisor's actions.

Common Characteristics of Balanced Scorecards

Performance measures used in the balanced scorecard approach tend to fall into the four groups illustrated in Exhibit 11–4: financial, customer, internal business processes, and learning and growth. Internal business processes are what the company does in an attempt to satisfy customers. For example, in a manufacturing company, assembling a product is an internal business process. For an airline, handling baggage is an internal business process. The basic idea is that learning is necessary to improve internal business processes, improving business processes is

EXHIBIT 11-4   From Strategy to Performance Measures: The Balanced Scorecard

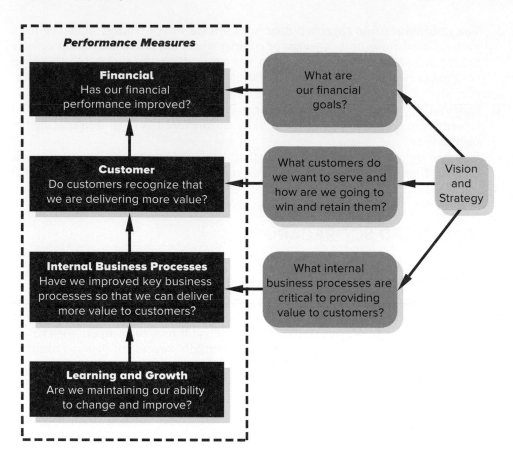

necessary to improve customer satisfaction, and improving customer satisfaction is necessary to improve financial results.

Note that the emphasis in Exhibit 11–4 is on *improvement*—not on just attaining some specific objective such as profits of $10 million. In the balanced scorecard approach, continuous improvement is encouraged. In many industries, this is a matter of survival. If an organization does not continuously improve, it will eventually lose out to competitors that do.

Financial performance measures appear at the top of Exhibit 11–4. Ultimately, most companies exist to provide financial rewards to owners. There are exceptions. Some companies—for example, The Body Shop—may have loftier goals, such as providing environmentally friendly products to consumers. However, these types of organizations must generate enough financial resources to stay in operation.

However, for several reasons, financial performance measures (even ROI or EVA®) are not sufficient in themselves—they should be integrated with non-financial measures in a well-designed balanced scorecard. First, financial measures are lagging indicators that report on the results of past actions. In contrast, non-financial measures of key success drivers, such as customer satisfaction, are leading indicators of future financial performance. Second, top managers are ordinarily responsible for the financial performance measures—not lower-level managers—so it may be easier for lower-level managers to have greater control and impact on non-financial than financial performance.

Consider the strategy of a regional airline with the following strategy: to uniquely position ourselves by focusing on being a short-haul, low-fare, high-frequency, point-to-point carrier in eastern North America. Exhibit 11–5 suggests how the airline might reflect this strategy in its balanced scorecard.

If the balanced scorecard is correctly constructed, the performance measures should be linked on a cause-and-effect basis. Each link can then be read as a hypothesis in the form "If we improve this performance measure, then this other

Vision: Continue building on our unique position—the *only* short-haul, low-fare, high-frequency, point-to-point carrier in Canada.

Simplified Strategy Map	Performance Measures	Targets	Initiatives
Financial Increase Profitability / Lower Costs / Increase Revenue	• Market value • Seat revenue • Plane lease cost	• 25% per year • 20% per year • 5% per year	• Optimize routes • Standardize planes
Customer More Customers / On-time Flights / Lowest Prices	• On-time arrival rating • Customer ranking • Number of customers	• First in industry • 98% Satisfaction • % change	• Quality management • Customer loyalty program
Internal Improve Turnaround Time	• On-ground time • On-time departure	• <25 minutes • 93%	• Cycle time optimization program
Learning Align Ground Crews	• % ground crew shareholders • % ground crew trained	• Yr. 1 70% Yr. 4 90% Yr. 6 100%	• Stock ownership plan • Ground crew training

Source: Developed from material by the Balanced Scorecard Collaborative and *Harvard Business Review* (Kaplan & Norton). © Balanced Scorecard Institute, a Strategy Management Group company.

performance measure should also improve." Starting from the bottom of Exhibit 11–5, we can read the links between performance measures as follows: If ground crews acquire the skills to perform better and become shareholders, they will perform better and be motivated to increase turnaround times, ensuring more on-time flights. More on-time flights when accompanied by low prices should increase customer satisfaction and loyalty, leading to increased revenues and decreased costs, resulting in an increase in profits.

In essence, the balanced scorecard illustrates a theory of how the company can attain its desired outcomes (financial, in this case) by taking concrete actions. While the strategy laid out in Exhibit 11–5 seems plausible, it should be regarded as only a theory that should be discarded if it proves to be invalid. One of the advantages of the balanced scorecard is that it can be used to continuously test the theories underlying management's strategy. If a strategy is not working, it should become evident when some of the predicted effects (i.e., more repeat customers) do not occur. Without this feedback, management may drift on indefinitely with an ineffective strategy based on faulty assumptions.

Exhibit 11–5 includes some examples of performance measures that can be found in the customer, internal business process, and learning and growth categories of the balanced scorecards of a regional airline. However, companies in other industries would likely highlight other performance measures that are of more relevance to organizations in their industries. Managers should carefully select the performance measures for their company's balanced scorecard, keeping the following points in mind. First, the performance measures should be consistent with, and follow from, the company's strategy. If the performance measures are not consistent with the company's strategy, people will find themselves working at cross-purposes. Second, the scorecard should not have too many performance measures. This can lead to a lack of focus and confusion.

While the entire organization will have an overall balanced scorecard, each responsible individual may have his or her own personal scorecard as well. This scorecard should consist of items the individual can personally influence that relate directly to the performance measures on the overall balanced scorecard (e.g., hours spent in training courses). The performance measures on this personal scorecard

Instant Quiz 11-4
Why does the balanced scorecard include financial performance measures as well as measures of non-financial performance? Why do the measures in a balanced scorecard differ from company to company?

should not be overly influenced by actions taken by others in the company or by events that are outside the individual's control. Also, the personal scorecard measures should not lead an individual to take actions that are inconsistent with the organization's objectives.

Tying Compensation to the Balanced Scorecard

Incentive compensation for employees, such as bonuses, can, and probably should, be tied to balanced scorecard performance measures. However, this should be done only after the organization has been successfully managed with the scorecard for some time—perhaps a year or more. Managers must be confident that the performance measures are reliable, sensible, understood by those who are being evaluated, and not easily manipulated. As Robert Kaplan and David Norton, the promoters of the balanced scorecard concept, argue, before linking compensation to achieving balanced scorecard targets, boards of directors must be sure that they are using the right measures and that the data collected concerning performance relative to target are reliable.

Advantages of Timely Feedback

Whatever performance measures are used, they should be reported on a frequent and timely basis. For example, data about defects should be reported to the responsible managers at least once a day so that action can be taken quickly if an unusual number of defects occur. In the most advanced companies, any defect is reported *immediately*, and its cause is tracked down before any more defects occur. Another common characteristic of the performance measures under the balanced scorecard approach is that managers focus on *trends* in the performance measures over time. The emphasis is on progress and *improvement* rather than on meeting any specific standard.

KNOWLEDGE IN ACTION

Managers can apply their knowledge about process costing when
- Using segmented reports to examine trends and results in each segment at a level of detail that allows them to better determine what may underlie results that are more positive or more negative than expected. Segment reports break down results of an organization into more manageable parts on the basis of product lines, geography, sales territory, etc.

- Accounting for the performance of their divisions. Responsibility centre managers are held accountable for the performance of their decentralized divisions. The results for which these managers are accountable depend on the degree to which they control costs, revenues, and investments for their division. Profit centre managers are held accountable for their division's achievement of profit targets, while investment centre managers are held accountable for their divisions' achievement of ROI or residual income targets.
- Accounting for their division's generation of profit or ROI. Managers may choose to use a balanced scorecard to communicate with employees in their organizations the means by which profit or ROI should be improved. The non-financial measures and targets included in the balanced scorecard provide guidance concerning the actions employees at the operational level in the division can take to help the division achieve its financial targets and for the organization as a whole to achieve its strategic objectives.

SUMMARY

- Segmented income statements provide information for evaluating the profitability and performance of divisions, product lines, sales territories, and other company segments. Under the contribution approach, variable costs and fixed costs are clearly distinguished from each other, and only those costs that are traceable to a segment are assigned to the segment. [LO1]
- A responsibility centre is any segment of an organization whose manager has control over and is accountable for cost, profit, or investments. Responsibility centre managers are evaluated based on what they can control. [LO2]
- A cost centre is a business segment whose manager has control over costs only. A profit centre is a segment whose manager controls revenues and costs but not investments in operating assets. An investment centre manager controls profits and investments in operating assets. [LO2]
- Return on investment (ROI), residual income, and economic value added (EVA®) can be used to evaluate investment centre performance. [LO3, LO4]
- The balanced scorecard consists of an integrated system of performance measures that are derived from and support the company's strategy. It has four main categories of performance measures: financial, customer, internal business processes, and learning and growth. Different companies will have different balanced scorecards because they have different strategies. [LO5]

REVIEW PROBLEM 1: SEGMENTED STATEMENTS

The business staff of the law firm Frampton, Davis, & Smythe have constructed the following report, which breaks down the firm's overall results for last month into two main business segments—family law and commercial law:

	Total	Family Law	Commercial Law
Revenues from clients	$1,000,000	$400,000	$600,000
Variable expenses	220,000	100,000	120,000
Contribution margin	780,000	300,000	480,000
Traceable fixed expenses	670,000	280,000	390,000
Segment margin	110,000	20,000	90,000
Common fixed expenses	60,000	24,000	36,000
Operating income	$ 50,000	$ (4,000)	$ 54,000

However, this report is not quite correct. The common fixed expenses, such as the managing partner's salary, selling and administrative expenses, and general firm advertising, have been allocated to the two segments based on revenues from clients.

Required:

1. Redo the segment report, eliminating the allocation of common fixed expenses. Would the firm be better off financially if the family law segment were dropped? (*Note:* Many of the firm's commercial law clients also use the firm for their family law requirements, such as drawing up wills.)
2. The firm's advertising agency has proposed an ad campaign targeted at boosting the revenues of the family law segment. The ad campaign would cost $20,000, and the advertising agency claims that it would increase family law revenues by $100,000. The managing partner of Frampton, Davis, & Smythe believes this increase in business could be accommodated without any increase in fixed expenses. What effect would this ad campaign have on the family law segment margin and on the firm's overall operating income?

Solution to Review Problem 1

1. The corrected segmented income statement appears below:

	Total	Family Law	Commercial Law
Revenues from clients.............................	$1,000,000	$400,000	$600,000
Variable expenses.................................	220,000	100,000	120,000
Contribution margin...............................	780,000	300,000	480,000
Traceable fixed expenses..........................	670,000	280,000	390,000
Segment margin	110,000	$ 20,000	$ 90,000
Common fixed expenses	60,000		
Operating income.................................	$ 50,000		

The firm would not be financially better off if the family law practice were dropped. The family law segment is covering all of its own costs and is contributing $20,000 per month to covering the common fixed expenses of the firm. While the segment margin for family law is much lower than for commercial law, it is still profitable.

2. The ad campaign would increase the family law segment margin by $55,000, as follows:

Increased revenues from clients....................................	$100,000
Family law contribution margin ratio ($300,000 ÷ $400,000)	× 75%
Incremental contribution margin....................................	$ 75,000
Less cost of the ad campaign......................................	20,000
Increased segment margin	$ 55,000

Since there would be no increase in fixed expenses (including common fixed expenses), the increase in overall operating income is also $55,000.

REVIEW PROBLEM 2: RETURN ON INVESTMENT AND RESIDUAL INCOME

Selected operating data for two divisions of Outback Brewing Ltd. are given below:

	Queensland	New South Wales
Sales	$4,000,000	$7,000,000
Average total operating assets...........................	$2,000,000	$2,000,000
Operating income......................................	$ 360,000	$ 420,000
Plant and equipment (net)	$ 950,000	$ 800,000

Required:
1. Compute the rate of return for each division using the ROI formula stated in terms of margin and turnover.
2. Compute residual income for each division, assuming the required rate of return is 15%.

Solution to Review Problem 2

1. ROI computations:

    ROI = Margin × Turnover

    $$= \frac{\text{Operating income}}{\text{Sales}} \times \frac{\text{Sales}}{\text{Average operating assets}}$$

    Queensland Division:

    $$\text{ROI} = \frac{\$360,000}{\$4,000,000} \times \frac{\$4,000,000}{\$2,000,000}$$
    $$= 9\% \times 2 = 18\%$$

    New South Wales Division:

    $$\text{ROI} = \frac{\$420,000}{\$7,000,000} \times \frac{\$7,000,000}{\$2,000,000}$$
    $$= 6\% \times 3.5 = 21\%$$

2. Residual income for each division is calculated as follows:
    Queensland Division:

    $$\$360,000 - (\$2,000,000 \times 15\%) = \$60,000$$

    New South Wales Division:

    $$\$420,000 - (\$2,000,000 \times 15\%) = \$120,000$$

DISCUSSION CASE

DISCUSSION CASE 11-1

Mason Paper Company (MPC) manufactures large quantities of standard white 8 ½ × 11 inch paper for use in computer printers and photocopiers. MPC has reported operating losses for the last two years due to intense price pressure from much larger competitors. The MPC management team is contemplating a change in strategy to reverse the trend of losses experienced over the last several years. The VP Finance, Don Townsend, has made the following argument concerning the new strategy:

> As we all know, the commodity paper manufacturing business is all about economies of scale. The largest competitors with the lowest cost per unit win. We have limited-capacity machines that keep us from producing high volumes of paper like our closest competitors. Therefore, I propose that we abandon cost reduction as a strategic goal and instead pursue manufacturing flexibility as the key to our future success.
>
> Manufacturing flexibility means we have to abandon our "crank out as many tonnes of paper as possible" mentality. Instead, we need to look for customers interested in lower-volume, specialty papers for which we can charge a higher price. To succeed in this new market, we first need to improve our ability to switch our equipment to produce different paper grades. Right now, we require an average of four hours to change over to another paper grade. Timely customer deliveries are a function of changeover performance. Second, we need to expand the range of paper grades that we can manufacture. Currently, we can manufacture only one paper grade. Our customers must perceive that we are a one-stop shop that can meet all of their specialty-grade paper needs. Third, we will need to improve our yields (e.g., tonnes of acceptable output relative to total tonnes processed) in the non-standard paper grades. Our percentage of waste within these grades will be unacceptably high unless we do something to improve our processes. Our variable costs will go through the roof if we cannot increase our yields!

Required:
Why would a company that changes its strategic goals need to change its performance measurement system as well? What are some examples of measures that would have been appropriate for MPC prior to its change in strategy? Why would those measures fail to support MPC's new strategy? What new measures would you suggest be adopted to support the new strategy at MPC?

GLOSSARY

 Review key terms and definitions on Connect.

QUESTIONS

11-1 What is meant by the term *decentralization*?

11-2 What is a segment of an organization? Give several examples of segments.

11-3 What costs are assigned to a segment under the contribution approach?

11-4 Explain how the segment margin differs from the CM.

11-5 Why aren't common costs allocated to segments under the contribution approach?

11-6 How is it possible for a cost that is traceable to a segment to become a common cost if the segment is divided into further segments?

11-7 Identify three inappropriate methods for assigning traceable costs among segments.

11-8 Identify three types of responsibility centres, and describe how performance is measured for each one.

11-9 What is meant by the terms *margin* and *turnover*?

11-10 What are the three approaches to improving ROI?

11-11 What is meant by the term *residual income*?

11-12 In what way can the use of ROI for investment centres lead to bad decisions? How does the residual income approach overcome this problem?

11-13 Should residual income be used to compare divisions of different sizes? Why or why not?

11-14 What are the four groups of performance measures typically included in a balanced scorecard?

EXERCISES

EXERCISE 11–1 Basic Segmented Income Statement [LO1]
Honeyville Hardware produces and sells two products for professional landscapers: shovels and rakes. Revenue and cost information relating to the products follow:

	Product	
	Shovels	**Rakes**
Selling price per unit	$ 10.00	$ 21.00
Variable expenses per unit	6.50	12.00
Traceable fixed expenses per year	8,000	25,000

Common fixed expenses in the company total $15,000 annually. Last year the company produced and sold 3,500 shovels and 5,000 rakes.

Required:
Prepare a contribution format income statement for the year, segmented by product lines.

EXERCISE 11–2 Segmented Income Statement [LO1]
Bovine Company, a wholesale distributor of umbrellas, has been experiencing losses for some time, as shown by its most recent monthly contribution format income statement:

Sales	$2,000,000
Variable expenses..................................	792,000
Contribution margin...............................	1,208,000
Fixed expenses.....................................	1,305,000
Operating loss......................................	$ (97,000)

In an effort to isolate the problem, the president has asked for an income statement segmented by geographic market. Accordingly, the Accounting Department has developed the following:

	Geographic Market		
	South	Central	North
Sales	$600,000	$800,000	$600,000
Variable expenses as a percentage			
of sales...	52%	30%	40%
Traceable fixed expenses....................................	$320,000	$530,000	$300,000

Required:
1. Prepare a contribution format income statement segmented by geographic market, as requested by the president.
2. The company's sales manager believes that sales in the Central geographic market could be increased by 15% if monthly advertising is increased by $25,000. Would you recommend the increased advertising? Show computations to support your answer.

EXERCISE 11–3 Working with a Segmented Income Statement [LO1]
Middleton Associates is a consulting firm that specializes in information systems for construction and landscaping companies. The firm has two offices—one in Toronto and one in Vancouver. The firm classifies the direct costs of consulting jobs as variable costs. A segmented contribution format income statement for the company's most recent year is given below:

			Office			
	Total Company		Toronto		Vancouver	
Sales	$750,000	100.0%	$150,000	100%	$600,000	100%
Variable expenses..............	405,000	54.0	45,000	30	360,000	60
Contribution margin............	345,000	46.0	105,000	70	240,000	40
Traceable fixed expenses.......	168,000	22.4	78,000	52	90,000	15
Office segment margin.........	177,000	23.6	$ 27,000	18%	$ 150,000	25%
Common fixed expenses						
not traceable to offices	120,000	16.0				
Operating income..............	$ 57,000	7.6%				

Required:
1. By how much would the company's operating income increase if Vancouver increased its sales by $75,000 per year? Assume no change in cost behaviour patterns.
2. Refer to the original data. Assume that sales in Toronto increase by $50,000 next year and that sales in Vancouver remain unchanged. Assume no change in fixed costs.
   a. Prepare a new segmented income statement for the company using the above format. Show both amounts and percentages.
   b. Observe from the income statement you have prepared that the CM ratio for Toronto has remained unchanged at 70% (the same as in the above data) but that the segment margin ratio has changed. How do you explain the change in the segment margin ratio?

EXERCISE 11–4 Working with a Segmented Income Statement [LO1]
Refer to the data in Exercise 11–3. Assume that Vancouver's sales by major market are as follows:

	Vancouver		Market			
			Construction Clients		Landscaping Clients	
Sales..........................	$600,000	100.0%	$400,000	100%	$200,000	100%
Variable expenses...............	360,000	60	260,000	65	100,000	50
Contribution margin..............	240,000	40	140,000	35	100,000	50
Traceable fixed expenses..........	72,000	12	20,000	5	52,000	26
Market segment margin...........	168,000	28	$ 120,000	30%	$ 48,000	24%
Common fixed expenses not traceable to offices........	18,000	3				
Office segment margin...........	$ 150,000	25%				

The company would like to initiate an intensive advertising campaign in one of the two markets during the next month. The campaign would cost $8,000. Marketing studies indicate that such a campaign would increase sales in the construction market by $70,000 or increase sales in the landscaping market by $60,000.

Required:
1. In which of the markets would you recommend that the company focus its advertising campaign? Show computations to support your answer.
2. In Exercise 11–3, Vancouver shows $90,000 in traceable fixed expenses. What happened to the $90,000 in this exercise?

EXERCISE 11–5 Decentralization and Responsibility Centres (LO2)
Listed below are terms relating to decentralization and responsibility centres.

Cost centre	Cost
Accountable	Investment
Profit	Flexible
Revenue	Residual income

Choose the term or terms that most appropriately complete the following statements. The terms can be used more than once. (Note that a blank can hold more than one word.)
1. A responsibility centre is any part of an organization for which a manager is _____ for performance.
2. A profit centre is a business segment where the manager has control over _____ and _____.
3. An investment centre manager is held responsible for the _____ of the segment.
4. A _____ is often evaluated using _____ budget variances.
5. _____ centre managers are responsible for initiating investment proposals.

EXERCISE 11–6 Computing and Interpreting Return on Investment [LO3]
Selected operating data on the two divisions of Prism Company are given below:

	Division	
	Eastern	Western
Sales...	$800,000	$1,850,000
Average operating assets.............................	300,000	400,000
Operating income	70,000	115,000
Plant and equipment	125,000	200,000

Required:
1. Compute the rate of return for each division using the ROI formula stated in terms of margin and turnover.
2. Which divisional manager seems to be doing the better job? Why?

EXERCISE 11–7 Contrasting Return on Investment and Residual Income [LO3, LO4]
Ferris Ltd. of Australia has two divisions, one in Perth and one in Darwin. Selected data on the two divisions follow:

	Division	
	Perth	Darwin
Sales...	$9,000,000	$20,000,000
Operating income	630,000	1,800,000
Average operating assets............................	3,000,000	10,000,000

Required:
1. Compute the ROI for each division.
2. Assume that the company evaluates performance using residual income and that the minimum required rate of return for any division is 16%. Compute the residual income for each division.
3. Is the Darwin Division's greater residual income an indication that it is better managed? Explain.

EXERCISE 11-8 Return on Investment and Residual Income Relationships [LO3, LO4]
A family friend has asked for your help in analyzing the operations of three companies operating in the same service sector industry. Supply the missing data in the following table:

	Company		
	A	B	C
Sales	$400,000	$750,000	$600,000
Operating income	$?	$ 45,000	$?
Average operating assets.....................	$160,000	$?	$ 150,000
Return on investment	20%	18%	?
Minimum required rate of return:			
Percentage	15%	?	12%
Dollar amount.................................	$?	$ 50,000	$?
Residual income.............................	$?	$?	$ 6,000

EXERCISE 11-9 Return on Investment Relationships [LO3]
Provide the missing data in the following table:

	Division		
	Fab	Consulting	IT
Sales	$800,000	$?	$?
Operating income	$ 72,000	$?	$40,000
Average operating assets.....................	$?	$130,000	$?
Margin.......................................	?	4%	8%
Turnover......................................	?	5	?
Return on investment	18%	?	20%

EXERCISE 11-10 Effects of Changes in Profits and Assets on Return on Investment [LO3]
FitPlus is a regional chain of health clubs. Each club's manager has the authority to make investments as needed and is evaluated based largely on ROI. FitPlus Club 52 reported the following results for the past year:

Sales.......................................	$500,000
Operating income.........................	15,000
Average operating assets	80,000

Required:
The following questions are to be considered independently. Carry out all computations to two decimal places.
1. Compute the club's ROI.
2. Assume that the manager of the club is able to increase sales by $80,000 and that as a result operating income increases by $6,000. Further assume that this is possible without any increase in operating assets. What would the club's ROI be?

3. Assume that the manager of the club is able to reduce expenses by $3,200 without any change in sales or operating assets. What would the club's ROI be?
4. Assume that the manager of the club is able to reduce operating assets by $20,000 without any change in sales or operating income. What would the club's ROI be?

EXERCISE 11–11 Evaluating New Investments Using Return on Investment and Residual Income [LO3, LO4]

Three divisions of Jameson Co. report the following sales and operating data:

	Fitness Training	Spa Services	Athletic Wear
Sales	$600,000	$750,000	$400,000
Average operating assets	$200,000	$250,000	$100,000
Operating income	$ 30,000	$ 37,500	$ 24,000
Minimum required rate of return	10%	12%	10%

Required:
1. Compute the ROI for each division, using the formula stated in terms of margin and turnover.
2. Compute the residual income for each division.
3. Assume that each division is presented with an investment opportunity that would yield a rate of return of 17%.
    a. If performance is being measured by ROI, which division or divisions will probably accept the opportunity? Reject it? Why?
    b. If performance is being measured by residual income, which division or divisions will probably accept the opportunity? Reject it? Why?

PROBLEMS

PROBLEM 11–12 Restructuring a Segmented Income Statement [LO1]

Brabant NV of the Netherlands is a wholesale distributor of Dutch cheeses that it sells throughout the European Union. Unfortunately, the company's profits have been declining, which has caused considerable concern. To help understand the condition of the company, the managing director of the company has requested that the monthly income statement be segmented by sales territory. Accordingly, the company's accounting department has prepared the following statement for March, the more recent month. (The Dutch currency is the euro, which is designated by €.)

	Sales Territory		
	Southern Europe	Middle Europe	Northern Europe
Sales	€300,000	€800,000	€700,000
Territorial expenses (traceable):			
Cost of goods sold	93,000	240,000	315,000
Salaries	54,000	56,000	112,000
Insurance	9,000	16,000	14,000
Advertising	105,000	240,000	245,000
Depreciation	21,000	32,000	28,000
Shipping	15,000	32,000	42,000
Total territorial expenses	297,000	616,000	756,000
Territorial income (loss) before corporate expenses	3,000	184,000	(56,000)
Corporate expenses:			
Advertising (general)	15,000	40,000	35,000
Selling and administrative	20,000	20,000	20,000
Total corporate expenses	35,000	60,000	55,000
Operating income (loss)	€(32,000)	€ 124,000	€(111,000)

Cost of goods sold and shipping expenses are both variable; other costs are all fixed. Brabant NV purchases cheeses at auction and from farmers' cooperatives, and it distributes them in the three territories shown in the statement above. Each of the three sales territories has its own manager and sales staff. The cheeses vary widely in profitability; some have a high margin and some have a low margin. (Certain cheeses, after having been aged for long periods, are the most expensive and carry the highest margins.)

Required:
1. List any disadvantages or weaknesses of the statement format illustrated above.
2. Explain the base that is apparently being used to allocate the corporate expenses to the territories. Do you agree with these allocations? Explain.
3. Prepare a new segmented contribution format income statement for May. Show a Total column as well as data for each territory. Include percentages on your statement for all columns. Carry percentages to one decimal place.
4. Analyze the statement that you prepared in (3) above. What points that might help to improve the company's performance would you bring to management's attention?

PROBLEM 11–13 Segment Reporting and Decision Making [LO1]
Creaston Limited's most recent monthly contribution format income statement is given below:

CREASTON LIMITED Income Statement For the Month Ended May 31		
Sales..	$900,000	100.0%
Variable expenses	408,000	45.3
Contribution margin	492,000	54.7
Fixed expenses....................................	465,000	51.7
Operating income	$ 27,000	3.0%

Management is disappointed with the company's performance and is wondering what can be done to improve profits. By examining sales and cost records, you have determined the following:
a. The company is divided into two sales territories—Central and Eastern. Central Territory recorded $400,000 in sales and $208,000 in variable expenses during May. The remaining sales and variable expenses were recorded in Eastern Territory. Fixed expenses of $160,000 and $130,000 are traceable to Central and Eastern Territories, respectively. The rest of the fixed expenses are common to the two territories.
b. The company is the exclusive distributor for two products—Kiks and Dows. Sales of Kiks and Dows totalled $100,000 and $300,000, respectively, in Central Territory during May. Variable expenses are 25% of the selling price for Kiks and 61% for Dows. Cost records show that $60,000 of Central Territory's fixed expenses are traceable to Kiks and $54,000 to Dows, with the remainder common to the two products.

Required:
1. Prepare contribution format segmented income statements, first showing the total company broken down between sales territories and then showing Central Territory broken down by product line. Show both Amount and Percentage columns for the company in total and for each segment. Round percentage computations to one decimal place.
2. Look at the statement you have prepared showing the total company segmented by sales territory. Which points revealed by this statement should be brought to management's attention?
3. Look at the statement you have prepared showing Central Territory segmented by product lines. Which points revealed by this statement should be brought to management's attention?

PROBLEM 11–14 Basic Segmented Statement; Activity-Based Cost Assignment [LO1]
Vega Foods Inc. recently purchased a small mill that it intends to operate as one of its subsidiaries. The newly acquired mill offers three products for sale—wheat cereal, pancake mix, and flour. Each product sells for $10 per package. Materials, labour, and other variable production costs are $3.00 per bag of wheat cereal, $4.20 per bag of pancake mix, and $1.80 per bag of flour. Sales commissions are 10% of sales for any product. All other costs are fixed.

The mill's income statement for the most recent month is given below:

| | | | Product Line | |
	Total Company	Wheat Cereal	Pancake Mix	Flour
Sales...	$600,000	$200,000	$300,000	$100,000
Expenses:				
Materials, labour, and other......................	204,000	60,000	126,000	18,000
Sales commissions..............................	60,000	20,000	30,000	10,000
Advertising....................................	123,000	48,000	60,000	15,000
Salaries......................................	66,000	34,000	21,000	11,000
Equipment depreciation.........................	30,000	10,000	15,000	5,000
Warehouse rent................................	12,000	4,000	6,000	2,000
Selling and administrative	90,000	30,000	30,000	30,000
Total expenses....................................	585,000	206,000	288,000	91,000
Operating income (loss)...........................	$ 15,000	$ (6,000)	$ 12,000	$ 9,000

The following additional information about the company is available:
a. The same equipment is used to mill and package all three products. In the above income statement, equipment depreciation has been allocated on the basis of sales dollars. An analysis of equipment usage indicates that it is used 40% of the time to make wheat cereal, 50% of the time to make pancake mix, and 10% of the time to make flour.
b. All three products are stored in the same warehouse. In the above income statement, the warehouse rent has been allocated on the basis of sales dollars. The warehouse contains 24,000 square metres of space, of which 8,000 square metres are used for wheat cereal, 14,000 square metres are used for pancake mix, and 2,000 square metres are used for flour. The warehouse space costs the company $0.50 per square metre to rent.
c. The selling and administrative costs relate to the administration of the company as a whole. In the above income statement, these costs have been divided equally among the three product lines.
d. All other costs are traceable to the product lines.
Vega Foods' management is anxious to improve the mill's 2.5% margin on sales.

Required:
1. Prepare a new contribution format segmented income statement for the month. Adjust the allocations as required.
2. After seeing the income statement in the main body of the problem, management has decided to eliminate the wheat cereal, because it is not returning a profit, and to focus all available resources on promoting the pancake mix.
   a. Based on the statement you have prepared, do you agree with the decision to eliminate the wheat cereal? Explain.
   b. Based on the statement you have prepared, do you agree with the decision to focus all available resources on promoting the pancake mix? Assume that an ample market is available for all three products. (*Hint:* Compute the CM ratio for each product.)

PROBLEM 11–15 Finely Segmented Income Statements [LO1]
Severo S.A. of Sao Paulo, Brazil, is organized into two divisions. The company's contribution format segmented income statement (in terms of the Brazilian currency, the real, R) for last month is given below:

	Total Company	Division Cloth	Division Leather
Sales...	R3,500,000	R2,000,000	R1,500,000
Variable expenses.................................	1,721,000	960,000	761,000
Contribution margin...............................	1,779,000	1,040,000	739,000
Traceable fixed expenses:			
Advertising..................................	612,000	300,000	312,000
Selling and administrative	427,000	210,000	217,000
Depreciation.................................	229,000	115,000	114,000
Total traceable fixed expenses....................	1,268,000	625,000	643,000
Divisional segment margin.........................	511,000	R 415,000	R 96,000
Common fixed expenses	390,000		
Operating income.................................	R 121,000		

Top management can't understand why the Leather Division has such a low segment margin when its sales are only 25% less than sales in the Cloth Division. As one step in isolating the problem, management has directed that the Leather Division be further segmented into product lines. The following information is available on the product lines in the Leather Division:

	Leather Division Product Line		
	Garments	Shoes	Handbags
Sales	R500,000	R700,000	R300,000
Traceable fixed expenses:			
Advertising..................................	R 80,000	R 112,000	R 120,000
Selling and administrative	R 30,000	R 35,000	R 42,000
Depreciation.................................	R 25,000	R 56,000	R 33,000
Variable expenses as a percentage			
of sales.....................................	65%	40%	52%

Analysis shows that R110,000 of the Leather Division's selling and administrative expenses are common to the product lines.

Required:
1. Prepare a contribution format segmented income statement for the Leather Division, with segments defined as product lines.
2. Management is surprised by the handbag product line's poor showing and would like to have the product line segmented by market. The following information is available about the markets in which the handbag line is sold:

	Handbag Markets	
	Domestic	Foreign
Sales..	R200,000	R100,000
Traceable fixed expenses:		
Advertising.......................................	R 40,000	R 80,000
Variable expenses as a percentage		
of sales	43%	70%

All of the handbag product line's selling and administrative expenses and depreciation are common to the markets in which the product is sold. Prepare a contribution format segmented income statement for the handbag product line with segments defined as markets.
3. Refer to the statement prepared in (1) above. The sales manager wants to run a special promotional campaign on one of the product lines over the next month. A marketing

study indicates that such a campaign would increase sales of the Garments product line by R200,000 or sales of the Shoes product line by R145,000. The campaign would cost R30,000. Show computations to determine which product line should be chosen.

PROBLEM 11–16 Comparison of Performance Using Return on Investment [LO3]

The following are comparative data submitted by three companies in the food services:

	Company		
	A	**B**	**C**
Sales...	$1,000,000	$300,000	$?
Operating income.................................	$ 140,000	$ 42,000	$?
Average operating assets	$ 500,000	?	$600,000
Margin..	?	?	4%
Turnover..	?	?	2
Return on investment.............................	?	7%	?

Required:

1. What advantages are there to breaking down the ROI computation into two separate elements, margin and turnover?
2. Fill in the missing information above, and comment on the relative performance of the three companies in as much detail as the data permit. Make *specific recommendations* about how to improve the ROI.

   (Adapted from National Association of Accountants, *Research Report No. 35*, p. 34.)

PROBLEM 11–17 Return on Investment and Residual Income [LO3, LO4]

Faced with headquarters' desire to add a new product line, Stefan Grenier, manager of Bilti Products' East Division, felt that he had to see the numbers before he made a move. His division's ROI has led the company for three years, and he doesn't want any letdown.

Bilti Products is a decentralized wholesaler with four autonomous divisions. The divisions are evaluated on the basis of ROI, with year-end bonuses given to divisional managers who have the highest ROI. Operating results for the company's East Division for last year are given below:

Sales..	$21,000,000
Variable expenses.......................................	13,400,000
Contribution margin.....................................	7,600,000
Fixed expenses	5,920,000
Operating income..	$ 1,680,000
Divisional operating assets	$ 5,250,000

The company had an overall ROI of 18% last year (considering all divisions). The new product line that headquarters wants Grenier's East Division to add would require an investment of $3,000,000. The cost and revenue characteristics of the new product line per year would be as follows:

Sales......................................	$9,000,000
Variable expenses..........................	65% of sales
Fixed expenses	$2,520,000

Required:

1. Compute the East Division's ROI for last year; also compute the ROI as it would appear if the new product line were added.
2. If you were in Grenier's position, would you accept or reject the new product line? Explain.
3. Why do you suppose headquarters is anxious for the East Division to add the new product line?
4. Suppose that the company's minimum required rate of return on operating assets is 15% and that performance is evaluated using residual income.

a. Compute East Division's residual income for last year; also compute the residual income as it would appear if the new product line were added.

b. Under these circumstances, if you were in Grenier's position, would you accept or reject the new product line? Explain.

PROBLEM 11–18 Return on Investment and Residual Income [LO3, LO4]
Financial data for Bridger Inc. for last year are as follows:

BRIDGER INC. Balance Sheet		
	Ending Balance	Beginning Balance
Assets		
Cash	$ 150,000	$ 145,000
Accounts receivable	500,000	360,000
Inventory	510,000	590,000
Plant and equipment, net	840,000	865,000
Investment in Brier Company	450,000	420,000
Land (undeveloped)	270,000	270,000
Total assets	$2,720,000	$2,650,000
Liabilities and shareholders' equity		
Accounts payable	$ 340,000	$ 380,000
Long-term debt	1,000,000	1,000,000
Shareholders' equity	1,380,000	1,270,000
Total liabilities and shareholders' equity	$2,720,000	$2,650,000

BRIDGER INC. Income Statement		
Sales		$4,180,000
Operating expenses		3,553,000
Operating income		627,000
Interest and taxes:		
Interest expense	$ 120,000	
Tax expense	200,000	320,000
Net income		$ 307,000

The company paid dividends of $197,000 last year. The "Investment in Brier Company" on the balance sheet represents an investment in the common shares of another company.

Required:
1. Compute the company's margin, turnover, and ROI for last year.
2. The board of directors of Bridger Inc. has set a minimum required return of 20%. What was the company's residual income last year?

PROBLEM 11–19 Cost–Volume–Profit Analysis; Return on Investment [LO3, LO4]
The Switch division of Tornax Inc. produces a small switch that is used by various companies as a component part in their products. Tornax operates its divisions as autonomous units, giving its divisional managers great discretion in pricing and other decisions. Each division is expected to generate a minimum required rate of return of at least 14% on its operating assets. The Switch Division has average operating assets of $700,000. The switches are sold for $5 each. Variable costs are $3 per switch, and fixed costs total $462,000 per year. The division has a capacity of 300,000 switches each year.

Required:
1. How many switches must the Switch Division sell each year to generate the desired rate of return on its assets?
   a. What is the margin earned at this level of sales?
   b. What is the turnover at this level of sales?

2. Assume that the Switch Division's current ROI equals the minimum required rate of 14%. In order to increase the division's ROI, the divisional manager wants to increase the selling price per switch by 4%. Market studies indicate that an increase in the selling price would cause sales to drop by 20,000 units each year. However, operating assets could be reduced by $50,000 due to decreased needs for accounts receivable and inventory. Compute the margin, turnover, and ROI if these changes are made.

3. Refer to the original data. Assume again that the Switch Division's current ROI equals the minimum required rate of 14%. Rather than increase the selling price, the sales manager wants to reduce the selling price per switch by 4%. Market studies indicate that this would fill the plant to capacity. In order to carry the greater level of sales, however, operating assets would increase by $50,000. Compute the margin, turnover, and ROI if these changes are made.

PROBLEM 11–20 Return on Investment Analysis [LO3]

The contribution format income statement for Smith & Company for its most recent period is given below:

	Total	Unit
Sales	$500,000	$50.00
Less variable expenses	300,000	30.00
Contribution margin	200,000	20.00
Less fixed expenses	160,000	
Operating income	40,000	
Less income taxes at 40%	16,000	
Net income	$ 24,000	

The company had average operating assets of $250,000 during the period.

Required:

1. Compute the company's ROI for the period using the ROI formula stated in terms of margin and turnover.

For each of the following questions, indicate whether the margin and turnover will increase, decrease, or remain unchanged as a result of the events described, and then compute the new ROI figure. Consider each question separately, starting in each case from the original ROI computed in (1) above.

2. The company achieves cost savings of $10,000 per period by using less costly materials.

3. Using lean production, the company is able to reduce the average level of inventory by $50,000. (The released funds are used to pay off bank loans.)

4. Sales are increased by $50,000; operating assets remain unchanged.

5. The company issues bonds and uses the proceeds to purchase $75,000 in machinery and equipment at the beginning of the period. Interest on the bonds is $2,000 per period. Sales remain unchanged. The new, more efficient equipment reduces production costs by $4,000 per period.

6. The company invests $50,000 in cash (received on accounts receivable) in a plot of land that is to be held for possible future use as a plant site.

7. Obsolete inventory carried on the books at a cost of $5,000 is scrapped and written off as a loss.

PROBLEM 11–21 Balanced Scorecards; Customer Metrics [LO5]

Many organizations focus their strategy on providing high-quality customer service and consequently place metrics concerning customer relationship management on their balanced scorecards. Consider Sam's Pita Pit and the Classic Steakhouse, two restaurants with different target markets and different strategies. Sam's Pita Pit is located near a college campus and serves mainly students looking for a healthy meal, quick service, and low prices. While there are several tables in the restaurant where customers can dine in, most of Sam's business is on a take-out basis. Classic Steak House, on the other hand, is an upscale restaurant targeting business lunches and special occasion dinners. Customers value good-quality food and service and spend on average $150 per table. Both restaurants are considering implementing balanced scorecards.

Required:
What kind of measures might Sam's Pita Pit and the Classic Steakhouse include in the customer category of their new balanced scorecards? Create a table with one column for each set of measures. Which measures would be similar and which would be different across scorecards and why?

PROBLEM 11–22 Balanced Scorecards and Incentives [LO5]

Smith's Family Fashions implemented a balanced scorecard performance measurement system several years ago. Smith's is a locally owned clothing retailer with fashions for men, women, teens, and children. At the beginning of the year, John Smith took over the management of the Women's Wear department from his mother when she retired. John recognized there was a need for trendy clothing appealing to fashionable local women. Since taking over the department, John has changed the fashion lines he carries to be more appealing to this new target market while still offering well-priced, high-quality clothing that appeals to the store's more traditional customers.

The management of Smith's Family Fashions is overseen by a board of directors, including several members of the Smith family. John and other department heads have agreed to be evaluated by the board on the basis of performance relative to targets set across balanced scorecard categories. John's targets and actual performance since taking over as department head are provided below. The board decides on year-end bonuses based on each department head's performance relative to target:

	Target	Actual
Return on assets employed by department	14%	15%
Proportion of repeat customers	60%	57%
Sales generated by new product lines as a percentage of total departmental sales	65%	58%
Average discount on goods sold	10%	18%

Required:
Take on the role of a member of the board of directors preparing for a board meeting at which decisions will be made about the payment of annual bonuses to department heads. Discuss the performance of the Women's Wear department as compared to actual based on the metric provided. Where has performance been better (worse) than actual? What do the actual results, taken together, say about the likely success of John's new strategy?

CASES

CASE 11–23 Creating Balanced Scorecards That Support Different Strategies [LO5]

The Performance Enhancement Group (PEG) helps companies to build balanced scorecards. As part of its marketing efforts, PEG conducts an annual balanced scorecard workshop for prospective clients. You are PEG's newest employee, so your boss has asked you to participate in this year's workshop by explaining to attendees how a company's strategy determines the measures that are appropriate for its balanced scorecard. Your boss has provided you with the excerpts below from the annual reports of two current PEG clients. She has asked you to use these excerpts in your portion of the workshop.

Excerpt from Applied Pharmaceuticals' annual report:

> The keys to our business are consistent and timely new-product introductions and manufacturing process integrity. The new-product introduction side of the equation is a function of research and development (R&D) yield (e.g., the number of marketable drug compounds created relative to the total number of potential compounds pursued). We seek to optimize our R&D yield and first-to-market capability by investing in state-of-the-art technology, hiring the highest possible percentage of the "best and the brightest" engineers, and providing world-class training to those engineers. Manufacturing process integrity is all about establishing world-class quality specifications and then relentlessly engaging in prevention and appraisal activities to minimize defect rates. Our customers must have an awareness of and respect for our brand image of being "first to market and first in quality." If we deliver on this pledge to our customers, then our financial goal of increasing our return on shareholders' equity should take care of itself.

Excerpt from Destination Resorts International's annual report:

> Our business succeeds or fails based on the quality of the service that our front-line em-
> ployees provide to customers. Therefore, it is imperative that we strive to maintain high
> employee morale and minimize employee turnover. In addition, it is critical that we train
> our employees to use technology to create one seamless worldwide experience for our
> repeat customers. Once an employee enters a customer preference (e.g., provide two extra
> pillows in the room, deliver fresh brewed coffee to the room at 8:00 A.M., etc.) into our
> database, our worldwide workforce strives to ensure that a customer will never need to
> repeat this preference at any of our destination resorts. If we properly train and retain a
> motivated workforce, we should see continuous improvement in our percentage of error-
> free repeat customer check-ins, the time taken to resolve customer complaints, and our
> independently assessed room cleanliness. This in turn should drive improvement in our
> customer retention, which is the key to meeting our revenue growth goals.

Required:
1. Based on the excerpts above, compare and contrast the strategies of Applied
    Pharmaceuticals and Destination Resorts International.
2. Select balanced scorecard measures for each company and link the scorecard measures
    using the framework from Exhibit 11–5. Use arrows to show the causal links between the
    performance measures and show whether the performance measure should increase or
    decrease over time. Feel free to create measures that may not be specifically mentioned in
    the chapter, but nonetheless make sense given the strategic goals of each company.
3. What hypotheses are built into each balanced scorecard? Why do the hypotheses differ
    between the two companies?

CASE 11–24 Balanced Scorecard [LO5]

Donnally Department Store is located in the downtown area of a medium-sized city in western
Canada. While the store had been profitable for many years, it is facing increasing competition from large national chains that have set up stores in the city's suburbs. Recently, the
downtown area has been undergoing revitalization, and the owners of Donnally Department
Store are cautiously optimistic that profitability can be restored.

In an attempt to accelerate the return to profitability, the management of Donnally
Department Store is designing a balanced scorecard for the company. Management believes the
company should focus on two key problems. First, customers are taking longer and longer to
pay the bills they incur on the department store's credit card, and they have far more bad debts
than are normal for the industry. If this problem were solved, the company would have more
cash to make much-needed renovations. Investigation has revealed that much of the problem
with late payments and unpaid bills is apparently due to disputed bills that are the result of
incorrect charges on the customer bills. These incorrect charges usually occur because salesclerks enter data incorrectly on the credit card machine. Second, the company has been incurring large losses on unsold seasonal apparel. Such items are ordinarily resold at a loss to
discount stores that specialize in such distress items.

The meeting in which the balanced scorecard approach was discussed was disorganized
and ineffectively led—possibly because no one other than you and one of the vice-presidents
had read anything about how to put a balanced scorecard together. Nevertheless, a number of
potential performance measures were suggested by various managers as follows.

Performance measures suggested by various managers:
*   Total sales revenue.
*   Percentage of salesclerks trained to correctly enter data on credit card machines.
*   Customer satisfaction with accuracy of charge account bills from monthly customer survey.
*   Sales per employee.
*   Travel expenses for buyers for trips to fashion shows.
*   Average age of accounts receivables.
*   Courtesy shown by junior staff members to senior staff members based on surveys of se-
    nior staff.
*   Unsold inventory at the end of the season as a percentage of total cost of sales.
*   Sales per square metre of floor space.
*   Percentage of suppliers making just-in-time deliveries.
*   Quality of food in the staff cafeteria based on staff surveys.
*   Written-off accounts receivables (bad debts) as a percentage of sales.
*   Percentage of charge account bills containing errors.

- Percentage of employees who have attended the city's cultural diversity workshop.
- Total profit.
- Profit per employee.

Required:
1. As someone with more knowledge of the balanced scorecard than anyone else in the company, you have been asked to build an integrated balanced scorecard. In your scorecard, use only performance measures suggested by the managers above. You do not have to use all of the performance measures suggested by the managers, but you should build a balanced scorecard that reveals a strategy for dealing with the problems with accounts receivable and with unsold merchandise. Construct the balanced scorecard following the format used in Exhibit 11–5. Do not be particularly concerned about whether a specific performance measure falls within the learning and growth, internal business process, customer, or financial perspective. However, use arrows to clearly show the causal links between the performance measures and decide whether the performance measures should show increases or decreases.
2. Assume that the company adopts your balanced scorecard. After a year, there are improvements in some performance measures but not in others. What should management do next?
3. *a.* Suppose that customers express greater satisfaction with the accuracy of their charge account bills but the performance measures for the average age of accounts receivable and for bad debts do not improve. Explain why this might happen.
    b. Suppose that the performance measures for the average age of accounts receivable, bad debts, and unsold inventory improve, but total profits do not. Explain why this might happen. Assume in your answer that the explanation lies within the company.

CASE 11–25 Return on Investment and Residual Income; Decentralization [LO3, LO4]
Kaiser Industries produces tool and die machinery for manufacturers. The company expanded vertically several years ago by acquiring Superior Steel Company, one of its suppliers of alloy steel plates. Kaiser decided to maintain Superior's separate identity and therefore established the Superior Steel Division as one of its investment centres.

Kaiser evaluates its divisions on the basis of ROI. Management bonuses are also based on ROI. All investments in operating assets are expected to earn a minimum required rate of return of 11%.

Superior's ROI has ranged from 14% to 17% since it was acquired by Kaiser. During the past year, Superior had an investment opportunity that would yield an estimated rate of return of 13%. Superior's management decided against the investment because it believed the investment would decrease the division's overall ROI.

Last year's absorption costing income statement for Superior Steel Division follows. The division's operating assets employed were $6,480,000 at the end of the year, which represents an 8% increase over the previous year-end balance:

SUPERIOR STEEL DIVISION Divisional Income Statement For the Year Ended December 31		
Sales.......................................		$15,600,000
Cost of goods sold		8,250,000
Gross margin................................		7,350,000
Less selling and administrative expenses:		
Selling expenses.........................	$2,810,000	
Administrative expenses.................	3,604,000	6,414,000
Operating income		$ 936,000

Required:
1. Compute the following performance measures for the Superior Steel Division:
    a. ROI. (Remember, ROI is based on the *average* operating assets, computed from the beginning-of-year and end-of-year balances.) State ROI in terms of margin and turnover.
    b. Residual income.
2. Would the management of Superior Steel Division have been more likely to accept the investment opportunity it had last year if residual income were used as a performance measure instead of ROI? Explain.

3.   The Superior Steel Division is a separate investment centre within Kaiser Industries. Identify the items Superior must be free to control if it is to be evaluated fairly by either the ROI or the residual income performance measure.

(CMA, adapted)

CASE 11-26 Service Organization; Segment Reporting [LO1]

The Canadian Association of Nutritionists, a fictional professional association for nutritional counsellors, has 10,000 members. The association operates from a central headquarters but has local chapters throughout Canada. The association's monthly journal, *Good Nutrition Today*, features recent developments in the field. The association also publishes special reports and books, and it sponsors courses that qualify members for the continuing professional education credit required by certification boards. The association's statement of revenues and expenses for the current year is presented below:

CANADIAN ASSOCIATION OF NUTRITIONISTS Statement of Revenues and Expenses For the Year Ended December 31	
Revenues	$970,000
Expenses:	
Salaries	440,000
Occupancy costs	120,000
Distributions to local chapters	210,000
Printing	82,000
Mailing	24,000
Continuing education instructors' fees	60,000
Selling and administrative	27,000
Total expenses	963,000
Excess of revenues over expenses	$ 7,000

The board of directors of the association has requested that you construct a segmented income statement that shows the financial contribution of each of the association's four major programs—membership service, journal, books and reports, and continuing education. The following data have been gathered to aid you:

a.   Membership dues are $60 per year, of which $15 covers a one-year subscription to the association's journal. The other $45 pays for general membership services.

b.   One-year subscriptions to *Good Nutrition Today* are sold to non-members and libraries at $20 per subscription. A total of 1,000 of these subscriptions were sold last year. In addition to subscriptions, the journal generated $50,000 in advertising revenues. The costs per journal subscription, for members as well as non-members, were $4 for printing and $1 for mailing.

c.   A variety of technical reports and professional books were sold for a total of $70,000 during the year. Printing costs for these materials totalled $25,000, and mailing costs totalled $8,000.

d.   The association offers a number of continuing education courses. The courses generated revenues of $230,000 last year.

e.   Salary costs and the cost of space occupied by each program and the central staff follow:

	Salaries	Space Occupied (square metres)
Membership services	$ 170,000	3,000
Journal	60,000	1,000
Books and reports	40,000	1,000
Continuing education	50,000	2,000
Central staff	120,000	3,000
Total	$440,000	10,000

f.   The $120,000 in occupancy costs incurred last year includes $20,000 in rental cost for a portion of the warehouse used by the Membership Services program for storage. The association has a flexible rental agreement that allows it to pay rent only on the warehouse space it uses.

g.   Printing costs are for printing the journal, books and reports, and continuing education materials.

h. Distributions to local chapters are for general membership services.

i. Selling and administrative expenses include costs relating to administration of the association as a whole. The association's central staff does some mailing of materials for selling and administrative purposes.

j. The expenses that can be traced or assigned to the central staff, as well as any other expenses that are not traceable to the programs, will be treated as common costs. It is not necessary to distinguish between variable and fixed costs.

Required:
1. Prepare a contribution format segmented income statement for the Canadian Association of Nutritionists for last year. This statement should show the segment margin for each program as well as results for the association as a whole.
2. Give arguments for and against allocating all costs of the association to the four programs.

(CMA, adapted)

CASE 11–27 Performance Evaluation; Return on Investment and Residual Income [LO3, LO4]

Convenient Food Markets (CFM) is a chain of more than 100 convenience stores. The company has faced increasing competition over the past several years, mainly because department store chains have been adding grocery departments and gas stations have been adding full-service convenience stores to their locations. As a consequence, the company has lost market share recently to competitors. The company has set a target minimum rate of return for its stores of 22%.

John Nicholson is the district manager of the 17 CFM stores in Bailingham. Nicholson's district happens to include the original store, the first in the CFM chain, which opened more than 40 years ago. In fact, Nicholson's first summer job was as a stock boy at the original store in the year that it opened. After university, he returned to CFM as a store manager, has worked his way up to district manager, and plans to retire in about five years.

CFM leases store buildings, investing significantly in the interior design, display, and decoration. The original CFM store remains profitable, in part because the fixtures and fittings are almost fully depreciated. While the company has invested in significant leasehold improvements in other newer stores, little has changed in the original store since opening day. While Nicholson has a sense of nostalgia for the original store, in reality, sales volumes have been falling and foot traffic has declined significantly in recent years. Fewer people are moving to the neighbourhood, as more and more people are moving to the suburbs.

All 17 stores in the district report to Nicholson, who is evaluated on the basis of average ROI for the stores in his district. For this calculation, the net book value of investment in furnishings and fixtures represents the operating assets of each of the stores. Operating income after depreciation on leasehold improvements represents the numerator for this calculation.

Nicholson is considering a proposal from a developer to open a new store in a newly developed residential neighbourhood. The developer has completed about 60% of the new homes planned for this neighbourhood and will complete the other 40% within the next 18 months. Due to limited capital to invest, Nicholson realizes that opening the new store would mean closing down an old store, and the original store seems to be the best candidate. To aid in his decision, Nicholson has collected the following information:

	Original Store (prior-year actual)	New Store (forecast)
Operating income less depreciation..........	$ 75,000	$145,000
Net book value of operating assets	195,000	475,000

Required:
1. Calculate the ROI and residual income for both the original store and the new store.
2. Take on the role of an internal auditor at CFM. Assume that your task is to evaluate the effectiveness of the performance evaluation system for CFM district managers. In this capacity, write a short memo to the CFO of CFM to discuss your findings. In the memo, you should indicate whether you believe Nicholson will want to open the new store, whether your analysis indicates that Nicholson should open the new store, and why or why not. You should also include your observations about the effect of the performance evaluation system on the decisions made by CFM district managers and what might be done to improve it.

INSTANT QUIZ SOLUTIONS

11–1

A traceable cost of a segment is a cost that arises specifically because of the existence of that segment. If the segment were eliminated, the cost would disappear. A common cost, by contrast, is a cost that supports more than one segment, but is not traceable in whole or in part to any one of the segments. If the departments of a company are treated as segments, then examples of the traceable costs of a department could include the salary of the department's supervisor, depreciation of machines used exclusively by the department, and the costs of supplies used by the department. Examples of common costs are the lease cost of the headquarters building, corporate image advertising, and periodic depreciation of machines shared by several departments.

11–2

Margin = Operating income ÷ Sales = \$3,600,000 ÷ \$12,000,000 = 30%
Turnover = Sales ÷ Average operating assets = \$12,000,000 ÷ \$24,000,000 = 0.5
Return on Investment = Margin × Turnover = 30% × 0.5 = 15%

11–3

Average operating assets (a)	£4,400,000
Net operating income	£ 600,000
Minimum required return: 9% × (a)	396,000
Residual income	£ 204,000

11–4

The balanced scorecard is constructed to support the company's strategy, which is a theory about what actions will further the company's goals. Assuming that the company has financial goals, measures of financial performance must be included in the balanced scorecard as a check on the reality of the theory. If the non-financial measures show improvement, but the financial outcomes do not improve, the theory may be flawed and the strategy should be changed. Since different companies have different strategies, their balanced scorecards should be different.

APPENDIX 11A: TRANSFER PRICING, QUALITY COSTS, AND SERVICE DEPARTMENT COST ALLOCATION

McGraw Hill Education connect   Appendix available on Connect.

connect   **LEARNSMART**   **SMARTBOOK**

SHORT-TERM AND LONG-TERM DECISIONS
Chapters 12 and 13

Two time frames are commonly used to characterize the types of decision analysis covered in this final section. **Chapter 12** presents a framework for making short-term decisions where the analysis involves examining those revenues and costs that differ across the alternatives under consideration. Several commonly encountered decision situations are presented, along with the approach used to identify and use relevant costs and benefits. However, the situations examined in this chapter do not involve long-term capital expenditures for items such as plant and equipment, so the time value of money

(cost of interest) does not need to be incorporated into the analysis.

Long-term decision analysis typically involves significant capital expenditures and requires explicit consideration of the time value of money. The approach presented in **Chapter 13** is commonly described as *capital budgeting*. The concept of using only relevant costs and benefits in the analysis still holds in this chapter. The chapter also introduces corporate income taxes to the analysis because of their effects on cash flows.

RELEVANT COSTS FOR DECISION MAKING

ENHANCING PRODUCT OFFERINGS TO STAY COMPETITIVE AT WESTJET

WestJet was founded in 1996 as an alternative airline to Air Canada for destinations in western Canada. WestJet's original strategy was to provide one class of efficient, low-cost, high-quality economy airfare to all customers. Today, WestJet is Canada's leading "high-value, low-fare" airline and has expanded its service to the United States and beyond. Even so, recent pressures on prices and the addition of Air Canada Rouge, a competing low-fare service, have forced WestJet to rethink its product offerings. WestJet has added two new product offerings to better compete in the business travel and regional airline markets. Specifically, WestJet has added a premium Economy Plus product to appeal to business customers. This fare type costs slightly more than a regular economy ticket but allows greater flexibility to change travel plans, added leg room in the first three rows of the plane, a second free checked bag, and priority boarding. WestJet's new Encore service, on the other hand, was created to provide affordable quick trips between Calgary, Vancouver, and Edmonton and relatively underserviced communities in western Canada including Grand Prairie, Nanaimo, Brandon, and Fort St. John. The strategy seems to be working, as WestJet reported a load factor of 79.2%, the second highest in the firm's history; capacity grew 8.1%; and the airline flew a record number of passengers in October 2013.

Which revenues and costs are relevant when evaluating the financial effects of adding or discontinuing a product line? This and other related topics are considered in this chapter.

Sources: Ross Marowits, "WestJet says efforts to attract business customers, Encore exceeding forecasts," *Montreal Gazette*, November 6, 2013; http://www.westjet.com.

Decision making is a critical aspect of managing an organization. Managers must constantly decide which products or services to offer, which production methods to use, whether to make or buy component parts, what prices to charge, whether to accept special orders at special prices, how to allocate limited resources, and so on. In each case, the decision should lead to outcomes that contribute to achieving the performance goals identified as part of the organization's strategic objectives (e.g., grow revenues, reduce costs, improve return on investment). However, decision making is a complex process. Numerous alternatives may exist for each decision situation, and large amounts of data must be analyzed, only some of which are relevant.

How can managers cope with these complexities in an effort to consistently make good decisions? The key is to identify and compare *only* the relevant costs and benefits for each alternative. A **relevant cost** is a cost that differs among the alternatives under consideration *and* that will be incurred in the future (i.e., the cost has not already been incurred). A key challenge for managers, and fundamental to good decision making, is differentiating between relevant and irrelevant costs. This is critical because consideration of irrelevant costs wastes managers' time and effort and can lead to the wrong decisions. Further complicating matters is the fact that the relevance of specific costs and benefits depends on the decision situation. For example, a product supervisor's salary is typically irrelevant in deciding whether or not to accept a special order from a customer but can be relevant when deciding whether to keep or drop that product line. The purpose of this chapter is to provide a framework for distinguishing between relevant and irrelevant costs by illustrating their use in a wide range of decision-making situations.

We begin the chapter by developing a general framework for identifying relevant costs and benefits. We then apply this framework to a variety of non-recurring situations to illustrate how the relevance of a cost or benefit depends on the type of decision being made. Next we turn our attention to analyzing situations where managers must decide how to allocate a limited resource such as labour-hours. Finally, the relationship between relevant costs and pricing issues is further examined in the appendix.

Two aspects of the decision situations and the related analysis presented in this chapter are important to emphasize. First, none of the situations involve capital expenditures (e.g., replacing production equipment), where the time value of money can be an important factor in the analysis. This type of analysis, termed *capital budgeting*, is covered in Chapter 13. Second, the key criterion used in the various decision situations presented in this chapter is the maximization of operating income. However, in practice, managers may also consider qualitative factors when making decisions. For example, when deciding whether to keep or drop a product or segment, the effect on employee morale and the impact on the company's reputation with its customers may be important but very difficult or costly to quantify. The extent to which qualitative factors influence a decision will vary from situation to situation, but these factors are often taken into account.

Relevant cost
A cost that differs among the alternatives in a particular decision and will be incurred in the future. In managerial accounting, this term is synonymous with *avoidable cost* and *differential cost*.

■ COST CONCEPTS FOR DECISION MAKING

Four cost terms discussed in Chapter 2 are particularly applicable to this chapter. These terms are *differential costs*, *incremental costs*, *opportunity costs*, and *sunk costs*. You may find it helpful to turn back to Chapter 2 and review the concepts before reading on.

Identifying Relevant Costs and Benefits

Because it is fundamental to the proper analysis of the various decision situations covered in this chapter, we begin by identifying the nature of relevant costs and benefits. Only those costs and benefits that differ in total among alternatives and that will be incurred in the future are relevant in a decision. If a cost will be the same regardless of the alternative selected, then it can be ignored. For example, if

LEARNING OBJECTIVE
Distinguish between relevant and irrelevant costs in decision making.

you are trying to decide whether to go to a movie or to download a movie for the evening, the lease payments on your car are irrelevant. Whether you go to a movie or stay home, the lease payments will be exactly the same and are therefore irrelevant in the decision. On the other hand, the cost of the movie ticket and the cost of downloading the movie are relevant in the decision because they are *avoidable costs*.

Avoidable cost

Any cost that can be eliminated (in whole or in part) by choosing one alternative over another in a decision-making situation. In managerial accounting, this term is synonymous with *relevant cost* and *differential cost*.

An **avoidable cost** is a cost that can be eliminated in whole or in part by choosing one alternative over another. By choosing the alternative of going to the movie, the cost of downloading a movie can be avoided. By choosing the alternative of downloading a movie, the cost of the movie ticket can be avoided. Therefore, the cost of the movie ticket and the cost of downloading a movie are both avoidable costs. On the other hand, the lease payments on the car are not an avoidable cost because you would continue to lease your car under either alternative. Avoidable costs are relevant costs. Unavoidable costs are irrelevant costs.

Two broad categories of costs are never relevant in decisions. These irrelevant costs are

1. sunk costs (e.g., a previously owned computer used to download the movie), and
2. future costs that do not differ between the alternatives (e.g., car lease payments when making a "go to a movie" versus "download a movie" decision).

As we learned in Chapter 2, a *sunk cost* is a cost that has already been incurred and that cannot be avoided, regardless of what a manager decides to do. Sunk costs do not change, regardless of the alternatives being considered, and they are therefore always irrelevant and should be ignored. Similarly, future costs that are the same under each alternative being considered are also irrelevant since they will not affect the decision. The cost of the car lease next month is a future cost but will be the same whether you go to the movie or download a movie. On the other hand, future costs that do differ between alternatives *are* relevant. For example, when deciding whether to go to a movie or download a movie, the cost of buying a movie ticket and the cost of downloading a movie have not yet been incurred. These are future costs that differ between alternatives when the decision is being made and therefore are relevant.

Along with sunk cost, the term *differential cost* was introduced in Chapter 2. In managerial accounting, the terms *avoidable cost*, *differential cost*, *incremental cost*, and *relevant cost* are often used interchangeably. To identify the costs and benefits that are relevant in a particular decision situation, these steps can be followed:

1. Eliminate costs and benefits that do not differ between alternatives. These irrelevant costs consist of (a) sunk costs and (b) future costs and benefits that do not differ between alternatives.
2. Use the remaining costs and benefits that do differ between alternatives in making the decision. The costs that remain are the differential, or avoidable, costs.

Different Costs for Different Purposes

It is important to recognize that costs that are relevant in one decision situation are not necessarily relevant in another. Simply put, this means that *the manager needs different costs for different purposes*. For one purpose, a particular group of costs may be relevant; for another purpose, an entirely different group of costs may be relevant. Thus, in *each* decision situation the manager must examine the data at hand and isolate the relevant costs. Otherwise, the manager runs the risk of being misled by irrelevant data.

The concept of "different costs for different purposes" is basic to managerial accounting; we will see its application frequently in the remainder of this chapter.

An Example of Identifying Relevant Costs and Benefits

Cynthia is currently a student in an MBA program in Halifax and would like to visit a friend in Moncton over the weekend. She is trying to decide whether to drive or take the train. Because she is on a tight budget, she wants to carefully consider the costs of the two alternatives. If one alternative is far less expensive than the other, that may determine her choice. By car, the distance between her apartment in Halifax and her friend's apartment in Moncton is 265 kilometres. Cynthia has compiled a list of items to consider in the table below:

	Item	Annual Cost of Fixed Items	Cost per Kilometre (based on 16,000 kilometres per year)
	Automobile Costs		
(a)	Annual straight-line depreciation on car [($24,000 original cost − $10,000 estimated resale value in 5 years)/5 years]	$2,800	$0.175
(b)	Cost of gasoline ($1.20 per litre ÷ 10 kilometres per litre)		0.120
(c)	Annual cost of auto insurance and licence	2,000	0.125
(d)	Maintenance and repairs		0.050
(e)	Parking fees at university ($45 per month × 8 months)	360	0.023
(f)	Tires ($600 to replace all 4 tires every 50,000 kilometres)		0.012
(g)	Total average cost per kilometre		$0.505

	Additional Data	
	Item	
(h)	Cost of round-trip VIA ticket	$85
(i)	Benefit of relaxing and being able to study during the train ride rather than having to drive	?
(j)	Cost of putting the cat in a kennel while gone	$40
(k)	Benefit of having a car available in Moncton	?
(l)	Hassle of parking the car in Moncton	?
(m)	Cost of parking the car in Moncton	$25 per day

Which costs and benefits are relevant in this decision? Remember, only those costs and benefits that differ between alternatives are relevant. Everything else is irrelevant and can be ignored. Starting at the top of the list, we consider the relevance of each item:

- Item (a): The original cost of the car is a sunk cost. This cost has already been incurred and therefore can never differ between alternatives. Consequently, it is irrelevant and can be ignored. The same is true of the accounting depreciation of $2,800 per year, which simply spreads the sunk cost across the useful life of the asset.

- Item (b): The cost of gasoline consumed by driving to Moncton is clearly a relevant cost in this decision. If Cynthia takes the train, this cost will not be incurred. Hence, the cost differs between alternatives and is therefore relevant.

- Item (c): The annual cost of auto insurance and licence is not relevant. Whether Cynthia takes the train or drives on this particular trip, her annual auto insurance premium and her auto licence fee will remain the same.[1]

- Item (d): The cost of maintenance and repairs is relevant. While maintenance and repair costs have a large random component, over the long run they are typically proportional to the amount the car is driven. Thus, the average cost of $0.05 per kilometre is a reasonable estimate to use.

- Item (*e*): The monthly fee that Cynthia pays to park at her university during the academic year is not relevant in the decision of how to get to Moncton. Regardless of which alternative she selects—driving or taking the train—she will still need to pay for parking at school.
- Item (*f*): The cost of replacing all four tires ($600) every 50,000 kilometres is relevant. The more often Cynthia uses her car, the sooner she will have to replace the tires. Therefore, the $0.012 per kilometre for tires is appropriate to use in deciding whether to drive or take the train.
- Item (*g*): Some elements of the total average cost of $0.505 per kilometre are relevant, but some are not relevant. Since it contains some irrelevant costs, it would be incorrect to estimate the cost of driving to Moncton and back by simply multiplying the $0.505 by 530 kilometres (265 kilometres each way × 2). This erroneous approach would yield a cost of driving of $267.65. Unfortunately, such mistakes are often made in both personal life and in business. Since the total cost is stated on a per kilometre basis, people are easily misled. Often people think that if the cost is stated as $0.505 per kilometre, the cost of driving 100 kilometres is $50.50. But it is not. Many of the costs included in the $0.505 cost per kilometre are sunk and/or fixed and will not increase if the car is driven another 100 kilometres. The $0.505 is an average cost, not an incremental cost. Study such unitized costs carefully (i.e., costs stated in terms of a dollar amount per unit, per kilometre, per direct labour-hour, per machine-hour, and so on)—they are often misleading.
- Item (*h*): The $85 cost of a round-trip ticket on VIA is clearly relevant in this decision. If Cynthia drives, she will not have to buy the ticket.
- Item (*i*): Although it is difficult to put a dollar value on relaxing and being able to study while on the train, this item is relevant to the decision. It is relevant because it is a benefit that is available only if she takes the train.
- Item (*j*): The cost of putting Cynthia's cat in the kennel while she is gone is clearly irrelevant to this decision. Whether she takes the train or drives to Moncton she will still need to put her cat in a kennel.
- Items (*k*) and (*l*): Like item (*i*), they are relevant to the decision even if it is difficult to measure their dollar impacts.
- Item (*m*): The cost of parking in Moncton is relevant to the decision since it will be incurred only if Cynthia takes her car.

Bringing together all of the relevant data, Cynthia would estimate the relative costs of driving and taking the train as follows:

Relevant financial cost of driving to Moncton:	
Gasoline (530 kilometres at $0.12 per kilometre)	$ 63.60
Maintenance and repairs (530 kilometres @ $0.05 per km)	26.50
Tires (530 kilometres @ $0.012 per km)	6.36
Cost of parking the car in Moncton (2 days @ $25 per day)	50.00
Total	$146.46
Relevant financial cost of taking the train to Moncton:	
Cost of round-trip VIA ticket from Halifax to Moncton	$ 85.00

What should Cynthia do? From a purely financial standpoint, it would be cheaper by $61.46 ($146.46 − $85.00) to take the train. Cynthia has to decide whether the benefit of having the car available in Moncton justifies the higher cost of driving.

In this example, we focused on identifying the relevant costs and benefits—everything else was ignored. In the next example, we will begin the analysis by including all of the costs and benefits—relevant or not. We will see that if we are very careful, we will still get the correct answer because the irrelevant costs and benefits will cancel out when we compare the alternatives.

Reconciling the Total and Differential Approaches

OfficeMate Company is considering a new labour-saving machine that rents for $3,000 per year. The machine will be used in the production of the company's best-selling heavy-duty stapler. Data concerning the company's annual sales and costs of producing these staplers with and without the new machine are shown in the following table:

	Current Situation	Situation with the New Machine
Units produced and sold.............................	5,000	5,000
Selling price per unit.................................	$ 40	$ 40
Direct materials cost per unit.........................	14	14
Direct labour cost per unit..........................	8	5
Variable overhead cost per unit......................	2	2
Fixed costs, other	62,000	62,000
Fixed costs, new machine............................	—	3,000

Given the annual sales and the price and cost data in this table, the operating income for the product under the two alternatives can be computed as shown in Exhibit 12–1.

Note that the operating income is higher by $12,000 with the new machine, so it is the better alternative. Note also that the $12,000 advantage for the new machine can be obtained in two different ways. It is the difference between the $30,000 operating income with the new machine and the $18,000 operating income for the current situation. It is also the sum of the differential costs and benefits as shown in the last column of Exhibit 12–1. A positive number in the Differential Costs and Benefits column indicates that the difference between the alternatives favours the new machine; a negative number indicates that the difference favours the current situation. A zero in that column simply means that the total amount for the item is exactly the same for both alternatives. So, since the difference in the operating incomes equals the sum of the differences for the individual items, any cost or benefit that is the same for both alternatives will have no impact on which alternative is preferred. This is why we stated earlier that costs and benefits that do not differ between alternatives are irrelevant and can be ignored. If we properly account for them, they will cancel out when we compare the alternatives.

	Current Situation	Situation with New Machine	Differential Costs and Benefits
Sales (5,000 units @ $40 per unit).............	$200,000	$200,000	$ 0
Less variable expenses:			
Direct materials (5,000 units @ $14 per unit)...	70,000	70,000	0
Direct labour (5,000 units @ $8 and $5 per unit)........................	40,000	25,000	15,000
Variable overhead (5,000 units @ $2 per unit)............................	10,000	10,000	0
Total variable expenses	120,000	105,000	
Contribution margin..........................	80,000	95,000	
Less fixed expenses:			
Other......................................	62,000	62,000	0
Rent of new machine........................	0	3,000	(3,000)
Total fixed expenses	62,000	65,000	
Operating income............................	$ 18,000	$ 30,000	$12,000

EXHIBIT 12–1   Total and Differential Costs

We could have arrived at the same solution more quickly by ignoring the irrelevant costs and benefits:

- The selling price per unit and the number of units sold do not differ between the alternatives. Therefore, the total sales revenues are exactly the same for the two alternatives, as shown in Exhibit 12–1. Since the sales revenues are exactly the same, they have no effect on the difference in operating income between the two alternatives. That is shown in the last column in Exhibit 12–1, which indicates a $0 differential benefit.
- The direct materials cost per unit, the variable overhead cost per unit, and the number of units produced and sold do not differ between the alternatives. Consequently, the direct materials cost and the variable overhead cost will be the same for the two alternatives and can be ignored.
- The "other" fixed expenses do not differ between the alternatives, so they can be ignored as well.

Indeed, the only costs that do differ between the alternatives are direct labour costs and the fixed rental cost of the new machine. Hence, these are the only relevant costs. The two alternatives can be compared based on just these relevant costs:

Net advantage to renting the new machine:	
Decrease in direct labour costs (5,000 units at a cost savings of $3 per unit)	$15,000
Increase in fixed expenses (rent)..	(3,000)
Net annual cost savings from renting the new machine...	$12,000

If we focus on just the relevant costs and benefits, therefore, we get exactly the same answer that we got when we listed all of the costs and benefits—including those that do not differ between the alternatives and hence are irrelevant. We get the same answer because the only costs and benefits that matter in the final comparison of the operating incomes are those that differ between the two alternatives and therefore are not zero in the last column of Exhibit 12–1. Those two relevant costs are both listed in the above analysis, showing the net advantage to renting the new machine.

Why Isolate Relevant Costs?

In the preceding example, we used two different approaches to analyze the alternatives. First, we considered only the relevant costs. Second, we considered all costs, both those that were relevant and those that were not. We obtained the same answer under both approaches. It would be natural to ask, "Why bother isolating relevant costs when total costs will do the job just as well?" Isolating relevant costs is desirable for at least two reasons.

First, only rarely will enough information be available to prepare a detailed income statement for both alternatives as we have done in the preceding examples. Assume, for example, that you are called on to make a decision relating to a *single product* of a multi-departmental, multi-product firm. Under these circumstances, it would be virtually impossible to prepare an income statement of any type. You would have to rely on your ability to recognize which costs are relevant and which are not in order to assemble the data necessary to make a decision.

Second, combining irrelevant costs with relevant costs may cause confusion and distract attention from the matters that are really critical. Furthermore, the danger always exists that an irrelevant piece of data may be used improperly, resulting in an incorrect decision. Indeed, research shows that managers will often attempt to use *all* information provided, relevant and irrelevant, when making a decision.[2] The best approach is to discard irrelevant data and base the decision entirely on the relevant data.

Relevant cost analysis, combined with the contribution approach to the income statement, provides a powerful tool for making decisions. We will investigate various uses of this tool in the remaining sections of this chapter.

Instant Quiz 12-1
"All future costs are relevant in decision making." Do you agree? Why or why not?

■ ANALYSIS OF VARIOUS DECISION SITUATIONS

LEARNING OBJECTIVE **2**
Prepare analyses for various decision situations.

Periodically, managers are faced with making non-routine or special decisions. Should a product line or segment be kept or dropped? Should a product component be made internally or purchased from an external supplier (outsourced)? Should special orders be accepted or rejected? Should a product be sold as is or processed further? While on the surface these may appear to be very different decision situations, the approach to the analysis is similar in each case. For each situation, the relevant costs and benefits must be quantified and the alternative with the most favourable impact on operating income selected. In some situations, the analysis will consist only of a comparison of relevant costs (make versus buy), while in others, both relevant benefits and relevant costs will be involved (keep or drop a product). As will be illustrated in the examples of each decision situation that follows, the challenge for managers is identifying and quantifying the relevant costs and benefits.

Adding and Dropping Product Lines and Other Segments

Decisions relating to whether existing product lines or other segments of a company should be dropped and new ones added are among the most difficult that a manager has to make. In such decisions, many qualitative and quantitative factors must be considered. Ultimately, however, any final decision to drop an old segment or to add a new one will hinge primarily on the impact the decision will have on operating income. To assess this impact, it is necessary to prepare a careful analysis of the costs involved.

Consider the three major product lines of AFM Electronics—plasma TVs, E-readers, and digital cameras. Sales and cost information for the preceding month for each separate product line and for the company in total are given in Exhibit 12–2.

What can be done to improve the company's overall performance? One product line—digital cameras—shows an operating loss for the month. Perhaps dropping this line would cause profits in the company as a whole to improve. In deciding whether the line should be dropped, management should employ the reasoning that follows.

If the digital camera line is dropped, then the company will lose $16,000 per month in contribution margin. By dropping the line, however, it may be possible to avoid some fixed costs by, for example, laying off certain employees or reducing advertising costs. If by dropping the digital camera line the company is able to avoid more in fixed costs than it loses in contribution margin, then it will be better off if the line is eliminated, because overall operating income should improve. On the other hand, if the company is not able to avoid as much in fixed costs as it loses

	Total	Product Line		
		Plasma TVs	E-readers	Digital Cameras
Sales....................	$340,000	$187,500	$112,500	$40,000
Less variable expenses.........	136,500	75,000	37,500	24,000
Contribution margin	203,500	112,500	75,000	16,000
Less fixed expenses:				
Salaries....................	69,400	44,250	18,750	6,400
Advertising	17,950	1,500	11,250	5,200
Utilities	2,300	750	750	800
Depreciation—fixtures	6,100	1,500	3,000	1,600
Rent.......................	27,200	15,000	9,000	3,200
Insurance	4,150	3,000	750	400
Selling and administrative....	40,800	22,500	13,500	4,800
Total fixed expenses	167,900	88,500	57,000	22,400
Operating income (loss)........	$ 35,600	$24,000	$18,000	$ (6,400)

EXHIBIT 12–2   AFM Electronics Product Lines

in contribution margin, then the digital camera line should be retained. In short, the manager should ask, "What costs can I avoid if I drop this product line?"

As we have seen from our earlier discussion, not all costs are avoidable. For example, some of the costs associated with a product line may be sunk costs. Other costs may be allocated common costs that will not differ in total regardless of whether the product line is dropped or retained. As discussed in Chapter 7, an activity-based costing analysis may be used to help identify the relevant costs.

To show how the manager should proceed in a product-line analysis, suppose that the management of AFM Electronics has analyzed the costs being charged to the three product lines and has determined the following:

1. The salaries expense represents salaries paid to employees working directly in each product-line area. All of the employees working in digital camera–related activities will be laid off if the line is dropped.
2. The advertising expense represents direct advertising of each product line and is avoidable if the line is dropped.
3. The utilities expense represents utilities costs for the entire company. The amount charged to each product line is an allocation based on space occupied and is not avoidable if the product line is dropped.
4. The depreciation expense represents depreciation on fixtures used for display of the various product lines. Although the fixtures are nearly new, they are custom built and will have little resale value if the digital camera line is dropped.
5. The rent expense represents rent on the entire building housing the company; it is allocated to the product lines on the basis of sales dollars. The monthly rent of $27,200 is fixed under a long-term lease agreement.
6. The insurance expense represents insurance carried on inventories within each of the three product-line areas.
7. The selling and administrative expense represents the costs of accounting, purchasing, and general management, which are allocated to the product lines on the basis of sales dollars. Total administrative costs will not change if the digital camera line is dropped.

With this information, management can identify costs that can and cannot be avoided if the product line is dropped:

	Total Cost	Not Avoidable*	Avoidable
Salaries	$ 6,400		$ 6,400
Advertising	5,200		5,200
Utilities	800	$ 800	
Depreciation—fixtures	1,600	1,600	
Rent	3,200	3,200	
Insurance	400		400
Selling and administrative	4,800	4,800	
Total fixed expenses	$22,400	$10,400	$12,000

*These costs represent either (1) sunk costs or (2) future costs that will not change if the digital camera line is retained or discontinued.

To determine how dropping the line will affect the overall profits of the company, we can compare the contribution margin that will be lost to the costs that can be avoided if the line is dropped:

Contribution margin lost if the digital camera line is discontinued (see Exhibit 12–2)	$(16,000)
Less fixed costs that can be avoided if the digital camera line is discontinued (see above)	12,000
Decrease in overall company operating income	$ (4,000)

In this case, the fixed costs that can be avoided by dropping the product line are less than the contribution margin that will be lost. Therefore, based on the data given, the digital camera line should not be discontinued unless a more profitable use can be found for the floor and counter space that it is occupying.

A Comparative Format

Some managers prefer to approach decisions of this type by preparing comparative income statements showing the effects on the company as a whole of either keeping or dropping the product line in question. A comparative analysis of this type for AFM Electronics is shown in Exhibit 12-3.

As shown by column 3 in the exhibit, overall company operating income will decrease by $4,000 each period if the digital cameras line is dropped. This is the same answer, of course, as we obtained in our earlier analysis.

Beware of Allocated Fixed Costs

Our conclusion that the digital camera line should not be dropped seems to conflict with the data shown earlier in Exhibit 12-2. Recall from the exhibit that the digital camera line is showing a loss rather than a profit. Why keep a line that is showing a loss? The explanation for this apparent inconsistency lies at least in part with the common fixed costs that are being allocated to the product lines. As we observed in Chapter 11, one of the great dangers in allocating common fixed costs is that such allocations can make a product line (or other segment of a business) *look* less profitable than it really is. By allocating the common fixed costs among all product lines, the digital camera line has been made to *look* as if it were unprofitable, whereas, in fact, dropping the line would result in a decrease in overall company operating income. This point can be seen clearly if we recast the data in Exhibit 12-2 by eliminating the allocation of the common fixed costs. This recasting of data—using the segmented approach from Chapter 11—is shown in Exhibit 12-4.

Exhibit 12-4 gives us a much different perspective of the profitability of the digital camera line compared to Exhibit 12-2. As shown in Exhibit 12-4, the digital camera line is covering all of its own traceable fixed costs and is generating a $2,400 segment margin toward covering the common fixed costs of the company. Unless another product line can be found that will generate a greater segment margin than

	Keep Digital Cameras	Drop Digital Cameras	Difference: Operating Income Increase or (Decrease)
Sales.......................	$40,000	$ 0	$(40,000)
Less variable expenses.................	24,000	0	24,000
Contribution margin	16,000	0	(16,000)
Less fixed expenses:			
Salaries...........................	6,400	0	6,400
Advertising	5,200	0	5,200
Utilities	800	800	0
Depreciation—fixtures	1,600	1,600	0
Rent..............................	3,200	3,200	0
Insurance	400	0	400
Selling and administrative............	4,800	4,800	0
Total fixed expenses	22,400	10,400	12,000
Operating income (loss)...............	$ (6,400)	$(10,400)	$ (4,000)

EXHIBIT 12-3   A Comparative Format for Product-Line Analysis

EXHIBIT 12-4   AFM Electronics Product Lines—Recast in Contribution Format (from Exhibit 12-2)

			Product Line	
	Total	**Plasma TVs**	**E-readers**	**Digital Cameras**
Sales.........................	$340,000	$187,500	$112,500	$40,000
Less variable expenses.........	136,500	75,000	37,500	24,000
Contribution margin	203,500	112,500	75,000	16,000
Less traceable fixed expenses:				
Salaries.....................	69,400	44,250	18,750	6,400
Advertising	17,950	1,500	11,250	5,200
Depreciation—fixtures	6,100	1,500	3,000	1,600
Insurance	4,150	3,000	750	400
Total fixed expenses	97,600	50,250	33,750	13,600
Product-line segment margin ...	105,900	$ 62,250	$ 41,250	$ 2,400*
Less common fixed expenses:				
Utilities	2,300			
Rent........................	27,200			
Selling and administrative....	40,800			
Total	70,300			
Operating income	$ 35,600			

*If the digital camera line is dropped, this $2,400 in segment margin will be lost to the company. In addition, we have seen that the $1,600 depreciation on the fixtures is a sunk cost that cannot be avoided. The sum of these two figures ($2,400 + $1,600 = $4,000) is the decrease in the company's overall profits if the digital camera line is discontinued.

this, the company would be better off keeping the digital camera line. By keeping the line, the company's overall operating income will be higher than if the product line is dropped.[3]

Additionally, we should note that managers may choose to retain an unprofitable product line if the line is necessary to the sale of other products or if it serves as a "magnet" to attract customers. Bread, for example, is not an especially profitable line in food stores, but customers expect it to be available, and many would undoubtedly shift their buying elsewhere if a particular store decided to stop carrying bread. Accordingly, to the extent that dropping a product line or segment results in decreases (or increases) to sales of other products or segments, the related impact on contribution margin should be included in the keep versus drop analysis.

LEARNING AID

KEEP OR DROP A PRODUCT/SEGMENT

Relevant Costs and Benefits
- Contribution margin (CM) lost if dropped
- Fixed costs avoided if dropped
- CM lost/gained on other products/segments

Irrelevant Costs
- Allocated common costs
- Sunk costs

Decision Rule:

Keep if   CM lost (all products/segments) > Fixed costs avoided + CM gained (other products/segments).

Drop if   CM lost (all products/segments) < Fixed costs avoided + CM gained (other products/segments).

Instant Quiz 12-1
Able Supply Co. is considering dropping a high-pressure water line from its product mix based on the following information:

Revenue from high-pressure water line	$100,000
Less: Direct costs	(83,000)
Indirect costs.......................	(22,000)
Loss from high-pressure water line	$ (5,000)

What factors should Able Supply consider before deciding to drop this product line?

The Make or Buy Decision

Many steps may be involved in getting a finished product into the hands of a consumer. First, raw materials may have to be obtained through mining, drilling, growing crops, raising animals, and so forth. Second, these raw materials may have to be processed to remove impurities and to extract the desirable and usable materials. Third, the usable materials may have to undergo some preliminary conversion so as to be usable in final products. For example, cotton must be made into thread and textiles before being made into clothing. Fourth, the actual manufacturing of the finished product must take place. And, finally, the finished product must be distributed to the ultimate consumer. Each of these steps is part of the value chain discussed in Chapter 1.

Separate companies may carry out each step in the value chain, or a single company may carry out several of the steps. When a single company is involved in more than one of these steps in the value chain, it is following a policy of **vertical integration**. Vertical integration is very common. Some firms control *all* of the activities in the value chain, from producing basic raw materials right up to the manufacture and final distribution of finished goods. Other firms integrate on a smaller scale by purchasing many of the parts and materials that go into their finished products.

A decision to produce internally, rather than to buy externally from a supplier, is called a **make or buy decision**. Indeed, any decision relating to vertical integration is a make or buy decision, since the company is deciding whether to meet its own needs internally or to buy externally.

Vertical integration
The involvement by a single company in more than one of the steps of the value chain, from production of basic raw materials to the manufacture and distribution of a finished product.

Make or buy decision
A decision as to whether an item should be produced internally or purchased from an outside supplier.

Strategic Aspects of the Make or Buy Decision

Integration provides certain advantages. An integrated firm is less dependent on its suppliers and may be able to ensure a smoother flow of parts and materials for production than a non-integrated firm. For example, a strike against a major parts supplier can interrupt the operations of a non-integrated firm for many months, whereas an integrated firm that is producing its own parts might be able to continue operations. Also, many firms feel that they can control quality better by producing their own parts and materials, rather than by relying on the quality control standards of outside suppliers.

The positive aspects of integration are counterbalanced by some advantages of using external suppliers. By pooling demand from a number of firms, a supplier may be able to realize economies of scale in research and development and in manufacturing. These economies of scale can result in higher quality and lower unit costs than would be possible if the firm were to attempt to make the parts on its own. However, companies must be careful to retain control over activities that are essential to maintaining their competitive position.

An Example of Make or Buy

To illustrate a make or buy decision, let's consider OSN Cycles. The company is now producing the heavy-duty gear shifters used in its most popular line of mountain bikes. The company's Accounting Department reports the following costs of producing the shifter internally:

	Per Unit	8,000 Units
Direct materials	$6	$ 48,000
Direct labour	4	32,000
Variable overhead	1	8,000
Supervisor's salary	3	24,000
Depreciation of special equipment	2	16,000
Allocated general overhead	5	40,000
Total cost	$21	$168,000

An outside supplier has offered to sell OSN Cycles 8,000 shifters per year at a price of only $19 each. Should the company stop producing the shifters internally and start purchasing them from the outside supplier? To approach the decision from a financial point of view, the manager should again focus on the differential costs. As we have seen, the differential costs can be obtained by eliminating those costs that are not avoidable—that is, by eliminating (1) the sunk costs and (2) the future costs that will continue regardless of whether the shifters are produced internally or purchased outside. The costs that remain after making these eliminations are the costs that are avoidable to the company by purchasing outside. If these avoidable costs are less than the outside purchase price, then the company should continue to manufacture its own shifters and reject the outside supplier's offer. That is, the company should purchase outside only if the outside purchase price is less than the costs that can be avoided internally as a result of stopping production of the shifters.

Looking at the data above, note first that depreciation of special equipment is listed as one of the costs of producing the shifters internally. Since the equipment has already been purchased, this depreciation is a sunk cost and is therefore irrelevant. If the equipment could be sold, its salvage value would be relevant. Or if the machine could be used to make other products, this could be relevant as well. However, we will assume that the equipment has no salvage value and that it has no other use except in making the heavy-duty gear shifters.

Also note that the company is allocating a portion of its general overhead costs to the shifters. Any portion of this general overhead cost that would actually be eliminated if the gear shifters were purchased rather than made is relevant in the analysis. However, it is likely that the general overhead costs allocated to the gear shifters are in fact common to all items produced in the factory and would continue unchanged even if the shifters were purchased from outside. Such allocated common costs are not differential costs (because they do not differ between the make and buy alternatives) and should be eliminated from the analysis along with the sunk costs.

The variable costs of producing the shifters (materials, labour, and variable overhead) are differential costs, because they can be avoided by buying the shifters from the outside supplier. If the supervisor can be laid off and her salary avoided by buying the shifters, then her salary will be a differential cost and relevant to the decision. Assuming that both the variable costs and the supervisor's salary can be avoided by buying from the outside supplier, the analysis takes the form shown in Exhibit 12–5.

Since it costs $5 less per unit to continue to make the shifters, OSN Cycles should reject the outside supplier's offer. However, there is one additional factor that the company may wish to consider before coming to a final decision. This factor is the opportunity cost of the space now being used to produce the shifters.

Opportunity Cost

If the space now being used to produce the shifters *would otherwise be idle*, then OSN Cycles should continue to produce its own shifters and the supplier's offer should be rejected, as stated above. Idle space that has no alternative use has an opportunity cost of zero.

EXHIBIT 12-5 OSN Cycles Make or Buy Analysis

	Production "Cost" per Unit	Per Unit Differential Costs		Total Differential Costs—8,000 Units	
		Make	Buy	Make	Buy
Direct materials.........................	$ 6	$ 6		$48,000	
Direct labour............................	4	4		32,000	
Variable overhead......................	1	1		8,000	
Supervisor's salary......................	3	3		24,000	
Depreciation of special equipment........	2	—		—	
Allocated general overhead..............	5	—		—	
Outside purchase price.................			$19		$152,000
Total cost	$ 21	$ 14	$19	$112,000	$152,000
Difference in favour of continuing to make...................		$ 5		$40,000	

But what if the space now being used to produce shifters could be used for some other purpose? In that case, the space has an opportunity cost that must be considered in assessing the desirability of the supplier's offer. What is this opportunity cost? It is the segment margin that could be derived from the best alternative use of the space.

To illustrate, assume that the space now being used to produce shifters could be used to produce disc brakes that would generate a segment margin of $60,000 per year. Under these conditions, OSN Cycles would be better off to accept the supplier's offer and to use the available space to produce the new product line:

	Make	Buy
Differential cost per unit (see Exhibit 12–5)...............................	$ 14	$ 19
Number of units needed annually.......................................	× 8,000	× 8,000
Total annual cost...	112,000	152,000
Opportunity cost–segment margin forgone on a potential new product line..	60,000	—
Total cost...	$172,000	$152,000
Difference in favour of purchasing from the outside supplier...		$ 20,000[4]

Opportunity costs are not recorded in the accounts of an organization because they do not represent actual dollar outlays. Rather, they represent economic benefits that are *forgone* as a result of pursuing a particular course of action. Because of this, opportunity costs are often erroneously ignored by managers when making decisions. The opportunity costs of OSN Cycles are sufficiently large in this case to make continued production of the shifters very costly from an economic point of view.

Special Orders

Managers must often evaluate whether a *special order* should be accepted, and if the order is accepted, what price should be charged. A **special order** is a one-time order that is not considered part of the company's normal ongoing business. The objective in setting a price for special orders is to achieve positive incremental operating income. To illustrate, OSN Cycles has just received a request from the police department of a

Instant Quiz 12-3
Susan Jones owns a local coffee shop. She and her staff have been producing baked goods in-house for several years. The bakery products are good sellers, but the margins are quite low. The owner has been approached by a large commercial bakery that can provide baked goods daily to the coffee shop at prices much below Jones's current production costs due to economies of scale rather than the use of poor-quality products. Jones has sampled the baked goods offered and has found them to be as good as her current product offering. What factors should Jones consider before deciding whether to accept the contract to outsource production of baked goods?

Special order
A one-time order that is not considered part of the company's normal ongoing business.

LEARNING AID

MAKE OR BUY

Relevant Costs

- Incremental costs of making the product (variable and fixed)
- Opportunity cost of utilizing space to make the product
- Outside purchase price

Irrelevant Costs

- Allocated common costs
- Sunk costs

Total relevant costs of making = Incremental costs + Opportunity costs

Decision Rule:

Make if　Total relevant costs of making < Outside purchase price.

Buy if　Total relevant costs of making > Outside purchase price.

large Canadian city to produce 100 specially modified mountain bikes at a price of $560 each. The bikes would be used to patrol some of the more densely populated residential sections of the city. OSN Cycles can easily modify its City Cruiser model to fit the specifications of the police department. The normal selling price of the City Cruiser bike is $700, and its unit product cost is $564, as shown below:

Direct materials.....................................	$372
Direct labour.......................................	90
Manufacturing overhead	102
Unit product cost	$564

The variable portion of the above manufacturing overhead is $12 per unit. The order would have no effect on the company's total fixed manufacturing overhead costs.

The modifications to the bikes consist of welded brackets to hold radios, nightsticks, and other gear. These modifications would require $34 in incremental variable costs per unit. In addition, the company would have to pay a graphic design studio $1,200 to design and cut stencils that would be used for spray painting the police department's logo and other identifying marks on the bikes.

IN BUSINESS

The entertainment industry is noted for rapid change in technology and consumer tastes. To deal with this, organizations must recognize opportunities to fine-tune their product offerings by adding profitable new products, dropping money-losing older products, and deciding when to produce products and services in-house and when to outsource production. For example, The Walt Disney Co. laid off 200 employees in its Interactive Division who were making console-based games as consumers shifted focus to online gaming in 2011. In 2013, Disney planned to change its strategy to focus on producing fewer films in-house in favour of relying more on outside producers, such as Steven Spielberg's Dreamworks Studio, that produce and finance their own films and then pay Disney a fee to market and distribute them. Each of these decisions requires identifying relevant costs, incremental costs/revenue, and opportunity costs, both financial and non-financial, as choices to make or buy and add, drop, or refocus a product line are made.

Source: Ronald Grover, "Disney looks for cost savings, ponders layoffs—sources," *Reuters*, January 7, 2013, http://www.reuters.com/article/2013/01/07/us-disney-layoffs-idUSBRE9060AH20130107.

This order should have no effect on the company's other sales. The production manager says that he can handle the special order without disrupting any of the regular scheduled production.

What effect would accepting this order have on the company's operating income?

Only the incremental costs and benefits are relevant. Since the existing fixed manufacturing overhead costs would not be affected by the order, they are not incremental costs and therefore are not relevant. The incremental operating income can be computed as follows:

	Per Unit	Total for 100 Bikes
Incremental revenue	$560	$56,000
Incremental costs:		
Variable costs:		
Direct materials	372	37,200
Direct labour	90	9,000
Variable manufacturing overhead	12	1,200
Special modifications	34	3,400
Total variable cost	$508	50,800
Fixed cost:		
Purchase of stencils		1,200
Total incremental cost		52,000
Incremental operating income		$ 4,000

Therefore, even though the price on the special order ($560) is below the normal unit product cost ($564) and the order would require incurring additional costs, it would result in an increase in operating income. In general, a special order is profitable as long as the incremental revenue from the special order exceeds the incremental costs of the order.

However, in performing the analysis it is important to make sure that there is indeed idle capacity and that the special order does not affect the company's ability to meet normal demand. For example, what if OSN Cycles is already operating at 100% of capacity and normally sells all the bikes it can produce for $700 each? What is the opportunity cost of accepting the order? Should the company accept the $560 price? If not, what is the minimum price it should accept? To answer these questions, the analysis can be conducted as follows:

	Per Unit
(a) Opportunity Costs:	
Normal selling price	$700
Less variable costs:	
Direct materials	372
Direct labour	90
Variable overhead	12
Total variable costs	474
Contribution margin forgone	$226*
(b) Total relevant costs:	
Incremental costs:	
Variable ($474 + $34)	$508
Fixed ($1,200/100)	12
	520
Opportunity costs	226
Total	$746

*If OSN Cycles is operating at 100% capacity, every bike it sells to the police department means forgoing the contribution margin of $226 the company would have earned on a sale to a regular customer. This is the per unit opportunity cost of accepting the special order.

LEARNING AID

ACCEPT OR REJECT A SPECIAL ORDER

Relevant Costs and Benefits
- Incremental costs of filling the order (variable and fixed)
- Opportunity cost of filling the order
- Incremental revenues from the order

Irrelevant Costs
- Allocated common costs
- Sunk costs

Total relevant costs = Incremental costs + Opportunity costs

Decision Rule:

Accept if   Incremental revenues > Total relevant costs.

Reject if   Incremental revenues < Total relevant costs.

Since the total relevant costs of $746 exceed the offer price of $560, OSN Cycles should decline the offer. Indeed, to be no worse off from a financial perspective, the minimum price that should be charged on the special order is $746 per bike. At this price, management should be indifferent between filling the special order and continuing to sell all it can produce to regular customers.

Joint Product Costs and the Sell or Process Further Decision

In some industries, a number of end products are produced from a single raw material input. For example, in the petroleum-refining industry, a large number of products are extracted from crude oil, including gasoline, jet fuel, home heating oil, lubricants, asphalt, and various organic chemicals. Another example is provided by the St. Thomas Wool Cooperative. The company buys raw wool from local sheepherders, separates the wool into three grades—coarse, fine, and superfine—and then dyes the wool using traditional methods that rely on pigments from local materials. Exhibit 12–6 contains a diagram of the production process.

As mentioned above, the St. Thomas Wool Cooperative produces coarse wool, fine wool, and superfine wool from one input—raw wool. Two or more products that are produced from a common input are known as **joint products**. The term **joint product costs** is used to describe those manufacturing costs that are incurred in producing joint products up to the split-off point. The **split-off point** is the point in the manufacturing process at which the joint products can be recognized as separate products. This does not occur at the St. Thomas Wool Cooperative until the raw wool has gone through the separating process. At the Cooperative, the joint costs are the $200,000 cost of the raw wool and the $40,000 cost of separating the wool. The undyed wool is called an *intermediate product* because it is not finished at this point. Nevertheless, a market does exist for undyed wool—although at a significantly lower price than finished dyed wool.

The Pitfalls of Allocation

Joint product costs are really common costs incurred to simultaneously produce a variety of end products. Traditional cost accounting books cover various approaches to allocating these common costs among the different products at the split-off point. A typical approach is to allocate the joint product costs according to the relative sales value of the end products.

Joint products
Two or more items that are produced from a common input.

Joint product costs
Costs that are incurred up to the split-off point in producing joint products.

Split-off point
That point in the manufacturing process where some or all of the joint products can be recognized as individual products.

EXHIBIT 12-6   Joint Products

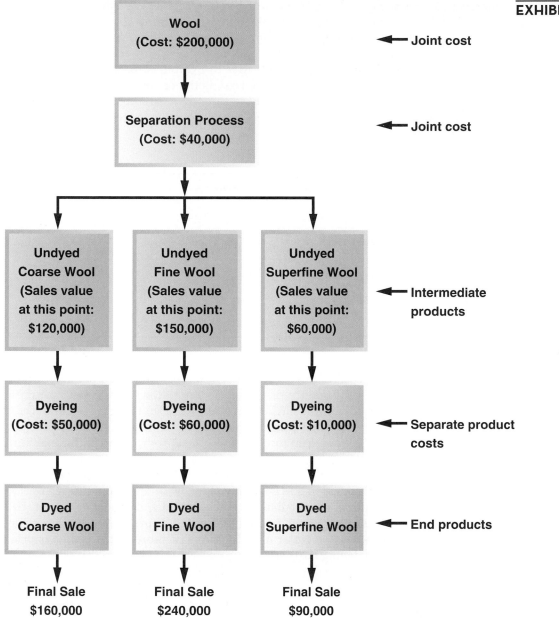

Although allocation of joint product costs is needed for some purposes, such as inventory valuation for financial reporting, allocations of this kind should be viewed with great caution *internally* in the decision-making process. As will be discussed in the next section, because allocated joint product costs are sunk costs, they should never be used when making decisions about what to do with the joint products beyond the split-off point (i.e., sell immediately or process further).

Sell or Process Further Decisions

Deciding what to do with a product from the split-off point forward is known as a **sell or process further decision**. Joint costs are irrelevant in these decisions because by the time the split-off point is reached, the joint product costs have already been incurred and therefore are sunk costs.

It will always be profitable to continue processing a joint product after the split-off point *as long as the incremental revenue from such processing exceeds the*

Sell or process further decision
A decision as to whether a joint product should be sold at the split-off point or processed further and sold at a later time in a different form.

incremental processing cost incurred after the split-off point. Joint product costs that have already been incurred up to the split-off point are sunk costs, which are irrelevant in decisions concerning what to do from the split-off point forward.

To provide a detailed example of the sell or process further decision, return to the data for the St. Thomas Wool Cooperative in Exhibit 12–6. We can answer several important questions using these data. First, is the company generating a profit if it runs the entire process from beginning to end? Assuming there are no costs other than those displayed in Exhibit 12–6, the company is indeed profitable, determined as follows:

Analysis of the profitability of the overall operation:		
Combined final sales value		
($160,000 + $240,000 + $90,000)		$490,000
Less costs of producing the end products:		
Cost of wool	$200,000	
Cost of separating wool	40,000	
Combined costs of dyeing		
($50,000 + $60,000 + $10,000)...	120,000	360,000
Profit..		$ 130,000

Note that the joint costs of buying the wool and separating the wool *are* relevant when considering the profitability of the entire operation. This is because these joint costs *could* be avoided if the entire operation were shut down. However, these joint costs are *not* relevant when considering the profitability of any one product. As long as the process is being run to make the other products, no additional joint costs are incurred to make the specific product in question.

Even though the company is making money overall, it may be losing money on one or more of the products. If the company buys wool and runs the separation process, it will get all three intermediate products. Nothing can be done about that. However, each of these products can be sold *as is* without further processing. It may be that the company would be better off selling one or more of the products prior to dyeing to avoid the dyeing costs. The appropriate way to make this choice is to compare the incremental revenues to the incremental costs from further processing, as done in Exhibit 12–7.

As this analysis shows, the company would be better off selling the undyed coarse wool as is rather than processing it further. The other two products should be processed further and dyed before selling them.

Note that the joint costs of the wool ($200,000) and of the wool separation process ($40,000) play no role in the decision to sell or further process the intermediate products. These joint costs are relevant in a decision of whether to buy wool and to run the wool separation process, but they are not relevant in decisions about what to do with the intermediate products once they have been separated.

Instant Quiz 12-5
The Corner Hardware Store sells barbecues in spring and summer. The store manager is trying to decide whether to sell the barbecues assembled or unassembled. An unassembled barbecue is purchased from the supplier for $100 and can be sold unassembled for $200. Assembly of the barbecue requires 30 minutes of labour time, and the store pays its employees $15 per hour. Corner Hardware can sell assembled barbecues for $225. Should the barbecues be sold assembled or unassembled?

EXHIBIT 12–7 Sell or Process Further Decision

	Coarse Wool	Fine Wool	Superfine Wool
Final sales value after further processing.......	$160,000	$240,000	$90,000
Less sales value at the split-off point	120,000	150,000	60,000
Incremental revenue from further processing ...	40,000	90,000	30,000
Less cost of further processing (dyeing)	50,000	60,000	10,000
Profit (loss) from further processing	$ (10,000)	$ 30,000	$20,000

LEARNING AID

SELL OR PROCESS FURTHER

Relevant Costs and Benefits
- Incremental costs of further processing
- Incremental revenues from further processing

Irrelevant Costs
- Allocated joint product costs

Decision Rule:

Process further if   Incremental revenues > Incremental costs of further processing.

Sell at split-off point if   Incremental revenues < Incremental costs of further processing.

◾ UTILIZATION OF A CONSTRAINED RESOURCE

Another decision situation that managers often face is the problem of how to utilize a constrained resource. When a limited resource of some type restricts a company's ability to fully satisfy demand for its products or services, the company is said to have a **constraint**. A convenience store has limited shelf space, so it must decide which products to sell. Manufacturing firms may have constraints on machine-hours, labour-hours, or the amount of raw materials available for production. The **theory of constraints** (TOC) maintains that effectively managing a constraint is important to the financial success of an organization. The challenge for managers is deciding how best to utilize the constrained resource to maximize the company's profits. As will be illustrated below, fixed costs are usually unaffected by the allocation of the constrained resource in the short run, so the focus will be on analyzing and maximizing contribution margin.

LEARNING OBJECTIVE ③
Determine the most profitable use of a constrained resource and the value of obtaining more of the constrained resource.

Constraint
A limitation under which a company must operate (such as limited machine time available or limited raw materials available) that restricts the company's ability to satisfy demand for its products or services.

Theory of constraints (TOC)
A management approach that emphasizes the importance of managing constraints.

Contribution Margin in Relation to a Constrained Resource

To maximize total contribution margin, a firm should not necessarily promote those products that have the highest *unit* contribution margin. Rather, total contribution margin will be maximized by promoting those products or accepting those orders that provide the highest unit contribution margin *in relation to the constrained resource*. To illustrate, OSN Cycles makes a line of panniers—saddlebags for bicycles. There are two models of panniers—a touring model and a mountain model. Cost and revenue data for the two models of panniers are given below:

	Model	
	Mountain Pannier	**Touring Pannier**
Selling price per unit.	$ 40	$ 50
Variable cost per unit.	30	42
Contribution margin per unit.	$ 10	$ 8
Contribution margin (CM) ratio	25%	16%

The mountain pannier appears to be much more profitable than the touring pannier. It has a $10 per unit contribution margin as compared to only $8 per unit for the touring model, and it has a 25% CM ratio as compared to only 16% for the touring model.

But now let's add one more piece of information—the plant that makes the panniers is operating at capacity. Ordinarily this does not mean that every machine and every person in the plant is working at the maximum possible rate. Because machines have different capacities, some machines will be operating at less than 100% of capacity. However, if the plant as a whole cannot produce any more units, some machine or process must be operating at capacity. The machine or process that is limiting overall output is called the *bottleneck*—it is the constraint.

At OSN Cycles, the bottleneck is a particular stitching machine. The mountain pannier requires four minutes of stitching time, and each unit of the touring pannier requires two minutes of stitching time. Since this stitching machine already has more work than it can handle, production will have to be cut back on one of the models. In this situation, which product is more profitable? To answer this question, the manager should look at the *contribution margin per unit of the constrained resource*, also known as the **profitability index**. This figure is computed by dividing the contribution margin by the quantity of the constrained resource required per unit. These calculations are carried out below for the mountain and touring panniers:

Profitability index
Contribution margin per unit ÷ Quantity of constrained resource required per unit

	Model	
	Mountain Pannier	**Touring Pannier**
Contribution margin per unit (a)	$10.00	$8.00
Time on the stitching machine required to produce one unit (b)	4 min.	2 min.
Contribution margin per unit of the constrained resource, (a) ÷ (b)......................	$2.50/min.	$4.00/min.

Using the profitability index, it is easy to decide which product is less profitable and should be de-emphasized. Each minute of processing time on the stitching machine that is devoted to the touring pannier results in an increase of $4 in contribution margin and profits. The comparable figure for the mountain pannier is only $2.50 per minute. Therefore, the touring model should be emphasized. Even though the mountain model has the larger per unit contribution margin and the larger CM ratio, the touring model provides the larger contribution margin in relation to the constrained resource.

To verify that the touring model is indeed the more profitable product when considering the constrained resource, suppose an hour of additional stitching time is available and that there are unfilled orders for both products. The additional hour on the stitching machine could be used to make either 15 mountain panniers (60 minutes ÷ 4 minutes) or 30 touring panniers (60 minutes ÷ 2 minutes), with the following consequences:

	Model	
	Mountain Pannier	**Touring Pannier**
Contribution margin per unit	$ 10	$ 8
Additional units that can be processed in one hour...	×15	×30
Additional contribution margin....................................	$150	$240

The analysis illustrated in this example generalizes well to situations where demand exceeds capacity and managers must allocate a constrained resource to three or more products. Demand should be fully satisfied for the product with the highest profitability index. Any capacity that remains should then be allocated to the product with the second-highest profitability index, and so on until all available capacity has been utilized. Simply looking at unit contribution margins alone is not enough when constraints exist; contribution margin per unit of the scarce resource must guide decision making.

Managing Constraints

Profits can be increased by effectively managing an organization's constraints. One aspect of managing constraints is to decide how best to utilize them. If the constraint is a bottleneck in the production process, the manager should select the product mix that maximizes the total contribution margin. In addition, the manager should take an active role in managing the constraint itself. Management should focus efforts on increasing the efficiency of the bottleneck operation (constraint) and on increasing its capacity. Such efforts directly increase the output of finished goods and will often pay off in an almost immediate increase in profits.

It is often possible for a manager to effectively increase the capacity of the bottleneck by what is called **relaxing (or elevating) the constraint**. For example, the stitching machine operator could be asked to work overtime. This would result in more available stitching time and hence more finished goods that can be sold. The benefits from relaxing the constraint in such a manner are often enormous and can easily be quantified. The manager should first ask, "What would I do with additional capacity at the bottleneck if it was available?" In the bicycle pannier example, the additional capacity was worth $4 ($2.50) per minute or $240 ($150) per hour because adding an hour of capacity would generate an additional $240 ($150) of contribution margin if it were used solely to process more touring (mountain) panniers. Based on the profitability indices, additional capacity should first be allocated to production of touring panniers, followed by mountain panniers if any capacity remains. Since overtime pay for the operator is likely to be much less than $240 (or $150 for that matter!), running the stitching machine on overtime would be an excellent way to increase the company's profits while satisfying its customers at the same time.

The implications are clear: managers should focus much of their attention on managing bottlenecks. As we have discussed, managers should emphasize products that most profitably utilize the constrained resource. They should also make sure that products are processed smoothly through the bottlenecks, with minimal lost time due to breakdowns and setups. And they should try to find ways to increase the capacity at the bottlenecks, which can be accomplished in a number of ways:

- Working overtime on the bottleneck.
- Subcontracting some of the processing that would be done at the bottleneck.
- Shifting workers from processes that are not bottlenecks to the process that *is* a bottleneck.
- Focusing business process improvement efforts such as total quality management and business process re-engineering on the bottleneck.
- Reducing defective units. Each defective unit that is processed through the bottleneck and subsequently scrapped takes the place of a good unit that could be sold.

The last three methods of increasing the capacity of the bottleneck are particularly attractive, because they are low-cost interventions and may even yield additional cost savings.

The Problem of Multiple Constraints

What does a firm do if it has more than one potential constraint? For example, a firm may have limited raw materials, limited direct labour-hours available, limited floor space, and limited advertising dollars to spend on product promotion. How would it proceed to find the right combination of products to produce? The proper combination or "mix" of products can be found using a quantitative method known as *linear programming*, which is covered in quantitative methods and operations management courses.

Relaxing (or elevating) the constraint
Increasing the capacity of a bottleneck.

Instant Quiz 12-6
How should the relative profitability of products be determined when trying to decide how to allocate a constrained resource such as machine-hours?

KNOWLEDGE IN ACTION

Managers can apply their knowledge about relevant costs when
- deciding whether to add or drop a product line or service offering
- deciding whether to make a product/offer a service or buy it from an outside source
- deciding whether to accept a one-time special order at a lower than usual price
- deciding whether to sell a product as-is or process it further
- making product mix decisions given capacity constraints and bottlenecks

SUMMARY

- A framework was presented for distinguishing between relevant and irrelevant costs. Relevant costs and benefits are those that will be incurred in the future and that differ among the alternatives under consideration. As such, sunk costs are irrelevant (incurred in the past), while avoidable, differential, and opportunity costs are all relevant. [LO1]
- Application of relevant cost concepts was illustrated in several different decision situations often faced by managers: adding or dropping product lines/segments, making versus buying decisions, accepting or rejecting special orders, and selling versus processing joint products further. A learning aid was presented for each type of decision, identifying the relevant and irrelevant costs and the decision rule. [LO2]
- A simple approach was illustrated for allocating a constrained resource when demand exceeds production capacity because of a production bottleneck in the short run. The allocation approach is based on calculating the contribution margin per unit of the constrained resource, which is known as the *profitability index*. Demand should first be fully satisfied for the product with the highest profitability index, and then for the product with the next highest index, and so on, until all of the available capacity has been used. [LO3]

REVIEW PROBLEM: RELEVANT COSTS

The St. Albert Cycle Company manufactures three types of bicycles—dirt bikes, mountain bikes, and racing bikes. Data on sales and expenses for the past quarter follow:

	Total	Dirt Bikes	Mountain Bikes	Racing Bikes
Sales	$300,000	$90,000	$150,000	$60,000
Less variable manufacturing and selling expenses	120,000	27,000	60,000	33,000
Contribution margin	180,000	63,000	90,000	27,000
Less fixed expenses:				
Advertising, traceable	30,000	10,000	14,000	6,000
Depreciation of special equipment	23,000	6,000	9,000	8,000
Salaries of product-line managers	35,000	12,000	13,000	10,000
Allocated common fixed expenses*	60,000	18,000	30,000	12,000
Total fixed expenses	148,000	46,000	66,000	36,000
Operating income (loss)	$ 32,000	$ 17,000	$ 24,000	$ (9,000)

*Allocated on the basis of sales dollars.

Management is concerned about the continued losses shown by the racing bikes and wants a recommendation as to whether or not the line should be discontinued. The special equipment used to produce racing bikes has no resale value and does not wear out.

Required:

1. Should production and sale of the racing bikes be discontinued? Explain. Show computations to support your answer.
2. Recast the above data in a format that would be more usable to management in assessing the long-run profitability of the various product lines.

Solution to Review Problem

1. No, production and sale of the racing bikes should not be discontinued. If the racing bikes were discontinued, then the operating income for the company as a whole would decrease by $11,000 each quarter:

Lost contribution margin		$(27,000)
Fixed costs that can be avoided:		
Advertising, traceable	$ 6,000	
Salary of the product-line manager	10,000	16,000
Decrease in operating income for the company as a whole.		$ (11,000)

The depreciation of the special equipment is a sunk cost and is not relevant to the decision. The common costs are allocated and will continue regardless of whether or not the racing bikes are discontinued; thus, they are not relevant to the decision.

Alternative Solution

	Current Total	Total if Racing Bikes Are Dropped	Difference: Operating Income Increase or (Decrease) if Dropped
Sales	$300,000	$240,000	$(60,000)
Less variable expenses.	120,000	87,000	33,000
Contribution margin.	180,000	153,000	(27,000)
Less fixed expenses:			
Advertising, traceable	30,000	24,000	6,000
Depreciation on special equipment	23,000	23,000	0
Salaries of product managers	35,000	25,000	10,000
Common allocated costs.	60,000	60,000	0
Total fixed expenses.	148,000	132,000	16,000
Operating income.	$ 32,000	$ 21,000	$ (11,000)

2. The segmented report can be improved by eliminating the allocation of the common fixed expenses. Following the format introduced in Chapter 11 for a segmented income statement, a better report is as follows:

	Total	Dirt Bikes	Mountain Bikes	Racing Bikes
Sales.	$300,000	$90,000	$150,000	$60,000
Less variable manufacturing and selling expenses	120,000	27,000	60,000	33,000
Contribution margin.	180,000	63,000	90,000	27,000
Less traceable fixed expenses:				
Advertising	30,000	10,000	14,000	6,000
Depreciation of special equipment.	23,000	6,000	9,000	8,000
Salaries of the product-line managers	35,000	12,000	13,000	10,000
Total traceable fixed expenses.	88,000	28,000	36,000	24,000
Product-line segment margin.	92,000	$35,000	$ 54,000	$ 3,000
Less common fixed expenses.	60,000			
Operating income.	$ 32,000			

DISCUSSION CASE

DISCUSSION CASE 12-1

One of the decisions facing managers illustrated in this chapter is whether to keep or drop an existing product, service, or operating segment. The analysis presented indicates that if the costs avoided by dropping the product or segment exceed the contribution margin lost, then "drop" is the correct decision from a financial perspective. However, when companies such as General Motors or Chrysler decide to drop a major product, service, or operating segment, there may be non-financial consequences involving suppliers, creditors, employees, and customers.

Required:
What non-financial consequences might General Motors or Chrysler face if they decided to drop their parts and service divisions and, instead, focus only on selling new and used cars?

GLOSSARY

 Review key terms and definitions on Connect.

QUESTIONS

12-1   What is a *relevant cost?*

12-2   Define the following terms: *incremental cost, opportunity cost,* and *sunk cost.*

12-3   Are avoidable costs always relevant costs? Explain.

12-4   Depreciation (as shown on the income statement) is an expense to a company, but this same expense is irrelevant in decision making. Explain why this is so.

12-5   "Sunk costs are easy to spot—they're simply the fixed costs associated with a decision." Do you agree? Explain.

12-6   Are variable costs always relevant in decision making? Explain.

12-7   Davis Company is considering dropping one of its product lines. What costs of the product line would be relevant to this decision? Irrelevant?

12-8   "If a product line is generating a loss, then that's pretty good evidence that the product line should be discontinued." Do you agree? Explain.

12-9   How does opportunity cost enter into the make or buy decision?

12-10 Which costs are relevant to special-order decisions?

12-11 What is a constraint?

12-12 List four ways to increase capacity at bottlenecks.

12-13 Define the following terms: *joint products, joint product costs,* and *split-off point.*

12-14 From a decision-making point of view, what pitfalls are there in allocating common costs among joint products?

12-15 What guideline can be used in determining whether a joint product should be sold at the split-off point or processed further?

12-16 Why should relevant costs be isolated when analyzing a decision situation?

EXERCISES

EXERCISE 12-1 Identifying Relevant Costs [LO1]

The management of Boehm & De Graaf A/S, a Danish furniture manufacturer, must determine whether certain costs are relevant in two different cases:

Case 1: The company chronically runs at capacity, and the old Model A3000 machine is the company's constraint. Management is considering purchasing a new Model B3800 machine to use in addition to the Model A3000 machine. The old Model A3000 machine would continue to be used to capacity as before, with the new Model B3800 being used to expand production. The increase in volume would be large enough to require increases in fixed selling expenses and in general administrative overhead, but not in the general fixed manufacturing overhead.

Case 2: The old Model A3000 machine is not the company's constraint, but management is considering replacing it with a new Model B3800 machine because of the potential savings in direct materials cost with the new machine. The Model A3000 machine would be sold. This change would have no effect on production or sales, other than some savings in direct materials costs due to less waste.

Required:

Place an X in the appropriate column to indicate whether each item is relevant or not relevant to each of the two cases. Consider the two cases independently.

	Case 1		Case 2	
Item	**Relevant**	**Not Relevant**	**Relevant**	**Not Relevant**
a. Sales revenue...................................				
b. Direct materials...............................				
c. Direct labour..................................				
d. Variable manufacturing overhead..............				
e. Book value—Model A3000 machine.............				
f. Disposal value—Model A3000 machine..........				
g. Depreciation—Model A3000 machine...........				
h. Market value—Model B3800 machine (cost)....				
i. Fixed manufacturing overhead (general)........				
j. Variable selling expense.......................				
k. Fixed selling expense..........................				
l. General administrative overhead...............				

EXERCISE 12–2 Dropping or Retaining a Segment [LO2]

Cumberland County Senior Services is a non-profit organization devoted to providing essential services to seniors who live in their own homes within the Cumberland County area. Three services are provided for seniors—home nursing, Meals on Wheels, and housekeeping. In the home nursing program, nurses visit seniors on a regular basis to check on their general health and to perform tests ordered by their physicians. The Meals on Wheels program delivers a hot meal once a day to each senior enrolled in the program. The housekeeping service provides weekly housecleaning and maintenance services. Data on revenue and expenses for the past year follow:

	Total	Home Nursing	Meals on Wheels	Housekeeping
Revenues...............................	$900,000	$260,000	$400,000	$240,000
Variable expenses.......................	490,000	120,000	210,000	160,000
Contribution margin....................	410,000	140,000	190,000	80,000
Fixed expenses:				
Depreciation............................	68,000	8,000	40,000	20,000
Liability insurance......................	42,000	20,000	7,000	15,000
Program administrators' salaries........	115,000	40,000	38,000	37,000
General administrative overhead*......	180,000	52,000	80,000	48,000
Total fixed expenses....................	405,000	120,000	165,000	120,000
Operating income (loss)................	$ 5,000	$ 20,000	$ 25,000	$(40,000)

*Allocated on the basis of program revenues.

The head administrator of Cumberland County Senior Services, Judith Ewa, is concerned about the organization's finances and considers the operating income of $5,000 last year to be razor-thin. (Last year's results were very similar to the results for previous years and are representative of what would be expected in the future.) She feels that the organization should be building its financial reserves at a more rapid rate in order to prepare for the next inevitable recession. After seeing the above report, Ewa asked for more information about the financial advisability of discontinuing the housekeeping program.

The depreciation in the housekeeping category is for a small van that is used to carry the housekeepers and their equipment from job to job. If the program were discontinued, the van would be donated to a charitable organization. Depreciation charges assume zero salvage value. None of the general administrative overhead would be avoided if the housekeeping program were dropped, but the liability insurance and the salary of the program administrator would be avoided.

Required:
1. Should the housekeeping program be discontinued? Explain. Show computations to support your answer.
2. Recast the above data in a format that would be more useful to management in assessing the long-run financial viability of the various services.

EXERCISE 12–3 Make or Buy a Component [LO2]
Current-Control Inc. manufactures a variety of electrical switches. The company is currently manufacturing all of its own component parts. An outside supplier has offered to sell a switch to Current-Control for $32 per unit. To evaluate this offer, Current-Control has gathered the following information relating to its own cost of producing the switch internally:

	Per Unit	12,000 Units per Year
Direct materials.	$ 12	$ 144,000
Direct labour.	10	120,000
Variable manufacturing overhead.	3	36,000
Fixed manufacturing overhead, traceable	8*	96,000
Fixed manufacturing overhead, common, but allocated	16	192,000
Total cost.	$49	$588,000

*25% supervisory salaries; 75% depreciation of special equipment (no resale value).

Required:
1. Assuming that the company has no alternative use for the facilities now being used to produce the switch, should the outside supplier's offer be accepted? Show all computations.
2. Suppose that if the switches were purchased, Current-Control could use the freed capacity to launch a new product. The segment margin of the new product would be $78,000 per year. Should Current-Control accept the offer to buy the switches from the outside supplier for $32 each? Show computations.

EXERCISE 12–4 Evaluating a Special Order [LO2]
Sato Jewellers has had a request for a special order for 10 gold bangles for the members of a wedding party. The normal selling price of a gold bangle is $389.95 and its unit product cost is $264.00, as shown below:

Direct materials.	$ 143.00
Direct labour.	86.00
Manufacturing overhead	35.00
Unit product cost.	$264.00

Most of the manufacturing overhead is fixed and unaffected by variations in how much jewellery is produced in any given period. However, $7 of the overhead is variable, depending on the number of bangles produced. The customer would like special filigree applied to the bangles. This filigree would require additional materials costing $6 per bangle and would also require acquisition of a special tool costing $465 that would have no other use once the special order was completed. This order would have no effect on the company's regular sales, and the order could be filled using the company's existing capacity without affecting any other order.

Required:
What effect would accepting this order have on the company's operating income if a special price of $349.95 is offered per bangle for this order? Should the special order be accepted at this price?

EXERCISE 12-5 Utilization of a Constrained Resource [LO3]

The following are the selling price, variable costs, and contribution margin for one unit of each of Banner Company's three products: A, B, and C:

	Product		
	A	**B**	**C**
Selling price	$60	$90	$80
Variable costs:			
Direct materials	27	14	40
Direct labour	12	32	16
Variable manufacturing overhead	3	8	4
Total variable cost	42	54	60
Contribution margin	$18	$36	$20
Contribution margin ratio	30%	40%	25%

Due to a strike in the plant of one of its competitors, demand for the company's products far exceeds its capacity to produce. Management is trying to determine which product(s) to concentrate on next week in filling its backlog of orders. The direct labour rate is $8 per hour, and only 3,000 hours of labour time are available each week.

Required:
1. Compute the amount of contribution margin that will be obtained per hour of labour time spent on each product.
2. Which orders would you recommend that the company work on next week—the orders for product A, product B, or product C? Show computations.
3. By paying overtime wages, more than 3,000 hours of direct labour time can be made available next week. Up to how much should the company be willing to pay per hour in overtime wages as long as there is unfilled demand for the three products? Explain.

EXERCISE 12-6 Sell or Process Further [LO2]

In a joint processing operation, Nolen Company manufactures three grades of sugar from a common input, sugar cane. Joint processing costs up to the split-off point total $80,000 per year. The company allocates these costs to the joint products on the basis of their total sales value at the split-off point. These sales values are as follows: raw sugar, $40,000; brown sugar, $40,000; and white sugar, $42,000.

Each product may be sold at the split-off point or processed further. Additional processing requires no special facilities. The additional processing costs and the sales value after further processing for each product (on an annual basis) are shown below:

Product	Additional Processing Costs	Sales Value
Raw sugar	$42,000	$80,000
Brown sugar	$28,000	$70,000
White sugar	$12,000	$82,000

Required:
Which product or products should be sold at the split-off point, and which product or products should be processed further? Show computations.

EXERCISE 12-7 Identification of Relevant Costs [LO1]

Hart Company sells and delivers office furniture across Western Canada.

The costs associated with the acquisition and annual operation of a delivery truck are given below:

Insurance.	$ 1,750
Licences.	$ 250
Taxes (vehicle).	$ 150
Garage rent for parking (per truck).	$ 1,350
Depreciation ($30,000 ÷ 5 years).	$6,000
Gasoline, oil, tires, and repairs	$0.16/km

Required:
1. Assume that Hart Company owns one truck that has been driven 50,000 kilometres during the first year. Compute the average cost per kilometre of owning and operating the truck.
2. At the beginning of the second year, Hart Company is unsure whether to use the truck or leave it parked in the garage and have all hauling done commercially. (The government requires the payment of vehicle taxes even if the vehicle isn't used.) What costs from the previous list are relevant to this decision? Explain.
3. Assume that the company decides to use the truck during the second year. Near year-end, an order is received from a customer over 1,000 kilometres away. What costs from the previous list are relevant in a decision between using the truck to make the delivery and having the delivery done commercially? Explain.
4. Occasionally, the company could use two trucks at the same time. For this reason, some thought is being given to purchasing a second truck. The total kilometres driven would be the same as if only one truck were owned. What costs from the previous list are relevant to a decision about whether to purchase the second truck? Explain.

EXERCISE 12–8 Dropping or Retaining a Segment [LO2]
Anderson Document Services, a document creation and copying company, has two departments, Design and Copying. The company's most recent monthly contribution format income statement follows:

		Department	
	Total	Design	Copying
Sales	$400,000	$75,000	$200,000
Variable expenses	250,000	50,000	120,000
Contribution margin	150,000	25,000	80,000
Fixed expenses	50,000	30,000	18,000
Operating income (loss)	$ 10,000	$(5,000)	$ 62,000

A study indicates that $14,000 of the fixed expenses being charged to the Design Department are sunk costs or allocated costs that will continue even if the Design Department is dropped. In addition, the elimination of the Design Department would result in a 5% decrease in the sales of the Copying Department.

Required:
If the Design Department is dropped, what will be the effect on the operating income of the company as a whole? Should the Design Department be dropped?

EXERCISE 12–9 Make or Buy a Component [LO2]
For many years, Comstock Company has produced an electrical part that it uses in the production of diesel tractors. The company's unit product cost for the part, based on a production level of 60,000 parts per year, is as follows:

	Per Part	Total
Direct materials	$ 4.00	
Direct labour	2.75	
Variable manufacturing overhead	0.50	
Fixed manufacturing overhead, traceable	3.00	$180,000
Fixed manufacturing overhead, common		
(allocated on the basis of labour-hours)	2.25	$135,000
Unit product cost	$12.50	

An outside supplier has offered to supply the electrical parts to Comstock Company for only $10.00 per part. One-third of the traceable fixed manufacturing cost is supervisory salaries and other costs that can be eliminated if the parts are purchased. The other two-thirds of the traceable fixed manufacturing costs consists of depreciation of special equipment that has no resale value. The decision to buy the parts from the outside supplier would have no effect on the common fixed costs of the company, and the space being used to produce the parts would otherwise be idle.

Required:
Prepare computations showing how much profits would increase or decrease as a result of purchasing the parts from the outside supplier rather than having the company make them.

EXERCISE 12–10 Special Order [LO2]

At the Kicher Company's current activity level of 8,000 units per month, the costs of producing and selling one unit of the company's only product are as follows:

Direct materials.	$2.50
Direct labour.	$3.00
Variable manufacturing overhead.	$0.50
Fixed manufacturing overhead.	$4.25
Variable selling and administrative expenses	$1.50
Fixed selling and administrative expenses	$2.00

The normal selling price is $15 per unit. The company's capacity is 10,000 units per month. An order has been received from a potential customer overseas for 2,000 units at a price of $12.00 per unit. This order would not affect regular sales.

Required:
1. If the order is accepted, by how much will monthly profits increase or decrease? (The order would not change the company's total fixed costs.)
2. Assume the company has 500 units of this product left over from last year that are inferior to the current model. The units must be sold through regular channels at reduced prices. What unit cost is relevant for establishing a minimum selling price for these units? Explain.

EXERCISE 12–11 Utilization of a Constrained Resource [LO3]

Westburne Company produces three products: Alpha, Omega, and Beta. Data (per unit) concerning the three products follow:

	Alpha	Omega	Beta
Selling price.	$160	$112	$140
Less variable expenses:			
Direct materials	48	30	18
Labour and overhead.	48	54	80
Total variable expenses	96	84	98
Contribution margin	$ 64	$28	$ 42
Contribution margin ratio.	40%	25%	30%

Demand for the company's products is very strong, with far more orders each month than the company can produce with the available raw materials. The same material is used in each product. The material costs $6 per kilogram, with a maximum of 10,000 kilograms available each month.

Required:
Which orders would you advise the company to accept first, those for Alpha, Omega, or Beta? Which orders second? Third?

EXERCISE 12–12 Sell or Process Further [LO2]

Senatory Limited produces several products from processing krypton, a rare mineral. Material and processing costs total $30,000 per tonne; one-third of the costs are allocated to the product Castingard. The Castingard produced from a tonne of krypton can be either sold at the split-off point or processed further at a cost of $13,000 and then sold for $60,000. The sales value of Castingard at the split-off point is $50,000.

Required:
Should Castingard be processed further or sold at the split-off point?

EXERCISE 12–13 Volume Trade-Off Decision [LO3]

Car Art makes miniature reproductions of classic sports cars. The bottleneck in the production process is the requirement to apply several coats of paint to each car. This process requires the attention of the shop's most experienced craftsperson. A total of 7,200 hours is available per year in this bottleneck operation. Data concerning the company's four products appear below:

	Corvette	Porsche	Ferrari	Jaguar
Unit contribution margin	$100	$ 64	$ 70	$ 144
Annual demand (units)	160	240	200	280
Hours required in the bottleneck operation per unit	10	8	14	16

No fixed costs could be avoided by modifying how many units are produced of any product or even by dropping any one of the products.

Required:
1. Is there sufficient capacity in the bottleneck operation to satisfy demand for all products?
2. What is the optimal production plan for the year?
3. What would be the total contribution margin for the optimal production plan you have proposed?

EXERCISE 12–14 Identification of Relevant Costs [LO1]

Jason brought home eight ducks from his last hunting trip in northern Ontario. His friend Harry dislikes any type of hunting, and to discourage Jason from further hunting, Harry has presented him with the following cost estimates:

Camper and equipment:	
Cost, $16,000; usable for eight seasons; 10 hunting trips per season	$200
Travel expense (pickup truck):	
100 kilometres at $0.35 per kilometre (gas, oil, and tires—$0.25 per kilometre;	
depreciation and insurance—$0.10 per kilometre)	35
Shotgun shells (two boxes)	20
Boat:	
Cost, $4,000, usable for eight seasons; 10 hunting trips per season	50
Hunting licence:	
Cost, $30 for the season; 10 hunting trips per season	3
Money lost playing poker:	
Loss, $40 (Jason plays poker every weekend)	40
Coffee beans:	
Cost, $20	20
Total cost of the trip	$368
Cost per duck ($368 ÷ 8 ducks)	$ 46

Required:
1. Assuming that the duck-hunting trip Jason has just completed is typical, what costs are relevant to a decision as to whether Jason should go duck hunting again this season?
2. Suppose that Jason gets lucky on his next hunting trip and shoots 10 ducks in the amount of time it took him to shoot 8 ducks on his last trip. How much would it have cost him to shoot the last 2 ducks? Explain.
3. Which costs are relevant in a decision of whether Jason should give up hunting? Explain.

EXERCISE 12–15 Dropping or Retaining a Segment [LO2]

Williams Products Inc. manufactures and sells a number of items, including school knapsacks. The company has been experiencing losses on the knapsacks for some time, as shown by the contribution format income statement below:

WILLIAMS PRODUCTS INC.
Income Statement—School Knapsacks
For the Quarter Ended June 30

Sales		$225,000
Variable expenses:		
Variable manufacturing expenses	$65,000	
Sales commissions	24,000	
Shipping	6,000	
Total variable expenses		95,000
Contribution margin		130,000
Fixed expenses:		
Salary of product-line manager	10,500	
General factory overhead	52,000*	
Depreciation of equipment (no resale value)	18,000	
Advertising–traceable	55,000	
Insurance on inventories	4,500	
Purchasing department	25,000†	
Total fixed expenses		165,000
Operating loss		$(35,000)

*Allocated on the basis of machine-hours.
†Allocated on the basis of sales dollars.

Discontinuing the knapsacks would not affect sales of other product lines and would have no noticeable effect on the company's total general factory overhead or total purchasing department expenses.

Required:
Would you recommend that the company discontinue the manufacture and sale of school knapsacks? Support your answer with appropriate computations.

EXERCISE 12–16 Make or Buy a Component [LO2]
Royal Company manufactures 20,000 units of Part R-3 each year. At this level of activity, the cost per unit for Part R-3 follows:

Direct materials	$ 4.80
Direct labour	7.00
Variable manufacturing overhead	3.20
Fixed manufacturing overhead	10.00
Total cost per part	$25.00

An outside supplier has offered to sell 20,000 units of Part R-3 each year to Royal Company for $23.50 per part. If Royal Company accepts this offer, the facilities now being used to manufacture Part R-3 could be rented to another company at an annual rental of $150,000. However, Royal Company has determined that $6 of the fixed manufacturing overhead being applied to Part R-3 would continue even if the part were purchased from the outside supplier.

Required:
Prepare computations showing how much profits will increase or decrease if the outside supplier's offer is accepted.

EXERCISE 12–17 Sell or Process Further [LO2]
The Fraser Paper Company produces large rolls of white paper weighing 1,000 kilograms for wholesalers for $1,500 each. The wholesalers then cut the paper into standard-sized sheets and package it in 2-kilogram packages. These packages are sold to printers for $4 per package. There is no waste in the cutting process. Fraser Paper currently produces 5 million kilograms of paper annually at a fixed cost of $1 million and a variable cost of $0.80 per kilogram.

If Fraser bypassed the wholesalers and cut its own paper for sale directly to printers, Fraser would have to add equipment and personnel with an annual fixed cost of $650,000. Incremental variable costs would be $0.10 per kilogram.

Required:
Should Fraser cut its own paper or continue to sell to wholesalers?

EXERCISE 12–18 Dropping a Product Line [LO2]

A firm makes two products: frying pans and saucepans. Frying pans sell for $30 each and saucepans sell for $20 each. The variable cost of making a frying pan is $20, and the variable cost of making saucepans is $8. The firm has additional manufacturing costs of $1 million.

Required:
1. If the firm sells 100 more saucepans, what is the additional profit to the firm?
2. If the firm could sell either one more saucepan or one more frying pan, which product would the firm prefer to sell? Why?
3. Under what conditions would the firm want to drop frying pans from the product mix?

EXERCISE 12–19 Make or Buy [LO2]

Electric Scooter Co. makes motorized scooters for city commuters. The scooters can be charged using a regular household plug, and the batteries hold their charge for 24 hours. The manufacturing plant is currently operating at 70% capacity. The plant manager is considering manufacturing headlights for the scooters, which are currently being produced by an outside company and purchased by Electric Scooter for $11 each. Electric Scooter has the equipment and the workforce to produce the headlights. The engineers have suggested a variable cost of $3 in direct labour and $4 in direct materials. The plant overhead rate is 200% of direct labour dollars, and 40% of the overhead is fixed cost.

Required:
Should Electric Scooter make the headlights in-house?

EXERCISE 12–20 Dropping a Product Line [LO2]

A doughnut shop makes three basic types of doughnuts: cream filled, chocolate filled, and jam filled. The doughnut shop manager is analyzing the product mix and has collected the following information:

	Chocolate Filled	Cream Filled	Jam Filled
Sales price per dozen	$ 4.00	$ 3.00	$ 2.50
Direct cost per dozen	(2.10)	(0.90)	(2.00)
Fixed overhead per dozen	(0.40)	(0.50)	(1.00)
Profit per dozen	$ 1.50	$ 1.60	(0.50)

The fixed costs are unavoidable and are allocated to each doughnut type based on the quantity produced. The doughnut shop has excess capacity.

Required:
1. Which product should the doughnut shop promote if the promotion will result in an increase in sales of 50 dozen of the promoted product?
2. Should the jam-filled doughnuts be dropped from the product line? Why or why not?
3. How does the decision to drop the jam-filled doughnuts change if the shop is currently producing at capacity?

PROBLEMS

PROBLEM 12–21 Dropping or Retaining a Tour [LO2]

A study has indicated that some of the bus tours operated by Clear Water Tours Inc. are not profitable. As a result, consideration is being given to dropping these unprofitable tours to improve the company's overall operating performance.

One such tour is a three-day Majestic Islands bus tour. Additional information and an income statement from a typical Majestic Islands tour are given below:

Ticket revenue (100 = seat capacity × 40% occupancy × $70 ticket price per person)	$2,800	100%
Variable expenses ($21.00 per person)	840	30
Contribution margin	1,960	70%
Tour expenses:		
Tour promotion	540	
Salary of bus driver	320	
Fee, tour guide	630	
Fuel for bus	110	
Depreciation of bus	410	
Liability insurance, bus	180	
Overnight parking fees, bus	50	
Room and meals, bus driver and tour guide	160	
Bus maintenance and preparation	270	
Total tour expenses	2,670	
Operating loss	$ (710)	

The following additional information is available about the tour:
a. Bus drivers are paid fixed annual salaries; tour guides are paid for each tour conducted.
b. The "Bus maintenance and preparation" cost in the statement is an allocation of the salaries of mechanics and other service personnel who are responsible for keeping the company's fleet of buses in good operating condition.
c. Depreciation of buses is due to obsolescence.
d. Liability insurance premiums are based on the number of buses in the company's fleet.
e. Dropping the Majestic Islands bus tour would not allow Clear Water Tours to reduce the number of buses in its fleet, the number of bus drivers on the payroll, or the size of the maintenance and preparation staff.

Required:
1. Prepare an analysis showing what the impact will be on the company's profits if this tour is discontinued.
2. The company's tour director has been criticized because only about 50% of the seats on Clear Water's tours are being filled, compared to an industry average of 60%. The tour director has explained that Clear Water's average seat occupancy could be improved considerably by eliminating about 10% of its tours, but that doing so would reduce profits. Explain how this could happen.

PROBLEM 12-22 Sell or Process Further [LO2]

Valley Meat Processing Corporation is a major processor of beef and other meat products. The company has a large number of T-bone steaks on hand, and it is trying to decide whether to sell the T-bone steaks as is or to process them further into filet mignon and New York–cut steaks.
   Management believes that a kilogram of T-bone steak would yield the following profit:

Wholesale selling price ($16.00 per kilogram)	$16.00
Less joint costs incurred up to the split-off point where T-bone steak can be identified as a separate product	12.00
Profit per kilogram	$ 4.00

As mentioned above, instead of being sold as is, the T-bone steaks could be further processed into filet mignon and New York–cut steaks. Cutting one side of a T-bone steak provides the filet mignon, and cutting the other side provides the New York cut. One 480-gram T-bone steak cut in this way will yield one 181-gram filet mignon and one 241-gram New York cut; the remaining grams are waste. The cost of processing the T-bone steaks into these cuts is $1.40 per kilogram. The filet mignon can be sold retail for $26 per kilogram, and the New York–cut can be sold wholesale for $22 per kilogram.

Required:
1. Determine the profit for each 480-gram T-bone steak processed further into filet mignon and New York–cut steaks.
2. Would you recommend that the T-bone steaks be sold as is or processed further? Why?

(Prepared from a situation suggested by Professor John W. Hardy.)

PROBLEM 12-23 Close or Retain a Store [LO2]
The Tilots Corporation's segmented absorption costing income statement for the last quarter for its three metropolitan stores is given below:

	Total	Uptown Store	Downtown Store	Westpark Store
Sales	$2,500,000	$900,000	$600,000	$1,000,000
Cost of goods sold	1,450,000	513,000	372,000	565,000
Gross margin	1,050,000	387,000	228,000	435,000
Selling and administrative expenses:				
Selling expenses:				
Direct advertising	118,500	40,000	36,000	42,500
General advertising*	20,000	7,200	4,800	8,000
Sales salaries	157,000	52,000	45,000	60,000
Delivery salaries	30,000	10,000	10,000	10,000
Store rent	215,000	70,000	65,000	80,000
Depreciation of store fixtures	46,950	18,300	8,800	19,850
Depreciation of delivery equipment	27,000	9,000	9,000	9,000
Total selling expenses	614,450	206,500	178,600	229,350
Administrative expenses:				
Store management salaries	63,000	20,000	18,000	25,000
General office salaries*	50,000	18,000	12,000	20,000
Utilities	89,800	31,000	27,200	31,600
Insurance on fixtures and inventory	25,500	8,000	9,000	8,500
Employee benefits	36,000	12,000	10,200	13,800
General office expenses–other*	25,000	9,000	6,000	10,000
Total administrative expenses	289,300	98,000	82,400	108,900
Total operating expenses	903,750	304,500	261,000	338,250
Operating income (loss)	$ 146,250	$ 82,500	$(33,000)	$ 96,750

*Allocated on the basis of sales dollars.

Management is very concerned about the Downtown Store's inability to show a profit, and consideration is being given to closing the store. The company has asked you recommend a course of action. Additional information available on the store is provided below:
a. The manager of the store has been with the company for many years; he would be retained and transferred to another position in the company if the Downtown Store were closed. His salary is $6,000 per month, or $18,000 per quarter. If the store were not closed, a new employee would be hired to fill the other position at a salary of $5,000 per month.
b. The lease on the building housing the Downtown Store can be broken with no penalty.
c. The fixtures being used in the Downtown Store would be transferred to the other two stores if the Downtown Store were closed.
d. Employee benefits are 12% of salaries.
e. A single delivery crew serves all three stores. One delivery person could be discharged if the Downtown Store were closed; this person's salary amounts to $7,000 per quarter. The

delivery equipment would be distributed to the other stores. The equipment does not wear out through use, but it does eventually become obsolete.

f.   One-third of the Downtown Store's insurance relates to its fixtures.

g.   The general office salaries and other expenses relate to the general management of the Tilots Corporation. The employee in the general office who is responsible for the Downtown Store would be discharged if the store were closed. This employee's compensation amounts to $8,000 per quarter.

Required:
1.   Prepare a schedule showing the change in revenues and expenses and the impact on the overall company operating income that would result if the Downtown Store were closed.
2.   Based on your computations in (1) above, what would you recommend to the management of the Tilots Corporation?
3.   Assume that if the Downtown Store were closed, sales in the Uptown Store would increase by $200,000 per quarter due to loyal customers shifting their buying to the Uptown Store. The Uptown Store has ample capacity to handle the increased sales, and its gross margin is 43% of sales. What effect would these factors have on your recommendation concerning the Downtown Store? Show computations.

PROBLEM 12-24 Make or Buy Decision [LO2]

Bastion Company, a manufacturer of several types of ballpoint pens, has just received an offer from an outside supplier to provide the ink cartridge for the company's Zappo pen line, at a price of $0.48 per dozen cartridges. The company is interested in this offer, since its own production of cartridges is at capacity.

Bastion Company estimates that if the supplier's offer were accepted, the direct labour and variable manufacturing overhead costs of the Zappo pen line would be reduced by 10% and the direct materials cost would be reduced by 20%.

Under current operations, Bastion Company manufactures all of its own pens from start to finish. The Zappo pens are sold through wholesalers at $4 per box. Each box contains one dozen pens. Fixed manufacturing overhead costs charged to the Zappo pen line total $50,000 each year. (The same equipment and facilities are used to produce several pen lines.) The present cost of producing one dozen Zappo pens (one box) is given below:

Direct materials.	$ 1.50
Direct labour.	1.00
Manufacturing overhead	0.80*
Total cost.	$3.30

*Includes both variable and fixed manufacturing overhead, based on production of 100,000 boxes of pens each year.

Required:
1.   Should Bastion Company accept the outside supplier's offer? Show computations.
2.   What is the maximum price that Bastion Company should be willing to pay the outside supplier per dozen cartridges? Explain.
3.   Due to the bankruptcy of a competitor, Bastion Company expects to sell 150,000 boxes of Zappo pens next year. As stated above, the company has enough capacity to produce the cartridges for only 100,000 boxes of Zappo pens annually. By incurring $30,000 in added fixed cost each year, the company could expand its production of cartridges to satisfy the anticipated demand for Zappo pens. The variable cost per unit to produce the additional cartridges would be the same as at present. Under these circumstances, how many boxes of cartridges should be purchased from the outside supplier and how many should be made by Bastion? Show computations to support your answer.
4.   What qualitative factors should Bastion Company consider in determining whether it should make or buy the ink cartridges?

(CMA, adapted)

PROBLEM 12–25 Relevant Cost Analysis in a Variety of Situations [LO2]
Ovation Company has a single product called a Bit. The company normally produces and sells 60,000 Bits each year at a selling price of $32 per unit. The company's unit costs at this level of activity are given below:

Direct materials...	$10.00	
Direct labour...	4.50	
Variable manufacturing overhead	2.30	
Fixed manufacturing overhead.................................	5.00	($300,000 total)
Variable selling expenses......................................	1.20	
Fixed selling expenses...	3.50	($210,000 total)
Total cost per unit	$26.50	

A number of questions relating to the production and sale of Bits follow. Each question is independent.

Required:
1. Assume that Ovation Company has sufficient capacity to produce 90,000 Bits each year without any increase in fixed manufacturing overhead costs. The company could increase its sales by 25% above the current 60,000 units each year if it were willing to increase the fixed selling expenses by $80,000. Would the increased fixed selling expenses be justified?
2. Assume again that Ovation Company has sufficient capacity to produce 90,000 Bits each year. A customer in a foreign market wants to purchase 20,000 Bits. Import duties on the Bits would be $1.70 per unit, and costs for permits and licences would be $9,000. The only selling costs that would be associated with the order are $3.20 per unit shipping cost. Compute the per unit break-even price on this order.
3. The company has 1,000 Bits on hand that have some irregularities and are therefore considered to be "seconds." Due to the irregularities, it will be impossible to sell these units at the normal price through regular distribution channels. What unit cost figure is relevant for setting a minimum selling price? Explain.
4. Due to a strike in its supplier's plant, Ovation Company is unable to purchase more material for the production of Bits. The strike is expected to last for two months. Ovation Company has enough material on hand to operate at 30% of normal levels for the two-month period. As an alternative, Ovation could close its plant down entirely for the two months. If the plant were closed, fixed manufacturing overhead costs would continue at 60% of their normal level during the two-month period and the fixed selling expenses would be reduced by 20%. What would be the impact on profits of closing the plant for the two-month period?
5. An outside manufacturer has offered to produce Bits and ship them directly to Ovation's customers. If Ovation Company accepts this offer, the facilities that it uses to produce Bits would be idle; however, fixed manufacturing overhead costs would be reduced by 75%. Since the outside manufacturer would pay for all shipping costs, the variable selling expenses would be only two-thirds of their current amount. Compute the unit cost that is relevant for comparison to the price quoted by the outside manufacturer.

PROBLEM 12–26 Shutting Down or Continuing to Operate a Plant [LO2]
(*Note:* This type of decision is similar to dropping a product line.) Nicholas Company manufactures a fast-bonding glue, normally producing and selling 40,000 litres of the glue each month. This glue, which is known as MJ-7, is used in the wood industry to manufacture plywood. The selling price of MJ-7 is $35 per litre, variable costs are $21 per litre, fixed manufacturing overhead costs in the plant total $230,000 per month, and the fixed selling costs total $310,000 per month.

Strikes in the mills that purchase the bulk of the MJ-7 glue have caused Nicholas Company's sales to temporarily drop to only 11,000 litres per month. Nicholas Company's management estimates that the strikes will last for two months, after which sales of MJ-7 should return to normal. Due to the current low level of sales, Nicholas Company's management is thinking about closing down the plant during the strike.

If Nicholas Company does close down the plant, fixed manufacturing overhead costs can be reduced by $60,000 per month and fixed selling costs can be reduced by 10%. Start-up costs at the end of the shutdown period would total $14,000. Since Nicholas Company uses lean production methods, no inventories are on hand.

Required:
1. Assuming that the strikes continue for two months, would you recommend that Nicholas Company close the plant? Explain. Show computations to support your answer.
2. At what level of sales (in litres) for the two-month period should Nicholas Company be indifferent between closing the plant and keeping it open? Show computations. (*Hint:* This is a type of break-even analysis, except that the fixed-cost portion of your break-even computation should include only those fixed costs that are relevant (i.e., avoidable) over the two-month period.)

PROBLEM 12–27 Make or Buy Analysis [LO2]

"That old equipment for producing carburetors is worn out," said Bill Seebach, president of Hondrich Company. "We need to make a decision quickly." The company is trying to decide whether it should rent new equipment and continue to make its carburetors internally or whether it should discontinue production of its carburetors and purchase them from an outside supplier. The alternatives follow:

Alternative 1: Rent new equipment for producing the carburetors for $120,000 per year.
Alternative 2: Purchase carburetors from an outside supplier for $16 each.

Hondrich Company's costs per unit of producing the carburetors internally (with the old equipment) are given below. These costs are based on a current activity level of 40,000 units per year:

Direct materials.	$ 5.50
Direct labour.	8.00
Variable overhead	1.20
Fixed overhead ($1.50 supervision, $1.80 depreciation, and $4 general company overhead)	7.30
Total cost per unit	$22.00

The new equipment would be more efficient and, according to the manufacturer, would reduce direct labour costs and variable overhead costs by 25%. Supervision cost ($60,000 per year) and direct materials cost per unit would not be affected by the new equipment. The new equipment's capacity would be 60,000 carburetors per year.

The total general company overhead would be unaffected by this decision.

Required:
1. Seebach is unsure what the company should do and would like an analysis showing the unit costs and total costs for each of the two alternatives given above. Assume that 40,000 carburetors are needed each year. Which course of action would you recommend to Seebach?
2. Would your recommendation in (1) above be the same if the company's needs were (*a*) 50,000 carburetors per year, or (*b*) 60,000 carburetors per year? Show computations in good form.
3. What other factors would you recommend that Seebach consider before making a decision?

PROBLEM 12–28 Accept or Reject a Special Order [LO2]

Moore Company manufactures and sells a single product called a Lop. Operating at capacity, the company can produce and sell 30,000 Lops per year. Costs associated with this level of production and sales are given below:

	Unit	Total
Direct materials	$15	$ 450,000
Direct labour	8	240,000
Variable manufacturing overhead	3	90,000
Fixed manufacturing overhead	9	270,000
Variable selling expense	4	120,000
Fixed selling expense	6	180,000
Total cost	$45	$1,350,000

The Lops normally sell for $50 each. Fixed manufacturing overhead is constant at $270,000 per year within the range of 25,000 through 30,000 Lops per year.

Required:
1. Assume that due to a recession, Moore Company expects to sell only 25,000 Lops through regular channels next year. A large retail chain has offered to purchase 5,000 Lops if Moore is willing to accept a 16% discount off the regular price. There would be no sales commissions on this order, so variable selling expenses would be slashed by 75%. However, Moore Company would have to purchase a special machine to engrave the retail chain's name on the 5,000 units. This machine would cost $10,000. Moore Company has no assurance that the retail chain will purchase additional units in the future. Determine the impact on profits next year if this special order is accepted.
2. Refer to the original data. Assume again that Moore Company expects to sell only 25,000 Lops through regular channels next year. The provincial government would like to make a one-time-only purchase of 5,000 Lops. The government would pay a fixed fee of $1.80 per Lop, and it would reimburse Moore Company for all costs of production (variable and fixed) associated with the units. Since the government would pick up the Lops with its own trucks, there would be no variable selling expenses associated with this order. If Moore Company accepts the order, by how much will profits increase or decrease for the year?
3. Assume the same situation as that described in (2) above, except that the company expects to sell 30,000 Lops through regular channels next year, so accepting the government's order would require giving up regular sales of 5,000 Lops. If the government's order is accepted, by how much will profits increase or decrease from what they would be if the 5,000 Lops were sold through regular channels?

PROBLEM 12–29 Utilization of a Constrained Resource [LO3]
Demand for Stuffin' Such stuffed animal shells and stuffing/finishing kits manufactured by RoseMarie Limited is increasing, and management requests assistance from you in determining the best sales and production mix for the coming year. The company has provided the following data:

Product	Demand Next Year (Units)	Selling Price per Unit	Direct Materials	Direct Labour
Teddy bear	10,000	$30	$4.50	$1.50
Polar bear	5,000	$32	$3.30	$2.00
Husky	6,000	$25	$2.50	$4.00
Tiger	3,000	$27	$3.10	$6.00
Stuffing/finishing kits	24,000	$12	$1.50	$1.00

The following additional information is available:
a.   The company's plant has a capacity of 8,500 direct labour-hours per year on a single-shift basis. The company's current employees and equipment can produce all five products.
b.   The direct labour rate of $10.00 per hour is expected to remain unchanged during the coming year.
c.   Fixed costs total $100,000 per year. Variable overhead costs are $2.00 per direct labour-hour.
d.   All of the company's non-manufacturing costs are fixed.
e.   The company's finished goods inventory is negligible and can be ignored.

Required:
1. Determine the contribution margin per direct labour-hour expended on each product (the profitability index).
2. Prepare a schedule showing the total direct labour-hours that will be required to produce the units estimated to be sold during the coming year.
3. Examine the data you have computed in (1) and (2) above. How would you allocate the 8,500 direct labour-hours of capacity to the various products?
4. What is the highest price, in terms of a rate per hour, that Stuffin' Such should be willing to pay for additional capacity (that is, for added direct labour time)?
5. Identify ways in which the company might be able to obtain additional production capacity in the short run so that it would not have to leave some demand for its products unsatisfied.

(CMA, adapted)

PROBLEM 12–30 Sell or Process Further [LO2]

Clean and Shine Corporation produces several types of industrial and household cleaning compounds and solutions. While most of its products are processed independently, a few are related, such as the company's Clean 236 and its Sparkle silver polish.

Clean 236 is a coarse cleaning powder with many industrial uses. It costs $3.20 a kilogram to make, and it has a selling price of $4.00 a kilogram. A small portion of the annual production of Clean 236 is retained in the factory for further processing. It is combined with several other ingredients to form a paste that is marketed as Sparkle silver polish. The silver polish sells for $8.00 per jar.

This further processing requires one-half kilogram of Clean 236 per jar of silver polish. The additional direct costs involved in the processing of a jar of silver polish are as follows:

Other ingredients	$1.30
Direct labour	2.96
Total direct cost	$4.26

Overhead costs associated with the processing of the silver polish are as follows:

Variable manufacturing overhead cost	25% of direct labour cost
Fixed manufacturing overhead cost (per month):	
Production supervisor	$6,000
Depreciation of mixing equipment	$2,800

The production supervisor has no duties other than to oversee production of the silver polish. The mixing equipment, purchased two years ago, is special-purpose equipment acquired specifically to produce the silver polish. Its resale value is negligible and it does not wear out through use.

Direct labour is a variable cost at Clean and Shine Corporation.

Advertising costs for the silver polish total $8,000 per month. Variable selling costs associated with the silver polish are 7.5% of sales.

Due to a recent decline in the demand for silver polish, the company is wondering whether its continued production is advisable. The sales manager feels that it would be more profitable to sell all of the Clean 236 as a cleaning powder.

Required:
1. What is the incremental contribution margin per jar from further processing Clean 236 into silver polish?
2. What is the minimum number of jars of silver polish that must be sold each month to justify the continued processing of Clean 236 into silver polish? Explain. Show all computations in good form.

CASES

CASE 12–31 Integrative Case: Relevant Costs; Pricing [LO1, LO2]

Double Duty, a combination fertilizer–weed killer, is Alanco's only product. It is sold nationwide through normal marketing channels to retail nurseries and garden stores.

Taylor Nursery plans to sell a similar fertilizer–weed killer compound through its regional nursery chain under its own private label. Taylor does not have manufacturing facilities of its own, so it has asked Alanco (and several other companies) to submit a bid for manufacturing and delivering a 25,000-kilogram order of the private-brand compound to Taylor. While the chemical composition of the Taylor compound differs from that of Double Duty, the manufacturing processes are very similar.

The Taylor compound would be produced in 1,000-kilogram lots. Each lot would require 30 direct labour-hours and the following chemicals:

Chemical	Quantity in Kilograms
CW–3	400
JX–6	300
MZ–8	200
BE–7	100

The first three chemicals (CW–3, JX–6, and MZ–8) are all used in the production of Double Duty. BE–7 was used in another compound that Alanco discontinued several months ago. The supply of BE–7 that Alanco had on hand when the other compound was discontinued was not discarded. Alanco could sell its supply of BE–7 at the prevailing market price less $0.10 per kilogram selling and handling expenses.

Alanco also has on hand a chemical called CN–5, which was manufactured for use in another product that is no longer produced. CN–5, which cannot be used in Double Duty, can be substituted for CW–3 on a one-to-one basis without affecting the quality of the Taylor compound. The CN–5 in inventory has a salvage value of $500.

Inventory and cost data for the chemicals that can be used to produce the Taylor compound are as shown below:

Raw Material	Kilograms in Inventory	Actual Price per Kilogram When Purchased	Current Market Price per Kilogram
CW–3	22,000	$0.80	$0.90
JX–6	5,000	0.55	0.60
MZ–8	8,000	1.40	1.60
BE–7	4,000	0.60	0.65
CN–5	5,500	0.75	(salvage)

The current direct labour rate is $14 per hour. The predetermined overhead rate is based on direct labour-hours (DLH). The predetermined overhead rate for the current year, based on a two-shift capacity of 400,000 total DLH with no overtime, is as follows:

Variable manufacturing overhead	$ 4.50 per DLH
Fixed manufacturing overhead	7.50 per DLH
Combined rate	$12.00 per DLH

Alanco's production manager reports that the current equipment and facilities are adequate to manufacture the Taylor compound. Therefore, the order would have no effect on total fixed manufacturing overhead costs. However, Alanco is within 400 hours of its two-shift capacity this month. Any additional hours beyond 400 hours must be done in overtime. If need be, the Taylor compound could be produced on regular time by shifting a portion of Double Duty production to overtime. Alanco's rate for overtime hours is 1½ times the regular pay rate, or $21 per hour. There is no allowance for any overtime premium in the predetermined overhead rate.

Required:
1. Alanco has decided to submit a bid for a 25,000-kilogram order of Taylor Nursery's new compound. The order must be delivered by the end of the current month. Taylor Nursery has indicated that this is a one-time order that will not be repeated. Calculate the lowest price that Alanco could bid for the order without reducing its operating income.
2. Refer to the original data. Assume that Taylor Nursery plans to place regular orders for 25,000-kilogram lots of the new compound during the coming year. Alanco expects the demand for Double Duty to remain strong. Therefore, the recurring orders from Taylor Nursery would put Alanco over its two-shift capacity. However, production could be scheduled so that 60% of each Taylor Nursery order could be completed during regular hours. As another option, some Double Duty production could be shifted temporarily to overtime so that the Taylor Nursery orders could be produced on regular time. Current market prices are the best available estimates of future market prices.

    Alanco's standard markup policy for new products is 40% of the full manufacturing cost, including fixed manufacturing overhead. Calculate the price that Alanco would quote Taylor Nursery for each 25,000-kilogram lot of the new compound, assuming that it is to be treated as a new product and this pricing policy is followed.

CASE 12–32 Special Order and Constrained Resource [LO2]
East Coast Digital (ECD) produces high-quality audio and video equipment. One of the company's most popular products is a high-definition personal video recorder (PVR) for use with digital television systems. Demand has increased rapidly for the PVR over the past three years,

given the appeal to customers of being able to easily record programs while they watch live television, watch recorded programs while they record a different program, and save dozens of programs for future viewing on the unit's large internal hard drive.

A complex production process is utilized for the PVR involving both laser and imaging equipment. ECD has a monthly production capacity of 4,000 hours on its laser machine and 1,000 hours on its image machine. However, given the recent increase in demand for the PVR, both machines are currently operating at 90% of capacity every month, based on existing orders from customers. Direct labour costs are $15 and $20 per hour to operate, respectively, the laser and image machines.

The revenue and costs on a per unit basis for the PVR are as follows:

Selling price		$320.00
Cost to manufacture:		
Direct materials	$50.00	
Direct labour—laser process	60.00	
Direct labour—image process	20.00	
Variable overhead	40.00	
Fixed overhead	50.00	
Variable selling costs	20.00	240.00
Operating profit		$ 80.00

On December 1, Dave Nance, vice-president of Sales and Marketing at ECD, received a special-order request from a prospective customer, Jay Limited, which has offered to buy 250 PVRs at $280 per unit if the product can be delivered by December 31. Jay Limited is a large retailer with outlets that specialize in audio and video equipment. This special order from Jay Limited is in addition to orders from existing customers that are utilizing 90% of the production capacity each month. Variable selling costs would not be incurred on this special order. Jay Limited is not willing to accept anything less than the 250 PVRs requested (i.e., ECD cannot partially fill the order).

Before responding to the customer, Nance decided to meet with Dianne Davis, the product manager for the PVR, to discuss whether to accept the offer from Jay Limited. An excerpt from their conversation follows:

Nance: I'm not sure we should accept the offer. This customer is really playing hardball with its terms and conditions.

Davis: Agreed, but it is a reputable company and I suspect this is the way it typically deals with its suppliers. Plus, this could be the beginning of a profitable relationship with Jay Limited since the company may be interested in some of our other product offerings in the future.

Nance: That may be true, but I'm not sure we should be willing to incur such a large opportunity cost just to get our foot in the door with this client.

Davis: Have you calculated the opportunity cost?

Nance: Sure, that was simple. Jay Limited is offering $280 per unit and we sell to our regular customers at $320 per unit. Therefore, we're losing $40 per unit, which at 250 units is $10,000 in lost revenue. That's our opportunity cost and it's clearly relevant to the decision.

Davis: I sort of follow your logic, but I think the fact that we're not currently operating at full capacity needs to be taken into consideration.

Nance: How so?

Davis: Well, your approach to calculating the opportunity cost ignores the fact that we aren't currently selling all of the PVRs that we could produce. So, in that sense we aren't really losing $40 per unit on all 250 units required by Jay Limited.

Nance: I see your point but I'm not clear on how we should calculate the opportunity cost.

Davis: This really isn't my area of expertise either, but it seems appropriate to start by trying to figure out how many of the 250 units required by Jay Limited we could produce without disrupting our ability to fill existing orders. Then we could determine how many units we would have to forgo selling to existing customers to make up the 250-unit order. That would then be our opportunity cost in terms of the number of physical units involved. Make sense?

Nance: I think so. So, to get the dollar amount of the opportunity cost of accepting the 250-unit order from Jay Limited we'd then simply multiply the number of units we'd have to forgo selling to existing customers by $40. Correct?

Davis: I'm not so sure about the $40. I think we somehow need to factor in the incremental profit we typically earn by selling each PVR to existing customers to really get to the true opportunity cost.

Nance: Now I'm getting really getting confused. Can you work through the numbers and get back to me?

Davis: I'll try.

Nance: Thanks. And by the way, Jay Limited is calling in an hour and wants our answer.

Required:

1. Is Davis's general approach to calculating the opportunity cost in terms of the physical units involved correct? Explain.

2. Assuming productive capacity cannot be increased for either machine in December, how many PVRs would ECD have to forgo selling to existing customers to fill the special order from Jay Limited?

3. Calculate the opportunity cost of accepting the special order.

4. Calculate the net effect on profits of accepting the special order.

5. Now assume that ECD is operating at 75% of capacity in December. What is the minimum price ECD should be willing to accept on the special order?

6. What are some qualitative issues that should be considered when accepting special orders such as that proposed by Jay Limited?

CASE 12–33 Sell or Process Further Decision [LO2]

Turnberry Tomatoes has a plant that can process vine-ripened tomatoes, along with other ingredients, into various tomato sauces and salsas. The company can sell all of its unprocessed vine-ripened tomatoes at a selling price of $6.15 per kilogram. In the past, the company has sold only part of its unprocessed vine-ripened tomatoes and has retained the rest for further processing into tomato sauces and salsas. The salsa has been selling for $8.75 per kilogram, but recently the price has become unstable and has dropped to $7.80 per kilogram. The costs and revenues associated with a kilogram of salsa follow:

		Per Kilogram of Salsa
Selling price		$ 7.80
Cost to manufacture:		
Raw materials:		
Extra salsa ingredients	$1.00	
Unprocessed tomatoes (1 kg)	5.90	6.90
Direct labour		0.25
Manufacturing overhead		0.75
Manufacturing profit (loss)		$(0.10)

Because of the weak price for the company's processed sauces and salsas, the sales manager believes that the company should discontinue processing the salsas and instead simply sell the unprocessed vine-ripened tomatoes. Current cost and revenue data on the unprocessed vine-ripened tomatoes follow:

		Per Kilogram of Tomatoes
Selling price		$ 6.15
Cost to manufacture:		
Seeds, pesticides, and fertilizers	$4.90	
Direct labour	0.25	
Manufacturing overhead	0.75	5.90
Manufacturing profit		$0.25

The sales manager argues that since the current $7.80 per kilogram price for the salsa results in a $0.10 per kilogram loss, the production of salsa should not be resumed until the price per kilogram rises above $7.90. The company assigns manufacturing overhead cost to the two products on the basis of labour-hours, but virtually all manufacturing overhead costs are fixed. Materials and labour costs are variable. The company can sell all of the unprocessed vine-ripened tomatoes and salsa it can produce at the current market prices.

Required:
1. Do you agree with the sales manager that the company should discontinue the processing of salsa and use the entire labour capacity to grow, sort, and package tomatoes if the price of salsa remains at $7.80 per kilogram? Support your answer with computations and explanations.
2. What is the lowest price that the company should accept for a kilogram of salsa? Again support your answer with computations and explanations.

CASE 12–34 Plant Closing Decision [LO1, LO2]

Automotive Interiors (AI) manufactures seats for automobiles, vans, trucks, and boats. The company has a number of plants, including the Woodstock Cover Plant, which makes seat covers.

Bill Rice is the plant manager at the Woodstock Cover Plant but also serves as the regional production manager for the company. His budget as the regional manager is charged to the Woodstock plant.

Rice has just heard that AI has received a bid from an outside vendor to supply the equivalent of the entire annual output of the Woodstock Cover Plant for $42 million. Rice was astonished at the low outside bid because the budget for the plant's operating costs for the coming year was set at $48.6 million. If this bid is accepted, the Woodstock operation will be closed down.

The budget for the Woodstock Cover Plant's operating costs for the coming year is presented below:

Materials		$ 16,000,000
Labour:		
Direct	$13,400,000	
Supervision	800,000	
Indirect plant	3,800,000	18,000,000
Overhead:		
Depreciation—equipment	2,600,000	
Depreciation—building	4,200,000	
Pension expense	3,200,000	
Plant manager and staff*	1,200,000	
Corporate expenses†	3,400,000	14,600,000
Total budgeted costs		$48,600,000

*Expense for Rice and his regional staff.
†Fixed corporate expenses allocated to plants and other operating units based on total budgeted wage and salary costs.

The following are additional facts regarding the plant's operations:
a. Due to the plant's commitment to use high-quality fabrics in all of its products, the Purchasing Department was instructed to place blanket purchase orders with major suppliers to ensure the receipt of sufficient materials for the coming year. If these orders were cancelled as a consequence of the plant closing, termination charges would amount to 25% of the cost of direct materials.
b. Approximately 350 employees would lose their jobs if the plant were closed. This includes all of the direct labourers and supervisors; management and staff; and the plumbers, electricians, and other skilled workers classified as indirect plant workers. Some of these workers would have difficulty finding new jobs. Nearly all of the production workers would have difficulty matching the plant's base pay of $12.50 per hour, which is the highest in the area. A clause in the plant's contract with the union may help some employees; the company must provide employment assistance and job training to its former employees for 12 months after a plant closing. The estimated cost to administer this service would be $1.6 million.

c.   Some employees would probably choose early retirement because AI has an excellent pension plan. In fact, $1.4 million of the annual pension expenditures would continue whether the plant is open or not.

d.   Rice and his regional staff would not be affected by the closing of the Woodstock plant. They would still be responsible for running three other area plants.

e.   If the plant were closed, the company would realize about $4 million salvage value for the equipment in the plant. If the plant remained open, there would be no plans to make any significant investments in new equipment or buildings. The old equipment is adequate for the job and should last indefinitely.

Required:

1.   Without regard to costs, identify the advantages to AI of continuing to obtain covers from its own Woodstock Cover Plant.

2.   AI plans to prepare a financial analysis that will be used in deciding whether or not to close the Woodstock Cover Plant. Management has asked you to identify the following:

a.   The annual budgeted costs that are relevant to the decision regarding closing the plant (show the dollar amounts).

b.   The annual budgeted costs that are not relevant to the decision regarding closing the plant and an explanation of why they are not relevant (again show the dollar amounts).

c.   Any non-recurring costs that would arise due to the closing of the plant and an explanation of how they would affect the decision (again show any dollar amounts).

3.   Looking at the data you prepared in (2) above, should the plant be closed? Show computations and explain your answer.

4.   Identify any revenues or costs not specifically mentioned in the problem that AI should consider before making a decision.

(CMA, adapted)

CASE 12–35 Make or Buy; Utilization of a Constrained Resource [LO1, LO2, LO3]
Drums, bins, boxes, and other containers that are used in the petroleum industry are sold by Holden Inc. One of the company's products is a heavy-duty, environmentally friendly, corrosion-resistant metal drum, called the STR drum, used to store toxic wastes. Production is constrained by the capacity of an automated welding machine that is used to make precision welds. A total of 4,500 hours of welding time is available annually on the machine. Since each drum requires 0.6 hours of welding time, annual production is limited to 7,500 drums. At present, the welding machine is used exclusively to make the STR drums. The accounting department has provided the following financial data concerning the STR drums:

STR Drums		
Selling price per drum		$225.00
Cost per drum:		
Direct materials	$ 78.15	
Direct labour ($27 per hour)	5.40	
Manufacturing overhead	6.75	
Selling and administrative expenses	44.70	135.00
Margin per drum.....................................		$ 90.00

Management believes that 9,000 STR drums could be sold each year if the company had sufficient manufacturing capacity. As an alternative to adding another welding machine, management has considered buying additional drums from an outside supplier of quality products, Anderson Industries Inc. Anderson would be able to provide up to 6,000 STR-type drums per year at a price of $207 per drum, which Holden would relabel and sell to its customers at its normal selling price.

Candace Burke, Holden's production manager, has suggested that the company could make better use of the welding machine by manufacturing wrought iron park benches, which would require 0.75 hours of welding time per bench and yet sell for far more than the drums. Burke believes that Holden could sell up to 2,400 wrought iron park benches per year to municipalities and conservation areas at a price of $360 each. The Accounting Department has provided the following data concerning the proposed new product:

Wrought Iron Park Benches		
Selling price per bench		$360.00
Cost per bench:		
Direct materials	$149.10	
Direct labour ($27 per hour)	43.20	
Manufacturing overhead.........................	54.00	
Selling and administrative expenses	71.70	318.00
Margin per bench..................................		$ 42.00

The park benches could be produced with existing equipment and personnel. Manufacturing overhead is allocated to products on the basis of direct labour-hours. Most of the manufacturing overhead consists of fixed common costs, such as rent on the factory building, but some of it is variable. The variable manufacturing overhead has been estimated at $2.00 per STR drum and $2.85 per park bench. The variable manufacturing overhead cost would not be incurred on drums acquired from the outside supplier.

Selling and administrative expenses are allocated to products on the basis of revenues. Almost all of the selling and administrative expenses are fixed common costs, but it has been estimated that variable selling and administrative expenses amount to $1.15 per STR drum whether made or purchased and $1.95 per park bench.

All of the company's employees—direct and indirect—are paid for full 40-hour workweeks and the company has a policy of laying off workers only in major recessions.

Required:
1. Should the financial analysis prepared by the company be used in deciding which product to sell? Why?
2. Compute the contribution margin per unit for
   a. Purchased STR drums.
   b. Manufactured STR drums.
   c. Manufactured park benches.
3. Determine the number of STR drums (if any) that should be purchased and the number of STR drums and/or park benches (if any) that should be manufactured. What is the increase in operating income that would result from this plan over current operations?

   As soon as your analysis was shown to the top management team at Holden, several managers got into an argument concerning how direct labour costs should be treated when making this decision. One manager argued that direct labour is always treated as a variable cost in textbooks and in practice and has always been considered a variable cost at Holden. After all, "direct" means you can directly trace the cost to products. "If direct labour is not a variable cost, what is?" Another manager argued just as strenuously that direct labour should be considered a fixed cost at Holden. No one had been laid off in over a decade, and for all practical purposes, everyone at the plant is on a monthly salary. Everyone classified as direct labour works a regular 40-hour workweek, and overtime has not been necessary since the company adopted just-in-time techniques. Whether the welding machine were used to make drums or park benches, the total payroll would be exactly the same. There is enough slack, in the form of idle time, to accommodate any increase in total direct labour time that the park benches would require.
4. Redo requirements (2) and (3) above, making the opposite assumption about direct labour from the one you originally made. In other words, if you treated direct labour as a variable cost, redo the analysis treating it as a fixed cost. If you treated direct labour as a fixed cost, redo the analysis treating it as a variable cost.
5. What do you think is the correct way to treat direct labour cost in this situation—as variable or as fixed?

INSTANT QUIZ SOLUTIONS

12–1
No. Only those future costs that differ between the alternatives under consideration are relevant costs in decision making.

12-2

Direct costs can usually be avoided, but some indirect costs might remain even after the product line is dropped. Another factor to consider is whether the company has an alternative use for the space taken up by the machinery and equipment used to produce this product. If so, then management needs to consider the opportunity cost of not putting the space to an alternative use in making a decision. Finally, management should also consider the effect of dropping this product on sales of Able's other products. Will customers expect to be able to buy this product from Able, and, if so, will they go elsewhere for all of their related needs since Able does not carry the full line of products that customers expect?

12-3

Jones must first consider which costs are avoidable by outsourcing baked goods production. For example, can some employees be laid off if products are no longer produced on-site? If so, how much cost savings will be generated? Jones should also consider the opportunity cost of the space currently taken up with bakery equipment. Could that space be put to a more productive use? For example, if she expanded her seating area, would she attract more customers to the shop? Factors other than potential cost savings must also be considered. For example, she would need to consider whether the supplier is dependable in terms of quality and delivery, and she should be concerned about the possibility that the supplier might raise the price soon after Jones signs the contract to a price greater than her original cost of production.

12-4

Smythe needs to consider the incremental costs of filling the special order. For example, will the additional cost of materials required to fill the special order be less than the $20 special price? Since Smythe's staff are paid fixed salaries, there should be no incremental fixed costs assuming they have time available to fill the order without working overtime. In addition, Smythe needs to consider the opportunity cost of filling this special order. Could he be generating more incremental revenue by filling a similar order at the regular price? If so, what is the likelihood a customer will place such an order before the end of the week?

12-5

The incremental revenue earned by assembling the barbecue is $225 − $200, or $25. The incremental cost is $15/hour × ½ hour = $7.50. Since the incremental revenue is greater than the incremental cost, Corner Hardware should sell the barbecues assembled.

12-6

When companies have a constraint on a production input such as labour-hours or machine-hours, the relative profitability of products should be determined by calculating the profitability index. The profitability index is determined by dividing the contribution margin per unit for each product by the amount of the good output. The result is the contribution margin per unit of the scarce resource. Production should be maximized for the product with the highest profitability index, and so on until all capacity has been utilized.

connect   LEARNSMART   SMARTBOOK

For more information on the resources available from McGraw-Hill Ryerson, go to www.mheducation.ca/he/solutions.

■ APPENDIX 12A: PRICING PRODUCTS AND SERVICES

Our consideration of special orders in the main body of this chapter focused on non-routine situations where companies receive an offer for a product or service at a specific price. By comparing to the offer price the relevant costs that would be incurred if the offer were accepted, managers can determine the incremental effect on operating income. In this appendix, we expand our discussion of the relationship between relevant costs and pricing issues to include two distinct pricing situations requiring ongoing analysis by managers. First, we examine situations where companies are faced with the problem of setting their own prices for products or services. In this setting, we present two approaches to setting prices based on costs. Second, we examine a setting where the company offers a product or service that competes with other similar products or services for which a market price already exists. In this setting, we introduce the concept of target costing. Importantly, in both settings managers must identify and use relevant cost information to make decisions that are in the best interests of the company. Setting prices is a critical decision for managers. If the price is set too high, customers will avoid purchasing the company's products. If the price is set too low, the company's costs may not be covered.

LEARNING OBJECTIVE ❹
Compute selling prices based on costs.

Cost-Plus Pricing

A common approach to pricing is to set prices based on a certain *markup* above cost.[5] A product's **markup** is the difference between its selling price and its cost. The markup is usually expressed as a percentage of cost. This approach is called **cost-plus pricing** because the predetermined markup percentage is applied to the cost base to determine a target selling price:

$$\text{Selling price} = \text{Cost} + (\text{Markup percentage} \times \text{Cost})$$

For example, if a company uses a markup of 50%, it adds 50% to the costs of its products to determine the selling price. If a product costs $10, then the company will charge $15 for the product.

There are two key issues when the cost-plus approach to pricing is used. First, what costs are relevant to the pricing decision? Second, how should the markup be determined? Several alternative approaches are considered in this appendix.

As discussed in Chapters 2 through 8 and Chapter 10, various definitions of *cost* exist, each of which could be used as the base for setting a selling price. To provide a coherent illustration of cost-plus pricing, absorption costing will be presented first. We will then present an example of cost-plus pricing using the total variable costing approach.

Markup
The difference between the selling price of a product or service and its cost. The markup is usually expressed as a percentage of cost.

Cost-plus pricing
A pricing method in which a predetermined markup is applied to a cost base to determine the target selling price.

Setting a Target Selling Price Using the Absorption Costing Approach

To illustrate, assume that the management of Roper Company wants to set the selling price on a product that has just undergone some design modifications. The Accounting Department has provided cost estimates for the redesigned product as shown below:

	Per Unit	Total
Direct materials..	$12	
Direct labour..	8	
Variable manufacturing overhead...............................	6	
Fixed manufacturing overhead..................................	—	$140,000
Variable selling and administrative expenses.................	4	
Fixed selling and administrative expenses....................	—	120,000

The first step in the absorption costing approach to cost-plus pricing is to compute the unit product cost. For Roper Company, this amounts to $40 per unit at a volume of 10,000 units, as shown in the first part of Exhibit 12A–1.

EXHIBIT 12A-1   Price Quotation Sheet—Absorption Basis (10,000 Units)

Direct materials	$ 12
Direct labour	8
Variable manufacturing overhead.	6
Fixed manufacturing overhead (based on 10,000 units)	14
Unit product cost	40
Markup to cover selling and administrative expenses and desired profit—50% of unit manufacturing cost	20
Target selling price.	$60

Roper Company has a general policy of marking up unit product costs by 50%. A price quotation sheet for the company prepared using the absorption approach is also presented in Exhibit 12A-1. Note that selling and administrative costs are not included in the cost base. Instead, the markup is set at a level that will cover these expenses.

Next we examine how some companies compute markup percentages.

Determining the Markup Percentage

How did Roper Company arrive at its markup percentage of 50%? This figure could be based on industry norms or just a company tradition that seems to work. The markup percentage may also be the result of an explicit computation. As we have discussed, the markup over cost should ideally be largely determined by market conditions. However, a popular approach is to at least start with a markup based on cost and desired profit. The reasoning is as follows: the markup must be large enough to cover selling and administrative expenses and provide an adequate return on investment (ROI). Given the forecasted unit sales, the markup can be computed as follows:

$$\text{Markup percentage on absorption cost} = \frac{\left(\begin{array}{c}\text{Required ROI}\\ \times \text{ Investment}\end{array}\right) + \text{Selling and administrative expenses}}{\text{Unit sales} \times \text{Unit product cost}}$$

To show how the formula above is applied, assume Roper Company must invest $200,000 to produce and market 10,000 units of the product each year. The $200,000 investment covers the purchase of equipment and the funds needed for working capital items such as inventory and accounts receivable. If Roper Company requires a 20% ROI, then the markup for the product is determined as follows:

$$\text{Markup percentage on absorption cost} = \frac{\left(\begin{array}{c}20\%\\ \times \$200,000\end{array}\right) + [(\$4 \times 10,000) + \$120,000]}{10,000 \times \$40}$$

$$\text{Markup percentage on absorption cost} = \frac{\$40,000 + \$160,000}{\$400,000} = 50\%$$

As shown earlier, this markup of 50% leads to a target selling price of $60 for the Roper Company product. As shown in Exhibit 12A-2, *if the company actually sells 10,000 units of the product at this price, and actual costs are as expected, the company's ROI on this product will indeed be 20%. If it turns out that more than 10,000 units are sold at this price, the ROI will be greater than 20%. If fewer than 10,000 units are sold, the ROI will be less than 20%. The required ROI will be attained only if the forecasted unit sales volume is attained or exceeded at the expected unit price (or higher),* and actual costs are equal to or less than expected costs for that level of sales activity.

Problems with the Absorption Costing Approach

Using the absorption costing approach, the pricing problem looks deceptively simple. All you have to do is compute your unit product cost, decide how much profit you want, and then set your price. It appears that you can ignore demand and arrive at a price that will safely yield whatever profit you want. However, as noted above, the absorption costing approach relies on a forecast of unit sales. Neither the markup nor the unit product cost can be computed without such a forecast.

EXHIBIT 12A-2   Income Statement and Return on Investment Analysis—Roper
Company Actual Unit Sales = 10,000 Units; Selling Price = $60

Direct materials	$ 12
Direct labour	8
Variable manufacturing overhead.	6
Fixed manufacturing overhead ($140,000 ÷ 10,000 units)	14
Unit product cost	$40

ROPER COMPANY
Absorption Costing Income Statement

Sales ($60 × 10,000 units).	$600,000
Less cost of goods sold ($40 × 10,000 units).	400,000
Gross margin.	200,000
Less selling and administrative expenses	
($4 × 10,000 units + $120,000).	160,000
Operating income	$ 40,000

ROI

$$ROI = \frac{\text{Operating income}}{\text{Average operating assets}}$$

$$= \frac{\$40,000}{\$200,000}$$

$$= 20\%$$

The absorption costing approach essentially assumes that customers *need* the forecasted unit sales and will pay whatever price the company decides to charge. However, customers have a choice. If the price is too high, they can buy from a competitor or they may choose not to buy at all. Suppose, for example, that when Roper Company sets its price at $60, it sells only 7,000 units rather than the 10,000 units forecasted. As shown in Exhibit 12A-3, the company would then have a loss of $50,000 on the product instead of a profit of $40,000. Some managers believe that the absorption costing approach to pricing is safe. This is not necessarily so. The absorption costing approach is safe only as long as customers choose to buy at least as many units as managers forecasted they would buy and costs behave as predicted or come in at lower levels.

Setting a Target Selling Price Using the Variable Costing Approach

Some companies use a variable costing approach to determine the target selling price based on either variable manufacturing costs or total variable costs. The key advantages of the variable costing approach are (1) it is consistent with the cost–volume–profit analysis presented in Chapter 4, which allows managers to determine the profit effects of changes in price and volume, and (2) it avoids the need to arbitrarily allocate common fixed costs to specific products.

To illustrate the use of the variable costing approach using total variable costs, we return to the Roper Company example.[6] The revised formula for calculating the markup is as follows:

$$\text{Markup percentage on total variable cost} = \frac{(\text{Required ROI} \times \text{Investment}) + \text{Total fixed expenses}}{\text{Unit sales} \times \text{Unit total variable costs}}$$

The numerator now includes fixed manufacturing overhead costs, and the denominator includes both manufacturing and selling and administrative variable expenses. The reason for

EXHIBIT 12A-3 Income Statement and ROI Analysis—Roper Company Actual Unit Sales = 7,000 Units; Selling Price = $60

Direct materials	$ 12
Direct labour	8
Variable manufacturing overhead.	6
Fixed manufacturing overhead ($140,000 ÷ 7,000 units)	20
Unit product cost	$46

ROPER COMPANY
Absorption Costing Income Statement

Sales ($60 × 7,000 units).	$420,000
Less cost of goods sold ($46 × 7,000 units)	322,000
Gross margin.	98,000
Less selling and administrative expenses	
($4 × 7,000 units + $120,000)	148,000
Operating income.	$ (50,000)

ROI

$$\text{ROI} = \frac{\text{Operating income}}{\text{Average operating assets}}$$

$$= \frac{\$50,000}{\$200,000}$$

$$= -25\%$$

this approach is that the markup must result in a contribution margin that covers all fixed expenses *and* leads to the required level of profit.

The calculations for the Roper Company data are as follows:

$$\text{Markup percentage on total variable cost} = \frac{(20\% \times \$200,000) + \$140,000 + \$120,000}{10,000 \times (\$12 + \$8 + \$6 + \$4)}$$

$$\text{Markup percentage on total variable cost} = \frac{\$40,000 + \$260,000}{\$300,000} = 100\%$$

A markup of 100% under the total variable costing approach results in the same $60 per unit selling price as the absorption costing approach: $30 + (100% × $30) = $60. By comparison, the markup required under the absorption costing approach is only 50% because the cost base ($40) is higher by virtue of including *all* manufacturing costs (variable and fixed). This highlights the need for managers using the total variable costing approach to remember that the markup must cover all costs, variable *and* fixed. While the ROI method of determining the markup explicitly incorporates all fixed costs in the calculations, other approaches, such as industry norms or company tradition, may not. Regardless of the method used to calculate the cost base or the markup percentage, managers must be diligent in ensuring that all costs are covered.

Setting a Target Selling Price for Service Companies Using Time and Materials Pricing

Time and materials pricing A pricing method, often used in service firms, in which two pricing rates are established— one based on direct labour time and the other based on direct materials used.

A variation of cost-plus pricing used by some companies, particularly in service industries, is called **time and materials pricing**. Under this approach, two pricing rates are established, one based on direct labour time and the other based on the cost of direct material used.

This pricing method is widely used in the service industry (e.g., repair shops and printing shops) and by many professionals, such as engineers and lawyers. The time and materials rates are usually market determined. In other words, the rates are determined by the interplay of supply and demand and by competitive conditions in the industry. However, some companies set the rates using a process similar to the process followed in the absorption costing approach to cost-plus pricing. In this case, the rates include allowances for selling and administrative expenses, for other direct and indirect costs, and for a desired profit. This section will show how the rates might be set using the cost-plus approach.

Time Component

The time component is typically expressed as a rate per hour of labour. The rate is computed by adding together three elements: (1) the direct costs of the employee, including salary and benefits; (2) a pro rata allowance for selling and administrative expenses of the organization; and (3) an allowance for a desired profit per hour of employee time. In some organizations (such as a repair shop), the same hourly rate will be charged regardless of which employee actually works on the job; in other organizations, the rate may vary by employee. For example, in a public accounting firm, the rate charged for a staff accountant's time will be less than the rate charged for an experienced senior accountant or for a partner.

Materials Component

The materials component is determined by adding a **materials loading charge** to the invoice price of any materials used on the job. The materials loading charge is designed to cover the costs of ordering, handling, and carrying materials in inventory, plus a profit margin on the materials themselves.

Materials loading charge
A markup applied to the cost of materials that is designed to cover the costs of ordering, handling, and carrying materials in inventory and to provide for some profit.

An Example of Time and Materials Pricing

To provide an example of time and materials pricing, we use data from The Quality Auto Shop. The following costs for repairs and parts have been budgeted for the coming year:

	Repairs	Parts
Mechanics' wages	$300,000	$ —
Service manager—salary	40,000	—
Parts manager—salary	—	36,000
Clerical assistant—salary	18,000	15,000
Employee benefits—		
16% of salaries and wages	57,280	8,160
Supplies	720	540
Utilities	36,000	20,800
Property taxes	8,400	1,900
Depreciation	91,600	37,600
Invoice cost of parts used	—	400,000
Total budgeted cost	$552,000	$520,000

The company expects to bill customers for 24,000 hours of repair time. A profit of $7 per hour of repair time is considered reasonable, given the competitive conditions in the market. For parts, the competitive markup on the invoice cost of parts used is 15%.

Exhibit 12A–4 shows the computation of the billing rate and the materials loading charge to be used for the next year. Note that the billing rate, or time component, is $30 per hour of repair time and the materials loading charge is 45% of the invoice cost of parts used. Using these rates, a repair job that requires 4.5 hours of mechanics' time and $200 in parts would be billed as follows:

Labour time: 4.5 hours × $30		$135
Parts used:		
Invoice cost	$200	
Materials loading charge: 45% × $200	90	290
Total price of the job		$425

EXHIBIT 12A-4   Time and Materials Pricing

	Time Component: Repairs		Parts: Materials Loading Charge	
	Total	**Per Hour***	**Total**	**Percent†**
Cost of mechanics' time:				
Mechanics' wages..............................	$300,000			
Employee benefits (16% of wages)...............	48,000			
Total cost	348,000	$ 14.50		
For repairs—other cost of repair service. For parts— costs of ordering, handling, and storing parts:				
Repairs service manager—salary.................	40,000		$ —	
Parts manager—salary	—		36,000	
Clerical assistant—salary	18,000		15,000	
Employee benefits (16% of salaries)...............	9,280		8,160	
Supplies..	720		540	
Utilities..	36,000		20,800	
Property taxes..................................	8,400		1,900	
Depreciation	91,600		37,600	
Total cost	204,000	8.50	120,000	30%
Desired profit:				
24,000 hours × $7	168,000	7.00		
15% × $400,000	—		60,000	15%
Total amount to be billed	$720,000	$30.00	$180,000	45%

*Based on 24,000 hours.

†Based on $400,000 invoice cost of parts. The charge for ordering, handling, and storing parts, for example, is computed as follows:
$120,000 cost ÷ $400,000 invoice cost = 30%.

Rather than using labour-hours as the basis for computing the time rate, a machine shop, a printing shop, or a similar organization might use machine-hours.

This method of setting prices is a variation of the absorption costing approach. As such, it is not surprising that it suffers from the same problem: customers may not be willing to pay the rates that have been computed. Further, if the actual volume of business is less than the forecasted 24,000 hours and $400,000 worth of parts, or actual costs exceed estimates, the profit objectives will not be met and the company may not even break even.

■ TARGET COSTING

LEARNING OBJECTIVE 5
Compute target costs based on selling prices.

Target costing
The process of determining the maximum allowable cost for a new product and then developing a prototype that can be profitably manufactured and distributed for that maximum target cost figure.

Our discussion so far has presumed that a product has already been developed, has been costed, and is ready to be marketed as soon as a price is set. In many cases, the sequence of events is just the reverse. That is, the company will already *know* what price should or can be charged, and the problem will be to *develop a product* that can be marketed profitably at the desired price. Even in this situation, where the normal sequence of events is reversed, cost is still a crucial factor. The company's approach will be to employ *target costing*. **Target costing** is the process of determining the maximum allowable cost for a new product and then developing a prototype that can be profitably made for that maximum target cost figure. Many companies use target costing, including Chrysler, Ford, Sharp, and Toyota.

The target cost for a product is computed by starting with the product's anticipated selling price and then deducting the desired profit, as follows:

$$\text{Target cost} = \text{Anticipated selling price} - \text{Desired profit}$$

The product development team is then given the responsibility of designing the product so that it can be made for no more than the target cost.

Reasons for Using Target Costing

The target costing approach was developed in recognition of two important characteristics of markets and costs. The first is that many companies have less control over price than they would like. The market (i.e., supply and demand) really determines prices, and a company that attempts to ignore this does so at its peril. Therefore, the anticipated market price is taken as a given in target costing. The second observation is that most of the cost of a product is determined in the design stage. Once a product has been designed and has gone into production, not much can be done to significantly reduce its cost. Most of the opportunities to reduce cost come from designing the product so that it is as simple to make as possible and uses cost-effective parts, while meeting the expectations of customers with respect to quality. If the company has little control over market price and limited control over cost once the product has gone into production, then it follows that the major opportunities for affecting profit come at the design stage, where valuable features for which customers are willing to pay can be added and where most of the costs are really determined. The difference between target costing and other approaches to product development is profound. Instead of designing the product, determining the cost, and setting the price, the target cost is set first and then the product is designed so that the target cost is attained.

Effective target costing requires a detailed understanding of what is valued by the customer; the full costs of production, including long-term investments; and a detailed breakdown of the target cost. A management philosophy of customer focus and cost reduction (Kaizen costing) will help a company to realize the full benefits of target costing.

An Example of Target Costing

For a simple numerical example of target costing, assume the following situation: AFM Electronics feels that there is a market niche for stereo headphones with certain new features. Surveying the features and prices of headphones already on the market, the Marketing Department believes that a price of $150 would be about right for the new headphones. At that price, Marketing estimates that 80,000 of the new headphones could be sold annually. To design, develop, and produce these new headphones, an investment of $8,000,000 would be required. The company wants a 30% ROI. Given these data, the target cost to manufacture, sell, distribute, and service one pair of headphones is $120, as shown below:

Projected sales (80,000 headphones × $150)	$12,000,000
Less desired profit (30% × $8,000,000)	2,400,000
Target cost for 80,000 headphones	$ 9,600,000
Target cost per pair of headphone ($9,600,000 ÷ 80,000 headphones)	$ 120.00

This $120 target cost would be broken down into target costs for the various functions: manufacturing, marketing, distribution, after-sales service, and so on. Each functional area would be responsible for keeping its actual costs within the target.

APPENDIX 12A SUMMARY

- Companies offering products and services where a market price is not readily available often use cost-plus pricing. One approach to cost-plus pricing uses absorption unit product costs as the cost base, with the markup calculated both to cover non-manufacturing costs and to provide an adequate return on investment (ROI). Another approach uses total variable costs as the base, with the markup covering all fixed costs and providing an adequate ROI. [LO4]
- Companies in the service industry often use a variation of the cost-plus approach called time and materials pricing. Two pricing rates are established: one for direct labour time and the other for direct material costs. [LO4]
- The degree to which either cost-plus pricing or time and materials pricing will lead to the desired profits critically depends on the accuracy of both the sales forecasts and the cost estimates. [LO4]

- Some companies develop and sell products or services for which an established market and price already exist. Target costing can be used in such situations. Desired profit is deducted from the estimated market price to determine the product's target cost. The product design and development team then has the responsibility of ensuring that the actual cost of the new product does not exceed the target cost. [LO5]

APPENDIX 12A EXERCISES AND PROBLEMS

EXERCISE 12A-1 Absorption Costing and Total Variable Costing Approaches to Setting a Selling Price [LO4]

Nolan Limited is considering introducing a new product. Management has gathered the following information:

Number of units to be produced and sold each year	10,000
Unit product cost	$ 16
Projected annual selling and administrative expenses	$ 40,000
Estimated investment required by the company	$400,000
Desired return on investment (ROI)	8%

Required:
1. Using the absorption costing approach to cost-plus pricing, compute the markup the company will have to use to achieve the desired ROI.
2. Assume that the $16 unit product cost includes $3 per unit for fixed manufacturing overhead based on producing and selling 10,000 units each year. Also assume that $26,000 of the total selling and administrative expenses of $40,000 is fixed. The remainder is variable. Use the total variable costing approach to calculate the markup the company will have to use to achieve the desired ROI.
3. Compute the target selling price per unit under each pricing approach from (1) and (2) above.

EXERCISE 12A-2 Target Costing [LO5]

Little River Cycles (LRC) produces and distributes carbon fibre road bikes. Management is eager to take advantage of the growing market for these bikes. To be competitive, LRC's sales manager estimates that the bike can't be priced at more than $2,000. At this price, management thinks the company can sell 1,000 bikes per year. Producing the bikes will require an initial investment of $2,000,000, and the company's target ROI is 25%.

Required:
Calculate the target cost of one carbon fibre road bike.

EXERCISE 12A-3 Time and Materials Pricing [LO4]

Ronnie's Repair Company provides repair services for small engines and uses time and materials pricing. The company has budgeted the following costs for next year:

Mechanics' wages and benefits	$900,000
Other repair costs, except for parts-related costs	$450,000
Costs of ordering, handling, and storing parts	40% of invoice cost

In total, the company expects to have 50,000 hours of billable repair time next year. According to competitive conditions, the company believes it should aim for a profit of $8 per hour of each mechanic's time. The competitive markup on parts is 40% of invoice cost.

Required:
1. Compute the time rate and the materials loading charge that would be used to bill jobs.
2. One of the company's mechanics has just completed a repair job that required 12 hours of time and $100 in parts (invoice cost). Compute the amount that would be billed for the job.

PROBLEM 12A-4 Standard Costs; Absorption Costing and Total Variable Costing Approach to Setting Prices [LO4]

Gerber Clothing Inc. has designed a rain suit for outdoor enthusiasts that is about to be introduced on the market.

A standard cost card has been prepared for the new suit, as follows:

	Standard Quantity or Hours	Standard Price or Rate	Standard Cost
Direct materials...................................	2.5 metres	$10.00 per metre	$25.00
Direct labour.....................................	1.0 hours	28.00 per hour	28.00
Manufacturing overhead (⅙ variable)............	1.0 hours	24.00 per hour	24.00
Total standard cost per suit			$77.00

a. The only variable selling and administrative costs will be $4 per suit for shipping. Fixed selling and administrative costs will be as follows (per year):

Salaries...	$ 45,000
Advertising and other	200,000
Total..	$245,000

b. Since the company manufactures many products, it is felt that no more than 10,000 hours of labour time per year can be devoted to production of the new suits.

c. An investment of $500,000 will be necessary to carry inventories and accounts receivable and to purchase some new equipment. The company wants a 20% ROI in new product lines.

d. Manufacturing overhead costs are allocated to products on the basis of direct labour-hours.

Required:

1. Assume that the company uses the absorption approach to cost-plus pricing.
   a. Compute the markup that the company needs on the rain suits to achieve a 20% ROI if it sells all of the suits it can produce using 10,000 hours of labour time.
   b. Using the markup you have computed, prepare a price quote sheet for a single rain suit.
   c. Assume that the company is able to sell all of the rain suits that it can produce. Prepare an income statement for the first year of activity, and compute the company's ROI for the year on the suits, using the ROI formula from Chapter 11.
2. Repeat 1(*a*) and 1(*b*) above, assuming that the company uses the total variable costing approach to cost-plus pricing.
3. After marketing the rain suits for several years, the company is experiencing a decrease in demand due to an economic recession. A large retail outlet will make a bulk purchase of suits if its company logo is affixed to each suit and if an acceptable price can be worked out. What is the minimum acceptable price per rain suit for this order?

PROBLEM 12A–5 Target Costing [LO5]

Free Riders Inc. is considering adding a scooter to its motorcycle line-up. Management will negotiate the price of the scooter with its manufacturer.

Management of Free Riders believes the scooters can be sold to its customers for $4,000 each. At that price, annual sales of the scooters should be 200 units. If the scooters are added to Free Riders' product lines, the company will have to invest $200,000 in inventories and special warehouse fixtures. The variable cost of selling the scooters will be $1,000 per unit.

Required:

1. If Free Riders requires a 20% ROI, what is the maximum amount the company would be willing to pay the manufacturer for the scooters?
2. After many hours of negotiations, management has concluded that the manufacturer is unwilling to sell the scooters at a low enough price for Free Riders to earn its 20% required ROI. Apart from simply giving up on the idea of adding the scooters to Free Riders' product lines, what could management do?

PROBLEM 12A–6 Time and Materials Pricing [LO4]

Computer Repair Inc. uses time and materials pricing, and each year it reviews its rates in light of the actual costs incurred in the prior year. Actual costs incurred last year in connection with repair work and in connection with the company's parts inventory are shown below:

	Repairs	Parts
Repair technicians—wages.	$480,000	
Repair service manager—salary	56,000	
Parts manager—salary.		$ 60,000
Repairs and parts assistant—salary	28,800	7,500
Retirement benefits (20% of salaries and wages).	112,960	13,500
Health insurance (5% of salaries and wages).	28,240	3,375
Utilities.	120,000	24,000
Truck operating costs	19,200	
Property taxes.	9,280	5,400
Liability and fire insurance	6,720	3,000
Supplies	1,200	225
Rent—building.	38,400	33,000
Depreciation—trucks and equipment.	59,200	
Invoice cost of parts used.		600,000
Total costs for the year.	$960,000	$750,000

Customers were billed for 20,000 hours of repair work last year.

The company has a target profit of $10 per hour of repair service time and a target profit of 40% of the invoice cost of parts used. During the past year, the company billed repair service time at $50 per hour and added a materials loading charge of 40% to parts. Management feels these rates may now be inadequate, since costs have risen somewhat over the last year.

Required:
1. Using the above data, compute the following:
   a. The rate that would be charged per hour of repair service time using time and materials pricing.
   b. The materials loading charge that would be used in billing jobs. The materials loading charge should be expressed as a percentage of the invoice cost.
2. Assume that the company adopts the rates that you have computed in (1) above. What should be the total price charged on a repair job that requires six hours of service time and parts with an invoice cost of $500?
3. If the company adopts the rates that you have computed in (1) above, would you expect the company's profits to improve?

CHAPTER 13

After studying Chapter 13, you should be able to

1. Evaluate the acceptability of an investment project using the net present value method.

2. Evaluate the acceptability of an investment project using the internal rate of return method.

3. Evaluate an investment project that has uncertain cash flows.

4. Rank investment projects in order of preference.

5. Determine the payback period for an investment.

6. Calculate the simple rate of return for an investment.

7. (Appendix 13A) Explain present value concepts and the underlying mathematics of interest.

8. (Appendix 13B) Incorporate income taxes into a capital budgeting analysis.

CAPITAL BUDGETING DECISIONS

◼ GOING FOR GOLD

Barrick Gold Corporation is the largest gold mining company in the world. Founded in the early 1980s, Barrick has its company headquarters in Toronto and has mining and exploration projects in numerous countries worldwide, including Canada, the United States, Australia, the Dominican Republic, Argentina, Peru, South Africa, Saudi Arabia, and Pakistan. The company had adjusted earnings before interest, taxes, depreciation, and amortization (EBITDA) of US$5.6 billion in 2013. To sustain growth in revenues and profits, Barrick must continuously make significant capital investments to develop new projects, expand existing projects, and sustain operations. Barrick's 2013 annual report shows the following details for capital expenditures:

	$US Millions
Project capital expenditures	$ 2,137
Expansionary capital expenditures	1,784
Sustaining capital expenditures	1,453
Total	$5,374

Some of these expenditures were necessary to comply with safety and environmental regulations, while others were undertaken because they are expected to generate positive net cash inflows in the future. According to the 2013 annual report, Barrick planned to incur capital expenditures in the range of US$2.4 billion to US$2.7 billion in 2014. The challenge for capital-intensive companies such as Barrick is deciding from among many alternatives which projects to invest in and when. For example, in any given year, Barrick has to decide whether to expand production capacity at existing locations, improve the efficiency of operations at existing locations, or develop new mines in new locations. Although these are not mutually exclusive alternatives, as is the case with most companies, Barrick is constrained by the amount of funds available for annual capital expenditures and so must undertake a thorough analysis of the costs and benefits of each option. The stakes are high for this type of analysis, as making good capital budgeting decisions can have a considerable impact on the long-term profitability of a company.

How do companies make capital budgeting decisions and choose from among the alternatives when funds are limited? These are the key topics covered in this chapter.

Source: Barrick Gold Corporation, *2013 Annual Report*. Reprinted with permission.

Managers often consider decisions that involve an investment today in the hope of realizing future profits. For example, Tim Hortons makes an investment when it opens a new restaurant. McCain Foods makes an investment when it expands production facilities to increase processing capacity. Paradigm makes an investment when it redesigns a stereo speaker model and must retool its production lines. All of these investments require spending now with the expectation of additional future net cash flows.

Capital budgeting
The process of planning significant outlays on projects that have long-term implications, such as purchasing new equipment or introducing a new product.

The term **capital budgeting** is used to describe how managers plan significant outlays on projects that have long-term implications, such as purchasing new equipment and introducing new products. Most companies have many more potential projects than can actually be funded, so managers must carefully select those projects that promise the greatest future return. How well managers make these capital budgeting decisions can affect the long-run profitability of the company, given the magnitude of the spending involved, as evidenced by Barrick Gold Corporation's capital expenditures discussed above.

■ CAPITAL BUDGETING—PLANNING INVESTMENTS

Typical Capital Budgeting Decisions

Any decision that involves an outlay now in order to obtain some return (increase in revenue or reduction in costs) in the future is a capital budgeting decision. Typical capital budgeting decisions are as follows:

1. *Cost-reduction decisions.* Should new equipment be purchased to reduce costs?
2. *Expansion decisions.* Should a new plant, warehouse, or other facility be acquired to increase capacity and production?
3. *Equipment selection decisions.* Which of several available machines should be purchased?
4. *Lease or buy decisions.* Should new equipment be leased or purchased?
5. *Equipment replacement decisions.* Should old equipment be replaced now or later?

Screening decisions
Decisions as to whether a proposed investment passes a pre-established profitability hurdle.

Capital budgeting decisions tend to fall into two broad categories—*screening decisions* and *preference decisions*. **Screening decisions** are those relating to whether a proposed project is acceptable—whether it passes a pre-established profitability hurdle. For example, a firm may have a policy of accepting projects only if they promise a return of at least 10% on the investment. The required rate of return is the minimum rate of return a project must yield to be acceptable.

Preference decisions
Decisions as to which of several competing acceptable investment proposals is best.

Preference decisions, by contrast, relate to selecting from among several acceptable alternatives. To illustrate, a firm may be considering several different machines to replace an existing machine on the assembly line. The choice of which machine to purchase is a *preference* decision.

In this chapter, we initially discuss screening decisions and then move on to preference decisions.

The Time Value of Money

Capital investments usually earn returns extending over fairly long periods of time. Therefore, when evaluating investment proposals, it is necessary to employ techniques that recognize the *time value of money*. A dollar today is worth more than a dollar a year from now. The same concept applies in choosing between investment alternatives. Projects that promise returns earlier in time are preferable to those that promise later returns.

IN BUSINESS

Sometimes a long-term decision does not have to involve present value calculations or any other sophisticated analytical technique. White Grizzly Adventures of Meadow Creek, British Columbia, needs two Snowcats for its powder skiing operations—one for shuttling guests to the top of the mountain and one to be held in reserve in case of mechanical problems with the first. Bombardier of Canada sells new Snowcats for $250,000 and used, reconditioned Snowcats for $150,000. In either case, the Snowcats are good for about 5,000 hours of operation before they need to be reconditioned. From White Grizzly's perspective, the choice is clear. Since both new and reconditioned Snowcats last about 5,000 hours, and the latter cost $100,000 less, the reconditioned Snowcats are the obvious choice. They may not have all of the latest bells and whistles, but they get the job done at a price a small operation can afford.

Bombardier Snowcats do not have passenger cabs as standard equipment. To save money, White Grizzly builds its own custom-designed passenger cab for about $15,000, using recycled Ford Escort seats and industrial-strength aluminum for the frame and siding. If purchased retail, a passenger cab would cost about twice as much and would not be as well suited to powder skiing.

Source: Brad and Carole Karafil, owners and operators of White Grizzly Adventures: http://www. whitegrizzly.com.

The capital budgeting techniques that recognize the time value of money involve *discounted cash flows*. We will spend most of this chapter illustrating the use of discounted cash flow methods in making capital budgeting decisions. If you are not already familiar with discounting and the mathematics underlying interest rates and discount factors, you should read Appendix 13A, The Concept of Present Value, at the end of this chapter, before proceeding any further.

■ DISCOUNTED CASH FLOWS—THE NET PRESENT VALUE METHOD

Two approaches to making capital budgeting decisions use discounted cash flows. One is the *net present value method*, and the other is the *internal rate of return method*. The net present value method is discussed in this section; the internal rate of return method is discussed in the following section.

LEARNING OBJECTIVE ①
Evaluate the acceptability of an investment project using the net present value method.

The Net Present Value Method Illustrated

Under the net present value method, the present value of a project's cash inflows is compared to the present value of the project's cash outflows. The difference between the present value of these cash flows, called the **net present value**, determines whether the project is an acceptable investment. To illustrate, assume the data outlined in Example 1 below.

Net present value
The difference between the present value of the cash inflows and the present value of the cash outflows associated with an investment project.

Example 1

Management at Harper Company is thinking about buying a machine to perform certain operations that are now performed manually. The machine will cost $50,000, and it will last for five years. At the end of the five-year period, the machine will have a zero scrap value. Use of the machine will reduce labour costs by $18,000 per year. Harper Company requires a minimum return of 20% before taxes on all investment projects.[1]

Should the machine be purchased? Management must determine whether a cash investment now of $50,000 can be justified if it will result in an $18,000 reduction in cost each year over the next five years. It may appear that the answer is obvious since the total cost savings are $90,000 ($18,000 per year × 5 years). However, the company can earn a 20% return by investing its money elsewhere. It is not enough that the cost reductions cover just the original cost of the machine; they must also yield at least a 20% return or the company would be better off investing the money elsewhere.

To determine whether the investment is desirable, the stream of annual $18,000 cost savings is discounted to its present value, which is then compared to the cost of the new machine. Since Harper Company requires a minimum return of 20% on all investment projects, this rate is used in the discounting process and is called the *discount rate*. Appendix 13A provides a discussion of the various formulas used to calculate discount rates and future value factors when doing analysis that incorporates the time value of money. Two of these formulas, the present value of a single cash flow paid or received in the future (A3) and the present value of a series of equal cash flows to be paid or received in the future (A4) are used extensively in capital budgeting analysis. Before software packages such as Microsoft Excel and handheld calculators with financial functions became so commonly used, preparers of capital budgeting analyses often relied on present value tables to provide the specific discount factors used in the calculations. These tables provided discount factors for a variety of required rates and time periods, based on the formulas presented in Appendix 13A. However, software packages and financial calculators are now readily available to perform the present value calculations quickly and without error, using these same formulas. Appendix 13A provides a list of Microsoft Excel formulas commonly used in net present value analysis. Because of its widespread use, Exhibit 13-1 shows the approach to the analysis with the present value of the annual cost savings calculated using the NPV formula in Microsoft Excel. We also use Microsoft Excel in our presentation of the examples that follow throughout the rest of the chapter.

According to the analysis, Harper Company should purchase the new machine. The present value of the cost savings is $53,831, compared to the present value of the required investment (cost of the machine) of only $50,000. Deducting the present value of the investment required from the present value of the cost savings gives a *net present value* of $3,831. Whenever the net present value is zero or greater, as in our example, an investment project is acceptable. Whenever the net present value is negative (the present value of the cash outflows exceeds the present value of the cash inflows), an investment project is not acceptable.

A full interpretation of the solution is as follows: The new machine promises more than the required 20% rate of return. This is evident from the positive net present value of $3,831. Harper Company could spend up to $53,831 for the new machine and still obtain the minimum required 20% rate of return. The net present value of $3,831, therefore, shows the amount of "cushion" or "margin of error."

EXHIBIT 13-1   Net Present Value Analysis of a Proposed Project

Initial cost	$50,000
Life of the project	5 years
Annual cost savings	$18,000
Salvage value	$ 0
Required rate of return	20%

Item	Year(s)	Amount of Cash Flow	Present Value of Cash Flows
Annual cost savings	1–5	$ 18,000	$ 53,831*
Initial investment	Now	$(50,000)	(50,000)
Net present value			$ 3,831

*Calculated using the NPV formula of Microsoft Excel and a required rate of return of 20%. Using formula (A4) in Appendix 13A to calculate the present value of an annuity (a series of equal cash flows) results in a discount factor of 2.9906, which is the same as that used in the Microsoft Excel calculations (i.e., $53,831 ÷ $18,000 = 2.9906, rounded).

One way to look at this is that the company could underestimate the cost of the new machine by up to $3,831, or overestimate the present value of the future cash savings by up to $3,831, and the project would still be financially attractive. If the present value of the cost savings was only $50,000 instead of $53,831, the project would still generate the required 20% return.

Emphasis on Cash Flows

In capital budgeting decisions, the focus is on cash flows and not on accounting income. Accounting income is based on accruals that ignore the timing of cash flows. From a capital budgeting standpoint, the timing of cash flows is critical, since a dollar received today is more valuable than a dollar received in the future. Therefore, instead of determining accounting income when making capital budgeting decisions, the manager must concentrate on identifying the specific cash flows associated with an investment project.

Although the specific cash flows will vary from project to project, certain types of cash flows tend to recur, as explained in the following paragraphs.

Typical Cash Outflows   Most projects will have at least three types of cash outflows. First, they often require an immediate cash outflow in the form of an initial investment in equipment or other assets. Any salvage value realized from the sale of old equipment can be recognized as a cash inflow or as a reduction in the required investment. Second, some projects require that a company expand its working capital. **Working capital** is current assets (cash, accounts receivable, and inventory) less current liabilities. When a company takes on a new project, the balances in the current asset accounts will often increase. For example, opening a new Future Shop location would require additional cash in sales registers and more inventory on hand to meet demand. These additional working capital needs should be treated as part of the initial investment in a project. Third, many projects require periodic outlays for repairs and maintenance and for additional operating costs. These should all be treated as cash outflows for capital budgeting purposes.

Typical Cash Inflows   Most projects will have at least three types of cash inflows. First, a project will normally increase revenues or reduce costs. In either case the amount involved should be treated as a cash inflow for capital budgeting purposes. Notice that from a cash flow standpoint, a reduction in costs is equivalent to an increase in revenues. Second, cash inflows are also frequently realized from selling equipment for its salvage value when a project is terminated, although the company may actually have to pay for the cost of disposing of some low-value or hazardous items. Third, any working capital that was tied up in the project can be released for use elsewhere at the end of the project and should be treated as a cash inflow. Working capital is released, for example, when a company sells off its inventory or collects its receivables.

In summary, the following types of cash flows are common in business investment projects:

Cash outflows:
Initial investment (including installation costs).
Increased working capital needs.
Repairs and maintenance.
Incremental operating costs.

Cash inflows:
Incremental revenues.
Reduction in costs.
Salvage value.
Release of working capital.

> **Instant Quiz 13-1**
> Calculate the net present value of a project that requires an initial investment of $100,000 and will generate $20,000 per year in cost savings for seven years. The required rate of return is 8%.

Working capital
The excess of current assets over current liabilities.

Initial cost		$3,170	
Life of the project		4 years	
Annual cost savings		$1,000	
Salvage value...............		$0	
Required rate of return		10%	

Item	Year(s)	Amount of Cash Flow	Present Value of Cash Flows
Annual cost savings	1–4	$ 1,000	$ 3,170*
Initial investment................	Now	$(3,170)	(3,170)
Net present value			$ 0

*Calculated using the NPV formula of Microsoft Excel and a required rate of return of 10%.

Recovery of the Original Investment

When computing the present value of a project, depreciation is not deducted for two reasons. First, depreciation is not a current cash outflow.[2] As discussed previously, discounted cash flow methods of making capital budgeting decisions focus on *cash flows*. Although depreciation is used in computing net income for financial statements, it is not relevant in an analytical framework that focuses on cash flows.

A second reason for not deducting depreciation is that discounted cash flow methods *automatically* provide for return of the original investment, thereby making a deduction for depreciation unnecessary. To demonstrate this point, consider the information given in Example 2.

Example 2

Carver Dental Clinic is considering purchasing an attachment for its X-ray machine that will cost $3,170. The attachment will be usable for four years, after which time it will have no salvage value. It will increase net cash inflows by $1,000 per year in the X-ray Department. The clinic's board of directors has decided that no investments are to be made unless these investments have an annual return of at least 10%.

A present value analysis of the desirability of purchasing the X-ray attachment is presented in Exhibit 13–2. Notice that the attachment promises exactly a 10% return on the original investment, since the net present value is zero at a 10% discount rate.

Each annual $1,000 cash inflow arising from use of the attachment is made up of two parts. One part represents a recovery of a portion of the original $3,170 paid for the attachment, and the other part represents a return on this investment. The breakdown of each year's $1,000 cash inflow between recovery *of* investment and return *on* investment is shown in Exhibit 13–3.

EXHIBIT 13-3 Carver Dental Clinic—Breakdown of Annual Cash Inflows

Year	(1) Investment Outstanding during the Year	(2) Cash Inflow	(3) Return on Investment (1) × 10%	(4) Recovery of Investment during the Year (2) − (3)	(5) Unrecovered Investment at the End of the Year (1) − (4)
1	$ 3,170	$1,000	$ 317	$ 683	$2,487
2..............................	2,487	1,000	249	751	1,736
3..............................	1,736	1,000	173	827	909
4..............................	909	1,000	91	909	0
Total investment recovered				$3,170	

The first year's $1,000 cash inflow consists of a return *on* investment of $317 (a 10% return *on* the $3,170 original investment), plus a $683 return *of* that investment. Since the amount of the unrecovered investment decreases over the four years, the dollar amount of the return on investment also decreases each year. By the end of the fourth year, the entire $3,170 original investment has been recovered.

Simplifying Assumptions

Two simplifying assumptions are usually made in net present value analysis.

The first assumption is that all cash flows other than the initial investment occur at the end of periods. This is somewhat unrealistic in that cash flows typically occur *throughout* a period—rather than just at the end. The purpose of this assumption is to simplify computations—it does not significantly affect the accuracy of the analysis in most cases.

The second assumption is that all cash flows generated by an investment project are immediately reinvested at a rate of return equal to the discount rate. Unless these conditions are met, the return computed for the project will not be accurate. We used a discount rate of 10% for the Carver Dental Clinic in Exhibit 13–2. Unless the funds released each period are immediately reinvested at a 10% return, the net present value computed for the X-ray attachment will be misstated.

Choosing a Discount Rate

A positive net present value means that the project's return exceeds the discount rate. Therefore, if the company's minimum required rate of return is used as the discount rate, a project with a positive net present value has a return that exceeds the minimum required rate of return and is acceptable. Conversely, a project with a negative net present value has a return that is less than the minimum required rate of return and is unacceptable.

The firm's *weighted-average cost of capital* is usually regarded as the most appropriate choice for the discount rate. The **weighted-average cost of capital** (WACC) is the average rate of return the company must pay to its long-term creditors and shareholders for the use of their funds. WACC is based on the different returns required by the various providers of capital (i.e., creditors and shareholders) and the proportion of capital provided by each. The detailed calculations and assumptions involved in determining the WACC are covered in finance texts and will not be considered here.

The WACC is the minimum required rate of return, because if a project's rate of return is less than the cost of capital, company earnings will not be enough to compensate its creditors and shareholders. Therefore, any rate of return less than the WACC should not be accepted. The WACC is known by various names. It is sometimes called the *hurdle rate*, the *cut-off rate*, or the *required rate of return*. Depending on the riskiness of the project under consideration, many companies may use a discount rate that differs from the WACC. For example, projects that are above the average level of risk taken on by the company will be analyzed using a discount rate that is higher than the WACC. The rationale for this approach is that riskier investments should generate higher returns. Decisions on the appropriate discount rate to use should be made on a project-by-project basis, taking the risk of the project's underlying cash flows into consideration.

An Extended Example of the Net Present Value Method

To continue our discussion, Example 3 presents an extended example of how the net present value method is used to analyze an investment proposal. This will help tie together and reinforce many of the ideas developed so far.

Weighted-average cost of capital (WACC)
The average rate of return companies must pay to long-term creditors and shareholders for the use of their funds.

Example 3

Under a special licensing arrangement, Swinyard Company has an opportunity to market a new product in western Canada for a five-year period. The product would be purchased from the manufacturer, with Swinyard Company responsible for all costs of promotion and distribution. The licensing arrangement could be renewed at the end of the five-year period at the option of the manufacturer. After careful study, Swinyard Company has estimated that the following costs and revenues would be associated with the new product:

Cost of equipment needed.....................................	$ 60,000
Working capital needed	100,000
Overhaul of the equipment in four years.......................	5,000
Salvage value of the equipment in five years	10,000
Annual revenues and costs:	
Sales revenues...	200,000
Cost of goods sold..	125,000
Out-of-pocket operating costs (for salaries,	
advertising, and other direct costs).......................	35,000

At the end of the five-year period, the working capital would be released for investment elsewhere if the manufacturer decided not to renew the licensing arrangement. Swinyard Company's discount rate and cost of capital are both 14%. Would you recommend that the new product be introduced?

This example involves a variety of cash inflows and cash outflows. The solution is given in Exhibit 13–4.

Notice how the working capital is handled in this exhibit. It is included as a cash outflow at the beginning of the project and as a cash inflow when it is released at the end of the project. Also notice how the sales revenues, cost of goods sold, and out-of-pocket costs are handled. **Out-of-pocket costs** are actual cash outlays for

Out-of-pocket costs
Actual cash outlays for operating costs.

EXHIBIT 13–4   The Net Present Value Method—An Extended Example

Sales revenues..............................	$200,000
Less cost of goods sold	125,000
Less out-of-pocket costs for	
salaries, advertising, etc.	35,000
Annual net cash inflows.....................	$ 40,000

Item	Year(s)	Amount of Cash Flow	Present Value of Cash Flows*
Purchase of equipment....................................	Now	$ (60,000)	$ (60,000)
Working capital needed...................................	Now	(100,000)	$(100,000)
Overhaul of equipment...................................	4	(5,000)	(2,960)
Annual net cash inflows			
from sales...	1–5	40,000	137,323
Salvage value of equipment	5	10,000	5,194**
Working capital released.................................	5	100,000	51,937
Net present value..			$ 31,494

*Calculated using the NPV formula of Microsoft Excel and a required rate of return of 14%.

**Using formula (A3) in Appendix 13A to calculate the present value of a single lump sum cash receipt results in a discount factor of 0.5194, which is the same as that used in the Microsoft Excel calculations (i.e., $5,194 ÷ $10,000 = 0.5194).

salaries, advertising, and other operating expenses. Depreciation is not an out-of-pocket cost, since it involves no current cash outlay. Since the net present value is positive, the new product is acceptable.

To illustrate all of the elements included in the net present value method, we separately show the present value of each cash flow in Exhibit 13–4 and in the other examples that follow. However, when using software tools such as Microsoft Excel, all cash flows in a particular year can be combined and the present value of the total calculated. For example, in Year 5 in Exhibit 13–4, the present value of the total inflows of $118,000 ($40,000 ÷ 5 + $10,000 + $100,000) would be calculated in Microsoft Excel rather than doing three present value calculations.

So far, all of our examples have involved only a single investment alternative. We will now expand the net present value method to include two alternatives. In addition, we will integrate the concept of relevant costs into the discounted cash flow analysis.

The net present value method can be used to compare competing investment projects in two ways: the *total-cost approach* and the *incremental-cost approach*. These approaches are illustrated in the following two sections.

Instant Quiz 13-2
Calculate the net present value of a project that requires an initial investment in new machinery of $500,000 and $50,000 in working capital, generates annual net cash inflows of $70,000 for 10 years, and will require maintenance spending of $25,000 at the end of year 5. All of the working capital will be released at the end of year 10, and the machine will have a salvage value of $50,000 at the end of the project. The required rate of return is 10%.

The Total-Cost Approach

The total-cost approach is the most flexible method for comparing competing projects. To illustrate the mechanics of the approach, assume the data provided in Example 4.

Example 4

Harris Ferry Company provides a ferry service across Harris Harbour. One of its ferryboats is in poor condition. This ferry can be renovated at an immediate cost of $200,000. Further repairs and an overhaul of the motor will be needed 5 years from now at a cost of $80,000. In all, the ferry will be usable for 10 years if this work is done. At the end of 10 years, the ferry will have to be scrapped at a salvage value of approximately $60,000. The scrap value of the ferry right now is $70,000. It will cost $300,000 each year to operate the ferry, and revenues will total $400,000 annually.

As an alternative, Harris Ferry Company can purchase a new ferryboat at a cost of $360,000. The new ferry will have a life of 10 years, but it will require some repairs at the end of 5 years. It is estimated that these repairs will amount to $30,000. At the end of 10 years, it is estimated that the ferry will have a scrap value of $60,000. It will cost $210,000 each year to operate the ferry, and revenues will total $400,000 annually.

Harris Ferry Company requires a return of at least 14% before taxes on all investment projects.

Should the company purchase the new ferry or renovate the old ferry? Using the total-cost approach, Exhibit 13–5 gives the solution.

Two points should be noted from Exhibit 13–5. First, *all* cash inflows and *all* cash outflows are included in the solution under each alternative. No effort has been made to isolate those cash flows that are relevant to the decision and those that are not relevant. The inclusion of all cash flows associated with each alternative gives the approach its name—the *total-cost* approach.

Second, notice that a net present value figure is computed for each of the two alternatives. This is a distinct advantage of the total-cost approach in that an unlimited number of alternatives can be compared side by side to determine the best action. For example, another alternative for Harris Ferry Company is to get out of the ferry business entirely. If management desired, the net present value of this alternative could be computed to compare with the alternatives shown in Exhibit 13–5. Still other alternatives might be open to the company. Once management has determined the net present value of each alternative that it wishes to consider, it can select the course of action that promises to be the most profitable. In this case, given only two alternatives, the data indicate that the most profitable course is to purchase the new ferry.[3]

EXHIBIT 13-5   The Total-Cost Approach to Project Selection

	New Ferry	Old Ferry
Annual revenue	$400,000	$400,000
Annual cash operating costs...........	210,000	300,000
Net annual cash inflows	$ 190,000	$ 100,000

Item	Year(s)	Amount of Cash Flow	Present Value of Cash Flows*
Buy the new ferry:			
Initial investment...	Now	$(360,000)	$(360,000)
Repairs in five years..	5	(30,000)	(15,581)
Net annual cash inflows	1–10	190,000	991,062
Salvage of the old ferry	Now	70,000	70,000
Salvage of the new ferry	10	60,000	16,185
Net present value...			701,666
Keep the old ferry:			
Initial repairs	Now	$(200,000)	(200,000)
Repairs in five years..	5	(80,000)	(41,549)
Net annual cash inflows	1–10	100,000	521,612
Salvage of the old ferry	10	60,000	16,185
Net present value...			296,248
Net present value in favour of buying the new ferry............			$ 405,418

*Calculated using the NPV formula of Microsoft Excel and a required rate of return of 14%.

The Incremental-Cost Approach

When only two alternatives are being considered, the incremental-cost approach offers a simpler and more direct route to a decision. Unlike the total-cost approach, it focuses only on differential costs.[4] The procedure is to include in the discounted cash flow analysis only those costs and revenues that *differ* between the two alternatives being considered. To illustrate, refer again to the data in Example 4 relating to Harris Ferry Company. The solution using only differential costs is presented in Exhibit 13–6.

Two things should be noted from the data in Exhibit 13–6. First, notice that the net present value of $405,418 in favour of buying shown in this exhibit agrees with

EXHIBIT 13-6   The Incremental-Cost Approach to Project Selection

Item	Year(s)	Amount of Cash Flow	Present Value of Cash Flows*
Incremental initial investment to buy the new ferry...	Now	$(160,000)	$(160,000)
Repairs in five years avoided...................................	5	50,000	25,968
Increased net annual cash inflows..............................	1–10	90,000	469,450
Salvage of the old ferry..	Now	70,000	70,000
Net present value in favour of buying the new ferry			$ 405,418

*Calculated using the NPV formula of Microsoft Excel and a required rate of return of 14%.

the net present value shown under the total-cost approach in Exhibit 13–5. This agreement should be expected, since the two approaches are just different approaches to analyzing the same underlying set of facts.

Second, notice that the costs used in Exhibit 13–6 are just the differences between the costs shown for the two alternatives in the prior exhibit. For example, the $160,000 incremental investment required to purchase the new ferry in Exhibit 13–6 is the difference between the $360,000 cost of the new ferry and the $200,000 cost required to renovate the old ferry shown in Exhibit 13–5. The other figures in Exhibit 13–6 were computed in the same way.

Least-Cost Decisions

Some decisions do not involve revenues. For example, a company may be trying to decide whether to lease or to buy an executive jet. In situations such as this, where no revenues are involved, the most desirable alternative will be the one that requires the *least total cost* from the present value perspective. Hence, these are known as *least-cost decisions*. To illustrate a least-cost decision, assume the data provided in Example 5.

Example 5

Val-Tek Company is considering replacing an old threading machine. A new threading machine is available that could substantially reduce annual operating costs. Selected data relating to the old and new machines are presented below:

	Old Machine	New Machine
Purchase cost when new...............................	$200,000	$250,000
Salvage value now.......................................	30,000	0
Annual cash operating costs	150,000	90,000
Overhaul needed immediately	40,000	0
Salvage value in six years...............................	0	50,000
Remaining life..	6 years	6 years

Val-Tek Company's cost of capital is 10%.

Exhibit 13–7 presents the alternatives using the total-cost approach. As shown in the exhibit, the new machine has the lower total cost when the present value of the net cash outflows is considered. An analysis of the two alternatives using the

EXHIBIT 13–7   The Total-Cost Approach (Least-Cost Decision)

Item	Year(s)	Amount of Cash Flow	Present Value of Cash Flows*
Buy the new machine:			
Initial investment	Now	$(250,000)	$(250,000)
Salvage of the old machine.........	Now	30,000	30,000
Annual cash operating costs........	1–6	(90,000)	(391,973)
Salvage of the new machine........	6	50,000	28,224
Present value of net cash outflows....			(583,749)
Keep the old machine:			
Overhaul needed now..............	Now	$ (40,000)	(40,000)
Annual cash operating costs........	1–6	(150,000)	(653,289)
Present value of net cash outflows...		100,000	(693,289)
Net present value in favour of			
buying the new machine............			$ 109,540

*Calculated using the NPV formula of Microsoft Excel and a required rate of 10%.

EXHIBIT 13-8   The Incremental-Cost Approach (Least-Cost Decision)

Item	Year(s)	Amount of Cash Flow	Present Value of Cash Flows*
Incremental initial investment to purchase the new machine	Now	$(210,000)	$(210,000)
Salvage of the old machine	Now	30,000	30,000
Savings in annual cash operating costs	1-6	60,000	261,316
Difference in salvage value in six years..................................	6	50,000	28,224
Net present value in favour of buying the new machine..................			$ 109,540

*Calculated using the NPV formula of Microsoft Excel and a required rate of return of 10%.

incremental-cost approach is presented in Exhibit 13–8. As before, the data in this exhibit represent the differences between the alternatives after all irrelevant cash flows have been eliminated, namely those that do not differ across the two alternatives.

DISCOUNTED CASH FLOWS—THE INTERNAL RATE OF RETURN METHOD

LEARNING OBJECTIVE **2**
Evaluate the acceptability of an investment project using the internal rate of return method.

The **internal rate of return** (IRR) is the return promised by an investment project over its useful life. The IRR is the discount rate that equates the present value of a project's cash outflows with the present value of its cash inflows. In other words, the IRR is the discount rate that results in a net present value of zero.

The Internal Rate of Return Method Illustrated

To illustrate the IRR method, assume the data shown in Example 6.

Internal rate of return (IRR)
The discount rate at which the net present value of an investment project is zero.

Example 6
Glendale School District is considering purchasing a large tractor-pulled lawn mower. At present, the lawn is mowed using a small hand-pushed gas mower. The large, tractor-pulled mower will cost $16,950 and will have a useful life of 10 years. It will have only a negligible scrap value, which can be ignored. The tractor-pulled mower would do the job much more quickly than the old mower and would result in a labour savings of $3,000 per year.

To compute the IRR promised by the new mower, we must find the discount rate that will cause the net present value of the project to be zero. How do we do this? As with the present value calculations discussed above, computer software programs such as Microsoft Excel can now be used to easily determine the IRR. The Microsoft Excel formula use to perform the calculation is IRR. Applying this formula to the cash flows related to the project, including the initial investment, will yield the discount rate that causes the net present value to be zero. For our example, the IRR is 12%.

Exhibit 13–9 shows that using a 12% discount rate equates the present value of the annual cash inflows with the present value of the investment required in the project, leaving a zero net present value. The 12% rate therefore represents the IRR promised by the project. Our example did not involve a salvage value, and the cash flows are constant at $3,000 per year. However, software programs such as Microsoft Excel can easily handle IRR calculations involving salvage values and uneven cash flows.

Instant Quiz 13-3
Calculate the IRR for a project that requires a $40,000 initial investment and is expected to generate annual net cash inflows of $10,000 for six years.

Using the Internal Rate of Return

Once the IRR has been computed, what does the manager do with the information? The IRR is compared to the company's *required rate of return*. The **required rate of return** is the minimum rate of return that an investment project must yield to be

Required rate of return
The minimum rate of return that an investment project must yield to be acceptable.

Initial cost		$16,950	
Life of the project		10 years	
Annual cost savings		$3,000	
Salvage value		$0	
Internal rate of return		12%*	

Item	Year(s)	Amount of Cash Flow	Present Value of Cash Flows**
Initial investment	Now	$(16,950)	$(16,950)
Annual cost savings	1–10	3,000	16,950
Net present value			$ 0

*Calculated using the IRR formula of Microsoft Excel.
**Calculated using the NPV formula of Microsoft Excel and a discount rate of 12%.

EXHIBIT 13-9   Evaluation of the Mower Purchase Using a 12% Discount Rate

acceptable. If the IRR is *equal* to or *greater* than the required rate of return, then the project is acceptable. If it is *less* than the required rate of return, then the project is rejected. As noted earlier, quite often, the company's WACC is used as the required rate of return. The reasoning is that if a project cannot provide a rate of return at least as great as the cost of the funds invested in it, then it is not profitable.

In the case of the Glendale School District example used earlier, assume that the district has set a minimum required rate of return of 15% on all projects. Since the large mower's IRR is only 12%, it does not meet the criterion and should be rejected as a project.

The Weighted-Average Cost of Capital as a Screening Tool

As we have seen in the examples, the WACC is often used to screen out undesirable investment projects. This screening is accomplished in different ways, depending on whether the company is using the IRR method or the net present value method in its capital budgeting analysis.

When the IRR method is used, the WACC is used as the *hurdle rate* that a project must clear for acceptance. If the IRR of a project is less than the WACC, then the project is ordinarily rejected. We saw the application of this idea in the Glendale School District example, where the hurdle rate was set at 15%.

When the net present value method is used, the WACC is the *discount rate* used to compute the net present value of a proposed project. Any project yielding a negative net present value is rejected unless other factors are significant enough to justify its acceptance. The use of the WACC as a screening tool is summarized in Exhibit 13–10.

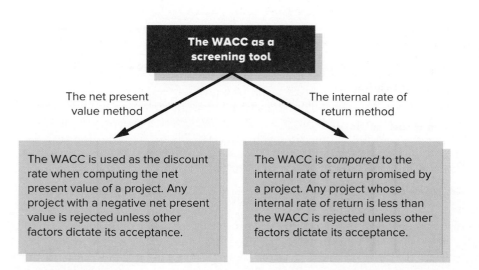

EXHIBIT 13-10   Capital Budgeting Screening Decisions

Comparison of the Net Present Value and Internal Rate of Return Methods

The net present value method offers a key advantage over the IRR method because of the assumption each method makes about the reinvestment of cash flows generated by the project. Both methods assume that cash flows generated by a project during its useful life are immediately reinvested elsewhere. The net present value method assumes that the rate of return is the discount rate, whereas the IRR method assumes that the rate of return is the IRR on the project. Specifically, if the IRR of the project is high, this assumption may not be realistic. Instead, it is generally more conservative and realistic to assume that cash inflows can be reinvested at a rate of return equal to the discount rate—particularly if the discount rate is the company's WACC. For example, if the discount rate is the company's WACC, this rate of return can actually be realized by paying off the company's creditors and buying back the company's shares with cash flows from the project. In short, when the net present value method and the IRR method do not agree concerning the attractiveness of a project, it is best to go with the net present value method. Of the two methods, it makes the more realistic assumption about the rate of return that can be earned on cash flows from the project.

Real Options

The analysis in this chapter has so far assumed that an investment cannot be postponed and that, once started, nothing can be done to alter the course of the project. In reality, investments can often be postponed. Postponement is a particularly attractive option when the net present value of the project is modest using current estimates of future cash flows, but the future cash flows involve a great deal of uncertainty that may be resolved over time.

Similarly, once an investment is made, management can often exploit changes in the business environment and take actions that enhance future cash flows. For example, buying a jet for use by company executives provides management with a number of options, some of which may become more attractive as time passes. Instead of just using the jet itself, the company may decide to rent it to other companies if the rental rates become high enough. In the case of an investment in automated equipment, management may initially buy only the basic model without costly add-ons, but keep the option open to add more capacity and capability later.

The ability to delay the start of a project, to expand it if conditions are favourable, and to otherwise modify usage plans as business conditions change, can add considerable value to many investments. These advantages can be quantified using what is called *real option analysis*, but the techniques are beyond the scope of this book.

LEARNING AID

NET PRESENT VALUE AND INTERNAL RATE OF RETURN METHODS

Relevant cash inflows:

- Incremental revenues; reduction in costs; salvage value; release of working capital.

Relevant cash outflows:

- Initial investment; increased working capital needs; incremental operating costs.

Decision Rule (for determining project acceptability):

Acceptable if	Net present value ≥ $0; Internal rate of return ≥ Required rate of return.
Not acceptable if	Net present value < $0; Internal rate of return < Required rate of return.

■ UNCERTAIN CASH FLOWS

The analysis to this point in the chapter has assumed that all of the future cash flows are known with certainty. However, future cash flows are often uncertain or difficult to estimate. A number of techniques are available for handling this complication. Some of these techniques are quite technical—involving computer simulations or advanced mathematical skills—and some are beyond the scope of this book. However, we provide a basic illustration of the approach in the next section.

LEARNING OBJECTIVE ❸
Evaluate an investment project that has uncertain cash flows.

An Example of Uncertain Cash Flows

As an example of difficult to estimate future cash flows, consider the case of investments in automated equipment. The up-front costs of automated equipment and the tangible benefits, such as reductions in operating costs and waste, tend to be relatively easy to estimate. However, the intangible benefits, such as greater reliability, greater speed, and higher quality, are more difficult to quantify in terms of future cash flows. These intangible benefits certainly affect future cash flows—particularly in terms of increased sales and perhaps higher selling prices—but the cash flow effects are difficult to estimate. What can be done?

A fairly simple procedure can be followed when the intangible benefits are likely to be significant. Suppose, for example, that a company with a 12% WACC is considering purchasing automated equipment that would have a 10-year useful life. Also suppose that a discounted cash flow analysis of just the tangible costs and benefits shows a negative net present value of $226,000. Clearly, if the intangible benefits are large enough, the company could turn this negative net present value into a positive net present value. In this case, the amount of additional cash flow per year from the intangible benefits that would be needed to make the project financially attractive can easily be computed using the PMT formula in Microsoft Excel (see Appendix 13A). This formula provides the annual amount of additional cash inflows for the 10-year life of the project that will have a present value of about $226,000 using a discount rate of 12%. The answer is an additional $40,000 per year (rounded), which as shown below has a present value of about $226,000:

Net present value excluding the intangible benefits (negative)	$(226,000)
Present value of $40,000 per year for 10 periods using a 12% discount rate	$ 226,009

So, if intangible benefits such as greater flexibility, higher quality of output, and avoidance of capital decline are worth at least $40,000 per year to the company, the automated equipment should be purchased. If, in the judgment of management, these intangible benefits are *not* worth $40,000 per year, then the automated equipment should not be purchased.

This technique can be used in other situations in which the future benefits of a current investment are uncertain or intangible. For example, this technique can be used when the salvage value is difficult to estimate. To illustrate, suppose that all of the cash flows from an investment in a supertanker have been estimated, other than its salvage value in 20 years. Using a discount rate of 12%, management has determined that the net present value of all these cash flows is negative $1,555,000. This negative net present value would be offset by the salvage value of the supertanker. How large would the salvage value have to be to make this investment attractive? This time, the solution can easily be obtained using the FVSCHEDULE formula in Microsoft Excel (see Appendix 13A). The objective is to find the amount to be received in 20 years that has a present value of $1,555,000, using a discount rate of 12%. As shown below, the amount is about $15,000,000:

Net present value excluding	
salvage value (negative).....................................	$(1,555,000)
Present value of $15,000,000	
to be received in 20 years using a discount	
rate of 12%..	$ 1,555,001

So, if the salvage value of the tanker in 20 years is at least $15,000,000, its net present value will be at least zero (or positive if the salvage value is higher) and the investment should be made. However, if management believes the salvage value is unlikely to be that large, the investment should not be made.

PREFERENCE DECISIONS—THE RANKING OF INVESTMENT PROJECTS

LEARNING OBJECTIVE 4

Rank investment projects in order of preference.

When considering investment opportunities, managers must make two types of decisions—screening decisions and preference decisions. Screening decisions, which come first, pertain to whether or not a proposed investment is acceptable. Preference decisions come *after* screening decisions and attempt to answer the following question: "How do the remaining investment proposals, all of which have been screened and provide an acceptable rate of return, rank in terms of preference? That is, which one(s) would be *best* for the firm to accept?"

Preference decisions are more difficult to make than screening decisions because investment funds are usually limited. This often requires that some (perhaps many) otherwise very profitable investment opportunities be forgone. Sometimes preference decisions are called *ranking decisions*, or *rationing decisions*, because they ration limited investment funds among many competing alternatives; hence, the alternatives must be ranked. Either the IRR method or the net present value method can be used in making preference decisions. However, as discussed earlier, if the two methods are in conflict, it is best to use the more conservative net present value method.

Internal Rate of Return Method

When using the IRR method to rank competing investment projects, the preference rule is simple: *the higher the IRR, the more desirable the project.* An investment project with an IRR of 18% is preferable to another project that promises a return of only 15%. Because of the simplicity and understandability of this approach, the IRR is widely used to rank projects.

Net Present Value Method

Unfortunately, the net present value of one project cannot be compared directly to the net present value of another project unless the required investments in the projects are of equal size. For example, assume that a company is considering two competing investments, as shown below:

	Investment	
	A	B
Investment required	$(10,000)	$(5,000)
Present value of cash inflows.........	11,000	6,000
Net present value...................	$ 1,000	$ 1,000

Although each project has a net present value of $1,000, the projects are not equally desirable if funds available for investment are limited. The project requiring an investment of only $5,000 is much more desirable when funds are limited than the project requiring an investment of $10,000. To compare the two projects on a valid basis, the present value of the cash inflows should be divided by the investment required. The result is called the **project profitability index**. The formula for the project profitability index is

$$\text{Project profitability index} = \frac{\text{Present value of net cash inflows}}{\text{Investment required}} \tag{1}$$

Project profitability index
The ratio of the present value of a project's cash inflows to the investment required.

The project profitability indexes for the two investments above are computed as follows:

	Investment	
	A	**B**
Net present value (a)	$ 1,000	$ 1,000
Investment required (b)..........................	$10,000	$5,000
Project profitability index, (a) ÷ (b)..............	0.10	0.20

When using the project profitability index to rank competing investment projects, the preference rule is as follows: *the higher the project profitability index, the more desirable the project.* Applying this rule to the two investments above, Investment B should be chosen over Investment A.

The project profitability index is an application of the techniques for utilizing scarce resources discussed in Chapter 12. In this case, the scarce resource is the limited funds available for investment, and the project profitability index is similar to the contribution margin per unit of the scarce resource.

A few details should be clarified with respect to the computation of the project profitability index. "Investment required" refers to any cash outflows that occur at the beginning of the project, reduced by any salvage value recovered from the disposal or sale of old equipment; it also includes any investment in working capital that the project may need.

Comparing the Preference Rules

The project profitability index is conceptually superior to the IRR as a method of making preference decisions. This is because the project profitability index will always give the correct signal as to the relative desirability of alternatives, even if the alternatives have different useful lives and different patterns of earnings. By contrast, if useful lives are unequal, the IRR method can lead the manager to make incorrect decisions. Assume the situation presented in Example 7.

Example 7

Parker Company is considering two investment proposals, only one of which can be accepted. Project A requires an investment of $5,000 and will provide a single cash inflow of $6,000 at the end of the first year. Therefore, it promises an IRR of 20%. Project B also requires an investment of $5,000. It will provide cash inflows of $1,360 each year for six years. Its IRR is 16%. Which project should be accepted?

Although Project A promises an IRR of 20%, compared to only 16% for Project B, Project A is not necessarily preferable to Project B. It is preferable only if the funds released at the end of the year under Project A can be reinvested at a high rate of return in some other project for the five remaining years. Otherwise, Project B, which promises a return of 16% over the entire six years, is more desirable.

Assume that the company in this example has an after-tax WACC of 12%. The net present value method, with the project profitability index, would rank the two proposals as follows:

	Project A	Project B
Present value of net cash inflows:		
$6,000 received at the end of one year at 12%	$5,357	
$1,360 received at the end of each year for six years at 12%		$5,592
Net present value (Investment — Net cash inflows)	357 (a)	592 (a)
Investment required	$5,000 (b)	$5,000 (b)
Project profitability index, (a) ÷ (b)	7.1%	11.8%

The project profitability index indicates that Project B is more desirable than Project A. This is in fact the case if the funds released from Project A at the end of one year can be reinvested at only 12% (the WACC). In short, the IRR method of ranking tends to favour short-term, high-yield projects, whereas the net present value method of ranking (using the project profitability index) tends to favour longer-term projects.

Post-audit of Investment Projects

A *post-audit* should be conducted after an investment project has been approved and implemented. A **post-audit** involves checking whether expected results are actually being realized. This is a key part of the capital budgeting process that helps keep managers committed to their investment proposals. Any tendency to inflate the benefits or understate the costs in a proposal should become evident after a few post-audits have been conducted. The post-audit also provides an opportunity to possibly expand successful projects or to cut losses on unsuccessful projects.

The same capital budgeting method should be used in the post-audit that was used in the original approval process. That is, if a project was approved on the basis of a net present value analysis, then the same procedure should be used in performing the post-audit. However, the data used in the post-audit analysis should be the *actual results* rather than the estimates used in the original proposal. This gives management an opportunity to compare how well the project has actually done relative to the original estimates. The accountability established by this approach also encourages managers to prepare realistic estimates when submitting capital budgets in the future, since they know that they will be compared to the actual results in the post-audit process.

The post-audit should be detailed enough to answer a variety of questions: Was the capital budgeting decision consistent with overall corporate strategy? Did the project meet the specifications that were set out in the original request? Were the financial estimates realistic versus excessively optimistic? Did unforeseen events occur that caused original estimates to vary from actual, such as an increase in installation costs? Have the estimated non-financial benefits (if any), such as improvements to quality, been realized? Were any additional expenditures properly authorized?

Post-audits are not without their challenges. A proper review may be time-consuming, and it is often difficult to attribute incremental costs and revenues to a specific project. This is especially true if several projects were implemented around the same time and there is overlap among them with respect to their impact on operating results. Also, to ensure objectivity, the post-audit should be performed by an individual or team that has not been directly involved in developing or implementing the actual project. Importantly, the post-audit should not be aimed at placing blame; instead the objective should be to improve control over the capital budgeting process and to facilitate a learning process that will improve the estimates developed in support of future projects.

Instant Quiz 13-4
Calculate the project profitability index of a project that requires an initial investment of $75,000 and is expected to generate cash inflows that will have a present value of $90,000.

Post-audit
Following up on a project that has been approved to see if expected results are being realized.

█ OTHER APPROACHES TO CAPITAL BUDGETING DECISIONS

Although conceptually inferior to the net present value or the IRR method, other techniques are used to make capital budgeting decisions. In this section, we examine two of these methods, known as *payback* and *simple rate of return*. Neither involves the use of discounted cash flows, but their popularity can be attributed to their simplicity.

LEARNING OBJECTIVE **5**
Determine the payback period for an investment.

The Payback Method

The payback method focuses on the *payback period*. The **payback period** is the length of time that it takes for a project to recover its initial cost from the net cash inflows that it generates. The basic premise of the payback method is that the more quickly the cost of an investment can be recovered, the more desirable the investment.

Payback period
The length of time that it takes for a project to recover its initial cost from the net cash inflows that it generates.

The payback period is usually expressed in years. *When the net annual cash inflow is the same every year*, the following formula can be used to compute the payback period:

$$\text{Payback period} = \frac{\text{Investment required}}{\text{Net annual cash inflow*}} \qquad (2)$$

> *If new equipment is replacing old equipment, this becomes incremental net annual cash inflow.

To illustrate the payback method, assume the data given in Example 8.

Example 8

York Company needs a new milling machine. The company is considering two machines: Machine A and Machine B. Machine A costs $15,000 and will reduce operating costs by $5,000 per year. Machine B costs only $12,000 but will also reduce operating costs by $5,000 per year.

Which machine should be purchased according to the payback method?

$$\text{Machine A payback period} = \frac{\$15,000}{\$5,000} = 3.0 \text{ years}$$

$$\text{Machine B payback period} = \frac{\$12,000}{\$5,000} = 2.4 \text{ years}$$

According to the payback calculations, York Company should purchase machine B, since it has a shorter payback period than machine A.

Evaluation of the Payback Method

The payback method is not a true measure of the profitability of an investment. Rather, it simply tells the manager how many years will be required to recover the original investment. Unfortunately, a shorter payback period does not always mean that one investment is more desirable than another.

To illustrate, refer to the example above. Since Machine B has a shorter payback period than Machine A, it *appears* that Machine B is more desirable than Machine A. But if we add one more piece of data, the conclusion will change. Now assume that Machine A has a projected 10-year life, and Machine B has a projected 5-year life. It would take two purchases of Machine B, costing $24,000 in total (assuming no inflation or other changes to the price) to provide the same length of service as would be provided by a single purchase of Machine A for $15,000. Under these circumstances, Machine A is a much better investment than Machine B, even though Machine B has a shorter payback period. Unfortunately, the payback method has no inherent mechanism for highlighting differences in useful lives between investments. Such differences can be very important, and relying on payback alone may result in incorrect decisions.

IN BUSINESS

Some companies use several of the techniques described in this chapter to evaluate the financial attractiveness of capital expenditures. A good example is **Rainy River Resources Ltd.**, a publicly owned Canadian mining company whose main asset is an advanced exploration stage gold project in northwestern Ontario. According to the company's website, total capital spending on the project is estimated to be around US$1.2 billion. A feasibility study of the gold project commissioned by Rainy River Resources and conducted by a consortium of consulting companies indicates that it has an after-tax net present value of US$931 million, an after-tax IRR of 23.7%, and an after-tax payback period of 3.2 years. These estimates are based on proven and probable reserves of 4 million ounces of gold and 10 million ounces of silver. The company has made these results available to the public by disclosing them on its website.

Source: http://www.rainyriverresources.com/properties/projects/default.aspx.

A further criticism of the payback method is that it does not adequately consider the time value of money. A cash inflow to be received several years in the future is weighed equally with a cash inflow to be received now. To illustrate, assume that for an investment of $8,000 you can purchase either of the two following streams of cash inflows:

Year...............	0	1	2	3	4	5	6	7	8
Stream 1............		$0	$0	$0	($8,000)	$2,000	$2,000	$2,000	$2,000
Stream 2		$2,000	$2,000	$2,000	($8,000)	$8,000	$0	$0	$0

Which stream of cash inflows would you prefer to receive in return for your $8,000 investment? Each stream has a payback period of 4.0 years. Therefore, if you relied on payback alone to make the decision, you would be forced to say that the streams are equally desirable. However, from the point of view of the time value of money, Stream 2 is much more desirable than Stream 1 because the return occurs sooner. You can check this logic by calculating the net present value of the two projects using the method discussed earlier in the chapter. Using any discount rate you like, Project B will always have a higher net present value than Project A.

On the other hand, under certain conditions, the payback method can be very useful. For one thing, it can help identify which investment proposals are in the ballpark. That is, the payback method can be used as an initial screening tool to help answer the question, "Should I consider this proposal further?" If a proposal doesn't provide a payback within some specified period, then there may be no need to consider it further. In addition, the payback period is often of great importance to firms that are cash poor. When a firm is cash poor, a project with a short payback period but a low rate of return might be preferred over another project because the company may simply need a faster recovery of its cash investment. Finally, the payback method is sometimes used in industries where products become obsolete very rapidly—such as consumer electronics. Since products may last only a year or two, the payback period on investments must be very short.

> **Instant Quiz 13-5**
> Calculate the payback period of a project that requires an initial investment of $275,000 and is expected to generate net annual cash inflows of $50,000.

An Extended Example of Payback

As shown by formula (2) above, the payback period is computed by dividing the investment in a project by the net annual cash inflows that the project will generate. If new equipment is replacing old equipment, then any salvage value to be received on disposal of the old equipment should be deducted from the cost of the new equipment, and only the *incremental* investment should be used in the payback computation. In addition, any depreciation deducted in arriving at the project's operating income must be added back to obtain the project's expected annual net cash inflow. To illustrate, consider the data in Example 9.

Example 9

Goodtime Fun Centres operates amusement parks. Some of the vending machines in one of its parks provide very little revenue, so the company is considering removing the machines and installing equipment to dispense soft ice cream. The equipment would cost $80,000 and have an eight-year useful life with no salvage value. Incremental annual revenues and costs associated with the sale of ice cream are as follows:

Sales	$150,000
Less cost of ingredients	90,000
Contribution margin	60,000
Less fixed expenses:	
Salaries	27,000
Maintenance	3,000
Depreciation	10,000
Total fixed expenses	40,000
Operating income	$ 20,000

The vending machines have a salvage value of $5,000. The company will not purchase equipment unless it has a payback period of three years or less. Does the ice cream dispenser pass this criterion?

Exhibit 13–11 shows the computation of the payback period for the ice cream dispenser. Several things should be noted. First, depreciation is added back to operating income to obtain the net annual cash inflow from the new equipment. Depreciation is not a cash outlay, so it must be added back to adjust operating income to a cash basis. Second, the payback computation deducts the salvage value of the old machines from the cost of the new equipment so that only the incremental investment is used to compute the payback period.

As Exhibit 13–11 shows, the proposed equipment has a payback period of less than three years, so the company's payback requirement has been met.

EXHIBIT 13–11 Computation of the Payback Period

Step 1: Compute the net annual cash inflow. Since the net annual cash inflow is not given, it must be computed before the payback period can be determined:

Operating income (given in Example 9)	$20,000
Add: Non-cash deduction for depreciation	10,000
Net annual cash inflow	$30,000

Step 2: Compute the payback period. Using the net annual cash inflow figure from above, the payback period can be determined as follows:

Cost of the new equipment	$80,000
Less salvage value of old equipment	(5,000)
Investment required	$ 75,000

$$\text{Payback period} = \frac{\text{Investment required}}{\text{Net annual cash inflow}}$$

$$= \frac{\$75,000}{\$30,000} = 2.5 \text{ years}$$

Payback and Uneven Cash Flows

When the cash flows associated with an investment project change from year to year, the simple payback formula provided earlier cannot be used. Consider the following data:

Year	Investment	Cash Inflow
1	$4,000	$1,000
2		0
3		2,000
4	2,000	1,000
5		500
6		3,000
7		2,000
8		2,000

What is the payback period on this investment? The answer is 5.5 years, but to obtain this figure it is necessary to track the unrecovered investment year by year. The steps involved in this process are shown in Exhibit 13–12. By the middle of the sixth year, sufficient cash inflows will have been realized to recover the entire investment of $6,000 ($4,000 + $2,000).

EXHIBIT 13–12 Payback Calculation and Uneven Cash Flows

Year	Investment (a)	Cash Inflow (b)	Unrecovered Investment* (c)
1	$4,000	$ 1,000	$3,000
2		O	$3,000
3		$2,000	$ 1,000
4	$2,000	$ 1,000	$2,000
5		$ 500	$ 1,500
6		$3,000	O
7		$2,000	O

*Year X unrecovered investment, column (c) = Year (X − 1) unrecovered investment (column c) + Year X investment (column a) − Year X cash inflow (column b). For example, the unrecovered investment in year 4 is calculated as follows: $1,000 (year 3 unrecovered investment) + $2,000 (year 4 investment) − $1,000 (year 4 cash inflow) = $2,000.

THE SIMPLE RATE OF RETURN METHOD

LEARNING OBJECTIVE 6
Calculate the simple rate of return for an investment

Simple rate of return
The rate of return computed by dividing a project's annual operating income by the initial investment required.

The **simple rate of return** method is another capital budgeting technique that does not involve discounted cash flows. The method is also known as the *accounting rate of return* or the *unadjusted rate of return*.

Unlike the other capital budgeting methods that we have discussed, the simple rate of return method does not focus on cash flows. Rather, it focuses on accounting-based operating income. The approach is to estimate the revenues that will be generated by a proposed investment and then deduct from these revenues all of the projected operating expenses associated with the project. This operating income figure is then related to the initial investment in the project, as shown in the following formula:

$$\text{Simple rate of return} = \frac{\overset{\text{Incremental}}{\text{revenues}} - \overset{\text{Incremental expenses,}}{\text{including depreciation}} = \overset{\text{Incremental}}{\text{operating income}}}{\text{Initial investment*}} \quad (3)$$

*The investment should be reduced by any salvage from the sale of old equipment.

Or, if a cost reduction project is involved, the formula becomes

$$\text{Simple rate of return} = \frac{\text{Cost savings} - \text{Depreciation on new equipment}}{\text{Initial investment*}} \qquad (4)$$

*The investment should be reduced by any salvage from the sale of old equipment.

The logic of deducting depreciation on the investment in new equipment is subject to potential confusion, given how the initial investment was handled earlier in the chapter. However, deducting depreciation expense in formula (3) or (4) makes the calculation of the simple rate of return conceptually similar to the return on investment (ROI) performance metric illustrated in Chapter 11. Examples 10 and 11 demonstrate the calculation of the simple rate of return.

Example 10

Brigham Tea Company is a processor of a low-acid tea. The company is contemplating purchasing equipment for an additional processing line. The additional processing line would increase revenues by $90,000 per year. Incremental cash operating expenses would be $40,000 per year. The equipment would cost $180,000 and have a nine-year life. No salvage value is projected.

The simple rate of return for this example is calculated as follows:

$$\text{Simple rate of return} = \frac{\left[\begin{array}{c}\$90,000 \\ \text{incremental} \\ \text{revenues}\end{array}\right] - \left[\begin{array}{c}\$40,000 \text{ cash operating expenses} \\ + \$20,000 \text{ depreciation}\end{array}\right]}{\$180,000 \text{ initial investment}}$$

$$= \frac{\$30,000}{\$180,000}$$

$$= 16.7\%$$

Example 11

Midwest Farms Limited hires people on a part-time basis to sort eggs. The cost of this hand-sorting process is $30,000 per year. The company is investigating purchasing an egg-sorting machine that would cost $90,000 and have a 15-year useful life. The machine would have negligible salvage value, and it would cost $10,000 per year to operate and maintain. The egg-sorting equipment currently being used could be sold now for a scrap value of $2,500.

A cost-reduction project is involved in Example 11. By applying formula (4), we can compute the simple rate of return as follows:

$$\text{Simple rate of return} = \frac{\$20,000 \text{ cost savings*} - \$6,000 \text{ depreciation on new equipment**}}{\$90,000 - \$2,500}$$

$$= 16\%$$

*$30,000 − $10,000 = $20,000 cost savings per year.
**$90,000 ÷ 15 years = $6,000 depreciation per year.

Criticisms of the Simple Rate of Return

The most damaging criticism of the simple rate of return method is that it ignores the time value of money—it considers a dollar received 10 years from now just as valuable as a dollar received today. Thus, the simple rate of return can be misleading if the alternatives being considered have different cash flow patterns. Also, many projects do not have constant incremental revenues and expenses over their useful lives. As a result, the simple rate of return will fluctuate from year to year, with the possibility that a project may appear to be profitable in some years and unprofitable in others. In contrast, the net present value method provides a single number that summarizes all of the cash flows over the entire useful life of the project and explicitly incorporates the time value of money.

> **Instant Quiz 13-6**
> Calculate the simple rate of return for an investment in automation equipment that would cost $660,000, have a 12-year useful life, have a salvage value of $60,000, and generate annual cost savings of $122,000.

▮ BEHAVIOURAL CONSIDERATIONS

So far, this chapter has emphasized the technical aspects of capital budgeting. Managers should also be cognizant of important behavioural considerations. An understanding of the functional and dysfunctional consequences of human behaviour can provide deeper insight into the capital budgeting process.

Estimates of cash flows, discount rates, and salvage values may be affected by the attitudes of individual managers toward risk. Risk-averse managers tend to be more conservative in their estimates than managers who tend to seek risk and take on projects that have riskier cash flows. Internal politics at an organization may also affect the capital budgeting process. Key managers may favour their own project ideas and bias the estimates of cash inflows and outflows to make the project look more attractive. This bias toward their own projects may also obscure managers' judgment as to when to abandon a particular project. Internal politics may also influence preference decisions. With only limited funds available for capital investments, a division with several good investment proposals may be denied approval of some proposals in favour of the less profitable projects of other divisions. Such allocations of resources (for non-financial reasons) may be deemed necessary to maintain harmony and to give the appearance of fairness across the organization.

The capital budgeting process may also create additional pressure on top management. Top management may be reluctant to reject projects already approved by managers at lower levels because doing so may be perceived as reducing the autonomy of those managers. On the other hand, some projects that have been rejected at lower levels, and thus not considered by top management, may actually be beneficial because they either help to diversify the firm's overall risk or may contribute to the operations of other business units in ways not considered by managers at the lower level. Thus, the hierarchical nature of the project approval process may result in some

IN BUSINESS

Not all capital expenditures incurred by companies are for projects expected to provide a positive net present value. Sometimes investments are made to improve environmental performance as part of a growing recognition by many companies that managing the "triple bottom line" of profits, people, and planet is essential. **Suncor Energy Inc.** is an example of a company undertaking significant capital expenditures in an effort to lessen the negative impact of its operations on the environment. Suncor is a Canadian energy company with headquarters in Calgary. One of its key activities is the production of synthetic crude oil from the oil sands in Fort McMurray, Alberta.

One of the by-products of extracting oil from oil sands is liquid tailings, a toxic mix consisting of water, sand, clay, and residual hydrocarbons. The tailings are held in ponds that occupy a considerable area of land, and because of the nature of their composition, the tailings do not readily evaporate nor are they solid enough (the consistency is akin to yogurt) to use as landfill. Indeed, using existing technology for consolidating tailings, it takes several decades for them to become firm enough for land reclamation to begin. So dealing with the tailings ponds presents an enormous environmental challenge for oil sands companies such as Suncor.

According to Suncor's 2012 annual report, capital expenditures for the year totalled $6.4 billion. Of that total, the company spent $496 million on infrastructure for a new process ("tailings reduction operations") that will reduce the tailings reclamation timeline by up to two decades. Although there will be long-term economic benefits arising from Suncor's ability to reclaim land currently occupied by the tailings pond, this is not the primary motivation for undertaking the capital expenditures. The key reason for the expenditures is to minimize the long-term environmental impact of oil sands development.

Source: Suncor Energy Inc., 2012 annual report; *Tailings Management*: http://www.suncor.com/en/responsible/3229.aspx. Reprinted with permission.

projects never being considered by those senior members of the organization best able to evaluate the projects' contribution to overall risk management or profitability.

Some projects are approved even though they may not generate a positive net present value. For example, projects involving employee, consumer, or environmental safety, or that otherwise impact a firm's ability to operate in a socially responsible manner, may have to be evaluated using non-financial criteria. Other projects that cannot be justified on financial grounds may have to be undertaken in order to conform to municipal, provincial or territorial, or federal laws.

In summary, the capital budgeting process often involves more than just the analytical techniques presented in this chapter. A purely quantitative approach to capital budgeting is not representative of what actually happens in practice. Important qualitative factors imposed on the process by the political, cultural, and social environment within the firm often strongly influence capital budgeting decisions.

KNOWLEDGE IN ACTION

Managers can apply their knowledge about capital budgeting when
- Deciding whether or not to proceed with an individual investment project
- Comparing and choosing projects to invest in when capital funds are limited
- Estimating the number of periods required to recover a project's initial investment
- Quantifying the intangible benefits necessary to make an investment project attractive

SUMMARY

- Capital budgeting decisions fall into two categories: screening decisions and preference decisions. Screening decisions involve determining whether a proposed investment meets a predetermined standard of acceptability. Preference decisions involve selecting from among two or more acceptable investment proposals.
- Investment decisions should take into account the time value of money, since a dollar today is more valuable than a dollar received in the future. The net present value and internal rate of return (IRR) methods both reflect this fact. In the net present value method, the difference between the present value of the cash inflows and the present value of the cash outflows is called the project's *net present value*. The discount rate used to calculate the net present value method is usually a minimum required rate of return, such as the company's weighted-average cost of capital (WACC). Software programs such as Microsoft Excel can be used to quickly and accurately calculate present value amounts. **[LO1]**
- The IRR is the rate of return that equates the present value of the cash inflows and the present value of cash outflows, resulting in a zero net present value. If the IRR is less than the company's minimum required rate of return, the project is rejected (if decisions are based solely on quantitative criteria). Software programs such as Microsoft Excel can be used to quickly and accurately calculate a project's IRR. **[LO2]**
- Some projects have cash flows that are difficult to estimate. Intangible benefits that may result from upgrading production equipment such as improved quality or reliability can be difficult to quantify with any degree of certainty. However, management can cope with this uncertainty by estimating the dollar amount of intangible benefits that would be required to make a project attractive. If management believes the value of the intangible benefits will meet or exceed the required amount, the project should proceed. **[LO3]**
- After identifying projects that are estimated to provide an acceptable rate of return, managers can rank them using either the project profitability index or their IRRs. The project profitability index is conceptually superior to the IRR approach and is computed by dividing the net present value of the project by the required initial investment. **[LO4]**
- After a project has been approved, a post-audit should be performed to see whether expected results are actually being realized. This is a key part of the capital budgeting process, since it tends to improve the quality of the estimates going into future investment proposals and provides management with an opportunity to recognize any developing problems or opportunities with existing projects. **[LO4]**

- Some companies prefer to use the payback period as an approach to making capital budgeting decisions. The payback period is the number of periods (usually expressed in years) required to recover the cost of the initial investment from the net cash inflows generated by the project. The payback approach ignores the time value of money. [LO5]
- The simple rate of return is another approach to making capital budgeting decisions that also ignores the time value of money. It is determined by dividing a project's accounting income (incremental revenues and costs) by the initial investment in the project. [LO6]

REVIEW PROBLEM: COMPARISON OF CAPITAL BUDGETING METHODS

Dawson Company is considering making a capital expenditure for a project that would have an eight-year life and require a $2,400,000 investment in equipment. At the end of eight years, the project would terminate and the equipment would have no salvage value. The project would provide operating income each year as follows:

Sales		$3,000,000
Variable expenses		1,800,000
Contribution margin		1,200,000
Fixed expenses:		
Advertising, salaries, and other		
fixed out-of-pocket costs	$700,000	
Depreciation	300,000	
Total fixed expenses		1,000,000
Operating income		$ 200,000

The company's discount rate is 12%.

Required:
1. Compute the net annual cash inflow from the project.
2. Compute the project's net present value. Is the project acceptable?
3. Find the project's IRR to the nearest whole percentage point.
4. Compute the project's payback period.
5. Compute the project's simple rate of return.

Solution to Review Problem

1. The net annual cash inflow can be computed by deducting the cash expenses from sales:

Sales	$3,000,000
Variable expenses	1,800,000
Contribution margin	1,200,000
Advertising, salaries, and	
other fixed out-of-pocket costs	700,000
Net annual cash inflow	$ 500,000

Or the net annual cash inflow can be computed by adding depreciation back to operating income:

Operating income	$200,000
Add: Non-cash deduction for depreciation	300,000
Net annual cash inflow	$500,000

2.   The net present value is computed as follows:

Item	Year(s)	Amount of Cash Flow	Present Value of Cash Flows*
Cost of new equipment	Now	$(2,400,000)	$(2,400,000)
Annual net cash inflows	1–8	500,000	2,483,820
Net present value			$ 83,820

*Calculated using the NPV formula of Microsoft Excel and a discount rate of 12%.

    Yes, the project is acceptable because it has a positive net present value.
3.   The IRR using the IRR formula in Microsoft Excel is 13%.
4.   The formula for the payback period is

$$\text{Payback period} = \frac{\text{Investment required}}{\text{Annual net cash flow}}$$

$$= \frac{\$2,400,000}{\$500,000} = 4.8 \text{ years}$$

5.   The formula for the simple rate of return is

$$\text{Simple rate of return} = \frac{\text{Annual incremental operating income}}{\text{Initial investment}}$$

$$= \frac{\$200,000}{\$2,400,000} = 8.3\%$$

GLOSSARY

Review key terms and definitions on Connect.

DISCUSSION CASE

DISCUSSION CASE 13–1
Many small and medium-sized companies tend not to use discounted cash flow techniques when analyzing capital expenditures. Instead, if any analysis of capital expenditures is performed, techniques such as the payback method or the simple rate of return are used.

Required:
1.   Why might smaller companies prefer to use techniques such as cash payback or the simple rate of return over discounted cash flow techniques?
2.   Do you think it is any less beneficial for smaller companies to use discounted cash flow techniques when analyzing capital expenditures than it is for larger companies? Why or why not?

QUESTIONS

13–1   What is the difference between capital budgeting screening decisions and capital budgeting preference decisions?
13–2   What is meant by the term *time value of money*?
13–3   What is meant by the term *net present value*?
13–4   Why isn't depreciation on any equipment acquired as part of a project proposal used in the net present value and IRR methods of making capital budgeting decisions?
13–5   Why are discounted cash flow methods of making capital budgeting decisions superior to other methods?
13–6   What are the two simplifying assumptions in net present value analysis?
13–7   What is a post-audit? What are some benefits of conducting post-audits?
13–8   "If a company has to pay interest of 14% on long-term debt, then its cost of capital is 14%." Do you agree? Explain.

13-9   How is the IRR used to determine whether a project is acceptable or not?

13-10   What are least-cost decisions? How are they evaluated?

13-11   "As the discount rate decreases, the present value of a given future cash flow also decreases." Do you agree? Explain.

13-12   Refer to Exhibit 13-4. Is the return on this investment proposal exactly 14%, more than 14%, or less than 14%? Explain.

13-13   How is the project profitability index computed, and what does it measure?

13-14   What is meant by the term *payback period*? How is the payback period determined? How can the payback method be useful?

13-15   How is the eventual salvage value of new equipment being purchased as part of a capital project treated when calculating the simple rate of return?

EXERCISES

EXERCISE 13-1 Net Present Value Method [LO1]

The management of Origami Company, a wholesale distributor of beachwear products, is considering purchasing a $30,000 machine that would reduce operating costs in its warehouse by $5,000 per year. At the end of the machine's eight-year useful life, it will have no scrap value. The company's required rate of return is 11%.

Required:

Ignore income taxes.

1. Determine the net present value of the investment in the machine.
2. What is the difference between the total undiscounted cash inflows and cash outflows over the entire life of the machine?

EXERCISE 13-2 Internal Rate of Return [LO2]

Billy Brown, owner of Billy's Ice Cream On-the-Go, is investigating purchasing a new delivery van that would contain a custom-built refrigeration unit. The van would cost $90,000, have an eight-year useful life, and generate cost savings of $15,000 per year compared to the van currently being used. Also, Billy estimates the new van would result in the sale of 2,000 more litres of ice cream each year, which has a contribution margin of $1 per litre.

Required:

Ignore income taxes.

1. What would be the total annual cash inflows associated with the new van for capital budgeting purposes?
2. Find the IRR promised by the new van, rounded to one decimal place.
3. Now assume that in addition to the cash flows described above, the van will have a $10,000 salvage value at the end of eight years. Calculate the IRR rounded to one decimal place.

EXERCISE 13-3 Uncertain Future Cash Flows [LO3]

Hanover Industries is investigating purchasing automated equipment that would save $100,000 each year in direct labour and inventory carrying costs. This equipment costs $750,000 and is expected to have a 10-year useful life with no salvage value. The company requires a minimum 15% rate of return on all equipment purchases. This equipment would provide intangible benefits (such as greater flexibility and higher-quality output) that are difficult to estimate and yet are quite significant.

Required:

Ignore income taxes. What dollar value per year would the intangible benefits have to be worth to make the equipment an acceptable investment?

EXERCISE 13-4 Preference Ranking [LO4]

Information on three potential projects is given below:

	Project		
	A	**B**	**C**
Investment required	$(170,000)	$(190,000)	$(220,000)
Present value of cash inflows	229,500	294,500	330,000
Net present value	$ 59,500	$ 104,500	$ 110,000

Required:
1. Compute the project profitability index for each project.
2. Rank the projects in terms of preference.

EXERCISE 13–5 Payback Method [LO5]

The management of Deitrich Inc., a civil engineering design company, is considering an investment in a high-quality blueprint printer with the following cash flows:

Year	Investment	Cash Inflow
1.	$28,000	$2,000
2.	$ 4,000	$3,000
3.		$6,000
4.		$8,000
5.		$9,000
6.		$8,000
7.		$6,000
8.		$5,000
9.		$4,000
10.		$4,000

Required:
1. Determine the payback period of the investment.
2. Would the payback period be affected if the cash inflow in the last year was several times as large?

EXERCISE 13–6 Simple Rate of Return Method [LO6]

The management of Stillford MicroBrew is considering purchasing an automated bottling machine for $80,000. The machine would replace an old piece of equipment that costs $33,000 per year to operate. The new machine would cost $10,000 per year to operate. The old machine currently in use could be sold now for a scrap value of $5,000. The new machine would have a useful life of 10 years with no salvage value.

Required:
Compute the simple rate of return on the new automated bottling machine.

EXERCISE 13–7 Comparison of Projects Using Net Present Value [LO1]

Mitchell Company has $30,000 to invest and has two alternative uses of the funds, as shown below. Mitchell Company uses an 8% discount rate:

	Invest in Project Alpha	Invest in Project Beta
Investment required	$30,000	$30,000
Annual cash inflows	$8,000	$0
Single cash inflow at the end of 10 years		$120,000
Life of the project	10 years	10 years

Required:
Ignore income taxes. Which investment would you recommend that the company accept? Show all computations using net present value. Prepare separate computations for each investment.

EXERCISE 13–8 Basic Net Present Value Analysis [LO1]

Sean Laarner paid $18,000 for 900 common shares of Acme Company on January 2, four years ago. Laarner received an $0.80 per share dividend on the shares at the end of each year for four years. At the end of four years, he sold the shares for $22,500. Laarner's goal is to earn a minimum return of 12% on all of his investments.

Required:
Ignore income taxes. Did Laarner earn a 12% return on the shares? Use the net present value method and the general format shown in Exhibit 13–1. Round all computations to the nearest whole dollar.

EXERCISE 13-9 Internal Rate of Return and Net Present Value [LO1, LO2]
Scotia Family Health Team is investigating purchasing an ultrasound machine for use in its patient clinic. The machine would cost $97,900, including invoice cost, freight, and the training of employees to operate it. Scotia has estimated that the new machine would increase the company's cash flows, net of expenses, by $17,000 per year. The machine would have a nine-year useful life with no expected salvage value.

Required:
Ignore income taxes.
1. Compute the machine's IRR rounded to one decimal place.
2. Compute the machine's net present value using a discount rate of 10%. Why do you have a zero net present value?
3. Suppose that the new machine would increase the company's annual cash flows, net of expenses, by only $15,000 per year. Under these conditions, compute the IRR rounded to one decimal place.

EXERCISE 13-10 Uncertain Future Life [LO3]
Willert Excavating Services has invested in certain equipment that cost the company $247,760. The equipment is expected to generate cash inflows of $40,000 each year.

Required:
How many years will the equipment have to be used in order to provide the company with a 12% return on its investment?

EXERCISE 13-11 Basic Payback Period and Simple Rate of Return Computations [LO5, LO6]
Colchester Company is considering purchasing a new piece of equipment. Relevant information concerning the equipment follows:

Purchase cost...	$180,000
Annual cost savings that will be	
provided by the equipment................................	$ 37,500
Life of the equipment	12 years

Required:
Ignore income taxes.
1. Compute the payback period for the equipment. If the company rejects all proposals with a payback period of more than four years, will the equipment be purchased?
2. Compute the simple rate of return on the equipment. Use straight-line depreciation based on the equipment's useful life, assuming $0 salvage value. Will the equipment be purchased if the company's required rate of return is 14%?

EXERCISE 13-12 Working with Net Present Value [LO1]
Piccadilly Hospital has purchased new lab equipment for $200,000. The equipment is expected to last for three years and to provide cash inflows as follows:

Year 1..........................	$60,000
Year 2..........................	$60,000
Year 3..........................	?

Required:
Assuming that the equipment will yield exactly a 10% rate of return, what is the expected cash inflow for year 3?

EXERCISE 13-13 Basic Net Present Value and Internal Rate of Return Analysis [LO1, LO2]
Consider each case below independently. Ignore income taxes.
1. Slade Company's required rate of return is 15%. The company can purchase a new machine at a cost of $40,350. The new machine would generate cash inflows of $15,000 per year and have a four-year life with no salvage value. Compute the machine's net present value. Is the machine an acceptable investment? Explain.
2. Western Products Inc. is investigating purchasing a new grinding machine that has a projected life of 15 years. It is estimated that the machine will save $20,000 per year in cash operating costs. What is the machine's IRR if it costs $111,500 new?
3. Sunset Press has just purchased a new trimming machine that cost $14,125. The machine is expected to save $2,500 per year in cash operating costs and to have a 10-year life.

Compute the machine's IRR. If the company's required rate of return is 16%, did it make a wise investment? Explain.

EXERCISE 13–14 Net Present Value Analysis of Two Alternatives [LO1]

Over the Rainbow Company has $300,000 to invest. The company is trying to decide between two alternative uses of the funds. The alternatives are as follows:

	A	B
Cost of equipment required	$300,000	$ 0
Working capital investment required	$ 0	$300,000
Annual cash inflows	$ 80,000	$ 60,000
Salvage value of equipment in seven years	$ 20,000	$ 0
Life of the project	7 years	7 years

The working capital needed for Project B will be released for investment elsewhere at the end of seven years. Over the Rainbow Company uses a 20% discount rate.

Required:

Ignore income taxes. Which investment alternative (if either) would you recommend that the company accept? Show all computations using the net present value format. Prepare separate computations for each project.

EXERCISE 13–15 Payback Period and Simple Rate of Return [LO5, LO6]

Jamieson Enterprises is considering the development of a go-kart track at an estimated total cost of $680,000. The go-karts would have a $50,000 salvage value at the end of their 10-year useful life. Estimated revenues and costs on an annual basis would be as follows:

Ticket revenues		$380,000
Less operating expenses:		
Maintenance and utilities	$ 71,000	
Salaries	130,000	
Depreciation*	63,000	
Insurance	43,000	
Total operating expenses		307,000
Operating income		$ 73,000

*($680,000 − $50,000) ÷ 10.

Required:

Ignore income taxes.
1. Jamieson Enterprises will not proceed with development of the go-kart track unless the payback period is less than six years. Should they proceed?
2. Compute the simple rate of return for the go-kart track. If Jamieson Enterprises requires a simple rate of return of at least 10%, does the go-kart track meet this criterion?

PROBLEMS

PROBLEM 13–16 Basic Net Present Value Analysis [LO1]

Delorian Mines Inc. owns a large tract of land, including the mining rights, in a mountainous area. The tract contains a mineral deposit that the company believes might be commercially attractive to mine and sell. An engineering and cost analysis has been done, and it is expected that the following cash flows would be associated with opening and operating a mine in the area:

Cost of equipment required	$850,000
Net annual cash receipts	$230,000*
Working capital required	$ 100,000
Cost of road repairs in three years	$ 60,000
Salvage value of equipment in five years	$200,000

*Receipts from sales of ore, less out-of-pocket costs for salaries, utilities, insurance, and so forth.

It is estimated that the mineral deposit would be exhausted after five years of mining. At that point, the working capital would be released for reinvestment elsewhere. The company's required rate of return is 14%.

Required:
Ignore income taxes. Determine the net present value of the proposed mining project. Should the project be accepted? Explain.

PROBLEM 13-17 Basic Net Present Value Analysis [LO1]
Sweetstuff Bakery would like to buy a special machine for icing and applying other toppings to pastries. These are now applied by hand. The machine that the bakery is considering costs $90,000 new. It would last the bakery for eight years but would require a $7,500 overhaul at the end of the fifth year. After eight years, the machine could be sold for $6,000.

The bakery estimates that it will cost $14,000 per year to operate the new machine. The present manual method of putting icing and other toppings on the pastries costs $35,000 per year. In addition to reducing operating costs, the new machine will allow the bakery to increase its production of pastries by 5,000 packages per year. The bakery realizes a contribution margin of $0.60 per package. The bakery requires a 16% return on all investments in equipment.

Required:
Ignore income taxes.
1. What net annual cash inflows will be provided by the new machine?
2. Compute the new machine's net present value. Use the incremental cost approach, and round all dollar amounts to the nearest whole dollar.

PROBLEM 13-18 Net Present Value Analysis; Uncertain Cash Flows [LO1, LO3]
Stirling Windows Inc. of Hong Kong is considering purchasing an automated cutting machine for use in the production of its stained-glass windows. The machine would cost $675,000. (All currency amounts are in Hong Kong dollars.) An additional $487,500 would be required for installation costs and for software. Management believes that the automated machine would provide substantial annual reductions in costs, as shown below:

	Annual Reduction in Costs
Labour costs.	$180,000
Material costs	$ 72,000

The new machine would require considerable maintenance work to keep it in proper adjustment. The company's engineers estimate that maintenance costs would increase by $3,200 per month if the machine were purchased. In addition, the machine would require a $67,500 overhaul at the end of the fifth year.

The new cutting machine would be usable for eight years, after which it would be sold for its scrap value of $157,500. It would replace an old cutting machine that can be sold now for its scrap value of $52,500. Stirling Windows requires a return of at least 16% on investments of this type.

Required:
Ignore income taxes.
1. Compute the net annual cost savings promised by the new cutting machine.
2. Using the data from (1) above and other data from the problem, compute the new machine's net present value. (Use the incremental-cost approach.) Would you recommend that the machine be purchased? Explain.
3. Assume that management can identify several intangible benefits associated with the new machine, including greater flexibility in shifting from one type of stained-glass window to another, improved quality of output, and faster delivery as a result of reduced throughput time. What dollar value per year would management have to attach to these intangible benefits in order to make the new cutting machine an acceptable investment?

PROBLEM 13-19 Preference Ranking of Investment Projects [LO4]
Information on four investment projects being investigated by Clenning Company is as follows:

	Project Number			
	1	**2**	**3**	**4**
Investment required	$(480,000)	$(360,000)	$(270,000)	$(450,000)
Present value of cash inflows at				
a 10% discount rate...........................	567,270	433,400	336,140	522,970
Net present value................................	$ 87,270	$ 73,400	$ 66,140	$ 72,970
Life of the project...............................	6 years	12 years	6 years	3 years
Internal rate of return...........................	16%	14%	18%	19%

Since the company's required rate of return is 10%, a 10% discount rate has been used in the present value computations above. Limited funds are available for investment, so the company can't accept all of the available projects.

Required:
1. Compute the project profitability index for each investment project.
2. Rank the four projects according to preference, in terms of
   a. Net present value.
   b. Project profitability index.
   c. IRR.
3. Which ranking do you prefer? Why?

PROBLEM 13-20 Simple Rate of Return; Payback [LO5, LO6]
Purchasing a large oven and related equipment for mixing and baking "crazy bread" is being considered by Perotti's Pizza. The oven and equipment would cost $120,000 delivered and installed. It would be usable for about 15 years, after which it would have a 10% scrap value. The following additional information is available:

a. Perotti, the owner, estimates that purchase of the oven and equipment would allow the pizza parlour to bake and sell 72,000 loaves of crazy bread each year. The bread sells for $1.25 per loaf.
b. The cost of the ingredients in a loaf of bread is 40% of the selling price. Perotti estimates that other costs each year associated with the bread would be as follows: salaries, $18,000; utilities, $9,000; and insurance, $3,000.
c. The pizza parlour uses straight-line depreciation on all assets, deducting salvage value from original cost.
d. Perotti would like all projects to provide a return of at least 12%.

Required:
Ignore income taxes.
1. Prepare a contribution format income statement showing the operating income each year from production and sale of the crazy bread.
2. Compute the simple rate of return for the new oven and equipment. Will this return be acceptable to Perotti? Explain.
3. Compute the payback period on the oven and equipment. If any of the equipment has less than a six-year payback, will Perotti purchase it?

PROBLEM 13-21 Keep or Sell a Property [LO1]
Ben Ryatt, professor of languages at a university in western Canada, owns a small office building adjacent to the university campus. He acquired the property 12 years ago at a total cost of $560,000: $52,000 for the land and $508,000 for the building. He has just received an offer from a real estate company that wants to purchase the property. However, the property has been a

good source of income over the years, so Ryatt is unsure whether he should keep it or sell it. His alternatives are as follows:

Keep the property. Ryatt's accountant has kept careful records of the income realized from the property over the past 10 years. These records indicate the following annual revenues and expenses:

Rental receipts...		$150,000
Less building expenses:		
Utilities	$28,600	
Depreciation of building	17,800	
Property taxes and insurance	19,500	
Repairs and maintenance	10,500	
Custodial help and supplies.....................	43,500	119,900
Operating income..................................		$ 30,100

Ryatt makes a $12,600 mortgage payment each year on the property. The mortgage will be paid off in 10 more years. He has been depreciating the building by the straight-line method, assuming a salvage value of $9,600 for the building, which he still thinks is an appropriate figure. He feels sure that the building can be rented for another 16 years. He also feels sure that 16 years from now the land will be worth 2.5 times what he paid for it.

Sell the property. A real estate company has offered to purchase the property by paying $150,000 immediately and $23,000 per year for the next 16 years. Control of the property would go to the real estate company immediately. To sell the property, Ryatt would need to pay the mortgage off, which could be done by making a lump-sum payment of $71,000.

Required:
Ryatt requires a 14% rate of return. Would you recommend he keep or sell the property? Show computations using the total-cost approach to net present value. Ignore income taxes.

PROBLEM 13–22 Simple Rate of Return; Payback; Internal Rate of Return [LO2, LO5, LO6]
Chateau Beaune is a family-owned winery headed by Gerard Despinoy and located in the Burgundy region of France. The harvesting season in early fall is the busiest part of the year for the winery, and many part-time workers are hired to help pick and process grapes. Despinoy is investigating purchasing a harvesting machine that would significantly reduce the amount of labour required in the picking process. The harvesting machine is built to straddle grapevines, which are laid out in low-lying rows. Two workers are carried on the machine just above ground level, one on each side of the vine. As the machine slowly crawls through the vineyard, the workers cut bunches of grapes from the vines, which then fall into a hopper. The machine separates the grapes from the stems and other woody debris. The debris is then pulverized and spread behind the machine as a rich ground mulch. Despinoy has gathered the following information relating to the decision of whether to purchase the machine:

a. The winery would save €190,000 per year in labour costs with the new harvesting machine. In addition, the company would no longer have to purchase and spread ground mulch—at an annual savings of €10,000. (The French currency is the euro, which is denoted by the symbol €.)
b. The harvesting machine would cost €480,000. It would have an estimated 12-year useful life and zero salvage value. The winery uses straight-line depreciation.
c. Annual out-of-pocket costs associated with the harvesting machine would be insurance, €1,000; fuel, €9,000; and a maintenance contract, €12,000. In addition, two operators would be hired and trained for the machine, and they would be paid a total of €70,000 per year, including all benefits.
d. Despinoy feels that the investment in the harvesting machine should earn at least a 16% rate of return.

Required:
Ignore income taxes.
1. Determine the annual net savings in cash operating costs that would be realized if the harvesting machine were purchased.
2. Compute the simple rate of return expected from the harvesting machine.
3. Compute the payback period on the harvesting machine. Despinoy will not purchase equipment unless it has a payback period of five years or less. Under this criterion, should the harvesting machine be purchased?

4.   Compute (to the nearest whole percentage point) the IRR promised by the harvesting machine. Based on this computation, does it appear that the simple rate of return is an accurate guide in investment decisions?

PROBLEM 13–23 Net Present Value; Uncertain Future Cash Flows; Post-Audit [LO1, LO3]

"If we can get that new robot to combine with our other automated equipment, we'll have a complete flexible manufacturing system (FMS) in place in our Northridge plant," said Hal Swain, production manager for Diller Products.

"Let's just hope that reduced labour and inventory costs can justify its acquisition," replied Linda Wycoff, the controller. "Otherwise, we'll never get it. You know how the president feels about equipment paying for itself out of reduced costs."

Selected data relating to the robot are provided below. Engineering studies suggest that using the robot will result in a savings of 20,000 direct labour-hours each year. The labour rate is $16 per hour. Also, the smoother work flow made possible by the FMS will allow the company to reduce the amount of inventory on hand by $300,000. The released funds will be available for use elsewhere in the company. This inventory reduction will take place in the first year of operation. The company's required rate of return is 20%:

Cost of the robot	$1,600,000
Software and installation	$ 700,000
Annual savings in labour costs	?
Annual savings in inventory carrying costs	$ 190,000
Monthly increase in power and	
maintenance costs	$ 2,500
Salvage value in 12 years	$ 90,000
Useful life	12 years

Required:

Ignore income taxes.

1.   Determine the net *annual* cost savings if the robot is purchased. (Do not include the $300,000 inventory reduction or the salvage value in this computation.)
2.   Compute the net present value of the proposed investment in the robot. Based on these data, would you recommend that the robot be purchased? Explain.
3.   Assume that the robot is purchased. At the end of the first year, Wycoff has found that some items didn't work out as planned. Due to unforeseen problems, software and installation costs were $125,000 more than estimated, and direct labour has been reduced by only 17,500 hours per year, rather than by 20,000 hours. Assuming that all other cost data were accurate, does it appear that the company made a wise investment? Show computations, using the net present value format as in (2) above. (*Hint:* It might be helpful to place yourself back at the beginning of the first year, with the new data.)
4.   On seeing your analysis in (3) above, the president stated, "That robot is the worst investment we've ever made and we'll be stuck with it for years."
    a.   Explain to the president what benefits other than cost savings might accrue from using the new robot and FMS.
    b.   Compute for the president the dollar amount of cash inflow that would be needed each year from the benefits in (a) above in order for the equipment to yield a 20% rate of return.

PROBLEM 13–24 Internal Rate of Return; Sensitivity Analysis [LO2]

Dr. Heidi Black is the managing partner of the Crestwood Dental Clinic. Black is trying to determine whether or not the clinic should move patient files and other items out of a spare room in the clinic and use the room for dental work. She has determined that it would require an investment of $142,950 for equipment and related costs of getting the room ready for use. Based on receipts being generated from other rooms in the clinic, Black estimates that the new room would generate a net cash inflow of $35,390 per year. The equipment purchased for the room would have a seven-year estimated useful life.

Required:

Ignore income taxes.

1.   Compute the IRR on the equipment for the new room to the nearest whole percentage point. Verify your answer by computing the net present value of the equipment using the IRR you have computed as the discount rate.

2. Assume that Black will not purchase the new equipment unless it promises a return of at least 14%. Compute the amount of annual cash inflow that would provide this return on the $142,950 investment.

3. Although seven years is the average life for dental equipment, Black knows that due to changing technology, this life can vary substantially. Compute the IRR to the nearest whole percentage point if the life of the equipment were (*a*) five years and (*b*) nine years, rather than seven years. Is there any information provided by these computations that you would be particularly anxious to show Black? Explain.

4. Black is unsure about the estimated $35,390 annual cash inflow from the room. She thinks that the actual cash inflow could be as much as 10% greater or less than this figure.
    a. Assume that the actual cash inflow each year is 10% greater than estimated. Recompute the IRR to the nearest whole percentage point using the seven-year life.
    b. Assume that the actual cash inflow each year is 10% less than estimated. Recompute the IRR to the nearest whole percentage point using the seven-year life.

5. Refer to the original data. Assume that the equipment is purchased and that the room is opened for dental use. However, due to an increasing number of dentists in the area, the clinic is able to generate only $30,000 per year in net cash receipts from the new room. At the end of five years, the clinic closes the room and sells the equipment to a newly licensed dentist for a cash price of $61,375. Compute the IRR to the nearest whole percentage point that the clinic earned on its investment over the five-year period. Round all dollar amounts to the nearest whole dollar.

PROBLEM 13–25 Net Present Value Analysis of a Lease or Buy Decision [LO1]
Brinsley Transport wants to upgrade its fleet of highway transport trucks. The new trucks that the company wants to acquire can be either purchased or leased from the manufacturer. The company has made the following evaluation of the two alternatives:

   Purchase alternative. If the new transport trucks are purchased, then the costs incurred by the company will be as follows:

Purchase cost of the trucks..............................	$680,000
Annual cost of servicing, licences, and taxes	$ 7,200
Repairs:	
First four years, per year	$ 2,400
Fifth year	$ 4,000
Sixth year..	$ 8,000

   The trucks would be sold after six years. Based on current resale values, the company would be able to sell them for about one-half of their original cost at the end of the six-year period.

   Lease alternative. If the new transport trucks are leased, then the company will have to make an immediate deposit of $40,000 to cover any damage during use. The lease will run for six years, at the end of which time the deposit will be refunded. The lease will require an annual rental payment of $140,000 (the first payment is due at the end of year 1). As part of this lease cost, the manufacturer will provide all servicing and repairs, license the trucks, and pay all taxes. At the end of the six-year period, the trucks will revert to the manufacturer, as owner.

Brinsley Transport's required rate of return is 16%.

Required:
Ignore income taxes.
1. Use the total-cost approach to determine the present value of the cash flows associated with each alternative.
2. Which alternative would you recommend that the company accept? Why?

PROBLEM 13–26 Preference Ranking of Investment Projects [LO4]
Since limited funds are available for investment, Yancy & Company must ration the funds among four competing projects. Selected information on the four projects follows:

Project	Investment Required	Net Present Value	Life of the Project (years)	Internal Rate of Return
A......................	$800,000	$ 221,615	7	18%
B......................	675,000	210,000	12	16%
C......................	500,000	175,175	7	20%
D......................	700,000	152,544	3	22%

The net present values above have been computed using a 10% discount rate. The company wants your assistance in determining which project to accept first, which to accept second, and so forth. The company's investment funds are limited.

Required:
1. Compute the project profitability index for each project.
2. In order of preference, rank the four projects in terms of
   a. Net present value.
   b. Project profitability index.
   c. IRR.
3. Which ranking do you prefer? Why?

PROBLEM 13–27 Simple Rate of Return and Payback Analysis of Two Machines [LO5, LO6]
Blue Ridge Furniture is considering purchasing two different items of equipment, as described below:

Machine A. A machine has just come onto the market that compresses sawdust into various shelving products. Currently, the sawdust is disposed of as a waste product. The following information is available about the machine:

a. The machine would cost $780,000 and would have a 25% salvage value at the end of its 10-year useful life. The company uses straight-line depreciation and considers salvage value in computing depreciation deductions.
b. The shelving products produced by the machine would generate revenues of $350,000 per year. Variable manufacturing costs would be 20% of sales.
c. Fixed annual expenses associated with the new shelving products would be advertising, $42,000; salaries, $86,000; utilities, $9,000; and insurance, $13,000.

Machine B. A second machine has come onto the market that would automate a sanding process that is now done largely by hand. The following information is available about this machine:

a. The new sanding machine would cost $220,000 and would have no salvage value at the end of its 10-year useful life. The company would use straight-line depreciation.
b. Several old pieces of sanding equipment that are fully depreciated would be disposed of at a scrap value of $7,200.
c. The new sanding machine would provide substantial annual savings in cash operating costs. It would require an operator at an annual salary of $26,000 and $3,000 in annual maintenance costs. The current hand-operated sanding procedure costs the company $85,000 per year.

Blue Ridge Furniture requires a simple rate of return of 16% on all equipment purchases. Also, the company will not purchase equipment unless the equipment has a payback period of four years or less.

Required:
Ignore income taxes.
1. For machine A:
   a. Prepare an income statement showing the expected operating income each year from the new shelving products. Use the contribution format.
   b. Compute the simple rate of return.
   c. Compute the payback period.
2. For machine B:
   a. Compute the simple rate of return.
   b. Compute the payback period.
3. According to the company's criteria, which machine, if either, should the company purchase?

PROBLEM 13-28 Net Present Value Analysis of a New Product [LO1]
Clarion Company is considering an opportunity to produce and sell a revolutionary new smoke detector for homes. To determine whether this would be a profitable venture, the company has gathered the following data on probable costs and market potential:

a. New equipment would have to be acquired to produce the smoke detector. The equipment would cost $100,000 and be usable for 12 years. After 12 years, it would have a salvage value equal to 10% of the original cost.

b. Production and sales of the smoke detector would require a working capital investment of $40,000 to finance accounts receivable, inventories, and day-to-day cash needs. This working capital would be released for use elsewhere after 12 years.

c. An extensive marketing study projects sales in units over the next 12 years as follows:

Year(s)	Sales in Units
1	4,000
2	7,000
3	10,000
4-12	12,000

d. The smoke detectors would sell for $45 each; variable costs for production, administration, and sales would be $25 per unit.

e. To gain entry into the market, the company would have to advertise heavily in the early years of sales. The advertising program follows:

Year(s)	Amount of Advertising
1-2	$70,000
3	50,000
4-12	40,000

f. Other fixed costs for salaries, insurance, maintenance, and straight-line depreciation on equipment would total $127,500 per year. (Depreciation is based on cost less salvage value.)

g. The company's required rate of return is 20%.

Required:
Ignore income taxes.
1. Compute the net cash inflow (cash receipts less yearly cash operating expenses) anticipated from sale of the smoke detectors for each year over the next 12 years.
2. Using the data computed in (1) above and other data provided in the problem, determine the net present value of the proposed investment. Would you recommend that Clarion Company accept the smoke detector as a new product?

PROBLEM 13-29 Net Present Value; Total-Cost and Incremental-Cost Approaches [LO1]
Clean Duds Laundromat has an industrial water softener that enhances the water quality used in its washing machines. The water softener is approaching the end of its useful life and must be either overhauled or replaced. Details of the two alternatives are shown below.

If the company overhauls its current water softener, then it will be usable for eight more years. If, instead, a new water softener is purchased, it will be used for eight years, after which it will be replaced. The new water softener will be considerably more energy efficient, resulting in a substantial reduction in annual operating costs, as shown below:

	Current Water Softener	New Water Softener
Purchase cost new	$8,000	$10,000
Remaining book value	$4,500	—
Overhaul needed now	$4,000	—
Annual cash operating costs	$6,000	$ 4,500
Salvage value now	$2,000	—
Salvage value eight years from now	$1,000	$ 3,000

Clean Duds computes depreciation on a straight-line basis. All equipment purchases are evaluated using a 12% discount rate.

Required:

Ignore income taxes.

1. Should Clean Duds Laundromat upgrade the old water softener or purchase the new one? Use the total-cost approach to net present value in making your decision.

2. Redo (1) above, this time using the incremental-cost approach.

CASES

CASE 13–30 Capital Budget Reviews and the Role of the Post-Audit [LO1]

Stephen Scott recently joined the Finance and Planning Division of the Carrigan Bank (Bassillo) Limited as an assistant chief financial officer (CFO). Scott is a certified management accountant and has spent the previous four years working in the accounting department of a large Canadian manufacturing company. He took the job at the bank because it provided an opportunity to get some international business experience.

One of Scott's responsibilities is to perform an initial review of the capital budgeting proposals developed by the various divisions at the bank. Because the bank's divisions are very large and have a high degree of operating autonomy, each division has its own divisional controller, who prepares the proposals with input from key managers in the division and other bank personnel. For 2015, the bank budgeted $500,000 for capital spending in each of the six major divisions for projects requiring less than $100,000 of expenditures. For projects of that size, the divisions are free to go ahead and spend the funds as they see fit, without the need for centralized review and approval. The bank budgeted a further $20 million in capital spending for 2015 to be allocated to the divisions on the basis of the project proposals submitted as part of the capital budget review process. These proposals are for individual projects requiring capital expenditures in excess of $100,000.

All project submissions are ranked from most to least profitable using the project profitability index: Net present value of project ÷ Investment required. The final review of the proposals is conducted by the CFO, the assistant CFO, and the vice-president of Finance (VPF). In addition to these three individuals, the review meeting is attended by the senior manager and controller of each division. Non-financial factors, such as the importance of the expenditure for maintaining the bank's competitive position and its impact on customer retention and growth, are considered as part of the review and approval process. However, these factors typically have a smaller impact on the final decision than the project profitability index, which senior management believes to be more objective and reliable.

As part of his initial review of the proposals, Scott was instructed by the CFO to evaluate the reasonableness of the assumptions and to check the accuracy of the calculations. Where necessary, he was to follow up with the divisional controllers if he had any questions about the details. As Scott began his review, he was struck by the relatively high project profitability index on the vast majority of the projects. Indeed, most of the proposals (about 75%) had a project profitability index in excess of 30%, while the remaining 25% had an index between 20% and 30%. In several instances, the assumptions underlying the proposal seemed very optimistic, so he decided to follow up with the individual divisional controllers.

Almost without fail, the controllers admitted to using highly optimistic cash inflows in order to make their proposals look as good as possible. The controllers also commented that the division managers viewed the capital budget review process as a game that they wanted to win by getting as many of their projects approved as possible. As one controller put it (but said he'd deny it if ever asked), "What's the harm in a little optimism as long as the estimates in all of the proposals are more or less equally overstated?" Scott also learned from the controllers that word had leaked out that last year only those projects with a project profitability index over 30% were funded, and that they had been instructed by their divisional managers to make sure the current-year proposals met that threshold. The divisional controllers also suggested that it was clear that senior management at the bank condoned the optimism included in their proposals since the use of post-audits had been discontinued several years ago after the CFO at the time (who has since been replaced) concluded that the cost of the audits exceeded their benefits.

As Scott sat in his office after a conversation with one of the divisional controllers, he wasn't sure what to do next. The divisional controllers told him he'd be wasting his time going to the CFO or the VPF, since they all knew how the capital budgeting game was being played. He was also concerned that rocking the boat would upset the divisional controllers, with whom he had to work closely on other aspects of his job. But he couldn't shake the feeling that this was an issue that deserved more attention.

Required:
1.   What should Scott do?
2.   Would the use of post-audits solve the problem of the overly optimistic project proposals being submitted at the bank? Why or why not?
3.   Who should be involved in conducting the post-audit process?

CASE 13–31 Net Present Value Analysis of Securities [LO1]
Anita Vasquez received $160,000 from her mother's estate. She placed the funds in the hands of a broker, who purchased the following securities on Vasquez's behalf:

a.   Common shares were purchased at a cost of $80,000. The shares paid no dividends, but they were sold for $180,000 at the end of four years.
b.   Preferred shares were purchased at their par value of $30,000. The shares paid a 6% dividend (based on par value) each year for four years. At the end of four years, the shares were sold for $24,000.
c.   Bonds were purchased at a cost of $50,000. The bonds paid $3,000 in interest every six months. After four years, the bonds were sold for $58,500. (*Note:* In discounting a cash flow that occurs semi-annually, the procedure is to halve the discount rate and double the number of periods. Use the same procedure in discounting the proceeds from the sale.)

The securities were all sold at the end of four years so that Vasquez would have funds available to start a new business venture. The broker stated that the investments had earned more than a 20% return annually, and he gave Vasquez the following computation to support his statement:

Common shares:	
Gain on sale ($180,000 − $80,000)............................	$100,000
Preferred shares:	
Dividends paid (6% × $30,000 × 4 years).....................	7,200
Loss on sale ($24,000 − $30,000).............................	(6,000)
Bonds:	
Interest paid ($3,000 × 8 periods)...........................	24,000
Gain on sale ($58,500 − $50,000).............................	8,500
Net gain on all investments......................................	$133,700
Return: ($133,700 ÷ 4) ÷ $160,000 = 20.9%	

Required:
Ignore income taxes.
1.   Using a 20% discount rate, compute the net present value of each of the three investments. On which investment(s) did Anita earn a 20% rate of return? (Round computations to the nearest whole dollar.)
2.   Considering all three investments together, did Anita earn a 20% rate of return? Explain.
3.   Anita wants to use the $262,500 in proceeds ($180,000 + $24,000 + $58,500 = $262,500) from sale of the securities to open a fast-food franchise under a 10-year contract. What net annual cash inflow must the store generate for Anita to earn a 16% return over the 10-year period? Anita will not receive back her original investment at the end of the contract. (Round computations to the nearest whole dollar.)

CASE 13–32 Comparison of Alternatives Using Net Present Value Analysis [LO1]
Hesselwood Company's market research division has projected a substantial increase in demand over the next several years for one of the company's products. To meet this demand, the company will need to produce units as follows:

Year(s)	Production in Units
1................................	10,000
2................................	15,000
3................................	20,000
4–10............................	22,500

At present, the company is using a single Model 2360 machine to manufacture this product. To increase its productive capacity, the company is considering two alternatives:

Alternative 1. The company could purchase another Model 2360 machine that would operate along with the one it now owns. The following information is available on this alternative:

a. The Model 2360 machine now in use was purchased for $82,500 four years ago. Its present book value is $49,500, and its present market value is $45,000.

b. A new Model 2360 machine costs $90,000 now and will have a negligible salvage value at the end of 10 years. The old Model 2360 machine will have to be replaced in six years at a cost of $100,000. The replacement machine will have a market value of about $50,000 when it is four years old.

c. The variable cost required to produce one unit of product using the Model 2360 machine is given in the "General information on the two alternatives" section below.

d. Repairs and maintenance costs each year on a single Model 2360 machine total $1,500.

Alternative 2. The company could purchase a Model 4720 machine and use the old Model 2360 machine as standby equipment. The Model 4720 machine is a high-speed unit with double the capacity of the Model 2360 machine. The following information is available on this alternative:

a. The cost of a new Model 4720 machine is $125,000.

b. The variable cost required to produce one unit of product using the Model 4720 machine is given in the "General information on the two alternatives" section below.

c. The Model 4720 machine is more costly to maintain than the Model 2360 machine. Repairs and maintenance on a Model 4720 machine and on a Model 2360 machine used as standby would total $2,300 per year.

General information on the two alternatives:

a. Both the Model 2360 machine and the Model 4720 machine have a 10-year life from the time they are first used in production. Straight-line depreciation is used by the company.

b. The two machine models are not equally efficient. Comparative variable costs per unit of product are as follows:

	Model 2360	Model 4720
Direct materials per unit	$0.54	$0.60
Direct labour per unit	0.75	0.33
Supplies and lubricants per unit	0.06	0.12
Total variable cost per unit	$1.35	$1.05

c. No other factory costs would change as a result of the decision between the two machines.

d. Hesselwood Company uses a 16% discount rate.

Required:

Ignore income taxes.

1. Which alternative should the company choose? Use the net present value approach. (Round to the nearest whole dollar.)

2. Suppose that the cost of direct materials increases by 50%. Would this make the Model 4720 machine more or less desirable? Explain. No computations are needed.

3. Suppose that the cost of direct labour increases by 25%. Would this make the Model 4720 machine more or less desirable? Explain. No computations are needed.

4. By how much would operating costs have to increase on average each year for the preferred alternative in part 1 to make the company indifferent between the two machines in terms of their net present values?

INSTANT QUIZ SOLUTIONS

13–1

Net present value = $(100,000) + $104,127* = $4,127

*Present value of $20,000 cost savings for seven years using an 8% required rate of return.

13–2

Item	Year(s)	Amount of Cash Flow	Present Value of Cash Flows
Purchase of equipment	Now	$(500,000)	$(500,000)
Working capital needed	Now	(50,000)	(50,000)
Overhaul of equipment................................	5	(25,000)	(15,523)
Annual net cash inflows	1–10	70,000	430,120
Salvage value of equipment	10	50,000	19,277
Working capital released	10	50,000	19,277
Net present value......................................			$ (96,849)

13–3

The IRR is 13% using the IRR formula in Microsoft Excel.

13–4

Net present value: $90,000 − $75,000 = $15,000 (a)
Investment required: $75,000 (b)
Project profitability index: $15,000 ÷ $75,000 = 20% (a) ÷ (b)

13–5

Initial investment = $275,000
Net annual cash inflows = $50,000
Payback: $275,000 ÷ $50,000 = 5.5 years

13–6

Simple rate of return = ($122,000 − $50,000*) ÷ ($660,000 − $60,000)
Simple rate of return = 12%
*Depreciation: ($660,000 − $60,000) ÷ 12 = $50,000 per year.

connect   LEARNSMART   SMARTBOOK

For more information on the resources available from McGraw-Hill Ryerson, go to www.mheducation.ca/he/solutions.

APPENDIX 13A: THE CONCEPT OF PRESENT VALUE

The point was made in the main body of the chapter that a manager would rather receive a dollar today than a dollar a year from now. There are two reasons why this is true. First, a dollar received today is more valuable than a dollar received a year from now. The dollar received today can be invested immediately, and by the end of the year it will have earned some return, making the total amount in hand at the end of the year *greater* than the initial investment. The person receiving the dollar a year from now will simply have a dollar in hand at that time.

Second, the future involves uncertainty. The longer people have to wait to receive a dollar, the more uncertain it becomes that they will actually get the dollar. As time passes, conditions change and future payment of the dollar might become impossible.

Since money has a time value, managers need a method of determining whether a cash outlay made now in an investment project can be justified in terms of the expected cash inflows from the project in future years. That is, the manager must have a means of expressing future receipts in present dollar terms so that the future receipts can be compared *on an equivalent basis* with whatever investment is required now in the project under consideration. The mathematics of interest provides managers with the means of making such a comparison. It is worth noting that some of the formulas that follow below (e.g., (A3) and (A4)) are used in software programs such as Microsoft Excel and financial calculators to perform the present value calculations discussed in the main body of the chapter.

The Mathematics of Interest

If a bank pays $102 one year from now in return for a deposit of $100 now, we say that the bank is paying interest at an annual rate of 2%. The relationships involved in this notion can be expressed in mathematical terms by means of the following equation:

$$F_1 = P(1 + r) \tag{A1}$$

where F_1 = the amount to be received in one year, P = the present outlay to be made, and r = the rate of interest involved. If the present outlay is $100 deposited in a bank savings account that is to earn interest at 2%, then $P = \$100$ and $r = 0.02$. Under these conditions, $F_1 = \$102$, the amount to be received in one year.

The $100 present outlay is called the **present value** of the $102 amount to be received in one year. It is also known as the *discounted value* of the future $102 receipt. The $100 figure represents the value in present terms of a receipt of $102 to be received a year from now when the interest rate is 2%.

Compound Interest   What if the investor leaves the money in the bank for a second year and continues to earn 2% per year? In that case, by the end of the second year, the original $100 deposit will have grown to $104.04:

Original deposit	$100.00
Interest for the first year:	
$100 × 0.02	2.00
Amount at the end of the first year	102.00
Interest for the second year:	
$102 × 0.02	2.04
Amount at the end of the second year	$104.04

Notice that the interest for the second year is $2.04, as compared to only $2 for the first year. The reason for the greater amount of interest earned during the second year is that during the second year, interest is being paid *on interest*. That is, the $2 interest earned during the first year has been left in the account and has been

LEARNING OBJECTIVE 7
Explain present value concepts and the underlying mathematics of interest.

Present value
The value now of an amount that will be received in some future period.

Compound interest
The process of paying interest on interest for an investment.

added to the original $100 deposit in computing interest for the second year. This concept is known as **compound interest**. The compounding we have done is on an annual basis. However, interest can be compounded on a semi-annual, quarterly, or even more frequent basis. Many financial institutions are now compounding interest on a daily basis. The more frequently compounding is done, the more rapidly the invested balance will grow.

How is the concept of compound interest expressed in equation form? It is expressed by taking equation (A1) and adjusting it to state the number of years, n, that a sum is going to be left deposited in the bank:

$$F_n = P(1 + r)^n \tag{A2}$$

where n = number of years.

If $n = 2$ years, then our computation of the value of F two years hence is as follows:

$$F_2 = \$100(1 + 0.02)^2$$
$$F_2 = \$104.04$$

Present Value and Future Value

Exhibit 13A–1 shows the relationship between present value and future value as expressed in the interest equations. As shown in the exhibit, if $100 is deposited in a bank at 2% interest, it will grow to $110.40 by the end of five years if interest is compounded annually.

Exhibit 13A–1 illustrates that an investment can be viewed in two ways: either in terms of its future value or in terms of its present value. We have seen from our computations above that if we know the present value of a sum (such as our $100 deposit), it is a relatively simple task to compute the sum's future value in n years by using equation (A2). But what if the tables are reversed, and we know the *future* value of some amount but we do not know its present value?

For example, assume that you are to receive $200 two years from now. You know that the future value of this sum is $200, since this is the amount that you will be receiving in two years. But what is the sum's present value—what is it worth *right now*? The present value of any sum to be received in the future can be computed by rearranging equation (A2) and solving for P:

$$P = F_n(1 + r)^{-n} \tag{A3}$$

EXHIBIT 13A–1   The Relationship between Present Value and Future Value

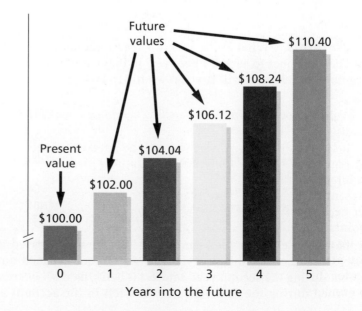

Suppose that in our example, $F = \$200$ (the amount to be received in the future), $r = 0.05$ (the rate of interest), and $n = 2$ (the number of years in the future that the amount is to be received):

$$P = F_n(1 + r)^{-n}$$
$$P = \$200(1 + 0.05)^{-2}$$
$$P = \$181.41$$

As shown by the computation above, the present value of \$200 to be received two years from now is \$181.41 if the interest rate is 5%. In effect, we are saying that \$181.41 received *right now* is equivalent to \$200 received two years from now if the rate of return is 5%. The \$181.41 and the \$200 are just two ways of looking at the same item at different points in time.

The process of finding the present value of a future cash flow, which we have just examined, is called **discounting**. We have *discounted* the \$200 to its present value of \$181.41. The 5% interest figure that we have used to find this present value is called the **discount rate**. As discussed in the chapter, companies typically use the weighted-average cost of capital (WACC) as the discount rate, with adjustments to the rate possible depending on the riskiness of the particular project under consideration. Discounting of future sums to their present value is a common practice in business. Knowing the present value of a sum to be received in the future can be very useful to a manager, particularly in making capital budgeting decisions.

Discounting
The process of finding the present value of a future cash flow.

Discount rate
The rate used to calculate the present value of future cash flows.

Some of the present value formulas we will be using are more complex and difficult to use. Fortunately, as discussed in the chapter, software programs such as Microsoft Excel and financial calculators incorporate these formulas, permitting fast and error-free calculations.

Example 1

A purchaser promises to pay \$100,000 two years from now for a lot of land. This amount includes interest at an annual rate of 5%. What is the selling price of the land today? Round to the nearest hundred dollars.

Using formula (A3), the answer is

$$P = \$100,000(1 + 0.05)^{-2}$$
$$P = \$90,700$$

Example 2

A woman in Vancouver plans to take a trip four years from now. She estimates that she will need \$18,000 at that time. At an annual interest rate of 4%, compounded semi-annually, how much must be deposited into a bank account today to accumulate the required \$18,000?

Because interest is compounded semi-annually in this example, the interest per period is 2% (the annual rate divided by 2) and the number of periods is 8 (the number of years times 2). The formula solution is $\$18,000 \times (1 + 0.02)^{-8} = \$15,363$.

Present Value of a Series of Cash Flows (Annuity)

The present value of an **annuity** is the present value of a series of equal payments or receipts discounted at compound interest and made at regular intervals. Stated differently, it is the total amount that allows the withdrawal of a series of equal amounts at regular intervals if the balance remaining after each withdrawal earns compound interest.

Annuity
A series of equal cash payments or receipts.

The present value of \$1 to be received at the end of each of four periods at 4% interest per period is shown graphically in Exhibit 13A-2.

Two points are important in connection with Exhibit 13A-2. First, notice that the farther we go forward in time, the smaller is the present value of the \$1 interest receipt. The present value of \$1 received a year from now is \$0.962, compared to only \$0.855 for the \$1 interest payment to be received four periods from now. This observation underscores the fact that money has a time value.

EXHIBIT 13A-2   Illustration of Present Value of an Ordinary Annuity

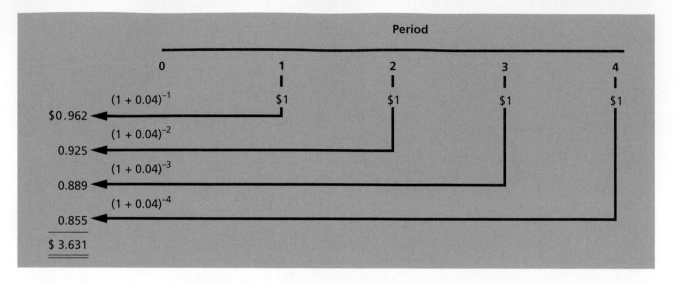

The formula for the present value (P_n) of an annuity of $1 per period compounded at the rate of r for n periods is

$$P_n = \frac{1 - (1 + r)^{-n}}{r} \tag{A4}$$

For the illustration in Exhibit 13A–2,

$$P_n = \frac{1 - (1 + 0.04)^{-4}}{0.04} = \$3.631$$

Example 3

What is the present value of receiving a series of six semi-annual payments of $2,000 at 4% interest compounded annually? Assume that it is now January 1, 2015, and the first payment is to be made on June 30, 2015.

The purpose of solving this problem could be to determine (1) the sum that will provide for six semi-annual withdrawals of $2,000 if invested at 2% per period (4% divided by two interest periods per year) and (2) the sum that is payable in settlement of a series of obligations of $2,000 that are due at six semi-annual intervals and discounted at 2% per period. Using formula (A4), the solution is

$$P_n = \frac{1 - (1 + 0.02)^{-6}}{0.02} \times \$2,000 = \$11,203$$

Example 4

How much money would a company be willing to invest in a project that would return $3,000 every three months for three years and, in addition, a lump sum of $20,000 at the end of the third year? The receipts begin three months from now. Interest is 8% per annum.

The $3,000 to be received at the end of each three-month period is an ordinary annuity. The number of interest periods is 12 (4 per year for 3 years), and the quarterly interest rate is 2% (8% ÷ 4 periods). The present value of the ordinary annuity of $3,000, using formula (A4), and the present value of the $20,000 lump sum, using formula (A3), are as follows:

$$P_n = \frac{1 - (1 + 0.02)^{-12}}{0.02} \times \$3,000 + \$20,000(1 + 0.02)^{-12}$$

$$P_n = \$31,726 + \$15,770$$

$$P_n = \$47,496$$

EXHIBIT 13A-3   Present Value of an Ordinary Annuity and an Annuity Due

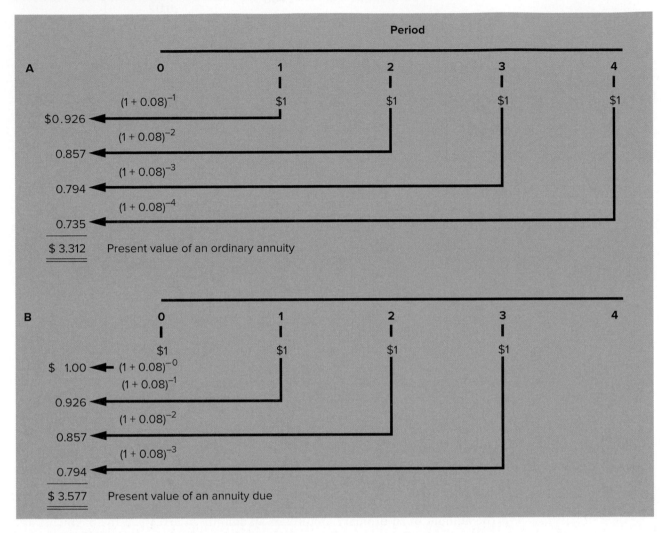

Present Value of an Annuity Due

An annuity due is one in which the payments or receipts occur at the *beginning* of each period. Exhibit 13A–3 compares the present value of an ordinary annuity of $1 for four periods with the present value of an annuity due for $1 for four periods. The interest rate is assumed to be 8%.

Note that part B of Exhibit 13A–3 can be interpreted as an ordinary annuity of $1 for three periods ($0.926 + $0.857 + $0.794) to which we add $1. We can calculate the present value of an annuity due by subtracting one period from n and calculating the present value of an ordinary annuity for $n - 1$ periods. We then add 1 to this annuity factor, because the first payment is received immediately.

Example 5

On February 1, 2015, Davis Company signed an 18-month lease with Kelly Leasing Company. The lease payments begin immediately. Calculate the present value of the lease, assuming that $2,000 is paid each quarter and that the annual interest rate is 8%.

To determine the present value, we use formula (A4) adjusted for the fact that we now have an annuity due, where n is equal to six periods (18 months = 6 quarters) and the quarterly interest rate is 2% (8% ÷ 4):

$$PV \text{(annuity due)} = \$2,000 \times \left[1 + \frac{1 - (1 + 0.02)^{-5}}{0.02}\right]$$
$$= \$2,000 \times (1 + 4.713)$$
$$= \$11,426$$

Deferred Annuities

A deferred annuity is one in which the first payment or receipt does not begin until more than one interest period has expired. This is common for capital expenditure decisions that may take several periods to become operational.

Example 6

What is the present value on January 1, 2015, of a series of five annual receipts of $1,000, the first of which is expected to be received on January 1, 2018? The interest rate is 5% per annum.

The easiest way of solving this problem is to think about it as having two steps:

Step 1.   Calculate the present value on January 1, 2017, of an ordinary annuity of a series of five receipts of $1,000 beginning January 1, 2018, using an interest rate of 5%.

$$\frac{1 - (1 + 0.05)^{-5}}{0.05} \times \$1,000 = \$4,329$$

Step 2.   The problem is now translated into a simple present value problem, where the present value on January 1, 2015, of the annuity beginning January 1 2018 can be computed by discounting the $4,329 back two interest periods (from January 1, 2017, to January 1, 2015):

$$PV \text{(January 1, 2015)} = \$4,329(1 + 0.05)^{-2}$$
$$= \$3,927$$

Future Value of an Annuity

Business transactions often involve a series of equal payments spaced evenly. As discussed earlier in this appendix, a series of equal payments at regular intervals is known as an *annuity*. The total that becomes due immediately after the last payment is the amount of an ordinary annuity or an annuity in arrears. If the payments are made or received at the beginning of the first interest period, the annuity is termed an *annuity due* or an *annuity in advance*.

The distinction between an ordinary annuity and an annuity due is presented graphically as follows:

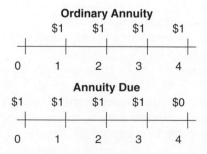

To illustrate how the future value of an ordinary annuity is determined, assume that $1 is deposited in a savings account at the end of each of four periods at 8% per period:

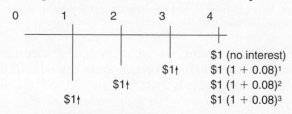

Thus, the value of an ordinary annuity of $1 due at the end of each period for four periods is

$$\$1 + \$1(1 + 0.08)^1 + \$1(1 + 0.08)^2 + \$1(1 + 0.08)^3$$
$$= \$1 + \$1.08 + \$1.1664 + \$1.2597$$
$$= \$4.5061$$

From the preceding illustration it can be seen that the $1 deposited at the end of the first year accumulates interest for a total of three periods, increasing to a value of $1.2597. The deposit at the end of the second year grows to $1.1664, and the $1 deposited at the end of the third period accumulates to $1.08. The $1 deposited at the end of the fourth period has not yet earned any interest. The series of four payments of $1 each period grows to $4.5061 at the end of the fourth period.

This problem can be solved quickly by using a mathematical expression based on a geometric progression. The future value of an annuity in arrears (F_n) compounded at an interest rate (r) for a given number of periods (n) is

$$F_n = \frac{(1 + r)^n - 1}{r} \tag{A5}$$

The value of a series of $1 deposits made at the end of each of four years compounded at 8% annually is

$$F_n = \$1 \times \frac{(1 + 0.08)^4 - 1}{0.08} = \$4.5061$$

The approach to finding the future value of an annuity of $1 where each payment is made at the beginning of each period is illustrated by the following diagram:

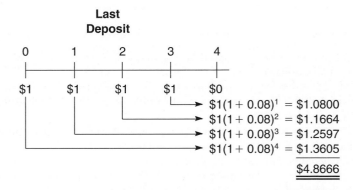

To find the future value of an annuity of $1 per period for four periods if each payment is made at the *beginning* of each period (an annuity due), we can modify the formula as follows:

$$F_n \text{ (annuity due)} = \$1 \times \frac{(1 + r)^n - 1}{r} \times (1 + r)$$

$$= \$1 \times \frac{(1 + 0.08)^4 - 1}{0.08} \times (1 + 0.08)$$

$$= \$4.867$$

Using Microsoft Excel

Microsoft Excel has numerous built-in formulas that can be used to quickly and accurately perform most of the calculations covered in the body of the chapter and the appendices. Some key formulas are as follows:

NPV(rate,value1,value2,. . .): net present value—allows for unequal cash flows.
PV(rate,nper,pmt,fv,type): present value—cash flows must be the same each period.
PMT(rate,nper,pv,type): the amount of an equal series of payments that will result in a specified present value.
FV(rate,nper,pmt,pv,type): future value—cash flows must be the same each period.
FVSCHEDULE(principal,schedule)
IRR(values,guess): IRR of a series of cash flows.
NPER(rate,pmt,pv,type): the number of periods required to yield a required rate of return.

where

- *rate* is the interest rate per period (e.g., the required rate of return for capital expenditures).
- *value1, value2,* . . . are the cash inflows and outflows related to the asset.
- *nper* is the total number of payment periods in an annuity.
- *pmt* is the payment made each period and cannot change over the life of the annuity.
- *pv* is the present value, the total amount that a series of future payments is worth now.
- *fv* is the future value, or a cash balance you want to attain after the last payment is made. If *fv* is omitted, it is assumed to be 0 (the future value of a loan, for example, is 0).
- *principal* is the amount to be invested now.
- *schedule* is the period and rate over which a given rate of return is to be compounded.
- *type* is the number 0 or 1 and indicates when payments are due (0 or omitted, payment is at the end of the period; 1, payment is at the beginning of the period).
- *values* are the cash inflows and outflows related to the project.
- *guess* is an estimate of the project's IRR (can be left blank).

APPENDIX 13A SUMMARY

- The concept of present value is based on the simple idea that a dollar received today is worth more than a dollar received in the future. This is so because a dollar received today can be invested immediately and will earn a positive return and because the future involves uncertainty. This uncertainty results in the possibility that the dollar will not be received in the future. [LO7]
- Several key concepts were covered in this appendix. *Present value* is the value now of an amount that will be received in some future period; an *annuity* is a stream of identical cash flows; *compound interest* is the process of paying interest on interest in an investment; and *discount rate* is the rate of return used to find the present value of future cash flows or the future value of amounts received now. [LO7]
- The factors used in the various present value and future value calculations can be determined by using the formulas presented throughout this appendix. However, financial calculators and spreadsheet programs such as Microsoft Excel are now commonly used to perform the calculations.

APPENDIX 13A REVIEW PROBLEM: PRESENT VALUE EXERCISES

Each of the following situations is independent.
1. Greg plans to retire in 12 years. When he retires, he would like to take an extended vacation, which he expects will cost at least $40,000. What lump-sum amount must he invest now to have $40,000 at the end of 12 years if the rate of return is
    a.   8%?
    b.   12%?

2. The Morganthalers would like to send their daughter to a music camp at the end of each of the next five years. The camp costs $1,000 a year. What lump-sum amount would have to be invested now to have $1,000 at the end of each year if the rate of return is
    a. 8%?
    b. 12%?
3. You have just received an inheritance from a relative. You can either receive a $200,000 lump-sum amount at the end of 10 years or receive $14,000 at the end of each year for the next 10 years.
    a. If your annual rate of return is 4%, which alternative would you prefer?
    b. If your annual rate of return is 8%, which alternative would you prefer?

Solution to Appendix 13A Review Problem

In the solutions below we use the formulas presented in the appendix to demonstrate the calculations underlying software packages and financial calculators. We suggest you check the answers using Microsoft Excel or a financial calculator.

1. a. The amount that must be invested now is the present value of the $40,000, using a discount rate of 8% and 12 periods. Using formula (A3), the answer is as follows:

$$P_n = \$40,000(1 + 0.08)^{-12}$$
$$P_n = \$15,885$$

    b. We will proceed as we did in (a) above, but this time we will use a discount rate of 12%.

$$P_n = \$40,000(1 + 0.12)^{-12}$$
$$P_n = \$10,267$$

    Notice that as the discount rate (desired rate of return) increases, the present value decreases.

2. This part differs from (1) above in that we are now dealing with an ordinary annuity rather than with a single future sum. The amount that must be invested now is the present value of the $1,000 needed at the end of each year for five years. Accordingly, we use formula (A4) to calculate the present values.

    a.

$$P_n = \frac{1 - (1 + 0.08)^{-5}}{0.08} \times \$1,000$$
$$P_n = \$3,993$$

    b.

$$P_n = \frac{1 - (1 + 0.12)^{-5}}{0.12} \times \$1,000$$
$$P_n = \$3,605$$

    Again, notice that as the discount rate increases, the present value decreases. When the rate of return increases, less must be invested today to yield a given amount in the future.

3. Whichever alternative has the higher present value is the one that should be selected.

    a. 4% rate of return:
        Present value of alternative 1 using formula (A3):

$$P_n = \$200,000(1 + 0.04)^{-10}$$
$$P_n = \$135,113$$

        Present value of alternative 2 using formula (A4):

$$P_n = \frac{1 - (1 + 0.04)^{-10}}{0.04} \times \$14,000$$
$$P_n = \$113,553$$

        Thus, you should prefer to receive the $200,000 at the end of year 10 rather than $14,000 per year as an annuity for 10 years if the annual return is 4%.

    b. 8% rate of return:
        Present value of alternative 1 using formula (A3):

$$P_n = \$200,000(1 + 0.08)^{-10}$$
$$P_n = \$92,639$$

Present value of alternative 2 using formula (A4):

$$P_n = \frac{1 - (1 + 0.08)^{-10}}{0.08} \times \$14,000$$

$$P_n = \$93,941$$

Now, you should prefer to receive the $14,000 annuity for 10 years if the annual return is 8% rather than the $200,000 lump-sum payment. Note how the preferred alternative is sensitive to the return that can be earned on an annual basis.

APPENDIX 13A EXERCISES

EXERCISE 13A–1 Basic Present Value Concepts [LO7]
Each of the following parts is independent. Ignore income taxes.
1. Express Delivery plans to build a new warehouse in four years to have more space for its products awaiting shipment. The warehouse will cost $500,000. What lump-sum amount should the company invest now to have the $500,000 available at the end of the four-year period? Assume that the company can invest money at
   a.   6%.
   b.   10%.
2. Washington Products Inc. can purchase a new electronic data storage server that will save $3,000 per year in paper storage and warehouse costs. The data server will last for five years and have no salvage value. What is the maximum purchase price that Washington Products would be willing to pay for the copier if the company's required rate of return is
   a.   9%?
   b.   15%?
3. Susan has just won the million-dollar Power Lottery jackpot at a gambling casino. The casino will pay her $50,000 per year for 20 years as the payoff. If Susan can invest money at a 5% rate of return, what is the present value of her winnings? Did she really win a million dollars? Explain.

EXERCISE 13A–2 Basic Present Value Concepts [LO7]
Consider each of the following situations independently.
1. Annual cash inflows from two competing investment opportunities are given below. Each investment opportunity will require the same initial investment. Compute the present value of the cash inflows for each investment using a 20% discount rate:

| | Investment | |
Year	X	Y
1	$ 1,000	$ 4,000
2	2,000	3,000
3	3,000	2,000
4	4,000	1,000
	$10,000	$10,000

2. At the end of three years, when you graduate from college, your parents have promised to give you a used car that will cost $12,000. What lump sum must they invest now to have the $12,000 at the end of three years if they can invest money at
   a.   6%?
   b.   10%?
3. Mark has just won the grand prize on the *Hoot 'n' Holler* quiz show. He has a choice between (*a*) receiving $500,000 immediately and (*b*) receiving $60,000 per year at the end of the year for eight years, plus a lump sum of $200,000 at the end of the eight-year period. If Mark can get a return of 10% on his investments, which option would you recommend that he accept? Use present value analysis, and show all computations.
4. You have just learned that you are a beneficiary in the will of your late Aunt Susan. The executor of her estate has given you three options as to how you may receive your inheritance:
   a.   You may receive $50,000 immediately.
   b.   You may receive $75,000 at the end of six years.
   c.   You may receive $12,000 at the end of each year for six years (a total of $72,000).
   If you can invest money at a 12% return, which option would you prefer?

■ APPENDIX 13B: INCOME TAXES IN CAPITAL BUDGETING DECISIONS

In our discussion of capital budgeting, we ignored income taxes in the chapter for two reasons. First, some organizations do not pay income taxes. Not-for-profit organizations, such as hospitals and charitable foundations, and government agencies are exempt from income taxes. Second, capital budgeting is complex and is best covered in small steps. Now that we have a solid groundwork in the concepts of present value, we can explore the effects of income taxes on capital budgeting decisions.

Canadian income tax regulations are very complex, so we cover only the basics in this appendix. To keep the material as easy to understand as possible, we have made many simplifying assumptions about the tax regulations throughout this appendix. Among the most important of these assumptions are (1) taxable income equals net income before income tax expense as computed for financial reports, and (2) the tax rate is a flat percentage of taxable income. The actual tax regulations are far more complex than this; however, the simplifications that we make throughout this appendix allow us to cover the most important implications of income taxes for capital budgeting without getting bogged down in too many details. It is also important to note that we focus on after-tax *cash* inflows and *cash* outflows in the discussion below. This is because capital project analysis, even on an after-tax basis, should be done using discounted cash inflows and outflows.

The Concept of After-Tax Cost

Businesses, like individuals, must pay income taxes. In the case of businesses, the amount of income tax that must be paid is determined by the company's net taxable income. Tax-deductible expenses (tax deductions) decrease the company's net taxable income and hence reduce the taxes the company must pay. For this reason, expenses are often stated on an *after-tax* basis. For example, if a company pays rent of $10 million per year but this expense results in a reduction in income taxes of $3 million (tax rate = 30%), the after-tax cost of the rent is said to be $7 million. The amount of an expenditure net of its tax effect is known as the **after-tax cost**.

After-tax cost
The net amount of cash outflow resulting from a tax-deductible cash expense after the income tax effects have been considered.

To illustrate, assume that a company with a tax rate of 30% is contemplating a training program that costs $60,000. What impact will this have on the company's taxes? To keep matters simple, let's assume the training program has no immediate effect on sales. How much does the company actually pay for the training program after taking into account the impact of this expense on taxes? The answer is $42,000, as shown in Exhibit 13B–1. While the training program costs $60,000 before taxes, it will reduce the company's taxes by $18,000, so its *after-tax* cost is only $42,000. This $18,000 reduction in taxes can also be calculated directly by simply multiplying $60,000 by the 30% tax rate.

EXHIBIT 13B–1 The Computation of After-Tax Cost

	Without Training Program	With Training Program
Sales....................................	$850,000	$850,000
Less tax-deductible expenses:		
Salaries, insurance, and other	700,000	700,000
New training program		60,000
Total expenses	700,000	760,000
Taxable income........................	$150,000	$90,000
Income taxes (30%).....................	$ 45,000	$ 27,000
Cost of new training program	$ 60,000	
Less reduction in income taxes		
($45,000 − $27,000).............................	18,000	
After-tax cost of the new training program	$ 42,000	

The after-tax cost of any tax-deductible cash expense can be determined using the following formula:[5]

$$\underset{\text{(net cash outflow)}}{\text{After-tax cost}} = (1 - \text{Tax rate}) \times \text{Tax-deductible cash expense} \qquad \text{(B1)}$$

We can verify the accuracy of this formula by applying it to the $60,000 training program expenditure:

$$(1 - 0.30) \times \$60,000 = \$42,000 \text{ after-tax cost of the training program}$$

This formula is very useful since it provides the actual amount of cash a company must pay after taking into consideration tax effects. It is this actual after-tax cash outflow that should be used in capital budgeting decisions.

Similar reasoning applies to revenues and other *taxable* cash inflows. Since these cash receipts are taxable, the company must pay out a portion of them in taxes. The **after-tax benefit**, or net cash inflow, realized from a particular cash receipt can be obtained by applying a simple variation of the cash expenditure formula used above:

$$\text{After-tax benefit (net cash inflow)} = (1 - \text{Tax rate}) \times \text{Taxable cash receipt} \qquad \text{(B2)}$$

We emphasize the term *taxable cash receipt* because not all cash inflows are taxable. For example, the release of working capital at the termination of a project is not a taxable cash inflow. It is not counted as income for either financial accounting or income tax reporting purposes since it is simply a recovery of the initial investment.

After-tax benefit
The net amount of cash inflow realized from a taxable cash receipt after income tax effects have been considered.

Capital Cost Allowance Tax Shield

Capital cost allowance (CCA) is the amount of depreciation expense allowed by the Canada Revenue Agency for tax purposes. Because CCA, like accounting depreciation, is not a cash outflow, it was ignored in the chapter in all discounted cash flow computations. However, CCA does affect the amount of taxes that must be paid and therefore has an indirect effect on the company's cash flows.

To illustrate the effect of CCA deductions on tax payments, consider a company with annual cash sales of $500,000 and cash operating expenses of $310,000. In addition, the company has a depreciable asset on which the CCA deduction is $90,000 per year. The tax rate is 30%. As shown in Exhibit 13B–2, the CCA deduction reduces

Capital cost allowance
The amount of depreciation expense allowed by the Canada Revenue Agency for tax purposes.

EXHIBIT 13B–2   The Effect of Capital Cost Allowance Deductions on Tax Payments

	Without CCA Deduction	With CCA Deduction
Sales...	$500,000	$500,000
Cash operating expenses.........................	310,000	310,000
Cash flow from operations........................	190,000	190,000
Capital cost allowance	—	90,000
Taxable income..................................	$ 190,000	$ 100,000
Income taxes (30%)	$ 57,000	$ 30,000
	$27,000 lower taxes with the CCA deduction	
Cash flow comparison:		
Cash flow from operations (above)..............	$ 190,000	$ 190,000
Income taxes (above)	57,000	30,000
Net cash flow.................................	$ 133,000	$ 160,000
	$27,000 greater cash flow with the CCA deduction	

the company's taxes by $27,000. In effect, the CCA deduction of $90,000 *shields* $90,000 in revenues from taxation and thereby *reduces* the amount of taxes that the company must pay. Because CCA deductions shield revenues from taxation, they are referred to as **capital cost allowance tax shields.**[6]

The reduction in tax payments made possible by the CCA tax shield illustrated in Exhibit 13B–2 is equal to the amount of the CCA deduction multiplied by the tax rate, as follows:

$$\text{Tax savings from the CCA tax shield} = \text{Tax rate} \times \text{CCA deduction} \qquad \text{(B3)}$$

We can verify this formula by applying it to the $90,000 CCA deduction in our example:

$$0.30 \times \$90,000 = \$27,000 \text{ reduction in tax payments}$$

In this appendix, when we estimate after-tax cash flows for capital budgeting decisions, we will include the tax savings provided by the CCA tax shield.

Rules for CCA are complex, and most companies take advantage of accelerated methods allowed under the tax regulations. These accelerated methods usually result in a reduction in current taxes because of higher CCA amounts and an offsetting increase in future taxes as CCA amounts fall. This shifting of part of the tax burden from the current year to future years is advantageous from a present value point of view, since tax savings received today are worth more than tax savings received in the future. A summary of the concepts we have introduced so far is given in the learning aid below.

Capital cost allowance tax shields
Reductions in tax payments caused by capital cost allowance deductions.

Capital Cost Allowance Instead of Depreciation

As noted above, CCA is the Canada Revenue Agency's counterpart to depreciation. Depreciation is the allocation of the cost of an asset over its useful life. The amount deducted each period for financial statement reporting purposes is based on generally accepted accounting principles (GAAP). For income tax purposes, however, depreciation is not an allowable expense. Instead, a CCA is permitted by regulations that accompany the Canadian Income Tax Act. A CCA deduction is allowed for business-related capital property such as equipment and automobiles.

The income tax regulations group assets into classes, and each class is then assigned a maximum CCA rate for tax purposes. Maximum CCA rates are prescribed by the regulations in the Income Tax Act for numerous classes or pools of assets. A company has the option of deducting CCA for each asset class for any amount ranging from zero to the maximum amount prescribed by the Act. The CCA rate applicable to each class is usually intended to reflect the economic life of the assets of that class.

LEARNING AID

Tax Adjustments Required in a Capital Budgeting Analysis

Item	Treatment
Tax-deductible cash expense*	Multiply by (1 — Tax rate) to get after-tax cost.
Taxable cash receipt*	Multiply by (1 — Tax rate) to get after-tax cash inflow.
CCA deduction	Multiply by the tax rate to get the tax savings from the CCA tax shield.

*Cash expenses can be deducted from the cash receipts and the difference multiplied by (1 — Tax rate). See the example at the top of Exhibit 13B-3.

These prescribed rates are subject to government change. Examples of these asset pools and maximum prescribed rates as per the 2013 Canadian Income Tax Act follow:

Asset	Class	Maximum Rate
Non-residential buildings	1	4%
Automobiles	10	30%
Computer hardware and software	52	100%
Assets not included in other classes	8	20%

Undepreciated capital cost (UCC)

The remaining book value of an asset class or pool of assets that is available for tax-deductible depreciation (capital cost allowance).

CCA is calculated by applying the prescribed rate to a declining balance called the **undepreciated capital cost** (UCC). The UCC of an asset class or pool of assets is the remaining book value that is available for tax-deductible depreciation (CCA). The maximum amount of CCA that may be deducted in a taxation year is the UCC multiplied by the CCA rate for that asset class. However, for net additions made to each asset class during the year, only one-half of the prescribed rate is permitted. Under this half-year rule, only half of the normal CCA for most assets is allowed as a tax-deductible expense in the year the asset is acquired.

Example 1

Saskatoon Ltd. has obtained a $30,000 loan to acquire a truck (Class 10 for CCA purposes). Assuming that the company will have taxable income for the foreseeable future, calculate the present value of the CCA tax shield for the first three years if the WACC is 10% and the tax rate is 40%.

(1) Year	(2) Undepreciated Capital Cost	(3) CCA (2) × 30%	(4) Tax Savings (3) × 40%	(5) Present Value of Tax Savings[†]
1	$30,000	$4,500*	$1,800	$1,636
2	25,500	7,650	3,060	2,528
3	17,850	5,355	2,142	1,609

*$30,000 × 0.30 × (½) = $4,500.
[†]Calculated using the NPV formula of Microsoft Excel and a required rate of return of 10%.

Because the CCA is calculated on the declining UCC balance of a pool of assets rather than on a single asset, a business is able to obtain tax savings from a project even after its disposition. As long as there are other assets in the pool and the proceeds from disposal are less than the UCC for the class, tax savings can be realized in perpetuity.

It can be shown mathematically that the present value of this perpetual stream of tax savings from a declining balance CCA is calculated by using the *CCA tax shield formula*:

$$PV = \frac{Cdt}{d + k} \times \frac{1 + 0.5k}{1 + k} \tag{B4}$$

where

C = The capital cost of the asset added to the asset pool.
d = CCA rate.
t = The firm's marginal income tax rate.
k = The weighted-average cost of capital.

$\dfrac{1 + 0.5k}{1 + k}$ = The correction factor to account for the provision that only one-half of the capital cost of an asset is included in UCC during the year of acquisition.

For the previous example, the present value of the CCA tax shield is

$$\frac{\$30,000 \times 0.3 \times 0.4}{0.3 + 0.10} \times \frac{1 + 0.5 \times 0.10}{1 + 0.10} = \$9,000 \times 0.95455 = \$8,591$$

Example 2
Using the data in the previous example, calculate the present value of the CCA tax shield, assuming that other assets remain in the pool and the asset is disposed of for $6,000 after five years' use.

The sale of the asset results in a cash inflow at the end of year 5. This disposal results in the asset pool balance (UCC) being reduced by the $6,000 proceeds. The present value of the CCA tax shield is also reduced, because from the end of year 5 onward, CCA will be applied to a smaller UCC balance than it otherwise would have been without the asset disposal. If S represents salvage value, the CCA tax shield formula must be adjusted by deducting

$$\frac{Sdt}{d + k} \times (1 + k)^{-n}$$

where

$$\frac{Sdt}{d + k}$$

calculates the present value of the lost tax shield at the end of year 5 ($n = 5$). This lost tax shield is then discounted to time period zero by multiplying it by $(1 + k)^{-n}$ (see Appendix 13A for the present value formula) or by using a software package or a financial calculator to perform the present value calculation. The present value of the tax shield lost is calculated as follows:

$$\frac{\$6,000 \times 0.3 \times 0.4}{0.3 + 0.1} \times (1 + 0.10)^{-5} = \$1,117.66$$

Therefore, the net present value of the CCA tax shields is $8,591 − $1,117.66 = $7,473.34.

Example of Income Taxes and Capital Budgeting

Now that we have reviewed after-tax costs, after-tax benefits, and the CCA tax shield, we can examine a comprehensive example of income taxes and capital budgeting that incorporates all of these concepts.

Example 3
The mineral rights to land that has a deposit of ore are owned by Englund Company. The company is uncertain whether it should purchase equipment and open a mine on the property. After careful study, the following data have been assembled by the company:

Cost of equipment needed	$300,000
Working capital needed	75,000
Estimated annual cash receipts from sales of ore	250,000
Estimated annual cash expenses for salaries, insurance, utilities, and other cash expenses of mining the ore	170,000
Cost of road repairs needed in 6 years	40,000
Salvage value of the equipment in 10 years	100,000

The ore in the mine would be exhausted after 10 years of mining activity, at which time the mine would be closed. The equipment would then be sold for its salvage value. Englund Company uses a 20% rate, assuming no salvage value, to compute CCA deductions for tax purposes. The company's after-tax WACC is 12% and its tax rate is 30%.
Should Englund Company purchase the equipment and open a mine on the property?

The solution to the problem is given in Exhibit 13B–3. We suggest that you carefully work through the solution noting the following points:

Cost of new equipment. The initial investment of $300,000 in the new equipment is included in full, with no reductions for taxes. This represents an *investment*, not an expense, so no tax adjustment is made. Only revenues and expenses are adjusted for the effects of taxes. However, this investment does affect taxes through the CCA deductions that are considered below.

Working capital. The working capital needed for the project is included in full, with no reductions for taxes. As with the cost of new equipment, working capital is an investment and not an expense, so no tax adjustment is made. Also observe that no tax adjustment is made when the working capital is released at the end of the project's life. The release of working capital is not a taxable cash flow, since it merely represents a return of investment funds to the company.

Net annual cash receipts. The net annual cash receipts from sales of ore are adjusted for the effects of income taxes, as discussed earlier in this appendix. Note at the top of Exhibit 13B–3 that the annual cash expenses are deducted from the annual cash receipts to obtain the net cash receipts. This simplifies the computations.

EXHIBIT 13B-3   Example of Income Taxes and Capital Budgeting

	Per Year
Cash receipts from sales of ore	$250,000
Less payments for salaries, insurance, utilities, and other cash expenses	170,000
Net cash receipts	$ 80,000

Items and Computations	Year(s)	(1) Amount	(2) Tax Effect*	After-Tax Cash Flows (1) × (2)	Present Value of Cash Flows†
Cost of new equipment.............	Now	$(300,000)	—	$(300,000)	$(300,000)
Working capital needed............	Now	(75,000)	—	(75,000)	(75,000)
Net annual cash receipts...........	1–10	80,000	1 − 0.30	56,000	316,412
Road repairs	6	(40,000)	1 − 0.30	(28,000)	(14,186)
Salvage value of equipment	10	100,000	—	100,000	32,197
Release of working capital	10	75,000	—	75,000	24,148
Subtotal					$ (16,429)

Present value of CCA tax shield:

$$PV = \left[\frac{Cdt}{d + k} \times \frac{1 + 0.5k}{1 + k} \right] - \left[\frac{Sdt}{d + k} \times (1 + k)^{-n} \right]$$

$$PV = \left[\frac{\$300{,}000 \times 0.2 \times 0.3}{0.2 + 0.12} \times \frac{1 + 0.06}{1 + 0.12} \right] - \left[\frac{\$100{,}000 \times 0.2 \times 0.3}{0.2 + 0.12} \times (1 + 0.12)^{-8} \right]$$

$$PV = (\$56{,}250 \times 0.9464) - (\$18{,}750 \times 0.3220)$$

$$PV = \$53{,}235 - \$6{,}037$$

$$PV = \$47{,}198$$

	47,198
Net present value	$ 30,769

*Taxable cash receipts and tax-deductible cash expenses are multiplied by (1 − Tax rate) to determine the after-tax cash flow. CCA deductions are multiplied by the tax rate itself to determine the after-tax cash flow (i.e., tax savings from the CCA tax shield).
†Except for the present value of the tax CCA shield, calculations use the NPV formula of Microsoft Excel and a required rate of return of 12%.

LEARNING AID

NET PRESENT VALUE AND INTERNAL RATE OF RETURN METHODS (WITH TAXES)

Relevant cash inflows:

- Incremental revenues (after tax); reduction in costs (after tax); salvage value; release of working capital; CCA tax shield.

Relevant cash outflows:

- Initial investment; increased working capital needs; incremental operating costs (after tax); CCA tax shield lost upon disposal of asset.

Decision Rule (for determining project acceptability):

Acceptable if	Net present value $\geq$ $0; Internal rate of return $\geq$ Required rate of return.
Not acceptable if	Net present value $<$ $0; Internal rate of return $<$ Required rate of return.

Road repairs. Since the road repairs occur just once (in the sixth year), they are treated separately from other expenses. Road repairs would be a tax-deductible cash expense, and therefore they are adjusted for the effects of income taxes, as discussed earlier in this appendix.

Capital cost allowance deductions. The tax savings provided by CCA deductions are essentially an annuity that is included in the present value computations using the CCA tax shield formula.

Salvage value of equipment. The salvage value of $100,000 results in the present value inflow of $32,200. However, later in the analysis, note that the present value of the tax shield is reduced. The value of $18,750 is the present value at the end of year 10 of the lost CCA tax shield from the salvage. This amount must therefore be discounted to *the present*. To illustrate, we have used the present value formula presented in Appendix 13A to calculate the amount.

Since the net present value of the proposed mining project is positive, the equipment should be purchased and the mine opened.

APPENDIX 13B SUMMARY

- Unless a company is a tax-exempt organization, such as a not-for-profit school or government unit, income taxes should be considered in making capital budgeting decisions. Tax-deductible cash expenditures and taxable cash receipts are placed on an after-tax basis by multiplying them by (1 − Tax rate). Only after-tax amounts should be used in determining the desirability of an investment proposal. [LO8]
- Although capital cost allowance (CCA; depreciation for tax purposes) is not a cash outflow, it is a valid deduction for tax purposes and therefore affects income tax payments. The CCA tax shield is computed by multiplying the CCA deduction by the tax rate and results in income tax savings. The present value of these tax savings is used in calculating the net present value of a project. [LO8]
- When an asset is sold, the undepreciated capital cost (UCC) is reduced by the amount of the sale proceeds. An adjustment must then also be made to the capital budgeting analysis to adjust for the present value of the CCA tax shields lost. [LO8]

APPENDIX 13B REVIEW PROBLEM: CAPITAL BUDGETING AND TAXES

Ace Company is considering investing $70,000 in a cargo van. The van is expected to generate net annual cash inflows of $13,500 over an eight-year period. The van will have a salvage value of $5,000 in eight years. The CCA is 30% and the income tax rate is 40%. Ace Company requires an after-tax return of 10% on all investments.

Required:
Compute the net present value of the investment in the van. Should the van be purchased?

Solution to Appendix 13B Review Problem

The net present value analysis is as follows:

Items and Computations	Year(s)	(1) Amount	(2) Tax Effect	(1) × (2) After-Tax Cash Flows	Present Value of Cash Flows[†]
Investment in cargo van	Now	$(70,000)		$(70,000)	$(70,000)
Net annual cash receipts	1–8	13,500	1 – 0.40	8,100	43,213
CCA tax shield*	1–8				19,345
Salvage value of the van	8	5,000		5,000	2,333
Net present value					$ (5,109)

*CCA tax shield calculations:

$$PV = \left[\frac{Cdt}{d+k} \times \frac{1+0.5k}{1+k} \right] - \left[\frac{Sdt}{d+k} \times (1+k)^{-n} \right]$$

$$PV = \left[\frac{\$70,000 \times 0.3 \times 0.4}{0.3+0.10} \times \frac{1+0.05}{1+0.10} \right] - \left[\frac{\$5,000 \times 0.3 \times 0.4}{0.3+0.10} \times (1+0.10)^{-8} \right]$$

$$PV = [\$21,000 \times 0.9545] - [\$1,500 \times 0.4665]$$

$$PV = \$19,345$$

[†]Except for the present value of the CCA tax shield, calculations use the NPV formula of Microsoft Excel and a required rate of return of 10%.

No, the investment project should not be undertaken. It has a negative net present value when the company's cost of capital is used as the discount rate.

APPENDIX 13B EXERCISES AND PROBLEMS

EXERCISE 13B–1 After-Tax Costs [LO8]
Solve each of the following parts independently.
1. Lowney Limited has hired a public accounting firm to identify opportunities to reduce their corporate income tax expense. The firm's tax advisory fee will be $250,000. What will be the after-tax cost of the firm's fee if Lowney's tax rate is 30%?
2. Cycling Accessories has introduced a new line of cold-weather apparel, and annual revenues have increased by $600,000. If the company's tax rate is 25%, what is the after-tax benefit from the increased revenues?
3. Solar Solutions has purchased new manufacturing equipment that cost $400,000. Calculate the yearly tax savings from the CCA tax shield for the next three years. Assume that the income tax rate is 30%, the CCA rate is 30%, and the weighted-average cost of capital (WACC) is 12%. Assume that CCA in the first year is subject to the half-year rule.

EXERCISE 13B–2 After-Tax Cash Flows in Net Present Value Analysis [LO8]
Draper Corporation is considering two investment projects, each of which would require a $60,000 initial investment. Cost and cash flow data concerning the two projects are given below:

	Project A	Project B
Investment in inventory scanning equipment	$60,000	
Investment in working capital		$60,000
Net annual cash inflows	$ 11,000	$ 11,000
Life of the project	10 years	10 years
CCA	20%	

The inventory scanning equipment would have a salvage value of $6,000 in 10 years. The equipment would be depreciated over 10 years. At the end of 10 years, the investment in working capital would be released for use elsewhere. The company requires an after-tax return of 12% on all investments. The tax rate is 30%.

Required:
Compute the net present value of each investment project. (Round to the nearest whole dollar.)

EXERCISE 13B–3 Net Present Value Analysis Including Income Taxes [LO8]

The Hub Store at a university in eastern Canada is considering purchasing a self-serve checkout machine similar to those used in many grocery stores and other retail outlets. Currently the university pays part-time wages to students totalling $55,000 per year. A self-serve checkout machine would reduce part-time student wages by $35,000 per year. The machine would cost $240,000 and has a 10-year useful life. Total costs of operating the checkout machine would be $5,000 per year, including maintenance. Major maintenance would be needed on the machine in five years at a total cost of $10,000. The salvage value of the checkout machine in 10 years would be $40,000.

The CCA rate is 30%. Management requires a 10% after-tax return on all equipment purchases. The company's tax rate is 30%.

Required:
1. Determine the before-tax net annual cost savings that the new checkout machine will provide.
2. Using the data from (1) above and other data from the exercise, compute the checkout machine's net present value. (Round all dollar amounts to the nearest whole dollar.) Would you recommend that the machine be purchased?

PROBLEM 13B–4 Basic Net Present Value Analysis Including Income Taxes [LO8]

Norris Property Management has been offered a six-year contract to provide grounds maintenance for various condominium corporations. To accept the contract, the company would have to purchase several pieces of equipment for both summer and winter grounds maintenance at a total cost of $280,000. Other data relating to the contract follow:

Net annual cash receipts (before taxes) from the contract...	$81,000
Cost of overhauling and rebuilding the mechanical equipment in four years........................	$33,000
Salvage value of the equipment at termination of the contract..............................	$15,000

If the contract is accepted, several old, fully depreciated pieces of equipment will be sold at a total price of $22,500. These funds will be used to help purchase the new equipment. For tax purposes, the company computes CCA deductions using the maximum rate of 20%. The company requires an 11% after-tax return on all equipment purchases. The tax rate is 30%.

Required:
Compute the net present value of this investment opportunity. Round all dollar amounts to the nearest whole dollar. Would you recommend that the contract be accepted?

PROBLEM 13B–5 A Comparison of Investment Alternatives Including Income Taxes [LO8]

Kim Huang, an expert in architectural design and restoration of historic buildings, has just received a $160,000 after-tax bonus for the successful completion of a project on time and under budget. Business has been so good that she is planning to retire in 15 years, spending her time travelling, enjoying outdoor activities, and doing charitable work. Huang is considering purchasing a small discount perfume shop that is available at a nearby factory outlet centre. The business can be purchased from its current owner for $160,000. The following information relates to this alternative:

a. Of the purchase price, $64,000 would be for fixtures and other depreciable items. The remainder would be for the company's working capital (inventory, accounts receivable, and cash). The fixtures and other depreciable items would have a remaining useful life of at least 15 years but would be depreciated for tax-reporting purposes using a CCA of 20%. Salvage value is expected to be negligible at the end of 15 years, but the working capital would be released for reinvestment elsewhere.

b.   Store records indicate that sales have averaged $325,000 per year and out-of-pocket costs have averaged $295,000 per year (before income taxes). These out-of-pocket costs include rent on the building, cost of goods sold, utilities, and wages and salaries for the sales staff and the store manager. Huang plans to entrust the day-to-day operations of the store to the manager.

c.   Huang's tax rate is 40%, and she wishes to use an after-tax discount rate of 10%, given the risk involved.

Required:

Should Huang purchase the perfume shop? Use the total-cost approach to discounted cash flow in your analysis and a discount rate of 10%. (Round all dollar amounts to the nearest whole dollar.)

PROBLEM 13B–6 Net Present Value Analysis Including Income Taxes [LO8]

The Perth Mining Company owns the mining rights to several tracts of land on which metals have been found in the past. The amount of precious metals on some of the tracts is somewhat marginal, and the company is unsure whether it would be profitable to extract and sell the precious metals that these tracts contain. Tract 420 is one of these, and the following information about it has been gathered:

Investment in equipment needed for extraction work..	$400,000
Working capital investment needed.............................	$ 55,000
Annual cash receipts from sale of precious metals, net of related cash operating expenses (before taxes)	$ 85,000
Cost of restoring land at completion of extraction work	$ 45,000

The precious metals in Tract 420 would be exhausted after eight years of extraction work. The equipment would have a useful life of 12 years, but it could be sold for only 20% of its original cost when extraction was completed. For tax purposes, the company would depreciate the equipment using a CCA rate of 20%. The tax rate is 30%, and the company's after-tax discount rate is 12%. The working capital would be released for use elsewhere at the completion of the project.

Required:

1.   Compute the net present value of Tract 420. Round all dollar amounts to the nearest whole dollar.

2.   Would you recommend that the investment project be undertaken?

EXTERNAL REPORTING AND ANALYSIS

Chapter 14

Online Chapter 14 presents a basis for conducting financial statement analysis that will be of use to an organization's external stakeholders, such as shareholders and creditors, and to internal users, such as managers. Shareholders are concerned about future earnings and dividends; creditors are concerned about the organization's ability to repay existing or new debt. Financial statement analysis, although based on historical information, can provide useful signals about an organization's prospects with respect to profitability and cash flow.

Financial statement analysis can also highlight areas in need of managerial attention, such as inventory turnover, liquidity management, and capital structure. Where possible, an effective approach to financial statement analysis also incorporates comparative information related to industry trends and specific results for leading competitors.

Chapter 14 is available on the *Managerial Accounting*, Tenth Canadian Edition, Connect site.

Endnotes

Chapter 1

1. These three customer value propositions were defined by Michael Treacy and Fred Wiersema in "Customer Intimacy and Other Value Disciplines," *Harvard Business Review*, January/February 1993, pp. 84–93.
2. *The CICA's Guide to IFRS in Canada, 2009 Edition*. Chartered Accountants of Canada, Toronto, ON.
3. CanWest News Service, "Bauer Recalling 100,000 Children's Hockey Sticks after Lead Paint Discovered," *National Post*, March 19, 2010.
4. Examples are the federal government sponsorship scandal, as well as those involving businesses such as Enron, WorldCom, Global Crossing, Arthur Andersen, and many others.
5. Certified Management Accountants (CMA) was one of the three independent professional accounting bodies in Canada that in 2013 were unified under one national organization, CPA Canada. Beginning in 2015, students wishing to become chartered professional accountants (CPAs) in Canada will all write the same national certification exam but as part of the professional education process can specialize in different technical areas, such as managerial accounting, auditing, finance, or tax.
6. This definition of corporate governance was adapted from the 2004 report entitled *OECD Principles of Corporate Governance*, published by the Organisation for Economic Co-operation and Development.
7. The insights presented in this paragraph and many of the examples in Exhibit 1–8 were drawn from Ronald W. Clement, "The Lessons from Stakeholder Theory for U.S. Business Leaders," *Business Horizons*, May/June 2005, pp. 255–264; and Terry Leap and Misty L. Loughry, "The Stakeholder-Friendly Firm," *Business Horizons*, March/April 2004, pp. 27–32.

Chapter 3

1. See calculus or statistics books for details of how these formulas are derived.
2. Newer versions of Microsoft Excel have a *Regression* function that automatically calculates the intercept, slope, R^2, and other statistics for least-squares regression models without requiring the use of a separate formula for each. The regression function is available as part of the *Analysis Toolpak* add-in for Excel.

Chapter 4

1. In economics, incremental analysis is often termed *marginal analysis* because of the assumptions used in economics about the behaviour of revenues and costs. Accountants tend to use a more general term, *incremental*, so that less restrictive assumptions about the behaviour of revenues and costs can be made, for example, step-variable costs.
2. The shortcut version of the equation is derived as follows:

Profit = (Sales − Variable expenses) − Fixed expenses
$0 = ($250Q − $150Q) − $35,000$
$35,000 = $100Q$
$Q = $35,000 ÷ 100
where $Q =$ Number (quantity) of speakers sold.

Chapter 7

1. Robin Cooper, "Cost Classification in Unit-Based and Activity-Based Manufacturing Cost Systems," *Journal of Cost Management*, Fall 1990, pp. 4–14.
2. Dan Swenson, "The Benefits of Activity-Based Cost Management to the Manufacturing Industry," *Journal of Management Accounting Research* 7, Fall 1995, pp. 165–180.
3. William T. Bonner, "Stormy Waters and the Canadian Coast Guard," *CMA Magazine*, February 1998, pp. 21–26; Michael Senyshen, "ABC/M in the Federal Government," *CGA Magazine*, December 1997, p. 19.
4. Kambiz Foroohar, "Rx: Software," *Forbes*, April 7, 1997, p. 114.
5. Philip Beaulieu and Anila Lakra, "Coverage of the Criticism of Activity-Based Costing in Canadian Textbooks," *Canadian Accounting Perspectives* 4, 2005, pp. 87–109, provides relevant comments on the proper treatment of organization-sustaining activities and idle capacity based on earlier analysis in the literature.

Chapter 9

1. Stan Davis, Todd De Zoort, and Lori Kopp, "The Effect of

Obedience Pressure and Perceived Responsibility on Management Accountants' Creation of Budgetary Slack," *Behavioural Research in Accounting* 18, 2006, pp. 19–36.

2. Joseph Fisher, Sean Peffer, and Geoff Sprinkle, "Budget-Based Contracts, Budget Levels, and Group Performance," *Journal of Management Accounting Research* 15, 2003, pp. 51–74.

Chapter 10

1. Soumitra Dutta and Jean-François Manzoni, *Process Reengineering, Organizational Change and Performance Improvement*, Chapter IV (New York: McGraw-Hill, 1999).

2. For further discussion, see Eliyahu M. Goldratt and Jeff Cox, *The Goal*, 2nd rev. ed. (Croton-on-Hudson, NY: North River Press, 1992).

3. Recall from Chapter 5 that using predetermined overhead application rates negates the need to track the actual quantity of variable overhead items used when assigning costs to products or services.

4. Normal costing systems are defined in Chapter 5.

5. Attiea Marie and Ananth Rao, "Is Standard Costing Still Relevant? Evidence from Dubai," *Management Accounting Quarterly*, Winter 2010, pp. 1–10.

6. Actual market shares for Deluxe and Standard video games are calculated as follows: Deluxe 16% = 12,000 ÷ 75,000; Standard 4.7% = 4,000 ÷ 85,000. Budgeted market shares for Deluxe and Standard video games are calculated as follows: Deluxe 14.3% = 10,000 ÷ 70,000; Standard 5.6% = 5,000 ÷ 90,000.

7. Because the sales quantity variance holds sales mix constant at the budgeted proportions, it can also be calculated using a weighted-average contribution margin approach. The weighted-average contribution margin, using the budgeted sales mix, is $29 per unit: (10/15 × $36) + (5/15 × $15). Total sales quantity variance = (Actual total sales quantity − Budgeted total sales quantity) × Budgeted average contribution margin per unit. Using the data from our example, (16,000 − 15,000) × $29 = $29,000 F.

Chapter 11

1. Some companies classify business segments that are responsible mainly for generating revenue, such as an insurance sales office, as *revenue centres*. Other companies consider this to be just another type of profit centre, since costs of some kind (salaries, rent, utilities) are usually deducted from the revenues in the segment's income statement.

Chapter 12

1. If Cynthia has an accident while driving to Moncton and back, this might affect her insurance premium when the policy is renewed. If the expected cost of the increase in the insurance premium could be estimated, it would be a relevant cost of this particular trip, but the normal amount of the insurance premium is not relevant in any case.

2. K. Siegel-Jacobs and F. Yates, "Effects of Procedural and Outcome Accountability on Judgment Quality," *Organizational Behaviour and Human Decision Processes* 65:1, 1996, pp. 7–17.

3. An alternative way of formulating the analysis is to start with the digital camera net loss of $(6,400) from Exhibit 12-2 and add back the non-avoidable (irrelevant) expenses of $10,400 to arrive at the relevant benefit (segment margin) of $4,000 that would be forgone if the product line were discontinued.

4. An alternative approach to the analysis is to add the incremental unit cost of continuing to make the shifters of $14 (see Exhibit 12-5) to the opportunity cost per unit of $7.50 ($60,000 opportunity cost ÷ 8,000 units), giving a total of $21.50. Since $21.50 is greater than the purchase price of $19 per unit, OSN Cycle should buy the shifters.

5. There are some legal restrictions on prices. Competition laws prohibit "predatory" pricing, which is generally interpreted by the courts to mean a price below average variable cost. "Price discrimination"—charging different prices to customers in the same market for the same product or service—is also prohibited by law.

6. The variable manufacturing cost approach would exclude variable selling and administrative expenses from the cost base and instead include them in the numerator. Otherwise, it is the same as the total variable costing approach.

Chapter 13

1. For simplicity, we ignore inflation and taxes. The impact of income taxes on capital budgeting decisions is discussed in Appendix 13B.

2. Although depreciation itself is not a cash outflow, it does have an effect on cash outflows for income taxes. We will take a look at this effect when we discuss the impact of income taxes on capital budgeting in Appendix 13B.

3. The alternative with the highest net present value is not always the best choice, although it is the best choice in this case. For further discussion, see the section Preference Decisions—The Ranking of Investment Projects, later in this chapter.

4. Technically, the incremental-cost approach is misnamed, since it focuses on differential costs (that is, on both cost increases and decreases) rather than just on incremental costs. As used here, the term *incremental costs* should be interpreted broadly to include both cost increases and cost decreases.

5. This formula assumes that a company is operating at a profit; if it is operating at a loss, the tax situation can be very complex. For simplicity, we assume in all examples, exercises, and problems that the company is operating at a profit.

6. The term *capital cost allowance (CCA) tax shield* may convey the impression that there is something underhanded about CCA deductions—that companies are getting some sort of a special tax break. However, to use the CCA deduction, a company must have already acquired a depreciable asset—which typically requires a cash outflow. Essentially, the tax regulations require companies to delay recognizing the cash outflow as an expense until CCA charges are recorded.

Photo Credits

Chapter 1: Page 2, PhotoAlto/Veer.
Chapter 2: Page 26, Kcphotos/Dreamstime.com.
Chapter 3: Page 65, Digital Vision/Getty Images.
Chapter 4: Page 103, Senohrabek/Dreamstime.com.
Chapter 5: Page 153, IceJerseys.com Team Outfitting: team.icejerseys.com. Photo courtesy of IceJerseys.com.
Chapter 6: Page 212, © Lester Lefkowitz/CORBIS; Page 215, © AP Photo/Yves Logghe.
Chapter 7: Page 249, Fotomilano011/Dreamstime.com; Page 253 (top & bottom), © Sandee Noreen; Page 254, Image Source/Javier Perini CM.
Chapter 8: Page 306, Jack Star/PhotoLink/Getty Images; Page 322, © PhotoDisc Collection/Getty Images.
Chapter 10: Page 399, Steve Cole/Getty Images.
Chapter 11: Page 480, Bjwynnyk/Dreamstime.com.
Chapter 12: Page 526, Icholakov/Dreamstime.com.
Chapter 13: Page 583, THE CANADIAN PRESS/Frank Gunn.

Company/Name Index

Subject Index